ROCK & ROLL

year by year

LUKE CRAMPTON & DAFYDD REES

ROCK &

in association with the Rock and Roll Hall of Fame and Museum

ROLL

year by year

DK

DK Publishing

DK

London, New York, Munich, Melbourne, Delhi

This book is dedicated to
Abby and Christiaan

Senior editor Nicki Lampon
US editor Margaret Parrish
Senior designer Alison Shackleton
DTP designers Gemma Casajuana Filella, Rajen Shah
Production controller Heather Hughes

Managing editor Adèle Hayward
Managing art editor Karen Self
Category publisher Stephanie Jackson
Art director Carole Ash

Produced for Dorling Kindersley by
PALAZZO EDITIONS LIMITED
15 Gay Street, Bath, BA1 2PH

Managing director Colin Webb
Design coordinater Sian Rance
Picture researcher Emily Hedges
Editor Beverley Jollands
Managing editor Sonya Newland
Indexer Tim Jollands

First American Edition, 2003
00 01 02 03 04 05 10 9 8 7 6 5 4 3 2 1

Published in the United States by
DK Publishing, Inc.
375 Hudson Street, New York, NY 10014

Library of Congress Cataloging-in-Publication Data

Crampton, Luke
Rock * roll year by year / Luke Crampton & Dafydd Rees
p. cm.

Includes index.
Contents: 1950s: the birth of rock 'n' roll – 1960s: from Mersey beat to flower power – 1970s: a blend of glam rock, glitter, and punk – 1980s: the decade of MTV and Live Aid – 1990s: from Seattle grunge to girl power – 2000s: the new breed
ISBN 0-7894-9649-6 (alk. paper)
1. Rock music – History and criticism. I. Rees, Dafydd. II. Title.

ML3534.C725 2003
781.66'09—dc21

2003051655

Reproduced by Colourscan, Singapore
Printed and bound in Italy by Graphicom SpA

See our complete catalog at
www.dk.com

contents

1950

1980

1960

1970

1990

2000

Louis Jordan's saxophone, early 1950s

Chuck Berry poster with added "N" to his name, 1953

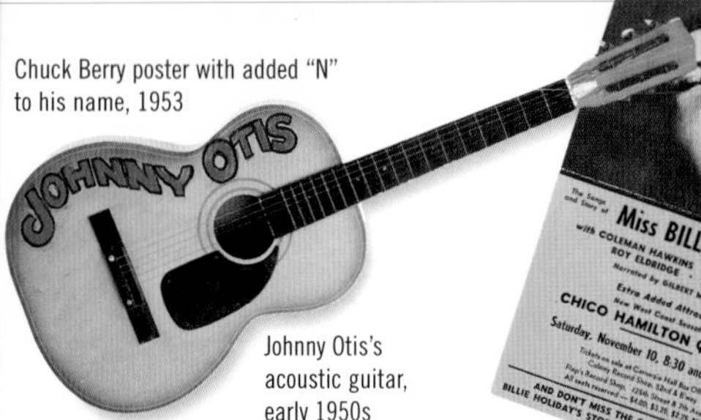

Johnny Otis's acoustic guitar, early 1950s

Billie Holiday Poster, 1957

Ray Charles's stage jacket, c.1955

Roy Orbison's sunglasses, c.1964

Jimi Hendrix poster, 1967

Foreword

Trying to untangle the twisted history of rock 'n' roll can be a daunting task. For one thing, there are no easy answers to some of the most basic questions. What is rock 'n' roll? When did rock 'n' roll begin? It depends on who you ask and what their prejudices are.

Most would agree that it was some time in the 1950s, yet its roots stretch back to the 1920s. What was the first rock 'n' roll record? Maybe *Rocket 88* by Ike Turner and Jackie Brenston. Maybe *Rock Around the Clock* by Bill Haley & His Comets. Maybe *That's All Right (Mama)* by Elvis Presley, Bill Black, and Scotty Moore. Like I said, it depends on who you ask.

But the difficulties don't end there. In the early days of rock, no one – not even the music's most fervent supporters – ever dreamed that rock 'n' roll would one day be studied in universities, or that entire museums would be devoted to "educating the world about the history and significance of rock and roll music," to quote from the Rock and Roll Hall of Fame and Museum's mission statement. As a result, little early history was recorded or kept in any methodical way. Few journalists covered rock 'n' roll. And those who did either covered it as a passing fad or as a horrible menace to established society. So even the most basic facts – the release date of a record, for example – are frequently hard to come by.

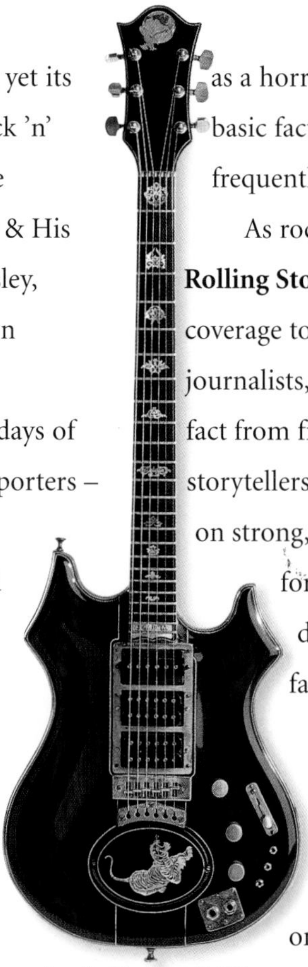

Jerry Garcia's guitar, mid 1970s

As rock 'n' roll came of age, magazines and newspapers like **Rolling Stone** and **New Musical Express** began devoting serious coverage to it. Still, most of the writers were fans, not trained journalists, and many had a hard time deciphering fact from fiction. And rock stars tend to be very talented storytellers. Some of the best writers from that era relied more on strong, opinionated literary voices than on facts. It made for great writing and reading, but, thirty years on, it doesn't necessarily aid someone trying to build a factual history of rock 'n' roll.

The nature of the music business hasn't helped either. Record companies are, by their very orientation, hit-driven. Their concern is the bottom line, and their effort, rightly or wrongly, is focused on getting hits – today. Until the relatively recent boom

David Bowie's collage jacket. c.1987

New Kids On The Block game, late 1980s

Bangles guitar, late 1980s

Zoo TV money, 1993

Partridge Family lunchbox, c.1970

George Clinton's boots, 1977

Spinners' jacket, c.1979

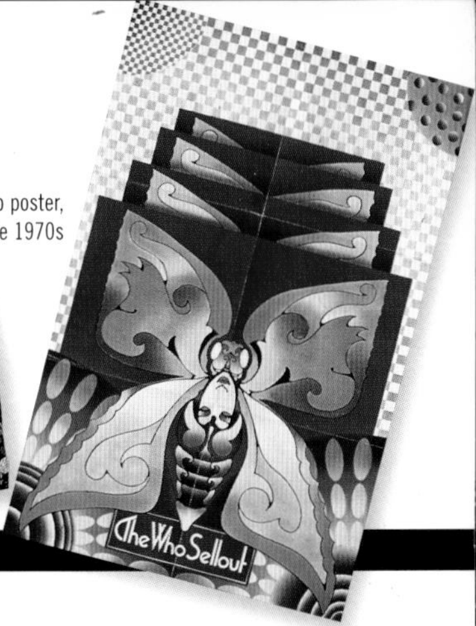

Who poster, late 1970s

in CD box sets, record labels paid very little attention to their history. As a former label employee, I can attest that history, in the form of documents and files, was routinely thrown away.

None of this, however, has stopped people from trying to write about the history of rock 'n' roll and its artists. Store shelves are filled with hundreds of books, ranging from A–Z encyclopedias to gushing fan bios. There are dense, academic tomes and lavish, heavily illustrated coffee-table books. There are some great biographies and some trashy biographies. Despite this deluge of books, if you are trying to locate or verify a fact about an event or a person in rock's history – as my staff at the Rock and Roll Hall of Fame and I do on a daily basis – good luck. You'll most likely have to search through several books, and, if you find any information at all, there's a good chance that the facts will be in conflict with each other.

That's why this day-by-day history fills a huge void. It is a straightforward, detailed telling of rock 'n' roll's evolution, from 1950 to the present. It has been carefully researched, and every effort has been made to ensure its accuracy. It is the perfect research tool for the rock scholar, and it's a fast, fun read for the rock fan. Naturally, not every band, every record, or every event gets a mention. But let's face it: love of rock 'n' roll is very subjective. One of the things we've found out at the Rock and Roll Hall of Fame is that virtually all of our visitors consider themselves experts on rock 'n' roll, and they all have their favorite groups, singers, songwriters, records, concerts, and so on. I regularly get e-mails from visitors asking why "so and so" isn't represented in the Museum. It's impossible to be absolutely inclusive, either in the Museum or in a book like this. Still, the authors, Luke Crampton and Dafydd Rees, come pretty damn close.

It's somewhat hard to fathom that rock 'n' roll – that unruly, rebellious music of the young – is now in its sixth decade. Somehow it has managed to survive, even thrive, despite the best efforts of its numerous detractors. The music that was created by poor, disenfranchised African-Americans and whites in the southern United States has become a universal language, heard and admired around the world. As the Grateful Dead once said, "It's been a long, strange trip," and this book is a great document of that journey.

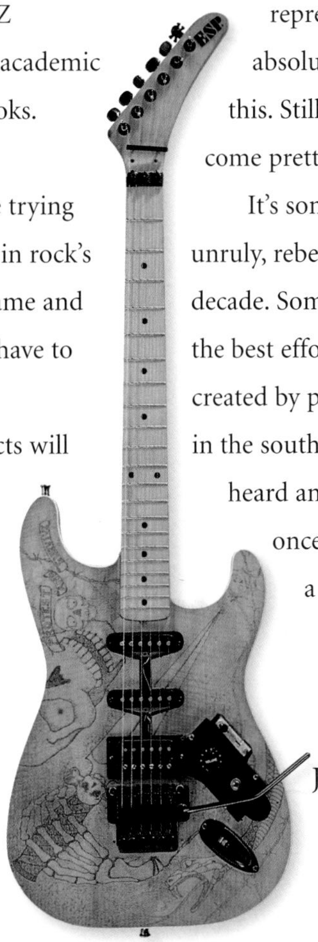

Joe Perry of Aerosmith's guitar, mid 1980s

JAMES HENKE

Vice President of Exhibitions and Curatorial Affairs

The Rock and Roll Hall of Fame and Museum

Cleveland, Ohio

Soundgarden poster, 1994

Alice in Chains Claymation dolls, c.1994

Alice Cooper's boots, c.1995

Spice Girls ticket, 1998

Madona ticket, 2000

TRL poster, 2000

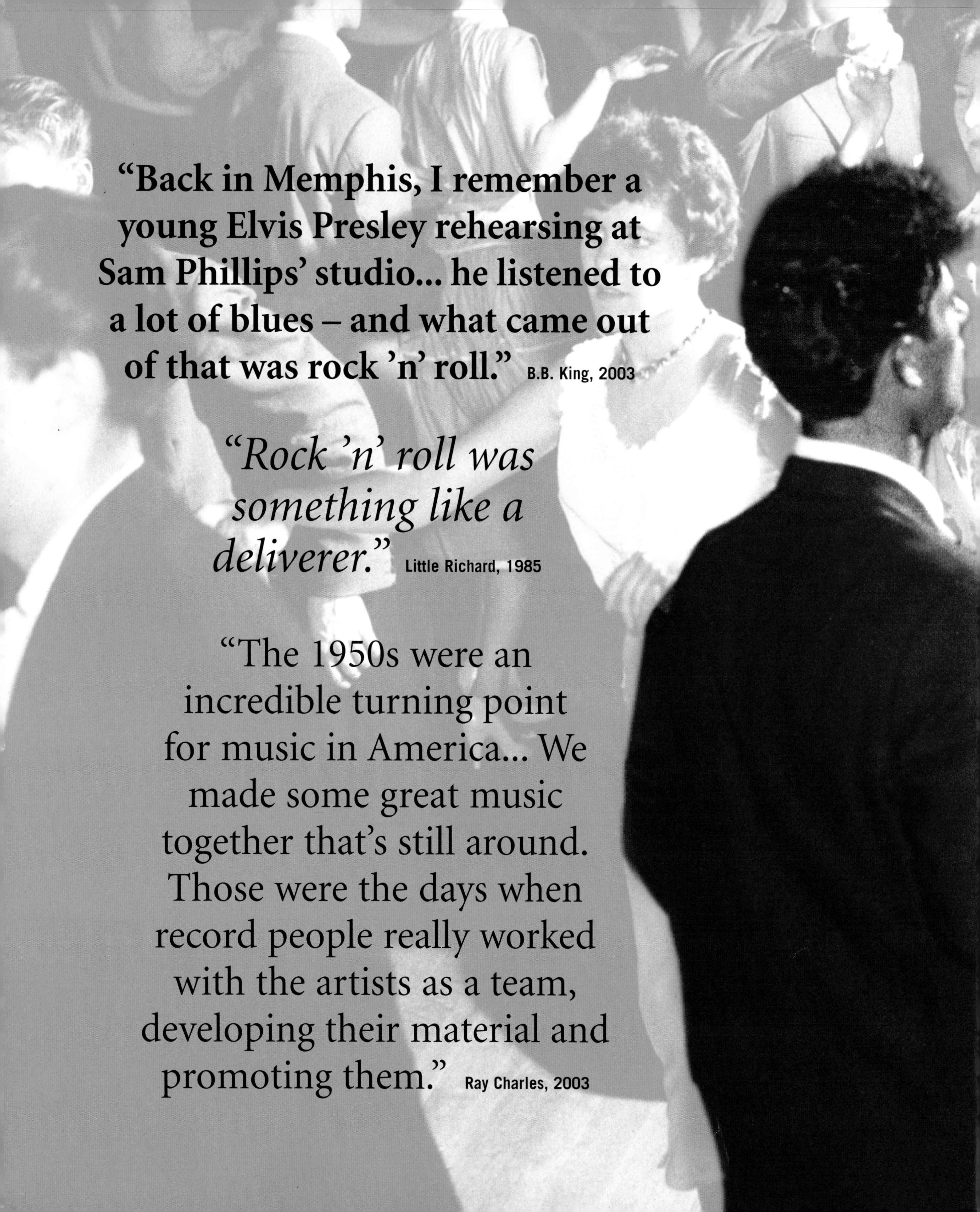

"Back in Memphis, I remember a young Elvis Presley rehearsing at Sam Phillips' studio... he listened to a lot of blues – and what came out of that was rock 'n' roll." B.B. King, 2003

"Rock 'n' roll was something like a deliverer." Little Richard, 1985

"The 1950s were an incredible turning point for music in America... We made some great music together that's still around. Those were the days when record people really worked with the artists as a team, developing their material and promoting them." Ray Charles, 2003

1950

Good Rockin' Tonight

1950-54

No.1 US SINGLES 1954

Jan 2	Oh, Mein Papa **Eddie Calvert**
Feb 27	Secret Love **Doris Day**
Mar 13	Make Love To Me! **Jo Stafford**
Mar 20	Secret Love **Doris Day**
Mar 27	Make Love To Me! **Jo Stafford**
Apr 10	Wanted **Perry Como**
June 5	Little Things Mean A Lot **Kitty Kallen**
Aug 7	Sh-Boom **Crew Cuts**
Sept 25	Hey There **Rosemary Clooney**
Nov 6	This Ole House **Rosemary Clooney**
Nov 13	Need You Now **Eddie Fisher**
Dec 4	Mr. Sandman **Chordettes**

No.1 UK SINGLES 1954

Jan 2	Answer Me **Frankie Laine**
Jan 9	Oh, Mein Papa **Eddie Calvert**
Mar 13	I See The Moon **Stargazers**
Apr 17	Secret Love **Doris Day**
Apr 24	I See The Moon **Stargazers**
May 1	Such A Night **Johnnie Ray**
May 8	Secret Love **Doris Day**
July 3	Cara Mia **David Whitfield with Chorus & Mantovani & His Orchestra**
Sept 11	Little Things Mean A Lot **Kitty Kallen**
Sept 18	Three Coins In The Fountain **Frank Sinatra**
Oct 9	Hold My Hand **Don Cornell**
Nov 6	My Son My Son **Vera Lynn**
Nov 20	Hold My Hand **Don Cornell**
Nov 27	This Ole House **Rosemary Clooney**
Dec 4	Let's Have Another Party **Winifred Atwell**

Hank Ballard & the Midnighters

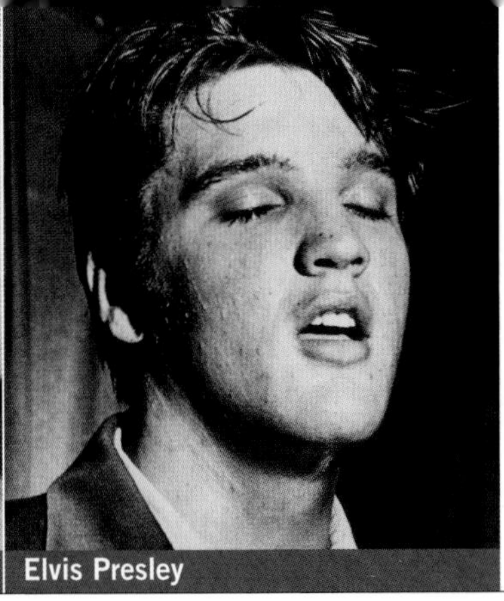
Elvis Presley

Hank Ballard worked on a car assembly line in Detroit before assembling the Midnighters in 1953... Elvis Presley was the perfect fusion of country and western, rhythm and blues, curled lips, and swiveling hips.

In the early 1950s America was a musical cauldron – reflecting a society that was diverse, vigorous, and emerging with optimism from the privations of World War II. The period saw the first challenges to racial segregation – sometimes led by musicians and music fans – a mixing of styles, the assertion of youth and with it, inevitably, rebellion. The charts were still dominated by the "safe" pop of artists such as **Rosemary Clooney**, **Perry Como**, and **Frank Sinatra**. **Nat King Cole** remained the doyen of pop balladry. But a new force was emerging. Increasingly, the mainstream artists were having to compete with energetic newcomers like **Bill Haley**, **Little Richard**, and **Chuck Berry**.

In its formative years, rock 'n' roll was a shameless borrower – from doo-wop and gospel, country and western, blues, bluegrass, and, above all, rhythm and blues. But it also developed its own trademarks: a pounding backbeat, loud guitars, youthful irreverence and energy. The cross-pollination was spurred by "crossover" records. While black R&B groups, such as the **Dominoes** and **Hank Ballard & the Midnighters**, found an audience among white teenagers, it wasn't all one-way traffic. **Alan Freed**'s radio shows in Ohio appealed to both black and white listeners, and **Johnnie Ray** had a No. 1 R&B hit in 1952. But in general, white artists were borrowing from black influences and succeeding, while black acts often saw little commercial return for their creativity.

Producers and promoters played a vital role in shaping rock 'n' roll. **Sam Phillips**, at the Memphis Recording Service, honed the sounds of **B.B. King**, **Howlin' Wolf**, and **Ike Turner** – who recorded *Rocket 88* in March 1951 – the template for hundreds of records to come. A year later, Phillips formed the pioneering label Sun Records, and a shy 18-year-old named **Elvis Presley** dropped in to cut a demo.

Ahmet Ertegun was building Atlantic Records into a formidable stable of blues and R&B artists. His signings included black groups such as the **Clovers** and the **Drifters**, and blues singer **Ruth Brown**. **Ray Charles** joined the roster in 1952. The **Chess Brothers** were also signing up future blues greats, such as **Muddy Waters** and **John Lee Hooker**. Vocal groups like the **Spaniels** spurred the growth of what would be the most successful black-owned label in the US, Vee-Jay Records.

Many of the seeds of rock 'n' roll were sown in the American south, with Memphis as the epicenter. The "Louisiana Hayride" radio show was an early vehicle for Elvis and many others. **Buddy Holly** auditioned for KDAV in Lubbock in 1953. The genre also benefited from new technology, as both the 45rpm disc and the long player gained popularity. Sadly, these early years even included the first rock 'n' roll obituaries. Country singer **Hank Williams** died in 1952, and **Johnny Ace** shot himself in 1954. But in the same month, Elvis recorded his third single – and the world was about to change.

"The most brutal, ugly, degenerate, vicious form of expression it has been my displeasure to hear."

Frank Sinatra on rock 'n' roll, **Western World**, 1958

Jan 1950

Sam Phillips sets up the Memphis Recording Service... Fats Domino's first hit... Tony Bennett debuts...

Sam Phillips

Sam Phillips, a former DJ, had dreams of turning rhythm and blues into rock 'n' roll... Miles Davis once said: "Don't play what's there, play what's not there"... Nat King Cole, originally a jazz pianist, was to become the doyen of pop balladry.

January

1 With the motto "We Record Anything – Anywhere – Anytime," 26-year-old **Sam Phillips** opens the doors of the storefront he is leasing for $150 a month at the corner of Union and Marshall in Memphis, to begin business as the Memphis Recording Service. Phillips, born in Alabama, began his career in radio in 1943. Having worked at the Memphis station WREC as an announcer and broadcast engineer, he recently secured a two-year loan from Buck Turner, one of the station's broadcasters, to buy recording and transcription equipment for his new venture. Although he is willing to record weddings, marching bands, funerals, and personal messages, and to make transcriptions for local radio stations, Phillips's principal goal is to tap into the wellspring of raw local talent that congregates around Beale Street, Memphis. This ambition will lead to sessions with artists such as **B.B. King**, **James Cotton**, and **Howlin' Wolf**.

4 Two years after Columbia Records introduced the "album" – a 12in microgroove long-playing vinylite record, developed by Peter Goldmark in 1947, that offers 23 minutes per side, spinning at 33⅓ revolutions per minute – established record label RCA Victor announces that it too will shortly begin manufacturing long-playing discs, having already introduced 7in 45rpm Extended Play vinylite records and record players in 1949. Another major label, Capitol Records, became the first to support all three recording speeds – 78, 45, and 33⅓rpm – last September.

February

4 Pioneering electric guitarist **T-Bone Walker**'s *Go Back To The One You Love* begins its only week on the Rhythm & Blues Records list. It is the last of a string of hits that started with *Bobby Sox Blues*, which made the top five of what was then known as the "Race Records" chart in 1947. One of the first blues artists to play electric guitar in the 1930s, the self-taught musician recorded the already influential *T-Bone Blues* and *Stormy Monday,* and his single-string guitar solos will influence future fretwork by artists such as B.B. King and Eric Clapton.

18 Innovative singer/pianist **Fats Domino** – influenced by Fats Waller and signed to Imperial Records last year – enters the R&B chart for the first time with *The Fat Man*. Taped last December

Johnny Otis spent much of 1950 fronting the Rhythm & Blues Caravan Show, featuring talent from his Barrelhouse club in Los Angeles.

Miles Davis

Nat King Cole

at Cosimo Matassa's J&M Studio in New Orleans, the record is a reworking of Champion Jack Dupree's composition, *Junker's Blues*. Domino is currently playing in honky-tonk bars around New Orleans for $3 a week, but the song introduces his unique rolling piano style to a wider audience and will spend nine weeks on the survey, hitting No. 2 and selling 800,000 copies by the end of the year. Its success will mark the beginning of a long and fruitful partnership with producer Dave Bartholomew and Imperial label head, Lew Chudd.

35:29-minute album of innovative "cool jazz" will be regarded as a landmark recording, influencing generations of musicians and composers beyond the jazz genre.

11 Though not particularly enthusiastic about the ballad on first hearing, **Nat King Cole** records *Mona Lisa* during a five-song session for Capitol Records. With an orchestral arrangement by Nelson Riddle, *Mona Lisa* – written by Jay Livingston and Ray Evans – will go on to hit US No. 1 on July 8, selling three million copies.

that combined to enormous popular effect, providing an important ingredient of the multigenre stew that will evolve into rock 'n' roll. Having begun as a "Barn Dance" show on WSM on November 28, 1925, the Grand Ole Opry invites a regular roster of "members" to perform on what is already America's longest-running weekly radio show. Its legacy, popularity, and influence – like that of the Carter Family – will extend into the next century.

"If I could find a white man who had the Negro sound and the Negro feel, I could make a million dollars." Sam Phillips, before meeting Elvis Presley

March

4 West Coast R&B pioneer **Johnny Otis** scores the first in a series of blues hits on the Savoy label, as *Double Crossing Blues* tops the R&B chart for the first of nine weeks. Credited to the Johnny Otis Quintette, it features **Little Esther** (soon to record as **Esther Phillips**). The cut also includes backing vocals by black male vocal quartet the **Robins**, whose line-up includes **Bobby Nunn**. (Later this year, Nunn will cut *That's What The Good Book Says* for the Modern label, the first recorded composition for young songwriting pair, **Jerry Leiber** and **Mike Stoller**. Nunn will also go on to become a founding member of the **Coasters**.) Several R&B-oriented record labels have noted Otis's ear for hot new artists, and he is becoming a top roving talent scout, on one occasion recommending to King Records three future major acts he has seen on the same night while visiting Detroit: **Jackie Wilson**, **Little Willie John**, and the **Royals** (later to become **Hank Ballard & the Midnighters**).

9 In the last of three recording sessions at the Capitol Recording Studio in New York, 23-year-old trumpet player **Miles Davis** completes four new cuts for inclusion on his upcoming ***Birth Of The Cool*** album. He is accompanied at this session by **Gerry Mulligan** (baritone sax), **J.J. Johnson** (trombone), **Lee Konitz** (alto saxophone), **John Barber** (tuba), **Gunther Schuller** (French horn), **Al McKibbon** (bass), **Max Roach** (drums), and **Kenny "Pancho" Hagood** (vocals). Davis served his apprenticeship playing alongside **Dizzy Gillespie**, **Charlie Parker**, and others, creating the bebop jazz style. The

April

15 Credited as the **Johnny Otis Orchestra**, Otis replaces himself at the top of the R&B chart, as *Mistrustin' Blues* – again featuring **Little Esther** – takes over from *Double Crossing Blues*.

17 In New York, 23-year-old jazz/pop vocalist **Tony Bennett** makes his first recording, *Boulevard Of Broken Dreams*, for Columbia Records. Bennett was given his performing name – and his break in show business – last year by comedian Bob Hope, who heard him singing at the Greenwich Village Inn in Manhattan. Hope suggested he change his name from Joe Bari and booked him on his own show at the Paramount Theater. Columbia's popular music director, **Mitch Miller**, on hearing an audition demo by Bennett of *Boulevard Of Broken Dreams*, has immediately brought him to the label. Bennett's first major hit, *Because Of You*, will become the top-selling record in the US next year.

May

29 At the invitation of country and western star George Morgan, the **Carter Sisters & Mother Maybelle** (Maybelle Carter and her three daughters, Helen, June, and Anita) join the Grand Ole Opry. They perform at the Ryman Auditorium in Nashville for live broadcast on radio station WSM, with itinerant guitarist **Chet Atkins** in their backing troupe. As the "First Family of Country," their history and influence stretches back to their original formation as the **Carter Family** in 1926. They introduced to the genre a harmony vocal style and gospel leanings

A steady stream of musical talent flowed around the Beale Street area of Memphis, but the gifted southern black blues artists who congregated there remained unrecorded until Sam Phillips set up his Memphis Recording Service.

June 1950

The Chess label makes its move... The Weavers – first superstar folk group... Muddy Waters records *Louisiana Blues*...

Leonard Chess was the co-founder of Chicago-based independent label, Chess Records.

June

3 Brothers **Leonard** and **Philip Chess** – two Polish immigrants who settled in Chicago in 1928 – reorganize their Aristocrat label (located on Maxwell Street at the end of Highway 61), and formally change its name to Chess Records. Concentrating on signing blues, jazz, and R&B artists, the Chess siblings entered into a partnership with Charles and Evelyn Aron in 1947 to form Aristocrat, and subsequently bought them out in 1949. One of their earliest successes has been McKinley Morganfield, who performs under the name **Muddy Waters**, and who has been with the label since its inception. Independent startups like Chess – along with Atlantic, King, Aladdin, Specialty, Imperial, and Modern – are serving the public with music that is missing from the rosters of the major record companies. In the late 1940s and early 1950s, Chess is discovering and recording several of the giants of postwar American blues, including **Memphis Slim**, **Jimmy Rogers**, **Sonny Boy Williamson**, **Howlin' Wolf**, **Little Walter**, **John Lee Hooker**, and **Willie Mabon**. It will also nurture the next generation of Chicago blues musicians – including **Buddy Guy**, **Koko Taylor**, and **Little Milton**.

August

19 *Hard Luck Blues* by **Roy Brown & His Mighty Mighty Men**, on the DeLuxe label, begins the first of three weeks at the top of the R&B chart. Brown has been a mainstay on the survey since 1948. His first charted composition, *Good Rockin' Tonight* – a historic precursor of the nascent rock 'n' roll sound – was one of that year's biggest hits, both in a version recorded by **Wynonie Harris** and the recording made by Brown himself. (The song will be widely covered by other artists, not least by Elvis Presley in 1954.) A gospel/blues singer-songwriter, Brown's writing and vocal style, alternately soulful and rocking, will influence dozens of upcoming artists during the 1950s, including Presley, Jackie Wilson, James Brown, and Junior Parker.

October

10 In New York, 19-year-old music entrepreneur **Jac Holzman** founds Elektra Records, which will focus on folk, ethnic, jazz, and gospel music. Its first release, in December, will be ***Songs By John Gruen***, recorded in one three-hour session, which Holzman will master and press at RCA. His next offering will be the 10in LP, ***Jean Ritchie Singing The Traditional Songs Of Her Kentucky Mountain Family***, which will eventually sell 2,000 copies: enough to keep his upstart company running. He will subsequently buy his own recording equipment, and Elektra will continue to issue folk-based material by the likes of **Cynthia Gooding**, **Shep Ginandes**, and **Frank Warner**, before

THE WEAVERS

Oct 21 ***Goodnight Irene* begins its tenth and final week at No. 1 on Billboard's Best Sellers in Stores chart. It is the first chart-topper for the Weavers, formed in 1948 by Pete Seeger (who will become an increasingly important folk mentor to singer-songwriters of the early 1960s). The song is a sweet revision of an old composition by Huddie Ledbetter – better known as Leadbelly. The legendary folk/blues singer-songwriter first recorded it in 1933 for folklorists John Lomax and his son Alan. As music archivists for the Library of Congress, the Lomaxes visited Leadbelly at the Angola Prison Farm in Louisiana (where he was serving time for assault with intent to murder), to record him on their Edison cylinder machine.**

***Goodnight Irene*'s success confirmed the Weavers' status as the first superstar folk group.**

Known as "Mr. Blues," Wynonie Harris began his career as a dancer and comedian, before becoming a pioneer of R&B.

broadening its scope to release its first blues titles – by **Sonny Terry** and **Brownie McGhee** – in 1954. These successes will enable Holzman to relocate his startup label to formal offices at 361 Bleecker Street.

23 Having recorded *Rollin' Stone* in February for Aristocrat, **Muddy Waters** now nails *Louisiana Blues* at a session featuring **Little Walter** (harmonica), **Elgin Evans** (washboard), and **Big Crawford** (bass). It will be his first single to chart on the Chess label, entering the R&B survey next January. He has made his name as Chicago's leading blues singer; his electrification of the blues and raw vocal style will make him a major influence during the dawn of rock 'n' roll.

November

5 The **Orioles**' guitarist **Tommy Gaither** is killed, and colleagues **George Nelson** and **Johnny Reed** are seriously injured, in a car accident in the early morning just outside Baltimore, while driving from a concert on Long Island to Washington D.C. The group's other two singers, **Sonny Til** and **Alex Sharp** are in another vehicle. **Ralph Williams** will be recruited to replace Gaither, and in a year's time the Orioles will score their third R&B chart-topper with *Crying In The Chapel* (a hit for Elvis Presley in 1965).

December

1 Replacing legendary lead tenor **Robert "R.H." Harris**, 19-year-old vocalist **Sam Cooke** – formerly with the Pilgrim Travelers and R.B. Robertson's Highway QCs – joins the line-up of star gospel group, the **Soul Stirrers**, in Pine Bluff, Arkansas. He will sing with the group for six years before launching a solo career.

9 Introduced by Duke Ellington to the burgeoning Atlantic Records label in 1948, blues singer **Ruth Brown** begins an 11-week tenure at the top of the R&B chart with *Teardrops From My Eyes*, her first No. 1. She first made the chart last year with *So Long*, and will become a major influence on upcoming blues and R&B singers. Brown's polished, pop-aimed, vocal style will also enable her to cross over into the emerging rock 'n' roll scene in the mid-1950s.

Leadbelly ironically died just ten months before the Weavers recorded their version of *Goodnight Irene*... The Orioles were considered by many to be the first true R&B vocal combo... Ruth Brown was Atlantic Records' top R&B singer.

Leadbelly

The Orioles

Ruth Brown

Jan 1951

Ike Turner and *Rocket 88*... Debuts for Johnnie Ray and Little Richard...

January

8 **B.B. King** – Memphis WDIA radio DJ, guitarist, and self-taught blues singer-songwriter – records *B.B. Blues* under the direction of Sam Phillips at the Memphis Recording Service. Riley B. King, also known as "Blues Boy," has recently shortened his nickname from "Bee Bee." He has been recommended by musician/talent scout Ike Turner to Saul, Joe, and Jules Bihari, the owners of Los Angeles-based Modern Records. They will issue the disc on their RPM Records imprint, for which King will record four R&B chart-toppers over the next four years.

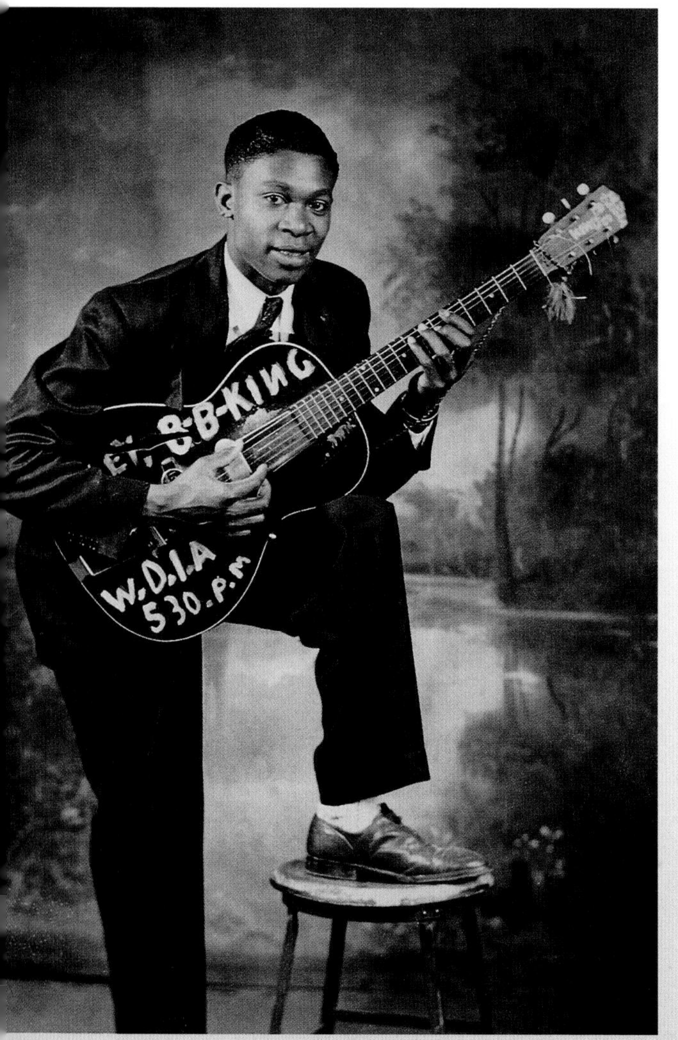

B.B. King was the master of "string-bending" – few other blues artists would have such a profound influence on rock 'n' roll.

February

22 Recently signed to Atlantic Records, the **Clovers** record their label debut, *Don't You Know I Love You*, a midtempo blues number written by label boss Ahmet Ertegun. This black R&B vocal quintet, which includes a guitarist (Bill Harris) in its ranks, recorded for the Rainbow label last year. The new song will become the group's first R&B chart No. 1 in September, but will be held off the top spot all summer by *Sixty-Minute Man* – on the Federal label – recorded by another innovative black male quintet, the **Dominoes**, featuring singer **Clyde McPhatter** in the line-up. Both groups are forging a previously unheard blend of R&B, pop, and rock 'n' roll, mixing a traditional soulful vocal style with often rollicking uptempo beat.

March

5 **Ike Turner** – traveling talent scout, songwriter/pianist, and DJ on the WROX station in Clarksdale, Mississippi – has driven to Memphis with his **Kings of Rhythm** band, featuring singer/saxophonist **Jackie Brenston**, guitarist **Willie Kizart**, and sax player **Ray Hill**. With Turner on piano, the troupe record *Rocket 88* – an ode to the joys of the Oldsmobile Rocket 88 automobile – with producer Sam Phillips at the Memphis Recording Service. A rocking blend of swing and raw jump blues, it also features an early example of distorted "fuzz guitar." Excited by the results, Phillips will lease the recording to Chess Records in Chicago. Though credited to **Jackie Brenston & His Delta Cats** – the label copy indicates that Brenston also wrote the song – *Rocket 88* is largely the work of Turner, notably as its actual writer and musical director. Turner makes it raw, insisting on a pounding backbeat, and superimposing Hill's tenor sax solos and Brenston's energetic vocal. *Rocket 88* will become a prototype for hundreds of other rock 'n' roll records, and will hit US R&B No. 1 on June 9.

April

26 **John Lee Hooker** records at the Chess Records studio for the first time, having already notched up a 1949 million-seller for Modern Records with *Boogie Chillen'*. In a marathon session, the blues singer-songwriter/guitarist from Clarksdale completes nine sides in one day, including *Union Station Blues* and *Ramblin' By Myself*. Unusually, Hooker is recording for a number of different labels in one-time deals, and will provide cuts to 21 labels over seven years.

May

14 In Memphis, Sam Phillips records *How Many More Years/Moanin' At Midnight*, the first single by **Howlin' Wolf** (who, as Chester Burnett, grew up on a Mississippi cotton plantation and learned to play guitar from blues pioneers **Charlie Patton** and **Willie Brown**). Phillips will license the recordings to Chess, though this will cause a rift with the Modern label, which claims exclusive rights to Wolf material. The double A-side will head into the R&B chart in November.

19 Veteran vocalist/saxophonist/songwriter **Louis Jordan** enjoys his last week on the R&B chart with his final hit, *Weak Minded Blues*. One of the most popular R&B artists of the last ten years, Jordan is a major influence on the aggregation of styles that will emerge as rock 'n' roll, and is one of the few already to have crossed over into the white record-buying market. His chart tenure – entirely with Decca ("Me and Bing Crosby, we made Decca Records") – includes dozens of influential hits, including *Five Guys Named Moe* and *Let The Good Times Roll*.

John Lee Hooker

Howlin' Wolf

Louis Jordan, the Arkansas-born prince of jump blues, was one of the earliest R&B artists to cross over into the white market.

21 With his latest hit, *Cold, Cold Heart*, still on the charts, 27-year-old **Hank Williams** is admitted to the North Louisiana Sanitarium, suffering from acute alcoholism. The troubled country superstar singer-songwriter has regularly resorted to alcohol and narcotics to ease severe back pain, which is now diagnosed as the result of a birth defect, spina bifida occulta.

29 **Johnnie Ray** makes his debut recordings for the mostly R&B-focused Okeh label in Detroit: *Whiskey & Gin*, a rousing R&B number, and *Tell The Lady I Said Goodbye*, both backed by **Maurice King & the Wolverines**. Ray, 24, has been partially deaf since childhood and has worn a hearing aid since the age of 14. He is currently performing regularly at Detroit's Flame Showbar, where he is the only non-black act. When the disc hits radio, listeners assume Ray to be a black blues singer, not a tall, fair, white man. Okeh's parent company, Columbia Records, will quickly decide to launch Ray on the main label, teaming him with producer Mitch Miller in October to record the ballad *Cry*.

The Rocket 88 automobile was launched in 1949... John Lee Hooker was the blues genius behind *Boogie Chillen'*... Howlin' Wolf was an electrifying pioneer of the Chicago blues scene.

July

11 **Alan Freed** – calling himself Moondog and adopting an energetic, upbeat, on-air style – makes his debut on WJW radio in Cleveland, introducing his "Moondog Rock 'n' Roll Party." Freed is an experienced radio broadcaster, having started at WKST in New Castle, Pennsylvania, in 1942 for $17 a week, before becoming a sports announcer at WKBN in Youngstown, Ohio. He began spinning hot jazz and pop records at WAKR, Akron, Ohio, in 1945, but quit radio after a dispute with the station in 1950 and has spent 18 months working at Cleveland's WXEL-TV. He is urged to return to radio by Leo Mintz, owner of the local Record Rendezvous store, who has noticed a surge of interest in the burgeoning R&B scene. Freed's nightly show mostly plays R&B records, and will soon be equally popular with both black and white listeners.

August

15 Appearing with celebrities such as Bob Hope, Jack Benny, Jimmy Durante, and Milton Berle, a temporarily recovered **Hank Williams** joins one of the largest US variety treks ever mounted: the Hadacol Tour (promoting its sponsor's product, a potent part alcohol, part laxative elixir).

October

16 Pianist/singer Richard Wayne Penniman – at 18, already performing as "**Little Richard**" – makes his first recordings at radio station WGST in Atlanta. Among other cuts for the RCA Camden label, he completes *Why Did You Leave Me*, *Taxi Blues*, *Every Hour*, and *Get Rich Quick*. Singer **Billy Wright** has introduced Richard to a local disc jockey – who has entered him in a radio audition contest at Atlanta's Eighty One Theater on Decatur Street. Wright, with his heavy make-up and gelled hair, will be a significant influence on Richard's own visual style.

November

3 While other performers continue to cover his songs, Mississippi-born blues singer-songwriter/guitarist **Arthur "Big Boy" Crudup**'s last chart record – *I'm Gonna Dig Myself A Hole*, issued by RCA Victor – enters the R&B survey.

Jan 1952

Sun Records is launched... Hardly a note gets played at the first Moondog Rock 'n' Roll concert... Johnnie Ray on the charts...

Although the first of Alan Freed's "Moondog" balls began and ended in mayhem, a profitable series of "Moondog" events became popular throughout Ohio.

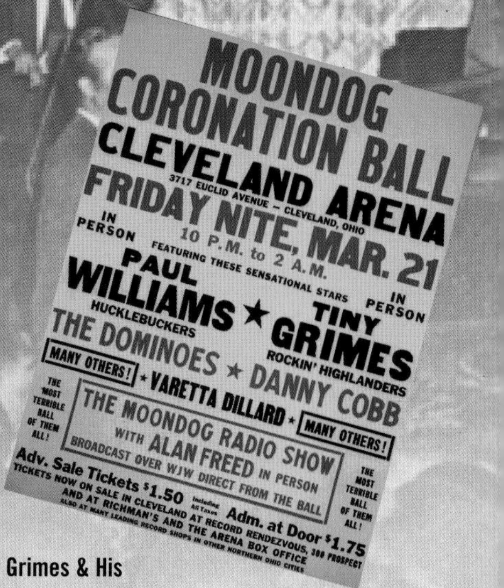

January

7 BBC television launches "Hit Parade," its first "pop" music show, with host Victor Barnard. It features the eight most popular songs of the moment, according to **Melody Maker** magazine, sung by **Eve Boswell**, **Carole Carr**, **Dick James**, **Lee Lawrence**, and the **Stargazers**, with **Cyril Stapleton & His Orchestra**.

24 In Corinth, Mississippi, 19-year-old singer/guitarist **Carl Perkins** marries Valda Crider, who is encouraging him to make a career in music. Perkins is from a poor sharecropping family in Ridgely, Tennessee, and has been picking cotton since the age of six. He assembled his first guitar from a broom handle and a cigar box, using baling wire for strings, and was taught to play by a black farm worker known as Uncle John Westbrooks. During their first year together, Perkins continues to pick cotton while Valda (who will give birth to their first child, Stan, on November 11) takes in laundry to make ends meet.

Carl Perkins started out playing bars and honky tonks around Mississippi with his brothers Jay and Clayton, as the Perkins Brothers Band.

February

2 With his eighth single released on the RPM label, **B.B. King** finally hits it big as *3 O'Clock Blues* tops the R&B chart.

March

1 Still running the Memphis Recording Service studio, **Sam Phillips** launches his own label, Sun Records, with the retail release of *Drivin' Slow* (Sun 175) by saxophonist **Johnny London**. An earlier single that was scheduled to introduce the label – *Blues in My Condition* by **Jackie Boy and Little Walter** (Sun 174) – has failed to hit stores, due to lack of interest from radio stations.

21 Deciding to cash in on the success of his "Moondog Rock 'n' Roll Party" radio broadcasts, **Alan Freed** has organized the first rock 'n' roll concert. The Moondog Coronation Ball, promoted by Freed and Lew Platt, and sponsored by Record Rendezvous, takes place at the 10,000-capacity Cleveland Arena on Euclid Avenue. Scheduled to perform are the **Dominoes**, **Paul Williams & His Hucklebuckers**, **Danny Cobb**, **Tiny Grimes & His Rockin' Highlanders**, **Varetta Dillard**, and others, with Freed himself set to broadcast live from the event on WJW radio. Tickets sell for $1.50 and $1.75. However, after 10,091 ticket holders have been admitted to the arena – and with another 20,000 youngsters still trying to gain access – Captain Emmett Porter of the Fire Preventive Bureau orders the doors to be closed, while police and firemen try to disperse the throng. Even with the doors closed, the fans go wild, both inside and outside the arena: doors are smashed, glass is broken, and fights break out while Paul Williams & His Hucklebuckers are on stage playing their first number. Finally, the fire marshals decide to close the whole thing down. At what will come to be widely regarded as the first major rock 'n' roll concert in music history, only one song is actually played. (In recalling the events of this historic night during an interview with the **New York Post** in October 1956, Alan Freed will remark: "Everybody had such a good time breaking into the arena they didn't ask for their money back.") Over the next two years, some 90,000 music fans will attend various "Moondog Balls" organized by Freed throughout Ohio.

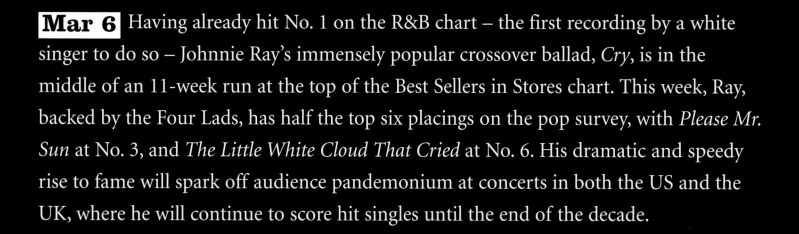

"Johnnie Ray raised more commotion than all the other crooners put together."

New York Daily News, April 1952

Mar 6 Having already hit No. 1 on the R&B chart – the first recording by a white singer to do so – Johnnie Ray's immensely popular crossover ballad, *Cry*, is in the middle of an 11-week run at the top of the Best Sellers in Stores chart. This week, Ray, backed by the Four Lads, has half the top six placings on the pop survey, with *Please Mr. Sun* at No. 3, and *The Little White Cloud That Cried* at No. 6. His dramatic and speedy rise to fame will spark off audience pandemonium at concerts in both the US and the UK, where he will continue to score hit singles until the end of the decade.

Johnnie Ray quickly managed to position himself as one of the leading pop balladeers of his day, despite having worn a hearing aid since the age of 14. He was alternately nicknamed the "Nabob of Sob" and the "Prince of Wails."

Ray Charles at Atlantic... The UK's first singles chart is published...

Harry Belafonte

Elmore James

Harry Belafonte had embarked on his singing career while studying drama in New York, discovering folk music in the early 1950s... Elmore James's mastery of the slide guitar would influence many future rock guitarists.

April

3 **Harry Belafonte**, the Harlem-born folk-calypso pioneer originally signed to Jubilee Records in 1949 as a pop vocalist, records his first songs for the RCA Victor label at the Manhattan Center in New York City, though he will have to wait until 1956 for his calypso-laced recordings of *Day-O (Banana Boat Song)* and *Mary's Boy Child* to catch on.

5 Electric guitar blues innovator **Elmore James**'s version of **Robert Johnson**'s *Dust My Broom* enters the R&B chart, set to hit No. 9 and become James's signature hit. It is the first of many popular cover versions of compositions by the legendary Johnson, made by both his contemporaries and future blues artists.

19 Hosted by Ed Sullivan, Willie Bryant, and Art Ford, the full network of the Mutual Broadcasting System presents "The Concert At Midnight," live from Carnegie Hall, New York City. This top-drawer jazz/blues event features **Dinah Washington** singing her current R&B hit, *Wheel Of Fortune*, and performances by **Sugar Ray Robinson**, **Louis Jordan**, **Sonny Parker**, **Lionel Hampton**, **Debbie Andrews**, **Lynn Hope**, and pianist **Eddie Heywood**.

July

10 Sam Phillips records the last of five **Howlin' Wolf** sessions. Offered a cash advance, Wolf will sign directly to Chess Records, taking his guitarists, **Hubert Sumlin** and **Willie Johnson**, with him to Chicago.

12 Rejected by the Imperial label (which favors **Fats Domino**), pianist, composer, and vocalist **Lloyd Price**'s re-recorded version of his own *Lawdy Miss Clawdy* – with Domino on piano – hits R&B No. 1 for the first of seven weeks. It will spawn numerous cover versions, including one by Elvis Presley.

Lloyd Price, a major new force in R&B, began leading an R&B quintet in New Orleans in 1950, while also writing and performing jingles and songs for local radio station, WBOK. *Lawdy Miss Clawdy* will be followed by two further R&B top five hits: *Oooh, Oooh, Oooh* and *Restless Heart*.

September

11 Atlantic Records having bought his contract from the Swingtime label in June for $2,500, 21-year-old singer-songwriter/pianist **Ray Charles** – who has been blind since the age of seven as a result of glaucoma – begins his first recording session for Atlantic at the label's office/studio at 234 West 56th Street, New York. Space in the room is tight, and those present have to pile one desk on top of another and push them into a corner to make room in the makeshift studio. In a three-hour session, with **Tom Dowd** engineering, **Jesse Stone** arranging, and label owners **Herb Abramson** and **Ahmet Ertegun** producing, Charles cuts *The Midnight Hour, The Sun's Gonna Shine Again, Roll With My Baby,* and *Jumpin' In The Morning. The Midnight Hour* will be released as the single, with *Roll With My Baby* – which will be reviewed by **Billboard** magazine as "Platter should do right fine in the coin boxes" – on the B-side. (With Charles as their most important signing to date, Atlantic Records has already become a significant independent label, having been formed in 1947 by Abramson and Ertegun, a Turkish immigrant, with financial backing from dentist, Dr. Vahdi Sabit. Both owners were eager to sign top jazz and blues talent like **Dizzy Gillespie**, **Sarah Vaughan**, **Professor Longhair**, **Leadbelly**, and **Sonny Terry**, before adding R&B performers such as **Ruth Brown** and **Joe Turner**. It will take two years – and the arrival of producer **Jerry Wexler** – before their signing of Charles begins to pay off.)

20 Having been arrested and jailed on August 18 for drunken behavior at the Russell Hotel in Alexander City, Alabama – and in an effort to restore his live credibility – **Hank Williams** begins his weekly Saturday night appearances on the "Louisiana Hayride," for a fee of $250 a week. Meanwhile, his *Jambayala* reaches US No. 20.

Regularly in trouble with the law, country and western superstar Hank Williams was haunted by the demons of alcohol.

Lloyd Price, based in New Orleans, pioneered a new strain of hard-rocking R&B.

27 **Johnny Ace**'s first single for the Duke label, *My Song*, which is credited to Johnny Ace with the Beale Streeters, tops the R&B chart, where it will remain for nine weeks. The 23-year-old Ace – who used his given name, John Alexander Jr., until signing with Duke earlier this year – is a fixture on the music scene of his native Memphis, having joined an R&B/blues combo run by Adolph Duncan as a pianist in 1949 before linking with **B.B. King**'s band. When King moved west to Los Angeles, and the group's singer, Bobby Bland, left to join the army, Ace took over vocals and renamed the band the **Beale Streeters**. *My Song* sets the style followed by most of Ace's subsequent releases: a sensitive baritone vocal with a subdued jazz, small-group backing, which will prove highly popular with black audiences.

> **"I was born with music inside me. Music was one of my parts. Like my ribs, my kidneys, my liver, my heart. It was a force already within me when I arrived on the scene."** Ray Charles, **Brother Ray**, 1978

October

7 "Bob Horn's Bandstand," a weekly popular music program, makes its television debut as a local show on WFIL-TV in Philadelphia, hosted by Bob Horn. Soon to become known as "American Bandstand," the series will get a new host in July 1956, in the form of a clean-cut 26-year-old named **Dick Clark**. He will relish the role, having already filled in as a substitute host during the previous year.

18 **Hank Williams** marries Billie Jean Jones in Minden, Louisiana, having divorced his first wife, Audrey, in May. He will pass out at the reception after drinking too much champagne. The couple will repeat their wedding vows twice tomorrow (Sunday), in front of a paying public, after the 3:00 pm and 7:00 pm shows that Williams is to perform at the Municipal Auditorium in New Orleans.

December

11 **Hank Williams** is arrested and jailed once again for drunken behavior, having discharged himself from the hospital in Shreveport, Louisiana, where he was admitted, suffering from acute alcohol intoxication, on October 31. Despite his rapidly deteriorating condition, Williams has been fulfilling several live engagements, meeting hostile crowds who are appalled by his drunkenness. Meanwhile, the ominously titled *I'll Never Get Out Of This World Alive* reaches US No. 20.

30 **Hank Williams** sets out from home in Montgomery, Alabama, for a New Year's Day performance at the Memorial Auditorium in Canton, Ohio, with 17-year-old Charles Carr driving the singer's blue Cadillac.

31 Needing a replacement for an ailing saxophonist in his **Johnnie Johnson Trio**, for a New Year's Eve show in St. Louis, pianist/bandleader Johnson asks a guitar-playing acquaintance, **Chuck Berry**, to fill in. The two will form a partnership that will last some 30 years.While playing evening gigs with Johnson, for the next three years the 25-year-old Berry – with a degree in cosmetology and tonsorial skills from the Poro School of Beauty Culture – will continue to work by day as a hairdresser and beautician.

31 After their plane is turned back because of bad weather in Knoxville, Tennessee, **Hank Williams** and Charles Carr book into the Andrew Johnson Hotel. Dr. Paul Cardwell is called after Williams suffers convulsions. Williams is helped into the back of the car and Carr continues driving at about 10:45 pm. In Blaine, Tennessee, Highway Patrolman Swann Kitts stops Carr and books him for reckless driving. He sees Williams slumped in the back seat and suggests he looks dead. Carr continues driving.

UK SINGLES CHART

Nov 14 **The first ever UK singles chart appears in the New Musical Express. Based on sales figures from 53 stores, mainly in London and southeast England, as well as Belfast and Glasgow, the chart is collated by Ted Hull, the paper's accountant.**

1	**Al Martino** (above), *Here In My Heart*
2	**Jo Stafford**, *You Belong To Me*
3	**Nat King Cole**, *Somewhere Along The Way*
4	**Bing Crosby**, *Isle Of Innisfree*
5	**Guy Mitchell**, *Feet Up (Pat Him On The Po-Po)*
6	**Rosemary Clooney**, *Half As Much*
7	**Vera Lynn**, *Forget Me Not*
	Frankie Laine, *High Noon*
8	**Doris Day & Frankie Laine**, *Sugarbush*
	Ray Martin, *Blue Tango*
9	**Vera Lynn**, *Homing Waltz*
10	**Vera Lynn**, *Auf Wiedersehen Sweetheart*
11	**Max Bygraves**, *Cowpuncher's Cantata*
	Mario Lanza, *Because You're Mine*
12	**Johnnie Ray**, *Walking My Baby Back Home*

Jan 1953

Hank Williams dies... Jerry Wexler joins Atlantic... Presley's first recording...

Willie Mae Thornton

Ray Charles

Frank Sinatra signed with Capitol and teamed up with Nelson Riddle in a pairing that would prove highly rewarding, both commercially and critically. The first results would be heard on Sinatra's first two Capitol album releases, *Songs For Young Lovers* and *Swing Easy*.

January

1 At 5:30 am, Charles Carr stops for directions at Burdette's Pure Oil station near Oak Hill, West Virginia. He notices that **Hank Williams**'s body feels cold, and drives to Oak Hill General Hospital where at 7:00 am Williams is pronounced dead. A note clutched in his hand reads: "We met, we lived and dear we loved, then comes that fatal day, the love that felt so dear fades away. Tonight love hathe [*sic*] one alone and lonesome, all that I could sing, I love you you [*sic*] still and always will, but that's the poison we have to pay." At 29, Hank Williams is the most successful artist in country music. At Canton Memorial Auditorium, where he was to have performed, a spotlight shines on the stage curtain as a weeping audience listens to the **Drifting Cowboys** perform *I Saw The Light* behind the drapes.

4 **Hank Williams**'s funeral is held at the City Auditorium in Montgomery. Roads into the city are thronged with 20,000 mourners. Williams leaves no will and, though the quality of his musical legacy will remain untouched, for the next 20 years his estate will be fought over by his mother, his wife, and his ex-wife. Both wives will begin touring as Mrs. Hank Williams.

"We met, we lived and dear we loved, then comes that fatal day, the love that felt so dear fades away." Note in Hank Williams's hand, January 1, 1953

April

2 **Frank Sinatra**, America's most popular actor/singer throughout the 1940s, records his first session for Capitol Records at KHJ Studios in Hollywood, taping *Lean Baby, I'm Walking Behind You, Day In Day Out,* and *Don't Make A Beggar Of Me*. The session marks the beginning of a new era for the performer, as Sinatra is emerging from a disastrous spell following a throat hemorrhage in April 1950, the death of his longtime publicist George Evans the same year, and his ill-fated marriage to actress Ava Gardner in 1951. Last year, Universal Pictures declined to renew his acting deal, CBS television canceled "The Frank Sinatra Show," and he was dropped by his longtime record label Columbia. A few months later, however, Capitol Records' A&R (Artist & Repertoire) executive Alan Livingston offered "the Voice" a renewable one-year contract (though with a meager five percent royalty rate). This first session for Capitol is under the guidance of Sinatra's longtime arranger, Axel Stordahl, but Livingston shrewdly introduces the singer to the label's youngest arranger, 32-year-old **Nelson Riddle**, who has already worked with Bing Crosby and Nat King Cole, among others.

"You ain't nothing but a Hound Dog," lamented ex-Hot Harlem Revue performer Willie Mae Thornton... Ray Charles said, "My music had roots which I'd dug up from my own childhood, musical roots buried in the darkest soil."

18 **Willie Mae "Big Mama" Thornton** spends the first of five weeks topping the R&B chart with *Hound Dog*, written by Jerry Leiber and Mike Stoller. Further down the chart, an "answer" record, *Bear Cat*, by local WDIA Memphis DJ **Rufus Thomas** (credited to Rufus Hound Dog Thomas Jr.) gives Sam Phillips's Sun Records its first chart entry.

May

5 Five students at Roosevelt High School in Gary, Indiana – bass vocalist **Gerald Gregory**, baritone **Opal Courtney**, tenors **Ernest Warren** and **Will Jackson**, and lead singer, **James "Pookie" Hudson** – initially performing as the Hudsonaires and now known as the **Spaniels**, record *Baby It's You, Sloppy Drunk, Since I Fell For You*, and *Bounce*, in the first ever sessions for the newly formed Vee-Jay label. The company has been created by **Vivian Carter** ("Vee") and her husband **James Bracken** ("Jay"). They run a record store in Gary – Vivian's Shop – and Vivian has a popular R&B show on local radio station WGRY. Convinced that the Spaniels have commercial potential, they have borrowed $500 to take the group into the studio and press enough copies for local distribution. *Baby It's You* (Vee-Jay 101) will make an immediate impact, forcing Vee-Jay to cut a national distribution deal with Chance Records

Jerry Wexler and Ahmet Ertegun

A new partnership began at Atlantic Records, with Jerry Wexler given an R&B brief by his boss Ahmet Ertegun... The Drifters became one of Wexler's earliest success stories.

The Drifters

in Chicago to meet demand. The record will make the R&B top ten in September, but more importantly it marks the first step by a tiny independent label that – within three years – will become the most successful black-owned record company in the US.

13 New Yorker **Jerry Wexler** joins Atlantic Records. A former **Billboard** music trade magazine journalist, he is credited with introducing the term "rhythm and blues" (replacing the increasingly controversial "race music") in an essay written for the **Saturday Review of Literature**. Through his work at **Billboard**, Wexler frequently met Atlantic boss **Ahmet Ertegun**, who asked him to come to work as a producer when label co-founder and producer **Herb Abramson** was summoned back to active duty by the US Army, to perform dental work in Germany. Wexler is made vice-president of the company, given the option to purchase 13 percent of the business for $2,063.25, and instructed by Ertegun to produce R&B music specifically targeted at the black market.

The close-harmony quintet, the Spaniels, made the first ever recordings for the fledgling Vee-Jay label.

17 **Ray Charles** returns to Atlantic's New York studio to cut six more sides: *It Should Have Been Me*, *Losing Hand*, *Heartbreaker*, *Sinner's Prayer*, *Mess Around*, and *Funny But I Still Love You*. Once again they feature Jesse Stone's arrangement, with Ertegun at the helm. During the recording of *Losing Hand*, the studio phone rings with news that Charles's mother has died.

23 The Essex Record label – a Philadelphia-based company established in 1951 by local media entrepreneur David L. Miller – enjoys its second big pop hit with *Crazy Man Crazy* by **Bill Haley & His Comets**. It enters the Best Sellers in Stores chart at No. 15, one place above the week's other new entry, **Mantovani**'s *The "Moulin Rouge" Theme (Where Is Your Heart)*. Having cut several commercially unsuccessful singles with his backing band, the Saddlemen, for Keystone Records, and for Miller's previous label, Holiday Records, over the past three years, 27-year-old Haley – who has been performing as a singer and guitarist since 1944 – has revised his earlier cowboy image and changed the name of his backing unit to the Comets. Fusing elements of country music, R&B, and western swing, *Crazy Man Crazy* is the first rock 'n' roll record to make the pop charts.

July

18 Having received his high school diploma from L.C. Humes High, Memphis, on June 14, and now employed by M.B. Parker Machinists' Shop, a shy, East Tupelo-born, 18-year-old singer, **Elvis Presley** – with his well-used acoustic guitar in hand – drops in at the Memphis Recording Service and asks Marion Keisker, office manager for Sam Phillips, if he can make a private recording. He pays $3.98 plus tax for one disc, and sings *My Happiness* – a reworking of a major 1948 hit for several artists, including Jon and Sandra Steele – and *That's When Your Heartaches Begin*, a song originally recorded by the Ink Spots in 1941, and revised in a country version by Bob Lamb. (Phillips and Keisker will report different recollections of the precise sequence of events: the former will insist that he was present at the session, while Keisker will maintain that he was not, and that she made the following memo for her absent boss, the misspelled note: "Elvis Pressley. Good ballad singer. Hold.")

August

9 At the suggestion of Atlantic Records head Ahmet Ertegun, his latest signing, the **Drifters** – an R&B vocal group formed to showcase lead singer, and ex-Dominoes vocalist, **Clyde McPhatter** – record the Jesse Stone-penned *Money Honey*. On November 21, the single will become the first of four US R&B chart-toppers for the group during the decade. The Drifters are also the first group to be produced by recently appointed label vice-president, Jerry Wexler.

September

1 Already a popular performing duo around their native Lubbock, Texas, **Buddy & Bob** audition for Lubbock country radio station KDAV's "Sunday Party," a show open to anyone who wishes to perform. The pairing comprises **Buddy Holly** – real name Charles Holley – and **Bob Montgomery**. Mixing bluegrass, country, and R&B, and adding **Larry Welborn** on bass, the group will earn a regular Sunday afternoon slot, a segment that will become known as "The Buddy and Bob Show."

November

6 The BBC places a restricted ban on the songs *Answer Me* – about to hit the top in successive weeks in two versions by **David Whitfield** and **Frankie Laine** – and **Lee Lawrence**'s *Crying In The Chapel*, following protests from religious groups. The ban means that every airing of either song must be approved by management, with the apparent goal of limiting the number of times they are played. Whitfield will re-record his version of *Answer Me* for Decca with revised lyrics, in the hope of overcoming the objections.

December

4 Having cut two sides in August at J&M Studios, New Orleans, **Ray Charles** – currently in residence at the city's Pelican Club – records four more tracks (*Don't You Know*, *Nobody Cares*, *Ray's Blues*, and *Mr. Charles Blues*) at radio station WDSU, with Ahmet Ertegun and Jerry Wexler producing.

1954

BILL HALEY & HIS COMETS

June 3 ***(We're Gonna) Rock Around The Clock*****, recorded on April 12, initially charts for a week in the US, at No. 23. With a current sales tally of some 75,000 copies, Decca decides to pick up its option on the group.**

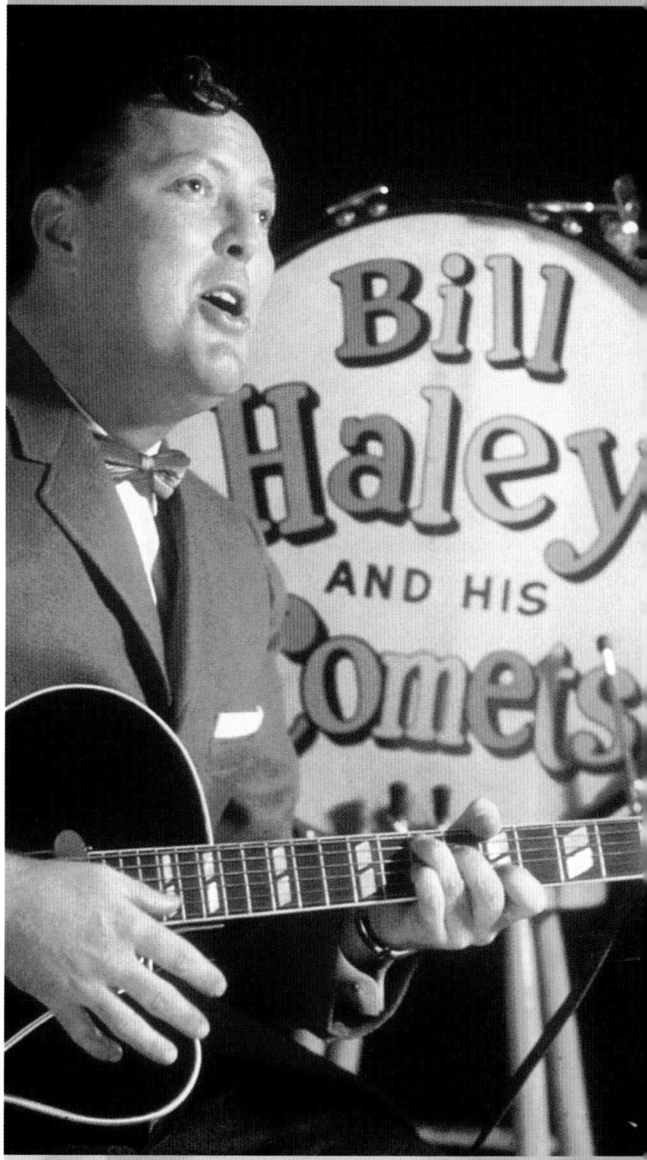

Bill Haley & His Comets had included *(We're Gonna) Rock Around the Clock*, originally recorded by Sunny Dae & His Knights, as an increasingly popular number in their live set over the previous six months.

Shake, Rattle And Roll... **Bill Haley & His Comets...** ***Sh-Boom*** **by the Chords – and the Crew Cuts...**

Muddy Waters, signed with Chess Records from the label's inception, recorded a seminal stream of electric blues classics.

January

4 **Elvis Presley** returns to the Memphis Recording Service to cut a second private record. He sings *It Wouldn't Be The Same Without You* – an old Jimmy Wakely number – and a cover of Joni James's *I'll Never Stand In Your Way*. This time, Sam Phillips asks for his address and a phone number, promising to contact him soon about trying something in the studio together.

7 **Muddy Waters** records *Hoochie Coochie Man* in Chicago with the illustrious session crew of **Little Walter** (harmonica), **Jimmy Rogers** (guitar), **Willie Dixon** (bass), and **Elgin Evans** (drums). Released on the Chess label, it will become Waters' biggest R&B hit, reaching No. 3.

February

1 **Big Joe Turner** cuts *Shake, Rattle And Roll*, written by Atlantic Records' arranger, Jesse Stone (under the name Charles Calhoun). It will top the chart on June 12. Turner, a 43-year-old blues vocalist from Kansas City, has been recording since the early 1940s. Signed with Atlantic in 1951, he enjoyed his first R&B No. 1 with *Honey Hush* last November.

4 In their fourth recording session for Atlantic Records, the **Drifters** cut four sides in what will turn out to be one of the most productive sessions in the history of popular music. The numbers are *Honey Love*, which will be banned from jukeboxes by the Memphis police for its suggestive lyrics, the gospel-driven *What'cha Gonna Do* (in the view of producer Jerry Wexler, the best Drifters record ever) and two Christmas tunes made famous by Bing Crosby in the 1940s: *The Bells Of St. Mary's* and one of the defining interpretations of *White Christmas*.

15 The **Platters**, a harmony-led vocal quartet, sign a management agreement with **Buck Ram**. Formed in Los Angeles last year, the group comprises lead singer **Tony Williams**, tenor **David Lynch**, bass **Herb Reed**, and baritone **Alex Hodge**. Ram will steer them to the Federal label, where – with **Paul Robi** replacing Hodge and a female singer, **Zola Taylor**, added to the line-up – they will record a Ram composition, *Only You*. Unsuccessful at Federal, Ram will sign the group to Mercury Records next year, where they will recut *Only You* and score their first million-seller.

March

20 **Billboard** reports that all the major record labels will introduce state-of-the-art "high fidelity" recordings by the end of 1954. During the year, the US market's $205 million sales will be divided: 52 percent for 78rpm discs, 28 percent for 45rpm, and 20 percent for the still relatively new LP format.

April

12 **Bill Haley & His Comets** make their first recordings for Decca Records at the Pythian Temple Studios in New York. Haley has left Essex and signed to Decca at the behest of songwriter Jimmy Myers. Using the pseudonym Jimmy DeKnight, Myers has co-written *(We're Gonna) Rock Around The Clock* with Max Freedman. He is eager for Haley to record it and has initiated an option deal with producer Milt Gabler, Decca's head of artist acquisition, who now directs the session. With the help of guitarist **Danny Cedrone**, who has played with Haley before, and studio drummer **Billy Guesack**, they record the beat-driven *(We're Gonna) Rock Around The Clock* – featuring Comets bassist **Al Rex**'s distinctive "slap-bass" style – and *Thirteen Women*, an R&B tune by Dickie Thompson.

May

8 On the grounds that the record is "too suggestive," the BBC bans **Johnnie Ray**'s cover version of the Drifters' *Such A Night*, following what it calls "a raft of complaints from listeners."

June

7 With **Big Joe Turner**'s original version set to hit No. 1 on the R&B chart, **Bill Haley & His Comets** record *Shake, Rattle And Roll* for Decca. The four-hour session at Pythian Temple Studios also yields *See You Later, Alligator* and *ABC Boogie*. During the recording, the suggestive lyrics of *Shake, Rattle And Roll* are slightly altered by Haley for the white market, although one line, "I'm like a one-eyed cat peeping in a sea-food store," remains unchanged.

July

3 *Sh-Boom* – recorded by Bronx-based R&B vocal quintet the **Chords**, and released by Atlantic's Cat label – enters the US R&B chart, set to hit No. 2. The Chords' only commercially successful disc, the infectious song has immediately been covered to even wider sales success by the **Crew Cuts**, an all-white male vocal quartet based in Toronto. This "white pop" revision of an essentially "black R&B" song is an early example of what will become common practice. The Crew Cuts will repeat it next February with their second million-selling single – their version of the **Penguins**' December 1954 hit, *Earth Angel*.

4 At the suggestion of Sam Phillips, **Elvis Presley** visits Memphis guitarist **Scotty Moore**, who runs the local club band Doug Poindexter's Starlite Wranglers and is keen to record new songs for Sun. Moore asks Presley to perform for him and his bass-playing friend **Bill Black**.

5 In the evening, Sam Phillips oversees a recording session with **Elvis Presley**, **Scotty Moore**, and **Bill Black**. They play Leon Payne's 1949 country ballad chart-topper, *I Love You Because*, and the 1950 Bing Crosby hit, *Harbor Lights*. During a break, Presley fools around with an uptempo romp through Arthur Crudup's blues number, *That's All Right*, and is joined first by Black, and then by Moore, in an impromptu jam session. Phillips – hearing in Presley the particular "something" for which he has been searching in vain for three years – has them repeat it with tapes running.

6 **Elvis Presley**'s recording session continues with further experimentation, including a tryout of Bill Monroe's *Blue Moon Of Kentucky*, which is accelerated with a racing tempo. **Scotty Moore** suggests the strange hybrid of (black) blues and (white) country will offend the southern radio and musical community, but Phillips hears commercial potential: he will couple a later version of *Blue Moon Of Kentucky* with *That's All Right* as the first Sun single.

The Chordettes' signature barbershop hit *Mister Sandman* would give the burgeoning Cadence Records its first No. 1 in November.

8 Sam Phillips takes acetates of **Elvis Presley**'s tracks to DJ **Dewey Phillips** at Memphis radio station WHBQ. He rates *That's All Right* highly and plays it on his R&B show, "Red Hot And Blue," just after 9:30 pm. The switchboard immediately lights up with requests for repeat spins. Dewey Phillips phones Presley's home to invite him to the studio for an interview, but Presley – warned by Sam Phillips of the single's likely airing and unable to bear hearing his voice on the radio – is at the Suzore No. 2 movie theater watching "Goldtown Ghost Riders." His parents go looking for him and take him to WHBQ, where Phillips puts him at his ease. Memphis learns that this hot new R&B singer is a local white 19-year-old, who will soon be given the title "King of Western Bop."

12 **Elvis Presley** signs a recording contract with Sun, and a one-year personal management deal with **Scotty Moore**, according to which Moore will receive "ten percent of all earnings from engagements, appearances and bookings made by him." Presley quits his day job.

17 The first Newport Jazz Festival is held at Newport's Casino Clubhouse in Rhode Island. **Eddie Condon** and his band open the world's first jazz festival with *Muskrat Ramble*. More than 6,000 people will see artists such as **Dizzy Gillespie**, the **Modern Jazz Quartet**, the **Gerry Mulligan Quartet**, **Ella Fitzgerald**, and **Pee Wee Russell** on the first of the two days.

18 Signed to Cadence Records in New York by its founder, **Archie Bleyer**, the **Chordettes** – Janet Ertel, her sister-in-law Carol Bushman, Lynn Evans, and Margie Needham – record *Mister Sandman*. They have been regulars since 1949 on the "Arthur Godfrey's Talent Scouts" radio show, for which Bleyer was musical director until December 1952. *Mister Sandman*, written by Pat Ballard and recently a B-side for Vaughn Monroe, is produced by Bleyer, who is also responsible for the lone male voice featured on the recording, saying "Yes."

Steered by manager/producer/songwriter Buck Ram and fronted by Tony Williams, the Platters became the era's No. 1 harmony vocal group.

July 1954

Presley hits the airwaves... LaVern Baker's first hit... Johnny Ace – an early casualty...

Elvis Presley

LaVern Baker

19 *That's All Right* and *Blue Moon Of Kentucky* is released as **Elvis Presley**'s Sun label debut. It will top the local chart by the end of the month, with action on both sides: Dewey Phillips plays *That's All Right*, while Sleepy Eye John, Uncle Richard, and most other Memphis DJs spin *Blue Moon Of Kentucky*.

20 **Elvis Presley**, **Scotty Moore**, and **Bill Black** perform in public for the first time – as the **Blue Moon Boys** – playing on a flatbed truck at the opening of a new drugstore on Lamar Avenue, Memphis, to a swelling and increasingly excited crowd. Local engagements at the Eagle's Nest and Bel Air clubs will follow, sometimes with the Starlite Wranglers, but Moore and Black will soon leave their band to work solely with Presley.

30 Local agent Bob Neal has booked **Elvis Presley** for two performances in Memphis, low on a bill headlined by **Slim Whitman**. After a polite reception given to two country ballads in the afternoon, Presley is advised by Dewey Phillips to perform uptempo material in the evening. He sings *Good Rockin' Tonight* and *That's All Right*, complete with rhythmic leg and body movements. The sensual performance drives the audience wild. Presley exits bewildered by screams and shouts that all but drown the music, and is pushed back by Phillips to encore, to a similar reception. Established country artist **Webb Pierce**, waiting to follow him, stands stunned and uncomprehending.

August

1 **Fats Domino**, **Muddy Waters**, **Buddy Johnson**, **Little Walter**, the **Clovers**, and the **Orioles** take part in **Alan Freed**'s Moondog Jubilee of Stars Under the Stars concert, at Ebbets Field in Brooklyn, New York.

6 Gale's Rhythm & Blues Show, a caravan tour featuring **Roy Hamilton**, the **Drifters**, and the **Spaniels**, begins its US itinerary in Cleveland.

13 **Chuck Berry** allegedly records solo for the first time, cutting *Oh Maria* and *I Hope These Words Will Find You Well* during sessions for Joe Alexander & the Cubans at the Premier Studios in St. Louis. The recordings will be released on the Ballad label, credited to Charles Berryn. Berry still plays with club combo the Johnnie Johnson Trio, with himself on guitar, Johnson on piano, and Ebby Harding on drums.

19 **B.B. King**, the **Platters**, and **Johnny Otis** top an all-star R&B bill at a sellout concert at the Savoy Ballroom in Hollywood.

21 Having returned to the Sun studio to record the Richard Rodgers and Lorenz Hart pop standard, *Blue Moon*, two days ago, **Elvis Presley** plays his first gig outside Tennessee in Gladewater, Texas.

September

8 **Alan "Moondog" Freed**, with a contract guaranteeing him an annual salary of $75,000 plus percentage rights, makes his first broadcast on the New York station WINS. The blind street musician Louis Hardin, who has been using the name "Moondog" since 1947, and who performs on the corner of 54th Street and 6th Avenue, will haul Freed into court in November and successfully enjoin the celebrity from using the name on his radio show.

October

2 Sam Phillips has secured a booking for **Elvis Presley** on Nashville's Grand Ole Opry show, broadcast live from the Ryman Auditorium. The singer is introduced by Hank Snow and sings *Blue Moon Of Kentucky*, but fails to impress the staid audience, or the talent booker Jim Denny, who suggests he should resume his job as a truck driver.

16 **Elvis Presley** performs on another country music radio show, the "Louisiana Hayride," broadcast live on KWKH from the Shreveport Municipal Auditorium. After singing *That's All Right* and *Blue Moon Of Kentucky* to an enthusiastic live audience, he is asked to return next week. Prior to his third appearance, station director Horace Logan will sign him to a year's contract, at $18 per weekly slot, with **Bill Black** and **Scotty Moore** earning $12 each per show. Presley will also be contracted to sing a commercial for one of the show's sponsors, Southern Made Doughnuts.

20 **LaVern Baker**, the latest signing to Atlantic, records *Tweedle Dee* – produced by Jerry Wexler and Ahmet Ertegun – in New York City. It will become her first hit record.

November

1 American crooners **Frankie Laine** (currently in the UK top 20 chart with three hits) and **Guy Mitchell** appear at the Royal Variety Performance, held at the London Palladium.

> **"Presley is a potent new chanter who can rock a tune for either the country or the R&B markets... A strong new talent."**
>
> **Billboard** review of Elvis Presley's debut single, August 7, 1954

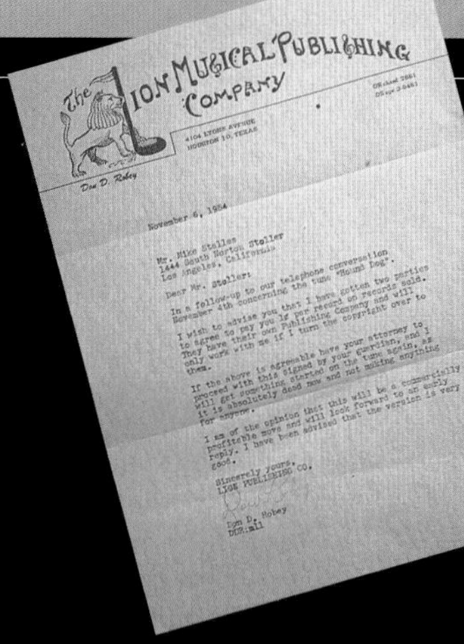

Sheet music remained a profitable business throughout the 1950s, particularly for vocal standards such as Sammy Cahn and Jule Styne's *Three Coins In The Fountain*... When Mike Stoller received a letter in November telling him that his song *Hound Dog* was "absolutely dead," little did he know that the up-and-coming Elvis Presley would record it in July 1956.

Ray Charles

Nat King Cole

Elvis Presley released his first single on the Sun label... The R&B diva LaVern Baker recorded her first hit for Atlantic, having signed with the label in 1953... Her labelmate Ray Charles found his true voice with *I Got A Woman*, which would top the R&B chart in summer 1955... Nat King Cole, known to jazz fans as a great swing pianist, was finding wider fame as a pop balladeer.

11 With the embryonic rock 'n' roll genre quickly gathering momentum, **Bill Haley**'s second Decca single, *Shake, Rattle And Roll*, hits US No. 7. (An American Hockey League team, the Springfield Indians, will adopt Haley's version, playing the disc before and after every home game and after each goal scored by the team.)

15 **Joan Weber**, an unknown 18-year-old, sings *Let Me Go, Lover* on the "Studio One" show on CBS-TV. Originally titled *Let Me Go, Devil*, it was recorded last year by Georgia Shaw, but Weber's performance will catapult it into one of the biggest one-hit wonders of the decade.

18 **Ray Charles** records four new tracks with his backing band, including saxophonist **David "Fathead" Newman**. *Blackjack*, *I Got A Woman*, *Greenbacks*, and *Come Back Baby* are cut at the city's WGST radio station. The musicians have to break at the top of each hour to allow the station to broadcast the news.

23 Agent Bob Neal, with Scotty Moore's agreement, informally assumes the management of **Elvis Presley**. He will book the trio (billed as Elvis Presley, the Hillbilly Cat, & His Blue Moon Boys), at Nashville's Country Convention, then get them one-night dates all over the south.

30 With his current hit, *Hajji Baba*, on its way to US No. 14, **Nat King Cole** performs the first of six concerts on consecutive nights at Harlem's Apollo Theater in New York.

Unlike the majority of early rockers, singer-songwriter/ guitarist Chuck Berry wrote all of his own hits.

December

17 **Bill Haley**'s *Shake, Rattle And Roll* becomes the first rock 'n' roll record to chart in the UK, set to peak at No. 4. The British pop chart is otherwise dominated by more mainstream pop imports like **Doris Day**, **Johnnie Ray**, **Frank Sinatra**, and **Rosemary Clooney**, and homegrown pop veterans such as **Vera Lynn** and **Winifred Atwell**.

25 Having been named earlier in the month as Most Promising Artist of 1954 by music trade publication **Cash Box**, **Johnny Ace** – who has been drinking vodka all evening – shoots himself shortly after 11:00 pm, during an intermission at a "Negro Christmas Dance" at the City Auditorium in Houston. He has already fired the gun at his girlfriend, Olivia Gibbs, and her friend Mary Carter, though it did not go off on either occasion. The cause of death will be given as "playing Russian roulette." (To embellish what is perhaps the first rock 'n' roll fatality, stories abound about a hired killer climbing through Ace's dressing room window.)

30 **Frank Sinatra** opens a scheduled four-week engagement at New York's Paramount Theater (though the shows will prove so popular that he will be booked for an additional month). Some 400 policemen are called out to curb crowd excitement, in what is an early example of pop fan hysteria – especially among young teenage girls.

ROOTS **During these years: Johnny Otis, a scouting talent for the King label, discovers Jackie Wilson – who has been singing with street corner group, the Thrillers – in a talent show at Detroit's Paradise Theater... at Pacoima Junior High, Ritchie Valens builds a solid-body electric guitar (which he will use until success pays for a Fender Stratocaster), after learning to play acoustic Spanish guitar (right-handed, despite being naturally left-handed) two years earlier... aspiring songwriters Neil Sedaka and Howard Greenfield meet for the first time, when Greenfield knocks on Sedaka's door; the first song they write together is *My Life's Devotion*... 12-year-old Paul Anka gives his first paid public performance, in a talent contest in which he impersonates Johnnie Ray... both sixth-graders at Forest Hills School in New York, Paul Simon plays the White Rabbit and Arthur Garfunkel the Cheshire Cat in a school production of "Alice in Wonderland"... and James Hendrix buys an acoustic guitar for $5 from a friend of his father Al; being left-handed, he turns it upside down and teaches himself to play by listening to records by bluesmen Muddy Waters, Elmore James, and B.B. King...**

(We're Gonna) Rock Around The Clock

1955

No.1 US SINGLES

- **Jan 8** Mr. Sandman **Chordettes**
- **Jan 29** Let Me Go, Lover **Joan Weber**
- **Feb 12** Hearts Of Stone **Fontane Sisters**
- **Feb 19** Sincerely **McGuire Sisters**
- **Apr 2** The Ballad Of Davy Crockett **Bill Hayes**
- **May 7** Cherry Pink And Apple Blossom White **Perez Prado**
- **July 16** (We're Gonna) Rock Around The Clock **Bill Haley & His Comets**
- **Sept 10** Yellow Rose Of Texas **Mitch Miller**
- **Oct 15** Love Is A Many-Splendored Thing **Four Aces**
- **Oct 22** Yellow Rose Of Texas **Mitch Miller**
- **Oct 29** Love Is A Many-Splendored Thing **Four Aces**
- **Nov 5** Autumn Leaves **Roger Williams**
- **Nov 19** Love Is A Many-Splendored Thing **Four Aces**
- **Dec 10** Sixteen Tons **Tennessee Ernie Ford**

No.1 UK SINGLES

- **Jan 8** Finger Of Suspicion **Dickie Valentine**
- **Jan 15** Mambo Italiano **Rosemary Clooney**
- **Jan 22** Finger Of Suspicion **Dickie Valentine**
- **Feb 5** Mambo Italiano **Rosemary Clooney**
- **Feb 19** Softly Softly **Ruby Murray**
- **Mar 12** Give Me Your Word **Tennessee Ernie Ford**
- **Apr 30** Cherry Pink And Apple Blossom White **Perez Prado**
- **May 14** Stranger In Paradise **Tony Bennett**
- **May 28** Cherry Pink And Apple Blossom White **Eddie Calvert**
- **June 25** Unchained Melody **Jimmy Young**
- **July 16** Dreamboat **Alma Cogan**
- **July 30** Rose Marie **Slim Whitman**
- **Oct 15** The Man From Laramie **Jimmy Young**
- **Nov 12** Hernando's Hideaway **Johnston Brothers**
- **Nov 26** (We're Gonna) Rock Around The Clock **Bill Haley & His Comets**
- **Dec 17** Christmas Alphabet **Dickie Valentine**

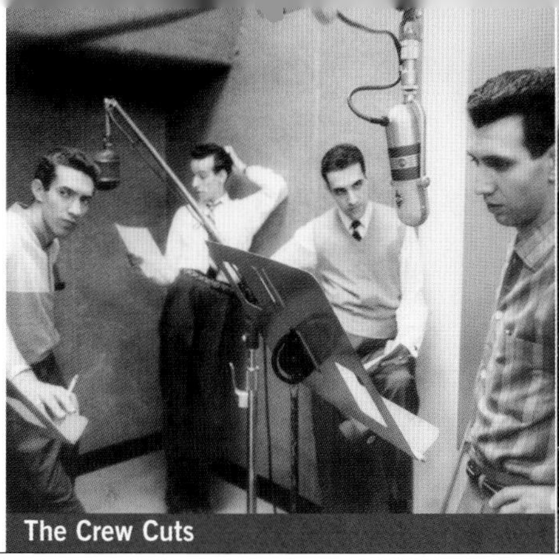
The Crew Cuts

The Penguins

Several white vocal acts borrowed heavily from the black originals, notably the clean-cut Crew Cuts... The Penguins, a Los Angeles-based vocal quartet, started the year with the chart-topping classic, *Earth Angel.*

To the horror of many – but the excitement of a growing fanbase – it became clear in 1955 that rock 'n' roll was no passing fad. On July 5, the mild-mannered **Bill Haley** reached US No. 1 with *(We're Gonna) Rock Around The Clock*. It became rock 'n' roll's first international hit, topping the British pop chart in November. Here was proof that a white artist could harness R&B to create an original rock 'n' roll sound – and reach a mass audience. Another budding rock 'n' roll talent also made his chart debut, as **Chuck Berry**'s *Maybellene* climbed to No. 5. (Both songs are on the Rock and Roll Hall of Fame's list of the 500 most influential songs.) Berry was on a roster of growing promise at Chess Records, having been introduced to the label by **Muddy Waters**, the most distinguished blues artist of the day, whose Mississippi-rooted, down-home style was to have a huge impact on generations to come – including Bob Dylan, Jimi Hendrix, Eric Clapton, and the Rolling Stones.

Bill Haley and Chuck Berry were veterans compared to the year's emerging stars. **Elvis Presley** turned 20 in January; **Buddy Holly** was still a teenager at the end of the year; **James Brown** was 22; **Johnny Cash**, **Carl Perkins**, and **Little Richard** all celebrated their 23rd birthdays during 1955. Elvis was rapidly building an audience of teenagers with his rockabilly songs and provocative stage presence.

R&B was highly influential in shaping many early rock 'n' roll artists, but its exponents rarely got the credit they deserved. Better record distribution and more radio airplay were crucial advantages for white artists. **Fats Domino**'s *Ain't It A Shame* (also among the Hall of Fame 500 influentials) was significantly outstripped by **Pat Boone**'s cover. The all-white **Crew Cuts** enjoyed huge success with the all-black **Penguins**' *Earth Angel* – although the latter's version has proved more enduring.

Unsurprisingly, R&B flourished more in the urban, less segregated, northern areas of the US, especially Chicago and New York. Early rock 'n' roll was a southern phenomenon – with Memphis as its pulse. Elvis recorded five songs at Sun's tiny Memphis studio in 1955; Carl Perkins recorded the seminal *Blue Suede Shoes*; and Johnny Cash cut *Cry, Cry, Cry* there.

The "package tour" began in earnest, with influential New York DJ **Alan Freed** assembling and promoting many shows. Segregation might have been outlawed in 1954, but concerts rarely included both white and black artists. Fats Domino, the **Drifters**, and the **Moonglows** toured together; Elvis, Johnny Cash, and Carl Perkins appeared on a different (all-white) bill.

Television – ever mindful of the youth audience – began to take notice of the new genre. But despite its growing popularity in the US, rock 'n' roll was still the upstart. Britain endured an even greater dearth, as it awaited a tidal wave of influential rock 'n' roll imports. But with *(We're Gonna) Rock Around The Clock* having opened a window in both countries, it wouldn't be long before rock 'n' roll took the door off its hinges.

"Hello everybody, how y'all tonight? This is Alan Freed, king of the Moondoggers!"

Alan Freed's trademark introduction on his radio show

The jukebox arrives in British coffee bars... Elvis meets "Col." Tom Parker...

Elvis Presley, performing in his regular weekly slot on the "Louisiana Hayride," was attracting a growing fanbase.

January

2 **Johnny Ace**'s funeral, at the Clayborn Temple African Methodist Episcopal Church in Memphis, is attended by 5,000 people. A host of blues contemporaries pay their respects: **Little Junior Parker**, **Roscoe Gordon**, and **Harold Conner** are pallbearers; **Don Robey**, **B.B. King**, and **Willie Mae Thornton** are honorary bearers.

8 **Elvis Presley** is still performing on the "Louisiana Hayride," broadcast Saturdays on KWKH. Tonight – on his 20th birthday – station DJ Frank Page tells the audience that Elvis is wearing crocodile-skin shoes with pink socks. Elvis sings *That's All Right, Hearts Of Stone, Blue Moon Of Kentucky,* and *Fool Fool Fool.*

14 **Alan Freed** stages his Rock 'n' Roll Ball at the St. Nicholas Arena in Harlem. **Fats Domino**, **Big Joe Turner**, the **Drifters**, **Buddy & Ella Johnson**, **Dakota Staton**, **Al Sears**, **Red Prysock**, the **Harptones**, **Babs Gonzales**, **Nolan Lewis**, the **Clovers**, the **Moonglows**, the **Moonlighters**, and the **Rivileers** perform.

15 Issued by RCA and credited to **Chet Atkins** and his Gallopin' Guitar, Atkins's first solo chart disc – an instrumental version of the Chordettes' current smash, *Mister Sandman* – enters the US Country chart, set to reach No. 13. It is taken from his debut solo album, *Chet Atkins' Gallopin' Guitar*, released last year. Atkins – a former country DJ, fired eight times by different stations over musical differences – was already an accomplished guitarist when he first performed at the Grand Ole Opry in 1946. His extensive, and intensive, recording career will see sales of 35 million-plus, and from 1957 he will also head the country division of RCA in Nashville, overseeing recordings by Presley, among others, in the 1960s.

17 EMI, Britain's biggest record company, signs a contract to buy Capitol Records in the US, issuing the following statement: "The Directors of EMI announce they have entered into a contract to purchase the majority of the 476,230 common shares of Capitol Records Incorporated of California U.S.A. at the price of 17.50 dollars per share." Capitol was the creation of songwriters Johnny Mercer and Buddy De Sylva in 1942, and its roster currently includes **Nat King Cole**, **Dean Martin**, **Peggy Lee**, **Les Paul & Mary Ford**, **Jo Stafford**, and the recently acquired **Frank Sinatra**.

22 **Carl Perkins** records *Movie Magg* and *Turn Around* at his first Sun recording session. They will be issued on Sam Phillips's new label, Flip Records, but will receive little attention. Even so, *Turn Around* will remain a favorite with Perkins, who will later say: "It is a song I wrote because I felt that way about the woman I married. I felt that if ever she was in trouble or ever she felt lonely, she'd just turn around, I'd be following her, I'd be there."

28 **Fats Domino** begins a 42-date US tour in New York on the Top Ten R&B Show. Other featured acts include the **Clovers**, **Big Joe Turner**, **Faye Adams**, and the **Moonglows** – an R&B vocal quintet from Louisville, who signed with Chess Records last year and are currently riding high with their recent chart-topper, *Sincerely*.

30 In Britain, the age of the jukebox arrives, accelerated by its appearance at the Amusement Trades Exhibition in London. John Haddock, president of the leading US manufacturer AMI, says an ideal location for jukeboxes would be the coffee bars that are fast becoming popular meeting places in London.

31 Electronics pioneer RCA demonstrates the first synthesizer to play musical sounds electronically. Developed by Herbert Belar and Harry Olsen – and officially known as the RCA Mark II synthesizer – it is the first full system created to produce "any sound." Using punched paper tape, it is based on the concept that sounds are formed by various parameters – amplitude, frequency, and spectrum – that can be manipulated using an electronic module.

"Mr. Art Rupe...you are now going to hear Little Richard and his Upsetters..." Little Richard introducing his demo tape for Specialty Records, February 1955

Newly arrived in the UK, jukeboxes were already an institution in the US, where more than half a million were said to be in use – one for every 300 people.

February

5 While recording a cover of Arthur Gunter's *Baby Let's Play House*, **Elvis Presley** creates a hiccuping, rockabilly vocal style – which many later impersonators will exaggerate. During the session, he also cuts versions of *I Got A Woman* and *Trying To Get To You.*

6 Now officially managed by Bob Neal, **Elvis Presley** has come to the attention of Oscar Davis – right-hand man to **"Col." Tom Parker**, talent entrepreneur and ex-manager of **Eddy Arnold**, who is currently managing **Hank Snow**. Davis first saw Presley perform last year at the Eagle's Nest Inn, Memphis Airport. Impressed by his onstage persona, good looks, and musical crossover potential, Davis has arranged a meeting this afternoon at Palumbo's Restaurant, between the 3:00 pm and 5:00 pm shows at the Ellis Auditorium in Memphis. Bob Neal, Sam Phillips, Elvis, Scotty Moore, and Parker will attend. In the meantime, Parker – initially ribbing Phillips about how a small label like Sun won't be able to offer Presley national distribution – negotiates with Neal to have the singer added to the line-up for his upcoming Hank Snow Jamboree. This package show of country acts – including the **Carter Sisters & Mother Maybelle** – will open in Roswell, New Mexico, on Valentine's Day.

13 **Elvis Presley** performs at the Fair Park Coliseum, Lubbock, Texas, where the bill is opened by a local act, young country and western duo **Buddy & Bob** (Buddy Holly and Bob Montgomery).

16 Tonight's two **Elvis Presley** gigs at the Odessa Senior High School Field House in Odessa, Texas, are attended by some 4,000 people, including teenage Texan singer, **Roy Orbison**.

17 **Art Rupe** – who founded Specialty Records in Los Angeles in 1944 with a largely black/blues/gospel roster – receives a demo tape from a Richard Penniman. Richard is currently washing dishes at a Greyhound bus station in his native Macon, Georgia, but – influenced by the "rolling" piano style of **Fats Domino** – he is also

Chet Atkins's debut album was the first of over 100 during his playing career... Belfast-born Ruby Murray broke through as the resident singer on BBC-TV's popular "Quite Contrary" show.

moonlighting as **Little Richard & the Upsetters.** He has been spotted by Specialty Records artist **Lloyd Price**, based in New Orleans, who suggested that Richard should send the demo to his label boss. Richard duly dispatched *Baby* and *All Night Long* – recorded at the WMBL Studio in Memphis. On first listen, Rupe and his A&R producer "Bumps" Blackwell are unimpressed, but after persistent telephone calling by Richard they will listen to the demo again and decide to offer the singer a contract (which will give him half a cent for each record sold). After initially canceling a recording session in Atlanta, the label will arrange for Richard to make his debut recordings for the company in New Orleans in September.

27 **Billboard** magazine reports that – for the first time – 45rpm singles are outselling 78s in the US.

March

2 Having brought demos of the songs to brothers Leonard and Phil Chess, owners of Chess Records, 26-year-old R&B guitarist/singer-songwriter **Bo Diddley** records his first session for the label at Bill Putnam's Universal Recording Studio at 111 East Ontario in Chicago, where he has lived since the age of eight. With **Jerome Green** on maracas, **Frank Kirkland** on drums, **Lester Davenport** on harmonica, and **Otis Spann** on piano, Diddley records *Bo Diddley*, *I'm A Man*, and *You Don't Love Me.* The double A-side disc, *Bo Diddley/I'm A Man* – released on the Chess imprint Checker Records – will hit US R&B No. 1 on June 25.

14 **Elvis Presley** is interviewed – but does not sing – on Jimmy Dean's "Town & Country Jubilee" television show, broadcast on WMAL-TV in Washington, D.C.

15 **Fats Domino** records the self-penned *Ain't It A Shame* for Imperial. It will begin an 11-week stretch topping the R&B chart on June 11. Subsequently regarded as a classic, the R&B/rock 'n' roll nugget will also hit No. 10 on the pop survey. (When **Pat Boone** records his version, later this year, he will call it *Ain't That A Shame*, because he thinks Domino's title is grammatically incorrect.)

19 Ten days shy of her 20th birthday, Irish songbird **Ruby Murray** celebrates by occupying five spots on today's UK top 20. *Softly, Softly* is at No. 2, *Let Me Go, Lover* at No. 5, *Happy Days And Lonely Nights* at No. 14, *Heartbeat* at No. 15, and *If Anyone Finds This I Love You* at No. 17.

22 One month after his 23rd birthday, singer-songwriter/guitarist **Johnny Cash** cuts five gospel/country tracks at the Memphis Recording Service, with **Luther Perkins** (bass) and **Marshall Grant** (guitar). He was auditioned by Sam Phillips late last year, both as a solo artist and with his group. The only track strong enough for future release is *Mr. Porter*, which Cash wrote on his return from Landsberg, Germany, where he was serving in the US Army as Radio Intercept Operator Cash. Needing an A-side, Phillips instructs Cash to go away and write a hit: he will duly oblige by penning *Cry, Cry, Cry*. Recorded in May, this will be Cash's first release on Sun.

23 **Elvis Presley**, his manager Bob Neal, Scotty Moore, and Bill Black fly to New York to audition for CBS-TV's "Arthur Godfrey's Talent Scouts" show. Playing at 2:30 pm, Presley's performance of *Good Rockin' Tonight* is below par. Godfrey's producers turn him down, and will instead decide to showcase the man who will become one of Presley's biggest 1950s rivals, **Pat Boone**.

April

9 Discovered by Johnny Otis and signed to Modern Records last year, 17-year-old blues singer **Etta James** hits No. 1 on the R&B chart with her first single, *The Wallflower*. The song, originally called *Roll With Me Henry*, is a re-titled "answer" record to **Hank Ballard**'s smash, *Work With Me Annie*. James will have one follow-up R&B hit with Modern, before re-emerging on the Argo label to score over 20 R&B/pop crossover hits in the 1960s – including the luscious and career-defining *At Last*.

Fats Domino, the affable dean of New Orleans R&B, easily made the transition into rock 'n' roll.

Chuck Berry's *Maybellene*... Elvis is mobbed by fans... *(We're Gonna) Rock Around The Clock*...

14 **Alan Freed**'s Rock 'n' Roll Easter Jubilee breaks the week-long attendance record at the Paramount Theater in Brooklyn – set in 1932 by Depression-era crooner Russ Columbo. The line-up features **LaVern Baker** (enjoying her first hit for Atlantic with *Tweedle Dee*), the **Three Chuckles**, **Danny Overbea**, the **Moonglows**, the **Moonlighters**, **Eddie Fontaine**, and the **Penguins**.

16 With an entrance fee of 60¢ for adults, **Elvis Presley** makes his first appearance – and tops the bill – on the "Big D Jamboree," a live Dallas radio show broadcast on KRLD, also featuring, among others, **Sonny James**, **Hank Locklin**, and the **Maddox Brothers**.

23 **Ray Charles** cuts *A Fool For You, This Little Girl Of Mine, Hard Times,* and *A Bit Of Soul* for Atlantic at Miami radio station WMAQ, with Jerry Wexler and Ahmet Ertegun producing.

25 John H. Walker, British delegate on the United Nations Commission on Narcotic Drugs, speaks of a "definite connection between increased marijuana smoking and that form of entertainment known as bebop and rebop." He says the British authorities are concerned about marijuana use among teenagers, particularly at bebop sessions when "excitement runs high."

Patsy Cline (born Virginia Patterson Hensley), a 22-year-old, starry-eyed, aspirant country and western singer, made her first recordings in June.

May

1 Chess Records signs **Chuck Berry**, who has been recommended to the label by **Muddy Waters**. Leonard Chess is particularly impressed with the singer's interpretation of the old country and western song *Ida Red*, now recast by Berry as *Maybellene*.

7 Six years after his first chart appearance, **Ray Charles** finally hits the top spot on the R&B survey with the self-penned *I Got A Woman*.

13 **Elvis Presley**'s stage act – in front of 14,000 fans – causes an audience riot for the first time, at a concert in Jacksonville. The trouble apparently starts after Elvis says to the females in attendance: "Girls, I'll see you backstage." He has much of his clothing ripped off, but escapes uninjured. When "Col." Tom Parker's assistant Oscar Davis reports what has happened to his boss, Parker – who is currently booking shows around the south for Presley's manager Bob Neal – reportedly resolves to find a way to become Presley's full-time representative.

22 Police in Bridgeport, Connecticut, cancel a show to be headlined by **Fats Domino** at the Ritz ballroom. They point to a "recent near-riot" at the New Haven Arena during a rock 'n' roll dance.

June

1 **Patsy Cline** makes her recording debut at producer Owen Bradley's Bradley Film & Recording Studios in Nashville (following an unsuccessful tryout at Decca's Pythian Temple Studios in New York last year). She cuts four sides: *Hidin' Out, Turn The Cards Slowly, A Church A Courtroom And Then Goodbye*, and *Honky Tonk Merry Go Round*, with **Harold Bradley** on acoustic guitar, **Owen Bradley** on piano, **Farris Coursey** on drums, **Don Helms** on steel guitar, **Tommy Jackson** on fiddle, **Grady Martin** on electric guitar and fiddle, and **Bob Moore** on acoustic bass. Cline is managed by bandleader Bill Peer, and signed a restrictive two-year recording deal last September with Four Star Records (which in turn is leasing to Decca).

17 "Col." Tom Parker and Bob Neal meet in Madison, Tennessee. They informally agree to Parker's suggestion that – though Neal will remain **Elvis Presley**'s manager – from July 24, all his show bookings and career strategy will be

CHUCK BERRY

May 21 **In Chicago, Chuck Berry records *Maybellene*, with Johnnie Johnson (piano), Willie Dixon (bass), Jasper Thomas (drums), and Jerome Green (maracas). It will go to No. 5 on the Best Sellers in Stores chart, and No. 1 on the R&B survey on August 20.**

Berry's unique style – uptempo blues-based with a country rockabilly infusion, driven by an insistent guitar rhythm – became legendary. Together with his inclination to write his own hits, it inspired thousands of artists over the next 30 years, and established him as a vital force in the evolution of rock.

Ruth Brown, Clyde McPhatter and LaVern Baker

Bo Diddley

Willie Dixon

While serving in the US military, popular Drifters' vocalist Clyde McPhatter decided to go solo... Bo Diddley and Willie Dixon were both making blues-based signature sounds in Chicago for Chess Records.

handled by Parker, who is also insistent that Presley should be moved from Sun to a nationally distributed, major record label.

July

9 Having been re-released, *(We're Gonna) Rock Around The Clock* by **Bill Haley & His Comets** storms back into the charts and begins an eight-week run at No. 1 in the US. Its reissue has been prompted by its inclusion – over the opening credits – in the film "The Blackboard Jungle," an MGM movie starring Glenn Ford as a high school teacher trying to control rowdy students. While the film sparks off nationwide controversy about the undisciplined behavior of youth, the song both reflects and engenders a rebellious fire. It will become one of the biggest-selling singles in chart history, spending 24 weeks in the US top 40 – 19 of them in the top ten. Although not the first rock 'n' roll record, it is certainly the most successful in the new genre – and a landmark in popular music history.

16 Lead singer **Clyde McPhatter**'s split with his group, the **Drifters**, which is not unexpected, becomes official. McPhatter was drafted into the army last year, but continued to front the R&B combo until April as he was stationed on Grand Island near Buffalo, New York. His replacement is teenage tenor **David Baughn**, recently a member of the **Checkers**.

"No singer is worth that much."

Mitch Miller, on the suggestion of a bid of $20,000 from RCA for Elvis Presley, August 15, 1955

16 **Elvis Presley** celebrates his first national chart placing, as *Baby Let's Play House* enters the US Country Best Sellers list on its way to No. 10. "Col." Tom Parker, who is promoting Presley heavily outside the south, impresses New York music publisher Arnold Shaw and top Cleveland DJ Bill Randle. Randle gives Elvis heavy airplay, which slowly spreads to New York.

***(We're Gonna) Rock Around The Clock* was co-penned by Max Freedman and publisher James E. Myers, aka Jimmy DeKnight, who copyrighted the song on March 31, 1953.**

August

15 At a meeting in Memphis attended by "Col." Tom Parker, **Elvis Presley**, Presley's father Vernon, and Bob Neal, Elvis signs a formal contract with Parker confirming him as his "special adviser." Parker has been growing increasingly irritated at what he views as management incompetence by Neal, and has also spread word that Presley's contract with Sun may be up for sale. Sun's owner Sam Phillips turns down Decca Records' bid of $5,000 and Dot Records' offer of $7,500. Parker tells Mitch Miller at CBS/Columbia that Mercury Records is considering a $10,000 bid; Miller responds that he is ready to pay $15,000. But when Parker says RCA may consider a bid of $20,000, Miller retorts that "no singer is worth that much." The bidding war continues, as Ahmet Ertegun of Atlantic is willing to risk $25,000, but Parker holds out for more.

20 **Bo Diddley** appears at the Apollo Theater in Harlem. By now he has a regular backing ensemble, comprising **Otis Spann** (piano), **Lester Davenport** (harmonica), **Frank Kirkland** (drums), and **Jerome Green** (maracas).

September

1 Alan Freed's First Anniversary Rock 'n' Roll Party opens at the Paramount Theater in Brooklyn. The one-week stint, six shows a day, will gross $155,000 – breaking the $147,000 record set by Dean Martin and Jerry Lewis in 1948. Gene Pleshette, the managing director of the theater, will state that in his 26 years in the business he has "never seen anything as exciting." Among those appearing are **Chuck Berry**, **Tony Bennett**, the **Nutmegs**, the **Rhythmettes**, the **Cardinals**, the **Four Voices**, the **Harptones**, **Nappy Brown**, **Red Prysock**, **Al Sears**, and the **Rock 'n' Roll Band** starring **Sam "The Man" Taylor**. Pop crooner Bennett will burst a blood vessel in his throat and have to pull out after two days, to be replaced by **Al Hibbler**.

10 **Willie Dixon**'s *Walking The Blues* enters the US R&B chart on its way to No. 6. Blues singer/composer/guitarist Dixon, based in Chicago, is Chess Records' inhouse songwriter, producer, and staff musician. Ironically it will be his only chart appearance as an artist – despite producing dozens of Chicago blues artists and writing several R&B classics. These include *Hoochie Coochie Man* and *I Just Want To Make Love To You* (for Muddy Waters); *Evil, Spoonful, I Ain't Superstitious, Little Red Rooster,* and *Back Door Man* (for Howlin' Wolf); Little Walter's hit *My Babe*; and *Bring It On Home* for Sonny Boy Williamson. Dixon's compositions will provide rich pickings for future British acts, such as Eric Clapton, Led Zeppelin, and the Rolling Stones.

Sept 1955

Billboard magazine launches the Top 100... Presley signs to RCA... Carl Perkins records *Blue Suede Shoes...*

Little Richard's *Tutti Frutti* would spend 22 weeks on the R&B chart, reaching No. 2, and peak on the pop survey at No. 17.

13 Now signed to Specialty Records by Robert "Bumps" Blackwell (who had been looking for a new Ray Charles, but found instead "this cat in this loud shirt, with hair waved up six inches above his head... talking wild"), **Little Richard** records his first session for the label at Cosimo Matassa's J&M Studios. With Blackwell producing, Richard and **Huey Smith** on piano, and **Earl Palmer** on drums, they swing their way through the blues numbers *Lonesome And Blue, Wondering, All Night Long,* and *Kansas City* (the last written by Jerry Leiber and Mike Stoller in 1952).

14 **Little Richard** continues his recording sessions with the Crescent City rhythm section (who feature on many of Fats Domino's discs), recording *Directly From My Heart, Maybe I'm Right, Baby, I'm Just A Lonely Guy (All Alone)*, and a version of a live number he has written called *Tutti Frutti* (with the lyrics cleaned up by local songwriter Dorothy La Bostrie). The histrionic vocal and pounding piano style cast the mold for Richard's image, as Blackwell insists on a live feel for the studio recordings.

19 Signed to Dot Records in January, 21-year-old singer and Jacksonville native **Pat Boone** hits US No. 1 with his (renamed) cover of **Fats Domino**'s *Ain't It A Shame*. A clean-cut antidote to the more rebellious Elvis Presley, Boone – who made his first recordings last year (four country tunes for Nashville's Republic label) – will soon settle into a comfortable and extremely successful niche. Aware that many current R&B hits are not seeing action on mainstream radio, Boone, who is married to Red Foley's daughter, Shirley, will cut cleaned-up pop versions of originals (by the likes of Domino, **Little Richard**, the **Flamingos**, and **Ivory Joe Hunter**), racking up an incredible five US No. 1s in two years.

24 In the UK, the new Independent Television – on what is only its third day of transmission – broadcasts "TV Music Shop," a new popular music program that features stars such as **Teddy Johnson and Pearl Carr**.

28 Under the songwriting and production guidance of Jerry Leiber and Mike Stoller, the **Robins**, an all-male vocal group, record *Smokey Joe's Café* and *Riot In Cell Block Number Nine* at Master Recordings studio in Los Angeles. Leiber and Stoller's Spark label will license the cuts to Atco Records. This in turn will lead to the group signing to Atco early next year, renaming themselves the **Coasters**.

29 **Billboard** magazine's review of **Little Richard**'s *Tutti Frutti* includes the observation: "A cleverly styled novelty with nonsense words, rapid fire delivery."

October

11 **Elvis Presley**, **Carl Perkins**, and **Johnny Cash** begin an 11-date Jamboree tour in Abilene, Texas. It is set to end on the 22nd in St. Louis.

14 **Buddy Holly**, **Bob Montgomery**, and **Larry Welborn** perform at the Fair Park Coliseum in Lubbock, Texas – in a show that also features **Bill Haley & His Comets**. The burgeoning success of Elvis Presley, and the growth of rockabilly, is tempting Holly away from his pure country base. His group is spotted by Nashville-based agent Eddie Crandall, who is traveling with the tour.

20 **Elvis Presley** (in his first show north of the Mason Dixon Line), **Bill Haley & His Comets**, **Pat Boone**, and the **Four Lads** perform before Brooklyn High School students in Cleveland. The show is filmed for the documentary "The Pied Piper of Cleveland: a Day in the Life of a Famous Disc Jockey," about DJ Bill Randle.

November

1 Secular R&B combo, the **Famous Flames** – led by 22-year-old singer **James Brown** and featuring **Bobby Byrd**, **Sylvester Keels**, and **Nafloyd Scott** – record an acetate dub of *Please, Please, Please* at radio station WIBB in Macon. It is supervised by DJ Hamp Swain, who will begin playing the song on air (while the group's manager, Clint Brantley, will send copies to Duke Records in Houston and the Chess label in Chicago). The Famous Flames have played gigs around Georgia through much of the year, blending gospel material with raucous jump-blues-based R&B. Their energetic, impassioned frontman – and main songwriter – has already led a varied existence, both as a juvenile delinquent and as an experienced singer/drummer and organ player with numerous R&B and gospel combos.

9 **Harry Belafonte** records *Jamaica Farewell* and *Come Back Liza* to complete the ***Calypso*** album, which will hit US No. 1 in 1956 and give Belafonte his nickname – "The Calypso King."

12 **Billboard** magazine introduces "The Top 100" – for the first time combining sales, airplay, and jukebox operation – for the survey week ending November 2. The first chart-topper is the **Four Aces**' *Love Is A Many-Splendored Thing*.

12 **Elvis Presley** is voted Most Promising Country and Western Artist in the annual US Disc Jockey Poll, with **Chuck Berry** hailed as Most Promising R&B Artist.

20 **Bo Diddley**, **LaVern Baker**, the **Five Keys**, and **Willis Jackson's Orchestra** appear on CBS-TV's "Toast Of The Town" show, hosted by Ed Sullivan, in a 15-minute R&B segment emceed by New York DJ Tommy "Dr. Jive" Smalls. Diddley plays his own *Bo Diddley*, despite having rehearsed *Sixteen Tons*.

James Brown

James Brown and Sam Cooke, who were making their way through the R&B ranks, both emerged from red-hot combos: Brown through the Famous Flames, and Cooke through the Soul Stirrers.

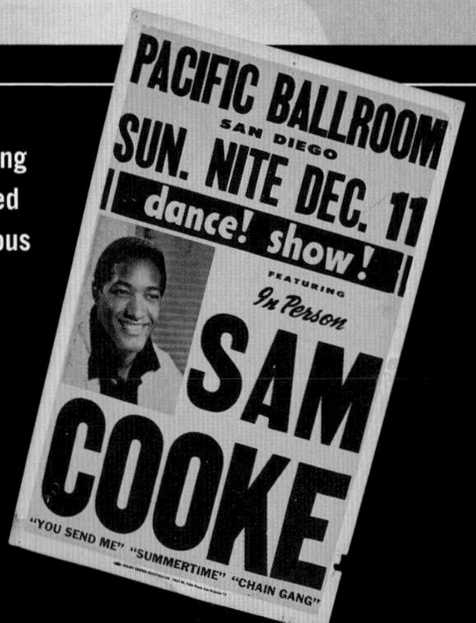

Nov 21 With Bob Neal's management contract about to expire, "Col." Tom Parker has taken up the negotiating power granted him by Elvis Presley's parents, and has worked out a deal with RCA Records executives Coleman Tily and Steve Sholes, and the publishing company Hill & Range. It is formally signed at the Sun studio in Memphis. Under the agreement, RCA will pay Sun and Sam Phillips's Hi-Lo Music $35,000 for the Presley contract and all previously recorded material, and Presley himself $5,000 for future royalties on existing Sun singles. RCA will reissue all five Presley singles on its own label, though Sun still has a selloff period for existing stock. In need of expansion capital (and with only one year of Presley's recording contract still to run), Phillips has accepted the offer. (He will begin investing in the fledgling Holiday Inn hotel chain, which will ultimately make him a bigger fortune than the record industry.)

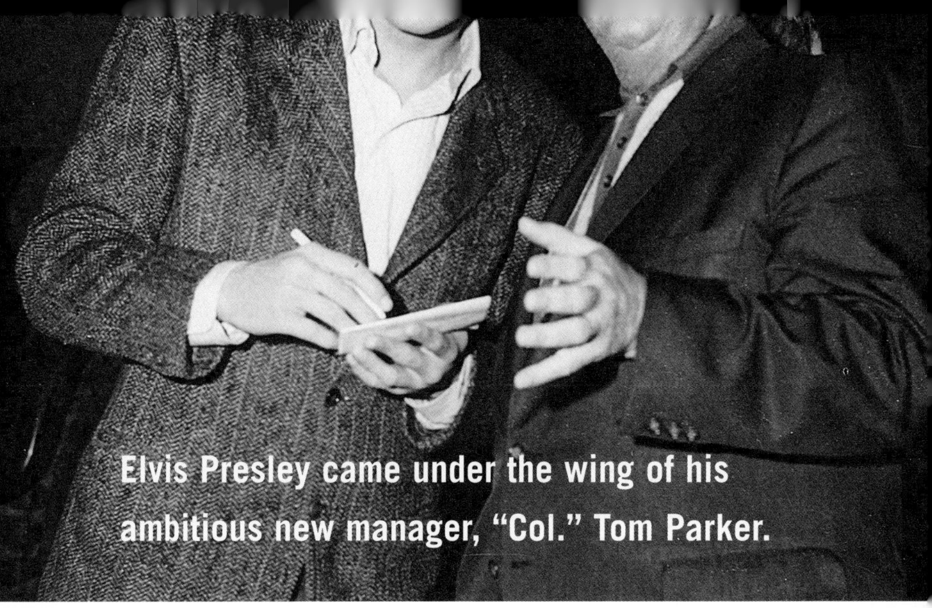

Elvis Presley came under the wing of his ambitious new manager, "Col." Tom Parker.

26 Released on the Brunswick label **Bill Haley & His Comets**' *(We're Gonna) Rock Around The Clock* is the first rock 'n' roll disc to hit UK No. 1.

December

3 Eddie Crandall, wires KDAV radio DJ Dave Stone in Lubbock. His telegram reads: "Have Buddy Holly Cut 4 Original Songs On Ascetate [*sic*] Don't Change His Style At All. Get These To Me As Soon As Possible." **Buddy Holly** will duly record the songs at Nesman Recording Studio in Wichita Falls, Texas, next week.

3 **"Tennessee" Ernie Ford**'s version of Merle Travis's *Sixteen Tons*, released by Capitol Records, begins the first of six weeks topping the **Billboard** Top 100 chart. The song is a massive crossover hit for the venerable country star, and the fastest-selling record in history, driving to No. 1 in just four weeks.

19 **Carl Perkins** and his band record his composition, *Blue Suede Shoes* (written at **Johnny Cash**'s suggestion and based on an actual incident spotted in a concert audience). Sensing its commercial potential, Sam Phillips will rush-release it on Sun with heavy promotion.

22 Alan Freed's Rock 'n' Roll Holiday Jubilee opens at the Academy of Music on East 14th Street, New York. The 12 days of shows – featuring the **Bonnie Sisters**, **Count Basie**, **LaVern Baker**, **Boyd Bennett**, the **Wrens**, the **Valentines**, **Don Cherry**, the **Chuckles**, the **Cadillacs**, the **Heartbeats**, **Gloria Mann**, **Joe Williams**, **Sam "The Man" Taylor**, and **Al Sears**, will close on January 2.

31 **Bill Haley & His Comets** end their phenomenal year performing at the Michigan State Fair Coliseum in Detroit, as *Burn That Candle* heads to its US No. 9 peak. By the end of the year, salaried band members **Joey Di'Ambrosia**, **Dick Richards**, and **Marshall Lytle** have left to form the **Jodimars**, signing a deal with Capitol Records. **Billy Williamson** and **Johnny Grande** – who are partners with Haley – continue in the band, with additional musicians hired for live performances: guitarist **Frank Beecher**, **Al Rex** (who rejoins), and newcomers **Rudy Pompilli** (formerly a sax player with the Ralph Marterie Orchestra), and **Don Raymond** on drums.

> "Without Elvis, none of us could have made it." Buddy Holly, **Billboard**

The Four Aces, a vocal quartet from Chester, Pennsylvania, led by Al Alberts, enjoyed their only No. 1 with *Love Is A Many-Splendored Thing*, the title theme from the movie starring William Holden and Jennifer Jones.

ROOTS During this year: child singing siblings Barry, Maurice, and Robin Gibb begin giving regular Saturday morning performances at local cinemas (the Gaumont, the Whalley Range Odeon, and the Palentine Theatre in Manchester), under the name the Rattlesnakes... Paul McCartney makes friends with fellow Liverpool Institute student George Harrison, although the latter is one year his junior... Roy Orbison makes his recording debut at Norman Petty's studio in Clovis, New Mexico, as a member of the Teen Kings... Willie Nelson begins broadcasting a radio show in Washington state, featuring a half-hour live set by his own band... 16-year-old Connie Francis signs to MGM Records and makes a series of demos, as well as dubbing Tuesday Weld's singing voice for Alan Freed's film "Rock Rock Rock"... Eddie Cochran, buying guitar strings in Bell Gardens Music Center, California, meets aspiring songwriter Jerry Capehart... and Don Everly places his song *Thou Shalt Not Steal* with a publisher for $600 (to be recorded by Kitty Wells) and, with his brother Phil, is offered a session with Columbia Records...

Roll Over Beethoven

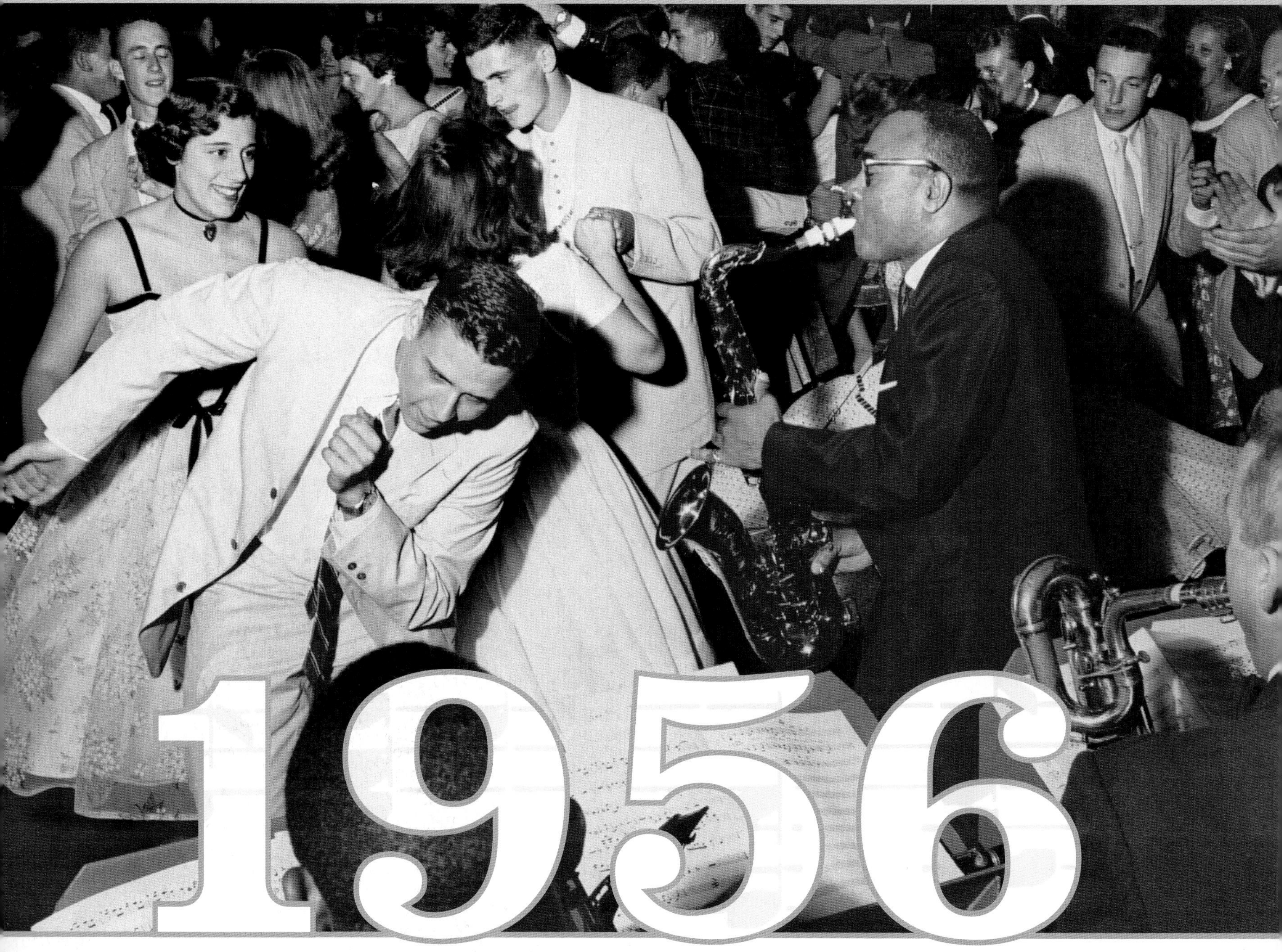

1956

No.1 US SINGLES

Jan 7 Sixteen Tons **Tennessee Ernie Ford**
Jan 21 Memories Are Made Of This **Dean Martin**
Feb 25 The Great Pretender **Platters**
Mar 10 Rock And Roll Waltz **Kay Starr**
Mar 31 Poor People Of Paris **Les Baxter**
May 12 Heartbreak Hotel **Elvis Presley**
June 30 The Wayward Wind **Gogi Grant**
Aug 11 I Almost Lost My Mind **Pat Boone**
Aug 25 My Prayer **Platters**
Sep 22 Don't Be Cruel **Elvis Presley**
Nov 10 Green Door **Jim Lowe**
Dec 1 Love Me Tender **Elvis Presley**
Dec 15 Singing The Blues **Guy Mitchell**

No.1 UK SINGLES

Jan 7 (We're Gonna) Rock Around The Clock **Bill Haley & His Comets**
Jan 21 Sixteen Tons **Tennessee Ernie Ford**
Feb 18 Memories Are Made Of This **Dean Martin**
Mar 17 It's Almost Tomorrow **Dreamweavers**
Mar 31 Rock And Roll Waltz **Kay Starr**
Apr 7 It's Almost Tomorrow **Dreamweavers**
Apr 14 Poor People Of Paris **Winifred Atwell**
May 5 No Other Love **Ronnie Hilton**
June 16 I'll Be Home **Pat Boone**
July 21 Why Do Fools Fall In Love **Teenagers featuring Frankie Lymon**
Aug 11 Whatever Will Be Will Be **Doris Day**
Sept 22 Lay Down Your Arms **Anne Shelton**
Oct 20 A Woman In Love **Frankie Laine**
Nov 17 Just Walkin' In The Rain **Johnnie Ray**

Pat Boone

Alan Freed's Holiday of Stars

Descendant of western pioneer Daniel Boone, singer Pat Boone took a less adventurous path... All-star package line-ups were all the rage, none more so than Alan Freed's bills at the Paramount.

Rock 'n' roll was finally breaking through to the young mainstream audience of America, as **Elvis Presley** built a massive following. His appeal was unique: the rebellious white kid who sang black music – with sex appeal. But amid the excitement, there was also controversy. Concerts by **Bill Haley & His Comets** were plagued by violence or banned altogether, and the movie "Rock Around the Clock" sparked off riots in Britain. Much of the music establishment both sneered at and feared rock 'n' roll. **Frank Sinatra** was quoted as saying of Elvis: "His kind of music is deplorable, a rancid-smelling aphrodisiac."

Presley quickly became the first "multimedia" star of the rock era, with his television appearances and his first film, "Love Me Tender," drawing huge audiences. His success influenced other emerging artists, such as **Buddy Holly** and **Gene Vincent**.

Presley shared the limelight in 1956 with Bill Haley – even if their images could not have been more different – and Haley's music also found a home in the movies, with "The Blackboard Jungle" and "Rock Around the Clock." Haley enjoyed even greater success in Britain – and much greater notoriety. Britain's youth was looking to the United States for musical stimulation. The only homebred talent to compare was Scotland's **Lonnie Donegan**, whose acoustic banjo "skiffle" sound made an impact on several emerging British songwriters.

R&B's chart presence was led by **Fats Domino**, whose uncluttered style and staid appearance contrasted with the frenetic **Little Richard**, perhaps the most exciting R&B star to break through in 1956. *Tutti Frutti* had an influence far beyond its modest No. 17 peak on the US chart, and not surprisingly, it was quickly covered by the clean-cut **Pat Boone**, whose version reached No. 12. Boone also covered Richard's *Long Tall Sally*, but failed to emulate his frenetic pace.

Chuck Berry was another songwriter whose contribution to the formative years of rock 'n' roll was greater than his chart success would suggest. *Roll Over Beethoven* struggled to No. 29 on the main **Billboard** pop survey, but not only was it an emblem of musical rebellion, it was later famously covered by the **Beatles**. John Lennon quipped: "If you tried to give rock 'n' roll another name, you might call it 'Chuck Berry.'"

In more sedate fashion, the **Five Satins** demonstrated a continuing market for doo-wop, as *In The Still Of The Night* reached No. 25. But the future lay with rock 'n' roll. Many more artists were in the wings, among them **James Brown** and Buddy Holly. Unusually among the rising white stars of rock, Holly was writing his own songs. In 1956, they included *Cindy Lou* – later to become famous as *Peggy Sue*.

In 1956, popular music became a true melting pot, as a dizzying mix of hillbilly, blues, gospel, folk, pop, and jazz set off a cultural revolution – a trail blazed by the curled lip and swiveling hips of Elvis Presley.

"...this cat in this loud shirt, with hair waved up six inches above his head...talking wild."

"Bumps" Blackwell, describing Little Richard in 1955

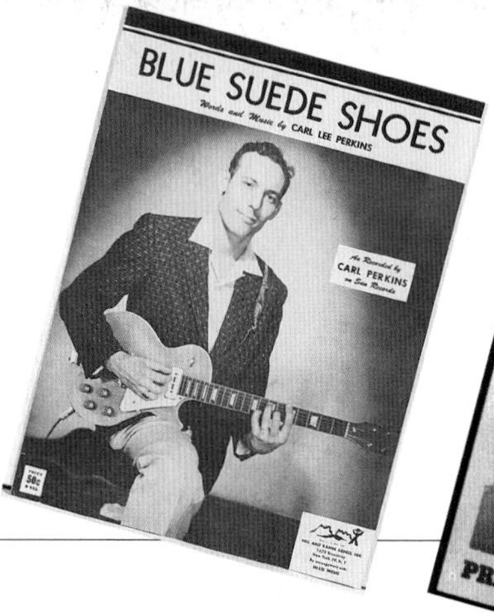

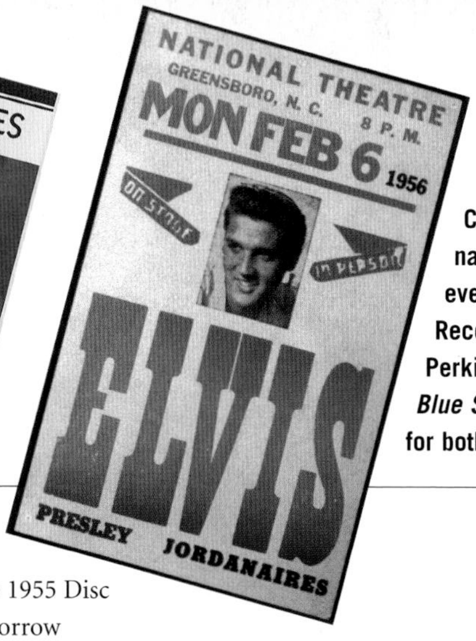

Causing a sensation nationwide, Elvis was everywhere... His ex-Sun Records labelmate, Carl Perkins, wrote the classic *Blue Suede Shoes*, a hit for both artists.

Buddy Holly tours... The Ivor Novello Awards... "Rock Around the Clock" opens...

January

9 **Buddy Holly & the Two-Tunes** – a new backing band – begin a 14-date US tour in Little Rock, Arkansas, set to end on the 23rd in Memphis. The tour is headlined by **Hank Thompson** and also features **George Jones**, **Cowboy Copas**, and **Wanda Jackson**. Columbia Records has recently turned down the opportunity to sign Buddy Holly, but Decca's Nashville office – through talent scout Jim Denny – has expressed interest in signing him as a solo artist. Fellow band member **Bob Montgomery** has insisted that Holly grab the opportunity. (Montgomery will stay in music, but will move into production and publishing.) Holly recruits guitarist **Sonny Curtis**, whom he met on the "Sunday Party" radio show when Curtis was a member of Ben Hall's country band. Bassist **Don Guess** – a friend from junior high school and recently with Holly in the Rhythm Playboys – completes the lineup.

10 **Elvis Presley** records his first RCA sessions, at the Methodist Television, Radio & Film Commission Studios in Nashville. His first cut is a cover of Ray Charles's recent R&B smash *I Got A Woman*. This is followed by a new composition, *Heartbreak Hotel*, written by Tommy Durden and Mae Boren Axton – Axton gave Presley the Glenn Reeves-recorded demo at the Andrew Jackson Hotel during the 1955 Disc Jockey Convention in Nashville. Tomorrow Presley will record *Money Honey*, *I'm Counting On You*, and *I Was The One*. Among the musicians during the two-day session are **Scotty Moore**, **Bill Black**, **Chet Atkins** on guitar, **Floyd Cramer** on piano, **Dominic "D.J." Fontana** on drums (the ex-house-drummer with the "Louisiana Hayride," he's been touring regularly with Presley), as well as brothers **Ben** and **Brock Speer**, and **Jordanaire Gordon Stoker** on backing vocals.

11 Under the production of songwriters Jerry Leiber and Mike Stoller, the newly named **Coasters** (previously the Robins) record their first sides for Atlantic Records in Hollywood: *Brazil, Down In Mexico, One Kiss Led To Another,* and *Turtle Dovin'.*

"We used humor to take off the edge. We'd have the Coasters in hysterics. The material was potent, the metaphors sometimes hidden, but the hook always dramatic." Jerry Leiber on recording with the Coasters

23 **James Brown & the Famous Flames** are signed by influential producer and talent scout Ralph Bass to his Federal label, a subsidiary of Syd Nathan's King label in Cincinnati. Bass has heard the band's recording of *Please, Please, Please* on an Atlanta radio station. He beats off Leonard Chess in Chicago, and signs them for a $200 advance.

26 **Buddy Holly & the Two-Tunes** record their first sessions for Decca at Bradley's Barn Studio in Nashville. With Owen Bradley producing, Grady Martin on rhythm guitar, and Doug Kirkham on percussion, they record *Blue Days Black Nights, Don't Come Back Knockin', Love Me,* and *Midnight Shift.*

27 Irvin Feld's Super Attractions R&B package trek opens in Pittsburgh. The ten-date all-star tour featuring **Bill Haley & His Comets**, the **Platters**, **LaVern Baker**, **Shirley & Lee**, the **Drifters**, **Joe Turner**, **Bo Diddley**, the **Five Keys**, **Roy Hamilton**, **Red Prysock**, and the **Turbans** will come to a close in Washington, D.C. on February 5.

28 Receiving $1,250 for each show, **Elvis Presley** makes the first of four appearances on the "Stage Show," hosted by Tommy and Jimmy Dorsey and aired live from CBS Studio 50 in New York. Introduced by Bill Randle, he performs *Shake Rattle And Roll, Flip Flop And Fly*, and *I Got A Woman*. Actor Jackie Gleason, whose company produces the show, says: "He can't last. I tell you flatly, he can't last." (Presley's four appearances will be increased to six by popular demand.)

30 **Elvis Presley** records his own version of **Carl Perkins**'s hit *Blue Suede Shoes* at RCA's New York studios, plus seven more tracks, over the next four days, for inclusion on his debut album.

Formerly the Robins, the newly named Coasters rode a popular wave under the guidance of songwriting/production team Leiber and Stoller.

LONNIE DONEGAN

Feb 4 British skiffle pioneer Lonnie Donegan's first hit, Rock Island Line (based on a Leadbelly-penned traditional American folk song) hits UK No. 8 during a 25-week chart run. Signed to Decca Records last year, Glasgow-born Donegan has performed in jazz bands as a guitarist and banjo player since 1949 – notably with Ken Colyer's Jazzmen, then Chris Barber's Jazz Band. Heavily influenced by American blues and folk, Donegan refocused both combos on playing blues work songs, one of which he has fashioned into Rock Island Line.

The acoustic banjo/washboard skiffle genre led by Lonnie Donegan – a precursor to British rock 'n' roll – would prove a strong influence on several emerging musicians, including Paul McCartney.

February

4 At the King Studios in Cincinnati, **James Brown**, with a **Famous Flames** lineup of **Bobby Byrd** (piano and backing vocals), **Nafloyd Scott** (guitar), and backing vocalists **Sylvester Keels**, **Johnny Terry**, and **Nashpendle Knox**, re-records *Please, Please, Please.* **Wilbert "Lee Diamond" Smith** and **Ray Felder** (tenor saxes), **Clarence Mack** (bass), and **Edison Gore** (drums) complete the lineup for the session.

18 Written by Dick Ware and Shorty Allen, pop vocalist **Kay Starr**'s unlikely smash *Rock And Roll Waltz* hits No. 1 on the US Top 100, completing a trio of firsts: the first chart-topper for RCA Records, the first to feature the words "rock" and "roll" in the title, and the first rock 'n' roll No. 1 by a female artist.

March

3 In his first showing on the Top 100 singles chart, **Elvis Presley**'s *Heartbreak Hotel* debuts at No. 68. Presley is introduced to a national audience via radio and, increasingly, television. The fusion of all his influences – country, gospel, R&B, blues, and pop – paired with his looks and unique stage manner, will bring unprecedented fame, as rock 'n' roll mania – led by Haley and Presley – takes off.

"He taught white America to get down." James Brown on Elvis Presley

10 Two weeks before **Lonnie Donegan**'s original enters the US Top 100 (set to hit No. 8), 19-year-old **Bobby Darin** sings *Rock Island Line* on his television debut on the "Stage Show." He is currently performing with the Decca-signed act, the **Jaybirds**, but will soon fly solo.

11 The presentation ceremony for the inaugural Ivor Novello Awards – the first meaningful music awards devoted solely to British songwriters – is held in London. *Ev'rywhere* by Tolchard Evans and Larry Kahn is named Most Popular Song, *In Love For The Very First Time* by Jack Woodman and Paddy Roberts is named Outstanding Popular Song, and their *Got'n Idea* is named Outstanding Comedy Song. To prove that not everyone is moving with the times, Julian Slade and Dorothy Reynolds's *Salad Days* is named Most Effectival Musical Play Score.

17 "Rock Around the Clock" has its world premiere in Washington. Produced by Sam Katzman, the film, which will receive wild reactions in both the US and Europe, features musical performances by **Bill Haley & His Comets**, the **Platters**, **Tony Martinez & His Band**, **Freddie Bell & His Bellboys**, and **Little Richard**.

Mar 1956

Carl Perkins is hospitalized...
The Capitol Tower lights up...
Alan Freed defends rock 'n' roll...

Southern teenagers listening to rock 'n' roll

21 Having made his first television appearance at the weekend on **Red Foley**'s country show "Ozark Jubilee," and with *Blue Suede Shoes* storming its way to No. 2 on the Top 100, **Carl Perkins** and his brother Jay leave Norfolk, Virginia, after playing on a bill with **Gene Vincent** and **Johnny Burnette**. They are on their way to New York for television appearances on "The Perry Como Show" (NBC) and "The Ed Sullivan Show" (CBS). But near Dover, Delaware, their car (driven by manager Dick Stuart) overturns after colliding with a pickup truck. Perkins suffers a spinal injury and numerous cuts, and will be transferred to a hospital in Memphis. Jay also sustains a spinal injury, as well as several broken ribs and internal injuries.

26 "Col." Tom Parker has moved in permanently to represent **Elvis Presley**, Bob Neal's management agreement having expired on March 15. Parker is formally confirmed as the "sole and exclusive advisor, personal representative and manager in any and all fields of public and private entertainment" – for a hefty 25 per cent commission.

29 The North Alabama White Citizens Council begins a campaign to persuade jukebox operators to throw out what executive secretary Asa Carter calls "immoral records in the new rhythm." Coin-music distributors respond that to do so would mean shutting out most of their hits. Carter claims the National Association for the Advancement of Colored Peoples has disseminated rock 'n' roll music among Southern white teenagers. NAACP executive secretary Roy Wilkins comments: "Some people in the South are blaming us for everything from measles to atomic fallouts."

30 Alan Freed's Easter Jubilee of Stars begins a ten-day sellout run at Brooklyn's Paramount Theater. Featuring the **Willows**, the **Platters**, the **Valentines**, the **Jodimars**, **Ruth McFadden**, the **Royaltones**, the **Cleftones**, **Cindy & Lindy**, the **Teenagers**, the **Flamingos**, the **Rover Boys**, and **Dori Anne Gray**, the package will gross $204,000 during its run.

31 **Brenda Lee**, who has been a professional singer since the age of five and recently signed to Decca Records, makes her television debut, aged 11. She sings on ABC's "Junior Ozark Jubilee" show, hosted by Red Foley – who saw her perform in Augusta when he presented a show from her parents' record shop. Lee has already performed at countless local talent contests – singing *Take Me Out To The Ball Game* at the age of five in her home town of Atlanta. After her appearance on ABC, Top Talent will offer her a five-year management deal. Dub Albritton will become her manager, a position he will retain until his death in 1972. Lee will also tour with Foley's roadshow, before making national television appearances on "The Perry Como Show" and "The Ed Sullivan Show."

> **"You can't call any music immoral. If anything is wrong with rock 'n' roll it is that it makes a virtue out of monotony."**
>
> Mitch Miller, April 15, 1956

April

1 **Elvis Presley** plays Jimmy Curry in a scene from "The Rainmaker" for his screen test at Paramount Studios in Hollywood. On the 6th, producer Hal B. Wallis will sign Presley to a three-film, seven-year contract with Paramount Pictures, worth $450,000.

1 The Rhythm and Blues of 1956 package tour begins a five-week North American trek in Richmond, Virginia. The bill features some of the hottest names in the R&B world, including **Fats Domino**, **Little Richard**, **Ruth Brown**, the **Cadillacs**, the **Clovers**, **Little Willie John**, the **Turbans**, the **Sweethearts**, **Al Jackson & the Fat Men**, **Joe Medlin**, and the **Choker Campbell Orchestra**. The show will travel through the East before heading to Toronto, where it will become the first of its kind in Canada.

Carl Perkins's accident saw him hospitalized for over a month, while his chance to capitalize on the success of *Blue Suede Shoes* slipped away.

Little Richard was a regular performer on wildly popular caravan package tours... Elvis Presley was simultaneously recording, performing live, appearing on television, and signing up for his first movie role.

SAM LEWIS presents:
FREDDY MARTIN
and His Orchestra
SHECKY GREENE
Extra Added Attraction
ELVIS PRESLEY
"The Atomic Powered Singer"
THE VENUS STARLETS • Choreography: Dorothy Dorben
CLOUD 9 LOUNGE
Rusty Draper
Billy Duke and His Dukes
Martha Davis & Spouse
NEW FRONTIER HOTEL
LAS VEGAS, NEVADA
OUT OF THIS WORLD!
RCA
RADIO CORPORATION OF AMERICA
RCA BUILDING
30 ROCKEFELLER PLAZA
NEW YORK
Dynamic Star of Television Radio · Movies and Records
thru
Sunday, May 6

3 An estimated 40 million people watch **Elvis Presley** on NBC's "The Milton Berle Show," live from the aircraft carrier USS *Hancock*, moored in San Diego. Around 25,000 people have applied for tickets, to see him sing *Heartbreak Hotel, Shake Rattle And Roll,* and *Blue Suede Shoes* – of which he performs two versions, one in a comedy routine with Berle playing Elvis's twin brother, Melvin. Presley earns $5,000 for the appearance.

6 The Capitol Tower in Hollywood – home to Capitol Records – is dedicated at a tour-and-reception party attended by 1,500 guests. The first circular office tower in America, the $2 million structure, 92ft in diameter and 13 storeys high, stands on the corner of Hollywood and Vine. Leila Morse, granddaughter of Morse code inventor Samuel Fulton Breeze Morse, taps a telegraph key to activate the red beacon at the top of the tower, which will blink the letters "H-O-L-L-Y-W-O-O-D" in Morse code at night.

7 "Rock 'n' Roll Dance Party" – the US's first nationally broadcast radio show devoted to the new genre – premieres on the CBS radio network, hosted by **Alan Freed.**

9 Sheriff Tex Davis, a DJ for WCMS in Norfolk, Virginia, takes 20-year-old singer **Gene Vincent** and his band into the station's studios to record three songs: *Be-Bop-A-Lula, Race With The Devil*, and the country ballad *I Sure Miss You*. Davis will send the demos to Ken Nelson at Capitol Records. Ex-Navy serviceman Vincent has recently left hospital after an extended stay following a motorcycle accident that seriously injured his legs. *Be-Bop-A-Lula* was reputedly co-penned by Vincent's fellow hospital patient, Donald Graves, who sells his share of the song to Vincent and Davis for $25.

10 Local authorities – fearing action from the White Citizens Council of Anniston, a town 60 miles east of Birmingham, Alabama – assign Detectives C.B. Golden and Carl Carruthers to look out for trouble prior to two shows being given tonight by **Nat King Cole** at the Municipal Auditorium in Birmingham. During the first (for a whites-only audience) Cole, backed by the **Ted Heath Orchestra** from England, is midway through *Little Girl* when white segregationists Kenneth Adams, Mike Fox, Orliss Clevenger, Willis Vinson, and his brother Edgar charge the stage. Willis Vinson punches Cole, mayhem ensues, and police rush in from the wings to arrest the assailants. In an attempt to quell the chaos, Cole's drummer Lee Young calls out to Ted Heath to play the national anthem. But instead of playing "The Star-Spangled Banner," Heath conducts his own country's national anthem, "God Save the Queen." Cole's publicist Dick LaPalm shouts, "The American anthem, the American one! To hell with the Queen!" Meanwhile, a shaken Cole recovers offstage and, on his return, tells the audience: "I was born here. I just came here to entertain you. That's what I thought you wanted." He is then examined by a doctor, and the "white" show is canceled. At 10:00 pm, he gives a brief performance in front of the black audience for the second show. Adams and Willis Vinson will be charged with assault with intent to murder, and Fox, Clevenger, and Edgar Vinson will be jailed on charges of conspiracy to incite a riot and disorderly conduct.

11 **Elvis Presley**'s plane makes an emergency landing in El Dorado, Arkansas, while flying from Amarillo, Texas, to Nashville. Although shaken, he records *I Want You, I Need You, I Love You* later in the day – though the incident will leave him with a fear of flying.

12 Bob Raiford, a DJ on North Carolina radio station WBT, is fired after he interviews Charlotte citizens about Tuesday's attack on **Nat King Cole.** WBT officials say it's against station policy to take a stand on controversial issues.

15 **Alan Freed** and Columbia Records' A&R producer and long-time executive **Mitch Miller** join two psychiatrists on Eric Sevareid's news program on CBS-TV to discuss the influence of rock 'n' roll on teenagers. Also featured are screen clips and interviews with teenagers taken from a recent rock 'n' roll show in Camden, New Jersey. Freed answers criticism of the genre and its effect on America's youth, and accuses the media of overreaction.

23 Billed as "The Nation's Only Atomic Powered Singer," **Elvis Presley** makes his debut in Las Vegas. He will earn $8,500 a week performing at the Venus Room of the New Frontier Hotel, opening for Freddie Martin & His Band and comedian Shecky Greene. He will, however, play only the first of two scheduled weeks, as the middle-aged audience's reaction is cool. Elvis won't return to Vegas for 13 years, but he will leave with an uptempo arrangement of R&B oldie *Hound Dog* from the hotel's lounge group, **Freddie Bell & the Bellboys.**

Nat King Cole was the subject of a racially motivated attack during a performance in Birmingham, Alabama.

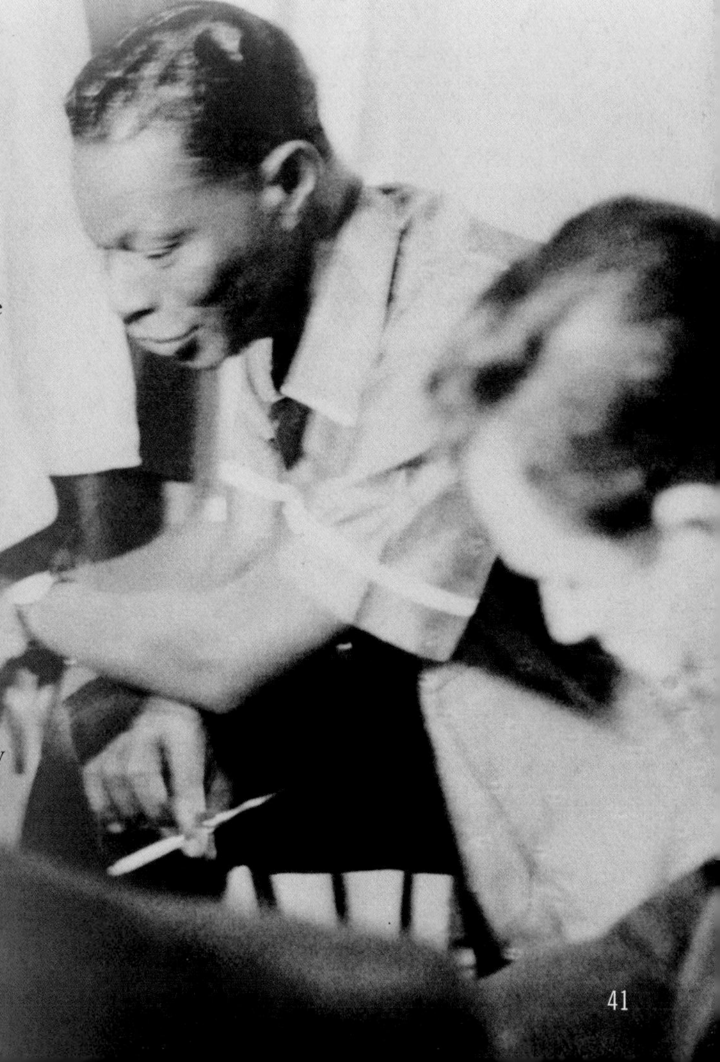

Heartbreak Hotel tops the charts... Elvis Presley's first film...

While Elvis would lead the celluloid charge of rock 'n' rollers performing in movies, many other new singers were in high demand in Hollywood.

May

2 The Biggest Rock and Roll Show of '56 caravan tour, a mixture of black and white acts, begins a 44-day North American swing in Hershey, Pennsylvania. Headlined by **Bill Haley & His Comets**, it features the **Platters**, **LaVern Baker**, **Joe Turner**, the **Drifters**, **Frankie Lymon & the Teenagers**, the **Teen Queens**, **Bo Diddley**, the **Colts**, the **Flamingos**, and **Red Prysock's Big Band**. The tour will gross over $100,000 on its first five dates.

4 **Gene Vincent** records a session at Owen Bradley's Nashville studio, with Ken Nelson producing. In his band: guitarists **"Galloping" Cliff Gallup** and **"Wee" Willie Williams**, bass player **"Jumpin'" Jack Neal**, and drummer **Dickie "Be-Bop" Harrell**. This lineup was to become the **Blue Caps**, taking their name from President Eisenhower's favorite blue golf cap. While the three demo songs from the April 9 session are re-recorded, the band also cuts the Jack Rhodes song *Woman Love*.

Frankie Lymon & the Teenagers were enjoying their first smash, the US No. 6 *Why Do Fools Fall In Love*.

5 *Heartbreak Hotel* begins a seven-week run heading the US Top 100. It will become **Elvis Presley**'s first million seller. It also hits C&W (country and western) No. 1 and R&B No. 5, and will prove to be the biggest-selling single of 1956. Presley's version of *Blue Suede Shoes*, released as the lead track on an EP, makes US No. 24 (while **Carl Perkins**'s original peaks at No. 4). Presley's debut album, ***Elvis Presley***, becomes the first rock 'n' roll album to top the US survey. With advance orders of 362,000, it becomes RCA's first million-dollar album by a solo artist, and the biggest-selling album to date, even before it is released. Next week, Presley will make his UK chart bow at No. 15 with *Heartbreak Hotel*.

19 Before beginning three weeks of US dates, **Lonnie Donegan** makes his US television debut, performing *Rock Island Line* on NBC-TV's "The Perry Como Show." The broadcast also features actor Ronald Reagan, who is appearing in some comedy sketches.

24 The first Eurovision Song Contest takes place in Lugano, Switzerland. Seven countries participate, each presenting two songs/performers. Lys Assia from Switzerland wins with *Refrain*, beating Belgium's marginally less cheerful *The Drowned Men Of The River Seine*.

30 Police go to a **Bill Haley & His Comets** concert at the Asbury Park Convention Hall in New Jersey, after a series of fights break out among the 2,700 fans at the beachfront hall. The city council will later ban rock 'n' roll concerts.

> **"When I met [Elvis] he only had about a million dollars' worth of talent. Now he has a million dollars."**
> "Col." Tom Parker

June

5 In his second appearance on "The Milton Berle Show," **Elvis Presley** performs a comedy routine with Berle, and sings *I Want You, I Need You, I Love You* and *Hound Dog*, in a hipshaking performance that initiates a storm of protest. The show features the **Jordanaires**, who are backing Presley on television for the first time: **Hoyt Hawkins** (baritone), **Gordon Stoker** (first tenor), **Neal Matthews** (second tenor), and **Hugh Jarrett** (bass). The Jordanaires are a gospel group from Springfield, Missouri, who met Elvis in October 1954 at the Ellis Auditorium in Memphis, where they were performing with Eddy Arnold.

July

1 **Elvis Presley** returns to NBC-TV, appearing on "The Steve Allen Show" in New York. The producers are looking for a less provocative act than on "The Milton Berle Show," and involve him in more comedy. Presley sings a sedate version of *I Want You, I Need You, I Love You*, followed by *Hound Dog* – the latter sung in white tie and tails to a real and unmoved basset hound called Sherlock. Allen presents the singer with an 18,000-signature petition from Tulsa, requesting him to be on television again, and Presley appears in "Range Roundup," a sketch with Allen and fellow guests Imogene Coca and Andy Griffith. After the show he also appears, from his hotel room, on local WRCA-TV's "Hy Gardner Calling" show.

2 **Elvis Presley** records *Hound Dog* – a 1953 hit for Willie Mae Thornton, written by Leiber and Stoller – at RCA's New York studio, finally satisfied after 31 takes. He also cuts quicker versions of *Don't Be Cruel* and *Any Way You Want Me (That's How I Will Be)*. For the first time, the Jordanaires supply backing vocals.

4 **Elvis Presley** returns to Memphis by train to appear at a charity concert for the **Memphis Press-Scimitar**'s Milk Fund and the Variety Club's Home for Convalescent Children. The venue is the 14,000-seater Russwood Park, the home of a minor league baseball team.

9 After the trouble at Asbury Park on June 30, **Bill Haley & His Comets** are banned from playing at the Roosevelt Stadium in Jersey City. Mayor Bernard Berry and the city commissioners are concerned that several recent rock 'n' roll concerts have ended in violence. They turn down appeals from concert promoter Ed Otto Jr. and bandleader Paul Whiteman, who was to have been master of ceremonies.

Whiteman maintains that the Friday show "was to be a concert" and therefore unlikely to result in a riot. A city ordnance reads: "Rock-and-roll music encouraged juvenile delinquency and inspired young females in lewd bathing suits to perform obscene dances on the city's beaches."

22 **Buddy Holly & the Three Tunes** (the third Tune is drummer **Jerry Allison**) cut a second Nashville session at Bradley's Barn. The song list from the session includes *I'm Changing All Those Changes*, *Girl On My Mind*, *Rock Around With Ollie Vee*, *Ting-A-Ling*, and *That'll Be The Day*. (Decca will sit on these recordings and release them in 1957, credited to Buddy Holly & the Three Tunes, on *That'll Be The Day*, after Holly has achieved success with the **Crickets.**) It will be more than a year before Buddy charts in the US, but *Blue Days, Black Nights* – his first recording, written by KDAV disc jockey Ben Hall – is currently enjoying airplay success in Britain.

23 In the UK, The Times newspaper's review of "Rock Around the Clock" describes it as a movie that cannot "profitably be discussed in the terms of normal criticism... There is one tremendous and solemn joke. Someone mentions the word 'waltz' and is immediately told to be careful with his language and to remember that there are ladies present."

August

14 Singer/guitarist **Eddie Cochran** is spotted by movie producer Boris Petroff while recording backing music for one of his low budget movies. Cochran will play a role in "The Girl Can't Help It," starring Jayne Mansfield and one of the first color rock 'n' roll movies, in which he sings *Twenty Flight Rock*. At 17, Cochran has been recording for Ekko Records and performed on television in 1955 as one half of the Cochran Brothers (with the unrelated Hank Cochran). He switched to rock 'n' roll after seeing Elvis Presley in Dallas late last year.

22 Filming begins in Hollywood on "The Reno Brothers," for which producer Hal Wallis has "loaned" his new movie property, **Elvis Presley**, to 20th Century Fox. The movie is a Civil War western, starring Richard Egan and Debra Paget, based on Maurice Geraghty's novel. It has been adapted to feature Presley, playing Clint Reno, and to include four period-style songs written by Ken Darby, whose trio backs Presley on the recordings. The producers will rename the movie "Love Me Tender" as Elvis's rendering of the ballad of that name (based on the 1861 folk ballad, *Aura Lee*), becomes its centerpiece.

24 Studio 51 in Great Newport Street, Soho – which is now billed as London's first rock 'n' roll club – begins its rock 'n' roll nights with a performance by **Rory Blackwell's Rock 'n' Rollers.**

28 **Alan Freed**'s annual ten-day rock 'n' roll show kicks off at the Paramount Theater in Brooklyn. It features **Fats Domino**, **Frankie Lymon & the Teenagers**, the **Cleftones**, the **Harptones**, and **Big Joe Turner**, together with doo-woppers, the **Moonglows** and the **Penguins**.

Sept **1956**

Elvis on "The Ed Sullivan Show"... Teenagers riot in British cities...

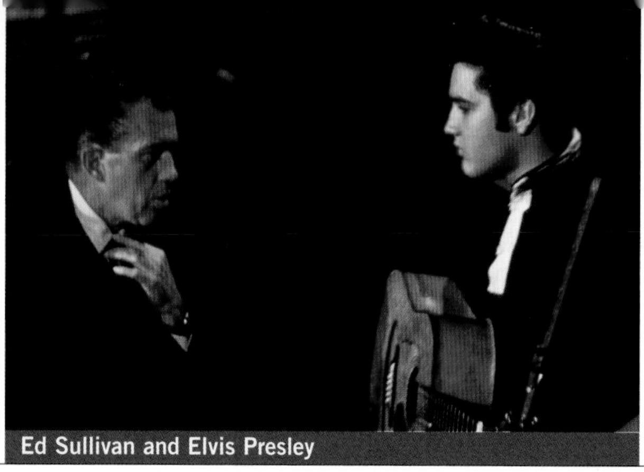
Ed Sullivan and Elvis Presley

September

1 Four weeks before his 20th birthday, rock 'n' roll aspirant, singer/pianist **Jerry Lee Lewis** – accompanied by his father Elmo – heads to Memphis from their home town in Ferriday, Louisiana, hoping to audition for Sam Phillips's Sun Records. (The Lewises have reportedly funded the trip by selling hundreds of eggs at Nelson's Supermarket in Ferriday.) When they arrive at the Memphis Recording Service, they find that Phillips is on vacation in Florida. Jerry Lee instead records some demos with recording engineer Jack Clement. Two months later, Sam Phillips will call Lewis back into the studio for another session.

9 An **Elvis Presley** segment aired from Hollywood is slotted into "The Ed Sullivan Show" transmitted from New York on CBS-TV. Sullivan is on record as saying he would never have Presley on his show, but Steve Allen's success in direct competition has changed his mind, and "Col." Tom Parker has negotiated a fee of $50,000 for three slots. The show features *Don't Be Cruel, Love Me Tender, Ready Teddy,* and *Hound Dog*, and is watched by an estimated 54 million people (a third of the US population and an 82.6 per cent viewing share). Sullivan himself is not presenting the show, having been injured in a car crash three days ago, and it is hosted by Charles Laughton. The following day, record stores are deluged with requests for copies of *Love Me Tender*, which is not scheduled for release for many weeks.

11 Following a showing of "Rock Around the Clock" at the Trocadero Cinema in the Elephant & Castle, London, two policeman are injured when called in to disperse a crowd "singing and jiving" in the New Kent Road. Bottles and fireworks are thrown and four shop windows are smashed. Nine youths are arrested and will appear at Tower Bridge Magistrates Court, where JP Miss Sybil Campbell will tell one defendant: "It's about time you realized you are grown up and stopped behaving like a silly little boy."

12 **The Times** newspaper publishes a letter from reader William Woolwich advocating the banning of the film "Rock Around the Clock" in the UK: "It was not pleasant to witness the rowdyism during and after the performance at a south London cinema in spite of the presence of police. It was still less pleasant on the way home to see a group outside another cinema which could only be dispersed with the aid of police dogs." He goes on to say, "The hypnotic rhythm and the wild gestures have a maddening effect on a rhythm-loving age-group and the result of its impact is the relaxing of all self-control."

> **"...it's a set of untalented twitchers and twisters whose appeal is largely to the zoot suiter and the juvenile department."**
>
> Billy Rose, songwriter and impresario, September 18, 1956

13 Authorities in the English cities of Birmingham, Blackburn, and Preston decide to ban the showing of the movie "Rock Around the Clock," following riots in other cities. A statement issued in Birmingham – Britain's second largest city – says the decision has been taken "on the ground that, if exhibited, the film would be likely to lead to disorder." Disturbances have been reported at showings in Manchester, Woolwich, Croydon, Chadwell Heath, Dagenham, Leyton, Peckham, West Ham, and

"Rock Around the Clock" was responsible for exporting rock 'n' roll around the globe, much to the delight of teenagers and the concern of the authorities. The film was also seen by Queen Elizabeth II.

Carl Perkins's guitar

Elvis Presley drew huge audiences for three appearances on the "Ed Sullivan Show"... While "Rock Around the Clock" was sparking riots in Britain, its sequel, "Don't Knock the Rock," opened in the US.

Twickenham. About a dozen arrests were made in Manchester after fans began jiving in the streets after the evening performance, while in Dagenham police ejected dancing youths from the Gaumont Cinema. Cinema manager, Mr. E.C. Carter, said, "We all enjoyed the first performance. Rowdies and troublemakers turned up for the next show and we had to call in the police." Alderman J. Shorrock, chairman of a "watch committee" in Blackburn, confirms, "After what has happened in Burnley and Manchester with these rock and roll teenagers, we are not prepared to agree to the showing of the film in Blackburn."

15 At Balmoral Castle in Scotland, Queen Elizabeth II asks to view "Rock Around the Clock" (she had been planning to see "The Caine Mutiny"). She is more fortunate than most of her loyal subjects: the Rank cinema chain cancels Sunday night showings of the film in several major UK cities, since Sunday has been chosen as the favored night out for the rock 'n' roll-inspired teddy boy gangs.

17 The BBC announces that it is banning **Bill Haley & His Comets**' *Rockin' Through The Rye* from the airwaves, on the grounds that it "tampers" with traditional British airs. The Haley record – currently standing at No. 5 in the UK charts – is based on the 18th-century Scottish folk tune *Comin' Thro' The Rye.*

18 A **Fats Domino** concert at a naval station in Newport, Rhode Island, ends in violence when the dancefloor is plunged into darkness. Ten sailors are injured and nine arrested. Rear Admiral Ralph Earle will ban rock 'n' roll music at the club for at least a month, after inspecting the wrecked room, strewn with broken bottles and chairs. His investigation concludes that, "The only cause of the melée among white and Negro sailors and marines and their wives and dates was the excitement accompanying the fever-pitched rock 'n' roll."

18 Songwriter and impresario Billy Rose blasts composition collecting agency Broadcast Music Inc. (BMI) at a congressional sub-committee hearing. It is looking into charges that television and radio networks, through the BMI, are controlling all pop songs heard by the public, both on air and on disc. Rose claims that BMI is publishing 74 per cent of the "top" songs, and observes: "It's the current climate on radio and television which makes Elvis Presley and his animal posturings possible. It used to be people like Al Jolson, Eddie Cantor and Nora Bayes who were the big salesmen of song. Now it's a set of untalented twitchers and twisters whose appeal is largely to the zoot suiter and the juvenile department."

24 Four days after Norwegian police had to use batons on a crowd of about 600 youngsters in an Oslo park, following the first showing in Norway of the film "Rock Around the Clock," Desmond Turrell is sentenced to six months in jail at High Wycombe Court, England, after pleading guilty to assaulting police Inspector Charles Currell. Turrell, described by police as the self-styled "King of the Teddy Boys," punched Currell in the eye during a disturbance at a local pub following a showing of the movie. A party of 23 – including Turrell – had gone to see the film in High Wycombe, because it had been banned in their home town of Reading.

29 **Bill Haley** equals a record set last year by **Ruby Murray**, with five songs simultaneously in the UK Top 30: *Rockin' Through The Rye* (No. 4), *The Saints Rock 'n' Roll* (No. 11), *(We're Gonna) Rock Around The Clock* (No. 13), *Razzle Dazzle* (No. 17), and *See You Later, Alligator* (No. 19).

"We took parts of four different types of music: dixieland, country and western, rhythm and blues, and our old jazz standards."

Bill Haley, BBC interview, September 14, 1956

October

12 The film "Don't Knock the Rock" opens in US theaters, featuring **Bill Haley & His Comets**, **Alan Freed**, and an irrepressible **Little Richard** (who is in stark contrast to a chubby, apparently middle-aged, Haley). Featured in the film are *Happy Baby, Rock-A-Beatin' Boogie, Razzle Dazzle, ABC Boogie, Mambo Rock, Rudy's Rock, R-O-C-K, See You Later Alligator,* and *Rock Around The Clock.*

TOMMY STEELE

Oct 15 **Having recently been scouted by several record companies and signed to Decca, 20-year-old singer/guitarist Tommy Steele makes his UK television debut on Jack Payne's "Off the Record" show, performing *Rock With The Caveman.***

Britain's first rocker, Bermondsey-born Tommy Steele, went from Cunard ship's steward to rocking the 2 i's coffee bar in London's Soho.

Sept 1956

Sept 26 Elvis Presley returns to Tupelo, to perform at the annual Mississippi-Alabama Fair and Dairy Show (the same fair at which he performed at the age of ten). Screaming teenagers are kept at bay by a cordon of the National Guard. The town declares "Elvis Presley Day," and Mayor James Ballard presents him with the key to the city. Elvis plays afternoon and evening open-air shows, donating his $10,000 fee to the Elvis Presley Youth Foundation. In future, he will donate $100,000 annually to the charity.

The set list for this afternoon's show in his hometown: *Heartbreak Hotel, Long Tall Sally, I Was The One, I Want You I Need You I Love You, I Got A Woman, Don't Be Cruel, Ready Teddy, Love Me Tender,* and *Hound Dog*.

"The young prince of rock 'n' roll...who is a guitar-playing Pied Piper..."

Tupelo Daily Journal, September 27, 1956

Oct 1956

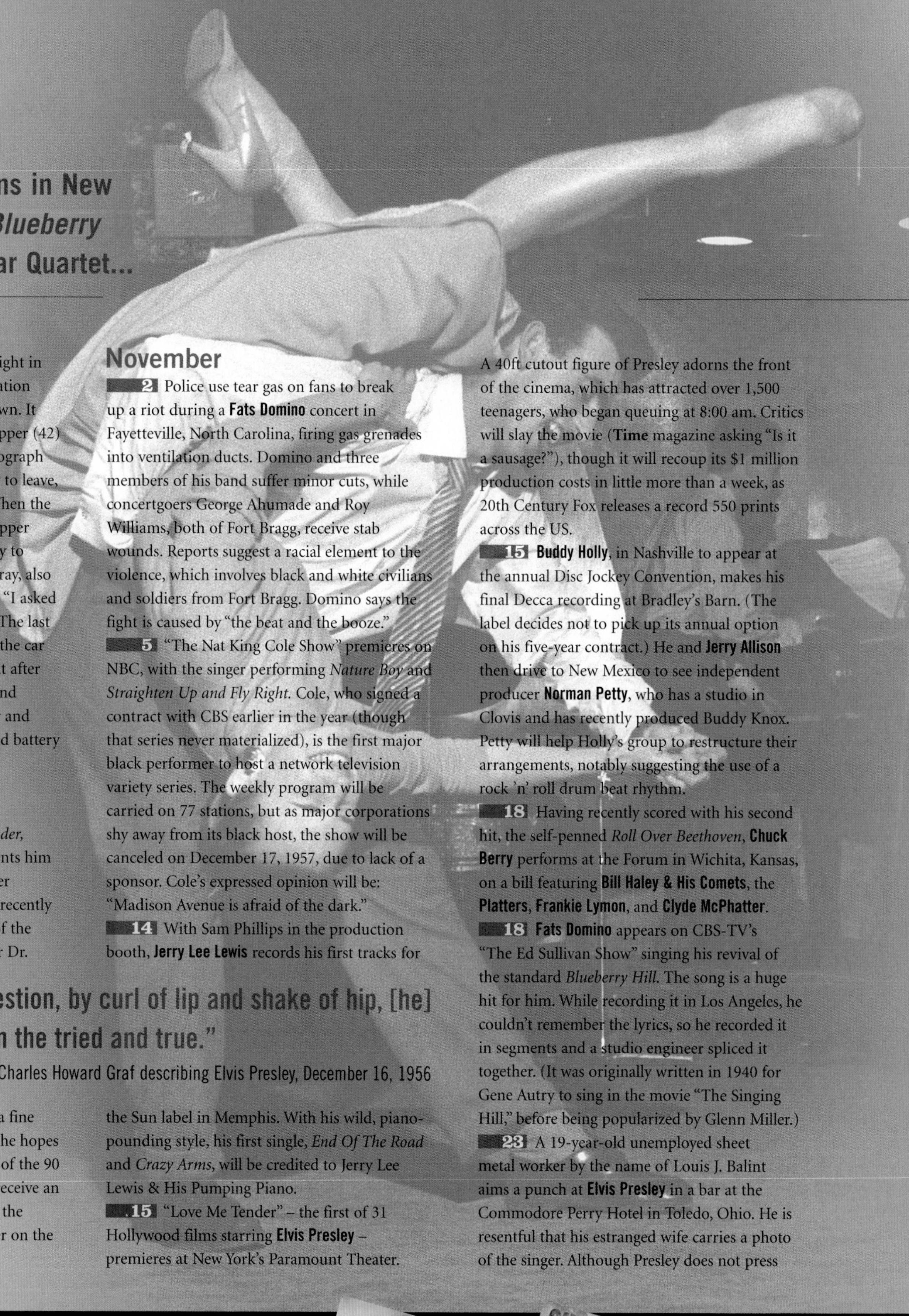

"Love Me Tender" opens in New York... Fats Domino's *Blueberry Hill*... The Million Dollar Quartet...

18 **Elvis Presley** gets involved in a fight in Memphis with Edd Hopper, a service station manager, and his employee, Aubrey Brown. It starts when 21-year-old Presley asks Hopper (42) to check his car's gas tank for leaks. Autograph hunters gather, and Hopper asks Presley to leave, so his station can get back to normal. When the singer continues to sign autographs, Hopper slaps him on the head, provoking Presley to punch him in the eye. Brown joins the fray, also receiving a punch. Hopper will later say, "I asked him three times to move, in a nice way. The last time I told him, he started to get out of the car and I shoved him back in. He started out after me." All three are charged with assault and battery, and disorderly conduct. Hopper and Brown will be found guilty of assault and battery and fined $25 and $15 respectively.

28 **Elvis Presley** makes his second appearance on "The Ed Sullivan Show," performing *Don't Be Cruel, Love Me Tender, Hound Dog,* and *Love Me*. Sullivan presents him with a gold disc for *Love Me Tender*. After rehearsals, Presley receives a shot of the recently developed Salk polio vaccine, courtesy of the City of New York. Health Commissioner Dr. Leona Baumgartner says: "He is setting a fine example for the youth of the country." She hopes that Presley's example will inspire some of the 90 per cent of New York's teenagers yet to receive an inoculation. Earlier, 1,000 fans attended the unveiling of a 40ft billboard of the singer on the Paramount Theater in Times Square.

November

2 Police use tear gas on fans to break up a riot during a **Fats Domino** concert in Fayetteville, North Carolina, firing gas grenades into ventilation ducts. Domino and three members of his band suffer minor cuts, while concertgoers George Ahumade and Roy Williams, both of Fort Bragg, receive stab wounds. Reports suggest a racial element to the violence, which involves black and white civilians and soldiers from Fort Bragg. Domino says the fight is caused by "the beat and the booze."

5 "The Nat King Cole Show" premieres on NBC, with the singer performing *Nature Boy* and *Straighten Up and Fly Right*. Cole, who signed a contract with CBS earlier in the year (though that series never materialized), is the first major black performer to host a network television variety series. The weekly program will be carried on 77 stations, but as major corporations shy away from its black host, the show will be canceled on December 17, 1957, due to lack of a sponsor. Cole's expressed opinion will be: "Madison Avenue is afraid of the dark."

14 With Sam Phillips in the production booth, **Jerry Lee Lewis** records his first tracks for the Sun label in Memphis. With his wild, piano-pounding style, his first single, *End Of The Road* and *Crazy Arms*, will be credited to Jerry Lee Lewis & His Pumping Piano.

15 "Love Me Tender" – the first of 31 Hollywood films starring **Elvis Presley** – premieres at New York's Paramount Theater. A 40ft cutout figure of Presley adorns the front of the cinema, which has attracted over 1,500 teenagers, who began queuing at 8:00 am. Critics will slay the movie (**Time** magazine asking "Is it a sausage?"), though it will recoup its $1 million production costs in little more than a week, as 20th Century Fox releases a record 550 prints across the US.

15 **Buddy Holly**, in Nashville to appear at the annual Disc Jockey Convention, makes his final Decca recording at Bradley's Barn. (The label decides not to pick up its annual option on his five-year contract.) He and **Jerry Allison** then drive to New Mexico to see independent producer **Norman Petty**, who has a studio in Clovis and has recently produced Buddy Knox. Petty will help Holly's group to restructure their arrangements, notably suggesting the use of a rock 'n' roll drum beat rhythm.

18 Having recently scored with his second hit, the self-penned *Roll Over Beethoven*, **Chuck Berry** performs at the Forum in Wichita, Kansas, on a bill featuring **Bill Haley & His Comets**, the **Platters**, **Frankie Lymon**, and **Clyde McPhatter**.

18 **Fats Domino** appears on CBS-TV's "The Ed Sullivan Show" singing his revival of the standard *Blueberry Hill*. The song is a huge hit for him. While recording it in Los Angeles, he couldn't remember the lyrics, so he recorded it in segments and a studio engineer spliced it together. (It was originally written in 1940 for Gene Autry to sing in the movie "The Singing Hill," before being popularized by Glenn Miller.)

23 A 19-year-old unemployed sheet metal worker by the name of Louis J. Balint aims a punch at **Elvis Presley** in a bar at the Commodore Perry Hotel in Toledo, Ohio. He is resentful that his estranged wife carries a photo of the singer. Although Presley does not press

> **"Using innuendo and suggestion, by curl of lip and shake of hip, [he] represents the revolt from the tried and true."**
>
> Rev. Charles Howard Graf describing Elvis Presley, December 16, 1956

Jerry Lee Lewis

The latest signing to Sun Records was rollicking singer-songwriter/pianist Jerry Lee Lewis, who sold eggs with his father to finance his first trip to Memphis... While Elvis became a movie star, Chuck Berry was in constant demand on tour.

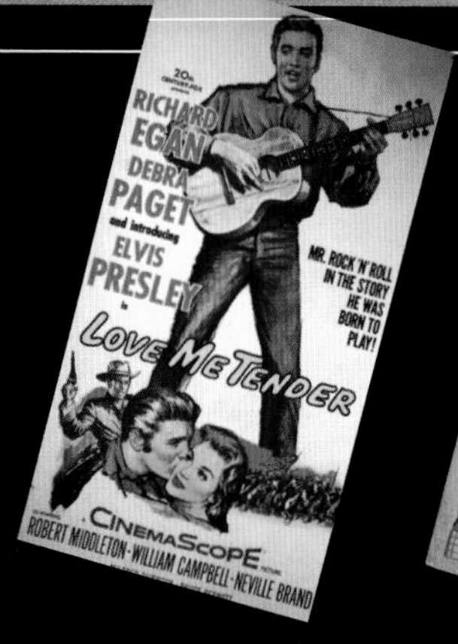

The legendary session was issued on disc after Presley's death.

charges, Balint is taken to the county workhouse to serve a seven-day sentence, because he is unable to pay the $19 fine and $9.60 costs.

December

7 **Tommy Steele** begins a series of concerts with a backing group known as the **Steelmen** (including **Roy Plummer** on guitar and **Alan Stewart** on saxophone). His first show at London's Finsbury Park Astoria gives rise to fan hysteria reminiscent of that being generated by **Elvis Presley** in the US. Steele's debut single, *Rock With The Caveman*, written with Mike Pratt and Lionel Bart, has already reached UK No. 13.

16 **Elvis Presley** makes his 50th and final appearance on the "Louisiana Hayride" at the Louisiana Fairgrounds, a benefit concert for the Shreveport YMCA. At the same time the Rev. Charles Howard Graf, rector of the Protestant Episcopal Church in Greenwich Village, New York, says the Elvis Presley craze will pass. "Basically I don't think youth wants this sort of thing. It is the result of the letdown that follows every war." Among other remarks, he describes Presley as "A lad who will probably earn more than the President and the entire Cabinet;" "A sad sack reminiscent of the late James Dean;" "A whirling dervish of sex;" and "An escape from reality in the form of a Pied Piper."

23 Alan Freed and His Rock 'n' Roll Christmas Show begins an eight-day residence at the Paramount Theater in Brooklyn. It is Freed's fifth event at the venue, and will gross $180,000. The show features **Shirley & Lee**, **Screamin' Jay Hawkins**, the **Moonglows**, the **Dells**, **Mac Curtis**, **Lillian Briggs**, **Eddie Cooley & the Dimples**, **George Hamilton IV**, the **Heartbeats**, the **Three Friends**, **Jesse Belvin**, the **G Clefs**, and **Bobbie Gaye**.

MILLION DOLLAR QUARTET

Dec 4 At home in Memphis for Christmas, Elvis Presley wanders into the Sun studios, where Carl Perkins and his group are recording, with Jerry Lee Lewis guesting on piano. Johnny Cash is also present initially, though his wife will draw him away to go shopping. The resulting jam session yields *Peace In The Valley*, *When God Dips His Love In My Heart*, *Brown-Eyed Handsome Man*, and *Don't Be Cruel*. Elvis, Carl, and Johnny also join Jerry Lee on *Crazy Arms*. Sam Phillips tapes what will become legendary as the "Million Dollar Quartet Session," a phrase coined by Robert Johnson, entertainment editor on the Memphis Press-Scimitar.

ROOTS During this year: Frank Zappa and Don Van Vliet meet at Antelope Valley High Scool in Lancaster, California, and form the Black-outs... 15-year-old Paul Anka forms his first group, the Bobbysoxers, with two classmates at Fisher Park High School in Ottawa, and begins work on *Diana*, a song inspired by his family's 18-year-old babysitter Diana Ayoub, for whom he has a passion... the Quintones, featuring the future Cliff Richard, debut at the Holy Trinity Youth Club in Waltham Cross, at an Anglo-French dance fundraiser... 14-year-old Aretha Franklin makes her first recordings, cutting live versions of Clara Ward hymns at her father's New Bethel Baptist Church in Detroit... brothers Steve and "Muff" Winwood perform in the Ron Atkinson Band alongside their tenor sax-playing father, Laurie... Leonard Cohen, having formed country and western squaredance band, the Buckskin Boys, at the start of the decade, has his first book of poems, Let Us Compare Mythologies, published... and Wayne Henderson joins Wilton Felder, Nesbert Hooper, and Joe Sample, who have been variously performing as the Chitterling Circuit, the Nite Hawks, and the Swingsters in their native Houston...

Let Me Be Your Teddy Bear

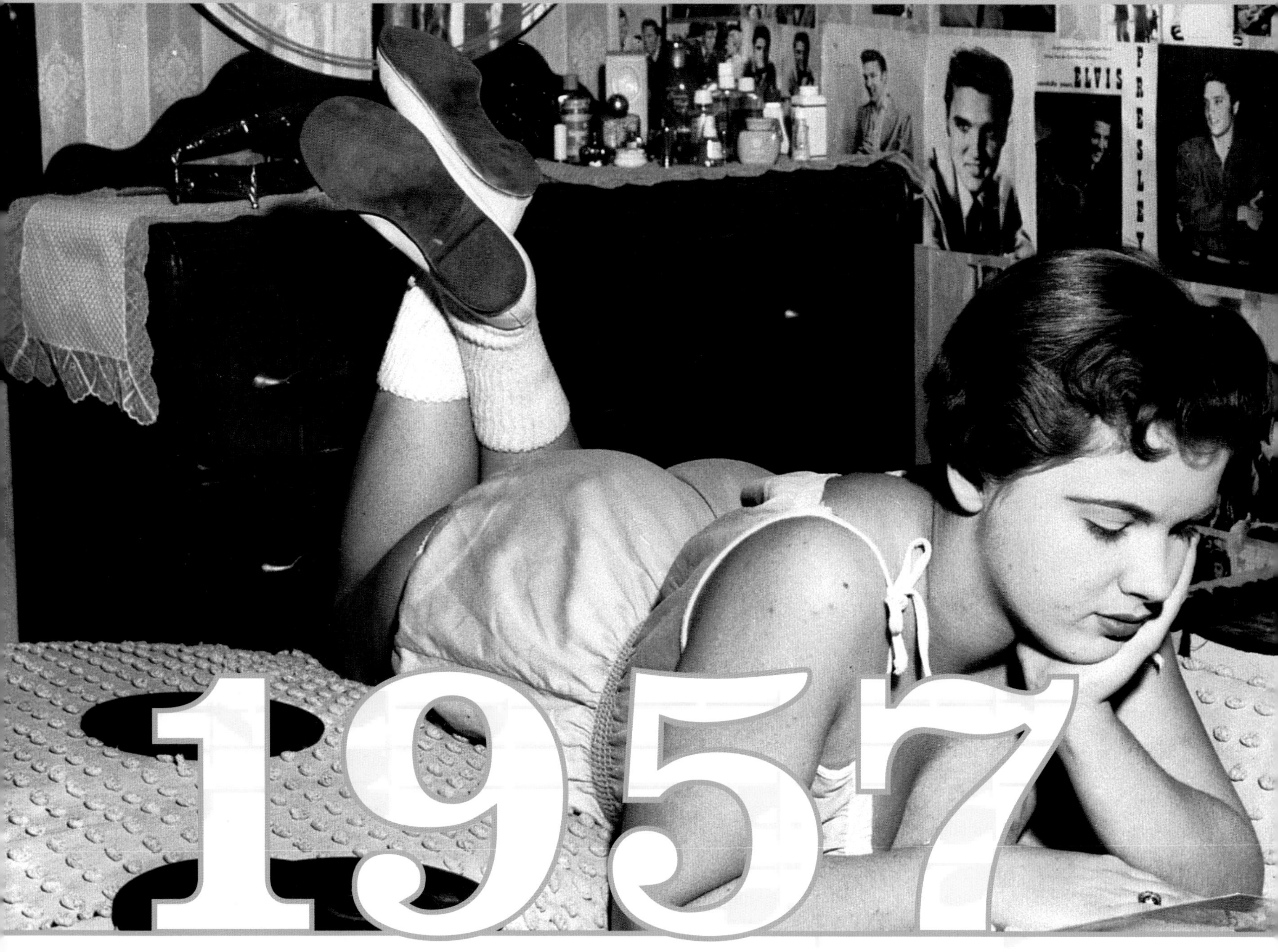

1957

No.1 US SINGLES

Jan 5	Singing The Blues	**Guy Mitchell**
Feb 16	Don't Forbid Me	**Pat Boone**
Feb 23	Young Love	**Tab Hunter**
Apr 6	Butterfly	**Andy Williams**
Apr 20	All Shook Up	**Elvis Presley**
June 15	Love Letters In The Sand	**Pat Boone**
July 20	Teddy Bear	**Elvis Presley**
Sept 7	Tammy	**Debbie Reynolds**
Oct 12	Honeycomb	**Jimmie Rodgers**
Oct 26	Wake Up Little Susie	**Everly Brothers**
Nov 9	Jailhouse Rock	**Elvis Presley**
Dec 21	You Send Me	**Sam Cooke**

No.1 UK SINGLES

Jan 5	Singing The Blues	**Guy Mitchell**
Jan 12	Singing The Blues	**Tommy Steele**
Jan 19	Singing The Blues	**Guy Mitchell**
Jan 26	Garden Of Eden	**Frankie Vaughan**
Feb 2	=Garden Of Eden	**Frankie Vaughan**
	=Singing The Blues	**Guy Mitchell**
Feb 9	Garden Of Eden	**Frankie Vaughan**
Feb 23	Young Love	**Tab Hunter**
Apr 13	Cumberland Gap	**Lonnie Donegan**
May 18	Rock-A-Billy	**Guy Mitchell**
May 25	Butterfly	**Andy Williams**
June 8	Yes Tonight Josephine	**Johnnie Ray**
June 29	Gamblin' Man/Putting On The Style	**Lonnie Donegan**
July 13	All Shook Up	**Elvis Presley**
Aug 31	Diana	**Paul Anka**
Nov 2	That'll Be The Day	**Crickets**
Nov 23	Mary's Boy Child	**Harry Belafonte**

Filming a skiffle band on "The Six-Five Special"

Bill Haley & His Comets

As rock 'n' roll's beat crossed the Atlantic, "The Six-Five Special" was the first rock music show in the UK... Bill Haley took the new sound even further afield, touring Australia.

By 1957, rock 'n' roll had spread far beyond the US, captivating teenagers as far afield as Australia, Japan, and Britain. **Bill Haley & His Comets** played a whistle-stop tour of Australia, and then moved on to the UK, where their reception verged on the hysterical. **Frankie Lymon & the Teenagers** – at the brief zenith of their popularity – also performed in Britain. **Elvis Presley** took his wildly successful show to Canada, where *All Shook Up* topped the new pop chart; it also became his first UK No. 1 hit. Britain began building its own rock 'n' roll roster, and first out of the gate – in what would become a five-year trend of copying America's lead – was **Tommy Steele**. Meanwhile, Scotsman **Lonnie Donegan** took skiffle music to Madison Square Garden in a rare transatlantic success for a Brit.

America's racial divide continued to spill over into popular music. A **Louis Armstrong** concert in Knoxville (for a segregated audience) was the target of a stick of dynamite, and black and white artists still played on separate bills in the Biggest Show of Stars of 1957 tour.

Increasingly, rock 'n' roll overshadowed what **Billboard** called the "good music" of **Pat Boone**, **Perry Como**, and **Debbie Reynolds**. **Elvis Presley** had four singles in the magazine's top 20 of the year; Boone had two. To the establishment on both sides of the Atlantic, rock 'n' roll was still a threat to society. But whether the establishment liked it or not, rock 'n' roll was becoming big business. On television, the "Ed Sullivan Show," the "Perry Como Show," and "Arthur Godfrey's Talent Scouts" program all competed for acts. **Jerry Lee Lewis**'s *Whole Lotta Shakin' Goin On* raced up the chart after he appeared on the "Steve Allen Show." Dick Clark's ratings-grabber, "American Bandstand," went nationwide. Elvis and Bill Haley were not the only ones to appear on the silver screen: **Little Richard** contributed to one of the more memorable movie sequences of the year, thrashing out *The Girl Can't Help It* while Jayne Mansfield strutted down a sidewalk clutching two bottles of milk to her ample bosom. No wonder he turned to God.

The roster of talent was growing fast. Presley, Haley, and **Chuck Berry** were joined on the charts by **Buddy Holly**, the **Everly Brothers**, Jerry Lee Lewis, and **Patsy Cline**. And they were so young. Another hot new act was **Paul Anka**. At the age of just 15, he wrote and recorded *Diana* – a boy's paean to an older teenage girl – flavored with cha cha and calypso, another sign of how genres were still being absorbed and mutated.

The finest songwriting team in rock 'n' roll also emerged: **Jerry Leiber** and **Mike Stoller**. Perfectly matching R&B with pop, they crafted some of the most memorable hit songs of the era. Another songwriting duo – who would soon begin making their own rock 'n' roll history – met for the first time in 1957: two teenagers named **John Winston Lennon** and **James Paul McCartney** were introduced at a Liverpool church fête. Fate indeed.

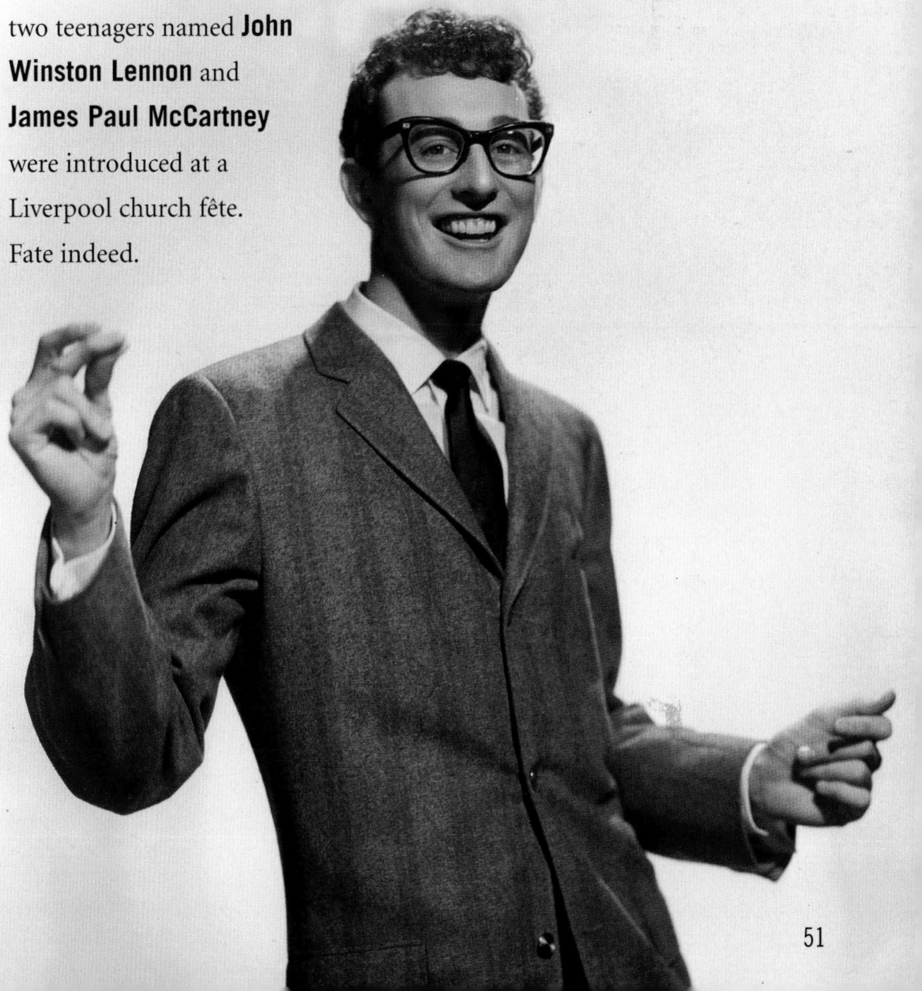

"Buddy Holly gave you confidence. He was like the boy next door."

Paul McCartney, **Rolling Stone**, 1980s

Bill Haley & His Comets visit Australia and Britain... The Cavern Club opens its doors...

January

1 Associated Rediffusion in London launches its first pop music television show, "Cool For Cats." The 15-minute program features host Kent Walton playing records and commenting on them, and sometimes includes visual interpretations of the music by the Dougie Squires Dancers. (The show will run until 1959.)

3 In New Orleans, **Fats Domino** cuts *I'm Walkin'* with sax players **Herb Hardesty** and **Lee Allen**, guitarist **Walter Nelson**, bassist **Frank Fields**, and drummer **Earl Palmer**. Dave Bartholomew produces.

4 Required to do his military service, **Elvis Presley** – dressed in a crimson jacket and black slacks – passes his pre-induction medical checkup at Kennedy Veterans Hospital Examination Station in Memphis. The commander of the Army's Memphis recruiting station says Presley's test scores place him in the 1-A Class. (His joining the army will be deferred until March 1958.)

8 **Bill Haley & His Comets** begin a world tour in Sydney, playing to two sellout crowds of 7,000 fans, which breaks the previous Australian attendance figure for a concert. **Freddie Bell & the Bellboys**, **Big Joe Turner**, **LaVern Baker**, and the **Platters** are the opening acts. This first ever rock 'n' roll tour of the country continues with two nights at the Brisbane Stadium, dates at the Tivoli Theatre, Adelaide, followed by gigs in Melbourne, then Victoria, and return visits to Melbourne and Sydney. During the group's visit to Australia, they will perform before more than 300,000 fans in all.

10 With the last of the **Crew Cuts**' 11 chart discs, *Young Love*, currently on the US survey, the Canadian vocal troupe perform the song on CBS-TV's "Dorsey Brothers Stage Show."

16 The Cavern Club opens on Mathew Street in Liverpool, with the aim of giving the city a top jazz cellar. The venue is owned by Alan Sytner – who has named it after the Paris jazz club, Le Caveau. The opening act is the **Merseysippi Jazz Band**, and over the coming years it will host many of the great names of British jazz. Ray McFall will buy the club from Sytner in 1959.

18 Mr. C.R. Seaton, headmaster of Nottingham Secondary Arts School, bans his students from attending twice-weekly lunchbreak rock 'n' roll dance sessions at a nearby dance hall. Writing to parents, he says, "I was shocked when I discovered that almost all the school had been to the sessions at some time or other. We used to run a lunchtime ballroom dancing session at the school which about sixty children attended. Now it's flopped completely."

21 **Elvis Presley**'s second film, and his first contracted movie for Hal Wallis, begins production at Paramount Studios. "Loving You" (originally titled "The Lonesome Cowboy," then "Running Wild," but now named after a Leiber and Stoller song) traces a working class lad's journey from gas station to recording studio. Elvis plays Deke Rivers, co-starring with Lizabeth Scott and Wendell Corey. During filming, he will receive his first screen kiss from Jana Lund, and the soundtrack will yield the hit *Let Me Be Your Teddy Bear*, which will begin a seven-week run at US No. 1 in June.

21 **Tommy Steele** makes his debut at the Café de Paris in London's upmarket Mayfair. Donning blue suede shoes, blue jeans, and matching canary-colored socks and scarf, the former ship's cabin boy stirs up the society crowd, which includes film star Douglas Fairbanks Jr. and stage designer Oliver Messel.

21 **Patsy Cline** appears on "Arthur Godfrey's Talent Scouts" television show, performing *Walkin' After Midnight* – written by Don Hecht and Alan Block – which will become her first US Country chart entry on March 2.

24 Swansea Corporation councillors turn down promoter Arthur Howes's request for skiffle king **Lonnie Donegan** to perform at the city's Brangwyn Hall. In a statement, committee member Mr. E.A.F. Smith says: "We felt this was a type of music that would attract an exuberant crowd of youngsters. We don't want that sort of thing because we cannot afford to take the risk of damage to the famous Brangwyn Panels in the Hall." Cardiff's civic leaders will allow the concert to go ahead there, at the Sophia Gardens Pavilion, on February 7. When asked whether they are concerned about the hall, 53-year-old Alderman Lawrence Doyle replies, "Not a bit."

31 Decca Records, UK distributor of the Brunswick label, announces that *(We're Gonna) Rock Around The Clock* has now sold over a million copies, mostly 10in 78s: the first time this feat has been achieved.

ELVIS PRESLEY

Jan 6 Wearing a gold lamé vest, Elvis appears on "The Ed Sullivan Show." Sullivan tells Presley that he's "never had a pleasanter experience on our *shew* with a big name than we've had with you," and says that he is a "real decent, fine boy."

During his uptempo numbers, Presley was shown on screen from the waist up only.

The Five Satins

Presley's second movie, "Loving You," was named after a Leiber and Stoller song... The Five Satins recorded the enduring radio favorite, ***In The Still Of The Night.***

February

1 On Don Everly's 20th birthday, the **Everly Brothers** – Don and his younger brother, Phil – are signed to Cadence Records on the recommendation of song publisher and manager Wesley Rose, for whom they are already staff writers at his co-owned Acuff-Rose publishing house. The harmonious country/pop singer-songwriter/guitarist siblings were born in Chicago, but moved to Shenandoah, Iowa, in 1945, and performed as children on the Earl May Seed Company radio show, where they were known as Little Donnie & Baby Boy Phil. They previously recorded four sides for Columbia Records, on November 9, 1955, but without success.

2 **Fats Domino** performs *Blue Monday* and *Blueberry Hill* on the "Perry Como Show." Como, already a highly popular television and music veteran who has scored more than 50 pop hits since 1943, continues to sidestep rock 'n' roll as he pursues his enormously successful, mainstream, ballad-led singing career.

4 **Daily Mirror** contest winners, teenager Madge Macbeth and her mother Ann, from Surrey, fly to Cherbourg in France to join **Bill Haley** on the last leg of his trip to England from New York aboard the venerable liner *Queen Elizabeth*. Macbeth named her mother in answer to the contest question: "Which square would you like to introduce to Haley?"

6 **Bill Haley & His Comets** make their UK bow at London's Dominion Theatre, before 3,000 screaming fans, who voice their disapproval when the band plays for little more than half an hour. The group – trussed in tartan tuxedos – open with *Razzle Dazzle*, followed by *Rudy's Rock* and *You Made Me Love You*, and end with *Rock Around The Clock*. Screams of "We want Bill" die away only when the national anthem is played. Even the reviewer for the staid, conservative newspaper **The Daily Telegraph** is caught up in the fervor, claiming, "I enjoyed the fun of the Haley type of entertainment. Let no cat call me square." The band will play 18 dates, with support acts the **Vic Lewis Band**, tin whistler **Desmond Lane**, and crooner **Malcolm Vaughan**, who also appears with **Kenny Earle** as comedy/singing duo **Earle & Vaughan**. The tour will end at the Gaumont Cinema in Southampton on the 23rd.

7 The movies "Rock Around The Clock" and "Bus Stop," the latter starring Marilyn Monroe, are banned in Iraq, judged by censors to be dangerous to teenagers and youths.

13 Dr. Ramon Vasconcelos, Cuba's Minister of Communications, announces a ban on all rock 'n' roll programs on television, citing rock 'n' roll as "immoral and profane" and "offensive to public morals and good customs." He will bow to public pressure and lift the ban in two days' time. As a compromise, television stations promise to have young performers remove three steps from a new dance that the minister considers "degrading to public morals."

15 **Chuck Berry**, **Fats Domino**, **Clyde McPhatter**, the **Five Satins**, the **Moonglows**, **LaVern Baker**, **Bill Doggett**, and others, embark on Irvin Feld's Greatest Show of 1957 package tour in Pittsburgh, which will run until May 5.

15 Filming begins in England on "The Tommy Steele Story," a cheap and cheerful depiction of the rise to fame of this humble London lad, with a script by Norman Hudis, directed by Gerard Bryant. Musical guest appearances in the movie include **Humphrey Lyttelton & His Band**, the **Chas McDevitt Skiffle Group with Nancy Whiskey**, the **Tommy Eytle Calypso Band**, and **Chris O'Brien's Caribbeans**.

15 In their second session for Atlantic, the **Coasters** record Leiber and Stoller's nuggets, *Sweet Georgia Brown, Searchin'* – which will become their first US top three hit in July (and their first British chart disc) – and *Young Blood*.

16 Disc jockey Pete Murray introduces a new music program on BBC television with the words: "Welcome aboard the Six-Five Special. We've got almost a hundred cats jumping here, some real cool characters to give us the gas, so just get on with it and have a ball." He's followed by Jo Douglas, adding: "Well, I'm just a square it seems, but for all the other squares with us, roughly translated what Pete Murray said was: 'We've got some lively musicians and personalities mingling with us here, so just relax and catch the mood with us.'" (Until this evening, BBC television has been "dark" between the hours of 6:00 and 7:00 pm – an arrangement affectionately known as the "toddlers' truce.")

> **"We've got almost a hundred cats jumping here, some real cool characters to give us the gas."**
>
> Pete Murray introducing "The Six-Five Special," February 16, 1957

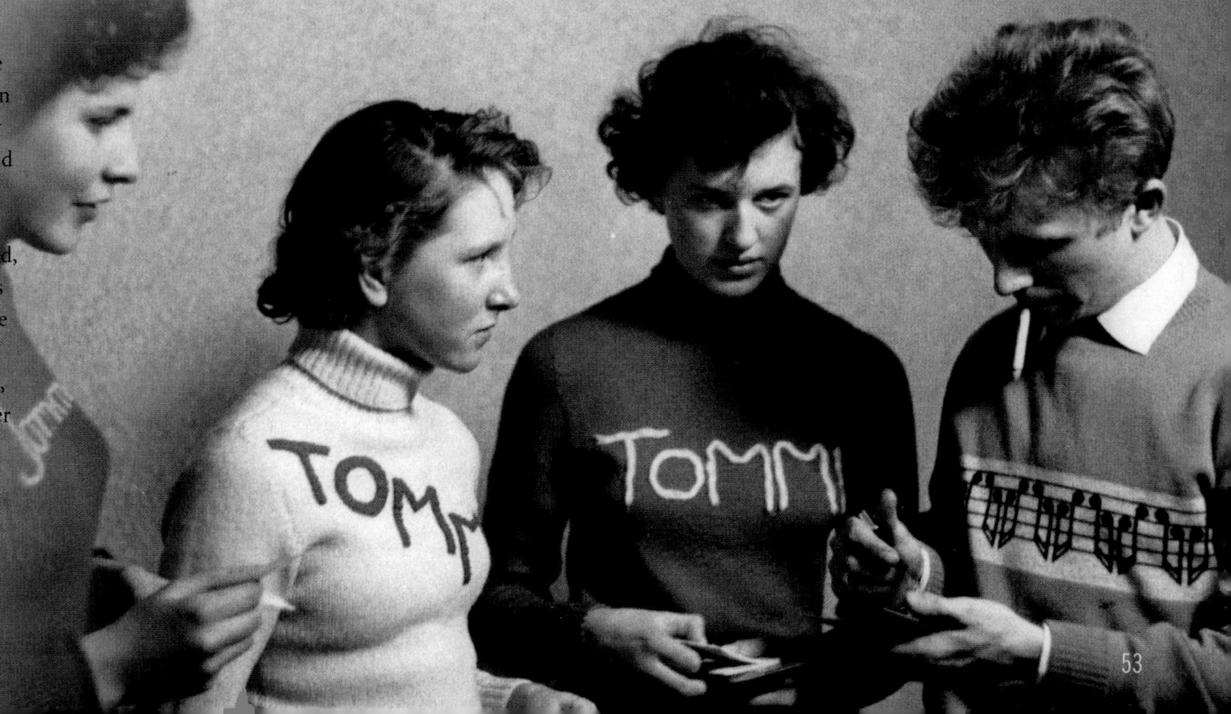

Former Cunard cruise line assistant steward Tommy Steele was one of three artists to hit UK No. 1 in 1957 with *Singing The Blues*.

Writing his daily diary, "Bill Haley's Column," for the Daily Mirror, Haley described having breakfast at teatime on board the transatlantic crossing "thanks to a guy called Caruthers."

"*(We're Gonna) Rock Around The Clock* has now sold over one million copies in Great Britain."

Decca Records, January 31, 1957

Feb 5 Bill Haley arrives at Southampton on the *Queen Elizabeth*, for his long-awaited British concert debut. He is greeted at the dock by a crowd estimated to number between 3,000 and 5,000. The first US rock artist to tour the UK, he is mobbed for 20 minutes by a further estimated 2,000 fans when his train reaches Waterloo station in London. Some fans break through the 50-strong cordon of police to pound on the windows and doors of the bandleader's car. One of tomorrow's newspaper reports will run: "Bowler-hatted commuters, their umbrellas at the ready, bravely fought their way through to their suburban trains."

Rocking in the aisles...
That'll Be The Day...
Elvis buys Graceland...

"...a composite of a teenage revival meeting and the Battle of the Bulge."

The New York Times review of "Don't Knock The Rock,"

19 **Louis Armstrong**, who is already a world-renowned jazz pioneer and – together with Nat King Cole – the most widely known black performer around, is performing at a hall in Knoxville, Tennessee. A single stick of dynamite is thrown from a passing car, landing some 200yd from the venue. Armstrong, who has just returned to the stage after an intermission, tells the segregated audience, estimated at 2,000 whites and 1,000 blacks, "That's all right folks. It's just the phone."

22 Arthur Murray, president of the venerable Arthur Murray Schools of Dancing, claims that the rock 'n' roll craze has led to a ten percent rise in the number of teenage pupils who have signed up for dance classes in the US since last summer. Meanwhile Edward Fields, president of rugmakers, E. Fields Inc., reveals that sales of small rugs have increased – a trend he attributes to the fact that parents of jiving youngsters prefer to buy small rugs because they are easy to roll up in preparation for dancing.

23 The New York Police Department assigns 279 officers to maintain order amid today's crowd of 16,000 at the Paramount Theater. An educational psychologist, who is attending a meeting of the American Psychopathological Association at the Park Sheraton Hotel nearby, suggests that what is happening at the theater is "very much like the medieval type of spontaneous lunacy where one person goes off and lots of other persons go off with him." The conference also hears of a study by Dr. Reginald Lourie of the Children's Hospital in Washington, which indicates that 10–20 percent of all children in 1949 did "some act like rocking or rolling." (In a more recent paper, Dr. Joost Meerlo, associate in psychiatry at Columbia University, has likened rock 'n' roll to St. Vitus Dance – the "contagious epidemic of dance fury" that "swept Germany and spread to all of Europe" toward the end of the 14th century, with its victims breaking into dancing and being unable to stop. Meerlo's thesis continues "The Children's Crusades and the tale of the Pied Piper of Hamelin remind us of these seductive, contagious dance furies.")

23 In a piece titled "Rock 'n' Roll Exported To 4 Corners of Globe," the **New York Times** reports on how the rock 'n' roll phenomenon is taking off all over the world. It even claims that recordings by **Elvis Presley** – cut on discarded X-ray plates – are selling in Leningrad for $12.50 each, while the film "Rock Around the Clock" has caused disturbances on every continent, even touching off a riot in Tokyo.

25 **Buddy Holly** records a new version of his composition *That'll Be The Day* at Norman Petty's studio in Clovis, New Mexico. (The title is taken from an oft-used phrase by John Wayne in the film "The Searchers.") Holly's backing crew comprises **Jerry Allison**, **Larry Welborn**, fellow Lubbock native **Niki Sullivan** (rhythm guitar), and **Gary** and **Ramona Tollet** (backing vocals). Holly will soon form a new band – which will be named the **Crickets** – with Allison, Sullivan, and **Joe Mauldin** (bass), a 16-year-old Lubbock high school student. They will tape several demos for Petty, of which two of the cuts – *Last Night* and *Maybe Baby* – will be sent to Roulette Records. While they wait for a reply, they will fail an audition for "Arthur Godfrey's Talent Scouts." After Roulette turns them down, Petty will contact Murray Deutch of publishers Peer-Southern, telling him he can have 50 percent of publishing royalties on *That'll Be The Day* if he can get the Crickets a recording deal. After they have been rejected by Atlantic, Columbia, and RCA, Deutch will persuade Bob Thiele, A&R chief at Coral (ironically a Decca subsidiary), to sign the band as a favor to him.

March

1 The **Everly Brothers** record *Bye Bye Love* and two other tracks (the self-penned *I Wonder If I Care As Much* and *Should We Tell Him*) at the RCA Victor studio in Nashville. The country/pop song *Bye Bye Love* has been written by **Felice** and **Boudleaux Bryant**, a middle-aged husband and wife songwriting team who have a gift for capturing teen emotion. The session is supervised by Everly family friend **Chet Atkins**, who also contributes guitar, with second guitarist **Ray Edent**, **Jimmy Day** on steel guitar, **Lightin' Chance** on bass, and **Buddy Harman** on

DON'T KNOCK THE ROCK

Feb 22 **Screaming teenagers cram into the US premiere of "Don't Knock The Rock" at New York's Paramount Theater. The accompanying Alan Freed package show includes the red-hot Platters, Ruth Brown, Jimmy Bowen, Nappy Brown, Frankie Lymon & the Teenagers, and the Cadillacs. The 8:30 am showing is almost halted when the building inspector insists that teenagers in the first four rows of the balcony sit down. The final showing is at 10:30 pm.**

drums. They record the song at the request of producer **Archie Bleyer** – also boss of Cadence Records – whose only country act is Gordon Terry. Some 30 acts (including Terry) have already turned down *Bye Bye Love*. The Everlys' version – featuring close Appalachian harmonies over acoustic guitars and a rock 'n' roll beat – establishes their trademark sound.

19 **Elvis Presley** buys Graceland, a 23-room, two-story mansion in 13.8 acres of ground at 3764 South Bellevue Boulevard, in the Memphis suburb of Whitehaven. He pays $102,500 for the property, built of Tennessee limestone and previously used as a place of worship by the Graceland Christian Church. The original house was built by S.E. Toof, who named it after his daughter Grace. It was rebuilt in the late 1930s by Grace's niece Ruth Moore, whose daughter now sells it to Presley.

22 **Elvis Presley** points a prop pistol at 18-year-old marine Private Hershel Nixon, who allegedly tried to start a fight with the singer. Afterwards, Nixon says: "I didn't try to fight with him and I wasn't drinking. I had no way of knowing the pistol was a toy. He didn't tell me the gun wasn't real or let me inspect it," adding, "Presley's lip curled and he snarled like a movie bad man, and said, 'I'll blow your brains out.'" Nixon says he won't complain to the police but will ask Presley for a personal apology. Presley claims Nixon walked up to him and said: "You bumped into my wife as she walked out of a restaurant about two months ago. She told me all about it. I want to get it straightened out right now." Next week Presley and Nixon will meet in a city judge's office and announce that "everything has been straightened out."

27 Still on a skiffle high, **Lonnie Donegan** performs at New York's Madison Square Garden, as part of a US tour arranged as an exchange with **Bill Haley & His Comets**.

31 Moscow newspaper **Soviet Culture** asserts that rock 'n' roll is not a musical but a financial phenomenon. It claims the real story is to be found "not in the scandal sections of newspapers where the exploits of its exponents are mentioned," but on the financial pages. "Rock 'n' roll is above all a tremendous goldbearing vein that brings enterprising, smart operators millions of dollars in profits."

31 In Little Rock, Arkansas, **Johnny Cash**, **Jerry Lee Lewis**, a now fully recovered **Carl Perkins**, **Onie Wheeler**, and **Glen Douglas** begin a country/rock 'n' roll tour of southern states.

> **"I was terrified. They put me on at Madison Square Garden and I was very aware of the fact that 17,000 people had come along to see the Harlem Globetrotters."**
>
> Lonnie Donegan, March 27, 1957

April

1 With dozens of rock 'n' roll acts now touring outside the US for the first time, **Frankie Lymon & the Teenagers** make their European debut at the London Palladium at the start of a 12-week continental trek.

10 **Ricky Nelson** sings his first single – a version of Fats Domino's current smash, *I'm Walkin'* – on ABC-TV's "The Adventures Of Ozzie and Harriet." Born in Teaneck, New Jersey, 16-year-old Ricky is the second son of showbiz couple Ozzie and Harriet Nelson (formerly a bandleader and band vocalist). He has already appeared in the movies "The Story Of Three Loves" and "Here Comes The Nelsons," after an even earlier start on "The Adventures Of Ozzie and Harriet" when it was a radio show in 1949. His television performance turns him into the next big music teen idol. Nelson told a girlfriend he wanted to record a single as a defensive reaction to her adulation of Elvis Presley. Through contacts at Verve Records, Ozzie Nelson gets the song recut in a studio session, arranged by guitarist Barney Kessel, with two other tracks. The renamed *I'm Walking* (with the final "g" added to distinguish it from the Domino original) will zoom to US No. 4 on June 3, one week before a second Nelson single, *A Teenager's Romance*, hits No. 2.

12 With his popular *Don't You Rock Me Daddy-O* still in the Top 10, **Lonnie Donegan**'s version of the traditional *Cumberland Gap* becomes the first skiffle disc to hit No. 1 on the UK singles chart.

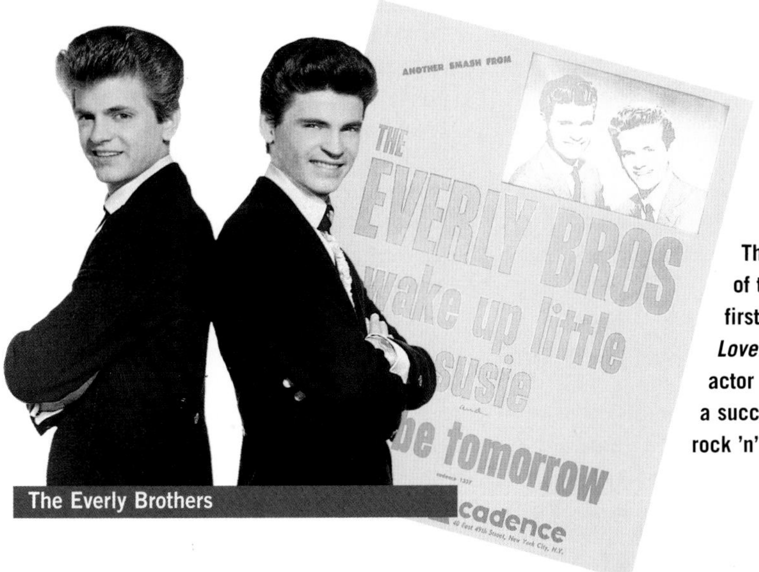

The Everly Brothers

The sweet harmonies of the Everly siblings first emerged on *Bye Bye Love...* Telegenic teenage actor Ricky Nelson made a successful transition to rock 'n' roll stardom.

Ricky Nelson

NARAS convenes... The height of the skiffle craze... John Lennon meets Paul McCartney...

Chas McDevitt's Skiffle Group

20 **Elvis Presley**'s *All Shook Up* begins an eight-week residence at the top of the US singles chart. The song has been written by **Otis Blackwell** (who was also responsible for *Don't Be Cruel*). He will later recount that the inspiration for *All Shook Up* came from a meeting with Shalimar Music executive Al Stanton. "He walked in with a bottle of Pepsi, shaking it as they did at the time. Al said, 'Otis, I've got an idea. Why don't you write a song called "All Shook Up"?' A couple of days later I brought the song in and said 'Look man, I did something with it!'" The record will sell two million copies in the US and become the biggest-selling single of 1957.

22 Second only to **Lonnie Donegan** in the current skiffle boom in Britain, **Chas McDevitt's Skiffle Group featuring Nancy Whiskey** perform at the Royal Festival Hall in London's first major skiffle concert. The bill also includes **Johnny Duncan, Ray Bush & the Avon Cities Jazz Band**, and **Bob Cort with Dickie Bishop**.

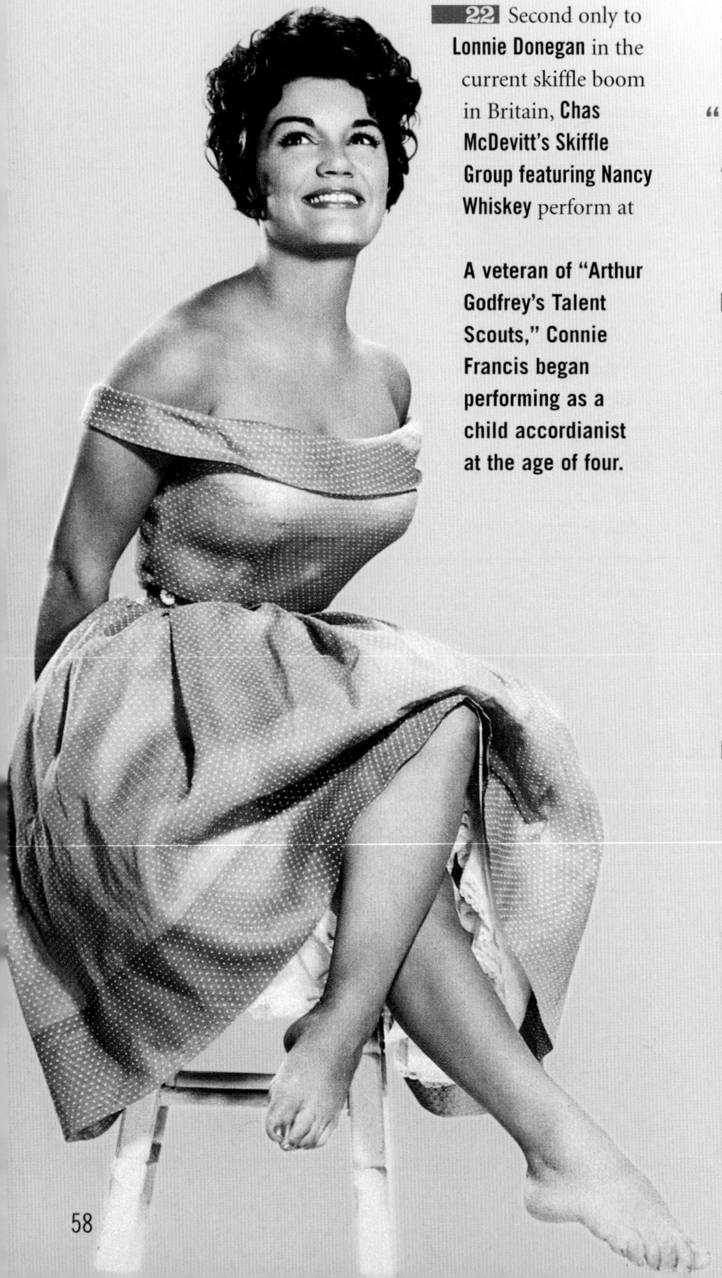

A veteran of "Arthur Godfrey's Talent Scouts," Connie Francis began performing as a child accordianist at the age of four.

27 **Elvis Presley** performs at Maple Leaf Gardens in Toronto, in his first concert outside the US, during a week-long tour that is taking in Detroit, Buffalo, New York, Ottawa, Philadelphia, and Wichita Falls.

May

4 **Alan Freed**'s "Rock 'n' Roll Revue" airs on ABC-TV, with the rather tame line-up of crooner **Guy Mitchell**, **June Valli**, **Sal Mineo**, **Martha Carson**, the **Del Vikings**, the **Clovers**, and the more boisterous **Screamin' Jay Hawkins**.

12 **Tommy Steele** opens at London's Dominion Theatre, headlining a variety bill that includes **Freddie Bell & the Bellboys**. **The Daily Telegraph** reports: "It may seem a far cry from the 12th-century troubadour to Mr. Steele, but the connection is there, though he may appear to some to be no more than a crazy mixed-up minstrel with ants in his pants. Honesty compels me to admit that the indescribable din let loose by these two turns caused – to put it mildly – something of a furore around me. In the modern idiom, this was an evening out for the 'cats'. Personally I'll take the more soothing, more civilised caterwaulings of the four-legged kind."

13 Production begins on **Elvis Presley**'s film "Jailhouse Rock" at MGM's Culver City Studios, co-starring Judy Tyler, Mickey Shaughnessy, Dean Jones, and Jennifer Holden. Presley plays Vince Everett, a misfit convicted of manslaughter who becomes a rock star.

14 **Elvis Presley** is rushed to Cedars of Lebanon Hospital in Los Angeles, suffering from chest pains. A porcelain cap from one of his front teeth – swallowed during a dance routine – is lodged in his right lung. He will remain in the hospital overnight, following an operation to remove the cap, and will recuperate at his hotel.

16 **Buddy Holly** formally signs with Bob Thiele of Coral Records; the agreement involves selling the master recordings of *Words Of Love* and *Mailman Bring Me No More Blues*. There are two separate recording contracts involving the singer: the first – with the Brunswick label – is for records issued under the name of the **Crickets**. The second – with Coral – is for tracks released under Buddy Holly's name. In 11 days, Brunswick will release *That'll Be The Day*.

21 Canadian **Paul Anka** cuts his first record for the ABC-Paramount label in New York: the self-penned *Diana*, about a girl back home in Ottawa. He recorded his first song, *I Confess*, for Modern last September. Only 15, Anka won an Easter trip to New York in a grocery store contest by collecting Campbell's soup can labels. He borrowed $100 from his father to return with four songs on tape. At the suggestion of his friends the **Rover Boys** (who are signed to ABC-Paramount), he visited the label's Don Costa, who signed him, impressed by his (at this time rare) singer-songwriting abilities – particularly in a boy so young.

28 The National Academy of Recording Arts and Sciences (NARAS) is established in Los Angeles by a group of label executives, recognizing the need for an organization to represent creative people in the music business and to put on an awards show. It has been prompted by requests from the Hollywood Beautification Committee (which puts "stars" in the sidewalks to honor leading talent) for recommendations of suitable celebrities from the music field. The committee contacted five top company bosses – Lloyd Dunn (Capitol), Paul Weston (Columbia), Sonny Burke (Decca), Dennis Farnon (RCA), and Jesse Kaye (MGM) – and today's meeting at the Brown Derby restaurant sees the founding of NARAS by these five, joined by their nomination for chairman, ex-Columbia head, Jim Conkling. Earlier, the separate idea for an "Oscars"-type award for music was also floated by Burke.

"He walked in with a bottle of Pepsi, shaking it as they did at the time. Al said, 'Otis, I've got an idea. Why don't you write a song called "All Shook Up"?'"

Otis Blackwell, **Time Barrier Express**, July 1979

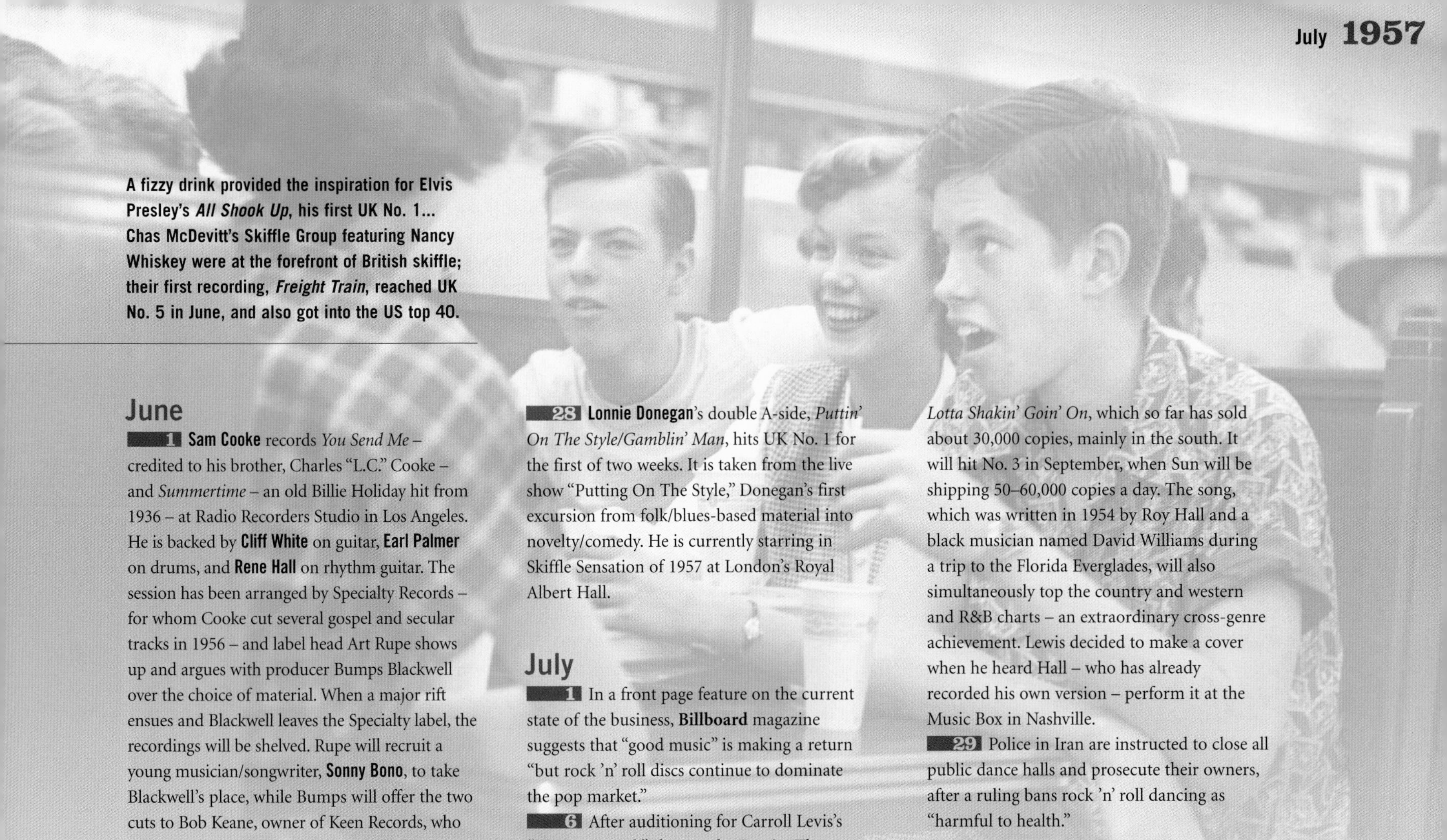

A fizzy drink provided the inspiration for Elvis Presley's *All Shook Up*, his first UK No. 1... Chas McDevitt's Skiffle Group featuring Nancy Whiskey were at the forefront of British skiffle; their first recording, *Freight Train*, reached UK No. 5 in June, and also got into the US top 40.

June

1 **Sam Cooke** records *You Send Me* – credited to his brother, Charles "L.C." Cooke – and *Summertime* – an old Billie Holiday hit from 1936 – at Radio Recorders Studio in Los Angeles. He is backed by **Cliff White** on guitar, **Earl Palmer** on drums, and **Rene Hall** on rhythm guitar. The session has been arranged by Specialty Records – for whom Cooke cut several gospel and secular tracks in 1956 – and label head Art Rupe shows up and argues with producer Bumps Blackwell over the choice of material. When a major rift ensues and Blackwell leaves the Specialty label, the recordings will be shelved. Rupe will recruit a young musician/songwriter, **Sonny Bono**, to take Blackwell's place, while Bumps will offer the two cuts to Bob Keane, owner of Keen Records, who will issue *Summertime* as the A-side, before DJs flip the disc to find the sweet joys of *You Send Me.*

1 At the height of the skiffle craze, and with four American vocalists above it in the chart, *Freight Train*, by Scotsman **Chas McDevitt's Skiffle Group featuring Nancy Whiskey**, hits UK No. 5. It was recorded in London at Levy's Sound Studios, New Bond Street, with Jack Baverstock producing.

15 **Elvis Presley**'s *All Shook Up* charts in the UK at No. 24, a week before its official release date: copies of the edition pressed for US servicemen in Britain have been made available to retailer HMV (whose parent company is currently releasing RCA material in the UK) and are being sold over the counter. It will disappear next week, before re-charting at No. 7 when the official pressing appears. (In August, the British outlet for Elvis Presley's recordings will change, as RCA's own label is launched through Decca. EMI, which has previously issued RCA products under its HMV label, will be given a lengthy selloff period for recordings already licensed, and the UK chart will be flooded by competing Presley singles on two labels.)

26 The Egyptian Ministry of the Interior announces that rock 'n' roll music is no longer to be played in public, because it is "against public morals." Citing the genre as an "imperialist plot," it also bans rock 'n' roll movies.

26 NARAS holds its first regular meeting at the Beverly Hilton hotel in Beverly Hills, where a board of governors is elected, including **Nat King Cole** and songwriter **Sammy Cahn**.

28 **Lonnie Donegan**'s double A-side, *Puttin' On The Style/Gamblin' Man*, hits UK No. 1 for the first of two weeks. It is taken from the live show "Putting On The Style," Donegan's first excursion from folk/blues-based material into novelty/comedy. He is currently starring in Skiffle Sensation of 1957 at London's Royal Albert Hall.

July

1 In a front page feature on the current state of the business, **Billboard** magazine suggests that "good music" is making a return "but rock 'n' roll discs continue to dominate the pop market."

6 After auditioning for Carroll Levis's "TV Star Search" show at the Empire Theatre in Liverpool last month, the **Quarry Men** skiffle group are playing the St. Peter's Parish Church garden fête in the Liverpool district of Woolton. **Ivan Vaughan** – who was a member of the group when they were known as the Black Jacks – introduces the group's lead singer, 16-year-old **John Lennon**, to another local musician, 15-year-old **Paul McCartney**, at the close of the band's set. McCartney impresses Lennon with his extensive knowledge of the lyrics of American rock 'n' roll hits of the day, in addition to his ability to tune a guitar.

12 The **Everly Brothers** appear on the premiere of **Alan Freed**'s "The Big Beat," singing *Bye Bye Love*. Also performing are **Frankie Lymon**, 23-year-old Texan **Buddy Knox**, and 18-year-old singer **Connie Francis**, from New Jersey. Knox recently enjoyed his first US chart-topper with *Party Doll* on Roulette Records – also the label's first hit – but Francis, signed to MGM Records two years ago and already a veteran of "Arthur Godfrey's Talent Scouts" show, is still trying for her first chart success.

15 **Elvis Presley**'s *All Shook Up* hits UK No. 1, becoming his first UK chart-topper (after ten previous releases failed to make the top spot). It will stay there for seven weeks, selling over half a million copies.

28 **Jerry Lee Lewis** makes his US television debut on "The Steve Allen Show." (His second appearance will be the only time Allen's show ever tops Ed Sullivan's in the national ratings.) Lewis's performance does wonders for *Whole Lotta Shakin' Goin' On*, which so far has sold about 30,000 copies, mainly in the south. It will hit No. 3 in September, when Sun will be shipping 50–60,000 copies a day. The song, which was written in 1954 by Roy Hall and a black musician named David Williams during a trip to the Florida Everglades, will also simultaneously top the country and western and R&B charts – an extraordinary cross-genre achievement. Lewis decided to make a cover when he heard Hall – who has already recorded his own version – perform it at the Music Box in Nashville.

29 Police in Iran are instructed to close all public dance halls and prosecute their owners, after a ruling bans rock 'n' roll dancing as "harmful to health."

Making the transition from radio to television, disc jockey Alan Freed's new show, "The Big Beat," premiered on ABC television in July.

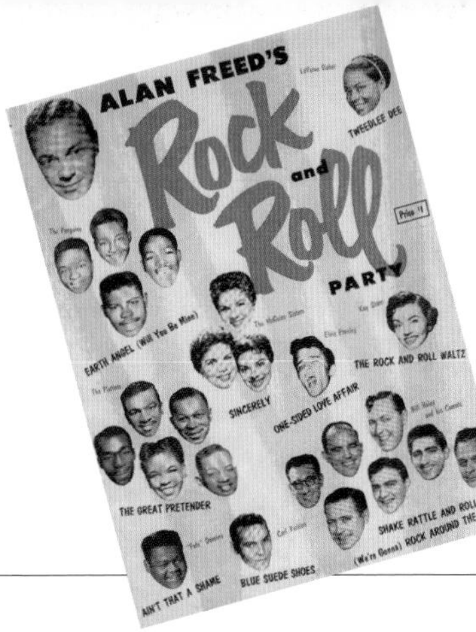

The Quarry Men play the Cavern... Paul Anka tops the charts...

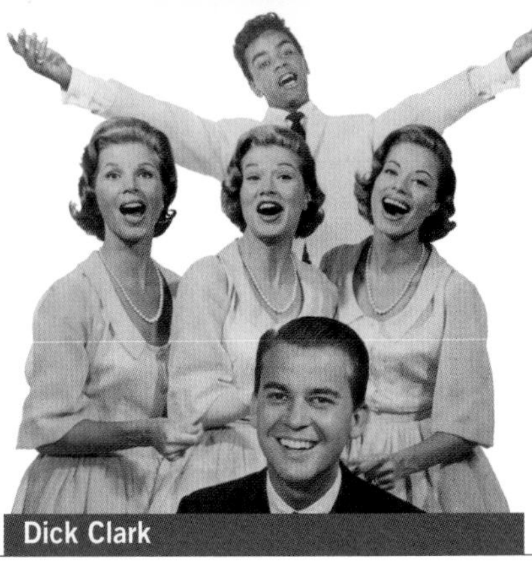
Dick Clark

The two most visible proponents of rock 'n' roll in the late 1950s were Alan Freed and the ever-youthful, clean-cut Dick Clark.

August

2 A multidate US tour gets under way, featuring **Buddy Holly & the Crickets**, **Clyde McPhatter**, the **Cadillacs**, **Otis Rush**, and others. It opens at the Howard Theater in Washington (where Holly will develop laryngitis and Niki Sullivan will pick up vocal duties for the concert on the 4th). Other dates will include the Royal Theater in Baltimore.

2 The Official UK **Elvis Presley** Fan Club is launched by Jeanne and Doug Saward. (In the US, there are already thousands of Presley fan clubs in existence.)

4 The **Everly Brothers** make their debut, to rapturous applause, on "The Ed Sullivan Show," performing their first and current hit *Bye Bye Love* (US No. 2) and its soon-to-be No. 1 follow-up, *Wake Up Little Susie* – which will also top the US R&B survey.

5 The first nationwide broadcast edition of the television show "American Bandstand" airs on ABC-TV. It is hosted by 26-year-old **Dick Clark**, an afternoon DJ on Philadelphia's WFIL radio station, who has replaced Bob Horn (host of the local Philadelphia show of the same name). Later, in his memoirs, Dick Clark will recall: "The studio was besieged by an angry crowd of students with picket signs. They were mad because I was replacing [Horn]. I understood their rage, but I had nothing to do with Horn leaving the show." Among the first guests are **Billy Williams** and the **Chordettes**, who are promoting their latest Cadence release, *Close Harmony*, and **Connie Francis**, who is still looking for that elusive first hit. (Making a national star of its host, "American Bandstand" will move to Los Angeles in 1964. It will briefly appear on the USA network with new host David Hirsh in the 1980s, before permanently going off the air in 1989.)

7 The **Quarry Men** make their debut at the Cavern jazz club in Liverpool, but without **Paul McCartney**, who is away at a scout camp in Hathersage, Derbyshire. Following their cover versions of *Hound Dog* and *Blue Suede Shoes*, club owner Alan Sytner dispatches the order: "Cut out the bloody rock!" (Last week, another Liverpool-based musician, 17-year-old drummer **Richard Starkey**, made his performing debut with the Eddie Clayton skiffle group.)

7 **Paul Anka** makes his first network television appearance in the US, on "American Bandstand," performing his fast-rising *Diana*. Also today, **Fats Domino**'s first album, ***This Is Fats***, is released by Imperial Records. (The record industry is still very much singles-driven, with their sales far outstripping most album releases.)

22 The **Crickets** end their US tour at the Apollo Theater in Harlem, and are the first all-white band to play this famous venue. (It is said that some of the audience were expecting to see the R&B group called the Crickets, led by Dean Barlow.)

30 Alan Freed's Third Anniversary Show takes place at the Paramount Theater in Brooklyn. Another extensive bill features **Buddy Holly & the Crickets**, **Little Richard**, the **Five Keys**, **Jimmie Rodgers** – whose fast-rising *Honeycomb* is currently heading to the top of the R&B chart – **Shaye Cogan**, the **Cleftones**, the **Moonglows**,

Fronted by John Lennon, young Liverpool-based skiffle combo the Quarry Men were picking up local gigs.

BUDDY HOLLY

Sept 23 The Crickets' era-defining *That'll Be The Day* – co-written by Buddy Holly, Jerry Allison, and Norman Petty – tops the US chart, on its way to becoming a million-seller. It will also become the Crickets' first UK chart entry and first No. 1 (on November 1). A second single is released on Brunswick's sister label Coral, credited only to Buddy Holly (the dual release ploy will continue for the next year). The song is *Peggy Sue*, originally written by Holly as *Cindy Lou*, but renamed after Allison's Lubbock High School girlfriend, Peggy Sue Gerron. Of the current crop of top stars, Holly, Paul Anka, Chuck Berry, Fats Domino, and Little Richard are almost unique as the writers of their own hits (unlike, for example, Elvis Presley). Holly and Berry in particular are setting new standards for artists who rely on their own compositional skills. They exemplify a fundamental change in the way popular music is being made (although many strictly R&B and blues artists have been writing their own material for decades).

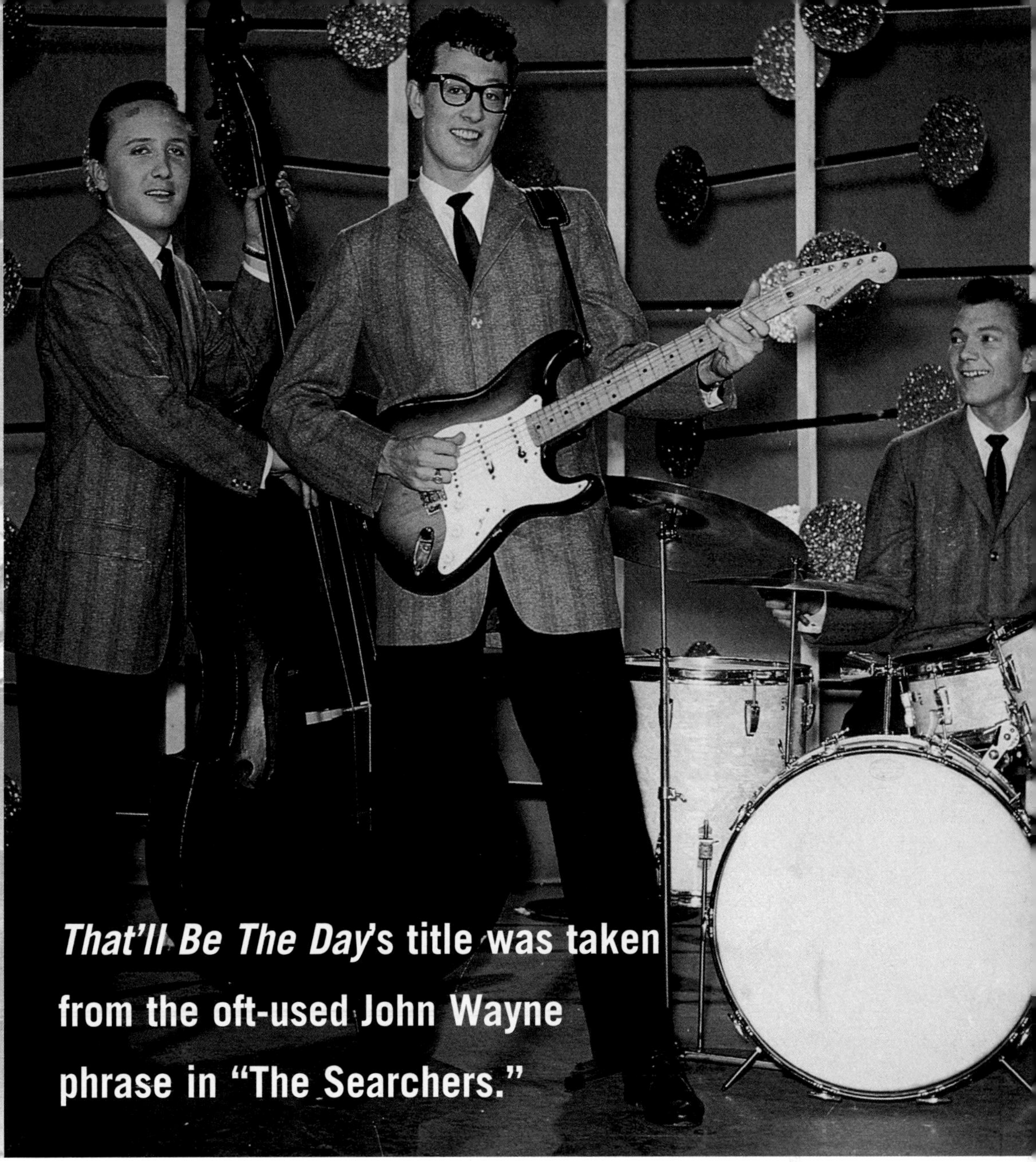

***That'll Be The Day*'s title was taken from the oft-used John Wayne phrase in "The Searchers."**

Ocie Smith, the **Del Vikings**, the latest vocal sensation the **Diamonds** (*Little Darlin'*), **Jo Ann Campbell**, **Mickey & Sylvia**, **Larry Williams**, **Alan Freed & His Rock 'n' Roll Orchestra featuring Sam "The Man" Taylor**, **Al Sears**, and **King Curtis**.

31 Within a month of its release – and prior to its US peak – **Paul Anka**'s *Diana* tops the UK chart, where it will stay for nine weeks. Worldwide sales of the record will eventually exceed nine million, and it will become one of the Top 10 best-selling singles of all time. In the US, *Diana* will hit No. 2 on September 2, and spend five weeks behind **Debbie Reynolds**'s chart-topper, *Tammy*. With the year's biggest teen anthem all the rage, Paul Anka is currently one of the hottest – and one of the youngest – international teen idols.

September

1 The Biggest Show of Stars for 1957 – a huge all-star caravan package tour – gets under way with the first of five nights at the Paramount Theater in Brooklyn, before heading out nationwide. Once again, **Buddy Holly & the Crickets** will feature prominently during this two-month extravaganza. They will be playing their first date in Norfolk, Virginia, next week, and subsequently performing in Waco, Texas, and Vancouver. Other acts appearing on the tour include **Chuck Berry**, **Paul Anka**, the **Drifters**, **Frankie Lymon & the Teenagers**, the **Everly Brothers**, and **Clyde McPhatter**. The tour will close on November 24 at the Mosque in Richmond, Virginia. (The white artists on the bill will be unable to play on several dates because of segregation laws, which forbid black and white acts performing on the same stage.)

19 In Hertfordshire, north of London, singer **Cliff Richard** joins the **Dick Teague Skiffle Group**, which is soon to begin playing pub venues around Ware, Cheshunt, and Hoddesdon. Born in India, but having returned to Britain and lived in Cheshunt since the age of eight, the 16-year-old is still known by his real name, Harry Webb, and is currently working during the day as a credit control clerk. He formed his own five-piece vocal group – the Quintones – in 1956, while he was still attending Cheshunt Secondary Modern School. Teague's father Walter writes in his diary tonight: "Harry introduced to group and enlisted right away. Good luck to the group's additional member."

21 **Bill Black** and **Scotty Moore**, **Elvis Presley**'s sidemen since the early days, quit over a salary dispute with "Col." Tom Parker. Black will form the Bill Black Combo, although he will play on three more Presley sessions next year.

24 **Alan Freed**'s self-congratulatory rockumentary film, "Mister Rock And Roll," receives its premiere at his favorite venue, the Paramount Theater in Brooklyn. Musical cameos in the movie include **Little Richard**, **Frankie Lymon**, **Clyde McPhatter**, the **Moonglows**, **Chuck Berry**, **LaVern Baker**, **Brook Benton**, **Ferlin Husky**, **Shaye Cogan**, **Teddy Randazzo**, and **Lionel Hampton & His Orchestra**.

27 **Elvis Presley** – now backed by **Hank Garland** and **Bob Moore** – plays a benefit concert for the Elvis Presley Youth Recreation Center at the annual Mississippi-Alabama Fair and Dairy Show in Tupelo.

Oct

1957

Little Richard turns to God... Sam Cooke sends you... Elvis is drafted...

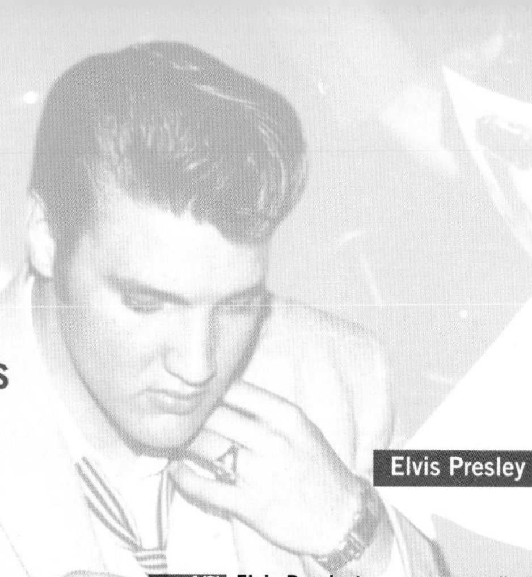

Elvis Presley

Elvis performed in Hawaii for the first time... Bill Haley charted 19 sides in the US between 1955–57 and, despite his born-again awakening, Little Richard continued to rack up hits to the end of the decade.

Bill Haley and Little Richard

October

2 **Connie Francis** is about to be dropped by M-G-M after releasing nine unsuccessful singles, and is at what is scheduled to be her last recording session for the label. At the insistence of her father, George Franconero, she spends four minutes cutting the Harry Ruby, Bert Kalmar, and Ted Snyder composition, *Who's Sorry Now?* Francis dislikes the song, thinking it "square," but, after a furious row with her persistent father, relents. It will become her first smash next March.

3 Having recently scored his fourth US chart-topper in two years with *Love Letters In The Sand*, pop crooner **Pat Boone**'s first television series, "The Pat Boone Chevy Showroom" – a weekly musical show sponsored by Chevrolet – begins airing on ABC-TV (and will run until mid-1960).

12 After a year of whirlwind success, **Little Richard** publicly renounces rock 'n' roll, and embraces God, while on stage in Sydney. He is quoted as saying, "If you want to live for the Lord, you can't take rock 'n' roll too. God doesn't like it." Richard's sax player, **Clifford Burks**, is reported to have dared Richard to prove his faith in God, whereupon Little Richard threw four diamond rings, valued at $8,000, into Sydney's Hunter River. (He will later tell the story of dreaming of his own damnation and praying to God after one of the engines in a plane he was in caught fire.)

13 Upon his return to the US, **Little Richard**'s label, Specialty, arranges a final eight-song session before he enters theological college. The label also tries to keep his conversion quiet. (His stablemate, Joe Lutcher, has been warning Richard for some time that pop music is "evil," and the pair will later tour the US as the "Little Richard Evangelistic Team.")

17 **Elvis Presley**'s new movie, "Jailhouse Rock" – filmed in May and June under the direction of Richard Thorpe, and co-starring Judy Tyler and Vaughn Taylor – premieres at Loew's State Theater in Memphis, where Presley worked back in 1952.

18 **Paul McCartney** – on lead guitar – makes his debut with the **Quarry Men** skiffle group at New Clubmoor Hall Conservative Club in Norris Green, Liverpool.

November

3 **Sam Cooke** makes his debut on CBS-TV's "The Ed Sullivan Show," but as he begins singing the fast-rising *You Send Me* he is cut off as the show runs out of time. (The R&B star will be invited back next month to complete a full performance.)

10 **Elvis Presley** makes his first concert appearance outside continental North America at Honolulu Stadium. (He will never perform in concert in Europe.)

11 The November issue of **Dance Teacher**, the official magazine of the Midland Dance Teachers Association, criticizes Princess Margaret for endorsing rock 'n' roll and in doing so hastening the demise of ballroom dancing: "From 1938 until last year rock (or jitterbug) was not respectable. Nice people did not do it." When news of Princess Margaret's approval became public, the magazine says taste shifted from "civilized" dance movements to "primitive capers." The article calls for rock 'n' roll to be discouraged, adding that the Princess will get "no bouquets" from ballroom dancing teachers.

12 The latest rock 'n' roll movie, "Jamboree," opens in Hollywood. It features **Carl Perkins**, **Fats Domino**, **Frankie Avalon** (an 18-year-old Philadelphia newcomer), country music veteran **Slim Whitman**, and **Connie Francis**. It is also the film debut of **Jerry Lee Lewis**.

17 Back from a recent tour of Australia, where he has been appearing with **Little Richard** and **Eddie Cochran**, **Gene Vincent** makes his television debut – with the **Blue Caps** – performing his new single *Dance To The Bop* on "The Ed Sullivan Show."

18 **Tommy Steele** performs at the Royal Variety Performance in London, singing *Long Tall Sally*. He has recently completed filming on his second movie, "The Duke Wore Jeans," and has also been named runner-up to Elvis Presley in the World Music Personality category in the **New Musical Express** annual readers' poll.

21 During the annual speech day at Weston Zoyland Secondary Modern School, near Bridgewater, Somerset, UK, the headmaster, Mr. L.H.B. Adams, reports that out of 30 students in a class of 14-year-olds, only four knew of Pandit Nehru, seven had heard of Nikita Khrushchev, and twelve of President Eisenhower, "But everyone was on Christian name terms with a **Mr. Presley**."

December

1 With *You Send Me* about to head the Top 100, and climbing to a million-plus domestic sales, **Sam Cooke** makes his quick return to "The Ed Sullivan Show." This time he is able to perform the entire number. Also appearing on tonight's broadcast are **Buddy Holly** (whom Sullivan interviews) **& the Crickets** playing *That'll Be The Day* and *Peggy Sue*, and **Jimmie Rodgers** performing *Honeycomb* and *Kisses Sweeter Than Wine*.

Pat Boone with Dinah Shore

Gene Vincent

Sidestepping rock 'n' roll, Pat Boone hosted his first television series... In Gene Vincent, Capitol Records hoped it had found its answer to Elvis Presley, but *Be-Bop-A-Lula* was followed by only one more top 20 hit, the 1957 release *Lotta Lovin'*.

The B-side to Bobby Helms's perennial favorite *Jingle Bell Rock* was the more ambitious *Captain Santa Claus (And His Reindeer Space Patrol).*

11 **Jerry Lee Lewis** secretly marries his 13-year-old second cousin Myra Gale Brown, who is the daughter of his bass player Jay, in Hernando, Mississippi. (She claims on the license to be 20.) However, on this day, Lewis is still married to his second wife, Jane Mitcham. His other cousins include future country singer Mickey Gilley and future televangelist, Jimmy Swaggart.

12 Al Priddy, a DJ at radio station KEX in Portland, Oregon, is fired for playing **Elvis Presley**'s version of *White Christmas*. The station's owner says: "It is not in the spirit we associate with Christmas. Playing Presley's version of that song is like having a stripper give my kids Christmas presents." Some radio stations have banned his Christmas album outright, while WCFL of Chicago has banned all records by Elvis.

"From 1938 until last year, rock (or jitterbug) was not respectable. Nice people did not do it."

Dance Teacher, November 11, 1957

19 Amid widespread teenage protest, Milton Bowers, chairman of the Memphis Draft Board No. 86, serves **Elvis Presley**'s draft notice for the US Army (at Graceland, where the star is to spend Christmas with his parents).

21 Frank Freeman, Paramount Studios' production chief, petitions the army for a 60-day deferment on **Elvis Presley**'s induction date, so that his latest movie, "King Creole," can be completed. Freeman is told that Presley will have to ask for the deferment personally. The draft board will in due course agree to a two-month delay, which will incur a barrage of comment from the public, alleging "special treatment."

23 *Jingle Bell Rock* – recorded by 22-year-old country singer/guitarist **Bobby Helms**, who has recently also scored with the crossover smash, *My Special Angel* – enters the US chart, set to peak at No. 6. It will soon become a yuletide standard.

25 Still packing them in with six shows a day – even at Christmas – the Alan Freed Christmas Jubilee package begins a 12-day run at the Paramount Theater in Brooklyn, again featuring **Buddy Holly & the Crickets** (who are now a trio after Niki Sullivan quit to sign a solo deal with Dot Records). Also on the bill are the red-hot **Paul Anka**, **Fats Domino**, **Jerry Lee Lewis**, the **Everly Brothers**, the **Rays**, **Danny & the Juniors**, the **Teenagers**, **Lee Andrew & the Hearts**, **Jo Ann Campbell**, the **Shepherd Sisters**, **Little Joe**, the **Dubs**, **Thurston Harris**, the **Twintones**, and **Terry Noland**.

27 Alan Freed's Christmas show grosses $37,000 – a one-day record for the Paramount Theater. The 20,000 fans begin lining up at 5:30 am, and by the time of the first show at 9:00 am Deputy Chief Inspector Thomas Burns is employing 33 policemen to hold the crowd in place. With girls outnumbering boys four to one, the store owners along 42nd Street are not happy. "If we were closed we would do as much business," says Louis Brook, the owner of Swank Shirt Shops. "We're not even getting window shoppers."

Elvis Presley's third movie vehicle, "Jailhouse Rock," opened in October. The film's hit title song – written by the ubiquitous Leiber and Stoller – hit US No. 1 on November 4, becoming Presley's fourth US chart-topper of 1957.

ROOTS During this year: schoolfriends Paul Simon and Art Garfunkel, billed as Tom & Jerry, sing *Hey Schoolgirl* on "American Bandstand" immediately after Jerry Lee Lewis performs *Great Balls Of Fire*... Welsh singer Thomas Woodward, soon to be known as Tom Jones, makes his singing debut as Tiger Tom the Twisting Vocalist, at the Treforest Working Men's Club in Glamorgan... Duane Eddy buys a Gretsch Chet Atkins 6120 at Ziggy's Music Store in Phoenix... south London timber yard laborer Reginald Smith is signed by impresario Larry Parnes, who changes his name to Marty Wilde... Brook Benton meets music publisher and Mercury Records A&R chief Clyde Otis (the first black in such a position at a major label) and joins him as a studio demo singer... the Impressions, with Jerry Butler as lead singer, are signed to Ewart Abner's Falcon Records, a subsidiary of leading R&B label Vee-Jay... and the Poquellos, an all-girl vocal quartet later to become the Shirelles, form at high school in Passaic, New Jersey, to sing at school parties and dances, where their specialty piece is the group-composed *I Met Him On A Sunday*...

Rock And Roll Is Here To Stay

No.1 US SINGLES

Jan 4	April Love **Pat Boone**
Jan 11	At The Hop **Danny & the Juniors**
Mar 1	Get A Job **Silhouettes**
Mar 15	Don't **Elvis Presley**
Mar 22	Tequila **Champs**
Apr 26	Twilight Time **Platters**
May 3	Witch Doctor **David Seville**
May 24	All I Have To Do Is Dream **Everly Brothers**
June 14	The Purple People Eater **Sheb Wooley**
July 26	Yakety Yak **Coasters**
Aug 2	Patricia **Perez Prado**
Aug 9	Poor Little Fool **Rick Nelson**
Aug 23	Volare (Nel Blu Dipinto Di Blu) **Domenico Modugno**
Aug 30	Little Star **Elegants**
Sept 6	Volare (Nel Blu Dipinto Di Blu) **Domenico Modugno**
Oct 4	It's All In The Game **Tommy Edwards**
Nov 15	It's Only Make Believe **Conway Twitty**
Nov 22	Tom Dooley **Kingston Trio**
Nov 29	It's Only Make Believe **Conway Twitty**
Dec 6	To Know Him Is To Love Him **Teddy Bears**
Dec 27	The Chipmunk Song **David Seville & the Chipmunks**

No.1 UK SINGLES

Jan 4	Mary's Boy Child **Harry Belafonte**
Jan 11	Great Balls Of Fire **Jerry Lee Lewis**
Jan 25	Jailhouse Rock **Elvis Presley**
Feb 15	The Story Of My Life **Michael Holliday**
Mar 1	Magic Moments **Perry Como**
Apr 26	Whole Lotta Woman **Marvin Rainwater**
May 17	Who's Sorry Now **Connie Francis**
June 28	On The Street Where You Live **Vic Damone**
July 5	=On The Street Where You Live **Vic Damone**
	=All I Have To Do Is Dream/Claudette **Everly Brothers**
July 12	All I Have To Do Is Dream/Claudette **Everly Brothers**
Aug 23	When **Kalin Twins**
Sept 27	Carolina Moon/Stupid Cupid **Connie Francis**
Nov 8	It's All In The Game **Tommy Edwards**
Nov 29	Hoots Mon **Lord Rockingham's XI**
Dec 20	It's Only Make Believe **Conway Twitty**

Elvis Presley

Neil Sedaka

Pvt. Presley, Elvis A., Serial No. US 53310761, was drafted into the US Army amid much attendant hoopla... Neil Sedaka, one of the young breed of Brill Building writers, had his first No. 1 with Connie Francis's *Stupid Cupid.*

Like a volcano, rock 'n' roll paused for breath in 1958. The perception that it was inseparable from juvenile delinquency, the sudden rise and decline of one-hit wonders, the payola scandal, **Elvis Presley**'s drafting into the US Army, all contributed to an unsettling year. With Presley in Germany (though still amassing pre-recorded hits), it was left to others to spread rock 'n' roll's beat abroad. Popular rock 'n' roll "package tours" in the US were dominated by **Irvin Feld**, who snapped up **Sam Cooke**, and the increasingly controversial **Alan Freed**. Some authorities reacted by banning live shows. Freed's own radio station banned him, and others dropped rock 'n' roll programing and returned to safer fare. Yet several seminal rock 'n' roll songs emerged, including **Buddy Holly**'s *Oh Boy!* **Chuck Berry** effortlessly produced two more outstanding discs: *Sweet Little Sixteen* and the uptempo *Johnny B. Goode*, the classic tale of country boy turned rock idol. **Danny & the Juniors** received a gold record for the party-anthem *At The Hop*. They followed it up with *Rock And Roll Is Here To Stay*. Of course, they were right.

Among the shooting stars that illuminated popular music in 1958 was 19-year-old **Eddie Cochran**. His *Summertime Blues* dominated the US singles chart during the summer, and he followed it with the equally enthralling *C'mon Everybody*. Both songs had a rebellious potency that was the essence of rock 'n' roll, and neatly encapsulated teenage yearnings. Cochran and his friend **Gene Vincent** were highly influential in Britain, where rock 'n' roll fans also welcomed **Buddy Holly & the Crickets**. **Paul McCartney** was just one youngster who watched Holly on television, keenly observing which chords he used. Britain was beginning to produce its own rock 'n' roll artists. **Billy Fury** was signed up by manager Larry Parnes who, with fellow impresario Jack Good, also brought **Tommy Steele**, **Terry Dene**, and **Marty Wilde** to the fore. Set to become the biggest star of all, 17-year-old **Cliff Richard** made his first move.

The rock 'n' roll instrumental emerged in 1958. The **Champs** scored the first No. 1 with *Tequila*, but the 20-year-old **Duane Eddy** would be more influential: *Rebel Rouser*, with its low, twangy riffs, was the first of a string of hits for Eddy, a pioneer of the electric rock guitar.

While the teenage **Neil Sedaka** nabbed his first No. 1 as a writer with *Stupid Cupid*, other notable songwriters seemed to come in pairs: while **Burt Bacharach** and **Hal David** were honing their softer style, **Jerry Leiber** and **Mike Stoller** showed their mastery with *Jailhouse Rock* for Elvis and *Yakety Yak* for the **Coasters** – the latter comically capturing the prevailing sense of adolescent rebellion.

Technological advances continued, as 78s were replaced by 45s, Gibson introduced the Flying V electric guitar, RCA offered the first stereo LPs, and home audio systems began incorporating stereo components, including headphones.

"Something told me, yes, he's going to be big. He's going to be really big."

John Foster, first manager of Cliff Richard & the Drifters, March 1958

Jan 1958

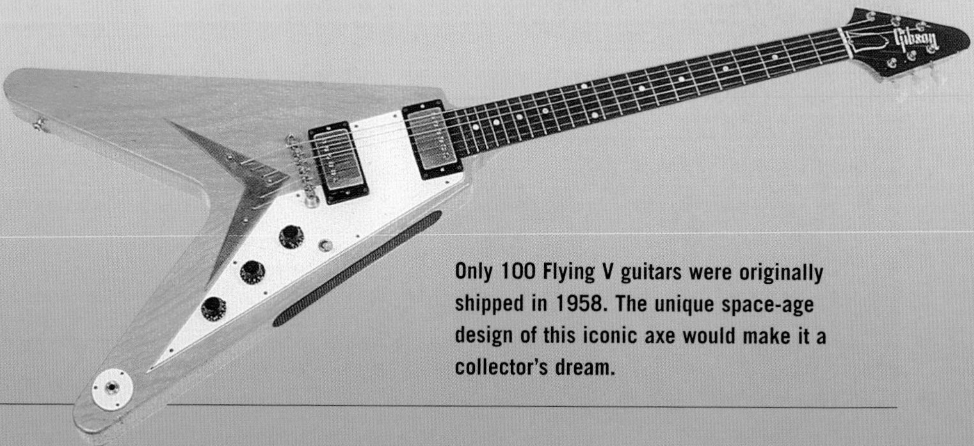

Only 100 Flying V guitars were originally shipped in 1958. The unique space-age design of this iconic axe would make it a collector's dream.

Danny and the Juniors' *At The Hop*... The Gibson Flying V... A chart champ – *Tequila*...

January

6 As it is being performed on the final day of the Alan Freed Christmas Jubilee in New York, **Danny & the Juniors**' *At The Hop* – a career-defining rock 'n' roll smash – is at US No. 1, at the beginning of a seven-week lock at the top. Fronted by Philadelphia native, Danny Rapp, this Italian-American vocal quartet formed in high school in 1955. They recorded *At The Hop* – co-written by label boss Artie Singer, Johnny Medora (aka John Madara), and the Juniors' first tenor, Dave White – after DJ Dick Clark suggested they revise the original composition, entitled *Do The Bop*.

7 The Flying V electric guitar, which will become the instrument of choice for legions of future rock musicians, is patented by the Gibson Guitar Company. (The pioneering firm was originally formed in 1894 in Kalamazoo, Michigan, by Orville H. Gibson, who began hand-building guitars and mandolins to sell to local musicians.)

9 **Carl Perkins** becomes the first rockabilly artist to sign to Columbia Records – which will issue his label debut, *Pink Pedal Pushers*, in May.

10 The British release of **Elvis Presley**'s single *Jailhouse Rock* is delayed for a week because Decca's pressing plant is unable to meet the advance orders of 250,000 copies. Two weeks later it will enter the chart at No. 1 (the first time a record has entered the UK survey in pole position) and will go on to sell 750,000 copies during a three-week stint at the top.

13 KWK radio in St. Louis, Missouri, decides that rock 'n' roll has had its day and begins breaking every record in its library – after playing them one last time. Having canvassed the station's DJs, KWK president Robert T. Convey says the genre has "dominated the music field long enough," and has "grown to such proportions as to alienate many adult listeners… The majority of listeners will be surprised and pleased how pleasant radio listening can be [without rock 'n' roll]."

13 Harry Webb (soon to become **Cliff Richard**) auditions at Studio 4, BBC Maida Vale in London for the "Saturday Skiffle Club" radio show. Later this week, he and **Terry Smart** will form a rock 'n' roll band – with **Norman Mitham** on guitar – calling themselves Harry Webb & the Drifters.

25 **Buddy Holly** records at Bell Sound Studios in New York with producer Milton De Lugg. Tomorrow, he and the **Crickets** will perform *Oh Boy!* during their second appearance on "The Ed Sullivan Show."

27 **Little Richard** embarks on a four-year course in religious studies at the Oakwood Theological College in Huntsville, Alabama, where he will receive a BA and be ordained as a Seventh Day Adventist minister – following in the footsteps of his father and his grandfather. Richard claims: "The Lord is on the side of the ballad singers. Rock 'n' roll is strictly Satan's music. Sure I made a lot of money out of rock 'n' roll. Now I want to make up for my sins for the rest of my life."

> **"The Lord is on the side of the ballad singers. Rock 'n' roll is strictly Satan's music."** Little Richard on entering theological college, January 27, 1958

29 Challenge Records releases the instrumental *Tequila*, the first single by a loose collection of studio musicians going by the name, the **Champs**. Its infectious rhythm and "Tequila" chant will immediately appeal to radio listeners and record buyers alike, with the song hitting US No. 1 within two months. By the end of this year the Champs' line-up will include sax player **Jimmy Seals** and drummer **Dash Crofts** (who will find success together in the 1970s as **Seals & Crofts**).

30 With *Peggy Sue* currently riding high in the US and UK charts, **Buddy Holly & the Crickets** begin a week-long tour of Australia, as part of the Big Show, presented by promoter Lee Gordon. They will play 12 gigs in Sydney, Newcastle, Brisbane, and Melbourne. Also on the package are **Jerry Lee Lewis**, Australian singer **Johnny O'Keefe**, **Jodie Sands**, and – topping the bill – **Paul Anka**.

February

1 **Elvis Presley** records four songs in his last studio session before enlisting in the US Army. They include his next single, *Wear My Ring Around Your Neck*, which will go to No. 3 in the US and UK, *Doncha Think It's Time*, *My Wish Came True*, and a cover of Hank Williams's *Your Cheatin' Heart* (which will not be released until 1965).

6 **Tommy Steele** and other rock 'n' roll musicians in the UK get a tongue-lashing during speech day at the Richard Hind Secondary Technical School for Girls in Stockton-on-Tees, from Miss Gwen Carr, the headmistress. She blames them for her schoolgirls' poor exam results: "We grew tired last year of hearing endless ecstatic appreciations of Tommy Steele and his rock 'n' roll companions in the entertainment world. This was out of all proportion to their value, and to the great hindrance of progress in school work. Their attitude to us, their teachers, might well have been expressed in the words of Tommy Steele himself, when it was suggested he needed a dramatic coach. He said 'I don't have no coach. I don't dig that stuff. Those people can't teach you nothing.' We are thankful that our insensitive pupils are in the minority." Steele will respond: "If I hindered your studies last term – like your headmistress says I did – then do me a favour and work hard for her – and me – next term. And if your exam results are better, I'll present a prize to the best pupil – if Miss Carr will let me! Fair enough?"

15 The young American writing team of **Burt Bacharach** and **Hal David** have their first UK chart-topper, as **Michael Holliday**'s *The Story Of My Life* hits No. 1. Proving they are no flash in the pan, in two weeks' time their song *Magic Moments*, sung by **Perry Como**, will knock Holliday off the top spot.

18 With two Top 20 UK hits already under his belt (including the popular *A White Sport Coat*), 19-year-old English rock 'n' roll singer **Terry Dene** is arrested in Southgate Street, Gloucester, after two plate-glass windows and a phone box window are broken, and the headlights and paintwork of several motorcycles are also damaged – at a total estimated cost of £114 ($320). Dene is charged with four counts of being drunk and disorderly and doing willful

Danny & the Juniors started out as the Juvenairs at John Bartram High School in Philadelphia.

Terry Dene performed at the 2 i's coffee bar in Soho, London – a hotspot for showcasing the city's burgeoning rock 'n' roll scene.

Canadian teen sensation Paul Anka's first single sold 300 copies; the follow-up, *Diana* – self-penned when he was 15 – sold nine million.

damage, and released on his own surety of £50 ($140) together with a further £50 from singer **Edna Savage**. Dene goes to Gloucester Royal Infirmary for treatment. Along with Tommy Steele, Dene is potentially one of Britain's fastest rising young stars, having been spotted performing at London's 2 i's coffee bar – the Soho venue that is hosting the early musical careers of Steele, **Adam Faith**, **Cliff Richard**, and others.

19 The matinee performance of the pantomime "Goldilocks" at the Royal Court Theatre in Liverpool is canceled during the intermission, as a group of students from Liverpool University heckle singer **Tommy Steele**. Upon his entrance, more than 100 students pretend to read newspapers, laugh, clap at inappropriate moments, and chant "I like Elvis." In turn, Steele's fans shower the students with orange peel and ice-cream cartons. In the words of theater manager Claude Mason: "I thought there might be trouble. The seats were booked in the name of a non-existent working men's club. It seems they were just bent on wrecking the show."

20 The Big Gold Record Stars tour, a six-day tour of Florida that features **Bill Haley**, the **Everly Brothers**, **Buddy Holly & the Crickets**, **Jerry Lee Lewis**, and **Jimmie Rodgers**, begins at the Kellogg Auditorium in Orlando. At the final date, in Fort Lauderdale, Jerry Lee Lewis will back Buddy Holly, playing piano on *Drown In My Tears*.

21 **Terry Dene**, following a court appearance where he has admitted to three charges of causing damage and has been fined £155 ($435) by Gloucester magistrates, says: "I am going away for some time to get straightened out. I am going to put myself in the hands of psychiatrists. I shall cancel my engagements and hope the treatment I get will settle me down." The charge of being drunk and disorderly was withdrawn. His lawyer, Mr. R.B.C. Purnell, poignantly adds: "He is a somewhat nervous and restless young man." Dene is banned from the Regal Cinema, where he was topping the bill with **Edna Savage**, and Tommy Steele's brother **Colin Hicks** replaces him. Following this widely reported incident, Dene will be unmercifully attacked by the establishment and the British media, portrayed as everything that's wrong about rock 'n' roll. When he tries to avoid military service later in 1958, his career will effectively be ruined.

22 *Don't Let Go* by R&B balladeer **Roy Hamilton** stands at US No. 13, significant as the first stereo single to make the US chart. (Stereophonic LPs became available in 1956 – with the Columbia-released original cast recording, ***My Fair Lady***, the first million-selling stereo album. In June 1958, Pye Records will be the first UK label to issue stereo discs.)

During their British tour, Buddy Holly and the Crickets had four records in the UK Top 30.

March

1 Perpetually in motion, **Buddy Holly & the Crickets** appear at the Trocadero, Elephant & Castle, London, to begin what will prove to be their only UK tour – a 25-date, twice-nightly package, with **Gary Miller**, the **Tanner Sisters**, **Des O'Connor**, and **Ronnie Keene & His Orchestra**.

1 Leading his nine-song set with *Tell Me That You Love Me*, Canadian teen star **Paul Anka** kicks off his second British trek at the Music Hall in Aberdeen.

6 At the RCA Victor Studio in Nashville, the **Everly Brothers** record a new Boudleaux Bryant ballad, *All I Have To Do Is Dream*, and the uptempo *Claudette*. The latter was offered to them by the Acuff-Rose publishing company, where singer-songwriter **Roy Orbison** is working. He wrote it about his wife Claudette Frady, and originally recorded it himself while with Sun Records, where he cut one chart single, the 1956 rockabilly number *Ooby Dooby*, which reached US No. 59. It will be four years before Orbison finds consistent success as a performer, when he signs to Fred Foster's Monument label.

11 As her husband has secretly married his 13-year-old cousin, **Jerry Lee Lewis**'s first wife, Jane Mitcham, files for divorce in Memphis.

ON THE STAGE
GAUMONT
DONCASTER
Prices 12/6, 10/-, 7/6, 5/-
BOX OFFICE NOW OPEN - BOOK NOW
MON 17TH MARCH
ONE DAY ONLY
6.25 TWO SHOWS 8.40
LEW & LESLIE GRADE Ltd. Presents
THE GREAT AMERICAN RECORDING STARS
BUDDY HOLLY
AND THE CRICKETS
HIT RECORDER OF 'PEGGY SUE'
FAMOUS FOR THEIR GREAT DISCS 'THAT'LL BE THE DAY' 'OH BOY' ETC. ETC.
GARY MILLER
THE PYE-NIXA RECORDING STAR
FEATURING HIS HIT RECORD 'THE STORY OF MY LIFE'
THE TANNER SISTERS
OF STAGE, RADIO & RECORDING FAME
DES O'CONNOR
COMEDIAN WITH THE MODERN STYLE
RONNIE KEENE AND HIS ORCHESTRA
BRITAIN'S NEW MUSICAL SENSATION

Mar 1958

The dawn of stereo... The first gold single... Elvis joins the army...

Eddie Cochran penned the seminal *Summertime Blues,* with co-writer Jerry Capehart, in 45 minutes.

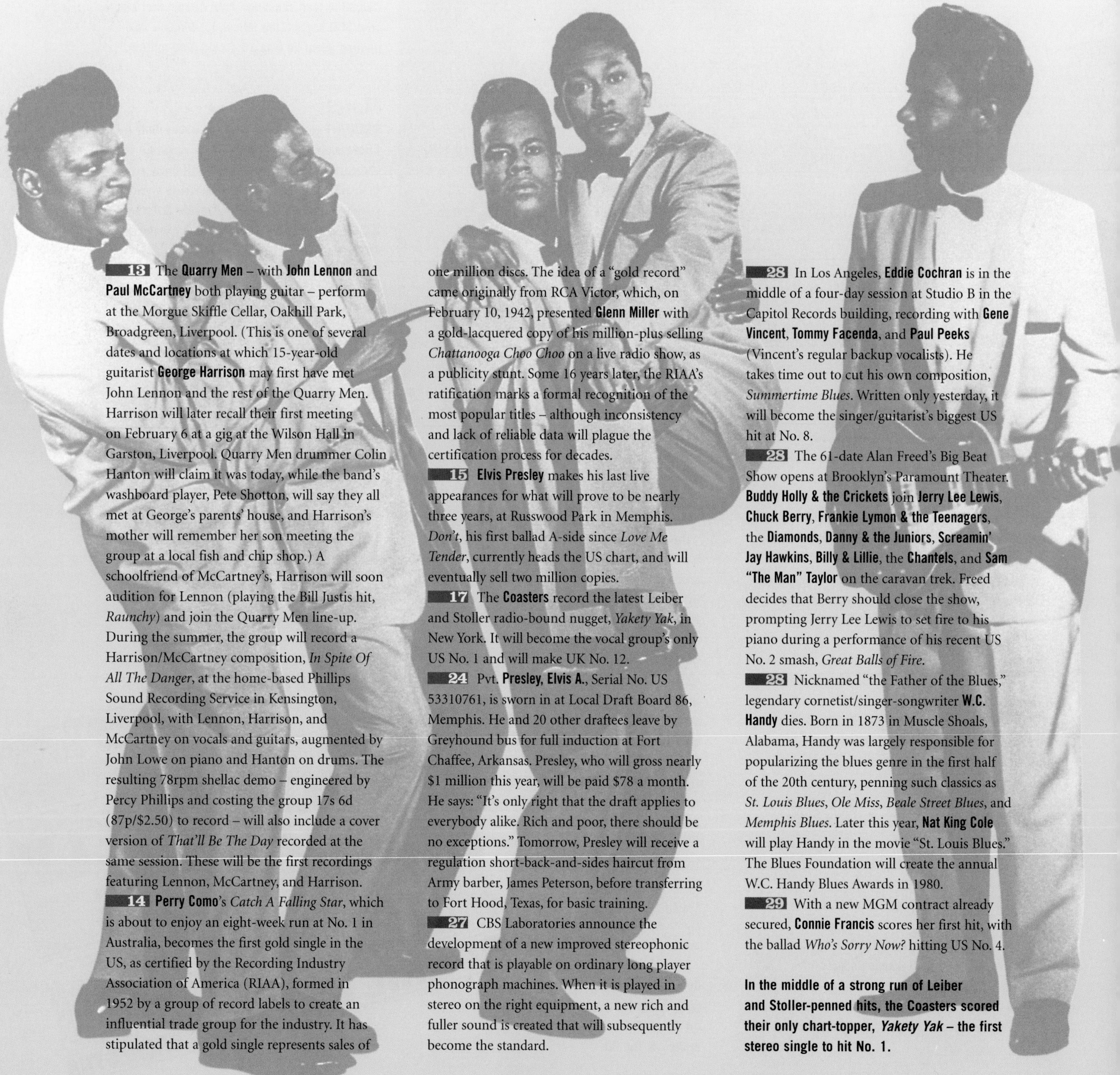

13 The **Quarry Men** – with **John Lennon** and **Paul McCartney** both playing guitar – perform at the Morgue Skiffle Cellar, Oakhill Park, Broadgreen, Liverpool. (This is one of several dates and locations at which 15-year-old guitarist **George Harrison** may first have met John Lennon and the rest of the Quarry Men. Harrison will later recall their first meeting on February 6 at a gig at the Wilson Hall in Garston, Liverpool. Quarry Men drummer Colin Hanton will claim it was today, while the band's washboard player, Pete Shotton, will say they all met at George's parents' house, and Harrison's mother will remember her son meeting the group at a local fish and chip shop.) A schoolfriend of McCartney's, Harrison will soon audition for Lennon (playing the Bill Justis hit, *Raunchy*) and join the Quarry Men line-up. During the summer, the group will record a Harrison/McCartney composition, *In Spite Of All The Danger*, at the home-based Phillips Sound Recording Service in Kensington, Liverpool, with Lennon, Harrison, and McCartney on vocals and guitars, augmented by John Lowe on piano and Hanton on drums. The resulting 78rpm shellac demo – engineered by Percy Phillips and costing the group 17s 6d (87p/$2.50) to record – will also include a cover version of *That'll Be The Day* recorded at the same session. These will be the first recordings featuring Lennon, McCartney, and Harrison.

14 **Perry Como**'s *Catch A Falling Star*, which is about to enjoy an eight-week run at No. 1 in Australia, becomes the first gold single in the US, as certified by the Recording Industry Association of America (RIAA), formed in 1952 by a group of record labels to create an influential trade group for the industry. It has stipulated that a gold single represents sales of one million discs. The idea of a "gold record" came originally from RCA Victor, which, on February 10, 1942, presented **Glenn Miller** with a gold-lacquered copy of his million-plus selling *Chattanooga Choo Choo* on a live radio show, as a publicity stunt. Some 16 years later, the RIAA's ratification marks a formal recognition of the most popular titles – although inconsistency and lack of reliable data will plague the certification process for decades.

15 **Elvis Presley** makes his last live appearances for what will prove to be nearly three years, at Russwood Park in Memphis. *Don't*, his first ballad A-side since *Love Me Tender*, currently heads the US chart, and will eventually sell two million copies.

17 The **Coasters** record the latest Leiber and Stoller radio-bound nugget, *Yakety Yak*, in New York. It will become the vocal group's only US No. 1 and will make UK No. 12.

24 Pvt. **Presley, Elvis A.**, Serial No. US 53310761, is sworn in at Local Draft Board 86, Memphis. He and 20 other draftees leave by Greyhound bus for full induction at Fort Chaffee, Arkansas. Presley, who will gross nearly $1 million this year, will be paid $78 a month. He says: "It's only right that the draft applies to everybody alike. Rich and poor, there should be no exceptions." Tomorrow, Presley will receive a regulation short-back-and-sides haircut from Army barber, James Peterson, before transferring to Fort Hood, Texas, for basic training.

27 CBS Laboratories announce the development of a new improved stereophonic record that is playable on ordinary long player phonograph machines. When it is played in stereo on the right equipment, a new rich and fuller sound is created that will subsequently become the standard.

28 In Los Angeles, **Eddie Cochran** is in the middle of a four-day session at Studio B in the Capitol Records building, recording with **Gene Vincent**, **Tommy Facenda**, and **Paul Peeks** (Vincent's regular backup vocalists). He takes time out to cut his own composition, *Summertime Blues*. Written only yesterday, it will become the singer/guitarist's biggest US hit at No. 8.

28 The 61-date Alan Freed's Big Beat Show opens at Brooklyn's Paramount Theater. **Buddy Holly & the Crickets** join **Jerry Lee Lewis**, **Chuck Berry**, **Frankie Lymon & the Teenagers**, the **Diamonds**, **Danny & the Juniors**, **Screamin' Jay Hawkins**, **Billy & Lillie**, the **Chantels**, and **Sam "The Man" Taylor** on the caravan trek. Freed decides that Berry should close the show, prompting Jerry Lee Lewis to set fire to his piano during a performance of his recent US No. 2 smash, *Great Balls of Fire*.

28 Nicknamed "the Father of the Blues," legendary cornetist/singer-songwriter **W.C. Handy** dies. Born in 1873 in Muscle Shoals, Alabama, Handy was largely responsible for popularizing the blues genre in the first half of the 20th century, penning such classics as *St. Louis Blues*, *Ole Miss*, *Beale Street Blues*, and *Memphis Blues*. Later this year, **Nat King Cole** will play Handy in the movie "St. Louis Blues." The Blues Foundation will create the annual W.C. Handy Blues Awards in 1980.

29 With a new MGM contract already secured, **Connie Francis** scores her first hit, with the ballad *Who's Sorry Now?* hitting US No. 4.

In the middle of a strong run of Leiber and Stoller-penned hits, the Coasters scored their only chart-topper, *Yakety Yak* – the first stereo single to hit No. 1.

SAM COOKE

Apr 5 **Having already racked up eight US radio hits and his first UK chart showing (*You Send Me*) in the past six months – Sam Cooke tops the bill on Irvin Feld's Greatest Show of Stars, which opens in Norfolk, Virginia, beginning an 80-date tour. The bill also includes the Everly Brothers, who will enjoy their second chart-topper during the tour with *All I Have To Do Is Dream*, Paul Anka, who is coming off his second Top 10 hit with *You Are My Destiny*, Frankie Avalon (whose second single for the Chancellor label, *You Excite Me*, has just been released), Clyde McPhatter, and Jimmy Reed. Reed is currently racking up hits for the Vee-Jay label, and has been one of a handful of influential black singer-songwriter/guitarists in the R&B genre to reach both black and white audiences effectively.**

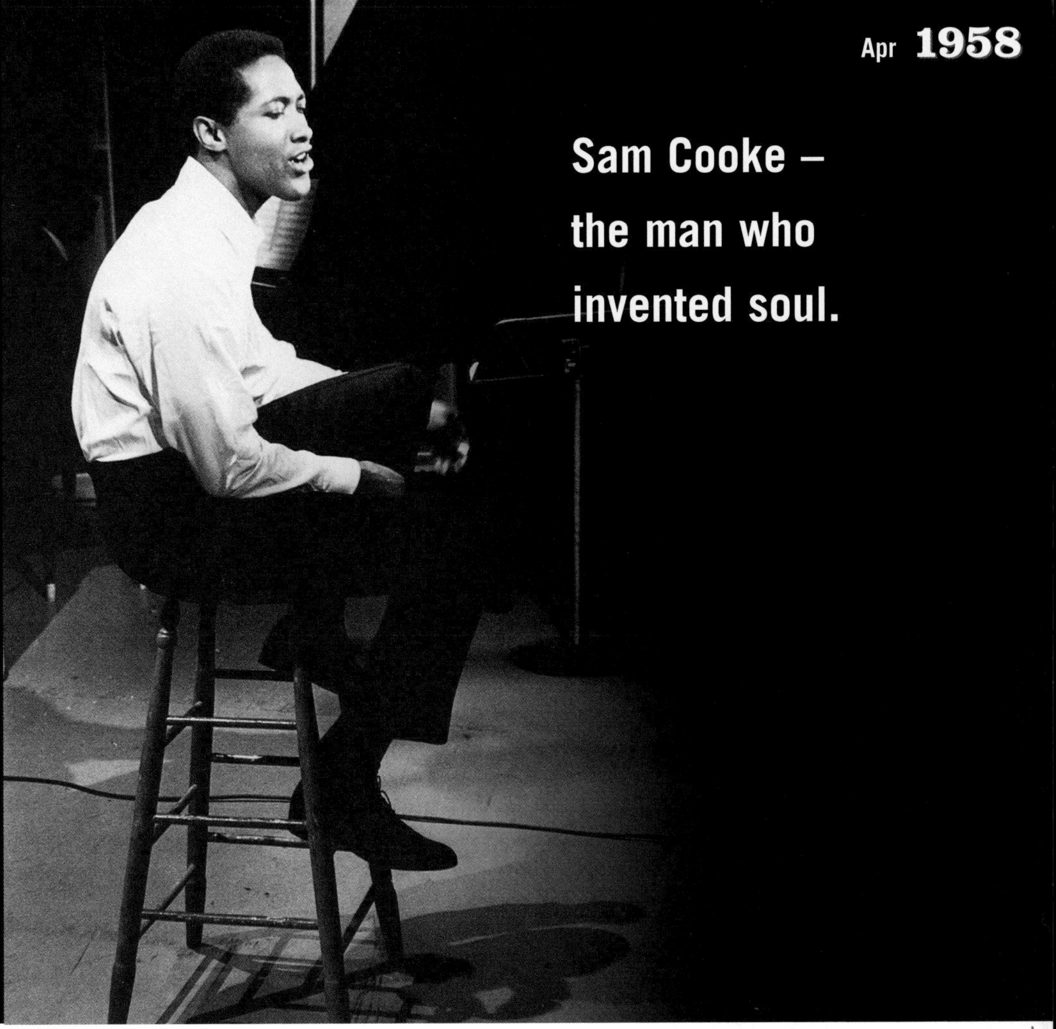

Sam Cooke – the man who invented soul.

Having finally made the chart, Francis won't leave easily, becoming its most consistent female resident, and racking up a staggering 55 US chart singles over the next ten years, including three No. 1s.

30 *A Handful Of Songs*, by **Tommy Steele** with Lionel Bart and Michael Pratt, is awarded Outstanding Song Composition at the Ivor Novello Awards. Steele's mother, Betty Hicks, collects the award on behalf of the singer, since he is on tour in South Africa. Russ Hamilton's *We Will Make Love* is named Best Selling Song.

31 Leading British newsagent and bookseller, W.H. Smith & Sons Ltd., opens its first record department at its branch in Kingsway, London. Company spokesman, Mr. S.P. Hyde, says: "The Kingsway record department will be the first of many at our shops throughout the country. We have extensive plans for the future, and intend to make this a full-scale development of our present organization."

W.C. Handy wrote one of the earliest blues compositions, *Memphis Blues*, in 1912.

April

6 Guitarist friends, **Hank Marvin** and **Bruce Welch**, both 16 years old, travel to London from their homes in Newcastle with their part-time skiffle quintet, the Railroaders. The group will come third in a national talent contest before they split next month. Remaining in the capital, Marvin and Welch will shortly join the Five Chesternuts, a new group led by drummer Pete Chester, son of radio comedian Charlie Chester. One of their first appearances will be backing comedian Benny Hill singing *Gather In The Mushrooms*, at a charity concert at the Town Hall in Stoke Newington, London.

7 Capitol Records formally abandons manufacture of the 78rpm disc in the UK market, and will now release only 45rpm singles. The first two singles released under the new policy are *Have Faith In Me* by the Blossoms, and the Four Freshmen's *Nights Are Longer*. Company sales manager, Arthur Muxlow, says: "Somebody's got to make the first move. With the marked increase in the sales of 45s and the decline of 78s in the past few months, we have decided to go ahead."

9 **Bill Haley & His Comets**' global itinerary finds them starting a four-week swing in South America, kicking off in Buenos Aires.

10 **Bobby Darin**, backed by a pickup band, cuts *Splish Splash*, produced by Herb Abramson and Ahmet Ertegun, and *Queen Of The Hop*, produced solely by Ertegun, in a recording session lasting less than two hours. Darin was picked up last year by Atlantic Records' subsidiary Atco, and is one of Ertegun's first non-black, non-R&B signings. *Splish Splash*, which the singer has written with Jean Murray – mother of New York DJ Murray the K – will become his first million-selling gold record in the US.

"He made it so easy to wear glasses. I was Buddy Holly."
John Lennon, 1960s

10 R&B singer-songwriter **Chuck Willis** dies at the age of 30, from a perforated ulcer, at the Hugh Spalding Hospital in his native Atlanta. Signed to Atlantic and nicknamed the "Sheik of the Blues" (with reference to the turban he wore on stage), Willis's R&B songs began crossing over into the mainstream in 1957 with *C.C. Rider* – the song that was the inspiration behind the year's "stroll" dance craze. His current single, the ironically titled *What Am I Living For?*, will shortly reach US No. 9, becoming his biggest hit.

78rpm R.I.P... Bobby Darin makes a splash... Alan Freed's Boston concert ends in rioting...

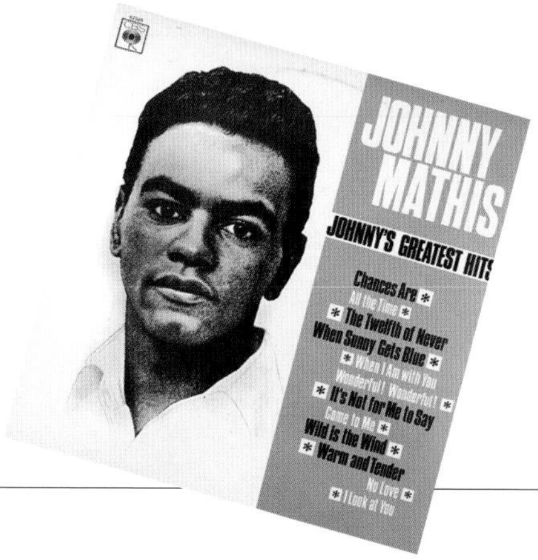

San Francisco native Johnny Mathis scored more than 60 chart albums in his 30-year career, with his *Greatest Hits* set staying charted for more than nine years in the US.

19 Signed to Columbia Records in 1956 at the age of 19, pop balladeer **Johnny Mathis** enters the US album chart for the first time with ***Johnny's Greatest Hits***. The LP, which will hit the top spot on June 14, will remain on the survey for a record 490 weeks. A gifted athlete, Mathis earned a track and field scholarship to San Francisco State College before choosing a career in music. He initially tried out as a jazz singer, but was styled into a pop vocalist by Columbia's Mitch Miller.

20 **The New York Times Magazine** covers the global popularity of rock 'n' roll, with location reports from Britain ("Popular But More Sedate"), France ("Past The Peak: It's Cha Cha Cha Now"), Germany ("A Sport, An Athletic Test"), Japan ("A Presley of Its Own" [19-year old **Masaaki Hirao**]), and even Egypt ("A Smuggled Pleasure").

30 On the opening night of his British tour, **Tommy Steele** – currently charting in the UK with *Happy Guitar* – is knocked unconscious when some 300 fans storm the stage at Dundee's Caird Hall, ripping off his shirt, pulling out tufts of hair, and twisting his right arm. An ambulance and doctor are summoned, and he regains consciousness in his dressing room. Police escort him from the hall after the show, when an estimated 500 fans gather outside the theater. Steele cancels appearances for the rest of the week, on the advice of his doctor.

May

3 Albert Reggiani, a 19-year-old sailor from Stoughton, Massachusetts, suffers multiple wounds to the chest during a riot at the end of an **Alan Freed** Big Beat Show at the Boston Arena. Several others of the estimated 5,000-plus fans are also injured. Reggiani, whose two companions, Jean Austin and Carol Wallace, are among those attacked, is taken to City Hospital for emergency treatment before being transferred to Chelsea Naval Hospital, where his condition is not regarded as serious. The Boston Arena will ban all future concerts, and Freed will later be charged with incitement to riot, destruction of property, and other violent behavior. The charges will be dismissed, though Freed will encounter more problems renewing his radio contract with WINS next week.

9 **Alan Freed** resigns from WINS, charging that the station's lack of support over his indictment in Boston has been a "hard thing to swallow," and adding, "they should have given me a little support after all the unproved publicity from Boston, but they ran all week refusing to say anything." In his resignation letter to vice-president and general manager of the station, Jock Fearnhead, Freed writes: "After

Alan Freed faced superior trouble, while Jerry Lee Lewis was in family trouble, as controversy raged over the circumstances of his marriage.

Alan Freed

Jerry Lee Lewis and his wife Myra

having come to New York and WINS almost four years ago, at which time WINS was one of the lesser important stations in the market, having diligently and earnestly striven to make my WINS program the most listened to radio show in New York, thereby helping WINS achieve the prominence of being the number one radio station in the market...I regret that I must hereby tender my resignation because I feel that you have failed to stand behind my policies and principles." Accepting the resignation, Fearnhead will state that Freed resigned and was not fired and that "the station's position in the Freed case up to last night had been one of a third party and a separate entity because the incident involved the non-radio activities of Mr. Freed."

19 Having passed an audition for Los Angeles-based Del-Fi (and Keen) Records' owner Bob Keane, 17-year-old singer-songwriter/guitarist **Ritchie Valens** – of Mexican/Indian parentage – records the self-penned *Come On, Let's Go*, together with a version of Leiber and Stoller's *Framed*, at his first session, held at the Gold Star Studios in Hollywood.

22 **Jerry Lee Lewis**'s unorthodox marriage to his then 13-year-old second cousin, Myra Gale Brown, causes a storm when the singer arrives in Britain, where he checks in – with Myra – to the Westbury Hotel in London. Waiting reporters ask who his young companion is. Lewis responds that she is his wife and cousin, and that he has been married twice before. The Home Office reveals that the Ministry of Labour and British child welfare organizations are investigating the scandal, while the National Society for the Prevention of Cruelty to Children will maintain that "This is a matter for the police."

27 The British media is in uproar over **Jerry Lee Lewis** (the most restrained headline, in the **Daily Sketch**, describes him as an "unappetizing fellow"). He is booed off stage and 34 of his scheduled 37 concerts are canceled, after two London shows at the Edmonton Regal and the Kilburn State. All this is despite a statement from the Rank company, which controls the Gaumont and Odeon cinemas: "When Jerry Lee Lewis was booked none of these facts concerning his private life were known. Because most seats have been sold in advance for these one night stands, it is unlikely that any cancellation of performances could take place – not even by an order from above. We booked Lewis as an act purely on his entertainment value and box office attraction." After reports that Lewis canceled the gigs, his manager, Oscar Davis, states that promoters Lew and Leslie Grade terminated the tour: "We didn't cancel the tour, or violate the contract, and so far, have not been told why it was stopped. Accordingly, I expect Jerry to be paid his full salary."

June

2 **Alan Freed** begins a new nightly rock 'n' roll broadcast on ABC's New York radio station WABC. The Monday to Friday show fills the 7:15 pm to 11:00 pm slot.

9 **Billboard** magazine includes a full-page ad taken out by **Jerry Lee Lewis** in an attempt to explain his recent problems. He writes: "I confess that my life has been stormy. I hope that if I am washed up as an entertainer, it won't be because of this bad publicity... I can't control the press or the sensationalism that these people will go to, to get a scandal started to sell papers." He also re-weds Myra in a ceremony of impeccable legality.

"We have more than enough rock 'n' roll entertainers of our own, without importing them from overseas." Sir Frank Medlicott, MP, June 25, 1958

10 On his first weekend's furlough from the Army, **Elvis Presley** begins a two-day recording session at RCA Studios in Nashville (which will provide his hit singles for late 1958 and 1959).

14 John Foster – manager of the newly named **Cliff Richard & the Drifters** – has arranged for the band to take part in a talent contest at the Gaumont Cinema on Shepherd's Bush Green in London, and has persuaded George Ganjou, a variety agent, to see the group perform. Even though Ganjou says he knows nothing about rock 'n' roll and is "square," he takes Richard's demo tape to Norrie Paramor, head of A&R at EMI Records' Columbia label, who will invite the combo to audition for him.

15 **Marty Wilde** is a featured act on the premiere edition of the ITV pop show "Oh Boy!" broadcast live from the Hackney Empire in London. (He will also appear on the last program, broadcast on May 30, 1959.) The 19-year-old Wilde was discovered by impresario Larry Parnes, who is developing a stable of teenage British male rock 'n' roll singers, including Tommy Steele, and has secured Wilde a recording deal with the Philips label. "Oh Boy!" is produced by Jack Good, who will also create the youth-oriented television series "Boy Meets Girls" and "Wham!" Good is the unofficial talent-spotter of early rock 'n' roll in Britain, backing artists such as Cliff Richard, Terry Dene, Wilde, and Billy Fury.

19 **Buddy Holly** records his first songs without the **Crickets**, at a session produced by Dick Jacobs at the Pythian Temple in New York – his first sides for the Coral label. He covers two **Bobby Darin** songs, *Early In The Morning* and *Now We're One*, backed by a small group (including saxophonist **Sam "The Man" Taylor**). Darin was to have released these, credited to the Ding Dongs, on the Brunswick label, but after the success of *Splish Splash*, Atco releases them under the name of the Rinky Dinks. In New York, Holly will meet his future wife – Puerto Rican Maria Elena Santiago – when visiting Murray Deutch at Peer-Southern publishers.

25 Sir Frank Medlicott, Independent MP for Norfolk Central, questions British Minister of Labour Iain MacLeod about the grounds on which a permit was given to **Jerry Lee Lewis** to tour the UK. Medlicott says: "Is my right honourable Friend aware that great offence was caused to many people by the arrival of this man with his 13-year-old bride, bearing in mind the difficulties other people have in getting permission to work here. We have more than enough rock 'n' roll entertainers of our own without importing them from overseas." MacLeod says the permit was issued under quota arrangements agreed with the Variety and Allied Entertainments Council, but agrees that it is "a thoroughly unpleasant case."

Marty Wilde was one of the rockers in the Larry Parnes talent stable, all of whom were given a "soft" forename and a "hard" surname.

The poster for a Jerry Lee Lewis show in Sheffield, which never happened.

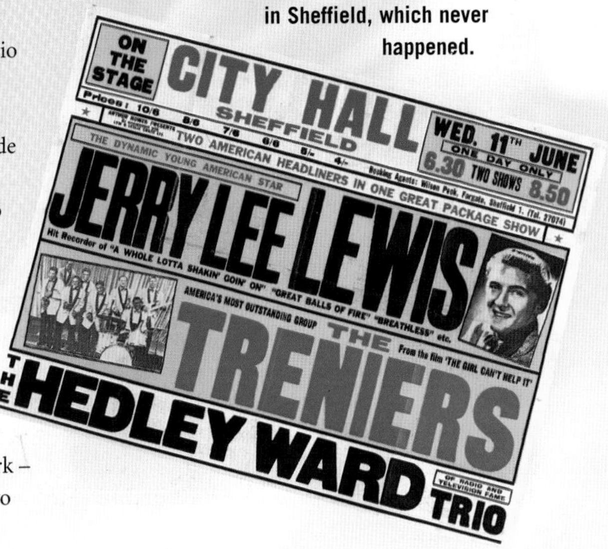

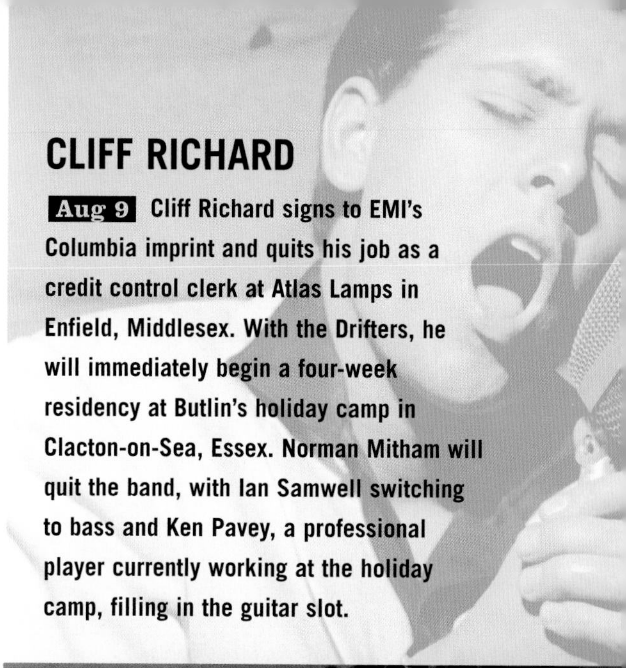

CLIFF RICHARD

Aug 9 Cliff Richard signs to EMI's Columbia imprint and quits his job as a credit control clerk at Atlas Lamps in Enfield, Middlesex. With the Drifters, he will immediately begin a four-week residency at Butlin's holiday camp in Clacton-on-Sea, Essex. Norman Mitham will quit the band, with Ian Samwell switching to bass and Ken Pavey, a professional player currently working at the holiday camp, filling in the guitar slot.

Prior to July's Abbey Road recording session, Richard had cut *Lawdy Miss Clawdy* and *Breathless* at HMV Records' Oxford Street recording facility, backed by Ian Samwell, Norman Mitham, Ken Pavey, and Terry Smart.

Hank Ballard and *The Twist*... Elvis Presley's mother dies... The Country Music Association is founded...

July

4 On Independence Day, **Buddy Holly & the Crickets** embark on an 11-date Summer Dance Party tour, with Tommy Allsup's Western Swing Band, in Angola, Indiana. Holly will drive his new Lincoln car from one date to the next.

5 The **Everly Brothers**' double A-side *All I Have To Do Is Dream/Claudette*, released on the London label, begins a seven-week run at UK No. 1, their first transatlantic chart-topper.

5 Following Atlantic's recent release of ***The Great Ray Charles***, **Charles** appears at the annual Newport Jazz Festival in Rhode Island. His performance is recorded by the label for release as a live album. With **Chuck Berry** also on the bill, the festival is inaugurating its first Blues Night, with performances by **Joe Turner** and **Big Maybelle**, among others.

7 The British Board of Trade announces that manufacturers' sales of gramophone records in April, totalling £1,040,000 ($2,912,000), were slightly higher than in March, and reflect a 22 percent increase over sales in the same month last year. Production of 78rpm discs, at 2,300,000, showed a 30 percent drop over the same period. The number of $33^1/_3$rpm records produced was 1,200,000 – 25 percent higher than in April last year.

8 Already a popular R&B singer-songwriter as front man with his group the **Midnighters**, with hits like *Work With Me Annie*, *Annie Had A Baby*, and the controversial *Sexy Ways*, **Hank Ballard** cuts his latest composition, *The Twist*, for Vee-Jay Records – his only recording for the label. On November 11 he will re-record the song in Cincinnati for King Records, for whom it will be a modest R&B hit in 1959, though its catchy dance-based theme will find global success only when adapted by **Chubby Checker** in 1960.

8 The first gold record album is awarded by the RIAA for the hugely popular soundtrack LP ***Oklahoma!*** The honor (granted on a different basis from the singles award) confirms that the album has reached $1 million in sales at "manufacturer wholesale prices based on one third of the list price for each record." In the same certification statement, 14-year-old singer **Laurie London** becomes the first British artist to earn a gold disc, for *He's Got The Whole World (In His Hands)*, based on a traditional gospel song. The London-born teenager has been discovered by EMI recording manager Norman Newell at a radio talent contest, and is backed on this recording by the Geoff Love Orchestra. The single will be London's only hit on both sides of the Atlantic.

9 Another former Sun Records artist, **Johnny Cash**, follows Carl Perkins in signing to Columbia Records. While Perkins's chart career will fade by the end of the 1950s, Cash will remain with the label for some 30 years.

12 Described as mirroring "the popular tastes of America as reflected by record sales," **Alan Freed**'s new half-hour TV series "The Big Beat" premieres on ABC. The program airs live, in front of an audience of 300, from ABC's Television Center at West 57th Street in Manhattan, and features the **Everly Brothers**, **Connie Francis**, **Ferlin Husky**, **Sunny Gale**, the **Billy Williams Quartet**, and **Johnnie & Joe**.

18 Alan Freed Enterprises, Inc. files a voluntary petition of bankruptcy, citing liabilities of $51,985 and no assets. The situation is largely caused by the cancellation of Freed's tour after the riots in Boston.

21 A popular staple on both radio and television during the 1950s, the last "Arthur Godfrey's Talent Scouts" program airs on CBS-TV. Among dozens of performers who got their start on the series are **Pat Boone**, **Tony Bennett**, the **McGuire Sisters**, and **Connie Francis**.

24 **Cliff Richard**, with **Ernie Shears** on guitar, **Frank Clarke** on bass, and **Terry Smart** on drums, records *Schoolboy Crush* and *Move It* in Studio 2 at the Abbey Road Studios in London. The session – running from 7:00 pm to 10:30 pm – is produced by Norrie Paramor, who will oversee all of Richard's early recordings.

> **"That was the new record from Cliff Richard & the Drifters. You can see them live tonight at the Rock 'n' Roll Ballroom."**
>
> Butlin's DJ, Tulah Tuke, to whom EMI sent a copy of *Move It*, August 1958

Elvis Presley was granted compassionate leave from the Army to visit his mother, Gladys, who had become ill on August 8. She died six days later.

August

2 **Buddy Holly**'s *Rave On* – by Norman Petty, Bill Tilghman, and Sunny West – hits UK No. 5. By now, Holly has successfully and uniquely bridged the gap between the raw energy of the early rock 'n' roll pioneers and the softer melodic sound of the teen-beat trend.

9 **Billboard** magazine changes the name of its weekly singles chart from "Top 100" to "Hot 100," a title that will stick until the end of 1996. The first No. 1 on the newly named list is **Ricky Nelson**'s *Poor Little Fool*.

11 **Elvis Presley**'s *Hard Headed Woman* single is confirmed gold – his first certification. (In August 2002, nearing the 25th anniversary of his death, the RIAA will certify 100 million US sales of his records.)

12 His mother, Gladys, having become ill with acute hepatitis last week, and having been admitted to the Methodist Hospital in Memphis the next day, **Elvis Presley** flies from Dallas, to see her and speak with Dr. Charles Clarke about her condition. After initial reluctance – the Army fears press allegations of "preferential treatment" – Presley has been granted compassionate leave.

13 In a letter to **Fats Domino**, his top artist, grateful Imperial Records head Lew Chudd writes on the occasion of the singer's tenth anniversary with the label: "I thought you would be interested in knowing that in the past ten years you have sold over 40,000,000 records, 3,000,000 albums and 4,000,000 EPs."

14 Having left Memphis Methodist Hospital a few hours earlier, **Elvis Presley** has returned to Graceland to rest when he gets a call from his father, Vernon, who confirms that Gladys Presley passed away at 3:15 am. She was 46. Her son is inconsolable.

15 With his solo LP ***Early In The Morning*** just released, **Buddy Holly** and Maria Elena Santiago are secretly married at the home of Holly's parents' in Lubbock, by pastor Ben Johnson.

16 Gladys Presley's funeral is held at the National Funeral Home in Forest Hill, Memphis. The **Blackwood Brothers** sing *Precious Memories* and *Rock Of Ages*, two of her favorite hymns. **Elvis Presley** is so overcome with grief that he is unable to stand for much of the proceedings and has to be supported. Meanwhile, 500 policemen keep a gigantic crowd at bay.

18 His second US chart-topper following the 1955 success of *Cherry Pink And Apple Blossom White*, 41-year-old **Perez Prado**'s *Patricia* single is certified gold by the RIAA. The Cuban-born bandleader and organist – who fronts his own orchestra – is known as "The King of the Mambo."

29 **Alan Freed** moves forward with his next event, as Alan Freed Presents the Big Beat opens in New York. The show switches from Freed's usual venue (the Paramount) to the Fox Theater in Brooklyn, and grosses more than $200,000 in ticket sales. The line-up features **Bill Haley & His Comets**, **Frankie Avalon**, the **Everly Brothers**, the **Kalin Twins** (currently enjoying a five-week spell at UK No. 1 with *When*), **Chuck Berry**, **Jimmy Clanton**, female pop-trio the **Poni Tails** (currently scoring with *Born Too Late*), **Teddy Randazzo**, **Ed Townsend**, **Jo Ann Campbell**, the **Elegants**, the **Royal Teens**, **Jack Scott**, the **Olympics**, **Bobby Freeman** (riding high with his first hit, the irresistible US No. 5, *Do You Wanna Dance*), the **Danleers**, **Bo Diddley**, **Larry Williams**, **Gino & Gina**, **Bobby Hamilton**, the **Cleftones**, **Alan Freed & his Rock 'n' Roll Orchestra** featuring **Sam "The Man" Taylor**, **King Curtis**, **Georgie Auld**, and 20-year-old newcomer **Duane Eddy**. Guitarist Eddy, a native of Corning, New York, has already recorded as one half of Jimmy & Duane (with Jimmy Delbridge), for Lee Hazlewood's Eb X. Preston label in 1955. Using a red Gretsch 6120 instrument bought in 1956, he is developing a unique "twangy" guitar sound that will become the trademark of an enormously successful career as America's leading rock 'n' roll instrumentalist. His style is already in evidence on his first three 1958 hits, *Moovin' 'N' Groovin'*, *Rebel Rouser*, and the current smash, *Ramrod*, on all of which he is backed by his band, the **Rebels**.

September

5 The Country Music Association is granted its charter in Nashville, the first trade organization formed to promote a particular genre of music. Initially consisting of only 233 members (which will grow to more than 6,000 organizational and individual constituents in 43 countries over the next 40 years), the objectives of the organization are to "guide and enhance the development of Country Music throughout the world...and to provide a unity of purpose for the Country Music industry." The CMA's first board of directors includes nine directors and five officers, with Wesley Rose – president of Acuff-Rose Publishing, Inc. – serving as its first chairman. Broadcasting entrepreneur Connie B. Gay is the founding president.

Newly signed to Columbia Records, country star Johnny Cash had his last No. 1 with Sun Records in June, with *Guess Things Happen That Way*.

Sept 1958

The hula-hoop craze... Cliff Richard and Eddie Cochran on television...

Cliff Richard was shadowed by Bruce Welch and Hank Marvin.

7 Providing the first national exposure for the current hula-hoop craze, **Georgia Gibbs** performs *The Hula-Hoop Song* on "The Ed Sullivan Show," which tonight also features **Johnnie Ray**. Her original recording of the song will make US No. 32, outpacing a rival chart version, by **Teresa Brewer**, by six places. Gibbs, aged 38, has already scored her biggest hit – in 1955 – with the US chart-topper, *Dance With Me Henry (Wallflower)*, a revised "answer" record to **Hank Ballard**'s *Work With Me Annie*.

13 **Cliff Richard** makes his British television debut on Jack Good's season-premiere "Oh Boy!" Good has heard the current Richard single, disregarded *Schoolboy Crush*, but raved over the B-side, *Move It*. He orders Richard to sing without his customary guitar and minus his sideburns. He also encourages a provocative stage act, instructing Richard to raise his eyes to the camera and grab his arm "as if stuck with a hypodermic syringe." The resulting newspaper reports will complain about television depravity and the corruption of Britain's youth, only helping to spur *Move It*, promoted to the A-side, to make its debut on the UK chart at No. 12. US rocker **Eddie Cochran** also makes his British bow on the show, which features resident singer **Marty Wilde**, who is booked for its entire 39-week run. The new season of "Oh Boy!" – launched in direct competition with the BBC's "Six-Five Special" – is hosted by Tony Hall and Jimmy Henney, and broadcast live from the Wood Green Empire in London, with musical director Harry Robinson and his band, **Lord Rockingham's XI**.

13 Cash Box, the American music trade publication, publishes its first expanded Top 100 Best Selling Tunes on Record (singles chart). The magazine started as a weekly coin machine and music industry publication in July 1942, and will flourish until closing in October 1996. Since the late 1940s, Cash Box has published both Best Sellers and Juke Box singles charts, though its weekly listings will largely live in the shadow of the **Billboard** charts throughout its history.

18 **James Brown** cuts four tracks at the Belltone Studios in New York, under producer Andy Gibson and arranger Gene Redd. They include the self-written, gospel-inflected *Try Me (I Need You)*, which will hit R&B No. 1 and give Brown and his backing band, the **Flames**, their first hit since *Please, Please, Please* in 1956.

22 After giving a press conference at the Military Ocean Terminal in Brooklyn, New York (by special dispensation of the US Army), **Elvis Presley** joins 1,170 others of the 3rd Armored Division on the USS *General Randall*, as she sets sail for Bremerhaven.

27 **Connie Francis** lands her second UK No. 1 with the double A-side *Carolina Moon* – her update of a Guy Lombardo standard – paired with *Stupid Cupid*. The latter hit was written by the young Brooklyn-based songwriting team of **Howard Greenfield** and 19-year-old **Neil Sedaka**, who have been working together for three years and originally offered the catchy tune to the **Shepherd Sisters**. Sedaka – who won a piano scholarship to New York's Juilliard School – is also trying to get his own recording career off the ground, having already cut discs for Legion Records and Decca.

October

1 From Bremerhaven, **Elvis Presley** is transported to the US Army base at Friedberg, near Frankfurt, where he joins his unit – Company D, 32nd Tank Battalion, 3rd Armored Division – to serve the remaining 16 months of his two years' military service. While on the base, he will be a jeep driver for his platoon sergeant, Billy Wilson. Presley will buy a house in nearby Bad Neuheim, taking advantage of a rule that allows him to live off camp if he has family to support. His father, grandmother, some friends, and staff will all move in.

2 At a press conference, **Elvis Presley** is asked whether he is afraid of being forgotten by his fans while he is in the Army. "It makes you wonder, but, if people forget me I can't complain. I had it once." On the subject of music he says: "I am not an expert on music. I don't even read it. Classical music is good for sending you to sleep."

2 **Buddy Holly** guests on **Alan Freed**'s "The Big Beat" show on WNEW-TV, where he is interviewed by the host and mimes to *It's So Easy* – a new non-charting release by the **Crickets** issued on the Brunswick label.

3 **Buddy Holly & the Crickets** begin the 19-date Biggest Show of Stars for 1958 – Autumn Edition tour, with **Frankie Avalon**, **Bobby Darin**, **Bobby Freeman**, **Clyde McPhatter**, the **Coasters**, and others. Also on the trek are **Dion & the Belmonts** – a fresh rock 'n' roll outfit from the Bronx, New York, led by 19-year-old singer-songwriter **Dion DiMuci** – who are currently scoring their second hit, *No One Knows*, for the new Bronx-based Laurie label. The tour starts at the Auditorium in Worcester, Massachusetts, and will conclude on the 19th at the Mosque in Richmond, Virginia. This marks the last tour for Holly & the Crickets, as Holly will decide to end his association with Norman Petty (with whom relations have soured) and base himself in New York. **Jerry Allison** (who has also recently been married – to Peggy Sue) and **Joe Mauldin** will

Dion & the Belmonts – fronted by Dion DiMucci – took their name from Belmont Avenue, which cuts through the area of the Bronx where they lived.

return to Texas, with Holly giving them full rights to the Crickets' name so that they can continue recording. Earl Sinks will replace Holly on vocals, while Tommy Allsup joins on guitar.

3 **Cliff Richard** cuts three sides at his second session for Columbia Records, once again in Studio 2 at Abbey Road with Norrie Paramor producing. He records *High Class Baby* (which will be his next single), *My Feet Hit The Ground*, and *Don't Bug Me Baby*.

4 R&B pianist/singer-songwriter **Tommy Edwards**, who has been recording since 1949, begins a six-week run at US No. 1 with *It's All In The Game* – based on a melody written in 1912 by Charles Dawes (who became US Vice-President in 1925). Its position at the top will be taken by *It's Only Make Believe* – a crossover smash by 25-year-old country singer, **Conway Twitty**, reflecting the ongoing popularity of both musical genres and the diversity of the public's taste. Both hits are available on the MGM label.

5 After manager John Foster has spotted guitarist Hank Marvin playing at London's popular 2 i's club, **Cliff Richard & the Drifters**, comprising Marvin (lead guitar), Bruce Welch (rhythm guitar, also brought in – at the insistence of Marvin), Ian Samwell (bass), and Terry Smart (drums), make their concert bow at the Victoria Hall in Hanley, Staffordshire. They are part of the **Kalin Twins**' UK tour, which also features trumpeter **Eddie Calvert** and the **Most Brothers**. Teen reaction to Cliff Richard will be such that, almost from the outset, the Kalin Twins will find him a hard act to follow.

6 As industry rumors surface about illegal payments to DJs and radio stations in return for airplay, **Billboard** magazine reports: "Payola, that under-the-turntable device whereby record companies win plugs and influence disc jockeys, is fast growing into a monster that may yet destroy its creators."

21 In what will prove to be his last session, **Buddy Holly** records four new tracks – *It Doesn't Matter Anymore, Moondreams, Raining In My Heart,* and *True Love Ways*, again at Pythian Temple in New York. *It Doesn't Matter Anymore* – written by **Paul Anka** (who is currently having less success with his own releases) – is recorded in one take. In his only session recorded in stereo, Holly is accompanied by a 12-piece string section from the Dick Jacobs Orchestra – a first for a rock 'n' roll artist.

26 **Bill Haley & His Comets** play the first rock 'n' roll concert in Germany, at the West Berlin Sportspalast, during a European tour. There is a major riot among the 7,000 fans. As Haley begins his German dates, East Germany's Minister of Defense, Willi Stoph, declares that Haley is promoting nuclear war by engendering fanatical, hysterical enthusiasm among the German youth, which will lead it to a mass rock 'n' roll grave.

27 **Tommy Steele** appears on BBC-TV's "This Is Your Life," hosted by Eamonn Andrews. Steele is at the height of his popularity: his crowded schedule includes an appearance at the Royal Variety Performance, a part in the pantomime "Goldilocks and the Three Bears" in Liverpool, recent tours of South Africa, Denmark, and Sweden, and three films.

Tommy Steele was making the transition from pop star to movie star, and starred in the rags-to-riches plotted "The Tommy Steele Story."

The UK's first album chart... The Kingston Trio... The Teddy Bears...

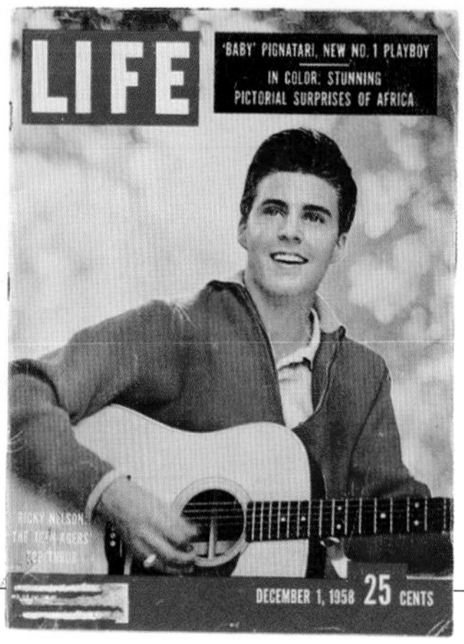

The pin-up favorite Ricky Nelson scored two top ten US chart albums this year, including the chart-topping *Ricky*.

28 **Buddy Holly & the Crickets** make what will prove to be their final television appearance on "American Bandstand" – miming to *Heartbeat* and *It's So Easy*.

29 **Elvis Presley** visits **Bill Haley & His Comets** backstage at the Kellesberg Hall in Stuttgart, on the final date of their German tour. While in Germany, the group also make the movie "Hier Bin Ich, Hier Bliebe Ich" ("Here I Am, Here I Stay") with Caterina Valente.

November

3 Superior Judge Charles Fairhurst refuses to quash the indictment charging **Alan Freed** with incitement to riot, in connection with the brawl that followed his concert at the Boston Arena on May 8. Freed has been free on $2,500 bail ever since the riot. The judge also refuses to rule on a second indictment, charging violation of the Massachusetts anti-anarchy law.

10 **Sam Cooke** and 22-year-old, Chicago-born singer **Lou Rawls**, a member of his tour backing group, the **Pilgrim Travelers Quartet**, suffer minor injuries in a car crash in Marion, Arkansas. Cooke's driver, Edward Cunningham, is killed in the accident.

10 The **Daily Sketch**, reporting on a rift that has opened up between **Marty Wilde** and his manager **Larry Parnes**, carries the following statement from Parnes: "I won't release Wilde from his contract. I think he's being a very stupid kid and he owes me an apology... Jealousy turned Marty's head. He's not jealous of Tommy Steele... Tommy is an established international entertainer. Marty Wilde is still in the napkin stage. He is just being plain childish. No, Wilde is jealous of Billy Fury. Record companies are already bidding against one another for him."

14 Backed for the first time in the studio by **Hank Marvin**, **Bruce Welch**, **Jet Harris**, and **Terry Smart**, **Cliff Richard** records *Livin' Lovin' Doll* and *Mean Streak* for his forthcoming single.

16 Violence breaks out among the audience during a **Cliff Richard** concert at the Trocadero Theatre, Elephant & Castle, in London. Richard is smuggled out of the building and into a waiting police car, which takes off at high speed. DJ Gus Goodwin is pelted with coins during the show and, following the concert, the stage door becomes completely blocked by a sea of screaming teenagers.

24 Folk-music pioneers the **Kingston Trio** become the first group to top the US album chart with their first album, ***The Kingston Trio*** – a revolutionary set of calypsos and sea shanties that includes the current chart-topping single, *Tom Dooley*, based on a late 18th-century folk song, *Tom Dula*. The group – **Dave Guard** on banjo, with guitarists **Bob Shane** and **Nick Reynolds** – formed last year in San Francisco and became popular in the region during an eight-month residence at the Purple Onion. Their music will prove enormously influential to a host of nascent folk singer-songwriters in the early 1960s, when singer-songwriter **John Stewart** will replace Guard.

December

5 With *Donna*, his second release on Del-Fi, already on its way to a US No. 2 peak, **Ritchie Valens** returns to his old school, San Fernando High, to play a concert that is recorded by

UK ALBUM CHART

Nov 8 **The first UK top ten album chart is published by music weekly Melody Maker:**

1. **Soundtrack** – *South Pacific* (below)
2. **Frank Sinatra** – *Come Fly With Me*
3. **Elvis Presley** – *Elvis' Golden Records*
4. **Elvis Presley** – *King Creole*
5. **Broadway cast** – *My Fair Lady*
6. **Johnny Mathis** – *Warm*
7. **Soundtrack** – *The King And I*
8. **Perry Como** – *Dear Perry*
9. **Soundtrack** – *Oklahoma!*
10. **Tom Lehrer** – *Songs By Tom Lehrer*

The New Musical Express – which introduced the first UK singles chart in 1952 – will stay out of the album chart fray for almost another four years, introducing its first top ten in June 1962. Trade paper Record Retailer will publish a top ten album chart when it launches in March 1960.

The Kingston Trio formed in 1957 in San Francisco, and their clean-cut folk harmonies prefaced a new folk wave in the early 1960s.

The Crests

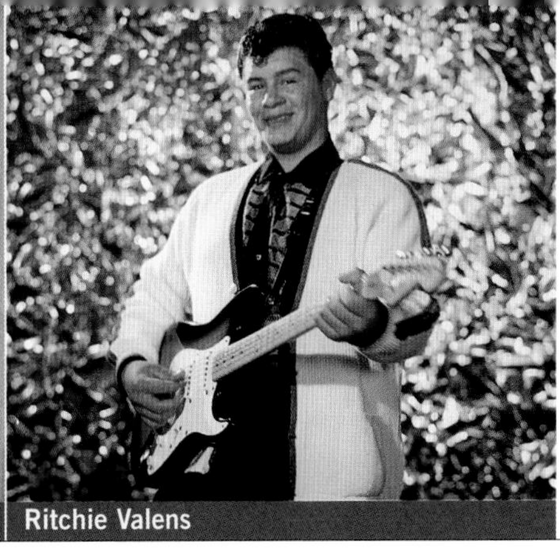

Ritchie Valens

Two hot acts on Alan Freed's annual Christmas package: vocal stylists the Crests, and fast-emerging Latino singer-songwriter/guitarist Ritchie Valens.

producer/label boss Bob Keane. During the performance, a cameo slot is also filmed for inclusion in Alan Freed's next rock 'n' roll movie, "Go, Johnny, Go!" with Valens lip-synching to *Ooh My Head*.

6 The **Teddy Bears** hit US No. 1 with their first outing, *To Know Him Is To Love Him*, issued on the Dore label (where Herb Alpert and Lou Adler are working in A&R). The song has been written, arranged, and produced by one of the trio's members, 17-year-old **Phil Spector**, who is joined by schoolfriend Marshall Lieb, and female vocalist Annette Kleinbard. Spector is also responsible for playing every instrument on the recording, except the drums, which are supplied by **Sandy Nelson** (who will launch his own career in 1959 with the percussive hit, *Teen Beat*). Born in the Bronx, Phil Spector moved with his mother to Los Angeles in 1953, after his father committed suicide. He was inspired to write this melodic pop nugget by the inscription – composed by his mother – engraved on his father's tombstone.

11 Following the No. 1 success of *Yakety Yak*, and with R&B saxophonist **King Curtis** guesting on his favored instrument, the **Coasters** record *Charlie Brown*, the latest composition by Leiber and Stoller. The session marks the first appearance of ex-**Cadets** vocalist **Will Jones**, who recently replaced Bobby Nunn in the line-up.

20 **George Harrison**, **Paul McCartney**, and **John Lennon** perform as the **Quarry Men** at the wedding reception of Harrison's brother Harry, held at the family house at 25 Upton Green, Speke, Liverpool.

25 **Alan Freed**'s Christmas Jubilee begins a ten-day seasonal run at New York's Loew's Theater in Manhattan. This year's bill features **Chuck Berry**, **Bo Diddley**, the **Everly Brothers**, **Jackie Wilson**, **Frankie Avalon**, **Eddie Cochran**, **Ritchie Valens**, **Johnnie Ray**, **Jimmy Clanton**, **Jo Ann Campbell**, **Harvey & the Moonglows** (whose recent Chess hit, *Ten Commandments of Love*, will prove to be their last), a new Chicago-based vocal group called the **Flamingos**, **Baby Washington**, the **Crests**, the **Nu-Tornadoes**, the **Cadillacs**, **Dion & the Belmonts**, **Inga**, **Ed Townsend**, **Gino & Gina**, **King Curtis**, **Sam "The Man" Taylor**, **Georgie Auld**, and **Earl Warren**. (The Crests are currently lighting up the charts with the US No. 2 hit *16 Candles*. The R&B group are led by **Johnny Maestro** and featured in their original line-up **Patricia Van Dross**, who has a younger brother named Luther.)

26 Promoting his first Columbia album release, ***The Fabulous Johnny Cash***, **Cash** performs at the Showboat Hotel, Las Vegas, topping a country bill that also features the Sons of the Pioneers and Tex Ritter.

27 **Buddy Holly** makes his first live appearance in Lubbock since gaining fame, at a KLLL radio event from the Morris Fruit & Vegetable Store. He also visits KLLL's studio to record *You're The One*, with station DJs Waylon Jennings and Ray "Slim" Corbin. The station has challenged Holly to write a song in 30 minutes, and the tune is duly recorded, with Holly on guitar and Jennings and Corbin adding "percussion" in the background: one claps his hands in the 1-2-1 beat, while the other slaps his knees – contributions that are enough to earn both a co-songwriting credit with Holly.

"I won't release Wilde from his contract. I think he's being a very stupid kid... Marty Wilde is still in the napkin stage. He is just being plain childish."

Larry Parnes, November 10, 1958

Although the Teddy Bears were a one-hit wonder, their success in 1958 introduced Phil Spector (bottom left) to the music world.

ROOTS During this year: young singer-songwriter Joan Baez performs at the first Newport Folk Festival... a staff writer at Keen Publishing with co-scribe Lou Adler, Herb Alpert scores his first chart hit as the co-composer of Sam Cooke's *Love You Most Of All*... Queen's College New York student Carole Klein meets Gerry Goffin, who is working in a pharmacy; they immediately embark on a songwriting and personal partnership... the Dave Clark Five, with Stan Saxon on vocals, make their debut at the South Grove Youth Club in Tottenham... soul singer Otis Redding goes on the road with the Upsetters, and then enters Hamp Swain's "Teenage Party" contest... Kris Kristofferson begins writing songs while studying as a Rhodes Scholar at Oxford University... Dick Clark sends Christmas greetings by way of a novelty recording, which features a former chicken plucker who will find fame as Chubby Checker... Ma and Pa Gilbert put together a new band – Charlie Johnson & the Big Little Show Band – for their Hi-Loc Club in Battle Creek, Michigan, fronted by Del Shannon... and tugboat deckhand Ronald Wycherley wangles his way into Marty Wilde's dressing room at the Essoldo Cinema in Birkenhead, where he immediately impresses impresario Larry Parnes; Parnes signs him, renaming him Billy Fury...

I Only Have Eyes For You

1959

No.1 US SINGLES

Jan 3 The Chipmunk Song **David Seville & the Chipmunks**
Jan 24 Smoke Gets In Your Eyes **Platters**
Feb 14 Stagger Lee **Lloyd Price**
Mar 14 Venus **Frankie Avalon**
Apr 18 Come Softly To Me **Fleetwoods**
May 16 The Happy Organ **Dave (Baby) Cortez**
May 23 Kansas City **Wilbert Harrison**
June 6 The Battle Of New Orleans **Johnny Horton**
July 18 Lonely Boy **Paul Anka**
Aug 15 A Big Hunk O' Love **Elvis Presley with the Jordanaires**
Aug 29 The Three Bells **Browns**
Sept 26 Sleep Walk **Santo & Johnny**
Oct 10 Mack The Knife **Bobby Darin**
Nov 21 Mr. Blue **Fleetwoods**
Nov 28 Mack The Knife **Bobby Darin**
Dec 19 Heartaches By The Number **Guy Mitchell**

No.1 UK SINGLES

Jan 3 It's Only Make Believe **Conway Twitty**
Jan 24 The Day The Rains Came **Jane Morgan**
Jan 31 One Night/I Got Stung **Elvis Presley**
Feb 21 As I Love You **Shirley Bassey**
Mar 21 Smoke Gets In Your Eyes **Platters**
Mar 28 Side Saddle **Russ Conway**
Apr 25 It Doesn't Matter Anymore **Buddy Holly**
May 16 A Fool Such As I/I Need Your Love Tonight **Elvis Presley with the Jordanaires**
June 20 Roulette **Russ Conway**
July 4 Dream Lover **Bobby Darin**
Aug 1 Living Doll **Cliff Richard & the Shadows**
Sept 12 Only Sixteen **Craig Douglas**
Oct 10 Here Comes Summer **Jerry Keller**
Oct 17 Mack The Knife **Bobby Darin**
Oct 31 Travellin' Light **Cliff Richard & the Shadows**
Dec 5 What Do You Want **Adam Faith**
Dec 19 = What Do You Want **Adam Faith**
= What Do You Want To Make Those Eyes At Me For? **Emile Ford & the Checkmates**
Dec 26 What Do You Want To Make Those Eyes At Me For? **Emile Ford & the Checkmates**

Bobby Darin

Dick Clark's "American Bandstand"

Bobby Darin scored a transatlantic chart-topper with a song from the "Threepenny Opera"... While his show was at an all-time ratings high, clean-cut Dick Clark would end the year embroiled in the payola scandal.

It might be termed the *annus horribilis* of rock 'n' roll – when rock lost many of its leading lights through tragedy, scandal, or simply absence.

On a frosty February morning in Iowa, the light aircraft that was carrying **Buddy Holly** – along with **Ritchie Valens** (whose *La Bamba* was the first hit of its kind to fuse rock 'n' roll with Latin music) and the **Big Bopper** – crashed into a cornfield, and all were killed. Holly was just 22 years old. Popular music had lost perhaps its finest singer-songwriter/guitarist, even if the media of the day didn't appreciate the fact. Despite the brevity of his musical career, Holly's songbook would influence generations of musicians to come – not least **John Lennon** and **Paul McCartney**.

Only **Chuck Berry**'s timeless songwriting skills and guitar hooks could rival Holly's, and his career was about to crash too – into scandal and a two-year prison sentence that virtually removed him from the musical radar. The man who had done much to promote Berry's career also fell foul of the law in 1959. **Alan Freed**, who had first given *Maybellene* airplay, and included Berry in his concert package tours, became embroiled in a Federal investigation of payola.

Elvis Presley, despite being stationed with the US Army in Germany, generated four hits: *(Now And Then There's) A Fool Such As I*, *I Need Your Love Tonight*, *A Big Hunk O' Love*, and *My Wish Came True*, but even he was beginning to lose that dangerous edge that had so appealed two years earlier. The year saw the further revival of white-bread pop music, served up by clean-cut idols. After Buddy Holly's death, 19-year-old **Frankie Avalon** took his place on tour. But for the biggest hit of his career – *Venus* – he forswore guitars and saxophone for orchestra, female vocals, and a soft calypso beat. **Bobby Darin** had huge hits with *Dream Lover* and *Mack The Knife*, and **Paul Anka** followed *Diana* with two more ballads of heartache: *Lonely Boy* and *Put Your Head On My Shoulder*.

Among R&B artists, **Sam Cooke**'s *Only Sixteen* had only modest chart success, but would go on to enjoy perennial airplay. **Jerry Leiber** and **Mike Stoller** were still churning out the hits, most notably the **Drifters**' *There Goes My Baby*, which broke new ground with its Latin rhythm and strings. Chiming with the tamer taste of 1959, vocal groups like the **Flamingos** and the **Platters** enjoyed an Indian summer with ephemeral covers of *I Only Have Eyes For You* and *Smoke Gets In Your Eyes*, though the Platters were also embroiled in scandal.

In Britain, **Cliff Richard** scored his first chart-topper with *Living Doll*, following up handsomely with *Travellin' Light*. Hot on his heels as a British heart-throb was **Adam Faith**, with the irresistible *What Do You Want*. On television, the fun "hit-picking" series "Juke Box Jury" began – a unique show on which celebrities critiqued the week's top new 45s.

Two significant fledgling operations began this year. **Berry Gordy Jr.** formed a record label, initially called Tamla, in Detroit, and the first Grammy Awards were held in Beverly Hills, though in typical mainstream industry fashion not a single rock 'n' roll record was nominated.

"You know you make me wanna shout."

The Isley Brothers' catchphrase, 1950s

Berry Gordy sets up his Tamla label... Buddy Holly dies in a plane crash...

Petula Clark

Berry Gordy

January

9 **Dion & the Belmonts** perform their soon-to-be-released *A Teenager In Love* on "American Bandstand" (which, in recent ARB television ratings, has been confirmed as the most watched US daytime broadcast). The song, set to become a career-defining US No. 5 hit for Dion, is the latest rock 'n' roll nugget from songwriting team **Doc Pomus** (lyricist) and **Mort Shuman** (pianist/composer). This pair, who sometimes also write with other teams such as Leiber and Stoller (*Young Blood* for the **Coasters**), are responsible for an increasingly impressive catalog of hit songs. Having penned cuts over the past four years for **Big Joe Turner**, **Ray Charles**, **Bobby Darin**, and **Fabian** (his new release, *Turn Me Loose*), among others, they are signed to the Hill & Range publishing house, and will continue to churn out hits for artists including the **Drifters**, **Gene McDaniels**, **Gary "U.S." Bonds**, and **Elvis Presley** – who will cut 20 of their compositions.

10 **Lonnie Donegan**, **Alma Cogan**, **Frankie Vaughan**, **Marty Wilde**, the **Mudlarks**, and the **King Brothers** take part in the annual **New Musical Express** Pollwinners Concert, held in London. Best New Singer winner, **Cliff Richard** (backed by the **Drifters**), **Joe "Mr. Piano" Henderson**, the **Ted Heath Orchestra**, the **Chris Barber Band**, the **John Barry Seven**, and **Petula Clark** – who has been established as one of Britain's top female vocalists since her chart debut in 1954 with *The Little Shoemaker* – are also featured.

12 The 29-year-old songwriter/producer **Berry Gordy Jr.** – using an $800 advance from his family's loan fund – forms his own record label. Named Tamla, it is based at 1719 Gladstone Street in his native Detroit. Berry has already co-written **Jackie Wilson**'s first chart single, *Reet Petite (The Finest Girl You Ever Want To Meet)* – which he penned in 1957 while still working on the Ford car assembly line in Detroit – and three follow-up hits, including the US No. 7 smash *Lonely Teardrops*. He has also begun dabbling in production, starting in 1957 with *Ooh Shucks* by the Five Stars, for George Goldner's Mark X label. Displaying an acute skill for finding and surrounding himself with talented singers and writers, Gordy has spotted a new R&B vocal group called the **Miracles** – including lead singer **William "Smokey" Robinson** – performing at a local talent show. He produced two singles for them in 1957, *Got A Job* and *I Cry*, both licensed to local labels, as well as separate solo singles last year for songwriter Eddie Holland and his brother Brian. The first release on Gordy's new Tamla label will be 20-year-old **Marv Johnson**'s *Come To Me* (Tamla 101) in March – which will be licensed to United Artists for national distribution, and will make US No. 30 in May. Gordy has also formed his own publishing company, Jobete, named by extracting the first two letters from the names of each of his three children: Hazel Joy (Jo), Berry IV (Be), and Terry (Te). He invites Robinson and the Holland siblings to help him with his dream of establishing Detroit's first major house of hits.

Already a seasoned entertainer in Britain, Petula Clark graced the New Musical Express Pollwinners Concert... High-school dropout Berry Gordy was the genius who created "Hitsville USA" in Detroit.

16 The **Everly Brothers** make a lightning visit to the UK. They appear on the television show "Cool For Cats," receive a **New Musical Express** award (they have been voted World No. 1 Vocal Group), and attend a Savoy Hotel reception in their honor – all within 24 hours, before flying on to Europe.

22 **Buddy Holly** makes what will prove to be his last recordings – on a tape recorder – in his apartment in the Brevoort Building on 8th Street in Greenwich Village, New York, adding to others he has demoed over the past few weeks. On the tape: *Crying Waiting Hoping*, *That's What They Say*, *What To Do*, *Peggy Sue Got Married*, *That Makes It Tough*, and *Learning The Game*.

The Drifters had the good fortune to record songs by Doc Pomus and Mort Shuman, as well as Jerry Leiber and Mike Stoller, Barry Mann and Cynthia Weil, and Gerry Goffin and Carole King.

23 **Buddy Holly** begins a 24-date Winter Dance Party tour at George Devine's Million Dollar Ballroom in Milwaukee, set to end on February 15 at the Illinois State Armory in Springfield. His backup band comprises **Tommy Allsup** (guitar), **Waylon Jennings** (bass), and **Carl Bunch** (drums). The bill also features Texas DJ and singer-songwriter the **Big Bopper**, **Ritchie Valens**, **Frankie Sardo**, and **Dion & the Belmonts**.

24 **Cliff Richard**, backed by the **Drifters**, begins his first headlining British tour at the Rialto Theatre in York. He is supported by **Wee Willie Harris** and **Tony Crombie & His Rockets**.

February

2 **Buddy Holly** plays the 11th date of his current tour at the Surf Ballroom in Clear Lake, Iowa, before an estimated crowd of 1,000–1,500. During the concert, Holly sits in on drums for several other acts, while the **Belmonts**' bass singer, **Carlo Mastrangelo**, plays drums on Holly's set, standing in for an ailing **Carl Bunch**, who is suffering from frostbite in his foot. Tired of bus travel (*en route* from Duluth to Green Bay yesterday, their bus broke down, resulting in a concert in Appleton, Wisconsin, being canceled), flight arrangements are made by Carroll Anderson, manager of the Surf Ballroom, for Holly and others to fly on to their next show in Moorhead, Minnesota.

"There was no fearful omen of tragedy Monday night when 1,100 teenagers and their parents packed the Surf Ballroom in Clear Lake... The entertainers were full of pep, reacting joyously to the big crowd of young people."

Clear Lake Mirror Reporter, February, 1959

Buddy Holly's remarkable legacy lived on long after his death – with chart albums in the US or UK every decade.

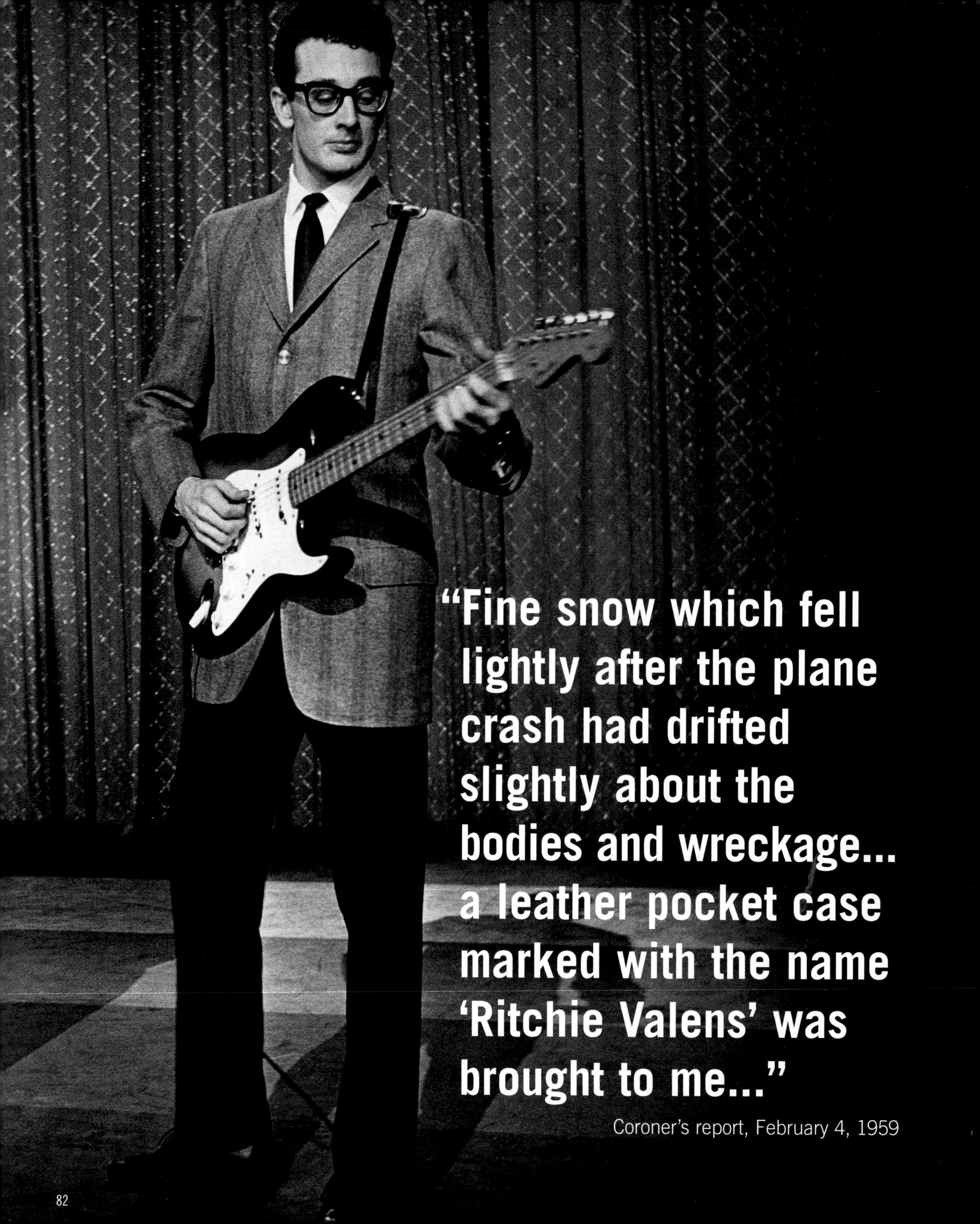

"Fine snow which fell lightly after the plane crash had drifted slightly about the bodies and wreckage... a leather pocket case marked with the name 'Ritchie Valens' was brought to me..."

Coroner's report, February 4, 1959

Feb 3 At approximately 1:00 am, Buddy Holly, Ritchie Valens (who has won a seat by tossing a coin with Tommy Allsup), and the Big Bopper (given the seat booked for Waylon Jennings), board a red Beechcraft-Bonanza light plane, No. N3794N, hired from Dwyer's Flying Service at Mason City Airport, Iowa, paying $36 each for their tickets. The flight is to take them

to Fargo, North Dakota, for their next tour date in Minnesota. Before takeoff, pilot Roger Peterson tries to persuade fellow pilot Dwayne Mansfield to fly, because he is too tired. Peterson apparently misreads the gyroscope, thinking the plane is climbing when it is in fact descending. In bad weather, the plane crashes about 8 miles northwest of the airfield, only minutes after takeoff – the main part of the craft coming to rest against a barbed wire fence at the north end of a stubble field. Holly, Valens, the Big Bopper, and pilot Peterson are all killed. The plane's owner, Jim Dwyer, spots the wreckage at around 9:00 am during an aerial search, since he hasn't been able to make contact with Peterson since takeoff. Deputy Sheriff Bill McGill is the first law enforcement officer to arrive at the scene. Later in the day, the two Moorhead shows are combined into one performance. Promoters audition for local talent to fill the bill, following an appeal on KVOX radio station. The band from Central High School, Fargo, gets the gig, with Bobby Velline – subsequently famous as Bobby Vee – singing, as he knows more lyrics than anyone else in the band. Tomorrow, singers Jimmy Clanton and Frankie Avalon will headline in Sioux City, Iowa, dropping other commitments in order to finish the Winter Dance Party tour. Buddy Holly's funeral, at the Tabernacle Baptist Church in Lubbock at the weekend, will be attended by over 1,000 people. The pallbearers will be Bob Montgomery, Jerry Allison, Joe Mauldin, Niki Sullivan, Sonny Curtis, and Phil Everly. Holly will be buried in Lubbock City Cemetery.

Fabian's *Turn Me Loose*... The Grammys ignore rock 'n' roll... "Juke Box Jury"...

8 **Johnny Cash** performs *Don't Take Your Guns to Town*, followed by **Frankie Laine** singing *You Can Depend On Me* and *Then I Should Fall In Love*, on the "Ed Sullivan Show."

10 **Link Wray & His Wraymen** make their second appearance on "American Bandstand," performing *Raw-Hide*, the follow-up to Wray's controversial US No. 16 hit, *Rumble*. Even though that single was an instrumental, it caused a furor when it was released in 1958 because both civic authorities and broadcasters were concerned that its title alone was encouraging teenage violence. Wray, a native of North Carolina, is credited with creating a unique "fuzztone" sound with his guitar – a distorted and "wicked-sounding" effect that was first heard on *Rumble*.

13 The **Skyliners**, a new white vocal quintet from Pittsburgh, make their debut on "American Bandstand" performing their rising smash, *Since I Don't Have You*.

March

3 With a revised line-up – and eschewing their old vocal style – the **Drifters** record *There Goes My Baby* for Atlantic, under the direction of Jerry Leiber and Mike Stoller in New York. The song has been co-written by Benjamin Nelson, lead singer with vocal group, the **Five Crowns**. Nelson – known as **Ben E. King** – has been recruited as the Drifters' new featured vocalist by the group's manager, George Treadwell. King's tenure with the act will last less than two years before his solo career begins in earnest on the Atlantic imprint, Atco Records.

5 **Chuck Berry** performs *Almost Grown* and *Little Queenie* – featured in the upcoming **Alan Freed** movie, "Go, Johnny, Go!" – on today's edition of "American Bandstand."

6 With reference to the riots at the Boston Arena concert on May 3 last year, prosecutors dismiss an anarchy charge against **Alan Freed**. Freed's attorney has argued that the anti-anarchy law – enacted during World War I – is unconstitutional, and Superior Judge Charles Fairhurst has asked the Massachusetts Supreme Court to rule on its consitutionality. On November 12, the charge of inciting a riot will be placed on file, effectively ending the case. Freed will be permitted to change his plea from not guilty to one of no contest.

The Fleetwoods were the most successful group of the year in the US.

11 With advance orders already topping one million in the US, RCA Records sends a gold disc of **Elvis Presley**'s new single, *I Need Your Love Tonight/A Fool Such As I*, to the singer at his Army base in Germany.

12 **Fabian**, a 15-year-old newcomer from Philadelphia, makes his television debut on "American Bandstand," performing his fast-rising hit *Turn Me Loose*. Fabian was discovered by Chancellor Records' boss Bob Maracucci, and has been signed up largely on the strength of his good looks and his unusual name. He will score his second Top 10 US hit in the summer, with *Tiger*, before making his film bow in "Hound Dog Man."

29 Irvin Feld's latest all-star revue begins a seven-week caravan trek in Richmond, Virginia. On the bill are the **Coasters**, **Bo Diddley**, **Clyde McPhatter**, **Little Anthony & the Imperials** (a Brooklyn-based R&B vocal group who have struggled to capitalize on their US No. 4 hit from last year, *Tears On My Pillow*), and **Lloyd Price**. Price – who achieved success in 1952 with the seminal *Lawdy Miss Clawdy* – has bounced back with the recent pop/R&B crossover smash and US chart-topper, *Stagger Lee*.

April

5 The **Fleetwoods** perform their current US No. 1, *Come Softly To Me*, on the "Ed Sullivan Show." This first release on the new Dolphin label (which has been formed by the group's manager, Bob Reissdorf) has been written by all three members of the trio: **Gretchen Christopher**, **Barbara Ellis**, and male singer **Gary Troxel**. Hailing from Olympia, Washington, the Fleetwoods will be the most successful American vocal act of 1959, logging a second chart-topper – *Mr. Blue* (which was originally offered to the Platters by writer Dwayne Blackwell) – in November.

11 Having banned the record two weeks ago because of the inclusion of the word "spitball," the BBC lifts its censorship of the **Coasters**' *Charlie Brown*. It is aired on David Jacobs's "Pick of the Pops" radio show (and will be the group's biggest UK hit at No. 6).

12 **Johnny Ray** sings *Alright, Okay* and *Here & Now* on the "Ed Sullivan Show" before **Brook Benton** makes his first network appearance, performing his recent US No. 3 breakthrough hit, the self-penned *It's Just A Matter Of Time*. Recently picked up by Mercury Records, 27-year-old R&B singer-songwriter Benton first recorded for the Okeh label in 1952 under his given name,

David Jacobs

Fabian shot to stardom, helped by legendary songwriters Doc Pomus and Mort Shuman... "Go Johnny Go" was Alan Freed's final movie production... David Jacobs hosted "Juke Box Jury," introducing each featured single with the catchphrase: "Let's hear what our panel thinks of this next record."

Benjamin Peay. Becoming one of the most prominent mainstream R&B singers of the era, he will notch up more than 40 hit singles for Mercury over the next six years.

16 A spokesman for British teen idol **Marty Wilde** announces that the 20-year-old singer has been found medically unfit for National Service. Although the War Office has given no reason, it is believed that Wilde is suffering from "defective feet, including fallen arches and severe corns." National Service doctors will send the singer to see a foot specialist immediately after finishing his medical examination.

22 The first major American rock 'n' roll package tour to Britain kicks off a three-week trek in London. With **Cliff Richard** invited to perform on a few dates, it features **Duane Eddy**, **Bobby Darin**, the **Poni Tails**, **Conway Twitty**, and **Dale Hawkins**.

22 **Alan Freed**'s latest (and last) rock 'n' roll movie, "Go, Johnny, Go!" opens, featuring **Jimmy Clanton**, **Jackie Wilson**, the **Cadillacs**, the **Flamingos**, **Ritchie Valens**, **Chuck Berry**, **Jo Ann Campbell**, and **Harvey Fuqua**.

24 Popular for more than two decades, the American radio show "Your Hit Parade" broadcasts for the last time. A countdown of each week's most popular songs, the series – which also spawned a television version – has been airing every Saturday night since its premiere on April 12, 1935.

27 **Cliff Richard & the Drifters** begin a twice-nightly, week-long run at London's Chiswick Empire, sharing the bill with the **Five Dallas Boys**, **Kay & Kimberley**, **Tommy Wallis & Beryl**, **Jean & Peter Barbour**, **Ray Alan & Steve**, and **Des O'Connor**.

May

3 **Cliff Richard** makes his West End debut at the Odeon Theatre in Tottenham Court Road, with fellow "Oh Boy!" stars **Cherry Wainer**, the **Dallas Boys**, **Cuddly Duddley**, and **Neville Taylor & the Cutters**.

4 Organized by the National Academy of Recording Arts and Sciences (NARAS), the first Grammy Awards ceremony takes place in the Grand Ballroom of the Beverly Hilton Hotel, Los Angeles, with 500 members of the music industry paying $15 each to attend the awards dinner. Comedian Mort Sahl is MC, with presenters **Frank Sinatra** (who is nominated in 12 categories but comes up empty except for Best Album Cover), **Dean Martin**, **Sammy Davis Jr.**, **Milton Berle**, **Peggy Lee**, **Jo Stafford**, **Henry Mancini**, **André Previn**, and **Johnny Mercer**. The nominees and winners of 28 statuettes have been voted for by 700 NARAS members. **Domenico Modugno**'s *Nel Blu Dipinto Di Blu (Volare)* wins the Record of the Year and Song of the Year categories, while **Henry Mancini**'s ***The Music From Peter Gunn*** is named Album of the Year. The **Champs**' *Tequila* is named Best Rhythm & Blues Performance, and the **Kingston Trio** win Best Country & Western Performance for *Tom Dooley* (both rather controversial awards, since neither belonged in these categories). Notably absent from both the trophy and guest list are all of the era's top rock 'n' roll stars: this "oversight" will often plague the annual ceremony during its first two decades. This week's **Variety** – the venerable entertainment trade paper – will report: "Over the pomp and circumstance of the festivities hung a cloud. The record academy has snubbed the rock. Not one rock 'n' roll record was nominated."

14 The film "Serious Charge," starring Anthony Quayle, premieres in London. It features **Cliff Richard** (who sings three songs, including *Living Doll*) appearing in the role of Curley Thompson, a young semidelinquent trying to make it as a rock singer.

23 R&B singer **Wilbert Harrison**'s jump-blues-based revision of Little Willie Littlefield's 1952 classic, *K.C. Lovin'* – issued as *Kansas City* – beats out several other competing versions to top the US chart. The North Carolina native made his first recordings for the DeLuxe label in 1952.

23 Singer/guitarist **Billy Fury**, the latest rock 'n' roll find of impresario/manager Larry Parnes, takes part in an "Oh Boy!" party at the Strand Ballroom in Islington, London. Recently signed to Decca Records, 19-year-old, Liverpool-born Fury will score 11 Top 10 UK hits over the next six years.

29 A crowd of more than 9,000 attends an open-air music festival – one of the first such events to take place – at the Herndon Stadium in Atlanta. **B.B. King**, **Jimmy Reed**, **Ray Charles**, the **Drifters**, and **Ruth Brown** perform.

> **"The record academy has snubbed the rock. Not one rock 'n' roll record was nominated."** **Variety**'s report on the first Grammy Awards, May 1959

30 **Billboard** magazine alters the name of its Best Selling Pop LPs chart, and splits the album list up into Best Selling Stereophonic LPs (Top 30) and the separate Best Selling Monophonic LPs (Top 50).

30 **Cliff Richard & the Drifters** top the bill on the last ever broadcast of the ITV pop music show "Oh Boy!" performing Richard's latest release, *Never Mind*. The program's regular star, **Marty Wilde**, also appears, together with **Billy Fury**, **Don Lang**, **Mike Preston**, **Dickie Pride**, **Bill Forbes**, **Cuddly Duddley**, **Peter Elliott**, resident artists the **Vernons Girls**, **Lord Rockingham's XI**, **Cherry Wainer**, the **Dallas Boys**, **Neville Taylor & the Cutters**, and hosts Jimmy Henney and Tony Hall.

June

1 BBC television airs "Juke Box Jury" for the first time, hosted by David Jacobs, who invites a panel of guests to critique the week's top new releases. The panel on the first edition consists of singers Alma Cogan and Gary Miller, DJ Pete Murray, and – according to the **Radio Times** – a "typical teenager," Susan Stranks (who will one day host the ITV television series for children, "Magpie").

June 1959

The Quarry Men get a regular booking... Bobby Darin's *Mack The Knife*...

Mike Stoller and Jerry Leiber

The Isley Brothers

3 **Elvis Presley** is admitted to Frankfurt Military Hospital suffering from an abscessed tonsil and a throat infection. (After being released next week, he will travel to Paris on two weeks' leave. One evening at the Lido nightclub – following the final set by music-miming act George and Bert Benard – Presley will sit down at the piano and play *Willow Weep For Me*, surrounded by the waiters, cleaners, bus boys, and commissionaires who work at the venue. He will play for half an hour, giving an impromptu performance that will prove to be his only European "gig.")

12 Police raid the New York hospital room of jazz/blues legend **Billie Holiday**, as she lies seriously ill with a kidney infection and cirrhosis of the liver. They find a tinfoil envelope of heroin and charge her with possession.

12 With his latest hit, *Only Sixteen*, climbing the US chart, **Sam Cooke** performs at the Norfolk Arena in Virginia, on a bill with **Jackie Wilson**. Cooke has insisted to the venue's management that they arrange to have integrated seating in the audience.

23 **Cliff Richard**, **Marty Wilde**, and **Lord Rockingham's XI** take part in an "Oh Boy!" segment during the Northern Royal Variety Show at Manchester's Palace Theatre, in the presence of the Queen Mother. The rest of the show features a typically conventional line-up of Liberace, Dickie Henderson, **Russ Conway**, Roy Castle, and others, but the Queen Mother will later be heard telling organist **Cherry Wainer**, "I thoroughly enjoyed 'Oh Boy!' I think it's wonderfully entertaining."

28 **Dick Clark**'s first prime-time television special is broadcast, featuring **Fats Domino**, **Fabian**, **Johnny Mathis**, **Les Paul & Mary Ford**, **Stan Freberg**, the **McGuire Sisters**, and **Stan Kenton**.

July

16 **Jerry Leiber** and **Mike Stoller** produce another session with the **Coasters** at Atlantic Recording Studios in New York, overseeing their most recent composition, *Poison Ivy*. Atlantic staff engineer, Tom Dowd, is at the desk.

29 The **Isley Brothers** – an R&B trio comprising **Ronald**, **Rudolph**, and **O'Kelly Isley** – record their second RCA single, *Shout* (following last month's *Turn To Me*), under the production guidance of Hugo Peretti and Luigi Creatore. It is an adaptation of the stage favorite *Lonely Teardrops*, with the intro line, "You know you make me wanna shout," and features the playing of the brothers' church organist, Professor Herman Stephens. The Cincinnati-born Isley Brothers started in 1955 as a gospel combo, and have already recorded one-off singles for a number of labels, including Teenage, Gone, Mark X, and Cindy Records.

August

1 *Living Doll*, which was written by Lionel Bart for the movie "Serious Charge," but has been revamped for single release as a midtempo, country-style song, tops the UK chart for the first of six weeks. It will eventually sell over 500,000 copies, and is the first UK chart-topper for **Cliff Richard & the Drifters**.

8 **Tommy Steele** cuts short his first visit to Russia to take part in a soccer game between the TV All-Stars XI and the Irish Press in Dublin. He flies from Moscow to Dublin, via Amsterdam and London – a journey of some 2,000 miles. During the game, skiffle king **Lonnie Donegan** will damage the big toe on his right foot.

10 The four male members of the **Platters** – Tony Williams, Paul Robi, David Lynch, and Alex Hodge – are arrested in Cincinnati, having been found *in flagrante delicto* with four 19-year-old women (three of

BILLIE HOLIDAY

July 17 **Revered as one of the great jazz vocalists, Billie Holiday dies from liver failure at the age of 44. In late 1956 during a television interview with Mike Wallace on WABD-TV in New York, Holiday – nicknamed Lady Day – prophetically said: "Why is it that so many great musicians die at a young age? The reason is they try to live 100 days in one day. Most of them have had so little when they were young, that when they do get something, they try to cram it all in. I'm like that too." In 1972, Diana Ross will play the role of the singer in the film "Lady Sings the Blues."**

The songs of rock 'n' roll and R&B *auteurs* Jerry Leiber and Mike Stoller defined the decade... After five years of trying, the Isley Brothers finally broke through in 1959... Cliff Richard scored the first of 13 UK No. 1s with *Living Doll*... Formed in Toledo, Ohio, and originally called the Orbits, Johnny & the Hurricanes were led by tenor saxophonist Johnny Paris.

Cliff Richard

Johnny & the Hurricanes

whom are white) at the Hotel Sheraton Gibson. They are charged with aiding and abetting prostitution, lewdness, and assignation. Wide media coverage will result in radio stations across the US removing Platters records from their playlists.

23 The Big Beat Show UK package tour opens at the Odeon Cinema in Southend. The bill features **Marty Wilde**, **Billy Fury**, **Terry Dene**, **Dickie Pride**, **Johnny Gentle**, **Duffy Power**, **Sally Kelly**, and the **Viscounts**.

29 On the opening day of the Casbah Coffee Club, run by Mona Best, in West Derby, Liverpool, an argument develops between Les Stewart and Ken Brown, members of the Les Stewart Quartet – which also includes **George Harrison** – who are scheduled to play tonight. Stewart walks out, and Brown asks Harrison if he knows anyone who can help out. Harrison rounds up **John Lennon** and **Paul McCartney**, and the **Quarry Men** give their first public performance since January. This will lead to a regular Saturday night spot at the Casbah until October 10, when Brown will go his own way.

September

4 The current **Bobby Darin** hit, *Mack The Knife*, is banned by WCBS radio in New York, in reaction to a recent spate of stabbing incidents in the city, one of which resulted in the deaths of two teenagers. The ban won't hurt, however: *Mack The Knife* will begin a staggering two-month residence at US No. 1 on October 10.

4 In Michigan, **Dick Clark**'s four-day State Fair show gets under way, an event that will pull in an audience of 15,000. The top performers featured include singer/actress **Annette** (Funicello) paired with **Frankie Avalon**, **Duane Eddy**, the **Coasters**, **LaVern Baker**, and a hot new vocal duo from California called **Jan & Dean**. Recently picked up by the Dore label after achieving two hits last year with Arwin Records, 18-year-old **Jan Berry** and 19-year-old **Dean Torrence** are currently climbing the US chart with *Baby Talk*.

6 **Johnny & the Hurricanes**, a rock 'n' roll instrumental band led by **Johnny Paris** on saxophone, make their debut on "American Bandstand" performing their current US No. 5 hit *Red River Rock*.

12 ATV launches its new music series "Boy Meets Girls" on British television. The Boy in question is **Marty Wilde**, and the Girls are the newly formed British female vocal trio, the **Vernons Girls**. (Wilde will subsequently marry one of the Girls, Joyce Baker.)

15 At the Odeon Cinema in Canterbury, **Cliff Richard & the Drifters** embark on a major UK concert tour of one-nighters, set to end on November 1 at the Gaumont Cinema in Doncaster. The line-up also includes **Al Saxon**, **Peter Elliott**, the **Jones Boys**, and **Roy Young**.

16 The first package caravan assembled by the newly formed Clark-Feld production company (**Dick Clark** and **Irvin Feld**) kicks off in the US with **Paul Anka**, the **Coasters**, **Lloyd Price**, **Duane Eddy**, the **Drifters**, **Annette**, **Phil Phillips**, and **LaVern Baker** on the bill.

27 In Glasgow, military police are called to assist the local city force when **Cliff Richard**'s concert at the Empire Theatre is oversold. Some fans are prevented from entering the hall; most disperse, but several storm the stage door.

28 With US rights snapped up by the ABC-Paramount label, **Cliff Richard**'s *Living Doll* enters the US chart. He is the first British rocker to make the survey, but will have to wait 17 years before he scores his first US Top 10 hit.

October

4 **Tommy Steele** signs a £100,000 ($280,000) deal to tour Australia in February 1960. Gordon Cooper, managing director of the Tivoli circuit, says: "This is the biggest single deal for an artist in the 58 years of our company's history."

9 With Atco having recently released his debut album, ***Bobby Darin***, the singer opens his first residency at the Copa Room in the Sands Hotel, Las Vegas – at the age of 21, he is the youngest performer to do so (beating **Johnny Mathis**'s previous record by two years).

10 *Bad Girl*, the **Miracles**' third single under Berry Gordy, enters the US chart for the first of only two weeks. It marks the first release (G-1) on Gordy's second label, Motown Records. Gordy has pressed a few copies for local sales before securing national distribution on the Chess Records label in Chicago. (All future Miracles singles will be issued on the companion Tamla label.)

18 Some 75 teenagers are arrested after fights break out at a rock 'n' roll concert at the Municipal Auditorium in Kansas City. Police manage to quell the disturbance among the crowd of 15,000, caused in part by liquor-laced soft drinks.

November

1 Following a modest run of chart placings on Atlantic, **Ray Charles** signs with the ABC-Paramount label. Within 12 months, Charles will finally score his first US chart-topper on the Hot 100.

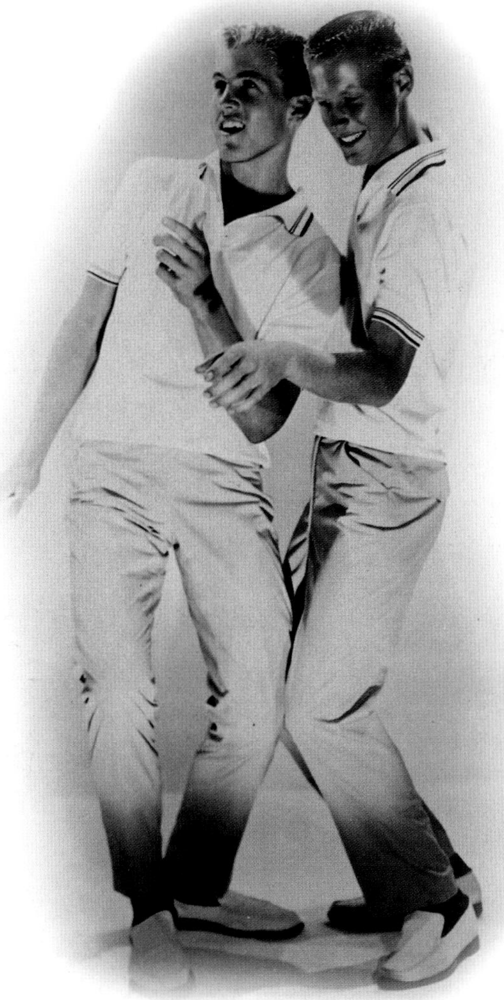

Discovering that the showers at Emerson Junior High School were a great place to sing, Jan & Dean were about to catch a wave.

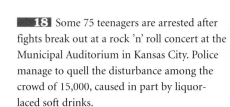

Nov 1959

Alan Freed

Payola... "Expresso Bongo"... Chuck Berry is arrested...

1 Following a **Cliff Richard** concert at the Lewisham Gaumont Cinema, manager B. Richardson tells the **New Musical Express**: "The fans were a bit naughty. They enjoyed the show but got carried away. Girls left their seats and rushed to the front of the stalls. One girl clambered past attendants on to the stage. The safety curtain had to be lowered while Cliff was still singing *A Whole Lotta Shakin'*."

2 Fifteen **Elvis Presley** fans are given prison sentences in Leipzig. They had marched through the city chanting "Long live Elvis Presley" while making derogatory comments about Communist Party leader Walter Ulbricht and denigrating East German music.

15 **John Lennon**, **Paul McCartney**, and **George Harrison** – who are currently calling themselves **Johnny & the Moondogs** – participate in the final round of talent-spotter Carroll Levis's "TV Star Search" at the Hippodrome Theatre in Ardwick, Lancashire. They perform *It's So Easy* and *Think It Over*.

20 As controversy builds over the practice of "payola" – whereby DJs accept under-the-table gifts from music publishers and record labels in exchange for airplay – **Alan Freed** is fired from the New York radio station WABC. He leaves the station while on the air (and is replaced in mid-record by DJ Fred Robbins). Freed has refused "on principle" to sign a statement, requested by the station, that he never received money or gifts for plugging certain records. (Two separate inquiries into payola have been gathering information for months: one conducted by the Harris House Special Subcommittee on Legislative Oversight in Washington, and another by the District Attorney's Office of Frank S. Logan. Recently fired Detroit DJ, Tom Clay – who has admitted accepting extra sums totalling $8,000 a year – defends the system as "part of the business," no different from "taking an apple to a teacher." Another Detroit DJ, Don McCloud, will resign next week.)

23 Following a two-hour meeting at WNEW-TV's offices in East 67th Street, New York, **Alan Freed** is fired for the second time inside a week, this time from his daily "Big Beat" television show. The US's top rock 'n' roll DJ continues to deny that he is guilty of any impropriety with regard to payola. WNEW issues a sworn statement signed by Freed that he has not at any time "committed any improper practice or done or omitted to do any act or thing for which I might properly be criticized." Freed states that he "signed this statement and not the one at WABC because nobody here tried to force me to do it." Station manager Bennet Korn releases a letter he has written to Freed, confirming that his contract will be terminated with effect from December 6, "except that you shall not be required to render any services in connection with any program scheduled to be broadcast after November 29."

24 As part of its inquiry into payola, the Harris Subcommittee in Washington sends an investigator and an attorney to question **Alan Freed** about alleged payola practices – and particularly about rival DJ/television host, **Dick Clark**. (On a separate issue, Clark has recently been ordered by ABC to divest himself of any conflict of interest regarding his alleged part-ownership in music publishing and record companies.) The investigators also quiz Johnny Brantley, Freed's talent coordinator, and Jack Hooke, a former associate. In tomorrow's newpapers, Freed will acknowledge that he was questioned about Clark, who he says "should be investigated." Government agents also seize $6,000 from Freed's salaries from WABC and WNEW to satisfy tax debts. His reaction: "This shows how rich I must be."

27 The British movie "Expresso Bongo" premieres in London. Based on a stage play by Wolf Mankowitz, it stars Laurence Harvey and features **Cliff Richard** as the manipulated teenage rock star, Bongo Herbert.

29 The year's second Grammy Awards ceremony (held just six months after the first, mainly due to overenthusiasm by the NARAS board) takes place at Los Angeles' Beverly Hilton Hotel, with a concurrent celebration party staged at New York's Waldorf-Astoria Hotel (starting a bicoastal tradition that will endure for the next ten years). Unlike the inaugural event on May 4, immediately after this ceremony a winners' show is broadcast live on NBC-TV from its Burbank studios. **Bobby Darin** takes home the Record of the Year trophy for *Mack The Knife*, which he sings on the show, and he is also named Best New Artist of 1959. Shut out in 11 of 12 categories in May – and not happy about it – **Frank Sinatra** does not attend this time. He wins big: ***Come Dance With Me*** is hailed Best Arrangement, Best Vocal Performance, Male, and Album of the Year. Song of the Year goes to writer Jimmy Driftwood for *The Battle Of New Orleans,* a No. 1 hit for **Johnny Horton** in June.

December

1 After performing in El Paso, **Chuck Berry** meets a 14-year-old Apache waitress, Janice Norine Escalanti, who is, unbeknown to Berry, working as a prostitute.

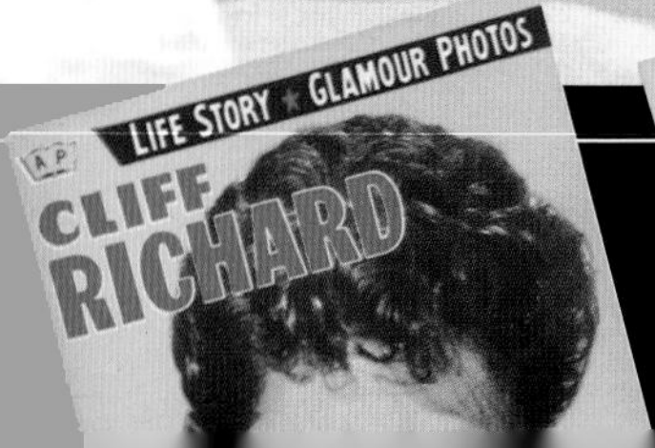

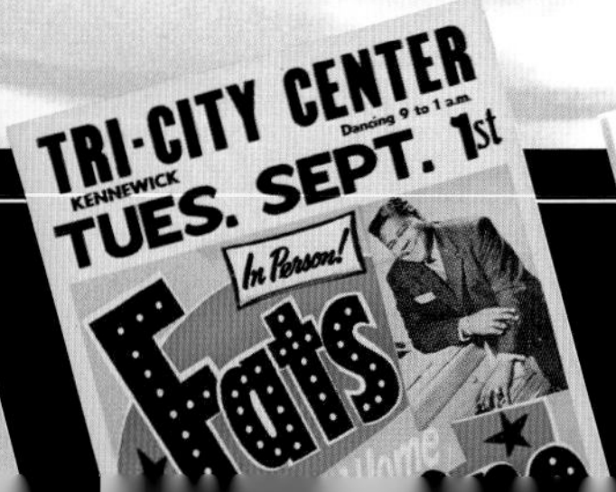

By the end of the decade, Cliff Richard was a household name in Britain, and Fats Domino had scored nine million-sellers in the US, while Gene Vincent had faded in America, but was still a top

Billy Fury

Bobby Darin

The movie "Expresso Bongo" featured Cliff Richard as a teenager plucked from a Soho coffee bar by an unscrupulous agent to be the next teen sensation.

5 **Adam Faith**'s *What Do You Want* hits UK No. 1 in only its third charted week. The first chart-topper for EMI Records' imprint, Parlophone, the single is selling 50,000 copies a day at its peak, and will shift a total of over 620,000 copies in Britain alone. The 19-year-old, London-born Faith is already a popular regular on BBC-TV's "Six-Five Special." This song establishes his vocal trademarks – his hiccuping, Hollyish phrasing and exaggerated pronunciation of "baby" ("buy-bee") – and begins a long partnership between the singer, songwriter **Johnny Worth** (under his pen-name, **Les Vandyke**), and arranger **John Barry** (whose pizzicato string arrangement is the record's other notable feature).

5 **Gene Vincent** arrives in the UK, where his reputation remains high despite three years without hits. He receives an enthusiastic welcome from fans at London's Heathrow Airport, and is met by television producer Jack Good. During his stay in Britain, Vincent will be interviewed on BBC Radio's "Saturday Club," make a special guest appearance on Larry Parnes's Big Beat Show at the Granada cinema in Tooting, south London – with some of Britain's best-known rockers including **Marty Wilde**, **Billy Fury**, **Terry Dene**, **Duffy Power**, and **Vince Eager** – and appear on Good's television show "Boy Meets Girls," before leaving for Germany to entertain US servicemen over Christmas.

10 The male group members of the **Platters**, who were arrested in Cincinnati on August 10, are acquitted of charges of lewdness, assignation, and aiding and abetting prostitution. However, Municipal Court Judge Gilbert Bettman lectures the singers in court about responsibility to their public. Despite the dismissal of the case, the scandal will severely impact on the group's career.

His star rapidly fading, Alan Freed was embroiled in the widening payola scandal... Billy Fury was a thoroughbred in Larry Parnes's stable of stars... Bobby Darin's *Mack The Knife* was named Record of the Year at the second Grammy Awards, held in 1959.

13 Impresario Larry Parnes's stable of artists begins a week-long run at the Finsbury Park Empire in north London, with **Billy Fury** headlining. **Duffy Power**, **Dickie Pride**, **Terry Dene & the Viscounts**, **Vince Eager**, **Johnny Gentle**, **Sally Kelly**, and **Julian X** make up the rest of the bill.

13 The **Everly Brothers** record their first session outside Nashville. *Let It Be Me*, an English translation of a French song, Gilbert Becaud's *J'Appartiens* (already a US hit for Jill Corey in 1957), is cut in Bell Sound Studios in New York. It is also the duo's first session with an orchestral backing: eight violins and a cello, conducted by Archie Bleyer.

23 **Chuck Berry** is arrested and charged with violating the Mann Act, having taken Janice Norine Escalanti to work as a hat-check girl in his nightclub in St. Louis. In the opinion of the police, he has committed the offense of transporting a minor across a State Line for immoral purposes. Berry allegedly fired the girl after he suspected her of working as a prostitute, and she has subsequently reported him to the police. Berry is initially convicted and sentenced to the maximum penalty of five years in jail and a fine of $2,000. However, after racist comments by case authority Judge George H. Moore Jr. are made public, Berry will be freed, prior to a retrial.

ROOTS

During this year: looking to complement his group the Primes, Milton Jenkins puts together a female trio, called the Primettes, who will soon become a quartet with the introduction of 15-year-old Diane Ross... schoolfriends Pete Townshend, John Entwistle, and Phil Rhodes form the Confederates at Acton County Grammar School... working in a bakery by day and singing with his own high school band by night, Mark Lindsay sees a band led by Paul Revere gigging at a local Elks hall, asks if he can sing with them and performs *Crazy Arms*... Robert Zimmerman, performing under the name Elston Gunn, joins Bobby Vee's band on piano for a gig in Gwinner, North Dakota; he will soon head to New York and emerge on the folk scene as Bob Dylan... Portola Junior High School colleagues John Fogerty, Stu Cook, and Doug Clifford form a rock 'n' roll trio, initially playing at local parties; Fogerty's older brother Tom soon joins, and the band becomes Tommy Fogerty & the Blue Velvets... and, initially known as the Mars Bars, until the chocolate maker insists on a name change, the Gerry Marsden-led Liverpool quartet make their debut at Holyoak Hall as the Pacemakers...

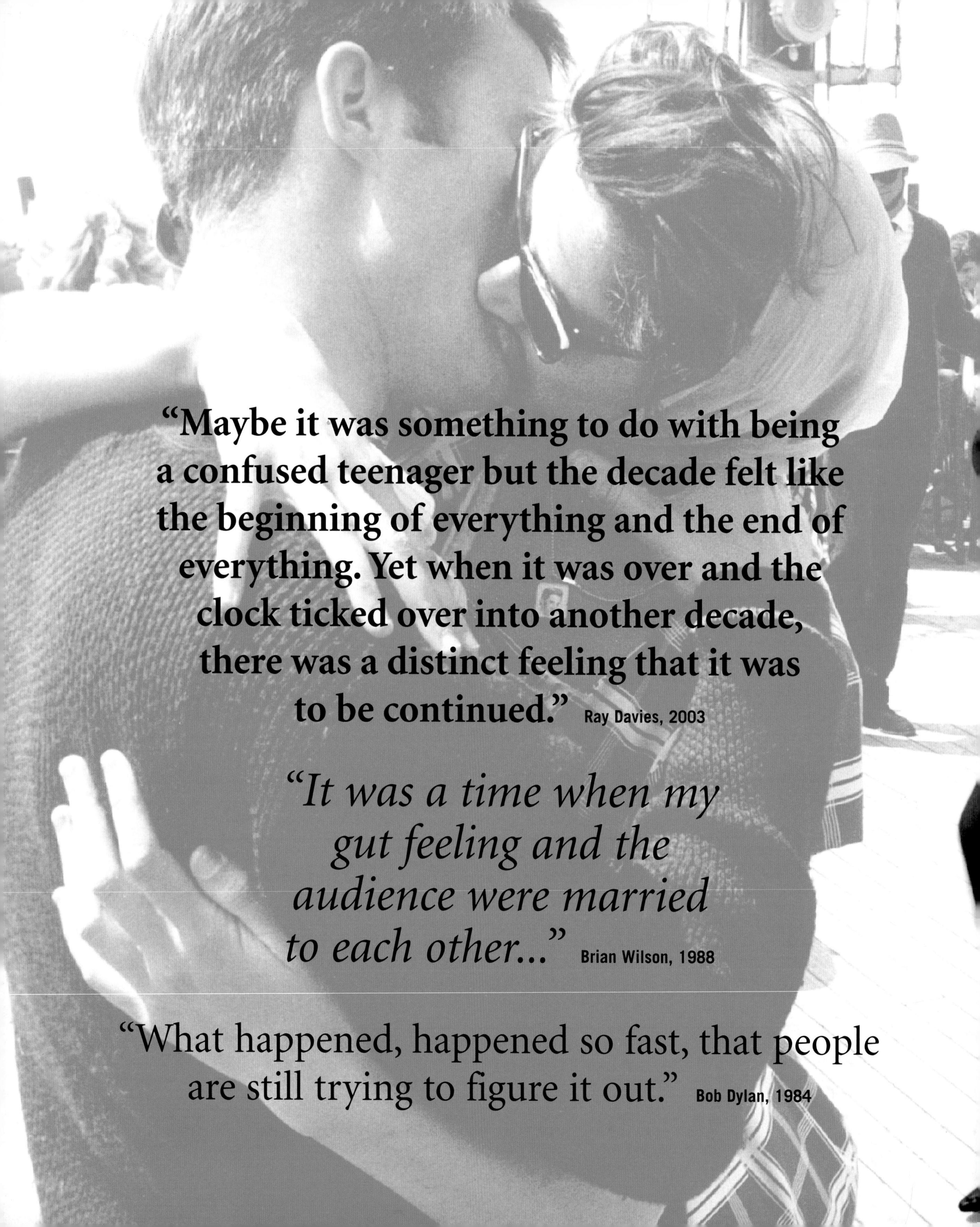

"Maybe it was something to do with being a confused teenager but the decade felt like the beginning of everything and the end of everything. Yet when it was over and the clock ticked over into another decade, there was a distinct feeling that it was to be continued." **Ray Davies, 2003**

"It was a time when my gut feeling and the audience were married to each other..." **Brian Wilson, 1988**

"What happened, happened so fast, that people are still trying to figure it out." **Bob Dylan, 1984**

1960

Baby (You've Got What It Takes)

1960

No.1 US SINGLES

Jan 2	Why	**Frankie Avalon**
Jan 9	El Paso	**Marty Robbins**
Jan 23	Running Bear	**Johnny Preston**
Feb 13	Teen Angel	**Mark Dinning**
Feb 27	Theme From A Summer Place	**Percy Faith**
Apr 30	Stuck On You	**Elvis Presley with the Jordanaires**
May 28	Cathy's Clown	**Everly Brothers**
July 2	Everybody's Somebody's Fool	**Connie Francis**
July 16	Alley-Oop	**Hollywood Argyles**
July 23	I'm Sorry	**Brenda Lee**
Aug 13	Itsy Bitsy Teenie Weenie Yellow Polka Dot Bikini	**Brian Hyland**
Aug 20	It's Now Or Never (O Sole Mio)	**Elvis Presley with the Jordanaires**
Sept 24	The Twist	**Chubby Checker**
Oct 1	My Heart Has A Mind Of Its Own	**Connie Francis**
Oct 15	Mr. Custer	**Larry Verne**
Oct 22	Save The Last Dance For Me	**Drifters**
Oct 29	I Want To Be Wanted	**Brenda Lee**
Nov 5	Save The Last Dance For Me	**Drifters**
Nov 19	Georgia On My Mind	**Ray Charles**
Nov 26	Stay	**Maurice Williams & the Zodiacs**
Dec 3	Are You Lonesome Tonight?	**Elvis Presley with the Jordanaires**

No.1 UK SINGLES

Jan 2	What Do You Want To Make Those Eyes At Me For?	**Emile Ford & the Checkmates**
Jan 30	Starry Eyed	**Michael Holliday**
Feb 6	Why	**Anthony Newley**
Mar 5	Poor Me	**Adam Faith**
Mar 19	Running Bear	**Johnny Preston**
Apr 2	My Old Man's a Dustman	**Lonnie Donegan**
Apr 30	Do You Mind	**Anthony Newley**
May 7	Cathy's Clown	**Everly Brothers**
June 25	Three Steps To Heaven	**Eddie Cochran**
July 9	Good Timin'	**Jimmy Jones**
July 30	Please Don't Tease	**Cliff Richard & the Shadows**
Aug 6	Shakin' All Over	**Johnny Kidd & the Pirates**

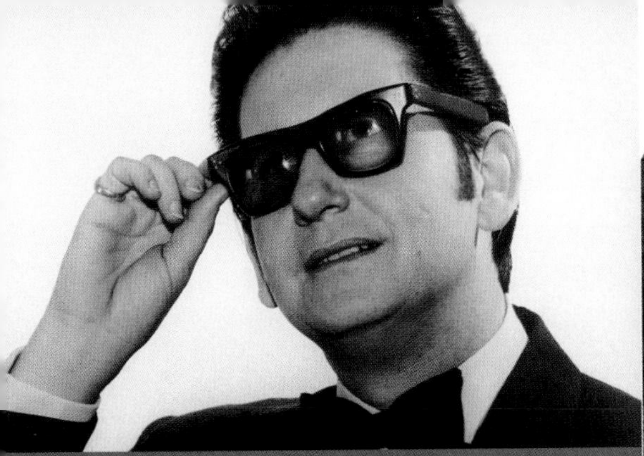

Roy Orbison

The Everly Brothers

Roy Orbison made his chart breakthrough in both the US and the UK with *Only The Lonely*, the first of a run of chart hits that brought him greater success in Britain than back home... After racking up sales of over 15 million on the Cadence label, the Everly Brothers signed a $1 million deal with Warner Bros.: their UK debut single was honored with the catalog number WB 1.

Elvis Presley was out of the US Army, the **Beatles** were learning the business in small clubs in England and Germany, and **Sam Cooke** and **Patsy Cline** recorded some of their most memorable numbers. Folk, country, jazz, and rock instrumentals all enjoyed a share of the limelight, but the headlines this year belonged to a new craze – and a new dance – the twist. The song of the same name, originally an R&B hit for **Hank Ballard & the Midnighters**, became a US chart-topper and a national phenomenon, and launched the career of a portly 18-year-old from Philadelphia, **Chubby Checker**.

After two pallid years, rock 'n' roll showed signs of revival in 1960, on both sides of the Atlantic. It was a year of memorable singles, not least **Roy Orbison**'s immortal *Only The Lonely*. **Neil Sedaka** followed up *Oh! Carol* with *Stairway To Heaven*, and the **Everly Brothers** found fans on both sides of the Atlantic with *Cathy's Clown*. Elvis emerged from the Army unscathed but also mellower and – dare one say it – respectable. Recording again within weeks, he adopted operatic airs with *It's Now Or Never* (the biggest hit of the year in Britain). He enjoyed similar success with *Are You Lonesome Tonight?*, cut his first gospel sides, and was soon in Hollywood to make "G.I. Blues."

Country music had a new standardbearer in 28-year-old Patsy Cline, for whom success came relatively late and would be tragically shortlived. But in 1960, she was admitted to the Grand Ole Opry, shrine of country music, while the success of *I Fall To Pieces* spilled over from the country to the pop charts. She was emulated by **Brenda Lee** (who shared her producer).

This was a fertile year for British rock 'n' roll, led by **Cliff Richard**, **Adam Faith**, and **Billy Fury**. Cliff enjoyed a sequence of top ten hits and was a huge draw on television light entertainment shows. The newly formed (Silver) Beatles were learning the music industry the hard way, turned down as a backing band for Billy Fury, and running into all sorts of trouble while working in Hamburg.

The year also provided some vintage R&B, with established talents finding their way into the pop charts and the 18-year-old **Aretha Franklin** cutting her first secular sides after earlier years in the gospel field. Perhaps energized by a label change, **Ray Charles** finally hit the top spot with the evergreen *Georgia On My Mind*. **Berry Gordy Jr.** was laying the foundations for the soul and Motown explosion with Tamla Records. **Barrett Strong**'s 1959 recording of the dance number *Money (That's What I Want)* – released on Gordy's sister Anna's label – enjoyed big sales.

The year was not without tragedy. The death of **Eddie Cochran** in a car accident in England deprived popular music of one of its most innovative performers. His parting gift was a posthumous UK No. 1: *Three Steps To Heaven*.

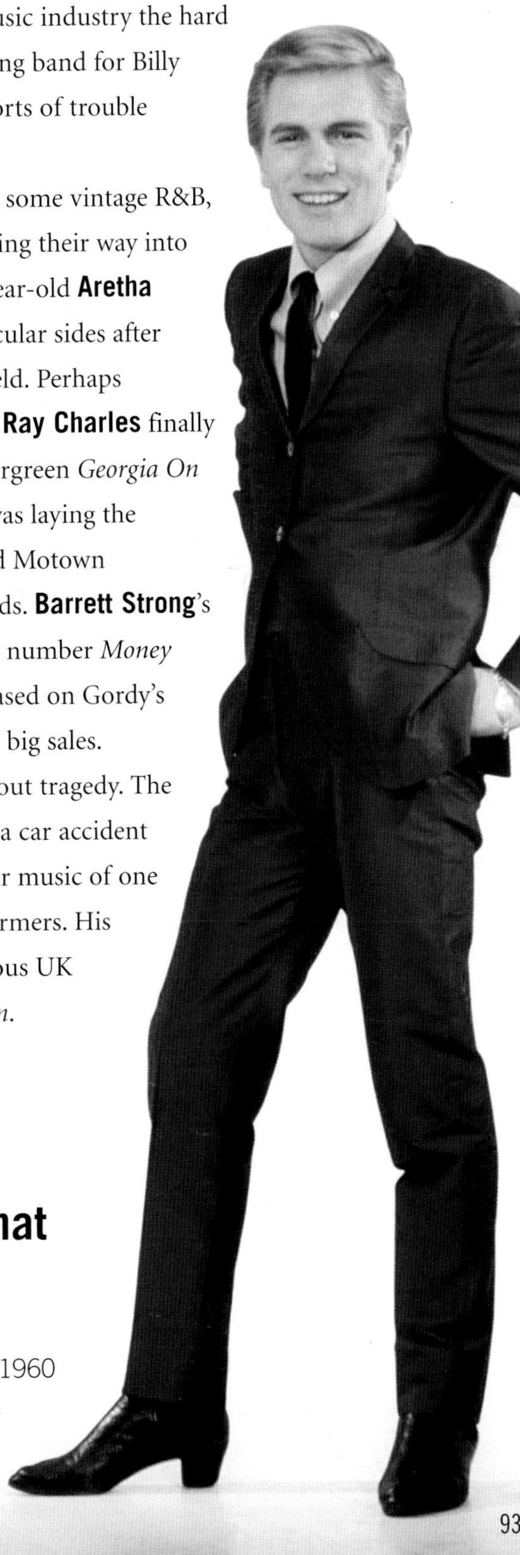

Aug 13	Please Don't Tease **Cliff Richard & the Shadows**
Aug 27	Apache **Shadows**
Oct 1	Tell Laura I Love Her **Ricky Valance**
Oct 22	Only The Lonely **Roy Orbison**
Nov 5	It's Now Or Never (O Sole Mio) **Elvis Presley with the Jordanaires**
Dec 31	I Love You **Cliff Richard & the Shadows**

"The most important thing in a teenager's life is love, which is what most of my songs are about."

Adam Faith, BBC-TV "Meeting Point," January 28, 1960

Jan 1960

Cliff Richard gets a record TV audience... Payola hearings... Elvis flies home...

Billy Fury had ambitions as a songwriter until impresario Larry Parnes threw him into the limelight and a star was born.

January

1 **Johnny Cash** plays the first of many free (and notable) jailhouse shows, in San Quentin Prison in California. Country singer **Merle Haggard** – who, at 22, is nearing the end of a three-year sentence for burglary – is among the captive audience.

9 **Eddie Cochran** flies to the UK to co-headline (with **Gene Vincent**) a sellout, ten-week, Larry Parnes package tour. The line-up also includes **Billy Fury** and 18-year-old newcomer **Joe Brown**, a chirpy singer/guitarist who will begin his UK chart career in March with *Dark Town Strutters' Ball*. Cochran has just completed what will prove to be his final recordings – one of the tracks is *Three Steps To Heaven* – at Goldstar Studios in Hollywood.

14 While enjoying five days' leave in Paris, **Elvis Presley** is promoted to Acting-Sergeant, receiving a $22.94 per month pay increase. He will take over command of a three-man platoon on his return to West Germany.

17 ATV's "Sunday Night at the London Palladium" – with **Cliff Richard and the Shadows** topping the bill – is seen by an estimated audience of some 19.5 million – the highest ever figure for a light entertainment show in British television history. Host Bruce Forsyth presents Richard with a gold disc for *Living Doll*.

22 Celebrating his 25th birthday, **Sam Cooke** signs to RCA Records, following successful negotiations by his new manager, Jess Rand. Under the deal, RCA acquires Cooke's Keen label back catalog, and pairs him with producers **Hugo Peretti** and **Luigi Creatore**.

22 **Frankie Avalon** (who has just scored his second US chart-topper with *Why*), **Freddy Cannon** (a 20-year-old newcomer from Lynn, Massachusetts, who recently debuted on the Swan label), **Bobby Rydell** (a 27-year-old Philadelphia native, whose new disc, *Wild One* will hit US No. 2 in March, and who cut his first sides for the Veko label two years ago, before being snapped up by Cameo Records), and **Clyde McPhatter** embark on a five-week North American package tour. When they reach Montreal they will be joined by special guests from Britain: **Cliff Richard and the Shadows**.

23 **Johnny Preston**'s *Running Bear* begins a three-week run topping the US chart. Preston, a 20-year-old singer from Texas, was a friend of the late J.P. Richardson – the **Big Bopper** – who wrote *Running Bear* and encouraged Preston to record it. The recording was made before Richardson's death last February, and he can be heard on backing vocals. The rock 'n' roll classic will reach the top spot in the UK in March.

February

6 Country singer-songwriter/guitarist, **Marty Robbins** – whose huge crossover hit *El Paso* spent two weeks at US No. 1 last month – performs at the Ryman Auditorium for the Grand Ole Opry. Having made his Opry debut on June 30, 1951, Robbins has since – with **Eddy Arnold** and **Jim Reeves** – been at the forefront of mainstream country/pop. Signed to Columbia, he also started his own Robbins label in 1958.

8 With investigations completed, the US Congress begins its payola hearings in the Senate, under the chairmanship of Oren Harris. They will focus heavily on radio station personnel from New York and Boston. WBZ DJ Dave Maynard will testify that he received over $6,000 in gifts and cash from Boston record companies for promoting discs outside the station, but will deny that this amounts to payola. Next week, WMEX president M. Richmond will admit that he received $14,000 for broadcasting one record for 13 weeks.

13 *Baby (You've Got What It Takes)*, recorded by two of the biggest names in R&B – **Dinah Washington** and **Brook Benton** – begins a ten-week lock at the top of the US Hot R&B singles chart. The pair will follow it with another

"I didn't particularly mind the heckling during my fast numbers. But when they tried to ruin my *Over The Rainbow* I couldn't take it any more." Gene Vincent after walking offstage at the Gaumont Cinema, Bradford, January 30, 1960

SAM COOKE

Jan 25 **In RCA's Studio A in New York Sam Cooke cuts what will become another career-defining song: *Chain Gang*. Written by Cooke, this will become a million-seller in the US, hitting No. 2 in September and UK No. 9 – his first top ten placing.**

Sam Cooke toured the West Indies in March, and his style was to be a major influence on a generation of Jamaican singers, including Bob Marley and Jimmy Cliff.

Bobby Rydell

Dinah Washington

Bobby Rydell, a 27-year-old from Philadelphia, was riding high with his fourth hit, *Wild One*, which reached US No. 2 in March... Performing with Lionel Hampton as a teenager, Dinah Washington was one of the most influential jazz-blues singers of her generation.

No. 1 crossover smash, *A Rockin' Good Way (To Mess Around And Fall In Love)* in June. These discs herald something of a return of R&B artists to the mainstream. With radio airplay stronger than ever, several R&B artists, including **James Brown** and **Etta James**, will see their first major crossover success this year.

17 Although all his album releases thus far have sold over one million domestic copies, **Elvis Presley** receives his first RIAA certified gold album for ***Elvis*** – originally released in 1956.

17 The **Everly Brothers** sign a ten-year contract, worth $1 million, with the Warner Bros. label. Part of the deal is rumored to include movie roles. During the duo's three-year tenure with Cadence Records, they have sold more than 15 million records.

19 Marking the end of an era, EMI Records' last new coarse-groove 78rpm record is issued in the UK: British pianist **Russ Conway**'s *Rule Britannia*, coupled with *Royal Event*.

March

2 **Elvis Presley** flies home from Rhein-Main airbase for discharge, with 79 other American servicemen. Possibly exceeding the "carry-on" limit, he has in his luggage 12 sacks of fan letters and 2,182 records. When the plane makes a refueling stop at Prestwick in Scotland, he talks to fans through an airport fence. This will prove to be the only occasion on which Presley sets foot on British soil, despite becoming the all-time dominant American artist on the UK charts. (The main reason that he never plays abroad is that "Col." Tom Parker – real name, Andreas van Kujik – is living in the US as an illegal alien from Holland, and will not risk having to re-enter the country.)

5 **Elvis Presley** is officially discharged from the US Army at Fort Dix, New Jersey, six weeks after being promoted to sergeant, receiving his last pay check of $109.54. Tennessee senator, Estes Kefauver, places a tribute to the star in the Congressional Record.

12 **Record Retailer**, Britain's first weekly music trade paper, is published. Its first No. 1 single is **Adam Faith**'s *Poor Me*, and its first chart-topping LP is **Freddy Cannon**'s ***The Explosive Freddy Cannon***. Statistical anomalies will plague chart-watchers, when singles topping the chart used by the BBC from 1962 for the Light Programme's "Pick of the Pops" and for television's "Top of the Pops" (beginning in 1964) never lead the **Record Retailer** list. Most notably, the **Beatles**' *Please Please Me* will spend three weeks at No. 1 for the BBC in February 1963, but peak at No. 2 in **Record Retailer**. The Allisons' *Are You Sure*, Bobby Vee's *Take Good Care Of My Baby*, Acker Bilk's *Stranger On The Shore*, Kenny Ball & His Jazzmen's *March Of The Siamese Children*, and Joe Brown's *A Picture Of You* will share the same fate.

18 A 22-date UK caravan trek, featuring American rockers **Bobby Darin** (whose *Mack The Knife* entered the UK chart this week for the third time in nine months), **Duane Eddy** (about to have his biggest US hit with *Because They're Young*), and **Clyde McPhatter**, opens at the Gaumont Theatre in Lewisham, south London.

20 **Elvis Presley**'s first post-Army recording session takes place at RCA Studios in Nashville, starting at 8:00 pm and lasting 12 hours, with **Scotty Moore** back in the band. Bassist **Bill Black**, who has started his own combo and is currently at US No. 9 with *White Silver Sands*, will never again play with Presley. His regular studio pianist is now **Floyd Cramer**, who will also become a hitmaker in his own right. Six tracks are nailed, including *Stuck On You* and *A Mess Of Blues*, all scheduled for rush-release by RCA.

25 **Ray Charles** cuts *Georgia On My Mind*, an update of Hoagy Carmichael's timeless ode to the southern state, at Capitol Studios in New York, under Sid Feller (who will become his longtime producer). After a string of modest chart placings for Atlantic, Charles is now recording for ABC-Paramount (who offered him a substantial advance last year). This, his second release for ABC, will be his first US chart-topper in November, become one of his signature songs, and establish his credentials in the pop mainstream.

April

2 With advance orders of 250,000 copies, **Lonnie Donegan**'s *My Old Man's A Dustman*, recorded live on stage in Doncaster, is the first single by a British act to enter the UK chart at No. 1, where it will stay for four weeks. (Only Elvis Presley has achieved this previously.)

3 Another Nashville session for **Elvis Presley**, this one lasting 11½ hours, proves highly productive, yielding material for ***Elvis Is Back***, and two million-selling singles, *It's Now Or Never* and *Are You Lonesome Tonight?*

On March 3, Elvis Presley landed in a snowstorm at McGuire Air Force Base, near Fort Dix. Nancy Sinatra was his official greeter as he stepped off the plane.

Eddie Cochran dies in a car crash... Presley and Sinatra together on television...

Johnny Kidd & the Pirates performed in pirate gear in front of a galleon backdrop, with Kidd wearing an eye-patch that, he later admitted, temporarily upset his eyesight after every show.

Nina Simone would have surprising UK hits at the end of the 1960s, with songs written by the Bee Gees, Jim Webb, and a medley from "Hair."

21 At US Senate hearings, Oren Harris, chairman of the subcommittee that began investigating payola last year, tells **Dick Clark** (who has by now shed his interests in several music-related businesses): "You're not the inventor of this system, or even its architect. You're a product of it. Obviously, you're a fine young man." Clark – introduced to the hearings as "the single most influential person in the music business" – testifies on his own behalf, admitting to having a financial interest in some of the records featured on "American Bandstand." Nonetheless, he will emerge from the proceedings relatively unscathed.

> **"You're not the inventor of this system, or even its architect. You're a product of it. Obviously, you're a fine young man."**
>
> Oren Harris to Dick Clark, Senate hearings on payola, April 21, 1960

23 ABC's new music show "Wham!" premieres on British television. Produced by Jack Good, its host is **New Musical Express** record reviewer Keith Fordyce. **Billy Fury**, **Joe Brown & the Bruvvers**, **Jess Conrad**, **Dickie Pride**, **Little Tony**, the **Four Jays**, and **Johnny Carson** appear on the first show.

25 In a private ceremony, **Eddie Cochran** is buried at Forest Lawn Memorial Park in Cypress, California, with only relatives and a few close friends present. On his gravestone is the simple tribute: "If mere words can console us for the loss of our beloved Eddie, then our love for him was a false one."

May

2 Having traveled with his father on Missouri Pacific Railroad's Texas Eagle Express from Memphis to Los Angeles, **Elvis Presley** begins filming "G.I. Blues" at Paramount Studios. The film, co-starring Juliet Prowse, typecasts Presley as Tulsa McLean, a US soldier in Germany serving in an entertainment unit.

8 **Nina Simone** makes her debut on the "Ed Sullivan Show." The 27-year-old, jazz-influenced singer/composer/pianist is a graduate of New York's Juilliard School, and scored her first hit – the crossover *I Loves You Porgy* – last year. Although major or consistent chart success will elude her, she will become a darling of music critics throughout her long career (notably recording with RCA), which will also include political activism in the 1970s.

11 After a short spell in hospital and a rest in the US, **Gene Vincent** has returned to London to make his first UK recording, at Abbey Road Studios. Backed by the **Beat Boys** (with **Georgie Fame** on piano), he cuts *Pistol Packin' Mama*.

12 **Elvis Presley** appears on ABC-TV's "The Frank Sinatra Timex Show – Welcome Home Elvis" special, taped in the Grand Ballroom of the Fontainebleau Hotel, Miami Beach, for which "Col." Tom Parker has negotiated a fee of $125,000. As well as Sinatra, the show features **Sammy Davis Jr.**, **Joey Bishop**, **Peter Lawford**, and Sinatra's daughter, **Nancy**. Presley sings *Fame And Fortune* and *Stuck On You*, and performs the Sinatra classic *Witchcraft*, a favor Sinatra returns by singing *Love Me Tender*. Presley also sings *It's Nice To Go Traveling*, dressed in army uniform, with the rest of the cast. The show captures an audience share close to 70 per cent. It will be Presley's last television appearance for eight years.

13 **Johnny Kidd & the Pirates** record *Shakin' All Over* (in one take) and *Yes Sir, That's My Baby* at EMI's studios in London. Like many of his contemporaries, 20-year-old, London-born Kidd has a background fronting a skiffle group, the Five Nutters. *Shakin' All Over*, written last night in six minutes, in the basement of the Freight Train nightclub owned by skiffle pioneer, **Chas McDevitt**, will become Kidd's only UK chart-topper (in August).

19 Currently working at KDAY in Los Angeles, **Alan Freed** is indicted by a Federal jury, along with seven others, on counts of payola. He is accused of accepting $30,650 in cash and gifts in return for airplay.

19 In a single New York recording session, with Jerry Leiber and Mike Stoller producing, the **Drifters** cut *Save The Last Dance For Me* (which will hit UK No. 2 in November and become the group's only US chart-topper), *Nobody But Me*, *I Count The Tears*, and *Sometimes I Wonder*.

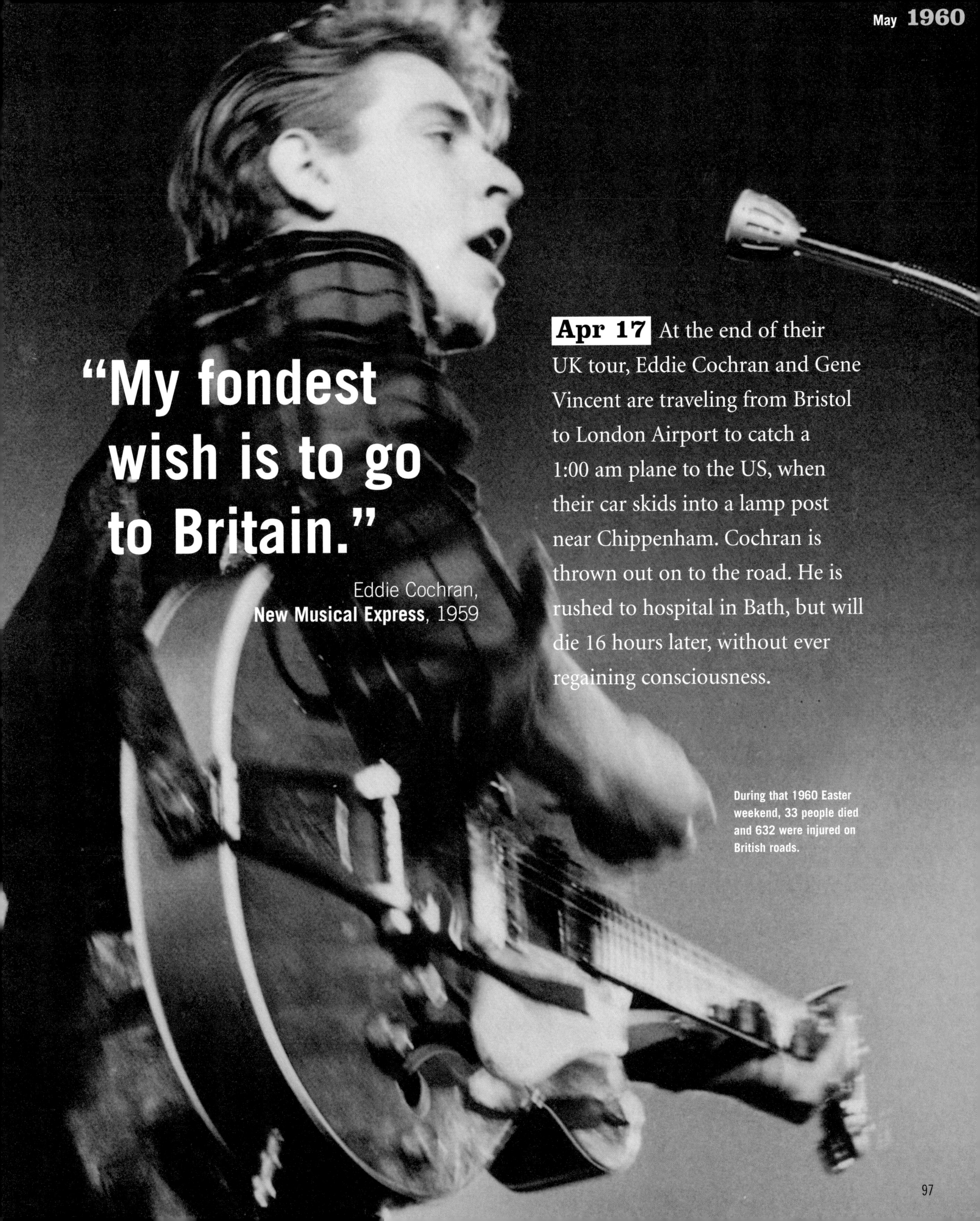

“My fondest wish is to go to Britain.”

Eddie Cochran,
New Musical Express, 1959

Apr 17 At the end of their UK tour, Eddie Cochran and Gene Vincent are traveling from Bristol to London Airport to catch a 1:00 am plane to the US, when their car skids into a lamp post near Chippenham. Cochran is thrown out on to the road. He is rushed to hospital in Bath, but will die 16 hours later, without ever regaining consciousness.

During that 1960 Easter weekend, 33 people died and 632 were injured on British roads.

May 1960

Joan Baez at the Newport Folk Festival... Aretha Franklin's first recordings... The twist...

Brenda Lee

Aretha Franklin

20 After a brief spell as the Beatals, the **Silver Beetles**, having failed an audition for Larry Parnes to be **Billy Fury**'s backing band, begin a seven-date tour of Scotland at the Alloa Town Hall, backing **Johnny Gentle**, another singer from the Parnes stable. **Tommy Moore** has been added to the line-up on drums, with Scotsman **Stuart Sutcliffe** (an art-school friend of **John Lennon**'s who joined the group in January) on bass. For the tour, **Paul McCartney** uses the pseudonym Paul Ramon, Sutcliffe calls himself Stuart da Staël, and **George Harrison** adopts the forename Carl.

23 **Cliff Richard** Fan Club members preview 21 newly recorded songs in the conference room at EMI's new Manchester Square headquarters in London. They vote for *Please Don't Tease*, written by Shadows guitarist Bruce Welch, to be Cliff's next single.

28 Already in the middle of a seven-week run at the top of the British chart, the **Everly Brothers**' irresistible *Cathy's Clown* – written by the siblings – begins a five-week stay at US No. 1.

June

5 While the American Grammy Awards (which do not take place this year) are still struggling to embrace rock 'n' roll, the fifth annual Ivor Novello Awards, held at the BBC Television Theatre, are suffering from the same problem. Contemporary teen fare is shut out in favor of traditional "safe" favorites. The winners include **Russ Conway**'s *Side Saddle* (Best Selling and Most Performed Work), **Eula Parker**'s *The Village of St. Bernadette* (Outstanding Song of the Year, Musically and Lyrically), and **Kenny Graham**'s *Beaulieu Festival Suite* (Outstanding Composition in the Jazz or Beat Idiom).

6 The Grosvenor Ballroom in Liscard, Wallasey, hosts a Whitsun bank holiday "jive and rock" session, featuring the **Silver Beetles** and **Gerry & the Pace-Makers** – both billed as "jive and rock specialists." The contract states "No local talent will be permitted from ballroom floor." (The Silver Beetles will play a weekly Saturday season until July 30, when complaints of rowdiness will force the Grosvenor to cancel the season and resume its "strict tempo" dances.) Gerry & the Pace-Makers are another Liverpool-based combo – formed last year from an earlier group, the skiffle-playing Mars Bars. They are led by 17-year-old singer/guitarist Gerry Marsden, and include his older brother Freddie on drums.

Raised in California, New York, Iraq, and Massachusetts, Joan Baez began playing in Boston coffee houses while her father was working at Massachusetts Institute of Technology.

19 **Gene Vincent** flies to New York, pulling out of his current UK variety tour and upcoming Blackpool summer season. He collapsed last week before his first show at the Glasgow Empire, then, during the week at the Nottingham Theatre Royal, he told the audience that he had received a telegram telling him that his 18-month-old daughter Melody had died from pneumonia. It will transpire that Vincent has made up the whole story.

24 The second annual Newport Folk Festival kicks off at Freebody Park in Newport, Rhode Island. A popular return act from the first event is 19-year-old folk singer-songwriter **Joan Baez**, who is gaining a strong following in the northeast, playing in coffee houses and nightclubs. Signed to Vanguard Records, her debut album, ***Joan Baez***, will be released to glowing reviews in September, and begin to establish her as a leading pioneer in the folk field. Also on today's bill are ex-Weavers singer-songwriter/guitarist **Pete Seeger**, the **Brothers Four** (a folk-pop quartet from the University of Washington, who scored the US No. 2 hit *Greenfields* in April), the **Tarriers**, the **Clancy Brothers & Tommy Makem**, and the **Limeliters**. Despite its title, the festival's diverse acts include bluesmen **John Lee Hooker** and **Muddy Waters**, gospel singer **Mahalia Jackson**, and country artist **Earl Scruggs**, with **Lester Flatt & the Foggy Mountain Boys**.

July

9 R&B singer and ex-Savoys frontman **Jimmy Jones** tops the UK chart with *Good Timin'* at the beginning of a three-week stay. It is the 23-year-old, Alabama-born artist's second hit of the year, following *Handy Man* (which will become a popular oldie, notably revised by James Taylor in 1977).

23 **Brenda Lee** tops the US chart for the first of four weeks with the country-style ballad *I'm Sorry*, written by Ronnie Self and Dub Allbritten. Originally promoted as "Little Miss Brenda Lee," she was subsequently nicknamed "Little Miss

Brenda Lee had a US No. 1 with *I'm Sorry*, and would go on to score more hit singles in the US than any other female artist of the 1960s... Although Aretha Franklin cut some fine material with Columbia Records, it wasn't until she came under the aegis of Jerry Wexler at Atlantic that she became the pre-eminent female soul singer.

Dynamite" after her August 1957 hit *Dynamite*. *I'm Sorry* will become Lee's second million-seller of 1960, following *Sweet Nothin's*, which hit US No. 4 in March. (*I Want To Be Wanted* will be her second and final US chart-topper in October.)

30 Having already hit US No. 2, **Elvis Presley** tops the UK LP chart (for the first time) with his first post-Army release, ***Elvis Is Back***.

30 *Only The Lonely*, originally offered to both Presley and the Everly Brothers, becomes 24-year-old singer-songwriter **Roy Orbison**'s breakthrough smash, hitting US No. 2. Written by the artist with Joe Melson, and featuring a "wordless" vocal accompaniment that will become a much-covered gimmick, it will eventually sell over one million copies, top the UK chart in October and position Orbison as one of America's leading pop songwriting/vocal stylists.

August

1 **Aretha Franklin** begins her first recording session for Columbia Records in New York, cutting four tracks, *Right Now*, *Over The Rainbow*, *Love Is The Only Thing*, and *Today I Sing The Blues*. The 18-year-old singer is the daughter of the Reverend C.L. Franklin, one of the most famous gospel preachers of the 1950s (dubbed the "Million Dollar Voice"). She was also taught to sing by other gospel greats (and family friends), Mahalia Jackson, James Cleveland, and most of all, Clara Ward. Franklin made her first recordings as a 14-year-old for Chicago's Checker label, singing live versions of Ward hymns at her father's church, which were released as ***The Gospel Sound Of Aretha Franklin***. She toured as a gospel vocalist after leaving school, but has been encouraged by Sam Cooke to tailor her extraordinary vocal gift to the secular field. Leaving home in Detroit, she has moved to New York, where Curtis Lewis – the writer of *Today I Sing The Blues* – has brought a Franklin demo to the attention of Columbia's veteran A&R executive John Hammond. He has signed her to a five-year deal following an audition arranged by Major "Mule" Holly, bassist with jazz pianist Teddy Wilson. Hammond produces Franklin on these first recordings for the label.

CHUBBY CHECKER

Aug 6 **Having released his debut album, *Chubby Checker*, the 18-year-old South Carolina-born singer (below, center, dancing with Conway Twitty, left, and Dick Clark) debuts his cover version of Hank Ballard's 1958 song, *The Twist*, on ABC-TV's "The Dick Clark Saturday Night Show." It is an immediate smash with teenagers. Born Ernest Evans, Checker adopted his stage name at the suggestion of Dick Clark's wife Bobbie, who saw a resemblance to a young Fats Domino (Chubby = Fats, Checker = Domino).**

Instructions for "doing the twist" were enclosed with every copy: "Imagine you are stubbing out a cigarette with both feet while drying your back with a towel." It would hit US No. 1 in September, launch a worldwide dance craze, inspire numerous spinoff records (by Checker and others), generate a "twist" industry that included movies ("Don't Knock the Twist" and "Rock Around the Twist," both starring Checker), and provide a career-defining brand for the singer that he would actively continue to promote into the next century.

Aug 1960

The Beatles in Hamburg... Elvis sings gospel – and sets a new UK chart record...

17 The **Beatles** – playing for the first time under that name – begin a 48-day residency at the Indra Club in Hamburg, playing four-and-a-half hours every night, and six hours every weekend. Their new drummer is 18-year-old **Pete Best** (son of Liverpool's Casbah Club owner Mona Best), who passed an audition to join the band on the 13th. On October 4, promoter Bruno Koschmider, heeding complaints about noise levels, will close the Indra as a music venue and move the Beatles into his other club, the Kaiserkeller, where they will play for a further 58 nights, alternating with another British rock 'n' roll group, **Rory Storm & the Hurricanes**.

22 Following an initial embargo on the sale of **Elvis Presley**'s *It's Now Or Never* in the UK, the single is cleared for release. It is a revival, with new lyrics, of Enrico Caruso's 1916 *O Sole Mio*, and was banned because copyright clearance could not be obtained. Already in poll position in the US, the Aaron Schroeder/Wally Gold adaptation will begin an eight-week run at UK No. 1 in November.

September

10 The Fall Edition of the Biggest Show of Stars for 1960 US tour begins, featuring **Brenda Lee**, the red-hot **Chubby Checker**, 25-year-old newcomer **Bobby Vinton**, **Fabian,** whose 21-month chart career is about to come to an end, and *Just A Dream* hitmaker **Jimmy Clanton**. Vinton is also touring throughout the year as leader of the backing band for Dick Clark's Caravan of Stars.

18 On his 21st birthday, **Frankie Avalon** receives the $600,000 he earned before coming of age. Although currently swarming both the UK and US charts, Avalon will soon focus on an acting career, a decision that will see him starring in more than ten movies during the 1960s, including several "Beach Party" films for American International Pictures.

24 After eight seasons on ABC-TV, "Ozark Jubilee" airs for the last time. A popular showcase of country talent, it introduced artists such as Brenda Lee, Porter Wagoner, Marvin Rainwater, and Wanda Jackson. It is being canned because host **Red Foley** has been indicted for alleged tax fraud. (He will be acquitted next year.)

October

11 **Aretha Franklin** gives her first live performance of non-gospel, secular material – singing blues and pop standards – at the Village Vanguard club in New York.

15 **Ringo Starr** – drummer with **Rory Storm & the Hurricanes** – fills in for Pete Best when the **Beatles** back Rory Storm guitarist **Wally Eymond** on a recording of George Gershwin's *Summertime* at the Akustik Studio in Hamburg. Best will continue as the Beatles' full-time drummer for two more years.

16 Having received more than 5,000 cards on his 20th birthday, **Cliff Richard** appears on ITV's "Birthday Honours," interviewed by Godfrey Winn. The program traces the careers of two men born on October 14, 1940 – the £1,000 ($2,800) per week Richard and a £6 ($17) per week Imperial College science student called Fred Chittenden.

Ben E. King departed the Drifters after complaining of low wages to the group's manager George Treadwell.

27 Having signed a solo deal with Atlantic subsidiary Atco, **Ben E. King** cuts four sides in three hours, with producers Leiber and Stoller and Phil Spector, and conductor Stan Appelbaum arranging the strings: *Spanish Harlem* (written by Spector and Leiber), *First Taste Of Love*, *Young Boy Blues*, and *Stand By Me* (based on the spiritual *Lord Stand By Me*). They will become the cornerstones of King's career.

30 At RCA Studio B in Nashville, **Elvis Presley** records his first lengthy gospel session. It will form much of his inspirational 1961 set, ***His Hand In Mine***. The 14-song marathon includes *Surrender* and *Crying In The Chapel*.

November

5 In the early hours of the morning, country singer **Johnny Horton** – who has had premonitions that he will soon die at the hands of a drunk – is killed when a truck crashes into his Cadillac in Milano, Texas, on his way to Shreveport, Louisiana. The truck driver is found to be drunk. Horton had just played at the Skyline in Austin, where **Hank Williams** played his last gig. They both leave the same widow, Billie Jean, who wed Horton after Williams's death.

5 With advance orders of 548,000 copies – the largest for any record released in Britain – **Elvis Presley** enters the UK chart at No. 1 with *It's Now Or Never (O Sole Mio)*, the first of four consecutive chart-toppers. On the first Saturday following its Friday release, many UK shops report selling more copies of this single than all other records combined.

Playing for 106 nights during three and a half months in Hamburg made the Beatles an unstoppable live force.

> **"We are taking it up with one of our patron MPs."**
>
> Miss Cynthia Arkle of the British Safety Council, claiming *Tell Laura I Love Her* will damage the Council's efforts to encourage road safety, October, 1960

Jerry Butler

Jerry Butler had the first of some 40 solo US chart hits... The Bronx-born Dion DiMucci, who split from the Belmonts in October but remained with the Laurie label, opened his solo account with *Lonely Teenager*.

Dion

7 One of the original founders and leader of the immensely influential Carter Family country group, **Alvin Pleasant "A.P." Carter** dies in Kingsport, Tennessee, at the age of 69. He will be buried at Mount Vernon Methodist Church Cemetery at Maces Spring, Virginia.

16 **Patsy Cline** records *Shoes*, *Lovin' In Vain*, and *I Fall To Pieces* for Decca at her favorite Bradley Studios in Nashville. *I Fall To Pieces*, a Hank Cochran/Harlan Howard composition, will prove to be a turning point in her career.

"You may think at 20 – how can I have a life story to tell? Well I haven't."

"It's Great To Be Young" – the Cliff Richard story, November 1960

19 **Jerry Butler**'s *He Will Break Your Heart* begins seven weeks at the top of the US Hot R&B singles chart. The 20-year-old singer, born in Mississippi and raised in Chicago, is already a veteran of the Northern Jubilee Gospel Singers – which he joined with childhood friend, singer-songwriter **Curtis Mayfield** – the **Quails**, and the **Roosters**, which became **Jerry Butler & the Impressions** in 1958. Nicknamed "The Iceman," Butler is now a solo act. He and Mayfield have co-written *He Will Break Your Heart*, and Mayfield is on backing vocals. Signed to Vee-Jay and then Mercury Records, Butler will be an ever-present R&B/pop hitmaker for the next 17 years, while Mayfield will steer the **Impressions** until 1970, before he too takes solo flight.

21 While the **Beatles** are performing at the Kaiserkeller in Hamburg (and also jamming – much to the irritation of club promoter Koschmider – with another British export, Tony Sheridan, at the rival Top Ten club), **George Harrison** is deported from West Germany, and heads back to England by train. Police have been tipped off (possibly by Koschmider) that the guitarist is not yet 18, and therefore not allowed to be in a nightclub after midnight. The rest of the group will play out their now shortened contract to the end of the month.

December

1 **Paul McCartney** and **Pete Best** are deported from West Germany, having spent last night in jail at the St. Pauli police station in Hamburg. They were arrested on suspicion of arson, after their hotel room mysteriously caught fire. **John Lennon** – uninvolved in the drama – will return home on December 10.

11 With his debut album, ***Adam***, heading to UK No. 6, **Adam Faith** appears on BBC-TV's "Face to Face," submitting to a penetrating interview by the incisive John Freeman, and acquits himself with aplomb.

13 **Elvis Presley**'s *It's Now Or Never* passes the million sales mark in Britain after just six weeks: the millionth copy leaving Decca's pressing plant at 3:30 pm. This sets a new record time for a disc achieving this total in the UK – the previous holder, Harry Belafonte's *Mary's Boy Child*, took eight weeks in 1957.

23 The week-long Christmas Rock 'n' Roll Show opens at New York's Brooklyn Paramount Theater, featuring 17-year-old **Bobby Vee**, **Neil Sedaka**, **Bo Diddley**, **Chubby Checker**, the **Drifters**, the **Skyliners**, **Dante & the Evergreens**, **Ray Charles**, **Johnny Burnette**, the **Coasters**, and **Dion**. Also in the line-up are the **Shirelles**, a Passaic, New Jersey-based R&B female vocal quartet who are heading to US No. 1 with *Will You Love Me Tomorrow* – written by 18-year-old **Carole King** and her boyfriend, **Gerry Goffin**.

27 On a lengthy break from Hamburg, the **Beatles** play a gig at Litherland Town Hall, Liverpool, to a reception that hints at the adulation they will receive in the future. (**Chas Newby** substitutes for **Stuart Sutcliffe**, who is still in Hamburg with his girlfriend, Astrid Kirchherr.)

Bobby Vee, the latest male teen-pop phenomenon, was bouncing up the US chart with his second top 10 smash, *Rubber Ball*.

ROOTS During this year: currently a member of the Gospelaires, Dionne Warwick enrolls at the Hartt College of Music in Hartford, paying for her tuition doing back-up work at the Apollo Theater in Harlem and New York sessions... having recently left the Sheffield Central Technical School, Joe Cocker buys a cheap drumkit and joins his brother Vic's skiffle group, the Cavaliers, making his first appearance at the Minerva Tavern... through his childhood friend Lenny Waronker, Randy Newman begins work as a staff writer at Metric Music... 10-year-old David Cassidy makes his stage debut in the chorus of a summer stock production of "The Pajama Game"... already a minor celebrity in his native Arkansas, Glen Campbell moves to Los Angeles at the urging of Albuquerque DJ Jerry Naylor, immediately finding work as a session guitarist... Nashville-born brothers, Gregg and Duane Allman, form the Kings – the first of several short-lived pop/dance bands featuring the siblings that will perform around Florida through the first half of the decade... relocated to Australia with their parents, the Rattlesnakes (brothers Barry, Maurice, and Robin Gibb) make their television debut on "Anything Goes" before making regular appearances on BQT7-TV's "Cottie's Happy Hour"... and Berry Gordy signs 10-year-old prodigy Stevie Wonder to a longterm deal with his Tamla label...

Let The Good Times Roll

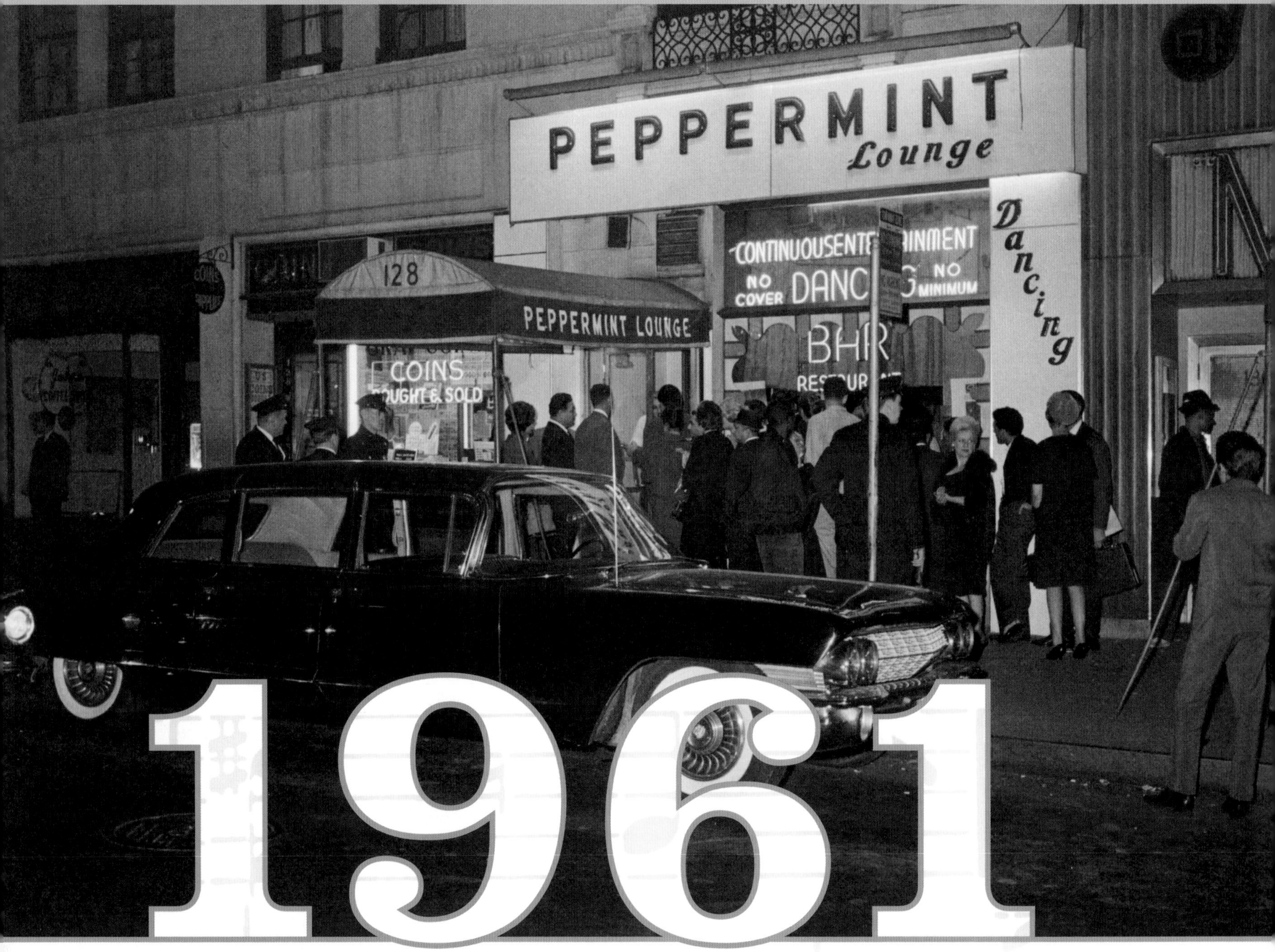

1961

No.1 US SINGLES

- **Jan 7** Are You Lonesome Tonight? **Elvis Presley with the Jordanaires**
- **Jan 14** Wonderland By Night **Bert Kaempfert**
- **Feb 4** Will You Love Me Tomorrow **Shirelles**
- **Feb 18** Calcutta **Lawrence Welk**
- **Mar 4** Pony Time **Chubby Checker**
- **Mar 25** Surrender **Elvis Presley**
- **Apr 8** Blue Moon **Marcels**
- **Apr 29** Runaway **Del Shannon**
- **May 27** Mother-In-Law **Ernie K-Doe**
- **June 3** Travelin' Man **Ricky Nelson**
- **June 10** Running Scared **Roy Orbison**
- **June 17** Travelin' Man **Ricky Nelson**
- **June 24** Moody River **Pat Boone**
- **July 1** Quarter To Three **U.S.Bonds**
- **July 15** Tossin' And Turnin' **Bobby Lewis**
- **Sept 2** Wooden Heart (Muss I Denn) **Joe Dowell**
- **Sept 9** Michael **Highwaymen**
- **Sept 23** Take Good Care Of My Baby **Bobby Vee**
- **Oct 14** Hit The Road Jack **Ray Charles**
- **Oct 28** Runaround Sue **Dion**
- **Nov 11** Big Bad John **Jimmy Dean**
- **Dec 16** Please Mr. Postman **Marvelettes**
- **Dec 23** The Lion Sleeps Tonight **Tokens**

No.1 UK SINGLES

- **Jan 7** I Love You **Cliff Richard & the Shadows**
- **Jan 14** Poetry In Motion **Johnny Tillotson**
- **Jan 28** Are You Lonesome Tonight? **Elvis Presley with the Jordanaires**
- **Feb 25** Sailor **Petula Clark**
- **Mar 4** Walk Right Back **Everly Brothers**
- **Mar 25** Wooden Heart **Elvis Presley**
- **May 6** Blue Moon **Marcels**
- **May 20** On The Rebound **Floyd Cramer**
- **May 27** You're Driving Me Crazy **Temperance Seven**
- **June 3** Surrender (Torna A Surriento) **Elvis Presley**
- **July 1** Runaway **Del Shannon**
- **July 22** Temptation **Everly Brothers**
- **Aug 5** Well I Ask You **Eden Kane**
- **Aug 12** You Don't Know **Helen Shapiro**
- **Sept 2** Johnny Remember Me **John Leyton**

Gene Pitney

David, Warwick, and Bacharach

At the age of 20, Connecticut native Gene Pitney was already established as a top songwriter – penning *Rubber Ball* for Bobby Vee and *Hello Mary Lou* for Rick Nelson... Burt Bacharach emerged as one of America's leading songwriters, penning hits for the Shirelles, the Drifters, and Gene McDaniels in 1961, before he and lyricist Hal David discovered their leading interpreter, Dionne Warwick.

In America, the musical center of gravity was shifting northward: to Detroit, home of Motown, and New York, where **Bob Dylan** was beginning to turn heads. On the west coast, the Wilson brothers were turning surfing into a musical style. By the end of the year they were the **Beach Boys**.

New York was home to a remarkable flowering of songwriting talent at the Brill Building on 1619 Broadway. Among its resident songwriting teams were **Carole King** and **Gerry Goffin**, who wrote the huge **Bobby Vee** hit *Take Good Care Of My Baby*, and **Barry Mann** and **Cynthia Weil**. Downtown in Greenwich Village, Dylan – just 19 – was playing the clubs and winning acclaim among "serious" music critics for his socially conscious folk music. By the end of the year he released his debut album and ignited a folk singer-songwriting fire.

This was a vintage year for R&B. **Ray Charles** dominated the Grammy Awards and wowed the French, **Bobby Lewis** enjoyed the biggest US hit of the year with *Tossin' And Turnin'*, and **Leiber** and **Stoller** wove their magic with the **Drifters** (*Please Stay* – written and arranged by **Burt Bacharach** – and *Sweets For My Sweet*). The Stax label in Memphis enlisted what would become the hottest rhythm section this side of heaven.

Phil Spector was making a name for himself as an innovative if temperamental producer/writer. His successes included the **Paris Sisters**' *I Love How You Love Me,* and *Spanish Harlem*, a giant hit for soulster **Ben E. King**. He produced **Gene Pitney**'s *Every Breath I Take* and **Curtis Lee**'s *Pretty Little Angel Eyes* – and by the end of the year had founded his own label. Harnessing state-of-the-art studio technology, he began overdubbing scores of musicians to create what he called "a Wagnerian approach to rock 'n' roll." The **Crystals**' *There's No Other* was a sign of the avalanche of hits to come.

The Crystals were one of a surge of female vocal groups. The **Shirelles** scaled the US charts and joined high-profile "package tours." The **Marvelettes** gave Motown its first US No. 1 single, **Mary Wells** appeared on "American Bandstand," and the **Primettes** became the **Supremes**.

Where was **Elvis**? He played just a handful of live appearances, though he remained busy in the studio and high in the charts on both sides of the Atlantic. But by now he was more movie idol than rock 'n' roll rebel.

Britain's pop scene seemed relatively conservative. Teenager **Helen Shapiro** dominated the charts with her extraordinarily mature pop-rock style. When she wasn't at the helm, **Cliff Richard** was. But the Mersey Sound was bubbling, with **Gerry & the Pacemakers** and the **Beatles** winning a growing following. A Decca talent spotter thought the Beatles worth watching. So did a local record dealer, **Brian Epstein**.

Sept 23	Reach For The Stars/Climb Ev'ry Mountain	**Shirley Bassey with Geoff Love & His Orchestra**
Sept 30	Johnny Remember Me	**John Leyton**
Oct 7	Kon-Tiki	**Shadows**
Oct 14	Michael	**Highwaymen**
Oct 21	Walkin' Back To Happiness	**Helen Shapiro**
Nov 11	Little Sister/(Marie's The Name) His Latest Flame	**Elvis Presley**
Dec 9	Tower Of Strength	**Frankie Vaughan**
Dec 30	Moon River	**Danny Williams with Geoff Love & His Orchestra & the Rita Williams Singers**

"Beautiful, lovely, talented..."

Murray the K on the Shirelles, 1961

Jan 1961

Del Shannon's *Runaway*... Jackie Wilson is shot... "Thank Your Lucky Stars"...

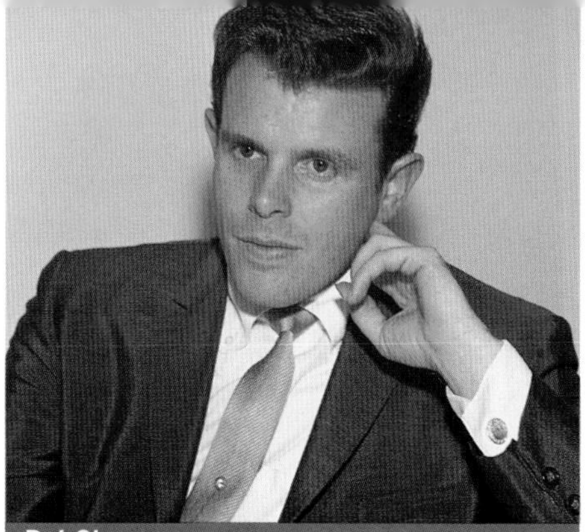

Del Shannon

The Primettes

January

12 The **Primettes** – a Detroit-based, R&B vocal quartet comprising **Diane Ross**, **Mary Wilson**, **Florence Ballard**, and **Barbara Martin** – sign to Motown Records, and label boss Berry Gordy encourages them to change their name to one suggested by Ballard: the **Supremes**. The group originally auditioned last summer at the Motown office (already called Hitsville USA), where they were introduced by Ross's friend, **Smokey Robinson**. Having entered the chart in December, the **Miracles** – fronted by Robinson – are on their way to US No. 2 with Motown's first million-selling disc, *Shop Around.*

16 Harry Balk, co-owner of another ambitious Detroit start-up label, Big Top Records, has sent 26-year-old Michigan carpet salesman **Del Shannon** to New York to record a song Shannon has co-written with his friend and drummer, Max Crook. At the end of an otherwise uneventful first session at Bell Sound Studios, Shannon and Crook nail *Runaway*. After producer Balk speeds up Shannon's vocal – which originally sounded a little flat – his first single will go on to top the US chart for four weeks in April.

Del Shannon's unique sound came courtesy of a specially designed keyboard called the musitron... The Primettes were formed as a female counterpart to the Primes: neither stayed that way for long, the Primettes becoming the Supremes and the Primes, the Temptations... The Beatles were now a four-piece with the departure of Stuart Sutcliffe.

16 At 14, **Helen Shapiro** records her first session for EMI's Columbia label. Born in Bethnal Green, London, she began writing songs with her schoolfriend Susan Heckman when she was nine, and sang with her brother Ron's trad jazz band last year. Shapiro is still attending Clapton Park Comprehensive School and is also taking weekly vocal classes at the Maurice Berman Singing Academy in Baker Street, London. With A&R head Norrie Paramor producing, she cuts *Don't Treat Me Like A Child* and *When I Am With You*. The former will hit No. 3 in May, followed by successive chart-toppers *You Don't Know* (August) and *Walkin' Back To Happiness* (October), establishing her as the youngest and most popular British singer of the early 1960s.

THE BRILL BUILDING

Feb 4 **Shirley Owens, Micki Harris, Doris Kenner, and Beverly Lee – the Shirelles – become the first all-girl group to hit US No. 1, with *Will You Love Me Tomorrow* on the New York-based Scepter label. It is the first chart-topper for writers Gerry Goffin and Carole King, who are part of a collective of young songwriters working at the Brill Building, at 1619 Broadway in New York's music district. The building itself is named after the Brill Brothers' clothing store at street level, but the Brill Building "sound" is being created in a number of music publishing offices along Broadway, between 49th and 53rd streets. After its completion in 1931, the owners of 1619 began renting space to publishers, the first three being Southern Music, Mills Music, and Famous-Music. In May 1958, the 21-year-old Don Kirshner installed Aldon Music, co-founded with Al Nevins, and Kirshner was behind the idea of employing teams of songwriters, including (pictured in front row, left to right) Barry Mann and Cynthia Weil, Goffin and King, and Neil Sedaka, whose partner is Howard Greenfield. Several other pairs, working in small offices with just a piano and two chairs – including Ellie Greenwich and Jeff Barry, and Burt Bacharach and Hal David – write songs, tape demos, take them round to publishers, have a string arrangement and a lead sheet written for $10, hire musicians, and record finished demos to present to record companies down the block.**

The Brill Building writers were responsible for creating an unrivaled canon of hit songs.

Beatles postcard

28 Despite several copies being returned to British stores by customers complaining that the disc is faulty, **Elvis Presley**'s latest ballad, *Are You Lonesome Tonight?* tops the UK chart. Owing to an unusual amount of bass in the recording, a worn stylus tends to make the record skip. Decca offers to replace the records returned to dealers, but many consumers simply buy new styluses.

February

4 Currently sliding down the US chart with his biggest hit, the No. 8-peaking teen anthem, *You're Sixteen*, **Johnny Burnette** undergoes an emergency appendectomy at Cedars Lebanon Hospital in Hollywood. It will force the postponement of a planned four-week tour of the UK, where *You're Sixteen* is heading to No. 3. Memphis-born Burnette – one of the earliest Tennessee rockabillies – formed the **Johnny Burnette Trio** with his older brother, Dorsey, in 1952, before writing three hits for **Ricky Nelson** in the late 1950s. Going solo in 1958, he signed to Liberty Records, where he has been paired with hit producer Snuff Garrett.

9 Having already played 30 shows this year, the **Beatles** make their first appearance at the Cavern Club in Liverpool. (They performed at the venue three years ago, but as the **Quarry Men**.) The fee for the lunchtime gig is £5 ($14).

15 **Jackie Wilson** is shot and seriously wounded by 28-year-old Juanita Jones in his apartment building at 408 West 57th Street, New York. He is confronted by Jones, whom he knows, when he answers the door. He sees she has a gun and grabs it, but two bullets are fired into his back and abdomen. Wilson stumbles on to the street, and is rushed to Roosevelt Hospital for surgery. A hysterical Jones tells police she went to the apartment intending to take her own life if Wilson spurned her again. "I didn't mean to hurt Jackie. I wanted to kill myself." He will spend 21 days in a coma, lose his left kidney to gangrene, and will never have the second bullet removed because it is so close to his spinal column.

25 **Elvis Presley** makes his first concert appearance since 1958, when he performs at the Ellis Auditorium in Memphis. The event raises $51,612 for local charities, which include the Elvis Presley Youth Center in Tupelo. During the show, he is presented with a plaque by RCA to mark worldwide record sales of 76 million. Before a crowd of about 10,000, Tennessee Governor Buford Ellington proclaims today Elvis Presley Day. (On March 8, Ellington will confer upon Presley the honorary title of Colonel, before the General Assembly of the State's legislature.)

March

10 Brill Building songwriter, 22-year-old **Jeff Barry**, signs an exclusive contract with Trinity Music in New York. Already the hit co-writer of *Tell Laura I Love Her*, Barry will marry **Ellie Greenwich** in 1962 and – working with producers Phil Spector and "Shadow" Morton – the pair will create top-drawer pop hits for the **Ronettes**, the **Crystals**, the **Shangri-Las**, the **Dixie Cups**, and **Manfred Mann**, among many others.

12 **Elvis Presley** cuts his first sides of the year – 12 tracks for his forthcoming LP ***Something For Everybody*** – at RCA's Studio B in Nashville, in a little under 12 hours.

25 **Elvis Presley** plays a benefit show at the Bloch Arena in Pearl Harbor, on an entertainment bill with Minnie Pearl and James Stewart, raising $62,000 for the USS *Arizona* Memorial Fund. (His 17-song set will be his last stage appearance for more than eight years.) Meanwhile, *Surrender* hits US No. 1 (displacing **Chubby Checker**'s latest dance effort, *Pony Time*). This dramatic adaptation by Doc Pomus and Mort Shuman, of the 1911 Italian ballad *Torna A Sorrento (Come Back To Sorrento)* is the only secular recording from Presley's October 1960 gospel session.

April

1 The **Beatles** begin a second spell in Hamburg, this time at the Top Ten club. Their run will be extended twice, with the result that the band will play for 92 consecutive nights before finishing the residency on July 1.

1 ITV's new music show "Thank Your Lucky Stars" airs for the first time. The premiere features **Anne Shelton**, the **Dallas Boys**, and Hughie Green, all introduced by regular host Pete Murray. Despite its "middle-of-the-road" beginnings, the series will run for five years and become one of the UK's seminal 1960s music shows. DJs hosting the show will include Keith Fordyce, Barry Alldis, Sam Costa, Alan Dell, Brian Matthew, Don Moss, Jimmy Savile, Kent Walton, and Jimmy Young. It will be Moss who introduces the "Spin a Disc" segment, which features a panel of teenagers awarding the latest releases a score out of five. In February 1962, a teenager called Janice Nicholls, on hearing **Brenda Lee**'s *Speak To Me Pretty*, will say, "Oi'll give it foive," in her thick Birmingham accent. She will become a fixture on the show and her simple critique, a national catchphrase.

With mohair suit and pompadour hairstyle, Jackie Wilson was perhaps the most riveting live act of his era.

Apr 1961

Dylan sings in Greenwich Village... The first issue of Mersey Beat... Mary Wells...

8 The **Marcels**' *Blue Moon* tops the US chart (and will also hit UK No. 1 next month). The Pittsburgh-based doo-wop quintet recorded only two takes of the Rodgers and Hart standard under the direction of Colpix Records' staff producer, Stu Phillips. WINS New York disc jockey Murray the K has championed the song.

11 **Bob Dylan** begins his first residency – a two-week booking – at Gerde's Folk City in Greenwich Village, opening for bluesman **John Lee Hooker**. He performs both traditional fare, such as *House Of The Rising Sun*, and his own songs, including *Song To Woody* – a tribute to **Woody Guthrie**. The son of a furniture store owner from Duluth, Minnesota, Dylan (born Robert Zimmerman) has taken his stage surname from Welsh poet Dylan Thomas. He arrived in New York on January 25, mainly to visit his idol Guthrie, the chief precursor of the folk boom, who has been increasingly disabled by Huntingdon's chorea for the past eight years. Greenwich Village, which is populated by a large student body and a strong artistic community, and has a growing number of coffee houses and small nightclubs, is fast becoming a magnet for members of the burgeoning folk singer-songwriter movement.

12 **Ray Charles** takes home four trophies at the third annual Grammy Awards ceremony, held at the Beverly Hills Hotel in Los Angeles and the Hotel Astor in New York. He wins Best Vocal Performance Album, Male for ***The Genius Of Ray Charles***; Best Vocal Performance Single Record or Track, Male and Best Performance by a Pop Single Artist for *Georgia On My Mind*; and Best R&B Performance for *Let The Good Times Roll*. **Marty Robbins** wins the award for Best Country & Western Performance for *El Paso*, and **Ella Fitzgerald** picks up two trophies for *Mack The Knife* (Best Vocal Performance, Single Record or Track, Female) and ***Mack The Knife, Ella In Berlin*** (Best Vocal Performance, Album, Female).

17 **Connie Francis** performs *Never On Sunday* at the 33rd Academy Awards ceremony at the Santa Monica Civic Auditorium. The tune, written by Manos Hadjidakis, is named Best Song, denying Jimmy Van Heusen and Sammy Cahn the opportunity of winning Best Song Oscars in consecutive years.

BOB DYLAN

Apr 5 Bob Dylan – a 19-year-old singer-songwriter – performs his first paid gig in New York City, at the Loeb Music Center, for New York University's Folk Society. Dylan began learning guitar and harmonica at the age of 12 (he never learned to read music), before traveling for a while with a Texas carnival when he was 13. In 1959 he began an art course at the University of Minnesota in Minneapolis, but left the campus in early 1961 to concentrate on a career in music. He was briefly employed as a pianist with Bobby Vee's backing group, the Shadows, under the name Elston Gunn.

At Hibbing High School in Minnesota Dylan formed several groups, including rock 'n' roll combos the Golden Chords and the Rock Boppers (and noted in the yearbook that he was leaving "to follow Little Richard").

Rick Nelson

Ray Charles

Bobby Lewis

Almost a permanent top ten chart fixture as Ricky Nelson, the change to Rick brought about only four more top tenners... Ray Charles became the first artist to pick up four awards at the Grammys... Indianapolis-born Bobby Lewis, adopted at the age of 12, topped the chart with the R&B classic *Tossin' And Turnin'*.

May

5 The **New Musical Express** reports on a Songwriters' Guild survey revealing that 104,472 discs were broadcast in 1960 – of which 39 percent were British. The BBC broadcast 20,232 discs – 2,875 more than 1959, nearly 27 percent of which were indigenous.

6 Staying at the Montowesi Hotel in Branford, Connecticut – and in town to perform at the Indian Neck Folk Festival – **Bob Dylan** makes a tape recording in his room of three Woody Guthrie songs: *Talking Columbia*; *Hangknot Slipknot*; and *Talking Fish Blues*.

8 On his 21st birthday, **Ricky Nelson** officially changes his performing name to Rick. His latest hit, *Travelin' Man* (originally offered by its writer Jerry Fuller to **Sam Cooke**), is currently heading to US No. 1.

20 **Cliff Richard** – who began shooting his latest film, "The Young Ones," at ABC's Elstree Studios last week – makes his debut on "Thank Your Lucky Stars," singing *A Girl Like You*.

31 **Chuck Berry** opens the gates to Berryland, his outdoor amusement park in Wentzville, Missouri, some 20 miles from St. Louis.

June

1 FM multiplex stereo broadcasting is heard for the first time on American radio, by listeners in Schenectady, Los Angeles, and Chicago. The Federal Communications Commission will adopt the standard next year.

3 In the biggest ever leap to the top of the UK charts, **Elvis Presley**'s *Surrender* vaults from No. 27 to No. 1. Decca has reported advance orders exceeding 461,500 for the single, Presley's third consecutive No. 1 (also a chart first).

6 Having made her home in France, **Petula Clark** participates in "La Nuit de la Chancellerie," a special stage show at the Palais de Chaillot, Paris, in the presence of Presidents John Kennedy and Charles de Gaulle.

14 **Patsy Cline** sustains near-fatal head injuries and a fractured right hip in a head-on car crash outside the Madison High School, Nashville. The accident kills a passenger in the other vehicle.

14 **Gene Vincent** is knocked unconscious after falling down 30 steps at the end of his performance at the Majestic, Newcastle. During the concert he has been mobbed by fans who rushed the stage.

16 Florida-born 22-year-old **Gary "U.S." Bonds** performs his first (and only) US chart-topper, *Quarter To Three* on "American Bandstand." The song will become a million-seller, and will be the subject of a $100,000 lawsuit in January 1963, when **Chubby Checker** will be accused of plagiarism for his hit *Dancin' Party*. The case will be settled out of court.

July

1 Having waited patiently at UK No. 2 for four weeks while Elvis Presley's *Surrender* ran out of steam, **Del Shannon** finally hits the top with *Runaway*. It will turn out to be the most successful of his 14 UK hits.

6 Created to document the vibrant and increasingly popular rock 'n' roll scene in Liverpool, the first issue of **Mersey Beat** is published in Britain. It includes an essay by **John Lennon** under the title, "Being a Short Diversion on the Dubious Origins of Beatles."

7 **Mary Wells**, Motown Records' first female signing, performs her second single, *I Don't Want To Take A Chance*, on "American Bandstand." The 18-year-old singer is a native of Detroit, and first met Berry Gordy in 1960 when she offered him a song she had written, *Bye Bye Baby*, to give to **Jackie Wilson**. Gordy suggested Wells cut it herself for his label.

15 R&B singer **Bobby Lewis** – an old friend of **Jackie Wilson** – finally makes it at the age of 28, after five years of trying: *Tossin' and Turnin'* hits US No. 1 at the beginning of seven weeks at the top. Released on New York's Beltone label, it will become the longest-running No. 1 smash of the year, also logging 10 weeks in pole position on the R&B survey.

"He is consciously trying to recapture the rude beauty of a Southern field hand musing in melody on his porch. All the 'husk and bark' are left on his notes and a searing intensity pervades his songs."

Robert Shelton on Bob Dylan, **The New York Times**, 1961

Gary "U.S." Bonds would enjoy a resurgence in his career in the late 1970s, when Bruce Springsteen and Steve Van Zandt co-produced a comeback album.

The "Stax Sound"... The Pendletones become the Beach Boys...

Booker T & the MG's provided the hallmark, rhythmic "Stax Sound" backbone to dozens of major hits... The Tokens recorded *The Lion Sleeps Tonight* – one of their audition songs for RCA Records – which would become the US No. 1 at Christmas.

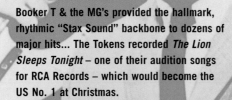

The Tokens

21 Already established as a top songwriter (penning *Rubber Ball* for Bobby Vee and *Hello Mary Lou* for Rick Nelson) 20-year-old singer **Gene Pitney** makes his debut on "American Bandstand," performing his new single, *Every Breath I Take* (written by Goffin and King, and produced by Phil Spector). While scoring a string of his own hit singles throughout the 1960s, Connecticut native Pitney will continue to write sterling material for other artists, notably next year's US chart-topper, the Spector-helmed *He's A Rebel*, for the **Crystals**.

27 *The Lion Sleeps Tonight* is recorded by Brooklyn-based vocal combo the **Tokens** at RCA's studios in New York. The group's debut cut for the label is a revised version of Paul Campbell's African folk-based composition *Wimoweh*. RCA Records inhouse producers, Hugo Peretti and Luigi Creatore, together with songwriting partner George Weiss, have written new English lyrics and given it a new title, and the song will become an enduring pop classic in its various guises. The Tokens learned it from the **Weavers**' 1951 cover of *Wimoweh* – itself based on a 1939 recording of the South African folk tune *Mbube*, by the Zulu group **Solomon Linda & the Evening Birds**. The Tokens – formed as the Linc-Tones in 1955, at Lincoln High School, Brooklyn, by longterm frontman **Hank Medress** – originally featured **Neil Sedaka**, **Eddie Rabkin**, and **Cynthia Zolitin**, though all three had left by 1958, to be replaced by new recruits **Jay Siegel** and brothers **Phil** and **Mitch Margo**.

29 **Bob Dylan** takes part in WRVR-FM radio's "Saturday of Folk Music" show, a 12-hour "Hootenanny" special, at the Riverside Church in New York. During a 27-minute performance he sings several traditional songs, including *Handsome Molly*, *Naomi Wise*, and *Poor Lazarus*.

August

12 *Last Night* by the **Mar-Keys** hits US No. 3. The Memphis-based R&B instrumental group have been signed to a small local label, Satellite Records, started by Jim Stewart in 1958. When he needed a cash investment for the venture, his sister – Estelle Axton – took out a second mortgage to buy Ampex recording equipment and lease premises, becoming an equal partner in the business. The operation was initially based in a small warehouse in Brunswick, but the siblings moved it back to Memphis in 1960, settling into an old movie theater at 926 East McLemore Street – where Axton also opened a record store. Among their first signings were **Rufus Thomas** (who recorded *Bear Cat* for Sun Records in 1953) and his teenage daughter **Carla**. Carla has already scored Satellite's first national hit (No. 10) in March, *Gee Whiz (Look At His Eyes)*, which they licensed to Atlantic as part of a five-year, $5,000 advance deal offered by Jerry Wexler. While the Mar-Keys hit has been climbing the chart, Stewart has learned of an existing Satellite Records in California, and changes his label name to Stax (gleaning "ST" from his name and "AX" from Axton). The printed copies of *Last Night* are switched from Satellite 107 to Stax 107, to become the first Stax release. Stewart has already lost a $100 bet with his sister that the record wouldn't be a hit. The Mar-Keys – formerly the Royal Spades – feature Estelle's son, **Charles "Packy" Axton** (tenor sax), **Jerry Lee "Smoochie" Smith** (keyboards), **Don Nix** (baritone sax), **Steve Cropper** (guitar), **Donald "Duck" Dunn** (bass), and **Terry Johnson** (drums). Cropper and Dunn will later team with local drummer Al Jackson, and a young pianist named Booker T. Jones. Collectively, these four will provide the hallmark, rhythmic "Stax Sound" backbone to dozens of major hits, as well as recording under their own group name: **Booker T. & the MG's**.

15 The **Kingston Trio** cut their first sides with new recruit, San Diego-born, 21-year-old singer/guitarist **John Stewart**, recording *Jesse James* and *The Whistling Gypsy*. They will continue sessions through the week, laying down the rest of the tracks that will make up their ***Close Up*** LP – a Grammy nominee next year for Best Performance by a Vocal Group.

30 **Gene Chandler** – a 24-year-old R&B singer-songwriter who finished three years in the Army last year – records a new song he has written, *Duke Of Earl*, for Vee-Jay Records in Chicago. Its A&R executive, Calvin Carter,

Booker T & the MG's

recently heard Chandler's demo, which was originally offered to Nat Records but turned down. Carter's enthusiasm prompted a call to Vee-Jay president Ewart Abner (in France), who green-lit the signing without hearing the song. *Duke Of Earl* – with its infectious "Duke, Duke, Duke, Duke of Earl" intro – will become the label's first million-seller and first chart-topper next February.

September

6 **Bob Dylan** performs six songs, including *Song To Woody* and Woody Guthrie's *Car, Car*, at hot New York folk venue, the Gaslight Café.

15 Hollywood-based music publisher Hite Morgan – for whom 19-year-old singer/guitarist **Al Jardine** has already auditioned as part of a folk group – records *Surfin'* by the **Pendletones** at World-Pacific Enterprises, his home studio at 8175 West Third Street, Los Angeles. The beach-themed song was written by Jardine's ex-high school friend, bassist/singer **Brian Wilson** (also 19), and Wilson's cousin, 20-year-old vocalist **Mike Love**. It was prompted by Brian's 16-year-old brother, **Dennis Wilson**, who is an avid surfer and also a drummer. In addition, they record *Luau* (written by Morgan's son Bruce), and a third cut, *Lavender* (written by Morgan's wife, Dorinda). The Pendletones – briefly known as **Carl & the Passions** – also include the youngest Wilson sibling, 14-year-old guitarist **Carl**. Morgan will sign *Surfin'* to his own Guild publishing company.

26 **Bob Dylan** begins another two-week engagement at Gerde's Folk City, opening for the **Greenbriar Boys**. **The New York Times** music critic Robert Shelton – in a review of the performer headlined, "Bob Dylan: A Distinctive Folk-Song Stylist" – will glowingly report that Dylan resembles "a cross between a choir boy and a beatnik...[with] a cherubic look and a mop of tousled hair he partly covers with a Huck Finn black corduroy cap..." and that he is "bursting at the seams with talent."

29 **Bob Dylan** plays harmonica on three tracks for folk singer **Carolyn Hester** at an album session in Studio 29 at Columbia Records' New York studios. Dylan once again impresses producer **John Hammond Sr.**, who recently met him at the home of a friend of Hester's, and will offer him a recording contract. (Hammond is already a legendary music maker, having discovered and produced records for, among many others, **Pete Seeger**, **Billie Holiday**, **Bessie Smith**, and **Count Basie**.)

October

2 On the anniversary of Gandhi's birth, the Asia Society presents Indian sitar master **Ravi Shankar** in concert at New York's Town Hall. The 41-year-old Shankar – already revered as his country's leading classical sitarist – shares the stage with **Kanai Dutta** on tabla and **N.C. Mullick** on tamboura. The performance precedes Shankar's first American tour, and is the first time western culture has been exposed to the ragas and talas on which Indian music is based.

3 The **Pendletones** return for a second session at Hite Morgan's home studio, re-recording *Surfin'* and *Luau*. Morgan will press both cuts as a single on his own X Record label, before taking the 45 to Herb Newman at the local Era Records, distributed through the larger Candix label. Newman will like the record, but not the group's name. Candix A&R man Joe Saraceno will play the song to Russ Regan, who works at Candix's Buckeye Record Distributors, and the three of them will coin the band's new name: the **Beach Boys**. Newman will have copies pressed on his Candix label, delivering them to Bill Angel at KFWB in Los Angeles.

"Certain adults have turned the twist into something more suggestive than it is. It's not a dirty dance. It shouldn't be turned into one."

Chubby Checker on the dance craze, 1961

14 **Ray Charles**, with his 16-piece band and the Raelets backing singers, begins a record-breaking seven-date run at the Palais des Sports in Paris. All 25,000 seats for the scheduled five concerts have already sold. **The New York Times** will report that this triumph is, "but the latest example of the popularity of American jazz here, which, even sixteen years after the end of World War II has given no evidence of waning." The shows come at a time when the French are particularly enamored of the twist, which is taking over from the cha cha and merengue as dance flavor of the month: 45 different twist records are on the market in France, with **Johnny Hallyday**'s version topping the national chart.

22 As the twist reaches fashionable nightspots like New York's Peppermint Lounge, **Chubby Checker** appears on the "Ed Sullivan Show" singing *The Twist* (with the Do-Re-Mi dancers twisting) and performing his new dance-themed hit, *The Fly*. The show also features upcoming British crooner **Matt Monro**.

28 Record-buyer Raymond Jones calls at Brian Epstein's NEMS record store in Liverpool, to enquire about the **Beatles**' German-only release *My Bonnie* (which was actually issued in August, under the name **Tony Sheridan & the Beat Brothers**). Epstein is unable to trace the record and, assuming the group to be German, promises to investigate further.

Chubby Checker's performance of *The Twist* on the "Ed Sullivan Show" in October re-sparked demand for the single. It would become the first record to reach No. 1 a second time around, on January 13, 1962.

Oct 1961

Phil Spector launches the Philles label... The Country Music Hall of Fame...

The Country Music Hall of Fame plaque for Hank Williams reads: "The simple beautiful melodies and straightforward plaintive stories in his lyrics of life as he knew it will never die."

29 Plugging an upcoming performance at Carnegie Chapter Hall in New York on November 4, **Bob Dylan** is interviewed by host Oscar Brand on WNYC radio. He also performs two songs: Woody Guthrie's *Sally Gal* and the traditional tune, *The Girl I Left Behind*.

30 **Phil Spector**'s own Philles label is launched in New York with the issue of the **Crystals**' *Oh, Yeah, Maybe Baby* and *There's No Other (Like My Baby)* (Philles 100). The label's name combines his first name with the first three letters of that of co-founder Lester Sill (who already owns Trey Records with Lee Hazlewood). As producer for all Philles releases, Spector will focus intensely on creating an entirely new recording architecture and sound, using the latest available studio technology.

An R&B trio from Inkster, Michigan, the Marvelettes chalked up 23 chart records in the 1960s, but none could top their debut, *Please Mr. Postman.*

November

3 The Country Music Association in Nashville announces the formation of the Country Music Hall of Fame. The first honorees are **Hank Williams**, **Fred Rose**, and **Jimmie Rodgers**, known as "The Father of Country Music." Although Rodgers died in 1933, his timeless influence stretched right through to the early roots of rock 'n' roll in the 1950s, as he was the first performer to merge hillbilly music with the blues.

4 Three weeks after its release – on his birthday – **Cliff Richard**'s ***I'm 21 Today*** tops the UK chart.

4 In a concert principally staged as a showcase for company executives, following his signing to Columbia on October 26, **Bob Dylan** performs seven songs (a mix of Bukka White, Leadbelly, Woody Guthrie, and Bessie Smith). However, he draws only 53 people to the event at Carnegie Chapter Hall's Folklore Center in New York – for which he reportedly earns $20. Tickets cost $2.

6 **Joey Dee & the Starliters** provide the music for a fund-raising dinner at the Four Seasons Hotel in New York. The dinner, called "The Twist," is one of the big social events of the year, and will benefit the Girls' Town charity. The New Jersey-based Starliters – led by Joseph DiNiola, a former classmate of the **Shirelles** – have for the last year been the house band at the Peppermint Lounge on 45th Street, between Broadway and 7th Avenue. The Lounge has become *the* in-spot for the high society in-crowd. **The New York Times** reports that "Café society has not gone slumming with such energy since its forays into Harlem in the Twenties. Greta Garbo, Noel Coward, Elsa Maxwell, Tennessee Williams, the Duke of Bedford and Countess Bernadotte – often in black tie or Dior gown – vie with sailors, leather-jacketed drifters and girls in toreador pants for admission to the Peppermint's garish interior." In two weeks time, Dee & the Starliters' *Peppermint Twist* – a pop cocktail mix blending the notoriety of the nightclub with the year's biggest dance craze – will enter the US chart on its way to No. 1.

7 Just after *Hit The Road Jack* has given **Ray Charles** his second US chart-topper, having reached No. 1 on October 14, the singer is arrested in Indianapolis, when police find heroin, marijuana, and drug-taking paraphernalia in his hotel room. A drug user since the age of 16, Charles was first arrested for possession in 1955.

9 Following up on Raymond Jones's October inquiry about the group's German-only release, record store owner **Brian Epstein** sees the **Beatles** perform for the first time, at a Cavern lunchtime session. In a subsequent interview on BBC radio, Epstein will recall his first impressions: "They were rather scruffily dressed in the most attractive way. Black leather jackets and jeans. Long hair of course, and rather untidy stage presentation. Not terribly aware and not caring very much what they looked like. I think they cared more even then in what they sounded like."

As positive word-of-mouth continued to spread, the Beatles topped the bill over some of Liverpool's brightest in "Operation Big Beat" in November... Their first gig in the south of England, in Aldershot, was billed as a "Battle of the Bands – Liverpool v. London." Only 18 people showed up.... Ray Charles was hailed "the most creative musical giant of this generation."

Ray Charles's drug habit caused the singer problems throughout the late 1950s and early 1960s.

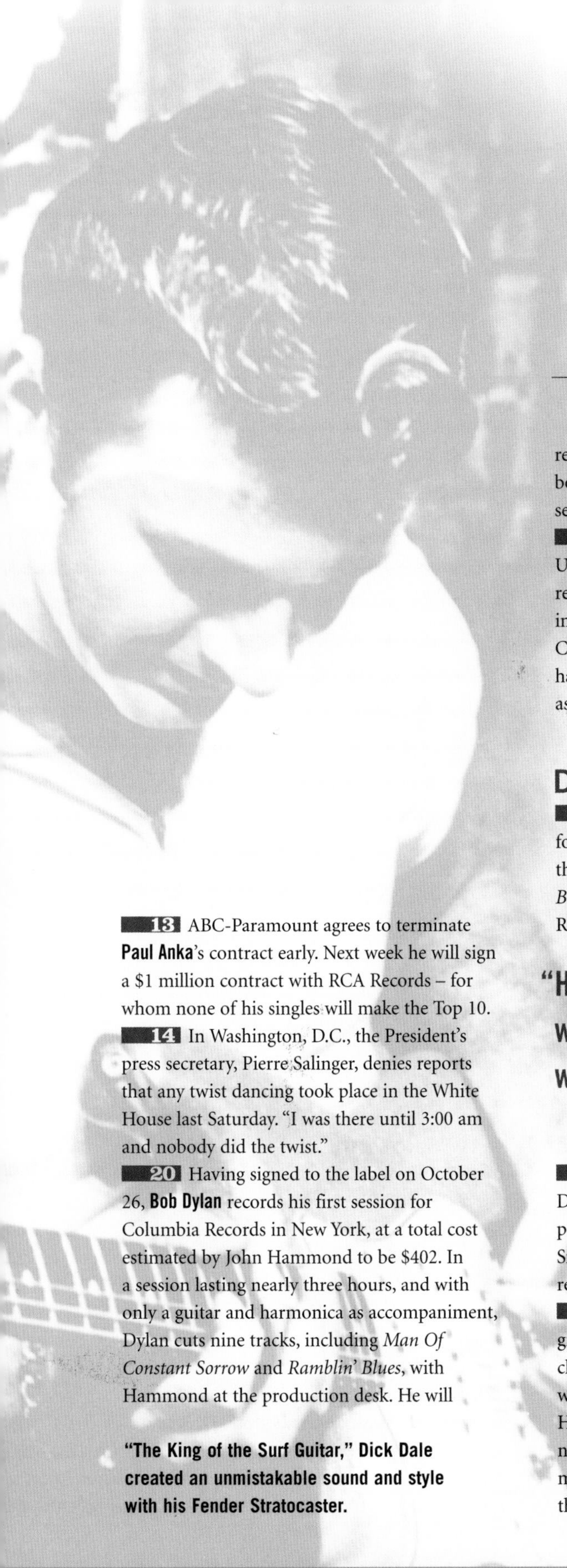

13 ABC-Paramount agrees to terminate **Paul Anka**'s contract early. Next week he will sign a $1 million contract with RCA Records – for whom none of his singles will make the Top 10.

14 In Washington, D.C., the President's press secretary, Pierre Salinger, denies reports that any twist dancing took place in the White House last Saturday. "I was there until 3:00 am and nobody did the twist."

20 Having signed to the label on October 26, **Bob Dylan** records his first session for Columbia Records in New York, at a total cost estimated by John Hammond to be $402. In a session lasting nearly three hours, and with only a guitar and harmonica as accompaniment, Dylan cuts nine tracks, including *Man Of Constant Sorrow* and *Ramblin' Blues*, with Hammond at the production desk. He will return in two days to record more tracks, and both sessions will comprise his debut LP, the self-titled ***Bob Dylan***.

25 Both **Everly Brothers** are sworn into the US Marine Corps Reserves in Nashville, and report to Camp Pendleton in San Diego for induction. After basic training in Oceanside, California, they will serve as artillerymen handling 105mm howitzers for the 8th Battalion, as part of a six-month period of duty.

"The King of the Surf Guitar," Dick Dale created an unmistakable sound and style with his Fender Stratocaster.

December

8 The **Supremes** – now trimmed to a trio following the departure of **Barbara Martin** – cut their second single for Motown, *Your Heart Belongs To Me*, written and produced by Smokey Robinson, in the company's Detroit studio.

"He said: 'They are four boys and I'd like to manage them. It wouldn't take any longer than two half days at a time.' He said it would never interfere with business."

Queenie Epstein, after her son Brian heard the Beatles playing at the Cavern, November 1961

13 Mike Smith, sent by his boss Dick Rowe, Decca's head of A&R, sees the **Beatles** performing at one of their regular Cavern gigs. Smith will suggest that Decca organizes a recording test for the group.

16 The **Marvelettes**' *Please Mr. Postman* gives Motown (via its Tamla imprint) its first US chart-topper. Co-written and produced by staff writers/producers Robert Bateman and Brian Holland, the song features 22-year-old Motown newcomer, **Marvin Gaye**, on drums, and will be much covered by many other artists (including the Beatles). The Marvelettes are an R&B vocal quintet who formed as the Casinyets at their high school in the Detroit suburb of Inkster, and won a talent contest sponsored by Motown. Label boss Berry Gordy changed their name.

29 With a surf music wave gathering strength in California, the **Beach Boys** perform two songs during the intermission at the Rendezvous Ballroom, on a bill with **Dick Dale**, the **Surfaris** (a teenage surf band from Glendora), and the **Challengers**. Dale is actually from Quincy, Massachusetts, but moved with his family to southern California as a teenager. A multi-instrumentalist, he has already fronted the **Del-Tones**, who took up a residency at the Rinky Dink Ice Cream Parlor and then the Rendezvous, originally playing country and rockabilly. As they became one of the most popular live acts in the area, Dale played lead guitar and developed a fast, heavily reverberated staccato style to simulate the rhythms of his favorite sport, surfing. This is now being much copied around southern California, but Dale created the first wave.

31 Local station KFWB has hired **Brian Wilson**'s group for a show where they debut on radio under their new name, the **Beach Boys**, on the bill of Ritchie Valens' Memorial Dance in Long Beach – a date for which they earn $300. It was on KFWB that Wilson first heard the **Four Freshmen**, a close harmony jazz vocal quartet formed in 1948, who are his main musical influence.

ROOTS **During this year: Beckenham lad Peter Frampton makes his stage debut at a Boy Scout variety show, singing *A Girl Like You* and *Poor Me*... Reginald Dwight, a student at the Royal Academy of Music in London, joins local R&B outfit the Corvettes, having already performed as a resident soloist at the Northwood Hills Hotel three nights a week, playing pub songs... Bob Marley, the son of English army captain Norval Sinclair Marley, comes to the attention of Jamaican music entrepreneur Leslie Kong, recording the self-penned single, *Judge Not (Unless You Judge Yourself)*, which when released is credited to Bob Morley... Liverpudlians John McNally and Mike Pender form an instrumental duo, performing at their local pub in Kirkdale, naming themselves the Searchers after John Ford's classic western... and former gospel singer Sam Moore is performing at the King of Hearts club in Miami, when one of the club's chefs, Dave Prater, spontaneously joins him onstage; their immediate rapport leads them to become a duo, known by their first names....**

You've Really Got A Hold On Me

1962

No.1 US SINGLES

Jan 6 The Lion Sleeps Tonight **Tokens**
Jan 13 The Twist **Chubby Checker**
Jan 27 Peppermint Twist **Joey Dee & the Starliters**
Feb 17 Duke Of Earl **Gene (Duke of Earl) Chandler**
Mar 10 Hey! Baby **Bruce Channel**
Mar 31 Don't Break The Heart That Loves You **Connie Francis**
Apr 7 Johnny Angel **Shelley Fabares**
Apr 21 Good Luck Charm **Elvis Presley**
May 5 Soldier Boy **Shirelles**
May 26 Stranger On The Shore **Acker Bilk**
June 2 I Can't Stop Loving You **Ray Charles**
July 7 The Stripper **David Rose & His Orchestra**
July 14 Roses Are Red **Bobby Vinton**
Aug 11 Breaking Up Is Hard To Do **Neil Sedaka**
Aug 25 The Loco-Motion **Little Eva**
Sept 1 Sheila **Tommy Roe**
Sept 15 Sherry **Four Seasons**
Oct 20 Monster Mash **Bobby (Boris) Pickett & the Crypt Kickers**
Nov 3 He's A Rebel **Crystals**
Nov 17 Big Girls Don't Cry **Four Seasons**
Dec 22 Telstar **Tornadoes**

No.1 UK SINGLES

Jan 6 Moon River **Danny Williams with Geoff Love & His Orchestra & the Rita Williams Singers**
Jan 13 The Young Ones **Cliff Richard & the Shadows**
Feb 24 Rock-A-Hula Baby/Can't Help Falling In Love **Elvis Presley with the Jordanaires**
Mar 24 Wonderful Land **Shadows**
May 19 Nut Rocker **B. Bumble & the Stingers**
May 26 Good Luck Charm **Elvis Presley**
June 30 Come Outside **Mike Sarne**
July 14 I Can't Stop Loving You **Ray Charles with the Jack Halloran Singers**
July 28 I Remember You **Frank Ifield**
Sept 15 She's Not You **Elvis Presley with the Jordanaires**
Oct 6 Telstar **Tornados**
Nov 10 Lovesick Blues **Frank Ifield with Norrie Paramor & His Orchestra**
Dec 15 Return To Sender **Elvis Presley with the Jordanaires**

George Martin

The Miracles

George Martin, who had made a name for himself producing comedy records for the likes of the Goons, recorded the first tracks by a young Liverpool quartet, the Beatles... The Miracles, distinguished by the remarkable voice of their leader Smokey Robinson, became one of Tamla Motown's earliest success stories.

British pop and rock had long been a pale imitation of US vibrancy. **Cliff Richard**, **Tommy Steele**, and **Helen Shapiro** all sold well at home but made no inroads in America, while **Lonnie Donegan** had managed only two US top ten positions in five years. But four lads from Liverpool – under the guidance of EMI producer **George Martin** – were about to change the transatlantic balance. In the first of many famous sessions, the **Beatles** cut *Please Please Me* and *Love Me Do* at Abbey Road for an increasingly excited Martin. And another quartet, from London, would not be far behind, as the **Rollin' Stones** were playing their first dates, covering blues standards.

In the US, Motown continued its ascendancy, putting together its own package tour of stars and savoring a million-seller with the **Miracles**' *You've Really Got A Hold On Me*. By the end of the year **"Little" Stevie Wonder** had released his first album, on which his composing skills, exuberant voice, and command of the harmonica suggested great things ahead. **Phil Spector** – at 21 – was both a brilliant producer and a ruthless businessman: by the end of 1962 he was the sole owner of his Philles record label, and a millionaire. **Bob Dylan** followed up his debut album by playing harmonica on **Harry Belafonte**'s ***Midnight Special*** and cutting several self-penned tracks – including *Blowin' In The Wind* and *Masters Of War*, an indictment of the military-industrial complex. Following in his footsteps, folk trio **Peter, Paul & Mary** signed to Warner Bros.

On the west coast, the **Beach Boys** cut several tracks, for which the subject matter was invariably a mix of surfing, girls and cars. **Brian Wilson** quickly established himself as the band's creative force, writing most of the songs and arranging their distinctive harmonies, set to a beat reminiscent of **Chuck Berry**. Led by strong sales in California, their first single, *Surfin' Safari*, made it into the US chart.

The first inkling of what the Caribbean would soon offer came from the fledgling Island Records, owned by **Chris Blackwell**. He would bring ska, reggae, and rocksteady to a global audience. **Bob Marley** was already writing songs for the Jamaican underclass, such as *Judge Not* – an attack on critics of the "rudeboy" culture prevailing among Kingston's youth.

The white heat of technology topped the charts on both sides of the Atlantic with the futuristic *Telstar* by the **Tornados** – a driving instrumental helmed by independent producer **Joe Meek**, who was inspired by the first communications satellite. The year saw its fair share of novelty records, including **Bobby Pickett**'s *Monster Mash*, a Boris Karloff spoof that has since sold four million copies, *Nut Rocker* by **B. Bumble & the Stingers**, and *Peppermint Twist* by **Joey Dee & the Starliters**. Of greater pedigree, if perhaps in the same category, **Little Eva** had a summertime US smash with *The Loco-Motion*. It was written by **Carole King**, for whom Eva babysat, proving there was more than one route to a hit – a point confirmed by trumpeter **Herb Alpert**, who started a small label named A&M Records in his garage.

"In scale and presence [Phil Spector] was to the record biz what Orson Welles was to Hollywood."

Andrew Loog Oldham, **Stoned**, 2001

Jan

1962

The Beatles audition unsuccessfully for Decca Records... "Pick Of The Pops"... Ray Charles sings country and western...

January

1 The **Beatles** audition for Decca Records, at the company's studios in West Hampstead, London, for producer Mike Smith (who will tell the **Liverpool Echo**'s Tony Barrow that "[I] think the Beatles are great.") They record 15 tracks in the space of an hour, mixing rock 'n' roll, R&B, and country numbers with three John Lennon and Paul McCartney originals: *Hello Little Girl*, *Like Dreamers Do*, and *Love Of The Loved*. At the end of the session, it's a case of "Don't call us – we'll call you." Afterward, **Brian Poole & the Tremeloes**, a five-piece combo based in Dagenham (much closer to Decca's London HQ than Liverpool), also audition. Decca will sign them, instead of the Beatles.

2 Veteran folk quartet the **Weavers** are barred from performing on NBC's "Jack Paar" television show, featuring substitute host Sam Levenson, after they refuse to sign loyalty oaths. They are approached by NBC lawyers at midday and asked to sign sworn statements that they are not and never have been members of the Communist party. They decline. NBC confirms that it has canceled the group's appearance, stating that company policy has long barred "the use of its facilities by performers identified with the Communist party... When questions concerning such association are raised, NBC seeks to obtain information as to the facts from the performers concerned. Two of the present four members of the singing group known as the Weavers have refused to testify before a Congressional committee on this matter."

Ironically, Brian Poole & the Tremeloes, whom Decca signed in preference to the Beatles, made their chart debut with *Twist And Shout*.

Cliff Richard began the year with *The Young Ones* and ended it with *Bachelor Boy* – two of more than 100 career UK hits.

4 **Mersey Beat** publishes its first group popularity poll. Not surprisingly, the **Beatles** are at No. 1, followed by **Gerry & the Pacemakers**.

7 "Pick Of The Pops" returns in a new hour-long format from 4:00 pm to 5:00 pm, with disc jockey Alan Freeman. Long part of the BBC Light Programme's radio schedule, it was most recently broadcast as part of "Trad Tavern" on Saturday nights. In this new Sunday afternoon slot, it will become the BBC's most listened-to music show, and will continue to be broadcast – albeit extended – into the 21st century, becoming "The Official UK Top 40" show. The program's first No. 1 is **Danny Williams**'s *Moon River*.

13 Re-released in the US, and with no sign of the dance craze ending, **Chubby Checker**'s *The Twist* tops the Hot 100 for the second time, for the first of two weeks – the only single ever to hit US No. 1 on two separate occasions.

26 In New York, Bishop Burke of the Buffalo Catholic Diocese issues a proclamation banning his parishioners and their children from performing, singing, listening to, or buying anything related to the twist dance phenomenon. (This follows a similar ban issued in Tampa, Florida, on January 3.)

28 **Adam Faith** appears on the BBC television Sunday discussion program, "Meeting Point," with Dr. Donald Coggan, Archbishop of York. Coggan made controversial comments about Faith last Saturday.

29 Folk trio **Peter** (Yarrow), **Paul** (Stookey), **& Mary** (Travers) are signed to Warner Bros. Records. Formed last year, and already popular on the Greenwich Village coffee-house circuit, they have been brought to the label by folk music impresario and entrepreneur, Albert Grossman.

February

1 The Thistle Café in West Kirby, Cheshire, UK, is anointed "The Beatle Club" for one night, to mark Brian Epstein's debut booking for the group. He reduces his usual commission to 10 percent of their earnings for the night – £18 ($50) – to mark the occasion. (Ironically, the **Beatles** will never play at the venue again.)

2 **Bob Dylan** plays harmonica on the title cut of **Harry Belafonte**'s forthcoming album, ***Midnight Special***. The recording session takes place at Webster Hall, New York with producer Hugo Montenegro. (Dylan's next session work will be on March 2, once again playing harmonica and adding backing vocals to four tracks by Victoria Spivey at Cue Recording Studios in New York.)

5 With dates at the Cavern at lunchtime and the Kingsway Club in Southport in the evening, and drummer **Pete Best** unwell, the **Beatles** need a replacement on drums. **John**, **Paul**, and **George**'s choice is **Ringo Starr**, who makes his first appearance with the group.

8 The **Beach Boys** record *Surfin' Safari, Surfer Girl, Judy*, and *Beach Boys Stomp (aka Karate)* for the Candix label at the World Pacific studio. Last year's debut *Surfin'* is set to enter the US chart in two weeks' time, and they are now gigging regularly at the Rainbow Gardens and Cinnamon Cinder clubs in Los Angeles.

15 **Ray Charles** cuts *I Can't Stop Loving You* (a 1958 country hit for its writer Don Gibson) and *You Don't Know Me*, at United Studios in Hollywood. The first track will top the US chart, also spending ten weeks at the top of the R&B survey, and give Charles his first UK No. 1. The second will hit US No. 2. Both are to form part of his groundbreaking album ***Modern Sounds In Country And Western Music***. A landmark release, helmed by Sid Feller, it sees R&B veteran Charles dig deep into country music, producing a critically and commercially successful crossover blend that will hog the top spot on the US album survey for 14 weeks from August 11.

16 As neither of the two big band albums he has cut over the past two years has sold well, **Bobby Vinton** is set to be dropped by Columbia imprint, Epic Records, but he still owes the label two single sides. In favor of a band arrangement, he records a country-style version of a song found on a demo, *Roses Are Red*, co-penned by Paul Evans and Al Byron, and produced by Bob Morgan. It is coupled with *Mr. Lonely*, written while he was in the Army. To promote the record, he will drive copies around to shops, and give away roses to radio stations. Vinton's grass-roots efforts will pay off when *Roses Are Red* tops the US chart in July, and reaches sales of one million in August. (He will stay with Epic, racking up more than 30 hits for the label by the end of the 1960s.)

18 Five days after completing their basic military training, the **Everly Brothers** appear – in full Marine uniform and with regulation cropped haircuts – on "The Ed Sullivan Show," singing their new single, *Crying In The Rain* and *Jezebel*.

19 **Chuck Berry** begins a three-year stretch – of which he will serve 20 months – in the Indiana Federal Penitentiary. Charged at the end of 1959 with transporting a minor across a state line for immoral purposes, his first conviction was quashed, and he was retried last October.

> **"No private business establishment such as NBC has the power or the right to require proof of any citizen's patriotism."**
>
> The Weavers' Fred Hellerman, January 2, 1962

March

8 The BBC Light Programme broadcasts "Teenager's Turn – Here We Go," recorded at the Playhouse Theatre in Manchester, and featuring the **Beatles** making their radio debut. Appearing for the first time in suits, white shirts, and ties, they perform Roy Orbison's *Dream Baby*, Chuck Berry's *Memphis, Tennessee*, and the Marvelettes' *Please Mr. Postman*.

13 At the annual Variety Club of Great Britain Awards, **Cliff Richard** is named Show Business Personality of 1961 "for his recordings, his performance in the film 'The Young Ones,' and his successful appearances in Britain and abroad." Receiving his Silver Heart, Richard says: "It frightens me tremendously for I know that I have a lot to live up to now. I don't know how long I have left but I hope to be able to make the best of it." His labelmate **Helen Shapiro** is voted joint Most Promising Newcomer of the Year (with actress Rita Tushingham) for her first three records. Receiving her award, Shapiro says: "I am greatly honored and sincerely hope I can live up to it." Meanwhile, the **Shadows** begin a six-day season at the Paris Olympia – becoming the first English rock group to headline a variety bill at the venue.

17 **Blues Incorporated** perform their first gig at London's Ealing Jazz Club. This loose collection of dedicated white British blues musicians, fronted by veteran guitarist **Alexis Korner** and harmonica player **Cyril Davies**, is becoming an apprentice shop for young blues players. Tonight's line-up is completed by pianist **Dave Stevens**, saxophonist **Dick Heckstall-Smith**, bass player **Andy Hoogenboom**, and a 20-year-old drummer born in Islington, London, by the name of **Charlie Watts**.

30 **Billy Fury** (who recently completed filming the musical "Play It Cool" at Pinewood Studios, near London, with first-time director Michael Winner) collapses backstage at the Adelphi in Slough, and is rushed to hospital, where he is suspected of having a recurrence of the kidney complaint he suffered in September last year. He will leave hospital next week. **Marty Wilde** will take over on the tour until Fury is well enough to rejoin.

30 "It's Trad Dad!" premieres at the London Pavilion, with **Helen Shapiro** – peaking at UK No. 2 this week with her LP ***Tops With Me*** – and Craig Douglas in featured acting roles. The film's flimsy plot is little more than an excuse to feature several current stars, notably **Gene Vincent** (*A Spaceship To Mars*), the **Brook Brothers** (*Double Trouble*), **Del Shannon** (*You Never Talked About Me*), **Gene McDaniels** (*Another Tear Falls*), **Chubby Checker** (*Lose-Your-Inhibitions Twist*), and **John Leyton** (*Lonely City*). It is the full-length feature debut of director Richard Lester, who will go on to direct two genre-defining music films of the 1960s: "A Hard Day's Night" and "Help!"

Island Records' first release... The Stones debut at the Marquee... *Telstar*...

The Tornados

Although he had already left the Beatles, Stuart Sutcliffe's influence on the group remained even after his death.

April

10 Having visited a doctor in February complaining of severe headaches, **Stuart Sutcliffe**, still living in West Germany, becomes ill at his fiancée Astrid Kirchherr's mother's house in the Hamburg suburb of Altona. He dies, at the age of 21, in his girlfriend's arms, in an ambulance on the way to the hospital. His body will be returned to Liverpool, to be interred at Huyton Parish Church Cemetery.

13 The **Beatles** begin another punishing schedule in Hamburg, performing for 48 nights, with only one day off, at the newly opened Star-Club. They will share the bill with **Gene Vincent** for two weeks, and during this time will also record two tracks backing **Tony Sheridan**, with producer Bert Kaempfert.

15 Unbeknown to the 10,000 fans at the annual **New Musical Express** Poll Winners Concert being held at the Empire Pool in Wembley, **Jet Harris** makes his final appearance with the **Shadows**. He will initially go solo, before teaming up with drummer **Tony Meehan**, another ex-Shadow, and will have three top-five hits in 1963, with *Diamonds*, *Scarlett O'Hara*, and *Applejack*. **Cliff Richard**, **Helen Shapiro**, **Brenda Lee**, **Adam Faith**, and **Billy Fury** take part in the all-star bill. Also appearing are the **Springfields**, a British folk trio signed to the Philips label last year. They include ex-**Lana Sisters**' singer/guitarist **Dusty Springfield**, on the eve of her 23rd birthday.

24 **Bob Dylan** returns to Columbia Records Studios, and cuts seven tracks – including the self-penned *Blowin' In The Wind*. He will continue tomorrow, and intermittently through the rest of the year, completing the recording of his second album ***The Freewheelin' Bob Dylan***. (It won't be until August next year that the album finally becomes Dylan's first chart disc.)

Bob Dylan's second LP, released in 1963, was his chart breakthrough, the first of more than 40 hit albums... The Tornados – session men formed as Billy Fury's backing band – became the unlikely hit recorders of *Telstar*, one of the best-known instrumentals of all time.

> **"Joe sent me a copy [of *Telstar*]. I listened and thought, 'God, I can't tell anybody I played on that.'"**
>
> Tornados drummer, Clem Cattini

29 Five days after his son Steve Allen drowned in the swimming pool of his family home (while his wife Myra Lewis was cooking Easter dinner), **Jerry Lee Lewis** makes a successful return to Britain for the first time in four years. Having previously been shunned by the British media, he now meets with favorable audience response at Newcastle City Hall. **Johnny Kidd & the Pirates**, **Vince Eager**, the **Viscounts**, the **Echoes**, **Mark Eden**, and the **Bachelors**, open for Lewis.

May

1 The first Cinebox – Britain's first visual jukebox – is installed at the Moka Bar, Frith Street in London. The 40-film unit features five "films" made in the UK, by **Eden Kane**, **Bobby Rydell**, the **Viscounts**, **Phil Fernando**, and the **Kentones**. All the rest are from Europe. Filmbox Equipment is expecting to install the machines at the rate of 50 a month. The Cinebox costs £1,250 ($3,500) and projects color film versions of hit songs on to a 21in screen. Each selection requires 1s (5p/14¢) in the slot.

8 During a trek around London visiting UK record companies Oriole, Philips, and Pye, **Brian Epstein** visits the HMV record store on Oxford Street, which has the facility to transfer recordings from tape to acetate. HMV engineer Ted Huntly, who converts the demo tape the **Beatles** made at Decca on to a disc, sees potential in the songs. He sends Epstein to see Sidney Coleman, director of publishers Ardmore & Beechwood. Coleman in turn arranges a meeting tomorrow with EMI producer **George Martin**.

13 **Helen Shapiro**, **Matt Monro**, **Anthony Newley**, **Tony Osborne**, **Ron Grainer**, and **Johnny Dankworth** perform at the seventh Ivor Novello Awards, broadcast from BBC Television Centre. The Special Award is presented to **Cliff Richard and the Shadows**, while Shapiro's *Walkin' Back To Happiness*, written by John Schroeder and Mike Hawker, is named Best Selling A-side.

14 **Helen Shapiro** begins two weeks at the London Palladium. She is the youngest person ever to head a variety bill at the venue.

19 **B. Bumble & the Stingers**' novelty instrumental, *Nut Rocker*, tops the UK chart for a single week – breaking the stranglehold at the top by **Cliff Richard**, the **Shadows**, and **Elvis Presley**. From January 13 to June 23, these three acts will otherwise hold off all comers, with *The Young Ones*, *Can't Help Falling In Love/Rock-A-Hula-Baby*, *Wonderful Land*, and *Good Luck Charm*.

29 **Chubby Checker** wins Best Rock & Roll Recording for *Let's Twist Again* at the fourth Grammy Awards, held at the Beverly Hills Hotel in Los Angeles and the Waldorf-Astoria Hotel in New York; **Ray Charles** wins Best Rhythm & Blues Recording for *Hit The Road Jack*. Otherwise, traditional safe voting continues, with wins for *Moon River* by **Henry Mancini** and Johnny Mercer (Record of the Year and Song of the Year), while **Judy Garland** nabs Best Solo Vocal Performance, Female for ***Judy At Carnegie Hall***, which is also named Album of the Year.

une

2 The Saigon apartment of US Embassy ecretary Patricia Ruth Clark is raided by police, nd Miss Clark is served with a warrant for llowing her guests to dance. The charge will e dropped next week, after Embassy officials pologize for the offense, which comes on the eels of a new morals law introduced in ietnam two weeks ago by President Ngo Dinh Diem. The law bans beauty contests, boxing, dancing, organized fights between animals, orcery, and birth control.

4 Jamaican singer **Owen Gray**'s *Twist Baby* is the first release by the fledgling Island Records label, for which entrepreneur owner **Chris Blackwell** – who started the Island/Blue Mountain company last year in his native amaica – has recently opened a small London office. Initially, Blackwell will focus on mporting and licensing Jamaican releases or sale in the UK, including records by **Jimmy Cliff** and the **Skatalites**. But he will soon begin negotiations to distribute records from the US via the New York-based Sue label, through which he will license material from Ace, Vee-Jay, and Kent.

6 Having signed a provisional demo contract with EMI on June 4, the **Beatles** make their first visit to the company's Abbey Road Studios in St. John's Wood, London, to record a test for the Parlophone label, under the direction of George Martin's assistant, Ron Richards. They perform *Besame Mucho* and impress Martin with three self-penned compositions, *Love Me Do*, *P.S. I Love You*, and *Ask Me Why*. Remembering his audition of the group, Martin will state: "They were pretty awful. I understand why other record ompanies turned them down...but when I met them, I liked them."

uly

12 Taking their name from an old Muddy Waters song, the **Rollin' Stones** play their first gig at the Marquee International Jazz Club on London's Oxford Street. The group comprises 19-year-olds **Mick Jagger** (vocals) and **Keith Richard** guitar), with guitarist Elmo Lewis (aka 20-year-old **Brian Jones**), bassist **Dick Taylor**, pianist **Ian Stewart**, and drummer **Mick Avory**. They will continue with this line-up to the end of the year. Jagger and Richard first met in February 1951, while both were at Maypole County Primary School in Wilmington, Kent, but lost contact until a chance meeting on a train two years ago. Their friendship was rekindled when they discovered a mutual love of R&B, particularly Chess label artists such as Waters and Chuck Berry. The pair subsequently joined R&B group **Little Boy Blue & the Blue Boys** (alongside **Dick Taylor, Bob Beckwith**, and **Allen Etherington**), and met Jones – who was performing with his own R&B band, which included Stewart – two months ago at the Ealing Jazz Club. Jagger has also become part-time vocalist with the Ealing club's resident group, **Alexis Korner**'s **Blues Incorporated**, which – unable to fulfill its scheduled gig tonight at the Marquee – has asked Jagger and his cohorts to fill in.

13 The **Everly Brothers** begin their first US tour since being discharged from the US Marines. Opening in Salt Lake City, it is set to end on August 27th.

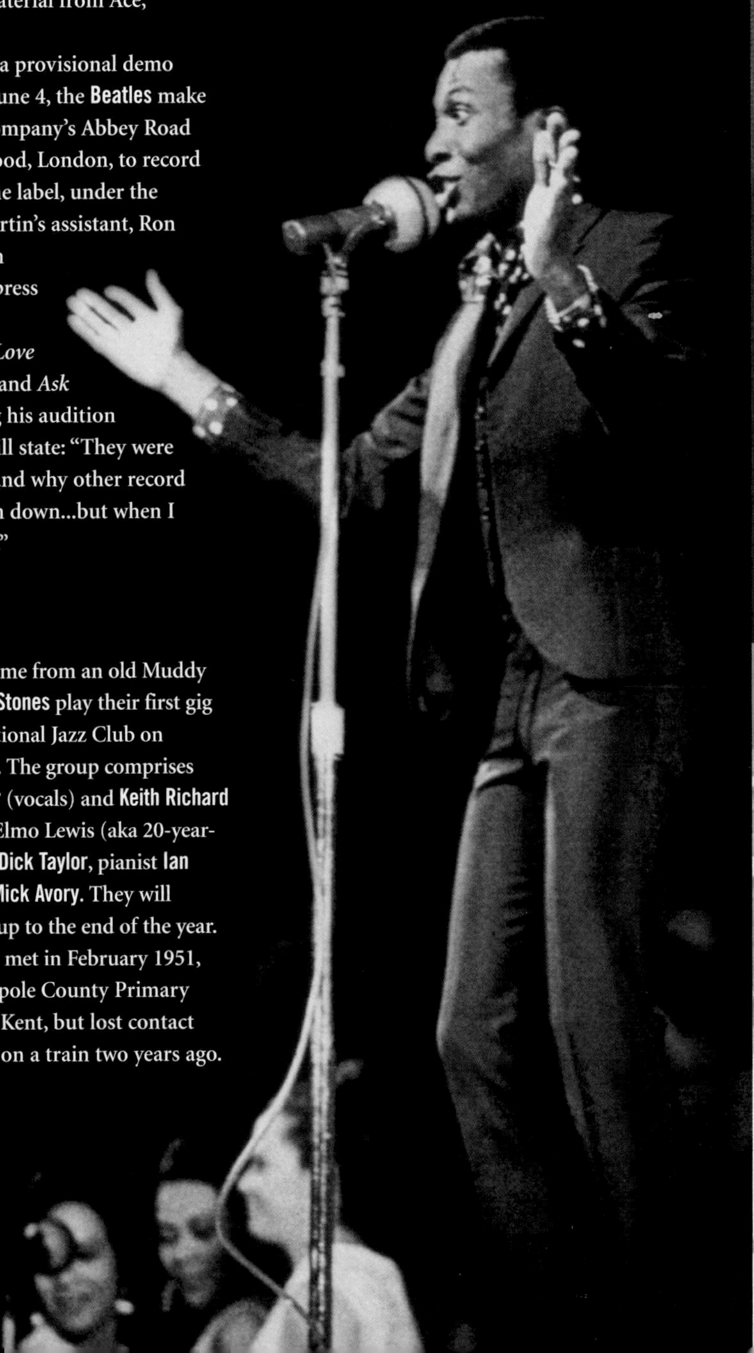

Jimmy Cliff made his recording debut as a 14-year old, cutting *Dearest Beverly* and *Hurricane Hattie* for Leslie Kong.

JOE MEEK

July 23 Joe Meek puts the finishing touches on *Telstar* by the Tornados, a group he recruited as session men to back his solo artists. He has brought in his favorite songwriter, Geoff Goddard, to add the tune's signature clavioline melody. The record will race to the top in October, enjoying a five-week stay at UK No. 1, and eventually selling 910,000 domestic copies. It will also enjoy a three-week run at the top of the US survey (released by the Tornadoes – with an added "e"), the first single by a UK group to do so. Global sales will eventually hit five million.

Joe Meek, Britain's first independent record producer, worked in a home-built studio above a leather goods shop at 304 Holloway Road in London. His best-known recording was inspired by the recently launched Telstar communications satellite.

A&M Records is launched... The Beach Boys climb the chart... The Beatles record at Abbey Road...

Isley Brothers

Little Eva

August

9 A&M Records releases its first single, *Lonely Bull*, by the **Tijuana Brass** featuring **Herb Alpert**. Trumpet-playing Alpert initially formed the label – with partner Jerry Moss, an ex-record promoter who moved from New York to Los Angeles in 1960 – as Carnival Records last year, each investing $100. When they discovered another label already trading as Carnival, they used the first letters of their last names to create A&M. Working out of his home-built recording studio in his garage at 419 Westbourne Drive in Los Angeles, Alpert has transformed a Sol Lake composition, *Twinkle Star*, into the Mariachi-flavored *Lonely Bull*, inspired by a bullfight he recently attended in Tijuana, Mexico. Following its US No. 6 success in December (with expert radio promotion by Moss), Alpert will record an equally popular debut album, relocate the A&M office to 8255 Sunset Boulevard, and establish one of the largest independent record labels in the business, also creating its own equally lucrative Rondor Music publishing arm.

11 After five years of trying to make the US Top 20, and currently signed to Wand Records, the **Isley Brothers** finally peak at No. 17 with *Twist And Shout*, their revision of a 1961 release by the **Top Notes**. Further down the chart is the **Beach Boys**' *Surfin' Safari*, on its way to becoming their first Top 20 success (making No. 14). A flipped B-side, the A-side is *409*, the group's first hot-rod car-themed song. With the closure of Candix Records, it is their first release for Capitol Records, where they have been signed at the behest of label producer Nik Venet. The band – now managed full-time by the Wilsons' father, Murry – recently met **Jan & Dean** at a teen hop in Los Angeles. They are occasionally opening for the duo, and both acts are becoming familiar with each other's repertoire. Jan & Dean have by now racked up ten US chart placings (none of them surf-themed).

15 Unbeknown to him, **Pete Best** plays his last gig with the **Beatles**, at the Cavern. The decision was made yesterday by Brian Epstein and the other three Beatles, long dissatisfied with Best's role in the group, to fire him. **Ringo Starr** – currently playing with **Rory Storm & the Hurricanes** at Butlin's Holiday Camp in Skegness – will be asked to replace him, after Epstein's choice, **Johnny Hutchinson** of the **Big Three**, has turned down the invitation.

16 **Pete Best** is fired from the **Beatles** by Epstein, only hours before the group's Riverpark Ballroom gig in Chester. (**Johnny Hutchinson** fills in for the night, as he will do tomorrow at gigs in Birkenhead and New Brighton.) Best will go on to join **Lee Curtis & the All Stars**.

18 **Ringo Starr** makes his debut as an official member of the Beatles, performing at Port Sunlight Horticultural Society's annual show in Birkenhead.

With their first hit single, *Surfin' Safari*, the Beach Boys fueled the surf-rock craze that was just beginning in southern California.

The Isley Brothers' *Twist And Shout* became a radio and dancehall standard (it would reach an even wider audience in 1963, when it was covered by the Beatles)... Little Eva's debut and No. 1 hit, *The Loco-Motion*, was another dance sensation... Meanwhile, Elvis, away from the concert stage, was working on his latest movie vehicle at the World's Fair in Seattle.

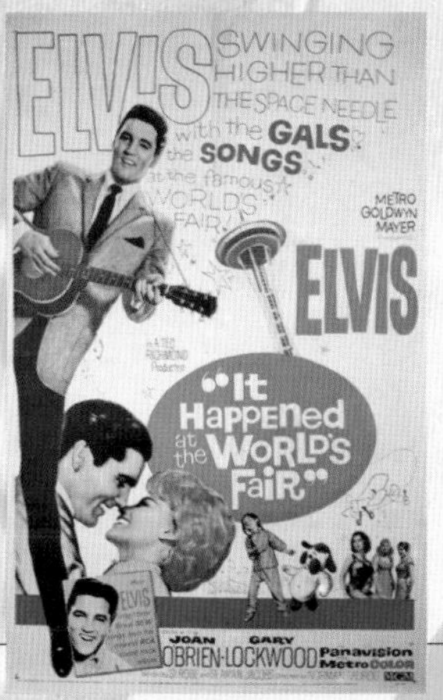

"Through a motion picture millions see Elvis. We are thinking in terms of the many rather than the few..."

"Col." Tom Parker, September 24, 1962

22 Fidelity's Duet Ampligram is launched at the Radio Show at Earl's Court, London. The machine integrates a microphone, guitar, tape, radio, and gram inputs, making it possible to sing and play along to records. It costs 27 guineas (£28.35/$79) and is the first of its kind in Europe. Also on display are the latest transistor radios, costing between £5 ($14) and £30 ($84), while the most expensive radiogram is priced at 750 guineas (£785.50/$2,200).

25 **The Times** of London reports that the Malayan Minister of Education, Inche Abdul Rahman Bin Haji Talib, has told women schoolteachers that they should not dance the twist because it is "an unhealthy and most un-eastern culture."

25 Eva Boyd – aka **Little Eva** – who babysits for songwriting couple Carole King and Gerry Goffin, hits US No. 1 with the Goffin-produced pop nugget and "brand new dance" sensation *The Loco-Motion*. The 17-year-old North Carolina-born Eva was asked by the Goffins to demo the song for presentation to R&B newcomer, **Dee Dee Sharp** (who has already scored two US top five hits this year: *Slow Twistin'* with Chubby Checker, and *Mashed Potato Time*). When Sharp's producers turned it down, Aldon Music publisher Don Kirshner – for whom Goffin and King work – decided to recut the song with Little Eva, and make it the first release on his new label, Dimension Records.

September

4 The **Beatles**' first recording session proper takes place at EMI's Abbey Road Studios. Following an afternoon rehearsal with Ron Richards, they record two sides: Mitch Murray's *How Do You Do It?* (originally intended for Adam Faith), and Lennon and McCartney's self-penned *Love Me Do*. George Martin decides the latter has the potential to become their first single.

11 The **Beatles** return to Abbey Road, recording *P.S. I Love You*, *Please Please Me*, and *Love Me Do*. Concerned about **Ringo Starr**'s inexperience in the studio, George Martin brings in the session-savvy **Andy White**. Starr helps out on maracas and tambourine.

14 Through a new licensing deal, Oriole-American releases its first three Tamla Motown Records in the UK: **Mary Wells**'s *You Beat Me To The Punch*, the **Marvelettes**' *Beechwood 4-5789*, and the **Contours**' *Do You Love Me*.

15 A newspaper in Canton reveals that the twist has reached south Communist China, citing "ugly displays" in Maoming Cultural Park.

22 Introduced by **Pete Seeger**, **Bob Dylan** takes part in the Carnegie Hall Hootenanny in New York, performing *Sally Gal*, *Highway 51*, *Talkin' John Birch Paranoid Blues*, *The Ballad Of Hollis Brown*, and *A Hard Rain's A-Gonna Fall*.

24 **Elvis Presley** receives an invitation to appear in this year's Royal Variety Performance. Declining the offer, "Col." Tom Parker will submit: "We have pointed out to newspapers that call us that it is true we have not been able to make personal appearances in Britain, but it is also true we have not appeared elsewhere. Through a motion picture, millions see Elvis. Through a personal appearance a very small fraction would see him. We are thinking in terms of the many rather than the few."

FOUR SEASONS

Sept 15 **A tune that took its writer, 19-year-old Bob Gaudio, 15 minutes to write, hits the US top spot: *Sherry* by the Four Seasons. Its title is a re-spelled nod to New York radio station WMCA DJ Jack Spector's daughter, Cheri. The demo was played to Vee-Jay west coast sales manager, Randy Wood, who passed it to local DJ Dick "Huggy Boy" Hugg. He played it on his show from the Dolphin's of Hollywood Record Store. With an immediately positive listener reponse to the pop diamond – highlighted by its tight harmonies, insistent beat, and the piercing falsetto end of Valli's three-octave tenor range – Crewe and Vee-Jay cut a deal. A No. 1 hit is born and begins a five-week run.**

Oct

1962

Little Richard returns... Phil Spector... The Beatles record *Please Please Me...*

October

2 **Cliff Richard** leaves for North America to start a tour in Cincinnati, followed by visits to Memphis, Houston, St. Louis, Detroit, Toronto, Buffalo, and New Orleans. He will make live appearances in movie theaters where his latest film, "Wonderful To Be Young," is being shown. He will also appear on "The Ed Sullivan Show" on the 21st, though none of this hard work will result in a US chart placing. The tour will come to an end on November 9 in Miami, before a convention for the Theatre Owners of America.

6 The **Beatles** make the first of many personal appearances, signing copies of *Love Me Do* – released yesterday by Parlophone/EMI – at Dawson's Music Shop in Widnes, UK.

8 The Reverend **Little Richard** returns to rock 'n' roll with a comeback tour – his first in the UK – with fellow American star **Sam Cooke**, promoted by Don Arden. During the 20-date series, two people will be treated in hospital after a Bristol show, an attendant will be injured when a crowd tries to storm the stage in Slough, and police with dogs will go on stage after a show in Walthamstow, London, to clear the audience. At tonight's opening, Cooke misses the first house because his plane arrives late. **Gene Vincent**, on hand to introduce Little Richard, sings *Be-Bop-A-Lula* from the auditorium, circumventing the ruling that the expiration of his work permit prevents him from singing on a British stage. Vincent and **Jet Harris**, one of the support acts on the tour, find time for a game of darts in a local pub before the second house.

10 Released in the US two months ago, *Monster Mash*, the novelty smash by **Bobby "Boris" Pickett & the Crypt-Kickers**, is banned from British radio and television by the BBC, whose policy is not to broadcast any music it deems "offensive." The ban works: the song won't chart in the UK until it is reissued in 1973, though it will top the US chart in time for Halloween.

12 The **Beatles** open for one of their rock 'n' roll idols, **Little Richard**, at the Tower Ballroom in New Brighton. The five-and-a-half-hour show also features the **Big Three**, **Pete MacLaine & the Dakotas**, **Lee Curtis & the All Stars**, **Billy Kramer & the Coasters**, **Rory Storm & the Hurricanes**, the **Undertakers**, the **Four Jays**, the **Merseybeats**, and **Gus Travis & the Midnighters**.

13 During a rehearsal for the **Everly Brothers**' 22-date, twice-nightly UK tour, older brother **Don** breaks down on stage at London's Prince of Wales Theatre, while singing *Crying In The Rain*. He is taken back to the Savoy Hotel to rest. Following a second collapse just after midnight, he is taken to Charing Cross Hospital. He will discharge himself six hours later, but will once again be hospitalized tomorrow afternoon. Younger brother **Phil** opens on his own at the Granada Cinema in East Ham, with the Everlys' guitarist, **Joey Page**, substituting on harmony vocals. Don will be discharged the day after tomorrow and fly to New York to receive treatment, and Phil will continue the tour solo.

24 **James Brown**'s now legendary stage act is taped at Harlem's Apollo Theater for future live album release. With LP sales becoming increasingly important in the record market, ***Live At The Apollo*** will eventually sell over one million copies after its release next year, giving Brown his first Top LP chart placing in **Billboard** and peaking at No. 2.

27 The **Rollin' Stones**, comprising **Mick Jagger**, **Keith Richard**, **Brian Jones**, **Ian Stewart**, and drummer **Tony Chapman** (a member of the **Cliftons**), make their first recordings at Curly Clayton Studios in Highbury, London. They tape covers of *Soon Forgotten* by Muddy Waters, Jimmy Reed's *Close Together,* and Bo Diddley's *You Can't Judge A Book (By Looking At The Cover)*. Over the next few weeks they will hawk the demo around London record companies with little success. **Blues Incorporated** drummer **Charlie Watts** has so far snubbed several requests to join the band as their permanent drummer, and continues with his day job as a designer with a Regent Street advertising agency.

November

1 **Little Richard** and the **Beatles** begin a 14-day stint at the Star-Club in Hamburg. (During the wildly popular engagement, **Paul McCartney** will reportedly ask Richard to teach him his singing style.)

3 With dance records all the rage, 19-year-old Latin-American singer **Chris Montez** – a young protégé of Ritchie Valens – begins a frustrating four-week stay at UK No. 2 with his US No. 4 hit, *Let's Dance*, behind the Tornados' *Telstar* and then British singer Frank Ifield's *Lovesick Blues*.

> **"You've just made your first number one."**
>
> George Martin, November 26, 1962

3 The Philles label celebrates its first US No. 1 with the **Crystals**' *He's A Rebel*. **Phil Spector**, who is seeking total control of the company, has returned to the west coast and established his recording base at Gold Star Studios, on the corner of Santa Monica Boulevard and Vine Street in Hollywood. He is recruiting some of the finest west coast session players, including

Although welcomed in California and New York, Cliff Richard couldn't duplicate his British success in the US. His biggest stateside hit would be the gold-selling *Devil Woman* in 1976.

The Miracles joined "Little" Stevie Wonder, Marvin Gaye, and the Supremes on Tamla Motown's two-month Motor Town Revue package tour, beginning in October.

STEVIE WONDER

Oct 16 The 12-year-old child prodigy "Little" Stevie Wonder – who recently made his live debut at Detroit's Latin Quarter club – joins the two-month Motown Records Motor Town Revue, opening in Washington. It features the Miracles, Mary Wells, the Marvelettes, Marv Johnson, the Contours, and the Supremes, and will conclude on December 16 with a ten-night stand at New York's legendary Apollo Theater. Weaned on the music of another blind, black R&B singer – Ray Charles – Wonder learned to play the piano, drums, and harmonica by the age of seven, and began writing songs at eight. Also on the bill for his first Motown tour is 23-year-old singer Marvin Gaye – already part of the Hitsville USA stable as a session drummer and songwriter, and now launching a solo career with the release of *Stubborn Kind Of Fellow*, which is on its way to US No. 46.

keyboardist **Larry Knechtel**, percussionist **Sonny Bono**, drummer **Hal Blaine**, and sax player **Steve Douglas**, along with arranger **Jack Nitzsche**. He has enlisted backing singers **Darlene Love**, **Gracia Nitzsche** (Jack's sister), and **Fanita James** (entirely replacing his New York-based **Crystals** line-up) to record the Gene Pitney-penned *He's A Rebel*. With its immediate success, Spector will use this blueprint – the Gold Star studio, a regular session team, and relatively unknown backing vocalists – to record an unbroken run of hit records over the next four years.

3 **Billboard** magazine drops the word "Western" from the title of its country music chart: the list will now be known as the Hot Country Singles chart.

26 The **Beatles** return to EMI's Abbey Road Studios to cut their second single. They record *Please Please Me*, re-arranged at the behest of producer George Martin from a slow, **Roy Orbison**-styled, number to an uptempo pleaser, and also nail *Ask Me Why*.

28 Following a three-week UK tour (their first since 1958) supporting **Bobby Vee**, the **Crickets** are given miniature cricket bats by Liberty label boss Roy Squires, who says, "They were in recognition of the group's friendliness and co-operation during its tour."

December

7 Bass player **Bill Wyman**, a 26-year-old, former Royal Air Force AC1 Air Craftsman First Class, and ex-member of the Cliftons with Tony Chapman, auditions for the **Rollin' Stones** at the Wetherby Arms at World's End in Chelsea. He will make his debut with the group at at the Ricky Tick Club in the Star and Garter Hotel in Windsor next week.

8 **Alan Freed** leaves radio station WQAM in Miami, and returns to New York to stand trial on December 10 on charges of payola. He is accused of accepting $2,000 from Cognat Distributors, and $700 from Superior Record Sales Company, to give preferential airplay to their respective releases. Refusing to testify at the trial, he will eventually be found guilty of payola, and will be fined $300 and given six months' probation.

9 The **Four Seasons** perform their current, and second straight, US chart-topper, *Big Girls Don't Cry*, on "The Ed Sullivan Show." It will be quickly followed up by their third US No. 1, *Walk Like A Man* (in March next year). Both songs are written by the team of Bob Crewe and Bob Gaudio.

18 Bound by their contract, the **Beatles** return to Hamburg for the fifth and final time, playing 12 more nights at the Star-Club supporting **Johnny & the Hurricanes. Ted Taylor**, of Liverpool group **King Size Taylor & the Dominoes**, tapes their final performance on New Year's Eve. (The recording will be released commercially in 1977.)

22 **Acker Bilk**'s *Stranger On The Shore* creates UK chart history when it drops out of the survey after 55 consecutive weeks, having peaked at No. 2 on the second chart of the year. (Bilk's achievement will stand until early 1968, when **Engelbert Humperdinck**'s *Release Me* notches up 56 consecutive weeks.)

27 **Gene Vincent** is admitted to Middlesex Hospital in London to have a bone-grafting operation on his injured leg, which has recently become inflamed. He will remain in the hospital for about three weeks. At recent one-nighters with **Adam Faith**, Vincent has performed sitting on a stool.

ROOTS During this year: guitarist and R&B aficionado Brian Jones advertises for fellow R&B enthusiasts... at the suggestion of record executive John Wimber, two Southern Californian bands – the Paramours and the Variations – join forces; the union is brief, but Bill Medley and Bobby Hatfield stay together, and are soon dubbed the Righteous Brothers... vocalist Eric Burdon joins the Alan Price Combo – a popular Newcastle-based R&B/rock 'n' roll group – and they gain a regular spot at the city's Downbeat club, picking up a new name, the Animals... New York University student Neil Diamond drops out six months before graduation, and becomes an apprentice songwriter at Sunbeam Music... studying stained-glass design at Kingston College of Art, Eric Clapton makes his first public appearance, as a busker... Stax sessions musicians Booker T. & the MG's cut *Green Onions* one summer Sunday afternoon, when rockabilly singer Billy Lee Riley fails to show to record a jingle by Dale Bowman... and the Paramounts, a strictly by-the-numbers R&B band led by Gary Brooker and Robin Trower, become the resident band at Shades in the English seaside town of Southend; while Trower will become a respected guitarist, Brooker will find lasting fame as the voice and writer of Procol Harum's *A Whiter Shade Of Pale...*

Dec

1962

Dec 22 Bob Dylan makes his first British appearance at the Singers' Club Christmas Party at the Pindar of Wakefield pub, Grays Inn Road, London. (Dylan is in the country to film a BBC-TV play.)

Dylan, who had legally changed his name from Robert Zimmerman to Bob Dylan during the summer, was also about to change the face of popular music, creating a new phenomenon:

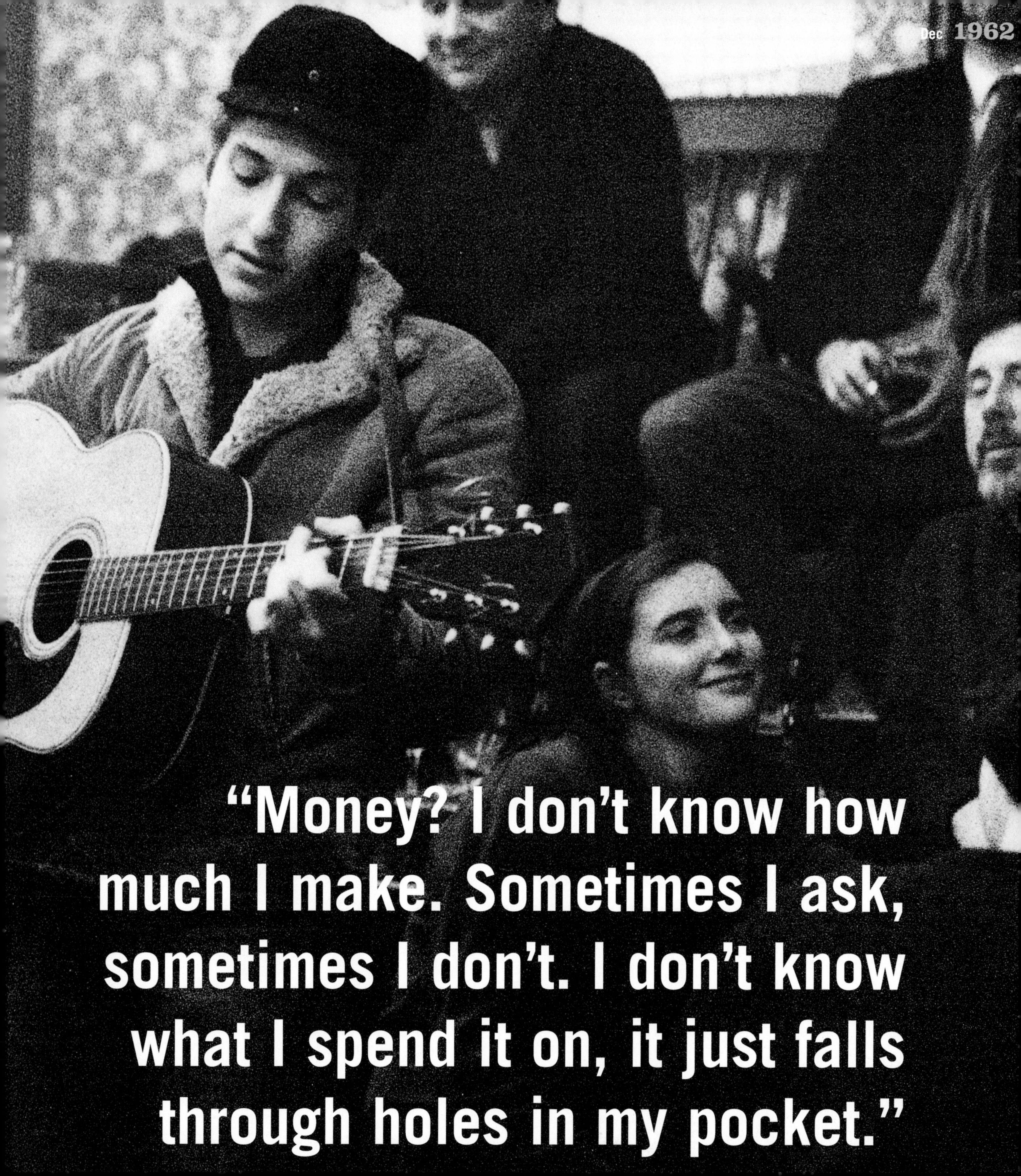

"Money? I don't know how much I make. Sometimes I ask, sometimes I don't. I don't know what I spend it on, it just falls through holes in my pocket."

I Want To Hold Your Hand

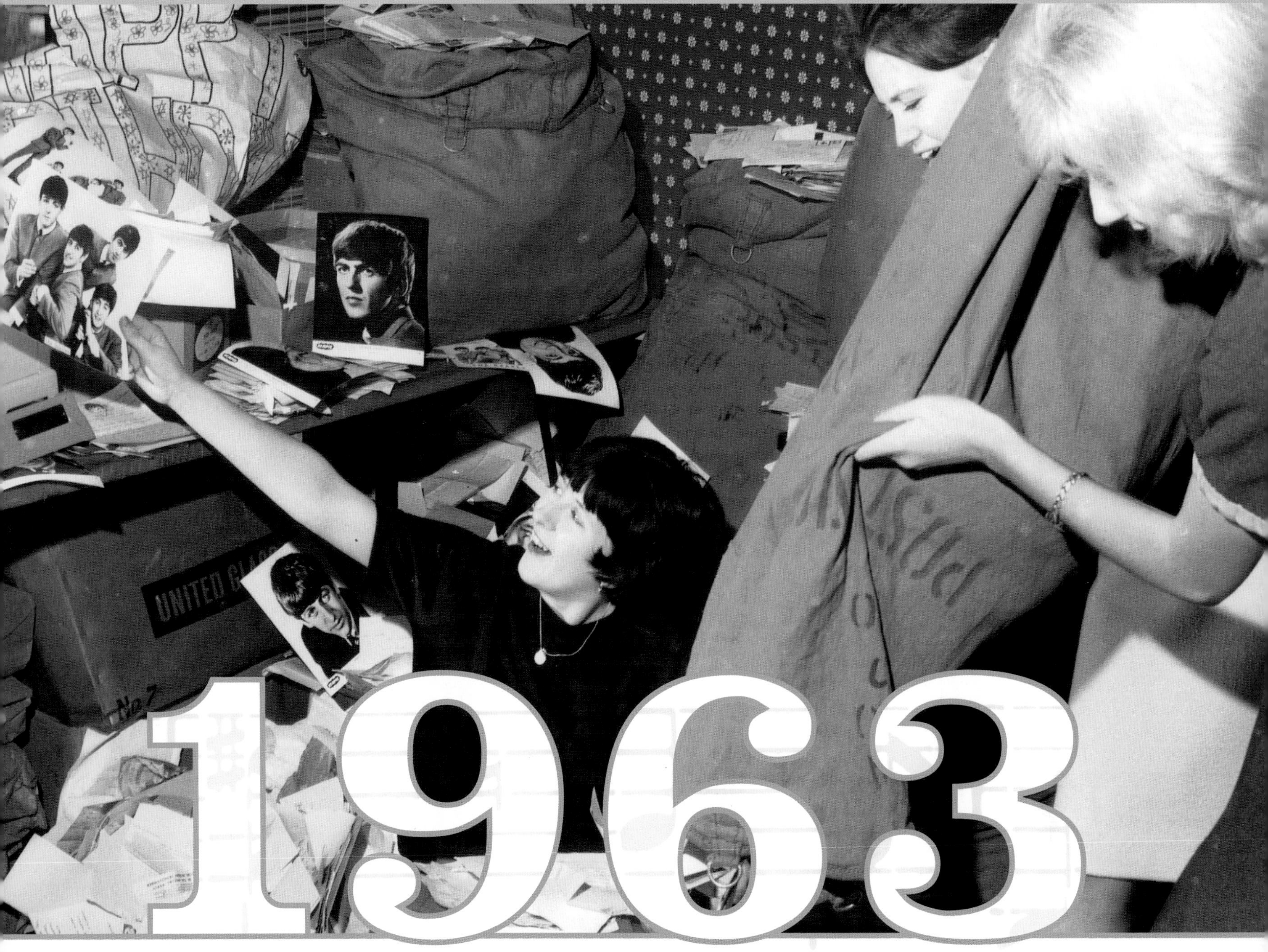

1963

No.1 US SINGLES

Jan 5 Telstar **Tornadoes**
Jan 12 Go Away Little Girl **Steve Lawrence**
Jan 26 Walk Right In **Rooftop Singers**
Feb 9 Hey Paula **Paul & Paula**
Mar 2 Walk Like A Man **Four Seasons**
Mar 23 Our Day Will Come **Ruby & the Romantics**
Mar 30 He's So Fine **Chiffons**
Apr 27 I Will Follow Him **Little Peggy March**
May 18 If You Wanna Be Happy **Jimmy Soul**
June 1 It's My Party **Lesley Gore**
June 15 Sukiyaki **Kyu Sakamoto**
July 6 Easier Said Than Done **Essex**
July 20 Surf City **Jan & Dean**
Aug 3 So Much In Love **Tymes**
Aug 10 Fingertips (Part 2) **Little Stevie Wonder**
Aug 31 My Boyfriend's Back **Angels**
Sept 21 Blue Velvet **Bobby Vinton**
Oct 12 Sugar Shack **Jimmy Gilmer & the Fireballs**
Nov 16 Deep Purple **Nino Tempo & April Stevens**
Nov 23 I'm Leaving It Up To You **Dale & Grace**
Dec 7 Dominique **Singing Nun**

No.1 UK SINGLES

Jan 5 The Next Time/Bachelor Boy **Cliff Richard & the Shadows**
Jan 26 Dance On **Shadows**
Feb 2 Diamonds **Jet Harris & Tony Meehan**
Feb 23 The Wayward Wind **Frank Ifield**
Mar 16 Summer Holiday **Cliff Richard & the Shadows**
Mar 30 Foot Tapper **Shadows**
Apr 6 Summer Holiday **Cliff Richard & the Shadows**
Apr 13 How Do You Do It? **Gerry & the Pacemakers**
May 4 From Me To You **Beatles**
June 22 I Like It **Gerry & the Pacemakers**
July 20 Confessin' (That I Love You) **Frank Ifield**
Aug 3 (You're The) Devil In Disguise **Elvis Presley**
Aug 10 Sweets For My Sweet **Searchers**
Aug 24 Bad To Me **Billy J. Kramer with the Dakotas**
Sept 14 She Loves You **Beatles**

Melody Maker poll winners

Joan Baez and Bob Dylan

Enjoying a knees-up with the Beatles: Billy J. Kramer and Susan Maughan. Kramer had much to thank Lennon and McCartney for, as he racked up three top five hits with their songs during the year. Maughan, coming off a top three hit with ***Bobby's Girl***, would never have major chart success again... Bob Dylan and Joan Baez were part of a movement that mixed politics and music.

It was, simply, rock 'n' roll's finest hour. The **Beatles**, the **Beach Boys**, **Stevie Wonder**, **Bob Dylan**, **Joan Baez**, **Peter, Paul & Mary**, and the **Ronettes**, among many others, made 1963 a milestone in contemporary music. The US saw a remarkable social breakthrough: more than a third of the year's top 100 singles featured female vocalists, and more than a third featured black artists. Above all, it was the Beatles' year – at least in Britain. Their roster of singles in 1963 included *Please Please Me, From Me To You, She Loves You*, and *I Want To Hold Your Hand* – immaculate conceptions as fresh now as when they were recorded under **George Martin**'s direction 40 years ago. Not since **Elvis** had one musical force arrived with such impact, though the fanfare initially made no impression in the US. Decca – anxious not to repeat their mistake in turning down the Beatles – signed the **Rolling Stones**. The band were not yet creating much original material, but gained greater notoriety for their anti-establishment rebelliousness.

The US charts featured the doo-wop-to-pop **Four Seasons**, and the Beach Boys enjoyed four US top 20 hit singles, distinguished by almost mathematically perfect harmonies and superb production. The **Surfaris** climbed on the bandwagon with the brilliant *Wipe Out*. **Phil Spector** continued to produce a string of hits – for the Ronettes, the **Crystals**, and **Darlene Love**. Outside the Philles stable, but with a similar sound, the **Chiffons** came up with *He's So Fine*. LPs were growing in importance, and **James Brown**'s legendary 1962 performance at Harlem's Apollo Theater became a million-seller, while "Little" Stevie Wonder became the first artist to have a No. 1 single with a live recording.

Folk music's combination of radical politics and poetry engendered a massive grassroots following, as hootenannys became the craze of American college campuses. ABC-TV's series of the same name ran into a political morass when it banned **Pete Seeger** – leading Bob Dylan and Joan Baez to boycott it. Within months, Dylan made his amazing debut at the Newport Folk Festival – joined on stage by other artists for the civil rights anthem *We Shall Overcome*. Rock's innocent adolescence was over; for much of the 1960s it would have an angry political edge.

"That vile-looking singer with the tire-tread lips."

Anonymous TV producer on Mick Jagger

Oct 12 Do You Love Me **Brian Poole & the Tremeloes**
Nov 2 You'll Never Walk Alone **Gerry & the Pacemakers**
Nov 30 She Loves You **Beatles**
Dec 14 I Want To Hold Your Hand **Beatles**

The Whisky A Go-Go club opens... The Beatles record their first album...

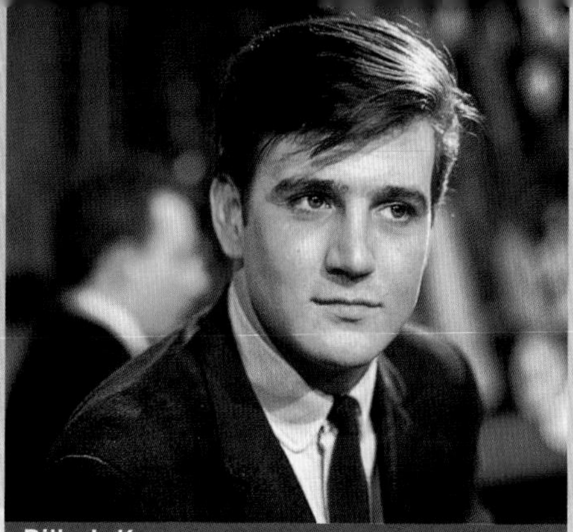
Billy J. Kramer

A photogenic British Railways apprentice by the name of William Howard Ashton became Billy J. Kramer... Giorgio Gomelsky turned a room at Richmond's Station Hotel into the Crawdaddy Rhythm & Blues Club, a focal point for the burgeoning blues and R&B scene in the UK.

January

3 Having flown back from Hamburg on New Year's Day, following their final stint at the Star-Club, the **Beatles** begin a five-date mini-tour of Scotland at the Two Red Shoes Ballroom in Elgin. Yesterday's opening show was canceled because of snowstorms. (At one date they will be billed as "The 'Love Me Do' Boys – The Beatles.")

3 Guaranteed to earn more than $1 million in sales revenue, **Rick Nelson**'s new 20-year contract with Decca Records comes into effect at 3:00 pm when the label signs. A separate agreement providing for two motion pictures is also confirmed. Nelson's deal with Lew Chudd's Imperial label – which has recently paid him some $400,000 in back royalties – ended on December 31.

4 Decca reports that sales of the **Tornados**' *Telstar* up to the last day of 1962 stand at 850,000 in Britain, and 922,000 in the US (where it is still at No. 1).

6 **Billy J. Kramer** signs a six-year management deal with Brian Epstein's NEMS management company. Formerly rhythm guitarist for the Phantoms, 19-year-old Liverpudlian Kramer was spotted by Epstein last December, singing at the Cavern club with the (British) **Coasters**, who were voted No. 3 favorite group in the Mersey Beat magazine poll. Failing to obtain the services of Liverpool's **Remo Four** as a backing group, Epstein will team Kramer with Manchester group, the **Dakotas**, who have been playing professionally for just under a year. They will remain separate entities, and the credit will always be "Billy J. Kramer with the Dakotas."

11 Elmer Valentine and Mario Maglieri's Whisky A Go-Go club – based on the trendy club of the same name in Paris – opens on Sunset Boulevard in Los Angeles. Mini-skirted dancers in cages complement the club's decor. It will soon be a must-play venue for aspiring west coast rock talent, eventually becoming one of the most venerable locations on the live circuit, and operating successfully into the next century.

12 **Sam Cooke** performs at the jam-packed, 2,000-capacity Harlem Square Club in Miami (playing a blinding, high-energy, raw set that will eventually be released as a live album in 1985). In the first show, which starts just after 10:00 pm, Cooke storms through versions of some of his best-known hits, including *Bring It On Home To Me*, *Cupid*, *Chain Gang*, and *Twistin' The Night Away*. A second performance will begin at 1:30 am.

13 BBC-TV broadcasts Evan Jones's play "Madhouse On Castle Street," starring Ursula Howells, Maureen Pryor, and David Warner. **Bob Dylan**, on his first visit to London, portrays a singing hobo, performing *Swan On The River*, *Blowin' In The Wind*, *Hang Me*, and *Cuckoo Bird*.

> **"I couldn't sing the damn thing, I was just screaming."**
>
> John Lennon, on recording *Twist And Shout*

17 **Mick Jagger**, **Keith Richard**, **Brian Jones**, **Bill Wyman**, **Ian Stewart**, and new recruit **Charlie Watts** (who finally acquiesced and joined the **Rollin' Stones** two days ago) perform together for the first time at the Marquee Jazz Club. The London venue will become one of several regular haunts for the Stones over the coming months.

19 The **Beatles** make their first national television appearance, on "Thank Your Lucky Stars." Featured at the bottom of a seven-act bill, they perform *Please Please Me* – which has entered the UK chart this week at No. 45.

21 Radio Luxembourg – the oldest continental European station broadcasting to Britain (since 1933) – devotes its entire "ABC Of The Stars" program to Cliff Richard. Broadcasting on 208khz on the medium wave from its headquarters at the Villa Louvigny, the commercial station has become established as a household name in Britain, and provided an apprentice shop for several top BBC disc jockeys, including Pete Murray, David Jacobs, Teddy Johnson, Alan Freeman, Jimmy Young, Jack Jackson, Brian Matthew, Sam Costa, Keith Fordyce, and Jimmy Savile.

22 **Gerry & the Pacemakers** record two sides at EMI's Abbey Road Studios, yielding the Mitch Murray-penned *How Do You Do It?* (already turned down by **Adam Faith**, and recorded and shelved by the **Beatles**), and Gerry Marsden and Les Chadwick's own *Away From You*. They are the second Liverpool act managed by Brian Epstein to be signed to EMI Records.

The Crawdaddy Club

February

2 The **Beatles** begin their first nationwide UK tour at the Gaumont Cinema in Bradford, on a bill headed by **Helen Shapiro**. By the time the tour closes on March 3, the group will have been promoted from opening the show to closing the first half. Their fee is £80 ($225) a week, shared among all four band members.

11 Taking two days off from their current tour (**Peter Jay & the Jaywalker**s fill in for them), the **Beatles** complete ten new tracks for their debut album, ***Please Please Me***, at EMI's Abbey Road Studios. The single session lasts 15 minutes short of ten hours. **John Lennon** – suffering from a heavy cold – finishes with a cover of the Isley Brothers' *Twist And Shout*, recorded in one take as an afterthought to complete the album.

24 The **Rollin' Stones** begin a Sunday residency at the Station Hotel in Richmond, near London, earning £24 ($67) and attracting an audience of 66. The venue will become the Crawdaddy Rhythm & Blues Club in April.

March

2 While *Walk Like A Man* begins a three-week run at US No. 1, the **Four Seasons** guest on Chubby Checker's "Limbo Party" show, staged at the Cow Palace in San Francisco. With their latest hit, the Four Seasons will have been in pole position for 13 of the last 27 weeks, becoming the first group to score three consecutive US No. 1s. With them are **Marvin Gaye**, the **Crystals**, **Paul & Paula**, 20-year-old newcomer **Lou Christie**, **Dick & Deedee** (*The Mountain's High* hitmakers from Santa Monica), **Bob B. Soxx & the Blue Jeans** (a new trio formed by Phil Spector), the **Alley Cats** (whose line-up includes moonlighting Bob B. Soxx vocalist, Bobby Sheen), actor-singer **Steve Alaimo**, **Dee Dee Sharp**, **Herb Alpert's Tijuana Brass**, and **Bobby Freeman** (an R&B singer who hit big with the rock 'n' roll anthem *Do You Wanna Dance*).

PATSY CLINE

Mar 5 At the age of 30, Patsy Cline is killed in a plane crash near Camden, Tennessee, when returning from a benefit performance in Kansas City for the widow of Cactus Jack Call, a disc jockey recently killed in an auto accident.

Best known for her crossover country hits, including *Walkin' After Midnight*, *I Fall To Pieces*, and her 1961 cover of Willie Nelson's *Crazy*, Cline – known as the Queen of Country – was posthumously inducted into the Country Music Hall of Fame in 1973 and was honored with a Grammy Lifetime Achievement Award in 1995.

Ray Hildebrand and Jill Jackson met at Howard Payne College in Brownwood, Texas. Taking the stage names Paul & Paula, they topped the US chart in February with the romantic *Hey Paula*.

2 Three hundred girls march to Tottenham Town Hall in north London with 4,500 signatures on a petition demanding that the **Dave Clark Five** return to the Royal Ballroom, Tottenham – theater-owner Mecca has switched them to its Basildon venue. Fronted by 20-year-old drummer **Dave Clark** – who formed the band at 17 while working as a film stunt man – the British rock 'n' roll combo recorded for Pye Records last year but have now been picked up by EMI's Columbia label.

5 The **Beatles** record *From Me To You* at EMI's Abbey Road Studios, five days after **John Lennon** and **Paul McCartney** wrote the song while traveling on a bus from York to Shrewsbury, during their tour with Helen Shapiro. The title was inspired by the regular **New Musical Express** letters column, "From You To Us."

8 The **Four Tops** sign to Berry Gordy's fast-moving Motown label, for a $400 advance. Their first recordings will be jazz-laced, with Gordy planning to put them on the specialist Workshop label. The R&B vocal quartet – **Levi Stubbs**, **Renaldo Benson**, **Abdul Fakir**, and **Lawrence Payton** – performed as the Four Aims from 1956. Renamed, they recorded non-charting sides for the Chess label, Red Top, and Columbia, before landing at Motown. They will spend the rest of 1963 singing backup on other Motown artists' records, including the **Supremes**' first Top 30 success, *When The Lovelight Starts Shining Through His Eyes*.

9 Having wound up their tour with **Helen Shapiro** last weekend, the **Beatles** embark on another at the Granada Cinema in East Ham, London, supporting "America's Exciting" **Chris Montez** and "America's Fabulous" **Tommy Roe**. As their fame rapidly spreads around the country, the group will eventually top the bill on the 21-date, twice-nightly tour. (**Lennon**, still suffering from a heavy cold, will miss the dates on the 12th, 13th, and 14th, and the band will play on as a trio.)

The Dave Clark Five won the Mecca Gold Cup as the British ballroom circuit's best band of 1963.

Mar 1963

Producer Quincy Jones's first hit... Bob Dylan's first major solo concert... Andrew Oldham becomes the Rolling Stones' manager...

Lesley Gore

Pete Seeger

9 R&B singer **Bobby "Blue" Bland** celebrates his third US R&B chart-topper with *That's The Way Love Is*. Having been a member of legendary Memphis band the **Beale Streeters**, in 1952, 33-year-old Bland is one of Duke Records' most enduring artists. He will eventually score 63 R&B chart hits in the US, including his biggest crossover success, *Ain't Nothing You Can Do*, next year.

11 The **Rollin' Stones** cut five sides at IBC Studios in Portland Place, London, with engineer Glyn Johns. Choosing material from Jimmy Reed, Bo Diddley, and Willie Dixon, they record *Baby What's Wrong*, *Bright Lights Big City*, *Diddley Daddy*, *I Want To Be Loved*, and *Road Runner*.

21 Having already recorded *Do You Want To Know A Secret?* last week, **Billy J. Kramer** and the **Dakotas** return to Abbey Road Studios to re-record the song, after it has been discovered that there are no vocals on the track. Signed to Parlophone by EMI's George Martin two weeks ago, Kramer and the group have been offered *She's My Girl* by Liverpool songwriter Ralph Bowdler but, because of the Epstein connection, they have access to Lennon and McCartney songs and have selected *I'll Be On My Way*, on which the **Beatles** have passed, and *Do You Want To Know A Secret?*, recorded by the Beatles last month for inclusion on their first album.

30 Having selected *It's My Party* from some 250 demos, **Quincy Jones** produces the cut with 16-year-old singer **Lesley Gore** at Bell Sound Studios, New York, with engineer Phil Ramone at the desk. It will be rush-released after Jones meets Phil Spector this evening on the steps of Carnegie Hall (where **Charles Aznavour** is performing) and learns that Spector intends to cut the same song with the Crystals. The 30-year-old Jones – a staff producer at Mercury Records – has already developed a top-drawer reputation as a gifted producer/arranger/conductor/composer, notably in the big-band field. Beginning as a trumpet player in jazz great **Lionel Hampton**'s combo in 1951, he has worked with **Count Basie**, **Frank Sinatra**, **Tommy Dorsey**, **Brook Benton**, **Dinah Washington**, **Johnny Mathis**, and his childhood friend, **Ray Charles**. He is proving equally comfortable in the pop arena. He spotted Gore singing with a college band in a cocktail lounge at the Prince George Hotel in Manhattan.

Lesley Gore's version of *It's My Party* would give producer Quincy Jones his first US chart-topper on June 1... Pete Seeger's political beliefs led to his being banned by US TV.

Originally a duo called the Two Teens, which grew into the Fourtones before evolving into the Deltas, the Hollies chose their final name as a tribute to Buddy Holly.

April

1 Chess label co-founder **Leonard Chess** unveils an all-black R&B radio station broadcasting on both AM (WVON) and FM (WHFC) in Chicago, and hires disc jockeys Al Benson, Ric Riccardo, Rodney Jones, Herb Kent, Franklyn McCarthy, Wesley South, Purvis Span, and the Reverend Bud Riley. Station manager Frank Ward describes the venture's format as a "pop R&B sound."

4 After recording a session for the BBC Light Programme series "Side By Side" at the Paris Studio in London, the **Beatles** give a late-afternoon performance – for £100 ($280) – at Stowe School in Buckinghamshire. They accepted a personal request from schoolboy Dave Moores, a fellow Liverpudlian.

4 The **Hollies** – based in Manchester, and formed in 1961 by former schoolfriends, singer **Allan Clarke** and guitarist **Graham Nash** – make a test recording for EMI at Abbey Road Studio 2. They cut a revival of the **Coasters**' *(Ain't That) Just Like Me*, which will be their first single, and two originals: *Hey What's Wrong With Me* and *Whole World Over*. They were spotted at Liverpool's Cavern Club by EMI producer Ron Richards, who is checking out the UK beat scene in the wake of the Beatles' success.

4 ABC-TV's "Hootenanny," the first weekly show devoted solely to folk music, premieres at 8:30 pm, featuring the **Limeliters**, **Bud & Travis**, **Bob Gibson**, and **Bonnie Dobson**. A traveling folk music jamboree taped at various college campuses, the show will stir considerable controversy when it blacklists both **Pete Seeger** and his former band, the **Weavers**, because of their political views. The genre's brightest stars – including the **Kingston Trio**, **Peter, Paul & Mary**, **Bob Dylan**, and **Joan Baez** – will boycott the series, which will run until September next year.

6 **Fats Domino** signs a new recording contract with ABC-Paramount, taking him away from Imperial Records, where he has notched up 60 million record sales since 1950. He will log his 60th US chart hit next month with his label debut *There Goes My Heart Again*.

12 **Bob Dylan** performs his first major solo concert at New York's Town Hall. It is recorded (though never released) by Columbia Records. A review of the gig in **Billboard** will opine: "Dylan is the stuff of which legends are made."

18 The BBC broadcasts "Swinging Sound '63" live from the Royal Albert Hall in London. One of a series of three live concerts at the venue, it features the **Beatles**, **Del Shannon**, the **Springfields**, **Kenny Lynch**, **Rolf Harris**, the **Vernons Girls**, **Shane Fenton & the Fentones**, **Lance Percival**, and **George Melly**. Meeting the Beatles, Shannon suggests covering a Lennon and McCartney song to help give them more exposure in the US.

23 Musical and social fraternization between the **Beach Boys** and **Jan & Dean** has led to **Brian Wilson** and **Jan Berry** writing *Surf City*. With the group's voices as backup, Jan & Dean record the song at United/Western Studios in Hollywood (without **Al Jardine**, who left the Beach Boys in January, and is replaced by guitarist **David Marks**). Produced by Berry, it will top the US chart for two weeks in July – a year before the Beach Boys' own first No. 1 – and sell over a million copies.

28 **Andrew Loog Oldham**, a 19-year-old ex-PR man for the Beatles, and a friend of Brian Epstein's, travels to Richmond with business associate Eric Easton to see the **Rollin' Stones** perform at the Crawdaddy Club, on the recommendation of **Record Mirror** journalist Peter Jones, and Beatle **George Harrison**.

> **"The celebrity business is for the birds. Respectability is nice, but consider whom do you most want to respect you?"**
>
> Pete Seeger, **Seventeen** magazine, 1963

May

1 Andrew Oldham and Eric Easton sign the **Rollin' Stones** to their new Impact Sound company, in a management contract that will become effective from May 6. The band become the **Rolling Stones** (adding the "g") at Oldham's insistence. **Ian Stewart** is moved to a backseat role of roadie and backing musician in the studio, as his straight image is seen by Oldham to be at odds with the style he intends to create for the group. Largely unseen by the public, Stewart will nonetheless remain an integral part of the band, and become known as the sixth Stone.

4 The **Beatles**' *From Me To You* tops the UK chart, where it will stay for seven weeks, selling over 650,000 copies. It begins a record-breaking run for the group of 11 No. 1s from now until August 1966.

9 The **Rolling Stones** sign a three-year recording contract with Impact. In turn, Impact concludes a tape/lease agreement with Decca Records – a deal ironically overseen by Dick Rowe, who turned down the Beatles.

10 At Olympic Sound in Barnes, west London, the **Rolling Stones** record *Come On*, an obscure Chuck Berry song, Leiber and Stoller's *Love Potion No. 9*, and versions of Willie Dixon's *I Want To Be Loved* and *Pretty Thing*. Decca will reject the initial recording as "dreadful," and the band will go back into the studio next week to recut the track *Come On*, in part to change the lyric "some stupid jerk" to "some stupid guy" to improve the chance of radio play.

Andrew Loog Oldham was an up-and-coming publicity agent who first saw the Rolling Stones at the recommendation of Record Mirror scribe Peter Jones.

May

1963

Please Please Me... The Monterey Folk Festival... The Crystals' *Da Doo Ron Ron*...

The advent of the Beatles curtailed the career of many a solo singer, but Cliff Richard went on indomitably, adding "movie star" to his résumé... The Searchers made their hit debut with a remake of the Drifters' *Sweets For My Sweet*.

11 In its sixth week on the UK chart, the **Beatles**' ***Please Please Me*** knocks **Cliff Richard and the Shadows**' ***Summer Holiday*** off the top spot. The album showcases the unique and timeless songwriting genius of **Lennon** and **McCartney**, who have penned eight of the twelve cuts, combined with simple vocal harmonies and an excellence in synchronized performing talent demonstrated by all four band members, who complement each other under the wise direction of producer George Martin. In changing the panorama of popular music in the short term, this first release sets the stage for the group's dramatic longterm influence, which will underpin popular culture throughout the decade.

12 Scheduled to perform *Talking John Birch Paranoid Blues* on "The Ed Sullivan Show," **Bob Dylan** is asked by CBS television executives to play a different song, because of the song's wry attacks on segregation and the military. Dylan declines the request, and walks off the set.

15 Columbia recording star vocalist **Tony Bennett**'s career-defining *I Left My Heart In San Francisco* wins Record of the Year and Best Solo Vocal Performance, Male at the fifth annual Grammy awards. **Ray Charles** wins the Best R&B Recording category for the third year running, with *I Can't Stop Loving You*, giving him his sixth award in total. **Peter, Paul & Mary**'s *If I Had A Hammer* is named Best Performance by a Vocal Group, and Best Folk Recording. Despite scoring three No. 1s over the past six months, the **Four Seasons** lose to Robert Goulet in the Best New Artist category. **Bent Fabric**'s novelty instrumental *Alley Cat* beats their *Big Girls Don't Cry* for Best Rock & Roll Recording, and also wins over the first ever Motown recording to be nominated for a Grammy: *You Beat Me To The Punch* by **Mary Wells**.

17 With protest folk singer-songwriters increasingly in vogue, two of the genre's most visible pioneers, **Joan Baez** and **Bob Dylan**, perform at the first Monterey Folk Festival in California, with Baez topping the bill. Today's line-up is completed by **Peter, Paul & Mary**, **Barbara Dane**, **New Lost City Ramblers**, and the **Andrews Sisters**.

18 The **Beatles** begin their third UK tour at the Adelphi Cinema in Slough, opening for **Roy Orbison**, with **Gerry & the Pacemakers**, **David Macbeth**, **Louise Cordet**, **Tony Marsh**, the **Terry Young Six**, **Erkey Grant**, and **Ian Crawford**. In response to audience reaction, the Beatles will again become bill-toppers.

24 Blues legend **Elmore James** dies of a heart attack in Chicago, at the age of 45. He will be remembered as one of the most creative electric guitar pioneers of his era, influencing a host of upcoming rock guitarists, including budding axmen **Keith Richard** and **Brian Jones**.

1963 was Peter, Paul & Mary's finest year, with three albums reaching the Top 10 and a Grammy award.

The Searchers

"Man, things like that shake up the other chicks"

Chubby Checker, denying he'll marry Dee Dee Sharp, June 1963

June

7 The **Rolling Stones** make their television debut, performing *Come On* on "Thank Your Lucky Stars." They have been coerced into wearing uniform check velvet collared jackets, with matching ties and trousers.

8 *Da Doo Ron Ron (When He Walked Me Home)* by the **Crystals**, with La La Brooks on lead vocal, hits US No. 3. Meticulously assembled by producer Phil Spector, it has been recorded over several days at Gold Star by members of the perfectionist's now regular session team, affectionately known as the Wrecking Crew: Larry Levine, engineer, and Jack Nitzsche, arranger, with **Hal Blaine** (drums), **Carol Kaye** and **Ray Pohlman** (bass), **Jimmy Bond** and **Lyle Ritz** (upright bass), **Glen Campbell**, **Barney Kessel**, **Bill Pitman**, **Billy Strange**, and **Tommy Tedesco** (all on guitars), **Al DeLory**, **Larry Knechtel**, **Don Randi**, and **Leon Russell** (pianos), **Steve Douglas** and **Nino Tempo** (sax), **Sonny Bono** and **Frank Capp** (percussion). Always recording in mono, Spector uses numerous musicians, echo effects, and multitrack recording techniques, to create his unique, layered "Wall of Sound" – an unrivaled signature style that will hallmark all future output on the Philles label.

15 A star in his home country for the past five years, **Kyu Sakamoto** becomes the first Japanese artist to top the US Hot 100, with *Sukiyaki.* Released by Capitol, the single is the retitled original Japanese hit, *Ue O Mui Te Aruko* ("Look Up When I Walk"). The song was first recorded outside Japan last year by British jazz artist **Kenny Ball**, and hit UK No. 10.

15 Billboard reports that Beach Boy **Brian Wilson** and his father Murry have formed their own Sea of Tunes Publishing Company, offering the license of pre-recorded surf music compositions to any interested parties. The company will become the home of Brian's valuable **Beach Boys** songs from 1961 to 1967, and will become the subject of much legal wrangling in the future, when Murry sells it to Irving Music in 1969 for a paltry $700,000.

16 With the **Beatles**' *From Me To You* holding off **Gerry & the Pacemakers**' *I Like It* at UK No. 2, and **Billy J. Kramer with the Dakotas** at No. 3 with *Do You Want To Know A Secret?,* all three Liverpool bands play the first of two consecutive dates at the Odeon Cinema in Romford, Essex. The remaining act on the bill – the **Vikings** – will fail to conquer the charts. No. 4 on this week's chart is the Liverpool-born **Billy Fury**, with *When Will You Say I Love You.*

24 While his first chart record, *These Arms Of Mine,* is still peaking on the US pop and R&B surveys, **Otis Redding** begins what is only his second full recording session at Stax studios in Memphis. The 21-year-old singer-songwriter/producer/pianist, from Dawson, Georgia, managed by Phil Walden, first recorded as lead singer with **Johnny Jenkins & the Pinetoppers** in 1960 for the Confederate label. Last October, Redding (who was also the band's driver) persuaded Stax label boss Jim Stewart to let him tape a couple of solo songs while he was waiting for Jenkins to finish his own recordings. Stewart was impressed by both *These Arms Of Mine* and a **Little Richard**-styled original, *Hey Hey Baby,* and has signed Redding to his new Stax imprint label, Volt.

29 "Lucky Stars Summer Spin," the summer spinoff of "Thank Your Lucky Stars," is devoted to the Mersey Sound. It features the **Beatles**, **Gerry & the Pacemakers**, **Billy J. Kramer with the Dakotas**, and the **Fourmost** – a new signing to Parlophone who are being launched with their first single, the Lennon and McCartney-penned *Hello Little Girl.* Also making their television debut are the **Searchers**, yet another Liverpool beat quartet (comprising **Mike Pender**, **Tony Jackson**, **John McNally**, and **Chris Curtis**) who have come up through the Hamburg/Liverpool club scene. Signed to Pye Records by A&R producer/songwriter Tony Hatch, the group's label debut, *Sweets For My Sweet,* enters the UK survey today.

29 Making good on his April promise to the Beatles, **Del Shannon**'s version of *From Me To You* becomes the first Lennon and McCartney composition to enter the US chart, set to peak at No. 77.

A high school dropout, Otis Redding's earliest influence was Little Richard, before he established himself as an influence on others.

The Beatles' last gig at the Cavern... "Ready Steady Go"... The Ronettes...

Cilla Black

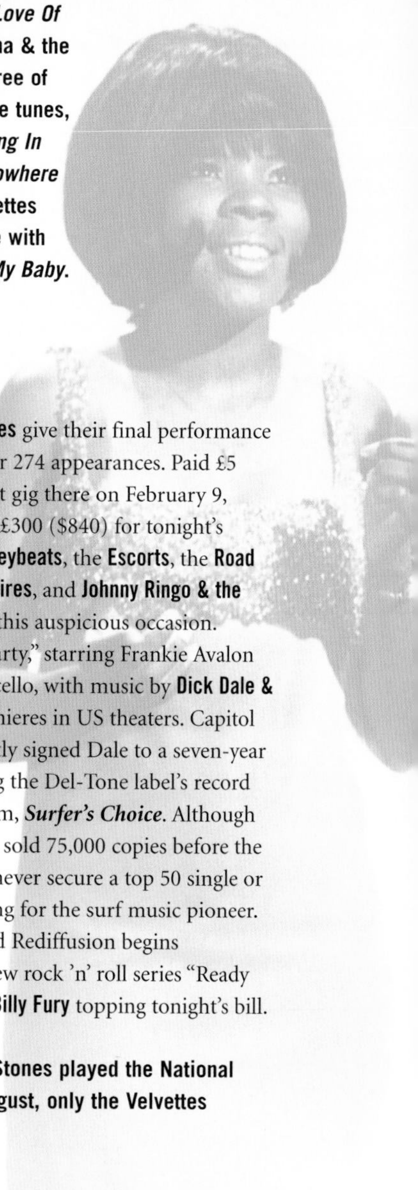

Cilla Black began her chart career with a Lennon/McCartney song, *Love Of The Loved*... Martha & the Vandellas sang three of Motown's signature tunes, *Heat Wave*, *Dancing In The Street*, and *Nowhere To Run*... The Ronettes burst on the scene with their seismic *Be My Baby*.

July

10 The Gordy label releases *Heat Wave* by **Martha & the Vandellas**. Motown's Mickey Stevenson spotted 21-year-old **Martha Reeves** in 1961, performing in a Detroit nightclub. On her audition day, she was instead hired as a secretary in the A&R department, working for Smokey Robinson, Robert Bateman, and the Holland/Dozier/Holland writing team. One of her jobs was to sing new lyrics on to tapes for artists, normally backup singers, who needed to learn the words. If a backing singer was absent from a session, the producer, familiar with Reeves's voice, would often suggest she fill the role – notably on the first few singles for **Marvin Gaye**. With **Annette Sterling** and **Rosalind Ashford** (her ex-high school friends, and backing singers in their earlier trio, the Del-Phis), Reeves finally got her own shot last September, recording *I'll Have To Let Him Go*. With *Heat Wave* set to hit US No. 4, Motown launches yet another successful act.

18 The **Beatles** start work on their second album in Studio 2 at EMI's Abbey Road Studios. The four tracks they record – *You Really Got A Hold On Me*, *Money (That's What I Want)*, *(There's A) Devil In Her Heart*, and *Till There Was You* – are all cover versions of American songs.

26 **Bob Dylan** performs at the three-day Newport Folk Festival, closing the opening day with a performance of *We Shall Overcome*, backed by a chorus comprising **Peter, Paul & Mary**, **Joan Baez**, **Theodore Bikel**, **Pete Seeger**, and the **Freedom Singers**.

29 With the hot-rod music scene moving into second gear – and promoting the current **Beach Boys** B-side single, *Little Deuce Coupe* (which will reach No. 15) – Capitol Records sends out a glossary of hip "hot-rod" words and phrases to disc jockeys and radio stations around the US. An entire album of the Boys' hot-rod material, ***Little Deuce Coupe***, will be released just a month after the October issue of a complete album of Beach Boys surf-only songs, ***Surfer Girl***. Both sets will be produced and largely written by **Brian Wilson**, and each will be trademarked by his remarkable talent in vocal harmony and melody. Thematically, Wilson is creating a steady stream of timeless, fun, summertime pop anthems.

August

3 The **Beatles** give their final performance at the Cavern, after 274 appearances. Paid £5 ($14) for their first gig there on February 9, 1961, they receive £300 ($840) for tonight's farewell. The **Merseybeats**, the **Escorts**, the **Road Runners**, the **Sapphires**, and **Johnny Ringo & the Colts** also play on this auspicious occasion.

7 "Beach Party," starring Frankie Avalon and Annette Funicello, with music by **Dick Dale & His Del-Tones**, premieres in US theaters. Capitol Records has recently signed Dale to a seven-year contract, acquiring the Del-Tone label's record master of his album, ***Surfer's Choice***. Although the LP has already sold 75,000 copies before the deal, Capitol will never secure a top 50 single or album chart placing for the surf music pioneer.

9 Associated Rediffusion begins broadcasting its new rock 'n' roll series "Ready Steady Go!" with **Billy Fury** topping tonight's bill.

When the Rolling Stones played the National Jazz Festival in August, only the Velvettes got lower billing.

Martha & the Vandellas

The Ronettes

With its "The weekend starts here!" catchphrase, the show – co-hosted by Keith Fordyce and demure mod Cathy McGowan – becomes the hippest music showcase on British television. Although the original theme tune is the **Surfaris**' current US No. 2 smash, *Wipe Out*, it will soon by replaced by *5-4-3-2-1*, by upcoming British beat group **Manfred Mann**, which becomes synonymous with the show. Its success will see a **Ready Steady Go** magazine launched in 1964, and a spinoff program called "Ready Steady Win!" that will search for new pop talent. The main series will run until December 1966.

11 Dashing from their regular lunchtime gig at London's Studio 51, the **Rolling Stones** play on the second day of the third National Jazz Festival at Richmond Athletic Grounds, for which they are paid £30 ($84). The festival still has a predominantly jazz line-up: the **Tubby Hayes Quintet**, **Chris Barber's Jazz Band**, the **Humphrey Lyttelton Band**, **Terry Lightfoot's Jazzmen**, and **Acker Bilk's Paramount Jazz Band** are among the featured acts. However, the presence of the Rolling Stones, **Long John Baldry**, and **Cyril Davies & His Rhythm and Blues All Stars**, begins a move to include other genres during the rest of the 1960s.

24 **"Little" Stevie Wonder**, age 13, becomes the first artist in US chart history to have an album – *Little Stevie Wonder/The 12 Year Old Genius* – and a single – *Fingertips Pt 2* – simultaneously hit the number No. 1 spot. This live version 45 also becomes Motown's second chart-topper.

28 **Joan Baez** performs at the Lincoln Memorial, at the end of a historic march on Washington, singing *Oh Freedom* and *We Shall Overcome*. Speaking from the steps of the Memorial to more than 200,000 people who have marched for jobs, justice, and peace, the Reverend Martin Luther King Jr. delivers an emotionally charged speech which includes the repeated refrain, "I have a dream..." With the Reverend recently signed to Motown, this historic moment is recorded to be released in October as ***The March on Washington***. Also lending support at the event are folk singers **Odetta**, **Peter, Paul & Mary**, **Bob Dylan**, and gospel great **Mahalia Jackson**.

29 Acerbic folk singer-songwriter **Phil Ochs** performs a "hoot" for shoppers at the Garden State Plaza mall in New Jersey. The craze for the hootenanny – an informal folk gathering – has reached the mainstream from its roots on college campuses.

September

6 **Cilla Black** – a 20-year-old Liverpudlian singer – signs a management contract with Brian Epstein at her parents' home in Liverpool. She auditioned for Epstein in a Birkenhead club, backed by the **Beatles**, and made a recording test for EMI on July 25, after George Martin spotted her while checking out **Gerry & the Pacemakers** in Liverpool last December. A former cloakroom attendant at the Cavern, Black (whose real name is Priscilla White – her performing name is the result of a mistake in an article in the **Mersey Beat**) is currently billed as "Swinging Cilla." Signed to Parlophone, she will soon become the leading female voice of the massive pop invasion emanating from Merseyside.

10 As the **Daily Mirror** publishes an interview under the heading "Four Frenzied Little Lord Fauntleroys Who Are Making £50,000 Every Week," the **Beatles** are honored with the Top Vocal Group of the Year award at the Variety Club of Great Britain luncheon at London's Savoy Hotel. As **John Lennon** and **Paul McCartney** are leaving the Savoy, a chance meeting with Andrew Oldham – who used to work for the Beatles – leads to their visiting Studio 51, where the **Rolling Stones** are rehearsing. The Stones are unable to decide on a second single, so Lennon and McCartney play part of a new song they are writing, *I Wanna Be Your Man*, and complete it within minutes. This puts the Stones in the privileged position of recording an unreleased Lennon/McCartney composition. (The Beatles will record their own version tomorrow, with Ringo on lead vocals.)

14 The Lennon and McCartney-penned instant pop classic *She Loves You*, tops the British chart. (With a reported advance order of 310,000 copies, it will sell 1.6 million in the UK alone, and remain Britain's best-selling single until 1977.) After a four-week stay at No. 1 – holding off **Cliff Richard**'s *It's All In The Game* for three weeks, it will be replaced by **Brian Poole & the Tremeloes**' *Do You Love Me*, followed by **Gerry & the Pacemakers**' *You'll Never Walk Alone*, but will return to the top slot on November 30, three days after passing the million mark.

28 The **Ronettes** perform *Be My Baby* on "American Bandstand." Formed in New York in 1958 as the Darling Sisters, **Veronica Bennett** (who will become the producer's wife, and thereafter be known as **Ronnie Spector**), her sister **Estelle**, and cousin **Nedra Talley** have been backing singers for Philles since 1962, and are now heading up the US chart with their archetypally Spector-sounding debut.

29 The **Rolling Stones** start their first British tour, a 32-date package supporting the **Everly Brothers** and **Bo Diddley** (on his first UK visit) at London's New Victoria Theatre. Out of respect for the blues legend, the Stones will drop Diddley's songs from their act.

"I have a dream that my four children will one day live in a nation where they will not be judged by the color of their skin but by the content of their character. I have a dream today."

Martin Luther King Jr, August 28, 1963

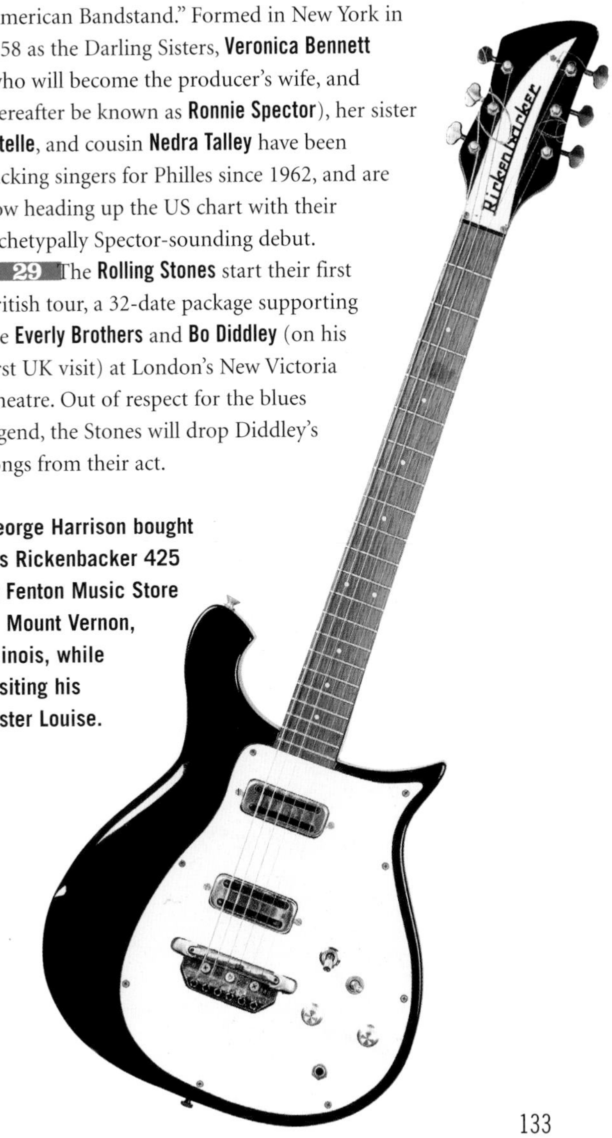

George Harrison bought his Rickenbacker 425 at Fenton Music Store in Mount Vernon, Illinois, while visiting his sister Louise.

Oct 1963

"Beatlemania" begins... Phil Spector's Christmas album... The Singing Nun...

The Beatles on "Ready Steady Go!"

October

4 The **Beatles** make their first appearance on "Ready Steady Go!" miming to *Twist And Shout*, *I'll Get You*, and *She Loves You*. They are briefly interviewed by fellow guest **Dusty Springfield**, whose solo career is about to begin in earnest with *I Only Want To Be With You*, which will zoom to UK No. 4 in December.

12 With the **Ronettes** at US No. 2 with *Be My Baby*, yet another girl group, the Bronx-based vocal quartet the **Chiffons**, perform their recent US chart-topper *He's So Fine*, and their follow-up hit, *One Fine Day*, on "American Bandstand." Underpinned by its infectious "doo-lang" backing chant, *He's So Fine* has spent four weeks in poll position.

13 The **Beatles** make their bill-topping debut on "Sunday Night At The London Palladium." Subsequent press stories will report scenes of hysteria among fans outside the venue, and the term "Beatlemania" will be coined. American R&B singer **Brook Benton** also appears on the show, which attracts a television audience of 15 million viewers.

19 The Greatest Record Show of 1963 UK tour, with hot American performers **Dion**, **Lesley Gore**, **Brook Benton**, and **Timi Yuro**, begins at London's Finsbury Park Astoria. Also on the bill is **Trini Lopez**, a pop-folk singer signed to Frank Sinatra's Reprise label. He is currently enjoying a No. 3 hit in the US with his version of Pete Seeger's *If I Had A Hammer*.

November

1 The **Beatles**' Autumn Tour opens at the Odeon Cinema, Cheltenham, as Beatlemania begins to grip the UK. The group returned yesterday from a six-date tour of Sweden, and their first official headlining trek is a 33-date, twice-nightly package, with **Peter Jay & the Jaywalkers**, the **Brook Brothers**, the **Vernons Girls**, the **Kestrels**, the **Rhythm & Blues Quartet**, and host Frank Berry.

2 **Gerry & the Pacemakers**' anthemic revival of Rodgers and Hammerstein's *You'll Never Walk Alone* (from the musical "Carousel") begins a four-week run at UK No. 1, and will prove to be their biggest UK seller (776,000 copies). Recorded on July 2, the record will become synonymous with the group, the city of Liverpool and particularly its soccer team, whose fans will subsequently adopt the song as their defining tribal chant. It also gives the group the unique distinction of having topped the UK chart with their first three singles, an achievement that will stand for 21 years.

2 Replacing themselves at US No. 1, **Peter, Paul & Mary**'s ***In The Wind*** takes over from their debut LP ***Peter, Paul & Mary***, which is at No. 2, with their second album, ***Moving***, still at No. 6. ***In The Wind*** features the Bob Dylan compositions *Blowin' In The Wind* and *Don't Think Twice, It's Alright*. (Meanwhile, Dylan's own album, ***The Freewheelin' Bob Dylan***, is having more modest success, having already peaked at US No. 22.) With folk music sales at an all-time high, Joan Baez's second live album, ***Joan Baez In Concert, Part 2***, will be released in December by Vanguard Records. It will begin its climb to US No. 7 while her first set is still only midway through its stay of over two years in the chart.

4 The **Beatles** receive a royal seal of approval from the Queen Mother, Princess Margaret, and Lord Snowdon, when the group perform in the Royal Variety Performance at London's Prince of Wales Theatre. John Lennon provokes major headlines in tomorrow morning's newspapers when he addresses the audience: "For our last number I'd like to ask your help. The people in the cheaper seats clap your hands, and the rest of you, if you'd just rattle your jewellery. We'd like to sing a song called *Twist And Shout*."

5 The **Daily Mirror** headlines an editorial "Yeah! Yeah! Yeah!" and continues: "You have to be a real sour square not to love the nutty, noisy, happy, handsome Beatles. If they don't sweep your blues away, brother, you're a lost cause. If they don't put a beat in your feet, sister, you're not listening."

8 **Dick Clark**'s latest Caravan of Stars package tour gets under way in Teaneck, New Jersey. The bill features the **Ronettes**, **Bobby Vee**, **Brian Hyland**, the **Dovells**, the locomoting **Little Eva**, **Paul & Paula**, the **Tymes**, **Jimmy Clanton**, **Linda Scott**, the **Essex** (hot off their US No. 1 summer smash *Easier Said Than Done*) the **Jaynettes**, the **Dixie Belles**, **Joe Perkins**, **Donald Jenkins**, and the **De-Lighters**.

20 The **Rolling Stones** begin the first of two days of recording at Regent Sound Studios in London. They cut ten tracks, including *That Girl Belongs To Yesterday*, which **Mick Jagger** and **Keith Richard** gave to American singer **Gene Pitney** at the recording of "Thank Your Lucky Stars" at the weekend. This marks the beginning of a songwriting partnership that will supply songs to other artists, though it will be almost a year before Jagger and Richard write an original for the Stones.

22 Pop vocal duo **Dale & Grace** (Dale Houston and Grace Broussard), currently at US No. 1 with the pop ballad *I'm Leaving It Up To You*, are touring as part of the latest Dick Clark Caravan of Stars package. Having played in Dallas last night, they are on Main Street watching President Kennedy's motorcade moments before he is assassinated.

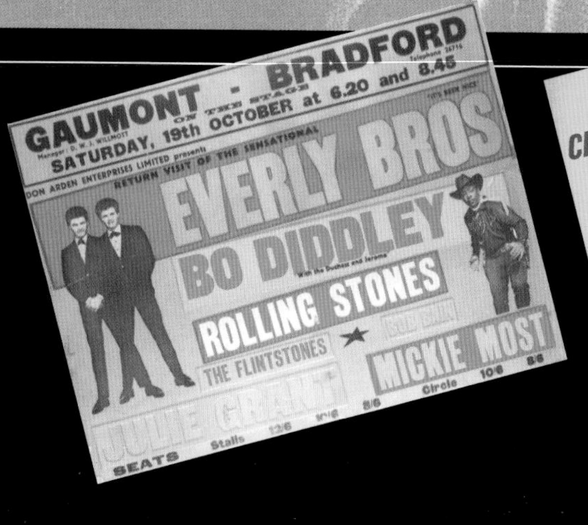

The Stones toured with the Everly Brothers and Bo Diddley... The Beach Boys, were only months away from their first worldwide hit, *I Get Around*... Beatles fans could have their heroes hanging from their Christmas trees.

Gerry & the Pacemakers

The Singing Nun

The Beatles ended 1963 at Nos. 1 and 2 with *I Want To Hold Your Hand* and *She Loves You*, two of Lennon/McCartney's 11 hit songs during the year... Unlike many Liverpool acts, Gerry & the Pacemakers didn't have to turn to the songs of Lennon/McCartney to have success, achieving three UK No. 1s... The Singing Nun initially recorded her song *Dominique* for personal use, mainly in order to give copies to friends.

22 The result of 14-hour days in the recording studio, **Phil Spector**'s ***A Christmas Gift For You*** is released by Philles. The album will fail to chart, as its sales prospects are seriously affected by weeks of national mourning following Kennedy's assassination, but it will be revered in later years as a seminal Christmas collection. It features a mix of seasonal standards and new Spector compositions performed by acts on the Philles label, all gift-wrapped in a "Wall of Sound."

14 Breaking sales and chart records at every turn, the **Beatles**' *I Want To Hold Your Hand* begins a five-week ride at UK No. 1. After an initial advance order of 940,000, it will sell 1.5 million copies in the UK and worldwide sales will total 15 million. It dethrones *She Loves You*, the first time an act has replaced itself at No. 1 in Britain. (**John Lennon** will posthumously equal this in 1981, when *Woman* replaces *Imagine* at No. 1.) *I Want To Hold Your Hand* is the ninth UK chart-topper from a Liverpool-based band during the year.

"You have to be a real sour square not to love the nutty, noisy, happy, handsome Beatles."

Daily Mirror, November 5, 1963

December

7 All four **Beatles** appear on "Juke Box Jury." They vote on the record that they will knock off the top in the US in eight weeks' time – **Bobby Vinton**'s *There! I've Said It Again* – declaring it a "miss." With advance orders of 270,000, and having entered at No. 2 last week, ***With The Beatles*** tops the UK chart, displacing ***Please Please Me***. (Combined, the two albums hold the top spot on the chart continuously from May 1963 to May 1964.) Once again mixing **Lennon** and **McCartney** originals with covers of a few of the group's favorite American R&B tracks (including *You Really Got A Hold On Me* and Chuck Berry's *Roll Over Beethoven*), ***With The Beatles*** will become the first million-selling album in the UK. It will even reach No. 11 in the **New Musical Express** singles chart, which includes all records irrespective of format.

14 Jazz-blues/R&B great **Dinah Washington** heads for "Soulville" – the title of her last hit – dying from a combination of weight-reduction pills and alcohol overdose in Detroit.

17 Carroll James Jr. becomes the first DJ to play a Beatles song in the US, on Washington station WWDC. A British flight attendant has brought a copy over from England. James will also host the Beatles' first US concert next year.

24 The **Beatles**' Christmas Show, a mix of music and pantomime, with **Rolf Harris**, the **Barron Knights**, **Tommy Quickly**, the **Fourmost**, **Billy J. Kramer with the Dakotas**, and **Cilla Black**, opens at London's Finsbury Park Astoria. The 100,000 tickets available for the 30-performance run sold out by November 16.

27 **The Times** music critic William Mann hails Lennon and McCartney as "the outstanding English composers of 1963." In an editorial, which Beatles fans may need a music dictionary to translate, Mann goes on to say, "one gets the impression that they think simultaneously of harmony and melody, so firmly are the major tonic sevenths and ninths built into their tunes, and the flat submediant key switches, so natural is the Aeolian cadence at the end of *Not A Second Time* (the chord progression which ends Mahler's 'Song of the Earth')." In this week's edition of **The Sunday Times**, journalist Richard Buckle will suggest that the songwriters are "the greatest composers since Beethoven."

28 Only four months after **"Little" Stevie Wonder** made US chart history, by simultaneously having an album and a single from that album at No. 1, the **Singing Nun** replicates the achievement. The LP, ***The Singing Nun***, and its extracted 45, *Dominique*, both hit the top spot. The album has so far sold 670,000 copies, and the single, 700,000. An unusual hitmaker, the Singing Nun is Sister Luc-Gabrielle (real name Jeanine Deckers) whose uplifting, melodic songs first became popular among the other Sisters at the Dominican Fichermont Convent in Belgium.

The Beatles's EPs and LPs were bought in such quantities that some of them sold enough to make the singles chart.

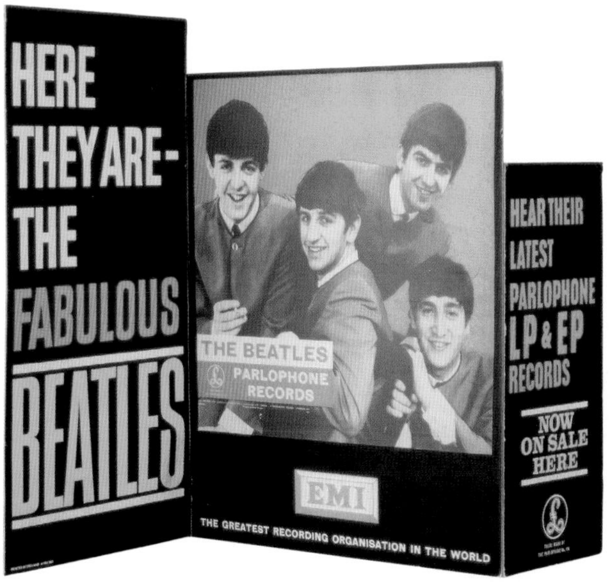

HERE THEY ARE- THE FABULOUS BEATLES
THE BEATLES
PARLOPHONE RECORDS
EMI
THE GREATEST RECORDING ORGANISATION IN THE WORLD
HEAR THEIR LATEST PARLOPHONE LP & EP RECORDS
NOW ON SALE HERE

ROOTS During this year: Edinburgh-born Ian Anderson and fellow blues-minded friends play their first gig as the Blades in Blackpool, for the princely sum of £2 ($5.60); they soon change their name to the John Evan Band, after their drummer, whose mother provided them with their van, but only a further name-change, to Jethro Tull, will bring them success... music industry jack-of-all-trades Sonny Bono meets aspiring actress Cherilyn La Piere Sarkisian at Aldo's Coffee Shop in Los Angeles... five-year-old Michael Jackson makes his debut with his brothers at a nightclub in Gary, Indiana, for which they are paid just $8, but collect more than $100 in coins and bills thrown on stage... teens James Taylor and Danny Kortchmar meet in Chilmark, Martha's Vineyard, and soon enter a local hootenanny contest, which they win... a disparate band of Bay Area bohemians come together in Palo Alto as Mother McCree's Uptown Jug Champions; led by Jerry Garcia, the nine-strong collective also includes Ron McKernan, Bill Kreutzmann, Bob Weir, and Robert Hunter... and R&B/beat group Them, featuring lead singer Van Morrison, secure a residency at the R&B club in Belfast's Maritime Hotel...

I'm Into Something Good

1964

No.1 US SINGLES

Jan 4 There! I've Said It Again **Bobby Vinton**
Feb 2 I Want To Hold Your Hand **Beatles**
Mar 21 She Loves You **Beatles**
Apr 4 Can't Buy Me Love **Beatles**
May 9 Hello, Dolly! **Louis Armstrong**
May 16 My Guy **Mary Wells**
May 30 Love Me Do **Beatles**
June 6 Chapel Of Love **Dixie Cups**
June 27 A World Without Love **Peter & Gordon**
July 4 I Get Around **Beach Boys**
July 18 Rag Doll **Four Seasons**
Aug 1 A Hard Day's Night **Beatles**
Aug 15 Everybody Loves Somebody **Dean Martin**
Aug 22 Where Did Our Love Go **Supremes**
Sept 5 The House Of The Rising Sun **Animals**
Sept 26 Oh, Pretty Woman **Roy Orbison**
Oct 17 Do Wah Diddy Diddy **Manfred Mann**
Oct 31 Baby Love **Supremes**
Nov 28 Leader Of The Pack **Shangri-Las**
Dec 5 Ringo **Lorne Greene**
Dec 12 Mr. Lonely **Bobby Vinton**
Dec 19 Come See About Me **Supremes**
Dec 26 I Feel Fine **Beatles**

No.1 UK SINGLES

Jan 4 I Want To Hold Your Hand **Beatles**
Jan 18 Glad All Over **Dave Clark Five**
Feb 1 Needles And Pins **Searchers**
Feb 22 Diane **Bachelors**
Feb 29 Anyone Who Had A Heart **Cilla Black**
Mar 21 Little Children **Billy J. Kramer with the Dakotas**
Apr 4 Can't Buy Me Love **Beatles**
Apr 25 World Without Love **Peter & Gordon**
May 9 Don't Throw Your Love Away **Searchers**
May 23 Juliet **Four Pennies**
May 30 You're My World **Cilla Black**
June 27 It's Over **Roy Orbison**
July 11 House Of The Rising Sun **Animals**
July 18 It's All Over Now **Rolling Stones**
July 25 A Hard Day's Night **Beatles**
Aug 15 Do Wah Diddy Diddy **Manfred Mann**
Aug 29 Have I The Right? **Honeycombs**
Sept 12 You Really Got Me **Kinks**
Sept 26 I'm Into Something Good **Herman's Hermits**
Oct 10 Oh Pretty Woman **Roy Orbison**

The Rolling Stones

The Temptations

On their arrival in New York for their first US tour, the Rolling Stones claimed that their long hair was "a style set by Charles I"... It was only with the arrival of David Ruffin's tenor vocals, that the Temptations had chart success with three hits in 1964, before hitting the top with *My Girl* in 1965.

"The British are coming." The **Beatles** kicked off the transatlantic invasion, arriving in New York to mass teenage hysteria – a scene that was repeated everywhere they went. Their exuberance and wit, and above all the fresh sound of the Lennon/McCartney compositions, filled a void for American teenagers, for whom the **Beach Boys, Motown**, and **Phil Spector**'s "Wall of Sound" weren't enough. The Beatles drew on the best of **Chuck Berry**, **Buddy Holly**, **Elvis**, and the **Everly Brothers**, while being in complete command of their own songs. Perhaps, also, America was looking for something to cheer it in the months following JFK's assassination.

The Beatles' success led US labels to snatch up other British groups, and the **Dave Clark Five**, the **Rolling Stones, Gerry & the Pacemakers**, the **Searchers**, and the **Animals** all enjoyed fervent favor. The Stones' blues-tinted rock found an immediate audience in the US – among the fans – though politicians and police chiefs were less enthusiastic. It was an uncomfortable year for the Establishment on both sides of the Atlantic. The Stones were condemned for everything from their unkempt hair to lack of neckties, and **Bill Wyman** and **Mick Jagger** spent a good deal of time in court. The radio monopoly (and respectability) of the BBC was challenged by "pirate" stations, broadcasting songs that the Corporation would not. And when the Beatles received MBEs, other recipients returned their medals in disgust. The cleavage between generations was perhaps at its greatest since Elvis had broken through.

American artists hadn't gone into hibernation. R&B enjoyed a golden year: the **Supremes** were the latest Motown act to sweep up the singles chart, and the **Temptations** had their breakthrough hit, as did **Dionne Warwick** with *Anyone Who Had A Heart*. This and her equally effortless second hit, *Walk On By*, were written by the Brill Building team of **Burt Bacharach** and **Hal David**. The year's greatest loss was an underrated R&B pearl: **Sam Cooke**, who was able to marry the perfect lyrical sentiment with the perfect melody, all wrapped up in a golden voice. In one all-night session in June, **Bob Dylan** cut his last entirely acoustic album for 30 years. Less polemical and more personal, it disappointed some in the folk movement. He was both influenced by and influenced the British new wave. As he said later: "[The Beatles] were doing things that nobody was doing. Their chords were outrageous, just outrageous, and their harmonies made it all valid."

"It's just rock and roll, it just so happens we write most of it." John Lennon, June 11, 1964

Oct 24	(There's) Always Something There To Remind Me **Sandie Shaw**
Nov 14	Oh Pretty Woman **Roy Orbison**
Nov 21	Baby Love **Supremes**
Dec 5	Little Red Rooster **Rolling Stones**
Dec 12	I Feel Fine **Beatles**

"Top of the Pops"... *Louie Louie* by the Kingsmen... The Beatles arrive in New York...

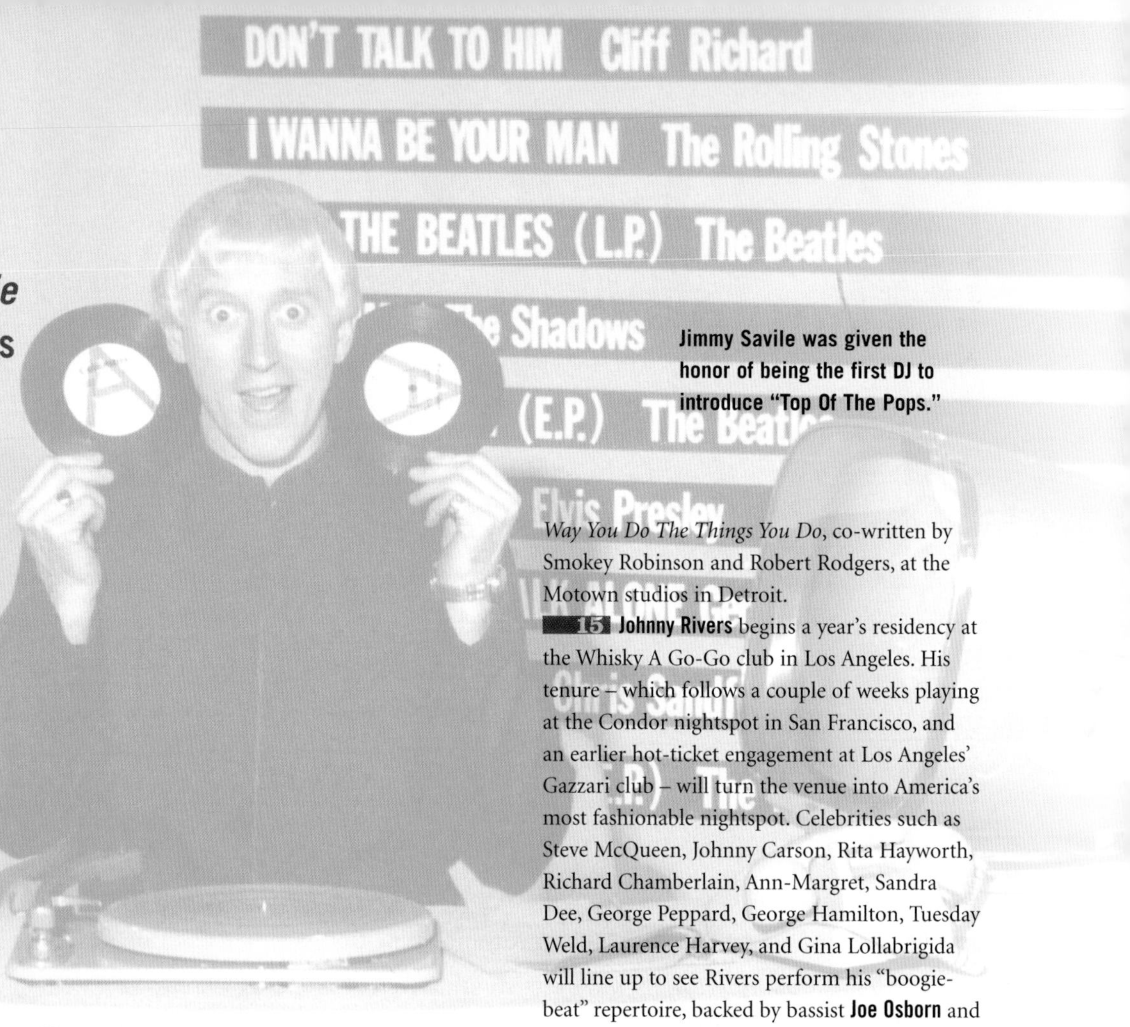

Jimmy Savile was given the honor of being the first DJ to introduce "Top Of The Pops."

January

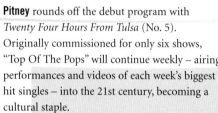

1 At 6:36 pm, "Top Of The Pops" airs on British television for the first time. Broadcast live from a converted church in Dickinson Road, Manchester, it is introduced by DJ Jimmy Savile, with Denise Sampey "spinning" the 45s. It opens with **Dusty Springfield** lip-synching to *I Only Want To Be With You*, currently at No. 4 in the BBC chart. She is followed in the studio by the **Rolling Stones** (performing *I Wanna Be Your Man*, which is at No. 11), the **Dave Clark Five** (*Glad All Over*, the BBC's No. 1), the **Hollies** (*Stay*, new at No. 12), and the **Swinging Blue Jeans** (*Hippy Hippy Shake*, No. 3 – the second single by yet another new Liverpool quartet). The rest of the show features **Cliff Richard and the Shadows** (*Don't Talk To Him*, No. 15), **Freddie & the Dreamers** on film performing *You Were Made For Me* (No. 4), followed by the **Beatles**' *She Loves You* (No. 6) and *I Want To Hold Your Hand* (joint No. 1 with the Dave Clark Five) on disc. **Gene Pitney** rounds off the debut program with *Twenty Four Hours From Tulsa* (No. 5). Originally commissioned for only six shows, "Top Of The Pops" will continue weekly – airing performances and videos of each week's biggest hit singles – into the 21st century, becoming a cultural staple.

6 The **Rolling Stones** begin their second British tour – their first as bill-toppers – on a 14-date Group Scene 1964 package, supported by the **Ronettes**, **Marty Wilde**, the **Swinging Blue Jeans**, **Dave Berry & the Cruisers**, and the **Cheynes**, at Harrow's Granada Theatre. The Stones are now attracting a major following, with screaming fans and press reports of their wild concerts (the **New Musical Express** describes the group as a "caveman-like quintet"). Their raucous image is a perfect counterpoint to the Beatles' more clean-cut presentation.

7 Harmonica player and pioneer of British blues **Cyril Davies** dies of leukemia at the age of 32. In 1961, Davies and **Alexis Korner** co-founded **Blues Incorporated**, which has nurtured several top musicians, including drummers **Ginger Baker** and **Charlie Watts**, and 22-year-old singer **Long John Baldry**.

9 Already a seasoned Motown act as the Elgins since 1961, the renamed **Temptations** – a five-piece vocal group featuring **Eddie Kendricks**, **Otis Williams**, **Paul Williams**, **Melvin Franklin**, and the recently recruited **David Ruffin** – record *The Way You Do The Things You Do*, co-written by Smokey Robinson and Robert Rodgers, at the Motown studios in Detroit.

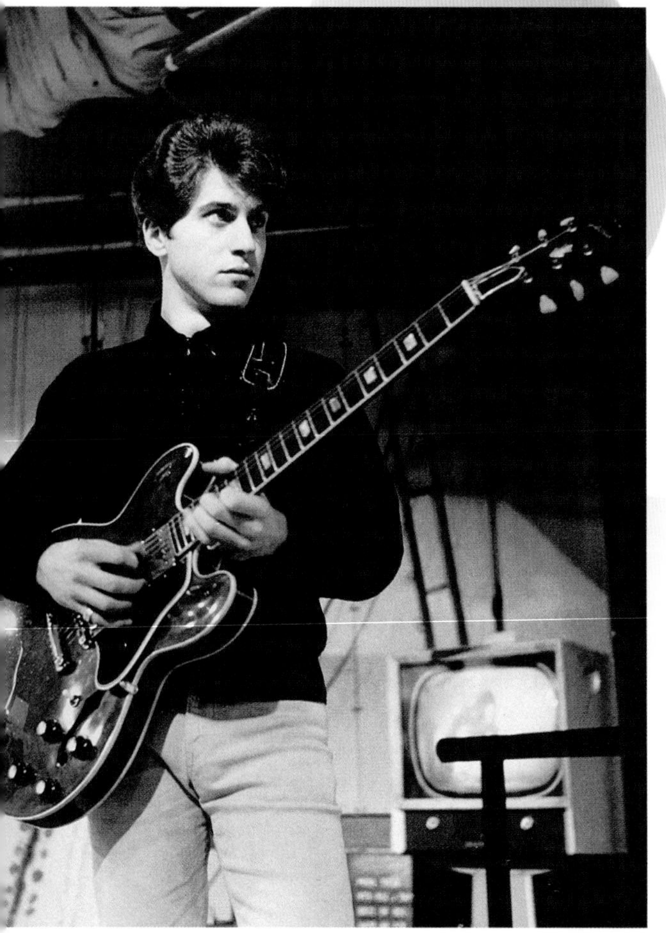

Hip-swinging "go-go" dancers moved provocatively to Johnny Rivers's every beat, sparking a new dance craze revolution.

15 **Johnny Rivers** begins a year's residency at the Whisky A Go-Go club in Los Angeles. His tenure – which follows a couple of weeks playing at the Condor nightspot in San Francisco, and an earlier hot-ticket engagement at Los Angeles' Gazzari club – will turn the venue into America's most fashionable nightspot. Celebrities such as Steve McQueen, Johnny Carson, Rita Hayworth, Richard Chamberlain, Ann-Margret, Sandra Dee, George Peppard, George Hamilton, Tuesday Weld, Laurence Harvey, and Gina Lollabrigida will line up to see Rivers perform his "boogie-beat" repertoire, backed by bassist **Joe Osborn** and jazz drummer **Eddie Rubin**. Accompanied by his red Gibson ES-335 guitar, Rivers's immaculate look is courtesy of hairdresser *du jour* Jay Sebring, with top tailor Giacomo of Hollywood supplying his trendy outfits. In about six weeks, Rivers and record producer Lou Adler will hire Wally Heider's mobile recording service to capture two consecutive beat-jumping nights for his first live album. It will be rejected by every major label before being snapped up by Imperial Records, and ***Johnny Rivers At The Whisky A Go Go*** will become a million-plus selling US album in the summer.

16 Having played a warm-up gig at the Cinéma Cyrano in Versailles, the **Beatles** begin an 18-day stint at the Olympia Music Hall in Paris, on a nine-act bill also featuring **Trini Lopez** and **Sylvie Vartan**. During the run, they will cut German versions of *She Loves You (Sie Liebt Dich)* and *I Want To Hold Your Hand (Komm, Gib Mir Deine Hand)* at EMI Pathé Marconi Studios in Paris – the only time they will record outside England.

18 With Liverpool acts having topped the charts for 20 of the past 23 weeks, Tottenham's own **Dave Clark Five** head the UK list with *Glad All Over*. Written by **Mike Smith** and **Dave Clark** (like most of the group's hits) the distinctive drum-heavy single replaces the **Beatles**' *I Want To Hold Your Hand* – which makes its bow in the US Hot 100 at No. 45 – and prompts "London Topples Liverpool"-type stories in the press.

21 New British vocal/guitar duo **Peter & Gordon** record the Lennon/McCartney composition *A World Without Love*, at EMI's

Peter and Gordon met at school and determined to pursue a music career together... Two days after their triumphant arrival in New York, the Beatles' US debut was broadcast live from CBS Studio 50 on Broadway and West 53rd Street, where they played in front of a studio audience of 703 people.

Peter and Gordon

The Beatles

Abbey Road Studios. **Peter Asher** – whose sister Jane is McCartney's girlfriend – and **Gordon Waller** met at Westminster School in 1959, where they were in a **Shadows**-like trio, and played at school events and in coffee bars. EMI's A&R chief Norman Newell spotted them at London's Pickwick Club and invited them to cut one of their own songs, *If I Were You*, before McCartney offered them one of his latest compositions, which will top the UK chart in June.

February

1 With *Louie Louie* having become a wildly popular US No. 2 hit last December, the **Kingsmen**, a Portland, Oregon-based five-piece rock combo fronted by **Jack Ely**, are in hot water. Widespread controversy, over whether Ely's indistinct vocal is masking off-color lyrics, comes to a head when Indiana Governor Matthew Welsh says his "ears tingled" when he first heard the 45, which he describes as "pornographic." He seems to be one of the few people in the world able to decipher the lyrics. Apparently a high school student from Frankfort, Indiana, sent him a copy of the record, after which students at Miami University in Athens, Ohio, sent him printed copies of "obscene lyrics." Welsh asks Reid Chapman, president of the Indiana Broadcasters Association, to ban the record from all radio stations in the state. Chapman, vice-president of WANE AM Fort Wayne, will pass the request on to his membership. Publisher Max Feirtag tells **Billboard** he will award a check for $1,000 to anyone finding anything suggestive in the lyrics. He can afford to: this update of **Richard Berry**'s 1956 R&B nugget, *Louie Louie*, based on **Ricky Rivera & the Rhythm Rockers**' *El Loco Cha Cha Cha*, cost just $50 to make in the small Northwestern Recording Studio in Portland – and has sold over a million domestic copies.

> **"Not in anyone's wildest imagination are the lyrics as presented on the Wand recording in any way suggestive, let alone obscene."**
>
> Wand Records spokesperson on the Kingsmen's *Louie Louie*, February 1, 1964

1 The **Beatles**' *I Want To Hold Your Hand*, described in a **Billboard** review as a "driving rocker with surf on the Thames sound," and first played on WWDC Radio in Washington, D.C., begins a seven-week run at US No. 1, displacing Bobby Vinton's *There! I've Said It Again*. (The first record by a UK act to top the US charts since the Tornadoes' *Telstar*, it is the first of three consecutive chart-toppers and a record-setting 20 US No. 1s; it will become the fastest ever UK million-seller in the US.) The Beatles will stay in pole position until May 9, when Louis Armstrong's *Hello Dolly* will topple *Can't Buy Me Love*. The only other British acts in this week's chart are Cliff Richard at No. 27, with *It's All In The Game*, and Dusty Springfield at No. 77, with *I Only Want To Be With You*.

Fellow northwestern band Paul Revere & the Raiders also cut *Louie Louie*, but it was the Kingsmen whose name was made by the infamous record.

9 The **Beatles**, with a flu-stricken **George Harrison** (who is not well enough to take part in this morning's rehearsal), make their US debut live on "The Ed Sullivan Show." Watched by an estimated 73 million viewers across North America (later described by McCartney as the "biggest showbiz town ever"), they perform five songs: *All My Loving, Till There Was You, She Loves You, I Saw Her Standing There*, and *I Want To Hold Your Hand*. Before the show they receive a cable from Hollywood: "Congratulations on your appearance on The Ed Sullivan Show and your visit to America. We hope your engagement will be a successful one and your visit pleasant give our best to r [*sic*] Sullivan sincerely Elvis & the Colonel."

11 The **Beatles**' US concert debut takes place at the Washington Coliseum, with **Tommy Roe**, the **Chiffons**, and UK pop duo the **Caravelles**. The 12-song set lasts half an hour, including the laborious moving of a primitive revolving set to accommodate the audience seated on all four sides of the stage.

15 Following a meteoric rise up the US chart, and already certified gold by the RIAA, ***Meet The Beatles!*** – a US-only collection, subtitled "The First Album by England's Phenomenal Pop Combo" – displaces the Singing Nun at No. 1. Things will never be the same again – especially for the Singing Nun. **Billboard** reports that "Great Britain hasn't been this influential in American affairs since 1775. The sensational impact of the Beatles on England's former colonies has had the explosive effect of sending major and independent firms here scrambling for more and more British product." More than a dozen acts have been snapped up by US labels in the past few weeks (often through their UK subsidiaries), including **Gerry & the Pacemakers**, the **Dave Clark Five**, the **Searchers**, the **Fourmost**, the **Swinging Blue Jeans**, and **Freddie & the Dreamers**.

Feb 7 Pan Am flight PA 101 touches down at 1:20 pm at New York's John F. Kennedy Airport, bringing the Beatles to the US for the first time. They experience near-riotous scenes, thanks to major publicity engineered by Capitol Records. On their way from the airport in their limousine, they tune into the radio and hear *I Saw Her Standing There.*

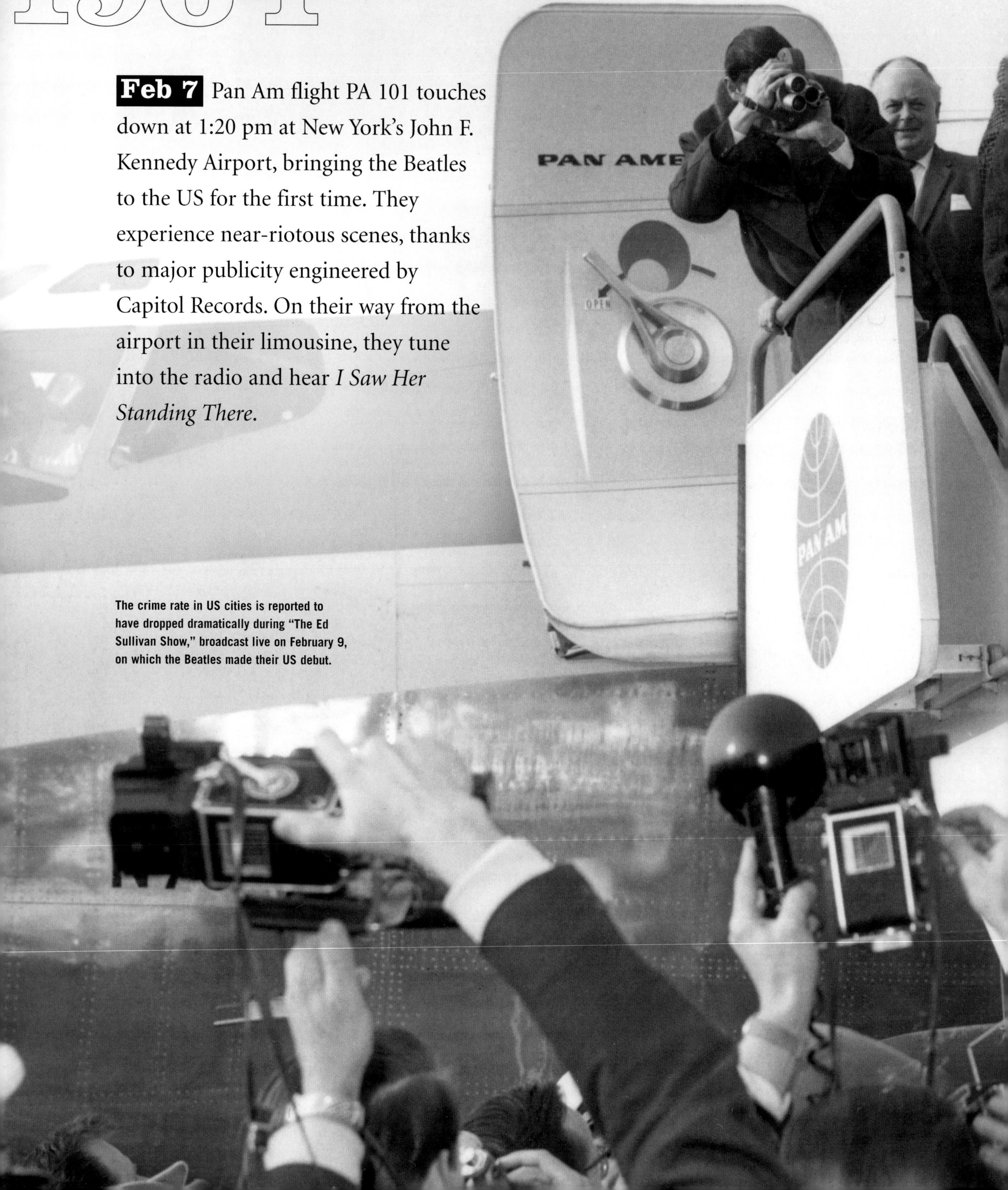

The crime rate in US cities is reported to have dropped dramatically during "The Ed Sullivan Show," broadcast live on February 9, on which the Beatles made their US debut.

"So this is America. They all seemed out of their minds."

Ringo Starr, February 7, 1964

Feb 1964

Simon & Garfunkel record *The Sounds of Silence*... Radio Caroline goes on air... Beatles' singles fill the charts...

16 One week after the **Beatles**' record-breaking debut on "The Ed Sullivan Show," they return, this time filmed at the Deauville Hotel in Miami Beach. At the afternoon rehearsal, McCartney is drowned out by screaming fans as he tries to announce the next number, and Lennon tells the audience, "Shut up while he's talking." With Mitzi Gaynor topping the bill, and comedians Marty Allen & Steve Rossi, standup comic Myron Cohen, and acrobats the Nerveless Nocks also appearing, an estimated 70 million people watch the show.

16 The **Crystals** embark on a six-week UK tour at the Coventry Theatre. Also on the bill are UK No. 5 *5-4-3-2-1* hitmakers, **Manfred Mann** – a London-based beat combo led by South African-born keyboard player, **Manfred Mann** (born Lubowitz) and featuring vocalist **Paul Jones**, guitarist **Mike Vickers**, bassist **Tom McGuinness**, and drummer **Mike Hugg** – with other tour openers **Johnny Kidd**, **Joe Brown**, and **Heinz**, a photogenic, 21-year-old from Germany who was formerly a member of the **Tornados**.

17 The **Tijuana Brass**, a group assembled by frontman trumpet player **Herb Alpert** to play in concert (on record he uses session players), is launched in concert in San Francisco. The line-up comprises **Bob Edmundson** (trombone), **Lou Pagani** (keyboards), **John Pisano** (rhythm guitar), **Tonni Kalash** (second trumpet), **Nick Ceroli** (drums), and **Pat Senatore** (bass). They will grow into one of the top-grossing live attractions in the US in the mid-1960s,

22 The **Beatles** arrive back from the US. BBC sports program "Grandstand" broadcasts their early-morning return during its afternoon schedule, including an interview with host David Coleman. The group are also interviewed by telephone by Brian Matthew, who broadcasts the conversation near the end of his "Saturday Club" show on the Light Programme. He follows it with a request to play the **Miracles**' *Shop Around* from a Mrs. Louise Harrison in Liverpool, for her son George's upcoming 21st birthday.

23 The **Beatles** appear for the third consecutive week on "The Ed Sullivan Show," in a taped segment featuring *Twist And Shout*, *Please Please Me*, and *I Want To Hold Your Hand*. Fellow British acts Morecambe & Wise, **Acker Bilk**, and puppets Pinky & Perky also feature. At the taping, Sullivan will presciently say, "All of us on the *shew* are so darned sorry, and sincerely sorry, that this is the third time and thus our last current *shew* with the Beatles, because these youngsters from Liverpool, England, and their conduct over here, not only as fine professional singers but as a group of fine youngsters, will leave an imprint on everyone over here who's met 'em."

March

2 The **Beatles** begin filming their major motion-picture debut, directed by Richard Lester and produced by Walter Shenson, at London's Paddington Station, on board a train that pulls out of Platform 5. The foursome are not members of Equity, the actors' union, so are quickly proposed and seconded by actors Wilfrid Brambell and Norman Rossington before filming starts.

8 The **Dave Clark Five** make their bow on "The Ed Sullivan Show," singing *Glad All Over*. They will become one of the show's favorite guests, and will be invited to perform 13 times (plus five repeats) over the next four years.

10 **Simon & Garfunkel** cut *The Sounds Of Silence* at Columbia Records' New York studios. Singer-songwriter **Paul Simon** and singer **Art Garfunkel**, both aged 22, attended Forest Hills High School in Queens, New York, and first recorded together as **Tom & Jerry**, scoring a modest hit in 1960 with *Hey Schoolgirl*. While Simon attended Queens College, Garfunkel went to Columbia University. Simon also recorded solo sides for the Warwick label and wrote songs for other singers. Reunited as a folk duo last year, the pair have signed to Columbia Records at the behest of label producer Tom Wilson. Further sessions to complete what will evolve into their first album, ***Wednesday Morning 3AM***, will be held on March 17 and 31, and April 5.

14 For the first time in chart history, not a single American record is featured in the UK top ten – which lists nine English acts and one Irish one (the Bachelors). However, perhaps more tellingly, eight of the songs are by American songwriters. The top ten lines up as:
1 Cilla Black – *Anyone Who Had A Heart*
2 The Dave Clark Five – *Bits And Pieces*
3 Billy J. Kramer with the Dakotas – *Little Children*
4 The Bachelors – *Diane*
5 The Rolling Stones – *Not Fade Away*

After recording *Wednesday Morning 3AM*, Simon & Garfunkel went their separate ways: Paul Simon to Britain, where he traveled the country performing at folk clubs, and Art Garfunkel to graduate school.

The Dave Clark Five's *Bits And Pieces* hit was banned in many ballrooms, for fear that dancers echoing its stomping beat would cause damage to the wooden dancefloors.

6 The Hollies – *Just One Look*
7 The Searchers – *Needles And Pins*
8 The Merseybeats – *I Think Of You*
9 Eden Kane – *Boys Cry*
10 Kathy Kirby – *Let Me Go Lover*

"This is Radio Caroline on 199, your all day radio station. We are on the air from six in the morning till six at night."

DJ Simon Dee, March 28, 1964

16 **Alan Freed**, who now lives in Palm Springs, is indicted by a Federal Grand Jury on charges of evading $37,920 in income taxes from 1957 to 1959, primarily stemming from his failure to declare payola income. He receives a six-month suspended sentence and a $300 fine.

19 Prime Minister Harold Wilson presents the **Beatles** with the award for Show Business Personalities of 1963 at the 12th annual Variety Club of Great Britain luncheon, held at London's Dorchester Hotel. In the evening, the group will tape their "Top Of The Pops" debut appearance – due to air on March 25 – miming to *Can't Buy Me Love* and *You Can't Do That.*

23 **John Lennon**'s book of nonsense verse, **In His Own Write**, is published in the UK by Jonathan Cape (it will win Foyle's Literary Prize). Lennon is interviewed by Kenneth Allsop on BBC TV's "Tonight" program. He then joins the other **Beatles** to attend the annual Carl-Alan Awards at the Empire Ballroom, Leicester Square. They are presented with awards for Best Beat Group of 1963 and Best Single for *She Loves You* by the Duke of Edinburgh. (The Duke will reportedly say later in the year that the band is "on the wane." Lennon's reply: "The bloke's getting no money for his playing fields from me.")

28 Pirate station Radio Caroline begins broadcasting off the British coast – circumventing the country's stringent broadcasting laws (BBC radio is the only station currently licensed). Founder Ronan O'Rahilly, also owner of London's Scene Club and manager of R&B pianist **Georgie Fame**, has anchored his ship – a Danish ferry called the *Fredericia* – off Harwich, and named the station after Caroline Kennedy. At noon, **Jimmy McGriff**'s *Round Midnight* is followed by the Caroline bell and the voice of disc jockey Simon Dee. As he hands over to Christopher Moore, the first record played is the **Rolling Stones**' *Not Fade Away.*

April

4 The **Beatles**' *Can't Buy Me Love* simultaneously tops the UK chart – having sold a record 1,226,000 copies in its first week and after a record-breaking 2.1 million advance sales – and the US list. Its advance sell-through of one million is the largest in UK record history. It makes a record leap from its US No. 27 chart debut, vaulting over *Twist And Shout* (which moves up one place to No. 2), selling two million copies in its week of release, after advance orders of 1,700,000. This week's **Billboard** chart reveals, without precedent before or since, five singles by the same act in the top five: No. 1 *Can't Buy Me Love*, No. 2 *Twist And Shout*, No. 3 *She Loves You*, No. 4 *I Want To Hold Your Hand*, No. 5 *Please Please Me.* The Beatles also occupy Nos. 31 (*I Saw Her Standing There*), 41 (*From Me To You*), 46 (*Do You Want To Know A Secret?*), 58 (*All My Loving*), 65 (*You Can't Do That*), 68 (*Roll Over Beethoven*), and 79 (*Thank You Girl*). (In next week's survey *There's A Place* and *Love Me Do* will make their debut.)

8 The **Supremes** – who have been struggling to secure a major hit – record the Holland/Dozier/Holland song *Where Did Our Love Go* at the Motown studios. It will begin an astonishing run of five US chart-toppers.

Within three weeks of its launch, pirate station Radio Caroline had gained an audience of nearly seven million, much to the chagrin of the BBC and the British government.

Apr 1964

Dionne Warwick

The Stones' release their first album... The Animals... Marianne Faithfull records *As Tears Go By*...

12 WINS' Murray the K's package opens at the Fox Theater in Brooklyn, New York, with the **Shirelles**, the **Kingsmen**, the **Chiffons**, **Johnny Tillotson**, **Bobby Goldsboro** (a 23-year-old singer-songwriter/guitarist from Florida), **Ben E. King**, **Dionne Warwick**, the **Tymes**, **Little Anthony**, **Dick & Deedee**, R&B star **Chuck Jackson**, the **Younger Brothers**, and **Earl Warren**'s band.

22 The **Daily Mirror** reports that Wallace Snowcroft, president of the National Federation of Hairdressers, is offering a free haircut to the next group to reach UK No. 1, claiming the **Rolling Stones** are the worst of all: "One of them looks as if he's got a feather duster on his head." The **Searchers** – the next group to top the charts – fail to take up this kind offer.

23 On Shakespeare's 400th birthday, **John Lennon** is guest of honor at a Foyle's Literary Lunch at the Dorchester Hotel, London. His speech is as follows: "Thank you very much. You've got a lucky face."

May

2 With 100,000 advance orders, the **Rolling Stones**' debut album, ***The Rolling Stones***, tops the UK chart, replacing ***With The Beatles*** (the first time in 51 weeks that the Beatles are not at No. 1). The Stones also make their first appearance on the US chart, at No. 98, with *Not Fade Away*, one place above Wayne Newton's *The Little White Cloud That Cried*. Certified gold on April 13, the Beatles' ***Second Album*** vaults to US No. 1, replacing ***Meet The Beatles!***

3 **Stevie Wonder** – who was scheduled to make his debut on "The Ed Sullivan Show" on January 5 – now appears on the show, performing *Fingertips*. **Gerry & the Pacemakers** also debut, singing *Don't Let The Sun Catch You Crying* and *I'm The One*.

6 "Around The Beatles" airs on ITV. Produced by Jack Good, it features **Cilla Black**, **P.J. Proby**, **Long John Baldry**, **Sounds Incorporated**, **Millie**, the **Vernons Girls**, the **Jets**, and the **Beatles**. In addition to performing half a dozen numbers, the Beatles participate in a spoof version of Act V Scene 1 from Shakespeare's "A Midsummer Night's Dream." American singer P.J. Proby, who has recently changed his stage name from Jet Powers, has been flown to England and given a style makeover

> **"Watch out USA... Here they come! The Rolling Stones! They're great! They're outrageous! They're rebels! They sell! They're England's hottest – but hottest – group!"**
>
> London Records ad, **Billboard**, May 14, 1964

Presented with flowers by a fan on their arrival in the US, the Rolling Stones failed to sell out many venues on their debut tour.

Signed to the Scepter label, former session singer Dionne Warwick was molded by Burt Bacharach and Hal David, who wrote and produced virtually all her material, including her first hit *Anyone Who Had A Heart*... Barbra Streisand won the Grammy for Album of the Year... Andrew Loog Oldham met his next protégée, the 18-year-old Marianne Faithfull, at a party in May.

Marianne Faithfull

by Good, which includes tight trousers, a loose smock top, and his hair tied in 18th-century fashion.

9 Released from jail in January – and much in demand – **Chuck Berry** begins his first UK tour at the Astoria Theatre in Finsbury Park, London: a 21-date, twice-nightly package, supported by **Carl Perkins**, the **Swinging Blue Jeans**, the **Nashville Teens**, **Karl Denver**, and others. Also on the bill are the **Animals**, yet another hot British group, formed in Newcastle two years ago, initially as the Alan Price Combo. The group features keyboardist **Price**, lead vocalist **Eric Burdon**, bassist **Chas Chandler**, guitarist **Hilton Valentine**, and drummer **John Steel**. They returned from the Hamburg Star-Club last year, relocated to London, and have come under the wing of rising producer Mickie Most. He spotted them performing at the Club A Go Go, and was instrumental in their signing to EMI's Columbia label, for whom they have recently recorded *The House Of The Rising Sun*, a Price rearrangement of a traditional folk-blues song. Helmed by Most, the song was recorded in 30 minutes at a cost of £4 10s (£4.50/$12.60).

11 In the middle of another UK tour, the **Rolling Stones** are refused lunch at the Grand Hotel in Bristol, where they are staying, because they are not wearing jackets and ties. They will be described in the **Daily Mirror** as appearing to have "everything... against them." The article calls them "the ugliest group in Britain," and says "They are not looked kindly upon by most parents or by adults in general."

12 At the sixth annual Grammy Awards, held jointly at Los Angeles' Beverly Hilton Hotel, New York's Waldorf-Astoria Hotel, and Chicago's Knickerbocker Hotel, **Henry Mancini** and Johnny Mercer's *The Days Of Wine And Roses* is named Song of the Year and Record of the Year. ***The Barbra Streisand Album*** is named Album of the Year, and 22-year-old, Brooklyn-born actress/pop vocalist **Barbra Streisand** also wins Best Vocal Performance, Female. **Nino Tempo & April Stevens** win Best Rock & Roll Recording with their revival of *Deep Purple*, and **Ray Charles**'s *Busted* is named Best Rhythm & Blues Recording. Folk trio **Peter, Paul & Mary** nab two awards – Best Vocal Performance by a Vocal Group and Best Folk Recording – for their version of Bob Dylan's *Blowin' In The Wind*. Nominated for both Record of the Year and Album of the Year, the **Singing Nun**'s *Dominique* wins in the Gospel or Other Religious Recording (Musical) category.

23 A ska-inflected pop smash, *My Boy Lollipop* (by 17-year-old Jamaican singer **Millie** Small) peaks at UK No. 2, behind the **Four Pennies**' *Juliet*. (It will also reach the same position in the US.) This evening, Millie's Island label boss, Chris Blackwell, in Birmingham with her for a BBC television appearance, goes to see **Carl Wayne & the Vikings** and then the **Spencer Davis Group**, signing the latter on the spot. As yet Blackwell lacks the resources to promote his acts, so will license the group's output to Philips' Fontana imprint – for which their debut is a revival of John Lee Hooker's *Dimples*. The band formed last year in Birmingham, and features guitarist **Davis**, drummer **Pete York**, bassist **Muff Winwood**, and his younger brother, 16-year-old **Steve Winwood**, on keyboard and vocals.

28 **Marianne Faithfull** – the daughter of a British university lecturer and an Austrian baroness, and an ex-pupil of St. Joseph's Convent School in Reading – makes her recording debut at Olympic Sound Studios. Taken to a party last month by her boyfriend, artist John Dunbar, she was introduced to Andrew Oldham. He was impressed by her striking looks and, learning that she wants to be a folk singer, has offered to record her and sign her to Decca Records. She is given a new Jagger/Richard song, *As Tears Go By*, and is also fortunate in being surrounded by a talented studio crew: producer Oldham, young engineers, Mike Leander and Gus Dudgeon, 20-year-old session guitarist **Jimmy Page**, and 17-year-old bassist **John Paul Jones**. In August, the single will become the first of Faithfull's four UK Top 10 hits.

June

1 The **Rolling Stones** arrive in New York for their first US tour. They will make their American television debut tomorrow evening on WABC's "The Les Crane Show."

3 **Ringo Starr** is rushed to University College Hospital, London, after collapsing at a photo session in Barnes. He is suffering from tonsillitis and pharyngitis.

The Animals made their chart debut with *Baby Let Me Take You Home*, an R&B version of the blues number *Baby Don't You Tear My Clothes*.

June 1964

The Rolling Stones in America... "A Hard Day's Night" opens... The Moody Blues debut on "Ready Steady Go!"...

The Zombies

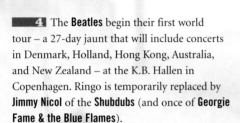

4 The **Beatles** begin their first world tour – a 27-day jaunt that will include concerts in Denmark, Holland, Hong Kong, Australia, and New Zealand – at the K.B. Hallen in Copenhagen. Ringo is temporarily replaced by **Jimmy Nicol** of the **Shubdubs** (and once of **Georgie Fame & the Blue Flames**).

10 The **Rolling Stones**, who are greatly influenced by the blues artists of the 1940s and 1950s, record at the now legendary Chess studios in Chicago – where they meet **Chuck Berry**, **Muddy Waters**, and **Willie Dixon**, among other stars on the Chess roster.

A former professional baseball player, disc jockey, and 1955 Grand Ole Opry inductee, Texan country singer Jim Reeves was killed in a plane crash in July.

12 Having won the opportunity to audition for Decca Records by topping the regional "Herts Beat" competition held at Watford Town Hall last month, the **Zombies**' first recording session takes place at Decca's West Hampstead Studio 2. The group was formed last year by three teenagers attending St. Alban's school – keyboardist **Rod Argent**, drummer **Hugh Grundy**, and lead vocalist **Colin Blunstone** – together with guitarist **Paul Atkinson** and 21-year-old bassist **Chris White**. At today's session, the band record *It's Alright With Me*, *You Make Me Feel Good*, *Summertime*, and *She's Not There*. The last is a song penned by Argent after being challenged by producer Ken Jones to write a hit record. He does: the single will make UK No. 12 in September, but will see phenomenal success in the US in December, hitting No. 2 and achieving million-plus sales.

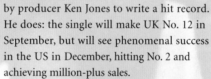

"There's more people here than came to see the Queen. I should think so, she didn't have any hit records."

George Harrison in Australia, June 1964

13 The **Rolling Stones** appear on ABC-TV's "The Hollywood Palace," performing *I Just Wanna Make Love To You*. They follow Bertha the Elephant and her daughter Tina, and are subjected to barbed quips from host Dean Martin. After comic acrobat Larry Griswold's act, Martin tells the audience: "That's the father of the Rolling Stones; he's been trying to kill himself ever since." He also comments, "They're challenging the Beatles to a hair-pulling contest. I could swear Jackie Coogan and Skippy were in that group somewhere."

14 In Melbourne, an estimated 300,000 people – the largest congregation of Australians ever assembled in one place – gather to meet the **Beatles**. Meanwhile, in Sunderland, UK, 12-year-old Carol Dryden is found by an observant railway clerk on a station platform, packed in a tea chest addressed to the Beatles.

15 Discharged from the hospital last week, **Ringo Starr** re-joins the **Beatles** as they play the first of three dates at the Festival Hall in Melbourne. During subsequent concerts in Sydney, **Paul McCartney** will complain to the media about fans throwing "jelly-babies" at them on stage. Mrs. Anita Lawrence, an acoustics expert from New South Wales University, will measure screams at the concerts at 112 decibels, between 10 and 20 decibels higher than the noise level of a Boeing 707 jet at 2,000ft.

The five members of the Zombies left school with 50 GCE "O" and "A" level passes between them... Them – fronted by ex-Monarchs vocalist, 18-year-old Belfast native Van Morrison – recorded their first sides for Decca in July.

20 The Summer Shower of Stars package tour gets under way at the Donnelly Theatre in Boston. The line-up features **James Brown** – the hardest-working man in showbusiness – 28-year-old preacher/soul singer **Solomon Burke**, who has already racked up more than a dozen crossover US R&B hits, gospel/R&B veterans Garnett Mimms and Joe Tex, and **Otis Redding**, whose first album, ***Pain In My Heart***, has just been released.

24 **Sam Cooke** begins a two-week residency at Manhattan's Copacabana club (where he debuted in 1958, opening for comedian Myron Cohen). He has paid $10,000 for a 20 x 100ft billboard, asking, "Who's the Biggest Cook in Town?" to be erected for a month in Times Square on the corner of Broadway and 43rd Street – a ploy dreamed up by his manager, Allen Klein. In a few days' time another billboard will be added, pronouncing: "Sam's the Biggest Cooke in Town."

27 After waiting patiently in the runner-up spot for three weeks, **Roy Orbison** tops the UK chart with *It's Over*. He is the first American artist to do so in almost a year – **Elvis Presley** had one week at No. 1 with *(You're The) Devil In Disguise* last August.

29 Britain's first commercial radio station based on land, Manx Radio, begins broadcasting from a movable trailer, initially parked on a hilltop in Onchan, near Douglas, Isle of Man. Licensed by the Isle of Man government, and with its first commercial plugging a local

Them

jeweller's store, the station is broadcasting on FM in stereo, and can be heard across the north coast of Wales, in Blackpool, and in parts of Cumbria. Beginning in October, it will also air on 188m Medium Wave (AM).

July

3 The **Beach Boys** headline "A Million Dollar Party," presented by radio station KPOI, at the International Center Arena in Honolulu. They share a bill with **Jan & Dean**, **Jimmy Clanton**, the **Kingsmen**, the **Rivingtons**, **Ray Peterson**, **Jody Miller**, **Jimmy Griffin**, **Mary Saenz**, **Peter & Gordon**, and **Bruce & Terry** – a new Columbia-signed surf-pop duo comprising future Beach Boy **Bruce Johnston** and Doris Day's son, **Terry Melcher** (who will go on to become a top record producer). Tomorrow, the Beach Boys' latest harmonic gem, *I Get Around*, will top the US chart. Its B-side, *Don't Worry Baby* – written by **Brian Wilson** for the **Ronettes** but rejected by Phil Spector – will peak at US No. 24.

4 The **Rolling Stones** appear on BBC-TV's "Juke Box Jury" – the only time the show has five panelists instead of its usual number of four – voting most of the songs "misses"- and cause controversy over their languid comments and appearance.

5 Formed in Belfast in 1963, and recently relocated to London, R&B/beat group **Them** record their first sides for Decca at the label's West Hampstead Studio. They cut *Don't Start Crying Now* and *One Two Brown Eyes*. With little radio interest, they will return to the studio in September to try again, nailing a passionate update of Big Joe Williams' *Baby Please Don't Go* which will crack the UK chart next year.

10 Around 200,000 people pack the route from Liverpool's Speke Airport to the city center, as the **Beatles** arrive in their home town for a civic reception at the Town Hall, and to attend the northern UK premiere of "A Hard Day's Night."

25 *A Hard Day's Night*, featuring a double-tracked vocal by **Lennon**, tops the UK chart. ***A Hard Day's Night*** also simultaneously hits UK (one week after entering) and US No. 1, and is unique in being the only album consisting entirely of **Lennon/McCartney** songs. It also features **Harrison** taking the lead vocal, normally the role of either Lennon or McCartney (or both), on *I'm Happy Just To Dance With You*. (The US version of the album also features four George Martin instrumentals).

31 Country-singing superstar **Jim Reeves** – piloting his own single-engine plane – and his pianist/road manager Dean Manuel are killed when the plane disappears from radar screens near Nashville airport, on a flight from Batesville, Arkansas. Thick fog will be cited as the cause. Reeves was one of the first country vocalists to cross over into the pop field, and notched up a dozen US Hot 100 hits, including the 1959 No. 2 smash, *He'll Have To Go*.

August

7 The **Moody Blues** make their television bow on "Ready Steady Go!" performing their first single, *Lose Your Money*. The Birmingham group was formed in May by 20-year-old singer-songwriter/guitarist **Denny Laine**, having disbanded his former **Diplomats** combo. He recruited ex-**Crewcats** members, flautist **Ray Thomas** and keyboard player **Mike Pinder**, drummer **Graeme Edge** (formerly with **Gerry Levene & the Avengers**), and guitarist **Clint Warwick** from the **Rainbows**. They secured a residency at the Carlton Ballroom in Birmingham, where the club's owners received £2,000 ($5,600) from brewers Mitchell & Butler for publicity purposes. In deference to the brewers, the band adopted the name the MB Five, but subsequently decided that the M should stand for Moody and the B for Blues, becoming the Moody Blues Five. They recently signed with London-based manager Tony Secunda, who secured them a season of Monday night gigs at the Marquee, which in turn has led to a contract with Decca.

9 **Joan Baez** and **Bob Dylan** take part in the Forest Hills Music Festival in Queens, New York, dueting on Dylan's *With God On Our Side*. **The New York Times** critic Robert Shelton, who was so unequivocal in his praise of Dylan in a 1961 article, is this time disappointed in Dylan's solo performance, "with the lack of control of his stage manner, his raucously grating singing and the somewhat declining level of his new composition."

10 After an appearance by the **Rolling Stones** in the Hague caused another riot at the weekend, **Mick Jagger** is fined £32 ($90) in Liverpool, for driving without insurance and breaking the speed limit.

THE BEATLES

July 6 **"A Hard Day's Night," featuring the Beatles in their "first full length, hilarious, action-packed film!" replete with six new songs, receives its world premiere at the London Pavilion. The group are introduced to Princess Margaret and the Earl of Snowdon. Twelve hours earlier, 200 policemen went on duty outside the venue to control a crowd of several thousand, mostly screaming girls. Time magazine's review, headlined "Beatles Blow It," suggests that readers "avoid this film at all costs." In sharp contrast, a future New York Post critique will hail it as "The greatest and most entertaining rock movie ever." It will get two Academy Award nominations.**

The Who, still known as the High Numbers, were spotted performing at the Railway Hotel in Harrow by their future manager Kit Lambert.

The "British Invasion" continues... The Who are gathering a following... Sandie Shaw and her bare feet...

12 Billed in the US as the "Queen of Bluebeat," **Millie Small** performs *My Boy Lollipop* (which recently hit US No. 2) at the ongoing World's Fair being staged in New York. Her success has prompted several US labels – notably Atlantic – to begin licensing ska music from Jamaica. The Jamaican government is trying to promote a mini ska boom, and has sent several local artists – including 26-year-old singer-songwriter **Jimmy Cliff** – to perform at the fair.

13 Sticking with their hugely successful formula, the **Supremes** – with **Diana Ross** becoming the focal point of the group as lead singer – cut another Holland/Dozier/Holland composition, *Baby Love*, in Detroit. The single will be released before the already recorded *Come See About Me*, to become a transatlantic chart-topper in both the UK and US in October, and the girl trio's signature hit.

15 Brill Building songwriters **Jeff Barry** and **Ellie Greenwich** – having already knocked the Beatles off the top spot in the US in June with the **Dixie Cups**' *Chapel Of Love* – do it again as **Manfred Mann**'s version of their infectious *Do Wah Diddy Diddy* replaces *A Hard Day's Night* at UK No. 1.

> "They don't seem to have the sense to realize we hate being the target for sweets coming like bullets from all directions."
>
> Paul McCartney, June 10, 1964

16 Having recently formed his own Magic Lamp record label, following a short spell with the small Sahara Records, 30-year-old rockabilly star **Johnny Burnette** falls from his boat while he is fishing on Clear Lake in California, and drowns.

19 The **Beatles**' North American tour, promoted as "The Beatles' First American Tour," opens at the Cow Palace in San Francisco, with the **Righteous Brothers** (the unrelated **Bill Medley** and **Bobby Hatfield**, who have recently been signed to Phil Spector's Philles label as its first white act), singer-songwriter **Jackie DeShannon**, R&B vocal quartet the **Exciters**, and **Bill Black's Combo**. The 25-date tour will end at the Dallas Memorial Auditorium on September 18. The Beatles will refuse to perform in Jacksonville until they receive assurances that the audience will not be segregated, and they will be paid a world record fee of $150,000 for a concert at the Municipal Stadium in Kansas City. Their performance at the Las Vegas Convention Center will be stopped twice, due to excessive jelly-baby hurling by fans, and the dates at the Forest Hills Tennis Stadium in New York will see 250 city police, 150 private guards, ten nurses, and one ambulance on duty. Most of the gigs will be hallmarked by fans simply drowning out the music – a problem that will contribute to their future decision to stop performing live.

Herman's Hermits' lead singer Peter Noone was named Herman because of his supposed likeness to Sherman, a TV cartoon character in the "Rocky and Bullwinkle Show."

September

4 With the "British Invasion" in full swing, the **Animals** make their American debut, beginning a 10-day engagement at Brooklyn's Paramount Theater. Preceded by the likes of **Dee Dee Sharp**, **Ronnie Dove**, **Ronnie & the Daytonas**, and fellow Brit, teenager **Elkie Brooks** – and the superfluous showing of a Jock Mahoney movie, "California" – the Animals witness at first hand the reaction to fellow UK performers: seasoned New York police officers holding screaming teenage girls at bay.

13 Murray the K's Big Holiday Show begins a ten-day run at the Brooklyn Fox Theater, with a Motown-heavy bill featuring **Marvin Gaye**, the **Miracles**, the **Supremes**, **Martha & the Vandellas**, the **Contours**, and the **Temptations**. Also on the bill are the **Searchers**, **Jay & the Americans** – formed by New York University students in 1959 and now scoring their biggest hit, *Come A Little Bit Closer* – the **Dovells**, **Little Anthony & the Imperials**, the **Newbeats**, the **Ronettes**, and the **Shangri-Las**.

15 At a **Beatles** show at the Public Auditorium in Cleveland, screaming fans rush down an aisle and try to reach the stage. Police

Jamaican Millicent Small introduced the masses to ska and bluebeat with her hit song *My Boy Lollipop*.

Inspector Carl Bear of Cleveland's Juvenile Bureau steps onstage and takes the microphone from **John Lennon** while he is still singing. The performance does not resume for another 15 minutes, until the girls calm down.

16 **Sam Cooke** stars in the first edition of ABC-TV's new half-hour music show "Shindig," created and produced by British television entrepreneur Jack Good. The episode also features the **Righteous Brothers**, the **Wellingtons**, **Bobby Sherman**, comic Alan Sues, and the **Everly Brothers**. Originally piloted in 1963 by Good as "Young America Swings the World," the show's dance-party atmosphere will be enhanced each week by pretty go-go dancers. It will be expanded to a full hour from next January, and will be produced by Dean Whitmore from July 1965 until coming off the air on January 8, 1966.

25 The **Temptations**, with **David Ruffin** on lead vocal, begin recording *My Girl* at Motown, a stepsister song to **Mary Wells**'s May US chart-topper *My Guy*. Both songs were written by Smokey Robinson, the latter with Ronald White.

26 **Herman's Hermits** top the UK chart with *I'm Into Something Good*, a perky, pure-pop cover of a Goffin and King composition that has already been a modest US summer hit for female singer **Earl-Jean**. Herman is baby-faced, 16-year-old Manchester singer Peter Noone, who has been signed – along with his backing group (previously known as the Heartbeats) – to EMI's Columbia label by independent producer Mickie Most. After recording the song, Most was unhappy with it and didn't want to release it until his wife heard the recording and convinced him he was on to something good. Most handed the master to the label, and yet another hot British group was launched. Herman's Hermits will also find enormous success in the US.

27 Following their first major US tour, the **Beach Boys** make their show debut on "The Ed Sullivan Show," singing *I Get Around* and *Wendy*.

October

9 After the British Musicians Union has declared an anti-apartheid embargo on the race-divided country, the **Rolling Stones** cancel their upcoming tour of South Africa.

18 The **Animals** begin their first British tour as headliners – with **Carl Perkins**, **Gene Vincent**, and the **Nashville Teens** among opening acts – at the beginning of a 28-date, twice-nightly UK tour at the Odeon Cinema, Liverpool.

22 John Burgess, assistant to EMI A&R manager Norman Newell, writes to Kit Lambert, a film director who is co-managing a new London-based band, the **High Numbers** (who have also been playing as the **Who** at pub and club dates around the city): "I have listened again and again, to the High Numbers' white labels, taken from our session, and still cannot decide whether or not they have anything to offer. You may, of course, in the meantime, have signed with another company, in which case, I wish you all the luck in the world. If you have not, I will be very interested to hear any other tapes you may have, featuring the group." The High Numbers are a spirited "mod-rock" teenage fourpiece, formed by guitarist **Pete Townshend** (son of Cliff Townshend, a sax-playing member of RAF dance band the Squadronaires), lead singer **Roger Daltrey** (formerly of the **Detours**), bassist **John Entwistle** (who played French horn with the Middlesex Youth Orchestra), and – the latest recruit – a wild and unpredictable drummer named **Keith Moon**. They are gaining a strong following for their high-octane performances around north London, particularly at the Railway Hotel in Harrow, where they often delight in smashing their equipment on stage.

24 Jumping from last week's No. 11, 17-year-old **Sandie Shaw**'s cover of Lou Johnson's US hit, *(There's) Always Something There To Remind Me*, tops the UK chart, where it will stay for three weeks, deposing Roy Orbison's *Oh, Pretty Woman*. Shaw can currently be seen on several British television shows, gaining notoriety from the fact that she sings barefoot (a gimmick dreamed up by her manager, Eve Taylor).

25 The **Rolling Stones** make their debut on "The Ed Sullivan Show," singing *Around And Around* and *Time Is On My Side*. After riotous scenes in the audience, Sullivan announces: "I promise you they'll never be back on our *shew*. It took me 17 years to build this *shew*; I'm not going to have it destroyed in a matter of weeks."

29 The "T.A.M.I. Show" (Teen Age Music International Show) is filmed at the Civic Auditorium in Santa Monica. It's a multiracial, multi-act spectacular, featuring the **Beach Boys**, the **Barbarians**, **Chuck Berry**, **Bo Diddley**, **James Brown**, **Marvin Gaye**, **Gerry & the Pacemakers**, **Lesley Gore**, **Jan & Dean**, **Billy J. Kramer with the Dakotas**, **Smokey Robinson & the Miracles**, the **Rolling Stones**, and the **Supremes**. Billed as the greatest rock special in television history, the project is produced by Steve Binder, who shoots it on video tape, and will transfer it to film for release in theaters via Electronovision. The world premiere is set for November 14.

31 **Ray Charles** is arrested by customs agents, charged with possession of narcotics, after landing at Logan Airport in Boston, scheduled to play at the Back Bay Theatre.

31 For the first time since January 18, the **Beatles** don't have a record on **Billboard**'s Hot 100, with *Matchbox* dropping off the survey. In April the group peaked with 14 entries on the list, on five different labels.

Diana Ross became the focal point of the Supremes, as the group's lead singer, when they recorded *Baby Love* in August.

Nov 1964

Tom Jones records *It's Not Unusual*... *Leader Of The Pack*... Sam Cooke is shot...

A crowd of 5,000 fans led to chaotic scenes at Sam Cooke's funeral. James Brown tried to attend, but when fans rushed his limousine he drove away rather than cause further disruption... It was the end of a great year for the Beatles.

Sam Cooke's funeral

November

4 Having appeared on BBC-TV's "Juke Box Jury" on October 31, commenting on one record, "I'd like it at a party if I was stoned," **Marianne Faithfull** collapses and pulls out of a scheduled 26-date British tour set to begin on November 7, with **Gerry & the Pacemakers** and others. US singer **Jackie DeShannon** steps in.

11 **Tom Jones** – a 24-year-old Welsh singer from a coal-mining community in Pontypridd – begins his second session for Decca Records, and nails a new Gordon Mills/Les Reed song, *It's Not Unusual.* Jones, who formed his first band in 1963 under a pseudonym, Tommy Scott & the Senators, recorded a number of tracks for EMI under producer Joe Meek. Having been spotted by Mills – an ex-member of UK vocal group the **Viscounts** – opening for Mandy Rice-Davies in Pontypridd, the singer has signed a management deal with him and signed to Decca.

21 Still releasing its records in Britain via the Stateside label, Tamla Motown has its first UK chart-topper, with the **Supremes**' *Baby Love.*

28 The **Shangri-Las**' *Leader Of The Pack,* written by Shadow Morton, Jeff Barry, and Ellie Greenwich, tops the US chart, and will become a million-seller. The unusual recording features a revving motorcycle, brought into the studio by its owner, recording engineer Joey Veneri. The all-girl group – lead singer **Mary Weiss**, her sister **Betty**, **Marge Ganser**, and her twin sister **Mary Ann** – were discovered by Morton singing at gigs while still attending Andrew Jackson High School in Cambria Heights, New York.

28 Texas-born 31-year-old country singer-songwriter **Willie Nelson** achieves a childhood ambition by making his debut at Nashville's Grand Ole Opry, initially performing as an opening act for **Roger Miller**.

"The world is better because Sam Cooke lived. He inspired many youths of all races and creeds." Lou Rawls, December 18, 1964

December

11 **Sam Cooke** is shot dead at the $3-a-night Hacienda Motel at 9137 S. Figueroa, Los Angeles, by its manager, 55-year-old Bertha Franklin, after spending last night at PJs nightclub and checking into the motel with 22-year-old Elisa Boyer. Franklin claims that Cooke – married to his high-school sweetheart, Barbara Campbell – had tried to rape Boyer, and then in anger to assault Franklin herself, when his intended victim fled to phone the police. By the time they arrive, the R&B legend is dead – at 34. The coroner will return a verdict of justifiable homicide.

15 Having sung to a multiracial audience at a cinema near Cape Town last night, **Dusty Springfield** is served with a deportation order by the South African Ministry of the Interior. On her departure from London last week, Springfield said that she would perform only in front of non-segregated audiences.

16 Another major new pirate radio station begins broadcasting from the M.V. *Galaxy,* anchored outside the 3-mile limit of British territorial waters. Inspired by reading about the success of Radio Caroline, Radio London's backers are Texas businessmen, headed by Don Pierson, mayor of Eastland, who intends to introduce American Top 40-style radio – similar to his local KLIF station – to British listeners.

Pirate radio DJs Kenny Everett and Dave Cash, brought their zany style to the daily "Kenny & Cash Show" on Radio London.

Beatlemania was generating an ever-growing catalog of merchandise, from wigs to wallpaper... The Mersey Beat newspaper, founded by local journalist Bill Harry in 1961, had become the source of all things musically Liverpudlian.

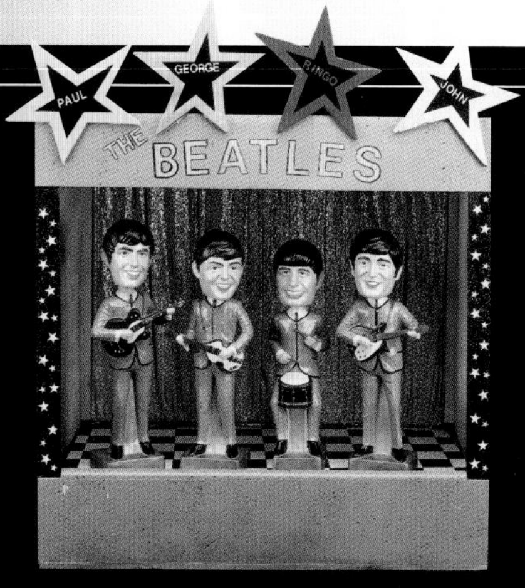

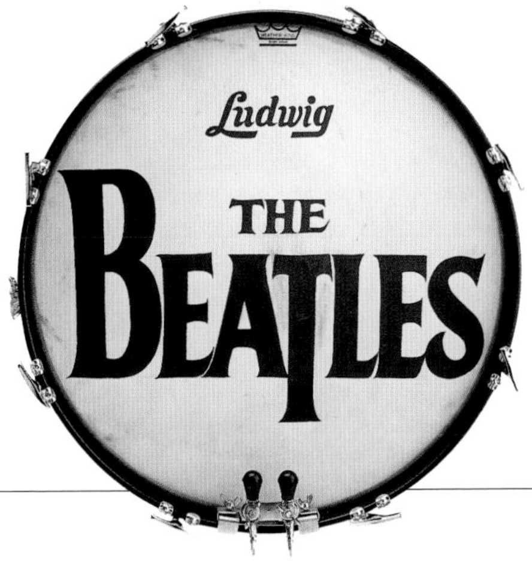

"Oh no, now they're saying the leader of the pack's dead and all that. This record's a load of rubbish. Turn it off"

Ringo Starr reviewing the Shangri-Las in **Melody Maker**, December 26, 1964

Among Radio London's first disc jockeys are Kenny Everett and Dave Cash. The station will stay on the air until August 14, 1967.

17 Thousands of mourners pay their last respects to **Sam Cooke** at the A.R. Leak Funeral Home in Chicago. His body is laid in a glass-topped coffin, and the fans file past in near-freezing temperatures. The numbers get out of hand, and the glass doors of the establishment are smashed before 50 policemen are called out to shepherd the overflow.

18 **Sam Cooke**'s funeral is held at the Mount Sinai Baptist Church in Chicago. The service, attended by many of his fellow musicians, becomes chaotic, despite **Ray Charles** singing *Angels Keep Watching Over Me*, and **Lou Rawls** and **Bobby "Blue" Bland** also performing gospel laments. On the gravestone is the inscription: "Sam Cooke. I Love You. 1930–1964. Until the day break, And the shadows flee away."

19 ***Beatles For Sale*** hits UK No. 1, displacing ***A Hard Day's Night*** after a run of 21 weeks. The new album includes eight new **Lennon/McCartney** compositions and six cover versions, including Buddy Holly's *Words Of Love* and Chuck Berry's *Rock And Roll Music* – on which Lennon, McCartney, and producer Martin all perform on one piano at the same time.

23 As the group's first appearance on "Shindig" airs (performing *Little Saint Nick*, *Johnny B. Goode*, *Dance Dance Dance*, and *Monster Mash*), the **Beach Boys' Brian Wilson** suffers a nervous breakdown (the first of three over the next 18 months), during a flight from Los Angeles to Houston at the start of a two-week tour. As he also suffers from partial deafness in one ear, he will retire from live performance with the group, and concentrate on writing and producing the records.

24 Another Beatles' Christmas Show opens at London's Hammersmith Odeon, also featuring **Freddie & the Dreamers**, Jimmy Savile, **Sounds Incorporated**, **Elkie Brooks**, the **Yardbirds**, **Michael Haslam**, the **Mike Cotton Sound**, and Ray Fell.

25 The US Labor Department's ruling that no more British artists will be granted H-1 work visas – because of concern over the number of groups "invading" the US – has resulted in the cancelation of tours by the **Zombies**, the **Nashville Teens**, and the **Hullabaloos**, but after a three-day wrangle, Murray the K's Big Holiday Show opens at the Fox Theater in Brooklyn, with all three bands on the bill. Also featured are **Chuck Jackson**, **Ben E. King & the Drifters**, the **Shirelles**, the **Shangri-Las**, Philadelphia-based R&B girl vocal group **Patti LaBelle & the Bluebelles**, and the **Vibrations**. (If the decision had stayed in force, tours by the Beatles and the Rolling Stones could have been canceled. Britain's Musicians Union insists that the regulations demand an exchange deal in every case. **Fats Domino**'s March dates have been canceled, as a "swap" for the Nashville Teens' US tour.)

26 In an advertisement placed in this week's **New Musical Express**, the **Rolling Stones** wish starving hairdressers and their families a Happy Christmas.

Rarely appearing as more than a trio, the Shangri-Las made the definitive "teen-death" record (storyline: girl meets boy, parents disapprove, boy dies on motorcycle) with *Leader Of The Pack*.

ROOTS **During this year: Levon Helm & the Hawks – with Robbie Robertson, Rick Danko, Richard Manuel, and Garth Hudson in the line-up – release their first record, *Leave Me Alone*, on the Toronto-based Ware Records label... 19-year-old guitarist Jeff Beck joins British band the Tridents for a 13-month apprenticeship before replacing Eric Clapton in the Yardbirds next year... 14-year-old piano savant Billy Joel is asked by producer Shadow Morton to play piano on tracks at a Red Bird session at Dynamic Studios in Levittown, New York... Journeymen veteran John Phillips, his girlfriend Michelle Gilliam, and Halifax Three veteran Denny Doherty come together as the New Journeymen on the Virgin Island of St. Thomas; they will soon be joined by ex-Mugwump, Cass Elliot... classically trained Welsh musician John Cale, in New York on a Leonard Bernstein scholarship, meets aspiring songwriter Lou Reed at a party... already with experience with the Decibels and the Town Criers, Bob Seger joins Doug Brown & the Omens – Ann Arbor, Michigan's top group... and aspiring singer-songwriter David Jones, working at an ad agency in London, joins former schoolfriend George Underwood to form the King Bees, whose first single, *Liza Jane* is released by Decca; it will be five years before he makes a chart impact as David Bowie....**

We've Gotta Get Out Of This Place

1965

No.1 US SINGLES

Jan 2 I Feel Fine **Beatles**
Jan 16 Come See About Me **Supremes**
Jan 23 Downtown **Petula Clark**
Feb 6 You've Lost That Lovin' Feelin' **Righteous Brothers**
Feb 20 This Diamond Ring **Gary Lewis & the Playboys**
Mar 6 My Girl **Temptations**
Mar 13 Eight Days A Week **Beatles**
Mar 27 Stop! In The Name Of Love **Supremes**
Apr 10 I'm Telling You Now **Freddie & the Dreamers**
Apr 24 Game Of Love **Wayne Fontana & the Mindbenders**
May 1 Mrs. Brown You've Got A Lovely Daughter **Herman's Hermits**
May 22 Ticket To Ride **Beatles**
May 29 Help Me, Rhonda **Beach Boys**
June 12 Back In My Arms Again **Supremes**
June 19 I Can't Help Myself **Four Tops**
June 26 Mr. Tambourine Man **Byrds**
July 10 (I Can't Get No) Satisfaction **Rolling Stones**
Aug 7 I'm Henry VIII, I Am **Herman's Hermits**
Aug 14 I Got You Babe **Sonny & Cher**
Sept 4 Help! **Beatles**
Sept 25 Eve Of Destruction **Barry McGuire**
Oct 2 Hang On Sloopy **McCoys**
Oct 9 Yesterday **Beatles**
Nov 6 Get Off Of My Cloud **Rolling Stones**
Nov 20 I Hear A Symphony **Supremes**
Dec 4 Turn! Turn! Turn! (To Everything There Is A Season) **Byrds**
Dec 25 Over And Over **Dave Clark Five**

No.1 UK SINGLES

Jan 2 I Feel Fine **Beatles**
Jan 16 Yeh Yeh **Georgie Fame & the Blue Flames**
Jan 30 Go Now **Moody Blues**
Feb 6 You've Lost That Lovin' Feelin' **Righteous Brothers**
Feb 20 Tired Of Waiting **Kinks**
Feb 27 I'll Never Find Another You **Seekers**
Mar 13 It's Not Unusual **Tom Jones**
Mar 20 The Last Time **Rolling Stones**
Apr 10 Concrete And Clay **Unit 4 + 2**

The Beatles filming "Help!"

The Who

The Beatles traveled to sunny climes to begin filming their second feature film, "Help!," which featured the chart-topping title track and *Ticket To Ride*, as well as Paul McCartney's masterpiece *Yesterday*... The Who began the year with memorable TV performances on "The Beat Room" and "Ready Steady Go!" and ended it with *My Generation*.

The British invasion would continue for the rest of the decade, and much that emerged from American artists this year was heavily influenced by the **Beatles**. British groups provided the year's signature songs, and the simplest is often cited as the greatest of the rock era: **Paul McCartney**'s *Yesterday* has become the most covered of all Beatles' songs (from **Marvin Gaye** to **Boyz II Men**), and for a time was the most played song in the history of American radio. In May, the **Rolling Stones** cut *(I Can't Get No) Satisfaction*, which quickly became an anthem for a generation at odds with its seniors.

But what has been dubbed the "most written-about performance in the history of rock" came from **Bob Dylan**: for 16 minutes at the Newport Folk Festival he abandoned the traditionalists and played electrified rock 'n' roll. His 1965 albums, ***Bringing It All Back Home*** and ***Highway 61 Revisited***, tore down barriers between folk and rock. It's not as though the Newport folkies had no warning. But when he strode on stage to embark on a three-song electric set, **Pete Seeger** reportedly tried to "unplug" him by attacking the generator with an ax.

One acoustic song Dylan performed at Newport was his *Mr. Tambourine Man* – which in a sweeter version had already become a big hit for the **Byrds**. Influenced by Dylan's lyrics and the Beatles' harmonies, the group introduced a smooth folk sound over tightly arranged rhythms, and a trademark in the jingle-jangle of **Jim McGuinn**'s 12-string Rickenbacker guitar. In turn, they influenced **George Harrison**'s *If I Needed Someone*, which appeared on ***Rubber Soul*** the same year. 1965 was the Byrds' most successful year.

The west coast rock scene was beginning to buzz. A new band called **Jefferson Airplane** played at the San Francisco nightclub the Matrix. The **Charlatans**, perhaps the first true psychedelic band, played the same club. A few months later, the **Grateful Dead** debuted at the Fillmore Auditorium, which was rapidly becoming the storefront for indigenous rock. Perhaps part of the buzz came from the growing popularity of LSD.

The business of making hits with timeless melodies looked almost mundane by comparison, but that's what Motown continued to do, and **Smokey Robinson** cut the perennial favorite, *The Tracks Of My Tears*. **James Brown** had a banner year, consolidating a stripped-down funk sound with pioneering hits like *Papa's Got A Brand New Bag* and his trademark song, *I Got You (I Feel Good)*, which sold more than a million copies.

"Ours is happy music - we haven't any message." Sonny Bono, Melody Maker, August 7, 1965

Apr 17	The Minute You're Gone	**Cliff Richard**
Apr 24	Ticket To Ride	**Beatles**
May 15	King Of The Road	**Roger Miller**
May 22	Where Are You Now (My Love)	**Jackie Trent**
May 29	Long Live Love	**Sandie Shaw**
June 19	Crying In The Chapel	**Elvis Presley**
June 26	I'm Alive	**Hollies**
July 3	Crying In The Chapel	**Elvis Presley**
July 10	I'm Alive	**Hollies**
July 24	Mr. Tambourine Man	**Byrds**
Aug 7	Help!	**Beatles**
Aug 28	I Got You Babe	**Sonny & Cher**
Sept 11	(I Can't Get No) Satisfaction	**Rolling Stones**
Sept 25	Make It Easy On Yourself	**Walker Brothers**
Oct 2	Tears	**Ken Dodd**
Nov 6	Get Off Of My Cloud	**Rolling Stones**
Nov 27	The Carnival Is Over	**Seekers**
Dec 18	Day Tripper/We Can Work It Out	**Beatles**

You've Lost That Lovin' Feelin' ... A defining recording session for Bob Dylan... The Byrds... Alan Freed and Nat King Cole pass away...

Black, Clark, and Shaw

January

3 Due to a tax dispute with the US Internal Revenue service, Brian Epstein says that future American visits by the **Beatles** are off, because income they have earned in the US is being blocked by Treasury officials. The group's take from American dates last year reportedly amounts to $2.8 million. (Under an Anglo-American tax treaty, artists have to pay taxes on all their earnings in both countries.)

4 CBS buys the Fender Guitar Company from its founder, Leo Fender, for $13 million. Together with the Gibson company, Fender has led the revolution in solid body guitars, with its Fender, Telecaster and Stratocaster models.

9 ***Beatles '65***, a US-only LP featuring eight tracks from ***Beatles For Sale*** and the No. 1 *I Feel Fine/She's A Woman*, jumps from No. 98 to No. 1: the biggest leap in **Billboard** chart history.

9 The **Righteous Brothers**' new single, *You've Lost That Lovin' Feelin'*, is featured on "Juke Box Jury," and voted a "miss" by all four panelists. Their collective decision will become a historic "miss," when the record tops both the US and UK charts next month, set to become the most played song in American radio history. It was written by Barry Mann and Cynthia Weil for the Righteous Brothers at the specific request of co-writer/producer **Phil Spector**, who has recently signed the duo to the Philles label. Even among a canon that includes *Da Doo Ron Ron*, *Be My Baby*, *Baby I Love You*, and *And Then He Kissed Me*, it is musical architect Spector's finest construction. With **Bobby Hatfield**'s high tenor countering **Bill Medley**'s rich baritone, and their vocal prowess surrounded by a Wall of Sound crescendo, *Feelin'* marks a defining moment in pop history.

12 "Hullabaloo," a new music-variety television series, debuts on NBC. The show features mini-skirted go-go girls known as the Hullabaloo Dancers, the voice-over announcements of disc jockey Johnny Holliday, and a different guest host each week. Its format includes the Top Pop Medley, in which the host and guests perform snippets of current chart hits, as well as the "Hullabaloo A Go-Go," on a set resembling a mod nightclub.

14 **Bob Dylan** begins the first of two recording sessions for his forthcoming LP, ***Bringing It All Back Home***, at Columbia's Studio A in New York. Once again produced by Tom Wilson, Dylan cuts some career-defining songs,

Influenced by the Beatles and covering Bob Dylan, the Byrds exploded on the scene with two No. 1 hits during the year.

The Righteous Brothers

With *Downtown*, veteran Petula Clark topped the US charts, something upstart British singers Cilla Black and Sandie Shaw were never able to do... Barry Mann and Cynthia Weil wrote *You've Lost That Lovin' Feelin'* for the Righteous Brothers at the Chateau Marmont Hotel in Hollywood.

including *Maggie's Farm, Subterranean Homesick Blues, If You Gotta Go Go Now, She Belongs To Me, Love Minus Zero/No Limit, Mr. Tambourine Man*, and *It's All Over Now, Baby Blue.*

17 The **Rolling Stones** record *The Last Time* in Los Angeles at RCA Hollywood Studios, along with its planned B-side, *Play With Fire*. The latter features **Phil Spector** on guitar.

20 Currently playing a residency at Ciro's in Los Angeles, the **Byrds** record Bob Dylan's *Mr. Tambourine Man* at Columbia's Hollywood Studios. The group recently signed to the label at the behest of jazz great Miles Davis. Although the line-up includes bassist/singer **Chris Hillman**, guitarist/singer **David Crosby**, percussionist/singer **Gene Clark**, and drummer **Michael Clarke**, the song's producer, Terry Melcher, allows only front man **Jim McGuinn** (a 22-year-old from Chicago) to play on the record. He uses top session men **Hal Blaine** on drums, **Larry Knechtel** on bass, **Jerry Cole** on rhythm guitar, and **Leon Russell** on electric piano. McGuinn's jangly introduction, played on his 12-string Rickenbacker guitar, will become a trademark sound for much future Byrds' material.

20 **Alan Freed**, the self-styled "Father of Rock 'n' Roll," dies – age 43 and virtually penniless – in Palm Springs. Credited with coining the phrase "rock 'n' roll" while a DJ at WJW Radio in Cleveland, Freed was one of the first radio personalities to program black music for white audiences. He became an extremely successful (and wealthy) promoter of rock 'n' roll package tours during the 1950s, but his later years have been plagued by payola scandals and lawsuits, following a congressional investigation that made him a scapegoat for what was a widespread industry practice. His ashes will be interred in Ferncliff Cemetery in Hartsdale, New York. (On March 21, 2002, they will be re-interred in a wall in the Rock and Roll Hall of Fame building in Cleveland.)

22 As the **Rolling Stones**' second album (again untitled, but known as ***Rolling Stones No. 2***) makes its UK bow at No. 9, they are greeted by 3,000 fans when they arrive in Sydney, at the start of a 16-date tour of Australia, New Zealand, and East Asia. About 300 youths tear down a fence, breaking into a quarantine area and ripping a rail in the customs hall. The busy tour, with **Roy Orbison**, **Rolf Harris**, and **Dionne Warwick** in support, will cover 36 shows in 16 days, and opens at the Manufacturers' Auditorium of the Agricultural Hall in Sydney.

"Already in the American Top 10, this is [Phil] Spector's greatest production, the last word in Tomorrow's sound Today, exposing the overall mediocrity of the Music Industry."

Ad by Andrew Loog Oldham for the Righteous Brothers' *You've Lost That Lovin' Feelin'*, January 1965

23 Stuck at No. 2 behind the **Beatles**' *I Feel Fine* for four weeks in the UK chart last month, **Petula Clark** manages to go one better in the US, as *Downtown* tops the Hot 100. The song was written by her producer Tony Hatch, and recorded last month at a session that the Paris-based Clark claimed would be her last English recording – if she couldn't get a hit.

28 The **Who** perform their first hit – the UK No. 8-peaking *I Can't Explain* – on "Ready Steady Go!" The studio audience consists mostly of mods: a stunt arranged by the group's manager, Kit Lambert.

February

1 **James Brown** records *Papa's Got A Brand New Bag* at the Arthur Smith Studios in Charlotte, North Carolina. He is backed by his regular crew: **Maceo Parker**, **St. Clair Pinckney**, **Al Clark**, **Eldee Williams**, **Jimmy Nolen**, **Alphonso Kellum**, **Melvin Parker**, **Lucas "Fats" Gander**, and trumpeters **Joe Dupars**, **Ron Tooley**, and **Levi Rasbury**. With its innovative, unconventional rhythm structure, and Brown's passionate signature vocal delivery, the record will give Brown his first US Top 10 hit (No. 8), top the R&B survey for two months, and open his UK chart account.

12 **Donovan**, an 18-year old folk/pop newcomer from Glasgow, marketed by his label, Pye Records, as "the British Bob Dylan," appears on "Ready Steady Go!" (He will return for the next two shows, becoming the first artist to make three consecutive appearances in the program's history). Amid media claims that he is little more than a pale imitation of Dylan – he wears a denim cap, racked harmonica, and a guitar inscribed "This machine kills" – Donovan performs his upcoming 45 debut, the self-penned *Catch The Wind*.

15 **Nat King Cole**, the most popular black performer of his era, dies from lung cancer in Santa Monica, at the age of 45. Some 400 friends and relatives will attend his funeral at St. James Church in Los Angeles in three days' time.

23 Filming of the second **Beatles** movie, as yet untitled, begins on New Providence in the Bahamas. After two weeks here, the Fab Four will head off to Obertauern in Austria for a further seven days of shooting, then home to England. Filming will continue on and off at Twickenham Film Studios, west London, until mid-May.

Feb 1965

The Walker Brothers... Solomon Burke nabs his first R&B No. 1... The Stones in America... *(I Can't Get No) Satisfaction*...

The Rolling Stones made their live UK television bow on ITV's "Ready Steady Goes Live!"

27 The **Seekers**, comprising **Judith Durham**, **Keith Potger**, **Bruce Woodley**, and **Athol Guy**, become the first Australian act to top the UK chart, with *I'll Never Find Another You*. The group, with six and 12-string acoustic guitar and stand-up bass accompanying one-time jazz singer Durham, will secure two further top three hits this year: *A World Of Our Own* and *The Carnival Is Over*. All three songs are penned by producer Tom Springfield.

March

13 A short article by journalist Chris Welch appears in **Melody Maker**, about the **Walker Brothers**, an American trio who have recently arrived in the UK, on a trip funded by a $10,000 loan from the father of drummer **Gary Leeds**. The group – completed by singers **Scott Engel** and **John Maus** – walked into the magazine's offices and buttonholed the writer, eager to impress him about their connection with P.J. Proby (for whom Leeds has been a regular drummer). They are already signed to Mercury Records' Smash imprint in the US. The Walker Brothers will become regular performers on "Ready Steady Go!" and find greater success in Britain than at home. Their third single, a cover of **Jerry Butler**'s *Make It Easy On Yourself*, will top the UK chart in September.

13 Having filled in for a sick **P.J. Proby** on a UK tour earlier in the week, **Tom Jones** makes his first major television appearance on BBC1's "Billy Cotton Band Show."

19 The **Tailor and Cutter** magazine carries a plea to the **Rolling Stones** to wear ties, to save tiemakers from financial disaster. Journalist William Marshall writes: "This article is triggered by the sartorial discrepancies of Mr. Mick Jagger (lead singer of the Rolling Stones) but the trend towards disregard for proper clothes for proper occasions is one shared in its instigation by other celebrities in the show business world. The Stones are not the only pebbles on the beach, but an authoritative lead from the Number One spot on the Top 20 would be clearly welcome. It might do more for the necktie than all the tie weeks from here to forever." Years later, **Tailor and Cutter** will name Jagger on its list of Hot Hundred Best Dressed Men.

19 Having left Roulette to sign with Atlantic Records, **Sam & Dave** make their first recordings at Stax Records' studios in Memphis. This is part of a deal, worked out between label heads Jerry Wexler and Jim Stewart, that sees the soul duo signed to Atlantic but loaned to Stax, so long as the label is distributed by Atlantic. Today they cut David Porter's *A Place Nobody Can Find* and the Porter/Steve Cropper song, *Good Night Baby*, backed by **Booker T. & the MG's**.

20 Tamla-Motown's Motor Town Revue opens a 21-date, twice-nightly UK tour, at the Finsbury Park Astoria in London, showcasing **Stevie Wonder**, **Martha & the Vandellas**, the **Miracles**, the **Supremes**, and the **Temptations**, with British guest stars **Georgie Fame & the Blue Flames**.

THE YARDBIRDS

Mar 13 Melody Maker reports that 19-year-old guitarist Eric Clapton has left the Yardbirds because he says they are becoming "too commercial." The popular London-based rock quintet recently signed to EMI's Columbia label, and *For Your Love* will enter the UK chart next week. Keith Relf, who met Clapton at Kingston College of Art, says: "It's very sad because we are all friends. There was no bad feeling at all, but Eric did not get on well with the business. He does not like commercialization. He loves the blues so much I suppose he did not like it being played badly by a white shower like us!" Clapton will go on to join John Mayall's Bluesbreakers, an apprentice shop for aspiring British blues musicians.

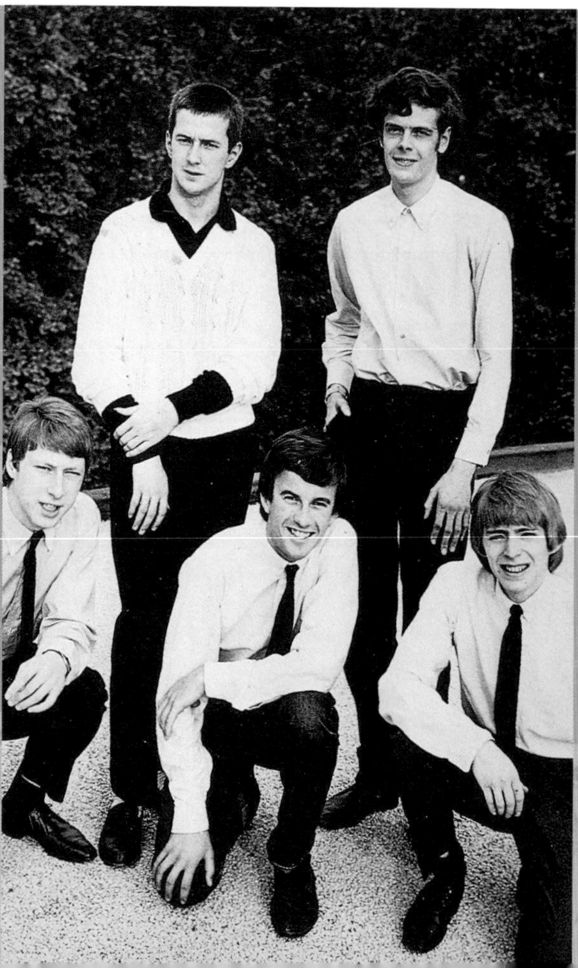

Another promising young guitarist, 19-year-old Jeff Beck, would replace Eric Clapton in the Yardbirds. Described by lead vocalist Keith Relf as "very, very good," he was recommended to the group by session man Jimmy Page, "who is the guv'nor."

Tom Jones

Tom Jones topped the UK chart in March with *It's Not Unusual* – the first solo act to do so since November 1964... "The Rolling Stones Book" was issued monthly from June 1964 until November 1966. The first publication was the only one to feature all five Stones on its cover.

April

3 Soul singer **Solomon Burke** – who has been recording for ten years and signed to Atlantic in 1960 – finally nabs a US R&B No. 1 with *Got To Get You Off My Mind*. Philadelphia-born Burke began his career as the "Wonder Boy Preacher," broadcasting from his own "Solomon's Temple" church from 1945 to 1955.

5 Songwriter/producer and Phil Spector sessioneer **Sonny Bono**, and his new bride, 18-year-old singer **Cher**, are signed to Atlantic Records' Atco imprint by Ahmet Ertegun. Cher has also worked for Spector as a backing singer for the Ronettes, and recorded one solo single – released on his Annette label – under the name **Bonnie Jo Mason**. As **Caesar & Cleo**, she and Sonny cut a one-off for Vault Records and two 45s for Mo Ostin's Reprise label last year.

13 **Roger Miller**, whose current crossover country smash *King Of The Road* (US No. 4) is also on its way to top the UK chart, sweeps the seventh annual Grammy awards. *Dang Me* wins the Best Country & Western Single, Best Country & Western Song and Best Country & Western Vocal Performance, Male categories. Miller is also named Best New Country & Western Artist, while ***Dang Me/Chug-a-Lug*** wins the Best Country & Western Album trophy. The **Beatles** nab just two awards, Best New Artist and Best Performance by a Vocal Group (for *A Hard Day's Night*), but are shut out in four other categories, losing to **Stan Getz and Astrud Gilberto**'s *The Girl From Ipanema* for Record of the Year, to *Hello, Dolly!* for Song of the Year, to **Petula Clark**'s *Downtown* for Best Rock & Roll Recording, and to the "Mary Poppins" soundtrack for Best Original Score Written for a Motion Picture or TV Show.

17 RCA Victor Records and the LearJet Corporation announce the development of an integrated car radio and stereo tape cartridge system. Expected to arrive in American vehicles by year's end, the new machine allows drivers to switch from Bach to the Beatles and back again at the push of a button. Irwin Tarr, RCA's manager of merchandising and planning, claims that "with only 400 feet of tape, listeners will be able to hear as much music as is now being carried on one or two long-playing records."

17 Murray the K's annual Easter package opens at the Fox Theater in Brooklyn, with the **Righteous Brothers**, the **Four Tops**, the **Temptations**, **Martha & the Vandellas**, the **Miracles**, **Marvin Gaye**, the **Marvelettes**, **Little Anthony & the Imperials**, the **Del Satins**, the **Rag Dolls**, **Cannibal & the Headhunters**, and **Gerry & the Pacemakers**, who are embarking on a US tour.

30 **Bob Dylan**'s eight-date UK Don't Look Back visit opens at Sheffield City Hall, and will be highlighted by two final sellout performances at the Royal Albert Hall on May 9 and 10.

May

2 Despite Ed Sullivan's comments after their first appearance last year, the **Rolling Stones** – who started their North American tour on April 23 in Montreal – return to "The Ed Sullivan Show," and perform *The Last Time*, *Little Red Rooster*, and *Everybody Needs Somebody To Love*. Also on the program are fellow Brits **Tom Jones** and **Dusty Springfield**. Following the Stones' appearance, Sullivan will send them a telegram: "Received thousands of calls from parents complaining about you but thousands from teenagers praising you. Best of luck on your tour."

6 **James Brown** records *I Got You (I Feel Good)* at Criteria Studios in Miami. It is set to become his biggest career hit at US No. 3, and sets new standards in soul music.

7 Following last night's gig at the Jack Russell Stadium in Clearwater, Florida, the **Rolling Stones**' **Keith Richard** wakes up in the Gulf Motel and discovers he left his tape recorder running last night while he was riffing. He finds he wrote a melody, to which **Mick Jagger** will add lyrics, creating *(I Can't Get No) Satisfaction*.

8 With **Bob Dylan**'s UK trip caught on film by director D.A. Pennebaker for a forthcoming *cinéma vérité* release, "Don't Look Back," the singer-songwriter makes a promotional clip for his current single, *Subterranean Homesick Blues*. Standing in a scaffolding-filled alleyway next to the Savoy Hotel in London, a virtually motionless Dylan flicks through themed "cards" that contain pertinent short words and phrases, effectively creating one of the first music videos. The cards have been written by **Joan Baez** and

> **"The trouble with a tie is that it could dangle in the soup... it is also something extra to which a fan can hang on when you are trying to get in and out of a theatre."**
>
> Mick Jagger, **Daily Mirror**, March 20, 1965

Sam & Dave (Samuel Moore and Dave Prater) first met at the King of Hearts club in Miami, where Dave was working as a chef.

Paul McCartney records *Yesterday*... Paul Revere & the Raiders...

"No more than four ugly faces, four long heads of hair, four sublime idiots, four barefoot bums." **Il Messaggero** on the Beatles, June 1965

Animals' keyboardist **Alan Price**. Allen Ginsberg and Bob Neuwirth can be seen in the background. Pennebaker's fly-on-the-wall documentary follows Dylan through jam sessions in hotels, confrontations with fans and journalists, limo rides, and stage performances.

12 The **Rolling Stones** lay down basic tracks for *(I Can't Get No) Satisfaction* at Chess Studios in Chicago. They will complete the recording in two days' time at the RCA Studios in Hollywood, where they will also finish more tracks for the forthcoming ***Out Of Our Heads.***

18 The publishers of "Who's Who in America" announce that the **Beatles** will be listed in the forthcoming edition, "now we're convinced they're stayers, at least for the period of our 1966–67 edition... The verve, freshness and rollicksome humor of their music and antics are refreshingly creative as well as commercially advantageous. Our policy is to recognize the unusual in the arts."

19 At a gig at the Capital Theatre in Cardiff, during the **Kinks**' UK tour, and having just finished playing *You Really Got Me*, guitarist **Dave Davies** is starting to play Little Richard's *Beautiful Delilah* when drummer **Mick Avory** hits him over the head with a cymbal. Davies is taken to the Cardiff Royal Infirmary for emergency treatment, and receives 16 stitches. Avory becomes *persona non grata* on discovering that the police want to arrest him on charges of causing grievous bodily harm. Fortunately, Davies refuses to press charges. The band will pull out of the rest of the tour, with the **Walker Brothers** filling in for them on the remaining dates.

"It was the song that really made the Rolling Stones, changed us from just another band into a huge, monster band..."

Mick Jagger on *(I Can't Get No) Satisfaction*

Bob Dylan's first UK tour was captured on film by D.A. Pennebaker. After the tour's final show in London, Dylan and the Beatles met for the first time.

25 **Sonny Boy Williamson** dies of a heart attack, at the age of 56, in Helena, Arkansas. The blues singer-songwriter/guitarist, who recorded for the Checker label in the mid-1950s, will also be remembered as one of the most influential blues harmonica players.

June

12 The **Beatles** each receive the MBE in the Queen's Birthday Honours List. Protests pour into Buckingham Palace, along with returned medals. Colonel Frederick Wragg returns 12 medals and former Canadian MP Hector Dupuis, MBE, claims, "The British house of royalty has put me on the same level as a bunch of vulgar numbskulls." (**John Lennon**'s only comment is, "I thought you had to drive tanks and win wars.")

14 **Paul McCartney**, accompanied by his own acoustic guitar, records *Yesterday* at EMI's Abbey Road Studio. Producer George Martin will add a string quartet arrangement later in the week. Although it will not be released as a single in the UK until 1976 (when it will hit No. 8), *Yesterday* will be featured on side 2 of the British issue of the forthcoming ***Help!*** soundtrack. The song will top the US chart for the first of four weeks on October 9 – where it is excluded from the album. The only **Beatles** hit recorded by only one member of the band, it will become – for a while – the most played song of all time on American radio, and the most covered tune (more than 2,500 versions) in the history of 20th-century music.

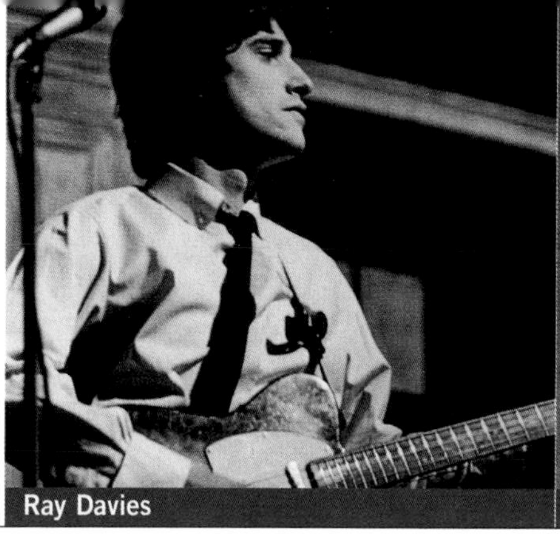

Ray Davies

The Hollies

Siblings Ray and Dave Davies were famous for their volatile relationship, but it was drummer Mick Avory who sent Dave to the hospital... The Hollies, one of the most consistent hitmakers of all time, had their first UK chart-topper in June.

15 Five months after laying down tracks for ***Bringing It All Back Home***, **Bob Dylan** returns to Columbia to record material for ***Highway 61 Revisited***. Today he cuts a new composition, *Like A Rolling Stone*, his first electric recording. He is accompanied by blues guitarist **Mike Bloomfield**, bassist **Harvey Brooks**, pianist **Paul Griffin**, **Bobby Gregg** on drums, and **Al Kooper** – whose rolling Hammond organ part will become one of rock music's most recognizable sounds.

20 **Ira Louvin**, who with his younger brother **Charlie** formed the influential country duo the **Louvin Brothers**, is killed, age 41, in a two-car collision in Williamsburg, Missouri. The accident takes the lives of six people, including Louvin's fourth wife, singer Anne Young. (Ira escaped death last year, when his previous wife, Faye, shot him. Charlie will continue to log up solo country hits for Capitol well into the 1970s.)

24 At the Stones' first concert in Norway, police armed with batons disperse rioting fans at the Messhallen in Oslo. With some 3,000 fans yelling "We want the **Rolling Stones**," one girl's plea comes true, when she climbs up on to the stage and embraces **Charlie Watts**. She immediately faints.

26 In a chart career that will span 30 years and 30 hits, the **Hollies** achieve their only UK chart-topper for the next two decades: the Clint Ballard-penned *I'm Alive*.

27 The **Beatles** play two shows at the Teatro Adriano in Rome, having begun a European tour in Paris on June 20. Their reception in Italy is a far cry from "Beatlemania." Neither house on this brief stop sells out, while newspapers make comments such as ***Il Messaggero***'s: "No more than four ugly faces, four long heads of hair, four sublime idiots, four barefoot bums."

28 ABC television launches **Dick Clark**'s new daily afternoon music show, "Where The Action Is," in essence an outdoor version of "American Bandstand." **Jan & Dean** (*Surf City* and *You Really Know How To Hurt A Guy*) and **Dee Dee Sharp** (*Ride* and *You'll Never Be Mine*) guest on today's opening edition, but it is **Paul Revere & the Raiders** who impress Clark with their showmanship, teen appeal, and their startling Revolutionary War stage outfits – a band trademark. He adopts them as the house band for the show. The resulting constant national exposure will turn the group into teen idols, particularly their photogenic lead singer, **Mark Lindsay**.

Racking up a string of pop/rock hits, Paul Revere & the Raiders became one of Columbia Records' biggest acts of the 1960s.

1965

Sonny & Cher

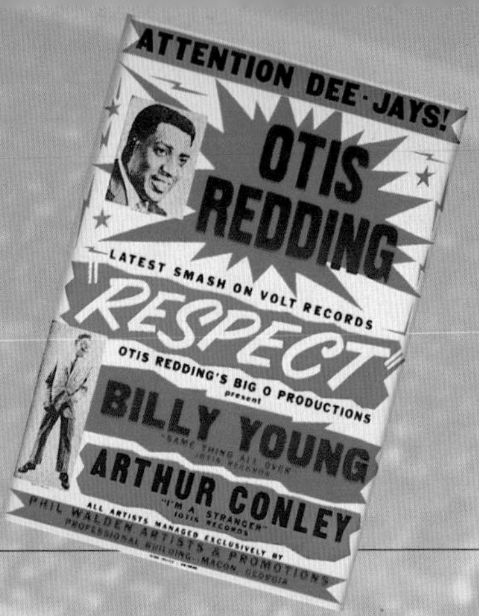

Otis Redding's seminal *Otis Blue*... Dylan goes electric... Elvis meets the Beatles...

July

7 **Sonny & Cher** sing their new single, *I Got You Babe*, on "Shindig." Written by Sonny at home in Laurel Canyon, Los Angeles, it was personally plugged by him during early promotion to Hollywood radio station, KHJ. The instant global smash will hit US No. 1 on August 14 and repeat the feat in the UK two weeks later.

9 Having cut the soul ballad *I've Been Loving You Too Long* on April 19, **Otis Redding** begins recording in earnest for what will emerge as ***Otis Blue***. He cuts *A Change Is Gonna Come* and *Shake* (both penned by Sam Cooke), *Rock Me Baby*, *You Don't Miss Your Water*, *Respect*, and a cover of the Rolling Stones' *(I Can't Get No) Satisfaction*. The last was recommended by guitarist **Steve Cropper** – Redding has not yet heard it.

13 The **Beatles** win two more Ivor Novello Awards at the tenth annual ceremony, held at the Savoy Hotel in London. *Can't Buy Me Love* is named the Most Performed Work of 1964 and also Best Selling "A" Side. (*A Hard Day's Night* is runner-up in two categories – Most Performed Work and the Year's Outstanding Theme from Radio, TV, or Film – and *I Feel Fine* is the Best Selling "A" Side runner-up.) **Paul McCartney**, who is the only Beatle to attend the ceremony, says, "Thanks. I hope nobody sends theirs back now." Tony Hatch's *Downtown* is named Outstanding Song of the Year.

22 Despite telling the magistrate that he suffers from a weak bladder, Rolling Stone **Bill Wyman** is fined £5 ($14), with joint costs of 15 guineas (£15.75/$44) imposed on fellow Stones **Mick Jagger** and **Brian Jones**. They are found guilty at West Ham Magistrates' Court, London, of insulting behavior by urinating "without taking steps to conceal this act" on March 18. Prosecutor Mr. Kenneth Richardson claims that Wyman asked the mechanic at the Francis Service Station on the Romford Road in Forest Gate, London, if he could go to the toilet – but was refused. When the mechanic asked Jagger to get the group off the garage forecourt he brushed him aside, saying, "We'll piss anywhere, man." Wyman, Jagger, and Jones were then seen to urinate against a wall. The car drove off with people inside sticking their hands through the windows making a well-known derogatory gesture. The magistrate rebukes the three of them for not setting a higher moral standard for their fans, and calls Wyman "a shaggy-haired monster."

25 Following an acoustic performance of *Mr. Tambourine Man* and *All I Really Wanna Do* at yesterday's afternoon workshop, **Bob Dylan** performs at the Newport Folk Festival. Backed by **Al Kooper**, **Barry Goldberg**, and the **Paul Butterfield Blues Band** rhythm section – **Mike Bloomfield**, **Jerome Arnold**, and **Sam Lay** – he plays his first electric set. Opinions will vary as to what happens next. Most media reports will allege that diehard acoustic folk "purists" in the audience tried to boo him offstage, while some firsthand accounts will claim that Dylan's electric experimentation was met by an enthusiastic response. What does clearly emerge is that Dylan is creatively restless, and eager to broaden his musical spectrum, a decision that will engender longterm respect and commercial return.

31 **Sonny & Cher** arrive in Britain, amid much publicity. They are barred from entering the London Hilton hotel, allegedly because of their attire. It will transpire that this is largely a publicity stunt, with film crews conveniently present to witness the barring, and a doorman's palm being greased with several crisp banknotes.

August

5 **Jan & Dean**'s **Jan Berry** breaks his leg on the first day of filming "Easy Come Easy Go" in Chatsworth, California, when a train rams a camera car on which he is standing. A total of 17 people are hurt in the accident, causing Paramount to cancel the film.

6 The 5th National Jazz & Blues Festival gets under way at Richmond Athletic Ground, west London. The three-day event is catering to a more rock-oriented audience – so much so that the jazz artists on the bill are placed in afternoon slots only. Today's line-up, titled "Ready, Steady, Richmond!," features the **Yardbirds**, the **Who**, the **Mike Cotton Sound**, and the **Moody Blues**.

7 *In The Midnight Hour* gives 24-year-old soul singer-songwriter **Wilson Pickett** his first US R&B chart-topper. Alabama-born Pickett, an ex-member of the **Falcons**, cut a few sides for the Double L label, before being snapped up by Atlantic's Jerry Wexler last year. *In The Midnight Hour* was recorded at the Stax studio in Memphis.

> **"It's all music: no more, no less. I know in my own mind what I'm doing. If anyone has imagination, he'll know what I'm doing. If they can't understand my songs they're missing something..."**
>
> Bob Dylan, **The New York Times**, August 28, 1965

The Beatles grossed a record-breaking $304,000 at Shea Stadium – home of the New York Mets baseball team – but declined an offer of $478,800 to play more dates in the city.

Wilson Pickett

bobcat vests... DJs were advised that Otis Redding's *Respect* was his latest smash on Volt... Wilson Pickett's hit, *In The Midnight Hour*, was written by him with Stax mainman Steve Cropper – in a Memphis hotel room over a bottle of Jack Daniel's.

"The fans went wild. I had to turn on the hose."

Security guard Harry Oldham at a Rolling Stones TV show, August 22, 1965

14 With the extracted title single topping the British survey last week, the **Beatles'** *Help!* debuts at US No. 1. It also enters at UK No. 1 (the first LP to do so in the seven-year history of the chart), displacing the soundtrack recording of *The Sound Of Music*. After nine weeks at No. 1, it will be replaced – by the same soundtrack. The next three Beatles albums will all be knocked off the top spot by the Von Trapps.

15 The **Beatles'** third North American tour begins at Shea Stadium in Flushing, before a record crowd of 55,600. With a security force numbering 2,000, the show grosses $304,000, a world record for a pop concert. The Beatles are supported by **Brenda Holloway and the King Curtis Band, Cannibal & the Headhunters, Sounds Incorporated**, and recent Atlantic Records signing, the **Young Rascals**. Led by ex-**Joey Dee & the Starliters** members, **Felix Cavaliere, Eddie Brigati**, and **Gene Cornish**, the Young Rascals are managed by Sid Bernstein, who flashes "The Rascals are Coming" on the scoreboard during the gig.

22 Security guards spray 200 screaming teenagers with water from a fire hose, when they break through a barrier at Granada Television's studios in Manchester. They have been waiting for the **Rolling Stones** to arrive for rehearsals for tomorrow night's "Scene at 6:30" program.

27 **Elvis Presley** plays host to the **Beatles**, who are on a break in Los Angeles during a US tour, at his rented house in Perugia Way, Bel Air. They talk and jam together late into the night, playing along to records, while their respective managers, "Col." Tom Parker and Brian Epstein, play pool in an adjoining room.

28 **Bob Dylan**'s fall tour begins at the Forest Hills Tennis Stadium, New York. For his first concert since the Newport Folk Festival, Dylan plays a solo set of seven numbers, opening with *She Belongs To Me* and ending with *Mr. Tambourine Man*. For the second half he is backed by keyboardist **Al Kooper**, bassist **Harvey Brooks**, and two members of the **Hawks**: 21-year-old Canadian **Robbie Robertson** on guitar, and 23-year-old Arizona native **Levon Helm** on drums. The eight-song set includes *Maggie's Farm* and *Like A Rolling Stone* among its highlights. This format, an acoustic followed by an electric set, will be followed throughout the tour, and during next year's world tour.

Otis Redding's *Otis Blue*, described as a "fusion of blues, pop and gospel," was subtitled "Otis Redding Sings Soul." In his sleeve notes, Bob Rolontz wrote: "Soul is not something that can be feigned – you either have it or you don't. Otis Redding has it."

Sept 1965

The Monkees are created... The Who record *My Generation*...

September

3 Another ten-day package promoted by Murray the K opens at Brooklyn's Fox Theater. It features the **Four Tops**, **Marvin Gaye**, the **Beau Brummels** (a new San Francisco-based rock quartet who have already scored two US Top 20 hits this year), **Stevie Wonder**, **Martha & the Vandellas**, the **Temptations**, the **Lovin' Spoonful** (a fresh New York City-based jug-band rock foursome, led by singer-songwriter/guitarist **John Sebastian**, who are taking off with *Do You Believe In Magic*), **Brenda Holloway**, **Patti LaBelle & the Bluebelles**, the **Del Satins**, and **Jordan Christopher**.

9 An ad appears in the **Hollywood Reporter** (followed tomorrow by the same notice in **Daily Variety**): "Madness!! Folk & ROLL Musicians Singers for acting roles in new TV series. Running parts for 4 insane boys, age 17 to 21. Want spirited Ben Frank's types. Have courage to work. Must come down for interview. Call: HO 6-5188." Television producers Bob Rafelson and Bert Scheider will audition 437 hopefuls, including 20-year-old, Dallas-born singer/guitarist **Stephen Stills** (who will allegedly be turned down because of bad teeth), songwriter **Paul Williams**, **Keith Allison**, **Jerry Yester**, and **Three Dog Night**'s future leader **Danny Hutton**, who makes the last eight. (Reports that Charles Manson auditions are inaccurate: he is currently serving time at Terminal Island prison.) The four who will be signed – to act in a new television pilot series named "The Monkees," are **Davy Jones** (19, the only Englishman), **Michael Nesmith** (22), **Mickey Dolenz** (20), and **Peter Tork** (21). Jones is an ex-apprentice jockey and actor, who played Ena Sharples' grandson Colin Lomax in the British TV show "Coronation Street," and the Artful Dodger in both London and New York productions of "Oliver." Nesmith is a member of the Los Angeles folk circuit, releasing singles under the name **Michael Blessing**. Dolenz, the son of Hollywood character actor George Dolenz, was the child star of the TV show "Circus Boy," and has been a member of **Micky & the One Nighters** and the **Missing Links**. Tork, recommended to the producers by his friend **Stephen Stills**, has also drifted around the Los Angeles folk circuit, playing in the **Au Go Go Singers**.

15 Ford Motors becomes the first car company to offer 8-track players as an option for their complete line of vehicles. Home players will not be introduced for another year, and 8-track prerecorded tapes will initially be sold only in auto parts stores and roadside truck stops.

16 The second season premiere of "Shindig" – reverting to a half-hour format and now scheduled twice a week – airs on ABC. The **Everly Brothers** sing a revival of **Mickey & Sylvia**'s *Love Is Strange*, while the **Byrds** perform *Feel A Whole Lot Better* and *The Bells Of Rhymney*. They join the **McCoys** – a new rock band formed in Indiana by **Rick Derringer** (born Zehringer) and his brother **Randy** – on *California Sun*, while the McCoys also perform their signature hit *Hang On Sloopy* (which is heading to US No. 1).

> **"I would rather take the program off in a blaze of glory than let it outstay its welcome."**
>
> Elkan Allan explaining why "Ready Steady Go" was coming to an end, **Billboard**, October 2, 1965

October

1 Following two concerts in Texas, **Bob Dylan** unveils his new touring band in New York at his Carnegie Hall show. Once again leading off with a solo acoustic set, he returns with **Robbie Robertson** on guitar, **Garth Hudson** on organ, **Rick Danko** on bass, **Richard Manuel** on piano, and **Levon Helm** on drums.

13 The **Who** record *My Generation*, at Pye Studios in London. **Pete Townshend** wrote the song – which neatly captures the theme of youth anger, frustration, and exuberance – on May 19 during a train journey to Southampton to appear on a television show. This version, completed at the fourth attempt, will become the group's 1960s highlight, hitting UK No. 2 in December.

21 **Bill Black** dies at Baptist Memorial Hospital Memphis, from cancer, aged 39. Black's upright bass playing was an integral part of **Elvis Presley**'s early success.

21 The **Spencer Davis Group** cut *Keep On Running* at Pye Studios in London, which will top the UK chart next January. With **Chris Blackwell** producing and **Jimmy Cliff** guesting on backing vocals, the record is driven by **Muff Winwood**'s pounding bass line, and highlighted by his teenage brother **Steve**'s husky R&B vocals.

November

1 More than 3,500 teenagers scream and hurl objects during a **Rolling Stones** performance at the Community War Memorial auditorium in Rochester, New York. Police stop the show, first in an effort to quiet the crowd, and again after the group has finished seven of their 11 numbers. During the melée, **Keith Richard** yells: "This is a hick town. You're too hard with them."

In late 1965 the Byrds went out on the Dick Clark Caravan Tour with Paul Revere & the Raiders, Bo Diddley, and the We Five, while Otis Redding spent the early part of 1966 on tour with Sam & Dave, Patti LaBelle & the Bluebelles, Percy Sledge, Garnett Mimms, and others.

THE BEATLES

Oct 26 The Queen presents the Beatles with their MBEs in the Great Throne Room at Buckingham Palace, watched by 182 other recipients. When the Queen asks Starr, "How long have you been together now?" he replies, "Forty years."

The Spencer Davis Group – who cut Jackie Edward's *Keep On Running* in October – became the launching pad for teenager Steve Winwood, whose raspy vocal style belied his years.

The Beatles later admitted to having smoked marijuana in the lavatories of Buckingham Palace.

20 Motown scores its fifth US chart-topper of the year, with *I Hear A Symphony* by the **Supremes**. The world's biggest girl group is also celebrating its sixth US No. 1 in seven releases.
22 **Ray Charles** pleads guilty in US Federal District Court in Boston, after a grand jury returned a criminal indictment against the singer in February, following his drug arrest in October 1964. The indictment was on four narcotics charges – two for possessing 3.17 ounces of heroin and 588 grains of marijuana, and two for bringing heroin and marijuana into the country. Judge George Sweeney, told that Charles has kicked his heroin habit during a stay at St. Francis Hospital in Lynwood, California, defers his decision.
26 Peter Eden and Geoff Stephens serve **Donovan** with a work injunction, after the singer's lawyers have announced that he has ended his management contract with them – and signed instead with Ashley Kozak as his business manager and his father as his personal manager. The injunction will be denied on November 29.
27 Author Ken Kesey and his accomplices, the Merry Pranksters, hold the first in a series of public acid tests at the Longshoreman's Hall in San Francisco. With willing participants tripping out on fruit drinks spiked with the still-legal hallucinogenic LSD (provided by chemist Owsley Stanley), they "move" to music provided by the **Grateful Dead**. Previously known as Mother McCree's Uptown Jug Champions, and more recently as the Warlocks, the Grateful Dead are a collection of chemically stimulated musicians, comprising lead guitarist **Jerry Garcia**, rhythm guitarist **Bob Weir**, organ/harmonica player **Ron "Pigpen" McKernan**, bassist **Phil Lesh**, and drummer **Bill Kreutzmann**. Psychedelic/acid rock is born.

December

3 The **Beatles** embark on what will prove to be their final British tour – a nine-date, twice-nightly show – at Glasgow's Odeon Cinema. Meanwhile, 40,000 ticket applications have been received for the concerts in two days' time at the Empire Theatre, Liverpool, which holds 2,550.
3 **Keith Richard** is knocked unconscious by an electric shock during the **Stones**' concert at the Memorial Hall in Sacramento, when his guitar makes contact with his microphone during a performance of *The Last Time*.
10 In San Francisco, 34-year-old concert promoter **Bill Graham** holds his first rock concert at the Fillmore Auditorium. A benefit gig for the San Francisco Mime Troupe (a street-theater company that Graham manages), the event features three of the city's most promising young bands, who are all emerging from its bohemian, "hippy" Haight-Ashbury district: the electric country/folk combo the **Charlatans**, **Jefferson Airplane** (led by founder, vocalist **Marty Balin**), and the **Grateful Dead**.

Keith Moon's platform shoes were conservative by his usual standards. The ad for the Who's *Won't Get Fooled Again* in 1971 had Moon in a blonde wig and corset and suspenders.

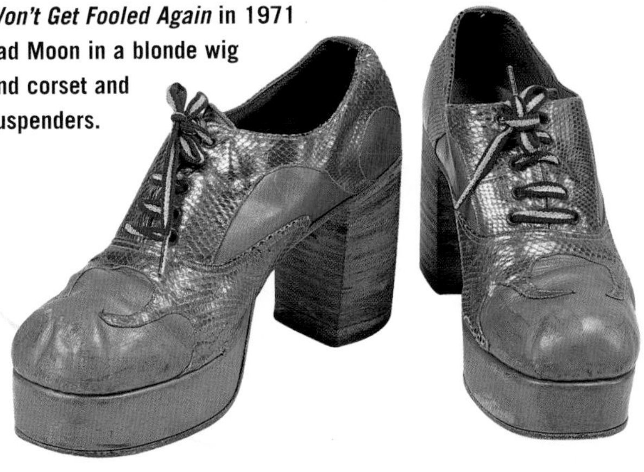

ROOTS During this year: Cortez High School friends in Phoenix form the Earwigs, playing mainly Rolling Stones and Who covers; changing their name to the Spiders next year, with lead vocalist Vincent Furnier, they will find their way to Los Angeles, initially to become the Nazz and then Alice Cooper... a troupe of art students at Goldsmith's College in south London form a whimsical, 1920s-inspired outfit called the Bonzo Dog Dada Band... having traveled through Denmark, France, and Spain, singer/songwriter Boz Scaggs records his debut album, *Boz*, in Stockholm... looking for a new member for their high school band, the Castiles take on 15-year-old Bruce Springsteen after he passes two auditions... Isaac Hayes, still holding down his day job in a Memphis meat-packing plant, meets insurance salesman and aspiring songwriter David Porter; they sign an exclusive writing and production partnership with Stax Records... on a US tour organized by the Jamaican government, Jimmy Cliff meets Island Records' boss Chris Blackwell, who persuades him to move to Britain... John Denver successfully auditions for the Chad Mitchell Trio, beating 250 other hopefuls... and Justin Hayward joins rock 'n' roll veteran Marty Wilde in the Wilde Cats; his songs also interest Lonnie Donegan, who signs him to a publishing deal...

(I'm) A Road Runner

1966

No.1 US SINGLES

Jan 1	The Sounds Of Silence **Simon & Garfunkel**
Jan 8	We Can Work It Out **Beatles**
Feb 5	My Love **Petula Clark**
Feb 19	Lightnin' Strikes **Lou Christie**
Feb 26	These Boots Are Made For Walkin' **Nancy Sinatra**
Mar 5	The Ballad Of The Green Berets **SSgt. Barry Sadler**
Apr 9	(You're My) Soul And Inspiration **Righteous Brothers**
Apr 30	Good Lovin' **Young Rascals**
May 7	Monday, Monday **Mamas & the Papas**
May 28	When A Man Loves A Woman **Percy Sledge**
June 11	Paint It Black **Rolling Stones**
June 25	Paperback Writer **Beatles**
July 2	Strangers In The Night **Frank Sinatra**
July 16	Hanky Panky **Tommy James & the Shondells**
July 30	Wild Thing **Troggs**
Aug 13	Summer In The City **Lovin' Spoonful**
Sept 3	Sunshine Superman **Donovan**
Sept 10	You Can't Hurry Love **Supremes**
Sept 24	Cherish **Association**
Oct 15	Reach Out I'll Be There **Four Tops**
Oct 29	96 Tears **? & the Mysterians**
Nov 5	Last Train To Clarksville **Monkees**
Nov 12	Poor Side Of Town **Johnny Rivers**
Nov 19	You Keep Me Hangin' On **Supremes**
Dec 3	Winchester Cathedral **New Vaudeville Band**
Dec 10	Good Vibrations **Beach Boys**
Dec 31	I'm A Believer **Monkees**

No.1 UK SINGLES

Jan 1	Day Tripper/We Can Work It Out **Beatles**
Jan 22	Keep On Running **Spencer Davis Group**
Jan 29	Michelle **Overlanders**
Feb 19	These Boots Are Made For Walkin' **Nancy Sinatra**
Mar 19	The Sun Ain't Gonna Shine Anymore **Walker Brothers**
Apr 16	Somebody Help Me **Spencer Davis Group**
Apr 30	You Don't Have To Say You Love Me **Dusty Springfield**

Brian Wilson

Mick Jagger

Brian Wilson, freed from the constraints of playing live with the Beach Boys, locked himself away in a studio to create his masterpiece, *Pet Sounds*... The Rolling Stones continued to move away from their R&B roots with the *Aftermath* album, entirely composed by Jagger and Richard, with Jack Nitzsche making an invaluable musical contribution.

This was "the year of living dangerously," artistically and literally. Drugs and anti-war protests fed a growing rift between rock and the Establishment – especially in the US. The **Beatles**, the **Beach Boys**, and others were experimenting with song structure and production techniques, and a psychedelic groove was emerging. Slamming the barn door long after the horse had bolted, the US authorities banned LSD in October. The Beatles learned that the public could be as hostile as it had been supportive, while opposition to the Vietnam draft presaged greater civil unrest. **Joan Baez** spent a while behind bars after an anti-Vietnam war protest.

And the music? The Beatles conjured with studio effects and eastern mysticism to produce their most daring LP yet – ***Revolver***, with **George Harrison** on the sitar betraying the influence of **Ravi Shankar**. The Stones' album ***Aftermath*** included experiments with heavy guitar distortion and often bizarre arrangements. In the US, music's center of gravity tilted toward the west coast, with the Beach Boys' ***Pet Sounds*** the most ambitious project of the year. With **Brian Wilson**'s meticulous production, the surf band had gone introspective: **Lennon** and **McCartney** were in awe.

The Haight-Ashbury district of San Francisco was emerging as the spiritual home of the hippie movement, and nurtured a kaleidoscope of musical and cultural styles. **Jefferson Airplane**, the **Grateful Dead**, and **Quicksilver Messenger Service** were joined on occasion by **Frank Zappa** and the **Mothers of Invention**. In the UK, **Pink Floyd** and **Soft Machine** played for the psychedelic underground scene. London was also launching American guitarist **Jimi Hendrix**, who became the hottest ticket in town.

Always to be relied upon to go his own way, **Bob Dylan** flavored his double album ***Blonde On Blonde*** with hints of country and western, and the album included some of his most emotional lyricism. Controversy still raged about the "plugged" rock that Dylan and his band the **Hawks** played at live gigs.

The year wasn't all drug-induced experimentation. Motown continued to make classic R&B songs and became the biggest-selling label in the US this year, thanks to the **Supremes, Stevie Wonder**, and the **Four Tops**. The Stax label, home of Memphis soul, also had another fruitful year.

Music's relationship with television was changing, underlined by the emergence of the **Monkees**, a group entirely made for television, who would enjoy huge chart success. Not quite the Mothers of Invention – but more acceptable early-evening viewing.

"The Monkees were not a musical act."

Michael Nesmith, **Off The Record**, 1988

May 7 Pretty Flamingo **Manfred Mann**
May 28 Paint It Black **Rolling Stones**
June 4 Strangers In The Night **Frank Sinatra**
June 25 Paperback Writer **Beatles**
July 9 Sunny Afternoon **Kinks**
July 23 Get Away **Georgie Fame & the Blue Flames**
July 30 Out Of Time **Chris Farlowe & the Thunderbirds**
Aug 6 With A Girl Like You **Troggs**
Aug 20 Yellow Submarine/Eleanor Rigby **Beatles**
Sept 17 All Or Nothing **Small Faces**
Sept 24 Distant Drums **Jim Reeves**
Oct 29 Reach Out I'll Be There **Four Tops**
Nov 19 Good Vibrations **Beach Boys**
Dec 3 Green, Green Grass Of Home **Tom Jones**

Jan 1966

Warhol and the Velvet Underground... *Pet Sounds*... Lennon's views on Jesus...

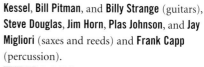

James Brown made his primetime TV debut on "The Ed Sullivan Show" after winning his first Grammy for *Papa's Got A Brand New Bag.* He would wait another 21 years before his next.

January

1 The year begins with folk/pop duo **Simon & Garfunkel** hitting US No. 1 for the first time, with *The Sounds Of Silence*, a song written by **Paul Simon** three years ago.

4 The **Temptations** begin recording *Ain't Too Proud To Beg* at the Motown Studios – with co-writer Norman Whitfield producing for the first time. The track will become their next single, and will begin an eight-week ride at No. 1 on the R&B chart on June 25, becoming the biggest genre hit of the year.

13 The **Velvet Underground** perform at the annual dinner of the New York Society for Clinical Psychiatry, held at the Hotel Delmonico on Park Avenue, New York, as part of a performance that is billed as "The Chic Mystique of Andy Warhol." **The New York Herald Tribune** reports that "a minority of old-fashioned Freudian analysts stormed out" but "the neo-Jungians, Harry Stack Sullivanites, Existentialists and just plain bread-and-butter head doctors got an electric shock treatment they'll never forget." **Newsweek** will report that one psychiatrist decided that it was "a spontaneous eruption of the id." The Velvet Underground is an experimental rock group formed two years ago by Long Island-born singer/guitarist **Lou Reed** and Welsh multi-instrumentalist **John Cale**. The line-up also includes **Sterling Morrison**, female drummer **Maureen Tucker**, and German-born vocalist **Nico**. They have come under the management wing of pop-culture artist Warhol, soon becoming the house band at his Factory arts collective in New York. Warhol will engage them in a number of increasingly avant-garde multimedia showcases, including next month's 70-minute "Exploding Plastic Inevitable," a mixed-media presentation that will debut at New York's Cinematique.

18 Having recorded the instrumental tracks *Trombone Dixie* and *Pet Sounds* last November, the Beach Boys' **Brian Wilson** begins work in earnest on what will be regarded as his recording zenith: the ***Pet Sounds*** project. *Let's Go Away For A While* is recorded at today's session at Gold Star Studios; *Wouldn't It Be Nice* will be laid down at the weekend and *You Still Believe In Me* next week. Like his mentor, **Phil Spector**, Wilson will use members of the Wrecking Crew to create the instrumental blocks of his aural masterpiece, namely **Hal Blaine** (drums), **Carol Kaye**, **Lyle Ritz**, and **Ray Pohlman** (basses), **Al DeLory**, **Larry Knechtel**, and **Don Randi** (piano and organ), **Glen Campbell**, **Al Casey**, **Jerry Cole**, **Barney Kessel**, **Bill Pitman**, and **Billy Strange** (guitars), **Steve Douglas**, **Jim Horn**, **Plas Johnson**, and **Jay Migliori** (saxes and reeds) and **Frank Capp** (percussion).

25 **Bob Dylan** cuts the first of two tracks – *One Of Us Must Know (Sooner Or Later)* and *Visions Of Johanna* – for inclusion on his forthcoming LP ***Blonde On Blonde***, at Columbia Studios in New York. He will record a further six days of sessions, but relocated at the Columbia Music Row Studios in Nashville, where he will be backed by the cream of the crop of Nashville musicians, including **Charlie McCoy**, **Hargus "Pig" Robbins**, **Kenny Buttrey**, **Jerry Kennedy**, and **Wayne Moss**.

Simon & Garfunkel found themselves with a surprise hit on their hands, after producer Tom Wilson added electric guitar, drums, and percussion to their acoustic *The Sounds Of Silence.*

February

3 During a visit to Britain, **Stevie Wonder** performs at the Scotch of St. James nightclub in Mason's Yard, London, and after the show meets audience member **Paul McCartney**.

6 London's Marquee club begins the "Spontaneous Underground," a Sunday afternoon psychedelic groove, with **Pink Floyd** as regulars. The all-English group – who last June took part in the **Melody Maker** National Beat Contest at the Wimbledon Palais – comprises 21-year-old vocalist/bassist **Roger Waters**, 20-year-old keyboardist **Rick Wright**, 21-year-old drummer **Nick Mason**, and 20-year-old vocalist/guitarist **Syd Barrett**. They have dropped their earlier blues sound and have begun playing extended psychedelic musical numbers, mostly written by Barrett.

16 **James Brown** cuts *It's A Man's, Man's, Man's World* at Talent Masters Studios in New York. It will become his third groundbreaking Top 10 US hit in 12 months.

17 At 11:30 pm, at Gold Star Studios, **Brian Wilson** begins laying down instrumental tracks for his new composition (with lyrics by **Mike Love**), *Good Vibrations*. It will eventually take the singer-songwriter/producer 11 lengthy sessions at Gold Star, Western Studios, RCA, and Columbia Studios before it is finished to his satisfaction. Multiple layered overdubs and exquisite harmonies will be meticulously refined. Wilson will elect not to include *Good Vibrations* on ***Pet Sounds***, despite its being the most expensive single recorded to date by any artist.

> **"Christianity will go... I needn't argue about that; I'm right and I will be proved right. We're more popular than Jesus now. I don't know which will go first – rock 'n' roll or Christianity."**
>
> John Lennon, **Evening Standard**, March 4, 1966

Critics and fans alike will make it Wilson's greatest pop triumph. It will hit UK No. 1 on November 17, and top the US chart on December 10 (curiously becoming the **Beach Boys**' last Top 10 US hit for ten years).

March

1 The **Byrds**' **Gene Clark** announces his decision to leave the band, reportedly due to his fear of flying (although he will later partially deny this). The group issue a press release: "He left not because of a row, and not because he was fired. He left because he was tired of the multitude of obligations facing successful rock 'n' roll groups. Tired of the travel, the hotels and the food. Tired of the pursuit of the most relentless autograph hunters, weary of the constant screaming. Bothered by the photographs and interviews, and exhausted by the whole punishing scene." Clark is not replaced, as the group is still fully stocked with three vocalists. He will go on to form the **Gene Clark Group** with the **Grass Roots**' **Joel Larson**, the **Leaves**' **Bill Reinhardt**, and the **Modern Folk Quartet**'s **Chip Douglas**.

3 The **Rolling Stones** begin a fresh round of recording sessions at RCA Studios in Hollywood. The tracks will appear on ***Aftermath*** – the first Stones album to consist entirely of **Jagger/Richard** originals. One track, *Paint It Black*, will become the first hit single to feature the sound of the sitar, played by **Brian Jones** (though **George Harrison** used the venerable Indian instrument on last year's **Beatles** album cut, *Norwegian Wood*).

4 An interview with **John Lennon** by Maureen Cleave is published in the **Evening Standard**, under the headline "How Does A Beatle Live? John Lennon Lives Like This." During a day spent with Cleave at his Weybridge mansion, Lennon made the comment that the **Beatles** were more popular than Jesus, which is reported in the article. The remark raises little media or fan rancor in Britain, but will have severe repercussions for the **Beatles** when the interview is reprinted in the US before their summer tour.

9 Polydor Records is served with an injunction, preventing any more copies of the **Who**'s *Substitute* being sold or distributed, until the court hears a complaint from the group's former recording manager, Shel Talmy. Polydor circumvents the injunction by pressing a new B-side to the single, namely *Waltz For A Pig*, performed by session musicians under the name of the Who Orchestra.

Pink Floyd quickly earned a reputation as the hippest band among London's early psychedelic set, experimenting with feedback and electronic soundscapes.

MAMAS AND PAPAS

Feb 19 **The Mamas & the Papas make their network television debut, performing *California Dreamin'* on "American Bandstand." This is their debut hit, on its way to its peak at US No. 4 next month.**

The west coast-based quartet formed in 1965, when folk singers John Phillips, his young bride Michelle (née Gilliam), Denny Doherty, and Cass Elliot were all vacationing, virtually penniless, in the Virgin Islands.

River Deep, Mountain High...
The Troggs' *Wild Thing...*
Buffalo Springfield...

11 Elektra Records – which has evolved into a fully-fledged multigenre label since its modest start in 1950 – releases the debut album ***Love*** by the progressive rock combo of the same name. Led by vocalist **Arthur Lee**, the Los Angeles-based **Love** is one of a growing number of rock acts – including the **Velvet Underground** (who will never secure a US chart single) – whose album success will outstrip their achievements on the singles survey.

15 In perhaps the most embarrassing Grammy Awards yet held, **Bob Dylan**, the **Beach Boys**, and the **Rolling Stones** are all snubbed, even as nominees. The eighth awards ceremony sees country singer **Roger Miller** collect six statuettes – the most ever bestowed on a single act – in part due to the influx of a bloc of new NARAS voters from Nashville. This trend runs throughout the proceedings: country outfit the **Statler Brothers** beat the **Beatles** for the Best Contemporary Performance by a Group (Vocal or Instrumental) trophy; Miller's *King Of The Road* wins Best Contemporary Vocal Performance, Male rather than **Paul McCartney**'s *Yesterday*; and the **Anita Kerr Quartet** is awarded the Best Performance by a Vocal Group for ***We Dig Mancini***, over the Beatles' *Help!* (Kerr is the current vice-president of the Nashville chapter of NARAS.) Nominated in nine categories, with *Yesterday* receiving five nods and *Help!* four, the Beatles come away empty-handed.

April

1 Raw British rock quartet the **Troggs** record their second single, *Wild Thing*, at Regent Sound Studio in London. Led by singer Reginald Ball – who will shortly change his name to **Reg Presley** at the suggestion of **New Musical Express** journalist Keith Altham – the group are managed by Kinks helmsman Larry Page, who has signed them to his Fontana-distributed Page One production company. *Wild Thing*, penned by US writer Chip Taylor (brother of actor Jon Voight) and cut (obscurely) in the US by **Jordan Christopher & the Wild Ones**, has been sent to Page by an American publishing associate. Before today's recording, the Troggs are sitting in a van outside the studio where the Larry Page Orchestra are in session,

IKE AND TINA TURNER

Mar 7 Ike Turner's wife, Tina, records her vocal for Phil Spector's latest epic at Gold Star Studios. The 26-year-old Tina, from Nutbush, near Brownsville, Tennessee, first performed with Ike as a backing singer in his Kings of Rhythm combo in St. Louis in 1956, and they married two years later. Having notched up six modest US chart singles for the Sue label since 1960, they were searching for a new deal, and signed with Spector in January. The producer offered Ike $20,000 to put Tina under a production contract (he admires her voice, but is underwhelmed by Ike's production skills, so the payment is on condition that Ike will not be involved in the sessions). Songwriters Jeff Barry and Ellie Greenwich have been called in to pen songs with Spector, one of them being *River Deep, Mountain High*. Spector has already spent another $22,000 creating the "Wall of Sound" backing track before adding Tina's part. Although the record will be a major hit in Britain at No. 3 in July, its disastrous showing in the US – where it will peak at No. 88 – will have a major impact on the legendary producer. Embittered by its poor reception, Spector will effectively withdraw from regular music-making, closing down his Philles label, and semi-retiring from production.

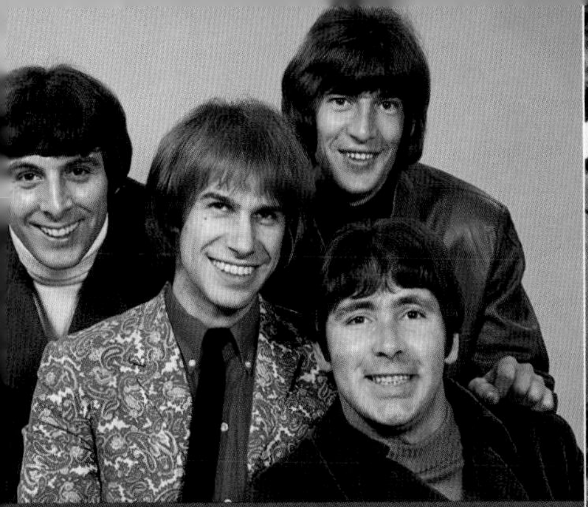

The Troggs

Buffalo Springfield

Formerly called the Troglodytes, the Troggs used a small egg-shaped instrument called an ocarina on their *Wild Thing* single, and found themselves with one of the biggest hits of 1966... Buffalo Springfield took their name from a steamroller they spotted resurfacing Fountain Avenue in Los Angeles.

having been told to wait in case any studio time opens up. They eventually have just 45 minutes to set up their equipment, test the levels, record the song and pack up. The single will hit UK No. 2 in May, before becoming a surprise chart-topper in the US on July 30, where it will sell over a million copies.

2 With all proceeds going to the Braille Institute, **Sonny & Cher** top a benefit bill at the Hollywood Bowl in Los Angeles. It also features **Jan & Dean**, **Otis Redding**, **Donovan** (who will score a US No. 1 in September with *Sunshine Superman*), **Bob Lind**, and the **Turtles** – a folk/pop/rock combo originally formed by teenagers **Mark Volman** and **Howard Kaylan** at Westchester High School, Los Angeles, in 1961. Also on the bill are the **Mamas & the Papas**, whose second release, *Monday, Monday*, will enter the US chart next week, set to become their first (and only) chart-topper.

6 The first session for what will become the **Beatles**' album ***Revolver*** begins at Studio 3 at Abbey Road in the evening, with the recording of the basic track for *Mark 1*, later retitled *Tomorrow Never Knows*.

9 **Eric Clapton**'s replacement in the **Yardbirds**, guitarist **Jeff Beck**, collapses on stage during a gig in Marseilles, France. He is admitted to hospital with suspected meningitis. It is a false alarm, however, and back in the UK he will resume playing with the band on the 16th in Southport, Lancashire.

12 **Jan & Dean**'s **Jan Berry**, who is perhaps preoccupied with the draft notice he has just received, plus an imminent medical school exam, crashes his Corvette Stingray into a parked truck on Whittier Boulevard in Los Angeles, and is almost killed. He will initially slip into a coma, and will then be totally paralyzed for several months, also suffering brain damage. He will take many years to recover and will be left partially paralyzed.

15 Having made their live debut at the Troubadour in Los Angeles earlier in the week, **Buffalo Springfield** open for the **Byrds** in the Swing Auditorium at the National Orange Showgrounds in San Bernardino, California. Although the group have been together for only a few weeks, they boast an experienced line-up: Canadian singer-songwriter **Neil Young** (**ex-Squires** frontman and **Mynah Birds** member), fellow Mynah Birds bassist **Bruce Palmer**, folk singer-songwriters **Stephen Stills** and **Richie Furay** (ex-**Au Go-Go Singers**), and ex-**Dillards** drummer **Dewey Martin**. Following a showcase residency at the Whisky A Go-Go, beginning next month, the group will be snapped up by Atlantic Records for a $22,000 advance.

22 With Andy Warhol as first-time producer, the **Velvet Underground** begin recording tracks, at the Scepter Records Studio in New York, which will evolve into their first LP, ***Velvet Underground & Nico***. The album will take only four days to record – two at Scepter and another two at T.T.G. Studios in Los Angeles – at a cost of some $1,500, of which $700 is supplied by Warhol. It will include songs subsequently regarded by music critics as seminal rock classics, including *Heroin* and *Venus In Furs*. Its distinctive cover art – a Warhol original – will feature a yellow banana which, when peeled, reveals a pink fruit. Problems with manufacturing the peelable sleeve will contribute to a long delay before the album's release next year by the M-G-M imprint, Verve Records – where it has been licensed from Warhol by Bob Dylan's former producer Tom Wilson.

> **"A most curious record, with words you really have to listen to, plus strange gaps in the sound."**
>
> **Record Retailer**'s review of the Troggs '*Wild Thing*', April 21, 1966

May

1 The **Beatles** play live for the first time since last December, albeit only a 15-minute spot, at the annual **New Musical Express** Poll Winners' Concert at the Empire Pool in Wembley, north London. They perform *I Feel Fine*, *Nowhere Man*, *Day Tripper*, *If I Needed Someone*, and *I'm Down*. It will prove to be the group's last ever British live concert. Making their first appearance at the event are new British Mod/beat combo, the **Small Faces**. Bassist **Ronnie Lane**, drummer **Kenney Jones**, singer/guitarist **Steve Marriott** (formerly a child actor), and organ-player **Ian McLagan**, all Londoners, formed last summer. Signed to Decca, their debut album ***Small Faces*** – which includes their upcoming UK No. 1 smash *All Or Nothing* – will be released tomorrow.

17 Following single concerts in Sweden, Denmark, and Ireland, and eight dates into his UK tour, **Bob Dylan** performs at Manchester Free Trade Hall. The concert is illegally recorded, and will become the most popular bootleg of all time (though incorrectly and mythically named "The Royal Albert Hall Concert"). Before Dylan performs *Like A Rolling Stone*, the final number of his second-half electric set, someone in the audience shouts "Judas," at which he turns to the band and instructs them to "Play f***ing loud."

The Small Faces were self-effacingly named because of the members' collective lack of height, but also for the cool Mod connotations of the word "Face."

The Grateful Dead... Cream form... The Beatles return to Hamburg...

19 The **Grateful Dead** debut at the Avalon Ballroom in San Francisco. Next month they will begin living communally at 710 Ashbury Street, in the center of the growing hippy movement. A one-off debut single, *Don't Ease Me In*, backed with *Stealin'*, will be recorded for the Scorpio label, a subsidiary of Berkeley-based Fantasy Records.

20 The **Who**'s **Keith Moon** receives a badly bruised eye and has three stitches in his leg after an altercation at the end of the group's set at the Ricky Tick Club in Newbury, Berkshire, UK. Moon and **John Entwistle** failed to show up on time for the gig, and **Pete Townshend** and **Roger Daltrey** – with a restless audience to deal with – go on with the supporting band. When Moon and Entwistle eventually show up, during *My Generation*, Moon gets whacked by Townshend, who later says: "At the end of our show we go mad in *Generation* and it annoyed me in the middle of the number when a cymbal from his drums fell and hit my leg. I wasn't hurt. I was just annoyed and upset." In a brief fit of pique, Moon informs the press that he and Entwistle are going to leave to form a duo. After a rest in a London nursing home, he will rejoin the group next week.

The Grateful Dead's communal home at 710 Ashbury Street became the base for an exhaustive series of free concerts.

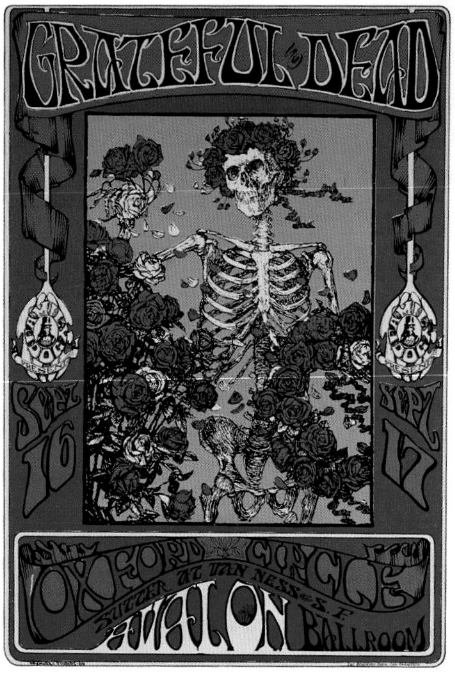

27 **Bob Dylan** plays the second of two dates at London's Royal Albert Hall, at the end of his British tour. Once again, purists in the audience conclude that the folk singer has "sold out" and make their feelings heard.

June

10 Having left her native Texas on June 4, 23-year-old blues/rock singer **Janis Joplin** makes her debut with **Big Brother & the Holding Company** – another burgeoning San Francisco-based rock combo – at the Avalon ballroom in San Francisco. Big Brother, formed last fall by bassist **Peter Albin** and guitarist **Jim Gurley**, who play their blues-based music around the Bay Area, recently decided to add a female singer to the line-up.

10 **Ray Charles**, the **Byrds**, the **Beach Boys**, **Stevie Wonder**, **Jerry Butler**, the **McCoys**, the **Marvelettes**, and the **Cowsills** (a new family-member pop group from Newport, Rhode Island) perform at the Soundblast '66 concert at Yankee Stadium, New York. The show features the teenage Go-Go Girls, 66 of whom ride out of the right-field bullpen on bicycles, then dismount along the baselines and perform a new dance called "The Bike," created by Jamaican-born musician Sir Lon de Leon. Other Go-Go Girls act as cheerleaders. The 9,000 fans in the 70,000-seat stadium enjoy what **The New York Times** describes as "the Isidore [sic] Duncans of frugdom."

11 **Melody Maker** reports the formation of the first "rock supergroup" – **Cream**. It means that **John Mayall's Bluesbreakers** will lose guitarist **Eric Clapton**, **Manfred Mann** will say goodbye to bassist **Jack Bruce**, and the **Graham Bond Organization** will forfeit drummer **Ginger Baker**. They will quickly secure a UK recording contract with Robert Stigwood's Reaction Records, and with Atlantic in the US.

Brian Epstein

Cat Stevens

Brian Epstein found himself in the middle of a diplomatic firestorm when the Beatles inadvertently upset Ferdinand and Imelda Marcos during a visit to the Philippines... Cat Stevens, born Steven Demetri Georgiou – the son of a Greek London restaurateur and a Swedish mother – began performing as Steve Adams.

14 Ron Tepper, of Capitol Records' publicity department, notifies the US media of the label's decision to withdraw the sleeve of the **Beatles**' newest LP ***Yesterday And Today***, which depicts smiling group members frolicking among several decapitated, blood-covered baby dolls. Capitol president Alan Livingston writes: "The original cover, created in England, was intended as 'pop art' satire. However, a sampling of public opinion in the United States indicates that the cover design is subject to misinterpretation." The original "butcher" cover – as it will come to be known – will become a hot collector's item.

21 Unable to reserve rooms at some of New York City's top hotels, the **Rolling Stones** sue 14 of them for a total of £1,750,000 ($4.9 million) over an alleged booking ban "injurious to the group's reputation, and discriminatory in violation of New York's Civil Rights law."

24 Three days after completing their new album, the **Beatles** begin a three-city tour of West Germany at the Circus-Krone-Bau in Munich. At the weekend they will return in triumph to Hamburg, in an eight-car motorcade escorted by a dozen motorcycle police, and play to two sellout crowds of over 11,000 at the Ernst Merck Halle. It is their first visit to the city since their final Star-Club date on December 31, 1962.

25 **Jackie Wilson** is charged with inciting a riot and refusing to obey a police order, after police are called to the Flamingo No. 2 club in Port Arthur, Texas. They find a crowd of between 200 and 400 in a "frenzy and tossing each other and the furniture around." Wilson refuses to stop singing, despite a request by police. The club's manager says that the crowd are angry because Wilson began his performance at 11:00 pm – three hours after the scheduled start. The singer will be convicted of drunkenness and fined $30.

July

4 Following three concerts at the Nippon Budokan Hall in Tokyo on June 30 and July 1 and 2 (with 500 crowd-control policemen drafted in for each show), the **Beatles** perform at the Rizal Memorial Football Stadium in Manila. Greeted by some 600 fans at the airport, the group play to a total of 80,000 people at two concerts.

5 Greeted with the headline "Imelda Stood Up" in this morning's **Manila Times**, the **Beatles** find themselves at the center of a diplomatic storm: an administrative mix-up apparently resulted in their failure to appear at a reception with President Ferdinand Marcos and his wife Imelda at the Malacanang Palace yesterday. A tax commissioner refuses to let the group leave the country until they have paid tax on yesterday's concert receipts. Brian Epstein pays the levy, and the Beatles leave for the airport, where they get involved in some pushing and shoving before belatedly leaving the Philippines.

"We're going to have a couple of weeks to recuperate before we go and get beaten up by the Americans." George Harrison, July 5, 1966

10 Singer-songwriter/guitarist **Cat Stevens** cuts *I Love My Dog* at Decca's studio in West Hampstead, London, with sessioneers **Nicky Hopkins** on piano and **John Paul Jones** on bass. Based on Yusef Lateef's *Plum Blossom*, the recording will be nailed after three hours and seven takes. Stevens, aged 18, successfully auditioned for manager/producer **Mike Hurst** (one-time **Springfields** guitarist) in Knightsbridge, London, on February 6. That has led to a deal with Decca's progressive rock label, Deram. *I Love My Dog* will become his first UK hit at No. 28 in November.

18 **Bobby Fuller** – who scored his only Top 10 US hit as leader of the **Bobby Fuller Four** with *I Fought The Law* in February – is found dead by his mother in her Oldsmobile car, outside the apartment they share at 1776 Sycamore in West Hollywood. His body has been badly beaten and reeks of gasoline. The circumstances of his death will never be uncovered. His label boss, Bob Keane, will release a statement dismissing the police report citing accidental death or suicide, but the question of foul play will never arise.

Melody Maker announced the formation of Cream, "a sensational new 'group's group' starring Eric Clapton, Jack Bruce, and Ginger Baker."

July 1966

The Cavern re-opens... The Beatles at Candlestick Park... Hendrix in London...

The Association – influenced more by the Limeliters and the Hi-Lo's than the Four Freshmen, on whose sound the Beach Boys based their harmony work – uniquely featured all six members as lead vocalists.

22 The **Association**, a six-piece harmony group from Los Angeles, perform at the Fillmore West, San Francisco, with **Quicksilver Messenger Service**, as they embark on their first national tour. They are currently riding high with *Along Comes Mary*, which has been banned by many radio stations for its alleged drug connotations. The Association will become one of the most popular live acts over the next three years, racking up three million-selling singles (*Cherish*, *Windy*, and *Never My Love*) and three million-selling albums (***Along Comes... The Association***, ***Insight Out***, and ***The Association's Greatest Hits***).

23 Prime Minister Harold Wilson re-opens the Cavern Club in Liverpool. He tells the assembled crowd: "The fact is that we all have got a job to do in this country. But it's not gloom we need. It's determination, hard work, liveliness and a sense of enjoyment, too." On the way up to Liverpool from London, **Dave Dee, Dozy, Beaky, Mick & Tich** – the British beat combo who have just released their first, self-titled album – have breakfast with the premier and his wife Mary. The Cavern closed down at the beginning of 1966, with debts of £10,000 ($28,000), and was bought by restaurateur Joseph Davey for £5,500 ($15,400) on April 18.

29 **Bob Dylan** suffers injuries (never fully detailed, but apparently involving a broken neck vertebra) when he crashes his Triumph 55 motorcycle at Albert Grossman's home in Woodstock, New York. His recuperation, purportedly on Cape Cod, will lead to a period of reclusive inactivity, interpreted by many as an attempt to escape into family life, away from the pressures of two heady years in the spotlight.

Scott and John Walker were the voices of the Walker Brothers – Gary Walker contractually could never play on any of the group's recordings.

31 Having played a warm-up gig at the Twisted Wheel in Manchester two days ago, **Eric Clapton**, **Jack Bruce**, and **Ginger Baker** – billed under their individual names – play their first major concert on the third and final day of the 6th National Jazz & Blues Festival in Windsor. The legend "Clapton is God" soon begins appearing in graffiti on London walls.

August

11 Two weeks after American **Datebook** magazine reprinted **John Lennon**'s March interview with Maureen Cleave, the three US television networks air the **Beatles**' press conference, held at the Astor Towers Hotel in Chicago, shortly after the group's arrival for their fourth US tour. Lennon publicly apologizes for his "Jesus" remarks: "If I had said television is more popular than Jesus, I might have got away with it, but I just happened to be talking to a friend and I used the words 'Beatles' as a remote thing, not as what I think – as Beatles, as those other Beatles like other people see us. I just said 'they' are having more influence on kids and things than anything else, including Jesus." The furor created by Lennon's remarks will result in several radio stations banning Beatles music forever, mass burnings of Beatles records and memorabilia, and several tour dates not selling out. Thurman H. Babbs, pastor of the New Haven Baptist Church in Cleveland, will vow to excommunicate any parishioner who goes to a Beatles concert or listens to their music.

11 As the **Beatles** bear the brunt of their notoriety, the **Rolling Stones** quietly continue to record new material at RCA Studios in Los Angeles, including *Have You Seen Your Mother, Baby, Standing In The Shadow?* and *Let's Spend The Night Together*. Both will create controversy: the latter for its obvious sexual connotations, the former for its sleeve, which will feature members of the group dressed in drag.

12 The **Beatles**' fourth – and final – North American tour, with the **Cyrkle**, the **Ronettes**, the **Remains**, and **Bobby Hebb** as opening acts, begins its 14-city run at Chicago's International Amphitheatre.

14 Radio station KLUE in Longview, Texas, which yesterday organized public bonfires of **Beatles** records, is knocked off the air when a

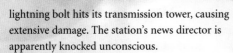

lightning bolt hits its transmission tower, causing extensive damage. The station's news director is apparently knocked unconscious.

15 **Scott Walker** is discovered unconscious in a gas-filled room in his London apartment at Marble Arch, by the group's road manager. He is rushed to St. Mary's Hospital in Paddington, but is released after treatment. The group's publicist will say tomorrow that Scott is "perfectly all right in mind and body. He is perfectly okay now except for a headache and he doesn't remember about last night."

19 At the **Beatles** concert in Memphis, the band receive an anonymous phone call stating that there will be an assassination attempt on one or all of them. During the second show, a firecracker is thrown on stage, among a mass of fruit and debris, including used flashbulbs. When the firecracker explodes, one audience member says, "They didn't miss a note." Six Ku Klux Klansmen picket outside the Coliseum.

20 Around 14,000 fans attend the Forest Hills Music Festival in Queens, New York, to see a triple threat of Motown's finest: the **Supremes**, the **Temptations**, and **Stevie Wonder**.

29 Seven years to the day since **John Lennon**, **Paul McCartney**, and **George Harrison** performed together for the first time at the opening of the Casbah Coffee Club in Liverpool, the final **Beatles** concert takes place, at Candlestick Park in San Francisco. Some 25,000 fans see their 11-song set, beginning with Chuck Berry's *Rock And Roll Music*, and closing with Little Richard's *Long Tall Sally* – the last song the group will ever perform live together in concert. Ironically, much of their subsequent decision to quit playing concerts is down to the fans, who make so much noise during their performances that it has been hard for the group to hear themselves or for the fans to hear the music.

September

6 Having flown to Celle, West Germany, yesterday to begin work on the Richard Lester-directed film "How I Won The War," in the role of Private Gripweed, Beatle **John Lennon** has a very public short-back-and-sides haircut from Klaus Baruck at the Inn on the Heath.

12 With the introductory musical phrase "Hey, hey we're the Monkees – and people say we monkey around," the **Monkees**' television show premieres on NBC. Modeled on the **Beatles**' "A Hard Day's Night" film, it will become one of the most popular music-based shows of all time. Each episode combines a (very) loose storyline, zany antics, and scripted comedy, along with mimed songs (the group sing on the recordings in the studio, but are rarely allowed to play their instruments). Songwriters Tommy Boyce and Bobby Hart – who have already supplied *Last Train To Clarksville* and *The Monkees Theme* – have been appointed musical producers, and Lester Sill is molding the Monkees' sound and musical personae. Songwriters Gerry Goffin and Carole King, Barry Mann and Cynthia Weil, 25-year-old Brooklyn-born Neil Diamond, and Neil Sedaka – all signed to Kirshner's Aldon Music company – have been brought in to write songs for the group. The series will air until 1969, and will become a popular staple in syndication for decades thereafter.

The Beatles finished their last ever live concert, appropriately, with Little Richard's *Long Tall Sally*.

24 Having traveled from the US on the 21st, the **Animals**' bass player **Chas Chandler** arrives in London with his protégé, 23-year-old, left-handed guitarist **Jimi Hendrix**, whom Chandler saw performing at the Café Wha in Greenwich Village, New York, in July. Legend has it that ex-Airborne Paratrooper Hendrix decided to change the spelling of his name from Jimmy to Jimi during the flight. Hendrix – who bought his first, right-handed, guitar (which he learned to play upside down) at the age of 12 – served his apprenticeship as a backing musician for a succession of early 1960s R&B acts, including the **Isley Brothers** (he appeared on all their 1964 recordings) and **Little Richard**. He checks into the Hyde Park Towers Hotel in Inverness Terrace, and later in the evening jams at the Scotch of St. James nightclub. Within a week, Hendrix will have auditioned and recruited two English musicians, bassist **Noel Redding** and drummer **Mitch Mitchell**, and formed the **Jimi Hendrix Experience**. Within a month, on October 18, they will open for French pop star **Johnny Hallyday** at the Olympia Music Hall in Paris.

Known as the Prefab Four, the Monkees were the first "manufactured" group, and were not allowed to play on their records. Mike Nesmith eventually complained publicly that "we're being passed off as something we aren't."

Oct 1966

Grace Slick joins Jefferson Airplane...
John and Yoko meet...
Jimi Hendrix cuts *Hey Joe*...

Jefferson Airplane

October

7 British rocker **Johnny Kidd** is killed at the age of 26, in a two-car accident on the A48 Bury New Road, near Radcliffe, UK. He is a passenger in the car, which is being driven by Wilf Isherwood, the husband of his fan club secretary, Chris. Isherwood and **Pirates** bass guitarist Nick Simper are injured.

7 Influential New Orleans R&B singer/guitarist **Smiley Lewis**, best known for his 1955 hit *I Hear You Knocking* (which will be much covered), dies from cancer at the age of 46.

8 **Cream**'s **Ginger Baker** collapses after playing a 20-minute drum solo during the group's concert at the University of Sussex. He is taken to hospital suffering from acute exhaustion and the flu. Bassist and singer **Jack Bruce** has also been ordered to take a break by his doctor, having missed four gigs last week through illness. The group's debut single, *Wrapping Paper*, is released today – one day late because 100,000 copies had to be re-pressed due to a technical fault.

14 Lead singer **Signe Toly Anderson**, scheduled to make her final appearance with **Jefferson Airplane**, fails to show up at the group's Fillmore Auditorium concert in San Francisco. Her replacement, 26-year-old **Grace Slick**, is already chosen and steps in, bringing with her two numbers she has performed with her old group, the **Great Society**: the bolero-like *White Rabbit* and *Somebody To Love*.

15 **The International Times** magazine is launched at an all-night rave, described as a Pop/Op/Costume/Masque/Fantasy-Loon/Blowout/Drag Ball, at the Roundhouse in Chalk Farm, London, with music provided by psychedelic rock combos **Pink Floyd** and **Soft Machine**. **The San Francisco Examiner** review of the event is unaware that Floyd played, taking them to be "a large pick-up band of assorted instruments on a small central platform."

23 Having returned from France, the **Jimi Hendrix Experience** record for the first time, at De Lane Lea Studios in London, cutting *Hey Joe* and *Stonefree* – both of which will become revered songs in the Hendrix canon. Based in England, Hendrix will find respect and success in the UK, where *Hey Joe* will open his chart account in January 1967, a full eight months before his home country takes notice.

28 Secretary of the Interior, Stewart Udall, proclaims Beale Street in Memphis – which was immortalized in **W.C. Handy**'s *Beale Street Blues* – a national landmark as the "Home of the Blues," despite its being home to some of the worst slums in the city.

November

2 **Mississippi John Hurt**, a deft, finger-picking, softly voiced bluesman who lived much of his life in obscurity before being rediscovered three years ago by folk-blues enthusiasts, dies of a heart attack in Grenada, Mississippi, age 73.

9 **John Lennon** meets 33-year-old Japanese conceptual artist **Yoko Ono** for the first time, at a private preview of Ono's avant-garde "Unfinished Paintings and Objects" exhibition at the Indica Gallery in Mason's Yard, London.

10 A fire breaks out near Gold Star Studios in Los Angeles, on the evening that **Brian Wilson** is recording a string segment for the track *Fire*. Superstitiously believing he is responsible for the blaze, Wilson will secure the tapes in a vault.

22 Exactly one year after the Federal Court deferred **Ray Charles**'s sentence for drug possession, the singer appears in a Boston court to receive his punishment. Following a court-ordered heroin check, he spent time in McLean Hospital in Belmont, Massachusetts, and was pronounced clean in April. He is fined $10,000 and receives four years' probation and a five-year suspended sentence.

24 Following a sabbatical during summer and fall, the **Beatles** reconvene in Abbey Road's Studio 2 to start work on new material. This evening they begin recording what will be their most complex single – *Strawberry Fields Forever*.

24 Several thousand teenagers go on the rampage in front of the Municipal Auditorium in Kansas City, where **James Brown** is performing. One woman is stabbed, another is cut by broken glass, several policemen are injured when they are hit by rocks, and at least 20 people are arrested. The disturbance began when police stopped the show because of "alleged obscene dances being performed on the stage."

25 The press is introduced to the **Jimi Hendrix Experience** when the trio perform at a media showcase at the Bag o' Nails club in Kingly Street, London. Their first UK interview, with the **Record Mirror**'s Peter Jones, will appear in the paper's December 10 issue.

December

1 **Tom Jones**'s sentimental ballad, *Green, Green Grass Of Home*, tops the UK chart for the first of seven weeks. A cover of last year's **Porter Wagoner** country hit, it will become the singer's all-time biggest-selling 45, eventually selling over 1,220,000 copies in Britain alone, and giving Decca Records its first UK million-selling single by a British artist. Writer Curly Putman will celebrate by spending some of his royalties on a green, green Cadillac.

The Who guested on the final edition of "Ready Steady Goes Live!" Their TV debut on the show in January 1965 did much to cement their increasing popularity... Tommy James formed his first band at the age of 12, and cut his first record – *Long Pony Tail* – at 15. He recorded *Hanky Panky* after hearing it in a nightclub in South Bend, Indiana.

Tommy James & the Shondells

Grace Slick joined Jefferson Airplane, leaving Great Society, a support act for the group during the past year... Tom Jones took a 1965 Porter Wagoner country smash and turned it into his only million-selling UK hit record... Jeff Beck quit the Yardbirds to form an unsuccessful alliance with Rod Stewart, Ron Wood, and Aynsley Dunbar.

The Yardbirds on "Ready Steady Go!"

3 The **Monkees** make their live debut, before a sellout crowd of 8,364, at the International Center Arena, Honolulu, with fan response confirming Beatlemania-like success.

5 **Buffalo Springfield** record *For What It's Worth* at Columbia Recording Studio in Los Angeles. Written by **Stephen Stills**, it was prompted by the Sunset Strip riots, when busloads of police showed up on Sunset Boulevard in response to merchants who thought teenagers hanging out on the street each night was detrimental to business. It will become a clarion call to young people experiencing similar treatment in other parts of the US.

6 Back at Abbey Road, the **Beatles** record *When I'm Sixty-Four* – which will prove to be the first track included on their upcoming project, ***Sgt. Pepper's Lonely Hearts Club Band***.

19 In response to a Los Angeles radio station announcement that **Mick Jagger** has died, Les Perrin, the **Rolling Stones**' press officer, tells **Melody Maker**: "I've had a hectic weekend with what seemed like the entire population of America on the phone." The front page of this week's paper will read "'Jagger dead' rumours sweep America."

23 Following a three-and-a-half-year run, "Ready Steady Go!" – retitled "Ready Steady Goes Live!" – airs for the last time, after an edict handed down by the Musicians Union bans the practice of miming. Guests on the last show include **Mick Jagger**, **Eric Burdon**, the **Spencer Davis Group**, **Dave Dee, Dozy, Beaky, Mick & Tich**, **Donovan**, **Paul Jones** (who has left **Manfred Mann** for a solo career), **Alan Price** (who has recently left the Animals following a rift with Burdon), and the **Who**.

23 Tamla-Motown's Motor Town Revue opens a week-long engagement at the Fox Theater in Detroit, with the **Temptations**, **Stevie Wonder**, **Martha & the Vandellas**, **Jimmy Ruffin**, the **Underdogs**, **Chris Clark**, **J.J. Barnes**, the **Earl Van Dyke Band**, and **Gladys Knight & the Pips** – Motown's latest signing, inked to its Soul Records imprint. The Pips trio, led by soul vocalist Knight, began performing in 1952 as an Atlanta-based family unit when she was just eight years old. They scored a one-off US No. 6 crossover hit, *Every Beat Of My Heart*, for Vee-Jay in 1961.

24 Having already notched up their first US chart-topper in July, with the Ellie Greenwich/Jeff Barry-penned *Hanky Panky*, **Tommy James & the Shondells**, led by 19-year-old James, a native of Dayton, Ohio, record their follow-up, *I Think We're Alone Now*, written by Ritchie Cordell.

31 **George Harrison** is refused admission to Annabel's nightclub in Berkeley Square, London, for not wearing a tie, so he and his party – including his wife Patti, Brian Epstein, and **Eric Clapton** – see in the New Year at Lyons' Corner House in Coventry Street.

"Mr. Jagger wished to deny that he is dead and say that the rumours have been grossly exaggerated."

Les Perrin, December 19, 1966

Tom Jones

ROOTS

During this year: Swedish piano player Benny Andersson and folk guitarist Björn Ulvaeus meet for the first time at a party in Västervik and decide to begin writing songs together... Walter Parazaider, Lee Loughnane, James Pankow, and Danny Seraphine – students at DePaul University in Chicago – form the Missing Links, immediately recruiting three more musicians; after a brief spell as the Big Thing, they will adopt the unwieldy name Chicago Transit Authority... Guyanian native Eddy Grant, who has formed a group at Acland Burghley School in Hornsey Rise, in his adopted England, adds Jamaican twins Derv and Lincoln Gordon and they emerge as the Equals... folk singer Tom Rush records *Urge For Going*, a song by Canadian songwriter Joni Mitchell, who has recently moved to New York after a spell working the northeastern US folk circuit with her former husband... Jimmy Seals and Dash Crofts, after going their separate ways after playing in the Champs, team up again with Louie Shelton and Joseph Brogan as the Dawnbreakers... teenage Army brat Jackson Browne begins creating a stir at the folk/rock Paradise venue in Los Angeles, leading to a short stint with the Nitty Gritty Dirt Band... and the Allman Joys – who include brothers Duane and Gregg Allman – record demos at Bradley's Barn studios in Nashville...

San Francisco (Be Sure To Wear Some Flowers In Your Hair)

1967

No.1 US SINGLES

Jan 7 I'm A Believer **Monkees**
Feb 18 Kind Of A Drag **Buckinghams**
Mar 4 Ruby Tuesday **Rolling Stones**
Mar 11 Love Is Here And Now You're Gone **Supremes**
Mar 18 Penny Lane **Beatles**
Mar 25 Happy Together **Turtles**
Apr 15 Somethin' Stupid **Nancy Sinatra & Frank Sinatra**
May 13 The Happening **Supremes**
May 20 Groovin' **Young Rascals**
June 3 Respect **Aretha Franklin**
June 17 Groovin' **Young Rascals**
July 1 Windy **Association**
July 29 Light My Fire **Doors**
Aug 19 All You Need Is Love **Beatles**
Aug 26 Ode To Billie Joe **Bobbie Gentry**
Sept 23 The Letter **Box Tops**
Oct 21 To Sir, With Love **Lulu**
Nov 25 Incense And Peppermints **Strawberry Alarm Clock**
Dec 2 Daydream Believer **Monkees**
Dec 30 Hello Goodbye **Beatles**

No.1 UK SINGLES

Jan 7 Green, Green Grass Of Home **Tom Jones**
Jan 21 I'm A Believer **Monkees**
Feb 18 This Is My Song **Petula Clark**
Mar 4 Release Me **Engelbert Humperdinck**
Apr 15 Somethin' Stupid **Nancy Sinatra & Frank Sinatra**
Apr 29 Puppet On A String **Sandie Shaw**
May 20 Silence Is Golden **Tremeloes**
June 10 A Whiter Shade Of Pale **Procol Harum**
July 22 All You Need Is Love **Beatles**
Aug 12 San Francisco (Be Sure To Wear Some Flowers In Your Hair) **Scott McKenzie**
Sept 9 The Last Waltz **Engelbert Humperdinck**
Oct 14 Massachusetts **Bee Gees**
Nov 11 Baby Now That I've Found You **Foundations**
Nov 25 Let The Heartaches Begin **Long John Baldry**
Dec 9 Hello Goodbye **Beatles**

The Beatles

Pink Floyd

The Beatles changed the face of music once again with the ground-breaking *Sgt. Pepper's Lonely Hearts Club Band...* Pink Floyd, already with a devoted following whenever they played live, emerged with their debut album *The Piper At The Gates Of Dawn* – a sign of things to come.

Rock musicians behaved badly, and pop music looked trite, innocent, and even irrelevant by comparison. While guerrilla war raged in Vietnam, the new counterculture took full shape, and rock became a social force and a weapon in a cultural war.

Despite the the drug-induced haze, the year was one of creative ferment and growing musical sophistication. The **Beatles**' epic ***Sgt. Pepper's Lonely Hearts Club Band*** had a seismic effect. On hearing it, **Brian Wilson** abandoned the **Beach Boys** album he was working on. The Beatles' masterpiece raised the creative bar to a previously unheard level – some would argue it has not been matched since.

Three of the **Rolling Stones** were charged with possessing banned substances this year, **Paul McCartney** acknowledged he used LSD, and all the members of the **Grateful Dead** were arrested for possession of marijuana. The **Doors** released their eponymous debut album, a powerful body of rock-blues music including the much-copied *Light My Fire,* with its line, "Girl, we couldn't get much higher." The band's driving force and lyricist, **Jim Morrison**, endured the first of many arrests for indecency.

At the first great outdoor rock festival – in Monterey – fans were urged to "dress as wild as you choose," and were treated to a lexicon of greats: **Jimi Hendrix**, **Simon & Garfunkel**, **Eric Burdon & the Animals**, the **Mamas & the Papas**, **Buffalo Springfield, Janis Joplin**... All accompanied by a San Francisco light show and a special batch of purple Owsley acid. No wonder **Ravi Shankar**'s long extended set was rapturously received. Rock's tectonic plates were shifting – the results would be a fracturing into progressive, symphonic, even "art-rock," and a list of other subgenres. **Velvet Underground** helped the year's narcotic flavor along with *Heroin* and *I'm Waiting For The Man.* **Pink Floyd** gave new meaning to the London underground, and pushed the progressive envelope with their debut album, ***The Piper At The Gates Of Dawn.*** Heard in the distance in 1967, heavy metal was helped along by the emergence of Jimi Hendrix. One of its leading progenitors **Jeff Beck** (formerly of the **Yardbirds**) founded the **Jeff Beck Group**, with vocalist **Rod Stewart** and bassist **Ron Wood**.

It must have been tough on teenagers. Too young for much of the heavier, more experimental rock, they looked increasingly to the Motown formula. The **Temptations** enjoyed chart success, and the **Supremes** quickly notched up two more hits. But it was to be the end of an era. **Holland/Dozier/Holland** left Motown to form their own label, and **Florence Ballard** quit the renamed **Diana Ross & the Supremes**. Perhaps the most tragic loss in 1967 was **Otis Redding**, killed in a plane crash soon after cutting *(Sittin' On) The Dock Of The Bay*, which became a posthumous No. 1.

"Jim Morrison writes as if Edgar Allan Poe had blown back as a hippie."

Vogue, 1967

The Doors on television... Aretha Franklin on the Atlantic label...

Van Morrison

Marvin Gaye

January

1 Signed to an unprecedented seven-album deal with Elektra Records last November by label boss Jac Holzman, Los Angeles-based rock quartet the **Doors** make their first live television appearance on KTLA Channel 5's "Shebang" show (a shortlived local Los Angeles music series produced by Dick Clark and hosted by Casey Kasem). The band – who played a three-month residency at the Whisky A Go-Go last year – comprises 23-year-old lead singer/lyricist and hallucinogenic fan **Jim Morrison**, guitarist **Robbie Krieger**, keyboardist **Ray Manzarek**, and drummer **John Densmore**. With Densmore's drums at center stage, winged by Morrison and Manzarek to the left, and Krieger to the right, they lip-synch to their first single, *Break On Through*, from their debut album, ***The Doors***, which will be released on the 4th. Having taken just six days to record, it will begin a two-year-plus US chart run in March.

9 Still living in at his childhood home in Belfast, ex-**Them** vocalist **Van Morrison** signs a solo recording deal with Bang! Records for an initial advance of $3,500.

14 The **Grateful Dead** and **Jefferson Airplane**, supported by three more San Francisco rock combos – **Country Joe & the Fish**, **Quicksilver Messenger Service**, and Janis Joplin's **Big Brother & the Holding Company** – perform at "The Human Be-In – A Gathering of the Tribes," at the Polo Grounds in Golden Gate Park. Some 25,000 people attend the event, whose free-spirited outdoor setting and large crowd prefigure future major rock festivals and the hippy "Summer of Love."

15 Around 2,000 fans wave goodbye to the **Walker Brothers** at London Airport, as they set off on a six-week tour of Australia and East Asia. Take-off is delayed for four hours – when the plane's hydraulics fail taxiing down the runway – during which **Scott Walker** has to be sedated.

22 Having performed *Let's Spend The Night Together*, *Ruby Tuesday*, *It's All Over Now*, and *Connection* on "Sunday Night At The London Palladium," the **Rolling Stones** refuse to join the other acts in the traditional farewall wave from the revolving stage. A media furor will ensue.

24 **Aretha Franklin** begins her first recording sessions for Atlantic Records – having signed to the label for a $25,000 advance. Overseen by producer Jerry Wexler, she cuts *I Never Loved A Man (The Way I Love You)* and *Do Right Woman – Do Right Man* at Rick Hall's Florence Alabama Music Emporium (FAME) studios in Muscle Shoals. At the end of the session, in the early hours, too much imbibing of alcohol results in a fist fight between Hall and Franklin's husband, Ted White. By noon tomorrow, White and Franklin will be on their way back to New York – where Wexler will take the Muscle Shoals Rhythm Section, excluding Hall, and resume sessions at Atlantic Studios.

The ever-changing, risk-taking Mothers of Invention were led by 26-year-old singer-songwriter/guitarist and activist Frank Zappa.

Van Morrison quit R&B combo Them to launch an enduring and constantly evolving solo career... Marvin Gaye teamed with Tammi Terrell to record a handful of Motown gems. He was by her side when she collapsed on stage later in the year, and was diagnosed with a brain tumor.

February

3 On the eighth anniversary of **Buddy Holly**'s death, legendary British record producer **Joe Meek** fatally shoots his landlady, Mrs. Violet Ethel Shenton, at 304 Holloway Road, London, before turning the gun on himself.

5 In a report headlined "Pop Stars And Drugs: Facts That Will Shock You," British Sunday tabloid **News of the World** names **Mick Jagger**, **Keith Richard**, and **Pete Townshend** among those who took LSD at a party held by the **Moody Blues**. Jagger, appearing later on ABC-TV's "Eamonn Andrews Show," announces he is to sue for libel. (He will file the suit on the 7th.)

6 Ten days after the **Beatles** signed a new nine-year contract with EMI, the company announces that the group has sold 180 million records worldwide in just four and a half years.

10 Using 40 session musicians to create the track's unique orchestral backdrop, the **Beatles** record *A Day In The Life* for their forthcoming album ***Sgt. Pepper's Lonely Hearts Club Band***.

12 Following tips from the **News of the World**, 15 Chichester police officers enter "Redlands," **Keith Richard**'s West Wittering farmhouse, under the authority of a warrant issued under the Dangerous Drugs Act, and take away various substances for forensic tests. Eight men and one woman are present at the time.

17 **Big Brother & the Holding Company** and **Quicksilver Messenger Service** play the first of two nights at San Francisco's Avalon Ballroom. Nearby, at the Fillmore – with opening acts **Canned Heat** and the **Blues Project** – the **Mothers of Invention** perform music from their debut set, ***Freak Out!*** The Mothers of Invention were signed last year for a $2,500 advance to Verve Records – MGM's jazz/R&B imprint – by ex-Dylan producer Tom Wilson, who was more interested in the group's R&B strengths than the musical social satire expounded by **Frank Zappa**.

22 **Marvin Gaye** – currently hitting US No. 14 with the Kim Weston duet, *It Takes Two* – performs at the opening of the re-appointed Ciro's club in Los Angeles. The long-time café-society bistro has been reopened as an R&B nightspot. Several of Gaye's subsequent releases will be duets with another new Motown female signing, **Tammi Terrell**, who will join him on hits written and produced by Motown staffers Nickolas Ashford and Valerie Simpson.

ARETHA FRANKLIN

Feb 14 **At Atlantic Studios in New York, Aretha Franklin completes the Wexler-produced recording of *Respect*, an update of Otis Redding's self-penned 1965 US No. 35 original. Rush-released – and hot on the heels of *I Never Loved A Man (The Way I Love You)*, her first Atlantic single, which peaked at No. 9 – *Respect* will become the Lady of Soul's signature 1960s hit, topping the US survey on June 3 and opening her UK chart account by hitting No. 10. It is a remarkable turnaround from her relatively unsuccessful years at Columbia.**

During the session, Franklin's sister Carolyn made suggestions regarding the tempo of her delivery of the letters "R-E-S-P-E-C-T," helping to create a timeless classic.

Traffic

The Bee Gees... Sinatra at the Grammys... Hendrix goes on tour... Elvis marries...

24 The **Bee Gees** sign a five-year management contract with Robert Stigwood (in partnership with Brian Epstein at NEMS Enterprises), having recently returned from Australia, where they've been playing for nine years and had ten Australian hits, including the No. 1, *Spicks And Specks*. The brothers Gibb – 19-year-old **Barry** and 17-year-old twins **Robin** and **Maurice** – began singing together in Manchester, UK in 1955, as the **Rattlesnakes**. They became popular on Australian television, and started writing songs in 1962, when they changed their name. Stigwood was impressed by their recent audition at the Saville Theatre in London (following a rejection by the Grade Organization) and will immediately secure them a longterm recording contract with Polydor.

27 Midway through an extensive UK club and college tour, **Pink Floyd** record their first single, *Arnold Layne*, with producer Joe Boyd at the Sound Techniques Studio in London. It will secure them a contract with EMI Records.

Legend has it that when they were introduced to label executives, Pink Floyd were asked: "Which of you is Pink?"

March

1 At the Coliseum in Ottawa, 3,000 fans riot after waiting nearly an hour for the **Animals** to go on stage. The stage is damaged, a set of drums and the loudspeaker system are trashed, windows smashed, and seats ripped. The concert is canceled without a single note being played.

2 **Frank Sinatra** wins big at the ninth annual Grammy Awards. He wins Record of the Year and Best Vocal Performance, Male for *Strangers In The Night*, and Album of the Year for ***Sinatra: A Man And His Music***. **Lennon** and **McCartney**'s *Michelle* beats out *Strangers In The Night* for Song of the Year. In a continuing trend of Grammy gaffes, the **Anita Kerr Quartet** wins Best Performance by a Vocal Group – a category that also features the **Association** (*Cherish*), the **Beach Boys** (*Good Vibrations*), and the **Mamas & the Papas** (*Monday, Monday*). Those three acts will also lose out in the Best Contemporary Rock & Roll Recording category to the **New Vaudeville Band**'s *Winchester Cathedral*. **Ray Charles** continues to dominate the R&B field, winning trophies for Best Rhythm & Blues Recording, and Best Rhythm & Blues Solo Vocal Performance, Male or Female, for *Crying Time*.

9 An inquest jury in St. Pancras, London, concludes that producer **Joe Meek** did indeed murder his landlady before shooting himself. Meek's friend, Mr. Patrick Pink, testifies that the deluded producer imagined that people were listening through the wall of his living room to steal song ideas for a rival recording company. Police reports confirm that amphetamine drugs, purple hearts, barbiturates, and dexedrine were found in Meek's flat. The pathologist confirms that a trace of an amphetamine-type drug was found in Meek's body: "I do not think the risk of these particular drugs is fully appreciated. You could get changes, including gross psychosis with delusions of persecution. Having taken an overdose they suddenly get an impression that somebody is following them."

11 Northern Songs – the publisher that owns Lennon/McCartney compositions – announces that 446 cover versions of **Paul McCartney**'s *Yesterday* have been recorded in the 18 months since the original appeared.

17 The Stax-packed bill of **Otis Redding**, **Sam & Dave** (who will shortly score with their signature hit *Soul Man*), *Knock On Wood* hitmaker **Eddie Floyd**, **Arthur Conley** (a Redding protégé whose Atco Records debut, *Sweet Soul Music* – written by Redding – is rising fast to hit US No. 2), **Carla Thomas**, the **Mar-Keys**, and **Booker T. & the MG's** embark on a 13-date UK Soul Concert Sensation '67 tour, at Finsbury Park Astoria in London.

18 Following an announcement two weeks ago by Island Records boss, Chris Blackwell, that the Winwood brothers are leaving the **Spencer Davis Group**, the **New Musical Express** reports that **Steve Winwood** is forming a new rock group with guitarist **Dave Mason**, drummer **Jim Capaldi**, and saxophonist **Chris Wood**. (They will choose the name **Traffic** and sign to Island.)

20 With ex-**Animal Alan Price**'s *Simon Smith And His Amazing Dancing Bear* new in this week's Top 20, BBC radio "Today" reporter Tim Matthews takes a "dancing bear" on a tour of London hotels and restaurants to see if, in fact, "a boy and a bear would be well accepted everywhere," as the lyrics claim. (The song is

Rolling Stones fans and police in Zurich

The Doors made their debut at the Avalon Ballroom on March 3 and 4 1967... Traffic signed to Island Records and retreated to a cottage in the English village of Aston Tirrold, Berkshire, to begin work on their debut album... The Rolling Stones' tour of Europe saw rioting in Sweden, Poland, and Switzerland.

penned by songwriter/pianist **Randy Newman**, who wrote several early 1960s hits, including songs for the **Fleetwoods** and **Jerry Butler**, and *I've Been Wrong Before* for **Cilla Black**.)

20 Timothy Hardacre, the lawyer representing **Mick Jagger** and **Keith Richard**, says that summonses have been served on his clients: Jagger for alleged offenses contrary to section one of the Drugs (Prevention of Misuse) Act, 1964, and Richard for alleged offenses contrary to section five (A) of the Dangerous Drugs Act, 1965. He adds, "These alleged offenses will be strenuously contested."

Alan Price's *Simon Smith And His Amazing Dancing Bear* instead of *Purple Haze*, to which Hendrix responds: "I don't know the words to that one, man."

31 **Jimi Hendrix** – beginning his first nationwide UK tour at the Finsbury Park Astoria – is taken to hospital after setting his guitar alight and suffering minor burns to his hands. In addition to his guitar distortion and feedback stage devices, Hendrix will make a nightly habit of playing the instrument with his teeth, and will occasionally set fire to it. Rank Theatres will warn Hendrix to tone down his act.

"I am bemused by the whole thing. All I want to do is sing and play guitar."

Jimi Hendrix, March 31, 1967

23 The **Beatles** win two more statuettes at the 12th annual Ivor Novello Awards. *Michelle* is named as the Most Performed Work of the Year, while *Yellow Submarine* is named the Best-Selling "A" Side of 1966. Geoff Stephens's *Winchester Cathedral* receives the award for International Song of the Year.

30 A photo session for the sleeve of ***Sgt. Pepper's Lonely Hearts Club Band*** takes place at Chelsea Manor Studios in Flood Street, London, with Michael Cooper as photographer. The design is a montage created by pop artist Peter Blake. EMI insists that permission must be granted by the many famous people the **Beatles** have selected as an imaginary audience, and all those known to be alive will be contacted before the album's release. Mae West rejected the idea of being in a lonely hearts club, but has been won over by a personal request from the group. Some of **Lennon**'s choices (including Jesus Christ, Gandhi, and Adolf Hitler) are removed from the final shot. **Bob Dylan** and **Dion** are the only two singers – apart from the Beatles – on the sleeve.

30 During an appearance by **Jimi Hendrix** on BBC1's "Top Of The Pops," a studio technician inadvertently puts on the backing track of

April

7 With pioneering DJ Tom Donahue at the turntables, San Francisco radio station KMPX-FM begins playing cuts from rock 'n' roll albums in a free-form format, 24 hours a day, marking the dawn of FM rock on US airwaves.

13 Polish police use batons and tear gas on several thousand teenagers trying to storm Warsaw's Culture Palace to see the **Rolling Stones** play their first concert behind the Iron Curtain.

29 **Cindy Birdsong**, replacing the increasingly unreliable **Florence Ballard**, makes her stage debut with the **Supremes** at the Hollywood Bowl, at a benefit for the United Negro College Fund and UCLA School of Music, which also features the **5th Dimension** and **Johnny Rivers**. Tamla Motown explains that Birdsong is filling in because Ballard is ill, but within weeks it will confirm that she has in fact taken Ballard's place.

29 The **International Times** presents the 14-Hour Technicolour Dream, a huge benefit event in the Great Hall of Alexandra Palace in north London. **Pink Floyd**, veteran London-based R&B/beat group the **Pretty Things**, the **Move**, **Savoy Brown**, **Soft Machine**, and British bluesman **Graham Bond** are among the 30 or so acts – although whatever's in the air tonight will make most people forget who performs.

May

1 Having purchased a wedding license for $15 at the Clark County Courthouse, **Elvis Presley** marries his girlfriend, Priscilla Beaulieu, at the Aladdin Hotel in Las Vegas, in room 246 – the private suite of its owner Milton Prell – at 9:41 am, before 100 invited guests. Presley's assistant, Joe Esposito, is the best man, and the bride's sister, Michelle, is the maid of honor.

Elvis and Priscilla Presley were married on May 1. After their reception at the Aladdin Hotel in Las Vegas, the newlyweds flew in Frank Sinatra's LearJet, *Christina*, to Palm Springs to begin their honeymoon.

Procol Harum... *Sgt. Pepper's Lonely Hearts Club Band*... The Monterey International Pop Festival...

1 The **Beach Boys**' **Carl Wilson**, having been arrested by the FBI in New York, is taken to Los Angeles to face charges of avoiding military call-up and refusing to take the Oath of Allegiance. He has refused to be sworn in on grounds of conscientious objection, after receiving his US Army draft notice in February. Wilson is released on bail, and charters a plane to fly to Dublin to join the rest of the band at the start of its British and Irish tour.

9 Recording of *Reflections* is completed at 2648 West Grand Boulevard, Detroit. It will be the first single released under the name **Diana Ross & the Supremes** (which will not sit well with **Mary Wilson**), and the 18th straight Holland/Dozier/Holland hit written for the group.

10 **Mick Jagger** and **Keith Richard** appear at Chichester Magistrates Court, charged with being in possession of pep pills and marijuana. With Robert Hugh Fraser, director of a Mayfair art gallery, they elect to go for trial at West Sussex Quarter Sessions on June 22. They plead not guilty and reserve their defense. They are committed for trial and granted bail, each on his own recognizance of £100 ($240). Meanwhile in London, their colleague **Brian Jones** and Prince Stanislas Klossowski de Rola, Baron de Watteville, are arrested at Jones's flat in Courtfield Road, South Kensington, for unauthorized possession of cannabis, being in possession of cocaine hydrochloride, and being in possession of methedrine.

11 With music press ads hailing them as "the most significant new musical talent of 1967," the **Bee Gees** make their "Top Of The Pops" debut, singing *New York Mining Disaster 1941*, and instantly showcasing their unique falsetto harmony vocal style.

June

4 **Procol Harum** make their London concert debut, supporting **Jimi Hendrix** at the Saville Theatre. Formed by 22-year-old pianist/singer-songwriter **Gary Brooker** – who auditioned members after placing an ad in **Melody Maker** – the London-based quintet's debut single, *A Whiter Shade Of Pale*, has taken Britain by storm. It will top the UK chart this week, having already sold over 356,000 copies in its first three weeks. Partly based on two themes by Johann Sebastian Bach, "Air on the G-string" and "Sleepers Awake," lead singer Brooker's timeless melody perfectly matches 20-year-old Keith Reid's surreal lyrics.

6 Columbia Records lays on a press junket for newly signed San Francisco rock combo **Moby Grape** at the Avalon Ballroom, to promote their debut album, ***Moby Grape***. Recorded at a cost of $11,000, its launch is accompanied by a marketing stunt involving the simultaneous release of five singles. In the early hours of the morning, band members **Peter Lewis**, **Jerry Miller**, and **Skip Spence** are arrested for contributing to the delinquency of minors, when they are allegedly caught with three underage girls in Marin County, California. The charges will be dropped.

9 **Love** begin recording their third album, ***Forever Changes***, at Sunset Sound Recorders in Los Angeles (they will also use **Leon Russell**'s Skyhill Studios), with session musicians **Hal Blaine**, **Billy Strange**, and **Don Randi** on hand.

10 **Jimi Hendrix** is refused admission to the Botanical Gardens in Kew, because "people in fancy dress aren't allowed."

16 Californian harmony group the **Association** open the Monterey International Pop Festival in California, followed by, among other

The Bee Gees returned from Australia and had their first No. 1 before the year was over... Procol Harum were only the sixth act in chart history to top the UK chart with their debut... Moby Grape's career was launched with five simultaneously released singles: only one made it – *Omaha* – albeit at US No. 88.

Bee Gees

Procol Harum

Moby Grape

THE BEATLES

June 10 The Beatles' *Sgt. Pepper's Lonely Hearts Club Band* hits UK No. 1. The landmark project – produced, as always, by George Martin – sets new standards in modern music, having cost £25,000 ($60,000) to produce and involving 700 hours of studio time. The sleeve is the first to print lyrics, and the inner sleeve is printed with a psychedelic design. At the group's insistence, the album has been given a simultaneous worldwide release date – and it is the first Beatles release by Capitol in the US to match the UK disc exactly. Its sophisticated musicality will cause Brian Wilson to abandon his plans to release the Beach Boys album on which he is currently working with Van Dyke Parks, which they have been recording under the working title *Smile*.

Sgt. Pepper **was critically revered by some as the seminal album of the rock era, and was seen by others as the climax of the Beatles' career.**

acts performing, the **Paupers**, **Lou Rawls**, **Beverly**, **Johnny Rivers**, **Eric Burdon & the Animals**, and **Simon & Garfunkel**. The event is the first of its kind in the rock field, and is the brainchild of Alan Pariser, who came up with the concept after attending last year's Monterey Jazz Festival. With seed money from the likes of Bill Graham and Harry Cohn Jr., the festival was co-opted by Lou Adler and the **Mamas & the Papas' John Phillips**. Pariser approached the Mamas & the Papas to headline the festival, and they have decided to turn it into a non-profit event. Pariser is paid $50,000 by Adler, John and **Michelle Phillips**, **Terry Melcher**, **Johnny Rivers**, and **Paul Simon** to take over ownership of the festival. They create the Monterey Pop Foundation, inviting **Paul McCartney**, **Mick Jagger**, **Brian Wilson**, **Smokey Robinson**, **Donovan**, **Jim McGuinn**, and others to join the board of governors. D.A. Pennebaker films the event (for subsequent release as "Monterey Pop"), which runs from midday to midnight over three days.

17 The second day of the Monterey Pop Festival features **Canned Heat** (whose appearance will lead to a contract with Liberty Records), **Big Brother & the Holding Company**, **Country Joe & the Fish**, **Al Kooper**, the **Butterfield Blues Band**, **Quicksilver Messenger Service**, the **Steve Miller Band** (another new San Francisco blues/rock band led by Milwaukee-born, 23-year-old singer-songwriter/guitarist Steve Miller), the **Electric Flag**, **Moby Grape**, exiled South African trumpet player **Hugh Masekela**, the **Byrds**, 19-year-old singer/songwriting newcomer **Laura Nyro**, **Jefferson Airplane**, **Booker T. & the MG's** with the **Mar-Keys**, and **Otis Redding**. Redding – a last minute replacement for the **Beach Boys** – closes the evening with a sterling five-song set. His appearance is seen as a move by the organizers to capture the attention of the predominantly young, white, rock audience. Redding's biggest asset is the passionate strength of his live performance, and he receives a rapturous reception from the largely hippy audience.

18 **Ravi Shankar**, the **Blues Project**, **Big Brother & the Holding Company**, the **Group With No Name**, **Buffalo Springfield**, the **Who**, the **Grateful Dead**, the **Jimi Hendrix Experience**, **Scott McKenzie** – who performs his current US Top 20 hit, the hippy-anthem *San Francisco (Be Sure To Wear Flowers In Your Hair)* – and the **Mamas & the Papas** play on the final day of the hugely successful Monterey event.

20 Having recently admitted in an interview in **Life** magazine that he has taken LSD and that the experience brought him closer to God – a claim he reiterated yesterday on television – **Paul McCartney** is criticized by evangelist Dr. Billy Graham, who says: "LSD should be shunned like the plague by young people. Paul says he came nearer to God. I would say to him I know the answer. There is only one way to find God and that is through Jesus Christ."

1967 June

All You Need Is Love by satellite... Jagger and Richard in court...

Paul McCartney and George Harrison were in the audience when Jimi Hendrix opened his set at the Saville Theatre, London, with *Sgt. Pepper's Lonely Hearts Club Band*.

24 Lead guitarist **Zal Yanovsky** quits the **Lovin' Spoonful** after the group's performance at the Forest Hills Music Festival, New York, following media indignation over a marijuana bust, when he allegedly incriminated others to avoid prosecution. His explanation for leaving? "I was getting bored. I want to look around and see what's been happening for the past two years. I feel I've lost touch, and there are so many things I want to do alone." His replacement will be ex-**Modern Folk Quartet** guitarist **Jerry Yester**.

25 The recording of the **Beatles**' singalong anthem *All You Need Is Love* at Abbey Road Studios in London is transmitted worldwide to an estimated audience of 400 million, as part of the first global satellite television linkup, "Our World." Among other musical segments, George Martin uses Glenn Miller's *In The Mood*, thinking it is no longer under copyright, but he will be successfully sued for a royalty settlement by Miller's publishers. As well as 13 session musicians, friends guesting on backing vocals are Mick Jagger, Keith Richard, Marianne Faithfull, Eric Clapton, Keith Moon, Jane Asher, McCartney's brother Mike McGear, the Walker Brothers' Gary Leeds, and Graham Nash and his wife, Rose.

29 **Keith Richard** stands trial for allowing his house to be used for the illegal smoking of cannabis. He claims that an American called David Sneidermann may have been in cahoots with the **News of the World**, which had been served with a libel suit by **Mick Jagger** for claiming that he had taken drugs, but is found guilty and sentenced to a year in jail and a £500 ($1,200) fine. Jagger is transferred to Brixton as Richard is locked up at Wormwood Scrubs.

30 **Jagger** and **Richard** are released on bail of £7,000 ($16,800) each, pending appeals.

July

1 **The Times** newspaper prints an editorial by William Rees-Mogg headlined "Who breaks a butterfly on a wheel?" He writes: "There are many people...who consider that Mr. Jagger has 'got what was coming to him.' They resent the anarchic quality of the **Rolling Stones**' performances, dislike their songs, dislike their influence on teenagers and broadly suspect them of decadence... There must remain a suspicion in this case that Mr. Jagger received a more severe sentence than would have been thought proper for any purely anonymous young man."

2 **The News of the World** denies tipping the police off to raid **Keith Richard**'s house in revenge for the libel suit brought by **Mick Jagger**, but asserts that it informed the police as "a public duty to assist the authorities... We believe that unauthorized drug-taking is a menace in Britain today and that we are right to bring any suspicion of this to public attention."

24 **The Times** prints a full page advertisement headlined "The law against marijuana is immoral in principle and unworkable in practice," advocating cannabis law reform. Among the 65 signatories – which include Graham Greene, David Hockney, Dr. R.D. Laing, jazz/blues performer **George Melly**, Kenneth Tynan, and MP Brian Walden – are all four **Beatles** and Brian Epstein.

31 The High Court quashes **Keith Richard**'s conviction after some evidence is deemed inadmissible. **Mick Jagger**'s sentence is reduced to a conditional discharge, with a warning that he must be of good behavior for 12 months.

> **"Jagger, who is perhaps more of a Cabbage White than a Red Admiral, was handled gingerly by his inquisitors."**
>
> Julian Critchley, "Who Breaks a Butterfly on a Wheel?," **The Times**, August 1, 1967

8 The **Monkees** begin a US tour in Jacksonville, Florida, with the **Jimi Hendrix Experience** in support. Hendrix's music and outrageous act are entirely inappropriate for the Monkees' teenybop audience and the group are dropped after only eight gigs. Manager Chas Chandler makes the dubious claim that protests from the right-wing Daughters of the American Revolution have brought this about, though he was aware that Hendrix would cause outrage.

22 The **Doors** perform *Crystal Ship* and *Light My Fire* on "American Bandstand." The **Bee Gees**, who are in London, are featured on film, singing their first US chart entry, *New York Mining Disaster 1941*, which recently hit US No. 14.

31 **Mick Jagger** appears on Granada's "World In Action" to talk about his trial, with William Rees-Mogg, editor of **The Times**, Dr. John Robinson, Bishop of Woolwich, leading Jesuit Fr. Thomas Corbishley, and former Home Secretary Lord Stow Hill. Flown in by helicopter to the garden of Spain's Hall in Finchingfield, Essex, Jagger discusses whether society is corrupt and the extent to which absolute freedom is desirable.

During the summer of love, fans got to see Cream, Pink Floyd, and the Jimi Hendrix Experience... The Doors' *Light My Fire* gave Jac Holzman's 17-year-old Elektra label its first No. 1 single, when it topped the US chart on July 29.

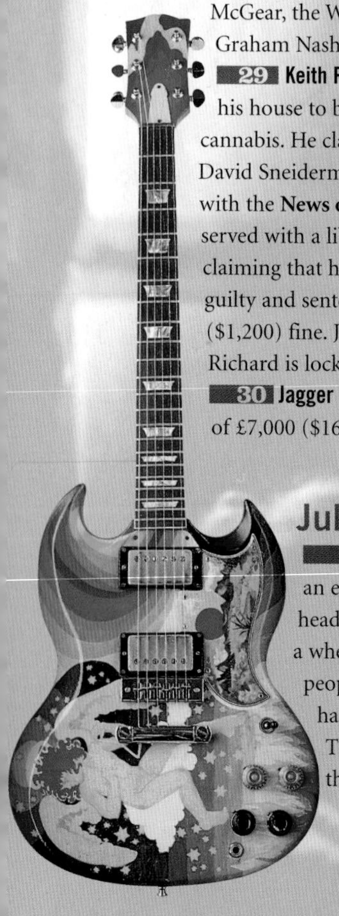

Eric Clapton's Guitar

The Doors

Despite his scholastic achievements – seven "O" level and two "A" level GCE passes – being mentioned in court, Mick Jagger spent a night in Lewes jail.

June 28 Mick Jagger is sentenced to three months imprisonment and £100 ($240) costs, for unlawfully possessing four benzedrine tablets containing amphetamine sulfate and methyl amphetamine hydrochloride, which he bought legally in Italy. The prosecution describes how police found a strong incense-like smell when they entered Keith Richard's house in February, where they encountered a "young lady sitting on the settee. All she was wearing was a light-coloured fur skin rug which from time to time she allowed to fall, disclosing her nude body. She was unperturbed and apparently enjoying the situation." Jagger is granted leave to appeal and remanded in Lewes jail overnight.

Brian Epstein dies... The launch of Radio 1... Woody Guthrie...

Tony Blackburn

Radio 1 went on air at 7:00 am on September 30, with its theme tune (written by George Martin) followed by controller Robin Scott introducing DJ Tony Blackburn, who played his signature tune – Johnny Dankworth's *Beefeaters* – followed by the Move's *Flowers In The Rain*... Strawberry Alarm Clock were one of many delectably named psychedelic rock bands who enjoyed their fifteen minutes of fame in 1967.

Brian Epstein had been due to join the Beatles and the Maharishi Mahesh Yogi in North Wales when he was found dead in his London home.

August

11 On the opening night of the seventh annual National Jazz, Pop, Ballads & Blues Festival in Windsor, headliners the **Small Faces** are plunged into darkness at midnight, 12 minutes into their set. The 6,000 booing fans discover that the power has been cut off by the local authorities. Despite its billing, there are no jazz acts this year, with rock taking center stage. Among those performing – in the pouring rain – over the next two days are progressive newcomers the **Nice** (featuring keyboardist **Keith Emerson**), the **Crazy World of Arthur Brown**, **Ten Years After** (a blues/rock outfit led by guitarist/singer **Alvin Lee**, and managed by Chris Wright of the nascent Chrysalis management company), R&B/beat combo **Amen Corner** (led by singer/guitarist **Andy Fairweather-Low**), the now solo **Jeff Beck**, **Chicken Shack**, and **Cream**. Tomorrow's bill will feature **Fleetwood Mac**, a new British blues/rock combo formed by ex-**John Mayall's Bluesbreakers** guitarist **Peter Green**, bassist **John McVie**, and drummer **Mick Fleetwood**, with ex-**Levi Set** guitarist **Jeremy Spencer**.

15 The Marine Offences Act becomes law in the UK after the Postmaster General, Tony Benn, argued last year that pirate radio stations violated international regulations, stole wavelengths, and paid no copyright fees on the records played. The government cited a dozen European countries, all signatories of the Strasbourg Treaty, that had registered complaints of interference with their own authorized broadcasts. Radio London closes at 3:00 pm, Radio 270 at 11:59 pm and Radio Scotland at midnight. Defiant to the last, Radio Caroline continues broadcasting.

15 **Joan Baez** says she has no gripe with the Daughters of the American Revolution, after the organization refuses to let her use its Constitution Hall for a concert, following what it considered her anti-nationalistic statements in Cleveland last week. She nevertheless gives a free outdoor concert for an estimated 30,000 people. The president general of the DAR, Mrs. William Sullivan Jr. says: "We are directly behind our Government's stand on Vietnam and we directly stand behind our boys who are dying there."

23 The **Rolling Stones**' promo film for their latest single, *We Love You*, is rejected by "Top Of The Pops" producer Johnnie Stewart, on the grounds that he does "not think it is suitable for the type of audience that watches the programme." The film is a parody of the trial of Oscar Wilde, in which **Mick Jagger** plays Wilde, **Marianne Faithfull** plays Bosie, and **Keith Richard** plays Lord Queensberry. The BBC points out that this is in no sense a ban, solely an individual's decision.

25 The **Beatles** attend a conference of the Spiritual Regeneration League at Normal College in Bangor, Wales, to study transcendental meditation with Indian guru Maharishi Mahesh Yogi. **Paul McCartney** will comment: "Young people who take drugs to broaden their minds should give them up and start meditating instead. I had given up drugs before becoming interested in the yogi's teachings. The only reason people take drugs is because they hear so much about experiences that can expand the mind. By meditating, this expansion can be done without drugs and without their ill effects. Meditation is a way of expanding the mind naturally."

26 Hippy culture having made its way across the Atlantic, the three-day Festival of the Flower Children begins at Woburn Abbey, with the notably un-hippy **Bee Gees**, the **Marmalade**, the **Alan Price Set**, and others. **The People** newspaper reports the blissfully unaware Duchess of Bedford saying, "I thought it was going to be a flower show with competitions, prizes and lots of flowers."

27 Beatles manager Brian Epstein is found dead in bed at his Belgravia home in London, apparently from a drug overdose following a long period of depression. In an obituary, **The New York Times** will call him, "the man who revolutionized pop music in our time."

> **"I think they have a different idea of freedom from what I have, and I think I threaten theirs, although they do not threaten mine."**
>
> Joan Baez on the Daughters of the American Revolution, August 15, 1967

September

1 British Prime Minister Harold Wilson is granted an interim injunction against the **Move** and their manager, Tony Secunda. It restrains the printing, publishing, circulating, or distributing of a postcard promoting the group's current single *Flowers In The Rain*. The card, depicting a nude caricature of Mr. Wilson lying in bed, is allegedly libelous.

2 The three-day Sound-Out festival in Woodstock begins, organized by local macrobiotic restaurateur "Jocko" Moffitt. An estimated 1,000 hippies – paying daily admission of $2.50 – are also encouraged to help with the building of the stage, fixing sound and lights, directing traffic, and clearing the field. **Eric Andersen**, **Richie Havens**, and **Phil Ochs** are all scheduled to take part on the 4th (Labor Day). Today's gathering – the first in the area – is described by the **New York Times** as "cool amid the bonfires."

Strawberry Alarm Clock

11 The **Beatles** begin shooting their television film, the bus-traveling "Magical Mystery Tour" in Teignmouth, while *All You Need Is Love* passes one million sales in the US.

14 **Mick Jagger** and **Keith Richard**, who arrived in New York yesterday for a series of business meetings, visit the immigration office of the Department of Justice in Manhattan to clarify their status under American law. The service says: "We were unable to determine the exact nature of their conviction record, if any. We have accordingly had to send abroad for particulars." The law – which details specific banned drugs – was designed to exclude any person trafficking in narcotics.

17 High jinks tonight on US television: the **Doors**, guesting on "The Ed Sullivan Show," have been requested during rehearsals to omit the line "Girl, we couldn't get much higher" from *Light My Fire*. They agree – but **Jim Morrison** sings it anyway. Immediately after that show, the **Who** appear on "The Smothers Brothers Comedy Hour." **Keith Moon** sets a flash powder explosion in his drum kit, not knowing the technical crew had already done so. The resultant explosion leaves **Pete Townshend** with singed hair and damaged ears, and Moon with a cut on his leg caused by a broken cymbal. Fellow guests Bette Davis and Mickey Rooney look on bemused.

23 West coast psychedelic rock group, **Strawberry Alarm Clock** perform their fast-rising debut hit, *Incense And Peppermints*, on "American Bandstand." With 16-year-old singer **Greg Munford** featured on lead vocal, the single will hit US No. 1 on November 25.

25 The current US No. 1, the **Box Tops**' *The Letter* – clocking in at a meager 1:58 – is certified gold by the RIAA. Recorded at Chips Moman's American Recording Studio, it required 30 takes to complete, with producer Dan Penn adding a jet-plane sound effect at the end. The Box Tops were assembled last year in Memphis by high-school student, singer/guitarist **Alex Chilton** (who will go on to form the power-pop band **Big Star**, with schoolmate **Chris Bell**, in 1970).

30 BBC Radio 1 is launched, scheduled to be on air 18 hours every day – from 5:30 am to 7:30 pm and 10:00 pm to 2:00 am. Kenny Everett, Dave Cash, Pete Murray, John Peel, Mike Raven, Emperor Rosko, and Ed Stewart are among the DJs – a mix of BBC and pirate radio announcers, all hired by controller Robin Scott.

October

2 All six **Grateful Dead** members are arrested at their communal base at 710 Ashbury Street, charged by police narcotics agents with possession of marijuana. They spend six hours in jail before being released on bail.

5 Arriving in Southampton from the US by ship, the **Mamas & the Papas** singer, **Cass Elliot**, is arrested and charged with the theft of two blankets and two keys, the property of Graham Dennis, in whose London apartment hotel Elliot stayed while touring with the group in February. She will be released tomorrow, and appear in court on the 9th – when the prosecution will offer no evidence against her.

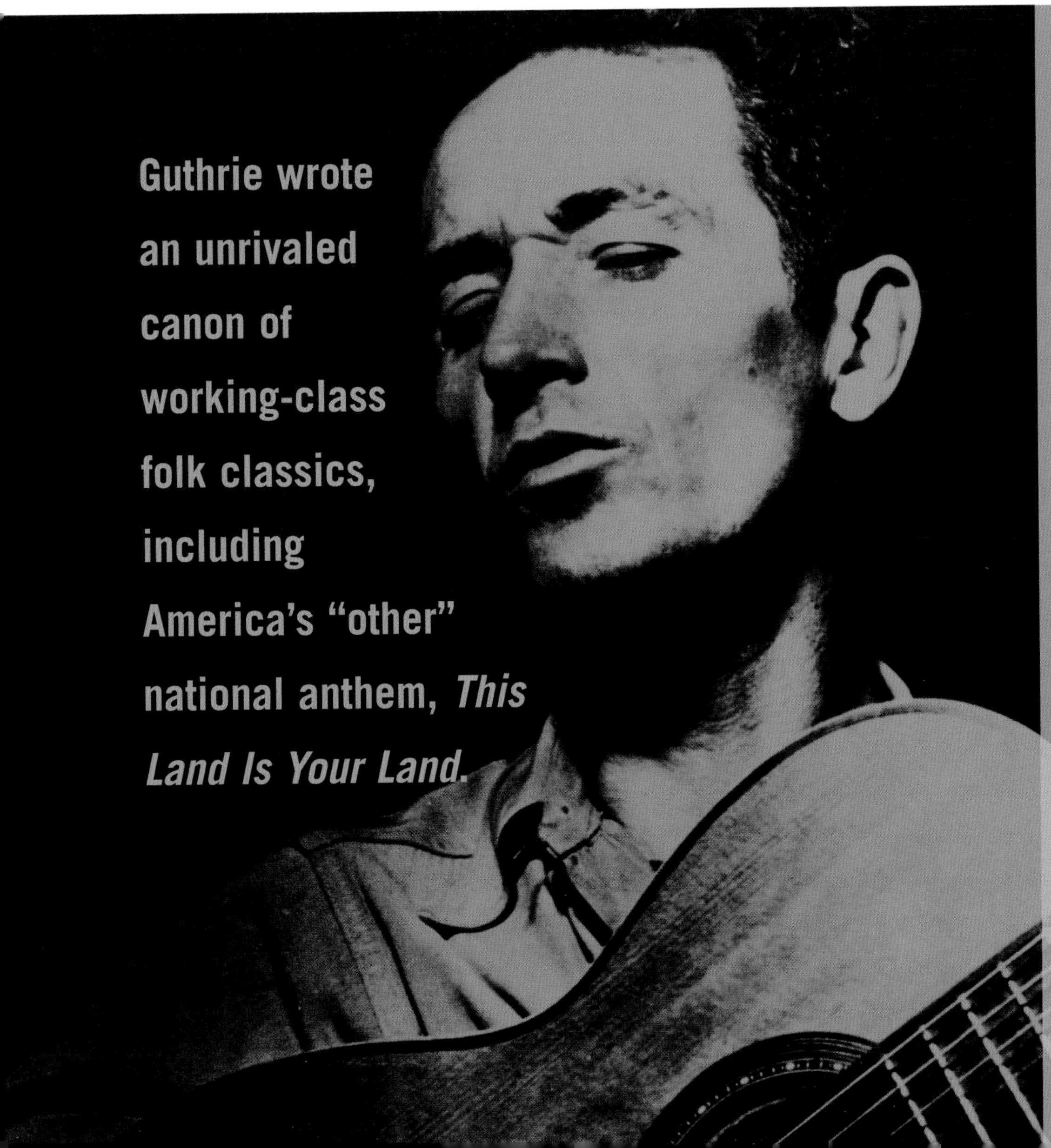

Guthrie wrote an unrivaled canon of working-class folk classics, including America's "other" national anthem, *This Land Is Your Land*.

WOODY GUTHRIE

Oct 3 **Hospitalized since 1961 with the inherited degenerative nerve disease, Huntington's chorea, folk legend Woody Guthrie dies in Queens, New York, age 55. His ashes will be scattered in the Atlantic. A prolific songwriter and itinerant performer, Guthrie rose through depression-era America and was a supporter of Roosevelt's "New Deal," and a literate guardian of the rights of union workers and dust-bowl farmers. Recording seminal sides for the Library of Congress archive in the 1930s (eventually released by Elektra), in 1940 he teamed with Pete Seeger to form the Almanac Singers. He completed his lauded autobiography "Bound for Glory" in 1943, before enlisting in the US Marines until the end of World War II. Guthrie made more than 200 recordings for the Folkways label, before becoming ill in the early 1950s. His influence on every artist of the 1960s folk boom has been incalculable, and his eldest son Arlo has already begun his own singer-songwriting career.**

Oct 1967

"Hair" the musical... The first issue of Rolling Stone... The death of Otis Redding...

The Move had five consecutive top five hits – all from the pen of Roy Wood – culminating in their only chart-topper, *Blackberry Way.*

7 New York concert promoter Sid Bernstein offers the **Beatles** $1 million to perform live again. It is the first of several lucrative offers the group will receive over many years, all of which they will decline.

11 Home Secretary Roy Jenkins rescinds expulsion orders on the **Bee Gees**' backing musicians **Vince Melouney** and **Colin Petersen**, which were due to come into effect on November 30, when their work permits expire. Jenkins cites the group's value to Britain during its economic crisis.

11 The **Move** apologize in the High Court for what is described as a "violent and malicious personal attack" on Harold Wilson. They agree to hand over all royalties from *Flowers In The Rain* – thought to be in excess of £7,000 ($16,800) – to the Spastics Society and Stoke Mandeville Hospital. *Cherry Blossom Clinic*, which was scheduled to be their next single, will be pulled from the release schedule, since its lyrics, concerning a mental asylum, are considered likely to create more unfavorable publicity. The track will appear on the group's first album.

16 Once again at the forefront of political agitation, **Joan Baez** is arrested, with 123 other anti-draft demonstrators, for blocking the entrance to an Armed Forces Induction Center in Oakland, California.

17 The New York Shakespeare Festival Public Theater's production of the rock musical "Hair" opens at the off-Broadway Anspacher Theatre. Written by Gerome Ragni (who will appear in the part of Berger) with James Rado and Galt MacDermot, it will transfer to the Cheetah Theater in December, closing there in January, before re-opening on Broadway at the Biltmore Theater on April 29 next year.

30 **Brian Jones** pleads guilty to charges of possessing cannabis and allowing his home to be used for the smoking of cannabis. He is sentenced to a nine-month prison sentence and ordered to pay 250 guineas (£262.50/$630) costs. He pleads not guilty to the charge of possessing cocaine and methedrine. He will be granted bail tomorrow, pending appeal, and undertakes to continue medical treatment until the hearing.

November

3 Scheduled to start a US tour last month, which was canceled because of visa problems, **Pink Floyd** finally make their American debut at the Winterland Ballroom, San Francisco. The tour will be cut short next week, when **Syd Barrett** reveals increasingly strange behavior: refusing to move his lips in time to *Arnold Layne* on "American Bandstand" tomorrow, and responding to questions on "The Pat Boone Show" in two days time with a blank stare. The band are promoting ***Pink Floyd*** (a trimmed-down collection of tracks from their British bow, ***The Piper At The Gates of Dawn***.)

> **"Not simply a music magazine but also about the things and attitudes that music embraces."**
>
> **Rolling Stone**, November 9, 1967

9 The first edition of **Rolling Stone** hits American newsstands, with a roach-clip attached as a freebie. The cover of the first issue features a photo of **John Lennon** from the film "How I Won the War." Based in New York, the magazine is the creation of 21-year-old Jann Wenner, a University of California at Berkeley dropout. Its title, which is derived from a **Muddy Waters** song, was suggested by Wenner's mentor, San Francisco music critic Ralph Gleason. The magazine will become a cornerstone of American rock culture.

11 **Van Morrison** performs *Brown Eyed Girl* – his first solo outing and already a US No. 10 smash – on "American Bandstand." He will fail to score a hit 45 in Britain until 1979.

December

2 The **Beatles** log their 15th US chart-topper as *Hello Goodbye* – featured on ***Magical Mystery Tour*** – begins a three-week lock.

6 At the start of a two-day session, **Otis Redding** records his latest composition – co-written with **Steve Cropper** – *(Sittin' On) The Dock Of The Bay* at the Stax/Volt studios in Memphis, under Cropper's production.

9 A **Doors** concert at the New Haven Arena is halted when **Jim Morrison** is arrested. This follows an earlier backstage incident: Lieutenant James Kelly, initially unaware of the singer's identity, has seen him making out with an 18-year-old girl in a shower stall near the dressing room. He asks Morrison to leave and a scuffle breaks out, with Kelly using mace on Morrison to try to subdue him. Morrison's manager Bill Siddons pleads with police to let the show go ahead, and they agree. However, midway through *Back Door Man*, Morrison stops to relate his version, replete with obscenities, of the event. At this point the lights come on and two officers drag him offstage. When Lieutenant Kelly tells the audience the show is over, fights

"Hair" opened off-Broadway on October 17. In April 1968 it would begin its Broadway run of 1,750 performances, becoming the sixth longest-running musical of all time, and spawning a hot-selling cast album and a 1978 film version.

break out between the police and the crowd. Morrison is charged with breach of the peace, giving an "indecent and immoral exhibition" backstage, and resisting arrest. He is released on a bond of $1,500.

9 **Otis Redding** flies to Cleveland in his new twin-engined Beechcraft H18 plane – owned by the Otis Redding Revue – to appear on "Upbeat," a syndicated television show hosted by Don Webster. He duets with **Mitch Ryder** on *Knock On Wood.*

10 Three years to the day that Sam Cooke died, and *en route* to a concert at the Factory in Madison, Wisconsin, **Otis Redding**'s plane is attempting an instrument landing in fog when it goes down at 3:28 pm into the icy waters of Lake Monoma, near Madison. Pilot Richard Fraser, 26-year-old Redding, his 17-year-old valet Matthew Kelly, and four members of his road band, the **Bar-Kays** – 18-year-old **Jimmy King** (guitarist), 19-year-old **Ronnie Caldwell** (organist), 18-year-old **Phalin Jones** (saxophone), and 18-year-old **Carl Cunningham** (drummer) – are all killed. The only survivor is 20-year-old trumpeter **Ben Cauley**. Police search the lake for three hours, until darkness falls. (At Redding's funeral at Macon's City Auditorium, the pall-bearers will be fellow soul singers **Joe Tex**, **Joe Simon**, who performs *Jesus Keep Me Near The Cross*, **Johnnie Taylor**, **Solomon Burke**, **Percy Sledge**, **Don Covay**, and **Sam Moore** of **Sam & Dave**. Jerry Wexler will read the eulogy. Redding will be buried at his family home at Round Oak, Jones County in Georgia. A notable absentee at the funeral will be his labelmate **Eddie Floyd**: having returned from a UK tour to Washington, D.C., to get a connecting flight to Atlanta, his plane's brakes will jam before take-off, resulting in a six-hour delay.)

12 **Brian Jones**'s appeal against his October 30 sentence is allowed. He is fined £1,000 ($2,400) and sentenced to three years' probation. The court hears evidence that he is emotionally unstable and has suicidal tendencies.

26 The **Beatles**' "Magical Mystery Tour" airs on BBC television and is castigated for its lack of plot and direction. **The Daily Express** critic claims never to have seen "such blatant rubbish." Reviewing the show for **The Times**, Henry Raynor writes "This was a programme to experience rather than to understand: I was unfortunate – I lacked the necessary key."

29 **Jim Webb** – a 21-year-old writer/arranger/producer who has already scored as the composer of the 5th Dimension's US No. 7 July hit *Up, Up And Away* – begins work at Sound Recorders in Hollywood on a three-part cantata, to be part of an album for Irish actor **Richard Harris**. The three segments – *In The Park*, *After The Loves Of My Life*, and *Allegro*, lasting 7:14 – will become one of the most talked about records of 1968, when Harris takes it, later titled *MacArthur Park*, all the way to US No. 2 in June. Its lyrics, heavy on symbolism, will remain a mystery, as the songwriter refuses to explain them.

31 Songwriter/producer **Bert Burns** dies in New York, age 38, following a heart attack. Burns (also sometimes known as Bert Russell), who was also president of Web 4 Music, wrote or co-wrote a slew of hits, including *Hang On Sloopy*, *Twist And Shout*, *Here Comes The Night*, *Brown Eyed Girl*, and *Cry To Me.*

Recorded three days before his death, *(Sittin' On) The Dock Of The Bay* gave Otis Redding his only US chart-topper.

ROOTS During this year: Birmingham, UK, schoolmates John Osbourne, Tony Iommi, Bill Ward, and Terry Butler form blues band Polka Tulk, soon changing their name to Earth; emerging as a successful live act, a further name-change to Black Sabbath will elevate them to a new level... siblings Richard and Karen Carpenter, with three friends, form the Summerchimes, recording nine tracks at the United Audio Studios in Orange County... pianist Reg Dwight auditions for the vacant spot in the Spencer Davis Group, but the job goes to Eddie Hardin... R&B combo the Mighty Mystics, comprising six students from the Tuskegee Institute, enter a talent contest to impress girls; teaming with another campus group, the Jays, they decide on a name-change, and with the help of a dictionary and the pointed finger of group member William King, they settle on the Commodores... Temple University students Daryl Hall and John Oates, both playing in bands – Hall in the Temptones and Oates in the Masters, meet at a dance at the Adelphi Ballroom in Philadelphia... and the Saxons – with brothers Alan and Derek Longmuir (future Bay City Rollers) in the line-up – make their live debut at a church hall in Edinburgh...

People Got To Be Free

1968

No.1 US SINGLES

- **Jan 6** Hello Goodbye **Beatles**
- **Jan 20** Judy In Disguise (With Glasses) **John Fred & His Playboy Band**
- **Feb 3** Green Tambourine **Lemon Pipers**
- **Feb 10** Love Is Blue **Paul Mauriat**
- **Mar 16** (Sittin' On) The Dock Of The Bay **Otis Redding**
- **Apr 13** Honey **Bobby Goldsboro**
- **May 18** Tighten Up **Archie Bell & the Drells**
- **June 1** Mrs. Robinson **Simon & Garfunkel**
- **June 22** This Guy's In Love With You **Herb Alpert**
- **July 20** Grazin In The Grass **Hugh Masekela**
- **Aug 3** Hello, I Love You **Doors**
- **Aug 17** People Got To Be Free **Rascals**
- **Sept 21** Harper Valley P.T.A. **Jeannie C. Riley**
- **Sept 28** Hey Jude **Beatles**
- **Nov 30** Love Child **Diana Ross & the Supremes**
- **Dec 14** I Heard It Through The Grapevine **Marvin Gaye**

No.1 UK SINGLES

- **Jan 6** Hello Goodbye **Beatles**
- **Jan 27** The Ballad Of Bonnie And Clyde **Georgie Fame**
- **Feb 3** Everlasting Love **Love Affair**
- **Feb 17** Mighty Quinn **Manfred Mann**
- **Mar 2** Cinderella Rockerfella **Esther & Abi Ofarim**
- **Mar 23** The Legend Of Xanadu **Dave Dee, Dozy, Beaky, Mick & Tich**
- **Mar 30** Lady Madonna **Beatles**
- **Apr 13** Congratulations **Cliff Richard**
- **Apr 27** What A Wonderful World/Cabaret **Louis Armstrong**
- **May 25** Young Girl **Union Gap featuring Gary Puckett**
- **June 22** Jumping Jack Flash **Rolling Stones**
- **July 6** Baby Come Back **Equals**
- **July 27** I Pretend **Des O'Connor**
- **Aug 3** Mony Mony **Tommy James & the Shondells**
- **Aug 17** Fire **Crazy World of Arthur Brown**
- **Aug 24** Mony Mony **Tommy James & the Shondells**
- **Aug 31** Do It Again **Beach Boys**

James Brown

Jimi Hendrix Experience

James Brown received a letter of thanks from the White House for his appeal for calm during race riots in US cities... With *Electric Ladyland*, Hendrix stretched the studio to the limit, conjuring with electronics and pioneering overdub techniques.

A revolution seemed entirely possible. The world was fraught with violent protests and scarred by political assassinations. The Summer of Love gave way to violence, alienation, and student unrest, as Abbie Hoffman and the confrontational "Yippies" pushed aside the doped-up flower power of Haight-Ashbury. Musicians were at the heart of this maelstrom. So tense were the times that the **Rolling Stones**' *Street Fighting Man* was banned from several US radio stations. Amid the riots that swept America after the assassination of Martin Luther King Jr., **James Brown** became the voice of calm, going on national television to make an emotional appeal. The **Rascals** recorded *People Got to Be Free*, an impassioned response to the assassinations of King and Robert Kennedy that was a worldwide hit.

The **Beatles** abandoned their brief flirtation with eastern mysticism, and were beginning to abandon each other. **Ringo Starr** walked out of a recording session; **John Lennon** was spending more time with **Yoko Ono** and less with the group. **Paul McCartney** was also embarking on solo efforts. Even so, the "White Album" was a richly diverse, often caustic double set that reflected the group's separate paths.

Meanwhile, the Rolling Stones came together triumphantly (despite **Brian Jones**'s continuing drug problems). After a US No. 1 with *Jumping Jack Flash* came the stunning ***Beggars Banquet***, on which they absorbed blues, R&B, gospel, and **Bob Dylan**, and spat out *Sympathy For The Devil*, *Factory Girl*, and *Stray Cat Blues*. The **Jimi Hendrix Experience** enjoyed success with ***Electric Ladyland***, one of only three studio albums released in Hendrix's lifetime, recorded at the end of a year of intensive touring. **Cream** offered up their final helping of heavy blues rock with the double album ***Wheels On Fire***, and by the time they packed up, **Led Zeppelin** and **Yes** were ready to pick up the respective torches for hard and progressive rock.

The success of the Beatles, Stones, and Hendrix helped solidify the trend that saw sales of LPs outstrip those of singles for the first time. Reflecting this in the US, there was a growing battle between the emerging, more album-orientated, FM radio stations, and AM stations. New federal regulations made it difficult for FM stations to control their own programming and compete. In June, the "father of progressive radio," Tom Donahue, and his fellow DJs organized a historic walkout at KMPX-FM in San Francisco, complaining of "government intimidation."

There were antidotes to the spirit of revolution (apart from Richard Nixon's election as US President). **Elvis** delivered more gospel, **Aretha Franklin**'s superlative ***Aretha: Lady Soul*** spawned four seminal Top 10 R&B singles, and **Simon & Garfunkel** graduated with the definitive film soundtrack hit, *Mrs. Robinson*.

Sept 7	I've Gotta Get A Message To You **Bee Gees**
Sept 14	Hey Jude **Beatles**
Sept 28	Those Were The Days **Mary Hopkin**
Nov 9	With A Little Help From My Friends **Joe Cocker**
Nov 16	The Good The Bad And The Ugly **Hugo Montenegro & His Orchestra**
Dec 14	Lily The Pink **Scaffold**

"It was the finest music of his life. If ever there was music that bleeds, this was it."

Greil Marcus, **Mystery Train**, remembering the 1968 TV special

Jan 1968

Albums outsell singles for the first time... Dylan once again plays live...

Syd Barrett

The Graduate

January

1 **Billboard** reports that Americans spent more than $1 billion on records last year, with albums (192 million) outselling singles (187 million) for the first time.

4 As the **Jimi Hendrix Experience** begin a four-date Scandinavian tour at Lorensberg Cirkus in Gothenburg, plugging a second album, *Axis: Bold As Love*, Hendrix is jailed overnight, and will be fined, for wrecking a hotel room, reportedly during a fight with **Noel Redding**.

6 "Happening '68" – a daytime music show produced by Dick Clark – begins on ABC television. Presented by **Mark Lindsay** and **Paul Revere**, and featuring the **Raiders**, the show will prove so popular that from July it will go out five times a week, Monday to Friday. The series will run until September 1969.

20 **Bob Dylan** – making his first public appearance since his motorcycle accident – takes part in the Woody Guthrie Memorial Concert at Carnegie Hall. **Pete Seeger**, **Arlo Guthrie**, **Odetta**, **Richie Havens**, **Judy Collins**, and **Ramblin' Jack Elliott** all pay their musical respects. Also appearing are the **Hawks**, already critically lauded as Bob Dylan's backing group on his 1965–6 world tour. Comprising singer/guitarist **Robbie Robertson**, pianist/singer **Richard Manuel**, bassist/singer **Rick Danko**, organist **Garth Hudson**, and drummer/singer **Levon Helm**, the Hawks – managed by Albert Grossman – have recently signed to Capitol as a stand-alone act.

26 As **Syd Barrett**'s behavior becomes increasingly unpredictable, the other members of **Pink Floyd** fail to pick him up for a gig at Southampton University. (**Roger Waters** will invite a friend of his, **David Gilmour**, to join the group, excusing Barrett from live appearances to concentrate on songwriting. Gilmour has been a member of local band the **Ramblers**, which became **Jokers Wild** – who once appeared on a bill with the **Pink Floyd Sound** and **Paul Simon**.)

28 The **Doors' Jim Morrison** taunts a security guard in the parking lot of an adult movie theater in Las Vegas by pretending to smoke a joint. Fellow guards attack Morrison, the police are called, and the singer is arrested on a charge of vagrancy and public drunkenness.

During a US tour, Jimi Hendrix performed at Garfield High, the school he attended as a boy, and was given the key to the city of Seattle.

The Maharishi Mahesh Yogi with the Beatles

Pink Floyd's Syd Barrett was being edged offstage by his fellow band members... Simon & Garfunkel recorded *Mrs. Robinson* for the Mike Nichols movie "The Graduate"... The Beatles flew to India to study further with the Maharishi... Hendrix walked off stage in Chicago when his amps started picking up radio signals.

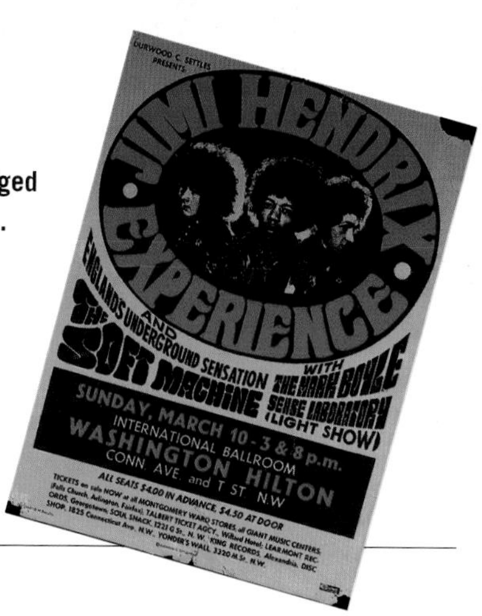

February

2 **Simon & Garfunkel**'s *Mrs. Robinson* is recorded in New York, with co-producer Roy Halee. The duo's trademark vocal synchronicity is a result of double-tracking both vocal parts to provide perfect overlaid harmony.

14 On a day off during their latest US tour, the **Hollies** give a free show at the Whisky A Go-Go in Los Angeles. The **Mamas & the Papas**, the **Beach Boys**, the **Doors**, **David Crosby**, **Stephen Stills**, and **Neil Young** are in attendance. Crosby, Stills, and Young don't rate the band, but are blown away by the harmony vocals of **Graham Nash**.

> "The Beatles have used their tremendous popularity not as a crutch but as a springboard to artistic growth; the fascinating thing has been that their fans have grown with them." **Downbeat**, January 1, 1968

15 The **Harrisons** and the **Lennons** fly to India to study meditation with the Maharishi Mahesh Yogi in Rishikesh. **Paul McCartney**, Jane Asher, and the **Starrs** will join them next week. Starr will soon become bored, and will return to London on March 1, comparing the retreat center to a Butlin's holiday camp. The others will depart because the Maharishi allegedly made amorous advances to actress Mia Farrow – or, as another rumor has it, because they don't like the food.

15 Blues singer **Little Walter** dies from a head injury, following a drunken brawl in Chicago. Born Marion Walter Jacobs, he moved to Chicago in the early 1950s, becoming a session player for Chess Records as both harmonica player and guitarist. After playing with the **Muddy Waters** band, he launched his own recording career, and cut a handful of blues classics.

27 On leave from his army post in Georgia, and scheduled to begin recording with Roulette Records tomorrow, **Frankie Lymon** is discovered dead in his grandmother's house in New York – where he grew up. A used syringe lies near his body. A star at 13, all but spent at 14, he is dead from a heroin overdose at 25. Lymon will be buried at St. Raymond's Cemetery in the Bronx – the same resting place as **Billie Holiday**.

29 Although the **Beatles**' ***Sgt. Pepper's Lonely Hearts Club Band*** picks up the major prize of Album of the Year – one of six nominations received – at the tenth Grammy Awards, the night belongs to a 21-year-old Oklahoma-born songwriter, **Jim Webb**. His composition *Up, Up And Away* is named Song of the Year, Record of the Year, Best Performance by a Vocal Group, Best Contemporary Single, and Best Contemporary Group Performance, Vocal or Instrumental for the **5th Dimension**, while the **Johnny Mann Singers**' version is named Best Performance by a Chorus. Webb's ballad *By The Time I Get To Phoenix* is named Best Vocal Performance, Male and Best Contemporary Male Solo Vocal Performance, both for **Glen Campbell** – whose solo career is finally soaring.

March

1 Following an admission from London-based pop quintet, **Love Affair**, that they didn't play on their recent UK chart-topping single *Everlasting Love*, the Musicians' Union adopts a code of fair practice to present to the recording industry. General secretary Hardie Ratcliffe says: "Some features of it are designed to bring an end to what has been described as 'ghosting' – the practice of using highly skilled musicians to stand in for those members of pop groups unable to do the work themselves."

2 **Cat Stevens** enters a London nursing home, after a cough is diagnosed as tuberculosis. Transferred to the King Edward VII Hospital, he will spend three months recuperating, followed by a further nine months resting at home.

2 **Big Brother & the Holding Company**, **Tim Buckley**, and **Albert King** play on the opening night of the Fillmore East, a converted movie theater on New York's Second Avenue and Sixth Street that becomes concert promoter Bill Graham's first East Coast venue.

20 Partying at **Stephen Stills**'s house, **Eric Clapton** and **Buffalo Springfield**'s **Neil Young**, **Jim Messina**, and **Richie Furay** are among eleven people busted by police on a charge of "being at a place where it is suspected marijuana was being used." They will plead guilty to disturbing the peace; all except Stills, who manages to escape through a window.

27 The **Bee Gees** open their first bill-topping UK tour at London's Royal Albert Hall, backed by a 67-piece orchestra, a choir, and the 50-strong Royal Air Force Band.

30 **The Times** reports that fears of a possible stampede – caused by people rushing to see **John Lennon** and **George Harrison** – have scuppered plans by the Maharashi Mahesh Yogi to take the two Beatles on a procession through Hardwar on the Ganges on April 13 – the most important day of the festival of Ard Khumb, when devout Hindus bathe in the sacred river.

April

4 The **Beach Boys**, who are scheduled to open a US college tour in Nashville with **Buffalo Springfield** and **Strawberry Alarm Clock**, cancel when they hear of Martin Luther King's assassination in nearby Memphis. **Jimi Hendrix**, **B.B. King**, and **Buddy Guy** learn the news in Virginia Beach, and gather to take part in an all-night blues session.

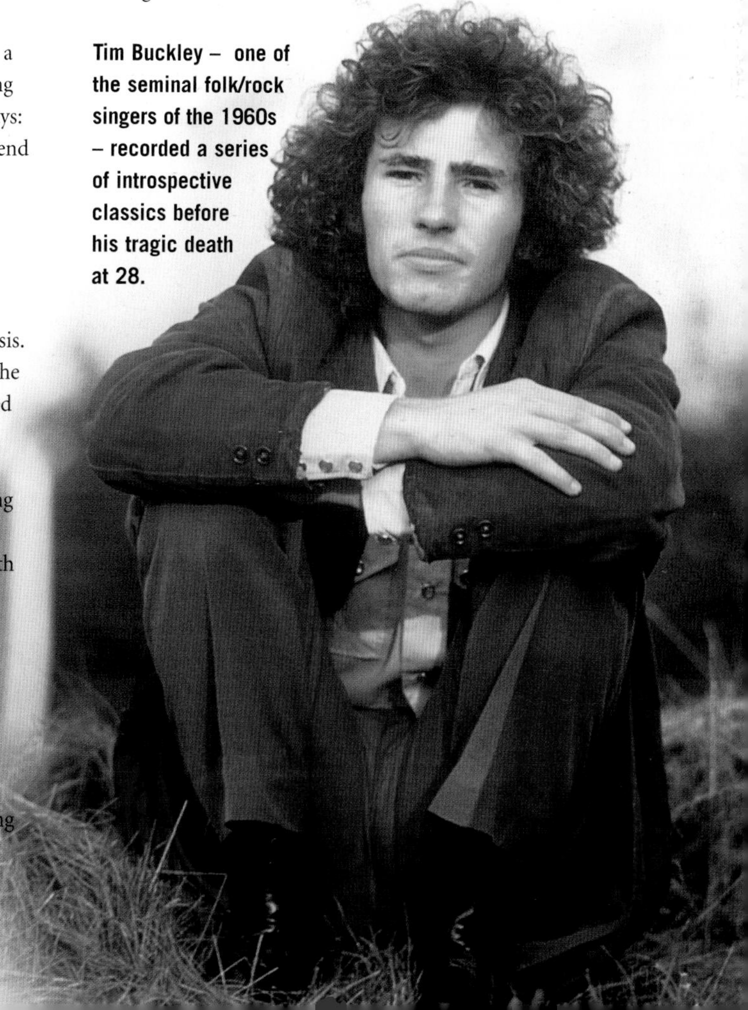
Tim Buckley – one of the seminal folk/rock singers of the 1960s – recorded a series of introspective classics before his tragic death at 28.

Apr

1968

Deep Purple's debut... The end of Buffalo Springfield... Bubblegum rock...

The Young Rascals' unique brand of blue-eyed soul was due to the band's two lead vocalists – Felix Cavaliere and Eddie Brigati.

Jim Morrison's increasing dependency on drugs and alcohol led to a series of arrests for lascivious behavior.

5 Following the assassination of Martin Luther King, which has spawned riots in 30 US cities, **James Brown** broadcasts on national television from the Boston Garden, appealing for calm and rational behavior. His efforts will receive official commendation from Vice-President Hubert H. Humphrey.

12 The **Mothers of Invention** play at the NARAS annual dinner in New York, with a performance which – unsurprisingly – pokes barbed fun at the assembled diners. **Frank Zappa** says: "All year long you people have manufactured this crap, now you're gonna have to listen to it." Meanwhile **Life** magazine's profile of the **Doors**, titled "Wicked Go the Doors," by Fred Powledge, describes **Jim Morrison** as "moody, temperamental, enchanted in the mind and extremely stoned on something."

20 The **Rolling Stones** record the latest **Jagger/Richard** rock nugget, *Jumping Jack Flash*, at Olympia Sound Studios in Barnes, London. It will hit US No. 3 and UK No. 1 in the summer.

20 Having recently changed their name from **Roundabout**, British hard-rock outfit **Deep Purple** make their concert debut under the new name in Tastrup, Denmark. The combo's fresh line-up comprises 23-year-old guitarist **Ritchie Blackmore**, 26-year-old keyboardist **Jon Lord**, 19-year-old drummer **Ian Paice**, 21-year-old bassist **Nick Simper**, and 23-year-old singer **Rod Evans**. Next month, they will be snapped up by EMI Records and record their first album ***Shades Of Deep Purple*** in one 18-hour session. It will be licensed in the US – where it will find greater success – to the Tetragrammaton label, owned by comedian Bill Cosby.

28 **Country Joe & the Fish** perform at Larry Van Over's farm in Duvall, Washington, after a piano is dropped from a helicopter to answer the question, "What does a piano sound like when dropped from a great height?" Although it lands with a less than resounding thud, enough fun is had by all to germinate the idea that will lead to the first Sky River Rock Festival and Lighter Than Air Fair at the beginning of September.

30 The Kaleidoscope Club – a self-proclaimed multimedia rock venue – opens on Sunset Boulevard in Hollywood, with **Canned Heat**, **Jefferson Airplane**, and **Fever Tree** playing.

May

3 The **Beach Boys** begin a US tour at Georgetown University in Washington, D.C., with the Maharishi Mahesh Yogi lecturing on spiritual regeneration. Tomorrow night's show at New York's Singer Bowl will be called off when only 300 people show up, and the Maharishi refuses to go on. The band's live show, based around an old-fashioned greatest hits presentation, is becoming an increasing anachronism in an era of progressive rock acts. **Al Jardine** will comment, "If anybody benefits from this tour, it'll be the florists." Half the tour dates will be canceled.

5 Confirming rumors that **Buffalo Springfield** are about to break up, **Stephen Stills** says, "This is it," as the band prepares to go on stage at the Long Beach Arena, for what will be its last performance. Stills will shortly combine with **David Crosby** and **Graham Nash**; **Bruce Palmer** will begin a short-lived solo career; **Neil Young** will achieve parallel success as both a solo artist for Reprise Records and as a fourth annex to **Crosby, Stills & Nash**, while **Richie Furay** will go on to form **Pogo**. With its successful offshoots, Buffalo Springfield will be revered in hindsight as a seminal folk-rock experiment.

12 The **Rolling Stones** make their first live appearance in more than a year – and their first on home soil since October 1966 – at the annual **New Musical Express** Poll Winners Concert at the Empire Pool, Wembley, premiering their new single *Jumping Jack Flash*. It will prove to be the last time **Brian Jones** plays with the band.

14 The **Rascals** (who recently dropped their "Young" prefix) record *People Got To Be Free*, set to become their fourth and last million-selling single. Written by **Felix Cavaliere** and **Eddie Brigati**, the former will claim that it was written in reaction to the assassinations of Martin Luther

> **"Don't terrorize. Organize. Don't burn. Give kids a chance to learn... the real answer to race problems in this country is education."**
>
> James Brown, April 5, 1968

STEPPENWOLF

May 4 Steppenwolf perform *Born To Be Wild* on "American Bandstand." Taking their name from a Hermann Hesse novel, the group were formed last year in Los Angeles by 24-year-old German-born frontman John Kay (born Joachim Krauledat). *Born To Be Wild* – written by drummer Jerry Edmonton's brother Dennis (aka Mars Bonfire), and featuring the lyric "heavy metal thunder" (which will help ignite the "heavy metal" scene) – will hit US No. 2, and become the archetypal biker song when it is used in the film "Easy Rider" next year. It will also boost the fortunes of the group's debut album, *Steppenwolf*, which cost $9,000 to record at American Recording Company, a converted Chinese restaurant on Ventura Boulevard, Studio City, California.

Like many acts from both the US and the UK, Steppenwolf followed Cream's lead in the burgeoning hard-rock genre.

King and Robert Kennedy, whose campaign the band had worked for – even though it is in fact being recorded the month before Kennedy's death. In March, while the group were on tour in Florida, their trailer broke down outside Fort Pierce, and they encountered heavy anti-rock and racist harassment from locals. In response, they have declared that they will no longer play on live bills that don't include at least one black act.

14 **John Lennon** and **Paul McCartney** appear on NBC-TV's "The Tonight Show," and announce the setting up of Apple Corps. With regular host Johnny Carson absent, former St. Louis Cardinals catcher Joe Garagiola sits in. Legendary actress Tallulah Bankhead also appears on the broadcast.

30 The **Beatles** convene at EMI's Abbey Road Studios to begin work on their forthcoming album – the first track they record is *Revolution*.

June

6 The day after Robert Kennedy is gunned down in Los Angeles, the **Rolling Stones** record *Sympathy For The Devil*, adding a passing reference to the assassination. In a more extensive tribute, **Stephen Stills** writes *Long Time Gone* – which will be recorded by **Crosby, Stills & Nash**.

7 Bubblegum meets Carnegie Hall, as Buddah Records' Jerry Kasenetz and Jeff Katz present the **Kasenetz-Katz Singing Orchestral Circus** – an aggregation of eight of their "bubblegum rock" acts, a novelty genre that sweetens the simplicity of garage rock. The acts featured are the **1910 Fruitgum Company**, **Ohio Express**, **Music Explosion**, the **Teri Nelson Group**, **Lt. Garcia's Magic Music Box**, **1989 Musical Marching Zoo**, **St. Louis Invisible Marching Band**, and **J.C.W Rat Finks**. There are 50 members in total, who also perform individually. **The New York Times**' Robert Shelton, reviewing the show, says: "If the bands had been as inventive as their names, the evening's music would have been more memorable... It was sort of a world's fair of rock, assembling not just the best, but the most of everything." The evening "suggested what might have happened had an electronic circus existed in the Weimar Republic."

9 Canadian singer/songwriter **Joni Mitchell** ends her first Los Angeles date: a six-day engagement at the Troubadour. Signed last year by Reprise Records, 24-year-old Mitchell is promoting her debut album, ***Joni Mitchell***.

10 Fire engines are called to Olympic Studios in Barnes, west London, when the building's roof goes up in flames while the **Rolling Stones** are filming a sequence for their "One By One" documentary.

11 With rifts emerging in the **Beatles**, and as a sign of things to come, **John Lennon** works solo on *Revolution 9* in Studio 3 at EMI Studios, while **Paul McCartney** records *Blackbird* in Studio 2. George and Ringo are currently in the US.

David Crosby spotted Joni Mitchell while she was performing in 1967 at the Gaslight Club in Coconut Grove, Florida.

The Hyde Park rock concert... Tim Hardin... The Beatles record *Hey Jude*...

14 With their debut album, ***Truth*** – produced by Mickie Most – on its way to US No. 15, the **Jeff Beck Group** make their US live debut. The popular guitarist's backing band comprises 21-year-old bassist **Ron Wood**, drummer **Aynsley Dunbar**, and 23-year-old London-born lead singer **Rod Stewart**.

28 **Aretha Franklin** – at US No. 2 with ***Aretha: Lady Soul***, and set to release its follow-up, ***Aretha Now***, next month – headlines the Soul Together concert at Madison Square Garden, with **Sam & Dave**, the **Rascals**, **Sonny & Cher**, **Joe Tex**, and **King Curtis**, to raise money for the Martin Luther King Memorial Fund. Audience member **Jimi Hendrix** donates $5,000 to the cause.

29 **Pink Floyd** top the bill at Britain's first ever, large-scale, free rock concert, staged in London's Hyde Park. The opening acts include **Jethro Tull**, a new progressive rock act led by flute-playing lead vocalist **Ian Anderson**, and managed by the Chrysalis booking agency (Chris Wright and Terry Ellis, who have combined "Chris" and "Ellis" to form their company name). Signed to Chris Blackwell's now flourishing Island label, for whom they are completing their debut album, ***This Was***, the group recently finished a residency at London's Marquee club. Also performing today are 27-year-old Mancunian singer/songwriter **Roy Harper**, and **Tyrannosaurus Rex**, led by a 20-year old singer/songwriter, born in Hackney, London, and previously singer/guitarist with **John's Children** – **Marc Bolan**.

July

3 *Baby Come Back* by the **Equals** – recently reissued as an A-side – tops the UK chart for the first of three weeks, deposing the **Rolling Stones**' *Jumping Jack Flash*. The London-based quintet was formed two years ago by Guyana-born songwriter/guitarist **Eddy Grant**, with **Derv Gordon** on lead vocals, Grant on lead guitar, **Lincoln Gordon** on rhythm guitar, **Pat Lloyd** on bass, and **John Hall** on drums. The Equals play a repertoire of ska-influenced R&B songs, mostly written by Grant, who will re-emerge in the 1970s as a highly successful solo artist.

7 Veteran blues/rock outfit the **Yardbirds** call it a day with a gig in Luton, UK, after a final US tour. They have consistently proved more popular in the US, scoring five charted albums.

ELVIS PRESLEY

June 27 Work begins at 6:00 pm at NBC's Studio 4 in Burbank, on a television special starring Elvis Presley, produced and directed by Steve Binder. Binder has won a lengthy battle with "Col." Tom Parker over the show's format, seeing it as a chance to relaunch Presley's magnetism as a live performer. (Parker had wanted Presley to sing 20 Christmas songs and say goodnight.) Two long jamming sessions are interspersed with choreographed set pieces, and the hours of tape will be edited into a one-hour program.

For two extended sessions, over two days, Presley, Scotty Moore, Charlie Hodge, and D.J. Fontana played with an audience gathered around them, jamming on familiar material.

Jethro Tull

Jethro Tull took their name from the 18th-century agriculturalist... Actors supplied the voices of the Beatles for the "Yellow Submarine" cartoon.

8 Two policemen are hurt, and seven juveniles and six adults arrested, following a concert by **Smokey Robinson & the Miracles** at Carter Playground in the South End of Boston. The disturbance starts during the show, when some of the crowd surge toward the stage. Police ask them to move back, the group leave the stage, and thousands stream out of the park, starting a rampage that results in broken store windows, stone-throwing, and the reported theft of a bus.

8 Plugging their new album ***A Saucerful Of Secrets***, **Pink Floyd** embark on a US tour of the same name, opening at the Kinetic Playground in Chicago. The 18 dates will take them to Detroit, New York, Philadelphia, Los Angeles, San Francisco, Seattle, and Sacramento.

16 **Tim Hardin** embarks on his first British tour, at London's Royal Albert Hall. Hailed a couple of years ago by **Bob Dylan** as one of America's greatest living singer/songwriters, the 26-year-old folk-blues performer has become a popular fixture at college campuses and blues festivals in the US, while **Bobby Darin** took his *If I Were A Carpenter* to US No. 8 in 1966. But Hardin's six-date visit will degenerate into farce, as he performs in an apparent drug-induced stupor, leaving his British backing musicians unable to play in time with him. Supporting act **Family** will invariably steal the limelight.

17 The **Beatles**' cartoon feature film "Yellow Submarine," animated by Heinz Edelman and directed by George Dunning, premieres at the London Pavilion. The screening is attended by all the members of the group except **Ringo**, who has a rare lead-vocal role on the movie's title theme.

28 **Robin Gibb** collapses, as the **Bee Gees** prepare to fly to the US for their first tour. He is admitted to Regent's Park Nursing Home suffering from "a severe attack of nervous exhaustion." He will be moved to a health farm in Sussex, and will be discharged next weekend.

29 On the eve of the South African leg of the **Byrds**' world tour, 21-year-old keyboardist/singer **Gram Parsons** – who joined the band in February – checks out of his London hotel and quits the group because he refuses to play to segregated audiences. He will be replaced for the remainder of the tour by ex-Byrds roadie, Carlos Bernal, and will soon form the **Flying Burrito Brothers** with another ex-Byrd, **Chris Hillman**.

31 The **Beatles** begin a two-day session to cut *Hey Jude* – written by **Paul McCartney** for **John Lennon**'s son **Julian** – at Trident Studios, off Wardour Street in London. It is recorded on eight-track tape, and a 36-piece orchestral accompaniment will be added tomorrow evening.

"At no time in American history has youth possessed the strength it possesses now. Trained by music and linked by music, it has the power for good to change the world. That power for good carries the reverse, the power of evil." Ralph J. Gleason, **Rolling Stone**, June 22 1968

August

6 **The Times** reports that the British Market Research Bureau is to begin compiling new weekly singles and album sales charts in November. Peter Meneer, its associate director, proposed the idea – which will involve 300 shops filling in daily diaries recording sales. The figures will be fed into a computer to produce the charts. Six record companies have already signed up, while others have until the 23rd to decide whether to participate.

9 Fans of rock 'n' roll legend **Jerry Lee Lewis** get out of hand at the eighth National Jazz and Blues Festival at Kempton Park in Sunbury-on-Thames, west of London. The opening night is brought to an end when headliners the **Herd** refuse to go on after a Lewis fan hurls a scaffolding coupling pin through **Andrew Steel**'s bass drum.

10 Justifying the name of the National Jazz and Blues Festival, the **Ronnie Scott Quintet**, **Jon Hendricks**, the **Mike Westbrook Band**, and others provide the afternoon's entertainment. The evening session reverts to type with performances from the **Nice**, **Ten Years After**, **Joe Cocker** (a 24-year-old, blue-eyed soul singer from Sheffield who recently cut his version of **Lennon/McCartney**'s *With A Little Help From My Friends*), the **Crazy World of Arthur Brown**, **Jeff Beck**, **Deep Purple**, **Tyrannosaurus Rex**, the **Spencer Davis Group**, and **Traffic** (who have just completed their second album, ***Traffic***).

The Equals were founded by Guyanian-born Eddy Grant at Acland Burghley School in Hornsey Rise, London.

The Isle of Wight Festival... John Peel on Radio 1... the New Yardbirds become Led Zeppelin...

Sly & the Family Stone

11 The bill on the second day of the National Jazz and Blues Festival highlights folk music, including performances by **Al Stewart**, the **Incredible String Band**, and Britain's newest folk-rock exponents, **Fairport Convention**, whose line-up includes guitarist **Richard Thompson**, vocalist **Ian Matthews**, and new lead vocal recruit, singer/songwriter **Sandy Denny**. Their first album, ***Fairport Convention***, produced by Joe Boyd, has just been released by Polydor. The evening session sees sets by **John Mayall's Bluesbreakers**, **Chicken Shack**, and **Jethro Tull**.

22 **Ringo Starr** walks out on the **Beatles** during the recording of their new album. While Ringo leaves the country (he'll return to the fold on September 3), the rest of the band will continue sessions, with **Paul McCartney** playing drums on *Back In The USSR*. Meanwhile, **John Lennon**'s wife Cynthia files for divorce on the grounds of his adultery with **Yoko Ono**.

24 **Country Joe & the Fish**'s **Joe McDonald**, **Barry Melton**, and **David Cohen** – in Chicago to perform for demonstrators outside the Democratic Party's National Convention – are attacked in the lobby of a Lake Shore Drive hotel, and go to the Wesley Memorial Hospital for treatment. Their three attackers are believed to be Vietnam vets.

31 An estimated 10,000 people attend the Great South Coast Bank Holiday Pop Festivity (forever known as the Isle of Wight Pop Festival) at Hayles Field near Godshill. Brothers Ray and Ron Foulk have planned it at their farm to raise funds for a swimming pool. Starting at 6:00 pm, and continuing non-stop until 10:00 tomorrow morning, 14 acts take part, introduced by disc jockey John Peel: **Jefferson Airplane** (the only American band on the bill), the **Move**, **Fairport Convention**, the **Pretty Things**, **Tyrannosaurus Rex**, **Aynsley Dunbar Retaliation**, **Plastic Penny**, **Smile**, **Orange Bicycle**, **Hunter's Muskett**, the **Mirage**, local bands **Halcyon Order** and **Harsh Reality**, and the **Crazy World of Arthur Brown**. Brown had planned to arrive by balloon, but had to abandon this idea because of high winds, which also prevent him from setting light to his headgear when performing *Fire*.

The first Isle of Wight festival was a fundraiser for the Isle of Wight Swimming Pool Association.

September

2 Currently on a European tour with **Jefferson Airplane**, the **Doors** have to perform as a trio at a concert in Amsterdam, after lead singer **Jim Morrison** passes out while dancing on stage during the Airplane's set.

4 The **Evening Standard** reports that several American radio stations have banned the **Rolling Stones**' latest single *Street Fighting Man*, on the grounds that it could incite further riots. **Mick Jagger** responds: "I'm rather pleased to hear they have banned [the single] as long as it's still available in the shops. The last time they banned one of our records in America, it sold a million."

7 The **New Yardbirds** make their live debut at Gladsaxe in Copenhagen, at the start of a 12-date Scandinavian tour. The new band was set up by **Jimmy Page** and **Chris Dreja**, but Dreja has quit the business to become a photographer. Page has recruited experienced session player/arranger and bassist, 22-year-old **John Paul Jones**, and 19-year-old ex-**Listen** vocalist **Robert Plant**, whom Page and manager Peter Grant recently saw perform with a band called **Hobbstweedle** in Birmingham. Plant has recommended 20-year-old drummer **John Bonham**, who completes the new quartet.

8 The **Beatles** perform *Hey Jude*, clocking in at 7:10, easily the longest song to hit UK No. 1, on David Frost's LWT show "Frost on Sunday."

11 As **Sly & the Family Stone** arrive in London to begin a tour, UK customs officials find bassist **Larry Graham** in possession of cannabis. The BBC will cancel a scheduled television appearance, and a week later the band will leave Britain without having performed. Ex-disc jockey and inhouse producer for Autumn Records, **Sly Stone** formed his multiracial psychedelic soul combo – a collision of funk, jazz, rock, R&B, and anarchic humor – last year in San Francisco, and signed to Epic Records. They will shortly record their third single, *Everyday People*, which will become Stone's first US chart-topper next February, having already scored a UK and US Top 10 smash with the funk-laden *Dance To The Music*.

14 Tragedy strikes **Roy Orbison**. While touring Britain, his home in Nashville catches fire, and the elder two of his three sons, Roy Jr. and Tony, die in the blaze.

Jim Morrison's downward spiral continued when he passed out on stage during a Jefferson Airplane performance in Amsterdam... Sly Stone was already a music veteran, as both producer (the Beau Brummels) and radio DJ (for KDIA in Oakland).

15 Featuring **Lou Rawls** and **Martha & the Vandellas** among others, NBC airs the first "Soul!" program – a weekly variety show aimed at black viewers.

23 On her first visit to Britain, **Joni Mitchell**, accompanied by the **John Cameron Group**, tapes a session for Radio 1's "Top Gear" show, which has been hosted from its inception last year by journeyman disc jockey, John Peel. It will evolve into his own, highly popular, late-night "John Peel Show." Peel spent some years in the US, working for WRR radio in Dallas and several other stations, including KOMA in Oklahoma City, and KMEN in California, then returned to Britain in 1967 and joined Radio London, where he hosted his eclectic show "The Perfumed Garden." On the air with BBC Radio 1 from day one, Peel is establishing himself as an eccentric on-air personality with a dry wit and a knack for being several years ahead of the record industry in discovering and exposing new talent. His taped "sessions" for hundreds of artists appearing on his program will become prized archival recordings that will see retail release.

26 **Brian Jones** is found guilty of unauthorized possession of cannabis and fined £50 ($120) with 100 guineas (£105/$252) costs at Inner London Sessions. Chairman R.E. Seaton tells Jones: "Do not get into trouble again. If you do there will be real trouble."

26 Newly signed to Atlantic Records, **Dusty Springfield** begins recording in Memphis, backed by the cream of local session talent, under the direction of label producers Tom Dowd, Arif Mardin, and Jerry Wexler. Her label debut, completed in less than a week, will be the critically revered ***Dusty In Memphis*** – a soulful classic that will include her biggest hit, *Son Of A Preacher Man*.

October

2 Alleging that the songwriting/production team of **Holland/Dozier/Holland** are in breach of their contract, by failing to have

Led Zeppelin

The Yardbirds, who had performed at the Fillmore Auditorium in October 1966, split in July, when Jimmy Page and Chris Dreja formed the New Yardbirds. They in turn evolved into Led Zeppelin, who adapted their name from a phrase – "going down like a lead Zeppelin" – often used to describe disastrous gigs.

written or produced any new material for the company since last year, Motown Records files a $4 (£1.7) million lawsuit against the trio.

7 Virtuoso acoustic guitarist **José Feliciano** (a 23-year-old blind Puerto Rican who hit US No. 3 with his cover of the Doors' *Light My Fire*) performs a controversial interpretation of the *Star-Spangled Banner* before the fifth World Series game between the Detroit Tigers and the St. Louis Cardinals at Detroit's Tiger Stadium.

17 After months of sessions at Abbey Road and Trident Studios, the **Beatles** finish their latest album. Thirty tracks of dizzying diversity will be featured on the double LP, due for release on November 22.

18 The **New Yardbirds** make their live UK debut at the Marquee Club. Two gigs later, at Surrey University next week, they will perform for the first time as **Led Zeppelin**.

18 **John Lennon** and **Yoko Ono** are taken to Paddington Green police station and charged with obstructing the police in execution of a search warrant, after cannabis is discovered in the London apartment where they are staying.

19 Guitarist **Peter Frampton** – 18 years old and currently a member of the **Herd** – sits in on guitar at a **Small Faces** gig in London, and strikes up a rapport with lead singer **Steve Marriott**. They begin to make plans to form a new group, which will emerge next April as **Humble Pie**.

22 Revolutionary street gang the Motherf***ers attempt to "liberate" the Fillmore East venue in New York. In justification, they claim that owner/promoter Bill Graham has "sucked the blood of the community and made himself rich off of rock, which belongs to the people." Graham counters: "Nobody wanted to liberate this place a year ago when it was a rat-infested dump. You can go liberate the opera house."

26 **Johnny Rivers**, **José Feliciano**, **Eric Burdon & the Animals**, the **Fraternity of Man**, **Rejoice**, and the **Buddy Miles Express** – led by 22-year-old R&B drumming vocalist **Buddy Miles**, who has come through the ranks playing for the likes of **Mike Bloomfield** and **Wilson Pickett** – perform on the first day of the San Francisco International Pop Festival, staged over the weekend at the Alameda County Fairgrounds in Pleasanton, California. Also on the bill are **Iron Butterfly**, a new heavy metal combo from San Diego, led by keyboardist/vocalist **Doug Ingle**. The group signed to Atco Records last year, and their second album, ***In-A-Gadda-Da-Vida*** – renamed from its original "In the Garden of Eden" through the band members' state of intoxication – will hit US No. 4 during a 140-week chart stay. It will be hailed by critics as the first true "heavy metal" album. Its title cut – which has been trimmed down to a four-minute edit from its original 17-minute album version – stands at US No. 30.

30 Detroit-based garage/punk unit **MC5**'s raucous performances tonight and tomorrow at the local Grande Ballroom are recorded by Elektra Records for subsequent release as ***Kick Out The Jams***. The fiercely anti-establishment, experimental rock group was originally formed in 1965 as the Motor City Five, comprising vocalist **Rob Tyner**, guitarists **Fred "Sonic" Smith** and **Wayne Kramer**, bassist **Michael Davis**, and drummer **Dennis Thompson**.

The MC5 were the house band for the radical White Panther Party and its associated Trans Love Commune.

Nov 1968

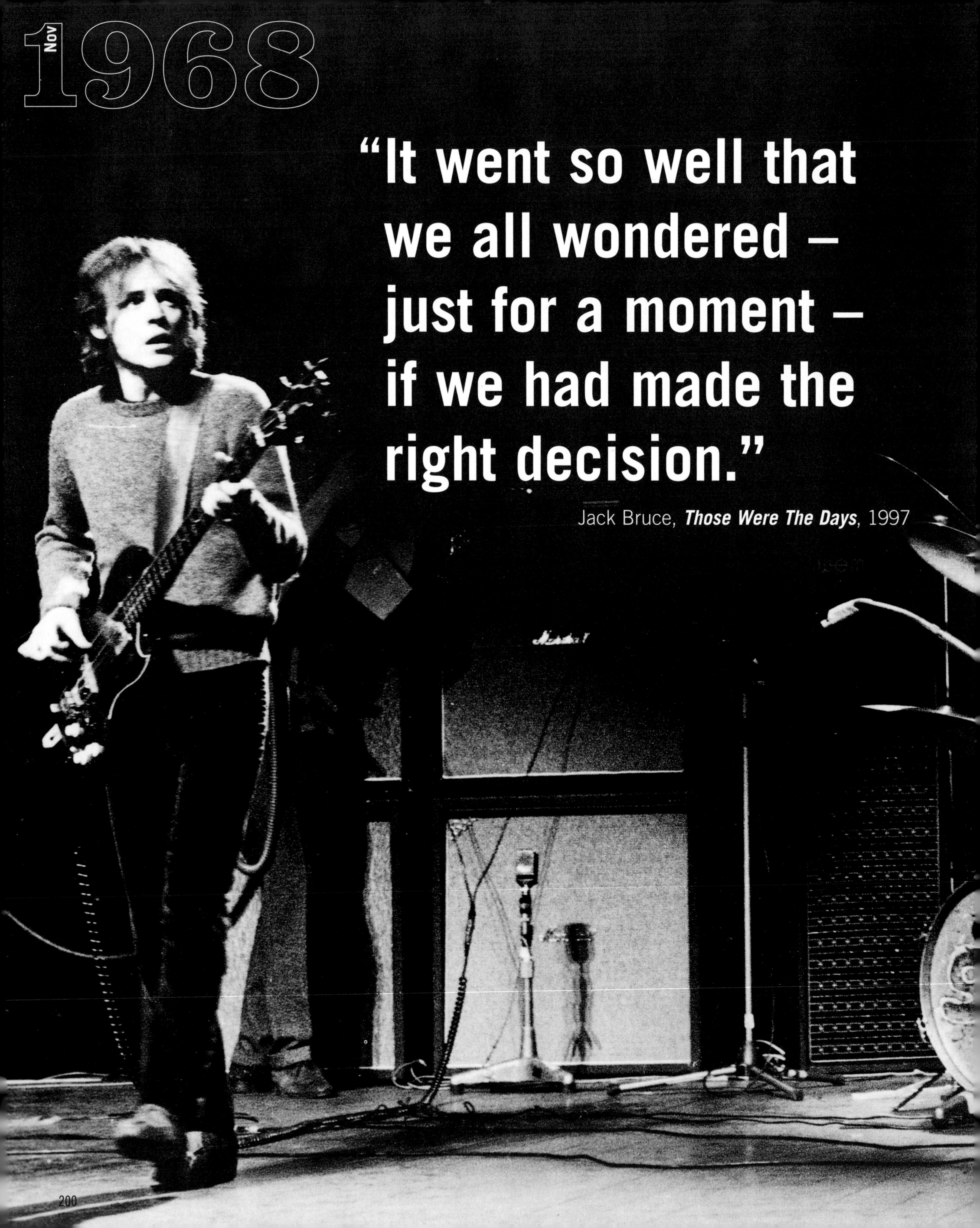

"It went so well that we all wondered – just for a moment – if we had made the right decision."

Jack Bruce, ***Those Were The Days***, 1997

Nov 18 A full house greets Cream at London's Royal Albert Hall, as they give their last ever performance, explaining that the band's music has gone as far as it can. In a career of two years and four months, the trio have played more than 300 live gigs. Filmmaker Tony Palmer documents the event for subsequent release as "Goodbye Cream."

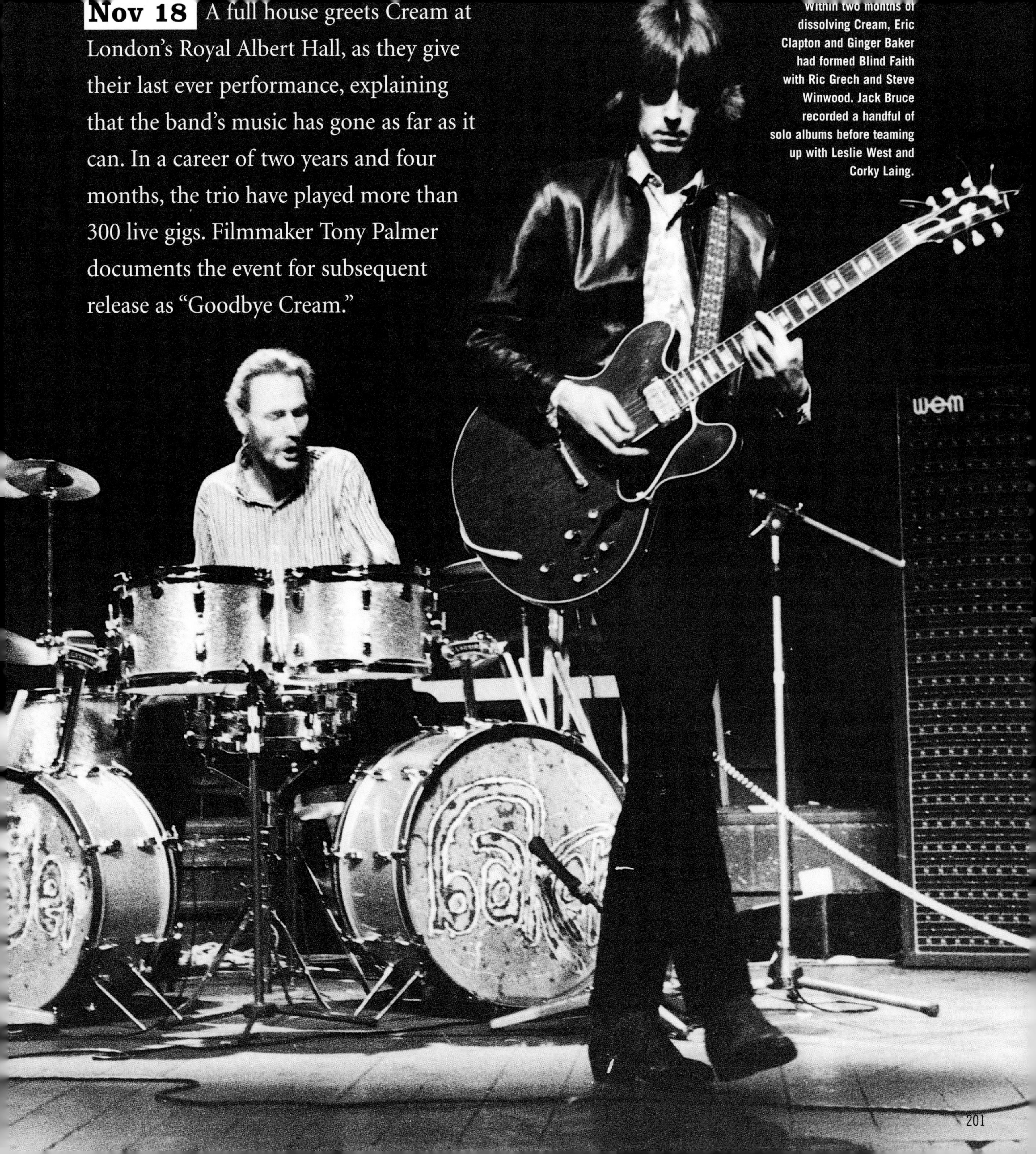

Within two months of dissolving Cream, Eric Clapton and Ginger Baker had formed Blind Faith with Ric Grech and Steve Winwood. Jack Bruce recorded a handful of solo albums before teaming up with Leslie West and Corky Laing.

Nov 1968

The Stones' *Beggars Banquet*... The "White Album"... Marvin Gaye makes it to No. 1...

The Monkees played their last dates as a quartet in Osaka, Japan, in October, before Peter Tork left the group at the end of the year.

November

1 The Apple label releases the first solo album by a Beatle: **George Harrison**'s ***Wonderwall Music***, the soundtrack to the movie "Wonderwall." This is not surprising: Harrison – bursting with musical ideas – has become increasingly frustrated at not being allowed to contribute enough compositions to Beatles albums.

6 The **Monkees**' feature film debut, "Head," premieres in New York. Given a budget of $750,000 by Columbia Pictures, Bob Rafelson was expected to deliver a standard teen flick, but has instead created a film about the manipulation of the group, mixed in with a tribute to classic Hollywood movies. His creative partner is actor Jack Nicholson, who has become part of the Monkees' clique. The resultant bizarre potpourri features a variety of guest appearances, from boxer Sonny Liston to beefcake actor Victor Mature as the Big Victor, a character representing "capitalism." There are scenes of the Monkees committing suicide by jumping from a bridge, and a concert intercut with Vietnam war atrocities. The film is a box-office disaster, and won't be shown in Britain until March 1977.

9 The **New Musical Express** publishes a world exclusive announcing that the **Beatles** are to play three concerts at the Roundhouse in Camden Town, London, next month. They won't.

10 **Jefferson Airplane** appear on the "Smothers Brothers Show," with **Grace Slick** in black face and giving the black power fist salute at the conclusion of *Crown Of Creation*.

18 The **Supremes**' **Diana Ross** – performing in the Royal Command Performance at the London Palladium – makes an impassioned plea for racial harmony after singing *Somewhere*. She tells the rapt audience: "There's a place for us. A place for all of us. Black and white, Jew and Gentile, Catholic and Protestant. So was the world of Martin Luther King and his ideal. If we keep this in mind, then we can carry on his work." Some believe her comments are provoked by the specter of the Black & White Minstrels – a British variety troupe popular on BBC television – causing her also to say: "Free at last! Great God Almighty, free at last!"

18 After rehearsing in Topanga Canyon for several weeks, Los Angeles-based country-rock band **Pogo** make their debut at the Troubadour's weekly "hoot" night. Comprising **Richie Furay**, **Rusty Young**, **Jim Messina**, and **Randy Meisner**, they play a five-song set, including Furay's *Nobody's Fool* and *What A Day*, and Young's instrumental *Grand Junction*.

28 Becoming the first Beatle to be convicted on a drug charge, **John Lennon** pleads guilty to cannabis possession and is fined £150 ($360) with 20 guineas (£21/$50) costs. **Yoko Ono** is cleared.

Diana Ross made an impassioned plea for racial harmony when the Supremes performed at the annual Royal Command Performance in London.

December

5 The press launch for the **Rolling Stones**' latest album, ***Beggars Banquet***, held at the Queensgate Hotel in London, is an actual banquet. It degenerates into a custard-pie fight between those present – Lord Harlech stands in for a late-arriving **Keith Richard**. Released in a

Bill Graham's Fillmore auditoriums – the East in New York and the West in San Francisco – became the defining live venues of the late 1960s. It was not unusual to see such eclectic bills as Led Zeppelin and Woody Herman, or Neil Young and Miles Davis.

Beggars Banquet party

John Lennon and Yoko Ono

Guests to the *Beggars Banquet* party were instructed to wear appropriate costumes... John Lennon's court appearance on a drugs charge was his second of the month, after his wife Cynthia had been granted a divorce because of his adultery with Yoko Ono.

plain white sleeve depicting an invitation, the LP will hit UK No. 3 by the end of the month. It is produced by Jimmy Miller and engineered by Glyn Johns, with mainly acoustic overtones. The album will be regarded by many as the Stones' creative zenith, and includes critics' favorite, *Sympathy For The Devil*. **Brian Jones** is gradually being excised from the group's activities, with drug abuse and life in the fast lane having taken their toll. The Stones' relationship with Decca Records has also worsened. (In July, Decca withdrew the album from its scheduled release date, objecting to the sleeve, which depicted a graffiti-covered toilet. When the label re-promotes the record in the 1980s, it will be available only in the infamous toilet sleeve.)

7 A richly diverse and experimental 30-track double set, including the use of a full orchestra, ***The Beatles*** tops the UK chart. It is referred to as the "White Album" because of its Richard Hamilton-designed plain white sleeve (in marked contrast to the lavish artwork of ***Sgt. Pepper***). For the first time, the **Beatles** have worked separately on different tracks, as cracks begin to appear in their creative union.

11 "The Rolling Stones' Rock and Roll Circus" – created by the group as a television show, and directed by Michael Lindsay-Hogg – is filmed at Intertel Studios, Stonebridge Park in north London. With **Mick Jagger** decked out in a ringmaster's costume, and assorted members of Sir Robert Fossett's Circus, the £50,000 ($120,000) special also features the **Who**, **Jethro Tull**, **Eric Clapton**, **Marianne Faithfull**, **Mitch Mitchell**, pianist **Julius Katchen**, violinist **Ivry Gitlis**, **John Lennon**, **Yoko Ono**, and **Julian Lennon**. (The show will never be transmitted.)

14 With his 30th US chart single, **Marvin Gaye** finally hits No. 1 – for the first of seven weeks – with *I Heard It Through The Grapevine*. The Norman Whitfield/Barrett Strong composition was a million-seller for labelmates **Gladys Knight & the Pips** last year. Recorded in February 1967, Gaye's dramatically restyled version becomes the biggest-selling single of Motown's ten-year history, and is featured on his latest album, ***In The Groove***.

> **"Arrogant as a barroom bully and erotic to the point of outright invitation."**
>
> Ed Ochs' **Billboard** review of the Jimi Hendrix Experience Thanksgiving concert at New York's Philharmonic Hall, December 14, 1968

21 Following an announcement in September by manager Albert Grossman that **Janis Joplin** will separate from **Big Brother** by the end of 1968, Joplin, backed by the **Kozmic Blues Band**, appears at the Stax-Volt Yuletide Thing for the company's annual convention in Memphis – the only non-Memphis act to perform.

23 The Apple office in London hosts a Christmas party for its employees' children, with **John Lennon** and **Yoko Ono** as Mr. and Mrs. Claus. Two weeks ago, the label released ***James Taylor***, its first album by a (non-Beatle) male singer/songwriter. In an attempt to overcome heroin addiction, 20-year-old Boston native Taylor recently relocated to London's Notting Hill, and has been signed to Apple Records by A&R executive **Peter Asher** (ex-Peter & Gordon), who produced Taylor's literate folk debut set.

26 Signed to Atlantic Records, and nearing completion of their debut album, **Led Zeppelin** begin their first North American tour with a concert at the Denver Auditorium Arena. The trek will include multiple dates at the Whisky A Go-Go in Los Angeles and the Fillmore West in San Francisco, where the band will receive greater audience response than headliners, **Vanilla Fudge**, a New York-based psychedelic rock combo who recently scored a US No. 6 smash with their reissued debut, *You Keep Me Hangin' On*.

Marvin Gaye's version of *I Heard It Through The Grapevine* became his first US chart-topper.

ROOTS During this year: Don McLean, an emerging singer/songwriter, is appointed "The Hudson River Troubadour" by the New York State Council... after auditioning as an understudy in the Broadway production of "Hair," Dorchester, England, native Donna Summer is offered a leading role in the Munich cast... Gerry Rafferty and Billy Connolly form the folk-based Humblebums... Ralf Hutter and Florian Schneider meet at an improvised music course at Dusseldorf Conservatory, and their fascination with electronic music leads to the formation of Kraftwerk... at a press conference to announce the creation of Apple, John Lennon and Paul McCartney cite singer Harry Nilsson as their favorite artist... taking their name from a make of fire engine, REO Speedwagon form in Champaign, Illinois, becoming the town's most popular act over the next few years... Decca Records executive Jonathan King books studio time to record an album for schoolboy band, Genesis, during their summer break from Charterhouse School... the New Yardbirds embark on a tour of Scandinavia... Vangelis Papathanassiou and Demis Roussos, refugees from the Greek Colonels' right-wing coup, team up as Aphrodite's Child in Paris... and 15-year-old multi-instrumentalist Mike Oldfield and his older sister, Sally, release their first album, *Children Of The Sun*, as Sallyangie...

Good Times, Bad Times

1969

No.1 US SINGLES

- **Jan 4** I Heard It Through The Grapevine **Marvin Gaye**
- **Feb 1** Crimson And Clover **Tommy James & the Shondells**
- **Feb 15** Everyday People **Sly & the Family Stone**
- **Mar 15** Dizzy **Tommy Roe**
- **Apr 12** Aquarius/Let The Sunshine In **5th Dimension**
- **May 24** Get Back **Beatles**
- **June 28** Love Theme From Romeo And Juliet **Henry Mancini & His Orchestra**
- **July 12** In The Year 2525 (Exordium & Terminus) **Zager & Evans**
- **Aug 23** Honky Tonk Women **Rolling Stones**
- **Sept 20** Sugar, Sugar **Archies**
- **Oct 18** I Can't Get Next To You **Temptations**
- **Nov 1** Suspicious Minds **Elvis Presley**
- **Nov 8** Wedding Bell Blues **5th Dimension**
- **Nov 29** Come Together/Something **Beatles**
- **Dec 6** Na Na Hey Hey Kiss Him Goodbye **Steam**
- **Dec 20** Leaving On A Jet Plane **Peter, Paul & Mary**
- **Dec 27** Someday We'll Be Together **Diana Ross & the Supremes**

No.1 UK SINGLES

- **Jan 4** Ob-La-Di Ob-La-Da **Marmalade**
- **Jan 11** Lily The Pink **Scaffold**
- **Jan 18** Ob-La-Di Ob-La-Da **Marmalade**
- **Feb 1** Albatross **Fleetwood Mac**
- **Feb 8** Blackberry Way **Move**
- **Feb 15** (If Paradise Is) Half As Nice **Amen Corner**
- **Feb 29** Where Do You Go To My Lovely **Peter Sarstedt**
- **Mar 29** I Heard It Through The Grapevine **Marvin Gaye**
- **Apr 19** The Israelites **Desmond Dekker & the Aces**
- **Apr 26** Get Back **Beatles with Billy Preston**
- **June 7** Dizzy **Tommy Roe**
- **June 14** The Ballad Of John And Yoko **Beatles**
- **July 5** Something In The Air **Thunderclap Newman**
- **July 26** Honky Tonk Women **Rolling Stones**
- **Aug 30** In The Year 2525 (Exordium & Terminus) **Zager & Evans**
- **Sept 20** Bad Moon Rising **Creedence Clearwater Revival**

Crosby, Stills & Nash...

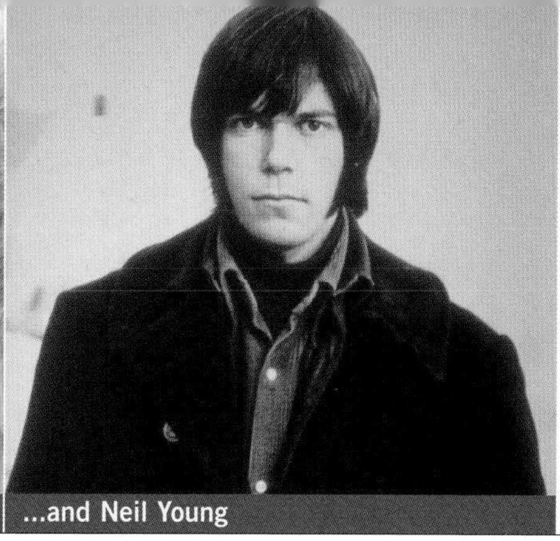
...and Neil Young

Crosby Stills & Nash had come together from the Byrds, Buffalo Springfield, and the Hollies, and were joined, initially on an ad hoc basis, by Neil Young at the suggestion of Atlantic boss Ahmet Ertegun. Young agreed, provided he could continue a parallel career with Crazy Horse. Their performance at Woodstock was only their second live appearance together.

This was the year of the festival: a hedonistic series of massive outdoor events, at which tens of thousands gathered to see the cream of rock. Most famously, it was the year of Woodstock. The organizers hoped to attract 150,000 fans, but more than 400,000 converged to see acts like the **Who**, **Jefferson Airplane**, **Janis Joplin**, **Creedence Clearwater Revival**, the **Grateful Dead**, and **Santana**. To keep the peace, thousands were admitted for free and the music played well into the night. Despite rain, bad acid, and appalling sanitation, the event was largely peaceful. But if Woodstock was the zenith, Altamont was the nadir. The last festival of the decade was bedeviled by violence, and a brutal riposte to flower power. The **Rolling Stones** fled the scene after a hurried set.

But there was music to celebrate. **Elvis Presley** enjoyed a brief return to form, and **Simon & Garfunkel** spent more than 800 hours recording the seminal *Bridge Over Troubled Water*. And then there was the pinball wizard, and the birth of the rock opera – the brainchild of **Pete Townshend**, "Tommy" broke new ground for rock music. **Led Zeppelin** announced their arrival with two LPs showcasing the dexterity of **Jimmy Page** and the beseeching voice of **Robert Plant**. This was the heyday of the rock supergroups, as musicians traded allegiances.

Graham Nash confessed to being terrified at Woodstock, not by the size of the crowd but by the fact that so many bands were there to listen to **Crosby, Stills, Nash & Young**. **Blind Faith** were another superstar confection, featuring **Eric Clapton** (ex-**Cream**) and **Steve Winwood** (ex-**Traffic**). The group's debut and only album was a transatlantic chart-topper, but they would disintegrate almost as soon as they formed. However, the success on disc of Blind Faith, the Who, and Led Zeppelin confirmed the sales supremacy of albums over singles.

The **Band** followed up *Music From Big Pink* with *The Band* – which landed them on the cover of **Time**. This was state-of-the-art rock, painting scenes from the American past (even though four members were Canadian) with virtuoso songwriting, and exceptional arranging and recording by producer John Simon. They played at the second most famous festival of 1969, on the Isle of Wight in England. So did **Bob Dylan** – in his first major stage appearance in three years.

For the Fab Four, the long and winding road was about to end. There was still time to release *Abbey Road*, but the **Beatles** spent little time working together. **George Harrison** stormed out of recording sessions, and **Lennon** and **Yoko Ono** celebrated marriage by staying in bed for the sake of world peace.

"It's nice to have any song that you write played in an elevator"

Paul Simon on *Bridge Over Troubled Water*, **Playboy**, 1984

Oct 11 Je T'Aime Moi Non Plus **Jane Birkin & Serge Gainsbourg**
Oct 18 I'll Never Fall In Love Again **Bobbie Gentry**
Oct 25 Sugar Sugar **Archies**
Dec 20 Two Little Boys **Rolf Harris**

Jan

1969

The Beatles' farewell... Creedence Clearwater Revival...

Creedence Clearwater Revival were offered $10,000 to perform at Woodstock, a month after *Proud Mary*, their exuberant tale of a Mississippi steamboat, hit No. 2.

January

2 Shooting begins at Twickenham Studios of the **Beatles** rehearsing for a back-to-the-roots album (which will evolve into the film and record project ***Let It Be***). Director Michael Lindsay-Hogg is behind the camera.

4 Perky Scottish lass **Lulu** hosts her "Happening for Lulu" variety show on BBC1, with special guests the **Jimi Hendrix Experience**. Hendrix causes production anxiety when he switches – in mid-act – to an unscheduled performance of Cream's *Sunshine Of Your Love*.

10 **George Harrison** walks out on the Beatles, following an argument between **Lennon** and **McCartney** at Twickenham Studios. He drives home to Esher, and will then visit his parents in Liverpool.

13 **Elvis Presley** begins ten days of sessions at Chips Moman's American Sound Studio in Memphis, the first time he has recorded in his home town since working with Sam Phillips on the Million Dollar Quartet tapes in December 1956. The 20 songs he records will form the basis of a highly rated series of singles (including *Suspicious Minds*) and an album.

15 **Crosby, Stills & Nash**, having recently rehearsed in Moscow Road, London, and then in **John Sebastian**'s house on Long Island, New York, sign to Atlantic after the label agrees "to assign to CBS all right, title, etc., to the exclusive services of Richard Furay" in exchange for acquiring **Graham Nash**, who is signed to Epic through the **Hollies**. This releases **Furay** to record for Epic as part of **Poco** (formerly **Pogo**). The trio will shortly fly to California to begin recording.

24 New Jersey's Union County Prosecutor Leo Kaplowitz issues a "don't sell or else" ultimatum to record dealers in connection with ***Two Virgins*** by **John Lennon** and **Yoko Ono**. This follows the impounding three weeks ago of 30,000 copies of the album by police at Newark Airport. Their justification is the album's sleeve, which features a nude photograph of John and Yoko, said to be "pornographic." Police also seize 22,300 covers – 300 with records inside – from Bestway Products Company in Mountainside.

30 Having conceived the idea at a meeting at the weekend, the **Beatles** – with 22-year-old "Shindig" regular, American R&B singer-songwriter/keyboardist **Billy Preston** guesting on organ – perform on the roof of the Apple building in Savile Row, London. They play for 42 minutes before they are halted by police, because the chief accountant of the nearby Royal Bank of Scotland has called to complain about the noise. Finishing with *Get Back*, it will prove to be the last time the Beatles perform together in public.

> **"I'd like to say 'thank you' on behalf of the group and ourselves, and I hope we passed the audition."**
>
> John Lennon, January 30, 1969

Jim Morrison's behavior offended some so much that a Rally for Decency concert, starring Anita Bryant, Kate Smith, the Lettermen, and the Miami Drum & Bugle Corps, took place in Los Angeles.

February

1 In the middle of sessions for her second album, ***Clouds***, **Joni Mitchell** performs for the first time at New York's Carnegie Hall.

3 With acrimony building, **John Lennon**, **George Harrison**, and **Ringo Starr** hire Allen Klein as their business adviser, while the dissenting **Paul McCartney** plays drums and sings backing vocals with the **Steve Miller Band**, recording *My Dark Hour* at AIR studios in London.

17 Having cut nine tracks last week that will find their way on to the upcoming ***Nashville Skyline***, **Bob Dylan** records with **Johnny Cash** in Nashville, although only one of their duet tracks, *Girl From The North Country*, will ever be issued.

24 On the verge of breaking up, the **Jimi Hendrix Experience** perform their last UK concert together – a sellout affair at London's Royal Albert Hall.

March

1 After a concert at the Dinner Key Auditorium in Miami, the Doors' **Jim Morrison** is charged with "lewd and lascivious behavior in public by exposing his private parts and by simulating masturbation and oral copulation," in addition to profanity, drunkenness, and other

Following their marriage, John and Yoko went to bed to promote world peace, and held a press conference in their pajamas.

minor offenses. The prospect of court appearances makes Doors tour bookings impossible for the next five months.

2 A big winner at last year's awards, **Glen Campbell** scoops the Album of the Year trophy for ***By The Time I Get To Phoenix*** at the 11th Grammy awards. In one of the most open contests in years, **Simon & Garfunkel**'s *Mrs. Robinson* is named Record of the Year and Best Contemporary, Pop Vocal Performance, Duo or Group; **Bobby Russell**'s *Little Green Apples* is Song of the Year, and **José Feliciano** picks up awards for Best New Artist and Best Contemporary, Pop Vocal Performance, Male for his interpretation of the Doors' *Light My Fire*. **Otis Redding**, **Aretha Franklin**, and the **Temptations** take the Rhythm & Blues prizes; **Mason Williams** wins two for his baroque instrumental *Classical Gas*; **Judy Collins** wins her first Grammy – Best Folk Performance for ***Both Sides Now***; ***Hair*** is named Best Score from an Original Cast Show Album; and **Jim Webb** adds yet another trophy to his collection, with *MacArthur Park* named Best Arrangement Accompanying Vocalist.

25 **John Lennon** and **Yoko Ono**, who were married in the British Consulate in Gibraltar last week, begin a seven-day "bed-in" to promote world peace, in the presidential suite on the ninth floor of the Hilton Hotel in Amsterdam.

29 The **Zombies**' *Time Of The Season*, recorded in August 1967 as part of the group's concept album ***Odessey And Oracle***, hits US No. 3. Released by Epic at the urging of **Al Kooper**, who heard it in England, it will become the group's second million-seller. Offers from the US flood in for a Zombies reunion, including one of $20,000 for a single concert. With keyboardist **Rod Argent** assembling his own band, **Argent**, all are resisted.

29 Even perkier than usual, **Lulu** represents the UK in this year's Eurovision Song Contest at the Teatro Real in Madrid with *Boom-Bang-A-Bang*. In the most bizarre result in the history of the contest, the song wins in a four-way tie with the entries from France, Spain, and Holland. Lulu has sung six entry nominations on her BBC television show "Happening For Lulu" over the past six weeks, including *I Can't Go On Living Without You*, penned by new writing team, 22-year-old singer/pianist/composer **Elton John** and 18-year-old lyricist **Bernie Taupin**. John has spent much of the 1960s playing for **Bluesology**, a UK blues/rock band latterly fronted by **Long John Baldry**. In 1967 he signed a short-lived solo deal with Liberty Records, who put him in touch with Taupin. Signed as songwriters to Dick James Music (DJM), they penned the B-side – *Lord You Made The Night Too Long* – to Baldry's 1967 UK No. 1, *Let The Heartaches Begin*. John has recently signed another short-term recording deal with Philips, while continuing to co-write with Taupin and search for solo success.

The one-time top session guitarist Glen Campbell proved to be the perfect voice for Jimmy Webb's songs.

April

1 Continuing their legal dispute with Capitol Records, the **Beach Boys** sue the label for over $2 million, alleging unpaid royalties and production fees – notably due to **Brian Wilson** – plus other losses incurred through general mismanagement. The group will shortly found their own Brother Records.

10 Currently the hottest San Francisco rock band, **Creedence Clearwater Revival** sign on to appear at the upcoming Woodstock Music & Art Fair. (**Canned Heat**, the progressive blues rocker **Johnny Winter**, and **Janis Joplin** will also all agree to perform at the festival over the next ten days.) Creedence are fronted by the **Fogerty** brothers – chief songwriter/vocalist/guitarist **John**, and rhythm guitar-playing **Tom** – who have been recording for the Fantasy label as the **Golliwogs** since 1964. They changed their name two years ago, and recently broke through with the US No. 2 smash, *Proud Mary*, written by John on the morning he was discharged from the US Army. The song will become the group's first million-seller and the most-covered Creedence song – with a 1971 version by **Ike & Tina Turner**, and covers by **Solomon Burke**, **Sonny Charles & Checkmates Ltd.**, and **Elvis Presley**. Its parent album, ***Bayou Country***, which develops the band's "swamp-rock" idiom, will shortly reach US No. 7, becoming their first million-selling LP.

Apr 1969

The Band's bassist Rick Danko found the rambling house, painted pink, in West Saugerties, New York, where the group recorded its landmark debut album.

The Who's rock opera... Blind Faith debut... Brian Jones quits the Stones...

14 With **Ringo Starr** filming "The Magic Christian" with Peter Sellers, and **George Harrison** unaccounted for, **John Lennon** and **Paul McCartney** head back into the studio to cut *The Ballad Of John And Yoko*. Over the coming weeks, recording will continue apace – but rarely with all four Beatles in the studio at the same time. When *The Ballad Of John And Yoko* is released, it will be banned on many US radio stations because of the lyric "Christ you know it ain't easy."

16 **MC5** are dropped by Elektra after placing an ad in a Detroit underground newspaper criticizing record chain Dayton Hudson for not stocking their album. Label head Jac Holzman explains: "Saying 'F**k Hudson's' with the Elektra logo stuck on it I thought was inappropriate." Dayton Hudson removes all Elektra records from its shelves, including MC5's ***Kick Out The Jams***, whose title track includes the incendiary lyric, "Kick out the jams, motherf***ers."

17 The **Band** – a New York-based, mostly Canadian rock quintet that evolved from being **Bob Dylan**'s backing group into a separate recording unit signed to Capitol Records – perform their first stand-alone concert at the Fillmore West in San Francisco, at the beginning of a US tour. It nearly doesn't happen: lead singer/guitarist, 24-year-old **Robbie Robertson**, has a high fever and has not eaten for two days. At the suggestion of promoter Bill Graham, he is hypnotized, and the hypnotist spends the gig in the wings continuing to hold his spell over Robertson. The Band's debut album ***Music From The Big Pink*** – named after the pink house in West Saugerties where the group spent much of 1967–8 jamming and recording with Bob Dylan – is still on the US album chart, having peaked at No. 30.

22 **John Lennon** makes his way back to the roof of the Apple building in Savile Row, London, where his middle name is legally changed by deed poll from Winston to Ono in a ceremony conducted by Commissioner of Oaths Señor Bueno de Mesquita.

Pete Townshend's "Tommy" project had its first live performance in the unlikely location of Bolton, Lancashire, England.

BLIND FAITH

June 7 Blind Faith – a rock supergroup formed by ex-Cream members Eric Clapton and Ginger Baker, with ex-Traffic alumni Steve Winwood and Ric Grech – make their debut at a free concert in London's Hyde Park. Signed to Polydor in the UK and Atco in the US, their soon-to-be-released debut album, *Blind Faith*, will formally confirm the commercial dominance of the album format: it will hit No. 1 in both countries without ever yielding a chart single. The album's initial, highly controversial, front cover – depicting a nude prepubescent girl – will quickly be replaced by a photo of the group.

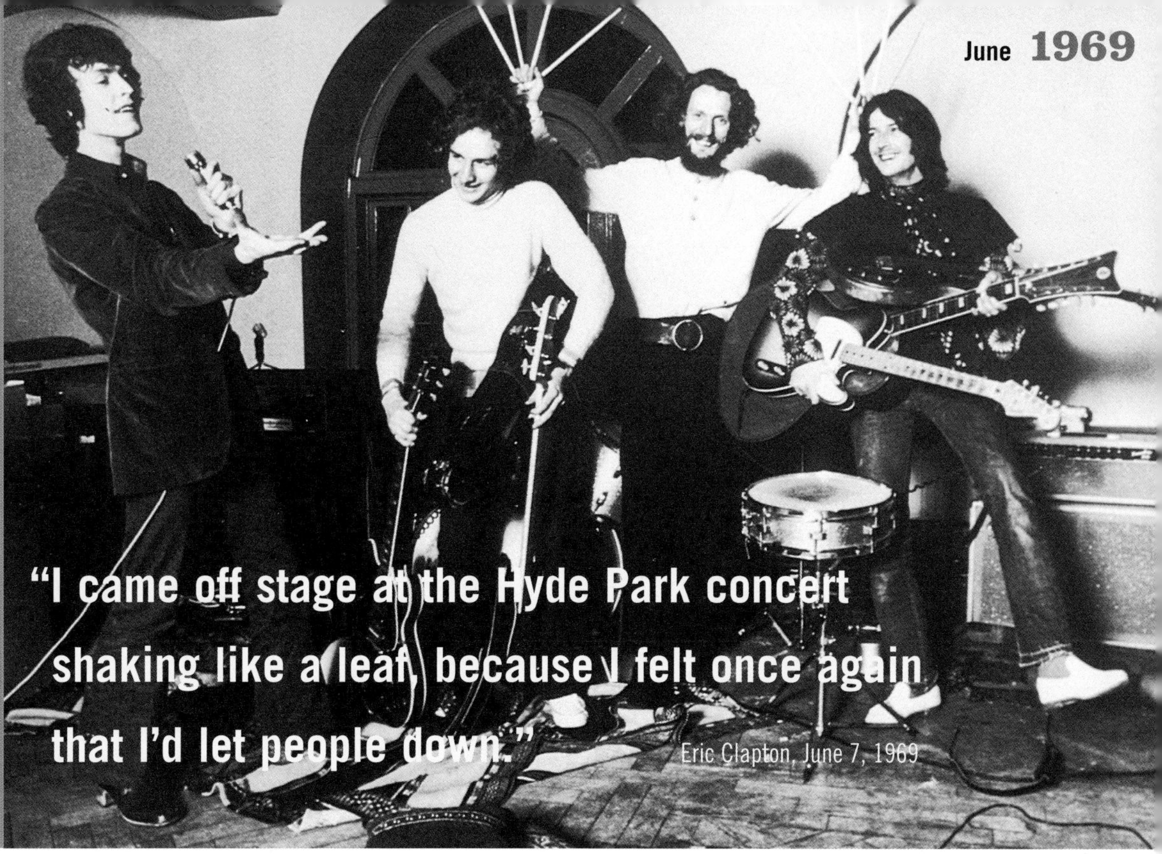

"I came off stage at the Hyde Park concert shaking like a leaf, because I felt once again that I'd let people down."

Eric Clapton, June 7, 1969

May

2 Conceived and written by **Pete Townshend**, the **Who**'s rock opera "Tommy" is given a press launch at Ronnie Scott's jazz club in Soho, London, at which the group perform the album in full. (Their first live performance of this ambitious project took place on April 22 at a gig in Bolton.) Critically acclaimed as a landmark recording, the groundbreaking "concept" album chronicles the story of a deaf, dumb, and blind boy who is also a pinball genius. He is elevated to prophet status, and then turned on by his followers.

3 **Jimi Hendrix** is arrested when he arrives at Toronto Airport, on his way to give a concert at the Maple Leaf Gardens, and charged with possession of heroin. Released on $10,000 bail, he will deny the use of hard drugs and will be acquitted in December.

5 **Billy Preston** records *That's The Way God Planned It* at Trident Studio, with **George Harrison** producing. To help out, Harrison has recruited the illustrious line-up of **Eric Clapton** (guitar), **Keith Richard** (bass), **Ginger Baker** (drums), and **Doris Troy** (backing vocals). They will finish the track tomorrow.

10 The **Temptations** – whose progressive, psychedelic, soul-grooving ***Cloud Nine*** is currently in the US Top 10 – and the **Turtles** play at a Masquerade Ball at the White House, as guests of Tricia Nixon. Media rumors will subsequently circulate that the Turtles' **Howard Kaylan** and **Mark Volman** snorted cocaine on Abraham Lincoln's desk.

12 British folk band **Fairport Convention** are returning from a gig in Birmingham, where they have performed with the **Mothers of Invention**, when their van crashes on the M1 motorway, killing 19-year-old drummer **Martin Lamble**, and **Richard Thompson**'s girlfriend, fashion designer Jeannie Franklyn.

16 **Pete Townshend** spends a night in jail, having been charged with assaulting a plain-clothes policeman during a **Who** concert at the Fillmore East in New York. The policeman – Daniel Mulhearn – was attacked by the guitarist while attempting to get to the microphone to warn fans of a fire that had broken out in a grocery store next to the venue.

17 The **New Musical Express** reports that, for the first time, album sales now outpace those of singles in the UK, a trend that began over a year earlier in the US.

22 The **Beatles**' *Hey Jude* is named the Best Selling A-side of 1968 at the 14th annual Ivor Novello Awards. The UK Eurovision entry, *Congratulations*, is named the Most Performed Work, while *Delilah* (a huge hit for **Tom Jones**) is named International Song of the Year. Special awards are also presented to the **Gibb** brothers' *Massachusetts (The Lights Went Out In)* and **Lennon/McCartney**'s *Fool On The Hill.*

26 The **Lennons** begin another eight-day "bed-in" to promote world peace, in Room 1742 of the Hotel Reine-Elizabeth in Montreal.

June

8 After a meeting with the other **Stones** at his Cotchford Farm home, **Brian Jones** is told he is surplus to requirements. Publicly it is announced that the guitarist is quitting. Jones issues a statement: "I want to play my kind of music, which is no longer the Stones' music. The music Mick and Keith have been writing is at a tangent, so far as my own taste is concerned."

9 The **Rolling Stones** announce that Jones will be replaced by **Mick Taylor**, currently the guitarist with **John Mayall's Bluesbreakers**.

13 **Aretha Franklin**, **Ray Charles**, **Sam & Dave**, the **Staple Singers**, and **Percy Sledge** are among those taking part in a major R&B music spectacular, Soul Bowl '69 – promoted as the biggest soul music festival ever staged – held at the Houston Astrodome.

The Temptations introduced their "psychedelic soul" style with *Cloud Nine*, at the recommendation of producer Norman Whitfield. The record won them their first Grammy.

June 1969

Festival fever in the US and the UK... The death of Brian Jones... Elvis back on stage...

ABC-TV broadcast a special from the Grand Ole Opry starring Bob Dylan and Johnny Cash, which featured several tracks from Dylan's *Nashville Skyline* album.

David Bowie recorded the innovative, astronomy-themed *Space Oddity*, featuring the memorable character "Major Tom."

14 R&B pioneer, singer/drummer **Wynonie Harris** dies of cancer at the age of 53 in Los Angeles. Pre-empting the rock 'n' roll era, Harris scored two US R&B chart-toppers, the seminal *Good Rockin' Tonight* (1948) and *All She Wants To Do Is Rock* (1949).

20 **David Bowie** records *Space Oddity* at Trident Studios in London. The session – a one-off production for the singer by Gus Dudgeon – is arranged by Bowie's main producer Tony Visconti, with Bowie on vocal, guitar, and stylophone, 20-year-old **Rick Wakeman** on keyboards, Visconti on bass, and **Terry Cox** on drums. Currently a camp cult figure around the London scene, Bowie has been trying to kickstart his music career since 1964 when – under his real name, David Jones – he formed the **King Bees** (recording for Decca's Vocalion label) then joined the **Manish Boys** (Parlophone), followed by the **Lower Third** (Pye Records) in 1965, the year he switched his surname. Going solo in 1966, he signed to another Decca imprint, Deram (which released his debut set ***David Bowie*** in 1967) before hooking up with producer Visconti. Recently signed to the Philips/Mercury label at the behest of Mercury employee Calvin Lee, singer/songwriter Bowie is actually re-recording *Space Oddity*, which he first recorded in February. It will be rush-released in the UK and US, to coincide with the first Apollo moon landing, and will become Bowie's first British hit, at No. 5.

20 Newport '69, the first large rock festival of the year – during a fertile period for festivals in general – gets under way at San Fernando Valley State College in California. Over the next three days, 150,000 attendees will see **Marvin Gaye**, **Johnny Winter**, **Joe Cocker**, **Jimi Hendrix**, **Janis Joplin**, **Spirit** (an eclectic Los Angeles-based rock troupe featuring lead singer **Jay Ferguson**, guitarist **Randy California**, bassist **Mark Andes**, keyboardist **John Locke**, and 46-year-old drummer **Ed Cassidy**), **Ike & Tina Turner**, the **Rascals**, **Poco**, **Steppenwolf**, **Three Dog Night** (another new Los Angeles rock combo led by singers **Danny Hutton**, **Cory Wells**, and **Chuck Negron** who are currently scoring big with their breakthrough US No. 5 smash, *One*), **Buddy Miles**, **Edwin Hawkins**, the **Full Tilt Boogie Band**, singer-songwriter **Tracy Nelson**, and a solo **Eric Burdon**.

27 Toronto having staged its first rock festival last weekend, cities all over North America are eager to hold their own events. Today the Denver Pop Festival begins its three days of fun, hosting the **Reverend Cleophus Robinson**, **Joe Cocker**, **Zephyr**, **Creedence Clearwater Revival**, the **Jimi Hendrix Experience**, **Big Mama Thornton**, **Sweetwater**, **Tim Buckley**, **Poco**, **Johnny Winter**, **Aum**, the **Flock**, **Iron Butterfly**, and the **Mothers of Invention**.

28 The festival bug has also hit Britain, where the Bath Festival of Blues is held on the city's Recreation Ground, with performances by **Fleetwood Mac**, **John Mayall**, **Ten Years After**, **Led Zeppelin**, **Nice**, **Chicken Shack**, Jon Hiseman's **Colosseum**, Mick Abraham's **Blodwyn Pig**, **Keef Hartley**, **Group Therapy**, **Liverpool Scene**, **Taste**, **Champion Jack Dupree**, **Savoy Brown**, **Clouds**, **Principal Edwards Magic Theatre**, **Babylon**, **Doop Blues Band**, **Just Slowing Down**, and disc jockey John Peel.

29 **Jimi Hendrix**'s gig on the final day of the Denver Pop Festival will prove to be the Experience's final concert together. Hendrix will spend the rest of the summer recording in New York, with **Electric Flag** drummer/vocalist **Buddy Miles** and bassist **Billy Cox**, a friend from his Army days.

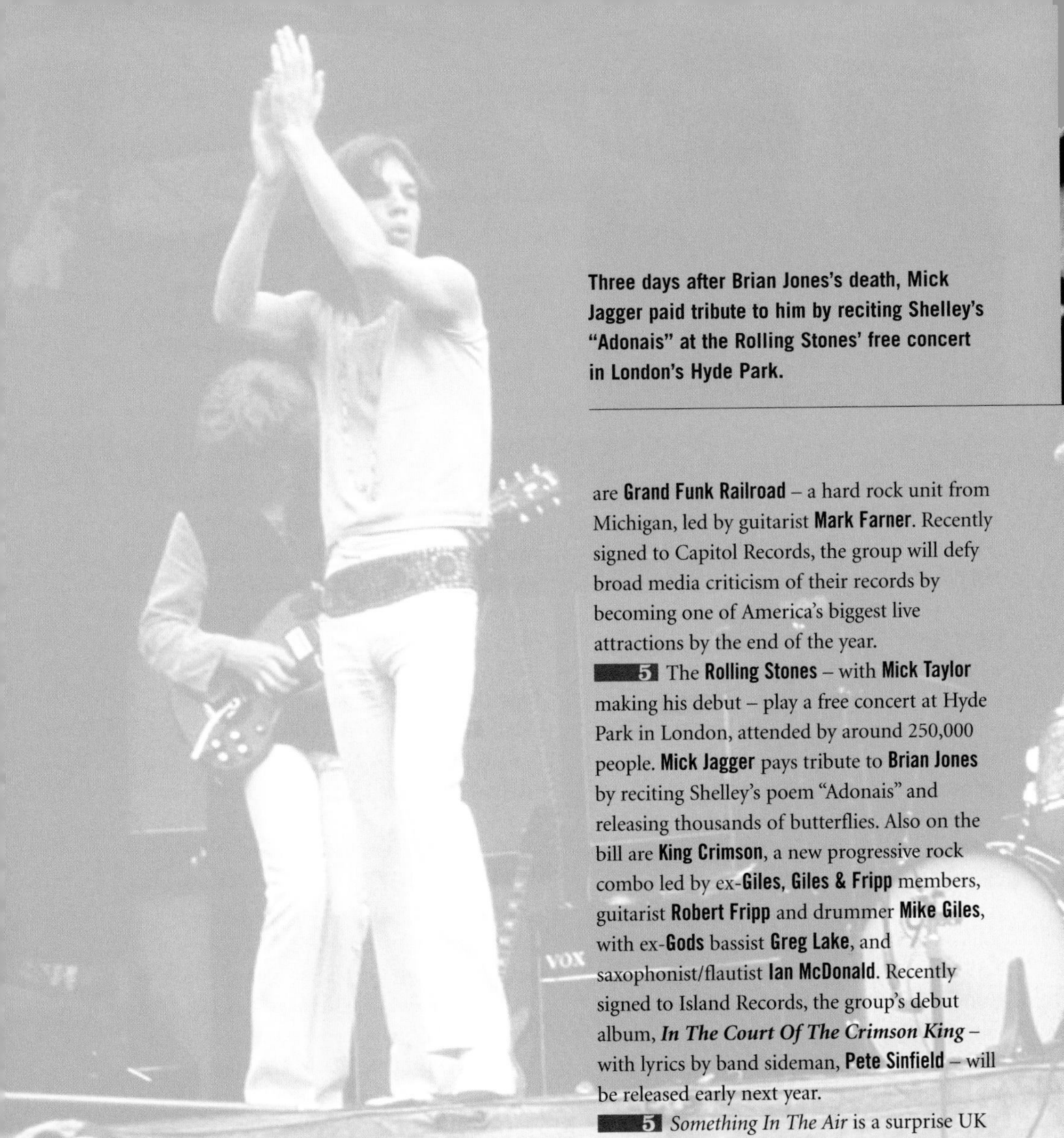

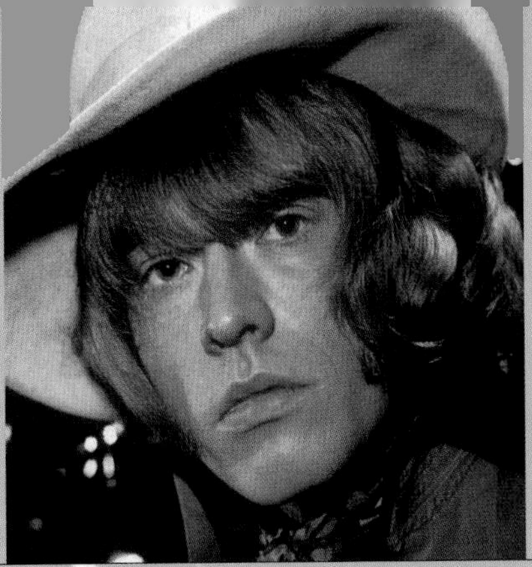

Three days after Brian Jones's death, Mick Jagger paid tribute to him by reciting Shelley's "Adonais" at the Rolling Stones' free concert in London's Hyde Park.

July

1 **John**, **Yoko**, **Julian Lennon**, and Yoko's son Kyoko, are taken to Lawson Memorial Hospital for treatment after a car accident in Golspie, Scotland. The remaining **Beatles** begin work in Studio 2 at Abbey Road, once again working with George Martin.

1 **Sam Phillips** sells his Sun Records label to Nashville music impresario Shelby Singleton, handing over master recordings by some of rock 'n' roll's foremost pioneers.

3 After an evening of heavy drinking with friends, 27-year-old ex-Rolling Stones guitarist **Brian Jones** is found dead in his swimming pool at Cotchford Farm, after taking a late-night swim, by girlfriend Anna Wohlin.

4 The two-day Atlanta Pop Festival, at the International Raceway in Hampton, gets under way in front of an estimated 125,000 people, with performances by **Led Zeppelin**, **Creedence Clearwater Revival**, **Canned Heat**, **Johnny Winter**, **Joe Cocker**, **Chuck Berry**, and **Blood, Sweat & Tears** – a jazz/rock combo formed by veteran keyboardist **Al Kooper** in 1967, with guitarist **Steve Katz**, bassist **Jim Fielder**, and drummer **Bobby Colomby**. The group are currently scoring their second straight US No. 2 smash with *Spinning Wheel*, written by Kooper's replacement, and new frontman, **David Clayton-Thomas**. Also appearing are **Grand Funk Railroad** – a hard rock unit from Michigan, led by guitarist **Mark Farner**. Recently signed to Capitol Records, the group will defy broad media criticism of their records by becoming one of America's biggest live attractions by the end of the year.

5 The **Rolling Stones** – with **Mick Taylor** making his debut – play a free concert at Hyde Park in London, attended by around 250,000 people. **Mick Jagger** pays tribute to **Brian Jones** by reciting Shelley's poem "Adonais" and releasing thousands of butterflies. Also on the bill are **King Crimson**, a new progressive rock combo led by ex-**Giles, Giles & Fripp** members, guitarist **Robert Fripp** and drummer **Mike Giles**, with ex-**Gods** bassist **Greg Lake**, and saxophonist/flautist **Ian McDonald**. Recently signed to Island Records, the group's debut album, ***In The Court Of The Crimson King*** – with lyrics by band sideman, **Pete Sinfield** – will be released early next year.

5 *Something In The Air* is a surprise UK chart-topper for London band **Thunderclap Newman**, featuring singer **Speedy Keen**, guitarist **Jimmy McCulloch**, and quirky pianist **Andy Newman**. An era-defining, revolution-themed pop nugget written by Keen, the single is produced by the Who's **Pete Townshend**.

7 The pathologist's report on **Brian Jones** states that his blood alcohol level at the time of his death was "approx. 7 whiskeys," and that an "amphetamine-like substance" was detected in his urine. According to the report, Jones was "seen to stagger on the Diving Board before jumping off into Swimming Pool, but managed to swim with other companion in Pool. Latter left to get Towel, returned to find deceased at bottom of pool." The East Grinstead coroner records a verdict of death by misadventure.

8 On the Australian set of the film "Ned Kelly," in which she is to co-star with **Mick Jagger**, **Marianne Faithfull** is discovered in a coma, suffering from a self-inflicted overdose, allegedly after Jagger has told her their relationship is over. She is fired from the production and enrolled in a drug treatment center for addiction to heroin.

10 **Brian Jones**'s funeral takes place at Hatherley Road Parish Church in Cheltenham – where he once sang as a choirboy – and he is buried in the Priory Road Cemetery in nearby Prestbury. The other **Stones**, excluding **Mick Jagger**, are present at the service. Canon Hugh Evan Hopkins reads Jones's own epitaph: "Please don't judge me too harshly."

12 Billed as "The Ultimate Supergroup," **Blind Faith** make their US concert debut at New York's Madison Square Garden. The engagement is the start of a sellout US stadium tour, which, despite being financially rewarding, will convince the band members that Blind Faith is musically unsatisfying, and that they should split when the tour is completed.

14 **Bob Dylan** makes a guest appearance – dressed in cowboy regalia – as "Elmer Johnson" during the encore of the **Band**'s concert at the Mississippi River Festival in Edwardsville, Illinois. They perform four songs together, including *I Ain't Got No Home*, *Slippin' And Slidin'*, and *In The Pines*.

20 **Pink Floyd** perform *What If It's Just Green Cheese?* live in the studio during an "Omnibus" Apollo 11 space mission special on BBC television.

31 In his first live concert since March 25, 1961, **Elvis Presley** opens at the Showroom of the International Hotel, Las Vegas. It is the first of 57 shows in a four-week engagement that will net him $1.5 million. The concerts will be universally acclaimed as a triumph, with the magnetic stage presence of old still intact, and Presley doing justice to both 1950s material and new songs. His new live back-up band includes **Rick Nelson**'s ex-guitarist **James Burton**, bassist **Jerry Scheff**, guitarists **John Wilkinson** and **Charlie Hodge**, keyboards player **Larry Muhoberac** (who will be replaced on future engagements by ex-**Cricket Glen D. Hardin**), and drummer **Ronnie Tutt**. Back-up vocals are provided by the Imperials (the **Jordanaires** having turned down the gig because of Nashville commitments) and the **Sweet Inspirations**.

> **"If Keith and Mick were the mind and body of the Stones, Brian was clearly the soul."**
>
> **Rolling Stone**, August 1969

Aug 1969

Woodstock... Paul McCartney lives... The Jackson 5 debut on television...

The 22-year-old actress Jane Birkin teamed up with her then new beau, 41-year-old French renaissance man Serge Gainsbourg, to make a banned UK No. 1.

August

2 A surprise attendee at the tenth-year reunion of the class of 1959 from Hibbing High School is **Bob Dylan**, who arrives with his wife Sara. The couple stay for an hour before a drunk partygoer attempts to pick a fight.

8 At 10:00 am a policeman holds up traffic while a photograph is taken of the **Beatles** walking across the pedestrian crossing outside EMI Studios in ***Abbey Road***, for use on the sleeve of the forthcoming Abbey Road. The album includes the ballad *Something*, which will become the first Beatles A-side (paired with **Lennon/McCartney**'s *Come Together*) to be written by **George Harrison**, when it is released as a single in October.

15 The Woodstock Music & Art Fair gets under way at 5:07 pm, with folk singer/guitarist **Richie Havens** taking the stage set up on Max Yasgur's farm in Bethel, Sullivan County, New York – 70 miles from the town of Woodstock. On its folk-rostered first day line-up, Havens's set is followed by performances from **Sweetwater**, **Bert Sommer**, **Tim Hardin**, **Ravi Shankar**, 22-year-old newcomer **Melanie**, **Arlo Guthrie**, and bill-topper **Joan Baez**. With the utopian hippie/peace movement at its zenith during the self-appointed "summer of love," an estimated 450,000 music fans will attend. Three (non-malicious) deaths, two births and four miscarriages, innumerable conceptions, the consumption of vast quantities of drugs and alcohol, the closure of the New York State Thruway, and one of the nation's worst traffic jams will all occur over the next four days.

16 With the crowd having swelled to 250,000, day two at Woodstock hosts **Quill**, **Country Joe McDonald**, **John B. Sebastian**, **Keef Hartley**, **Santana**, **Incredible String Band**, **Canned Heat**, the **Grateful Dead**, **Creedence Clearwater Revival**, **Janis Joplin**, **Sly & the Family Stone**, with the **Who** and **Jefferson Airplane** playing well into the night. The festival has been created and organized by four young entrepreneurs who together formed Woodstock Ventures Inc. in March: Joel Rosenman, Artie Kornfeld, Michael Lang, and John Roberts. Roberts, who is heir to a drugstore and toothpaste manufacturing business, has bankrolled much of the event.

17 **Joe Cocker**, **Country Joe & the Fish**, **Leslie West & Mountain**, **Ten Years After**, the **Band**, **Johnny Winter**, **Blood, Sweat & Tears**, and **Crosby, Stills, Nash & Young** perform during Woodstock's third day, with the audience size now estimated at its 450,000 peak.

18 The Woodstock festival closes after morning performances by the **Paul Butterfield Blues Band**, retro-1950s combo **Sha Na Na**, and finally, at 9:00 am, **Jimi Hendrix**, who launches into *Star-Spangled Banner*.

Santana, led by Mexican-born Carlos Santana, released their debut album the same month they made an impressive appearance at Woodstock.

20 **Frank Zappa** disbands the **Mothers of Invention** (whose line-up had recently included singer **Lowell George**) at the end of a short tour of Canada, reportedly "tired of playing for people who clap for all the wrong reasons" (and also because of the considerable expense of keeping the large outfit on the road).

20 All four **Beatles** are together for the last time at EMI's Abbey Road Studios, as they complete *I Want You (She's So Heavy)* for their forthcoming ***Abbey Road*** album.

September

6 At the end of a Memphis concert, **James Brown**, the "hardest working man in show business," announces his intention to retire from the road after the next Independence Day: "I'm tired man. My brain seems to get much heavier."

13 **John Lennon**'s **Plastic Ono Band** makes its debut at the University of Toronto. Having initially planned a rock 'n' roll revival show, also featuring **Chuck Berry**, **Bo Diddley**, **Fats Domino**, **Jerry Lee Lewis**, **Little Richard**, and **Gene Vincent**, Lennon puts together an ad hoc band, comprising **Eric Clapton**, bassist **Klaus Voormann**, and drummer **Alan White**.

17 Drake University's **Times-Delphic** publishes an article, written by Tim Harper, which speculates that **Paul McCartney** was killed in a car crash in Scotland on November 9, 1966 (despite the fact that he and his then girlfriend, Jane Asher, were vacationing in Kenya at the time), and has been replaced by former Beatle-look-a-like competition winner William Campbell, who has undergone plastic surgery. The rumor will mushroom when Northern Illinois University's **Northern Star** picks up on Harper's story, followed by Detroit radio station WKNR disc jockey Russ Gibbs breaking it on air, and major print articles perpetuating the myth. **Sunday People** journalist Hugh Farmer will track McCartney down to his Scottish farm near Campbeltown, to be greeted with the comment, "Do I look dead? I'm as fit as a fiddle."

> **"Do I look dead? I'm as fit as a fiddle."**
>
> Paul McCartney, 1969

ISLE OF WIGHT

Aug 30 **The second annual Isle of Wight Festival begins in Wootton on the Isle Of Wight. More than 100,000 attendees show up to see Bob Dylan, the Moody Blues, the Nice, Joe Cocker, Richie Havens, British pop/comedy troupe the Bonzo Dog Doo-Dah Band, the Pretty Things, Fat Mattress, Julie Felix, Marsha Hunt and White Trash, Eclection, Third Ear Band, Family, Aynsley Dunbar, Blodwyn Pig, Gypsy, Free (a new British rock band featuring lead vocalist Paul Rodgers, guitarist Paul Kossoff, bassist Andy Fraser, and drummer Simon Kirke), the Edgar Broughton Band (another fresh UK rock outfit), Blonde on Blonde, Mighty Baby, folk singer/songwriter Tom Paxton, Pentangle, Gary Farr, Liverpool Scene, Indo-Jazz Fusions, and the Who.**

Backed by the Band, Dylan – who had declined to perform at Woodstock – played for scarcely an hour. He told a news conference before his performance: "I don't want to protest any more. I never said I'm an angry young man."

19 **Neil Young** – whose debut solo album for Reprise Records, ***Everybody Knows This Is Nowhere***, was released in June – performs at New York's Fillmore East during his current tour with **Crosby, Stills & Nash**. Their liaison has come about at the suggestion of Atlantic label boss Ahmet Ertegun, and is made on the condition that Young is free to continue working solo and with his band, **Crazy Horse**. Although **The New York Times** critic Mike Jahn compliments CSN&Y on their "exquisitely wrought vocal leaders," he also feels that "it's almost too pretty and too lacking in basic enthusiasm."

21 Reggae pioneers **Desmond Dekker**, **Johnny Nash**, **Jackie Edwards**, **Jimmy Cliff**, and **Max Romeo** participate in the first Caribbean Music Festival, held at the Empire Pool in Wembley.

25 **John Lennon**, **Yoko Ono**, **Eric Clapton**, **Klaus Voormann**, and **Ringo Starr** record the **Plastic Ono Band**'s *Cold Turkey* in Studio 3 at EMI's Abbey Road Studios.

October

9 For the first time in its five-year history, "Top Of The Pops" does not feature this week's No. 1 – the banned *Je T'Aime Moi Non Plus*, by **Jane Birkin & Serge Gainsbourg**. Philips Records has pulled copies of the erotic song off the market following media outcry, with indie label Major Minor picking up the license to retail what has become a rare French hit in Britain.

16 R&B pioneer **Leonard Chess**, who founded the seminal Chess label in 1948 with his brother **Phil**, dies of a heart attack in Chicago.

18 **Bill Haley** is given an eight-minute ovation at Richard Nader's first Rock 'n' Roll Revival concert, held at the Felt Forum in Madison Square Garden, New York. It also features **Chuck Berry**, the **Platters**, the **Coasters**, the **Shirelles**, **Jimmy Clanton**, and **Sha Na Na**.

18 Relocated to Los Angeles, groomed by Berry Gordy, and billed by Motown as the protégés of **Diana Ross**, the **Jackson 5** make their network television debut on "Hollywood Palace." An R&B quintet from Gary, Indiana, they are brothers **Jackie** (18), **Tito** (15), **Jermaine** (14), **Marlon** (12), and ten-year-old lead singer, **Michael**. They were introduced by **Gladys Knight** and **Bobbie Taylor**, and brought to Berry Gordy's attention by label staffer Suzanne De Passe.

20 The **Who** begin a six-night stand at the Fillmore East in New York, performing "Tommy." The rock opera is proving significantly more popular here than in the UK, and ***Tommy*** will spend over two years on the US chart – compared with a meager nine weeks back home.

November

7 The **Rolling Stones** begin their first North American tour in three years (their sixth overall) at the State University in Fort Collins, Colorado. The 17-date trek will end on the 30th at the Miami Pop Festival in West Palm Beach. In **The New York Times**, Albert Goldman compares **Jagger** to Hitler.

An estimated 450,000 music fans, most without tickets, attended Woodstock, the largest rock festival/cultural exposition held to date.

Nov 1969

Bridge Over Troubled Water... Lennon returns his MBE.. Blood, Sweat & Tears...

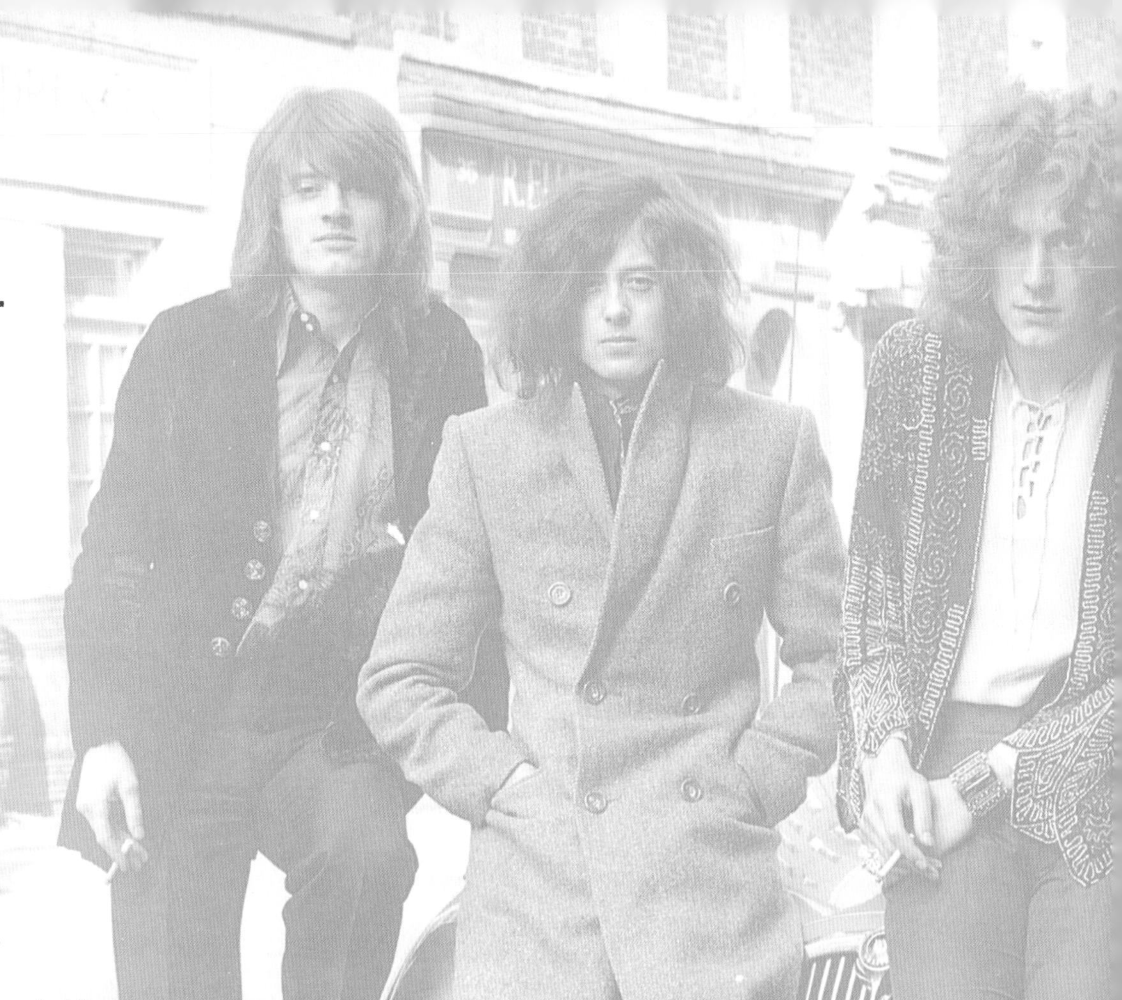

Simon & Garfunkel were said to have spent over 800 hours recording their album *Bridge Over Troubled Water.*

Led Zeppelin were honored at the Board of Trade Awards in London by Parliamentary Secretary to the UK Board of Trade, Mrs. Gwyneth Dunwoody.

9 **Simon & Garfunkel** record *Bridge Over Troubled Water* at Columbia Studios in New York. Composed (as always) by **Paul Simon**, and co-produced by regular helmsman Roy Halee, the ballad – highlighted by **Art Garfunkel**'s angelic tenor – will become the duo's signature song and a global chart-topper, hitting US No. 1 for six weeks and UK No. 1 for three. The album of the same name, despite becoming their bestselling LP, will also lead to the demise of the pairing by the time of its release in February 1970.

11 Fresh from a three-week North American tour, **Led Zeppelin** attend the Board of Trade Awards at the Savoy Hotel in London, where they are presented with two platinum discs and a gold disc. Last week, the group's second album, ***Led Zeppelin II***, entered both the UK and US album charts, set to top both lists. Critically hailed as a landmark work, its blues-brushed brand of heavy metal, led by **Robert Plant**'s unique vocal chops and **Jimmy Page**'s dextrous guitar work, will influence dozens of hard rock/heavy metal bands for decades to come. It contains their first and only US Top 10 hit (Zeppelin 45s will never be issued in Britain) – the No. 4-peaking *Whole Lotta Love.*

16 **Janis Joplin** is arrested at a gig at Curtis Hixon Hall in Tampa, for using "vulgar and indecent language," having allegedly badmouthed a policeman during her concert.

25 **John Lennon** returns his MBE to Buckingham Palace with a note: "Your Majesty, I am returning this MBE in protest against Britain's involvement in the Nigeria-Biafra thing, against our support of America in Vietnam, and against *Cold Turkey* slipping down the charts. With love, John Lennon of Bag."

29 **Jefferson Airplane** complete a three-day stint at the Fillmore East in New York, with **Grace Slick** dressing up as Adolf Hitler, and actor Rip Torn making an appearance as Richard Nixon.

30 The **Monkees** make their last live appearance at the Oakland-Alameda County Coliseum in Oakland. During the performance, **Mike Nesmith** announces his plans to form a new group called the **First National Band**, while **Mickey Dolenz** and **Davy Jones** state their intention to continue as the Monkees. (It will be another 15 years before the band play live again.)

December

1 **Barry Gibb** announces he has left the **Bee Gees**, explaining that he is "fed up, miserable, and completely disillusioned."

Although Levon Helm was the Band's drummer, his mandolin playing added a distinctive sound... It was on the Rolling Stones 1969 US tour that the phrase "the greatest rock 'n' roll band in the world" was coined... Although Jefferson Airplane wanted to love everyone, not everybody felt the same – Jack Casady and Paul Kantner were arrested for drug possesssion, Grace Slick had to have a throat operation, and the group played at Altamont

Following **Robin**'s recent decision to go it alone, this leaves the Bee Gees – once a quintet – as a solo act, comprising **Maurice Gibb**.

2 **George Harrison**, having seen **Delaney & Bonnie & Friends**' opening date of their UK tour last night at London's Royal Albert Hall, joins the band anonymously at their second show. The American married couple of **Delaney** and **Bonnie Bramlett** – accompanied by a loose aggregate of musician friends – recently opened for **Blind Faith** on their US trek, which led to ad-hoc jams and recordings with **Eric Clapton**.

10 After eight hours of deliberation, a Toronto jury finds **Jimi Hendrix** not guilty on charges of possession of heroin and marijuana. He has testified that he has experimented with pot, hashish, and LSD, but has since "outgrown" the Jimi Hendrix "experience."

15 The **Plastic Ono Band** make their UK performance debut, headlining the UNICEF Peace for Christmas concert at London's Lyceum Ballroom. Put together at 48 hours' notice, Ono Band veterans **Lennon**, **Ono**, **Clapton**, **Voormann**, and **White** are augmented by **George Harrison**, **Bobby Keyes**, **Billy Preston**, **Keith Moon**, **Jim Gordon**, and **Delaney & Bonnie**. The concert sees two Beatles on stage together for the first time since May 1, 1966 – with Lennon making what will prove to be his last live appearance in Britain.

20 At the end of an astonishingly successful year for the band, the **Los Angeles Times** publishes the following summary: "**Blood, Sweat & Tears** may just be the most important new pop music group of the decade. Profound though the influence of the Beatles has been, their work represented an escape from everything B, S & T is bringing into rock; an orchestral sound, warm harmonic concepts and improvized jazz solos of high caliber."

20 The **Rolling Stones**' ***Let It Bleed*** enters the UK chart at No. 1, replacing the Beatles' ***Abbey Road***. It includes guest artists ranging from the prodigious 22-year-old Los Angeles guitarist **Ry Cooder**, to American singer **Merry Clayton**. It is highlighted by *Midnight Rambler* – with **Jagger** portrayed in the role of the Boston Strangler, Albert de Salvo – and *Country Honk*, the original country conception of *Honky Tonk Women* (which has already been a US and UK No. 1 summer smash).

21 **Diana Ross & the Supremes** make their last television appearance together on "The Ed Sullivan Show," singing a Supremes' medley and *Someday We'll Be Together*, as part of a review of the decade titled "The Swinging, Soulful Sixties." Ross is solo bound.

21 **The Rolling Stones** close the year with the last of four live appearances in London – at the Lyceum Ballroom. Peter Smith, the Lyceum's manager, says: "This is Christmas and we thought we would give everyone a surprise; although this came earlier than anticipated." The line of hopeful fans stretches back along the Strand, where there are dozens of police on duty.

31 **Jimi Hendrix** introduces bassist **Billy Cox** and drummer **Buddy Miles** as his new band, the **Band of Gypsys**, when they perform a New Year's Eve gig at New York's Fillmore East. The show is recorded for release as ***Band of Gypsys***.

Blood, Sweat & Tears were conceived by Al Kooper (far right), but only found success when David Clayton-Thomas took over as lead singer.

ROOTS

During this year: Bonnie Raitt, a recent graduate of Radcliffe College, begins playing at small coffee houses in the Boston area, before enjoying increasing success on the east coast folk and blues scene... after being homeless in Greenwich Village for a couple of weeks, Nils Lofgren puts together Paul Dowell & the Dolphin, successfully auditioning for Sire Records... Dutch millionaire Stanley August Miesegaes sponsors a new band led by Rick Davies, who recruits the other players through a music paper ad, offering a "genuine opportunity" to form a new group; they take their name from "The Autobiography of a Supertramp"... Mickie Most, in Detroit to produce Jeff Beck, sees Cradle at a local club and, impressed with their lead singer, Suzi Quatro, invites her to London to record for his RAK label... Birmingham combo the 'N Betweens, a covers band on the Midlands club circuit, move to London, where they are seen by manager/producer Chas Chandler. They become Ambrose Slade, finding fame after they drop the "Ambrose"... and two Texas bands – American Blues and the Moving Sidewalks – split, and the latter's Billy Gibbons recruits drummer Frank Beard, who brings on board American Blues' Dusty Hill; after rejecting Z.Z. Hill and Z.Z. Brown, they settle on the name Z.Z. Top...

Dec 1969

"It was just obvious he wasn't going to make it. There was no equipment there to treat him."

Robert Hiatt, a medical resident at San Francisco's Public Health Hospital, and the first doctor to reach Meredith Hunter, **Rolling Stone**, January 30, 1970

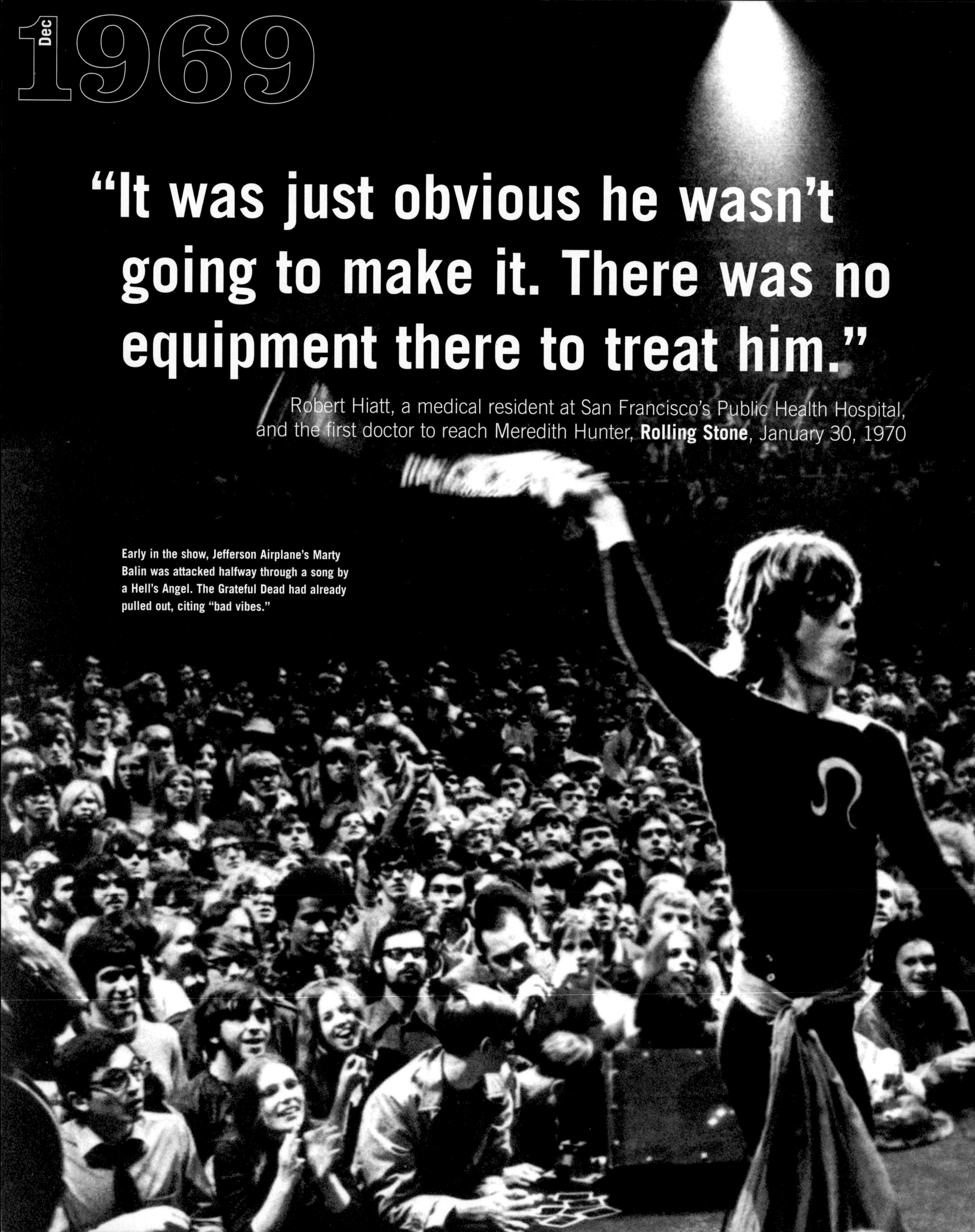

Early in the show, Jefferson Airplane's Marty Balin was attacked halfway through a song by a Hell's Angel. The Grateful Dead had already pulled out, citing "bad vibes."

Dec 6 Aiming to repeat the success of their Hyde Park concert in July, the Rolling Stones close their US tour headlining a free concert, also featuring Santana, the Flying Burrito Brothers, and Jefferson Airplane, at the Altamont Speedway track in Livermore, California, attended by a crowd of some 300,000. (The intended venue was the Sears Point Raceway, but this was made unavailable 20 hours before the scheduled start.) Having employed British Hell's Angels to act as security men in London, the group have hired their San Francisco counterparts for tonight's event. They prove to be less placid and, fueled by a mixture of alcohol and drugs, provoke angry, violent scenes. In a confused atmosphere, 18-year-old black youth Meredith Hunter, wearing a lime green suit, is stabbed to death by Hell's Angels when he pulls a gun at the front of the stage midway through the Stones' performance of *Under My Thumb*. The group rush through their numbers before fleeing in a helicopter. Three other attendees die during the evening: two people are run over in their sleeping bags, and one other person drowns in a nearby lake. The disastrous concert will be viewed by many as an epitaph to the peace and love "flower power" movement of the late 1960s, and the end of an ideological era.

"The Seventies were the best time for rock music... Bowie, Floyd, Hendrix, the Who... Led Zepelin, the Sex Pistols, Queen, Elton... the list is incredible. Their... recordings stand on their own and stand the test of time." Bryan Adams, 2003

"We were all hippies... We felt we were all in this together." Joni Mitchell, 1988

"1965–1975 was, in my opinion, a stellar period for music. Artists from Britain... American R&B... Southern soul... American pop, rock, and folk... some good disco and jazz were wonderful. All these forces came together and became part of that fabulous musical mosaic during that time." Arif Mardin, 2003

THE SEVENTIES
1970

Let's Work Together

1970

No.1 US SINGLES

Jan 3	Raindrops Keep Fallin' On My Head **B.J. Thomas**
Jan 31	I Want You Back **Jackson 5**
Feb 7	Venus **Shocking Blue**
Feb 14	Thank You (Falettinme Be Mice Elf Agin)/ Everybody Is A Star **Sly & the Family Stone**
Feb 28	Bridge Over Troubled Water **Simon & Garfunkel**
Apr 11	Let It Be **Beatles**
Apr 25	ABC **Jackson 5**
May 9	American Woman/No Sugar Tonight **Guess Who**
May 30	Everything Is Beautiful **Ray Stevens**
June 13	The Long And Winding Road **Beatles**
June 27	The Love You Save **Jackson 5**
July 11	Mama Told Me (Not To Come) **Three Dog Night**
July 25	(They Long To Be) Close To You **Carpenters**
Aug 22	Make It With You **Bread**
Aug 29	War **Edwin Starr**
Sept 19	Ain't No Mountain High Enough **Diana Ross**
Oct 10	Cracklin' Rosie **Neil Diamond**
Oct 17	I'll Be There **Jackson 5**
Nov 21	I Think I Love You **Partridge Family**
Dec 12	The Tears Of A Clown **Smokey Robinson & the Miracles**
Dec 26	My Sweet Lord **George Harrison**

No.1 UK SINGLES

Jan 3	Two Little Boys **Rolf Harris**
Jan 31	Love Grows (Where My Rosemary Goes) **Edison Lighthouse**
Mar 7	Wand'rin' Star **Lee Marvin**
Mar 28	Bridge Over Troubled Water **Simon & Garfunkel**
Apr 18	All Kinds Of Everything **Dana**
May 2	Spirit In The Sky **Norman Greenbaum**
May 16	Back Home **England World Cup Squad "70"**
June 6	Yellow River **Christie**
June 13	In The Summertime **Mungo Jerry**
Aug 1	The Wonder Of You **Elvis Presley**
Sept 12	The Tears Of A Clown **Smokey Robinson & the Miracles**
Sept 19	Band Of Gold **Freda Payne**
Oct 31	Woodstock **Matthews Southern Comfort**
Nov 21	Voodoo Chile **Jimi Hendrix Experience**
Nov 28	I Hear You Knocking **Dave Edmunds**

Yoko Ono and John Lennon

Phil Spector and George Harrison

John Lennon wrote most of the material on his *John Lennon And The Plastic Ono Band* album after an intensive six-month course in primal scream therapy... George Harrison emerged with his triple album boxed set *All Things Must Pass*, co-produced by Phil Spector, and featuring Eric Clapton, Ringo Starr, Billy Preston and others.

The roller-coaster 1960s were over. By comparison, 1970 seemed like a cold shower – a year laced with tragedy, in which popular music fragmented into subgenres.

Within days of each other, two of the leading lights of rock died, as **Jimi Hendrix** and **Janis Joplin** both succumbed to the ravages of drugs. Joplin died of a heroin overdose in a Hollywood motel. Hendrix was under financial pressure, exhausted, and confused by the conflicting demands of musicianship and showmanship. There would be protracted legal wrangling over his musical legacy, but it is beyond dispute that he revolutionized guitar-playing.

The **Beatles** had revolutionized popular music altogether, but friction within the group spilled over to their final album, ***Let It Be***, by their supreme standards a patchy offering. It seemed a fusion of four individuals, rather than a group effort. **Lennon** spent much of 1970 promoting peace and predicting that the mantra "Make love not war" would "resurrect itself." His album ***Plastic Ono Band*** was notable for protest songs such as *Working Class Hero*, and for uncharacteristic minimalist production by **Phil Spector**. **McCartney** released his solo album in April; by the end of the year he was suing the rest of the group.

Diana Ross and the **Supremes** were also breaking up. But Motown was more preoccupied with its latest hit-machine, the **Jackson 5**. R&B was in something of a transition, with a more political edge reflecting a growing black consciousness. The **Temptations**' *Ball of Confusion* tackled social ills such as riots and "white flight," and **James Brown** had already recorded *Say It Loud, I'm Black and Proud.*

An intriguing array of artists and discrete genres emerged. Reggae was migrating from the slums of Kingston, Jamaica, into the mainstream (at least in Britain) with **Desmond Dekker** and **Jimmy Cliff** in the vanguard. **Bob Dylan** described Cliff's *Vietnam* as the best protest song he'd ever heard, and two years later **Paul Simon** would use it as the template for *Mother and Child Reunion*. But in 1970 *Bridge Over Troubled Water*'s soothing sensibility was probably the right antidote to the upheaval of the later 1960s. **James Taylor** contributed to the more introspective mood, returning to the studio to produce ***Sweet Baby James***.

An even gentler sound emanated from the **Carpenters**, propelled into the limelight by the success of *(They Long To Be) Close To You*. Neither **Dionne Warwick** nor **Dusty Springfield** had much success with this **Burt Bacharach** song, but the Carpenters sent the song to US No. 1.

The year's high notes included **Eric Clapton**'s first recording of the seminal *Layla*, while **Elton John** received the best possible notices at his US debut in Los Angeles. "And you can tell everybody, This is your song..." Indeed it was.

"The Carpenters are youthful musical craftsmen who build their act on a solid foundation called talent."

Billboard December 19, 1970

Jan 1970

Blood Sweat & Tears

Diana Ross and the Supremes part... Reggae music makes a splash... *Bridge Over Troubled Water*...

January

3 The **Beatles**' last group recording session takes place at EMI's Abbey Road Studio 2, with Paul, George, and Ringo overdubbing some harmony vocals and re-recording a new guitar and drum part for inclusion on what will prove to be their final album, ***Let It Be***.

4 The **Who**'s **Keith Moon**, after presiding over the opening of a disco at the Cranbourne Rooms in Hatfield, England, is confronted by skinheads as he leaves the venue. The skinheads surround his Bentley, throwing coins and stones. When his chauffeur Neil Boland gets out to try to clear a path for the car, Moon – a non-driver – puts his foot on the accelerator pedal, sending the car careering down the road. Boland is caught under the wheels, and dies on his way to the hospital. The death will be ruled accidental.

14 After scoring 12 US chart-topping singles since 1964, **Diana Ross & the Supremes** make their final live appearance together at the Frontier Hotel in Las Vegas. Ross introduces her replacement, **Jean Terrell**, on stage. Fellow Motown singer **Marvin Gaye** is a surprise guest.

27 Recorded in ten takes, **John Lennon**'s *Instant Karma* is written, recorded, and mixed in a session lasting nine hours from beginning to end. Lennon plays acoustic guitar and **George Harrison** is on lead guitar, with **Plastic Ono Band** regulars **Billy Preston** (electric piano), **Klaus Voormann** (bass), and **Alan White** (drums). **Phil Spector** produces.

31 With reggae music now a huge crossover success in the UK, its top Jamaican protagonists begin a package tour at the Royal Albert Hall in London. On the bill: 27-year-old singer/songwriter, **Desmond Dekker** – whose *The Israelites* hit UK No. 1 last April; 22-year-old **Jimmy Cliff** – who began as a ska singer for legendary producer Leslie Kong in 1963, and scored his debut smash with *Wonderful World Beautiful People* for the pioneering UK reggae label, Trojan Records; **Max Romeo**, who hit UK No. 10 last summer with *Wet Dream*; and three reggae groups: the **Upsetters** (who hit UK No. 5 with *Return of Django/Dollar In The Teeth*), **Harry J's All Stars**, and the **Pioneers**.

February

2 Guitarist **Ronnie Wood**, bassist **Ronnie Lane**, keyboard player **Ian McLagan**, and drummer **Kenney Jones**, now fronted by lead singer **Rod Stewart** – who joined the band last autumn, after leaving the **Jeff Beck Group** – play at the Top Rank, Southampton, UK. This is their first gig as the **Faces** (having dropped the "Small" prefix). They have recently signed a long-term recording contract with Warner Bros., though it allows for Stewart to honor his recent solo deal with Mercury Records.

17 **Joni Mitchell**, who recently completed recording ***Ladies Of The Canyon***, announces that she is quitting live performance during a concert at the Royal Festival Hall – her fifth live appearance in London. This will turn out to be a premature decision, as she will return in August to take part in the Isle of Wight Festival.

21 **Simon & Garfunkel**'s ***Bridge Over Troubled Water*** enters the UK chart at No. 1, where it will stay for 13 consecutive weeks. It will return to the top spot regularly over the next 18 months, eventually spending 41 weeks there, including an 11-week run beginning next January. Becoming one of the biggest-selling albums of the decade, it will also begin a ten-week ride at US No. 1 in two weeks' time.

No longer "small", the Faces recruited Rod Stewart as their lead singer. He has a highly successful parallel career as a soloist.

Jimmy Cliff

Peter Green

Blood, Sweat & Tears joined Jimi Hendrix, The Rascals and others at a Vietnam Monatorium Committee benefit at Madison Square Garden... Jimmy Clift scored his UK debut smash *Wonderful World, Beautiful People*... with the pressure of stardom proving intolerable, Peter Green decided to quit Fleetwood Mac.

28 The **New Musical Express** runs a story headlined "Why **Peter Green** Wants To Give His Money Away." The **Fleetwood Mac** lead guitarist, "looking every day more like a character out of the massive bound Bible that sits on a shelf in the middle of his extensive stereo collection," makes plain his intention that he will give away any excess money he earns: "There must be no starvation. Just because somebody is born on the other side of the world that is no reason why they should be starving for it."

28 Heeding a warning from Eva von Zeppelin – a relative of airship designer Ferdinand von Zeppelin – to sue the group if her family name is used in Denmark, **Led Zeppelin** play a gig in Copenhagen billed as the Nobs.

March

11 **Blood, Sweat & Tears**' self-titled second album takes Album of the Year honors at the 12th annual Grammy awards. The band, leading the pack with ten nominations, also collects the Best Contemporary Instrumental Performance prize for *Variations On A Theme By Erik Satie*. Grammy favorites the **5th Dimension** continue their winning ways, receiving Record of the Year and Best Contemporary Vocal Performance, Group for *Aquarius/Let The Sunshine In* – the **Bones Howe**-conceived medley from the musical "Hair." In an unusually strong Best New Artist field, **Crosby, Stills & Nash** holds off nominees **Chicago** and **Led Zeppelin**. **Joe South**'s *Games People Play* picks up two awards, including Song of the Year.

16 Motown singer **Tammi Terrell** dies in Graduate Hospital, Philadelphia, at the age of 24. She has undergone eight operations over the past 18 months, following the diagnosis of a brain tumor. She will be buried at Mount Lawn Cemetery in Sharon Hill, Pennsylvania. Grief-stricken, her singing partner **Marvin Gaye** will retire from the public eye for the rest of the year.

27 **Joe Cocker**'s Mad Dogs & Englishmen concert tour reaches the Fillmore East in New York for the first of two nights. The climax of an intensive schedule – playing 65 concerts in 57 days – these two shows are filmed and recorded for subsequent release under the same (Noël Coward-inspired) title, which will give Cocker his biggest-selling album at US No. 2. The 43 musicians in his entourage include **Leon Russell** and **Rita Coolidge** (a Nashville-born singer recently signed to A&M Records, and girlfriend of **Kris Kristofferson**).

> **"The Band is far and above the best American rock group working today."**
>
> **Billboard**, January 17, 1970

BLACK SABBATH

Mar 9 **Birmingham-based heavy metal quartet Black Sabbath – who changed their name from Earth last year – make their London concert debut at the Roundhouse in Camden Town. The group, managed by Jim Simpson, was formed in 1967 by schoolfriends Ozzy Osbourne (lead vocal), Tony Iommi (lead guitar and keyboard), Geezer Butler (bass), and drummer Bill Ward. They have signed to nascent progressive rock label, Vertigo Records, and their self-penned debut album, *Black Sabbath*, was released on Friday, February 13. Costing £600 ($1,440) to record, it was nailed in just three days. The group will begin sessions for an equally quick follow-up LP at Regent Sound and Island studios in London over the summer, set for release in September as *Paranoid*.**

Crosby, Stills, Nash & Young

The Beatles break up... Derek & the Dominos... the American Top 40 bows...

April

1 The last session for a **Beatles** album takes place, with only **Ringo Starr** in attendance. He overdubs drum parts on *Across The Universe, I Me Mine,* and *The Long And Winding Road* – three tracks featured on the forthcoming Phil Spector-helmed *Let It Be.*

4 On the release of British rock group **Brinsley Schwarz**'s self-titled debut album (which is fronted by guitarist Brinsley Schwarz, and contains six compositions by 21-year-old bass player **Nick Lowe**), PR company Famepushers tries to launch the group by flying a planeload of 133 UK music journalists and photographers to New York, at a cost of £30,000 ($72,000), to see the band open for **Van Morrison** at the Fillmore East. The hype will inevitably backfire, the band will be panned, and the stunt will go down in history as one of the most disastrous – and expensive – promotional gimmicks of all time.

10 **Paul McCartney** announces the break-up of the **Beatles**. In a prepared statement, he reveals that he doesn't know "whether the break will be temporary or permanent," and that he does not "foresee a time when the Lennon/McCartney partnership will be active again in songwriting." In response to the news, Ringo says it is "all news to me"; a friend of George's says, "He just wants to be left alone"; while Lennon – in typical style – says jokingly, "He didn't quit. He was fired." Although the decision to break up is unanimous, McCartney will forever be saddled with the press's description of him as the "man who broke up the Beatles." His first solo album, *McCartney*, will be released next week by Apple.

17 **Johnny Cash** performs at the White House, at the invitation of President Nixon. The Commander-in-Chief makes a special request for *Okie From Muskogee* and *Welfare Cadillac,* but Cash respectfully declines and sings *A Boy Named Sue* instead.

24 **Grace Slick** and her date, activist Abbie Hoffman – who is currently on trial for his part in conspiring to riot at the 1968 Democratic convention in Chicago – are turned away at the gates of the White House, although Slick has been invited by the President's daughter, Tricia, to attend a tea party for alumni of Finch College, a prestigious New York finishing school, where both girls studied between 1957 and 1958.

May

1 **Bob Dylan** and **George Harrison** spend the day jamming at Columbia Studio B in New York, backed by **Charlie Daniels, Bob Johnston,** and **Billy Mundi**. They cut eight songs in the session, including versions of *Don't Think Twice It's All Right, Just Like Tom Thumb's Blues,* and *One Too Many Mornings,* as well as *Da Doo Ron Ron* and **Paul McCartney**'s *Yesterday.*

Iggy (James Jewel Osterberg) & the Stooges made their live debut at a Halloween party in Ann Arbor, Michigan.

8 The **Beatles**' final album of new material, *Let It Be,* is released as a deluxe boxed set, with a photographic record of last year's sessions. The New Musical Express describes the album as "a cardboard tombstone," and a "sad and tatty end to a musical fusion." While their contemporaries, the **Rolling Stones** and the **Who**, will continue recording and touring into the next century, the Beatles' astonishing recording legacy has been built in just seven years: 20 US and 18 UK No. 1 singles, 13 US and 11 UK No. 1 albums – an unrivaled canon of legendary recordings.

10 In California, the **Stooges** begin a two-week recording session for their second album, *Fun House,* at Elektra Sound Recorders in Los Angeles, under producer Don Gallucci. The three-year-old raw-rock combo, led by their emaciated, drug-fueled frontman, 23-year-old Michigan native **Iggy Pop**, signed to Elektra Records last year. Earlier Iggy pal **James Williamson** joins the sessions as an extra guitarist.

15 Having played at the Fillmore East last week, the re-formed **Mothers of Invention** premiere **Frank Zappa**'s latest offering, "200 Motels," with Zubin Mehta conducting the Los Angeles Philharmonic Orchestra, at UCLA's Pauley Pavilion (a 13,000-capacity sports hall) as part of a contemporary music festival. The program also includes Mel Powell's "Immobiles 1–4" and Edgar Varèse's "Intégrales."

21 **Crosby, Stills, Nash & Young** – whose second album, the career-defining *Déjà Vu*, hit US No. 1 last week – record *Ohio* at the Record Plant in Los Angeles. **Neil Young** was inspired to write the song by graphic media reports of the killing of four people by National Guard troops at Kent State University in Ohio on May 4, during student protests against the United States's involvement in Vietnam and Cambodia.

24 The two-day Hollywood Festival, staged on land rented from farmer Ted Askey at Leycett, near Newcastle-under-Lyme, closes with a performance by **Traffic**. The Sunday line-up also features a three-and-a half hour set by the **Grateful Dead** (who are making their first UK appearance), San Francisco-based rock quintet **Flamin' Groovies, Jose Feliciano, Black Sabbath, Free,** and **Mungo Jerry** – whose breakthrough performance is the highlight of the festival (their first hit, *In The Summertime*, will top the UK chart in three weeks' time.)

The first Crosby, Stills, Nash & Young album *Deja Vu* took a reputed 800 hours to record and then hit the top during a 97-week chart stay in the US... The Allman Brothers were put together at the instigation of Phil Walden, who had founded his Capricorn record label in 1969.

The Allman Brothers

26 **George Harrison** – long frustrated at not being allowed to contribute more songs to Beatles albums – begins recording tracks for his solo debut at EMI's Abbey Road studios, with producer **Phil Spector**. The sessions will evolve into his epic masterpiece ***All Things Must Pass*** – a triple album that will include the global chart-topper, *My Sweet Lord*.

June

6 **Eric Clapton** tells **Melody Maker** that he will "vote for **B.B.King**" in the upcoming British general election: "The first thing any new MP should do is apply the mind to producing a self-tuning electric guitar."

7 The **Who** performs "Tommy" at the prestigious Metropolitan Opera House in New York, at the start of a month-long coast-to-coast US tour. A spokesman for the group says it is likely that this will be the last time they perform the rock opera live, "After all, how can you possibly follow the Met?"

9 **Bob Dylan** is awarded an honorary Doctorate in Music by Princeton University.

14 **Eric Clapton** plays a charity concert at London's Lyceum Ballroom, in aid of the Dr. Spock Civil Liberties Defense Fund to aid Vietnam War dissenters. Clapton calls on **Carl Radle** (bass), Bobby Whitlock (keyboards), Jim Gordon (drums), and **Traffic**'s **Dave Mason** (guitar) to back him. After one day's rehearsal – and ten minutes before taking the stage – they adopt the name **Derek & the Dominos**.

22 Following last night's concert at the Ellis Auditorium in Memphis, the **Who**'s **Pete Townshend** is pulled off a plane and detained by FBI agents for using the word "bomb." He tells the authorities that the word is English slang. In fact, while the group were stuck on the plane waiting for it to take off, Townshend reacted to a persistent high-pitched whine coming from the cabin speakers by shouting, "I'll tell where the bomb is!" When he is released the band flies to Atlanta, arriving late to perform.

28 At an eventful Bath Festival of Blues & Progressive Music, staged in Shepton Mallet, **Canned Heat** – who were scheduled to appear at 8:45 pm yesterday – finally get on at 5:00 am and then play for three hours. Later in the day, audience member **Donovan** gives a two-hour impromptu performance while the announced act is held up in traffic. **Led Zeppelin**, the **Mothers of Invention**, **Pink Floyd**, and **John Mayall** are among the other acts who have performed over the three-day weekend. Not bad for £2 10s (£2.50/$6).

"I want to say here and now, that it's all utter rubbish. We're all happier now than ever have ever been and I want everyone to know it." John Bonham, **New Musical Express** June 27, 1970 on rumors of a Led Zeppelin split

July

3 "The American Top 40" – a radio chart show hosted by disc jockey Casey Kasem – begins broadcasting from KDEO in El Cajon, San Diego, at 7:00 pm, and is initially syndicated in 11 markets across the US, including Boston and San Francisco. In the three-hour program, Kasem counts down the 40 biggest hits from **Billboard**'s Hot 100 singles chart. (The show's popularity will take off, and by the early 1980s it will be heard on over 500 stations. Kasem's final "AT40" will air on August 6, 1988, after which he will join the Westwood One radio network and create the adult contemporary-based "Casey's Top 40.")

3 The second annual three-day Atlanta International Pop Festival gets under way at the Middle Georgia Raceway in Byron. The A-list bill features **Jimi Hendrix**, **Jethro Tull**, **B.B. King**, **Procol Harum**, **Led Zeppelin**, and **Mountain**, among many others. Also appearing are the **Allman Brothers**, a new local band managed by Phil Walden, who is setting up his own Capricorn Records label. The rock quintet, led by Nashville-born siblings, **Duane** and **Gregg Allman**, are already popular in the south, and are touring to promote their debut album, ***The Allman Brothers Band***. Not all goes well during the festival, however: with rampant drug-taking reported throughout the event, local doctors and law-enforcement officials will plead with State authorities to declare it a "health disaster area."

11 Already certified gold, ***Woodstock*** – which documents the historic, utopian music event of last summer – becomes the first triple LP to top the US chart.

31 The day after announcing that Allen Klein no longer represents them – which begins a round of litigation between the two parties – the **Rolling Stones**' Decca contract, which has grossed over £60 million ($144 million) over seven years, expires. In order to fulfill their contract with Decca, the Stones will deliver *Cocksucker Blues*.

Having toured Iceland and turned down $200,000 to play two US concerts, Led Zeppelin returned to play at the Bath Festival.

Aug 1970

Clapton's *Layla*... The Isle of Wight Festival... Jimi Hendrix dies...

August

6 **Paul Simon**, **Janis Joplin**, **Steppenwolf**, **Poco**, and **Johnny Winter** are among the acts participating in the 12-hour anti-war Concert for Peace, at New York's Shea Stadium, on the 25th anniversary of the dropping of the first atomic bomb on Hiroshima.

8 **Janis Joplin** buys a headstone for the grave of her greatest influence, **Bessie Smith**, having discovered that Smith's grave at the Mount Lawn Cemetery in Philadelphia is unmarked. The epitaph is provided by Columbia Records' executive **John Hammond** (Smith's producer), and reads: "The greatest blues singer in the world will never stop singing Bessie Smith 1895–1937." (Smith died on September 26, 1937, following a car accident, and it was rumored that she bled to death having been refused admission to a whites-only hospital.)

14 While on a **Crosby, Stills, Nash & Young** US tour, **Stephen Stills** is arrested on suspected drugs charges at a San Diego motel, after being found crawling along a corridor in an incoherent state. He is freed on $2,500 bail.

23 Progressive rock supergroup **Emerson, Lake & Palmer** make their live debut at the Guildhall in Portsmouth, England.

23 **Lou Reed** plays his last two gigs with the **Velvet Underground**, at Max's Kansas City in New York. Both concerts are recorded for posterity and will be released in May 1972. He will spend much of the rest of the year at his parents' home in Freeport, Long Island – working as a typist in his father's accounting firm for $40 a week – before signing a solo deal with RCA Records.

26 **Derek & the Dominos** begin recording sessions at Criteria Studios in Miami. **Eric Clapton** invites **Duane Allman** to join in, after seeing him play nearby with the **Allman Brothers**. A double album is finished in less than ten days. Clapton will later say that Allman was the "catalyst" of the whole project, which will become the ***Layla*** album. Allman's guitar dueting with Clapton on the title track will become his most famous work outside the brothers' band.

Ralph McTell – one of the many acts to perform at the Isle of Wight festival – has been a consistently popular live act. His UK chart career amounted to a meager two hits, including his signature tune *Streets Of London*.

ELTON JOHN

Aug 25 **On the first stop of a tour to promote his debut solo album, and opening with *Your Song*, Elton John makes his live US debut at the 20th-anniversary celebrations for Doug Weston's Troubadour club in Los Angeles. With Leon Russell and Quincy Jones in the audience, the singer-songwriter/pianist is accompanied by regular sidemen, bassist Dee Murray and drummer Nigel Olsson. He plays seven songs co-written with Bernie Taupin, before closing with covers of the Stones' *Honky Tonk Women* and the Beatles' *Get Back*.**

Elton John received top-drawer reviews for his live US debut – critical reverence that he later claimed changed his life.

Ex-Nice keyboard whiz Keith Emerson, ex-Gods and ex-King Crimson bassist/vocalist Greg Lake, and ex-Crazy World of Arthur Brown and ex-Atomic Rooster drummer Carl Palmer united to form Emerson, Lake & Palmer.

28 After a two-day free warm-up, the Isle of Wight Festival gets under way with **Arrival** (a seven-piece combo from Liverpool), followed by Irish blues-rock band **Taste**. Then **Chicago** (a four-year-old jazz-laced pop/rock octet currently scoring their first US top five hit with *25 Or 6 To 4*) make their first UK appearance. The day climaxes with a long-awaited set from **Procol Harum**, and closes with the **Voices of East Harlem**.

29 Following conjecture about the **Beatles**' future in the August 15 issue of **Melody Maker**, the paper's mailbag section prints the following correspondence: "Dear Mailbag, In order to put out of its misery the limping dog of a news story which has been dragging itself across your pages for the past year, my answer to the question, 'Will the Beatles get together again?' ...is no. **Paul McCartney**."

29 The second day of the Isle of Wight Festival opens with a performance by now solo singer-songwriter **John Sebastian** (ex-**Lovin' Spoonful**), highlighted by an impromptu appearance by his erstwhile colleague **Zal Yanovsky**. They sing together for the first time in three years. **Emerson, Lake & Palmer** make their festival bow, followed by **Ten Years After** and the **Doors**. **Joni Mitchell**'s set is interrupted when a festivalgoer jumps on stage and yells: "This is just a hippy concentration camp."

30 The final day of the Isle of Wight Festival sees performances from **Kris Kristofferson** (whose *Me And Bobby McGee* was recently cut by **Janis Joplin**), British folk singer-songwriter **Ralph McTell**, **Heaven**, **Free**, **Donovan**, **Pentangle**, the **Moody Blues**, **Jethro Tull**, the **Jimi Hendrix Experience**, **Joan Baez**, **Richie Havens**, and 35-year-old Canadian poet/singer-songwriter **Leonard Cohen & His Army**. Assessing the event's overall success, Douglas Osmond, Chief Constable of Hampshire, says: "One of the good things has been the absense of violence. There is far less violence here than at a normal league football match," despite the attitude of "the lunatic fringe" toward the police. Osmond says he found it "very pleasant."

September

3 While his colleagues in the band wait for him at Los Angeles Airport, scheduled to fly to Berlin, 27-year-old **Canned Heat** member **Al Wilson** is found dead in a sleeping bag in a redwood forest in Topanga Canyon, California. A bottle of barbiturates is found next to the singer/guitarist, who has been suffering from deep depression.

6 After bad experiences in Denmark (where he left the stage with the words, "I've been dead for a long time") and in Germany (where the audience booed his late appearance), **Jimi Hendrix** makes what will prove to be his last major concert appearance at the Love and Peace Festival in Puttgarden, on the Isle of Fehmarn in Germany. Cutting short a European tour after **Billy Cox** flies back to the US, Hendrix leaves the festival by helicopter for Hamburg, and then returns to London.

25 "The **Partridge Family**," loosely based on real-life family singing group, the **Cowsills**, premieres on ABC television. Although its star is **Shirley Jones**, playing the matriarch of the performing family, it launches the career of 20-year-old singer/actor **David Cassidy**. Cassidy is the son of actor Jack Cassidy and stepson of his screen mother Shirley Jones. He has previously had small roles in several shows, but his role as Keith Partridge will turn him into a major pop star. The storyline in the first episode sees the Partridge family kids asking their mother to help out on a song they're recording called *I Think I Love You* – which they then sell to a record label, scoring their first No. 1. In real life – and within two months – the Partridge Family's *I Think I Love You* will top the US chart.

26 Having returned from New York two days ago, **John Lennon** begins recording sessions at Abbey Road Studios with producer Phil Spector. The songs, already demoed in Los Angeles while Lennon was undergoing primal therapy, will form the basis of his ***John Lennon/Plastic Ono Band*** LP.

"Rejoice. Rock music...has a new star. He's Elton John, a 23-year-old Englishman, whose debut Tuesday night at the Troubadour was, in almost every way, magnificent." Robert Hilburn, **Los Angeles Times**, August 27, 1970

JIMI HENDRIX

Sept 18 An ambulance is called to the basement apartment of Jimi Hendrix's German-born girlfriend, Monika Dannemann, at the Samarkand Hotel in Bayswater, London, where ambulancemen find the motionless body of Jimi Hendrix with vomit around his mouth. Dannemann dialed the emergency 999 number after being unable to wake her boyfriend, who has apparently taken nine of her sleeping pills. He is placed in the back of the ambulance and driven to St. Mary Abbot's Hospital in Kensington, where he is pronounced dead on arrival. He had left the message, "I need help bad, man," on Chas Chandler's answering machine in the early hours of the morning. The cause of death, following an inquest next Monday, will be given as: "Inhalation of vomit, Barbiturate intoxication (quinalbarbitone), Insufficient evidence of circumstances, open verdict." The coroner will estimate that Hendrix – age 27 – died in his sleep at approximately 5:30 am.

Berry Gordy said: "The Jackson 5 are bigger than any race issue" after three concerts were blacklisted in Texas.

Janis Joplin dies... The Jackson 5 – four No. 1s... Elvis at the White House...

October

1 Following a funeral service at the Dunlap Baptist Church in Renton, King County, Washington, (where his aunt played the organ during his childhood), **Jimi Hendrix** is buried at Greenwood Memorial Park. His gravestone bears the inscription, "Forever In Our Hearts James 'Jimi' Hendrix 1942–1970." **Miles Davis**, **Johnny Winter**, **Noel Redding**, and **Mitch Mitchell** are among those attending the service.

4 After partying at Barney's Beanery at 8447 Santa Monica Boulevard, 27-year-old **Janis Joplin** is found dead in room 105 of the Landmark Hotel on Franklin Avenue in Hollywood. (She was scheduled to record the vocal for *Buried Alive In The Blues* tomorrow.) An autopsy will be conducted tomorrow by Thomas Noguchi from the Los Angeles County Medical Examiner's Office – who also performed autopsies on Marilyn Monroe, Robert F. Kennedy, and Sharon Tate. He will conclude "accidental death" by "acute heroin-morphine intoxication due to injection of overdose," and will report numerous needle marks in both arms.

17 The **Jackson 5** ballad, *I'll Be There* – co-written by label boss Berry Gordy and producer Hal Davis with Willie Hutch, and hallmarked by **Michael**'s now familiar treble vocal – gives the R&B quintet their fourth US No. 1 of the year. Motown recently reported that the group has already sold ten million copies worldwide.

30 In Miami, **Jim Morrison** is found guilty of using profanity in public and indecent exposure, but acquitted on charges of lewd behavior and public drunkenness. He is sentenced to six months in jail and fined $500.

31 *Fire And Rain*, written and recorded by **James Taylor** in three segments – the first in London, the second in a Manhattan hospital room, and the third at Austin Riggs, a mental hospital, all during 1968 – hits US No. 3. Its parent album, ***Sweet Baby James***, is certified gold in the US. The album – featuring musical contributions from **Carole King**, **Randy Meisner**, **Red Rhodes**, and **Chris Darrow** – will also hit No. 3 during a two-year run. It includes the follow-up single, *Carolina In My Mind*, with **Paul McCartney** on bass.

November

4 **Jethro Tull**, touring to promote their third album, ***Benefit***, lives up to its title by headlining a fundraiser concert at Carnegie Hall, New York, for the Phoenix House drug rehabilitation center.

5 During the **Beach Boys**' four-night stint at the Whisky A Go-Go in Los Angeles, **Brian Wilson** joins the band on stage for only the

Five days after performing in the humble surroundings of the Marquay Club in Torquay, Derek & the Dominos began recording their debut album in Miami, Florida... Janis Joplin died of a heroin overdose in a Hollywood motel, leaving behind an unfinished album, *Pearl*, which included an acclaimed version of Kris Kristofferson's *Me And Bobby McGee*, and her tortured vocals on other tracks.

Janis Joplin

Ian Anderson of Jethro Tull

Jethro Tull's Carnegie Hall benefit held was in the presence of the Duke and Duchess of Bedford and raised $10,000. Billboard described Ian Anderson as "looking like a carnival magician gone wild."

second time in five years. In a fragile mental state, and with his recurring ear problem getting worse, he will not play with them again for some time.

17 **Elton John** performs a live concert for radio station WPLJ-FM at the WABC Studios in New York. The set is recorded (by studio engineer Phil Ramone) for subsequent release as *11-17-70* in the US, and as *17-11-70* in the UK.

December

5 On "American Bandstand" brother-sister duo the **Carpenters** perform their recent US chart-topper, a cover of Bacharach/David's *(They Long To Be) Close To You*, and their current US No. 2 follow-up, *We've Only Just Begun*. Songwriter/keyboard player **Richard** and his younger sister, drummer/singer **Karen**, born in New Haven, Connecticut, were briefly signed to RCA Records four years ago before inking a deal – at the behest of label boss Herb Alpert – with A&M last year. Their smooth blend of romance-laced adult contemporary balladry is in stark contrast with both the politically themed hippy movement of the late 1960s, and the heavy metal and progressive rock genres that are currently dominating FM radio in America.

10 **Desmond Dekker** – who recently hit UK No. 2 with *You Can Get It If You Really Want It* – is back in Jamaica to receive the Musgrave Award from the island's Prime Minister, Hugh Shearer. Dekker also performs a special charity show.

16 The RIAA certifies gold sales of eleven **Creedence Clearwater Revival** records – the singles *Bad Moon Rising, Down On The Corner, Lookin' Out My Back Door, Travelin' Band*, and *Up Around The Bend*, and the albums ***Bayou Country***, ***Cosmo's Factory***, ***Creedence Clearwater Revival***, ***Green River***, ***Pendulum***, and ***Willy And The Poor Boys***.

21 **Elvis Presley**, staying at a Washington hotel under the name Joe Burrows, meets President Richard Nixon in the Oval Office of the White House. Nixon presents him with the badge of a Federal Agent of the Bureau of Narcotics and Dangerous Drugs. Two months ago, he also received a CNOA Membership Certificate that read: "This is to certify that Elvis A. Presley is a member in good standing of the California Narcotic Officers Association."

31 With **Melody Maker** reporting that the **The Beatles** are searching for a new bassist, **Paul McCartney** files suit in the High Court of Justice, Chancery Division, Group – assigned case number 1970 No. 6315 – against the rest of the Beatles. He is attempting to dissolve the Beatles & Co. partnership and seeks the appointment of a receiver to handle the group's affairs. He also ends links with Allen Klein. The writ seeks that "a declaration under the name of The Beatles & Co., and constituted by a deed of partnership dated 19 April 1967 and made between the parties hereto, ought to be dissolved and that accordingly the same be dissolved."

"[Elton] John, gaudily attired, is a magnetic performer in blues, boogie and rock." **Billboard** review of his November 20, 1970 Fillmore East show

THE DOORS

Dec 12 Following a triumphant performance in Dallas last night – where they previewed a new cut, *Riders On The Storm* – the Doors play at the Warehouse in New Orleans. Morrison repeatedly smashes his microphone on to the stage, before tossing the broken pieces into the audience. It will prove to be the last time the Doors play together live.

Three months after this concert, Jim Morrison moved to Paris

ROOTS During this year: Swedish musicians/singers, Benny Andersson, Björn Ulvaeus, Agnetha Fältskog, and Frida Lyngstad give their first public performance together, under the name Festfolk Quartet, at a restaurant in Gothenburg... rock singer Steven Tyler meets guitarist Joe Perry in an ice-cream parlor called The Anchorage in Sunape, New Hampshire; Perry invites Tyler to sing with his group Jam Band at a local club, the Barn... American singer-songwriters Dewey Bunnell and Gerry Beckley form the acoustic folk-quintet, Daze, in London... Tanzanian-born Freddie Mercury joins Brian May and Roger Taylor in Smile... songwriting duo Walter Becker and Donald Fagen answer an ad in the *Village Voice* from guitarist Denny Dias, who is looking for "musicians with jazz chops"... taking their name from their old school gym teacher, Lynyrd Skynyrd cuts demos in Sheffield, Alabama, at the suggestion of Capricorn Records boss, Phil Walden... Maurice White brings his band, the Salty Peppers, to Los Angeles, changing their name to Earth, Wind & Fire... Yorkshireman Robert Palmer joins Lancastrian Elkie Brooks in avant-garde jazz rockers DaDa... and Ray Parker Jr. becomes a guitarist with the house band in Detroit's biggest club, the Twenty Grand. ..

Thin Line Between Love And Hate

1971

No.1 US SINGLES

Jan 2 My Sweet Lord **George Harrison**
Jan 23 Knock Three Times **Dawn**
Feb 13 One Bad Apple **Osmonds**
Mar 20 Me And Bobby McGee **Janis Joplin**
Apr 3 Just My Imagination (Running Away With Me) **Temptations**
Apr 17 Joy To The World **Three Dog Night**
May 29 Brown Sugar **Rolling Stones**
June 12 Want Ads **Honey Cone**
June 19 It's Too Late **Carole King**
July 24 Indian Reservation (The Lament Of The Cherokee Reservation Indian) **Raiders**
July 31 You've Got A Friend **James Taylor**
Aug 7 How Can You Mend A Broken Heart **Bee Gees**
Sept 4 Uncle Albert/Admiral Halsey **Paul & Linda McCartney**
Sept 11 Go Away Little Girl **Donny Osmond**
Oct 2 Maggie May/Reason To Believe **Rod Stewart**
Nov 6 Gypsys, Tramps & Thieves **Cher**
Nov 20 Theme From Shaft **Isaac Hayes**
Dec 4 Family Affair **Sly & the Family Stone**
Dec 25 Brand New Key **Melanie**

No.1 UK SINGLES

Jan 2 I Hear You Knocking **Dave Edmunds**
Jan 9 Grandad **Clive Dunn**
Jan 30 My Sweet Lord **George Harrison**
Mar 6 Baby Jump **Mungo Jerry**
Mar 20 Hot Love **T. Rex**
May 1 Double Barrel **Dave & Ansil Collins**
May 15 Knock Three Times **Dawn**
June 19 Chirpy Chirpy Cheep Cheep **Middle of the Road**
July 24 Get It On **T. Rex**
Aug 21 I'm Still Waiting **Diana Ross**
Sept 18 Hey Girl Don't Bother Me **Tams**
Oct 9 Maggie May **Rod Stewart**
Nov 13 Coz I Luv You **Slade**
Dec 11 Ernie (The Fastest Milkman In The West) **Benny Hill**

Marvin Gaye

Ravi Shankar

Marvin Gaye's *What's Going On* is now regarded as a landmark work in his storied career... Ravi Shankar made a personal plea to George Harrison, who then organized the Concert for Bangla Desh to aid victims of famine and war in that country.

If the late 1960s was dominated by protest songs and counterculture, 1971 saw another form of musical protest. America's leading black artists wrote of troubled times in the cities, and ambiguity and unease stalked the land. The year also saw the emergence of **Rod Stewart**, **Elton John**, and **David Bowie** as a new generation of rock icons.

Motown didn't want to release **Marvin Gaye**'s ***What's Going On***, which somehow didn't fit the hit factory formula. But the artist prevailed, and some of the period's most socially powerful lyrics went straight to the hearts of those perturbed by poverty, discrimination, pollution, and corruption. The songs combined layers of his sensuous, beseeching vocals, and a fluid instrumental style that would influence **Stevie Wonder**, **Curtis Mayfield**, and many more. To many, it remains the most significant soul record ever made. While Gaye held out the prospect of redemption, **Sly & the Family Stone**'s No. 1 album, ***There's A Riot Goin' On***, was darker and more disturbed, a reflection of drug-induced inner turmoil as much as America's social ills. Soul and funk artists didn't corner the market in social causes. **George Harrison** mobilized fellow artists for the Concert for Bangla Desh, featuring **Ringo Starr**, **Eric Clapton**, **Billy Preston**, and **Ravi Shankar** – as well as an unannounced appearance by **Bob Dylan**.

Rod Stewart's *Maggie May* ushered him into the limelight as a solo artist. Already successful with the **Jeff Beck Group** and the **Faces**, Stewart's musical impact was magnified by constant tabloid gossip. Capable of raucous R&B-flavored rock and introspective ballads, he would enjoy nearly 30 years of chart success around the globe. So would Elton John, whose *Your Song* became the first self-performed success of his partnership with lyricist **Bernie Taupin**. Drawing on country, progressive rock, and pure pop, and imbuing all with unique melodic skills, John was the definition of versatility.

The year brought the first glint of glam rock, courtesy of **Marc Bolan** and **T. Rex**. Bolan claimed the glitter began as a joke, but it worked. Another exponent was David Bowie, whose outrageous costumes, hints of gender-bending, and glitzy cosmetics established his persona. The music wasn't bad either.

After the passing of **Janis Joplin** and **Jimi Hendrix** in 1970, **Doors**' singer **Jim Morrison** died of similar causes this year. Jazz legend **Louis Armstrong** and early rocker **Gene Vincent** also departed.

The year had its lighter side. **Three Dog Night** enjoyed a No. 1 with the relentlessly cheerful *Joy To The World*, and **Benny Hill**'s *Ernie (The Fastest Milkman in the West)* topped the final British survey in December. Strange kind of year.

"I believe in the visual media very strongly. I'm a media man."

Marc Bolan, **Sounds**, April 3, 1971

Jan

1971

Judy Collin's *Amazing Grace*...
The Osmonds (and Donny)...
Led Zeppelin's thank-you tour...

With the singer/songwriter movement at its creative and commercial zenith, James Taylor appeared on the cover of *Time* magazine.

January

3 **James Taylor** begins recording a new album at Crystal Recording Studios in Hollywood, with **Peter Asher** once again producing. The sessions will yield ***Mud Slide Slim And The Blue Horizon*** (which will hit US No. 2 and UK No. 4, boosted by the chart-topping success of the **Carole King**-penned *You've Got A Friend*, which features **Joni Mitchell** on backing vocals).

31 The **Jackson 5** plays a benefit concert at Westside High School in Gary, Indiana, in support of Mayor Richard Hatcher's re-election campaign. Jackson Street is renamed Jackson 5 Boulevard for the day, and the group is given the keys to the city.

"I haven't really listened to *Layla*. I listened to some of it, though, and I didn't dig it too much."

Paul Kossoff, **Sounds**, March 20, 1971

19 The case to dissolve the **Beatles**' partnership begins in the High Court in London. Under oath, **Ringo** claims that "Paul behaved like a spoiled child." Nonetheless, the judge will rule in **McCartney**'s favor on March 12.

27 **David Bowie** arrives in the US for his first visit. He is not to perform live during this trip because of work permit restrictions, but he attracts publicity by deciding to wear dresses at a number of promotional events in Texas and California.

February

8 **Frank Zappa** is forced to cancel a planned **Mothers of Invention** performance of his work "200 Motels," with the Royal Philharmonic Orchestra, at London's Royal Albert Hall, after venue officials declare the libretto to be obscene. Undaunted, Zappa will proceed with the making of the "200 Motels" movie, a fictionalized documentary about the Mothers, with guest appearances by **Ringo Starr** and **Keith Moon** of the **Who**, among others.

15 **Pete Townshend**'s "Lifehouse" – a multimedia project devised to "completely negate anybody's desire to see rock in its current form" – begins a short run on Monday nights at the Young Vic theater in London. Townshend has written the music for the **Who**'s next double album, but will scrap the idea, retaining a few songs for what will emerge as the single LP, ***Who's Next***.

The lyrics to *Amazing Grace*, sung by Judy Collins, were written in 1772 by John Newton after his conversion from slave trader to abolitionist.

THE OSMOND BROTHERS

Feb 21 **The Osmond Brothers perform their current US No. 1, *One Bad Apple*, on CBS-TV's "The Glen Campbell Goodtime Hour." The five siblings – Alan, Wayne, Merrill, Jay, and 13-year-old Donny – born in Ogden, Utah, to devout Mormons George and Olive Osmond, are already seasoned television veterans. Last year they were signed to M-G-M Records by label president Mike Curb, who is eager to market them as a new Jackson 5. Aware of Donny's teen-idol appeal, Curb has also signed him to a parallel solo contract, and Donny will score two million-selling singles before the end of this year: *Sweet And Innocent* (US No. 7) and *Go Away Little Girl*, his first No. 1.**

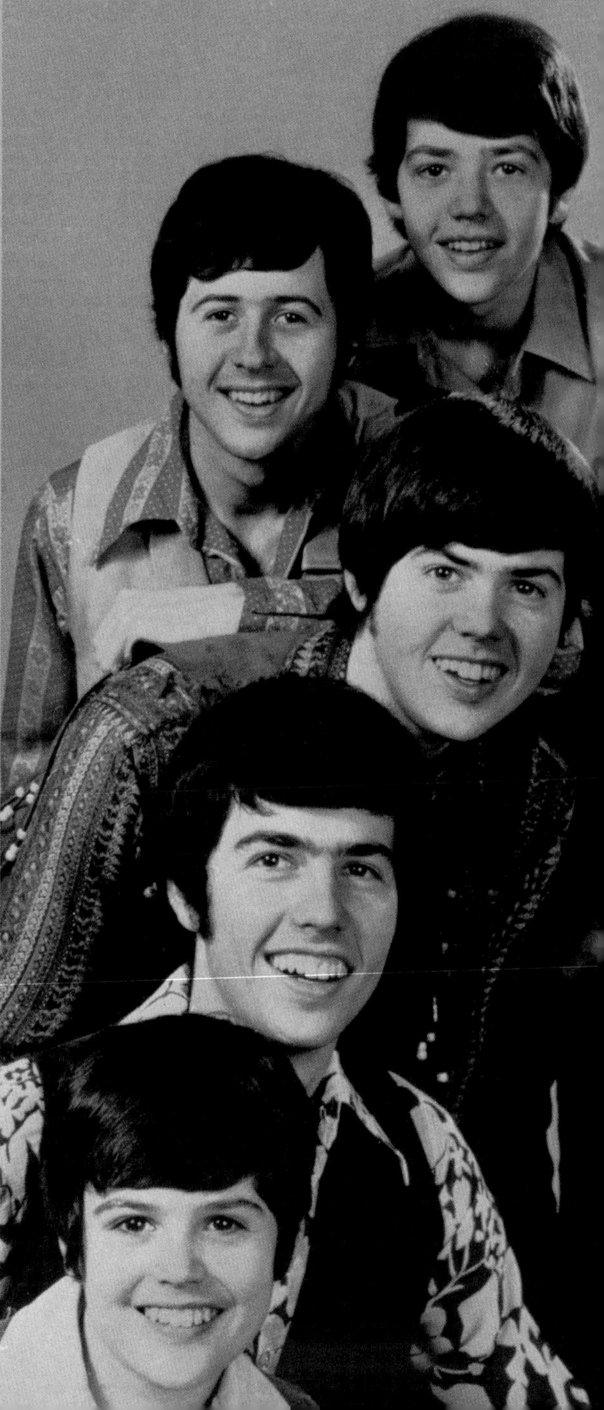

Frank Zappa recorded *200 Motels* with the help of the Los Angeles Philharmonic Orchestra and its conductor Zubin Mehta.

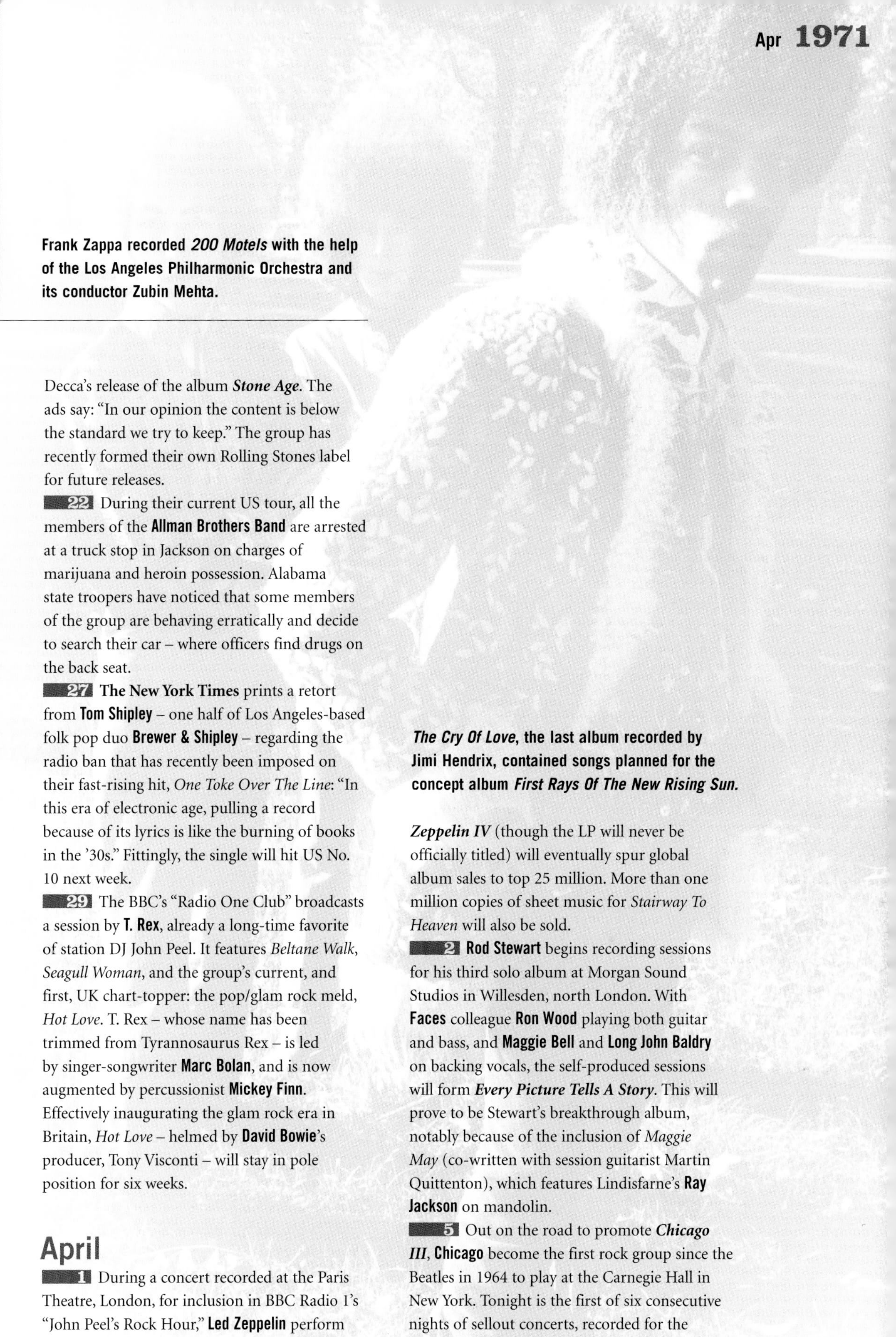

The Cry Of Love, the last album recorded by Jimi Hendrix, contained songs planned for the concept album *First Rays Of The New Rising Sun.*

20 **Judy Collins**'s arrangement of the traditional standard *Amazing Grace*, recorded in St. Paul's Chapel at Columbia University and taken from her current album, ***Whales And Nightingales***, reaches US No. 15 and hits UK No. 5. It is her biggest UK hit, and will enjoy one of the longest runs in UK chart history. Initially on the survey for 32 weeks, and continuing in the lower regions via constant re-entries, it will move up to No. 20 in mid-1972 and finally exit in January 1973, after 67 weeks.

March

3 **Elton John** performs a 21-song set before a capacity crowd at London's Royal Festival Hall. The event is billed as "The first major London concert appearance of Elton John with Orchestra," and is filmed for subsequent television broadcast. John and his band play with the Royal Philharmonic Orchestra, conducted by Paul Buckmaster.

5 Having performed at the Royal Albert Hall on January 9, **Led Zeppelin** begins a "thank you" tour for their British fans, appearing in the clubs and ballrooms of their early days in 1968. They have also agreed to play for their original 1968 performance fees – if the promoters charge that year's ticket price.

8 WPAX Hanoi, a radio station created in New York by Abbie Hoffman and his fellow Yippies (members of the Youth International Party), who make tape recordings for transmission via Radio Hanoi to US troops in Vietnam, opens its first broadcast with **Jimi Hendrix**'s *Star-Spangled Banner*.

16 As expected, **Simon & Garfunkel** dominate the 13th annual Grammy Awards, held at the Hollywood Palladium. *Bridge Over Troubled Water* is named Record of the Year, Song of the Year, and Best Contemporary Song. Its companion album picks up the main prize, Album of the Year, beating out the **Carpenters**, **Chicago**, **Crosby, Stills, Nash & Young**, **Elton John**, and **James Taylor**. The Carpenters are named Best New Artist, and *Close To You* wins them Best Contemporary Vocal Performance by a Duo, Group, or Chorus.

20 At their own expense, the **Rolling Stones** place full-page advertisements in all the UK's music papers disclaiming any connection with Decca's release of the album ***Stone Age***. The ads say: "In our opinion the content is below the standard we try to keep." The group has recently formed their own Rolling Stones label for future releases.

22 During their current US tour, all the members of the **Allman Brothers Band** are arrested at a truck stop in Jackson on charges of marijuana and heroin possession. Alabama state troopers have noticed that some members of the group are behaving erratically and decide to search their car – where officers find drugs on the back seat.

27 **The New York Times** prints a retort from **Tom Shipley** – one half of Los Angeles-based folk pop duo **Brewer & Shipley** – regarding the radio ban that has recently been imposed on their fast-rising hit, *One Toke Over The Line*: "In this era of electronic age, pulling a record because of its lyrics is like the burning of books in the '30s." Fittingly, the single will hit US No. 10 next week.

29 The BBC's "Radio One Club" broadcasts a session by **T. Rex**, already a long-time favorite of station DJ John Peel. It features *Beltane Walk*, *Seagull Woman*, and the group's current, and first, UK chart-topper: the pop/glam rock meld, *Hot Love*. T. Rex – whose name has been trimmed from Tyrannosaurus Rex – is led by singer-songwriter **Marc Bolan**, and is now augmented by percussionist **Mickey Finn**. Effectively inaugurating the glam rock era in Britain, *Hot Love* – helmed by **David Bowie**'s producer, Tony Visconti – will stay in pole position for six weeks.

April

1 During a concert recorded at the Paris Theatre, London, for inclusion in BBC Radio 1's "John Peel's Rock Hour," **Led Zeppelin** perform a new **Page/Plant** composition, *Stairway To Heaven*. When the show airs on the weekend, it will be the first time the song is played on the radio. The group has already recorded it at their Headley Grange studio, and at Island Studios in London, during sessions for their upcoming fourth album. *Stairway To Heaven* – a mystical 7:55 minute rock opus – will become the most played rock song ever on FM radio in the US. Its inclusion on what will become known as ***Led Zeppelin IV*** (though the LP will never be officially titled) will eventually spur global album sales to top 25 million. More than one million copies of sheet music for *Stairway To Heaven* will also be sold.

2 **Rod Stewart** begins recording sessions for his third solo album at Morgan Sound Studios in Willesden, north London. With **Faces** colleague **Ron Wood** playing both guitar and bass, and **Maggie Bell** and **Long John Baldry** on backing vocals, the self-produced sessions will form ***Every Picture Tells A Story***. This will prove to be Stewart's breakthrough album, notably because of the inclusion of *Maggie May* (co-written with session guitarist Martin Quittenton), which features Lindisfarne's **Ray Jackson** on mandolin.

5 Out on the road to promote ***Chicago III***, **Chicago** become the first rock group since the Beatles in 1964 to play at the Carnegie Hall in New York. Tonight is the first of six consecutive nights of sellout concerts, recorded for the forthcoming four-album set ***Chicago At Carnegie Hall***.

6 **Carly Simon**, a 25-year-old New Yorker newly signed to Elektra Records, performs her first concert. Currently promoting her maiden release, ***Carly Simon***, she opens for **Cat Stevens** at the Troubadour in Los Angeles, with backing band members **Jim Ryan**, **Paul Glanz**, and **Russ Kunkel**. At the end of her set, **James Taylor** goes backstage to meet her.

Stevie Wonder turns 21... *American Pie*... Jim Morrison dies...

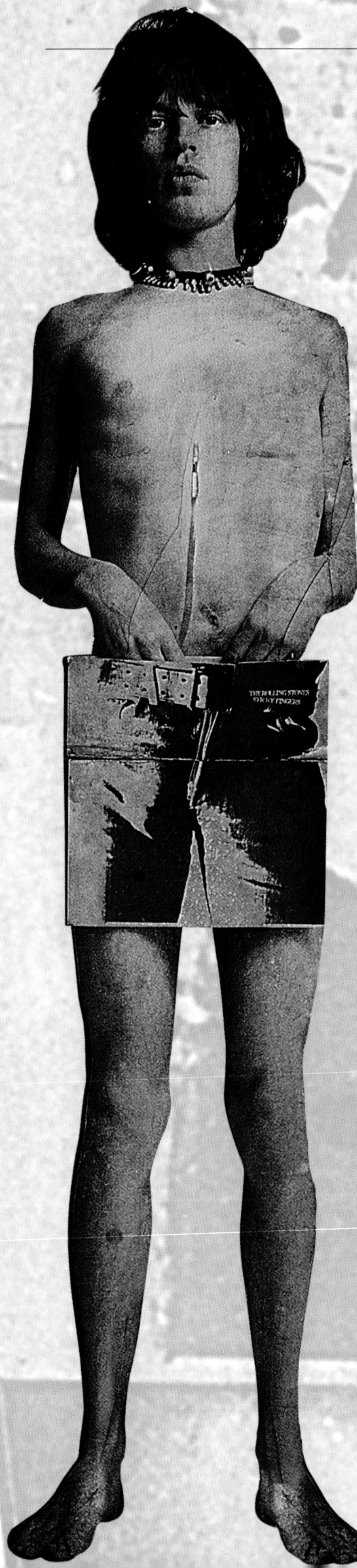

23 The **Rolling Stones** launch their record label, and introduce ***Sticky Fingers***, their latest album, with a media reception on the French Riviera. The album has an Andy Warhol-designed sleeve showing a male torso clad in jeans, complete with a real zipper. It features musical guests **Billy Preston**, **Jim Price**, **Bobby Keyes**, **Ry Cooder**, **Jack Nitzsche**, and the ever-present **Ian Stewart**, and is highlighted by the label's first single, *Brown Sugar*.

26 **John Lennon**, **George Harrison**, and **Ringo Starr** drop their planned appeal against **Paul McCartney**'s moves to dissolve the **Beatles**.

"Sticky Fingers may well plunge the [Rolling] Stones into a controversy over rock lyrics now raging between the Federal Government and American radio stations." ***Time***, 1971

May

12 **Mick Jagger** marries Bianca Perez Morena de Macias at Chapelle St. Anne in St. Tropez. The guest list includes assorted **Stones**, **Paul McCartney**, **P.P. Arnold**, **Ringo Starr**, **Eric Clapton**, **Michael Shrieve** and **David Brown** of **Santana**, and **Stephen Stills**. Police chief Jean-Pierre Harambourne recruits two **Daily Mirror** reporters to help the couple make their way through the attendant throng.

13 On his 21st birthday **Stevie Wonder** receives all his childhood earnings; despite having grossed in excess of $30 million, he receives only $1 million. His contract re-negotiations with Motown will result in the formation of his autonomous Taurus Productions and Black Bull Publishing companies.

20 **Chicago**'s lead singer **Peter Cetera** is involved in a serious brawl with four men – who allegedly object to the length of his hair– at a Los Angeles Dodgers home baseball game against the Chicago Cubs. Cetera loses four teeth and has to undergo five hours of emergency dental surgery.

29 At a **Grateful Dead** Winterland Ballroom concert in San Francisco, 36 fans require medical attention after unknowingly drinking cider laced with LSD.

Ticket scalpers charged up to £10 for tickets to the Rolling Stones farewell concert. If only they knew...

Grand Funk Railroad fired their manager, Terry Knight, in 1972, setting off an acrimonious series of multi-million dollar lawsuits.

June

1 **Elvis Presley**'s birthplace in Tupelo is opened to tourists. Meanwhile, his new album, ***Love Letters From Elvis*** – recorded last year in Nashville – is released this week, and will shortly become his 52nd charted LP in the US.

5 Breaking the **Beatles**' box-office record, an appearance at New York's Shea Stadium by **Grand Funk Railroad** – booked by legendary promoter Sid Bernstein – sells out in only 72 hours, grossing $306,000 in ticket sales. The group is currently on the road to promote their fourth straight platinum-selling album, ***Survival***.

10 Before a 10,000-plus crowd, **Jethro Tull** – promoting its current smash album, ***Aqualung*** – play in a cloud of tear gas at the Red Rock Amphitheater in Denver, after police fire canisters into the audience.

20 **David Bowie** plays a solo acoustic set at the hippy-attended Glastonbury Fayre Festival, held at Worthy Farm, Pilton, Somerset, UK.

26 *American Pie* – written and performed by 25-year-old singer-songwriter/guitarist **Don McLean**, and recorded last month – receives its first radio play, on New York station WNEW-FM. The title track from his forthcoming second album, ***American Pie***, it is – against all convention – an 8:36 minute single divided into two parts, a musical opus that documents rock 'n' roll Americana, most notably referencing **Buddy Holly**'s death as "the day the music died."

July

3 **Jim Morrison** is found dead by his girlfriend, Pamela Courson, at an apartment at 17, Rue Beautreillis, Paris, where they are staying during a sabbatical in France. They went out to see a movie last night, returned home, and went

CAROLE KING

June 18 Carole King performs at New York's Carnegie Hall, with guest James Taylor. Tomorrow, her double A-side *It's Too Late/I Feel The Earth Move* will hit US No. 1, at the beginning of a five-week run. Its parent album, the landmark *Tapestry*, will also top the album survey. The self-penned set, featuring Taylor and her regular sidemen, bass player Charles Larkey, guitarist Danny "Kootch" Kortchmar, and drummer Russ Kunkel, has been produced by Lou Adler. It will stay at No. 1 for 15 weeks during a phenomenal 302-week chart tenure, eventually selling over 15 million copies worldwide (although its certification by the RIAA will be overlooked until the late 1990s).

Before Carole King topped the US chart with *It's Too Late* she had accumulated 72 hits as a writer.

Graffiti near Jim Morrison's grave

Don McLean

Jim Morrison's tombstone reads "Kata ton daimona eay toy", Greek for "True to his own spirit"... Don McLean spent the latter part of the 1960s as the New York State Council of the Arts' "Hudson River Troubadour".

to bed. Morrison – complaining of chest pains during the night – rose early to take a bath. Courson has woken to find his motionless body still in the bathtub. The official cause of death is given as "heart failure," but the authorities will fail to perform an autopsy, leading to much speculation as to whether drugs were involved. Morrison's personal effects are given to Courson. A copy of his death certificate will be sent to his father, Admiral George S. Morrison, at the Pentagon, on August 11.

6 The most widely known and best-loved jazz performer in the world, **Louis Armstrong**, suffers a heart attack one month before his 70th birthday, and dies in New York. An enormously popular entertainer, singer, trumpet player, and actor, "Satchmo" even scored No. 1 pop crossover hits on both sides of the Atlantic – *Hello Dolly* in the US in 1964, and *What A Wonderful World* in the UK four years later. His funeral in New York will attract a crowd of 25,000, and a traditional funeral march will be performed in his honor through the streets of New Orleans, his home town. He will be buried at Flushing Cemetery in Queens.

9 His family having disowned him, **Jim Morrison** is buried in the cemetery of Père Lachaise in Paris, which contains the remains of such luminaries as Oscar Wilde, Edith Piaf, Frédèric Chopin, and Honoré de Balzac.

12 Recorded by the Australian/British pop vocal group the **New Seekers** on an Italian hilltop last year, and already broadcast as a jingle on radio, a Coca-Cola television commercial based on the lyric *I'd Like To Buy The World A Coke* begins airing in the US. It features 200 young people clutching bottles of Coke and miming to the recording. Spurred by phenomenal viewer response, the song's British writers, **Roger Greenaway** and **Roger Cook**, will amend the lyrics and the New Seekers will hastily re-record the nugget. With all references to Coke removed, the song will begin charting around the world in December – billed as *I'd Like To Teach The World To Sing*.

17 **John Lennon** and **Yoko Ono** are guests on the fifth edition of the BBC's new late night talk show, "Parkinson." Lennon intercepts and refutes host Michael Parkinson's question to Yoko: "Recently, another reason for people taking a dislike to you, is because you're known, again through the newspapers, as the woman who broke up the Beatles." Lennon retorts: "That's not true. I tell you, people on the streets and kids do not dislike us. It's the media. I'm telling ya. We go on the streets and the lorry drivers wave, 'Hello John, hello Yoko,' all that jazz, and I judge it by that. My records still sell well. Her records sell all right." He adds: "The British press actually called her ugly. I've never said that about any woman or man, even if the person is ugly."

22 During a year of non-stop gigging, **Slade** play their first London gig at the Marquee club. The Wolverhampton-based quartet, comprising singer/guitarist **Noddy Holder**, guitarist **Dave Hill**, bassist/pianist/violinist **Jim Lea**, and drummer **Don Powell**, first played together as the **'N Betweens** in 1966. They changed their name to **Ambrose Slade** before being picked up in 1969 by manager **Chas Chandler**, who launched **Jimi Hendrix**'s career in Britain. After cutting a few sides for Fontana Records, the band signed to Polydor, and is scoring with its first hit, *Get Down And Get With It*. In an attempt to cash in on the UK's current skinhead cult, Chandler has decked the group out in "bovver" boots and suspenders to complement their short-cropped hair.

"I think we are what a lot of kids in Britain have been looking for. A pop band who play their music well; we play songs and not long extended pieces, and we look OK."

Sweet's Andy Scott, **Melody Maker**, July 1971

July

1971

Marvin Gaye's *What's Going On*...
The Concert for Bangla Desh...
Bowie and Warhol meet...

Gilbert O'Sullivan

31 **Marvin Gaye**'s ***What's Going On*** hits US No. 6. The critically lauded album has been solely produced and mostly written by Gaye – with the notable exception of the million-selling, peace-themed title cut, which hit US No. 2 on April 10. *What's Going On* was conceived by **Four Tops** singer **Renaldo Benson** in 1969, after he witnessed violent clashes between protesters and San Francisco police over a disused urban area called People's Park. When Gaye heard the song – augmented by co-writer Al Cleveland – he immediately empathized with its lyrical bent and added the finishing touches. Its soul-dripping parent album is a creative tour de force, and a major change in direction for Gaye. It addresses themes of urban survival, war, and the environment – and spins off two further US hits: *Mercy Mercy Me (The Ecology)*, and *Inner City Blues (Make Me Wanna Holler)*.

August

1 After a personal plea from his friend **Ravi Shankar**, **George Harrison** has organized the Concert for Bangla Desh, in aid of its victims of famine and war. It is the largest benefit concert to date, with two shows held in one day at Madison Square Garden in New York. The line-up includes **Eric Clapton**, **Bob Dylan**, **Billy Preston**, **Leon Russell**, **Ringo Starr** (who fluffs the lines to his current hit, *It Don't Come Easy*), and Shankar, with musical backing from **Badfinger**, **Jesse Ed Davis**, **Jim Horn**, **Jim Keltner**, **Don Nix**, and **Carl Radle**. Legal problems will result in the proceeds being frozen, and Harrison will write his own check to maintain the fund. The event is filmed for posterity, and recorded for release as Harrison's second triple album set, ***The Concert For Bangla Desh***, which will hit US No. 2 and UK No. 1 early next year.

3 **Paul McCartney** announces the formation of his new band, **Wings**, comprising himself and his wife **Linda**, ex-Moody Blues guitarist **Denny Laine**, and **Denny Seiwell** on drums.

7 The **Bee Gees**' plaintive ballad *How Can You Mend A Broken Heart*, written by **Barry** and **Robin** when they were reconciled after a

Bob Dylan made his only live appearance of the year at the Concert for Bangla Desh, organized by George Harrison.

Gilbert O'Sullivan played in a band called Rick's Blues, led by future Supertramp founder Rick Davies... Isaac Hayes's Shaft opened with the memorable line, "Who's the black private dick that's a sex machine to all the chicks?"

15-month rift, hits US No. 1, where it will stay for four weeks, becoming another million-seller and a long-term US radio staple.

8 Irish singer-songwriter/pianist **Gilbert O'Sullivan** performs his new UK hit, *We Will*, on "It's Lulu," a weekly variety series on BBC1 hosted by the perky Scottish lass. Sporting a bowl haircut, the singer performs in his familiar garb: vest, tie, old shirt, suspenders, knee-length trousers, hobnail boots, and a cloth cap. O'Sullivan has been signed by impresario Gordon Mills, who manages **Tom Jones** and **Engelbert Humperdinck**, to his newly formed MAM label.

13 R&B saxophone great **King Curtis** – who contributed the memorable sax line to the Coasters' hit *Yakety Yak* – is stabbed to death during an argument outside his apartment building on West 86th Street in New York City.

30 Having spent the morning together at their estate, Tittenhurst Park in Sunningdale, **John Lennon** and **Yoko Ono** fly from Heathrow Airport to New York. The singer will never set foot on British soil again.

31 Bringing their second lawsuit in six weeks, the **Rolling Stones** and **Brian Jones**'s father file a High Court writ against their former manager Andrew Oldham, and Eric Easton, for "royalty deprivation." The band is alleging that the two men made a secret deal with Decca Records in 1963, and that Oldham persuaded Brian Jones to accept 6 percent of the wholesale record price as the Stones' share, while Decca was paying Oldham and Easton 14 percent. At the same time, Oldham retained a 25 percent group management contract.

"If we hadn't been related, we would probably never have gotten back together." Robin Gibb of the Bee Gees on the group's reconciliation, **Time**, 1971

September

8 **Elvis Presley** receives the Bing Crosby Award from the National Academy of Recording Arts and Sciences. It is given to performers who "during their lifetimes, have made creative contributions of outstanding artistic or scientific significance to the field of phonograph records." He is the sixth recipient, following **Bing Crosby**, **Frank Sinatra**, **Duke Ellington**, **Ella Fitzgerald**, and **Irving Berlin**.

9 **David Bowie** signs to RCA records in New York, the day before he meets Andy Warhol for the first time at the artist's Factory complex.

17 **Pink Floyd** – the only non-classical act at a music festival in Montreux – performs its latest progressive opus, "Atom Heart Mother."

21 Recently signed to Warner Bros., the acoustic folk/rock trio **America** – comprising **Dewey Bunnell**, **Gerry Beckley**, and **Dan Peek** (all sons of US air force officers stationed in the UK), perform on the first edition of a new BBC2 rock show, "The Old Grey Whistle Test." Hosted by the reverential, softly spoken, "whispering" Bob Harris, the series will distinguish itself from "Top Of The Pops" by its earnest selection of acts, all of whom perform live. Initially produced in a tiny studio on the fourth floor of Broadcasting House in London, it will become a popular and influential television fixture until 1987.

24 "Shaft," a movie starring Richard Roundtree as private detective John Shaft, premieres in American theaters. The most prominent of a number of "blaxploitation" films, it is directed by Gordon Parks, who enlisted 29-year-old ex-Stax session man and R&B songwriter/keyboardist/saxophonist/producer/arranger **Isaac Hayes** – who was turned down for the lead role – to write and perform the score. Featuring an instantly memorable wah-wah guitar lick and staccato brass hooks, *Theme From Shaft* will top the US chart for the first two weeks in November, becoming a million-selling single and a signature hit for Hayes.

30 **Yes** begin a 23-date UK tour at the De Montfort Hall in Leicester, with ex-**Strawbs** keyboard player **Rick Wakeman** making his live debut with the band. The progressive rock quintet formed in 1968 around lead vocalist **Jon Anderson**, bassist **Chris Squire**, and drummer **Bill Bruford**, and they got their biggest break when they opened for **Cream** at the latter's farewell concert at the Royal Albert Hall in London. They subsequently recruited guitarist **Steve Howe** and signed to Atlantic Records, and recently finished recording their third album, ***Fragile***.

October

2 "Soul Train" – a new weekly R&B show set in a club-like atmosphere with dancers – begins national syndication on US television, initially picked up in seven markets. This first broadcast features **Gladys Knight & the Pips**, ex-**Temptations** singer – and now solo – **Eddie Kendricks**, **Honey Cone** (a Los Angeles-based vocal trio who recently scored the US No. 1 smash, *Want Ads*), and newcomer **Bobby Hutton**. The series is hosted and produced by ex-WVON Chicago radio announcer Don Cornelius, who filmed a pilot in 1969 that appealed to the Sears Roebuck Company. He was offered funding in exchange for the rights to use "Soul Train" to promote a new line of record players. With this investment, Cornelius launched the show on WCIU-TV, a Chicago UHF station, before relocating to Hollywood with the help of a new sponsor, the Johnson Products Company, which manufactures Afro-Sheen hair products.

Marvin Gaye's *What's Going On?* was conceived by the Four Tops' Renaldo Benson after he had witnessed clashes between protestors and the police.

Oct 1971

Rod Stewart's transatlantic chart-topper... Duane Allman dies... Ziggy Stardust... John Lennon's *Imagine*...

9 **Rod Stewart** becomes one of a select number of artists to achieve a chart-topping single and album in both the UK and US in the same week. *Maggie May*, flipped to the A-side following its release as the B-side to his cover of Tim Hardin's *Reason To Believe*, begins five weeks at UK No. 1, having hit pole position in the US at the beginning of a six-week ride last week. Its parent album, ***Every Picture Tells A Story***, is in its second week astride both the US and UK album surveys.

12 Having returned to the US to scrape some money together, and now staying with his parents in Saugus, California, rock 'n' roll pioneer **Gene Vincent** – who has suffered severe leg pains ever since a motorcycle accident in 1955 – trips and falls, causing his stomach ulcers to hemorrhage. He is taken to Inter-Valley Hospital in Newhall, where he dies, age 36.

15 **Rick Nelson** is booed for playing new material alongside his old hits at the seventh annual Rock 'n' Roll Revival concert at Madison Square Garden, where he is sharing a bill with **Gary "US" Bonds**, the **Coasters**, the **Shirelles**, **Bobby Rydell**, **Bo Diddley**, and **Chuck Berry**. In response, he will pen *Garden Party* – his first Top 10 US hit in nine years.

David Bowie revealed his bisexuality in a January 1972 interview with Melody Maker.

23 Making his network television debut on "American Bandstand," 24-year-old Arkansas-born soul/gospel singer-songwriter **Al Green** performs his current hit, *Tired Of Being Alone* and its follow-up, *Let's Stay Together*. Meanwhile, on "Soul Train," 26-year-old **Freda Payne**, an R&B singer from Detroit, sings her UK No. 1 and US No. 3 smash, *Band Of Gold*. Her slot follows R&B veteran family group the **Staple Singers** – fronted by 55-year-old **Roebuck "Pops" Staples** and signed to Stax – performing their current crossover hit, *Respect Yourself*. Although their family name is Staples, the group's name is the Staple Singers.

29 Riding his motorcycle home from a birthday party for band colleague **Berry Oakley**'s wife, Linda, 24-year-old guitarist **Duane Allman**, founding member of the **Allman Brothers Band**, crashes when trying to avoid a truck just outside Macon. He is pronounced dead after three hours of surgery at the Macon Medical Center.

November

1 The **Allman Brothers Band** perform *Stormy Monday*, *In Memory of Elizabeth Reed*, and *Statesboro Blues* at **Duane Allman**'s funeral, at the Memorial Chapel in Macon, joined by **Thom Doucette** (harmonica), **Dr. John** (guitar), **Bobby Caldwell** (drums), and **Delaney Bramlett** (vocals). Allman is buried at Rose Hill Cemetery.

8 **Paul McCartney** launches ***Wings Wildlife*** with a bash at the Empire Ballroom, Leicester Square, London, with music provided by **Ray McVay & His Band of the Day**, and dancing by the Frank & Peggy Spencer Formation Team.

8 **David Bowie** begins work on a new album at Trident Studios in London's Soho, recording *Rock 'n' Roll Star* (later retitled *Star*)

JOHN LENNON

Oct 30 Already widely acclaimed as his most rounded solo work, *Imagine* by John Lennon tops both the US and UK charts in the same week. The album was produced by John and Yoko with Phil Spector, and recorded in a series of sessions in May, using an eight-track studio installed in Lennon's Tittenhurst Park mansion. The set, which contains two thinly veiled attacks on Paul McCartney – *Crippled Inside* and *How Do You Sleep?* – features the backing unit of Nicky Hopkins (piano), Jim Keltner and Alan White (drums), and Klaus Voormann (bass). Guest musicians include George Harrison on guitar, Badfinger, the late King Curtis, Mike Pinder (Moody Blues) on tambourine, Jim Gordon on drums, and the ubiquitous Spector. The (white) piano-led, utopian-themed title ballad, *Imagine*, will hit US No. 3, and will be revered as the artist's signature solo moment.

Freehold, New Jersey singer/songwriter Bruce Springsteen founded his 10-piece *The Bruce Springsteen Band* with a horn section and girl singers.

"I cannot see how the single is such a big hit. It has no melody."

Rod Stewart on his transatlantic chart-topper *Maggie May*, **New Musical Express**, October 9, 1971

Deep Purple's *Machine Head* topped the UK chart in April 1972. It also became the band's only multi-platinum-selling record in the US.

and *Hang On To Yourself*. Most of the project will be wrapped up in two weeks, to emerge as the expression of Bowie's first conceptual incarnation, "Ziggy Stardust." The final version of *Ziggy Stardust* will be nailed later this week.

18 Following a series of brain operations, blues singer/harmonica player **Little Junior Parker** dies, age 39, in Blue Island, Illinois. Parker scored a major R&B hit for Sun Records with *Feelin' Good* in 1953, and also wrote the classic *Mystery Train*, covered by **Elvis Presley** the following year.

18 **Procol Harum** perform with the Edmonton Symphony Orchestra and the Da Camera Singers, at the Jubilee Auditorium in Edmonton, Alberta. The show mainly consists of newly arranged versions of earlier album tracks, and is recorded for a live album release next year.

23 With their second hit, the foot-stomping pop-rock anthem *Coz I Luv You* currently at UK No. 1 (they will deliberately misspell all the titles of their next six hits), **Slade** finally arrive in Bremerhaven, Germany, 26 hours behind schedule. They set out for a week of promotional television appearances in Europe two days ago, but their ferry caught fire in a Force 9 gale, and several passengers had to be taken off the ship on stretchers.

December

3 **Deep Purple** – whose current album is entitled ***Fireball*** – are recording in Montreux Casino, when the building burns to the ground during a set by **Frank Zappa**'s **Mothers of Invention**. The British group will immortalize the incident in *Smoke On The Water*, which will appear on their next album, ***Machine Head***.

4 **Sly & the Family Stone**'s third US chart-topper – *It's A Family Affair*, written and produced by **Sly** – begins a three-week reign at US No. 1. The track is taken from the critically revered ***There's A Riot Goin' On***, which will also hit the top spot in two weeks' time.

10 **Frank Zappa** is playing in London and has just finished an encore of *I Want To Hold Your Hand* when he is pushed off the stage into the orchestra pit by 24-year-old Trevor Howell, the jealous boyfriend of an ardent female Zappa fan. Zappa breaks a leg in several places, and suffers a fractured skull. His recuperation will involve nine months in a wheelchair, and three more in a surgical brace.

30 **Bob Marley** – a 26-year-old Jamaican reggae singer-songwriter – visits Island Records' founder, Chris Blackwell, at his London office. Marley, the son of British army captain Norval Sinclair Marley, who came from Liverpool, is already a major star in Jamaica as lead singer/guitarist with the **Wailin' Wailers**, a group he co-founded in 1964 with guitarist/singer **Peter Tosh** and percussionist/singer **Bunny Wailer**. During the 1960s he has been working with Jamaica's top reggae producers, including **Leslie Kong** and **Lee "Scratch" Perry**. Blackwell will sign Marley and the Wailers to a long-term recording deal via their own Tuff Gong label, formed in Jamaica earlier in the year. The Wailers have been brought over to Europe by American singer **Johnny Nash** – who is fusing reggae into his repertoire – to form his backing band for a UK tour of high schools.

While Slade were enjoying their first No. 1 with *Coz I Luv You*, they performed at the Black Prince Pub in Bexley Kent.

ROOTS **During this year: Alan Gorrie and "Molly" Duncan invite fellow Scots Roger Ball and Onnie McIntyre to form a soul group that also play instruments; adding more Scots later, they become the Average White Band... Peter Criss places an ad in *Rolling Stone*: "Drummer willing to do anything to make it." Gene Simmons and Paul Stanley contact him... Kraftwerk make their TV debut on "Beat Club," performing *Truckstop Gondolero*... Gram Parsons meets an aspiring country/folk singer, Emmylou Harris, at Clyde's, a Washington, D.C. bar... Canvey Island R&B/rock band Dr. Feelgood back former Tornado, Heinz, as they begin to gain favor on the burgeoning UK pub-rock circuit... waitress Annie Lennox meets Dave Stewart in Pippins restaurant in Hampstead, London... Mudcrutch, led by Tom Petty, make their first recordings, financed by Gerald Maddox, a bell pepper farmer from Bushnell, Florida, at Miami's Criteria Studios, under the tutelage of producer Ron Albert... Linda Ronstadt books Glenn Frey, Don Henley, Bernie Leadon, and Randy Meisner to back her on a three-month road trip... and singer-songwriter/pianist Tom Waits is spotted by his future manager, Herb Cohen, performing at Los Angeles' famous Troubadour haunt, playing his own subterranean brand of songs on "Amateur Hoots Nights"...**

Children Of The Revolution

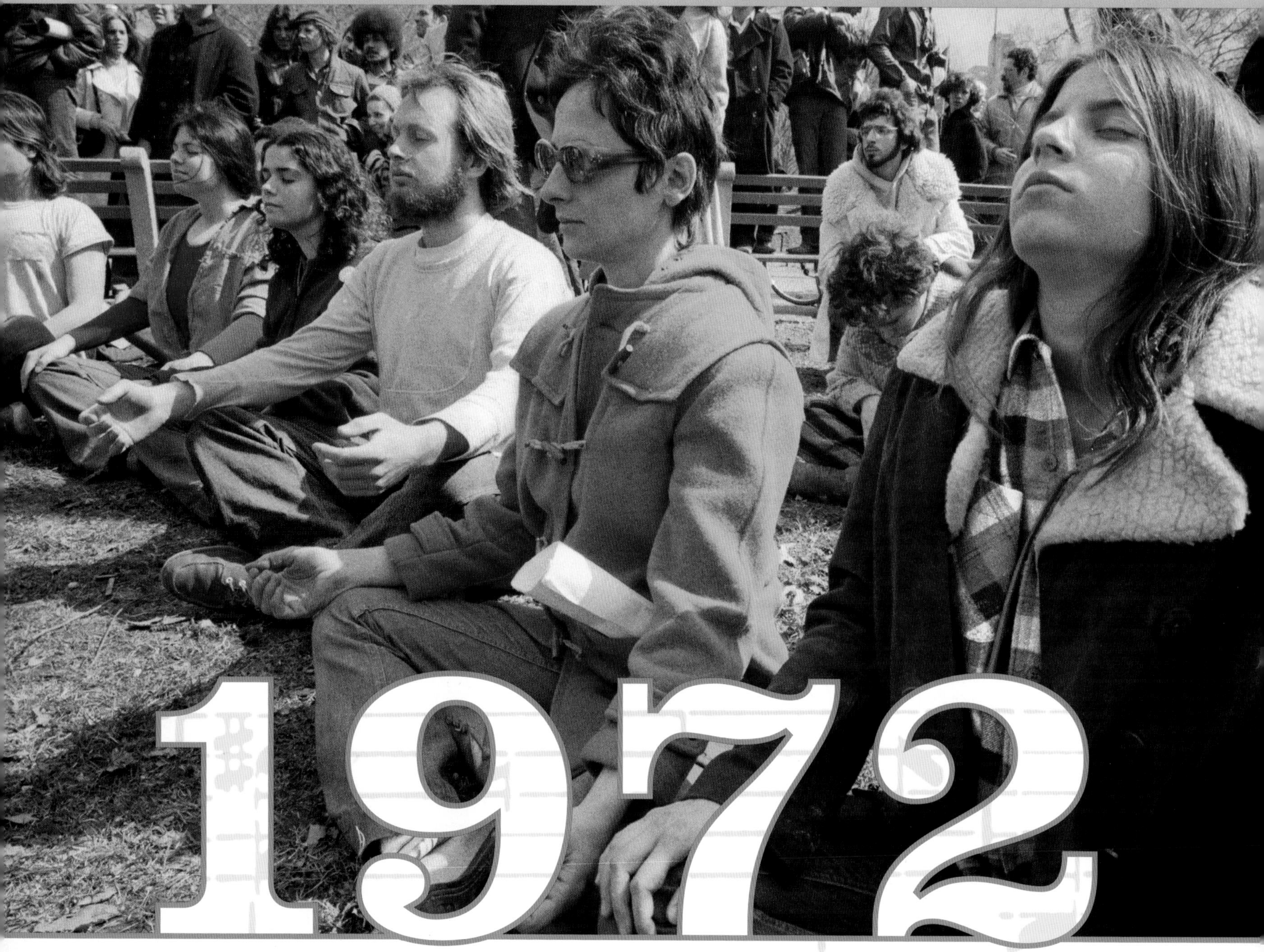

1972

No.1 US SINGLES

Jan 1 Brand New Key **Melanie**
Jan 15 American Pie – Parts I & II **Don McLean**
Feb 12 Let's Stay Together **Al Green**
Feb 19 Without You **Nilsson**
Mar 18 Heart Of Gold **Neil Young**
Mar 25 A Horse With No Name **America**
Apr 15 The First Time Ever I Saw Your Face **Roberta Flack**
May 27 Oh Girl **Chi-Lites**
June 3 I'll Take You There **Staple Singers**
June 10 The Candy Man **Sammy Davis Jr.**
July 1 Song Sung Blue **Neil Diamond**
July 8 Lean On Me **Bill Withers**
July 28 Alone Again (Naturally) **Gilbert O'Sullivan**
Aug 26 Brandy (You're A Fine Girl) **Looking Glass**
Sept 2 Alone Again (Naturally) **Gilbert O'Sullivan**
Sept 16 Black & White **Three Dog Night**
Sept 23 Baby Don't Get Hooked On Me **Mac Davis**
Oct 14 Ben **Michael Jackson**
Oct 21 My Ding-A-Ling **Chuck Berry**
Nov 4 I Can See Clearly Now **Johnny Nash**
Dec 2 Papa Was A Rollin' Stone **Temptations**
Dec 9 I Am Woman **Helen Reddy**
Dec 16 Me And Mrs. Jones **Billy Paul**

No.1 UK SINGLES

Jan 1 Ernie (The Fastest Milkman In The West) **Benny Hill**
Jan 8 I'd Like To Teach The World To Sing **New Seekers**
Feb 5 Telegram Sam **T. Rex**
Feb 19 Son Of My Father **Chicory Tip**
Mar 11 Without You **Nilsson**
Apr 15 Amazing Grace **Pipes & Drums of the Royal Scots Dragoon Guards**
May 20 Metal Guru **T. Rex**
June 17 Vincent **Don McLean**
July 1 Take Me Bak 'Ome **Slade**
July 8 Puppy Love **Donny Osmond**
Aug 12 School's Out **Alice Cooper**
Sept 2 You Wear It Well **Rod Stewart**
Sept 9 Mama Weer All Crazee Now **Slade**
Sept 30 How Can I Be Sure **David Cassidy**
Oct 14 Mouldy Old Dough **Lieutenant Pigeon**

Cat Stevens

Pink Floyd

1972 gave Cat Stevens his first chart-topper with *Catch Bull At Four* – the first of four consecutive Top 10 albums... Pink Floyd premiered a new work entitled *Eclipse* in February. It evolved into *Dark Side Of The Moon.*

Glamor, self-indulgence, and camping it up – these were the watchwords of a musical year when the political and social conscience of the 1960s already seemed a generation away. Maybe escapism was excusable in a year that included the killings at the Munich Olympics, the Watergate burglary, and the biggest B-52 bombing raids yet on Vietnam.

David Bowie outraged (most) parents across Britain by announcing his bisexuality and then delivering a limp-wristed *Starman* on TV. But this would be his blue-ribbon year, with ***The Rise And Fall Of Ziggy Stardust And The Spiders From Mars*** album and tour. Theatrical ephemera and outlandish costumes were part of the package offered by **Alice Cooper**, **Elton John**, and **T. Rex.** Shock-rocker Cooper used a guillotine and electric chair as props, and a live snake as part of his wardrobe. The mutinous *School's Out* was his breakthrough anthem. **Roxy Music** showed up with **Brian Eno** on keyboards to perform *Virginia Plain* – the first hit for **Bryan Ferry**, highly influenced by Warhol's pop art. There were cheap imitations, as always. **Gary Glitter** burst upon the British stage with the chant of *Rock 'n' Roll* – all chest-hair and tinsel costumes.

"Serious" rock bands also embraced theatrics. **Genesis** added symphonic overtones to their brand of progressive rock. Fittingly, the group made its US debut at New York's Philharmonic Hall, displaying the full range of **Peter Gabriel**'s costume (and mood) changes. Fellow British acts **Yes** and **Emerson, Lake & Palmer** also took their popular progressive rock brands across the pond. **Carly Simon**'s *You're So Vain* (with **Mick Jagger** on backing vocals) seemed an apt riposte to the posing. Supposedly addressed to a composite of friends and lovers (including husband **James Taylor**), it typified the laid-back, autobiographical material so popular with songwriters in 1972.

Folk-rock provided an alternative for those who couldn't stomach the showmanship. **Cat Stevens**'s *The Teaser and The Firecat* made its full impact worldwide this year – the reflective antidote to the times from a reclusive 23-year-old. The **Eagles** branded a much less tortured combo of West Coast rock, folk, and country, with their debut album and lead-off single, *Take It Easy*. It was left to two ex-Beatles to wear a social conscience. The BBC banned **Paul McCartney**'s *Give Ireland Back To The Irish*, while US radio gave similar treatment to **John Lennon** and **Yoko Ono**'s *Woman Is The Nigger Of The World*, a bold advocacy of women's rights betraying the influence of hippie-radical Jerry Rubin.

While glam took center stage in 1972, **Pink Floyd** labored long and hard in the Abbey Road studios vacated by the **Beatles**. By the end of the year the work was nearly complete. **Roger Waters** remarked: "I'm obsessed with truth and how the futile scramble for material things obscures our path to a more fulfilling existence. That's what ***The Dark Side Of The Moon*** is about."

Nov 11 Clair **Gilbert O'Sullivan**
Nov 25 My Ding-A-Ling **Chuck Berry**
Dec 23 Long-Haired Lover From Liverpool **Little Jimmy Osmond**

"I think [people] see me as a new kind of woman, very strong, very, very liberated... big smile, big teeth..."

Carly Simon, **Rolling Stone**, January 20, 1972

Jan

1972

Paul McCartney's Wings on the road... Grammys for Carole King...

January

13 **Stevie Wonder** begins a British tour at London's Hammersmith Odeon, having recently completed his new album, ***Music Of My Mind***, which sees him moving in a more serious and soulful direction.

22 In this week's **Melody Maker**, **David Bowie** – who married Mary Angela Barnett two years ago – reveals his bisexuality in an interview with journalist Michael Watts, claiming: "I'm gay." He says he always has been, "even when I was David Jones." He also predicts: "I'm going to be huge, and it's quite frightening in a way." Discussing his penchant for wearing women's clothes, Bowie says: "I just don't like the clothes that you buy in shops. I don't wear dresses all the time, either. I change every day. I'm not outrageous. I'm David Bowie."

22 **Curtis Mayfield**, who recently left the Impressions and has set up his own Curtom label, performs his debut solo single *Move On Up* on "Soul Train." The R&B giant is currently working on the film soundtrack ***Superfly***, which will bring him two top ten US hits by the end of the year.

31 On the theme of the long-standing conflict in Northern Ireland, **Paul McCartney** finishes writing and recording *Give Ireland Back To The Irish*, less than 24 hours after the events of "Bloody Sunday," during which British paratroopers fired into a civil rights demonstration in Derry, killing 13 Catholics. The record will instantly be banned by the BBC.

February

9 With **Paul McCartney** eager to take a grassroots approach, **Wings** embark on their first British tour, arriving at colleges unannounced and asking social secretaries if they would like the band to perform in their hall that evening. Tonight's opening gig is at Nottingham University. With new recruit ex-**Grease Band** guitarist **Henry McCullough** added to the line-up, the 11-date series will finish at the end of the month at Oxford University.

10 Currently Britain's biggest pop band, **T. Rex** begin their first headlining US tour in Seattle. They will score two UK chart-topping singles, including the anthemic *Metal Guru*, with another pair hitting UK No. 2 before the end of the year.

THE EAGLES

Mar 13 The Eagles – a country rock quartet formed last year in Los Angeles and recently signed to Asylum Records – begin recording sessions for their debut album with producer Glyn Johns at Olympic Studios in London. The ten songs, recorded in three weeks by singer/guitarist Glenn Frey, drummer Don Henley, bassist Randy Meisner, and guitarist Bernie Leadon, will be issued as *Eagles* on June 1, and will immediately find favor on American FM radio, eventually reaching US No. 22. Two of the tracks – *Nightingale* and *Take It Easy* (their first hit single) – were co-written by Jackson Browne, a 23-year-old singer-songwriting friend whose *Jackson Browne* debut has recently been issued as Asylum's second album release. Both acts were signed to the nascent label by its founder, David Geffen, an ambitious impresario/manager from Brooklyn who has already helped to steer the careers of Joni Mitchell and Crosby, Stills, Nash & Young.

The Eagles recorded their debut album – the epitome of California soft/rock – in the leafy suburbs of Barnes in south-west London.

Curtis Mayfield

John Lennon at Immigration

Neil Young

Curtis Mayfield's *Superfly* was the singer's first gold record... The authorities were more concerned with John Lennon's anti-war stance than his four-year-old drug conviction... Neil Young's *Harvest* featured Crosby and Nash but not Stills.

11 Introducing his new Ziggy Stardust stage persona, flamboyant rocker **David Bowie** embarks on a lengthy UK tour at the Lanchester Arts Festival in Coventry. His regular backing band – led by guitarist **Mick Ronson**, with **Trevor Boulder** on bass and **Woody Woodmansey** on drums – performs as the **Spiders from Mars**.

14 **John** and **Yoko Lennon** begin a five-day run as guest hosts of the US syndicated television talk show, "The Mike Douglas Show." They interview libertarian Ralph Nader and actor Louis Nye, and music is provided by the Chambers Brothers and the Lennons themselves, who perform *It's So Hard* with their new backing band, **Elephant's Memory**. Increasingly eclectic groups of guests will appear during the week, including the US Surgeon General, a macrobiotic chef, and **Chuck Berry**.

17 **Pink Floyd**'s new work, ***The Dark Side Of The Moon*** (working title "Eclipse"), written by Roger Waters, is previewed at the Rainbow Theatre, Finsbury Park, London, in the first of four consecutive nightly shows.

19 **Nilsson**'s epic ballad *Without You* tops the US chart for the first of four weeks. While recording in the UK last year with producer **Richard Perry**, Brooklyn-born singer-songwriter Harry Nilsson heard **Badfinger**'s original rendering, written by the group's **Pete Ham** and **Tom Evans**, and decided to record his own version. Its Perry-helmed parent album, ***Nilsson Schmilsson***, also hits US No. 3. Both will be certified gold by the RIAA on March 3, before *Without You* goes on to spend five weeks at UK No. 1 on March 11.

March

1 **John Lennon** is threatened with deportation from the US when his immigration visa runs out. It is the start of a long battle with the authorities, which will involve secret investigations by the FBI. The Immigration and Naturalization Service is claimed to be concerned about his 1968 conviction for drug possession.

10 Allen Klein presents a $1 million check to UNICEF in New York – the first royalty revenue from sales of ***The Concert For Bangla Desh***.

11 **Neil Young**'s fourth solo album, ***Harvest***, hits US and UK No. 1. Its success is spurred by the global smash, *Heart Of Gold* – featuring 25-year-old ex-**Stone Poneys** singer **Linda Ronstadt**, and **James Taylor** on backing vocals – which will top the US Hot 100 next week. A mostly acoustic affair, the album includes the anti-redneck *Southern Man* (which will prompt Southern rock combo **Lynyrd Skynyrd** to respond with *Sweet Home Alabama*), and the ballad *A Man Needs A Maid*, written about his girlfriend, actress Carrie Snodgress. Variously co-produced with Elliot Mazer, Henry Lewy, and Jack Nitzsche, it also features contributions from **David Crosby** and **Graham Nash**.

14 **Carole King**'s ***Tapestry***, the best-selling album of 1971, is named Album of the Year at the 14th annual Grammy Awards, held at New York's Felt Forum in Madison Square Garden. King dominates the ceremony, also winning Record of the Year (*It's Too Late*), Song of the Year (*You've Got A Friend*) and Best Pop Vocal Performance, Female (*Tapestry*). **James Taylor**'s version of *You've Got A Friend* wins him Best Pop Vocal Performance, Male, and **Quincy Jones**'s *Smackwater Jack* is named Best Pop Instrumental Performance. Although **Bill Withers** – a 33-year-old soul singer-songwriter/guitarist from West Virginia, signed to Sussex Records – is edged out by **Carly Simon** as Best New Artist, his *Ain't No Sunshine* is named Best Rhythm & Blues Song.

> **"We were locked into an image and style of music and there was nothing for us to look forward to."**
>
> John Kay, on the announcement of Steppenwolf's break-up, February 14, 1972

16 **John Lennon** lodges an appeal with the US Immigration and Naturalization Service in New York, after being served with a deportation order arising from his 1968 conviction for possession of cannabis. If he leaves the country – either voluntarily or by force – it is unlikely that he will be allowed to return. As a result, New York will become his permanent home.

18 **T. Rex** plays the first of two sellout dates at the Empire Pool, Wembley – the venue's first rock concerts. The event is filmed by first-time director, **Ringo Starr**, for inclusion in the Apple documentary on the group's success, "Born to Boogie," which will also feature **Elton John**.

18 The **Chi-Lites** – an R&B vocal group from Chicago, fronted by Eugene Record – make their second appearance on "Soul Train" singing their fast-rising soul nugget, *Oh Girl*, which will hit US No. 1 on May 27.

Nilsson was a computer specialist at the Security First National Bank in Van Nuys, California, before he began a career in music.

1972

Columbia signs Bruce Springsteen... *The Dark Side Of The Moon*... Roxy Music...

April

7 The **Grateful Dead** opens a European trek at the Empire Pool, Wembley, beginning a 22-date tour that will also take in Denmark, West Germany, France, Holland, and Luxembourg.

10 Draped in chains and emerging from beneath the stage in clouds of smoke, **Isaac Hayes** performs *Theme From Shaft* – winner of the Best Original Song category – at the 44th annual Academy Awards, held at the Dorothy Chandler Pavilion of the Music Center in Los Angeles. His complete soundtrack to the film loses out to *Summer Of '42* by **Michel Legrand** as Best Music, Original Dramatic Score.

16 The **Electric Light Orchestra** makes its live debut at the Greyhound pub in Croydon England. It marks the demise of popular English beat group the **Move**, as the new classical/rock/pop fusion ensemble has been assembled by **Move** frontman **Roy Wood** and his fellow Brummies, 24-year-old lead singer-songwriter/guitarist **Jeff Lynne**, and drummer **Bev Bevan**. Central to the band's mini-orchestral sound is a string section currently led by cellist **Hugh McDowell**. Wood will leave the group in July to form the more pop-aimed **Wizzard**.

May

3 **Les Harvey** – 25-year-old co-founder and lead guitarist with British blues-rock combo, **Stone the Crows**, and younger brother of Scottish rock singer **Alex Harvey** – is fatally electrocuted on stage during a gig at Swansea University in Wales. Touching a loose connection on a microphone lead, he receives a massive jolt and is tossed into the air. He dies three hours later in a local hospital. Singer **Maggie Bell** – Harvey's girlfriend and co-founder of the group – is hospitalized suffering from shock.

11 Currently at No. 2 in the UK and promoting his recently released debut solo album, *Cherish*, **David Cassidy** is featured bare-chested on the cover of **Rolling Stone**.

18 The New York Times reports that **Paul McCartney** and the **Beatles** have reached an out-of-court settlement – in part to release about £10 million ($23 million) currently held in escrow because of their legal fight.

June

3 The **Rolling Stones** begin a sellout eight-week North American tour in Vancouver, in support of their new double album *Exile On Main Street*. With **Stevie Wonder** and **Martha Reeves** as the opening acts, the Stones play for an hour and 40 minutes in front of 17,000 fans; 30 policemen are injured by gatecrashers.

5 **George Harrison** and **Ravi Shankar** are honored with the "Child is Father to the Man" award by UNICEF, in thanks for their efforts to aid famine relief in Bangla Desh.

9 At the behest of label executive John Hammond, 22-year-old singer-songwriter/guitarist **Bruce Springsteen** signs a worldwide, ten-year, ten-album recording contract with Columbia Records for an advance of $25,000, with a $40,000 recording budget. The deal follows intense negotiations by his manager Mike Appel. Springsteen, based in New Jersey, has played in several bands over the past seven years, including the **Castles**(in high school), **Earth**, **Child**, **Steel Mill**, and **Dr. Zoom & The Sonic Boom**. Nine months ago, he formed the **Bruce Springsteen Band**, with local musicians **David Sancious** (keyboards), **Garry Tallent** (bass), guitarist **Steve Van Zandt**, drummer **Vini Lopez**, keyboard player **Danny Federici**, and saxophonist **Clarence Clemons**. Columbia sees him as a solo folk performer but Springsteen will take his band into 914 Sound Studios in Blauvelt, New York, to record his first album in three weeks' time.

13 **Clyde McPhatter**, former lead singer of **Billy Ward & the Dominoes**, and the **Drifters**, dies in Teaneck, New Jersey, following long-time addictions to alcohol and drugs. He is 39.

17 During a gig at Oxford Town Hall, a photographer takes a picture of **David Bowie** erotically "licking" **Mick Ronson**'s guitar.

David Bowie walked on stage at London's Royal Festival Hall for a Save The Whales benefit in July and proclaimed "I'm Ziggy."

PINK FLOYD

June 1 **Pink Floyd begins recordings for the group's first concept album, the epic *The Dark Side Of The Moon.* Taking eight months to complete – and with a theme of "madness" prominent – many of its quirky vocal snippets will be from interviews of people around Abbey Road Studios, including the doorman, Jerry Driscoll, who will contribute its final spoken words: "There is no dark side of the moon, really. Matter of fact, it's all dark." The engineer, 22-year-old Alan Parsons (who previously worked on Beatles cuts), will add many sound effects, notably the clock montage leading into track 3, *Time.* The prismic sleeve artwork is created by the Hipgnosis design team.**

To Ronson's displeasure, the photo will appear in **Melody Maker**, before finding its way into the tabloid press.

20 Currently opening for **Rory Gallagher** on a UK tour, **Roxy Music** makes its television debut on "The Old Grey Whistle Test," performing the group's first single, *Virginia Plain*. The art-rock combo was formed last year by stylish frontman and vocalist **Bryan Ferry**, saxophonist **Andy Mackay**, and electronics expert and synthesizer player**Brian Eno**. They recently signed to Island Records, via a production deal with London-based E.G. Management. With guitarist **Phil Manzanera** added to the core line-up in February, the group recorded their first album, ***Roxy Music***, in March at Command Studios in London. The recording cost £5,000 ($11,500), and was produced by ex-King Crimson lyricist **Pete Sinfield**.

20 Mississippi's Tallahatchie Bridge collapses. The landmark has been a popular attraction since it was immortalized in **Bobbie Gentry**'s 1967 US chart-topper *Ode to Billie Joe*.

22 **Rolling Stone** publishes a rare interview by notoriously media-shy singer-songwriter **Van Morrison** (who recently wound up a US tour with two nights at the Winterland in San Francisco). He reflects on his upcoming album: "Y'know, I had planned to quit working for several months after this [tour], but now I'm not so sure. First I gotta finish up the album so they can get it out by July. We changed the title from ***Green*** to ***Saint Dominic's Preview***. I've still got two more songs I've got to put together and right now I don't know where they're gonna come from. I'm pretty confused right now, but, y'know, I've got a feeling that everything's starting to come together. I think it's all gonna work out."

July

1 In Philadelphia, the **Spinners** (known in Britain as the Detroit Spinners, to avoid confusion with the British folk group) record *I'll Be Around* and *How Could I Let You Get Away* at the Sigma Sound Studios. The R&B vocal group began in 1955 as the **The Domingos**, and spent much of the 1960s in the frustrating position of being one of the few virtually hitless acts at Motown. They recently recruited a new lead singer, **Philippe Wynne**, and were brought to Atlantic Records at the suggestion of **Aretha Franklin**. The label has paired them with songwriter/producer **Thom Bell**, who is working (freelance) at Sigma with **Kenny Gamble** and **Leon Huff**, founders of the Philadelphia International label. The double A-side recording will reverse the group's fortunes, becoming a million-seller and the first of 19 US chart hits garnered by the Spinners/Bell combination over the next six years. Bell is using a similar formula at the same studio with another soul quintet, the **Stylistics**, who have scored with *You Are Everything* and *Betcha By Golly, Wow*, written and produced by him.

Roxy Music opened for Alice Cooper at the Empire Pool, Wembley in July, garnering most of the positive press reviews.

July 1972

Trouble for the Rolling Stones... Peter Frampton's solo debut... Philadelphia soul...

Paul and Linda McCartney were arrested for possession of cannabis hours before performing a concert in Gothenberg, Sweden.

3 In Memphis, **"Mississippi" Fred McDowell** dies from abdominal ulcers and cancer, at the age of 68. The influential singer-songwriter/guitarist performed in a traditional Delta blues style with a bottleneck twist, continuing a legacy begun by **Charlie Patton** and **Son House**, and was a popular fixture at blues/folk festivals during the 1960s. McDowell's *You Gotta Move* was covered by the **Rolling Stones** on last year's ***Sticky Fingers*** album, while the slide guitar style of 22-year-old blues-rock newcomer **Bonnie Raitt** – learned from listening to McDowell – will be in evidence on her upcoming second album, ***Give It Up***.

9 **Wings** makes their formal concert debut at the Théâtre Antique in Chateauvallon, France, at the start of a 25-date European and Scandinavian tour. The band is traveling in a converted double-decker London bus.

16 At the end of a six-month farewell US tour, **Smokey Robinson**, who since 1970 has wanted to leave the **Miracles** to pursue his own projects, makes his last appearance with the group at the Carter Barron Amphitheater in Washington. He tells reporters: "We've had a gas." He will stay at Motown to launch his solo career.

23 **Mick Jagger**, **Keith Richards**, and three members of the Rolling Stones' retinue – Stanley Moore, Marshall Chess, and Robert Frank – are arrested at T.F. Green Airport in Warwick, Rhode Island, on their way to a concert at Boston Garden, after an altercation with **Providence Journal** photographer Andy Dickerman. Boston Mayor Kevin White, interceding on their behalf, phones the Rhode Island governor to get them released on bail. The show eventually starts at 12:30 am. Richards and Moore will file suit against the newspaper.

August

5 The first Rock 'n' Roll Revival Show is held at Wembley Stadium near London, and features **Bill Haley**, **Chuck Berry**, **Little Richard**, **Emile Ford**, **Heinz**, **Billy Fury**, **Jerry Lee Lewis**, **MC5**, **Wizzard**, and **Bo Diddley**. The 50,000 people who attend the event, mostly "Teddy boys" and greasers, give the performers a poor reception, and even boo Little Richard off the stage. Also on the bill is rising British glam-pop star **Gary Glitter**, whose dance-chant pop anthem, *Rock 'n' Roll*, hit UK No. 2 in June. The 30-something Glitter – real name Paul Gadd – has been performing, with little success, since 1958, under a succession of pseudonyms including Paul Russell, Paul Raven, Paul Monday, and even Rubber Bucket. Last year's image switch introduced glitter bodysuits and huge platform shoes, and – teamed with co-writer, producer, and long-time collaborator, **Mike Leander** – Glitter's first single success will also hit No. 7 in the US (where it will eventually become a popular crowd chant at sporting events).

19 The first edition of NBC television's "Midnight Special" is broadcast, featuring **War** performing their recent US No. 16 million-selling hit, *Slippin' Into Darkness*. Last year, ex-**Animals** frontman **Eric Burdon** quit the seven-piece blues-based rock outfit, which he had recruited as his new backing band in 1969.

> **"Slade handle their music with the delicacy of a demolition gang on a works outing ... They are everything parents must hate in modern society."**
>
> **The Times**, September 8, 1972

21 **Grace Slick** is maced, and **Paul Kantner** slightly injured, when a scuffle ensues after **Jefferson Airplane**'s equipment manager calls police "pigs" during a show at the Rubber Bowl in Akron, Ohio. Police also arrest a protesting **Jack Casady** and drag him off stage.

30 **John** and **Yoko Lennon** host a One To One benefit concert in New York's Madison Square Garden. Guests **Stevie Wonder** and **Roberta Flack** join Lennon and **Elephant's Memory** for a rousing *Give Peace A Chance* finale. Over $250,000 is raised to aid mentally handicapped children.

September

7 In the week that **Slade** achieves a third UK No. 1 in four releases, with *Mama Weer All Crazee Now*, the band flies home to London during a US tour, to headline the opening of the Sundown concert venue in the Mile End Road.

10 **Iggy Pop** and the **Stooges** – **Ron** and **Scott Asheton**, and **James Williamson** – begin four weeks of sessions at London's CBS Studios that will

In a career spanning more than 35 years, Leon Huff and Kenny Gamble have written more than 100 US hits – five of which topped the charts.

evolve into Raw Power. The recordings will be mixed by Bowie and Pop, with Williamson producing.

16 Ex-**Humble Pie** Pie guitarist **Peter Frampton** makes his solo stage debut in New York City, opening for the **J.Geils Band**, and backed by his own new backing band, **Frampton's Camel**. He is on the road to promote his solo debut, *Wind Of Change.*

27 **Rory Storm** (real name, Alan Caldwell), one-time leader of Merseybeat band, **Rory Storm & the Hurricanes**, commits suicide using alcohol and pills at his home in Liverpool. His mother is also found dead in the house, which will lead to speculation about a suicide pact.

October

10 All remaining lawsuits between the **Rolling Stones**, Allen Klein's company ABKCO, Decca, Eric Easton, and Andrew Oldham are finally settled.

14 British music trade paper Music Week reports that, according to EMI, ten years after the release of *Love Me Do*, worldwide record sales by the **Beatles** and the group's solo ex-members stand at a total of 545 million.

16 **Creedence Clearwater Revival** issues a press statement announcing their decision to split: "We will devote our time to individual rather than group projects." The group has racked up six multimillion-selling albums in four short years, but **Tom Fogerty** left in February last year, and his brother, frontman and chief songwriter **John Fogerty**, is increasingly at odds with both the band and their record label, Fantasy. He will continue recording, adopting a bluegrass/country-rock style that he will market under the name the **Blue Ridge Rangers**.

21 On "Soul Train," the **O'Jays** – a veteran R&B vocal trio from Canton, Ohio, comprising **Eddie Levert**, **Walter Williams**, and **William Powell** – perform their breakthough crossover US No. 3 hit, *Back Stabbers*. The group is signed to the two-year-old Philadelphia International label, formed by **Kenny Gamble** and **Leon Huff**, who are quickly becoming the new Holland/Dozier/Holland. Gamble and Huff are writing and producing a slew of top-drawer, catchy, R&B hits – collectively known as the "Sound of Philadelphia" – for recent signings **Harold Melvin & the Blue Notes** (fronted by **Teddy Pendergrass**), who are currently scoring with the US No. 3 smash ballad, *If You Don't Know Me By Now*, the O'Jays, and local singer **Billy Paul** – whose single *Me And Mrs. Jones* will give the label its first chart-topper in December.

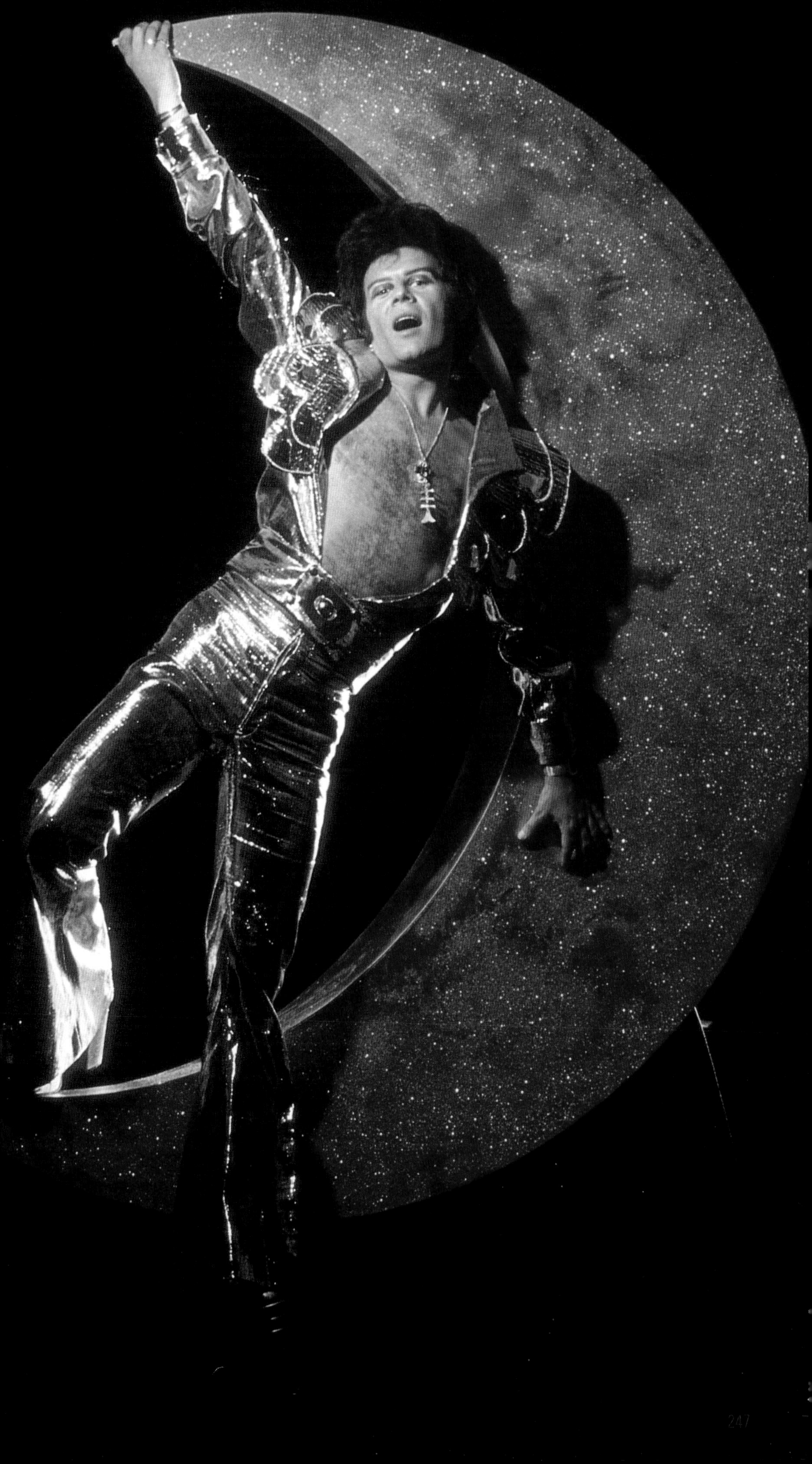

Gary Glitter buried his Paul Rave persona in January 1973 by placing all vestiges of his form self in a coffin and released it to the bottom of the Thames.

Carly and James marry... Genesis' concert debut... MC5 bow out...

Drummer Billy Murcia was the first New York Doll to succumb to a drug-related death – he wouldn't be the last.

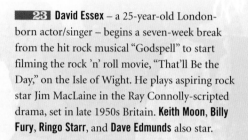

23 **David Essex** – a 25-year-old London-born actor/singer – begins a seven-week break from the hit rock musical "Godspell" to start filming the rock 'n' roll movie, "That'll Be the Day," on the Isle of Wight. He plays aspiring rock star Jim MacLaine in the Ray Connolly-scripted drama, set in late 1950s Britain. **Keith Moon**, **Billy Fury**, **Ringo Starr**, and **Dave Edmunds** also star.

November

1 Following a live debut last month at Under the Ice House in Glendale, California, **Steely Dan** begins a week-long residency at Max's Kansas City in New York. Steered by producer **Gary Katz**, who recently relocated them to Los Angeles, the two songwriters – keyboard player/singer **Donald Fagen** and bass player **Walter Becker** – are augmented by guitarists **Jeff "Skunk" Baxter** and **Denny Dias**, vocalist **David Palmer**, and drummer **Jim Hodder**. Next week they will return to Los Angeles to finish recording their debut album, ***Can't Buy A Thrill***, during exacting and meticulous sessions at the Village Recorder studios, for release by ABC Records next March.

3 **Carly Simon** marries singer-songwriter **James Taylor** in her Manhattan apartment. This evening she joins him on stage during the encore at New York's Radio City Music Hall, and announces the happy event to his audience.

6 Following a performance at Imperial College in London, the **New York Dolls**' 21-year-old drummer, **Billy Murcia**, dies in a Chelsea apartment, suffocating on coffee administered by his girlfriend – who is trying to wake him up. The coroner will also cite severe exhaustion as the cause of death. Reveling in a glam rock/punk image, and musically influenced by the raw vitality of the **Stooges** and **MC5**, the New York Dolls formed earlier this year in New York, around flamboyant 22-year-old frontman, vocalist **David Johansen**, and 20-year-old guitarist **Johnny Thunders**.

11 **Allman Brothers** bass player **Berry Oakley** is killed when his motorcycle collides with a bus, hurling him down the road. The accident happens in Macon, only three blocks from the site of **Duane Allman**'s death a year ago. Oakley will be buried in Macon's Rose Hill Cemetery, where Allman also lies. Both were 24.

18 **Bill Withers** makes his second appearance on "Soul Train," singing his summer US chart-topper, the self-penned ballad *Lean On Me*, and its recent US No. 2 follow-up, *Use Me*. **Harold Melvin & the Blue Notes** also appear, performing their ballad smash *If You Don't Know Me By Now*.

23 **Bob Dylan** arrives in Durango, Mexico, to start filming his role as the outlaw Alias in Sam Peckinpah's cowboy movie "Pat Garrett and Billy the Kid." Dylan will contribute three songs to the soundtrack album, including a new composition, *Knockin' On Heaven's Door*.

24 Taped earlier in the day at Hofstra University in Long Island, "Don Kirshner's Rock Concert" – created by the hugely successful

> **"Frank Zappa Sr. will give private instruction in craps, roulette, keno, and blackjack taught through mathmatics, your place or his."**
>
> **Variety**, December 8, 1972

Bob Dylan played the role of Alias and wrote the soundtrack music for Sam Peckinpah's "Pat Garrett And Billy The Kid."

David Essex started out as a drummer in a semi-pro band in East London called The Everons. Ringo Star was also a drummer... Alexander's department store in New York stayed open after hours to let Alice Cooper do his Christmas shopping.

David Essex and Ringo Starr

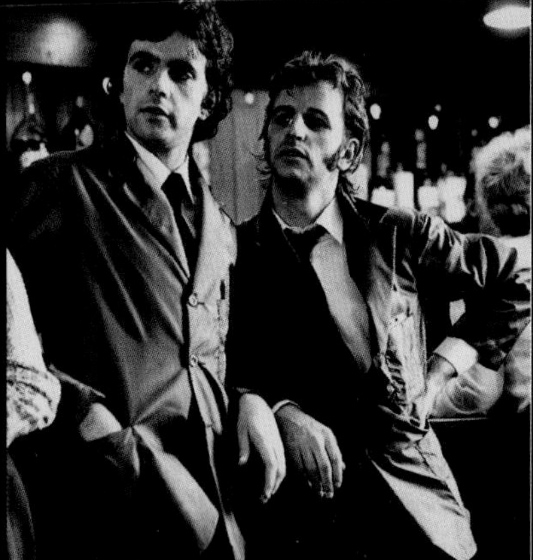

Alice Cooper

GENESIS

Dec 11 **Genesis – a progressive British art-rock group formed in 1966 by Charterhouse schoolfriends Peter Gabriel, Tony Banks, and Mike Rutherford – makes its US concert debut at Brandeis University in Waltham, Massachusetts. Their variable early line-up was finalized in 1970, with the recruitment of ex-Quiet World guitarist Steve Hackett, and drummer Phil Collins (a former child actor who appeared in a crowd scene in the Beatles' "A Hard Day's Night"). Genesis has already developed a solid following in Britain for their highly theatrical stage shows – highlighted by Gabriel's growing fondness for using theatrical props and masks – which has helped the group's recently released fourth album, *Foxtrot*, to become their first chart album at UK No. 12.**

music publisher and TV producer – premieres on ABC television. The first edition features shock-rocker **Alice Cooper**, who fronts his own band of the same name. The 24-year-old Detroit-born preacher's son scored a global smash over the summer with the rock anthem, *School's Out*. The other guests include the **Allman Brothers**, **Chuck Berry**, **Poco**, and **Seals & Crofts** – the pop duo **Jim Seals** and **Dash Crofts** – whose debut hit, *Summer Breeze*, is still charting in the US.

24 Having returned from their second short (seven-date) tour of the UK, the **Eagles** appear on the first day of the weekend-long Woodstock of the West festival in Los Angeles, sponsored by KROQ radio. Despite heavy promotion, and an impressive all-star bill that includes **Sly & the Family Stone**, **Stevie Wonder**, the **Bee Gees**, and **Mott the Hoople**, the event attracts only 32,000 people to the 100,000-seater Memorial Coliseum.

30 For the second time in ten months, the BBC bans a **Paul McCartney** single – this time the newly released *Hi Hi Hi* – after it is played once on Radio 1's "Tony Blackburn Breakfast Show."

December

6 In Nice, France, the Public Prosecutor's Office confirms that arrest warrants have been issued for **Keith Richards** and his girlfriend Anita Pallenberg, in connection with their violation of French drug laws. Richard comments: "The first that I heard of the warrant for my arrest was when I read it in the newspaper here this morning."

9 An all-star cast, including **Roger Daltrey** playing the central role, **Rod Stewart**, **Steve Winwood**, Peter Sellers, **Merry Clayton**, and **Richie Havens**, with the **Who**, give a performance of "Tommy" with full orchestra at the Rainbow Theatre in London.

11 After a concert in Knoxville, Tennessee, **James Brown**, while talking to fans about drug abuse, is arrested and charged with disorderly conduct when an informant tells police that he is trying to incite a riot. Brown subsequently threatens the Knoxville authorities with a million-dollar lawsuit, and the incident is hastily written off as a "misunderstanding."

23 In the middle of **Grand Funk Railroad**'s rehearsals for an "in concert" recording at New York's Madison Square Garden, the group's ex-manager, Terry Knight, with his attorney and two deputy sheriffs, turns up with a furniture van and a court order giving him the right to seize $1 million in money or equivalent assets, pending the settlement of outstanding lawsuits. The band's equipment is confiscated after the show.

31 **MC5** plays its last ever gig, fittingly at the Grande Ballroom in Detroit, after which the band permanently dissolves. Their fee for the night's work is $200.

ROOTS **During this year: Gordon Sumner, a St. Paul's First School teacher in Newcastle, England, joins the Newcastle Big Band; fellow jazzman Gordon Soloman gives him the nickname Sting, because of a yellow-and-black-striped soccer jersey he is prone to wear... Bernard Edwards and Nile Rodgers hook up with Tony Thompson to form rock-fusion combo, the Big Apple Band... multimedia artist Laurie Anderson makes her live debut on the town green in Rochester, Vermont, with the townsfolk beeping car, truck, and motorcycle horns... drummer Charles Smith invites his cousin Prince Rogers Nelson to join his junior high school band Grand Central... answering an ad placed in the Brighton Evening Argus, Patches – led by impish lead singer Leo Sayer – audition at the Pavilion Theater for David Courtney; impressed, Courtney signs the band and takes on Sayer as his co-writer... with financial backing from Virgin record shops' owner Richard Branson, who is planning his own record label, 19-year-old Mike Oldfield begins work at Abbey Road Studios in London on a 50-minute quasiclassical instrumental composition... and underground poet Patti Smith is making $5 a night working as an opening act at the Mercer Art Center in New York...**

Do You Wanna Touch Me (Oh Yeah)

1973

No.1 US SINGLES

Jan 6 You're So Vain **Carly Simon**
Jan 27 Superstition **Stevie Wonder**
Feb 3 Crocodile Rock **Elton John**
Feb 24 Killing Me Softly With His Song **Roberta Flack**
Mar 24 Love Train **O'Jays**
Apr 7 The Night The Lights Went Out In Georgia **Vicki Lawrence**
Apr 21 Tie A Yellow Ribbon Round The Ole Oak Tree **Dawn featuring Tony Orlando**
May 19 You Are The Sunshine Of My Life **Stevie Wonder**
May 26 Frankenstein **Edgar Winter Group**
June 2 My Love **Paul McCartney & Wings**
June 30 Give Me Love – (Give Me Peace On Earth) **George Harrison**
July 7 Will It Go Round In Circles **Billy Preston**
July 21 Bad, Bad Leroy Brown **Jim Croce**
Aug 4 The Morning After **Maureen McGovern**
Aug 18 Touch Me In The Morning **Diana Ross**
Aug 25 Brother Louie **Stories**
Sept 8 Let's Get It On **Marvin Gaye**
Sept 15 Delta Dawn **Helen Reddy**
Sept 22 Let's Get It On **Marvin Gaye**
Sept 29 We're An American Band **Grand Funk Railroad**
Oct 6 Half-Breed **Cher**
Oct 20 Angie **Rolling Stones**
Oct 27 Midnight Train To Georgia **Gladys Knight & the Pips**
Nov 10 Keep On Truckin' (Part 1) **Eddie Kendricks**
Nov 24 Photograph **Ringo Starr**
Dec 1 Top Of The World **Carpenters**
Dec 15 The Most Beautiful Girl **Charlie Rich**
Dec 29 Time In A Bottle **Jim Croce**

No.1 UK SINGLES

Jan 6 Long Haired Lover From Liverpool **Little Jimmy Osmond**
Jan 27 Blockbuster! **Sweet**
Mar 3 Cum On Feel The Noize **Slade**
Mar 31 The Twelfth Of Never **Donny Osmond**
Apr 7 Get Down **Gilbert O'Sullivan**
Apr 21 Tie A Yellow Ribbon Round The Ole Oak Tree **Dawn featuring Tony Orlando**
May 19 See My Baby Jive **Wizzard**
June 16 Can The Can **Suzi Quatro**
June 23 Rubber Bullets **10cc**

David Bowie

David Cassidy

David Bowie announced in July that he was retiring from live performance. It was in fact the last performance of the Ziggy Stardust persona... BBC-TV's "Top Of The Pops" banned teenybopper acts from appearing live on the program after a riot following David Cassidy's performance.

The theme was the depravity and meaninglessness of life; the album was dotted with snatches of dialogue and sonic fireworks: in ***The Dark Side Of The Moon*** **Pink Floyd** had created *the* concept album – whose precocity made it a staple ingredient of every college-goer's record collection.

It cast a long shadow in a year not renowned for its depth. Pretty-boy singers, such as **Donny Osmond** and **David Cassidy**, were cleverly marketed to teenage girls, and 1973's most successful example of pop-pulp was *Tie A Yellow Ribbon Round The Ole Oak Tree*, sung by **Tony Orlando & Dawn**.

R&B provided some of the most sensual sounds: **Roberta Flack**'s *Killing Me Softly With His Song* was destined to become a classic, **Marvin Gaye** switched from politics to pillow talk with *Let's Get It On*, and **Gladys Knight** was on the *Midnight Train To Georgia*. An entire album of "soul's greatest hits" could be comfortably filled without straying from 1973. **Barry White** fused catchy pop/soul melodies and sweeping arrangements to his husky growl. Disco was coming.

Not that rock was in hibernation. Some 600,000 people converged on Watkins Glen in New York – the biggest rock crowd ever assembled. The **Grateful Dead** played for five hours, the **Band** for three hours, and the **Allman Brothers** for four. Now that the Vietnam war was over, musicians rallied around less dramatic causes: the emerging **Bruce Springsteen** featured in concerts "for a non-nuclear future," and the **Rolling Stones** raised funds for the victims of Nicaragua's earthquake. Heavy rock continued to build its fan base. **Lynyrd Skynyrd** recorded the guitar-driven classic *Freebird*, which became their ticket to supporting the **Who** on tour. **Led Zeppelin** broke box office records throughout their US tour. **David Bowie**, who had sold eight million records in Britain, announced at the end of his Ziggy Stardust tour that he'd no longer play live – a typically melodramatic put-on. Significantly, he went on to mix **Iggy & the Stooges**' ***Raw Power*** – their final and most influential work. A cult band, the Stooges were exponents of an anarchic, often dirty and bluesy rock. Their stripped-down aggression would plant seeds in the minds of many a putative punk rocker.

Drugs – of one form or another – continued to be part of the fabric of rock music. **Keith Richards** was convicted of possessing marijuana. **Paul McCartney** was fined for growing it. Worse still, country-rock pioneer **Gram Parsons** – formerly of the **Byrds** and the **Flying Burrito Brothers** – died of an overdose soon after recording *Fallen Angel* with **Emmylou Harris**. **Elvis Presley** was becoming dangerously addicted to prescription drugs, but he started 1973 in spectacular fashion, with nearly 1.5 billion people around the world tuning into his "Aloha from Hawaii" concert.

June 30	Skweeze Me, Pleeze Me **Slade**
July 21	Welcome Home **Peters & Lee**
July 28	I'm The Leader Of The Gang (I Am!) **Gary Glitter**
Aug 25	Young Love **Donny Osmond**
Sept 22	Angel Fingers (A Teen Ballad) **Wizzard**
Sept 29	Eye Level (Theme from "Van Der Valk") **Simon Park Orchestra**
Oct 27	Daydreamer/Puppy Song **David Cassidy**
Nov 17	I Love You Love Me Love **Gary Glitter**
Dec 15	Merry Xmas Everybody **Slade**

"We love you Donny, oh yes we do."

The perfunctory supplication of Osmonds fans in Britain

Jan 1973

Eric Clapton's comeback... Elvis says hello from Hawaii... The Byrds break up...

January

5 Signed last November to EMI Records, **Queen** tapes its first radio session, for BBC Radio 1, in the Langham 1 studio at Broadcasting House in London. They play four songs – including their upcoming debut single *Keep Yourself Alive* – which will be broadcast on John Peel's show on February 15. Queen formed two years ago, when guitarist **Brian May** and drummer **Roger Taylor** (both ex-**Smile** members) recruited Zanzibar-born lead singer **Freddie Mercury** and bassist **John Deacon**. EMI will officially launch the group with a showcase gig at London's Marquee club on April 9.

"Lou's a changed man... like he's cut down on his drinking drastically and eats watercress sandwiches now."

A secretary at Lou Reed's Management office in New York, **New Musical Express**, April 28 1973

7 "Fanfare for Europe" is staged at the London Palladium to celebrate Britain's entry into the European Economic Community. The bill is topped by **Slade**, at the personal invitation of Prime Minister Edward Heath, purportedly a fan.

13 An all-star comeback concert for **Eric Clapton**, who has been battling heroin addiction, takes place at London's Rainbow Theatre, organized by **Pete Townshend**. Those recruited to play alongside Clapton include **Ron Wood**, **Steve Winwood**, and **Jim Capaldi**. The concert is recorded and will be released as ***Eric Clapton's Rainbow Concert***. Despite this show of support by his contemporaries, Clapton will once again retreat from the public eye.

14 "Elvis: Aloha from Hawaii" – a global **Elvis Presley** showcase – is aired live from Honolulu International Center Arena via the Intelsat IV satellite to Japan, Australia, New Zealand, South Vietnam, Thailand, Philippines, Hong Kong, Singapore, and Malaysia. The US and Europe will see a taped version, but British broadcasters decline to license it. Its worldwide audience is estimated as one billion – the largest ever for a television show. The concert raises $75,000 for the Kuiokalani Lee Cancer Fund, and Presley performs a version of Lee's best-known song, *I'll Remember You*, during the telecast.

18 The **Rolling Stones** host and perform in a benefit show at the Los Angeles Forum in aid of victims of the recent earthquake in Nicaragua (Jagger's wife Bianca is Nicaraguan). The event raises $200,000 – to which the group will add a further donation of $150,000. The 18,625 fans who show up also enjoy the music of support act, **Santana**, and the comedy of Cheech & Chong.

23 **Neil Young** stops in the middle of a Madison Square Garden concert to pass on news to the audience that an accord has been reached for peace in Vietnam. Reading a message handed to him on stage, he begins with "Peace has come" – and then has to wait ten minutes while the crowd celebrates the announcement.

Roberta Flack's *Killing Me Softly With His Song* sat atop the US chart. The singer picked up the Record of the Year at the Grammys.

Free played their last gig in February, with Osibisa's Wendell Richardson replacing Paul Kossoff on guitar.

30 Formed last year as Wicked Lester, the New York-based hard-rock quartet of bassist **Gene Simmons**, guitarist **Paul Stanley**, guitarist **Ace Frehley**, and drummer **Peter Criss** play their first show under their new name, **KISS**, at the Popcorn Club in Queens.

February

11 **Aretha Franklin**, **Roberta Flack**, **Ray Charles**, and **Chicago** appear on CBS-TV's "Duke Ellington... We Love You Madly" variety show.

13 **Elvis Presley** becomes ill during a concert in Las Vegas, and is attended by Dr. Sidney Bowers (who will receive a white Lincoln Continental in appreciation). Meanwhile, ***Aloha From Hawaii Via Satellite*** is certified gold by the RIAA.

14 During the US leg of his current world tour, an exhausted **David Bowie** – wearing a white dress for tonight's Valentine's Day gig – collapses, soon after being attacked by a male fan who tries to kiss him during a two-hour concert at Radio City Music Hall in New York.

17 **Free** – promoting their swansong album ***Heartbreaker*** – play their last gig at Florida's Hollywood Sportatorium, with **Osibisa**'s **Wendell Richardson** replacing guitarist **Paul Kossoff**. Frontman **Paul Rodgers** and drummer **Simon Kirke** will move on to form **Bad Company**.

24 The **Byrds** make their final live appearance – with **Chris Hillman** invited back to the line-up and his **Manassas** colleague **Joe Lala** filling in on drums – at the Capitol Theater in Passaic, New Jersey, after which **Roger McGuinn** will dissolve the band.

24 **Roberta Flack** scores her second US No. 1 as the soulful ballad, *Killing Me Softly With His Song*, begins a five-week run. Flack heard the original version – by singer **Lori Lieberman** – while on a TWA flight from Los Angeles to New York. It was written for Lieberman by Norman Gimbel and Charles Fox, who were inspired by her story of how emotional she felt while listening to **Don McLean** at a concert at the Troubadour in Los Angeles. Flack spent three months in the studio meticulously perfecting her version under the production of Joel Dorn.

Eric Clapton

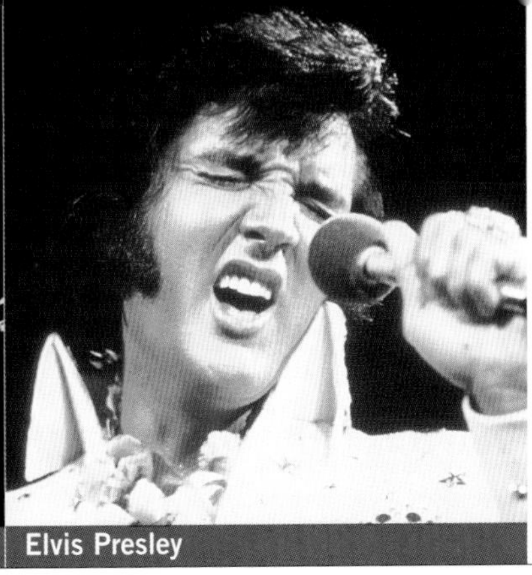

Elvis Presley

Eric Clapton (center) was enticed back onstage by Pete Townshend (right) for an all-star concert at the Rainbow Theatre in London, which also featured Ron Wood (left)... Elvis Presley won only his second Grammy – in the Religious Album category.

26 **Alice Cooper** poses for surrealist artist Salvador Dali, wearing over a million dollars' worth of diamonds loaned by Harry Winston Jewellers, and beside an anatomical model of a brain that includes the Daliesque symbols of a soft watch, a coffee eclair, and some ants. Cooper also holds a microphone in the shape of a sectioned Venus de Milo, representing "the shattering of antiquity by this rock star's voice." The sitting is filmed using a holographic process, involving a laser beam and refracted light. The three-dimensional portrait will be presented on April 3 at the Knoedler Gallery in New York City.

March

3 ***The Concert For Bangla Desh***, the recording of the August 1971 concert organized by **George Harrison**, takes the prize for Album of the Year at the 15th annual Grammy Awards. **Roberta Flack**'s *The First Time Ever I Saw Your Face* is named Record of the Year, and brings its composer, **Ewan MacColl**, the Song of the Year trophy. The Best Pop Vocal Performance award is given to **Nilsson**, for his career-defining recording of *Without You*. **Don McLean** is shut out in all four categories in which he is nominated. **Helen Reddy**, accepting the award for Best Pop, Rock and Folk Vocal Performance, Female for her US No. 1 feminist anthem, *I Am Woman*, thanks "everyone at Capitol Records, my husband and manager Jeff Wald...and God because She makes everything possible."

7 **Bruce Springsteen** plays at Max's Kansas City in New York. During the show, Columbia A&R executive **John Hammond** – who brought the singer-songwriter to the label – suffers his third (non-fatal) heart attack. His doctor will insist it was caused by Hammond's over-excitement at seeing Springsteen perform.

8 **Ron "Pigpen" McKernan** dies, aged 27, from a stomach hemorrhage and liver failure brought on by alcohol poisoning, in the yard of an apartment in Corte Madera, California. He was a founding member of **Mother McCree's Uptown Jug Champions**, who became the **Warlocks** and then the **Grateful Dead**.

17 **David Cassidy** – already an even bigger solo star in Britain than in America – performs the first pair of four shows over two days at the Empire Pool, Wembley, during a UK tour.

21 The BBC issues a ban on "teenybopper" acts appearing live on "Top Of The Pops," after a small riot accompanies today's pre-taped appearance by **David Cassidy**.

23 The Immigration and Naturalization Service orders **John Lennon** to leave the US within 60 days, beginning a new round of litigation and applications to gain the necessary "green card" to enable him to remain in the country. Lennon issues a press statement: "Having just celebrated our fourth wedding anniversary, we are not prepared to sleep in separate beds. Love and peace, John and Yoko."

24 **Lou Reed** is bitten on the butt by a fan who leaps on stage at a concert in Buffalo, New York, shouting "Leather!" The man is seized and ejected by bouncers. Reed is touring the US in support of his just-released and highly rated second solo album, ***Transformer***, which was produced in London by his fans and friends, **David Bowie** and **Mick Ronson**. It includes the hit single, *Walk On The Wild Side*, which fails to receive the expected BBC ban, despite the inclusion of the lyric "giving head."

29 New Jersey-based pop-rock combo, **Dr. Hook & the Medicine Show** – led by eyepatch-wearing singer **Ray Sawyer** – fulfill the ambition implicit in their second US smash, *The Cover Of Rolling Stone* – by appearing on the cover of the current issue of **Rolling Stone**. In the UK, the BBC is refusing to play the single because of the mention of the magazine, as it is against its charter to promote a commercial enterprise. This prompts the band to re-record the song as *The Cover Of Radio Times* (the BBC's own weekly publication). It is the group's second US million seller, following last year's No. 5 hit, *Sylvia's Mother*. Both songs were written by humorist/songwriter/author Shel Silverstein.

April

21 Don Kirshner protegés **Tony Orlando & Dawn** perform *Tie A Yellow Ribbon Round The Ole Oak Tree* on "American Bandstand." The song is the act's second US chart-topper (following 1970's *Knock Three Times*), and is spending the first of four weeks simultaneously astride both the US and UK charts. New Yorker Orlando has been encouraged to record the story-song by producers Hank Medress (ex-**Tokens**) and Dave Appell (ex-**Applejacks**), who received it from writers Irwin Levine and L. Russell Brown. It is based on the true story of a prisoner who wrote to his wife asking her to tie a yellow ribbon around an oak tree in the square of their home town – White Oak, Georgia – if she still loved him. He would look out for the ribbon as his bus rolled in.

After being bitten on the bottom by an over-zealous fan in Buffalo, New York, Lou Reed made the comment, "America seems to breed animals."

Apr 1973

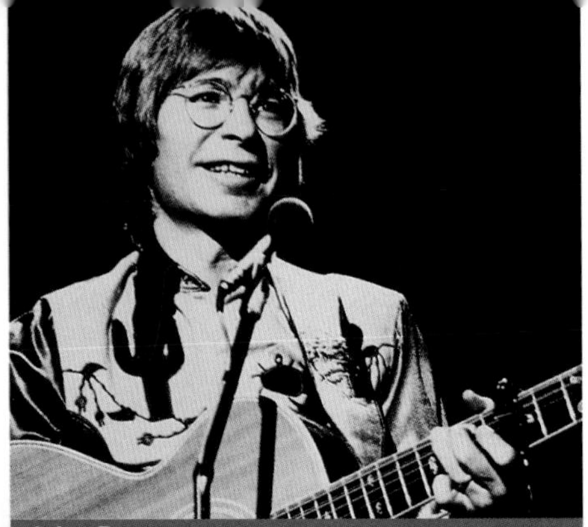
John Denver

Elton's Rocket is launched... Washington celebrates Marvin Gaye Day ... *Tubular Bells*... Watkins Glen...

26 **Elton John**'s new Rocket Records label is launched with a press junket aboard a British Rail soccer special train on a trip to the Cotswold village of Moreton-in-the-Marsh. The Moreton brass band launches into *Congratulations* in the village hall when the party arrives. Rocket signings **Mike Silver** and **Longdancer** perform, before Elton John himself takes part in an impromptu jam. The company is co-owned with lyricist Bernie Taupin, producers Gus Dudgeon and Steve Brown, and manager John Reid. Its first signing is British chanteuse

Deep Purple's *Smoke On The Water* was the group's only million-seller in the US.

Bread

Mike Oldfield

Rolling Stone magazine was of the opinion that John Denver was "completely devoid of human characteristics... Bread split amid rumors of a disagreement between David Gates and James Griffin, who was apparently upset that his songs had not be released as singles... Mike Oldfield had released his first record *Children Of The Sun* as one half of Sallyangie with sister Sally when he was 15.

Kiki Dee. John himself is still signed to DJM in the UK and MCA in the US, and his own recordings won't appear on Rocket until 1976.

27 The **Wailers** begin their first British tour as headliners at Nottingham's Coleman Club. The month-long trek will take in such venues as Mr. B's in Peckham, Boobs in Bristol, Hitchin Town Hall, and Fantasia in Northampton.

29 **John Denver**, a 29-year-old American singer-songwriter who is already a rising country-pop star back home, begins a weekly live television special, "The John Denver Show," broadcast from the BBC's Shepherds Bush Green studios.

"A record that quite genuinely covers new and uncharted territory... combines logic with surprise, sunshine with rain."

John Peel describing Mike Oldfield's *Tubular Bells*

May

1 As Washington, D.C. proclaims "Marvin Gaye Day," the artist sings *What's Going On* at the city's Cardoza High School auditorium, before performing at the Kennedy Center this evening.

6 **Paul Simon** begins his first solo tour since splitting with **Art Garfunkel**, at the Music Hall in Boston. He is joined toward the end of his acoustic set by Latin American quartet **Urubamba**, and gospel group the **Jessy Dixon Singers**.

10 "James Paul McCartney" airs on ITV. A musical extravaganza, the television special features **Paul McCartney** leading a sing-along in a crowded Liverpool pub, and performing a Fred Astaire-style dance routine. It ends with a solo performance of *Yesterday*.

23 Columbia Records president **Clive Davis** is fired during tax investigations, during which it is alleged that he has used corporate money for non-business items, including $20,000 for his son's bar mitzvah and $53,700 on remodeling his New York apartment. An indomitable figure, Davis – who steered Columbia to great heights in the 1960s, and owns one of the best pairs of ears in the industry – will re-emerge to form Arista Records.

25 ***Tubular Bells*** is issued in Britain, as the first release by the fledgling Virgin Records label started by entrepreneur and Virgin music retailer Richard Branson. It is the first project of its creator, 20-year-old composer and multi-instrumentalist **Mike Oldfield**. Using 20 instruments and some 2,000 tape overdubs, the mainly instrumental recording is almost entirely the work of Oldfield, apart from contributions from ex-Bonzo Dog Doo-Dah Band vocalist **Viv Stanshall** as the narrator, **Mundy Ellis** (vocals), **Steve Broughton** (drums), and **Jon Field** (flute). A unique, landmark work – assembled at both Abbey Road and Branson's new Manor Studios – it will find both critical and commercial acclaim. It will hit US No. 3 – spurred by its main theme being used in the score for the horror movie, "The Exorcist" – and will log more than five years on the UK album chart.

June

1 At a party in London, **Soft Machine** drummer/vocalist **Robert Wyatt** falls five stories from an open window, breaking his back. He is left paralyzed from the waist down.

5 Following appearances at country-rock festivals in Baltimore and Philadelphia, in support of his groundbreaking country-rock solo debut album, ***GP***, **Gram Parsons** gives what will prove to be his last performance, at Philadelphia's Tower Theater, before returning to the studio with his girlfriend, 26-year-old country singer **Emmylou Harris**, to self-produce his next album.

21 **Bread** perform what they say will be their final show together, before a capacity crowd of 13,000 at the Salt Palace in Salt Lake City. They have to play with borrowed equipment because their tour truck rolled over following a blowout in Flagstaff, en route to the gig, and equipment worth $30,000 was wrecked.

29 **Deep Purple**'s lead vocalist, **Ian Gillan**, quits after a show in Osaka at the end of a tour of Japan, despite the success of their current – and biggest – album, ***Smoke On The Water***. Former **Marbles** singer **Graham Bonnet** will briefly replace him, before **David Coverdale** becomes the band's permanent new lead singer. **Roger Glover** will also leave, initially to become the new Purple label's A&R man. He will be replaced by **Glenn Hughes**.

July

3 **David Bowie**'s UK tour closes at the Hammersmith Odeon. At the end of the concert – which has featured special guest **Jeff Beck** – Bowie announces that he is to retire from live performing: "This show will stay the longest in our memories, not just because it is the end of the tour, but because it is the last show we'll ever do." Although he is genuinely exhausted, it eventually transpires that the Ziggy Stardust fantasy stage persona is being retired, not Bowie.

13 The personal conflict that has built up between the **Everly Brothers** finally comes to a head during a concert at the John Wayne Theater at Knott's Berry Farm in Hollywood. Entertainment manager Bill Hollinghead, unhappy with **Don**'s performance, stops the show midway through the second set. **Phil** smashes his guitar and storms off stage. Don performs the third set solo and announces the break-up with the caustic remark, "The Everly Brothers died ten years ago." The siblings will not perform together again until 1984.

14 Ex-**Byrds** guitarist **Clarence White**, age 29, is killed by a drunk driver while loading equipment after a gig in Palmdale, California.

28 MCA Records holds a press launch for its latest signing, Southern rock group **Lynyrd Skynyrd**, announcing the release of their debut album, ***Lynyrd Skynyrd (pronounced leh-nerd skin-nerd)***, and their opening slot on a forthcoming US tour by the **Who**.

28 The **Allman Brothers Band**, the **Grateful Dead**, and the **Band** take part in the largest ever rock festival – in poor weather – before a crowd of 600,000 at the Grand Prix Racecourse at Watkins Glen Raceway in upstate New York.

30 **Led Zeppelin**'s concert at Madison Square Garden – the last of three consecutive nights – is filmed for the forthcoming Zeppelin movie, "The Song Remains the Same." Last night the group was robbed of $180,000 – which included receipts from the first two shows – from a deposit box at New York's Drake Hotel.

July 1973

July 18 Bruce Springsteen and the E Street Band – now augmented by keyboardist David Sancious – co-headline the first of six consecutive nightly shows with Bob Marley & the Wailers at Max's Kansas City club in New York. Springsteen performs several new songs, including *4th July Asbury Park (Sandy).*

Bruce Springsteen's debut album *Greetings From Asbury Park* sold a miserly 25,000 copies initially.

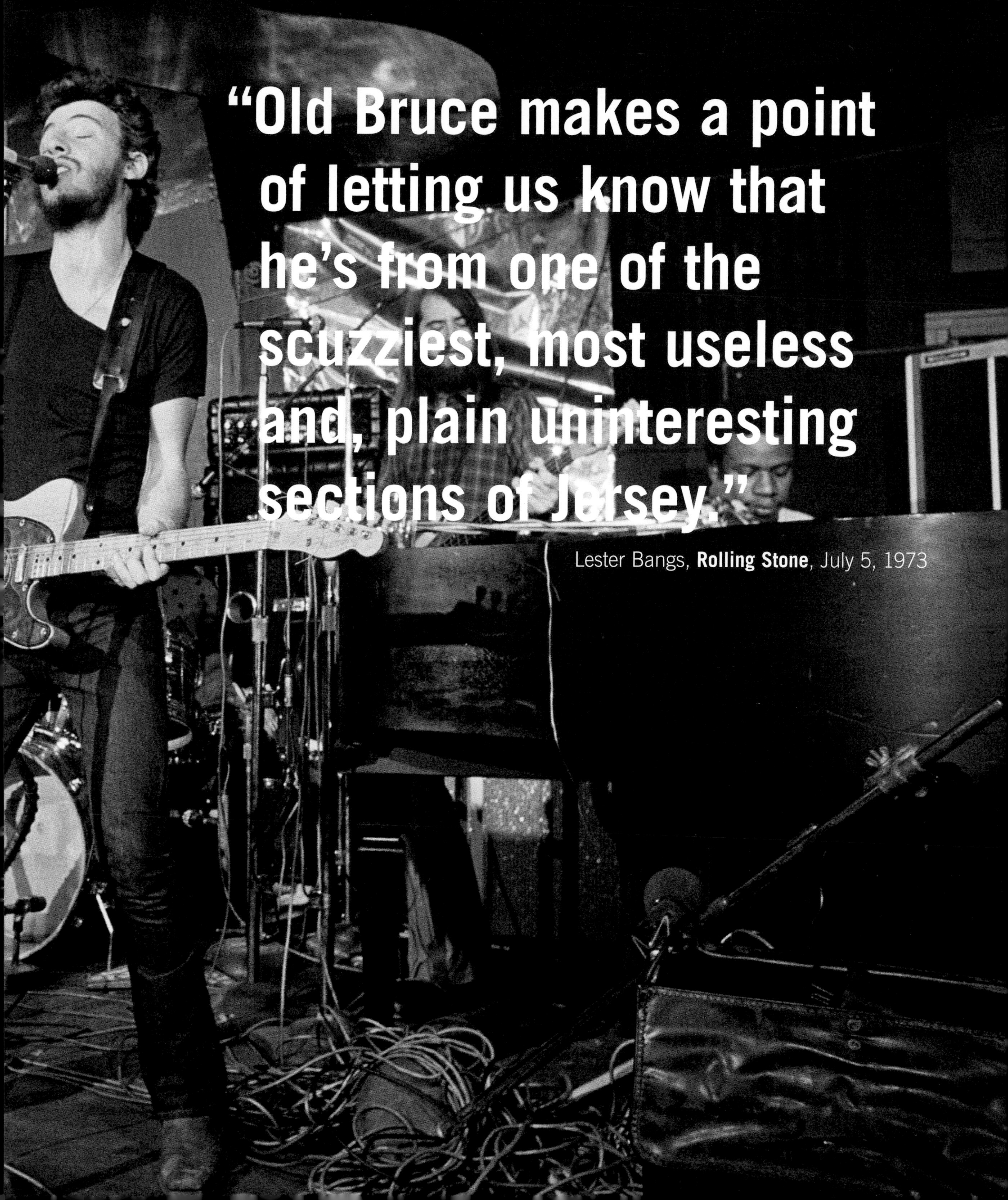

"Old Bruce makes a point of letting us know that he's from one of the scuzziest, most useless and, plain uninteresting sections of Jersey."

Lester Bangs, **Rolling Stone**, July 5, 1973

Stevie Wonder seriously injured... Gram Parsons dies... 10cc debut...

10CC

10cc initially came together working for the Kasenatz–Katz production team... Two American singer/songwriters died within 24 hours of each other – one (Parsons) from a drug overdose, the other (Croce) in a plane crash.

August

1 On his 31st birthday, **Jerry Garcia** is greeted by a naked dancer bursting out of a gigantic birthday cake during a **Grateful Dead** concert at the Roosevelt Stadium in Jersey City.

6 While traveling from Greenville to Durham, North Carolina, during a US tour, **Stevie Wonder** is seriously injured when his car crashes into a logging truck near Winston-Salem. He suffers multiple head injuries (which will rob him of his sense of smell), and will lie in a coma for four days. Wonder has scored two straight US chart-toppers this year, *Superstition* in January and *You Are The Sunshine Of My Life* in May, both taken from his US No. 3, multimillion-selling ***Talking Book***.

17 The **Temptations**' co-founder and baritone **Paul Williams** – in ill health since leaving the group in 1971 (though he continued to supervise their choreography) – shoots himself through the forehead while sitting in his car, wearing only bathing trunks. He is parked a few blocks from the Motown offices in Detroit. Dead at the age of 34, Williams owes $80,000 in taxes, and his Celebrity Boutique business had recently failed.

25 With **Rod Stewart**'s solo career soaring, and with recently recruited Japanese bassist **Tetsu Yamauchi**(who replaced **Ronnie Lane**) unable to get a UK work permit from the Musicians Union, the **Faces** announce they are splitting up.

26 At the beginning of a UK tour to promote their self-titled first album, **10cc** makes its stage debut at the Douglas Palace Lido on the Isle of Man. The four Manchester-born musicians who make up the group already boast illustrious careers: they are singer-songwriter/guitarist **Graham Gouldman**, who has penned hits for the **Yardbirds**, including *For Your Love*, the **Hollies** (*Bus Stop*), and **Herman's Hermits**, ex-**Wayne Fontana & the Mindbenders** guitarist **Eric Stewart**, ex-**Whirlwind** guitarist/songwriter **Lol Creme**, and ex-**Mockingbirds** drummer **Kevin Godley**. Before signing to British impresario **Jonathan King**'s UK label last year, the quartet scored a two million-selling worldwide hit, *Neanderthal Man*, under the name **Hotlegs** in 1970. After being renamed by King, they scored their first UK No. 1 with *Rubber Bullets* on June 23.

September

1 **Paul McCartney**, his wife **Linda**, and **Denny Laine** begin three weeks of sessions at an eight-track studio owned by EMI in Lagos. The highly productive sessions will yield **Wings**' third album, ***Band On The Run***, set for release before Christmas.

9 **Todd Rundgren** – a 25-year-old singer-songwriter, virtuoso musician, and producer, whose *Hello It's Me* single will hit US No. 5 in November to become his biggest hit – records 1,000 voices during a huge taping session conducted at the Golden Gate Park in San Francisco. He will use the combined sound on

ELTON JOHN

Sept 7 At the beginning of his sellout US tour, Elton John plays to a crowd of 25,000 at the Hollywood Bowl. He is introduced by porn-actress Linda Lovelace as "the biggest, largest, most gigantic man and co-star of an upcoming joint venture." His onstage flamboyance reaches new heights: the stage is furnished with five colored grand pianos which, with their tops raised, spell out ELTON, a staircase, and palm trees. Hundreds of white doves are released during the *Your Song* finale. John performs 16 numbers, including the title cut from his forthcoming double album, *Goodbye Yellow Brick Road* (recorded in France in May), and his UK No. 5 and US No. 1 smash, *Crocodile Rock*. For the latter he is accompanied by his sound engineer, Clive Franks, playing one of the pianos dressed as a crocodile, while a live crocodile crawls across the stage.

Gram Parsons

Jim Croce

the left channel of *Sons Of 1984*, a track he is preparing for his next album, *Todd*. The right channel has already been completed, featuring 5,000 voices recorded in Central Park, New York.

19 His body having been found in a room at the Joshua Tree Inn, **Gram Parsons** is pronounced dead at the Hi Desert Memorial Hospital in Yucca Valley, California, at 12:15 am. He is the second ex-member of the **Byrds** to die in the past two months. The cause of death is listed as, "Drug toxicity, days, due to multiple drug use, weeks."

20 Having performed earlier today at Northwestern State University, Louisiana, 30-year-old folk/pop singer-songwriter **Jim Croce** is due to perform a second gig tonight, some 70 miles away in Sherman, Texas. His chartered plane hits a tree on take-off, killing Croce and five others, including his long-time guitarist, **Maury Muehleisen.** Croce's career has soared in the past two years. His debut solo album, *You Don't Mess Around With Jim* – released in June last year – is still climbing the US chart on its way to No. 1, and *Bad Bad Leroy Brown*, taken from his still-rising second effort, *Life And Times*, topped the US Hot 100 in July.

21 As **Gram Parsons** has already indicated that, "If I go, I want to be in Joshua Tree and my ashes scattered there," his road managers, Phil Kaufman and Michael Martin, drive to Van Nuys Airport in a hearse and successfully persuade a Western Airlines baggage loader to release the body and coffin of the dead musician to them. They drive to Cap Rock in the California desert, pour gasoline over Parsons' body and cremate him. His ashes will be flown to New Orleans and buried in the Garden of Memories in Metairie.

October

4 **David Crosby** and **Graham Nash** join **Stephen Stills** – who is playing with his side-venture combo, **Manassas** (which includes ex-Byrds guitarist **Chris Hillman**) – on stage at the Winterland Ballroom, San Francisco. **Neil Young** arrives later in the set, and the result is a full 50-minute **CSN&Y** reunion. Next week, rumors will sweep Britain that Young has died of a drug overdose, even making the BBC radio news.

15 At the age of 49, **Chet Atkins** becomes the youngest inductee into the Country Music Hall of Fame, at its annual awards in Nashville. During tonight's ceremony, **Patsy Cline** becomes the first female solo performer to be inducted into the venerable institution.

24 **John Lennon** begins a new round of litigation against the US government, accusing it of illegal surveillance, and of wire-tapping his phone and that of his attorney, Leon Wildes – activity that has undermined the likelihood that he will receive a fair deportation trial.

30 The **Osmonds**, coming to the UK to promote their new album, *The Plan*, are greeted at Heathrow Airport by 10,000 screaming fans, mostly teenage girls. As with **David Cassidy**, the group – and **Donny** in particular – are receiving mania-like attention in the UK, and greater success on the charts than in their home country: this year alone, **Little Jimmy** greeted the New Year at UK No. 1, Donny has scored his second and third UK chart-toppers with ballad covers of *The Twelfth Of Never* and *Young Love*, and the group's latest single *Let Me In* is on its way to UK No. 2.

November

1 **Fleetwood Mac**'s manager Clifford Davis, who is angered at the group's decision to cut short a recent tour to promote their latest album, *Mystery To Me*, sends a letter to guitarist **Bob Welch** (who replaced **Jeremy Spencer** in 1971), informing him that he intends to take a new Fleetwood Mac to the US in January, and asking whether he might be interested in being a part of its line-up. Welch contacts his band colleagues at Benifolds, their UK base (though **Mick Fleetwood** is currently in Africa), to alert them to their manager's plan. Nonetheless, Davis will go ahead and assemble a bogus Fleetwood Mac to fulfill the dates, resulting in a bitter legal battle.

There were rumors in late 1973 that Mick Jagger had been approached to star in the film version of Tommy.

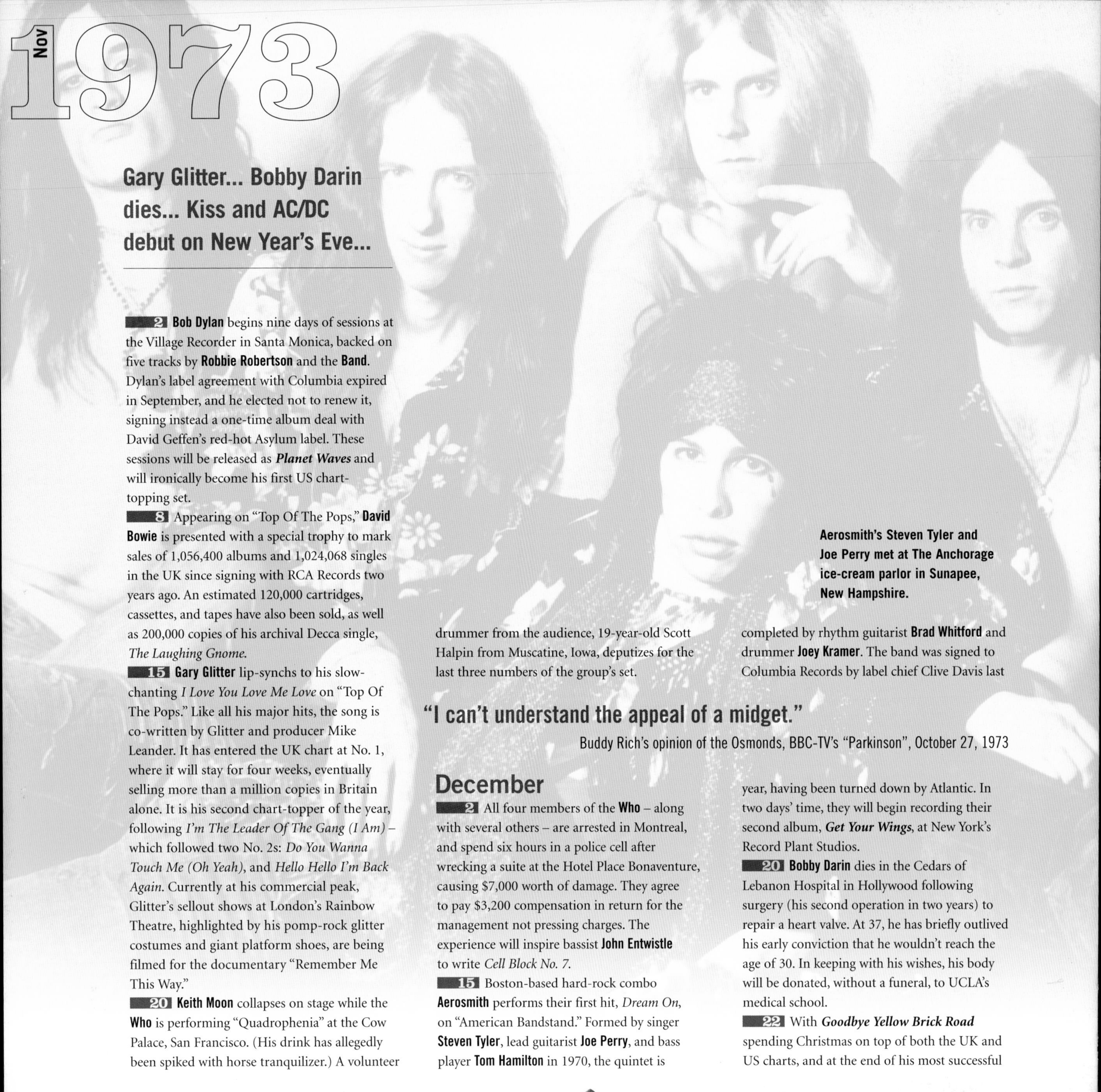

Nov 1973

Gary Glitter... Bobby Darin dies... Kiss and AC/DC debut on New Year's Eve...

2 **Bob Dylan** begins nine days of sessions at the Village Recorder in Santa Monica, backed on five tracks by **Robbie Robertson** and the **Band**. Dylan's label agreement with Columbia expired in September, and he elected not to renew it, signing instead a one-time album deal with David Geffen's red-hot Asylum label. These sessions will be released as ***Planet Waves*** and will ironically become his first US chart-topping set.

8 Appearing on "Top Of The Pops," **David Bowie** is presented with a special trophy to mark sales of 1,056,400 albums and 1,024,068 singles in the UK since signing with RCA Records two years ago. An estimated 120,000 cartridges, cassettes, and tapes have also been sold, as well as 200,000 copies of his archival Decca single, *The Laughing Gnome*.

15 **Gary Glitter** lip-synchs to his slow-chanting *I Love You Love Me Love* on "Top Of The Pops." Like all his major hits, the song is co-written by Glitter and producer Mike Leander. It has entered the UK chart at No. 1, where it will stay for four weeks, eventually selling more than a million copies in Britain alone. It is his second chart-topper of the year, following *I'm The Leader Of The Gang (I Am)* – which followed two No. 2s: *Do You Wanna Touch Me (Oh Yeah)*, and *Hello Hello I'm Back Again*. Currently at his commercial peak, Glitter's sellout shows at London's Rainbow Theatre, highlighted by his pomp-rock glitter costumes and giant platform shoes, are being filmed for the documentary "Remember Me This Way."

20 **Keith Moon** collapses on stage while the **Who** is performing "Quadrophenia" at the Cow Palace, San Francisco. (His drink has allegedly been spiked with horse tranquilizer.) A volunteer drummer from the audience, 19-year-old Scott Halpin from Muscatine, Iowa, deputizes for the last three numbers of the group's set.

Aerosmith's Steven Tyler and Joe Perry met at The Anchorage ice-cream parlor in Sunapee, New Hampshire.

"I can't understand the appeal of a midget."

Buddy Rich's opinion of the Osmonds, BBC-TV's "Parkinson", October 27, 1973

December

2 All four members of the **Who** – along with several others – are arrested in Montreal, and spend six hours in a police cell after wrecking a suite at the Hotel Place Bonaventure, causing $7,000 worth of damage. They agree to pay $3,200 compensation in return for the management not pressing charges. The experience will inspire bassist **John Entwistle** to write *Cell Block No. 7*.

15 Boston-based hard-rock combo **Aerosmith** performs their first hit, *Dream On*, on "American Bandstand." Formed by singer **Steven Tyler**, lead guitarist **Joe Perry**, and bass player **Tom Hamilton** in 1970, the quintet is completed by rhythm guitarist **Brad Whitford** and drummer **Joey Kramer**. The band was signed to Columbia Records by label chief Clive Davis last year, having been turned down by Atlantic. In two days' time, they will begin recording their second album, ***Get Your Wings***, at New York's Record Plant Studios.

20 **Bobby Darin** dies in the Cedars of Lebanon Hospital in Hollywood following surgery (his second operation in two years) to repair a heart valve. At 37, he has briefly outlived his early conviction that he wouldn't reach the age of 30. In keeping with his wishes, his body will be donated, without a funeral, to UCLA's medical school.

22 With ***Goodbye Yellow Brick Road*** spending Christmas on top of both the UK and US charts, and at the end of his most successful

"Y'know he learned a lot more from us than we did from him."

Kelly Isley on Jimi Hendrix, **Melody Maker**, November 3, 1973

The outrageous platform shoe – the higher the better – became the rock and roller's sartorial symbol of the 1970s. Everyone from Elton John to Gene Simmons of KISS (whose shoes are shown here) wanted to stand tall.

SLADE

Dec 15 Slade's *Merry Christmas Everybody* enters the UK chart at No. 1, becoming the group's third chart-topper of the year. Hallmarked by Noddy Holder's intense "It's Christmas" scream at the end of the record, it will become a perennial seasonal favorite in Britain, re-charting every year from 1981 to 1986.

Merry Christmas Everyone was recorded in New York at the height of summer.

year to date, **Elton John**'s third concert – during a run of six Christmas shows at the Hammersmith Odeon in London – is broadcast live on BBC Radio 1. The show climaxes with *Saturday Night's Alright For Fighting*.

24 **Doobie Brothers** singer/guitarist **Tom Johnston** is arrested for marijuana possession in Visalia, California. A hearing date will be set for January 10. Fittingly, the group – formed in San Jose three years ago by Johnston and guitarist/singer **Patrick Simmons**, and signed to Warner Bros. – named themselves after the California slang for a marijuana joint. They have just finished recording their upcoming fourth album, ***What Were Once Vices Are Now Habits***. Already a staple on FM radio in the US, the group's breakthrough hit, *Listen To The Music*, hit US No. 11 in November last year.

29 Recorded over two years ago, the ironically titled, self-penned ballad, *Time In A Bottle*, posthumously hits US No. 1 for **Jim Croce**. It is taking over from country singer **Charlie Rich**'s romantic ode to *The Most Beautiful Girl*.

31 After some two dozen gigs during the year, **KISS** perform at the Academy of Music, New York, on a bill with Long Island-based hard-rock quintet **Blue Öyster Cult** (led by singer **Eric Bloom** and lead guitarist **Donald "Buck Dharma" Roeser**), **Iggy Pop & the Stooges**, and **Teenage Lust**.

31 Scottish-born brothers **Angus** and **Malcolm Young** debut their new hard-rock combo, **AC/DC**, at the Chequers club in Sydney, Australia, (to where the Young family emigrated in 1963). They spotted their band name – the abbreviation for Alternating Current/Direct Current – on the back of a vacuum cleaner.

Gary Glitter claimed that Brian Eno went to see his show to trash it, but instead thought it was the best thing he'd ever seen.

ROOTS During this year: Harry Casey and Richard Finch form KC & the Sunshine Junkanoo Band, playing locally around the Miami area, with a variable line-up of as many as 11 performers... Akron native Chrissie Hynde, now domiciled in England, becomes a contributing writer to the New Musical Express; her first published work is a review of Neil Diamond's *Rainbow*... Chris Stein sees former Playboy bunny waitress Debbie Harry perform in all-girl group, the Stilettos, at the Boburn Tavern in New York... Declan McManus forms his own band, Flip City, while working for the Elizabeth Arden cosmetics company; he takes the name D.P. Costello, before trying Elvis instead... Kirshner Records vice-president Wally Gold attends a White Clover showcase at the Opera House in Ellinwood, Kansas; suitably impressed, he recommends that Don Kirshner sign the band, who have the good sense to change their name to Kansas... Donna Summer meets Italian-born, German-based producer Giorgio Moroder, who hears her singing background vocals at a Blood, Sweat & Tears demo session... Joe Jackson joins pub band Arms & Legs... and Chicago native Rickie Lee Jones, now based in Los Angeles, begins waitressing in an Echo Park-area Italian restaurant and starts playing her own songs, some spoken as monologues, at local clubs, including the Troubadour...

Love Me For A Reason

1974

No.1 US SINGLES

Jan 5 Time In A Bottle **Jim Croce**
Jan 12 The Joker **Steve Miller Band**
Jan 19 Show And Tell **Al Wilson**
Jan 26 You're Sixteen **Ringo Starr**
Feb 2 The Way We Were **Barbra Streisand**
Feb 9 Love's Theme **Love Unlimited Orchestra**
Feb 16 The Way We Were **Barbra Streisand**
Mar 2 Seasons In The Sun **Terry Jacks**
Mar 23 Dark Lady **Cher**
Mar 30 Sunshine On My Shoulders **John Denver**
Apr 6 Hooked On A Feeling **Blue Swede**
Apr 13 Bennie And The Jets **Elton John**
Apr 20 TSOP (The Sound Of Philadelphia) **MFSB**
May 4 The Loco-Motion **Grand Funk Railroad**
May 18 The Streak **Ray Stevens**
June 8 Band On The Run **Paul McCartney & Wings**
June 15 Billy, Don't Be A Hero **Bo Donaldson & the Heywoods**
June 29 Sundown **Gordon Lightfoot**
July 6 Rock The Boat **Hues Corporation**
July 13 Rock Your Baby **George McCrae**
July 27 Annie's Song **John Denver**
Aug 10 Feel Like Makin' Love **Roberta Flack**
Aug 17 The Night Chicago Died **Paper Lace**
Aug 24 (You're) Having My Baby **Paul Anka**
Sept 14 I Shot The Sheriff **Eric Clapton**
Sept 21 Can't Get Enough Of Your Love, Babe **Barry White**
Sept 28 Rock Me Gently **Andy Kim**
Oct 5 I Honestly Love You **Olivia Newton-John**
Oct 19 Nothing From Nothing **Billy Preston**
Oct 26 Then Came You **Dionne Warwicke and the Spinners**
Nov 2 You Haven't Done Nothin' **Stevie Wonder**
Nov 9 You Ain't Seen Nothing Yet **Bachman-Turner Overdrive**
Nov 16 Whatever Gets You Thru The Night **John Lennon with the Plastic Ono Nuclear Band**
Nov 23 I Can Help **Billy Swan**
Dec 7 Kung Fu Fighting **Carl Douglas**
Dec 21 Cat's In The Cradle **Harry Chapin**
Dec 28 Angie Baby **Helen Reddy**

No.1 UK SINGLES

Jan 5 Merry Xmas Everybody **Slade**
Jan 19 You Won't Find Another Fool Like Me **New Seekers**

CBGB Club

New York Dolls

Journalist Charles Shaar Murray described CBGBs, situated at 315 Bowery in New York's East Village, as "a toilet." Patti Smith was one of its earliest discoveries... Fellow scribe Nick Kent described the New York Dolls as if: "Donny Osmond ditched the brothers, started taking downers and grew fangs, picked up with a bunch of heavy-duty characters down off 42nd Street."

In a year that meandered musically, both punk and disco were germinating – though disco would surface far more quickly. Rock relied on the old standards and a growing following for **Bruce Springsteen**; **Abba** broke the Anglo-Saxon monopoly on pop; and a surfeit of banal and forgettable singles found a surprising number of buyers.

They may have had "rock" in the title, but **George McCrae**'s *Rock Your Baby*, and the **Hues Corporation**'s *Rock The Boat*, were all about dancing. Both were huge hits, as was **Barry White**'s *You're The First, The Last, My Everything*. **Gloria Gaynor** became the first of many disco divas. Soul music was being dressed up for a predominantly white audience, in the year that a black model graced the cover of a major fashion magazine for the first time. The disco-zation of funk (*Pick Up The Pieces* by the **Average White Band** and *Jungle Boogie* by **Kool & the Gang**), and one-hit wonders such as **Bimbo Jet**'s *El Bimbo*, helped to set the glittering ball turning. The success of **Carl Douglas**'s *Kung Fu Fighting* demonstrated the new influence of the dance clubs, and it was a good deal more fun than most pop offerings this year. **Terry Jacks**'s *Seasons In The Sun* and **Paper Lace**'s *Billy Don't Be A Hero* dripped with sap. At least there was Abba, soon to become Sweden's second most important export after Volvo. *Waterloo*'s victory at the usually embarrassing Eurovision Song Contest launched the quartet on a global conquest, and played well with a neglected adult audience that appreciated unadventurous but well-produced pop.

That audience definitely wouldn't appreciate the punk revolution now on the horizon. There is much debate as to whether the first seeds were sown in the US, by bands like the **Ramones** and **Television**, and in clubs like CBGBs, or even by glam-punksters the **New York Dolls** (managed by British impresario **Malcolm McLaren**) – or in Britain, where a raw, working-class brand would soon emerge. For now, punk stayed underground – and rock was safe.

A more conventional, blue collar rock was emanating from New Jersey, where Bruce Springsteen already had a passionate following. He was beginning to tour nationwide with the **E Street Band**, and getting rave reviews in the process. But his label, Columbia, was getting tired of Springsteen's lack of commercial success. 1975 would be his make-or-break year.

"Freddy [sic] Mercury... is a rather endearing person... curveting and prancing." **The Times**, November 21, 1974

- **Jan 26** Tiger Feet **Mud**
- **Feb 23** Devil Gate Drive **Suzi Quatro**
- **Mar 9** Jealous Mind **Alvin Stardust**
- **Mar 16** Billy – Don't Be A Hero **Paper Lace**
- **Apr 6** Seasons In The Sun **Terry Jacks**
- **May 4** Waterloo **Abba**
- **May 18** Sugar Baby Love **Rubettes**
- **June 15** The Streak **Ray Stevens**
- **June 22** Always Yours **Gary Glitter**
- **June 29** She **Charles Aznavour**
- **July 27** Rock Your Baby **George McCrae**
- **Aug 17** When Will I See You Again **Three Degrees**
- **Aug 31** Love Me For A Reason **Osmonds**
- **Sept 21** Kung Fu Fighting **Carl Douglas**
- **Oct 12** Annie's Song **John Denver**
- **Oct 19** Sad Sweet Dreamer **Sweet Sensation**
- **Oct 26** Everything I Own **Ken Boothe**
- **Nov 16** Gonna Make You A Star **David Essex**
- **Dec 7** You're The First, The Last, My Everything **Barry White**
- **Dec 21** Lonely This Christmas **Mud**

1974

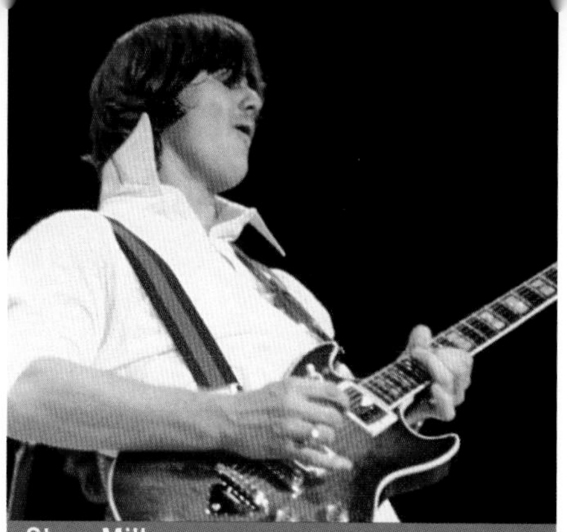
Steve Miller

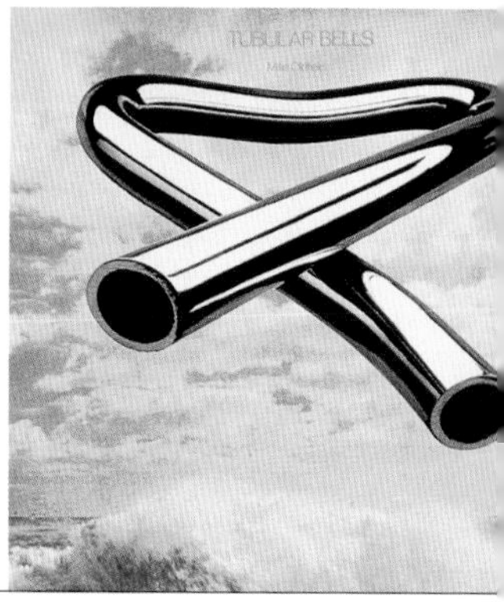

First American Music Awards... Television and Bad Company debut... Chinnichap...

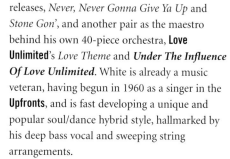

January

1 **Mike Oldfield**'s ***Tubular Bells*** becomes the first record to be certified gold by the British Phonographic Industry, while **Gary Glitter**'s *I Love You Love Me Love* is the first ever platinum single. By the end of 1974, 257 records will have been ratified: two platinum, 72 gold, and 183 silver; 76 singles and 181 albums.

3 **Bob Dylan** and the **Band** – who also play their own stand-alone set – open a 39-date US tour (Dylan's first in nearly eight years) at Chicago Stadium. The tour will reach Madison Square Garden in New York City on January 30. More than five million applications were received for the 660,000 tickets available, and several dates will be recorded for a live double album ***Before The Flood***, to be released in June.

4 **Marvin Gaye** makes his first concert appearance in five years, at the Oakland-Alameda County Coliseum in California. He is backed by **Ray Parker Jr.**, **James Jamerson**, **Joe Sample**, **Ernie Watts**, **Ed Greene**, **David T. Walker**, and others.

12 **Steve Miller** hits US No. 1 with the self-penned acoustic guitar-led FM radio favorite, *The Joker*, certified gold yesterday by the RIAA. Meanwhile, on "American Bandstand," **Kool & the Gang** perform their breakthrough hit, the US No. 4 dance smash, *Jungle Boogie* and *Funky Stuff*. A veteran R&B group, the band originally came together in high school in 1964 as the Jazziacs, formed around bassist **Robert "Kool" Bell** and his sax-playing brother, **Ronald**.

20 After a five-month absence following his near-fatal car accident, **Stevie Wonder** makes his first public appearance at the annual MIDEM music festival in Cannes.

26 **Ringo Starr** scores his second US No. 1 with *You're Sixteen* – featuring **Paul McCartney** on kazoo and **Nilsson** on backing vocals. Like *Photograph*, it was produced by Richard Perry, and both tracks are featured on the ***Ringo*** album. The only ex-Beatle not to have nabbed two solo US chart-toppers thus far is **John Lennon**.

February

7 **Barry White**, 29-year-old R&B singer-songwriter/producer/arranger, receives four gold discs for his recent work: two for his own releases, *Never, Never Gonna Give Ya Up* and *Stone Gon'*, and another pair as the maestro behind his own 40-piece orchestra, **Love Unlimited**'s *Love Theme* and ***Under The Influence Of Love Unlimited***. White is already a music veteran, having begun in 1960 as a singer in the **Upfronts**, and is fast developing a unique and popular soul/dance hybrid style, hallmarked by his deep bass vocal and sweeping string arrangements.

13 **Stevie Wonder** jams with **Johnny Winter** and **Dr. John** at the opening of the new 500-seat Bottom Line club in New York. Also at the inaugural party are **Mick Jagger** and **Carly Simon**.

18 **David Essex** begins filming "Stardust," the sequel to "That'll Be The Day." The movie chronicles his character, Jim MacLaine's rise and fall as a pop star, and co-stars **Adam Faith** and Larry Hagman. Essex recently scored his second UK Top 10 hit with *Lamplight*, the follow-up to *Rock On*, which is now heading to US No. 5.

19 Created by television veteran Dick Clark as a populist alternative to the Grammys, the inaugural American Music Awards are staged. The event – in which the winners are decided by a mix of record sales, airplay, and popular vote – will become a successful annual staple, regularly gaining higher viewing figures than its more formal, industry-led competitor. This year's winners include: the **Carpenters** (Favorite Band, Duo or Group, Pop/Rock); **Jim Croce** (Favorite Male Artist, Pop/Rock); **Roberta Flack** (Favorite Female Artist, Soul/Rhythm & Blues); **Al Green** (Favorite Album for ***I'm Still In Love With You***, Soul/Rhythm & Blues); **Tony Orlando & Dawn** (Favorite Single Pop/Rock for *Tie A Yellow Ribbon Round the Ole Oak Tree*); **Stevie Wonder** (Favorite Single Soul/Rhythm & Blues for *Superstition*, and Favorite Male Artist Soul/Rhythm & Blues). **Bing Crosby** receives the Special Award of Merit.

23 With the opening sentences "Face it. The era of tits 'n' asses is coming to an end," journalist **Chrissie Hynde**'s interview with glam-rock starlet **Suzi Quatro** – who scores her second UK chart-topper today – appears in this week's New Musical Express.

Suzi Quatro received an invite from Elvis Presley after he heard her version of *All Shook Up*. She was too nervous to take up the offer.

Steve Miller received his first guitar at age five from family friend, Les Paul... *Tubular Bells* followed its UK gold certification with the same award in the US... Barry White enjoyed his best year in 1974, with *Love's Theme* and *Can't Get Enough Of Your Love, Babe*, both topping the US singles chart – two of four million-selling singles of the year.

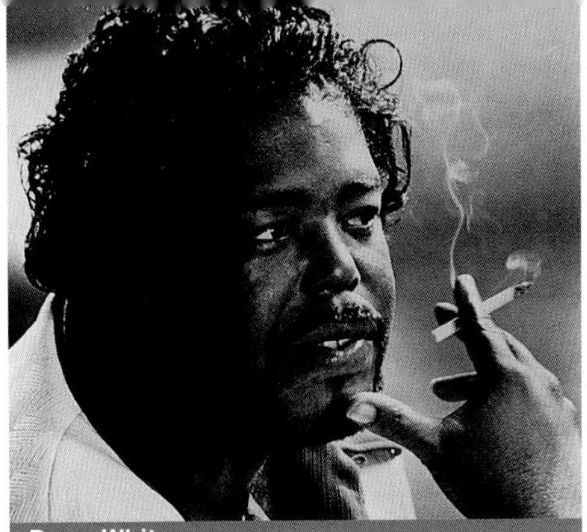
Barry White

March

1 With *Seven Seas Of Rhye* set to become their debut chart single next week, **Queen** hit the road as headliners for the first time, beginning a British tour at the Winter Gardens in Blackpool, in support of their album, ***Queen 2.***

2 **Stevie Wonder**'s groundbreaking work ***Innervisions*** scoops five awards at the 16th annual Grammys. It is named Album of the Year (beating out Paul Simon's ***There Goes Rhymin' Simon***) and Best Engineered Recording, Non-Classical for **Robert Margouleff** and **Malcolm Cecil**. Of the individual tracks, *You Are The Sunshine Of My Life* is hailed Best Pop Vocal Performance, Male; *Superstition* is named Best Rhythm & Blues Song, and also wins Wonder the trophy for Best Rhythm & Blues Vocal Performance, Male. **Roberta Flack**, following her Record of the Year last year with *The First Time Ever I Saw Your Face*, repeats the achievement with *Killing Me Softly With His Song*. It also wins Song of the Year honors for **Norman Gimbel** and **Charles Fox**, and Best Pop Vocal Performance, Female for Flack. **Bette Midler** is named Best New Artist.

2 **Television** make their live debut at New York's Townhouse Theater. The local unsigned group was formed last December by singer/guitarist **Tom Verlaine**, bassist **Richard Hell**, rhythm guitarist **Richard Lloyd**, and drummer **Billy Ficca**. The band will quickly earn a sufficient following on the New York underground scene for Verlaine to convince the owner of CBGBs – a small club on the Bowery – to feature live bands, thus establishing an important base for the city's burgeoning new wave of alternative rock acts.

9 **Paul Rodgers** and drummer **Simon Kirke**, ex-members of **Free**, with guitarist **Mick Ralphs** and bassist **Boz Burrell**, make their live debut as **Bad Company** at the City Hall in Newcastle-upon-Tyne, England. They are contracted to Island Records (which signed Free) in the UK, but will appear on **Led Zeppelin**'s new Swan Song label in the US.

> **"I feel that if there are 13- and 14-year olds hooked on Alice Cooper, and they see dolls mutilated onstage, then its bound to have a bad effect."**
>
> Cliff Richard **New Musical Express**, February 23, 1974

In addition to his solo success in 1974, Marvin Gaye had a pair of hits duetting with Diana Ross.

CHINN AND CHAPMAN

Feb 23 Songwriters Nicky Chinn and Mike Chapman replace themselves at UK No. 1, as Suzi Quatro's *Devil Gate Drive* takes over from Mud's *Tiger Feet*. This remarkable feat also marks consecutive UK No. 1s for producer Mickie Most and his label, RAK. With glam rock at its British peak, much of its poppier fare has been supplied by the "Chinnichap" partnership. Australian-born Chapman linked with Chinn under Most's supervision in 1971, and they wrote their first hits for pop combo New World. They have since racked up more than 20 UK smashes.

The acts proved only as durable as their link with the prolific hit-making machine of Chinn and Chapman.

Mar 1974

Abba win Eurovision... Eric Clapton returns to the studio... Dolly Parton's second country chart-topper...

Eric Clapton

Bruce Springsteen

13 Following a temporary split from **Yoko Ono**, an inebriated **John Lennon** (who has recently been seen in the company of his former personal assistant, May Pang) is forcibly removed in the early hours from the Los Angeles Troubadour club with drinking pal **Harry Nilsson**, after hurling insults at the performing Smothers Brothers, and punching their manager and a cocktail waitress.

26 The **Spinners** and **Dionne Warwicke** (who has recently added an **"e"** to her surname) record *Then Came You* at Sigma Sound Studios in Philadelphia, under the candied production of **Thom Bell**. Following the session, Bell is concerned that Warwicke – hitless for some years – doesn't like the results. He will later recall: "She didn't like it much, but I knew we had something. So we ripped a dollar in two, signed each half and exchanged them. I told her, 'If it doesn't go to number one, I'll send you my half.' When it took off, Dionne sent hers back. There was an apology on it."

28 **Arthur "Big Boy" Crudup** dies from a stroke at the age of 69, in Nassawadox, Virginia. The revered R&B pioneer was the writer behind 1945's *Rock Me, Mama* and **Elvis Presley**'s hit, *That's All Right*. Dying in poverty, he is one of the clearest examples of seminal influences who have been repeatedly ripped off by the record industry.

April

6 The California Jam festival is held at the Ontario Motor Speedway near Los Angeles, with a crowd of 200,000 showing up to see **Deep Purple**, **Black Sabbath**, **Black Oak Arkansas** (a Southern rock sextet led by **Jim "Dandy" Mangrum**), Detroit-based rock combo **Rare Earth**, **Emerson Lake & Palmer**, **Seals & Crofts**, and the **Eagles** – who are now a five-piece with the addition of a second guitarist, **Don Felder**. Also on the bill are the Los Angeles-based R&B troupe, **Earth, Wind & Fire**, formed by producer/songwriter/singer/percussionist and expert kalimba player, **Maurice White** – an ex-Chess Records sessioneer and member of the **Ramsey Lewis Trio**. After a fallow period with Warner Bros., the group's fortunes have been steadily improving since signing with Columbia Records in 1972.

Eric Clapton's comeback album 461 *Ocean Boulevard* gave the guitarist his first US No. 1... Rock critic Jon Landau saw Bruce Springsteen open for Bonnie Raitt in Harvard Square, Cambridge, Massachusetts.

10 After **Eric Clapton** has informed RSO label boss Robert Stigwood that he is ready to return to recording, Stigwood throws a party at a Chinese restaurant in London's Soho. He has invited producer Tom Dowd to oversee Clapton's forthcoming project, which they will begin recording next month in Miami at Criteria Studios, while staying in a rented house at 461

ABBA

Apr 6 **The instantly catchy *Waterloo* by Swedish foursome, Abba, wins the Eurovision Song Contest, held in Brighton, England. (The accompanying orchestra is conducted by Sven-Olof Walldoff – dressed as Napoleon.) Co-written with the group's manager, Stig Anderson (who has bet on them to win with odds of 20/1), the tune was penned by keyboardist Benny Andersson and guitarist Björn Ulvaeus, who formed Abba in 1971, initially as the Festfolk Quartet, with their wives and co-lead singers, Frida Lyngstad and Agnetha Fältskog. They are already a popular fixture in Scandinavia, where their (rejected) submission for last year's contest, *Ring Ring*, was a major hit. *Waterloo* will hit UK No. 1 in May and mark their US chart debut at No. 6 in August.**

Ocean Boulevard. They will assemble a backing band comprising bassist **Carl Radle**, **Jamie Oldaker** (drums), **Dick Sims** (keyboards), **George Terry** (guitar), and **Yvonne Elliman** and **Marcy Levy** (vocals), and this unit will form the basic line-up for Clapton's next four albums.

20 *TSOP* (*The Sound Of Philadelphia*) by **MFSB** tops the US chart, marking the high-water mark for the "Philly Sound" of **Kenny Gamble** and **Leon Huff**. Also used as the title theme for the television series, "Soul Train," it features the **Three Degrees**, a recent female trio signing to the Philadelphia label. They recorded *When Will I See You Again*, another Gamble and Huff nugget, which will hit US No. 2 and top the UK chart in the summer.

(whose first single, *Can't Get Enough Of Your Love* will be released in the UK next week), and **Humble Pie**, who are currently charting in the US with ***Thunderbox***.

18 In a year that will see a high number of novelty records top the Hot 100, the veteran master of the "genre," **Ray Stevens** (who reached No. 5 in 1962 with *Ahab, The Arab*, and US No. 8 in 1969 with *Gitarzan*) hits US No. 1 with his ultimate novelty smash, the self-written and produced *The Streak*. It celebrates the current fad for running around naked at public gatherings. Other US novelty chart-toppers this year are *Hooked On A Feeling* by **Blue Swede** (the first Swedish group to top the survey), **Paper Lace**'s *The Night Chicago Died*, *Billy Don't Be A Hero* by **Bo Donaldson & the Heywoods**, and **Carl Douglas**'s *Kung Fu Fighting*. Mercifully, none of these acts, including Stevens, will ever return to pole position.

"I saw rock and roll's future – and its name is Bruce Springsteen."

Jon Landau, **The Real Paper**, May 1974

May

8 The 36-year-old keyboardist **Graham Bond**, who recently suffered a nervous breakdown aggravated by heroin abuse, jumps in front of a subway train at Finsbury Park station in London. Bond was a pioneer of the early 1960s British blues boom, and the **Graham Bond Organization** proved a top training ground for the likes of **Jack Bruce**, **John McLaughlin**, and **Ginger Baker**. Last year he attempted to form one final unit – the short-lived **Magus** – with British folk-singer **Carolanne Pegg**.

9 **Bruce Springsteen** opens for **Bonnie Raitt** at the Harvard Square Theater in Cambridge, Massachusetts. His set includes the premiere of a new composition, the anthemic *Born to Run*. In the audience is influential rock critic, 26-year-old Jon Landau, a scribe for **Rolling Stone** and the Boston-based **The Real Paper**. He is moved to write: "I saw rock and roll's future – and its name is Bruce Springsteen." The often misquoted sentence will spark intense efforts at Columbia, which will re-promote Springsteen's first two albums. In addition, a long-term friendship will develop between the artist and Landau – who will become Springsteen's co-producer for his next album.

18 The **Who** top the bill at an open-air concert at Charlton Athletic Football Club in London, supported by **Lou Reed**, **Bad Company**

26 Tragedy occurs during a UK concert by teen heart-throb **David Cassidy** at the White City Stadium in London. Over 1,000 fans in the frenzied crowd have to be treated by attendant ambulance workers. Six girls are taken to the hospital, and 14-year-old Bernadette Whelan will die in four days from heart failure. Cassidy will admit he is shaken by the tragedy and feels some responsibility.

June

5 **Sly Stone** marries 21-year-old Kathy Silva, on stage, before a gig at New York's Madison Square Garden. "Soul Train" host Don Cornelius is master of ceremonies, while **Eddie Kendricks** is the opening act. (Kathy will file for divorce on October 30.)

8 Unhappy with **Yes**'s recent album, ***Tales From The Topographic Ocean***, and happy with the already successful launch of his solo career (the UK No. 1 album, ***Journey To The Centre Of The Earth***), keyboardist **Rick Wakeman** announces that he is leaving the group. He will be replaced in August by ex-**Refugee** keyboardist, **Patrick Moraz**.

DOLLY PARTON

June 8 **Dolly Parton scores her second US Hot Country Singles chart-topper with *I Will Always Love You*, following the success of *Jolene* in February. Both gems were written by the 28-year-old singer-songwriter/guitarist, who made her Grand Ole Opry debut in 1958 (she was invited to join in 1969). Raised in poverty in the Smokey Mountains of Tennessee, she started performing on Cass Walker's radio show in Knoxville, at the age of ten. Of her glamorous country star image, she says: "When I wear fancy outfits and hairdos and sparkling jewelry, people might think I'm showing off. But I'm not. When I was a little girl I liked toys but I didn't have any. I was always very impressed when I saw someone dressed real fine. I used to sigh and say: someday, girl, someday."**

1974

June

Mama Cass dies... The Ramones at CBGBs... Tragedy for the Average White Band...

John Denver

Joni Mitchell promotional poster

14 **David Bowie**'s Diamond Dogs North American tour opens in Montreal. It is an elaborate, highly choreographed stage show, complete with a ten-member backing band and a three-dimensional cityscape stage set designed by Mark Ravitz, drawing on concepts from Bowie's hit album, ***Diamond Dogs***. The album cover has been created by Dutch painter Guy Peellaert, who transformed the chameleon artist into a dog (initially including genitalia, an idea scotched by Bowie's label, RCA).

29 Canadian folk-pop singer-songwriter/guitarist **Gordon Lightfoot** scores his first US No. 1 with *Sundown*. Its parent album of the same name is spending its second week topping the album survey. Lightfoot has been recording since the early 1960s, and two of his earlier compositions – *For Lovin' Me* and *Early Morning Rain* – were hits for **Peter, Paul & Mary** in 1965.

July

4 **Steely Dan** perform an Independence Day gig at the Civic Center in Santa Monica, after which they retire from live work, and will not tour again for more than 18 years. Perfectionists in the studio, **Walter Becker** and **Donald Fagen** are currently enjoying the platinum US success of ***Pretzel Logic*** and its No. 4 hit, *Rikki Don't Lose That Number*.

17 **Cat Stevens** ends his Bamboozle tour of North America at Madison Square Garden, with a benefit concert for UNICEF. Stevens will shortly be named the organization's first pop music ambassador.

20 **George McCrae**, a 29-year-old soul singer from Florida, sings his fast-rising, falsetto smash, *Rock Your Baby*, on "American Bandstand." Hitting both US and UK No. 1, the song is proving extremely popular in dance clubs and discotheques. It was written and produced by T.K. Records labelmates, singer/keyboardist **Harry Wayne Casey** and bassist **Richard Finch**, who formed **KC & the Sunshine Band** in Miami last year. Also on tonight's show are **Rufus & Chaka Khan** – another hot R&B/soul band led by singer **Chaka Khan**, a 21-year-old Illinois native – performing their first breakout dance hit, *Tell Me Something Good*, written by **Stevie Wonder**.

27 *Annie's Song*, a loving ode from **John Denver** to his wife Ann, inspired by a temporary rift in their marriage, tops the US chart for the first of two weeks. The ballad was written by Denver in ten minutes while riding on a ski-lift. It will also top the UK survey on October 12.

29 **Cass Elliot** dies, aged 32, while staying in London at singer **Harry Nilsson**'s apartment. Following initial reports by police – one of whom saw a sandwich on a nightstand near the body – tomorrow's post mortem will suggest that "she died as a result of choking on a sandwich while in bed and from inhaling her own vomit." The story will be seized upon by the media. However, a subsequent autopsy will debunk the sandwich theory, concluding that Elliot succumbed to a heart attack brought about by obesity.

> **"I am still number one... my only rival is David Bowie."**
>
> Mark Bolan, **Record Mirror**, July 20, 1974

John Denver's *Greatest Hits* topped the US chart in March and went on to sell nine million copies... *Court And Spark* was Joni Mitchell's first fully-electric album, with help from Larry Carlton, Joe Sample, Wilton Felder, Robbie Robertson and the L.A. Express.

August

1 The **Carpenters**' ***The Singles 1969-1973*** becomes the first album ever to be certified platinum in the UK. Meanwhile in the US, **Bruce Springsteen** begins recording sessions at 914 Sound Studios for his third album, which will be highlighted by its title cut, *Born To Run*.

1 **Eric Clapton**'s current single, *I Shot The Sheriff* – a laid-back version of the **Bob Marley** reggae pearl – and its parent album ***461 Ocean Boulevard*** are both rapidly heading to US No. 1 as Clapton, now drug-free, reaches Atlanta on his

David Bowie's two concerts at the Tower Theater, Philadelphia in July were recorded for release as *David Live*.

The Average White Band were an authentic-sounding soul band from Scotland. Singer Alan Gorrie said the group set out "to be the (Detroit) Spinners, but play instruments at the same time."

US tour. Here he is joined on stage by **Pete Townshend** and **Keith Moon** to perform *Layla*, during which Townshend hits "God" over the head with a plastic ukulele.

3 **Bruce Springsteen & the E Street Band** open for 29-year-old Canadian songbird **Anne Murray** at the Schaefer Festival in New York City. It is the final gig for E Streeters **Ernest Carter** (who early on replaced **Vini Lopez**) and **David Sancious**. They will be replaced by long-term recruits, drummer **Max Weinberg** and pianist **Roy Bittan**.

12 The **Osmonds** begin six evenings of live primetime television shows, broadcast from the BBC Television Theatre in Shepherd's Bush, London. With *I'm Leaving It All Up To You* – a duet by **Donny** and his 14-year-old sister **Marie** (who started her solo career last year with the US million-selling *Paper Roses*) – already on its way to UK No. 2, the group's latest ballad, *Love For Me For A Reason*, is due for release next week. It will become the group's first UK No. 1 on the 31st.

16 The **Ramones** begin a residency at New York's hot new-wave venue, CBGBs. With a "punk" attitude and a small repertoire of fever-paced, rapid-fire, garage-rock songs, the group recently formed in Forest Hills, Queens, and had their first gig at a private party on March 30 at the Performance Studio, a rehearsal facility on East 23rd Street in Manhattan. The (unrelated) members all take the stage name Ramone: lead vocalist **Joey** (**Jeffrey Hyman**), guitarist **Johnny** (**John Cummings**), bassist **Dee Dee** (**Douglas Glenell Colvin**), and drummer/manager **Tommy** (Hungarian-born **Thomas Erdelyi**).

23 The three-day 13th annual Philadelphia Folk Festival gets under way in Schwenksville, Pennsylvania. Its performance highlights include sets from 28-year-old country-folk singer-songwriter/guitarist **John Prine** (an Atlantic Records signing), 26-year-old singer-songwriter/guitarist **Steve Goodman** (who has recently been snapped up by Asylum), **Arlo Guthrie**, folk songwriter **David Bromberg**, and Canadian singer-songwriter **Bruce Cockburn**.

24 Having recently wrapped up recording their last album, ***When The Eagle Flies***, **Traffic** make their final live appearance in Britain at the 14th annual National Jazz, Blues, Folk & Rock Festival, near Reading. Also on today's bill, hard-rocking combo **Thin Lizzy**, led by singer/bassist **Phil Lynott**, reveal their two new lead guitarists: Scotsman **Brian Robertson** and California native **Scott Gorham**. (This line up follows the departure of temporary member **Gary Moore**, who quit in January.) The band was formed in Dublin five years ago by Lynott and drummer **Brian Downey**. After three non-charting albums for Decca (but a big debut hit single last year, *Whisky In The Jar*), the group will shortly sign with Phonogram's progressive rock imprint, Vertigo.

28 **Television** begin a five-night residency at Max's Kansas City, opening for 27-year-old underground poet **Patti Smith**. Having been accompanied at previous reading gigs by her guitarist friend **Lenny Kaye**, the Chicago-born music journalist has recently formed the **Patti Smith Group**, with guitarist **Ivan Kral** and drummer **Jay Dee Daugherty**. They recorded the double A-side *Hey Joe/Piss Factory* for artist Robert Mapplethorpe's Mer label, initially licensed by Seymour Stein's Sire Records.

September

9 The **Grateful Dead** begin a three-day stint at London's Alexandra Palace, at the start of a week-long European tour.

13 With his latest work, ***Fulfillingness' First Finale***, spending its first week at US No. 1, **Stevie Wonder** begins a US tour – his first concert series since his accident – at the Nassau Veterans Memorial Coliseum in Uniondale, New York.

14 **Joni Mitchell** – whose recent ***Court And Spark*** album for Asylum is proving her most commercially successful US release at No. 2 – performs in the UK at Wembley Stadium, on a bill with **Crosby, Stills, Nash & Young** (who re-formed for a US tour in July) and the **Band**.

23 After a week-long booking at the Troubadour club in Los Angeles, 24-year-old **Average White Band** drummer **Robbie McIntosh** dies from a strychnine-laced heroin overdose, which he snorts, believing it to be cocaine. He is at a party being held for **Gregg Allman** at the Los Angeles home of millionaire Kenneth Moss. Band colleague **Alan Gorrie** has taken the same poisoned drug, but his life is saved by the alertness of singer **Cher**, who keeps him conscious. The group – uniquely a blue-eyed R&B/funk-styled soul combo from Scotland – are in the States touring behind their smash second album, ***AWB***. Produced by Atlantic Records' Arif Mardin, it is already heading to US No. 1, with its extracted single, *Pick Up The Pieces*, set for a similar destiny on the Hot 100. The band will replace McIntosh with their long-time friend and ex-**Bloodstone** drummer, **Steve Ferrone**, who will ironically become the only black member of the Average White line-up.

974

aylor quits Stones... Nick)rake dies... Buckingham and Vicks join Fleetwood Mac

Al Green

)ctober

5 Los Angeles-based singer-songwriter/ ianist **Randy Newman** – whose new album, the ypically dry-humored *Good Ole Boys*, features he **Eagles' Don Henley** and **Glenn Frey** – performs t the Atlanta Symphony Hall, accompanied by n 87-piece orchestra conducted by his uncle, Emil Newman.

18 While **Al Green** is taking a shower at his Aemphis home, ex-girlfriend Mary E. Woodson ursts in, pours boiling hot grits over him and hen fatally shoots herself with his gun. She has eft a suicide note that reads: "The more I trust ou, the more you put me down. I can't take it ny more, please forgive me. You don't know ow deep my love is for you but you turn your ack on me without hearing the facts." Green is ospitalized with second-degree burns on his ack, neck and arms. Rumors will persist that he incident prompted Green to become a born- gain Christian, but he will claim his spiritual ebirth had already taken place last year. His aith will, however, be more prominent from his point: he will soon join the ministry, ecoming an ordained pastor of the Full Gospel abernacle in Memphis.

25 Reclusive English folk singer-songwriter **lick Drake** dies from an overdose of tryptasol, n antidepressant, in a bedroom of his parents' ouse in Tanworth-in-Arden. He is 26. The oroner's verdict will be death by suicide, the ulmination of prolonged mental illness, though is parents, Molly and Rodney Drake, dispute his, claiming that it was not a deliberate act. He vill be buried in Tanworth churchyard. Drake eaves behind three albums, two produced by oe Boyd, which – with their languid, melancholic tyle – will be increasingly revered as an nfluential and accomplished body of work.

Al Green had had six consecutive Top 10 hits in the US in the two years prior to 1974... Nick Drake's introspective songs found fame long after his death.

November

2 **George Harrison** becomes the first member of the **Beatles** to undertake a solo world tour, when the 30-date North American leg of his George Harrison and Friends global trek gets under way at the Pacific Coliseum in Vancouver. The friends include **Ravi Shankar** and **Billy Preston** – who recently scored a US No. 1 with *Nothing From Nothing*. The US portion of the tour will climax on December 20 at New York's Madison Square Garden. A-list members of Harrison's backing band on the tour include **Tom Scott**, **Chuck Findley**, **Jim Horn**, and **Andy Newmark**.

8 R&B singer-songwriter/pianist **Ivory Joe Hunter** dies of lung cancer in Memphis, age 63. Hunter switched from a successful pop/R&B career in the 1940s and 1950s (*I Almost Lost My Mind*) to a new one in country music in the 1960s, becoming a regular performer on the "Grand Ole Opry."

8 After an appearance at the Westbury Music Fair in Westbury, New York, singer **Connie Francis** is attacked and raped at knifepoint in a second-floor room at a Howard Johnson's Lodge motel in Long Island. She will be awarded $3,055,000 in damages. Emotionally scarred, she will retreat from public view and will not perform again until 1981.

9 Canadian hard rockers, **Bachman-Turner Overdrive**, top the US chart with the stuttering smash, *You Ain't Seen Nothing Yet*. The song was written by frontman and ex-**Guess Who**

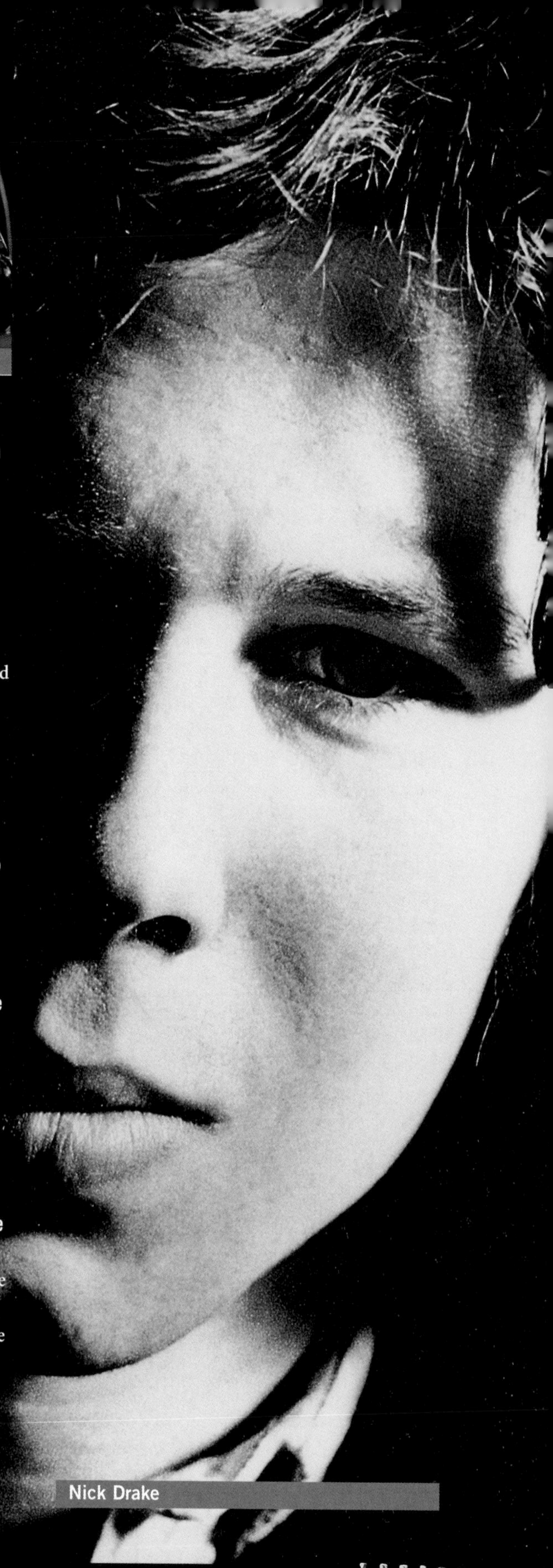

Nick Drake

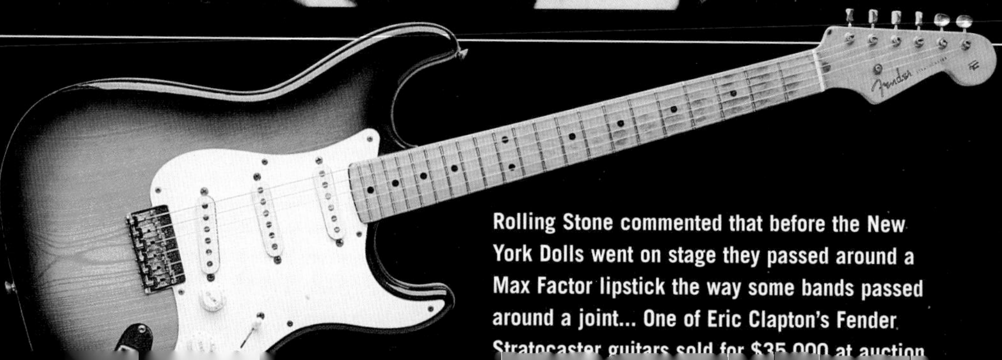

Rolling Stone commented that before the New York Dolls went on stage they passed around a Max Factor lipstick the way some bands passed around a joint... One of Eric Clapton's Fender Stratocaster guitars sold for $35,000 at auction

Elton John and John Lennon

Fleetwood Mac

During his 44-date US tour, which saw him joined on stage by John Lennon, Elton John wandered on stage at a Stooges gig in Atlanta wearing a gorilla suit... Mick Fleetwood became aware of Buckingham and Nicks when producer Keith Olsen played a track of theirs as a demonstration at the Sound City Studios.

guitarist/singer, **Randy Bachman**, for his brother, erstwhile band manager, Gary – who suffers from stuttering.

17 **Abba** begin their first European tour at the Falkontheater, Copenhagen, playing dates outside Sweden for the first time. The tour will also take in Germany, Austria, and Switzerland.

28 On Thanksgiving Day, **John Lennon** makes what will prove to be his final concert appearance, at Madison Square Garden, joining **Elton John** for three songs: *Whatever Gets You Thru The Night* (Lennon's first solo US No. 1), and covers of the **Beatles**' *Lucy In The Sky With Diamonds* and *I Saw Her Standing There.* Following the gig, he and Yoko are reunited backstage.

new album. Taylor says: "The last 5½ years with the Stones have been very exciting and proved to be a most inspiring period. And as far as my attitude to the other four members is concerned, it is one of respect for them, both as musicians and people. I have nothing but admiration for the group, but I feel now is the time to move on and do something new." **Mick Jagger** adds: "After 5½ years, Mick wishes a change of scene and wants the opportunity to try out new ventures, new endeavors. While we are all most sorry that he is going, we wish him great success and much happiness." The subsequent Stones sessions for what will become ***Black And Blue*** will feature three guitarists: **Ron Wood**, **Wayne Perkins**, and **Harvey Mandel**.

21 **Harry Chapin**'s *Cat's In The Cradle* – his second hit single of the year following *WOLD,* a song about the life of a DJ – tops the US chart. A native New Yorker, 32-year-old singer-songwriter/guitarist Chapin will later say: "I always got a kick out of *Kung Fu Fighting* by **Carl Douglas**. Following it at No. 1 says a thing or two about variations in popular music."

"She pretends I'm not hers."

David Bowie on being asked by Dick Cavett what his mother thinks of him, Wide World Of Entertainment TV show, December 1974

December

9 With his second album having already topped the UK chart in September, **Mike Oldfield** performs "Orchestral Hergest Ridge Parts 1 & 2" at the Royal Albert Hall, London, with help from conductor **David Bedford** and **Gong** guitarist **Steve Hillage**, among others.

12 After more than five years with the group, **Mick Taylor** quits the **Rolling Stones**, in the middle of recording sessions in Munich for their

31 Singer-songwriting lovers 27-year-old **Lindsey Buckingham** and 26-year-old **Stevie Nicks**, are both invited to join **Fleetwood Mac**, completing the group's tenth line-up since 1967. **Mick Fleetwood** was recently introduced to them while visiting Sound City Studios in Van Nuys, California. Previously members of San Francisco Bay area group **Fritz**, the pair moved to Los Angeles in 1971 and recorded their debut album, ***Buckingham Nicks***, for Polydor.

BRYAN FERRY

Dec 19 **After spending much of the year on a Roxy Music world tour promoting the UK No. 1 albums, *Stranded* and *Country Life*, a dapper Bryan Ferry performs a black-tie solo date at London's Royal Albert Hall, with a backing band and an orchestra conducted by Martyn Ford. The suave dinner-jacket look has become Ferry's solo trademark (even though his current image with Roxy Music is military chic). He performs 18 songs from his two solo top five UK chart LPs: last year's *These Foolish Things* and the recent *Another Time, Another Place*, both torch albums filled with stylish cover versions of pop standards.**

ROOTS **During this year: Kent State University art students Jerry Casale and Mark Mothersbaugh form a deliberately anonymous quartet with additional Mothersbaughs, Bob and Jim and another Casale, Bob; this will evolve into De-Evolution and then Devo... Nancy Wilson joins her older sister Ann in the hard-rock combo Heart, who have been playing small venues on the Pacific Northwest circuit... working for a Savile Row tailor, Trinidadian Billy Ocean releases his first single under the group name Scorched Earth... Los Lobos Del Este De Los Angeles, a quartet eager to rediscover and revitalize traditional Chicano folk music, make their first recording as a backup group on *Si Se Puede*, a benefit disc for the Hispanic United Farm Workers Union... 11-year-old Sealhenry Samuel makes his first stage appearance at a school talent show, performing *I Can See Clearly Now*... Graham Parker places an ad in Melody Maker, which – by a circuitous route – leads him to Dave Robinson, who will sign him to his Stiff label at the end of the decade... Alan Parsons, an engineer and producer at Abbey Road Studios, hooks up with Eric Woolfson to create the Alan Parsons Project... Joe Strummer forms the 101ers with Alvaro Pena-Rojas... and former New Christy Minstrel, Kim Carnes, releases her solo debut, *Rest On Me*, on the Amos label...**

I Wanna Dance Wit Choo

1975

No.1 US SINGLES

Jan 4 Lucy In The Sky With Diamonds **Elton John**
Jan 18 Mandy **Barry Manilow**
Jan 25 Please Mr. Postman **Carpenters**
Feb 1 Laughter In The Rain **Neil Sedaka**
Feb 8 Fire **Ohio Players**
Feb 15 You're No Good **Linda Ronstadt**
Feb 22 Pick Up The Pieces **Average White Band**
Mar 1 Best Of My Love **Eagles**
Mar 8 Have You Never Been Mellow **Olivia Newton-John**
Mar 15 Black Water **Doobie Brothers**
Mar 22 My Eyes Adored You **Frankie Valli**
Mar 29 Lady Marmalade **LaBelle**
Apr 5 Lovin' You **Minnie Riperton**
Apr 12 Philadelphia Freedom **Elton John Band**
Apr 26 (Hey Won't You Play) Another Somebody Done Somebody Wrong Song **B.J. Thomas**
May 3 He Don't Love You (Like I Love You) **Tony Orlando & Dawn**
May 24 Shining Star **Earth, Wind & Fire**
May 31 Before The Next Teardrop Falls **Freddy Fender**
June 7 Thank God I'm A Country Boy **John Denver**
June 14 Sister Golden Hair **America**
June 21 Love Will Keep Us Together **Captain & Tennille**
July 19 Listen To What The Man Said **Wings**
July 26 The Hustle **Van McCoy & the Soul City Symphony**
Aug 2 One Of These Nights **Eagles**
Aug 9 Jive Talkin' **Bee Gees**
Aug 23 Fallin' In Love **Hamilton, Joe Frank & Reynolds**
Aug 30 Get Down Tonight **KC & the Sunshine Band**
Sept 6 Rhinestone Cowboy **Glen Campbell**
Sept 20 Fame **David Bowie**
Sept 27 I'm Sorry **John Denver**
Oct 4 Fame **David Bowie**
Oct 11 Bad Blood **Neil Sedaka**
Nov 1 Island Girl **Elton John**
Nov 22 That's The Way (I Like It) **KC & the Sunshine Band**
Nov 29 Fly, Robin, Fly **Silver Convention**
Dec 20 That's The Way (I Like It) **KC & the Sunshine Band**
Dec 27 Let's Do It Again **Staple Singers**

Earth, Wind & Fire

Peter Frampton

Earth, Wind and Fire broke through in 1975 with their first US chart-topping single and album... Peter Frampton would emerge as a massive solo success when he recorded *Frampton Comes Alive!* over two summer's nights in California.

From the 1950s, black music had been appropriated by white artists. Now it was being bought by a white audience in greater volume than at any time since Motown's heyday. Disco was upon us. **Donna Summer**, **KC & the Sunshine Band**, **Tavares**, **Van McCoy**, and many others crowded the pop charts. The stand-out disco track was probably Donna Summer's *Love To Love You Baby* – disco's answer to *Je T'aime*. Taking disco to greater heights, and redefining funk, were **Earth, Wind & Fire**. Their 1975 album ***That's The Way Of The World*** was an assemblage of tight horns, percussion, and lush vocals, with immaculate balance as well as soul. The success of disco was not lost on white artists. The **Bee Gees** hit the dance floor with *Jive Talkin'*, which began their spectacular comeback.

Rock fans were revolted by the glitter, banal lyrics, and synthesized beat of disco. They took refuge with **Led Zeppelin**, who had wildly popular US and British tours. **Bruce Springsteen**'s high-octane *Born To Run* catapulted him to superstardom and the front cover of the news magazines. His subject matter spoke to millions: the lure of the road; the threat and promise of the night; the thin line between despair and delight. **Patti Smith** made her debut with *Horses* – which had intellectual pretensions that Springsteen would never aspire to, but also a raw three-chord emotion. This was also the year of **Aerosmith**'s breakthrough, with ***Toys In The Attic***. Though sneered at by some as formulaic heavy rock, it boasted an evergreen hard-rock number in *Walk This Way* – the perfect antidote to disco (but, ironically, a future stalwart of rap).

Mainstream pop-rock did well in 1975. **Elton John**'s ***Captain Fantastic And The Brown Dirt Cowboy*** marked the apogee of his partnership with **Bernie Taupin**. The **Eagles** also demonstrated their versatility and selling power with ***One Of These Nights***. There was the hint of a waltz in *Take It To The Limit*, and the perfect smooth country rocker in *Lyin' Eyes*.

Fleetwood Mac were joined by Americans **Lindsey Buckingham** and **Stevie Nicks**. It worked. This was a new Californian rock sound, combining excellent vocal harmonies and irresistible melodies, establishing **Christine McVie** and Nicks among the finest pop vocalists of the time.
And **Peter Frampton** recorded
Frampton Comes Alive!.

"What is impressive... about Led Zeppelin is their lack of conceit. The inner concord that one sees in their existence." Philip Norman, **The Times**, May 26, 1975

No.1 UK SINGLES

Jan 4	Lonely This Christmas **Mud**
Jan 18	Down Down **Status Quo**
Jan 25	M/S Grace **Tymes**
Feb 1	January **Pilot**
Feb 22	Make Me Smile (Come Up And See Me) **Steve Harley & Cockney Rebel**
Mar 8	If **Telly Savalas**
Mar 22	Bye Bye Baby **Bay City Rollers**
May 3	Oh Boy **Mud**
May 17	Stand By Your Man **Tammy Wynette**
June 7	Whispering Grass **Windsor Davies & Don Estelle**
June 28	I'm Not In Love **10cc**
July 12	Tears On My Pillow **Johnny Nash**
July 19	Give A Little Love **Bay City Rollers**
Aug 9	Barbados **Typically Tropical**
Aug 16	Can't Give You Anything (But My Love) **Stylistics**
Sept 6	Sailing **Rod Stewart**
Oct 4	Hold Me Close **David Essex**
Oct 25	I Only Have Eyes For You **Art Garfunkel**
Nov 8	Space Oddity **David Bowie**
Nov 22	D.I.V.O.R.C.E. **Billy Connolly**
Nov 29	Bohemian Rhapsody **Queen**

Jan 1975

Beatles and Co. dissolves... Stevie Wonder sweeps the Grammys... *J-J-J-Jive Talkin'*...

Little Feat were named after the shoe size of their prodigiously talented leader Lowell George.

January

6 More than 2,000 impatient **Led Zeppelin** fans – waiting overnight outside Boston Garden to buy tickets for the group's show next month – throw beer bottles at the building, resulting in damage estimated at $75,000. Mayor Kevin White immediately cancels the show. The 60,000 tickets for Zeppelin's upcoming three concerts at Madison Square Garden, New York, will sell out in a record four hours.

9 The Beatles & Co. partnership is officially dissolved at a private hearing in the London High Court. However, the four **Beatles** still remain directors of Apple, so company law may require all of them to meet for future board meetings.

16 **Paul McCartney & Wings** begin a new round of recording sessions (which will yield ***Venus And Mars***) with producer Allen Toussaint at his Sea Saint Studio in New Orleans.

17 A-list celebrities attend a reception hosted by Warner Bros. Records UK and the US Embassy Cultural Affairs Office, at the US Embassy in London's Grosvenor Square, to promote the Warner Bros. Music Show. This nine-city, 18-show European tour features **Little Feat** who are promoting their breakthrough (US No. 36) album, ***Feats Don't Fail Me Now***, the **Doobie Brothers**, heavy-metal combo **Montrose** (led by **Ronnie Montrose**), **Tower of Power** (an interracial R&B group consisting of top session musicians), and **Graham Central Station**, the new R&B unit assembled by ex-**Sly & the Family Stone** bassist, **Larry Graham**.

23 British rock/pop quintet **Supertramp** begin a 13-date UK tour to introduce their third album, ***Crime Of The Century***. The group formed in 1969, but founding members **Rick Davies** (vocals, keyboards, harmonica) and **Roger Hodgson** (vocals, guitar, pianos) have recently revised the line-up, recruiting drummer **Bob C. Benberg**, saxophonist **John Anthony Helliwell**, and bassist **Dougie Thomson**. Their first chart single, *Dreamer*, will enter the UK survey next month.

30 Marking a major new musical direction for the band, the **Bee Gees** begin recording the funky, trio-penned, *Jive Talkin'* – with its stuttered "J-J-J-Jive talkin'" intro – at Criteria Recording Studios in Miami, with lead vocal taken by **Barry Gibb**. The brothers are midway through sessions for what will emerge as the chart-busting ***Main Course***, under the production guidance of Atlantic Records' Arif Mardin.

The Bee Gees were about to resurrect their career after spending part of 1974 performing at the Batley Variety Club in the north of England.

February

4 **Louis Jordan** dies from a heart attack, at the age of 66, in Los Angeles. The singer/alto saxophonist was a prime mover in the nascent R&B scene in the 1940s and 1950s, influencing a host of upcoming performers, including **Chuck Berry**. Jordan also holds the record for the most weeks – 113 – spent topping the US R&B chart, including an extraordinary 18-week run in 1946, with *Choo Choo Ch'Boogie*.

8 R&B combo **Ohio Players**' *Fire* hits US No. 1, while its parent album of the same name also heads the album list. The seven-member group, formed 15 years ago in Dayton, have altered their earlier traditional R&B leanings into a popular brand of funk inspired by **Sly & the Family Stone**.

13 With funk music generating an increasingly popular buzz, both on radio and in concert, the **Ohio Players**, **Graham Central Station**, and **Parliament/Funkadelic** play at New York's Radio City Music Hall. Parliament/Funkadelic are an already influential and prolific funk aggregation of up to 40 musicians, assembled and led by lead singer and veteran R&B producer/songwriter, **George Clinton**, who originally formed the **Parliaments** as a doo-wop group in 1955. A separate rhythm section, Funkadelic, was created in 1968, and both units often share the same personnel.

16 Following a riot at **Lou Reed**'s gig in Milan on the 13th – at which the singer was struck in the face by a brick during an attempt by a political group to stop the show – his concert at the Sports Palace in Rome is abandoned after police use tear gas on an unruly section of the crowd.

27 Having already scored three Top 10 singles and two top five albums in his native Britain, 26-year-old singer **Leo Sayer** begins his second US tour with a residency until March 3 at the Bottom Line in New York. Unlike his first visit, when he was dressed as a pint-sized pierrot, Sayer appears in regulation blue jeans.

March

1 **Stevie Wonder** sweeps the Grammy Awards for a second time, picking up four more Grammys at the 17th ceremony. He wins Album of the Year and Best Pop Vocal Performance, Male for ***Fullfillingness' First Finale***, Best Rhythm & Blues Song (*Living For The City*), and Best Rhythm & Blues Vocal Performance, Male (*Boogie On Reggae Woman*). **Olivia Newton-John**'s *I Honestly Love You* is named Record of the Year, and she also picks up the trophy for Best Pop Vocal Performance, Female. **Marvin Hamlisch** is named Best New Artist – over **Bad Company**, R&B singer-songwriter **Johnny Bristol**, and singer-songwriter/guitarist **Phoebe Snow** – who recently hit US No. 5 with her breakthrough *Poetry Man*.

8 With the headline "Stones Choose Wayne," the **New Musical Express** announces that the **Rolling Stones** have decided on a permanent replacement for **Mick Taylor**. He is American guitarist **Wayne Perkins**, formerly of **Smith, Perkins & Smith**. He has been rehearsing with **Keith Richard** at **Ron Wood**'s home studio in Richmond for the past month.

16 London's esteemed rock venue, the Rainbow Theatre, closes down with the Over the Rainbow concert, headlined by **Procol Harum**. It also features mellow Scottish folk singer-songwriter **John Martyn**, ex-**Fairport Convention** co-founder **Richard Thompson** and his wife **Linda**, and singer-songwriter, **Kevin Coyne**.

22 Brooklyn-born singer/pianist **Barry Manilow** performs his melodramatic US chart-topping breakthrough smash, *Mandy*, and his new single, *It's A Miracle*, on "American Bandstand," following a performance by 27-year-old soul songbird, **Minnie Riperton**, who sings her fast-rising ballad *Loving You*, which will hit US No. 1 in two weeks.

April

5 On the road to support their new album, ***The Original Soundtrack***, **10cc** begin their first European tour at the Gothenburg Concert House in Sweden. The LP's second single, *I'm Not In Love*, will be released next month. Written by **Eric Stewart** and **Graham Gouldman**, and created at the group's own Strawberry Recording Studios in Stockport, it features 256 vocal overlays assembled by three voices recorded 16 times each on a 13-note chromatic scale, an innovative device that sets it apart from any previous pop ballad. The "Big boys don't cry" recitative was voiced by the studio's receptionist, Kathy Redfern. Becoming an instant radio favorite, *I'm Not In Love* will top the UK chart on June 28 and hit US No. 2 on July 26, becoming a multi-million seller worldwide and the group's signature song.

6 Veteran R&B vocal trio, **LaBelle** – fronted by soul belter **Patti LaBelle**, with **Nona Hendryx** and **Sarah Dash** – perform their provocative smash, *Lady Marmalade*, on "Cher." Last week's US No. 1 and also a US R&B chart-topper, the song's fortunes have been boosted by its saucy invitation, "Voulez-vous coucher avec moi ce soir?"

12 Following the recent premiere of Ken Russell's film adaptation of "Tommy," starring the **Who**, Oliver Reed, Ann-Margret, Jack Nicholson, and **Elton John**, its soundtrack (No. 27), a new classical interpretation of the work by the **London Symphony Orchestra** (No. 78), and the original double album by the Who (No. 124) all appear on this week's US chart.

24 The day after meeting **Badfinger** co-founder **Tom Evans** for a drink in a local pub, and four days before his 28th birthday, **Pete Ham** is found hanged in the garage of his Woking home by his girlfriend. Found near his body is a suicide note: "Stan Polley is a soulless bastard." Polley has been Badfinger's manager since 1970, and is in litigation with the group over their finances.

> "Mr. [Duke] Ellington contributed more music than I ever could in a thousand years."
>
> Stevie Wonder at the Grammys, March 1, 1975

A week after winning four Grammys, Stevie Wonder was awarded the NARM Presidential Award, "In tribute to a man who embodies every facet of the complete musical artist."

LINDA RONSTADT

Mar 27 **Having topped the US Hot 100 singles and album charts simultaneously on February 15 (with her revival of Betty Everett's *You're No Good* and *Heart Like A Wheel*), 28-year-old singer Linda Ronstadt appears on the cover of Rolling Stone. Born in Tucson of Mexican/German parentage, Ronstadt began performing in 1964, with her brother Mike and sister Suzi, as the Three Ronstadts. She signed a deal with Capitol in 1966 as a member of folk trio, the Stone Poneys, before going solo in 1968. Her backing band in 1971 included future Eagles, Bernie Leadon, Glenn Frey, Randy Meisner, and Don Henley, which led to her signing with Asylum Records in 1973, though she still owed Capitol one more album – which became *Heart Like A Wheel*. She is now managed and produced by ex-Peter & Gordon star, Peter Asher.**

May 1975

Bay City Rollers mayhem...
Tim Buckley dies...
Epic sign the Jackson 5...

Peter Gabriel

Tammy Wynette

May

13 **Bob Wills** dies at the age of 70 in Fort Worth, following several heart attacks. Backed by the **Texas Playboys**, Wills was a pioneer of western swing, an uptempo hybrid of country and western, jazz, swing, and blues. In his will, he leaves his fiddle to country singer **Merle Haggard**, who will continue to play it on stage.

17 **Tammy Wynette**'s *Stand By Your Man* begins a three-week stand at UK No. 1. Its success in Britain – rare for a country record – is even more surprising given that it originally topped the US Country chart in 1968 (to the chagrin of the then active feminist movement), the same year her first trademark ballad, *D.I.V.O.R.C.E.*, also headed the US Country list.

18 During an appearance by the **Bay City Rollers** at a BBC Radio 1 Fun Day at Mallory Park racetrack near Leicester, England, 40 girl fans need to be rescued from a lake, having tried to swim out to meet their heroes, who are being ferried from an island in the middle of the track onto the event site. The event attracts a crowd of 47,000, and foam and water fire extinguishers have to be used to quell the screaming hordes. Four girls are taken to hospital, and 35 are treated on site. The group leave by helicopter without performing. A spokesman says, "Unfortunately it got out of hand and it was decided to close the roadshow."

21 The British Airports Authority informs Polydor Records that the **Osmonds** – who are due to arrive in the UK at the weekend for a concert tour – will not be allowed to land at Gatwick Airport. The officials are unhappy that Polydor has announced their arrival in advance. On the group's last visit, 20 teenage girls were injured at Heathrow, when a balcony wall collapsed.

23 At the end of a highly successful sojourn performing the concept album, ***The Lamb Lies Down On Broadway***, **Peter Gabriel** plays what will prove to be his last show with **Genesis** at the Palais des Sports in St. Etienne, France. Despite rumors of his departure, his intention to pursue a solo career will not become official until August.

24 **Barry White** takes over "Soul Train" for the evening, performing a slew of recent solo and **Love Unlimited** hits: *Can't Get Enough Of Your Love Babe*, *You're the First The Last My Everything*, *What Am I Gonna Do With You*, and **Love Unlimited Orchestra**'s *Love's Theme*, *Making Believe That It's You*, and *Wanna Stay*.

June

2 UK Member of Parliament Marcus Lipton complains about "the mass hysteria deliberately created by the promoters of pop concerts," following scenes at yesterday's **Bay City Rollers**' concert at Hammersmith Odeon. At tonight's show at the New Theatre in Oxford, a hysterical girl jumps into the orchestra pit, and fighting breaks out when two St. John Ambulance Brigade members grab her. More than 60 girls need first aid, mostly for hysteria and shock, and three are treated in hospital.

14 Tonight's concert by **Peter Frampton** at the Winterland Ballroom in San Francisco is recorded, like last night's gig at the Marin Civic Center in San Rafael, for release next January as the double-album set, ***Frampton Comes Alive!*** Commenting on what will prove to be historic

LaBelle enticed their way to the top of the US charts in April with the saucy invitation "Voulez-vous couchez avec moi ce soir?"

Leaving Genesis to pursue a solo career, Peter Gabriel's first album wasn't released until 1977... Originally a US Country No. 1 in 1968, Tammy Wynette's *Stand By Your Man* became an unlikely UK chart-topper in May 1975.

recordings, Frampton will say: "The night that the album was recorded was really the first time we had headlined a show... and it was just one of those great nights when you think 'I wish we had recorded tonight!' Well, thank God, we did!"

16 **John Lennon** files suit in Manhattan Federal Court against government officials, including former Attorney General John Mitchell, charging that "deportation actions directed against [him] were improper."

23 In the middle of his Welcome to My Nightmare tour, **Alice Cooper** falls off the stage in Vancouver during the opening number, breaking six ribs and cutting his scalp.

24 In a sweeping move, the New Jersey District Attorney indicts 19 record company executives following a two-year investigation into industry practices. Among those charged on various counts alleging tax evasion and payola are Clive Davis (who recently formed Arista Records), **Kenny Gamble** and **Leon Huff**, and seven staffers at the Brunswick label.

29 Singer-songwriter/guitarist **Tim Buckley** dies in Santa Monica Hospital, having been found unconscious in his apartment. He is 28. UCLA research assistant Richard Keeling tells hospital staff that the singer took an overdose of barbiturates. Keeling will be arraigned on one count of murder and one count of furnishing heroin to Buckley, who took the drug at his house, apparently believing it to be cocaine.

30 A press conference is convened to announce the **Jackson 5**'s new recording deal with Epic Records, effective from March 10, 1976, which signifies the end of their Motown contract. It is revealed that the group recorded 469 songs for the label, of which only 174 were released; they received only 2.7 per cent royalties on Motown sales, and were not allowed to write their own material. Berry Gordy will file a $5 million lawsuit for breach of contract, and will in turn be countersued, because the group had to pay full costs of $500,000 on tracks that were not released. The Jacksons will refuse to record any more material for Motown, and Gordy will receive $600,000 in the final, compromise, settlement. The group will also discover that Gordy registered a patent on their name on March 30, 1972, and they will change their name to the Jacksons for Epic releases.

KRAFTWERK

May 11 Kraftwerk play the final night of a 24-date US tour – their first American visit – at the Keystoke Club in Berkeley. The uniquely repetitive 22:30 minute title track from their latest album *Autobahn* – relaying a journey on a German highway – has received unexpected UK and US airplay, with an edited version reaching UK No. 11 and US No. 25 this month. The album is already on its way to UK No. 4 and US No. 5. Its hi-tech, rhythmic, synthesized style will greatly influence futurist, electronic, and Eurodisco acts over the next 20 years.

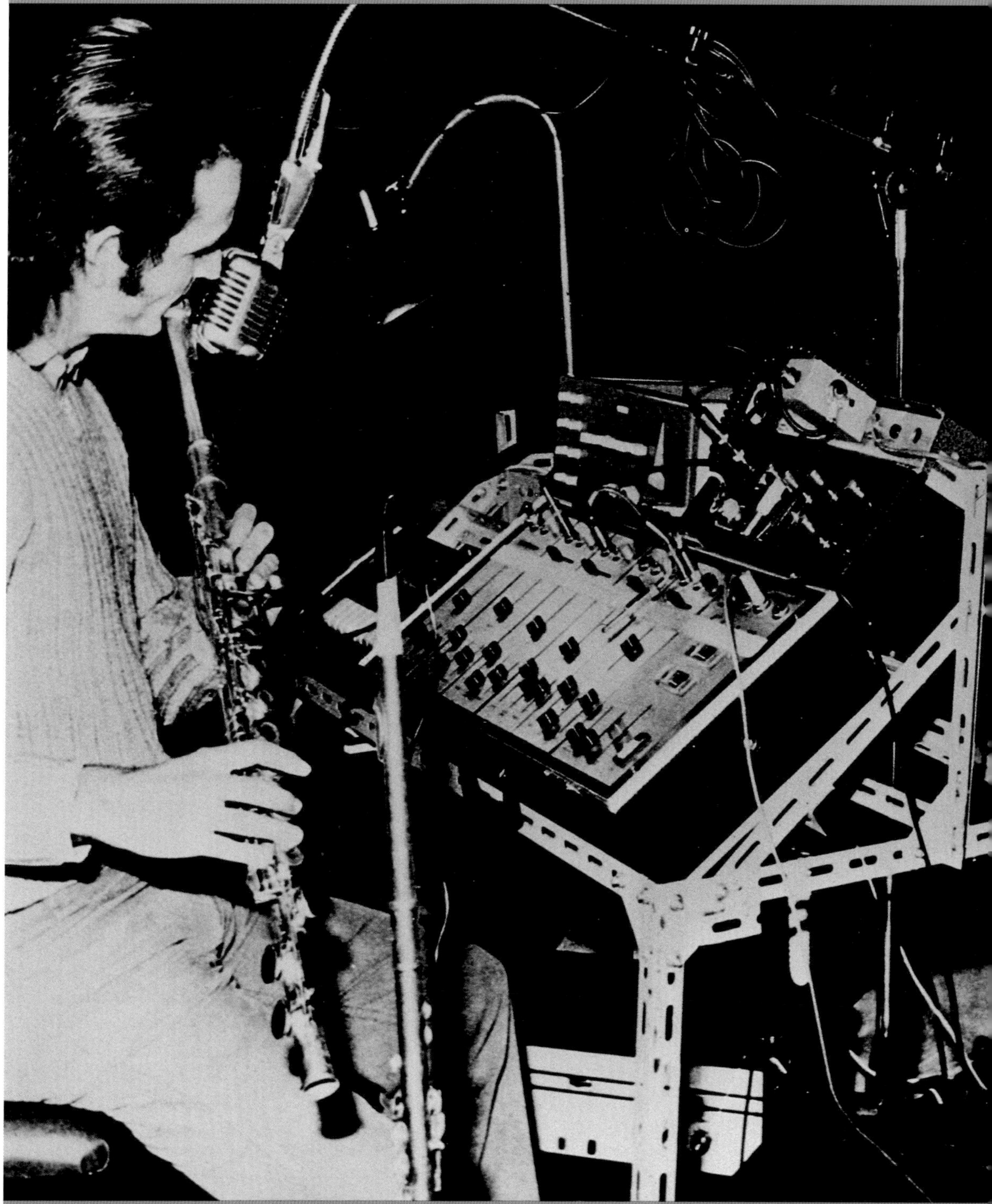

The innovative group was formed in 1970 in Düsseldorf by keyboardists Ralf Hütter and Florian Schneider-Esleben, who almost singlehandedly pioneered an avant-garde form of electronic rock.

July 1975

Irish band victims of terrorism... Robert Plant seriously injured... Saturday Night Live debuts...

July

18 Nearing completion of what will prove to be their breakthrough set, *Natty Dread*, **Bob Marley & the Wailers** perform the first of two shows at the Lyceum Ballroom in London.

26 **Van McCoy**'s *The Hustle* – which hit No. 1 on the US R&B chart two weeks ago – becomes the first disco record to reach No. 1 on the Hot 100. Writer/producer/arranger, and conductor of the **Soul City Symphony**, McCoy recorded the mostly instrumental track in one hour as an afterthought, for inclusion on his latest album, *Disco Baby*.

28 **Bob Dylan** cuts tracks at Columbia Studios in New York, for what will become next year's *Desire* album. Helping out on *Romance In Durango* is a dobro-playing **Eric Clapton**.

30 **Tom Waits** – a critically revered 25-year-old singer-songwriter/pianist from California – begins the first of two nights of recording at the Record Plant in Hollywood. The tracks, played before a select group of friends to give the aura of a live performance, will emerge as his third album, *Nighthawks At The Diner*. Waits has already seen success as a songwriter, penning *Ol' 55*, which was featured on last year's **Eagles** album, *On The Border*.

31 During "the troubles" in Northern Ireland, gunmen belonging to the Ulster Volunteer Force, a loyalist paramilitary group, murder three members of top Irish rock band, the **Miami Showband**, when an attempted ambush goes awry. Posing as an Army patrol, the loyalists stop the band near Newry, as they are returning to Dublin from a concert in Banbridge. They order the group out of their Volkswagen van and line them up against a hedge. Two of the gunmen are killed when a bomb they are placing in the van explodes, and the Showband members are gunned down as they attempt to flee the scene. Lead singer **Fran O'Toole**, **Tony Geraghty**, and **Brian McCoy** are killed, while **Steve Travers** is shot in the chest and stomach. The fifth band member, **Desmond McAlea**, manages to escape and raises the alarm.

> **"It was the suspicious habit of the program to give awards to almost everybody who showed up and performed."**
>
> **The New York Times**, August 9, 1975, commenting on the First Annual Rock Music Awards

August

2 The **Eagles** achieve their second US Hot 100 No. 1 of the year with *One Of These Nights*, written by **Don Henley** and **Glenn Frey**, as its parent album of the same name begins a second week at the top of the US album list.

5 **Robert Plant** and his wife Maureen are badly injured in a car crash while on holiday in Rhodes. They are airlifted back to London by specially chartered jet, with two Harley Street doctors and a supply of plasma on board. They have both sustained multiple fractures and are placed under intensive care, but when it is discovered that Plant is close to overstaying his welcome in the eyes of the taxman, he flies out, encased in plaster casts, to Jersey in the Channel Islands. Maureen remains in intensive care.

5 **Stevie Wonder** and Motown Records agree to the richest record deal to date, eclipsing **Elton John** 's $8 million deal with MCA and **Neil Diamond**'s $5 million re-signing with Columbia. Wonder's contract guarantees him $13 million over a seven-year period, during which time he must deliver one album per year.

13 **Bruce Springsteen and the E Street Band** perform the first of five twice-nightly gigs at the Bottom Line in New York, showcasing their upcoming release *Born To Run*.

Bob Marley's breakthrough hit in the UK in 1975 – *No Woman, No Cry* – was his only non self-penned chart record. It was by Vincent Ford.

Van McCoy

Bay City Rollers

Sha-La-La (Make Me Happy), certfied in January 1975, was the last of Al Green's eight gold singles... Van McCoy penned 34 US hits – *The Hustle* was the only one to top the chart... The Bay City Rollers guested on Howard Cosell's Saturday Night Variety Show on ABC-TV on a bill with John Wayne.

30 Ex-**Free** guitarist **Paul Kossoff** "dies" for 35 minutes, and is brought round by electric shock treatment, at Northwick Park Hospital in north London. He will spend the next ten days in intensive care, before being transferred to the Grayshott Nursing Home near Hindhead for a further month.

September

6 **Rod Stewart**'s ballad *Sailing* – written by **Gavin Sutherland** – begins a four-week run at UK No. 1. It is taken from ***Atlantic Crossing***, which is in the second of an initial five weeks topping the UK album list.

9 **Wings** begin a 13-month world tour at the Gaumont Cinema in Southampton. They will play to over two million people in ten countries. In Australia, faux chat-show host Norman Gunston will ask **Linda McCartney** whether the only reason she is in the band is because she sleeps with the group's lead singer.

29 Just after singing the line "My heart is crying..." from *Lonely Teardrops*, **Jackie Wilson** suffers a heart attack during Dick Clark's Good Ol' Rock 'n' Roll revue at the Latin Casino in Cherry Hill, New Jersey, hitting his head as he falls to the stage. He is immediately hospitalized but lapses into a four-month coma, and will suffer severe brain damage due to oxygen starvation: all his faculties will be impaired.

30 The **Bay City Rollers**, arriving at Kennedy Airport, are greeted by film crews, reporters and some 200 fans. Promoter Sid Bernstein announces he will be showcasing the band at both Yankee and Shea Stadiums next June, thereby going one better than his success with the **Beatles** a decade ago. He became interested in the band when he was told that **Eric Faulkner** and **Woody Wood** were the next **Lennon** and **McCartney**, reportedly saying, "That was enough for me. I was on the next plane." The hype will extend to one US chart-topper, *Saturday Night*, next January – written, like most of the group's UK hits, by **Bill Martin** and **Phil Coulter**.

October

1 **Al Jackson**, 39, **Booker T. & the MG's**' drummer, and a key member of the Stax label house band, is shot dead by an intruder at home in Memphis. He had already been shot in the chest by his wife Barbara, during an incident in July.

4 **Bob Marley**, **Bunny Wailer**, and **Peter Tosh** reunite for their last performance together as the **Wailers**, at a concert at Kingston's National Stadium, to benefit the Jamaican Institute for the Blind. **Stevie Wonder** also takes part, joining Marley in *I Shot The Sheriff* and *Superstition*.

7 The New York State Supreme Court of Appeal votes by a two to one majority to overturn the Immigration Department's deportation order served on **John Lennon**. A previous UK drug bust is deemed unjust by American standards. In two days time, **Yoko** will give birth to Sean Ono Lennon.

11 NBC launches "Saturday Night Live," a weekly satirical television show produced by Lorne Michaels and broadcast from Rockefeller Center in New York. In a premiere hosted by comedian George Carlin, that sees comic actor Andy Kaufman sing *Mighty Mouse*, and introduces the likes of **John Belushi** and Chevy Chase to American homes, the musical guests are singer-songwriter **Janis Ian**, performing her recent US No. 3 introspective ballad, *At Seventeen*, and **Billy Preston**.

13 Having performed at a UNESCO benefit at New York's Radio City Music Hall last night, **Marvin Gaye** is commended at the United Nations by the US Ambassador to Ghana, Shirley Temple Black, and UN Secretary General, Kurt Waldheim.

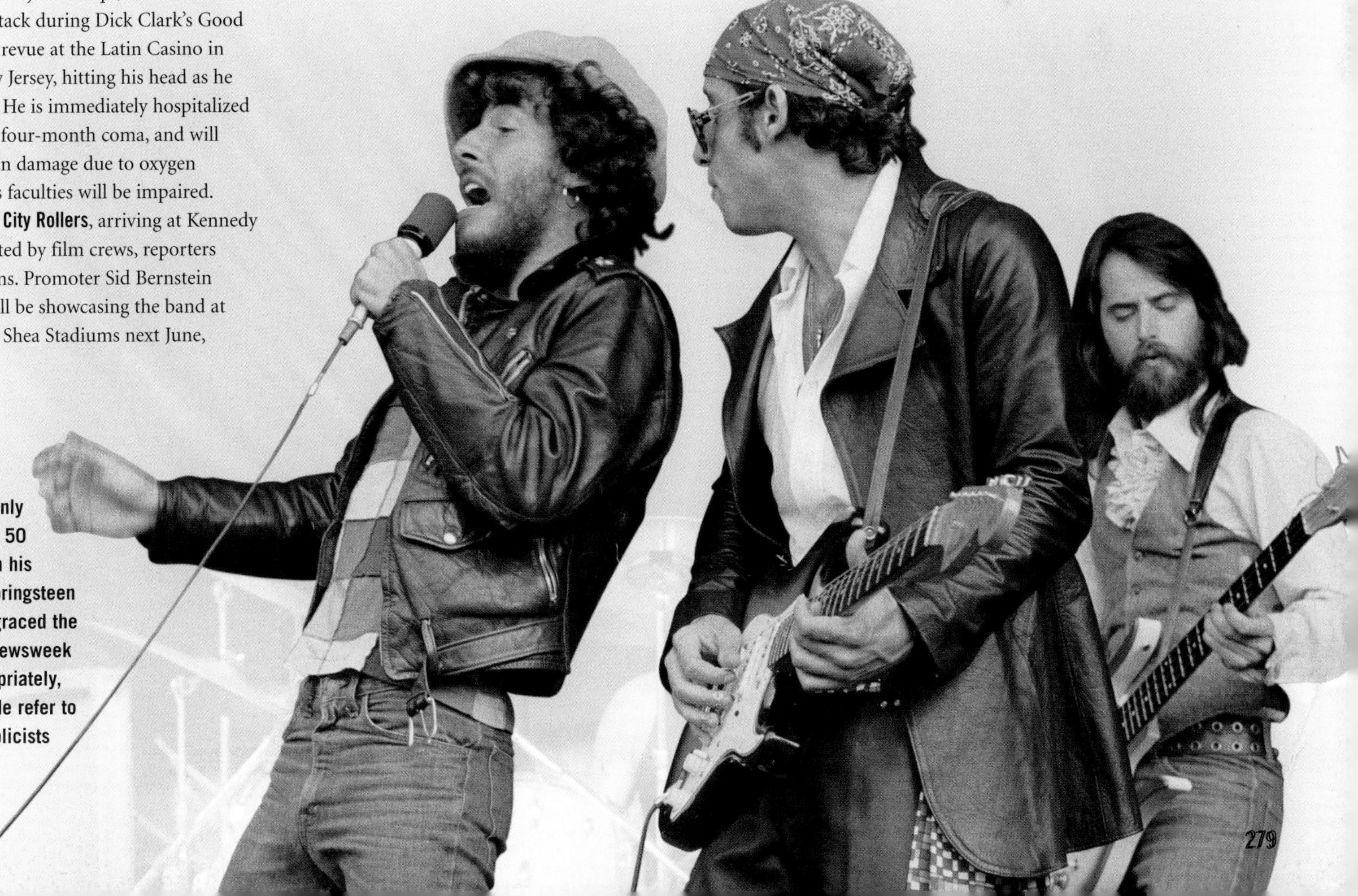

Despite having only secured one Top 50 album thus far in his career, Bruce Springsteen simultaneously graced the covers of both Newsweek and Time. Appropriately, the articles inside refer to the power of publicists in making stars.

1975

Oct 26 **Elton John** concludes his West of the Rockies US tour at the Dodger Stadium in Los Angeles. He is the first artist to play there since the **Beatles** in 1966, and by way of tribute he sings *Lucy In The Sky With Diamonds* and *I Saw Her Standing There*, dressed in a sequined Dodgers uniform. He is also joined on stage by lyricist **Bernie Taupin** (wearing a kilt), tennis star Billie Jean King, and a church choir.

Elton John received a star on Hollywood's Walk of Fame during Elton John Week. For the first time, the organizing committee was forced to block off the streets.

Oct

1975

Dylan's Rolling Thunder Revue tour... The Sex Pistols' debut... *Bohemian Rhapsody*...

Bob Dylan

KC & the Sunshine Band

18 **Paul Simon** (whose new album, ***Still Crazy After All These Years***, is released this week in the US) hosts the second edition of "Saturday Night Live," with fellow music guests **Randy Newman**, **Phoebe Snow**, and the **Jessy Dixon Singers**. To the audience's surprise, Simon is joined by **Art Garfunkel** (whose ***Breakaway*** has also just hit retail and includes the UK chart-topper, *I Only Have Eyes For You*) to sing their classics, *The Boxer* and *Scarborough Fair*.

23 **David Essex** – currently at UK No. 1 with his second chart-topper, *Hold Me Close* – makes his live debut in the US with a performance at the Bottom Line in New York, cheered by fellow Brits, **Ian Hunter** and three members of **Slade**.

30 **Bob Dylan**'s North American Rolling Thunder Revue tour, initially low-key and spontaneous, starts at the Memorial Hall in Plymouth, Massachusetts. Tonight's opening show features **Joan Baez**, **Roger McGuinn**, **Mick Ronson**, **Ramblin' Jack Elliott**, **Bobby Neuwirth**, **Ronee Blakley**, and Allen Ginsberg, who all make their entrance wearing Lone Ranger masks.

November

1 Following five years of constant recording and touring, **Karen Carpenter**, now weighing only 90lb after an extensive slimming program, is taken ill and will take two months off to recuperate, forcing the cancellation of a scheduled British tour.

6 The **Sex Pistols** play their first gig: a performance lasting less than 20 minutes, in the common room at St. Martin's School of Art in London. Guitarist **Steve Jones**, bassist **Glen Matlock**, drummer **Paul Cook**, and the recently recruited lead singer, **John Lydon**, who is given the name **Johnny Rotten** by Jones, have been assembled by **Malcolm McLaren**, ex-**New York Dolls** manager and co-owner of Sex, a boutique on London's King's Road. McLaren is intent on introducing a new brand of raw, musically unsophisticated "punk" music, with an accompanying anarchistic culture and lifestyle, carefully orchestrated to shock and offend.

Paul Simon's *Still Crazy After All These Years* featured the song *My Little Town*, a duet with Art Garfunkel.

Bob Dylan's Rolling Thunder Revue tour ended in December with a benefit for convicted murderer Rubin "Hurricane" Carter... KC & the Sunshine Band's original name was the unwieldy KC & the Sunshine Junkanoo Band.

10 The video for **Queen**'s latest single, *Bohemian Rhapsody*, is shot in four hours at Elstree Studios at a cost of about £4,000 ($8,000). The unique 5:52 minute single – lavishly produced by Roy Thomas Baker, and cut down from its 7:00 minute original version – brings writer **Freddie Mercury**'s epic operatic bent to the fore, and establishes a landmark recording for the group. Released two weeks ago, after which it was broadcast 14 times over two weekend shows by Capital Radio DJ, Kenny Everett, *Bohemian Rhapsody* will begin a nine-week stay at UK No. 1 on November 29. Its tenure will be helped considerably by the equally innovative accompanying mini-film – a promotional tool that sets a new standard for music video production.

18 **Bruce Springsteen** embarks on his first European tour with a debut performance in Britain – the first of two dates at London's Hammersmith Odeon. Posters across the capital proclaim the legend: "Finally London is ready for Bruce Springsteen." One wag adds the graffito: "If not, CBS has blown this year's budget."

20 Bay City Roller **Les McKeown** is cleared of causing the death of 76-year-old Euphemia Clunie by driving dangerously. The jury at Scotland's Edinburgh Sheriff's Court finds him guilty of driving recklessly and dangerously. He is fined £150 ($300) and disqualified from driving for a year. McKeown hit Ms. Clunie after she had apparently changed direction four times while crossing Corstorphine Road last May.

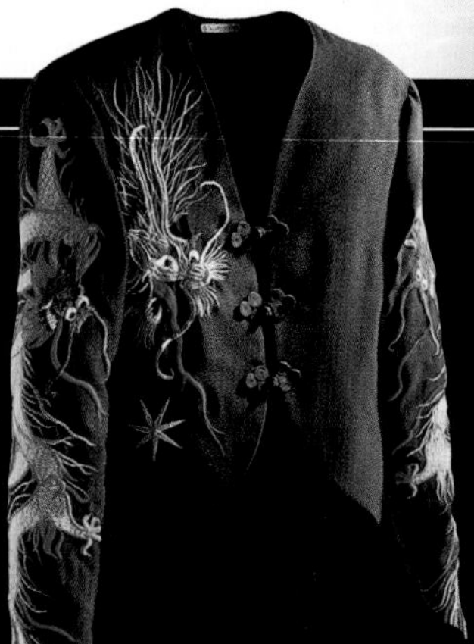

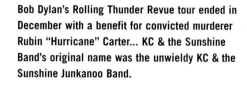

Jimmy Page's sartorial elegance demonstrated his fascination for symbols and mythology, especially the Zoso sign used on Led Zeppelin's fourth album... John Entwistle said of his self-designed bass guitar, "If there is a bass guitar Batman plays, this is it."

22 As disco music explodes around the US, **KC & the Sunshine Band** score their second US chart-topper of the year, with the career-defining *That's The Way I Like It.*

December

6 A preacher in Tallahassee pronounces **Rolling Stone** records to be "sinful," after conducting a survey of 1,000 unmarried mothers, and discovering that 984 of them had conceived to the sound of rock music (although not necessarily the Stones). His congregation enjoys a bonfire fueled by Rolling Stones and **Elton John** records.

13 The Chilean government rejects a request by the **Rolling Stones** to perform on Easter Island, in part because "the whole future of the island" would be "damaged," in the opinion of the Bureau of Tourism. Easter Island, famous for its giant stone statues, is about 2,300 miles from the South American coast. The promoters had planned to charter planes and boats to ferry some 100,000 fans to a three-day festival in February.

19 The **Faces**' split becomes official, when the **Daily Mirror** runs a story headlined "Why Rock Star Rod is Quitting the Faces." **Rod Stewart** says he is severing all connections with the group, complaining that **Ron Wood** is permanently "on loan" to the **Rolling Stones**. Stewart plans to form a new backing band, as he prepares to record his new solo album with his regular producer, Tom Dowd, in the New Year.

20 **Led Zeppelin** – with **Robert Plant** still on crutches – give an impromptu 45-minute set at Behan's West Park, a 350-seat venue on Jersey. Keeping a promise to resident pianist Norman Hale, they play a mix of their own material and rock classics, including *Blue Suede Shoes.* (On the final date of their most recent US tour, they played before a crowd of 85,000.)

24 **Queen**'s most successful year to date ends with their album, ***A Night At The Opera***, at UK No. 1, and a simultaneous live broadcast tonight on "The Old Grey Whistle Test" and BBC Radio 1 of their Hammersmith Odeon show.

Freddie Mercury acknowledged to Melody Maker that "in certain areas we always feel that we want to go overboard."

ROOTS During this year: John Mellencamp, recently laid off from his job at a telephone company, heads to New York, with a demo he has made of Paul Revere & the Raiders' *Kicks*. He meets MainMan management company's Tony De Fries, who agrees to sign him... German record label Metronome sign five-piece Hanover rockers, the Scorpions, making the decision to release their records in English and not in German... Bob Geldof, having interviewed the likes of Elton John and Little Richard for the New Musical Express and other publications, forms the Nightlife Thugs in Dun Laoghaire, near Dublin... Pink Floyd's Dave Gilmour hears songs written by St. Joseph's Convent Grammar School student Kate Bush and is keen to help her career... looking for a lead singer, Malcolm McLaren recommends ex-Television front man Richard Hell to the Swankers; a name-change to the Sex Pistols, and the addition of one Johnny Rotten will do the trick however... Ian Dury & the Kilburns form, and with Dave Robinson as manager, secure a regular gig at the Hope & Anchor pub in Islington, London... and 16-year-old country singer/guitarist Randy Travis wins a talent contest at the Country City USA club in Charlotte, North Carolina, becoming one of the venue's regular performers under the wing of its (and subsequently Travis's) manager, Lib Hatcher...

Love Really Hurts Without You

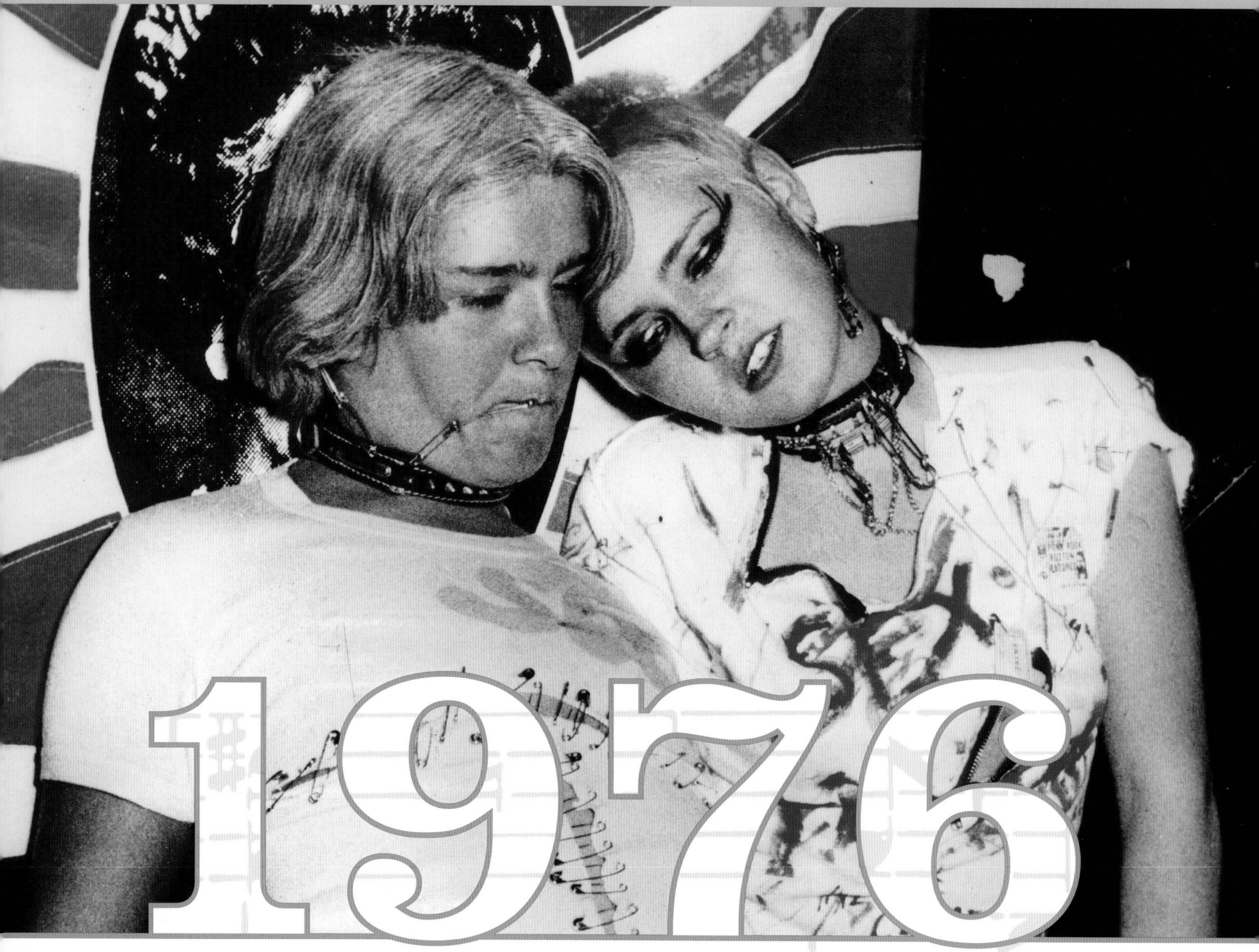

1976

No.1 US SINGLES

Jan 3 Saturday Night **Bay City Rollers**
Jan 10 Convoy **C.W. McCall**
Jan 17 I Write The Songs **Barry Manilow**
Jan 24 Theme From Mahogany (Do You Know Where You're Going To) **Diana Ross**
Jan 31 Love Rollercoaster **Ohio Players**
Feb 7 50 Ways To Leave Your Lover **Paul Simon**
Feb 28 Theme From S.W.A.T. **Rhythm Heritage**
Mar 6 Love Machine (Part 1) **Miracles**
Mar 13 December, 1963 (Oh, What A Night) **Four Seasons**
Apr 3 Disco Lady **Johnnie Taylor**
May 1 Let Your Love Flow **Bellamy Brothers**
May 8 Welcome Back **John Sebastian**
May 15 Boogie Fever **Sylvers**
May 22 Silly Love Songs **Wings**
May 29 Love Hangover **Diana Ross**
June 12 Silly Love Songs **Wings**
July 10 Afternoon Delight **Starland Vocal Band**
July 24 Kiss And Say Goodbye **Manhattans**
Aug 7 Don't Go Breaking My Heart **Elton John & Kiki Dee**
Sept 4 You Should Be Dancing **Bee Gees**
Sept 11 (Shake, Shake, Shake) Shake Your Booty **KC & the Sunshine Band**
Sept 18 Play That Funky Music **Wild Cherry**
Oct 9 A Fifth Of Beethoven **Walter Murphy & the Big Apple Band**
Oct 16 Disco Duck (Part 1) **Rick Dees & His Cast of Idiots**
Oct 23 If You Leave Me Now **Chicago**
Nov 6 Rock'n Me **Steve Miller**
Nov 13 Tonight's The Night (Gonna Be Alright) **Rod Stewart**

No.1 UK SINGLES

Jan 3 Bohemian Rhapsody **Queen**
Jan 31 Mamma Mia **Abba**
Feb 14 Forever And Ever **Slik**
Feb 21 December, 1963 (Oh, What A Night) **Four Seasons**
Mar 6 I Love To Love (But My Baby Loves To Dance) **Tina Charles**
Mar 27 Save Your Kisses For Me **Brotherhood of Man**
May 8 Fernando **Abba**
June 5 No Charge **J.J. Barrie**

The Ramones

George Benson

The Ramones' debut album was recorded on a $6,400 budget. The band reportedly took its name from one-time Paul McCartney pseudonym Paul Ramon... George Benson had been recording for a decade – with albums for A&M and CTI charting – but it took the three-million selling *Breezin'* to give him his only US chart-topper.

Rock music was beginning to look a little tired: it seemed to have lost its spirit of adolescent rebellion. FM radio tended to favor established artists and was not wildly adventurous. The recording process had become more sophisticated, and rough edges could be effortlessly discarded. There was a uniformity about the sound of rock that invited trouble.

And it came, in the shape of punk. Item one: a scruffy quartet from Forest Hills, New York, called the **Ramones**. Their unpolished two-minute songs majored on boredom and broken homes, and drove rock back into the garage. They may not have generated a single hit, but they influenced many of the next generation of rock musicians. And they touched contemporaries in Britain – only to be eclipsed by them. Bands like the **Sex Pistols** and the **Clash** tapped into the seething resentment of working-class British youth, against unemployment, snobbery, and inner-city decay. The music was rough, the musicians untrained, the rhythms forced; the songs started and finished abruptly. So what? It was attitude that counted.

Punk took off with the Sex Pistols' *Anarchy In The UK*, though another London band, the **Damned**, offered the first widely available UK punk single, issued on the nascent Stiff Records label. Punk was a rude awakening for an industry dominated by disco, heavy-metal, progressive rock, and easy listening. The **Eagles**' ***Their Greatest Hits 1971–1975*** became the first platinum album, while they checked their laid-back country rock into the ***Hotel California*** to record an adult contemporary classic, just as **Fleetwood Mac** was creating another. **Boston**'s technical skills in the studio, and **Peter Frampton**'s prowess in concert, became hotly rotated FM fodder. Southern soul artist **Johnnie Taylor** emerged from the wreckage of the bankrupt Stax label to make *Disco Lady* – which became the first platinum single. Disco was in full flood: even **Abba** got in on the act, with perhaps their most cherished single, *Dancing Queen*.

One genre immune from the disco craze was reggae. But it influenced the emerging punk culture – with which it shared a sense of alienation and injustice. The best known of the Caribbean's reggae exports, the **Wailers**, had signed to Island Records in 1971 – giving the band access to state-of-the-art recording facilities and a formidable publicity machine – and in 1974 **Eric Clapton** took leader **Bob Marley**'s *I Shot The Sheriff* to No.1 in the US. Renamed **Bob Marley & the Wailers**, they were hailed as **Rolling Stone**'s "band of the year" for 1976.

"...Abba are the classiest pop outfit around Europe at the moment." **Melody Maker**, December 4, 1976

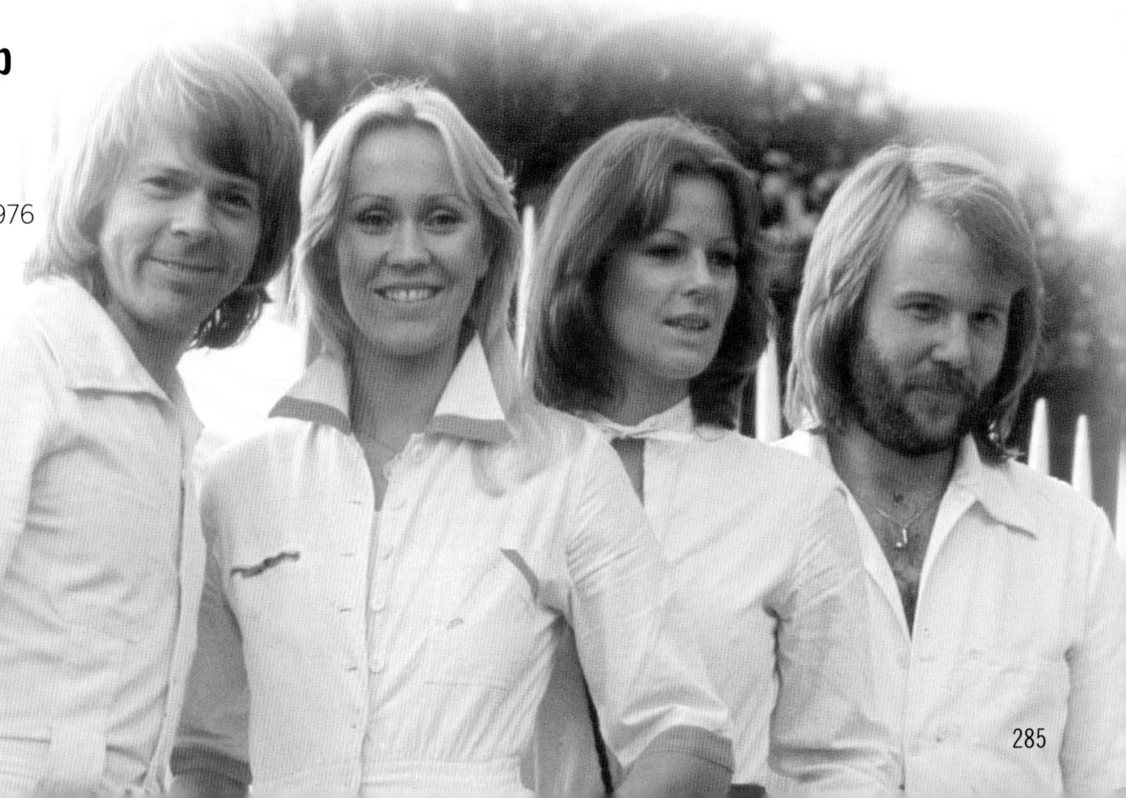

June 12 The Combine Harvester (Brand New Key) **Wurzels**
June 26 You To Me Are Everything **Real Thing**
July 17 The Roussos Phenomenon (EP) **Demis Roussos**
July 24 Don't Go Breaking My Heart **Elton John & Kiki Dee**
Sept 4 Dancing Queen **Abba**
Oct 16 Mississippi **Pussycat**
Nov 13 If You Leave Me Now **Chicago**
Dec 4 Under The Moon Of Love **Showaddywaddy**
Dec 25 When A Child Is Born (Soleado) **Johnny Mathis**

Jan 1976

Joe Walsh joins the Eagles... Gary Glitter "retires"... RIAA certifies first platinum disc...

Graham Parker, who had just come back from a spell picking tomatoes in Guernsey in the Channel Islands, sent a demo tape of original R&B numbers to the Hope & Anchor pub, drawing the attention of future Stiff Records boss Dave Robinson.

January

3 Newly signed to Warner Bros. Records, **George Benson** begins his first session for the company at Capitol Records Studio in Hollywood. Switching labels, and teaming with producer Tommy LiPuma, will provide a dramatic change of fortunes for the former child prodigy. Already highly rated as a jazz guitarist, Benson is encouraged by LiPuma to record a jazz/R&B/pop fusion that also showcases his considerable, and previously underused, vocal chops. The resulting ***Breezin'*** will hit US No. 1 in July, propelled by his hit versions of *This Masquerade*, written by **Leon Russell**, and the **Bobby Womack**-penned title cut.

9 **Graham Parker** – a 25-year-old London-born singer-songwriter with an R&B/rock background – signs to Vertigo Records, after A&R chief Nigel Grainge heard demos of *Between You And Me* and *Nothing's Gonna Pull It Apart* on Charlie Gillett's influential BBC Radio London show "Honky Tonk."

10 After years of deteriorating health, blues great **Howlin' Wolf** dies of complications from kidney disease in the Veterans Administration Hospital in Hines, Illinois.

15 Following a press announcement confirming that **Bernie Leadon** has left the **Eagles**, successful solo rock singer-songwriter/guitarist **Joe Walsh** (ex-**James Gang** and **Barnstorm**) makes his live debut as a permanent member of the group at the first of a series of dates in Australia, New Zealand, and Japan.

19 US promoter Bill Sargent makes the **Beatles** a public offer (via newspaper ads) of $30 million if they will re-form for one night only on July 5, at the venue of their choice. Sargent (who is currently involved in promoting closed-circuit TV rights to a "death match" between Australian shark-hunter Wally "Crowd-pleasing Lightweight" Gibbins and a super-shark known as the "Scourge of Samoa") says the Beatles are welcome to do solo sets, as long as they play together for at least 20 minutes.

26 The **Beatles**' nine-year contract with EMI expires.

27 At the age of 31 (and counting), **Gary Glitter** announces that he is to retire "for strong personal reasons." Speculation about those reasons includes the **Evening Standard**'s suggestion that he is "quitting for the love of his children." He will tell the **Sunday People**: "I have no intention of doing a Frank Sinatra and making a comeback in a few months' time." He will bow out with a farewell tour next month. Tax problems will later spur his return to the stage.

February

12 The **Sex Pistols** begin a tour, opening for **Eddie & the Hot Rods**, at the Marquee Club. It is the band's first major London date, and as a sign of things to come, the gig features two scantily clad girls dancing in the audience, and furniture flying through the air. The Pistols are summarily dismissed from the tour. Under **Malcolm McLaren**'s guidance, they are building a cult following in London, playing a novel, volatile, nihilistic brand of seemingly unrehearsed garage rock, and pioneering the new punk rock scene. McLaren is also cultivating the group's anti-social attitude, and an anti-fashion image that includes bondage clothing, safety pins through

Johnny Rotten auditioned for the Sex Pistols by standing next to a jukebox in Malcolm McLaren's King's Road shop, Sex, and singing along to Alice Cooper's *School's Out*.

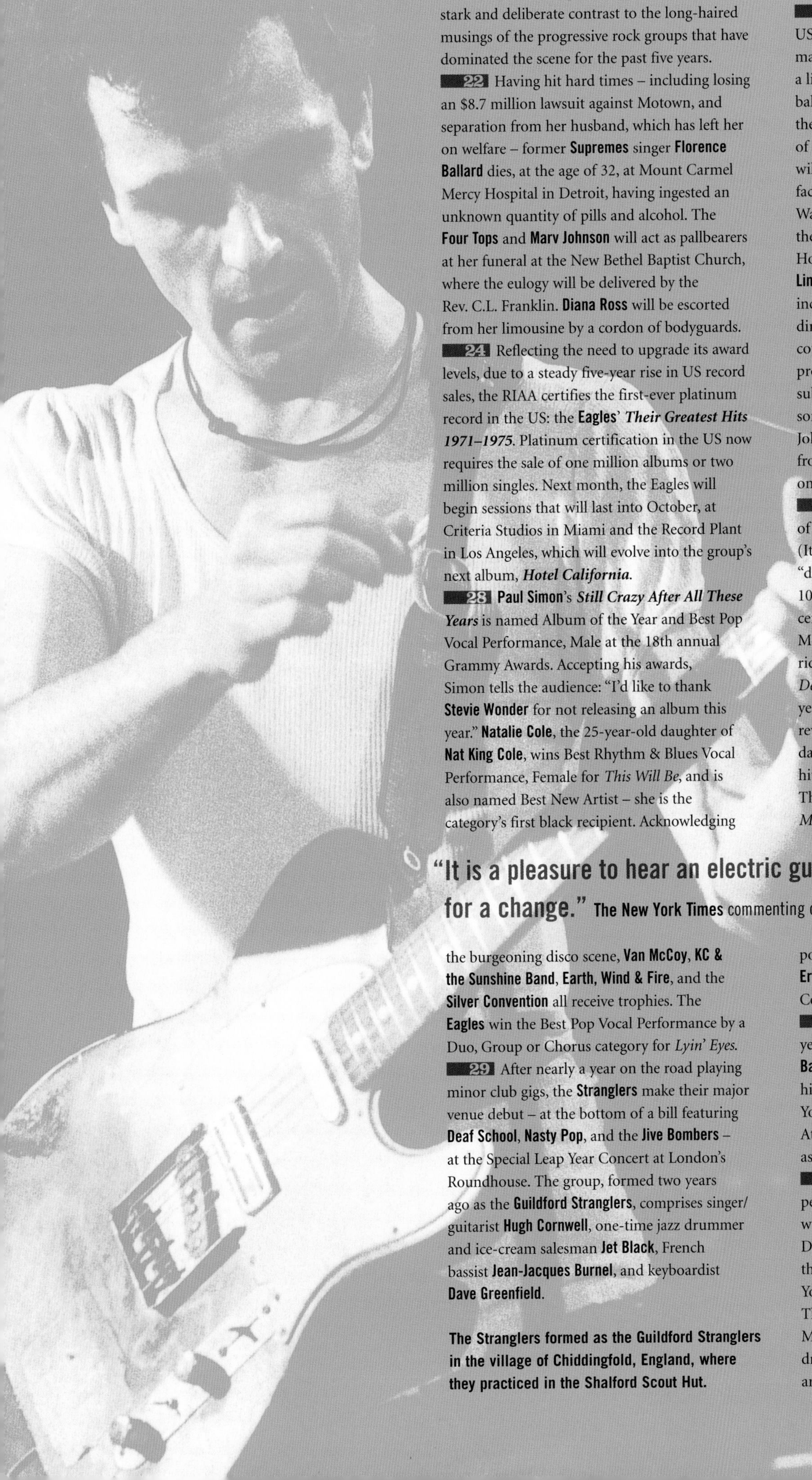

the skin and short, spiked, dyed hair – all in stark and deliberate contrast to the long-haired musings of the progressive rock groups that have dominated the scene for the past five years.

22 Having hit hard times – including losing an $8.7 million lawsuit against Motown, and separation from her husband, which has left her on welfare – former **Supremes** singer **Florence Ballard** dies, at the age of 32, at Mount Carmel Mercy Hospital in Detroit, having ingested an unknown quantity of pills and alcohol. The **Four Tops** and **Marv Johnson** will act as pallbearers at her funeral at the New Bethel Baptist Church, where the eulogy will be delivered by the Rev. C.L. Franklin. **Diana Ross** will be escorted from her limousine by a cordon of bodyguards.

24 Reflecting the need to upgrade its award levels, due to a steady five-year rise in US record sales, the RIAA certifies the first-ever platinum record in the US: the **Eagles**' ***Their Greatest Hits 1971–1975***. Platinum certification in the US now requires the sale of one million albums or two million singles. Next month, the Eagles will begin sessions that will last into October, at Criteria Studios in Miami and the Record Plant in Los Angeles, which will evolve into the group's next album, ***Hotel California***.

28 **Paul Simon**'s ***Still Crazy After All These Years*** is named Album of the Year and Best Pop Vocal Performance, Male at the 18th annual Grammy Awards. Accepting his awards, Simon tells the audience: "I'd like to thank **Stevie Wonder** for not releasing an album this year." **Natalie Cole**, the 25-year-old daughter of **Nat King Cole**, wins Best Rhythm & Blues Vocal Performance, Female for *This Will Be*, and is also named Best New Artist – she is the category's first black recipient. Acknowledging the burgeoning disco scene, **Van McCoy**, **KC & the Sunshine Band**, **Earth, Wind & Fire**, and the **Silver Convention** all receive trophies. The **Eagles** win the Best Pop Vocal Performance by a Duo, Group or Chorus category for *Lyin' Eyes*.

29 After nearly a year on the road playing minor club gigs, the **Stranglers** make their major venue debut – at the bottom of a bill featuring **Deaf School**, **Nasty Pop**, and the **Jive Bombers** – at the Special Leap Year Concert at London's Roundhouse. The group, formed two years ago as the **Guildford Stranglers**, comprises singer/guitarist **Hugh Cornwell**, one-time jazz drummer and ice-cream salesman **Jet Black**, French bassist **Jean-Jacques Burnel**, and keyboardist **Dave Greenfield**.

The Stranglers formed as the Guildford Stranglers in the village of Chiddingfold, England, where they practiced in the Shalford Scout Hut.

March

3 With ***Fleetwood Mac*** still rising on the US album chart, the group is assembling material for their next album, and today record a live version of the **Christine McVie**-penned ballad *Songbird* at the Zellerbach Auditorium at the University of California, Berkeley. The rest of the new set (which will become ***Rumours***) will be cut at a variety of studios: Record Plant facilities in both Sausalito and Los Angeles, the Wally Heider Recording Studios in Los Angeles, the Davlen Recording Studio in North Hollywood, and Criteria Studios in Miami. As **Lindsey Buckingham** and **Stevie Nicks** play an increasingly important role in **Fleetwood Mac**'s direction, the personal frictions between the couple, and between Mr. and Mrs. McVie, are proving musically fruitful. Buckingham will subsequently remark: "Stevie and I were writing songs about each other... as Christine was about John. And there were just these dialogs shooting from member to member which really crackled on the record."

13 **Johnnie Taylor**'s *Disco Lady* begins a run of six weeks at No. 1 on the US R&B survey. (It is the first chart-topper to feature the word "disco" in its title.) It will also top the US Hot 100 on April 3, and become the first single to be certified platinum by the RIAA on April 22. Meanwhile, the **Four Seasons** begin a three-week ride topping the Hot 100 with the nostalgic *December, 1963 (Oh, What A Night)*, some 12 years after their last No. 1, *Rag Doll*. The group's revival as a top pop act began last year with the dance-flavored smash, *Who Loves You*, their first hit via a new recording deal with Warner Bros. Their current chart-topper holds off *All By Myself* at No. 2, a lushly orchestrated, dramatic pop ballad by ex-**Raspberries** lead vocalist, **Eric Carmen**, based on Rachmaninoff's Piano Concerto No. 2 in C Minor.

19 Following a brush with death late last year, **Paul Kossoff**, the 25-year-old ex-**Free** and **Back Street Crawler** guitarist, dies – apparently in his sleep – on a flight from Los Angeles to New York to meet executives at his record company, Atlantic. The cause of death will be confirmed as cerebral and pulmonary edema.

21 **David Bowie** – whose current stage persona is "the Thin White Duke" – is arrested with **Iggy Pop** (booked in under the name James Dituberg), Dwain Vaughns, and Chivah Soo at the Flagship Americana Hotel in Rochester, New York, charged with possession of marijuana. They are released on bail set at $2,000, except for Ms. Soo, who pays $1,000. The charges will be dropped on condition that none of them is arrested again within the next year.

"It is a pleasure to hear an electric guitar handled without distortion for a change." The New York Times commenting on a George Benson concert, February 28, 1976

Stevie Wonder had five US No. 1 hit singles during the 1970s.

Talking Heads live at CBGBs... *Frampton Comes Alive*... The Who make the Guinness Book of Records...

25 **Talking Heads**, by now fixtures at New York's new-wave venue CBGBs, begin a three-night headlining run at the club. Initially a trio comprising ex-Rhode Island School of Design students, **David Byrne** (guitar/vocals), **Tina Weymouth** (bass), and **Chris Frantz** (drummer), they continued with their day jobs when they started out: Byrne worked in an advertising agency cum art studio, Frantz was a stock boy at Design Research, and Weymouth worked in the shoe department of Henri Bendel. In September, the group will become a permanent quartet with the addition of ex-**Jonathan Richman & the Modern Lovers** keyboardist, **Jerry Harrison**, before signing a record deal with Sire Records at the behest of label boss, Seymour Stein.

27 After a trip to Moscow, **David Bowie** is detained for several hours on a train at the Russian/Polish border, by customs officers who take exception to Nazi books and mementoes found in his luggage. They are apparently research material for a film on Joseph Goebbels, Minister of Propaganda during the Nazi regime.

30 At 3:00 am, after a gig at the Ellis Auditorium in Memphis, **Bruce Springsteen**, **Stevie Van Zandt**, and publicist Glen Brunman ask a Memphis cab driver to take them to **Elvis Presley**'s home, Graceland. Springsteen climbs over the wall, but a security guard – assuming him to be just another crank fan – apprehends him. He is escorted off the premises while still trying to explain who he is.

> **"I've always wanted to be known as the best guitarist in the world."**
>
> Peter Frampton, **Los Angeles Times**, May 23, 1976

28 With their third UK chart-topping album, ***Blue For You***, still at No. 1, **Status Quo**'s **Francis Rossi**, **Rick Parfitt**, and **Alan Lancaster** are arrested during an incident at Vienna Airport. Lancaster is charged with assaulting an airport official, and the other two with resisting arrest. They are released on bail.

April

9 Protest folk singer and contemporary of **Bob Dylan**, **Phil Ochs** hangs himself at his sister Sunny's Far Rockaway house in New York City. He has been suffering from depression for over six months. He is 35.

10 After four average-selling studio albums, **Peter Frampton**'s double set, ***Frampton Comes Alive!***, recorded in June last year, tops the US chart at the beginning of a broken ten-week run, which will climax with a straight five-week stay in October. With blanket US rock radio support, it will become the most successful live album in rock history, eventually selling over 25 million copies worldwide. The album introduces Frampton's unique "talkbox" guitar technique – forming words by channeling the sound through a mouthpiece – and includes three massive pop-rock hits: *Show Me The Way*, *Baby I Love Your Way*, and an edited version of the 13:46-minute FM anthem, *Do You Feel Like We Do*.

Talking Heads resisted offers from Arista, CBS, RCA, and Berserkley, before signing with Sire Records – after initially turning them down.

May

12 **Keith Relf**, 33-year-old former lead singer with the **Yardbirds**, and co-founder of **Renaissance**, is found dead by his eight-year-old son at home in Hounslow, west London. He is thought to have been electrocuted by the guitar that he is still holding.

19 **Keith Richards** falls asleep at the wheel of his Bentley and veers off the southbound section of the M1 near Newport Pagnell, plowing into a field through a hedge and a fence. When police arrive, they find drug paraphernalia in the car. Richards will appear in court next January.

20 The **Sex Pistols** cut three demos at Majestic Recording Studios in London, with producer Chris Spedding: *No Feelings*, *Pretty Vacant*, and *Problems*.

31 The **Who**'s Who Put the Boot In concert, at Charlton Athletic Football Club in southeast London, is attended by 65,000 fans. **Little Feat**, the **Sensational Alex Harvey Band**, the **Outlaws**, **Streetwalkers**, and **Widowmaker** are also on the ticket. The concert will enter **The Guinness Book of Records** as the loudest performance (at

STEVIE WONDER

Apr 14 **Motown Records holds a press conference with Stevie Wonder to announce his signing to a $13 million contract renewal, eight months after the agreement was initially reached. It will immediately pay off: Wonder is midway through recording his latest opus, the double album (with a bonus four-track EP), *Songs In The Key Of Life*. The album will ascend to US No. 1 on October 16, eventually holding pole position for 14 weeks, the longest (non-consecutive) chart-topper since Carole King's album *Tapestry* in 1971. The milestone set will yield back-to-back US No. 1 singles, *I Wish* and *Sir Duke* (a tribute to Duke Ellington), and will also spend more than a year on the UK survey.**

Paul McCartney bought the Edwin H. Morris Music publishing company in July, with the entire Buddy Holly catalog... The Buzzcocks released their debut, *Spiral Scratch,* on their own New Hormones label, set up with a £500 loan. They joined the mainstream, however, signing with United Artists on the day Elvis Presley died in August 1977.

Wings

The Buzzcocks

120 decibels) by a rock group. The band will turn the sound down for two further soccer stadium gigs in Glasgow, Scotland, and Swansea, Wales.

June

7 The **Steve Miller Band** embark on a 16-date Summer Serenade '76 tour in Dallas. Miller is promoting his new album, ***Fly Like An Eagle***, containing the upcoming US chart-topper *Rock'n Me*, and its No. 2 follow-up title track.

10 With **Paul McCartney**'s latest pop ditty, *Silly Love Songs*, at US No. 1, and during a record-breaking tour of North America – his first in nearly ten years – **Wings** establish a new world attendance record for an indoor crowd: 67,100 paying customers see them at the Kingdome in Seattle. During the trek, concerts will be recorded and edited down to the 30-track triple album, ***Wings Over America***, which will hit US No. 1 next January.

15 Delayed after an exhausting trek of the US, the **Electric Light Orchestra** begin their first major British tour at Bristol's Colston Hall. **Jeff Lynne** is currently putting the finishing touches to the group's sixth album, ***A New World Record***.

18 **Abba** give a Royal Performance in Stockholm for Sweden's King Carl XVI Gustaf and Silvia Sommerlath, on the eve of their wedding.

July

4 The **Ramones** – in Europe to promote their debut album, the furious-paced, bare-bones punk set, ***The Ramones*** – celebrate the US bicentennial by making their debut at London's Roundhouse, with fellow patriots the **Flamin' Groovies** and the very British **Stranglers**. In September, the Stranglers will open a short UK tour for punk poet **Patti Smith**.

20 Named after a word used in a **Time Out** magazine review of the musical "Rock Follies," the **Buzzcocks** make their live debut, supporting the **Sex Pistols** and the **Damned**, at the Lesser Free Trade Hall in Manchester. The Buzzcocks have been formed by their lead singer, philosophy student **Howard Devoto**. Having seen the Sex Pistols in High Wycombe in February, and after promoting a Pistols gig in Manchester two months later, Devoto has teamed with guitarist/singer **Pete Shelley**, ex-member of the **Jets of Air**, whom he met at the Bolton Institute of Higher Education, with bassist **Steve Diggle** and drummer **John Maher** completing the band's initial line-up. The **Damned**, another new punk combo, are only a few weeks into their career, having made their live bow – again opening for the Pistols – on the 6th at the 100 Club, with **Dave Vanian** on lead vocals, **Brian James** on guitar, **Captain Sensible** on bass, and **Rat Scabies** on drums. None of the groups on this punk line-up is yet signed to a label.

Electric Light Orchestra's *A New World Record* was the first of four US top five chart albums and five platinum albums.

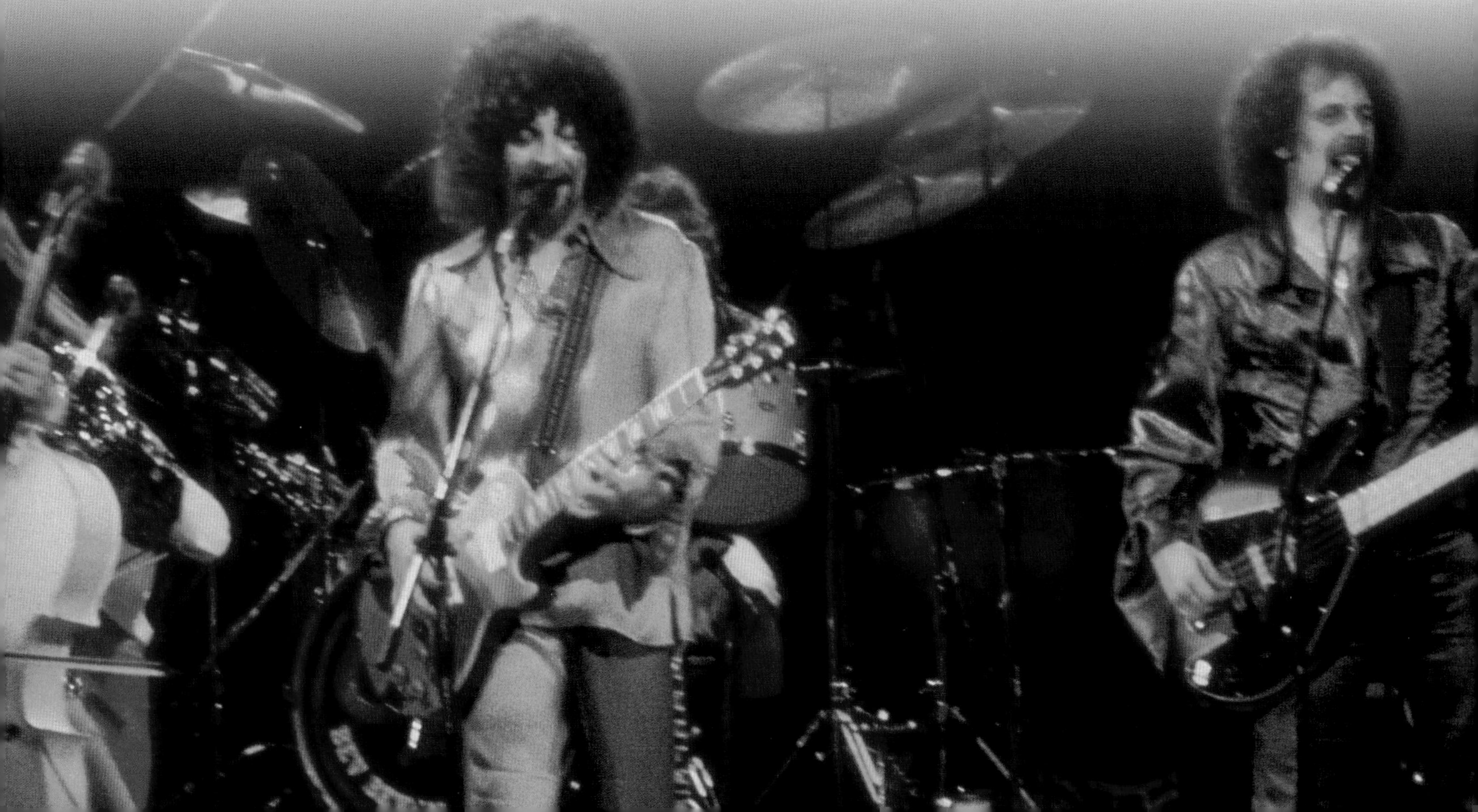

John Lennon gets the green card... The Clash debut... Fleetwood Mac hit the top...

Born William Royce Scaggs, the soulful singer-songwriter met Steve Miller while at St. Mark's Preparatory School in Dallas and joined his band the Marksmen on vocals and tambourine.

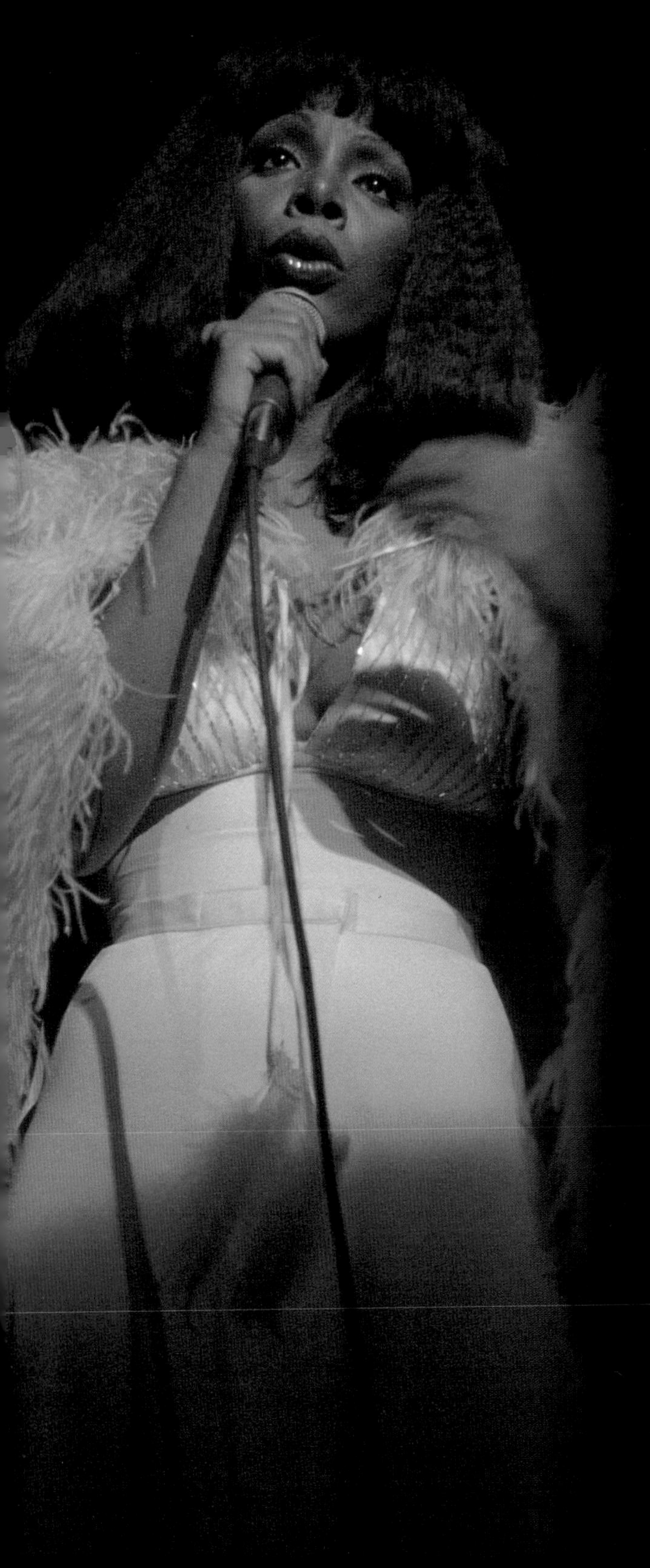

Donna Summer was discovered singing at a Blood, Sweat & Tears demo session in Munich. She had moved to Europe after being offered a

20 The **Allman Brothers Band**'s former road manager and bodyguard, John "Scooter" Herring, is sentenced to a maximum term of 75 years in jail, after being found guilty of supplying cocaine and pills to **Gregg Allman**. Allman was in court to give two days of testimony last month, acting as a prosecution witness. Federal Judge Wilbur Owens Jr. says he will review the sentence after three months' observation, and that "the public tells me that Mr. Herring is nothing but a scapegoat – that the person who ought to be prosecuted is Mr. Allman." However the public is overlooking "the gigantic difference between those who use drugs and those who traffic in them." Allman will be ostracized by other band members, who claim he has betrayed their fraternal loyalty.

27 At a 90-minute hearing in the New York offices of the US Immigration and Naturalization Service, Judge Ira Fieldsteel approves **John Lennon**'s application for his green card (no: A17-597-321), which will allow him permanent residence in the US. Gloria Swanson, Norman Mailer, Geraldo Rivera, and sculptor Isamu Noguchi appear at the hearing as character witnesses. To celebrate the decision, John and **Yoko** retire to Serendipity's, an ice-cream parlor on the Upper East Side.

August

10 As his pop duet with **Kiki Dee**, *Don't Go Breaking My Heart*, begins a month at US No. 1 (it is also enjoying a six-week ride at the top in the UK – curiously, his only domestic chart-topper), **Elton John** plays the first of seven nightly shows at Madison Square Garden, dressed as the Statue of Liberty. The series will take $1.25 million in ticket receipts, breaking the house record set a year ago by the **Rolling Stones**.

11 EMI signs a deal with Soviet record company Melodiya to release **Wings**' *Band On The Run* in the Soviet Union.

13 The **Clash** perform their first concert: a media showcase at a rehearsal hall in Chalk Farm, London. Managed by Bernie Rhodes – who works in Malcolm McLaren's Sex boutique – they were assembled in June by guitarist **Mick Jones**, who had spent nine abortive months with early punk outfit **London SS**. Jones has recruited bassist **Paul Simonon**, drummer **Terry Chimes**, and ex-**101ers** lead vocalist, **Joe Strummer**.

14 Singer-songwriter **Nick Lowe**'s debut single *So It Goes*, coupled with *Heart Of The City*, co-produced with Jake Riviera, is the first release – with the catalog number BUY 1 – on the UK independent label Stiff. Lowe and Riviera have borrowed £600 ($1,020) from **Lee Brilleaux** of **Dr. Feelgood** (for whom Riviera was tour manager) to start up the label, and Lowe's single was recorded as a publisher's demo at a cost of £45 ($77). Lowe will become an in-house producer, responsible for the **Damned**'s debut album and **Elvis Costello**'s first single, *Less Than Zero*. Aside from his label duties, he will also produce *Chicken Funk* by **Clover** (including **Huey Lewis** and future **Doobie Brother John McFee**), and **Dave Edmunds**'s *Get It*.

18 The launch issue of the first punk fanzine, Sniffin' Glue, is published in Britain. Edited by Mark P., the alternative rag will quickly establish itself as a must-read for the burgeoning blank generation, and will continue to appear until September of next year.

26 **Donna Summer** performs her disco smash, *Love To Love You Baby*, on "American Bandstand." The erotic song – featuring Summer's overtly climactic sighs and groans – hit US No. 2 and UK No. 4 in February, having been edited down from its 16:48-minute album version. Massachusetts-born, 25-year-old Summer met **Pete Bellotte**, owner/producer of Munich's Musicland Studios, while she was performing in "Godspell" in Germany, and he co-wrote her maiden hit with producer **Giorgio Moroder**, who licensed it to Neil Bogart's Casablanca label in the US.

29 The Screen on the Green, a favored art movie house in Islington, north London, holds a Midnight Special punk event, with performances by the **Sex Pistols**, the **Clash**,

September

4 ***Fleetwood Mac*** finally hits US No. 1, 15 months after entering the chart. In Britain, **Abba** score their third chart-topper of the year with *Dancing Queen*, following *Mamma Mia* and *Fernando*. Like all their hits, it is written and produced by the quartet's male contingent, **Benny Andersson** and **Björn Ulvaeus**, with group manager Stig Anderson.

18 **Queen** perform at a free concert in London's Hyde Park, preceded by opening acts **Kiki Dee** and **Supercharge**, before an estimated crowd of 150,000.

20 The **Sex Pistols** headline a punk rock festival at the 100 Club in London. It sees the debuts of **Subway Sect** and **Siouxsie & the Banshees**, featuring 19-year-old **John Beverly** – aka **Sid Vicious** – on drums. At a subsequent festival gig, featuring the **Damned**, a girl will lose an eye when hit by a broken bottle, believed to have been thrown by Vicious. The Damned will visit the girl in the hospital.

25 American singer-songwriting duo **Kenny Loggins** and **Jim Messina** split, following a concert in Hawaii at the end of a 34-city US tour. Both artists will remain individually signed to Columbia Records, for whom they have notched up five Top 20 US chart albums as a pair over the past four years. Meanwhile, on US television, blue-eyed soul singer-songwriter, **Boz Scaggs**, is the music guest on "Saturday Night Live." He performs his breakthrough smash, *Lowdown*, taken from his US No. 2-peaking, soul-pop fused ***Silk Degrees*** album, which is six months into a 115-week chart run.

27 The **Runaways**, on their first European tour to promote their maiden album, ***The Runaways***, are detained by police in Dover, England, as they are about to board a cross-channel ferry. Several items allegedly stolen from London's White House Hotel – including hotel keys and a hairdryer – are found in one of the cars in which the group is traveling. They spend the night in jail. The glam-punk band has been assembled by impresario/producer, **Kim Fowley**, with the all-girl line-up of lead singer **Cherie Currie**, guitarists **Joan Jett** and **Lita Ford**, bassist **Jackie Fox**, and drummer **Sandy West**.

October

1 **David Bowie** moves to the Schöneberg district of West Berlin, where he will live as a semi-recluse for the next three years. He has relocated with **Iggy Pop** in a mutual (and successful) attempt to kick their drug addiction.

2 **Joe Cocker**, making his first appearance on "Saturday Night Live," has to put up with cast member **John Belushi**'s spot-on impersonation of him as they duet on **Traffic**'s *Feelin' Alright*. **Eric Idle** is hosting the program, having promised to bring the **Beatles** with him if producer Lorne Michaels pays him $3,000.

8 A week after **Johnny Rotten** appeared on the cover of the **New Musical Express**, the **Sex Pistols** are signed by EMI Records for a £40,000 ($68,000) advance, following bids by Chrysalis, RAK, and Polydor. Polydor had been expecting the band to show up at a recording session with producer Chris Parry. An EMI spokesman says, "Here at last is a group with a bit of guts for younger people to identify with."

23 Three days after the London premiere of their film, "The Song Remains the Same," **Led Zeppelin** make their first-ever appearance on US television. They perform the songs *Black Dog* and *Dazed And Confused* on "Don Kirshner's Rock Concert."

29 A sign of things to come, a **Sex Pistols** gig at Lancaster Polytechnic is banned by the local authority, which doesn't want "that sort of filth in the town limits."

The Runaways were put together by veteran record producer and entrepreneur Kim Fowley, who was looking to form a female Ramones.

BOSTON

Aug 9 **Epic Records release Boston's debut album in the US. *Boston* has been almost entirely written and recorded by 29-year-old guitarist/keyboardist Tom Scholz, while working as a product designer for Polaroid. Brad Delp has contributed lead vocals and two compositions. Scholz comes from Toledo, Ohio, but is a graduate of MIT, with a master's degree in mechanical engineering. The album was assembled as a collection of sophisticated rock demos in a self-constructed basement studio in Swampscott, Massachusetts.**

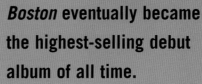

Boston **eventually became the highest-selling debut album of all time.**

Nov 1976

The Band say goodbye... The Sex Pistols on TV... Attempt made on Bob Marley's life...

George Harrison and Paul Simon

November

13 Having left the top spot on the Hot 100 last week, **Chicago**'s breezy ballad, *If You Leave Me Now*, begins a three-week run at UK No. 1. Their first chart-topper in both territories, the song was written by lead singer, **Peter Cetera**, and helmed by their long-time manager/ producer, James William Guercio.

19 **Van Morrison** is awarded his first gold record in the US, for ***Moondance***. Released more than six years ago, the album failed to make either the US or UK Top 30, but is increasingly revered as his seminal work, becoming a strong-selling catalog item for Warner Bros.

20 Ex-**Lovin' Spoonful**'s **John Sebastian** – who scored a US No. 1 solo hit with *Welcome Back* in May – tops the bill with **Joni Mitchell** at the California Celebrates the Whales benefit organized by Governor Jerry Brown, at the Memorial Auditorium in Sacramento.

20 **Paul Simon** hosts "Saturday Night Live" for a second time, this time with musical guest **George Harrison**. The duo sing *Here Comes The Sun* and *Homeward Bound* together, and Simon performs *Still Crazy After All These Years* dressed in a turkey costume. Harrison asks producer Lorne Michaels whether he can have the $3,000 the show is promising for the **Beatles** to reunite. Michaels replies: "If it was up to me, you could have the money, but NBC wouldn't agree." **Paul McCartney** is apparently staying with **John Lennon** in New York, and both are watching the show.

25 After 16 years together, the **Band** make their farewell appearance on Thanksgiving Day, at San Francisco's Winterland Ballroom – the

KISS began the year having their footprints placed on the sidewalk outside Grauman's Chinese Theater and ended it with a Top 30 hit.

The Jamie Reid-designed artwork featured a picture of Her Royal Highness, Queen Elizabeth II, with God Save The Queen and Sex Pistols respectively superimposed on her eyes and mouth. The Sex Pistols tour was doomed from the start with only three of the original 19 dates going ahead.

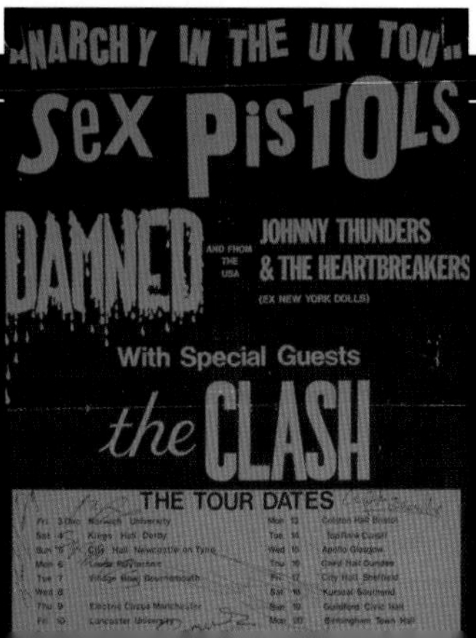

The Band plus guests

George Harrison thought that he should get a quarter of the money offered for a Beatles reunion for his solo appearance on "Saturday Night Live", while Paul Simon suffered the ignominy of singing *Still Crazy After All These Years* in a turkey costume... The Los Angeles Times' Robert Hilburn described The Last Waltz as the most prestigious lineup of rock talent ever to assemble for a single event.

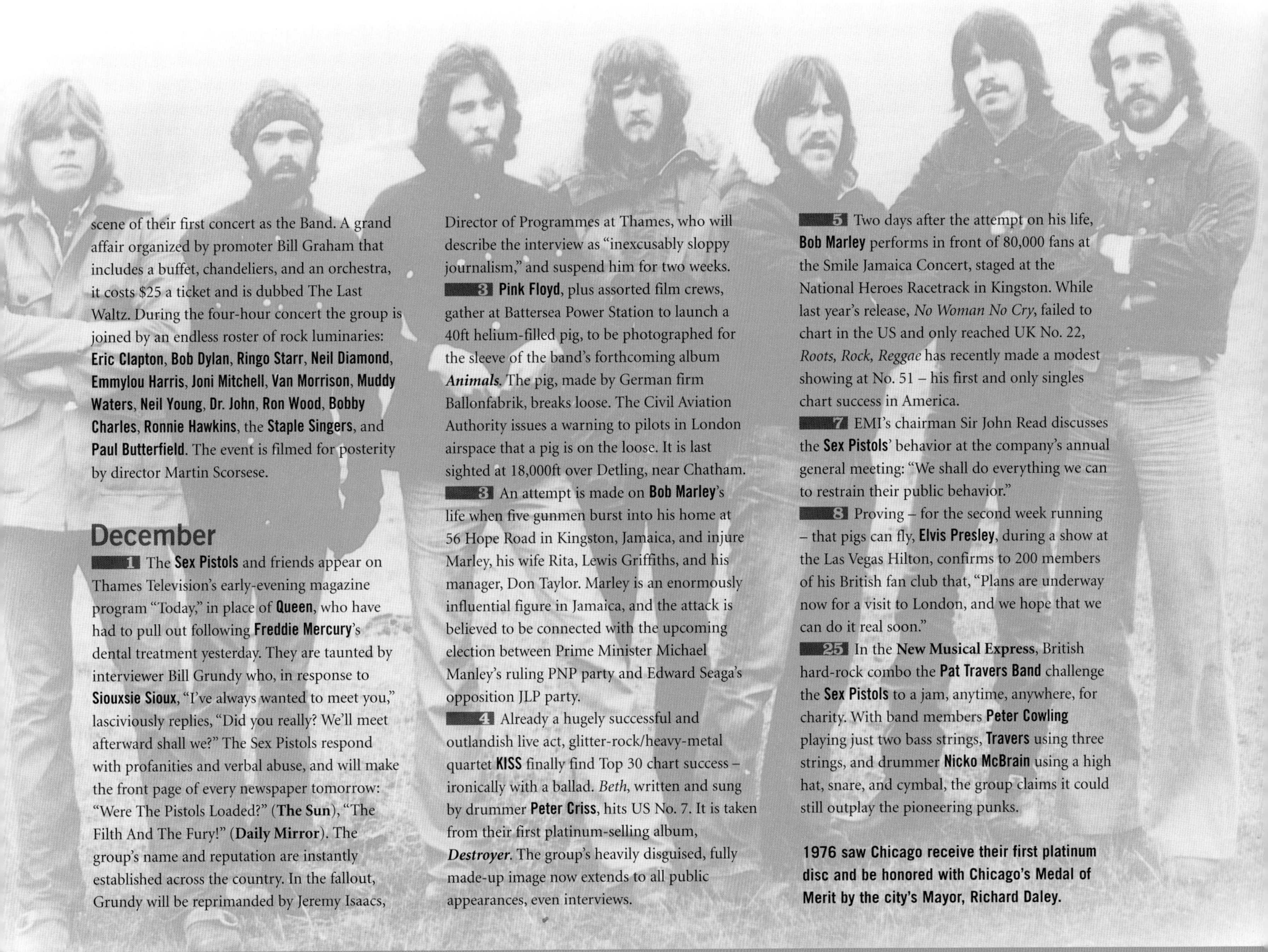

scene of their first concert as the Band. A grand affair organized by promoter Bill Graham that includes a buffet, chandeliers, and an orchestra, it costs $25 a ticket and is dubbed The Last Waltz. During the four-hour concert the group is joined by an endless roster of rock luminaries: **Eric Clapton**, **Bob Dylan**, **Ringo Starr**, **Neil Diamond**, **Emmylou Harris**, **Joni Mitchell**, **Van Morrison**, **Muddy Waters**, **Neil Young**, **Dr. John**, **Ron Wood**, **Bobby Charles**, **Ronnie Hawkins**, the **Staple Singers**, and **Paul Butterfield**. The event is filmed for posterity by director Martin Scorsese.

December

1 The **Sex Pistols** and friends appear on Thames Television's early-evening magazine program "Today," in place of **Queen**, who have had to pull out following **Freddie Mercury**'s dental treatment yesterday. They are taunted by interviewer Bill Grundy who, in response to **Siouxsie Sioux**, "I've always wanted to meet you," lasciviously replies, "Did you really? We'll meet afterward shall we?" The Sex Pistols respond with profanities and verbal abuse, and will make the front page of every newspaper tomorrow: "Were The Pistols Loaded?" (**The Sun**), "The Filth And The Fury!" (**Daily Mirror**). The group's name and reputation are instantly established across the country. In the fallout, Grundy will be reprimanded by Jeremy Isaacs, Director of Programmes at Thames, who will describe the interview as "inexcusably sloppy journalism," and suspend him for two weeks.

3 **Pink Floyd**, plus assorted film crews, gather at Battersea Power Station to launch a 40ft helium-filled pig, to be photographed for the sleeve of the band's forthcoming album *Animals*. The pig, made by German firm Ballonfabrik, breaks loose. The Civil Aviation Authority issues a warning to pilots in London airspace that a pig is on the loose. It is last sighted at 18,000ft over Detling, near Chatham.

3 An attempt is made on **Bob Marley**'s life when five gunmen burst into his home at 56 Hope Road in Kingston, Jamaica, and injure Marley, his wife Rita, Lewis Griffiths, and his manager, Don Taylor. Marley is an enormously influential figure in Jamaica, and the attack is believed to be connected with the upcoming election between Prime Minister Michael Manley's ruling PNP party and Edward Seaga's opposition JLP party.

4 Already a hugely successful and outlandish live act, glitter-rock/heavy-metal quartet **KISS** finally find Top 30 chart success – ironically with a ballad. *Beth*, written and sung by drummer **Peter Criss**, hits US No. 7. It is taken from their first platinum-selling album, *Destroyer*. The group's heavily disguised, fully made-up image now extends to all public appearances, even interviews.

5 Two days after the attempt on his life, **Bob Marley** performs in front of 80,000 fans at the Smile Jamaica Concert, staged at the National Heroes Racetrack in Kingston. While last year's release, *No Woman No Cry*, failed to chart in the US and only reached UK No. 22, *Roots, Rock, Reggae* has recently made a modest showing at No. 51 – his first and only singles chart success in America.

7 EMI's chairman Sir John Read discusses the **Sex Pistols**' behavior at the company's annual general meeting: "We shall do everything we can to restrain their public behavior."

8 Proving – for the second week running – that pigs can fly, **Elvis Presley**, during a show at the Las Vegas Hilton, confirms to 200 members of his British fan club that, "Plans are underway now for a visit to London, and we hope that we can do it real soon."

25 In the **New Musical Express**, British hard-rock combo the **Pat Travers Band** challenge the **Sex Pistols** to a jam, anytime, anywhere, for charity. With band members **Peter Cowling** playing just two bass strings, **Travers** using three strings, and drummer **Nicko McBrain** using a high hat, snare, and cymbal, the group claims it could still outplay the pioneering punks.

1976 saw Chicago receive their first platinum disc and be honored with Chicago's Medal of Merit by the city's Mayor, Richard Daley.

ROOTS **During this year: Dublin schoolboys Paul Hewson, David Evans, Adam Clayton, Larry Mullen, and Dick Evans form as Feedback, at Mullen's parents' home, in response to his recruitment note left on a noticeboard at the Mount Temple High School... aspiring singer-songwriter Bryan Adams replaces Nick Gilder as lead singer in Canadian rock combo, Sweeney Todd... Gary Kemp forms the Makers, with fellow Owens Grammar School friends, Tony Hadley and John Keeble, Steve Norman and Richard Miller (it will evolve into Spandau Ballet)... on the way to forming Air Supply, Graham Russell and Russell Hitchcock work for the first time together as cast members of "Jesus Christ Superstar" in Melbourne... Bronx DJ, Kevin Donovan (aka Afrika Bambaataa) forms Zulu Nation, an Afro-centric musical and cultural collective... 11-year-old Icelandic child singer Björk signs a record deal with the local Fálkkin label and records her maiden album, which includes a cover version of Syreeta's *Your Kiss Is Sweet*... Billy MacKenzie and Alan Rankine form a cabaret duo called the Absorbic Ones in MacKenzie's native Dundee; continuing with a series of ad hoc bands over the coming years, they will have success at the end of the decade as the Associates... and Adam Ant places an ad in Melody Maker: "Beat On A Bass With The B-Sides"...**

Dec 1976

Less than two months after signing to EMI Records, the company's Chairman Sir John Reed apologized for the group's behavior at the AGM.

"There is no way we are going to be prevented from playing in Britain."

Malcolm McLaren, **Melody Maker**, December 11, 1976

Dec 6 The **Sex Pistols**' Anarchy in the UK tour, also featuring the **Clash**, the **Damned**, and the **Heartbreakers**, begins at Leeds Polytechnic (which is the tour's fourth scheduled date). Only three out of 19 planned gigs will go ahead. The Damned will be thrown off the tour after agreeing to play for Derby councilors in private (to assess their suitability for Derby youth). Capable of upsetting just about everyone – **Johnny Rotten** complains to one audience: "You're not wrecking the place. The **News Of the World** will be really disappointed" – the Sex Pistols will be vilified at every turn. Conservative London Councilor Bernard Brook-Partridge, one of the many they offend, says, "I think most of these groups would be vastly improved by sudden death. The worst are the Sex Pistols and they are the antithesis of humankind, and the whole world would be vastly improved by their total and utter non-existence."

Dance, Dance, Dance (Yowsah, Yowsah, Yowsah)

1977

No.1 US SINGLES

Jan 1	Tonight's The Night (Gonna Be Alright) **Rod Stewart**
Jan 8	You Don't Have To Be A Star (To Be In My Show) **Marilyn McCoo & Billy Davis Jr.**
Jan 15	You Make Me Feel Like Dancing **Leo Sayer**
Jan 22	I Wish **Stevie Wonder**
Jan 29	Car Wash **Rose Royce**
Feb 5	Torn Between Two Lovers **Mary MacGregor**
Feb 19	Blinded By The Light **Manfred Mann's Earth Band**
Feb 26	New Kid In Town **Eagles**
Mar 5	Love Theme From "A Star Is Born" (Evergreen) **Barbra Streisand**
Mar 26	Rich Girl **Daryl Hall & John Oates**
Apr 9	Dancing Queen **Abba**
Apr 16	Don't Give Up On Us **David Soul**
Apr 23	Don't Leave Me This Way **Thelma Houston**
Apr 30	Southern Nights **Glen Campbell**
May 7	Hotel California **Eagles**
May 14	When I Need You **Leo Sayer**
May 21	Sir Duke **Stevie Wonder**
June 11	I'm Your Boogie Man **KC & the Sunshine Band**
June 18	Dreams **Fleetwood Mac**
June 25	Got To Give It Up (Pt. I) **Marvin Gaye**
July 2	Gonna Fly Now (Theme From "Rocky") **Bill Conti**
July 9	Undercover Angel **Alan O'Day**
July 16	Da Doo Ron Ron **Shaun Cassidy**
July 23	Looks Like We Made It **Barry Manilow**
July 30	I Just Want To Be Your Everything **Andy Gibb**
Aug 20	Best Of My Love **Emotions**
Sept 17	I Just Want To Be Your Everything **Andy Gibb**
Sept 24	Best Of My Love **Emotions**
Oct 1	Star Wars Theme/Cantina Band **Meco**
Oct 15	You Light Up My Life **Debby Boone**
Dec 24	How Deep Is Your Love **Bee Gees**

The Clash

Blondie's Debbie Harry

Three months after signing with CBS Records, the Clash debuted with their punk classic *White Riot*... Chrysalis Records presciently signed Blondie away from the Private Stock label, acquiring all rights to their previously recorded material before releasing *Plastic Letters*.

In the year that **Elvis** died, the **Sex Pistols** led the punk rebellion, disco met celluloid in "Saturday Night Fever," and bands such as **Foreigner**, **Journey**, and **Rush** demonstrated rock's staying power: not an easy time to be a teenager.

The **Eagles**' lyric, "You can check out any time you like, But you can never leave," could apply to no one more aptly than **Presley**. His legend and music would generate more income after his death than while he was alive. One of the top-selling artists in the world even in 2003, Elvis will never truly "leave."

With the Sex Pistols' manager maestro, **Malcolm McLaren**, playing the record industry like a violin, Virgin Records released *God Save The Queen*: it got no radio play but was still a British No. 2 hit. They followed up with their first and last album, which rocketed to UK No. 1. The band promptly imploded.

The Sex Pistols had the highest profile, but they were certainly not the most talented punk band. The **Clash**, the **Stranglers**, the **Damned**, and several others had more to give. And offering a more literate musical angst were artists like **Elvis Costello & the Attractions**. The British bands acquired a cult US following, but there was no comparable US demographic to propel them to chart success. New York bands such as **Blondie**, **Television**, and **Talking Heads** pursued a more esoteric and musical path, soon to be simplistically bracketed as New Wave. The mainstream was best represented by **Fleetwood Mac**, whose masterpiece ***Rumours*** was the essence of California pop-rock. Personal problems within the group gave the lyrics real emotion, and the melodies were timeless – both elements connecting with a more mature audience, who were turned off by disco and punk. The album spent longer at the top of the US charts than any other since *West Side Story*.

And through it all, disco sailed on. **Donna Summer** fronted another teutonic mega-hit with *I Feel Love*, and a slew of classics filled the dancefloors and the charts. Above all, there was "Saturday Night Fever," and the unlikely marriage of disco and the **Bee Gees**. One unkind critic described them as "former **Beatles** clones singing like mechanical mice with an unnatural sense of rhythm." But their nervous energy, chugging beats, and trademark falsetto harmonies helped to make the double album the bestselling soundtrack to date. In a fractured year, the **Clash** presented their White Riot tour in the UK, and the velvet rope made its debut at Studio 54 in New York. *C'est chic.*

"The band's appeal is awful... many find it irresistible."

Melody Maker on the Stranglers, May 14, 1977

No.1 UK SINGLES

Jan 1	When A Child Is Born (Soleado) **Johnny Mathis**
Jan 15	Don't Give Up On Us **David Soul**
Feb 12	Don't Cry For Me Argentina **Julie Covington**
Feb 19	When I Need You **Leo Sayer**
Mar 12	Chanson D'Amour **Manhattan Transfer**
Apr 2	Knowing Me, Knowing You **Abba**
May 7	Free **Deniece Williams**
May 21	I Don't Want To Talk About It/First Cut Is The Deepest **Rod Stewart**
June 18	Lucille **Kenny Rogers**
June 25	Show You The Way To Go **Jacksons**
July 2	So You Win Again **Hot Chocolate**
July 23	I Feel Love **Donna Summer**
Aug 20	Angelo **Brotherhood of Man**
Aug 27	Float On **Floaters**
Sept 3	Way Down **Elvis Presley**
Oct 8	Silver Lady **David Soul**
Oct 29	Yes Sir, I Can Boogie **Baccara**
Nov 5	The Name Of The Game **Abba**
Dec 3	Mull Of Kintyre/Girls' School **Wings**

1977

EMI terminate the Sex Pistols... CBS sign the Clash... Fleetwood Mac's *Rumours* is released...

***Hotel California* proved to be the Eagles' bestselling original album, eventually shifting over sixteen million copies in the US alone.**

The Jam signed with Polydor Records following a month's residency at the Red Cow pub, where they auditioned for, and were rejected by, EMI.

January

1 While London's revered rock venue, the Rainbow Theatre, relaunches with a concert by **Genesis**, the smaller – and hipper – Roxy Club in Covent Garden officially opens with a concert by the **Clash**, having hosted a gig for new punks on the block, **Siouxsie & the Banshees** and **Generation X** (fronted by **Billy Idol**) on December 14.

4 The **Sex Pistols** fly out of Heathrow Airport, for a 24-date tour of Holland, Denmark, Norway, Sweden, and Finland, and delight in offending as many people as possible on the plane. A flight attendant observes: "These are the most revolting people I've ever seen. They called us filthy names and insulted everyone in sight. One of them was sick in a corridor."

6 Prior to a scheduled meeting between the **Sex Pistols**' representatives and EMI Records, the label issues a statement: "EMI and the Sex Pistols group have mutually agreed to terminate their recording contract. EMI feels it is unable to promote this group's records internationally in view of the adverse publicity which has been generated over the last two months."

10 **Keith Richard** is tried at Aylesbury Crown Court on two counts of drugs possession for his latest bust last May. He will be found guilty of cocaine possession and fined £750 ($1,425) with £250 ($475) costs, but acquitted on the charge of LSD possession. He is also fined £25 ($47.50) for driving without an MOT or car tax. When questioned by Sir Peter Rawlinson, his defense counsel, about playing lead guitar for a living, he replies: "It means I make a lot of noise."

10 The **Bee Gees** begin work on vocal and bass touch-ups and mixing of live tracks for their upcoming ***Here At Last... Bee Gees Live!***, at Le Château Hérouville studio in France. During the week, they will receive a call from their manager Robert Stigwood, founder of the RSO label, asking them to write and record four songs for a film he is producing based on a New York magazine article, "Tribal Rites Of The New Saturday Night," about Brooklyn's blue-collar disco culture. They will produce five songs: *Stayin' Alive*, *How Deep Is Your Love*, *Night Fever*, *More Than A Woman* (which they will give to R&B combo, **Tavares**), and *If I Can't Have You* (for Hawaiian-born singer, **Yvonne Elliman**).

15 Certified platinum in the US last month, the Bill Szymczyk-produced ***Hotel California*** tops the US chart for the **Eagles**. Mostly written by **Don Henley** and **Glenn Frey**, it will spin off three hit singles, including two US chart-toppers, *New Kid In Town* and the career-defining 6:30-minute title track, hallmarked by guitar solos by **Joe Walsh** and **Don Felder**.

22 The **Sex Pistols** and EMI make their divorce official. The band receives £30,000 ($57,000), plus £10,000 ($19,000) from its publishing deal.

23 In the middle of singing *Ain't It Strange*, **Patti Smith** falls 15ft off the stage at a gig in Tampa, Florida, where her group is opening for **Bob Seger**, breaking a bone in her neck. Seger's set goes ahead. The 31-year-old, Michigan-born, rock singer-songwriter/guitarist is touring to support his breakthrough Capitol album, ***Night Moves*** (which will hit US No. 8 and be certified platinum in March).

26 The **Clash** sign a worldwide contract with CBS Records, in a deal said to be worth £100,000 ($190,000) for six albums – despite widespread industry concerns over the volatile punk movement.

30 With their first single, *(Get A) Grip (On Yourself)*, released yesterday, the **Stranglers**' gig at London's Rainbow Theatre – supporting the **Climax Blues Band** – is brought to an abrupt end because of singer **Hugh Cornwell**'s obscene T-shirt. Defying an agreement made between the Greater London Council and Rainbow management, that certain words "would not appear on their apparel or over the amplification," Cornwell – who is wearing the T-shirt with the offending word on the back – takes it off and puts it back on the other way round.

February

12 The **Police** – who have yet to play a gig – record their first single, *Fall Out*, backed by *Nothing Achieving*, at Pathway Studios in Islington. The session costs them £150 ($285).

FLEETWOOD MAC

Feb 15 **Lyrically documenting personal problems within the group – the McVies are separating, the Buckingham and Nicks relationship is unsettled, and Mick Fleetwood's divorce proceedings are under way – Fleetwood Mac's *Rumours* is finally released in the US. With songwriting divided between Lindsey Buckingham, Stevie Nicks, and Christine McVie (except the group-penned *The Chain*), it has been co-produced by the band with Richard Dashut and Ken Caillat. A landmark set – both for the group and for popular music in general – the soft-rock album will yield four major hits: *Go Your Own Way*, the US No. 1 smash *Dreams*, *Don't Stop*, and *You Make Loving Fun*.**

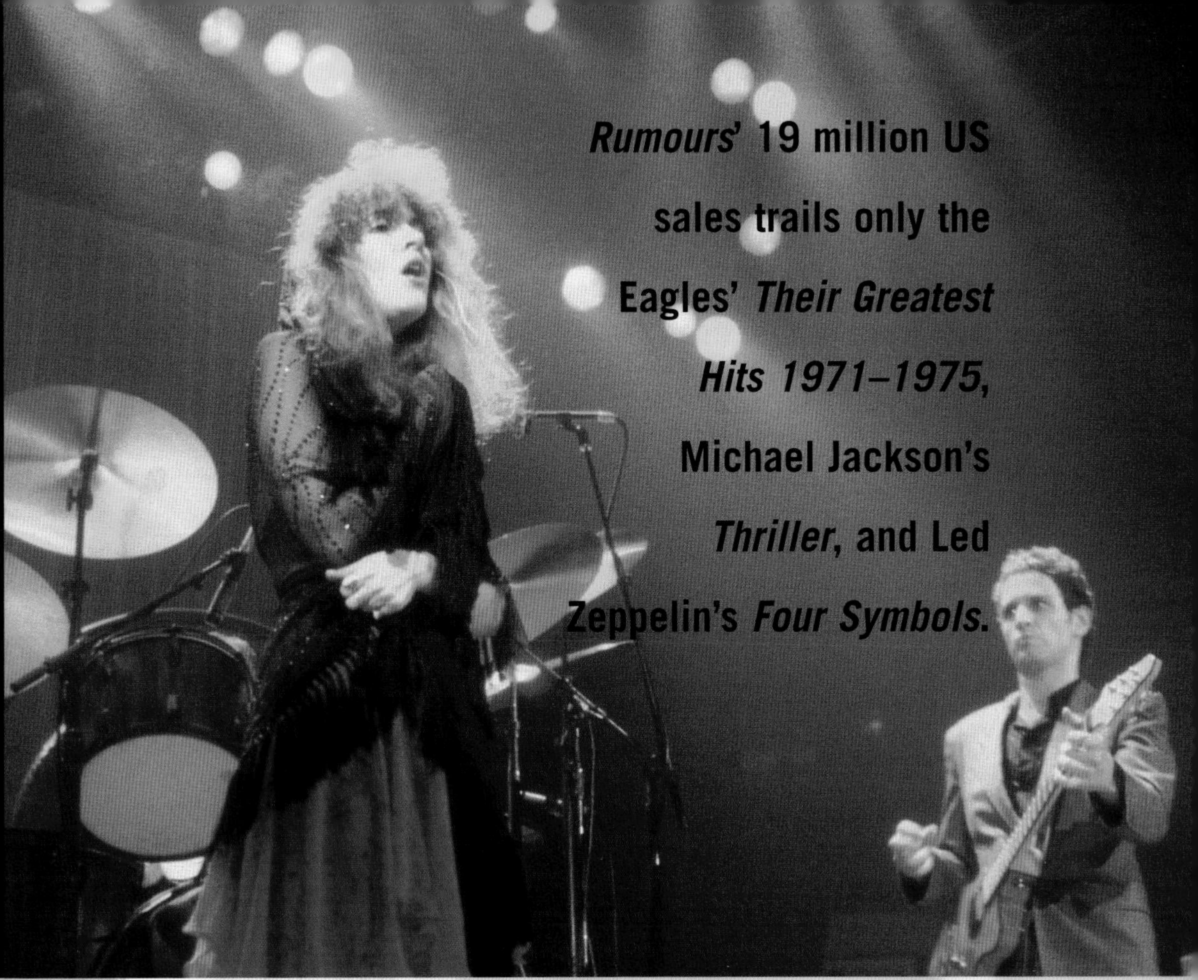

***Rumours'* 19 million US sales trails only the Eagles' *Their Greatest Hits 1971–1975*, Michael Jackson's *Thriller*, and Led Zeppelin's *Four Symbols*.**

They were formed last month by ex-**Curved Air** drummer, 24-year-old Virginia-born **Stewart Copeland** (the son of a CIA agent) and 25-year-old British **Last Exit** singer/bass player **Gordon Sumner**, nicknamed **Sting** because he regularly wears a bee-like black and yellow striped jersey. The third member of the trio is guitarist **Henri Padovani**.

14 Formed last October following a drunken evening at a Chinese restaurant, the **B-52's** – comprising **Fred Schneider** on keyboards/vocals, **Kate Pierson** on organ/vocals, **Keith Strickland** on drums, **Cindy Wilson** on guitar/vocals, and her older brother **Ricky Wilson** on guitar – play their first gig at a Valentine's Day house party in a greenhouse in Athens, Georgia.

19 **Stevie Wonder** wins the Album of the Year category – for the third time – for ***Songs In The Key Of Life*** at the 19th annual Grammy Awards. He also picks up trophies for Producer of the Year, Best Pop Vocal Performance, Male (***Songs In The Key Of Life***), and Best R&B Vocal Performance, Male (*I Wish*). (During a live satellite linkup with Wonder from Lagos, the sound is lost, and host Andy Williams says "Well, if you can't hear us, I hope you can see us.") **George Benson** collects three awards, including Record of the Year for *This Masquerade*, while **Chicago** win Best Pop Vocal Performance by a Duo, Group or Chorus for *If You Leave Me Now*, which also wins Best Arrangement Accompanying Vocalists for Jimmie Haskell and James William Guercio.

19 **Bruce Springsteen** enjoys his first US No. 1 – albeit as a songwriter – as **Manfred Mann's Earthband** takes *Blinded By The Light* to the top.

22 **Rose Royce**'s *Car Wash* is certified platinum by the RIAA. The group has been assembled by the song's writer and producer, **Norman Whitfield**, an ex-Motown marvel who helmed five US chart-toppers before setting up on his own. Whitfield was commissioned to provide songs for last year's "Car Wash," which became the first film to feature a complete disco soundtrack.

25 Polydor Records announces the signing of new mod/punk trio, the **Jam**, for a £6,000 ($11,400) advance offered by A&R staffer Chris Parry, who was urged to see them by **Shane MacGowan**, lead singer with the startup punk combo, the **Nipple Erectors**. **Paul Weller** (singer/guitarist and main songwriter), drummer **Rick Buckler**, who met Weller at Sheerwater Secondary Modern School, and bassist **Bruce Foxton** are managed by Weller's father, John, who is at present making business calls from a building site where he is working. Currently sporting mohair suits and using Rickenbacker guitars, the Jam will establish their own niche within the burgeoning punk/new wave genres.

March

5 The **Rolling Stones** give the second of two performances at the 350-capacity El Mocambo nightclub in Toronto, Canada. The two-hour set, with an audience of contest winners picked by radio station CHUM, is the first the band has given in a club setting since it played in Bristol, England, in 1964. **Jagger** will say that, although it was "fun," it wouldn't be financially feasible to do it again. "We made $371 from our take from the bar last night," he says. Some of tonight's songs will be included on the group's forthcoming ***Love You Live*** album, to be released in September.

7 Atlantic Records releases the eponymous ***Foreigner*** in the US. The transatlantic band, formed last year, features experienced British musicians, lead guitarist/founder **Mick Jones** (who began his career more than a decade ago in **Nero & the Gladiators**) and multi-instrumentalist **Ian McDonald**, with four relative newcomers: British drummer **Dennis Elliott**, and Americans, bassist **Ed Gagliardi**, lead vocalist **Lou Gramm**, and keyboardist **Alan Greenwood**. The album will yield two hits: *Feels Like The First Time* and *Cold As Ice*.

> **"We got a little more into rock 'n' roll, a little more into rhythm 'n' blues… But that's not to say we've given up country. We're only exploring a bit of new territory for a while."**
>
> Don Henley on ***Hotel California***, interview in **Country Rambler**, January 1977

The Damned

The Sex Pistols are hired and fired by A&M... *Rumours* makes No. 1... Studio 54 opens in New York City...

9 After two months of negotiations, the **Sex Pistols** – with "bassist" **Sid Vicious** having replaced **Glen Matlock** – sign with A&M Records at the label's publishing arm, Rondor Music, in London. They will receive £150,000 ($285,000) over two years, with 18 songs required in each year. Commenting on the decision to sign the controversial group at Rondor, label MD Derek Green will say: "I did it there because I wanted to keep the band away from A&M as long as possible. As much as I loved the music, I wanted to delay any clash between them and my staff as long as possible. It came as quite a shock, when the signing took place, that Glen Matlock wasn't in the band. It had been Matlock's name all the way through negotiations, and then on the day there was Sid Vicious, an unknown quantity."

12 "The Old Grey Whistle Test" host Bob Harris is accosted at the Speakeasy club in London by musician **Jah Wobble**, asking when he is going to play the **Sex Pistols**' new record on the show. Harris ignores the question, and is punched. In the ensuing melée, **Johnny Rotten** allegedly attacks Harris's studio engineer George Nicholson, shattering a beer mug over his head.

16 Amid rumors that fellow A&M acts have put pressure on the company to get rid of the **Sex Pistols**, although it is more likely that the incident at the Speakeasy last weekend is responsible, the label announces that their contract has been terminated, and that production of their single *God Save The Queen* has been canceled. When **Malcolm McLaren** contacts label chief Jerry Moss in America, he is told that the decision was based on "humane grounds." He will tell the **New Musical Express** that A&M were glad to have the band on the label and that they "didn't just have to work with the **Captain & Tennille** all the time." The band collect a further £75,000 ($142,500) without passing Go, causing McLaren to comment later: "I keep walking in and out of offices being given cheques!"

18 Debut singles by the **Clash** (*White Riot*) and **Elvis Costello** (*Less Than Zero*) are released in the UK. The former is featured on the debut ***Clash*** album – a 14-song punk battle cry that rails against the establishment – due for release next month by CBS. The latter is produced by **Nick Lowe** and issued by Stiff Records.

21 The **Sex Pistols** play their first London date of the year, at the Notre Dame Halls – an annex to a Roman Catholic church – near Leicester Square. Hastily organized for the benefit of an NBC television crew shooting a documentary on the punk scene, it marks **Sid Vicious**'s debut with the group. In the audience are **Dave Vanian** of the **Damned**, punk upstarts **TV Smith**, the **Adverts**' lead singer, **Gaye Advert**, and Nancy Spungen, a well-to-do American girl, whose future will be inexorably tied to Vicious.

April

2 The latest headlining tour by **Kansas** – in support of their fourth album, ***Leftoverture***, peaking at US No. 5 – climaxes at the Palladium in New York. Formed by guitarist **Kenny Livgren** and drummer **Phil Ehart** in Topeka, Kansas, in 1969, the rock sextet recently scored their first hit with FM radio favorite, *Carry On Wayward Son*, penned by Livgren.

2 ***Rumours*** hits US No. 1 for **Fleetwood Mac**, and will spend a record 31 weeks topping the US survey. Worldwide sales will eventually

THE SEX PISTOLS

Mar 10 **The Sex Pistols' signing to A&M Records is restaged at a 7:00 am press conference, on a trestle table outside Buckingham Palace. Commenting on the group's first single for the label, *God Save The Queen*, manager Malcolm McLaren says: "It's not a punk rock version of the National Anthem, but the boys' own genuine tribute to the Queen." In a meet-and-greet with A&M staff this afternoon, they celebrate by smashing a window in the ladies' toilet, assaulting a female member of staff, throwing up on the floor, and leaving a trail of blood on the carpet.**

oomtown Rats

Dave Vanian was a gravedigger and Rat Scabies a drummer for the musical "Puss In Boots" prior to joining the Damned... Before founding the Boomtown Rats, Bob Geldof was a music journalist interviewing the likes of Elton John and Little Richard for the New Musical Express.

exceed 25 million, with 134 weeks on the US survey and more than 400 weeks on the UK listing – though only one of those will be at No. 1 (next January).

7 The **Damned** – the first British punk group to play US dates – open a four-night stint at CBGBs, home of the New York punk scene.

26 With the popularity of disco music reaching its peak in the US, Studio 54 opens in a converted television studio at 254 West 54th Street in New York. Owned and managed by Steve Rubell and Ian Schrager, it will quickly become *the* disco nightspot. With glittering chic decor, intimate alcoves, top celebrities, and an "anything goes" environment that celebrates drug-taking and sexual liberation, the club's elitist velvet rope admissions policy will be much copied around the world, as it becomes the hedonistic hotspot for the rich, famous, and just plain weird.

29 During the final concert of his British tour at London's Rainbow Theatre, **Eric Clapton** abruptly walks off stage before the end of his set, and the house lights come up. Ten minutes later he returns and tells the audience euphemistically that he is "tired and emotional," before completing the gig, with **Pete Townshend** joining him on *Layla* and *Crossroads*.

May

6 Dublin pop-punk band, the **Boomtown Rats** (named after a gang in the movie "Bound For Glory," based on the life of **Woody Guthrie**), make their British debut at London's Studio 51, before a group of Phonogram Records employees. They have been signed to the Ensign imprint, after a bidding war involving five other companies. Lead singer, 22-year-old **Bob Geldof**, says: "We are in this to get rich, to get famous, and to get laid."

8 London Weekend Television's "The London Programme" alleges that the **Sex Pistols** are in cahoots with ultra-right political movement the National Front. A retort by Malcolm McLaren is published in London's **Evening Standard**: "The Sex Pistols are not into any political party, least of all the loathsome National Front. I think it is extraordinarily irresponsible and dumb to give that scummy organization a load of free publicity by connecting them with us. Anarchy is not fascism but self-rule and a belief in following one's own way of life without recourse to any form of dictatorship of nationalism. We hate this kind of army nonsense."

10 Newly formed London punk act, **Adam & the Ants**, make their official live debut at London's Institute of Contemporary Arts restaurant at lunchtime. **Ant** (22-year-old singer **Stuart Goddard**) has told the ICA they are a country and western band. He makes his entrance dressed in leather gear with a hood and chains, and breaks into *Beat My Guest*. After this one number, the booker pays them their £8 ($15) and asks them to leave quietly.

12 Virgin Records announces it has signed the **Sex Pistols**. The group's third recording contract in eight months is worth an initial sum of £15,000 ($28,500) to the band, paid on the understanding that they will deliver an album during the coming year. Next month, Virgin will pay a further £50,000 ($95,000) advance for worldwide rights to Pistols material. Quotable as ever, **Johnny Rotten** will say: "I've always liked Richard Branson because, pompous rich twat that he is, he has a great sense of rebelliousness."

13 The **Damned** begin a major UK tour at the Porterhouse in Retford, England, supported by the **Adverts**. The tour posters confirm: "The Damned can now play three chords, the Adverts can play one. Hear all four of them at..." The tour will degenerate into farce when several dates are canceled or re-scheduled. Fellow punksters the **Jam** and the **Stranglers** will find venues banning them as well.

> **"As an outré avant-garde experience it had its definite charms. But it's hardly an experience one would want to repeat very often."**
>
> John Rockwell on the Damned, **The New York Times**, April 8, 1977

Elvis Costello was still working as a computer operator at an Elizabeth Arden cosmetics factory when his first single was released.

Punk in full swing... Sex pistols in fights... The Clash arrested... Elvis Costello busks...

The Clash headlined the appropriately titled Britain's Burning – The Last Big Event Before We All Go To Jail concert at the Rag Market in Birmingham, England.

19 The **Jam** become the first punk band to appear on "Top Of The Pops," performing their current chart single *In The City*.

22 The American New Wave hits the UK, with two New York underground bands, **Blondie** and **Television**, embarking on their first British tour at the Apollo Theatre in Glasgow, Scotland. Blondie is supporting its self-titled debut album, released on the independent US label, Private Stock. The band was formed in 1974 by guitarist **Chris Stein** and his singer girlfriend, **Debbie Harry**, a former beautician and Playboy bunny.

27 The **Sex Pistols**' *God Save The Queen* is released by Virgin Records in the UK, and will reportedly sell 150,000 copies in five days, despite being banned from leading stores and by the BBC, which "has no intention of playing the record, because it is in gross bad taste." (The last hit to suffer a blanket ban by Radio 1 was **Max Romeo**'s *Wet Dream*, always referred to as "a record by Max Romeo.") Producer Robin Nash says *God Save The Queen* "is quite unsuitable for an entertainment show like 'Top Of The Pops.'"

June

1 Closing a four-month US tour, **Billy Joel** performs the first of four nightly shows at the Carnegie Hall in New York. Having had a false start in 1974 with his first hit, *Piano Man*, the 28-year-old pop singer-songwriter/pianist – born in Hicksville, Long Island – will shortly complete sessions for his fifth solo album, ***The Stranger***. This first collaboration with producer Phil Ramone will include the signature ballad, *Just The Way You Are*.

5 **Alice Cooper**'s boa constrictor, long a co-star of his live act, suffers a mortal bite from the rat it is being fed for breakfast. Next week, the distraught artist will hold a public audition – judged by **Flo & Eddie** – at the ABC Entertainment Center in Century City, California, to find a new performing boa. A snake named Angel will get the gig.

7 The **Sex Pistols**' River Party on the Thames – on the aptly named *Queen Elizabeth* – degenerates into mayhem, with a fracas breaking out between a French cameraman and Sex Pistols' cohort **Jah Wobble**. The skipper calls the River Police, who are following the boat, and when it ties up 11 people are arrested. They are hauled off to Bow Street police station.

11 *God Save The Queen* peaks at UK No. 2, behind **Rod Stewart**'s *I Don't Want To Talk About It/First Cut Is The Deepest*. Despite a widespread broadcasting ban, and many outlets not advertising or stocking it, *God Save The Queen* has been the bestselling single of the week. However, the British Market Research Bureau, compiler of the official chart, makes an arbitrary ruling that as it was on Virgin Records, all sales figures from Virgin stores are to be left out of the final calculations. The establishment wins this round, making sure that the reviled **Sex Pistols** are not topping the British chart during the week of the Queen's Silver Jubilee.

13 After being picked up by police in London on Friday and taken to Newcastle, England, where they spent the weekend in jail, the **Clash**'s **Joe Strummer** and **Topper Headon** are in Morpeth Magistrates Court on petty theft charges relating to the disappearance of Holiday Inn pillowcases and a key, during their recent stay in Seaton Burn. They failed to appear before the Morpeth Magistrates last week, because they were in London being fined £5 ($9.50) each at Kentish Town Court for spray-painting "Clash" graffiti on a wall. The group's UK tour, which starts later this week, is duly named Out on Parole.

18 Taking a break from recording at Wessex Studio in Highbury, north London, **Johnny Rotten**, producer Chris Thomas, and studio manager Bill Price are attacked outside the New Pegasus pub by a gang wielding knives and razors. Rotten has two tendons severed in his left arm, and is also slashed in the face. Thomas receives a cut to his face, and Price is cut on his arm.

19 **Sex Pistols**' drummer **Paul Cook** is beaten up outside London's Shepherd's Bush tube station, by six men who club him with a crowbar. He is taken to hospital where his head wounds require 15 stitches. He comments: "I was attacked by some old Teds. Apparently they didn't like the fact I was wearing brothel creepers!"

30 While the **Boomtown Rats** perform at the Music Machine in Camden Town, London, – and in keeping with the current rash of punk violence – lead singer **Bob Geldorf** is attacked on stage. He soldiers on with a bloody face and loose teeth.

After racking up 14 self-penned hits since 1970, Hot Chocolate turned to the pen of Russ Ballard, who wrote them their only UK No. 1 – *So You Win Again...* CBS Records held a reception in London for Billy Joel, at which he was carried around dressed as a boxer by British pugilists Terry Downes, Alan Minter, Colin Powes, and John H. Stracey.

July

2 **Hot Chocolate**, a multiracial London pop/soul sextet, enjoy their only UK No. 1 with *So You Win Again*. It is their 15th British hit, though their signature song will remain the 1975 global smash, *You Sexy Thing*. Formed in 1970, the group of mostly Caribbean-born musicians, led by Jamaican singer-songwriter **Errol Brown**, are signed to producer Mickie Most's RAK label.

14 **Elvis Costello** and his backing band the **Attractions** – supporting his debut album, ***My Aim Is True*** – play their first gig together as a support act to **Wayne** (yet to become **Jayne**) **County & the Electric Chairs** at the Garden in Penzance. The line-up is bassist **Bruce Thomas** (ex-**Sutherland Brothers & Quiver**), keyboardist **Steve Nieve** (a Royal College of Music graduate), and drummer **Pete Thomas** (ex-**Chilli Willi & the Red Hot Peppers**).

16 *Easy* by the Motown-signed **Commodores** becomes the group's third US R&B No. 1 smash, and their second chart-topper written by singer/keyboardist **Lionel Richie**. Originally formed as R&B combo the **Mighty Mystics**, by Richie and lead guitarist **Thomas McClary** while students at Tuskegee Institute in Alabama, the group's fortunes are gradually becoming dependent on Richie's compositional skills as a soulful balladeer. The exception will be *Easy*'s follow-up hit, the funk-driven, group-written *Brick House*, which will hit US No. 5 in October.

23 Yet to be released in the US, but already a massive disco hit across Europe, **Donna Summer**'s *I Feel Love* begins the first of four weeks at UK No. 1. It is underpinned by a furious bpm (beats per minute) groove, built around a mesmeric electronic sequencer rhythm, provided by producer **Giorgio Moroder**.

26 **Elvis Costello** busks outside the London Hilton Hotel, where Columbia Records is holding its annual sales conference. With a Voxx practice amp strapped over one shoulder, he performs for the arriving conventioneers, singing *Welcome To The Working Week, Waiting For The End Of The World*, and *Less Than Zero*. A confrontation between hotel security staff and Costello's manager, Jake Riviera, leads to the arrival of the police. Riviera protests: "He's not busking, he's just singing in the street. You can't stop people from singing!" When Costello is asked to move along, he continues to sing and is arrested. He is taken to Vine Street police station where he is charged with obstruction, and will subsequently be fined £5 ($9.50).

"We're not pretending the record isn't there. We mention it when announcing our chart listings, but we refuse to play it."

Radio 1 spokesman James Conway, commenting on the Sex Pistols' *God Save the Queen*, May 27, 1977

After three consecutive US Top 10 ballad hits, the Commodores returned to their familiar uptempo funk style with *Brick House*. A return to their softer style in 1978 brought them their biggest hit – *Three Times A Lady*.

977

Aug 18 **Elvis Presley**'s funeral service, arranged by singer **J.D. Sumner** and conducted by the Rev. C.W. Bradley, is held at Graceland, with 150 people attending, and 75,000 outside the gates. Presley died two days ago, after being discovered unconscious in a bathroom by his girlfriend Ginger Alden at 2:20 pm. He had been sitting on the toilet, reading **The Scientific Search For The Face Of Jesus**, but was found lying on the floor, with his gold pajama bottoms around his ankles, and his swollen face in a pool of vomit on the shagpile carpet. Alden called bodyguard Al Strada and aide Joe Esposito, who had been playing racquet ball with Presley earlier in the day. Presley failed to respond to Esposito's attempts at resuscitation and was rushed to Baptist Memorial Hospital, where he was pronounced dead at 3:30 pm in Trauma Room No. 1. (Bio Science Laboratories will subsequently reveal that at the time of his death, Presley's body contained butabarbital, codeine, morphine, pentobarbital, Placidyl, Quaalude, Valium, and Valmid.) His death at 42, by "cardiac arrythmia due to undetermined heartbeat," has immediately made headlines throughout the world. Thousands of fans from all over the US, and overseas, arrived in Memphis yesterday to pay their respects to the King. Some 25,000 people filed past his coffin at Graceland. Teenagers Alice Hovatar and Juanita Johnson are killed during an all-night vigil at the mansion after a

Elvis's body – in a copper casket – was taken in a 19-Cadillac cortege to Memphis' Forest Hill cemetery, for internment at 4:30 pm in a mausoleum alongside his mother, surrounded by thousands of floral tributes which required over 100 vans to take them from Graceland to the burial site. The King was buried still wearing his TCB

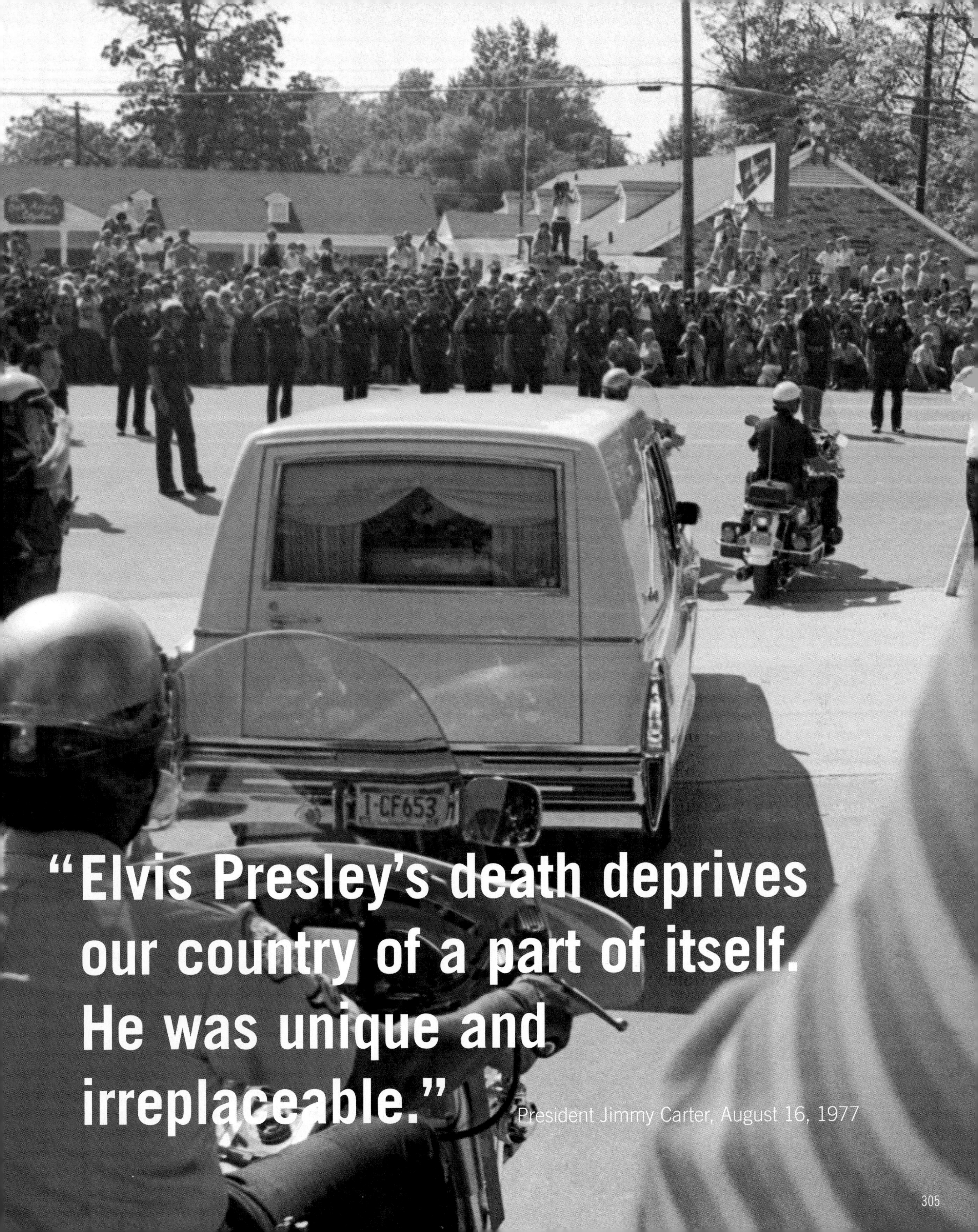

"Elvis Presley's death deprives our country of a part of itself. He was unique and irreplaceable."

President Jimmy Carter, August 16, 1977

1977

Elvis dies... Dire Straits debut... Brit record industry celebrates Queen's Silver Jubilee...

David Soul parlayed his popularity as Ken Hutchinson in the cop series "Starsky And Hutch" into a brief, but successful, singing career, scoring three consecutive UK smashes.

August

1 Ballantine Books publishes **Elvis: What Happened?**, a scurrilous, tell-all account of life with **Presley** by former bodyguards Sonny and Red West and Dave Hebler, with help from **National Star** editor, Steve Dunleavy. Portraying the King as an increasingly neurotic, overweight recluse, the book will be derided by most critics – and sell more than three million copies.

11 In an ill-advised meeting of cultures, the **Clash**, the **Damned**, and **Elvis Costello** play before jazz fans and hippies on "punk" night at the Bilzen Festival in Liège, Belgium. Overreacting to the reputation of punk bands and their fans, the organizers have erected a 10ft fence between the stage and the crowd. The audience, more interested in the barrier than the music, merrily while away the time digging up the concrete posts that support it. Several people are injured by being crushed against the wire.

19 The **Sex Pistols**, undertaking an "undercover" UK tour as the **S.P.O.T.S.** ("Sex Pistols On Tour Secretly"), play the Lafayette Club in Wolverhampton, England. They will also play under the pseudonyms the **Tax Exiles**, **Special Guest**, the **Hamsters**, and **Acne Rebble**.

26 Stiff Records releases **Ian Dury**'s *Sex And Drugs And Rock And Roll* in the UK, nimbly connecting the pub-rock scene of the early 1970s, in which Dury was a leading protagonist as frontman for **Kilburn & the High Roads**, with the exploding new wave/punk movement. (The 35-year-old singer-songwriter contracted polio from a swimming pool in Southend, England, at the age of seven, which left him with a stricken leg and hand). His new album, the critically revered ***New Boots And Panties!***, will be regarded as a seminal work – adding to Stiff Records' burgeoning reputation as an imaginative and innovative independent label.

"Elvis was dead before he died and his gut was so big it cast a shadow over rock 'n' roll in the last few years." Johnny Rotten, August 1977

4 Following the kidnapping of West German industrialist Hanns-Martin Schleyer in Cologne yesterday, British punk band the **Vibrators** – temporarily domiciled in Germany – are rudely awakened at dawn by 30 police at a farm outside Hamburg. The police search the farm and the band's van, only to discover that the Vibrators are indeed nothing more than a punk band, and not a terrorist faction.

9 **David Bowie** appears on **Marc Bolan**'s Granada television show "Marc," singing *Heroes* (the title track from his highly rated second album of the year) and a duet with Bolan, *Standing Next To You*. (In a less conventional pairing, Bowie will team up with **Bing Crosby** on US television in "Bing Crosby's Merrie Olde Christmas" on the 28th, dueting on *The Little Drummer Boy* and *Peace On Earth*. Curiously, both Bolan and Crosby will die within weeks.)

16 After a long night out at a London club, **Marc Bolan** and girlfriend **Gloria Jones** are on their way home when, at 5:00 am, their car (driven by Jones) leaves the road at a bend on Barnes Common in London, and crashes into a tree. Jones is badly injured, and Bolan is killed, two weeks before his 30th birthday. (The car, a purple Mini 1275 GT, had a tyre replaced and its wheels balanced earlier in the week. It is found after the crash that the offside tyre pressure was 16psi, instead of 26psi, and that two nuts on the offside front wheel were only finger tight.) Bolan will be cremated on the 20th at London's Golders Green Crematorium.

September

3 **Elvis Presley** posthumously scores his 17th UK No. 1 with *Way Down* beginning a five-week run.

October

3 The 24-date Stiff tour package, Stiff Live Stiffs, with eccentric stablemates **Elvis Costello**, **Nick Lowe**, **Ian Dury & the Blockheads**, ex-pub-rocker turned pop-punker **Wreckless Eric**, and journeyman guitarist and ex-**Pink Fairie**, **Larry Wallis**, begins at High Wycombe Town Hall, England. At the end of the trek, Costello and Lowe will leave Stiff to join Jake Riviera's newly formed Radar Records.

6 One of the few punk bands still without a record deal, **Siouxsie & the Banshees** wake up to find that someone has sprayed "Sign The Banshees Do It Now" on the walls of 15 different record companies around London. The group deny all knowledge of the stunt – which was undertaken by Les Mills, a friend of theirs.

8 While punk dominates the UK music scene, the most unlikely chart-topper, American "Starsky & Hutch" actor, **David Soul**, scores his second UK No. 1 of the year with *Silver Lady*, following the platinum-selling *Don't Give Up On Us* (which also hit US No. 1 in April).

12 After just a handful of gigs, **Dire Straits** make their debut at the Rock Garden in Covent Garden. They are led by singer-guitarist **Mark Knopfler**, a part-time teacher, pub-rock player

25 years after his death, fans still maintain a shrine at the tree on Queen's Ride, Putney, where Marc Bolan died.

and songwriter, and formerly a journalist on the **Yorkshire Evening Post**. His cohorts are his guitarist brother **David** (a social worker), sociology undergraduate **John Illsley**, and session drummer **Pick Withers**. Given their name by a friend of Knopfler's, who noted their financial plight, they scraped together £120 ($228) to record a five-song demo tape at London's Pathway studios in July. A copy was given to DJ Charlie Gillett, who featured the songs on his weekly BBC Radio London show, "Honky Tonk." Phonogram Records' A&R man John Stainze, one of many impressed by the broadcast demos, will track down the band, and after a short bidding war, will sign them to Phonogram's Vertigo imprint in December.

18 To celebrate the Queen's Silver Jubilee, the BPI hold the British Record Industry Britannia Awards at Wembley Conference Centre, honoring the best in British music since 1952. The **Beatles** win the Best British Pop Album (for ***Sgt. Pepper's Lonely Hearts Club Band***) and Best British Pop Group categories. **Cliff Richard** is named Best British Male Solo Artist. **Procol Harum**'s *A Whiter Shade Of Pale* and **Queen**'s *Bohemian Rhapsody* are named joint winners as Best British Pop Single. (Procol Harum re-form for the occasion to perform the song live.) **Simon & Garfunkel** appear together, in tuxedos, and, due to a camera fault, have to do six takes of *Bookends/Old Friends*. ***Bridge Over Troubled Water*** has been voted the Best International (Non-UK) Album and Single.

20 **Lynyrd Skynyrd**'s lead vocalist **Ronnie Van Zant**, guitarist **Steve Gaines** (who joined the group last year), his sister **Cassie Gaines** – one of the group's three backing singers – and personal manager Dean Kilpatrick are among six passengers killed when the band's rented plane, short of fuel, crashes into a swamp in Gillsburg, Mississippi, en route from Greenville, South Carolina, to Baton Rouge, where the group is scheduled to play at Louisiana University. **Gary Rossington**, **Allen Collins**, **Billy Powell**, and **Leon Wilkeson** are all seriously injured. MCA withdraws the sleeve of ***Street Survivors***, released on Monday, which pictures the group standing amid flames.

20 The Belgian Travel Service launches a lawsuit against the **Sex Pistols** and Virgin Records for doctoring a brochure for the group's *Holidays In The Sun* picture sleeve.

28 During a special three-night run at the 600-seat Old Waldorf in San Francisco, 24-year-old Californian singer **Steve Perry** – dressed entirely in white – walks on stage for the first time to join **Journey** for their encore song *Lights*. Recruited by the band's manager, Herbie Herbet, after he heard him singing on a demo tape with his former group, **Alien Project**, Perry's permanent addition to the hard-rock combo will dramatically change their fortunes, beginning with their next album, ***Infinity***.

Siouxsie Sioux was working as a waitress when she took part in the 100 Club Punk Festival in 1976 – a 20-minute set that included a recitation of The Lord's Prayer.

Bat Out Of Hell... "Saturday Night Fever" premieres... Elvis Costello on "Saturday Night Live"...

November

3 During a concert at London's Empire Pool in Wembley, **Elton John** – who collapsed during two recent concert performances – announces, "I have made a decision tonight. This is going to be the last show." (He will return to the live arena on February 3, 1979, in Sweden.)

5 PC Julie Dawn Storey – on patrol duty in Nottingham, England, – sees an ad for the **Sex Pistols**' ***Never Mind The Bollocks Here's The Sex Pistols*** album in the Virgin Record store. She notifies manager Christopher Seale that he could be prosecuted for contravening the Indecent Advertising Act. Seale takes down the offending poster, but after Storey leaves, he puts it back up again. Storey returns and arrests him. When Seale goes to trial, he will have noted barrister, John Mortimer, as his QC. The album will hit UK No. 1 next week. In the US – where it is released by Warner Bros. – it will stall at No. 106, though it will eventually reach platinum status as a punk classic and strong catalog seller.

The Ramones' 1977 album *Leave Home* featured 13 tracks, five of which were less than two minutes in duration.

16 **Rush** – a Canadian progressive hard-rock combo formed in 1973 by singer/guitarist **Alex Lifeson** and bassist **Geddy Lee**, with drummer **Neil Peart** recruited a year later – receive three US gold discs for ***2112***, ***All the World's A Stage***, and ***A Farewell To Kings***.

19 The **Ramones**' **Joey Ramone** suffers second degree burns when a makeshift humidifier explodes backstage before a concert at the Capitol Theater in Passaic, New Jersey. He undergoes emergency treatment and carries on with the show. After the last encore he is rushed to New York Hospital Burn Center, where he will stay for a week. A "Get Well" message will appear on the Jumbotron screen in Times Square.

22 A strong showcase of diverse new British talent, the three-week Front Row Festival begins at the Hope & Anchor pub in Upper

"If he is, as is claimed, the father of punk rock, then all I can say is I should love to meet the

MEAT LOAF

Nov 28 **As *Bat Out Of Hell* continues its inexorable rise up the charts (it will chart for 82 weeks in the US, and a monstrous 472 weeks in the UK), a Meat Loaf concert from the Bottom Line in New York is broadcast live on WNEW-FM. *Bat Out Of Hell* producer/composer Jim Steinman, and larger-than-life singer Meat Loaf (Marvin Lee Aday), started rehearsing the project last January. Steinman originally intended the songs for "Neverland," his futuristic musical version of "Peter Pan." They signed a deal with RCA Records, but pulled out when the label refused to include producer Todd Rundgren as part of the package. Their manager David Sonenberg approached the fledgling Cleveland International company, which persuaded Epic Records to release the project. It will amass global sales of over 20 million, becoming one of the most successful albums of the rock era.**

Street, Islington, England. It features the **Stranglers**, **Dire Straits**, reggae outfit **Steel Pulse**, recent Virgin Records new wave signing **XTC** (fronted by erudite singer-songwriter/guitarist, **Andy Partridge**), the **Tom Robinson Band** (who signed to EMI on August 9 and are led by openly gay, socio-politically motivated singer-songwriter Robinson) and the **Wilko Johnson Band** (ex-**Dr. Feelgood**).

26 Highlighting the polarization and diversity of current British music taste, the 20-track compilation album ***The Sound Of Bread*** – which will eventually achieve double-platinum status – hits No. 1 for the first of two weeks, replacing the **Sex Pistols**' ***Never Mind The Bollocks Here's The Sex Pistols***. The timeless collection will regain pole position in January.

December

1 Topping the UK chart, **Wings**' *Mull Of Kintyre* is certified platinum by the BPI. With nine weeks at the top, it will become the biggest-selling UK single to date, overtaking the **Beatles**' *She Loves You*. Written by **Paul McCartney** with **Denny Laine**, the waltz is inspired by the tip of the Kintyre peninsula, 11 miles from McCartney's Scottish farmhouse. It will fail to score in the US, though its B-side, *Girls School*, will reach No. 33.

14 "Saturday Night Fever" – a disco-themed movie starring **John Travolta** as Tony Manero, a working-class, 19-year-old Italian living in Bay Ridge, Brooklyn, whose Saturday nights revolve around dancing (superbly) at his local club – receives its world premiere in New York City. The screenplay, by British writer Nik Cohn, is based on his own original **New York** magazine story, and the film will become the global commercial icon of the disco movement. The double album soundtrack features music by the **Trammps**, **Kool & the Gang**, **K.C. & the Sunshine Band**, **Ralph McDonald**, **Walter Murphy & the Big Apple Band**, **Yvonne Elliman**, **MFSB**, **Tavares**, **David Shire**, and five new recordings by the **Bee Gees**. It will hit US No. 1 on January 21, staying for a record-breaking 24 weeks, and will spend 18 consecutive weeks at the top of the UK survey. Global sales will eventually exceed 20 million, making it the biggest-selling soundtrack to date. With five compositions by the **Gibb** brothers – four of which will hit US No. 1 – the project will also inexorably tie the trio to the disco era, much to their future frustration.

15 The **Sex Pistols** are denied entry visas into the US because of their criminal records. They were scheduled to start a US tour in Homestead, Pennsylvania, in two weeks' time. Even without entering the country, the band upset the producers of "Saturday Night Live" by pulling out of this week's show three days ago, saying they'd rather play a gig in England. **Elvis Costello** will take their place.

17 Popping down to his local pub, the Row Barge in Henley-on-Thames, England, **George Harrison** plays an unannounced live set.

Of the 17 tracks on the *Saturday Night Fever* soundtrack album, 11 made the Hot 100 and seven topped the charts.

17 Deputizing for the **Sex Pistols** on "Saturday Night Live," **Elvis Costello & the Attractions**, who made their New York City debut at the Bottom Line this week, stop in the middle of *Less Than Zero* as Costello says, "I'm sorry ladies and gentlemen, there's no reason to do this song," and launches into *Radio Radio*, which he has previously been told not to sing by the show's producers.

22 **Heatwave**'s *Boogie Nights* is certified platinum by the RIAA, having already hit both US and UK No. 2. The floor-filling disco classic was written by the band's keyboard player, **Rod Temperton**, who will retire from live work with the group next year to concentrate on writing.

23 **Cat Stevens** formally embraces Islam on Muharram 16, 1398, and changes his name to Yusuf Islam.

25 The **Sex Pistols** play what will be their last ever UK gig, at Ivanhoe's in Huddersfield, England – a charity performance before an audience mainly consisting of children.

30 At the end of one of the most controversial years in British rock history, the US Immigration Service reverses its decision not to issue entry visas to the **Sex Pistols**. Warner Bros. attorney Ted Jaffe has argued that the group's UK convictions would be considered only as misdemeanors in the US.

ROOTS **During this year: music journalist Martin Fry launches a fanzine, Modern Drugs... R&B combo Manchild – whose ranks include young guitarist/backing vocalist Kenneth "Babyface" Edmonds – score a minor US R&B hit with *Especially For You* ... aspiring classical pianist Tom Bailey forms the Thompson Twins with Peter Dodd and John Roog in Chesterfield... Green Gartside, inspired by a Sex Pistols' gig in Leeds, England, forms Scritti Politti, the name taken from a political pamphlet by Gramsci... Madonna Ciccone moves to New York City, at the urging of her ballet teacher, initially finding work in a Times Square doughnut shop... Suzanne Vega, working as an office receptionist by day, begins performing on New York City's Greenwich Village folk circuit... German record giant Hansa places an ad in Melody Maker headed "Wanna Be A Recording Star?" – Easy Cure are among the hundreds of bands who reply, and Hansa signs them for £1,000 ($1,900), which they spend on equipment... Stephen Morris auditions for the vacant drum seat in Joy Division outside Strangeways prison in Manchester, England... and Chris Rea quits the Beautiful Losers, who won Melody Maker's Best Newcomers of 1975 award, to sign with Magnet Records as a solo artist...**

You're The One That I Want

1978

No.1 US SINGLES

Jan 7 How Deep Is Your Love **Bee Gees**
Jan 14 Baby Come Back **Player**
Feb 4 Stayin' Alive **Bee Gees**
Mar 4 (Love Is) Thicker Than Water **Andy Gibb**
Mar 18 Night Fever **Bee Gees**
May 13 If I Can't Have You **Yvonne Elliman**
May 20 With A Little Luck **Wings**
June 3 Too Much, Too Little, Too Late **Johnny Mathis/Deniece Williams**
June 10 You're The One That I Want **John Travolta & Olivia Newton-John**
June 17 Shadow Dancing **Andy Gibb**
Aug 5 Miss You **Rolling Stones**
Aug 12 Three Times A Lady **Commodores**
Aug 26 Grease **Frankie Valli**
Sept 9 Boogie Oogie Oogie **A Taste of Honey**
Sept 30 Kiss You All Over **Exile**
Oct 28 Hot Child In The City **Nick Gilder**
Nov 4 You Needed Me **Anne Murray**
Nov 11 MacArthur Park **Donna Summer**
Dec 2 You Don't Bring Me Flowers **Barbra & Neil**
Dec 9 Le Freak **Chic**
Dec 16 You Don't Bring Me Flowers **Barbra & Neil**
Dec 23 Le Freak **Chic**

No.1 UK SINGLES

Jan 7 Mull Of Kintyre/Girls' School **Wings**
Feb 4 Up Town Top Ranking **Althia & Donna**
Feb 11 Figaro **Brotherhood of Man**
Feb 18 Take A Chance On Me **Abba**
Mar 11 Wuthering Heights **Kate Bush**
Apr 8 Matchstalk Men And Matchstalk Cats And Dogs **Brian & Michael (Burke & Jerk)**
Apr 29 Night Fever **Bee Gees**
May 13 Rivers Of Babylon/Brown Girl In The Ring **Boney M**
June 17 You're The One That I Want **John Travolta & Olivia Newton-John**
Aug 19 Three Times A Lady **Commodores**
Sept 23 Dreadlock Holiday **10cc**
Sept 30 Summer Nights **John Travolta & Olivia Newton-John**
Nov 18 Rat Trap **Boomtown Rats**
Dec 2 Da' Ya' Think I'm Sexy? **Rod Stewart**
Dec 9 Mary's Boy Child – Oh My Lord **Boney M**

The Sex Pistols

Boney M

When the Sex Pistols went their separate ways in January 1978, Steve Jones and Paul Cook went to visit Great Train Robber, Ronald Biggs, in Rio de Janeiro... Boney M were 'assembled' by Frank Farian after his single *Baby Do You Wanna Bump?* took off in Holland and he needed a group to perform the song live. And then came Milli Vanilli.

Dance, dance, dance. Reverberating across the dancefloor came the music of **Chic**, brainchild of producers **Bernard Edwards** and **Nile Rodgers**. *Le Freak* was released on a promotional disc to club DJs, and would become Atlantic Records' bestselling single to date. Disco was everywhere – even the **Rolling Stones** succumbed with *Miss You*, and **Rod Stewart** got silly in spandex with the equally genre-chasing *Da' Ya' Think I'm Sexy?* Trying to reclaim the night, **Funkadelic** responded with *One Nation Under A Groove*. The synthesis of guitars, bass, rhythm, and horns declared the power of funk – and the lyrics were rather more challenging than those of German producer **Frank Farian**'s hugely successful dance/pop creation, **Boney M**.

The **Sex Pistols** may have grabbed headlines in Britain, but in the US they could generate audiences of only a few hundred. After their show at the Winterland Ballroom in San Francisco, **Rolling Stone** commented: "You could reach out and touch every jagged note." But the performance was more ragged than jagged. The band broke up a few days later, and the venerable Winterland Ballroom closed at the end of the year.

Back in the UK, there was better punk on offer. The **Clash** produced an album of brute force, emblematic of a sour and polarized society. But their music was also becoming more "rock-friendly" – which gave the band wider appeal if less credibility with hardcore punks. **Sham 69** played a more raucous version, and were also heavily involved in the Rock Against Racism circuit. Much of the best British talent was signed to Stiff Records. Witness the astute lyrics of **Ian Dury & the Blockheads**, who melded punk and funk together in such gems as *Sex And Drugs And Rock 'n' Roll* and *Hit Me With Your Rhythm Stick*. Also on Stiff, **Elvis Costello & the Attractions**, whose debut album ***My Aim Is True*** was one of the few from the stable to make an impact in the US.

By the fall, the **Police** were performing on British television and appearing at CBGBs in New York. **Dire Straits** were another British band breaking through, at least at home. Their blues-rock may have swum against the prevailing tide, but **Mark Knopfler**'s fluent guitar on *Sultans Of Swing* gave them a unique sound and a hit single.

New Wave – the acceptable face of punk – was gaining traction in America. **Talking Heads** cut ***More Songs About Buildings and Food***, an arty pop-funk confection produced by **Brian Eno**. Powered by the alluring **Debbie Harry**, **Blondie** recorded their mainstream breakthrough album ***Parallel Lines***. The **Cars**' debut album became a permanent fixture in the charts.

Rock music had more than its share of loss in 1978, including **Chicago** guitarist **Terry Kath**, **Who** drummer **Keith Moon**, and **Sid Vicious**, who allegedly killed his girlfriend in a rapid downward spiral of destruction.

"[Talking Heads are] one of the most interesting idiosyncratic rock bands to emerge in the last few years." **Newsweek**, August 21, 1978

Sex Pistols in the US... *Wuthering Heights*... Bee Gees dominate US charts...

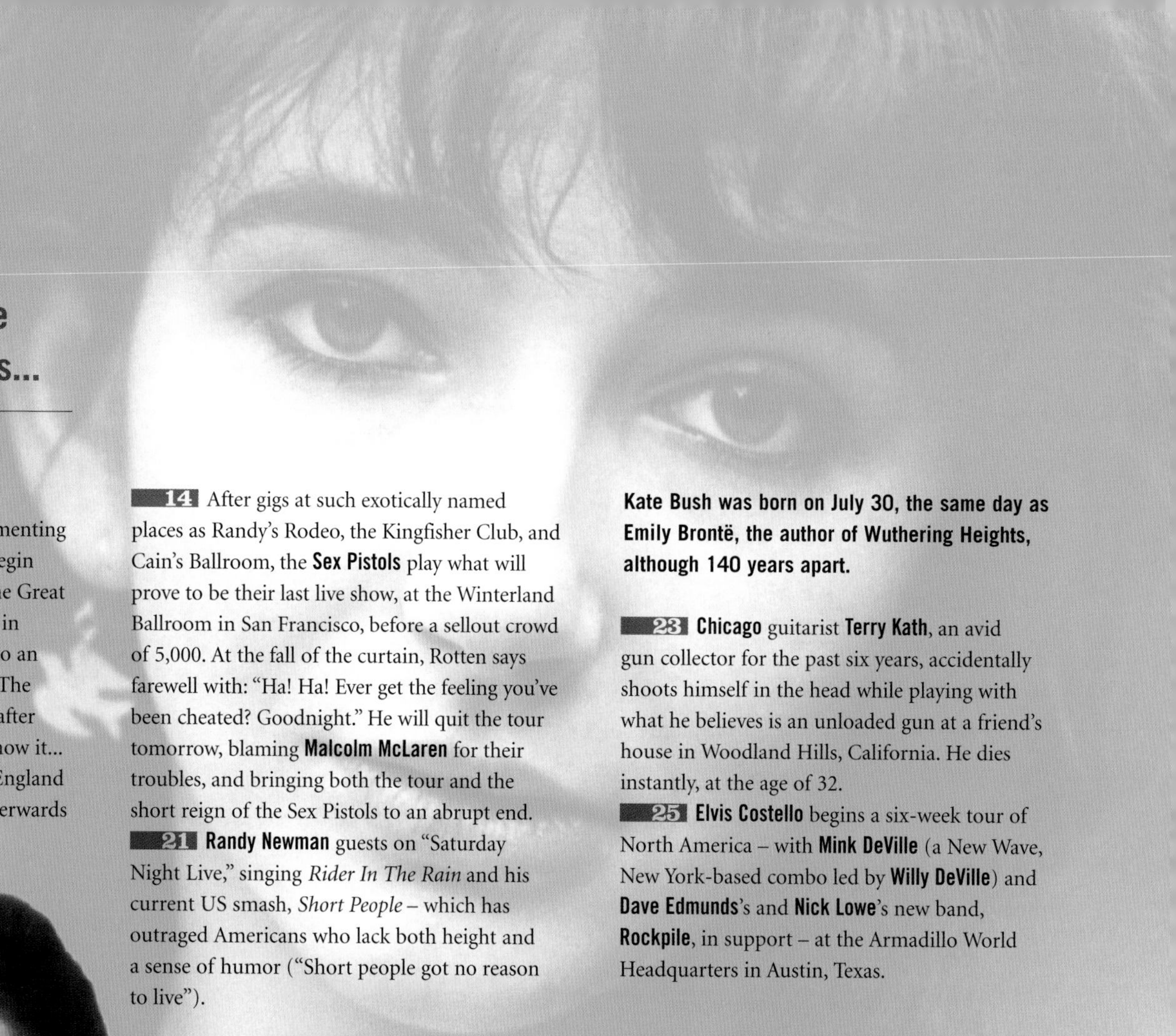

January

5 With the American media documenting their every move, the **Sex Pistols** finally begin their US tour before a packed house at the Great Southeast Music Hall in a shopping mall in Atlanta. Johnny Rotten's opening words to an American audience? "Where's my beer?" The band kick off with *God Save The Queen*, after which Rotten says: "We're ugly and we know it... See what kind of fine upstanding youth England is chucking out these days?" They will afterwards claim that it was their worst ever gig.

The Bee Gees had six US No. 1s between December 24, 1977, and June 9, 1979.

14 After gigs at such exotically named places as Randy's Rodeo, the Kingfisher Club, and Cain's Ballroom, the **Sex Pistols** play what will prove to be their last live show, at the Winterland Ballroom in San Francisco, before a sellout crowd of 5,000. At the fall of the curtain, Rotten says farewell with: "Ha! Ha! Ever get the feeling you've been cheated? Goodnight." He will quit the tour tomorrow, blaming **Malcolm McLaren** for their troubles, and bringing both the tour and the short reign of the Sex Pistols to an abrupt end.

21 **Randy Newman** guests on "Saturday Night Live," singing *Rider In The Rain* and his current US smash, *Short People* – which has outraged Americans who lack both height and a sense of humor ("Short people got no reason to live").

Kate Bush was born on July 30, the same day as Emily Brontë, the author of Wuthering Heights, although 140 years apart.

23 **Chicago** guitarist **Terry Kath**, an avid gun collector for the past six years, accidentally shoots himself in the head while playing with what he believes is an unloaded gun at a friend's house in Woodland Hills, California. He dies instantly, at the age of 32.

25 **Elvis Costello** begins a six-week tour of North America – with **Mink DeVille** (a New Wave, New York-based combo led by **Willy DeVille**) and **Dave Edmunds**'s and **Nick Lowe**'s new band, **Rockpile**, in support – at the Armadillo World Headquarters in Austin, Texas.

February

3 **Harry Chapin** – who has spent four months successfully lobbying the US Senate and House of Representatives to create a commission on hunger – meets with President Carter in the White House. At a gathering in the Cabinet Room, Carter announces the establishment of a Presidential Commission on Domestic and International Hunger and Malnutrition.

14 **Dire Straits** begin recording their first album at Basing Street Studios in west London, with producer **Muff Winwood**. The cost of the sessions – which will yield their lead-off hit, *Sultans Of Swing*, and its parent album, ***Dire Straits*** – will total £12,500 ($25,000). Due for release in May, the **Mark Knopfler**-penned ***Dire Straits*** will showcase his distinctive and skillfully fluid guitar work and blues-tinged vocal style, both reminiscent of reclusive American singer-songwriter **J.J. Cale** (who will one day remark, "My hope is that someday [Knopfler] covers one of my songs, instead of sounding like them").

14 Having made her first ever television appearance last week in a disused tram depot in West Germany for the popular "Bio's Bahnhof" show, 19-year-old

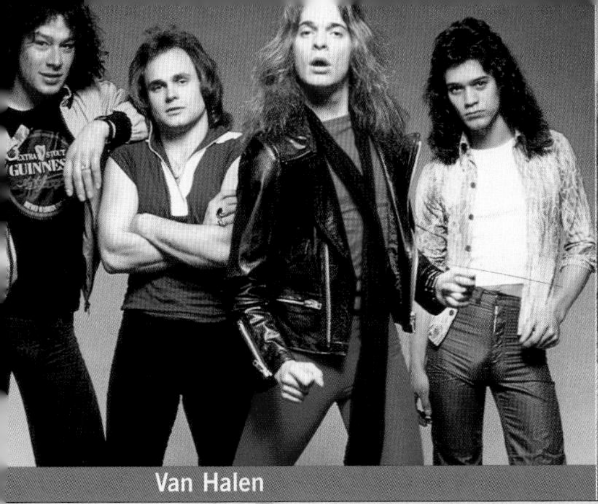

Van Halen

Heart

Contracts for Van Halen's tours stipulated that their M&M confectionery provision did not include any brown ones... Heart, a Seattle-based rock band led by sisters Ann and Nancy Wilson broke through with *Dreamboat Annie* in 1979.

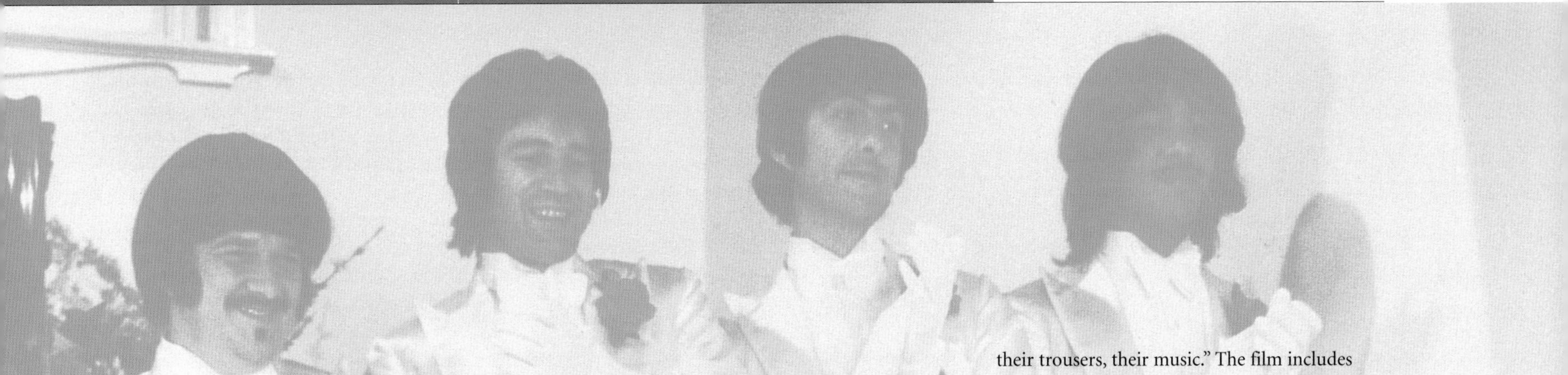

English singer-songwriter **Kate Bush** performs her maiden hit *Wuthering Heights* on "Top Of The Pops." Startlingly different from its chart contemporaries, with its lush orchestral backing framing her uniquely ethereal soprano vocal style, the song will begin a four-week run at UK No. 1 on March 11, and will quickly establish her as a major new British talent.

22 A Wrigley's chewing gum commercial featuring the **Police** premieres on US television. The band have been required to dye their hair blond for the shoot, and will mine their new image for the rest of the year.

23 In a year dominated by punk music in the UK, adult contemporary American rock acts are the big winners at the 20th annual Grammy Awards. **Fleetwood Mac** and the **Eagles** pick up the two major prizes: Album of the Year (***Rumours***), and Record of the Year (*Hotel California*). The man who had a hand in discovering the Eagles, 39-year-old country-pop singer **Kenny Rogers**, picks up the Best Male Country Performance trophy for last year's smash story ballad *Lucille*.

23 **Sid Vicious**, currently in New York playing solo gigs at Max's Kansas City and CBGBs, is arrested with his American girlfriend Nancy Spungen for possession of drugs.

March

3 **Van Halen** embark on their first nationwide US tour at the Aragon Ballroom in Chicago, in support of their debut album ***Van Halen*** (helmed by Warner Bros. Records in-house producer, **Ted Templeman**, who brought them to the label last year). A hard-rock/heavy-metal quartet, the group are named after the Dutch-born **Van Halen** brothers – guitarist **Eddie** and drummer **Alex** – who recruited wild-boy lead singer **David Lee Roth**, and ex-**Snake** bassist **Michael Anthony**, in 1973.

17 After playing pub and club gigs in Dublin, spunky local rock band **U2** – who are still in their final year at school and who have recently changed their name from the **Hype** – win the Limerick Civic Week Pop '78 Competition, sponsored by the **Evening Press** and Guinness Harp Lager. They win £500 ($1,000) and the chance to audition for CBS Ireland at Keystone Studios in June. The quartet was originally formed as a covers band called **Feedback**, by singer **Paul Hewson** (who has adopted the name **Bono** from a billboard advertising a hearing-aid retailer, Bono Vox), guitarist **David Evans** (who has chosen the nickname **The Edge**), bassist **Adam Clayton** (who was kicked out of Dublin's Mount Temple Comprehensive School last week), and drummer **Larry Mullen Jr**.

18 An estimated 350,000 people attend the California Jam II festival in Ontario. It features **Aerosmith**, **Heart**, French synthesizer whiz **Jean Michel Jarre** (who made a significant global breakthrough last year with his instrumental opus, ***Oxygène***), Canadian hard-rock trio **Frank Marino & Mahogany Rush**, ex-**Fleetwood Mac** singer-songwriter/guitarist **Bob Welch**, ex-**Traffic** guitarist **Dave Mason**, **Ted Nugent**, and **Santana**.

18 At the peak of their commercial success, the **Bee Gees**' disco classic *Night Fever* replaces younger brother **Andy Gibb**'s *(Love Is) Thicker Than Water* at US No. 1. It is the RSO label's fifth consecutive US chart-topper, while the trio's *Stayin' Alive* is still alive at US No. 2. The Bee Gees also wrote and produced the current No. 3, *Emotion* by **Samantha Sang**.

22 Interest is re-awakened in legendary Liverpool band, the **Rutles**, through the NBC-TV broadcast of the biographical documentary "All You Need Is Cash" – "Their lives, their loves, their trousers, their music." The film includes allegations by blues singers, Blind Lemon Pye and Rambling Orange Peel, that the Rutles plagiarized their music. Even less likely claims are made by the media, who report that the Rutles are little more than a spot-on satire on the **Beatles**, created by ex-Monty Python co-founder **Eric Idle** and ex-**Bonzo Dog Doo Dah Band** member, **Neil Innes**, who recruited ex-**Beach Boys** sideman, **Ricky Fataar**, and rock session drummer **John Halsey** to form a fictional group whose story and songs closely mirror those of the Fab Four. **Mick Jagger**, **Paul Simon**, and **George Harrison** all appear in the documentary to prove the absurdity of this scurrilous notion.

30 The **Clash**'s **Paul Simonon** and **"Topper" Headon** are arrested in Camden Town, London, for criminal damage after shooting down racing pigeons with airguns from the roof of Chalk Farm Studios. Four police cars and a helicopter are required to make the arrest. The pair, by now used to handing over money in fines, will find themselves £800 ($1,600) poorer.

April

1 With *Because The Night*, co-written with **Bruce Springsteen**, currently at UK No. 5 and US No. 13, **Patti Smith** plays the first of three sellout dates at London's Rainbow Theatre in support of her latest critics' favorite, ***Easter***, which has been helmed by emerging producer Jimmy Iovine.

14 Post-punk underground band **Joy Division**, formed last year in Manchester by **Ian Curtis** (lead vocals), **Bernard Albrecht** (guitar), **Peter Hook** (bass), and drummer **Stephen Morris**,

Leggy Mountbatten, a one-legged retail chemist from Bolton, England, became the Rutles' manager when he fell in love with the fit of their trousers.

Apr 1978

Boney M's *Rivers Of Babylon*... Dylan and Clapton together... Keith Moon dies...

Gerry Rafferty

Steely Dan

perform at the Stiff Test/Chiswick Challenge, an audition night organized by the two UK independent labels at Manchester's Rafters club. They go on last, at 2:00 am, but impress in-house DJ – and their future manager – Rob Gretton. Television journalist Tony Wilson, boss of the recently formed Factory Records, is also taken by the band's performance.

21 Former **Fairport Convention** lead singer, 31-year-old **Sandy Denny**, dies of a cerebral hemorrhage, after falling downstairs at a friend's house in London three days ago. After leaving Fairport in 1969, Denny formed **Fotheringay**, with her husband-to-be **Trevor Lucas**, making a self-titled album in 1970. She then recorded three critically revered solo albums, before rejoining Fairport Convention for a year in 1975.

22 **Bob Marley & the Wailers** headline the One Love Peace Concert in Kingston, Jamaica, which also features top local reggae acts **Dennis Brown**, **Culture**, **Inner Circle**, the **Mighty Diamonds**, and a now solo (and openly spliff-smoking) **Peter Tosh**. Marley unites Prime Minister Michael Manley and opponent Edward Seaga on stage, in avowals of common purpose.

28 **Cheap Trick** make what will prove to be a career-changing appearance at the Budokan Hall, Tokyo. The American rock quartet – fronted by guitarist founder **Rick Nielsen** and featuring lead singer **Robin Zander** – are currently more popular in Japan, where "Trickmania" rages, than in the US. A live recording of tonight's gig is made for future release as ***Cheap Trick At Budokan***.

Boney M are the only act to have two singles in the Top 10 alltime UK bestsellers list, with *Rivers Of Babylon/Brown Girl In The Ring* selling 1,985,000 copies and *Mary's Boy Child - Oh My Lord* 1,790,000.

Gerry Rafferty was a founder member of Stealers Wheel, hitmakers in 1973 with *Stuck In The Middle With You*... Steely Dan took their name from William Burroughs' novel The Naked Lunch.

"Among the most talented rock 'n' roll drummers in contemporary music."
From **The Times** obituary of Keith Moon, September 9, 1978

May

1 **Boney M**'s double A-side, *Rivers Of Babylon/Brown Girl In The Ring*, is certified platinum by the BPI. The group is the brainchild of German producer Frank Farian, who assembled four Munich-based Caribbean session singers to front his electronic dance/pop creations in 1976, employing a stylized female/bass male vocal combination. Following their breakthrough hit last year with *Daddy Cool*, the group are taking Europe by storm with a string of catchy singles. *Rivers Of Babylon* is set to hit UK No. 1 on May 13, and will be flipped during the summer, with the B-side keeping the disc alive at UK No. 2. The group – the biggest-selling singles act in Europe this year – will also hit UK No. 2 with *Rasputin* in October, before spending December back on top with their update of Harry Belafonte's 1957 hit, *Mary's Boy Child*.

3 "FM," a movie depicting day-to-day life at an American radio station, premieres in Los Angeles. Although the film is a commercial flop, its soundtrack will become a US No. 5 platinum-selling smash. It features A-list material from the current giants of FM radio, including the **Eagles**, **Neil Young**, **Billy Joel**, 31-year-old rock singer-songwriter/pianist **Warren Zevon** (who is currently scoring with his signature hit *Werewolves Of London*), **Steve Miller**, **Foreigner**, the **Doobie Brothers**, **Bob Seger**, 26-year-old singer/songwriter **Dan Fogelberg** (who has already quietly crafted three platinum-selling US hit albums in the past four years), **Queen**, **Joe Walsh** (still with the Eagles but also recording solo and about to release his biggest hit, *Life's Been Good*), and **B.B. King** – all topped off by a title theme from **Steely Dan**.

13 **Chic**, a new disco unit signed to Atlantic Records and formed by singer-songwriter/producers, bassist **Bernard Edwards** and guitarist **Nile Rodgers**, perform their second hit, *Everybody Dance*, on today's "American Bandstand." Stylish blue-eyed soul/rock singer and ex-**Vinegar Joe** frontman, Yorkshire-born **Robert Palmer**, follows with his breakthrough 45, *Every Kinda People*.

13 Five years after his last hit, 32-year-old R&B singer **Donny Hathaway** reaches US No. 2 for the first of two weeks, behind **Yvonne Elliman**'s *If I Can't Have You*. Hathaway's new hit is his fourth duet with **Roberta Flack**, the slow, soulful *The Closer I Get You*, a **James Mtume/Reggie Lucas** composition from her album ***Blue Lights In The Basement***. Hathaway is an accomplished musician/singer/producer who has worked for several labels over the past ten years, including Chess, Stax, and **Curtis Mayfield**'s Curtom Records. He and Flack won a Grammy for their 1972 smash, *Where Is The Love*.

26 The **Cure** – a new art-punk band formed by 19-year-old Lancashire-born singer/guitarist **Robert Smith**, keyboardist **Lol Tolhurst**, and guitarist **Porl Thompson** – record *Boys Don't Cry* at the Chestnut Studios in Sussex, adding to an armory of demos that will result in their signing to Fiction Records, a new label set up by ex-Polydor Records A&R staffer, Chris Parry.

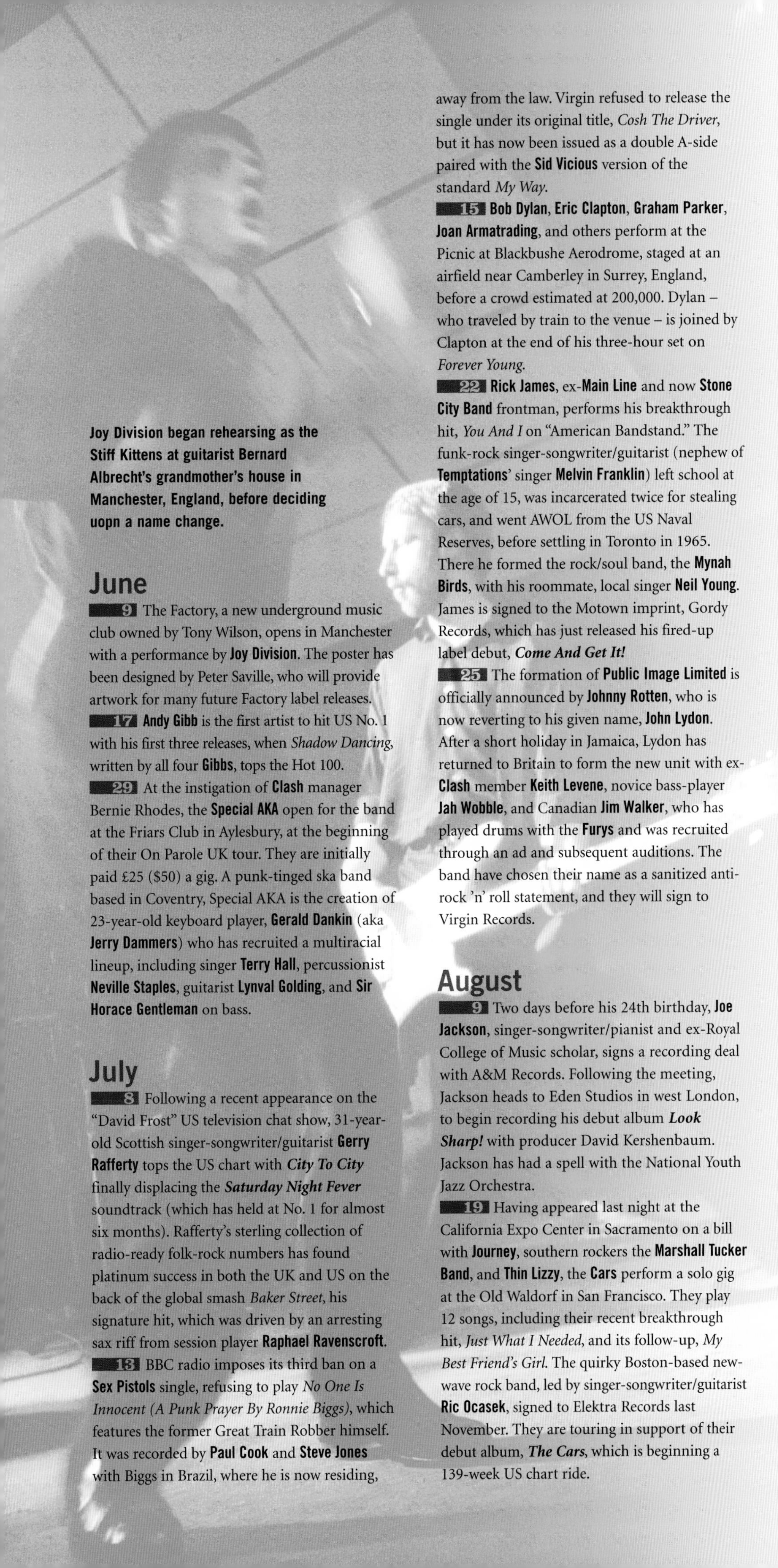

Joy Division began rehearsing as the Stiff Kittens at guitarist Bernard Albrecht's grandmother's house in Manchester, England, before deciding uopn a name change.

June

9 The Factory, a new underground music club owned by Tony Wilson, opens in Manchester with a performance by **Joy Division**. The poster has been designed by Peter Saville, who will provide artwork for many future Factory label releases.

17 **Andy Gibb** is the first artist to hit US No. 1 with his first three releases, when *Shadow Dancing*, written by all four **Gibbs**, tops the Hot 100.

29 At the instigation of **Clash** manager Bernie Rhodes, the **Special AKA** open for the band at the Friars Club in Aylesbury, at the beginning of their On Parole UK tour. They are initially paid £25 ($50) a gig. A punk-tinged ska band based in Coventry, Special AKA is the creation of 23-year-old keyboard player, **Gerald Dankin** (aka **Jerry Dammers**) who has recruited a multiracial lineup, including singer **Terry Hall**, percussionist **Neville Staples**, guitarist **Lynval Golding**, and **Sir Horace Gentleman** on bass.

July

8 Following a recent appearance on the "David Frost" US television chat show, 31-year-old Scottish singer-songwriter/guitarist **Gerry Rafferty** tops the US chart with ***City To City*** finally displacing the ***Saturday Night Fever*** soundtrack (which has held at No. 1 for almost six months). Rafferty's sterling collection of radio-ready folk-rock numbers has found platinum success in both the UK and US on the back of the global smash *Baker Street*, his signature hit, which was driven by an arresting sax riff from session player **Raphael Ravenscroft**.

13 BBC radio imposes its third ban on a **Sex Pistols** single, refusing to play *No One Is Innocent (A Punk Prayer By Ronnie Biggs)*, which features the former Great Train Robber himself. It was recorded by **Paul Cook** and **Steve Jones** with Biggs in Brazil, where he is now residing, away from the law. Virgin refused to release the single under its original title, *Cosh The Driver*, but it has now been issued as a double A-side paired with the **Sid Vicious** version of the standard *My Way*.

15 **Bob Dylan**, **Eric Clapton**, **Graham Parker**, **Joan Armatrading**, and others perform at the Picnic at Blackbushe Aerodrome, staged at an airfield near Camberley in Surrey, England, before a crowd estimated at 200,000. Dylan – who traveled by train to the venue – is joined by Clapton at the end of his three-hour set on *Forever Young*.

22 **Rick James**, ex-**Main Line** and now **Stone City Band** frontman, performs his breakthrough hit, *You And I* on "American Bandstand." The funk-rock singer-songwriter/guitarist (nephew of **Temptations**' singer **Melvin Franklin**) left school at the age of 15, was incarcerated twice for stealing cars, and went AWOL from the US Naval Reserves, before settling in Toronto in 1965. There he formed the rock/soul band, the **Mynah Birds**, with his roommate, local singer **Neil Young**. James is signed to the Motown imprint, Gordy Records, which has just released his fired-up label debut, ***Come And Get It!***

25 The formation of **Public Image Limited** is officially announced by **Johnny Rotten**, who is now reverting to his given name, **John Lydon**. After a short holiday in Jamaica, Lydon has returned to Britain to form the new unit with ex-**Clash** member **Keith Levene**, novice bass-player **Jah Wobble**, and Canadian **Jim Walker**, who has played drums with the **Furys** and was recruited through an ad and subsequent auditions. The band have chosen their name as a sanitized anti-rock 'n' roll statement, and they will sign to Virgin Records.

August

9 Two days before his 24th birthday, **Joe Jackson**, singer-songwriter/pianist and ex-Royal College of Music scholar, signs a recording deal with A&M Records. Following the meeting, Jackson heads to Eden Studios in west London, to begin recording his debut album ***Look Sharp!*** with producer David Kershenbaum. Jackson has had a spell with the National Youth Jazz Orchestra.

19 Having appeared last night at the California Expo Center in Sacramento on a bill with **Journey**, southern rockers the **Marshall Tucker Band**, and **Thin Lizzy**, the **Cars** perform a solo gig at the Old Waldorf in San Francisco. They play 12 songs, including their recent breakthrough hit, *Just What I Needed*, and its follow-up, *My Best Friend's Girl*. The quirky Boston-based new-wave rock band, led by singer-songwriter/guitarist **Ric Ocasek**, signed to Elektra Records last November. They are touring in support of their debut album, ***The Cars***, which is beginning a 139-week US chart ride.

26 The first Canada Jam festival takes place in Ontario, before a crowd of 80,000, with the **Commodores** (who are currently flying high at US No. 1 with their signature ballad, the **Lionel Richie**-penned *Three Times A Lady*), **Earth, Wind & Fire**, **Kansas**, **Dave Mason**, and the **Village People** – the latter an unabashedly camp disco-pop combo created by New York-based French producer/songwriter, Jacques Morali. The actor/singers in the line-up visually represent six American male gay stereotypes: a cowboy, a Native American, a policeman, a biker, a G.I., and a construction worker. Their breakthrough hit, *Macho Man*, will enter the US survey next week.

September

2 Having left **Harold Melvin & the Blue Notes** for a solo career in 1976, soul crooner **Teddy Pendergrass** – promoting his already platinum-certified second set, ***Life Is A Song Worth Singing*** – performs a midnight concert, For Women Only, at Avery Fisher Hall in New York. Audience members are given white chocolate and teddy-bear-shaped lollipops – and some reciprocate by offering the singer their underwear. Further "ladies only" concerts, invariably standing room-only affairs, will follow, in a PR exercise devised by manager Shep Gordon to capitalize on the perception of Pendergrass as an aural seducer.

7 The **Who**'s **Keith Moon**, having returned to Flat 9, 12 Curzon Place – the same London apartment in which **Mama Cass** died four years ago – with his girlfriend Annette Walter-Lax, after attending a party hosted by **Paul McCartney** for the UK movie premiere of "The Buddy Holly Story," watches a video, "The Abominable Dr. Phibes," until approximately 4:00 am. He then takes some Heminevrin (prescribed to combat alcoholism) and goes to sleep, only to wake again at around 7:30 am. He eats a steak, watches the movie again, and takes more Heminevrin before nodding off once more. At 3:40 pm, Walter-Lax finds him unconscious and calls his doctor, Dr. Geoffrey Dymond. Moon is pronounced dead on arrival at Middlesex Hospital. An autopsy will reveal that 28 undissolved pills lay in Moon's stomach – some 14 times the recommended dosage.

9 The **Tubes** – a highly theatrical rock aggregation from San Francisco, led by singer **Fee Waybill** – close their performance at the Oh God, Not Another Boring Old Knebworth... festival with a **Who** medley in tribute to **Keith Moon**. **Peter Gabriel**, **Frank Zappa**, the **Boomtown Rats**, **Rockpile** – featuring **Dave Edmunds** and **Nick Lowe** – and **Wilko Johnson's Solid Senders** round out the bill. Mr. Pruett, the licensing officer for the event, says of the festival's noise level: "I know of nothing to equal it since the artillery barrage at the crossing of the Rhine during the last World War."

June 16 "Grease," the comedy/musical movie, opens in US theaters nationwide. Based on the Broadway hit, it co-stars **John Travolta** as leather-clad Danny Zuko and **Olivia Newton-John** as the virginal Sandy Olsen, with Stockard Channing as Rizzo. The film takes a nostalgic look at adolescent life at an American high school in the 1950s and is produced by Robert Stigwood and directed by Randall Kleiser. Although slammed by critics, it will be adored by moviegoers. Its soundtrack will become a multiplatinum success, spending 12 weeks topping the US chart and 13 on the UK list, and spinning off the global chart-topper, *You're The One That I Want*, which hit US No. 1 last week. The **Barry Gibb**-penned title song also reignites the solo career of **Four Seasons**' lead vocalist, **Frankie Valli**: it will become his second US No. 1 in August.

The original stage version of "Grease" ran for more than eight years and 3,388 performances to become the eighth longest-running musical of all time. Barry Bostwick was the original Danny Zuko and Richard Gere a later one.

"Grease is the word."

Barry Gibb

Sept 1978

Grateful Dead in Egypt... Cars first to release picture-disc in UK... Chic and *Le Freak*...

14 The **Grateful Dead** perform the first of three dates at the Sound & Light Amphitheatre in the shadow of the Great Pyramid in Giza, the last of which will be timed to coincide with a lunar eclipse. Proceeds from the concerts go to the Egyptian Department of Antiquities and the Faith & Hope Society for the Handicapped.

October

5 **Jeff Wayne**'s *War Of The Worlds* – an epic rock musical interpretation of the H.G. Wells literary classic – is certified platinum by the BPI. The double album will become one of the biggest-selling albums of the 1980s, at four times platinum. It features **Julie Covington** as Beth, **David Essex** as the Artilleryman, **Phil Lynott** as the Parson, and **Jo Partridge** as the Heat Ray, with actor Richard Burton providing the narration as the Journalist. The **Moody Blues' Justin Hayward** has contributed two songs, including the recent UK No. 5 hit, *Forever Autumn.*

9 Renaissance man **Jacques Brel** dies, aged 49, two days after being admitted to the Franco-Musulman Hospital in Bobigny, France, suffering from a pulmonary embolism. The Brussels-born singer-songwriter/actor/director influenced artists ranging from **David Bowie** to **Leonard Cohen**, and **Rod McKuen** (who wrote English lyrics to many of his songs) to **Scott Walker**. *If You Go Away*, translated from the original *Ne Me Quitte Pas*, became a standard, cut by **Frank Sinatra**, **Neil Diamond**, **Tom Jones**, **Dusty Springfield**, and **Glen Campbell**, among others.

14 All four members of **KISS** chart simultaneously with eponymous solo albums. Launched in a high-profile campaign, each LP cover features a matching portrait of the respective artist in full make-up, forming one section of a four-part KISS mural. (Buy all four albums and you get the full mural.) Each disc has already shipped platinum, but sales will fail to match the expected demand. **Gene Simmons** will fare best, eventually reaching US No. 22, followed by **Ace Frehley** (No. 26), **Paul Stanley** (No. 40), and **Peter Criss** (No. 43). On a chutzpah level, Simmons takes the prize, using **Helen Reddy**, **Cher**, and **Janis Ian** as backing vocalists, and closing the album with his take on Disney's classic, *When You Wish Upon A Star.*

20 Having flown to New York on the budget Laker Skytrain earlier today, carrying their instruments as hand luggage, **Sting** and **Andy Summers** join drummer **Stewart Copeland** (who arrived yesterday) in New York, to make the **Police**'s US debut at CBGBs, at the start of a 23-date North American trek.

November

4 **Van Morrison** guests on "Saturday Night Live," singing *Kingdom Hall* and *Wavelength* – the title cut from his critically revered new album. Meanwhile, on "Soul Train," the **Trammps** get the party started with their signature hit, *Disco Inferno.* They are followed by **Shalamar** –

Record producer Dick Griffey recruited two dancers from the "Soul Train" TV show – Jody Watley, whose godfather was Jackie Wilson, and Jeffrey Daniel, whose spectacular body-popping moves were a focal point of the group.

SID VICIOUS

Oct 12 Sid Vicious, who is currently living with his girlfriend, Nancy Spungen, in room 100 at the Chelsea Hotel, 222 West 23rd Street, New York, calls for help after finding her dead. Detective Gerald Thomas, Sgt. Thomas Kilroy, and police officer William Sportiello arrive to find her sitting on the bathroom floor in blood-soaked underwear, fatally stabbed in the stomach with a hunting knife. Vicious is arrested, charged with murder in the second degree and placed in the detox unit of a New York prison. In an often contradictory "voluntary disclosure sheet" subsequently released by the police, Vicious will claim to detectives that, "I stabbed her but I didn't mean to kill her. I loved her, but she treated me like shit." During a four-day spell at Rikers Jail, he will attempt suicide twice. Malcolm McLaren will eventually bail him out of jail with $50,000 supplied by Virgin.

an R&B trio formed by Dick Griffey and Simon Soussan last year, comprising singer/ dancers, **Jody Watley** and **Jeffrey Daniel**, with singer **Gerald Brown** – who perform their R&B smash, *Take That To The Bank*, and *Tossin', Turnin', Swingin'*. (Brown will be replaced early next year by new lead singer **Howard Hewett**.)

16 During **Queen**'s performance of *Fat Bottomed Girls* at New York's Madison Square Garden, the audience is treated to the sight of semi-nude female cyclists (a device also used in the video). The group are awarded the venue's Gold Ticket for playing to over 100,000 fans.

25 The **Cars**' new single, *My Best Friend's Girl* – notable as the first picture-disc single commercially released in the UK – hits No. 3. The group will have to wait three years before collecting their first Top 10 hit back home.

December

4 The **Cure** perform *Killing An Arab* on Radio 1's John Peel show. It was scheduled for release on the 22nd, but Polydor Records, concerned about issuing it so near Christmas in case its title causes a fuss, strike a deal whereby indie label Small Wonder will release the first 15,000 copies, after which their Fiction imprint will take over. It will be released in February.

8 **Sid Vicious** is charged with first degree assault and possession of a dangerous instrument, after smashing a beer glass into the face of **Patti Smith**'s brother **Todd** and kicking him in the genitals. Smith requires medical treatment. The attack takes place at the Hurrah club in New York, while Vicious is out on bail for the alleged murder of Nancy Spungen.

23 *C'Est Chic*, containing *Le Freak*, Atlantic's best-selling single to date, hits US No. 4. Subsequently regarded as a landmark dance album, it has been entirely written and produced by **Bernard Edwards** and **Nile Rodgers**, and features guest vocalists **David Lasley** and **Luther Vandross. Chic** were initially rejected by every record label in New York, including Atlantic – who eventually signed them at the behest of executive Jerry Greenberg. Rodgers' chopping disco-rhythm guitar bars, underpinned by Edward's dextrous bass playing and **Tony Thompson**'s drumming, and offset by the twin female vocals of **Alfa Anderson** and **Luci Martin**, with melodic string arrangements by **Gene Orloff**, will become Chic's trademark sound – and make Edwards and Rodgers the hottest writing/production team around. Their next project – for Philly-based R&B quartet, **Sister Sledge** – is already in the can.

Ex-**Box Tops** and **Big Star** singer-songwriter/guitarist and power-pop pioneer, **Chris Bell**, is killed in the early hours, when his Triumph TR6 hits a telephone pole on Poplar Avenue in Memphis. He is 27.

31 The **Grateful Dead** play their 48th, and last, gig at the Winterland Ballroom, San Francisco, before promoter Bill Graham permanently closes it down. Sharing the bill are the **New Riders of the Purple Sage** and the **Blues Brothers**, namely **John Belushi** (**Joliet Jake Blues**) and **Dan Aykroyd** (**Elwood Blues**), who have taken their popular "Saturday Night Live" sketch/ musical characters on the road – and on to the charts: their Atlantic-released debut album, *Briefcase Full Of Blues*, will hit No. 1 within six weeks.

Chic started out as the Big Apple Band, and then Allah & the Knife-Wielding Punks, before wisely settling on their hit-making name.

ROOTS During this year: Boy George and DJ Mikey Craig form In Praise Of Lemmings, name-changing to Sex Gang Children, when guitarist John Suede joins... ten-year-old Damon Albarn moves with his parents to Colchester, where he becomes a schoolmate of German-born Graham Coxon at Stanway Comprehensive School; by the end of the next decade, they will be the driving force behind BritPoppers, Blur... local Austin, Texas, record label, BF Deal, releases *There's A Light Beyond These Woods*, the debut album by local folk singer/songwriter, Nanci Griffith... 14-year-old singer/guitarist Roddy Frame performs in UK punk band, the Forensics... Belinda Carlisle and Jane Wiedlin form the Misfits, which after a year of gigging earnestly around the Los Angeles punk club scene will become the Go-Go's... brothers Bruce and Bobby Hornsby, with drumming buddy John Molo, form the Bruce Hornsby Band, which will begin a seemingly endless tour of bars and lounges around the southern states and seven years of recording demo tapes of original material, all of which will be rejected by the record industry... and DJ Neal Kay, of the Bandwaggon Soundhouse in London, receives a demo from a heavy metal band, Iron Maiden; his interest sparked, the band will play regularly at the venue and the record will become a major rock club hit...

He's The Greatest Dancer

1979

No.1 US SINGLES

- **Jan 6** Too Much Heaven **Bee Gees**
- **Jan 20** Le Freak **Chic**
- **Feb 10** Da' Ya' Think I'm Sexy? **Rod Stewart**
- **Mar 10** I Will Survive **Gloria Gaynor**
- **Mar 24** Tragedy **Bee Gees**
- **Apr 7** I Will Survive **Gloria Gaynor**
- **Apr 14** What A Fool Believes **Doobie Brothers**
- **Apr 21** Knock On Wood **Amii Stewart**
- **Apr 28** Heart Of Glass **Blondie**
- **May 5** Reunited **Peaches & Herb**
- **June 2** Hot Stuff **Donna Summer**
- **June 9** Love You Inside Out **Bee Gees**
- **June 16** Hot Stuff **Donna Summer**
- **June 30** Ring My Bell **Anita Ward**
- **July 14** Bad Girls **Donna Summer**
- **Aug 18** Good Times **Chic**
- **Aug 25** My Sharona **Knack**
- **Oct 6** Sad Eyes **Robert John**
- **Oct 13** Don't Stop 'Til You Get Enough **Michael Jackson**
- **Oct 20** Rise **Herb Alpert**
- **Nov 3** Pop Muzik **M**
- **Nov 10** Heartache Tonight **Eagles**
- **Nov 17** Still **Commodores**
- **Nov 24** No More Tears (Enough Is Enough) **Barbra Streisand/Donna Summer**
- **Dec 8** Babe **Styx**
- **Dec 22** Escape (The Pina Colada Song) **Rupert Holmes**

No.1 UK SINGLES

- **Jan 6** Y.M.C.A. **Village People**
- **Jan 27** Hit Me With Your Rhythm Stick **Ian Dury & the Blockheads**
- **Feb 3** Heart Of Glass **Blondie**
- **Mar 3** Tragedy **Bee Gees**
- **Mar 17** I Will Survive **Gloria Gaynor**
- **Apr 14** Bright Eyes **Art Garfunkel**
- **May 26** Sunday Girl **Blondie**
- **June 16** Ring My Bell **Anita Ward**
- **June 30** Are "Friends" Electric? **Tubeway Army**

Michael Jackson

The Doobie Brothers

Michael Jackson's *Off The Wall* was certified platinum in December 1979. It was just a sign of things to come. His seven solo albums have sold a total of more than 37 million copies in the US alone... The Doobie Brothers had two distinct incarnations – both of which brought them US No. 1s.

Sid's vicious cycle of destruction was complete; disco received a new injection of energy; ska emerged as a force in the British charts; and the first rap record charted. 1979 was a veritable musical smorgasbord. With 11 disco singles certified platinum in the US, it seemed nothing could exterminate the genre, not even the "Disco Sucks" movement. Disco's enemies had not reckoned with the selling power of **Bernard Edwards** and **Nile Rodgers**, the producers behind **Chic** and **Sister Sledge**. The **Bee Gees** won five Grammys, and **Michael Jackson** also got in on the act with ***Off The Wall.*** **Donna Summer** reclaimed her throne as the queen of disco with *Hot Stuff* and *Bad Girls.*

Long brewing in the clubs of Harlem and the streets of the Bronx, hip-hop finally made it to vinyl. The **Sugar Hill Gang**'s multiplatinum *Rapper's Delight* revealed a popular taste for it. Soon, **Grandmaster Flash and the Furious Five**, **Funky 4+1**, and **Sequence** were developing the genre.

Punk was on its shortlived last legs in Britain, where new genres were jostling for center stage, including synthesizer-based pop/rock (**Joy Division**, **Human League**) and the New Wave of British Heavy Metal (**Iron Maiden**). Perhaps the most interesting arrival was a revival – of Caribbean ska – by bands like the **Specials**. Founded by **Jerry Dammers**, 2-Tone Records became one of the most innovative startups in the UK, also briefly boasting acts like the (**English**) **Beat**, **Madness,** and the **Selecter**.

The US was largely immune to postpunk meanderings, and remained a redoubt of rock (despite the prevalence of disco). **Bruce Springsteen** consolidated his reputation as the Boss of American rock; in stadia and arena, **Aerosmith**, **Boston**, and **Foreigner** were joined by Australian heavy rock combo **AC/DC**. British newcomers **Dire Straits** added commercial to critical success with a soldout debut US tour. **Bob Dylan** attended the band's Los Angeles gig and afterwards asked **Mark Knopfler** and drummer **Pick Withers** to guest on his forthcoming album. The resultant ***Slow Train Coming*** was his first as a born-again Christian, but also re-affirmed his commitment to social justice. The almost-forgotten **Doobie Brothers** added a funky edge and bounced back with their bestselling album ***Minute By Minute***, spurred by the distinctive touch and sound of **Michael McDonald**. Also using keyboards to good effect, **Supertramp** issued their sixth and most successful album ***Breakfast In America.***

1979 was also a year of technical achievement. While electronic advances were making keyboards so versatile that entire acts could be synth-driven (to wit, **Kraftwerk** and **Gary Numan**), Sony introduced the Walkman portable audio cassette player. And **Ry Cooder** made the first entirely digitally recorded album, the soul/R&B flavored ***Bop Till You Drop.***

July 28 I Don't Like Mondays **Boomtown Rats**
Aug 25 We Don't Talk Anymore **Cliff Richard**
Sept 22 Cars **Gary Numan**
Sept 29 Message In A Bottle **Police**
Oct 20 Video Killed The Radio Star **Buggles**
Oct 27 One Day At A Time **Lena Martell**
Nov 17 When You're In Love With A Beautiful Woman **Dr. Hook**
Dec 8 Walking On The Moon **Police**
Dec 15 Another Brick In The Wall Part II **Pink Floyd**

"I think the fans have come to expect me to wear it."

AC/DC's Angus Young on his trademark schoolboy outfit, **Melody Maker**, November 10, 1979

1979

Blondie break through with their first chart-topper... Sid Vicious dies... the 2-Tone label...

Blondie's Chris Stein and Debbie Harry penned the group's 1979 transatlantic chart-topper *Heart Of Glass*. Stein also wrote their UK No. 1 follow-up, *Sunday Girl*.

Sid Vicious's murder trial opened in New York on January 2. A month later he was dead.

January

1 **Bruce Springsteen**'s seven-month Darkness at the Edge of Town tour – which set out from the Shea Theatre in Buffalo back in May – ends at the Richfield Coliseum in Cleveland, after 109 sellout shows in 86 cities.

4 Jazz giant **Charles Mingus** dies from a heart attack, age 56, in Cuernavaca, Mexico, having long suffered from a form of motor neurone disease. A gifted pianist/bassist and composer, one of his last projects was contributing songs to **Joni Mitchell**'s forthcoming ***Mingus*** set, which will include her version of one of his best-remembered titles, *Goodbye Pork Pie Hat.*

9 The Music for UNICEF Concert – an all-star fundraiser staged to raise both awareness and $500,000 to help relieve world hunger during the International Year of the Child – takes place in the General Assembly Hall of the United Nations in New York. Top acts include the **Bee Gees**, **Abba**, **Elton John**, **Kris Kristofferson**, **Rita Coolidge**, **Donna Summer**, **Olivia Newton-John**, **Rod Stewart**, **John Denver**, **Earth Wind & Fire**, and **Andy Gibb**. It will be broadcast tomorrow on NBC television as "A Gift Of Song."

13 Soul singer **Donny Hathaway** dies at 33, after falling out of a window on the 15th floor of the Essex House Hotel in New York. Police find his room door has been locked from the inside, and the window's safety glass removed and laid on the bed. The coroner's verdict will be suicide. Hathaway's funeral will be held in St. Louis, with **Roberta Flack**, **Stevie Wonder**, and the Rev. Jesse Jackson among the mourners.

29 Brenda Spencer – a 16-year-old student – kills school principal Burton Wragg and custodian Mike Suchar, and wounds nine others, with a .22-caliber rifle, during a shooting spree in the playground of Grover Cleveland Elementary School in San Diego. When asked by a reporter why she committed the crime, Spencer responds, "I don't like Mondays, this livens up the day." She will be sentenced to 25-years-to-life. **Boomtown Rats** frontman, **Bob Geldof**, is particularly intrigued by the incident.

February

1 **Blondie**'s pop breakthrough, *Heart Of Glass* – featured on tonight's "Top Of The Pops" – is certified platinum by the BPI, as it begins a four-week stay at UK No. 1. It will also rise to the top spot in the US for one week on April 28. Co-written by **Debbie Harry** and **Chris Stein**, it marks a radical departure from the band's early New Wave leanings, fully embracing pop/disco under the direction of glam-pop veteran Mike Chapman. The feature track on the parent ***Parallel Lines*** (which will hit UK No. 1 on February 17, and US No. 6), the hit elevates Blondie – and particularly their striking cover-girl lead singer – into rock's A-league. In May, the band will secure a second UK chart-topper from the album, with *Sunday Girl.*

1 Released on bail (having served seven weeks at Rikers Island for his December 8 fracas), **Sid Vicious** meets up with his mother, Anne Beverly, a few New York junkie acquaintances, and his new girlfriend Michelle Robinson. They all go back to Robinson's apartment in Greenwich Village to celebrate his temporary freedom. His mother has bought him some heroin and is present when he injects it. (She will claim she was fearful that he would be arrested if he bought the drug himself.)

2 Shortly after midnight – having collapsed on the bed throughout the evening – **Sid Vicious** loses consciousness. Medics are called and the 21-year-old **Sex Pistol** dies on the way to the hospital. The death certificate will confirm accidental death caused by "acute intravenous narcotism, pending chemical examination." Vicious will be cremated, and the location of his ashes will remain unknown.

9 After six months of rehearsals, multiracial reggae outfit **UB40** – named after the number on UK unemployment benefit forms – make their debut at the Horse and Hounds pub in King's Heath, in their native Birmingham,

THE SPECIALS

Mar 23 **The Special AKA begin recording the Jerry Dammers-penned *Gangsters*, a tribute to Prince Buster's ska classic, *Al Capone*, which will be released on the group's own independent 2-Tone label. Dammers creates a striking black and white checkerboard logo, which will hallmark all future releases. With a licensing deal with indie distributor Rough Trade, 5,000 copies will be pressed before Chrysalis Records steps in to cut a longterm agreement, which uniquely allows 2-Tone complete creative independence.**

Jerry Dammers, the Special AKA, and the independent 2-Tone label spearheaded a rapidly built, rock-steady, ska revival craze in Britain, infused with a left-leaning political stance and a DIY punk sensibility.

Dire Straits

Elvis Costello

sharing the bill with another new local band, the **Au Pairs**. Most of the eight-member group – led by lead vocalist/guitarist **Ali Campbell** and his lead guitarist brother **Robin Campbell** (sons of Scottish folk singer **Ian Campbell**) – have known each other for up to ten years, and several attended art school together. Despite major label interest, the group will sign to the independent Graduate Records, run by David and Susan Virr from their record shop in Dudley.

15 Nominated in six categories, the **Bee Gees** win five awards, including Album of the Year, at the 21st annual Grammys. **Billy Joel**'s *Just The Way You Are* is named Record of the Year and Song of the Year. Sixteen years into their recording career, the **Rolling Stones** receive their first nomination: Album of the Year for ***Some Girls***. In a category in which the other nominations are the **Cars**, **Elvis Costello**, **Chris Rea**, and **Toto**, disco quartet **A Taste of Honey** – who scored with last year's disco nugget *Boogie Oogie Oogie* – are named Best New Artist. (In the hotly contested Best Spoken Word Recording, Orson Welles beats out Richard Nixon.)

17 The **Clash**, during the US portion of their Pearl Harbor '79 tour, open their show at New York's Palladium Theater with *I'm So Bored With The USA*. **Bo Diddley** is the opening act.

23 **Dire Straits** begin their first North American tour – 51 sellout shows over 38 days – at the Paradise Club in Boston.

24 **Bonnie Pointer** having left the R&B group to start a solo career with Motown, the remaining **Pointer Sisters** trio of **June**, **Anita**, and **Ruth** (who recently signed to producer Richard Perry's new Planet label) score their biggest hit with *Fire* – written by **Bruce Springsteen** – reaching US No. 2.

March

16 Currently on his Armed Funk US tour, **Elvis Costello** is at the Holiday Inn in Columbus, enjoying a late-night drink with **Bonnie Bramlett** and **Stephen Stills** after last night's concert at the Agora Club. Alleged derogatory remarks by Costello about **Ray Charles**, **James Brown**, and American music in general, anger Bramlett, who takes a punch at him. The ensuing brawl will be explained away by Costello as "bringing a silly argument to a quick end... and it worked too."

Dire Straits' self-titled debut album cost £12,500 to record and became multi-platinum in both the US and UK... During Elvis Costello's 1979 US tour, he played three gigs in three clubs – the Great Gildersleeves, the Lone Star Cafe, and the Bottom Line – in one night in New York.

17 Veteran traditional Irish folk/Celtic roots aggregate, the **Chieftains**, guest on "Saturday Night Live," performing *If I Had Maggie In The Woods* and *Morning Dew*. Formed in 1963 by uilleann pipes and tin whistle-player **Paddy Maloney**, and fiddle-player **Martin Fay**, the group featured on **Mike Oldfield**'s 1975 opus, ***Omnadawn***, and on the soundtrack to Stanley Kubrick's 1976 film "Barry Lyndon." They will perform as the opening act for the Pope at an outdoor mass held before 1.35 million people, at Dublin's Phoenix Park, in September.

> "Elvis is no racist. His mother and I were always very strict on that point."
>
> Elvis Costello's father, Ross McManus, **New Musical Express**, April 4, 1979

April

3 **Kate Bush** makes her first live appearance at the Empire Theatre in Liverpool, for the first concert of the 28-date Tour of Life. The show – a 2½ hour act, strong on dance, image, and theatrical choreography (including 17 costume changes) – will play throughout Europe, with the UK segment set to climax at the London Palladium. Exhausted by the experience, Bush will never tour again.

7 Following a limited showcase US tour of small clubs to introduce her first, self-titled, album, **Rickie Lee Jones** appears on "Saturday Night Live," despite arguing with the producers over her choice of song. She wins out, performing *Coolsville*, as well as her forthcoming single, *Chuck E.'s In Love*. The 24-year-old Chicago-born singer/songwriter is currently receiving high praise for her literate-hobo compositions, jazz-folk leanings, and distinctive vocal style.

Supertramp

Elton plays in Russia... Lowell George dies... The Sony Walkman...

22 **Keith Richards** (who has reverted to his given name) plays two charity concerts for the Canadian National Institute for the Blind at the Civic Auditorium in Oshawa, as ordered by the court that sentenced him for heroin possession in October 1978. There are performances by both the **Rolling Stones** and the **New Barbarians**, a group assembled by Richards with **Ron Wood** (guitar), **Ian McLagan** (keyboards), **Stanley Clarke** (bass), **Ziggy Modeliste** (drums), and **Bobby Keyes** (sax), who are about to embark on a US tour.

May

1 Following a three-month bible class at the Vineyard Christian Fellowship's School of Discipleship in Los Angeles, the born-again **Bob Dylan** begins recording an album of original gospel songs in Muscle Shoals. Guest musicians, **Dire Straits' Mark Knopfler** and **Pick Withers**, work alongside Muscle Shoals regulars, **Barry Beckett** (who co-produces with **Jerry Wexler**) and **Tim Drummond**. The 11 days of sessions will result in ten new tracks, which will make up Dylan's new album, ***Slow Train Coming***.

2 The **Who** play their first concert since the death of **Keith Moon** at the Rainbow Theatre, with former **Face Kenney Jones** on drums, and **John "Rabbitt" Bundrick** on keyboards. **Roger Daltrey** introduces **Pete Townshend** and **John Entwistle** as the two new members in the band. During concerts in France in two weeks' time, the band will attend premieres of "The Kids Are Alright" (a Who documentary feature) and "Quadrophenia" (a movie based on the group's 1973 double album opus, which includes a cameo by **Sting**) at the Cannes Film Festival.

4 **Kate Bush** wins the Outstanding British Lyric category for *The Man With The Child In His Eyes* at the 24th annual Ivor Novello Awards, at London's Grosvenor House Hotel. The **Electric Light Orchestra** – whose double album epic, ***Out Of The Blue*** became a multimillion-selling global success last year – are honored with the Outstanding Contribution to British Music.

21 **Elton John** becomes the first major British solo artist to perform in Russia, kicking off an eight-show, two-city visit at the Bolshoi Concert Hall in Leningrad. The concerts are to be filmed for the television documentary "To Russia...With Elton." The Russian diplomats assigned to oversee the shows request that John refrains from kicking over his piano stool during *Bennie And The Jets*.

23 **Tom Petty** files for Chapter 11 Bankruptcy (giving him the right to work out a reorganization of his debts.) This has arisen partly from a record company dispute: Shelter – to which he is signed – was recently sold to ABC, which has now been bought by MCA Records. Petty is said to owe MCA $575,000, which will be automatically repaid only if he remains one of its acts and cuts six further albums. MCA has sued for breach of contract, but Petty's bankruptcy declaration, revealing assets of only $56,000, renders the suit pointless. A solution will quickly be reached via the formation of the new MCA-controlled label, Backstreet Records, to be run by Danny Bransom

Sting played the part of Ace in "Quadrophenia", having apparently turned down several other movie roles, including a villain in the James Bond film "For Your Eyes Only."

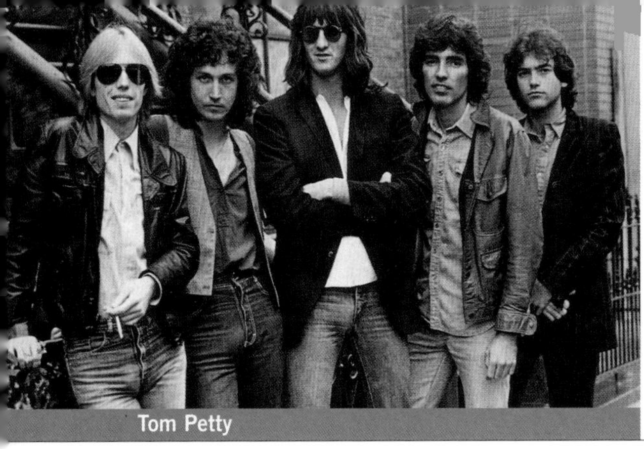
Tom Petty

Sony initially manufactured 30,000 Walkmans – they were ultimately to sell 100 million in the US alone... Two Supertramp albums were certified gold in the US in 1977. Then along came the four-million selling *Breakfast In America* and their only chart-topper... Tom Petty & the Heartbreakers' *Damn The Torpedoes* was stuck at No. 2 for seven weeks behind Pink Floyd's *The Wall*.

GARY NUMAN

July 7 Two dramatically different acts hold the top two spots on this week's UK chart: at No. 1 is *Are "Friends" Electric*, the fourth single by Tubeway Army, an electronic/synthesizer-based vehicle for 21-year-old London-born singer-songwriter Gary Numan, whose robotic visual and musical style is much influenced by Kraftwerk. It holds off *Up The Junction*, by quirky new wave British quintet, Squeeze, formed in 1974 by literate songwriters Chris Difford and Glenn Tilbrook, and featuring 24-year-old keyboardist Jools Holland. This is the London-based group's second consecutive runner-up, following the title cut from *Cool For Cats*, which hit No. 2 in April.

and devoted wholly to Petty and the **Heartbreakers**. It will issue their breakthrough album, ***Damn The Torpedoes***, in November.

31 With their smash album ***Breakfast In America*** in the middle of a six-week run at US No. 1, **Supertramp** perform for the first time at New York's Madison Square Garden. During the sellout concert they receive a platinum disc for one million US copies sold. Less popular in the UK (where it has peaked at No. 3), the album – recorded last year at Los Angeles' Village Recorders Studio – is yielding three huge FM hits: *The Logical Song*, *Goodbye Stranger*, and *Take The Long Way Home*, all co-written by **Rick Davies** and **Roger Hodgson**.

> "Disco in America is mindless and disgusting... I can go to a disco for maybe half an hour and then I have to run to the bathroom."
>
> Hot Chocolate's Errol Brown, **Feature**, May 1979

June

10 Following several weeks of recording at Compass Point Studios in Nassau, Bahamas, in January and February, the **Rolling Stones** begin a month of sessions at the Pathé Marconi Studios in Boulogne-Billancourt near Paris.

12 *Born To Run* is adopted by the New Jersey State Legislature as its unofficial Youth Rock Anthem.

28 **Elton John** receives the prestigious Nordoff-Robbins Silver Clef Award at its fourth annual lunch in London. Nordoff-Robbins is an organization that seeks to help "disabled children and individuals under psychiatric care" by using "creative music therapy... based upon the belief that there is an inborn musicality residing in every human being that can be activated in the service of personal growth and development."

29 Two months after the break-up of **Little Feat**, and the day after a sellout solo performance in Washington, D.C., 34-year-old **Lowell George** is found dead from a heart attack, brought on by drug abuse, in a motel room in Arlington.

July

2 The first portable audio cassette player, developed by Sony and called the Walkman, goes on sale. The electronics giant initially manufactures 30,000 of the TPS-L2 units to test the market. Their success inaugurates a new era of personal music listening: over the next 20 years, more than 100 million units will be sold in the US alone.

8 Signed to Island Records in the UK (where they will find initial success) and to Warner Bros. in the US, offbeat new wave group the **B-52's** make their live British debut at London's Lyceum Ballroom. It is the first date of a short tour to introduce their **Chris Blackwell**-produced first album, ***The B-52's***. They are opening for the **Tourists**, a British pop-rock combo led by ex-**Catch** members, 24-year-old Scottish singer **Annie Lennox**, and 26-year-old keyboardist/guitarist **Dave Stewart**. The Tourists will hit UK No. 4 next month with their revision of **Dusty Springfield**'s *I Only Want To Be With You*.

12 With the "Disco Sucks" backlash beginning in the US, anyone bringing a disco record to Comiskey Park gets to see the doubleheader between the Chicago White Sox and the Detroit Tigers for 98 cents. Local DJ Steve Dahl invites the crowd to toss their records on a pyre, causing so much damage to the field that the second game can't be played.

22 Now calling himself the Rev. Richard Penniman, **Little Richard** preaches at a revival meeting in North Richmond, California, saying, "If God can save a old homosexual like me, he can save anybody."

23 The Ayatollah Khomeini outlaws rock 'n' roll in Iran, citing it as a corrupting influence.

28 Before a crowd of 70,000, the World Series of Rock concert gets under way at the Municipal Stadium in Cleveland, with an A-list bill of **Aerosmith**, **Journey**, **Ted Nugent**, **Thin Lizzy**, and German metal quintet the **Scorpions** (led by vocalist **Klaus Meine**, and featuring guitarist siblings **Rudolf** and **Michael Schenker**). Australian-based heavy-metal combo **AC/DC** receive a rapturous welcome; they are touring the US in support of their sixth album, the high-voltage ***Highway To Hell***.

Echo and the Bunnymen replaced their drum machine, "Echo" with a human being, Pete de Freitas.

The Knack's *My Sharona*... The MUSE concert... Rapper's Delight...

31 The Lee Herschberg-produced ***Bop Till You Drop***, by blues-rock guitarist/composer **Ry Cooder**, is released, the first rock album to be recorded using a fully digital process. It was assembled at Warner Bros. Recording Studios in North Hollywood, using 3-M multitrack digital equipment, which samples sound 50,000 times/second and records its characteristics numerically. It features singers **Chaka Khan**, **Bobby King**, and **David Lindley**, among others.

Police's *Message In A Bottle* topped the UK chart in September – the first of five No. 1s. Only *Every Breath You Take* managed to reach the top in the US.

August

4 Following two warm-up shows in Copenhagen, **Led Zeppelin** headline the Knebworth Festival – their first British date in over four years – before a crowd of 120,000.

10 *The Prince*, 2-Tone's second single release, and the first single by London newcomers **Madness**, hits UK retail. Recorded at Pathway Studios in north London, with *Madness* and *My Girl*, for a mere £200 ($440), it will be the first of countless hits for the seven-member white ska band from Camden Town. Their lead singer, **Suggs**, struck up a friendship with the **Specials** after seeing them perform at the Hope & Anchor pub in Islington in March, which led Madness to sign a one-off deal with 2-Tone. Following their UK No. 16 success, they will ink a longterm agreement with Dave Robinson's Stiff Records, where they will be paired with producers Clive Langer and Alan Winstanley for their smash debut album, ***One Step Beyond***.

18 With their **Chic** technique becoming more polished with each release, the instant disco classic, *Good Times*, written and produced by **Bernard Edwards** and **Nile Rodgers**, tops the US chart. Built around a distinctive Edwards bass line, it will become one of pop's most imitated songs (most prominently copied by **Queen** for next year's US chart-topper, *Another One Bites The Dust*). It is also currently the hottest track played by New York-based club/party DJs, notably in Harlem, where MCs are using it as the basis for sampling and live rapping. *Good Times* – trimmed down from its 8:03-minute album version – follows the US No. 2 success earlier in the summer of Edwards and Rodgers's equally infectious dancefloor filler, *We Are Family*, created for **Sister Sledge**. Their in-demand skills as a one-stop shop for hit compositions/productions will lead to commissions for **Sheila B. Devotion** (*Spacer*), and albums for **Diana Ross**, **Debbie Harry**, and **David Bowie**, among others.

25 **Cliff Richard** scores his first UK No. 1 in over 11 years, with the pop smash *We Don't Talk Anymore*, written and produced by **Alan Tarney**.

25 **Knack**'s debut single, *My Sharona*, written about Sharona Alperin, a 17-year-old senior at Los Angeles' Fairfax High, is an instant US smash. It sells over a million copies inside two weeks, and will add a second million in less than a month in the US, becoming the bestselling 45 of the year. It also hits UK No. 6. Its parent album, ***Get The Knack***, performs similarly, having already topped the US chart two weeks earlier for the first of five weeks. It will sell over five million copies worldwide by the end of 1979. The Los Angeles-based quartet are heavily influenced by the music and style of the Fab Four. They were formed in May last year by lead singer/guitarist **Doug Fieger** and lead guitarist **Berton Averre**, co-writers of *My Sharona*, with the intention of presenting a tight update of the mid-1960s beat group/power-pop style. The accuracy of their execution will prove both a blessing – with the huge success of this first hit – and a curse, when the group prove unable to live up to constant comparisons to the **Beatles**. At least they won't blow too much cash on their relatively unsuccessful follow-up album, which will cost $10,000 to make. Within just three years of *My Sharona*'s success, the group will split up.

The MUSE concerts were described by Rolling Stone as a "stunning testimony to the depth of the shared beliefs of the generation that came of age in the Sixties."

SUGAR HILL

Sept 18 Sugar Hill Records releases *Rapper's Delight* by the Sugar Hill Gang. Sylvia Robinson (below) has created the label as an outlet for the burgeoning rap genre, which has been percolating around Harlem since 1969, when the Last Poets played sessions for Jimi Hendrix's producer Alan Douglas. The technique has long been present in American black culture, appearing in early rural music, blues, gospel, ragtime, and even vaudeville. More recently, DJs in Harlem and the Bronx have been voicing ad-libbed rhymes over the instrumental "breaks" in records, and some have compiled their own mix tapes. Issued as a 12in single, *Rapper's Delight* will immediately find favor in northeastern clubs and on R&B radio, also picking up novelty plays on Top 40 stations. It will sell over two million copies and bring rap to the forefront of the music business – where it will be written off as little more than a fad.

September

3 Post-punk British quartet **Bauhaus** – lead singer **Pete Murphy**, guitarist **Daniel Ash**, and brothers **David** (bass, aka **David Jay**) and **Kevin Haskins** (drums) – record their first song, the sonorously brooding *Bela Lugosi's Dead*, for less than £50 ($110), in the English town of Wellingborough. Written by the group, the do-it-yourself cut will be released as a 12in single, via a one-off deal with indie label Small Wonder in London. Though failing to chart on the pop survey, it will sell consistently in the UK for years, becoming an enduring fixture on the new UK Independent chart and a substantial cult release. It will endear the group to the alternative UK music press, and link them inextricably with the emerging punk-Goth movement.

8 The two-day Futurama '79: The World's First Science Fiction Music Festival begins at the Queen's Hall in Leeds, England, featuring a slew of pioneering alternative/indie bands currently creating a buzz: **Public Image Limited**, **Joy Division**, **Cabaret Voltaire**, **Orchestral Manoeuvres in the Dark**, and **A Certain Ratio**. Also appearing are the psychedelia-influenced **Teardrop Explodes**, a new Liverpool combo led by outspoken frontman **Julian Cope**, and **Echo & the Bunnymen**, formed last year by lead singer **Ian McCulloch** – Cope's ex-colleague in the **Crucial Three** (with **Wah!** founder **Pete Wylie**) – with guitarist **Will Sergeant**, and bassist **Les Pattinson**.

23 The final show of a five-day concert series takes place at Madison Square Garden, organized by Musicians United for Safe Energy (MUSE), an alliance of artists and activists pledged to put an end to atomic power plants and nuclear weapons. **Bruce Springsteen**, celebrating his 30th birthday, takes part in tonight's concert, at **Jackson Browne**'s invitation. Over the past five days the all-star bill has included the **Doobie Brothers**, **Crosby, Stills & Nash**, **James Taylor**, **Carly Simon**, **Bonnie Raitt**, **Tom Petty & the Heartbreakers**, **Raydio** (an R&B group based around 25-year-old session guitarist/singer-songwriter **Ray Parker Jr.**, who broke through last year with *Jack And Jill*), **Nicolette Larson**, **Poco**, **Chaka Khan**, **Ry Cooder**, and **Gil Scott-Heron**.

29 The **Police** perform at New York's Diplomat Hotel at the start of a two-month US tour, which will include a visit to Kennedy Space Center in Houston to film a video for their forthcoming US and current UK No. 1, *Walking On The Moon*.

October

10 "Fleetwood Mac Day" is celebrated as the group receive a star on the Hollywood Walk of Fame (located in front of famed lingerie store, Frederick's of Hollywood). ***Tusk*** will be released next week, a double album that has cost more than $1 million to produce.

Iron Maiden

New Wave of British Heavy Metal... Dylan finds God... The Kampuchea concerts...

13 Having signed a solo deal with Epic Records last year, **Michael Jackson** scores his first US No. 1 in five years with the red-hot dance smash, *Don't Stop Till You Get Enough.* Released on July 28, the Jackson-penned number, originally demoed in his 24-track home studio with brother **Randy**, is taken from ***Off The Wall***, his second collaboration with veteran composer/producer/arranger, **Quincy Jones** (they teamed on last year's movie soundtrack for "The Wiz," starring Jackson and **Diana Ross**). Jones, flush from his first successful foray into disco/dance with the **Brothers Johnson**, has assembled a top-notch crew of session musicians, guest vocalists, and hit-potential material for this project (including songs by ex-**Heatwave** writer, **Rod Temperton**). It will eventually sell over ten million copies worldwide – much to the surprise of Epic, which was very resistant to the idea of the Jones/Jackson combination.

27 **Iron Maiden** appear for the first time on the front cover of **Sounds** newspaper. Inside is an article by journalist Geoff Barton, summarizing what he calls the "New Wave of British Heavy Metal." He uses the term to describe a burgeoning batch of hardcore UK rock bands, who play a ferocious, speeded-up brand of heavy metal. Barton first heard it at the Heavy Metal Crusade concert at London's Music Machine in May, featuring Iron Maiden (formed by lead guitarist **Dave Murray** and bassist **Steve Harris** in 1976), **Samson** (fronted by future Maiden lead singer, **Bruce Dickinson**), and **Angel Witch**.

November

1 **Bob Dylan**'s Slow Train Coming gospel tour opens, with the first of 14 dates at the Fox Warfield Theater in San Francisco. Although upcoming shows in Santa Monica will be well received – partly due to the presence of members of World Vision International, a non-denominational Christian charity organization – much of the tour will be resisted by fans because of Dylan's insistence on performing only his new gospel material.

Iron Maiden recorded four tracks at Spaceward Studios in Cambridge, England, in December 1978 but couldn't afford to pay for the master tape. When they went back later to buy them, the tape had been wiped.

6 **Paul Simon** begins a UK tour – during which he will offer to buy drinks for each audience (a gesture that will cost him around £1,000 ($2,200) a night) – at London's Hammersmith Odeon. It is his first live appearance in Britain for five years.

11 The **Human League** – a Sheffield-based electronic/synthesizer-based combo founded by **Martyn Ware** and **Ian Craig Marsh**, with lead vocalist **Philip Oakey** – play their last gig as a quartet at the Lyceum Ballroom in London. Oakey and visual stylist **Adrian Wright** will continue with a reconstituted Human League, recruiting bassist **Ian Burden** and two female singers – **Joanne Catherall** and **Suzanne Sulley** – while Marsh and Ware will go on to create the **British Electric Foundation** (and subsequently **Heaven 17**).

24 Having already hit No. 1 with *Hot Stuff* in June and *Bad Girls* in July, **Donna Summer** scores her third US chart-topper of the year, a duet with **Barbra Streisand** on *No More Tears (Enough Is Enough).* It is the 12th disco-tinged single to head the US survey in the past 11 months. Even veteran trumpet-player **Herb Alpert** has found dancefloor favor with *Rise.*

THE PRETENDERS

Oct 26 **The Pretenders begin four consecutive Monday night gigs at the Marquee club in London, while their third chart single, *Brass In Pocket*, begins its climb to UK No. 1. With a perfect rock pedigree – which has included playing in Saturday Sunday Matinee alongside future Devo keyboardist Mark Mothersbaugh in 1967, a spell as a music scribe at the New Musical Express, and a part-time job at punk guru Malcolm McLaren's Chelsea boutique, Sex, in 1974 – 28-year-old American singer-songwriter/guitarist Chrissie Hynde formed the Pretenders last year with three Hereford-based musicians: guitarist James Honeyman-Scott, bassist Pete Farndon, and drummer Martin Chambers.**

Joe Strummer is rumored to have faxed Paul Simonon to dig out his old bass guitar to join a reunion for the Clash's induction into the Rock and Roll Hall of Fame. Hopefully it wasn't the one pictured here.

December

1 Having made their bow on the cover of UK magazine **Record Mirror** on November 10, **U2** perform for the first time outside Ireland, playing the first of 11 London dates at West Hampstead's Moonlight Club. Their gig on the 4th at the Hope & Anchor in Islington (billed as "The U2s") will be attended by nine people.

3 Three dates into the **Who**'s current US tour, and hours before tonight's concert at the Riverfront Coliseum in Cincinnati, fans are assembling outside the venue in freezing cold weather. While the group are performing their soundcheck at around 6:00 pm, the sizeable crowd begin pushing hard against the four locked doors, which are not opened until 7:15 pm. A disastrous bottleneck results as fans try to rush into the arena. The first body is found at 7:54 pm, and 11 people are crushed or trampled to death outside the venue. The group play on, unaware of the carnage. When the emergency services arrive, the fire marshal requests that the concert be stopped, but the group's manager argues that a cancellation might spark further trouble. The band members are informed about the tragedy after the show. Deeply shocked, they will hold a press conference tomorrow morning, expressing sympathy for the relatives of those who died, and rebutting charges that their stage act encouraged violence, or that they were involved in security issues at the Coliseum.

"You all heard what happened yesterday. We feel totally shattered. We lost a lot of family yesterday. This show's for them."

Roger Daltrey, December 4, 1979 at the Buffalo Memorial Auditorium

8 Written by lead singer **Dennis DeYoung**, **Styx**'s rock ballad, *Babe*, tops the US chart for the first of two weeks, becoming their bestselling signature hit. The released version is a scarcely embellished reissue of DeYoung's original demo.

15 Known principally as an albums band (they haven't scored a UK chart single since 1967), **Pink Floyd** top the UK chart for the first of five weeks with *Another Brick In The Wall Part II*, which will be certified platinum on January 1.

18 Midway through a 12-date UK tour, the **Police** perform at two different venues in London on the same night. They are transported in an armored personnel carrier from the Hammersmith Odeon gig – which begins at 6:00 pm – to the nearby Hammersmith Palais for a 10:00 pm show.

29 The last of four benefits entitled Concert for the People of Kampuchea, staged at London's Hammersmith Odeon, sees bill-topper **Paul McCartney** assemble **Rockestra**, an ad hoc band comprising **Robert Plant**, **Pete Townshend**, **Billy Bremner**, **Dave Edmunds**, **James Honeyman-Scott**, **John Paul Jones**, **Ronnie Lane**, **Bruce Thomas**, **Kenny Jones**, **Gary Brooker**, and **John Bonham**.

Johnny Rotten, reviewing Human League's *Being Boiled* single for the New Musical Express in 1978, described the group as "trendy hippies."

Michael Jackson's Epic career began inauspiciously with his single *You Can't Win* only managing to reach No. 81 in the US chart.

ROOTS **During this year: Duran Duran cut a demo tape with local indie producer Bob Lamb; newly recruited vocalist Andy Wickett will leave almost immediately, as will guitarist John Curtis; Andy Taylor will be recruited by way of an ad for a "live wire guitarist"... after being told by doctors two years ago that she would never sing again, and forming Blue Angel with John Turi last year, Cyndi Lauper now signs with Polydor Records... schoolfriends George Michael, Andrew Ridgeley, Paul Ridgeley, David Austin, and Andrew Leaver form the Executive, a ska-modeled band, at Bushey Meads Comprehensive School... Colin Hay and Ron Strykert, who met performing in the musical "Heroes" in Sydney, form Men at Work, initially as an acoustic duo... Michael Timmins and Alan Anton form the Hunger Project in Toronto, auditioning but rejecting Timmins' sister Margo; it will be another eight years before they re-emerge as the Cowboy Junkies... Silmarillion, named after the novel by J.R.R. Tolkien, now recruit Steve Rothery and Brian Jelliman, truncate their name and go into the studio to make their first recording, *The Web*... and the daughter of Australian accountant father Ron and Welsh mother Carol, 11-year-old actress Kylie Minogue secures her first acting role, as a Dutch girl in the Australian TV soap opera "The Sullivans"...**

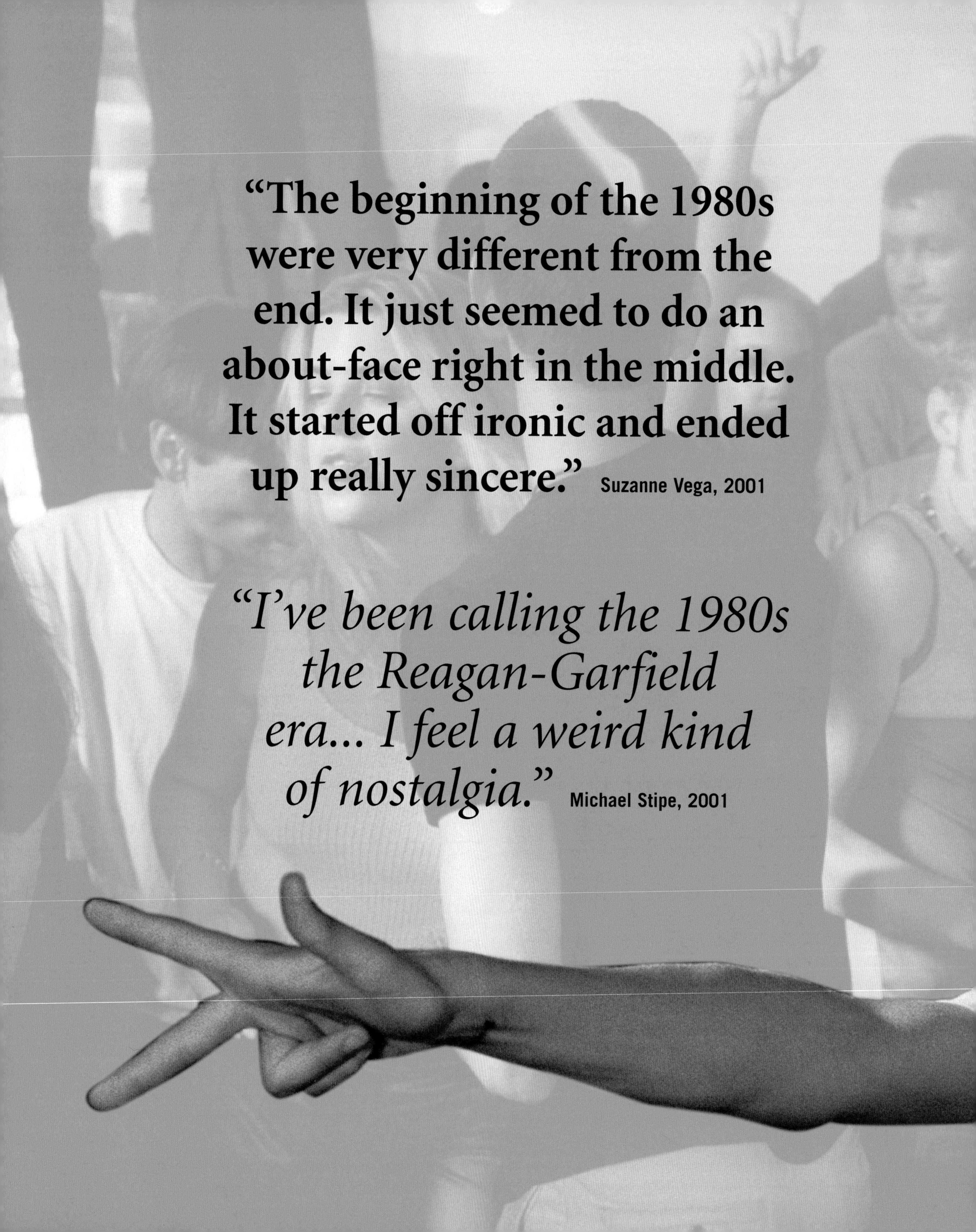

“The beginning of the 1980s were very different from the end. It just seemed to do an about-face right in the middle. It started off ironic and ended up really sincere.” Suzanne Vega, 2001

“I’ve been calling the 1980s the Reagan-Garfield era... I feel a weird kind of nostalgia.” Michael Stipe, 2001

THE EIGHTIES

1980

(Just Like) Starting Over

1980

No.1 US SINGLES

- **Jan 5** Please Don't Go **KC & the Sunshine Band**
- **Jan 19** Rock With You **Michael Jackson**
- **Feb 16** Do That To Me One More Time **Captain & Tennille**
- **Feb 23** Crazy Little Thing Called Love **Queen**
- **Mar 22** Another Brick In The Wall Part II **Pink Floyd**
- **Apr 19** Call Me **Blondie**
- **May 31** Funkytown **Lipps, Inc.**
- **June 28** Coming Up (Live At Glasgow) **Paul McCartney**
- **July 19** It's Still Rock And Roll To Me **Billy Joel**
- **Aug 2** Magic **Olivia Newton-John**
- **Aug 30** Sailing **Christopher Cross**
- **Sept 6** Upside Down **Diana Ross**
- **Oct 4** Another One Bites The Dust **Queen**
- **Oct 25** Woman In Love **Barbra Streisand**
- **Nov 15** Lady **Kenny Rogers**
- **Dec 27** (Just Like) Starting Over **John Lennon**

No.1 UK SINGLES

- **Jan 5** Another Brick In The Wall Part II **Pink Floyd**
- **Jan 19** Brass In Pocket **Pretenders**
- **Feb 2** Special A.K.A. Live! (EP) **Specials**
- **Feb 16** Coward Of The County **Kenny Rogers**
- **Mar 1** Atomic **Blondie**
- **Mar 15** Together We Are Beautiful **Fern Kinney**
- **Mar 22** Going Underground/The Dreams Of Children **Jam**
- **Apr 12** Working My Way Back To You – Forgive Me Girl **Detroit Spinners**
- **Apr 26** Call Me **Blondie**
- **May 3** Geno **Dexy's Midnight Runners**
- **May 17** What's Another Year **Johnny Logan**
- **May 31** Theme From M*A*S*H (Suicide Is Painless) **Mash**
- **June 21** Crying **Don McLean**
- **July 12** Xanadu **Olivia Newton-John/Electric Light Orchestra**
- **July 26** Use It Up And Wear It Out **Odyssey**
- **Aug 9** The Winner Takes It All **Abba**
- **Aug 23** Ashes To Ashes **David Bowie**
- **Sept 6** Start **Jam**
- **Sept 13** Feels Like I'm In Love **Kelly Marie**
- **Sept 27** Don't Stand So Close To Me **Police**

Yoko Ono and John Lennon

Prince

Announcing his return to the music world on his 40th birthday, John Lennon said: "God willing, there are another 40 years of productivity to go." Sadly, it was not to be... Prince was at the forefront of a new sound emanating from Minneapolis.

A year that began with **Paul McCartney**'s incarceration in Japan became more calamitous as it wore on. The lifestyle that went with rock stardom deprived music of some its greatest talent. **John Bonham**, hard-living and hard-drinking – a vodka binge killed him in 1980. Unlike many other groups who lost a member, the dignified **Led Zeppelin** simply called it quits. Bonham was the godfather of hard-rock drumming – his improvised jams and famous *Moby Dick* solo were a staple of Led Zep gigs. **Tim Hardin** was one of the finest folk-blues songwriters of his generation – but was also crippled and eventually killed by addiction – in his case to heroin. The suicide of **Joy Division's Ian Curtis** put a premature end to a band that was influential beyond its slim output, with a glacial distillation of romance and alienation, and alternative rock lost one of its most promising talents. However, the most grievous loss was that of **John Lennon**, gunned down in New York City by a deranged fan on a December evening. Ten years after the **Beatles**' break-up, the death of one of them could still wipe all other news from the front pages.

So much for the sad news. Meanwhile, the **Specials** and the (**English**) **Beat** were purveying their politically laced 2-Tone, ska-driven energy. **Madness** took a less political route, logging up hit after hit of mainstream ska-pop, and the **Jam** emerged from punk's debris to become a serious musical force under the literate leadership of **Paul Weller**.

The award for most spectacular live event went to **Pink Floyd**. The cost of staging "The Wall" – the final epic masterpiece from Pink Floyd's main architect, **Roger Waters** – was so prohibitive that the band played just 12 concerts in the US, at two venues. The double album, released in 1979, was full of malevolence and rage. The single, *Another Brick In The Wall Part II*, with its chorus of (unpaid) London kids, became a global No. 1 hit – surprising for a band deeply rooted in album success.

R&B had a new champion in a 21-year-old from Minneapolis. Influenced by **James Brown** and **Jimi Hendrix**, **Prince** broke through this year with the single *I Wanna Be Your Lover*. He wrote and played most of the instruments on the album ***Prince***, which was crammed with irresistible hooks and overt sexuality. As **Rolling Stone** noted: "With a trace more sophistication, he could become a solo Bee Gees of the libido."

The record industry was beginning to take rap seriously, with Mercury Records releasing an influential eponymous debut album by **Kurtis Blow**, who had built up a reputation as a flamboyant MC in Harlem. It was unusual for a rap artist to release an album in a genre that was still singles-driven.

But, unavoidably, the year is most remembered for the event of December 8: "Man shot. One West 72nd."

Oct 25 Woman In Love **Barbra Streisand**
Nov 15 The Tide Is High **Blondie**
Nov 29 Super Trouper **Abba**
Dec 20 (Just Like) Starting Over **John Lennon**
Dec 27 No One Quite Like Grandma **St. Winifred's School Choir**

"Madness pop is... the perfect soundtrack for contemporary teenagers."

Garry Bushell, **Sounds**, September 27, 1980

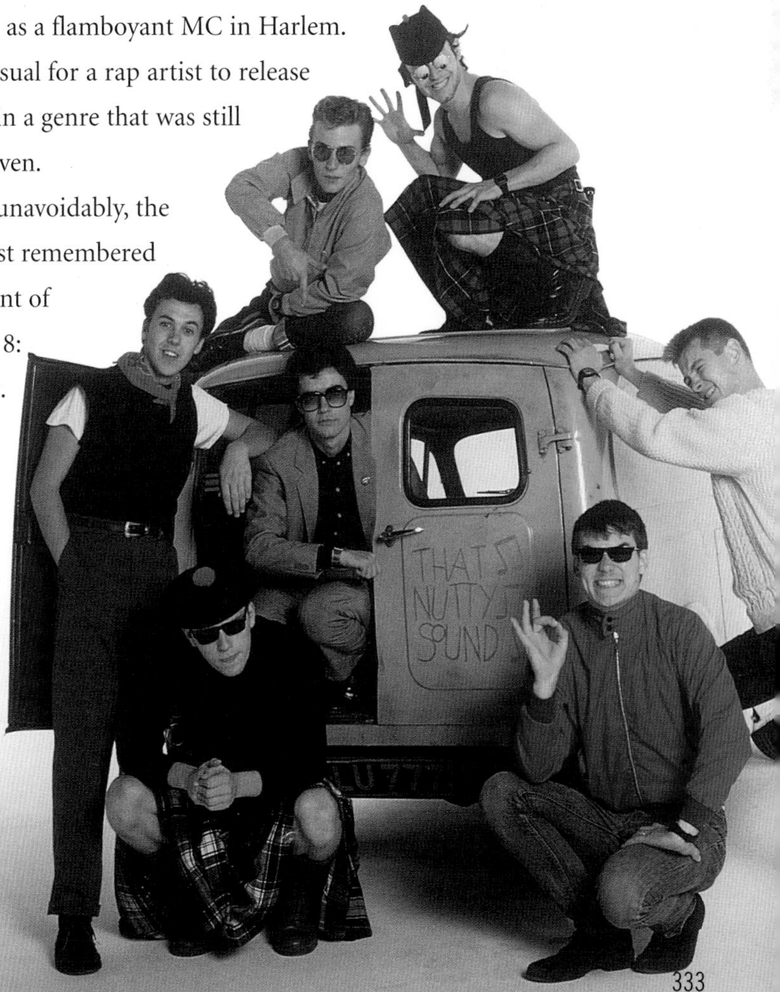

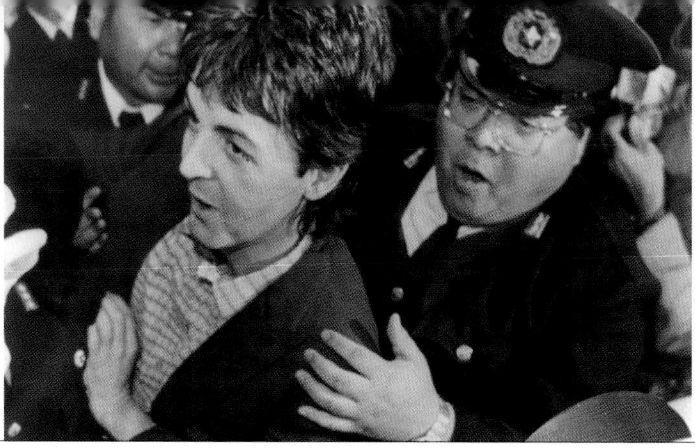

Paul McCartney is busted... Joy Division's *Love Will Tear Us Apart*... Dylan thanks the Lord...

January

2 Rock 'n' roll singer-songwriter/pianist **Larry Williams**, whose 1950s compositions *Bad Boy*, *Dizzy Miss Lizzy*, and *Slow Down* were all recorded by the **Beatles**, is found by his mother, dead, with what appears to be a self-inflicted gunshot wound. The verdict will be suicide.

8 **Joy Division** record *These Days* and *Love Will Tear Us Apart*, at Pennine Sound Studios in Oldham, near London. In March they will re-record *Love Will Tear Us Apart* at **10cc**'s Strawberry Studios in Stockport, England, and the haunting, career-defining song will become the Factory label's biggest hit to date, reaching UK No. 13 in July. Regarded by many alternative rock critics as the finest single of the year, it will feature on their equally well-received second album, ***Closer***, a visionary collection of despair-filled, post-punk songs written by the group, propeled by **Ian Curtis**'s intense vocal style and bassist **Peter Hook**'s compulsive bass lines.

16 **Paul McCartney** is arrested at Narita International Airport in Tokyo, after customs officials find 7.7oz of marijuana in his suitcase. A scheduled 11-date **Wings** Japanese tour is immediately canceled.

25 A six-week US tour by the **Specials** opens at New York's Hurrah club. It is set to end with four soldout dates at the Whisky A Go-Go in Los Angeles, where many fans sport "2-Tone" black-and-white clothing.

26 **Prince** makes his national television debut on "American Bandstand," performing his first US R&B chart-topper *I Wanna Be Your Lover*. The 21-year-old singer-songwriter/guitarist/pianist/producer, born and still based in Minneapolis, immersed himself in music and surrounded himself with top local talent even before leaving Minneapolis Central High School at 16. He signed a long-term contract with Warner Bros. three years ago. A prodigious writer and performer, he is notably influenced by **James Brown**, whom he first saw perform in 1968. Despite having trouble breaking through to the mainstream – mainly because of his overtly sexual material – his second album, ***Prince***, has fared well enough to earn him a platinum disc next month, though crossover success will elude him for two more years.

28 With the first incarnation of his backing band having split up following disagreements with former manager Malcolm McLaren, **Adam Ant** and ex-**Models** and **Siouxsie & the Banshees** guitarist **Marco Pirroni** meet in a cake shop in London's Covent Garden and agree to establish a songwriting partnership to create "antmusic." They will shortly team up with new manager Falcon Stewart, and recruit drummer/producer **Chris Hughes**.

30 New Orleans R&B pianist **Professor Longhair** dies in his home city at the age of 62. He first recorded in 1949, signing with the fledgling Atlantic label, and was a major influence on the likes of **Fats Domino**, **Huey "Piano" Smith**, **Allen Toussaint**, **James Booker**, and **Dr. John**, but remained a cherished secret in the Crescent City. Longhair quit the music business in 1964, but came out of retirement to play at the 1971 New Orleans Jazz & Heritage Festival, closing the show each year thereafter.

Prisoner No. 22 Paul McCartney was jailed for a mandatory ten days in January before the Japanese authorities decided not to prosecute.

> **"I only got into rock 'n' roll for a bit of fun and to see the world for a couple of years."**
>
> Bill Wyman, announcing his intention to leave the Rolling Stones, **Daily Express**, February 18, 1980

February

7 In the third of 15 consecutive weeks topping the US album chart with their double album, ***The Wall***, **Pink Floyd**'s live production of the opus begins its US visit at the Sports Arena in Los Angeles. The band will play six more dates here, followed by five at Nassau Veterans Memorial Coliseum in Uniondale. In one of the

Pink Floyd's *The Wall* was largely written by Roger Waters, who was at the time the group's main creative force. Their classic *The Dark Side Of The Moon* became the longest consecutive-charting album in Billboard chart history when it racked up its 303rd week in March.

most celebrated stage spectaculars in rock history, a wall, 160ft wide and 30ft high, is built out of 5lb styrofoam blocks between the group and the audience during the first half of the show, and then ceremoniously destroyed after the intermission. Due to its enormous cost, the show will be performed only 29 times – at a financial loss that is more than offset by the multiplatinum success of the album and its globally chart-topping extract, *Another Brick In The Wall Part II*, with its rebellious children's chorus chant, "We don't need no education."

12 Signed last year to the 2-Tone label for their first single, but having recently set up their own Go-Feet label, the (**English**) **Beat** begin recording *Mirror In The Bathroom* at the Roundhouse Studio in London. The record is notable as the first digitally recorded British single, and the session is not without its problems: hardware manufacturers 3M assign an engineer (who sleeps at the studio) to help fix teething problems. The line-up of the Birmingham-based ska/pop fusion combo features the four founding members – singer/guitarist **Dave Wakeling**, guitarist **Andy Cox**, bassist **David Steele**, and drummer **Everett Morton** – recently augmented by post-punk rapper **Ranking Roger**, and Jamaican-born saxophonist **Saxa**.

13 **John Lydon**'s London house is raided by the police, who smash open the front door to find him waving a ceremonial sword at them from the top of the stairs. The only illegal item found on the premises is a canister of tear gas, claimed to be for defense against intruders.

19 While recording in Britain, **AC/DC**'s lead singer **Bon Scott** and his musician friend Alisdair Kinnear spend the evening at the Music Machine in Camden Town, London, watching **Protex** and the **Trendies** while consuming vast quantities of alcohol. Kinnear drives Scott back to his house in East Dulwich, and leaves him asleep in the car.

20 Kinnear returns to the car to find **Bon Scott** unconscious, and drives him to the nearby King's College Hospital, where he is pronounced dead. The coroner will record a verdict of "death by misadventure – acute alcoholic poisoning," stating that Scott has literally "drunk himself to death." Scott's body will be flown out to Fremantle, Australia, and cremated, and his ashes buried in the cemetery's Memorial Garden.

27 In an attempt to move with the times, NARAS awards an all-time high of 57 Grammys at the 22nd ceremony, most notably reviving the Best Rock Vocal Performance, Male category, which goes to **Bob Dylan** – surprisingly a first-time winner – for the gospel-tinged *Gotta Serve Somebody*. Dylan, saying, "I didn't expect this. The first person I want to thank is the Lord," is one of seven artists who choose to thank Jesus or God during the evening. The **Doobie Brothers** – with the most nominations, at six – win Record of the Year for *What A Fool Believes*, which also gives its writers, **Michael McDonald** and **Kenny Loggins**, the prize for Song of the Year. **Rickie Lee Jones** is Best New Artist, and **Gloria Gaynor**'s *I Will Survive* is Best Disco Recording.

29 The glasses that **Buddy Holly** was wearing when he died – along with the wristwatch worn by the **Big Bopper** – are discovered in a police file in Mason, Georgia, unnoticed for over 21 years.

March

3 Sotheby's, the London auction house, holds its first ever auction of pop memorabilia. Among the items under the hammer are four dollar bills signed by the **Beatles**, which go for £220 ($528), and a paper napkin signed by **Elvis Presley** at the Riviera Hotel in Las Vegas, which fetches £500 ($1,200). It will be some years before more substantial items – such as musical instruments – start to be auctioned off, but the rock memorabilia industry will become big business, led by the burgeoning and acquisitive Hard Rock Café chain.

7 Setting their own style, with an emphasis on extravagant clothing, make-up, and nightclubbing (at trendy new London hotspots like Blitz, Billy's, Le Kilt, and Le Beat Route), **Spandau Ballet** – wearing kilts – perform at London's Scala Cinema. This is the latest in a number of unusual single live dates booked by manager Steve Dagger to intrigue the music media. Spearheading the nascent "New Romantic" movement, the quintet was formed last year by Islington-based songwriter/guitarist **Gary Kemp**, whose brother **Martin** is on bass. They are fronted by lead singer **Tony Hadley**.

23 **Jacob Miller** is killed, age 27, in a car crash on Hope Road in Kingston, Jamaica. Miller came under the tutelage of Coxsone Dodd while still a teenager, cutting *Love Is A Message*, before recording with **Augustus Pablo** in the mid-1970s. Becoming reggae troupe **Inner Circle**'s lead singer from 1976, he was the voice of Jamaica's ghetto class.

26 In the middle of their Reggatta de Blanc world tour, the **Police** become the first Western pop group in ten years to play in Bombay, when they perform to 5,000 fans at the open-air Homi Bha Bha Auditorium. (**Hawkwind** played there in 1970.) The concert, which raises $12,000 for sick children, has been organized by the Time and Talents Club, a group of 48 middle-aged ladies. Promotional banners around the city proclaim: "Police – Not Cops but Pops."

28 Following a concert at the Zurcher Hallenstadion in Zurich, the **Who**'s **Pete Townshend** decides to quit the music business. He sets off on foot for Berne, carrying just his passport, wallet, and a bottle of brandy, to visit the bears in the city's famous zoo. On arrival, he finds it's the off-season and the bears are hibernating. He passes out in the bear enclosure. Waking, he makes his way to Vienna, to perform with the Who at the weekend.

April

1 **Iron Maiden** embark on their first headlining tour with a performance at the Rainbow Theatre in London, having just finished a 19-date UK tour, opening for fellow metal purveyors **Judas Priest** (a Birmingham band led by **Rob Halford**, who have just released *British Steel*, their most successful album to date). Iron Maiden will play their first show outside the UK at the weekend, during the Wheel Pop Festival in Belgium and will open for **KISS** on a European tour at the end of the year.

17 **Bob Marley** performs at the Zimbabwe Independence Day celebrations at the Rufaro Stadium in Salisbury, in front of Prince Charles and President Robert Mugabe. Marley and the **Wailers** will shortly begin a major European tour to promote their new album, *Uprising*, playing in Switzerland, West Germany, France, England, Norway, Sweden, Denmark, East Germany, Belgium, Holland, Spain, Ireland, and Scotland, with a 100,000 sellout show at the San Siro Stadio in Milan.

On March 22, the Jam's *Going Underground/The Dreams Of Children* became the ninth record to enter the UK chart at No. 1.

Joy Division's Ian Curtis dies... Donna Summer becomes Geffen's first signing... Led Zeppelin perform for the last time...

19 The **New Musical Express** reports that ex-**Geordie** singer **Brian Johnson** has been named as the replacement for lead vocalist **Bon Scott** in **AC/DC**. He will shortly join them at Compass Point Studios in Nassau, the Bahamas, where they are recording a new album with South African producer Robert John "Mutt" Lange. The seven weeks of sessions will yield their landmark album, ***Back In Black***.

25 The **Stranglers**' lead singer, **Hugh Cornwell**, is released from Pentonville Prison, after serving six-weeks for heroin possession.

May

2 At Birmingham University, **Joy Division** play what will prove to be their final gig, during which **Ian Curtis** – who was hospitalized last month after overdosing on phenobarbitone – has to be helped offstage, clearly in pain.

2 **Pink Floyd**'s *Another Brick In The Wall Part II* is banned in South Africa, on the grounds that it is "prejudicial to the safety of the state." Black schoolchildren have adopted the song to protest at their inferior standard of education.

3 **Dexy's Midnight Runners**' *Geno* – a tribute to 1960s British soul singer **Geno Washington** – tops the UK chart for the first of two weeks. It is the first triumph for the group's founder, frontman, and guiding force, 26-year-old singer-songwriter/guitarist **Kevin Rowland**. Rebellious and outspoken, he has recently taken advertising space in UK music papers to publish controversial ranting essays berating both fans and the music industry. Constantly at odds with EMI Records, Rowland recently seized the master tapes of the group's debut album, ***Searching For The Young Soul Rebels***, from its producer, **Pete Wingfield**, and is refusing to return them until the label agrees to more favorable contract terms. The stand-off will be resolved in July, when the well-received set hits UK No. 6.

4 In an incongruous billing, Hispanic band **Los Lobos** open for **Public Image Ltd.** at a concert at the Olympic Auditorium in Los Angeles. Their acoustic set receives a hostile reception from the hardcore punk audience, which pelts the group with bottles, coins, and spit, forcing them to give up after ten minutes. (Unfazed by the experience, the pioneering group will continue performing locally and come to the attention of the local Anglo-American music industry, as it integrates an electric sound into the previously acoustic-only Spanish and American tune Latin genre.)

17 **Paul** and **Linda McCartney** guest on "Saturday Night Live," singing **Wings**' new single *Coming Up*. The studio version A-side is being flipped by American DJs, who prefer the B-side live version of the same song, recorded in Glasgow on December 17 last year – a move that will give McCartney his seventh solo/Wings US chart-topper on June 28. *Coming Up* has already reached UK No. 2, spurred by its ironic accompanying video clip, in which McCartney takes the roles of five musicians: **Frank Zappa**, **Ron Mael** (of eccentric synth duo **Sparks**), **Buddy Holly**, **Roxy Music**'s **Andy Mackay**, and himself – as a **Beatle** with a collarless suit in a group dubbed the Plastic Macs.

18 The two members of **Buggles** (who hit UK No. 1 last year with the infectious synth-based pop nugget, *Video Killed The Radio Star*), production whiz **Trevor Horn** (vocals and guitar), and **Geoff Downes** (keyboards), join **Yes**, replacing the outgoing **Jon Anderson** and **Rick Wakeman**. They will stay for only one album, ***Drama***, but it will yield the group's biggest hit, *Owner Of A Lonely Heart*.

27 With **Van Halen** in Europe to promote their new album ***Women And Children First***, **David Lee Roth** collides with low-hanging stage lights during the execution of a flying leap from **Alex Van Halen**'s drum riser, fracturing his nose and suffering multiple contusions and concussion during the recording of an Italian television special at the Piper Club in Rome.

30 **Carl Radle** – notable session man and bass player to **Leon Russell**, **J.J. Cale**, and **Derek & the Dominos** – dies of kidney disease in a hospital in Tulsa, Oklahoma. He is 37.

> **"It's the most depressing, demoralizing, inhuman place I have ever spent any time in."** The Stranglers' Hugh Cornwell on release from prison, April 25, 1980

JOY DIVISION

May 18 In the early hours of the morning, with Iggy Pop's *The Idiot* still on his turntable and Werner Herzog's "Strojek" in the video player, Joy Division's Ian Curtis hangs himself at the age of 23, four days before the group is due to fly to the US. He reportedly leaves a note: "At this moment I wish I was dead, I just can't cope anymore." He will be buried in Macclesfield Cemetery near Manchester, with "Love Will Tear Us Apart" inscribed on his headstone. Joy Division's greatest commercial success will come after Curtis's death, and he, through the group's legend and music, will influence many alternative rock acts over the next 20 years. During the weeks ahead, *Love Will Tear Us Apart* and *Closer* will be released as scheduled, while the remaining group members resolve to continue, remaining on Tony Wilson's Factory label but recording under a new name. At a brainstorming session in a pub, they will suggest Khmer Rouge and the Witch Doctors of Zimbabwe, finally choosing New Order at the insistence of Bernard Sumner and Peter Hook.

Born Patricia Andrzejewski, Pat Benatar – who briefly studied music at the Juilliard School – was spotted singing in a cabaret at the Catch a Rising Star in New York.

June

13 American rocker **Pat Benatar** performs on a temporary stage erected on the infield before tonight's Philadelphia Phillies baseball team home game. During the performance she dances with the team's green duck mascot. At 27, Benatar – who signed with Chrysalis Records last year – is about to nab her first major US smash with *Hit Me With Your Best Shot*.

14 With ***Peter Gabriel*** topping the UK chart, the former **Genesis** frontman sets out on a 20-date US tour at the Clubhouse in Santa Ana, California. In the fall, he will wend his way through Sweden, Germany, France, Switzerland, Italy, and Portugal on a 31-date European tour, making his last live appearances until 1982.

19 **Donna Summer** is the first act signed by David Geffen to his new Geffen label. He will quickly add other star names to his roster, including **Elton John** and **Neil Young** – though his biggest signing will come in September.

21 **The Stranglers** are arrested in Nice, after allegedly inciting a riot when a concert at the University is canceled because a generator has not been supplied. The band apparently told fans to "take it out on the University, not us." **Jean-Jacques Burnel** is allowed out on £10,000 ($24,000) bail, while the other band members are released unconditionally.

25 With his current album ***Glass Houses*** midway through a six-week stay at US No. 1, and with the extracted *It's Still Rock 'n' Roll To Me* also heading to the top spot, **Billy Joel** is awarded the Gold Ticket for playing to over 100,000 fans at New York's Madison Square Garden.

27 **Led Zeppelin**'s concert in Nuremberg is halted after three numbers, when drummer **John Bonham** collapses.

July

2 **Sheena Easton** – a 21-year-old pop singer from Glasgow, Scotland – is featured in tonight's edition of "The Big Time," a BBC television show that gives ordinary people an opportunity to live out their fantasies. Easton is filmed auditioning for EMI Records, recording her first single and undergoing the grooming and marketing process that the label normally undertakes when launching a new act. The exposure will shoot her debut single, the jaunty pop ditty *Morning Train (Nine To Five)*, to UK No. 3 next month.

4 The **Beach Boys** give a free performance before half a million people in Washington, D.C., on Independence Day. An annual Fourth of July concert will become a regular date on the group's calendar throughout the decade.

7 **Led Zeppelin** play at the Eissporthalle in Berlin, at the end of a 14-date European tour, and on the 12th anniversary of the **Yardbirds**' break-up. The gig – which closes with *Whole Lotta Love* – will prove to be their final concert.

14 **Roxy Music**'s lead singer **Bryan Ferry** collapses in his hotel room in Port Barcares in southwest France. Tomorrow he will be flown to London and hospitalized with a kidney infection. The band's ***Flesh And Blood*** is currently between two separate peaks at UK No. 1.

Roxy Music were at the start of a 60-date European tour when lead singer Bryan Ferry became ill.

John Lennon begins recording again... The first Monsters of Rock festival...

When Mercury signed Kurtis Blow, he became the first rapper to be signed to a major record label... Led Zeppelin's John Bonham allegedly consumed 40 shots of vodka during a drinking binge that led to his death.

Kurtis Blow

14 **Malcolm Owen** – lead singer with reggae-laced punk combo the **Ruts**, and a leading voice in the Rock Against Racism movement – is found dead in his bathtub at home. His death follows a long-standing addiction to heroin.

25 Following the departure on May 17 of drummer **Peter Criss**, his replacement, **Eric Carr** – cosmetized into a fox (Criss was a cat) – makes his live debut with **KISS** at the Palladium Theater in New York City.

28 The Dalymount Festival takes place in Dublin, boasting performances by the **Police**, **U2**, and **Squeeze**.

August

4 **Pink Floyd** begin a week-long series of concerts – their first in the UK since March 1977 – performing "The Wall" at London's Earls Court. Down the road at the Hammersmith Odeon, the Greater London Council refuses permission for US punk band the **Plasmatics** – led by bare-breasted, leather-clad punkette, **Wendy O. Williams** – to blow up a car on stage during tonight's debut UK performance. It is the latest of a number of increasingly outrageous stunts planned by the band during their shows.

4 After a recording hiatus of more than five years, during which he has become Mr. Mom to his son Sean, **John Lennon** – with **Yoko** – begins recording songs he wrote recently while vacationing in Bermuda, in sessions at the Hit Factory in New York City. The co-producer is Jack Douglas, and the musicians include **Hugh McCracken** and **Earl Slick** (guitars), **Tony Levin** (bass), **George Small** (keyboards), and **Andy Newmark** (drums). The sessions – which include today's takes of *(Just Like) Starting Over* and the Ono-penned *Kiss Kiss Kiss*, *I'm Moving On*, and *Every Man Has A Woman Who Loves Him* – will produce 22 completed songs.

16 **Rainbow** headlines the first Monsters of Rock festival at Castle Donington in Leicestershire, England. Both lead singer **Graham Bonnet** and journeyman drummer **Cozy Powell** are making their last appearance with the band. Also featured on the bill are **Judas Priest**, the **Scorpions**, Canadian rockers **April Wine**, **Saxon**, **Riot**, and **Touch**.

19 Still climbing the US survey, **Kurtis Blow**'s *The Breaks (Part 1)* is certified gold by the RIAA. It is the first certified million-selling rap disc, and the first 12in single to go gold. (The **Sugar Hill Gang**'s million-plus selling *Rapper's Delight* has not been certified – one of many inconsistencies that plague the RIAA certification process, often because of poor record-keeping by labels.) Blow is a 21-year-old New Yorker named Kurt Walker, who began rapping as a DJ in Harlem clubs in 1976, honing his craft over the next three years at local clubs like Small's Paradise, and working with fellow rap pioneer **Grandmaster Flash**.

23 **David Bowie**'s *Ashes To Ashes* tops the British chart – his first UK No. 1 single since the re-released *Space Oddity* in 1975. Fittingly, the song continues the "Major Tom" saga introduced in *Space Oddity*. Its success is spurred by a visually striking and innovative video produced by David Mallet.

> **"Bowie's performance was startling on opening night – his speech was halting and slurred yet inquisitive, and his angular body defined [John] Merrick's grotesque physical stature."**
>
> Review of David Bowie in "The Elephant Man" in Denver, Colorado, **Record Mirror**, August 9, 1980

September

6 **Diana Ross** scores her first US No. 1 in five years with *Upside Down*, written and produced by **Bernard Edwards** and **Nile Rodgers**.

21 After performing in a pair of concerts with co-headliners the **Commodores** at Madison Square Garden in New York yesterday and the day before, **Bob Marley** collapses while jogging with his friend Skilly Cole in Central Park. His wife Rita wants the rest of the tour canceled, but Marley insists it should go ahead.

22 **John Lennon**, all of whose solo releases to date have been issued on the Beatles' Apple label, signs with Geffen Records, after David Geffen offers to release his album without hearing any of the material.

23 **Bob Marley** collapses on stage at the Stanley Theater in Pittsburgh. He is flown to New York and admitted to Sloan-Kettering Hospital, where a brain tumor is diagnosed and he is given one month to live. The remainder of his tour is canceled.

25 On the eve of a US tour, **Led Zeppelin**'s drummer **John Bonham** dies at the age of 32, at **Jimmy Page**'s home, the Old Mill House in Windsor, England. The cause is inhalation of vomit after a heavy drinking session. A private

The magic touch of Bernard Edwards and Nile Rodgers brought Diana Ross her fifth solo chart-topper in the US.

John Bonham

funeral will be held in Rushock church, near Worcester. A cymbal will be placed in front of his grave.

October

1 **Paul Simon**'s semi-autobiographical film "One-Trick Pony" opens in US movie theaters, but will achieve only modest box-office success. It includes brief appearances by the **B-52's**, a specially re-formed **Lovin' Spoonful**, and **Lou Reed**.

3 **Bruce Springsteen** begins the River tour, at the University of Michigan's Crisler Arena in Ann Arbor, to promote his upcoming fifth album, ***The River***. He opens – for the first time ever – with *Born To Run*, and later Michigan's favorite son, **Bob Seger**, joins him on *Thunder Road*. The critically lauded double-LP set, trimmed from an original choice of 60 songs, will become Springsteen's first US No. 1 release.

4 **Lindsey Buckingham**, **Stevie Nicks**, and **Mick Fleetwood** present the University of Southern California Trojan Marching Band with a platinum disc, for its contribution to ***Tusk***, at half-time during a game at Dodger Stadium in Los Angeles.

4 Heavily borrowing its bassline from **Chic**'s *Good Times*, **Queen**'s *Another One Bites The Dust* tops the US chart. It is their second Stateside No. 1 of the year, following the popabilly smash, *Crazy Little Thing Called Love*.

6 **John Lydon** is arrested for assault after a pub brawl in Dublin. He will be sentenced to three months in jail for disorderly conduct, but acquitted on appeal.

9 **John Lennon** celebrates his 40th birthday, with Geffen Records releasing *(Just Like) Starting Over*, his first single in five years.

27 In London, **Steve Peregrine Took**, **Marc Bolan**'s co-founding partner in **Tyrannosaurus Rex**, spends a royalty check on the purchase of morphine and magic mushrooms. He chokes to death on a cherry after the mushrooms numb any sensation in his throat. He is 31.

November

4 **Bob Marley** is baptized at the Ethiopian Orthodox Church, Kingston, converting to a Christian Rastafarian and taking the new name Berhane Selassie ("Light of the Holy Trinity").

BLONDIE

Nov 15 Blondie's *The Tide Is High*, a lilting reggae number written by John Holt and previously recorded by the Paragons, heads the UK chart, becoming the group's third British chart-topper of the year – its fifth to date – following the earlier success of *Atomic* in March and *Call Me* in April. *The Tide Is High* is taken from the group's new *Autoamerican* album, their third collaboration with producer Mike Chapman, and will also top the US chart in January.

While Blondie was at its career peak, Debbie Harry was already eyeing a solo career, which would begin the following year with *Koo Koo*.

1980

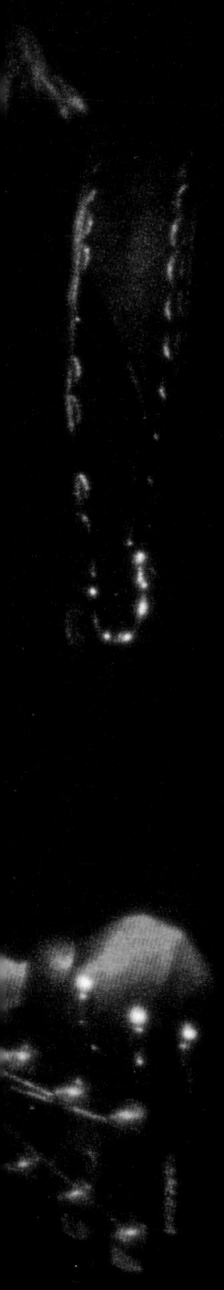

Dec 8 John Lennon and Yoko Ono leave the Record Plant studio in New York at 10:30 pm. They enter the West 72nd Street entrance of the Dakota building, where they live, and Lennon turns around when he hears a voice say, "Mr. Lennon." He is shot four times by 25-year-old Mark David Chapman, before struggling up six stairs into the alcove of the guard area, where he collapses at approximately 10:50 pm. Two bullets have hit him in the back, piercing his lung and passing through his chest. Two more have hit him in the shoulder, one shattering his left shoulder bone, the other ricocheting inside his chest and severing his aorta. A fifth bullet missed. The police receive a five-word report: "Man shot. One West 72nd." When they arrive at the Dakota, they find Lennon bleeding profusely. He is placed in the back of Police Officer James Moran's patrol car and driven to the Roosevelt Hospital 15 blocks away, where he is pronounced dead from a massive loss of blood at 11:30 pm. Lennon is 40 years old. Earlier today, at around 5:00 pm, he had autographed Chapman's copy of ***Double Fantasy*** with the inscription: "John Lennon 1980."

"Man shot. One West 72nd." Police dispatcher, December 8, 1980

Sportscaster Howard Cosell broke the news of Lennon's death during a "Monday Night Football" game between the Miami Dolphins and the New England Patriots.

Nov

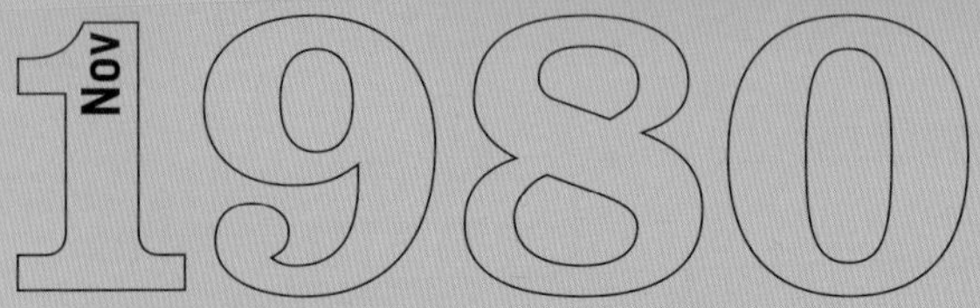

U2 make their US debut... The Clash's *Sandinista!*... John Lennon is murdered...

Motörhead

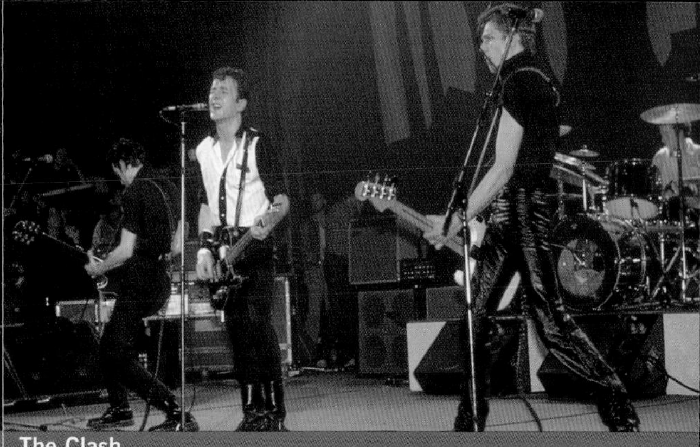

The Clash

21 **Eagles**' singer/drummer **Don Henley** is arrested and charged with drug offenses (allegedly marijuana, cocaine, and Quaaludes) and "contributing to the delinquency of a minor," when a naked 16-year-old girl is found in his Los Angeles home, suffering from a drug overdose. He will be fined $2,000, given two years' probation, and ordered to attend a drug counseling course.

26 **Motörhead** – promoting ***Ace Of Spades***, the group's breakthrough album, which will peak at UK No. 4 – begin a four-night run at London's Hammersmith Odeon. The performance is recorded and edited down for release as ***No Sleep Till Hammersmith*** (which will hit UK No. 1 next year). They were formed five years ago by ex-**Jimi Hendrix** roadie and ex-**Hawkwind** bassist **Lemmy**, who has proudly stated: "We're the kind of band that if we moved in next to you, your lawn would die." Pioneering a furious brand of high octane heavy metal (that will become known as both thrash and speed metal) and spurred by Lemmy's relentless hellbent lifestyle and approach to music, Motörhead has reached a unique position: while following the do-it-yourself ethics and anarchic style of punk, they are also the most endearing purveyors of the New Wave of British Heavy Metal. With the live album neatly capturing such ear-shattering audience favorites as *Ace Of Spades*, *Overkill*, *Bomber*, and *Motörhead*, the group will have enormous influence on successive waves of speed/thrash metal groups and new punk bands alike, in both the UK and US.

In an unlikely coupling of artists, U2 opened for Slade at the Lyceum Ballroom in October following a week-long tour of the Netherlands.

December

2 Country/pop veteran **Kenny Rogers**' ***Greatest Hits*** – on the way to the top spot in the US – is certified platinum by the RIAA. It is his third million-selling album of the year, following ***Kenny*** (January 16) and ***Gideon*** (May 28). Having amassed dozens of US country hits, both as a solo artist and as former leader of the **First Edition**, the 42-year-old Texan is also in his third week at No. 1 on the Hot 100 with *Lady*, a ballad written and produced (in just four hours) by **Commodores**' frontman **Lionel Richie** – who is lining up his own solo career at Motown.

4 **Jimmy Page**, **Robert Plant**, and **John Paul Jones** announce **Led Zeppelin**'s decision not to continue after "the loss of our dear friend," in the wake of **John Bonham**'s death in September.

6 **U2** play their first dates in North America: a nine-date visit that opens tonight at the Ritz in New York. They are promoting their debut album, ***Boy***, which was produced by Steve Lillywhite and recorded at the Windmill Lane Studios. (The photogenic "boy" featured on the album cover is Peter Rowan, the brother of **Virgin Prunes** vocalist, **Guggi**.)

10 **John Lennon**'s body, having been taken from the hospital morgue to the Frank E. Campbell Funeral Chapel at Madison and 81st Street, is cremated at the Ferncliff Mortuary in Hartsdale, New York. (Lennon's killer, Mark Chapman, quit his job as a maintenance man in Honolulu, in October, and on October 27 purchased a five-shot Charter Arms .38 special from J&S Sales Ltd. for $169. After a brief visit to Atlanta, where he used to attend high school, he returned to Hawaii, before finally leaving on December 5. He arrived in New York on the 6th, checking into a $16.50 a night room at a YMCA, nine blocks from the Dakota. On the 7th, he moved to a $82 a day room at the Sheraton Center Hotel. He had married a Japanese woman several years his senior, covered his ID badge at his job with the name John Lennon, and constantly played **Beatles** songs on his guitar. In the opinion of one forensic psychiatrist: "He had already tried to kill himself and he was unsuccessful, so he decided to kill Lennon. The homicide was simply a suicide turned backward.")

14 While fans the world over are still coming to terms with **John Lennon**'s death, **Yoko Ono** requests that all who wish to remember him should observe ten minutes' silence from 2:00 pm Eastern Standard Time. With hundreds of people still keeping vigil outside the Dakota building, approximately 100,000 gather in New York's Central Park, with another 30,000 converging outside St. George's Hall on Lime Street, Liverpool.

20 The **Clash**'s triple album set ***Sandinista!***, having received mixed reactions due to its sprawling contents, reaches UK No. 19. CBS has

Afrika Bambaataa, Soulsonic Force, and Kurtis Blow were among the pioneers of the rap/electro/hip-hop genre, initially gaining enormous popularity in their Bronx neighborhoods.

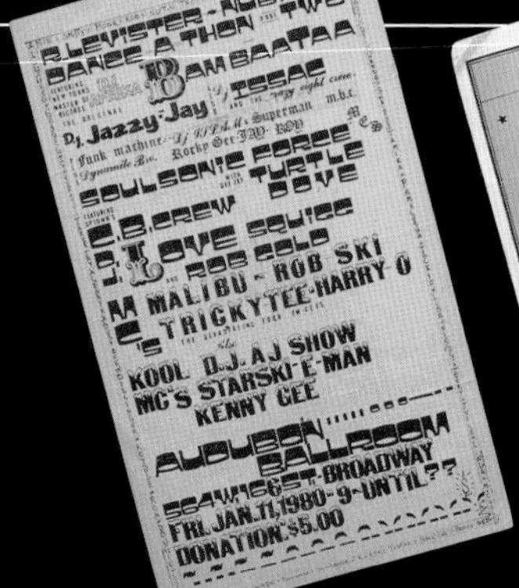

Motörhead were led by Ian Kilminster, aka Lemmy, a minister's son from Stoke-on-Trent, England... The Clash released their ambitious double-album project, *Sandinista!*

"I can't tell you how much it hurts to lose him. His death is a bitter, cruel blow – I really loved the guy."

Paul McCartney, December 9, 1980

issued the ambitious project at a double-album price at the band's insistence, on condition that they agreed to relinquish royalties on the first 200,000 copies. Commenting on the album's musical content, **Mick Jones** says: "Listen, the bottom line on ***Sandinista!*** is that you can dance all the way through it. The only thing is that you have to dance a certain way."

21 Back in England five months after the start of their Zenyatta Mondatta World Tour, the **Police** play the first of two charity Christmas concerts in a large tent on Tooting Bec Common in South London.

27 With the irony-laced *(Just Like) Starting Over* already in its second week at UK No. 1 (holding off the reissued *Happy Xmas (War Is Over)* at No. 2), **John Lennon**'s first posthumous hit tops the US chart, with its parent album, ***Double Fantasy***, also heading the US album list. The LP won't reach the UK summit until February 7.

29 His partner Susan having left him in September, folk/blues singer-songwriter **Tim Hardin** dies from "acute heroin-morphine intoxication due to overdose" in his Los Angeles apartment. He is 39. An enormously talented singer and writer, best known for his compositions *If I Were A Carpenter* (covered by the likes of **Bobby Darin**, the **Four Tops**, **Johnny Cash**, **Bob Seger**, and **Leon Russell**) and *Reason To Believe* (a popular nugget in **Rod Stewart**'s canon), Hardin's career has been dogged by a chronic drug problem.

Mourners sang *Give Peace A Chance* at the Lincoln Memorial in Washington, D.C., a candlelit celebration of Lennon's life took place in Los Angeles, and thousands visited the scene of his death in New York.

ROOTS During this year: Lead vocalist with R&B outfit, Chapter 8, soul singer Anita Baker quits the group to settle into an office job in Detroit... John Bongiovi, at second cousin Tony's request, records *R2-D2 We Wish You A Merry Christmas* for the album *Christmas In The Stars: Star Wars Christmas*... Enya Ni Bhraonain joins her siblings in the band Clannad on vocals and keyboards, appearing uncredited on *Cran Ull*... Michael Dion sends a demo tape of his sister Celine to an address on the back of an album by her idol French singer, Ginette Reno... Sade Adu, attending St. Martin's School of Art in London, joins her first group, Arriva, while continuing to develop her own songs... Roland Orzabal and Curt Smith join pop/ska band, Graduate... Joan Osborne graduates from high school, before spending 18 months studying theater arts and working for a short time at the Burt Reynolds Dinner Theater in Jupiter, Florida... Simon Le Bon joins nascent synth-pop combo Duran Duran, having been recommended by ex-girlfriend Fiona Kemp... Michael Stipe, a student at the University of Georgia in Athens, and guitarist Peter Buck, who first met in the Wuxtry Records store two years ago, form R.E.M. with Bill Berry and Mike Mills, whom they met at a party... and Thom Yorke writes his first song, *Mushroom Cloud*...

Don't Stand So Close To Me

1981

No.1 US SINGLES

Jan 3	(Just Like) Starting Over **John Lennon**
Jan 31	The Tide Is High **Blondie**
Feb 7	Celebration **Kool & the Gang**
Feb 21	9 To 5 **Dolly Parton**
Feb 28	I Love A Rainy Night **Eddie Rabbitt**
Mar 21	Keep On Loving You **REO Speedwagon**
Mar 28	Rapture **Blondie**
Apr 11	Kiss On My List **Daryl Hall & John Oates**
May 2	Morning Train (Nine To Five) **Sheena Easton**
May 16	Bette Davis Eyes **Kim Carnes**
June 20	Medley **Stars On 45**
July 25	The One That You Love **Air Supply**
Aug 1	Jessie's Girl **Rick Springfield**
Aug 15	Endless Love **Diana Ross & Lionel Richie**
Oct 17	Arthur's Theme (Best That You Can Do) **Christopher Cross**
Nov 7	Private Eyes **Daryl Hall & John Oates**
Nov 21	Physical **Olivia Newton-John**

No.1 UK SINGLES

Jan 3	No One Quite Like Grandma **St. Winifred's School Choir**
Jan 10	Imagine **John Lennon**
Feb 7	Woman **John Lennon**
Feb 21	Shaddup You Face **Joe Dolce Music Theatre**
Mar 14	Jealous Guy **Roxy Music**
Mar 28	This Ole House **Shakin' Stevens**
Apr 18	Making Your Mind Up **Bucks Fizz**
May 9	Stand And Deliver **Adam & the Ants**
June 13	Being With You **Smokey Robinson**
June 27	One Day In Your Life **Michael Jackson**
July 11	Ghost Town **Specials**
Aug 1	Green Door **Shakin' Stevens**
Aug 29	Japanese Boy **Aneka**
Sept 5	Tainted Love **Soft Cell**
Sept 19	Prince Charming **Adam & the Ants**
Oct 17	It's My Party **Dave Stewart with Barbara Gaskin**
Nov 14	Every Little Thing She Does Is Magic **Police**
Nov 21	Under Pressure **Queen & David Bowie**
Dec 5	Begin The Beguine (Volver A Empezar) **Julio Iglesias**
Dec 12	Don't You Want Me **Human League**

Simon & Garfunkel

Grandmaster Flash

Hello darkness my old friend: Simon & Garfunkel performed for the first time in more than a decade... Grandmaster Flash, born Joseph Saddler in Barbados, began working as a mobile DJ in the Bronx, to where his parents had emigrated in the early 1960s.

With **John Lennon**'s posthumous hits casting a shadow worldwide, 1981 was off to a solemn start. And it would get worse. The music world said farewell to two more legends: **Bill Haley** died in February, and **Bob Marley** in May, leaving markedly different legacies. Haley was the first white artist to meld country and western with R&B at the dawn of rock 'n' roll, but his career was spent by 1960. Marley became the world's first legitimate reggae superstar, spreading a message of peace and spiritual growth in a more complicated world. While Haley's pioneering contribution will never be forgotten, Marley's impeccable canon of work has become even more popular since his death.

More bad news plagued the music community. With both the disco and punk bubbles now finally burst, record sales fell worldwide, and many blamed the rise in home taping. One mischievous record company boss – Island's Chris Blackwell – released "1+1" cassettes, with music on one side and blank "recordable" space on the other. Concerns about cassette taping did not seem to affect the phenomenal sales of FM-based US adult rock acts: **REO Speedwagon** racked up the best-selling album of the year in the US, and were followed by a slew of other melody-based hard rock bands, such as **Styx**, **Survivor**, and **Journey**. Adult contemporary fare also dominated American radio, with **Chicago** and newcomer **Christopher Cross** seemingly on car radios all day, every day.

The American situation presented a dramatic contrast with the UK scene, where the "New Romantic" movement hit the mainstream. Synthesizers were the order of the day, as groups like **Duran Duran** and **Ultravox** struck poses in capes, ruffled shirts, and full make-up. On a more serious note, Britain was "coming-like-a-ghost town," as documented by the **Specials** (who broke up in 1981, marking the end of the ska revival). With race riots and high unemployment, a nasty postscript to the punk era arose in the form of the skinhead-led, racist "Oi" movement. The New Wave of British Heavy Metal also emerged, as **Motörhead**, its most authentic pioneers, **Iron Maiden**, and **Saxon** moved out of the clubs and on to the charts.

Perhaps the year's most memorable reunion was that of **Simon & Garfunkel**, who temporarily put aside their differences to perform in New York's Central Park.

Rap music was spreading out from its New York roots to gain wide appeal, and breaking new ground with each new year. As rap pioneer **Grandmaster Flash** took sampling and DJ dexterity to new heights, **Blondie** brought the genre to a mass audience with the **Debbie Harry**-voiced *Rapture.*

"A really important thing, next to the sound and the look, was to create an audience, not to cater for one."

Adam Ant, **Smash Hits**, 1981

Jan 1981

Phil Collins's first solo release... Oi!... Christopher Cross sweeps the Grammys...

Ultravox

Christopher Cross

January

9 **Jerry Dammers** and **Terry Hall** of the **Specials** are fined £400 ($760) each, and ordered to pay £133 ($253) costs, at Cambridge Magistrates Court, England, convicted of using "threatening words and behavior" at a gig in the town last October. They had attempted to stop fans from fighting with security guards, which the authorities had misinterpreted, charging them instead with provoking the crowd. Dammers says: "The evidence just didn't stand up. The 3,000 people at the concert will see the injustice of this. We detest violence at our concerts." Guitarist **Roddy Radiation** will say: "What started out as a big party ended up like 'One Flew Over the Cuckoo's Nest.'"

10 **Genesis** drummer/lead singer **Phil Collins** records a session on "The Old Grey Whistle Test," playing drums and singing backing vocals on *Sweet Little Mystery* for his chum, Scottish folk singer-songwriter **John Martyn**. Collins signed last year to Virgin Records in Britain and Atlantic in the US for a parallel solo career, which is about to explode with this week's release of *In The Air Tonight* and the confessional debut album ***Face Value***, which will hit UK No. 1 on February 21, at the beginning of a 193-week chart run. It will also rack up four-million US sales during 164 weeks on the US chart.

12 The RIAA donates some 800 rock albums – including the **Sex Pistols**' ***Never Mind The Bollocks... Here's The Sex Pistols***, **Bob Dylan**'s *Blonde On Blonde* and **KISS**'s *Alive!* – to the Library of Congress.

14 With their breakthrough smash, *Vienna*, entering the UK chart this week on its way to No. 2, **Ultravox** – emerging as part of the burgeoning New Romantic movement with their melodramatic, synthesized sound, created by ex-**Visage** members **Midge Ure** (guitar, lead vocals) and **Billy Currie** (keyboards), **Chris Cross** (synthesizer, bass), and **Warren Cann** (drums) – are featured live giving a 40-minute performance "In Concert" on BBC Radio 1.

16 **Stevie Wonder** speaks on Capitol Hill in Washington, D.C., in support of the Martin Luther King, Jr., Holiday Bill, to make King's birthday on January 15 a national holiday (a bill will be passed in 1983). Wonder also gives a concert in the capital, premiering a new song, *Happy Birthday*, a musical tribute to the civil rights leader that is featured on his recently released ***Hotter Than July***.

Ultravox had been around since 1976 with little success, but a re-formed line-up, fronted by former Slik leader Midge Ure, took off after signing with Chrysalis Records... Christopher Cross professed that housewives doing their ironing found it easy to listen to his music.

17 **Echo & the Bunnymen** fans with concert tickets are ferried to a secret location by bus or given a map to the mystery Peak District venue. It turns out to be the Pavilion Gardens in Buxton, England, a 23-acre public park designed by Edward Milner in 1871. The concert is filmed by Bunnymen lighting designer Bill Butt for release as "Shine So Hard" (its title taken from a line in the band's *Stars Are Stars*).

19 **Plasmatics**' lead singer **Wendy O. Williams** is arrested at the end of a gig at the Palms nightclub in Milwaukee, charged with

DURAN DURAN

Jan 16 **Duran Duran record their first BBC Radio 1 session for the "Peter Powell Show," performing *Planet Earth*, *Anyone Out There*, *Friends Of Mine*, and *Sound Of Thunder*. Assembled three years ago in Birmingham by schoolmates, keyboardist Andy Rhodes and bassist John Taylor, and leaving behind early members (including singer Stephen Duffy), the photogenic group has settled into a solid quintet with the recruitment of (unrelated) guitarist Andy Taylor, drummer Roger Taylor, and 22-year-old lead vocalist Simon Le Bon. They have taken their name from the character played by Milo O'Shea in Roger Vadim's 1968 sci-fi movie version of Jean-Claude Forest's "Barbarella." *Planet Earth*, set for release by EMI as their first single on February 2, will immediately establish them as front runners in the New Romantic movement, which is rapidly spreading in Britain as a backlash against punk-originated new wave. The style is hallmarked by synthesizer-based music and a highly stylized, flamboyant, richly clothed look.**

Depeche Mode settled on their name – a phrase seen in a French fashion magazine – after wisely rejecting Peter Bonetti's Boots, the Lemon Peels, the Runny Smiles, and the Glow Worms.

"simulating masturbation with a sledgehammer in front of an audience." Denying the charge, a resistant Williams is manhandled by police, receiving a cut above her eye that will require several stitches, and is further charged with resisting arrest. The band is released on $2,000 bond and driven to its next show in Cleveland, where Williams is arrested again for "pandering obscenity." (In March, local bands in Milwaukee will play a Plasmatics Defense Fund Raising Benefit at the Metropole Theatre.)

24 This week's **Sounds** magazine includes a special two-page feature on Oi! – a hardcore genre derived from latter-day punk bands like **Sham 69** and the **Angelic Upstarts**. With its strictly working-class roots and anti-establishment political bent, it is attracting a new generation of extreme right-wing British skinheads and fascist National Front members. The increasingly violent and controversial movement is spearheaded by the **4-Skins**, **Last Resort**, and **Infa Riot**. Its short-lived popularity among inner-city youth – documented by its proponent, **Sounds** journalist Garry Bushell – is fueled by the UK's record unemployment and urban unrest.

31 Some Bizzare – a new wave label established by music impresario Stevo – releases ***Some Bizzare*** in the UK. The pioneering compilation album features various "Futurist" bands, all of whom have performed in concert/club events organized by Stevo. It includes *Photographic*, the first recording by Basildon synth band **Depeche Mode**. Formed last year by keyboardists **Vince Clarke** and **Martin Gore**, bassist **Andy Fletcher**, and lead singer **Dave Gahan**, they recently entered into a long-term recording arrangement with innovative indie label Mute, which is run by producer Daniel Miller. Other hot acts featured on the album include **The The** – aka singer-songwriter/guitarist **Matt Johnson** – and **Soft Cell**, a synth-based unit formed by singer **Marc Almond** and keyboardist **David Ball**: both acts are signed to Some Bizzare.

February

7 Veteran R&B band **Kool & the Gang** finally celebrate their first US chart-topper with *Celebration* – which greeted American hostages when they returned home on January 26, after 444 days of captivity in Iran. The group's fortunes have been steadily improving since the arrival in 1978 of new lead singer and songwriter **James "J.T." Taylor**.

8 At the London Palladium, **Adam & the Ants** perform their current UK No. 2 smash, *Antmusic*, for the Royal Children's Variety Performance, and are presented to Princess Margaret after the show. Currently at UK No. 1 with ***Kings Of The Wild Frontier***, Ant has finally hit a commercial vein with his Burundi-styled percussion pop nuggets, boosted by a new swashbuckling pirate image in video clips directed by Steve Barron.

9 **Bill Haley**, age 56, is found dead, fully clothed, on his bed at home in Harlingen, Texas. He has been suffering from a brain tumor for some years, and played his final tour dates in South Africa last year. Haley sold an estimated 60 million records during his pioneering rock 'n' roll career.

13 "1+1" cassettes are launched in Britain by Island Records. One side of the tape features an album, and the other side is left blank to allow the consumer to record on it – a gimmick that flies in the face of current industry bleating about how home taping is damaging record sales. The first title to be released in the series is **Steve Winwood**'s ***Arc Of A Diver***, the debut album by the ex-**Spencer Davis Group**, ex-**Blind Faith**, ex-**Traffic** veteran, who is now embarking on what will become an equally successful solo career.

"Home taping is gradually killing the music industry in this country and it is particularly unfortunate that Island should embark on this venture at this time." BPI in response to Island's "1+1" cassettes, February 11, 1981

15 Blues guitarist **Mike Bloomfield** is found dead at the age of 36 in his car in San Francisco, apparently of an accidental drug overdose. A key member of the **Paul Butterfield Blues Band**, he was perhaps best known for backing **Bob Dylan** at his 1965 Newport Folk Festival appearance, when the singer went electric. Bloomfield recently completed his final album, ***Living In The Fast Lane***.

25 Amid predictions that veterans **Frank Sinatra** and **Barbra Streisand** will win the top prizes at the 23rd Grammys, the biggest upset in the history of the awards takes place, when a debut artist sweeps the ceremony. **Christopher Cross**, a 29-year-old singer-songwriter/guitarist, who a year ago was playing a fraternity party in Austin, Texas, but has since been snapped up by Warner Bros. and paired with producer Michael Omartian, wins five awards: Album of the Year (for ***Christopher Cross*** – an adult contemporary best-seller that features backing singers **Michael McDonald**, **Nicolette Larson**, **Don Henley**, and **J.D. Souther**), Record of the Year (*Sailing*), Song of the Year (*Sailing*), Best New Artist, and Best Arrangement Accompanying Vocalist (*Sailing*). Sinatra and Streisand receive one award between them – Best Pop Performance by a Duo or Group with Vocal, won by Streisand for *Guilty*, her duet with **Barry Gibb**.

The Adventures of Grandmaster Flash... Bob Marley dies... The Glastonbury Festival...

Named after a Marvel comic caption, the psychedelia-influenced group Teardrop Explodes came from Liverpool and were led by Welshman Julian Cope.

March

7 Robert W. Morgan's "Special Of The Week" radio show, broadcast in the US by Watermark, features the first of a two-part interview with **Daryl Hall & John Oates** (the second show will be broadcast tomorrow). Having failed to capitalize on their 1977 US chart-topper, *Rich Girl*, the pop/soul duo – who teamed up in 1972 and spent several years at Atlantic before signing with RCA in 1976 – are one month from scoring their second US No. 1, with *Kiss On My List*.

14 Eight dates into his Another Ticket US tour, following yesterday's concert at the Dane County Exposition Center in Madison, **Eric Clapton** is admitted to United Hospital in St. Paul, suffering from bleeding ulcers. The 60-date tour has to be canceled. Clapton will not play live again until September.

19 Having postponed some dates due to ill-health, **Bruce Springsteen** – on the road for most of the year – returns to Britain for his first dates since 1975, opening with two nights in London.

19 **Teardrop Explodes** performs *Reward* – the group's biggest hit at UK No. 6 – on "Top Of The Pops." Featuring **"Hurricane" Smith** on trumpet, the anthemic song has recently been added to their reissued debut album, the **Julian Cope**-devised ***Kilimanjaro***.

21 **Blondie**'s *Rapture* tops the US chart. Featuring a non-stop rap by singer **Debbie Harry** (written with partner **Chris Stein**), it is produced by the ubiquitous **Mike Chapman**, and features jazz saxophonist **Tom Scott**. It is largely responsible for introducing rap music to Top 40 radio, mainstream America, and music buyers around the world. Not for the first time in music history, a white act has adapted a quintessentially black sound, and made it acceptable to a multicolored audience. Meanwhile, the **Sugar Hill Gang** become the first rap act to appear on national television in the US, performing *Rapper's Delight* and *Bad News Don't Bother Me* on "Soul Train."

April

4 Bubbly British quartet **Bucks Fizz** win the "Eurovision Song Contest" in Dublin, with the perky *Making Your Mind Up* (co-written and produced by Andy Hill). It will shoot to UK No. 1, launching a successful European career that will last into mid-decade.

5 **Canned Heat**'s lead singer/harmonica player **Bob Hite** dies from a heart attack, age 36, after becoming ill between sets at the Palamino Club in North Hollywood. The blues band is best remembered for its hits *On The Road Again*, *Going Up The Country*, and *Let's Work Together*.

15 Having made their debut recordings on February 8 at Bombay Studios in Smyrna, Georgia, **R.E.M.** (which stands for "Rapid Eye Movement") record with producer Mitch Easter for the first time, re-cutting *Sitting Still*, *Radio Free Europe*, and two versions of *White Tornado* at his Drive-In studio in Winston-Salem. The quartet – **Michael Stipe**, guitarist **Peter Buck**, bassist **Mike Mills**, and drummer **Bill Berry** – got together last year, making their debut on April 5 as the **Twisted Kites**, at a party given by a friend, Kathleen O'Brien, at the Steeplechase, a converted Episcopalian church on Oconee Street in Athens. They will use today's recordings (which mark the beginning of a long collaboration with Easter) to make ***Cassette Set***, of which they will duplicate 400 copies to be sent out to clubs, magazines, and record companies.

24 **New Order** begin two weeks' recording at Strawberry Studios with producer Martin Hannett, for their first album. They also film a TV special for Granada Television, for whom Factory supremo Tony Wilson moonlights.

28 As he plays the last of three sell-out shows at London's Wembley Arena, UK, **Gary Numan** announces his retirement from live work. He will return with the Assassin Tour – an 18-date US tour – in October of next year.

May

5 Created by Bronx-based pioneering rap DJ/producer Joseph Saddler, aka **Grandmaster Flash**, *The Adventures Of Grandmaster Flash On The Wheels Of Steel* is released in the US by Sugar Hill Records. The 12in single will fail to chart on the Hot 100 and will make only a modest impression on the US R&B survey, though it will later be revered as a definitive entry in the progress of the hip-hop/rap genre. It features harshly mixed samples of **Blondie**'s *Rapture*, **Chic**'s *Good Times*, the **Furious Five**'s own *Birthday Party*, **Spoonie Gee**'s *Monster Jam*, **Queen**'s *Another One Bites The Dust*, and the **Sugar Hill Gang**'s *8th Wonder*, a medley selected by label head **Sylvia Robinson**.

15 **Public Image Ltd.**, now going by the acronym **PiL**, play a show at New York's Ritz club (deputizing for **Bow Wow Wow**). They pose behind a video screen while the music is played from tapes. They are showered with missiles and booed off the stage by the audience of 1,500, who are reviled by **John Lydon** and **Jah Wobble**. The band consider the event successful, videotaping the debacle for movie use. A second show tomorrow night will be canceled.

16 *Bette Davis Eyes*, an update of a 1974 **Jackie DeShannon** track from ***New Arrangement*** by 34-year-old Californian singer **Kim Carnes**, tops the US chart for the first of nine weeks. It displaces EMI America-labelmate **Sheena Easton**'s *Morning Train* (whose title has been amended for the US market, to avoid confusion with **Dolly Parton**'s film-theme song, *9 To 5*, which hit US No. 1 in March). During its run, and after its first five chart-topping weeks, *Bette Davis Eyes* will be nudged from No. 1 for one week by the Dutch novelty hit medley *Stars On 45*, but will return to the top spot for a further four weeks. It will also hit UK No. 10.

21 A Jamaican legend, **Bob Marley** is buried (with his Bible and Gibson guitar) with full state honors in Nine Miles, St. Ann's, Jamaica, following an Ethiopian Orthodox Festival funeral at the National Heroes Arena in Kingston. The service is attended by thousands, including Prime Minister Edward Seaga. Jamaican Governor General Michael Manley says of Marley: "His message was a protest against injustice, a comfort for the oppressed. He stood there, performed there, his message reached there and everywhere. Today's funeral service is an international right of a native son. He was born in a humble cottage nine miles from Alexandria in the parish of St. Ann. He lived in the western section of Kingston as a boy where he joined in the struggle of the ghetto. He learned the message of survival in his boyhood days in Kingston's west end. But it was his raw talent, unswerving discipline, and sheer perseverance that transported him from just another victim of the ghetto to the top ranking superstar in the entertainment industry of the third world."

29 The second night of the **Clash**'s 17-date stint at Bond's in New York, with **Grandmaster Flash** opening, is canceled because the Fire Department and Manhattan Building Inspector won't allow 3,500 people into the club.

Kim Carnes took a Jackie DeShannon album track and, with a radical arrangement by Bill Cuomo, found herself with a worldwide best-seller.

June

16 The nine-day Noise Festival gets under way at New York's White Columns Gallery on Spring Street, showcasing alternative acts that have grown out of the late 1970s No Wave movement in New York's East Village. The event is co-organized by **Thurston Moore**, lead singer/guitarist of new alt-rock combo **Sonic Youth**, who will take the stage for the first time on June 18.

20 The Glastonbury Festival in England–which began a decade ago as the "Glastonbury Fayre" – takes place, benefiting the Campaign for Nuclear Disarmament. The 18,000 attendees enjoy an eclectic bill, with **New Order**, **Hawkwind**, **Taj Mahal**, and British reggae pioneers, **Aswad**.

30 **Jerry Lee Lewis** is admitted to Memphis Methodist Hospital with a bleeding stomach ulcer. From his bed, he countersues Elektra Records for $5 million, as a label dispute ends his contract. On July 9, he will undergo the first of two serious operations, after which his doctors will estimate his chances of survival at 50/50. He will be back on the road within four months, and recording for MCA Records.

BOB MARLEY

May 11 **Having flown into Miami yesterday from Germany, where he was receiving treatment for cancer from controversial specialist Dr. Josef Issels at the Cancer Treatment Centre in Rottach-Egern, Bob Marley dies at approximately 11:30 am at the Cedars of Lebanon Hospital in Miami. The cancer had spread to his brain and liver. His mother Cedella Booker and lawyer Diane Jobson are present. He is 36. Marley was scheduled to receive the Special Order of Merit from Jamaican Prime Minister Edward Seaga next week. He leaves behind 11 children and an estate with a current estimated value of $30 million.**

Returned to Jamaica, Marley's body lay in state for two days at Kingston's National Arena.

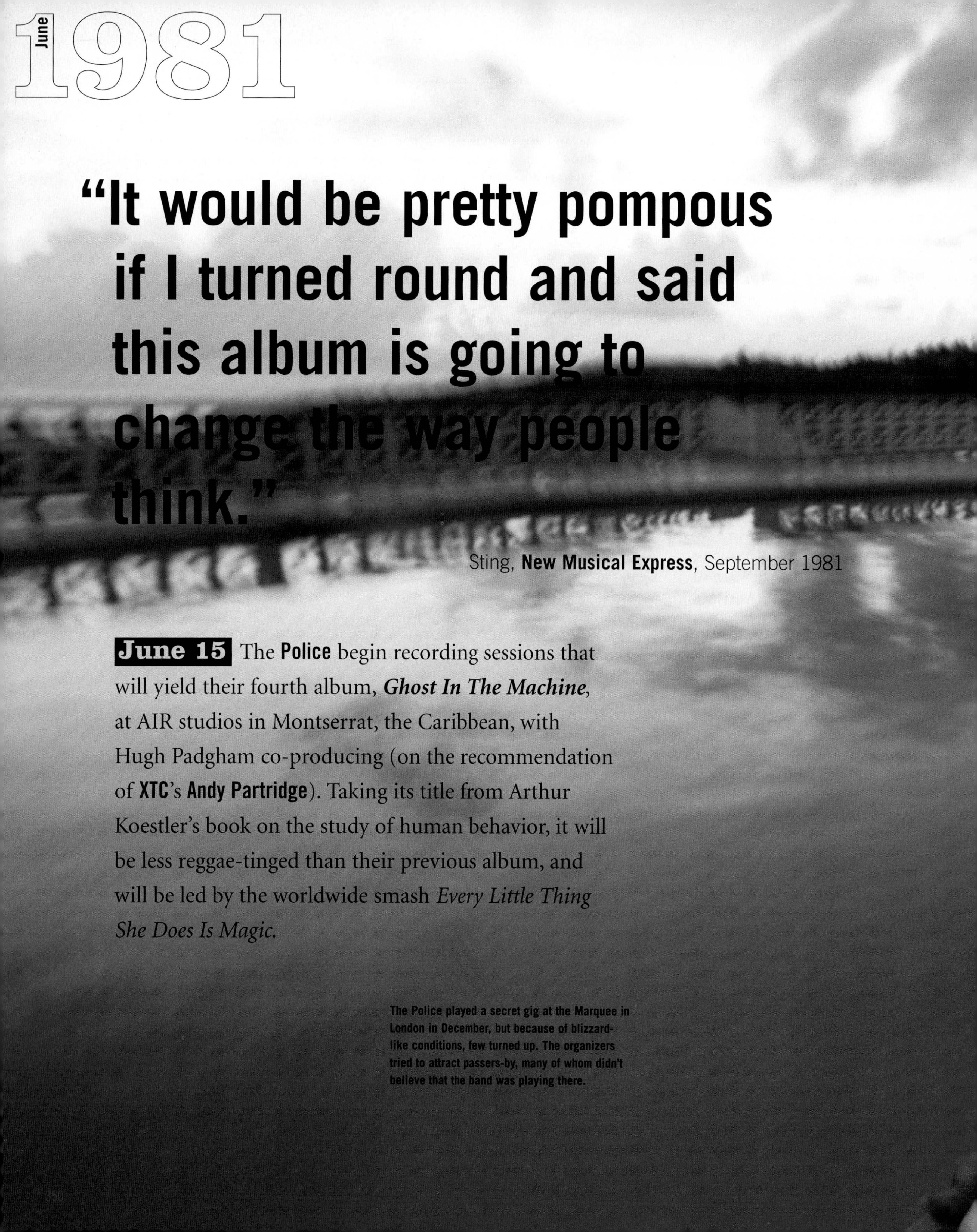

"It would be pretty pompous if I turned round and said this album is going to change the way people think."

Sting, **New Musical Express**, September 1981

June 15 The **Police** begin recording sessions that will yield their fourth album, ***Ghost In The Machine***, at AIR studios in Montserrat, the Caribbean, with Hugh Padgham co-producing (on the recommendation of **XTC**'s **Andy Partridge**). Taking its title from Arthur Koestler's book on the study of human behavior, it will be less reggae-tinged than their previous album, and will be led by the worldwide smash *Every Little Thing She Does Is Magic.*

The Police played a secret gig at the Marquee in London in December, but because of blizzard-like conditions, few turned up. The organizers tried to attract passers-by, many of whom didn't believe that the band was playing there.

The Jacksons' Triumph tour... MTV goes on air... Soft Cell's *Tainted Love*...

"That was really my thing, repairing TVs, washing machines. Then for some reason... I got into DJing."

Grandmaster Flash, **New Musical Express**, September 26, 1981

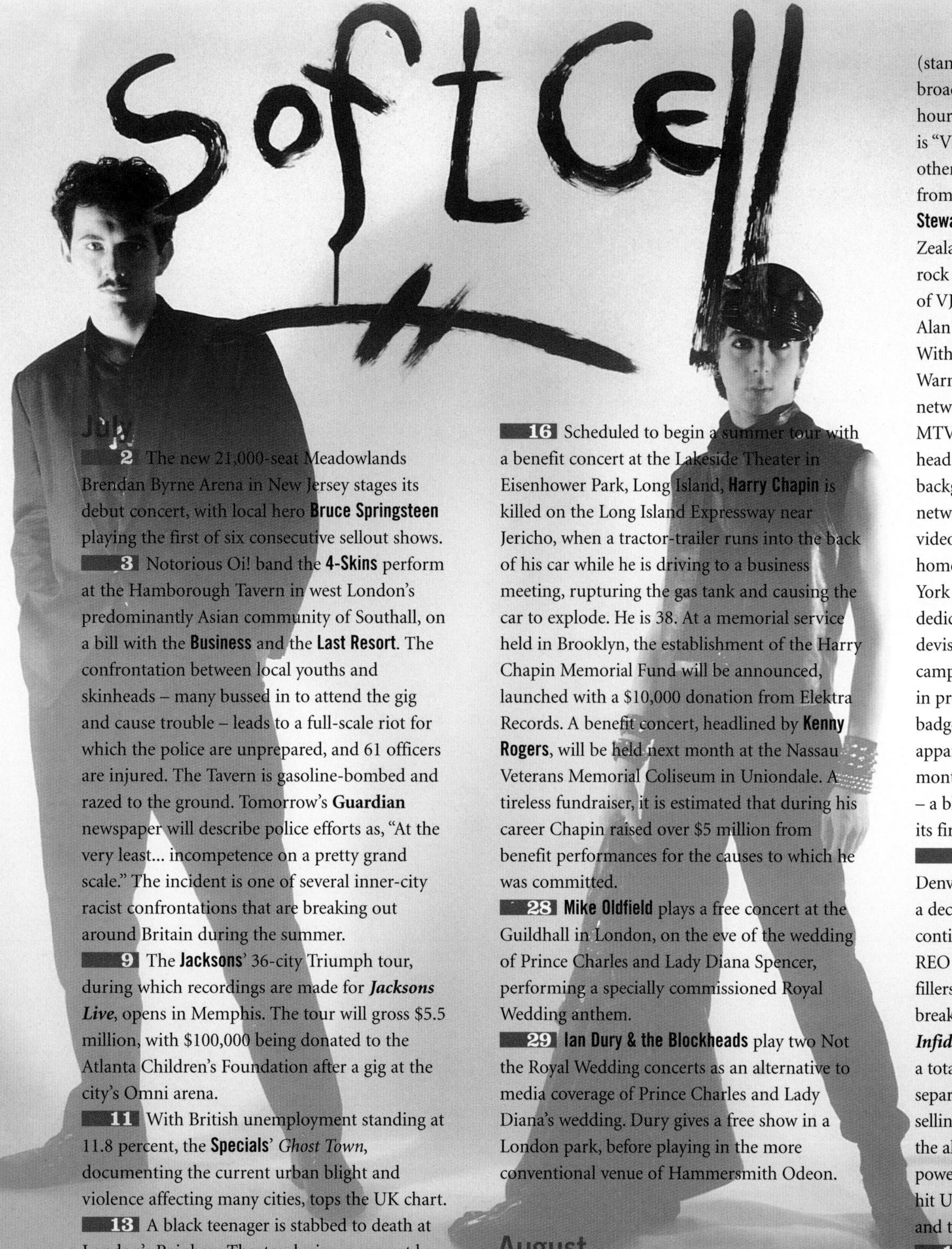

July

2 The new 21,000-seat Meadowlands Brendan Byrne Arena in New Jersey stages its debut concert, with local hero **Bruce Springsteen** playing the first of six consecutive sellout shows.

3 Notorious Oi! band the **4-Skins** perform at the Hamborough Tavern in west London's predominantly Asian community of Southall, on a bill with the **Business** and the **Last Resort**. The confrontation between local youths and skinheads – many bussed in to attend the gig and cause trouble – leads to a full-scale riot for which the police are unprepared, and 61 officers are injured. The Tavern is gasoline-bombed and razed to the ground. Tomorrow's **Guardian** newspaper will describe police efforts as, "At the very least... incompetence on a pretty grand scale." The incident is one of several inner-city racist confrontations that are breaking out around Britain during the summer.

9 The **Jacksons**' 36-city Triumph tour, during which recordings are made for ***Jacksons Live***, opens in Memphis. The tour will gross $5.5 million, with $100,000 being donated to the Atlanta Children's Foundation after a gig at the city's Omni arena.

11 With British unemployment standing at 11.8 percent, the **Specials**' *Ghost Town*, documenting the current urban blight and violence affecting many cities, tops the UK chart.

13 A black teenager is stabbed to death at London's Rainbow Theatre during a concert by Jamaican reggae band **Black Uhuru**.

Soft Cell's *Tainted Love*, long a cult favorite on the Northern Soul circuit, was written by ex-Four Preps and Piltdown Men member Ed Cobb.

16 Scheduled to begin a summer tour with a benefit concert at the Lakeside Theater in Eisenhower Park, Long Island, **Harry Chapin** is killed on the Long Island Expressway near Jericho, when a tractor-trailer runs into the back of his car while he is driving to a business meeting, rupturing the gas tank and causing the car to explode. He is 38. At a memorial service held in Brooklyn, the establishment of the Harry Chapin Memorial Fund will be announced, launched with a $10,000 donation from Elektra Records. A benefit concert, headlined by **Kenny Rogers**, will be held next month at the Nassau Veterans Memorial Coliseum in Uniondale. A tireless fundraiser, it is estimated that during his career Chapin raised over $5 million from benefit performances for the causes to which he was committed.

28 **Mike Oldfield** plays a free concert at the Guildhall in London, on the eve of the wedding of Prince Charles and Lady Diana Spencer, performing a specially commissioned Royal Wedding anthem.

29 **Ian Dury & the Blockheads** play two Not the Royal Wedding concerts as an alternative to media coverage of Prince Charles and Lady Diana's wedding. Dury gives a free show in a London park, before playing in the more conventional venue of Hammersmith Odeon.

August

1 At 12:01 am, with its logo superimposed over the image of an astronaut sticking a flag into the moon's surface, and the words "Ladies and gentlemen, rock and roll," spoken on camera by John Lack, new television cable network MTV (standing for Music Television) begins broadcasting in the United States, offering a 24-hour stream of music videos. The first clip to air is "Video Killed the Radio Star" by **Buggles**, and others featured in the first hour include those from the **Who**, **Cliff Richard**, **Pat Benatar**, **Rod Stewart**, **Styx**, the **Pretenders**, **Todd Rundgren**, New Zealand new wave combo **Split Enz**, and southern rock group, **.38 Special**. The network's first batch of VJs are Nina Blackwood, Mark Goodman, Alan Hunter, J.J. Jackson, and Martha Quinn. With $20 million seed money supplied by Warner Amex Satellite Entertainment, the network's launch has been masterminded by MTV founders Tom Freston and programing head Bob Pittman, a WASEC executive with a background in radio, who is targeting the network at 12–34-year-olds. Initially the music video channel is available in only 2.1 million homes, and cannot yet be seen in either New York City or Los Angeles. The world's first dedicated music broadcaster will, however, soon devise its highly successful "I Want My MTV" campaign, enlisting music stars to use the tagline in promos to encourage potential viewers to badger their local cable operators. What will apparently go largely unnoticed for many months is MTV's "white rock/pop only" playlist – a black artist will not appear on MTV during its first year of operation.

8 MTV features **REO Speedwagon** live from Denver for its first stereo concert broadcast. After a decade as one of the busiest and most continually mobile support bands in the US, REO Speedwagon are now bill-topping stadium-fillers in their own right, mostly thanks to the breakout success of the group's current album, ***Hi Infidelity***, which held pole position in the US for a total of 15 weeks to the end of June (in three separate runs beginning in February). Eventually selling more than ten million domestic copies, the album has yielded the **Kevin Cronin**-penned, power-rock ballad, *Keep On Loving You* – which hit US No. 1 on March 21, *Take It On The Run*, and their current hit *Don't Let Him Go*.

15 **Stevie Wonder** gives his recently received ***Hotter Than July*** gold disc to Tami Ragoway, whose boyfriend, Randy Burrell, was shot and killed while returning home after Wonder's concert at the Great Western Forum in Inglewood California on December 12 last year.

FOREIGNER

Aug 22 **With the group trimmed to a core quartet of Lou Gramm, Mick Jones, Rick Wills, and Dennis Elliott, Foreigner's *4*, the epitome of adult rock, tops the US chart for the first of ten weeks. Co-helmed by Jones and magic-touch rock producer Robert John "Mutt" Lange, it will become the group's most successful project, eventually selling over six million in the US. It includes FM staple radio hits, *Urgent*, *Juke Box Hero*, and an uncharacteristic ballad, *Waiting For A Girl Like You*, written by Jones and Gramm, which will begin an unprecedented ten weeks at No. 2 in November, becoming a US million seller, and will also become their first UK Top 10 hit in January.**

Wonder is performing at the Black Family Fair, an outdoor festival at the Rose Bowl in Pasadena. It also features *Shame* disco hitmaker **Evelyn King**, **Third World**, and jazz/R&B saxophonist great **Grover Washington, Jr.**, among others.

20 **Bruce Springsteen** gives a Night for the Vietnam Veteran concert at the Los Angeles Sports Arena, to benefit the Vietnam Veterans of America Foundation and Mental Health Association.

26 **Lee Hays**, co-founder of the **Weavers** and co-writer of *If I Had A Hammer* – dies at his home in upstate New York, age 67, from a heart attack following a long battle with diabetes.

"We were a load of misfits. That's the only reason we're together."

UB40's Jim Brown, **Melody Maker**, July 4, 1981

September

3 **Soft Cell** perform their current UK No. 1 electro-pop smash *Tainted Love* on "Top Of The Pops." It will become their signature hit, and will spend 43 weeks on the US chart next year. Produced by Mike Thorne, it was recorded at London's Advision Studios in July, resurrecting **Gloria Jones**'s little-known original.

5 Undertaking a parallel solo career, with the new Modern Records label established mainly for her releases, **Stevie Nicks**'s first solo single, the adult oriented rock/pop *Stop Draggin' My Heart Around*, with help from **Tom Petty & the Heartbreakers**, hits US No. 3 and UK No. 50. In the same week, her maiden album, the largely self-written ***Bella Donna***, produced by Jimmy Iovine – and with the Heartbreakers providing the rhythm section – tops the US chart.

12 With ***Escape*** topping the US chart, **Journey** perform the first of six nightly concerts at Pine Knob Music Theatre in Clarkston, Michigan, opened by the **Greg Kihn Band** (the latest signing to the quirky new-wave label, Berserkley Records). Journey are at the beginning of a sprawling 88-date North American trek, and have – together with **REO Speedwagon** and **Foreigner** – become the darlings of US FM radio, notably scoring with trademark power ballads (and ***Escape*** cuts), *Who's Crying Now*, *Don't Stop Believin'*, and *Open Arms* – written by group members **Steve Perry**, **Jonathan Cain**, and **Neal Schon**.

14 Bottleneck blues guitarist **Walter "Furry" Lewis** dies of heart failure, age 88, in Memphis, where he has been cleaning streets for 44 years during the day, and performing in clubs at night. Lewis, regarded as a seminal Delta blues influence, was the subject of **Joni Mitchell**'s 1976 song, *Furry Sings The Blues*.

15 Following a month's rehearsal at Long View Farm in Brookfield, Massaschusetts, the **Rolling Stones** play a warm-up gig in the early hours of the morning, as Blue Sunday & the Cockroaches, at the 350-capacity Sir Morgan's Cave in Worcester. When word of the show leaks out, ticketless fans – estimated as anywhere between 1,500 and 4,000 – show up at the venue.

19 **Simon & Garfunkel** reunite for a concert in New York's Central Park, after 11 years apart. Over 400,000 attend the performance, which features a 22-song set led by *Mrs. Robinson*. Following this success (documented on film, television – for HBO – and video), the duo will undertake a 12-month world tour, beginning next spring, although there will be press reports of growing personal friction between them. Today's event is recorded for release as the double live album, ***The Concert In Central Park***.

25 With their latest record, ***Emotional Rescue***, spending its first week at No. 1 on the US album chart, the **Rolling Stones**, with **Tina Turner** in support, begin their tenth US tour at JFK Stadium in Philadelphia, before a sellout crowd of 90,000. The 50-date sojourn, which will be attended by more than two million people and gross over $50 million, will be dogged by offstage controversy: thieves will try to steal tickets for forthcoming concerts in Maryland, killing one man and injuring another; 22-year-old Wesley Shelton will be murdered by a teenager near a concession stand at the Astrodome in Houston (in 1986, his family will be awarded $4.7 million, alleging that security at the concert was inadequate); and 12 people will be hurt and 56 arrested at a Hartford concert.

Journey, fronted by the distinctive voice of Steve Perry, had three top ten hits in six months during 1981 and 1982.

1981

Jean Michel Jarre in China... Olivia Newton-John gets *Physical*... The million-selling *Don't You Want Me*...

Daryl Hall & John Oates

Haircut 100

October

1 The **Pretenders**' current tour of the US is canceled, after drummer **Martin Chambers** is injured when he puts his hand through a window in a Philadelphia hotel room. Asked about the incident years later, Chambers will reveal the truth about it: "At the time, we said I was opening a window. I just took a swing at a porcelain lampstand for no particular reason. I'd just had a lovely dinner. I wasn't drunk. I hadn't taken anything. The lampstand went into pieces and I cut 50 percent of the tendon at the top of my middle finger."

10 **Duran Duran** wind up their first American tour at the Underground Club in New York. Hitless in the US this year, the group – who are pioneering the music video genre, with increasingly glossy and stylized clips accompanying each successive single – will have scored four UK chart hits with their first four releases by the end of the year: *Planet Earth*, *Careless Memories*, *Girls On Film* (spurred to No. 5 by a particularly provocative clip), and *My Own Way*.

16 **Diana Ross** and **Lionel Richie**'s *Endless Love* is certified platinum by the RIAA – one of only two singles to reach that plateau officially this year (the other being **Kool & the Gang**'s *Celebration*). The Richie ballad was commissioned by film producer Franco Zeffirelli, who needed a song for his movie "Endless Love," starring Brooke Shields. Zeffirelli also suggested Diana Ross as a co-vocalist. With Ross tied up on a concert trek, and Richie still occupied with the **Commodores**, the busy stars had to meet in April to record the song in Reno (while Ross was performing in nearby Lake Tahoe). The session began at 3:00 am, and the final version was nailed by 5:00 am. Since August, *Endless Love* has spent nine weeks topping the US chart, becoming Motown's 47th US No. 1, its most successful single to date and the longest-running chart-topper by a duo in US chart history.

19 Multimedia artist **Laurie Anderson**, a 34-year-old singer-songwriter/violinist from Chicago, records an interview for BBC radio at the Riverside Studios in London. The subject is her seven-hour musical work "United States," and its extracted piece, *O Superman* – which, despite its eight-minute length, hits UK No. 2 this week. The oddly monotone, electronically treated recording – based on *O Souverain*, an aria from Jules Massenet's 1885 opera "Le Cid" – was originally pressed in a limited edition of 5,000 copies for New York independent label One Ten (funded by a grant from the National Endowment for the Arts). It has since been licensed to Warner Bros., found its way on to British airwaves, and become a surprise novelty hit around Europe.

21 **Jean Michel Jarre** becomes the first western rock artist to perform in China, with the first of five major concerts in Beijing, backed by 35 Chinese musicians. The event, in front of 400,000 spectators, is filmed by Andrew Piddington for a television special, and is recorded for album release (***The Concerts In China***) to offset the phenomenal costs involved. Some 15 tons of equipment, packed in 30 army trucks, have been shipped to China for the five gigs, which will climax in Shanghai on November 15.

> **"I think of John's death as a war casualty – it is a war between the sane and the insane."**
>
> Yoko Ono in a letter to **Rolling Stone** on the anniversary of John Lennon's death, December 8, 1981

Daryl Hall and John Oates, with 16 Top 10 US hits, are the most successful duo of all time... Haircut 100's clean-cut, harmonious pop sound and ingenuous Ivy League image led to a scramble by UK record companies for their signatures.

November

2 With lead singer **Terry Hall** and colleagues **Neville Staples** and **Lynval Golding** having already left the troupe to form **Fun Boy Three**, the **Specials** announce their intention to split.

7 **Daryl Hall & John Oates**'s *Private Eyes*, the title track from their new album, becomes their second US No. 1 of the year. They are currently the hottest duo in pop music, on their way to outpacing the **Everly Brothers** as the most successful pairing in American chart history. The perky *Kiss On My List*, written by Janna Allen who, reputedly, had never written a song before and is the younger sister of Hall's girlfriend (and regular songwriting partner) Sara, topped the US chart for three weeks in April. ***Private Eyes*** the LP, self-produced in four months of sessions at the Electric Lady Studios in New York, has become their first US Top 10 album, while another extract – the pop-soul fused *I Can't Go For That (No Can Do)* – is set to become their fourth US chart-topper in February. It will also

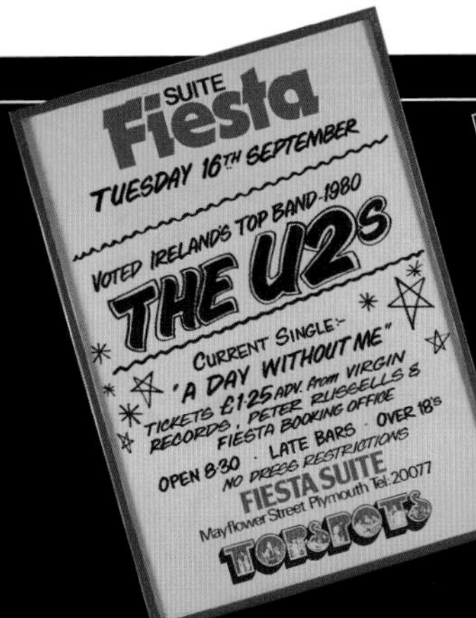

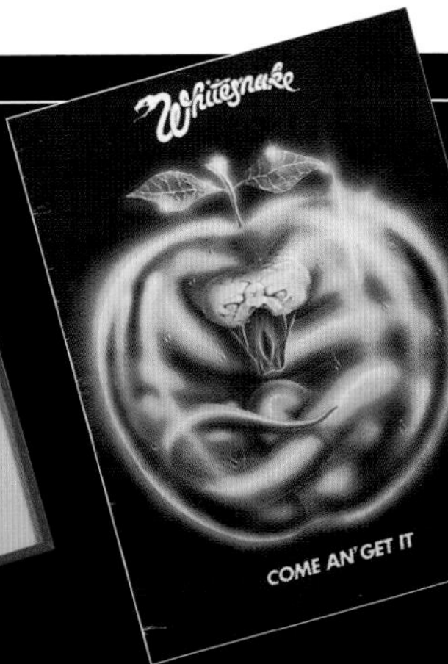

During a 1981 US tour, U2 were the supporting attraction at a Miss Wet T-shirt contest in Dallas... Whitesnake were led by former Deep Purple lead singer David Coverdale, who sometimes called on his old bandmates to play in the band... The Go-Gos began as the all-girl new-wave outfit, the Misfits.

The Go-Gos

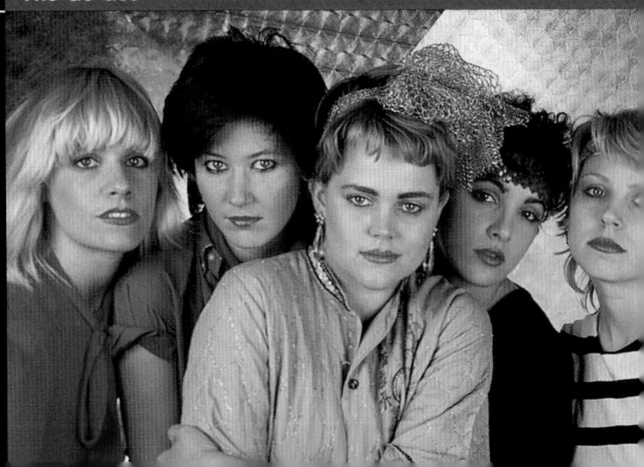

find unexpected crossover success, hitting US R&B No. 1, an extremely rare feat for a white act – only the fourth instance since 1965 – but perfectly in synch with Hall & Oates's long-held, blue-eyed soul-based vision.

12 **Haircut 100** perform their debut single, the UK No. 4-peaking *Favourite Shirts (Boy Meets Girl)*, on "Top Of The Pops." Led by telegenic singer-songwriter **Nick Heyward**, the in-demand British group signed to Arista Records in September.

14 The **Go-Go's** – an all-female Los Angeles-based new wave/pop quintet signed to Miles Copeland's emerging I.R.S. label – make their US television debut on "Saturday Night Live." Comprising lead singer **Belinda Carlisle**, guitarists **Jane Wiedlin** and **Charlotte Caffey**, bassist **Kathy Valentine**, and drummer **Gina Schock**, they perform their first hit, *Our Lips Are Sealed* (written by Wiedlin and **Fun Boy Three** frontman **Terry Hall**, and produced by **David Byrne**) and its smash follow-up, *We Got The Beat* (which will hit US No. 2 next March).

21 **Olivia Newton-John**'s *Physical*, written by Steve Kipner and Terry Shaddick, and banned by some radio stations for its supposed sexual innuendo, hits US No. 1 for the first of ten weeks, equaling the second longest holding chart-topper in pop history, behind **Elvis Presley**'s 11 weeks with *Hound Dog*. It will also hit UK No. 7, and become one of the first and most identifiable aerobic workout themes.

21 **George Benson** performs his two biggest crossover hits, *Give Me The Night*, written by **Rod Temperton** (US No. 4), and the current US No. 5 smash *Turn Your Love Around*, on "Soul Train." Both songs are featured on the multiplatinum ***Give Me The Night***, produced by Quincy Jones.

22 During the band's latest US trek, **Rolling Stones Mick Jagger**, **Keith Richard**, and **Ron Wood** jam with **Muddy Waters** (whose *Rollin' Stone* song inspired the group's name), **Buddy Guy**, and **Junior Wells** at the Checker Board Lounge in Chicago. They play several blues classics – including *Hoochie Coochie Man*, *Mannish Boy*, and *Got My Mojo Working*.

December

9 The **Orioles**' lead singer **Sonny Til** dies of a heart attack at the age of 56 in Washington, D.C. As lead vocalist on such hits as *Crying In The Chapel* and *It's Too Soon To Know*, Til fronted the band once referred to as "the first R&B vocal group."

10 The video for **Madness**'s current single, *It Must Be Love*, which shows the band jumping into a swimming pool with guitars, is broadcast on "Top Of The Pops." DJ host Jimmy Savile warns viewers not to try this at home.

12 **Human League**'s *Don't You Want Me* tops the UK chart for the first of five weeks. Written by frontman **Phil Oakey**, **Adrian Wright**, and **Jo Callis**, the synth-pop classic, featuring traded vocals between Oakey and **Joanne Catherall**, is aided by a popular film-within-a-film video clip. It will be the biggest-selling UK single of the year, topping a million sales, as the group's synthesizer-led sound revolutionizes British pop music. It also marks the first UK No. 1 single for Virgin Records. The hit is taken from the parent album ***Dare!***, which was co-helmed by the band with producer du jour Martin Rushent, and which topped the UK chart two weeks ago. Containing a batch of hit singles, it will eventually sell over five million copies worldwide, while *Don't You Want Me* will also reach US No. 1 the next summer.

Virgin Records showed its appreciation for achieving its first ever No. 1 by giving Human League's Phil Oakey a BMW motorcycle.

25 Christopher Tyrer, a 15-year-old heavy metal fan, dies after attending a **Saxon** concert in Wolverhampton, England, on December 17, when he subjected himself to three hours of "head-banging." He regained consciousness the following day, paralyzed on one side and unable to talk. The coroner will return a verdict of death by misadventure.

25 **Michael Jackson** makes a Christmas Day telephone call to **Paul McCartney** and suggests they write and record together (which will prompt the ex-**Beatle** to fly to Los Angeles to cut *The Girl Is Mine*).

25 The **J. Geils Band** – heading to US No. 1 with *Centerfold* – perform a Christmas concert for inmates at the Norfolk Correctional Center in Massachusetts. Lead singer **Peter Wolf** tells the audience: "We wanna be the first to buy you all a free drink on the outside."

27 Legendary singer-songwriter/pianist **Hoagy Carmichael** dies at the Eisenhower Medical Center in Rancho Mirage, following a heart attack at his home. He is 92. Included in his substantial canon of work: *Georgia On My Mind*, *Heart And Soul*, *I Get Along Without You Very Well*, *In The Still Of The Night*, *Lazy Bones*, *Rockin' Chair*, *Skylark*, and, for a time, the most recorded song in music history, *Stardust*.

31 **Elvis Costello** performs at the Palladium, New York, during a three-city mini US tour. In the first half of the concert he performs selections from his recent country album, ***Almost Blue*** (recorded with legendary producer Billy Sherrill in Nashville), while the second half rocks with songs from Costello's earlier catalog.

ROOTS **During this year: Would-be singer-songwriter Myra Ellen Amos plays a residency at the Hilton Hotel in Myrtle Beach, South Carolina... Michael Diamond, a member of the Young Aborigines, meets Adam Yauch at a Bad Brains gig; they team up as the Beastie Boys – an acronym for Boys Entering Anarchistic States Towards Internal Excellence... Neneh Cherry joins alternative jazz/funk/punk collective Rip, Rig & Panic... Natalie Merchant joins Still Life while studying at Jamestown Community College in Jamestown, New York; with the addition of John Lombardo, they change their name, mistakenly taking it from a B-movie horror flick called "2,000 Maniacs"... after placing an ad in Los Angeles newspaper *The Recycler* ("loud, rude, aggressive guitarist available"), Bob Deal, changing his name to Mick Mars, is recruited by Mötley Crüe... San Franciscan Ron Quintana, who had thought of using it for a forthcoming fanzine, recommends the name Metallica to some friends of his, who have just started a heavy-metal band... keyboard whiz Thomas Dolby performs for more than 24 hours in the foyer of the Bloomsbury Theatre in London, during the "Marathon Music Quiz" charity event, broadcast on Radio 1... and the Cocteau Twins, armed with two demo tapes, travel to London from their native Falkirk in Scotland...**

Young Guns (Go For It)

1982

No. 1 US Singles

Jan 2	Physical **Olivia Newton-John**
Jan 30	I Can't Go For That (No Can Do) **Daryl Hall & John Oates**
Feb 6	Centerfold **J. Geils Band**
Mar 20	I Love Rock 'n Roll **Joan Jett & the Blackhearts**
May 8	Chariots Of Fire – Titles **Vangelis**
May 15	Ebony And Ivory **Paul McCartney (with Stevie Wonder)**
July 3	Don't You Want Me **Human League**
July 24	Eye Of The Tiger **Survivor**
Sept 4	Abracadabra **Steve Miller Band**
Sept 11	Hard To Say I'm Sorry **Chicago**
Sept 25	Abracadabra **Steve Miller Band**
Oct 2	Jack And Diane **John Cougar**
Oct 30	Who Can It Be Now? **Men At Work**
Nov 6	Up Where We Belong **Joe Cocker & Jennifer Warnes**
Nov 27	Truly **Lionel Richie**
Dec 11	Mickey **Toni Basil**
Dec 18	Maneater **Daryl Hall & John Oates**

No. 1 UK Singles

Jan 2	Don't You Want Me **Human League**
Jan 16	The Land Of Make Believe **Bucks Fizz**
Jan 30	Oh Julie **Shakin' Stevens**
Feb 6	Computer Love/The Model **Kraftwerk**
Feb 13	Town Called Malice/Precious **Jam**
Mar 6	The Lion Sleeps Tonight **Tight Fit**
Mar 27	Seven Tears **Goombay Dance Band**
Apr 17	My Camera Never Lies **Bucks Fizz**
Apr 24	Ebony And Ivory **Paul McCartney (with Stevie Wonder)**
May 15	A Little Peace **Nicole**
May 29	House Of Fun **Madness**
June 12	Goody Two Shoes **Adam Ant**
June 26	I've Never Been To Me **Charlene**
July 3	Happy Talk **Captain Sensible**
July 17	Fame **Irene Cara**
Aug 7	Come On Eileen **Dexy's Midnight Runners & the Emerald Express**
Sept 4	Eye Of The Tiger **Survivor**
Oct 2	Pass The Dutchie **Musical Youth**
Oct 23	Do You Really Want To Hurt Me **Culture Club**
Nov 13	I Don't Wanna Dance **Eddy Grant**
Dec 4	Beat Surrender **Jam**
Dec 18	Save Your Love **Renée & Renato**

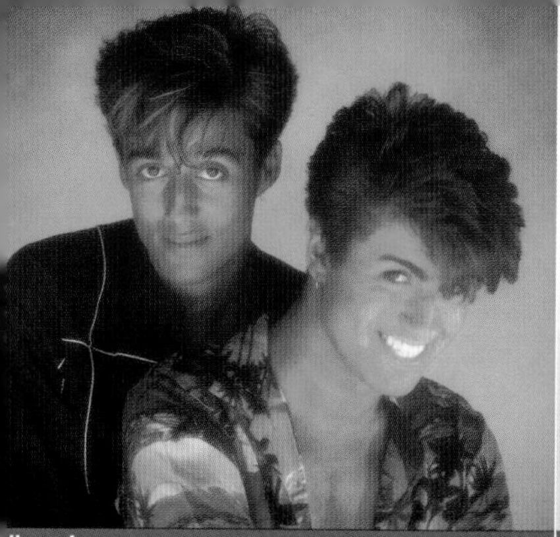
ham!

Duran Duran

Friends from Bushey Meads Comprehensive School, George Michael and Andrew Ridgeley would have three No. 1 singles in both the UK and the US in 1984 and 1985... Duran Duran's videos, lavishly directed by Russell Mulcahy, played an important part in their success.

This was the year of MTV in the US, and the synthesizer in the UK. The music world embraced one British band after another, as the "new wave" took hold. Record sales continued to decline worldwide in a harsh economic climate, yet the gloom did not prevent Philips and Sony from spending lavishly on creating the CD format.

Acts jostled for airplay and chart places in Britain, from the pure pop of **Wham!** to the much grittier **Smiths**. The cause of the New Romantics was helped by the dawning of music television, making the look as influential as the sound. Inspired by **David Bowie** and **Roxy Music**, the androgynous pin-ups **Duran Duran** somehow described themselves as "the **Sex Pistols** meet **Chic**." Rather more than androgynous, **Boy George** and **Culture Club** crashed the charts and bemused the British public. The best of British was heralded with the inaugural BPI Awards, the British version of the Grammys. UK acts honored included the flamboyant **Adam & the Ants**, **Soft Cell**, and the **Human League**, whose *Don't You Want Me* put British synth-pop/rock firmly on the world map.

Trying to escape the "New Romantics" tag, **Depeche Mode**, boasting three members on synthesizers and the vocals of **Dave Gahan**, began a series of sellout concerts in Britain and Europe. Also majoring on synthesizers, but in much gloomier tones, the **Cure** finally nabbed a Top 10 album in Britain with ***Pornography***, and further extended a devoted fan base. **XTC** enjoyed critical and commercial success with their double album ***English Settlement***. Veterans compared to many British acts, the **Jam** combined inner turmoil with stunning UK chart success, but **Paul Weller** was emotionally and professionally restless. After a farewell tour, the band split and Weller went off to form the equally political, though more R&B-laced, **Style Council**. The last quarter of the year belonged to a band of high-spirited Australians. **Men at Work** was the surprise hit package of the year, helped by the endless rotation on MTV of the playful video for *Who Can It Be Now?* – a sure sign of the growing impact of videos and music television. MTV was proving adept at converting inherently eclectic fare, such as **Talking Heads** and even the quirky offerings from the ever-inventive **Devo**, into mainstream popularity.

Metal remained popular in the US. **Ozzy Osbourne** played an extensive tour, and **Iron Maiden**'s ferocious live performances and demonic dabblings provoked hostility among the Christian right in the US. Still mostly underground – and mostly in New York – rap was diversifying and experimenting. Pioneering cuts like **Afrika Bambaataa & the Soul Sonic Force**'s *Planet Rock* were proving that the genre would be more than a fleeting novelty for adventurous radio programs and block parties.

"Now we can't do anything right. I suppose at the beginning we were flavor of the month."

Depeche Mode's Dave Gahan, **Melody Maker**, October 2, 1982

Jan 1982

Ozzy goes to bat... The first BPI awards... I Want My MTV...

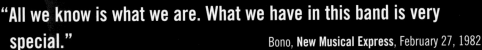

Ozzy Osbourne

Bob Dylan

January

7 In a race-motivated attack at a Coventry disco, **Lynval Golding** of **Fun Boy Three** is slashed with a knife on the right side of his face and neck, and requires 29 stitches. While still a member of the **Specials**, he was previously the victim of a racist assault in south London.

12 Signed to RCA Records last year, and following their nine-date maiden UK tour last month, **Eurythmics** – comprising former **Tourists**, **Annie Lennox** and **Dave Stewart** – play at the Barracuda Club in London. Lennox, wearing black leather and a long black wig, and Stewart, wearing a suit and playing a double-necked guitar hung from the ceiling, perform accompanied by backing tapes.

20 At the beginning of a US tour, **Ozzy Osbourne** bites the head off a bat thrown on stage by a fan during a show in Des Moines, Iowa. Apparently confused by the bright lights, the bat lies still. Osbourne, confused by virtually everything and thinking it is a fake rubber bat, picks it up and takes a bite. The bat bites back, and Osbourne has to undergo a series of rabies injections.

23 Hiring a Portastudio for £20 ($32), **Wham!** – 18-year-old clubbing enthusiasts and schoolfriends **George Michael** and **Andrew Ridgeley** – record demos of their self-penned pop/dance songs, *Wham Rap!*, *Come On*, *Club Tropicana*, and *Careless Whisper* at Ridgeley's parents' home in Bushey. When they hawk the tape around London record companies – who will be universally uninterested – the duo will be introduced to ex-Phonogram employee Mark Dean, who is setting up his own dance-based label, Innervision. Through a loan arrangement with CBS, Dean will offer Wham! a contract (which will later prove highly restrictive) and Michael and Ridgeley will sign a songwriting deal with publishers Morrison Leahy in April.

30 Texas blues singer and guitarist **Lightnin' Hopkins** dies of cancer in Houston at the age of 69. He made his first instrument, a cigar-box guitar with chicken-wire strings, when he was eight, and within two years was playing music with his cousin, **Alger Alexander**, and **Blind Lemon Jefferson**. After World War II, having been given his Lightnin' nickname by pianist **Wilson Smith**, he made his first records for Aladdin Recordings in Los Angeles. In 1959, he hooked up with producer Sam Chambers and began to reach a mainstream white audience. He began the 1960s performing at Carnegie Hall with **Pete Seeger** and **Joan Baez**, and closed it opening for rock acts such as the **Grateful Dead** and **Jefferson Airplane**. Among more than 85 albums, his seminal recordings include *Big Mama Jump*, *Short Haired Woman*, and *Blues Is A Feeling*.

30 Quietly creating his own niche as Britain's singular "popabilly" singer, 33-year-old Welshman **Shakin' Stevens** scores his third UK No. 1 in two years with his first self-penned hit, *Oh Julie*. It follows his earlier cover triumphs of Stuart Hamblen's *This Ole House* and the Jim Lowe/Frankie Vaughan 1956 hit, *Green Door*.

Ozzy bit a bat and got married – nothing unusual there... Bob Dylan continued on his evangelical theme with the Shot of Love tour.

The androgynous Annie Lennox and mysterious Dave Stewart scored with a string of synthesizer-heavy, radio-friendly melodies.

> **"All we know is what we are. What we have in this band is very special."**
>
> Bono, **New Musical Express**, February 27, 1982

February

4 Former frontman of the **Sensational Alex Harvey Band**, hell-raising rock 'n' roller Harvey dies of a heart attack in Zeebrugge, Belgium, a day before his 47th birthday, when about to board a ferry back to Britain. His bandmates hear this halfway across the English Channel.

4 Britain's own version of the Grammys is launched with the first British Phonographic Industry (BPI) Awards, held at the Grosvenor House Hotel in London. The relatively low-key affair is highlighted by the Outstanding Contribution to British Music honor being posthumously awarded to **John Lennon**. **Soft Cell**'s *Tainted Love* wins Best British Single, and **Adam & the Ants**' *Kings Of The Wild Frontier* wins Best British Album. The **Police** take the Best British Group prize, and **Human League** the Best British Newcomer. **Cliff Richard** is Best British Male Solo Artist, and **Randy Crawford** (born in Macon, Georgia) is Best British Female Solo Artist. Martin Rushent picks up Best Producer.

6 Reissued, and by now a club and airplay favorite, the teutonic double A-side *Computer Love/The Model* (the latter track is four years old) tops the UK chart for **Kraftwerk**, confirming their influence over the plethora of synth-based/electropop bands that have emerged in Britain over the past 12 months.

Adam Ant turned down an offer to star on stage in "The Pirates of Penzance," explaining that he'd "been through the pirate thing already."

12 **Depeche Mode** begin a 15-date UK tour, in support of the new single *See You*, at the Top Rank in Cardiff, Wales. Playing only his fourth date with the band is **Vince Clarke**'s replacement, 22-year-old vocalist and synth player **Alan Wilder**. Meanwhile Clarke, looking for a singer to work with him in a new duo, answers an ad placed by **"Alf" Moyet** (born Genevieve Alison Jane Moyet): "Powerful female singer, experienced gigs, studio, seeks semi-pro R&B, soul, blues band. – Alison, Basildon 44115." Moyet has been a vocalist with Southend R&B acts, including the **Vicars** and the **Screaming Abdabs**. The pair will become **Yazoo**, releasing their debut single, *Don't Go*, on Mute Records in July, before embarking on their Guided Tour in November.

14 With an increasingly outrageous stage act – which includes chainsawing mannequins and setting their pants on fire – and playing regularly at Los Angeles venues, including the Roxy and the Troubadour, **Mötley Crüe** play their tenth and final gig at a favorite venue, the Whisky A Go-Go. The hell-raising metal quartet – singer **Vince Neil**, guitarist **Mick Mars**, bassist **Nikki Sixx**, and drummer **Tommy Lee** – formed last year and will be snapped up by Elektra Records (beating out Virgin) in June.

20 Veteran jingles singer and soul singer-songwriter, sessioneer, and producer, 30-year-old New Yorker **Luther Vandross** – who was an integral part of **David Bowie**'s 1974 ***Young Americans*** project, and can also be heard on hits by **Chic**, **Sister Sledge**, and current post-disco unit, **Change** – performs his current crossover smash, *Never Too Much* on "Saturday Night Live." It is taken from his debut solo album of the same name, released by Epic.

23 **Paul McCartney** is the 40th anniversary guest on BBC Radio 4's "Desert Island Discs." The long-running program invites guests to choose eight records and one luxury item they would want with them if they were stranded on a desert island. McCartney's selections are **Elvis Presley**'s *Heartbreak Hotel*, **Chuck Berry**'s *Sweet Little Sixteen*, **Gene Vincent**'s *Be Bop A Lula*, **John Lennon**'s *Beautiful Boy*, the **Coasters**' *Searchin'*, **Little Richard**'s *Tutti Frutti*, the **Country Hams**' *Walking In The Park With Eloise*, and Julian Bream's *Courtly Dances* from Benjamin Britten's "Gloriana." His luxury item is a guitar. He will subsequently describe the program as conjuring "traditional British pleasures like the Great British Breakfast, Billy Cotton's Band Show – very downbeat, very relaxed. I love its homeliness."

24 **John Lennon**'s ***Double Fantasy*** is named Album of the Year at the 24th Grammys. **Kim Carnes**'s *Bette Davis Eyes* is named Record of the Year, and brings its writers, **Jackie DeShannon** and Donna Weiss, the award for Song of the Year – despite being written five years ago. **Sheena Easton** is named Best New Artist, somehow topping **Luther Vandross** and soul singer **James Ingram**. In another upset, 64-year-old **Lena Horne** wins Best Pop Vocal Performance, Female for her ***Lena Horne: The Lady And Her Music Live On Broadway***. It is the album's producer, however, who is the evening's biggest winner. Nominated in 11 categories, **Quincy Jones** wins the coveted Producer of the Year, as well as three further awards for his own album, ***The Dude***. Continuing their fine tradition of making poor decisions, the NARAS voters give **Rick Springfield** Best Rock Vocal Performance, Male for *Jessie's Girl*, over **Bruce Springsteen**'s ***The River***.

25 **Prefab Sprout**, a trio from Consett in northeast England, led by Newcastle University student **Paddy McAloon**, with his brother **Martin** and drummer **Mick Salmon**, begin their first studio sessions, cutting *Lions In My Own Garden*, *Exit One*, and *Radio Love*. The band will soon be augmented by singer **Wendy Smith**, playing pub gigs in the Durham area and being rejected by all the major labels they approach. After releasing 1,000 copies of the tracks on their own Candle label ("The Wax That Won't Get On Your Wick"), they will come to the attention of Keith Armstrong, manager of Newcastle's HMV record store. He will sign them to his Kitchenware Records, which will strike a distribution deal with CBS in October.

March

1 MTV launches its "I Want My MTV" marketing campaign, enlisting **Pete Townshend**, the **Police**, **Mick Jagger**, **Stevie Nicks**, **Adam Ant**, **Pat Benatar**, and **David Bowie**.

15 **Bob Dylan** is inducted into the Songwriters Hall of Fame at the 13th annual awards dinner held at New York's Hilton Hotel.

18 On the way home from a basketball game in Philadelphia, ex-**Harold Melvin & the Bluenotes** singer and hugely popular solo soul swooner **Teddy Pendergrass** crashes his Silver Spirit Rolls Royce. He will be paralyzed from the neck down for some time and his injuries will prevent him from working for over two years.

18 **XTC**'s **Andy Partridge**, never comfortable performing live, walks off stage 30 seconds into a performance at Le Palace in Paris, suffering from acute stage fright. The band – on the road to promote its UK No. 5 hit album ***English Settlement*** – will cancel the rest of the European tour. Following a sole American date in San Diego, the group will never perform live again.

"I think this is pretty amazing because I can't read or write a note of music. Thank you."
Bob Dylan, Songwriters Hall of Fame, March 15, 1982

19 In town to perform at the Tangerine Bowl's annual "Rock Superbowl XVI," **Ozzy Osbourne** and his retinue are hit by tragedy. During high jinks, the band's tour plane is buzzing their bus when its wing clips the vehicle, splinters a tree and slams into the side of a house, killing 25-year-old guitarist **Randy Rhoads** (named last year's Best New Talent in **Guitar** magazine), Osbourne's hairdresser Rachel Youngblood, and pilot Andrew Aycock. Osbourne escapes the flames without injury.

28 Driving to an anti-nuclear rally near San Clemente, **David Crosby** crashes his car under the influence of cocaine. Police, finding the drug and a loaded .45 caliber pistol, book him on weapons and drug charges. He gives his reason for carrying the gun in two words: "**John Lennon**."

Apr 1982

The Clash

Joe Strummer goes AWOL... The second "British Invasion"... The first WOMAD...

April

26 On the eve of the **Clash**'s Know Your Rights UK tour, **Joe Strummer** disappears, causing its cancellation. Tracked down in Paris, France, Strummer will claim he went there because his girlfriend's mother was in jail, and that he ran in the Paris Marathon. Initially thought to be a publicity stunt, his behavior will be attributed to the less interesting cause of exhaustion. The Clash will play their next gig at the Lochem Festival in Holland, on May 20.

29 **John Lennon**'s *Woman* wins the Outstanding British Lyric category at the 27th Ivor Novello Awards. **Sting** wins his second Ivor, as *Every Little Thing She Does Is Magic* is named Best Pop Song, while **Phil Collins**'s *In The Air Tonight* nabs International Hit of the Year. **Adam Ant** and **Marco Pirroni** are named Songwriters of the Year, with *Stand And Deliver* being confirmed Best Selling A-Side. The **Who** are honored with the Outstanding Contribution to British Music.

30 Respected rock critic Lester Bangs – a frequent contributor to **Rolling Stone**, **Creem** and the **Village Voice** – dies of a heart attack in New York, age 33. His **Blondie – An Unauthorized Biography** was published last year.

May

8 Record executive **Neil Bogart** dies of lymphoma at the age of 38. Born Neil Bogarz in Brooklyn, Bogart began his career as a singer, scoring a minor hit as **Neil Scott** in 1961 with *Bobby*. He went from **Cashbox** magazine advertising salesman to vice-president of Cameo Parkway in three years. At only 24, he became general manager and then president of Buddah Records, where he oversaw the label's domination of the "bubblegum" market, hitting the charts with the **1910 Fruitgum Company**, the **Ohio Express**, and the **Lemon Pipers**. But it was his founding of Casablanca Records in 1973 that established Bogart as one of the most important characters in the industry – signing **KISS**, **Donna Summer**, **Village People**, **Cher**, and **Parliament**.

11 The six-month North American leg of **Iron Maiden**'s Beast on the Road tour begins in Flint, Michigan. Supporting **Rainbow**, **.38 Special**, and the **Scorpions**, as well as headlining some dates, they will play 103 shows, including a sellout date at the Palladium in New York, where their onstage mascot, the larger-than-life Eddie, holds aloft the bitten-off "head" of **Ozzy Osbourne**. For six weeks of the tour, lead singer **Bruce Dickinson** will have to wear a neck brace, the result of too much head-banging.

15 **Asia**'s self-titled debut album tops the US album chart. The progressive British rock supergroup comprises ex-**Yes** guitarist **Steve Howe**, ex-**King Crimson**/**Roxy Music** bassist **John Wetton**, ex-**ELP** drummer **Carl Palmer**, and ex-**Buggles**/**Yes** keyboardist **Geoff Downes**.

22 Having already logged up ten tongue-in-cheek UK Top 10 hits in three years, **Madness**'s first highlights compilation, ***Complete Madness***, tops the UK chart while their latest cut, *House Of Fun*, enters the singles survey, set to become their first UK No. 1 next week.

27 An already tense relationship between the **Cure**'s **Robert Smith** and **Simon Gallup** worsens during the band's Fourteen Explicit Moments tour in Europe, which Smith will describe as "more like a rugby tour than a Cure tour." Following a performance at the Tivoli Hall in Strasbourg, France, Gallup punches Smith in a club. When they return to England, Gallup will becomes a "former" member of the group, while Smith will go camping in Wales.

> **"I'm not so hung up on being number one and staying on top that it's going to drive me crazy."**
>
> Billy Joel, **Playboy**, May 1982

29 **Paul McCartney** snags his seventh post-**Beatles** US No. 1 album, with ***Tug Of War***. It has already become his fifth chart-topper in the UK on May 1 – its global success spurred by the No. 1 hit duet with **Stevie Wonder**, *Ebony And Ivory*.

29 The synthesizer-driven ***Rio*** hits UK No. 2 for **Duran Duran**, its fortunes enhanced by another trio of hit singles and exotic accompanying videos, filmed on location in Antigua and Sri Lanka by in-demand director, Russell Mulcahy.

June

6 **Stevie Wonder**, **Jackson Browne**, **Crosby, Stills & Nash**, **Bob Dylan**, **Joan Baez**, who duets with Dylan on *Blowin' In The Wind* and *With*

Asia

The Cure

The Clash said goodbye to drummer Topper Headon, who cited "difference of political direction" for his departure... Asia's self-titled debut album, released by Geffen Records, stayed at US No. 1 for two months and sold four million copies... The Cure started out in 1977, answering an ad headed "Wanna Be a Recording Star?"

Madness, profoundly English in every respect, managed only one US Top 10 hit, with *Our House*.

God On Our Side, **Linda Ronstadt**, **Dan Fogelberg**, and **Tom Petty** participate in the Peace Sunday: We Have a Dream anti-nuclear concert, to launch Peace Week, at the Rose Bowl in Pasadena, before a crowd of 85,000. There will be further concerts over the seven days, including the final event in New York's Central Park, attended by an estimated 750,000.

16 Two days after the **Pretenders**' bassist **Pete Farndon** was fired because of his increasing unreliability due to drug addiction, guitarist **James Honeyman-Scott** is found dead in his London apartment, age 25. The official cause of death is "cocaine-related heart failure."

26 **Van Halen** hold the first of two days of rehearsals in Francis Ford Coppola's Zoetrope Studios in Hollywood, in preparation for the Hide Your Sheep tour.

27 An out-of-court settlement is reached between **Sting** and Virgin Music over a contract signed in 1977, concerning the copyright to Sting's early compositions. He is granted a 100 percent royalty for his first solo album, copyright of his songs will be returned to him within 7½ years, and he receives an immediate payment of £200,000 ($320,000).

July

3 Given his current performing name **John Cougar** by **David Bowie**'s manager Tony DeFries, 29-year-old rock singer-songwriter/guitarist **John Mellencamp** gives a free concert in Fort Wayne for 20,000 high-school students who sandbagged for eight days in March, during Indiana's worst flood crisis. His breakthrough hit *Hurts So Good* will reside at US No. 2 throughout August.

3 The second "British Invasion" takes hold in the US, as the **Human League**'s *Don't You Want Me* tops the Hot 100. **Soft Cell** stands at No. 9 with *Tainted Love*, **Kim Wilde** (daughter of **Marty Wilde**) is at No. 41 with *Kids In America*, **Haircut 100**'s *Love Plus One* is at No. 43, ex-**Generation X** lead singer **Billy Idol** – now solo – is at No. 65 with *Hot In The City*, **Bow Wow Wow** have *I Want Candy* at No. 76, and synth-pop combo **A Flock of Seagulls** are at No. 86 with *I Ran*. Established acts such as **Paul McCartney**, **Elton John**, the **Rolling Stones**, and **Queen** also fly the flag.

3 Former **Damned** bassist and singer, **Captain Sensible**, tops the UK chart with his individual interpretation of Rodgers and Hammerstein's *Happy Talk*, from the musical "South Pacific." His first solo release, it has broken the record for the biggest jump to the top (from an entry at No. 33). On the album list, **ABC**'s ***The Lexicon Of Love*** enters at No. 1. The debut set by Sheffield-based duo **Martin Fry** and **Mark White** includes their two recent Top 10 hits, *Poison Arrow* and *The Look Of Love*, and showcases the rich, multilayered production skills of in-demand producer Trevor Horn.

4 Having left his wife Thelma in 1981, **Ozzy Osbourne** marries Sharon, daughter of rock manager and impresario Don Arden, in Maui, Hawaii. His drummer **Tommy Aldridge** is best man. The drugs and booze-soaked rocker will credit Sharon, who is now his personal manager, with saving his life.

18 The first World Of Music, Arts & Dance (WOMAD) Festival, comes to an end at the Royal Bath & West Showground in Shepton Mallet. Household names such as the (**English**) **Beat**, the **Chieftains**, **Echo & the Bunnymen**, and **Simple Minds** have been joined by an eclectic gathering of musicians from 25 countries, including Nigeria's **Prince Nico Mbarga**, Gambia's **Konte Family**, and perhaps the festival highlight, the 15-strong **Drummers of Burundi**. WOMAD, organized by **Peter Gabriel**, will become an annual (and personally costly) event.

21 **Phil Collins**, **Kate Bush**, **Pete Townshend**, **Robert Plant**, **Midge Ure**, and **Gary Brooker** join an all-star band taking part in the inaugural Prince's Trust Rock Gala at the Dominion Theatre in London. £72,000 ($115,200) is raised for the Trust, founded in 1976 by Prince Charles, which will become the UK's leading youth charity. **Madness**, wearing matching kilts, open the proceedings performing *God Save The Queen* on kazoos. They are followed by **Joan Armatrading** – who flies in from Sweden to take part – and **Jethro Tull** (with Collins taking the drumstool).

24 **Survivor**'s rock-pop anthem *Eye Of The Tiger* tops the US chart for the first of six weeks (and will be certified platinum on August 23). The little known Chicago-based hard-rock quintet was asked by "Rocky" creator/actor Sylvester Stallone to write and record a theme song for "Rocky III." After hearing their last album, ***Premonition***, he contacted his friend Tony Scotti, founder of the Scotti Bros. label to which the group are signed.

Kim Wilde outscored her father Marty's UK Top 10 tally 8–6, as well as topping the US charts with *You Keep Me Hangin' On*.

Aug 1982

Global record sales in decline... The US Festival... Launch of the CD player...

The custom Fender electric guitar owned by John Mellencamp, still known as John Cougar, who topped the US chart in October with the guitar-led *Jack and Diane* – one of ten Top 10 hits.

August

6 "Pink Floyd The Wall," a surreal two-hour movie based on the band's 1979 album, premieres in New York. Directed by Alan Parker, with **Bob Geldof** in the lead role of Pink, it has cost $10 million and will be largely panned by critics. (Parker's last music-related effort, 1980s "Fame" – inspired by New York's High School of the Performing Arts – has latently spawned a UK No. 1 this year with **Irene Cara**'s title cut.)

7 The **Cocteau Twins**' debut album ***Garlands*** bows at No. 14 on the UK Independent album chart. Singer **Elizabeth Fraser** and multi-instrumentalist **Robin Guthrie** traveled to London from their native Falkirk in Scotland, armed with two demo tapes. They gave one to receptive BBC Radio 1 DJ John Peel, the other to keyboardist **Simon Raymonde** (son of **Chucks**' *Loo Be Loo* hitmaker, 1960s arranger/ producer Ivor Raymonde, who also co-wrote **Dusty Springfield**'s *I Only Want To Be With You*), who was working in a store beneath the offices of new indie record company, 4AD. Label manager Ivo Watts-Russell, impressed by their ethereal material, signed them up.

13 Atlantic, Capitol, Columbia, Elektra/ Asylum, and Warner Bros. all shed employees as the US record industry plunges into the "worst shape in its history."

28 Taking a two-week break from their current US tour, **Iron Maiden** – playing small club dates in Chippenham two days ago and Poole last night – are tonight's headliner at the Reading Rock Festival. A virtual smorgasbord of heavy metal acts, the festival is also hosting **Praying Mantis**, **Diamond Head**, **Budgie**, **Gary Moore**, **Blackfoot**, **Tygers of Pan Tang**, **Twisted Sister** (led by larger-than-life frontman **Dee Snider**), **Y&T**, and the **Michael Schenker Group** from Germany.

28 Anarchistic post-punk combo, the **Crass**, score their only UK chart record, with ***Christ The Album*** reaching No. 26. Formed in 1978, when they debuted at a squatters' free festival, they set up their own label after releasing an album for indie label Small Wonder. Releasing records that are part music, part anarchist propaganda, the band never wavers from its political beliefs, causing enough establishment concern to keep it off the national charts despite topping the independent charts. Music historian Barry Lazell will say: "Crass probably lived and espoused the minimalist punk lifestyle more than any other band before or since."

September

3 The US Festival, financed by Apple Computers founder Steve Wozniak, gets under way at the Glen Helen Regional Park in Devore, near San Bernardino, California. An estimated 400,000 people will attend the three-day event – the first to bring together music and new technology, with five large tents housing the US Festival Technology Exposition. The sound system – at 400,000 watts – is the largest ever constructed, and enormous video screens flank the stage. The event is the first of its kind to be broadcast live on cable television (on MTV). Today's opening is headlined by the **Police**, with **Talking Heads**, the **B-52's**, **Oingo Boingo**, the (**English**) **Beat**, the **Ramones**, and **Gang of Four**. Tomorrow, **Tom Petty & the Heartbreakers**, **Pat Benatar**, the **Kinks**, the **Cars**, **Santana**, **Eddie Money**, and **Dave Edmunds** will perform. The Labor Day festival will climax in two days' time, with performances by **Fleetwood Mac**, **Jackson Browne**, **Jimmy Buffett**, *Mr. Bojangles* hitmaker **Jerry Jeff Walker**, and the **Grateful Dead**. Wozniak will reportedly lose $12.5 million on the event.

"The band as a horse has run its course, and the jockeys are now considering new mounts." Squeeze, announcing their decision to split, September 28, 1982

DEXY'S MIDNIGHT RUNNERS

Aug 7 **The rousing, fiddle-led *Come On Eileen* by Dexy's Midnight Runners hits UK No. 1, where it will remain for four weeks, eventually selling over a million copies in Britain, while its parent album, *Too-Rye-Ay*, hits UK No. 2. Under Kevin Rowland's direction, the group has adopted a new musical stance, fusing traditional soul with Irish folk, and adding a three-piece fiddle section that shares billing as the Emerald Express. The original "Mean Streets" look, and the more recent anoraks, balaclavas, and sports gear, have been discarded for overalls and gypsy accoutrements. The changes work: *Come On Eileen* will top charts around the world, even reaching US No. 1 next spring, a remarkable achievement for the outspoken, eccentric, and thoroughly British Rowland.**

Queen

The striking visual images for "Pink Floyd The Wall" were the work of artist Gerald Scarfe... Queen would play their last date in August 1986, having performed 658 concerts.

11 **Chicago**'s *Hard To Say I'm Sorry* tops the US chart. It is co-written by songwriter/producer David Foster, lead vocalist **Peter Cetera** (who recently began a parallel solo career with his eponymous debut album), and keyboardist **Robert Lamm**. With the recent addition of another vocalist, ex-**Sons of Champlin**'s **Bill Champlin**, a label switch to Blue Moon Records, and the teaming up with Foster, it sets the tone for a slew of successful Foster-helmed Chicago hits that will continue to the end of the decade.

11 As the self-penned, co-produced (with Don Gehman) ***American Fool*** tops the US chart for **John "Cougar" Mellencamp**, the midwestern adolescent tale *Jack And Diane* (with major input from **Mick Ronson**) moves up to US No. 4, and *Hurts So Good* falls to US No. 8. This makes Mellencamp the only male artist to have two US Top 10 hits and a No. 1 album simultaneously. With saturation airplay on FM radio, ***American Fool*** will stay at US No. 1 for nine weeks, eventually achieving multiplatinum sales.

16 **Afrika Bambaataa & the Sonic Soul Force**'s *Planet Rock* is certified gold by the RIAA. In an innovative hip-hop/electronic blend, pioneering Bronx DJ Bambaataa has sampled sections from **Kraftwerk**'s *Trans-Europe Express*, with overlaid rap from Sonic Soul Force MCs.

20 Bromley Magistrates order the forfeiture of 8,816 copies of *So What*, the single by post-punk combo the **Anti-Nowhere League**, under the Obscene Publications Act, in what is believed to be the first court case of its kind. WXYZ label boss John Curd, who released it, announces his intention to appeal, on the grounds that the record was not heard in open court, as is the case with books and films.

22 The **Who** embark on a farewell US stadium tour at the Capital Center in Landover, Maryland, with **Santana** and the **Clash** in support. The 40-date trek, on which **Eddie Money** and **David Johansen** will open on some dates, will end at Toronto's Maple Leaf Gardens a week before Christmas, and will be the most successful tour of 1982, grossing $23 million. (The band won't play together again until July 1985.)

25 **Queen** – who played what will prove to be their last ever US show at the Great Western Forum in Inglewood on the 15th – guest on "Saturday Night Live," singing *Crazy Little Thing Called Love* and *Under Pressure*.

27 The CBS distribution plant reports orders of 102,000 copies (90,000 of them before lunch) of this week's UK No. 1, **Musical Youth**'s *Pass The Dutchie*. Record label MCA reveals that it is probably the fastest-selling UK single since **Art Garfunkel**'s *Bright Eyes* three years ago. The single is a cover version of the **Mighty Diamonds**' *Pass The Kutchie* (with the title changed from "kutchie," a pot-smoking device, to "dutchie," a cooking pot), and will sell over four million copies worldwide. It will also become the biggest reggae hit in the US since **Johnny Nash**'s *I Can See Clearly Now* ten years ago, hitting No. 8. The five-piece group – all aged between 13 and 15 – will score five more Top 30 hits before disappearing as quickly as they arrived.

30 **Dexy's Midnight Runners** perform their new chart single, *Jackie Wilson Said*, on "Top Of The Pops." The TV production team, unaware that **Van Morrison**'s song is a tribute to the soul legend, places a larger-than-life picture of portly, beer-drinking, darts legend Jocky Wilson behind the faux-gypsy troupe.

October

1 In Tokyo, Sony unveils the first commercially available compact disc player, the CDP-101 (priced at ¥168,000/$650), with **Billy Joel**'s hit album ***52nd Street*** becoming the first CD to go on sale in Japan. It will be available in Europe later this month, with a North American rollout scheduled for next spring. Digital compact disc technology has been pioneered by electronics firm Philips, which standardized the format and specifications with Sony in 1980. The new technology will revolutionize (and financially save) the music industry, dramatically changing buying habits worldwide.

2 **Genesis** and its former lead singer **Peter Gabriel** reunite for a one-off performance at the Six of the Best WOMAD benefit concert held at the Milton Keynes Bowl in the UK. Former guitarist **Steve Hackett** also joins in the fun, playing on the encore, *I Know What I Like*. The benefit helps offset some of the losses of July's WOMAD Festival.

4 The **Smiths** play for the first time at the Ritz in Manchester, supporting **Blue Rondo à la Turk**. The group centers on the music of 18-year-old guitarist **Johnny Marr** (a veteran of several Manchester-based bands, including **Freaky Party**, **Paris Valentinos**, **Sister Ray**, and **White Dice**), and fellow Mancunian, 23-year-old lyricist **Morrissey**, to whom he was introduced by Steve Pomfret on May 18, at Morrissey's home, 384 King's Road. Morrissey, whose book **James Dean Isn't Dead** has been published by local company Babylon Books, has also been the UK president of the **New York Dolls** fan club. (Musically, he has played for seven weeks in the **Nosebleeds**, and auditioned to join **Slaughter & the Dogs**.) The pair has recruited bassist **Andy Rourke**, a former schoolfriend of Marr's, and drummer **Mike Joyce**. Rejecting an offer from the local Factory label, they will sign with seminal London-based indie label, Rough Trade, next spring.

Billy Joel's 1978 multimillion-selling *52nd Street* was afforded the honor of being the first commercially available CD.

Oct

1982

Men At Work come from down under... The Beatles' 20th anniversary... *Thriller*...

5 On the 20th anniversary of its original release, the **Beatles**' *Love Me Do* is reissued by EMI Records. It will hit UK No. 4 by the end of the month. All their singles will be subsequently re-released on their matching dates, the majority achieving respectable chart placings.

15 **Eddie Van Halen**'s left wrist is X-rayed at Hand Surgery Associates in New York. A fracture is found that results in the cancellation of three shows on **Van Halen**'s current Diver Down tour, promoting the band's fifth straight platinum album, ***Diver Down***. Next week, Van Halen Day will be declared in Worcester, Massachusetts, after radio station WAAF sponsor a 25,000-signature petition to get the band to add a third show at the local Centrum venue.

21 **Culture Club** perform their first UK No. 1, *Do You Really Want To Hurt Me*, on "Top Of The Pops." Emerging from the dressy New Romantic London club scene at venues like Hell and Blitz, the pop/soul quartet crystalized last year into the line-up of guitarist/keyboardist **Roy Hay**, bassist **Mikey Craig**, and drummer **Jon Moss**, who provide the rhythm section for flamboyant lead singer **Boy George**. The 21-year-old **George O'Dowd** is proving a strong focal point, with his androgynous, cross-dressing look (designed by Sue Clowes), complemented by heavy make-up and dreadlocks. Signed to Virgin Records in the spring, Culture Club hastily wrote their breakthrough hit when asked to come up with a fourth song for inclusion in a Radio 1 Peter Powell session in June.

November

3 Ever-creative new wave *Whip It* hitmakers **Devo** (led by the **Mothersbaugh** brothers **Bob** and **Mark** and the **Casale** brothers **Bob** and **Jerry**) begin a US tour in Minneapolis. They perform in front of a 50ft rear projection video screen, which continually reveals animations, lyrical snippets, and abstract computer graphics, with which the band playfully interact throughout the show.

4 With **Wham!**'s *Young Guns (Go For It)* at UK No. 42, "Top Of The Pops" producer Michael Hurll makes the rare decision to feature a group from outside the Top 40 on this week's show. Wham! reciprocate with an upbeat performance that will spur the disc to UK No. 3.

5 The **Jam** appear on the premiere edition of Channel 4's "The Tube." Devised by Malcolm Gerrie and Andrea Wonfor, the all-live show will quickly gain a reputation as the most adventurous and stylish music show on UK television. Becoming a popular outlet for new talent, its most visible early success will be next month's airing of a rough, Tube-shot video of new Liverpool pop/rock quintet, **Frankie Goes To Hollywood**, performing its self-penned *Relax*. This appearance will attract record company interest, particularly from Trevor Horn, composer of the show's theme music.

9 **Eddy Grant** appears on "Top Of The Pops" performing this week's UK chart-topper, the self-penned *I Don't Wanna Dance*. Having last year relocated his Ice recording studio/record company operation back to his home in St. Phillip, Barbados, Grant's new album ***Killer On The Rampage*** includes a Caribbean Airways logo on its cover – part of a deal he struck with the airline in return for flying over a group of UK journalists for a press junket.

11 **Marvin Gaye** scores his 13th (and final) US R&B chart-topper, as *Sexual Healing* begins a ten-week run. A sensual return to form, it is his first release since a new deal signed with CBS/Columbia Records earlier in the year, and is featured on ***Midnight Love***, recorded during the fall at Studio Katy in Ohaine, Belgium.

Paula Yates and former Squeeze keyboard player Jools Holland hosted "The Tube", the UK's hippest TV music show.

13 **Soft Cell**'s *Tainted Love* drops off the Hot 100 after 43 weeks, surpassing **Paul Davis**'s longevity record for *I Go Crazy* by three weeks. (Since 1955, these two singles are the only two to have reached 40 weeks. In the next 20 years, 51 will achieve the feat.) Meanwhile, **Diana Ross**'s *Muscles* – written and produced for her by **Michael Jackson** – peaks at No. 10. The song's title is also the name of Jackson's pet snake, one of his increasing number of unusual animal companions. He has recently completed sessions for his second Epic Records album, again under the production of Quincy Jones.

22 Highly stylized British art-pop electronic band, **Japan**, announces its breakup following a final concert at Hammersmith Odeon in London. Virgin Records – which released the group's five albums – will stick by lead singer **David Sylvian** for the next 20 years, issuing a succession of increasingly avant garde and critically lauded solo albums.

27 The finale of the three-day Jamaica World Music Festival takes place in Montego Bay. An eclectic group of artists, including the **Grateful Dead**, the **B-52's**, **Squeeze** (playing a final gig together), **Joe Jackson**, **Jimmy Cliff**, **Peter Tosh**, the **Beach Boys**, **Aretha Franklin**, **Toots & the Maytals**, **Gladys Knight**, and **Black Uhuru**, have entertained 45,000 festivalgoers. **Rick James**, the **Clash**, **Jimmy Buffett**, and island favorites **Yellowman** and **Rita Marley & the Melody Makers**, close the festival.

Culture Club

U2

Culture Club became the first act since the Supremes in 1965 to score three US Top 10 hits from a debut album... U2's *Sunday Bloody Sunday* "peace in Northern Ireland" message became a live focal point for the band.

MEN AT WORK

Oct 23 Australian pop/rock quintet Men at Work performs *Who Can It Be Now?* – which will hit US No. 1 next week, followed by the group's current Australian chart-topper *Down Under* (which will make No. 1 in both the US and UK in January) on "Saturday Night Live." Formed in Melbourne by lead singer and principal songwriter, Scottish-born Colin Hay, in 1979, the group signed to CBS in Australia in 1980 and recently opened a US tour for Fleetwood Mac. Its debut album, *Business As Usual*, will begin a 15-week hold at US No. 1 on November 13, while the band begins its first, 50-date, headlining North American trek.

Down Under is the only hit record to include the lyric "vegemite sandwich," a culinary delight unique to Australians.

December

1 Epic Records releases ***Thriller*** by **Michael Jackson**, produced in just eight weeks by Quincy Jones. With demos originally recorded at Jackson's Encino home, some with British songwriter **Rod Temperton** present, it includes four tracks written by Jackson. The rest were chosen from 600 songs submitted to Jones, including the title cut by Temperton. The album is engineered by Bruce Swedien and boasts Jones's topflight session crew, including keyboardist **Greg Phillinganes**, trumpet player/arranger **Jerry Hey**, bassist **Louis Johnson**, drummer **John Robinson**, and percussionist **Paulinho DaCosta**. Breaking all sales records, it will become the most successful chart album of all time, selling over 50 million copies worldwide (over one million copies in Los Angeles alone) and hitting No. 1 in every Western country, including the UK and the US (it will spend a record 37 weeks at US No. 1). It will also yield an unprecedented seven Top 10 US hit singles, and receive a record 12 Grammy nominations. Its first extract is the current smash *The Girl Is Mine*, a playfully feuding duet with **Paul McCartney**, though *Thriller*'s full sales potential won't be fully realized until the release of its second single, *Billie Jean*.

2 **David Blue**, a contemporary of **Bob Dylan** in the 1960s Greenwich Village folk scene, dies from a massive heart attack while jogging in Washington Square Park in New York. Blue recorded eight albums for Elektra, Reprise, and Asylum between the mid 1960s and mid 1970s, becoming one of the music world's great secrets – ignored by the many, loved by the few.

8 The country world loses a giant as **Marty Robbins** dies, age 57, in Nashville, after a third round of heart surgery. A Grammy, ASCAP, and BMI award-winner, and a member of the Songwriters Hall of Fame, he is best known for his 1959 smash, *El Paso*. He was inducted into the Country Music Hall of Fame in October.

11 Finally embarking on a solo career with the launch of ***Lionel Richie*** in October, **Richie** guests on "Saturday Night Live." He sings the album's first two singles, *You Are* and *Truly*, last week's US chart-topper and a trademark ballad indistinguishable from those he wrote and sang for the **Commodores**.

11 The **Jam** play their last ever date, at the Conference Centre in Brighton, at the end of the Dig the New Breed tour, during which the group played five sellout shows at the Wembley Arena. Frontman **Paul Weller** will sign a solo deal with Polydor, before teaming up with **Mick Talbot** as the **Style Council**.

17 Blues legend **Big Joe Williams** dies in Macon, age 79. A Delta blues traditionalist, the singer-songwriter/guitarist is best known for *Baby Please Don't Go*, *Crawlin' King Snake*, and *Sugar Hill*.

20 During a concert at the Maysfield Leisure Centre in Belfast, Bono introduces a new **U2** song, *Sunday, Bloody Sunday*. Written principally by **The Edge** and **Bono**, it highlights their ongoing socio-political lyrical stance.

29 As the single *Allentown* continues its climb up the Hot 100, and following a benefit concert in the Pennsylvania town about which it is written, **Billy Joel** gives another at the Nassau Veterans Memorial Coliseum in Uniondale, raising $125,000 for his own Charity Begins at Home organization, which will distribute the sum between over 60 different causes.

ROOTS During this year: having bought his way out of the British Army last year after just 90 days, Billy Bragg embarks on a UK tour via bus and train... the Southern Death Cult make their debut at the Heaven club in London... New Edition audition, initially unsuccessfully, for impresario Maurice Starr... signed to the Cherry Red label, Ben Watt puts out a message on Hull University's paging system to meet labelmate Tracey Thorn in reception... the Vortex Motion make their live debut at Clydebank Community Centre in Scotland, subsequently taking a new name – Wet Wet Wet – from a line in a song by Scritti Politti... Janet Jackson signs with A&M Records, promoting her debut album (including a duet with Cliff Richard) by touring high schools and encouraging children to stay in school... Shane MacGowan and Jem Finer busk at Finsbury Park tube station, before teaming up with "Spider" Stacy to play Irish rebel songs at the Cabaret Futura in London... 12-year-old Debbie Gibson wins $1,000 in a songwriting contest for *I Come From America*... and Pulp signs with indie label, Red Rhino, which releases the group's first album *It*...

Is There Something I Should Know?

1983

No.1 US SINGLES

- **Jan 1** Maneater **Daryl Hall & John Oates**
- **Jan 15** Down Under **Men At Work**
- **Feb 5** Africa **Toto**
- **Feb 12** Down Under **Men At Work**
- **Feb 19** Baby, Come To Me **Patti Austin (with James Ingram)**
- **Mar 5** Billie Jean **Michael Jackson**
- **Apr 23** Come On Eileen **Dexy's Midnight Runners**
- **Apr 30** Beat It **Michael Jackson**
- **May 21** Let's Dance **David Bowie**
- **May 28** Flashdance...What A Feeling **Irene Cara**
- **July 9** Every Breath You Take **Police**
- **Sept 3** Sweet Dreams (Are Made Of This) **Eurythmics**
- **Sept 10** Maniac **Michael Sembello**
- **Sept 24** Tell Her About It **Billy Joel**
- **Oct 1** Total Eclipse Of The Heart **Bonnie Tyler**
- **Oct 29** Islands In The Stream **Kenny Rogers with Dolly Parton**
- **Nov 12** All Night Long (All Night) **Lionel Richie**
- **Dec 10** Say Say Say **Paul McCartney & Michael Jackson**

No.1 UK SINGLES

- **Jan 1** Save Your Love **Renée & Renato**
- **Jan 15** You Can't Hurry Love **Phil Collins**
- **Jan 29** Down Under **Men At Work**
- **Feb 19** Too Shy **Kajagoogoo**
- **Mar 5** Billie Jean **Michael Jackson**
- **Mar 12** Total Eclipse Of The Heart **Bonnie Tyler**
- **Mar 26** Is There Something I Should Know? **Duran Duran**
- **Apr 9** Let's Dance **David Bowie**
- **Apr 30** True **Spandau Ballet**
- **May 28** Candy Girl **New Edition**
- **June 4** Every Breath You Take **Police**
- **July 2** Baby Jane **Rod Stewart**
- **July 23** Wherever I Lay My Hat (That's My Home) **Paul Young**
- **Aug 13** Give It Up **KC & the Sunshine Band**
- **Sept 3** Red Red Wine **UB40**
- **Sept 24** Karma Chameleon **Culture Club**
- **Nov 5** Uptown Girl **Billy Joel**
- **Dec 10** Only You **Flying Pickets**

Metallica

Mötley Crüe

Metallica and Mötley Crüe were two of the leaders in the evolving heavy metal scene, racking up US album sales of more than 70 million between them over two decades.

It was a fertile year for popular music, powered by the worldwide success of **Michael Jackson**'s *Thriller*, a vibrant British pop scene, the explosion of the **Police** in the US, yet another incarnation for **David Bowie**, and the emergence of a 25-year-old from Bay City, Michigan, called **Madonna**.

Released late in 1982, ***Thriller*** conquered charts around the world, and picked up a record 12 Grammy nominations. Its impact was heightened by cutting-edge videos, more like short movies, which were so innovative that MTV gave up its undeclared reluctance to air videos by black artists. With signature singles such as *Billie Jean* and *Beat It* (the latter backed by **Eddie Van Halen**'s guitar solo), Jackson monopolized dancefloors, invented the moonwalk, and singlehandedly revived the fortunes of Epic Records.

With his own brand of erotically charged lyrics, **Prince** confirmed himself as a major all-around talent with the release of the double opus *1999*. It was a rich fusion of funk, pop and rock, by turns elegant, sleazy, and fragile, from the pop nugget *Little Red Corvette* to the hot and heavy sexuality of tracks like *Lady Cab Driver*.

This was also the year of dance-pop. **Bowie**'s ***Let's Dance*** was just that – the chameleon's venture into danceable disco-infused rock (created with **Chic** founder **Nile Rodgers**), and his most successful album. **Culture Club** just couldn't avoid having hits in both Europe and the US, and the debut album from **Wham!** produced four Top 10 hits in Britain. Already queen of the dance charts with *Holiday*, provocative newcomer Madonna's debut album began its three-year chart run.

Synthesized pop and the New Romantics were still very much in vogue in Britain, perhaps as an escape from record unemployment and a sour social mood. Offering slick and stylish white "soul," **Spandau Ballet** produced its biggest chart success on both sides of the Atlantic with ***True*** and its timeless title cut. But it was the **Police** who led the British invasion – with the biggest-selling single of the year, *Every Breath You Take*, and the multiplatinum ***Synchronicity***. They were now able to fill American arenas, but it would be their last tour and last album, as personal and creative tensions took hold.

Irish rock band **U2** also made an impact in the US following the chart success of *Sunday Bloody Sunday*. Their ability to tackle sectarian hatred and drug abuse in a musical setting began to set them apart from the pack. The album ***War*** also boasted the anthemic *New Year's Day* (inspired by the Solidarity movement in Poland) and *Two Hearts Beat As One*.

A completely different audience lapped up heavy metal. **Metallica**'s ***Kill 'Em All*** unleashed "thrash" metal. **Mötley Crüe**'s heaviest offering yet, ***Shout At The Devil***, played to teenage angst and aggression, and was their breakthrough set. The equally thunderous **Quiet Riot** took the prize for the first metal album (***Metal Health***) to reach US No. 1, before disappearing almost as fast as they'd emerged.

"Life is about sex and risk but that doesn't mean that's all that life is."

David Bowie, **Musician**, May 1983

Jan 1983

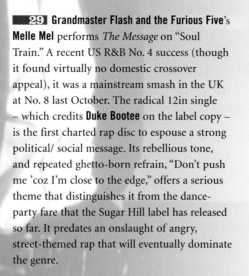

Bowie signs to EMI... Karen Carpenter passes away... Toto sweep the Grammys...

Toto

January

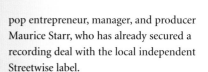

5 **Everything But The Girl** (a name taken from a secondhand furniture store in Hull) make their live debut as a duo at the Institute for Contemporary Arts in London. **Tracey Thorn** and **Ben Watt** have already been separately signed to Ian McNay's London-based indie label Cherry Red. They were both students at Hull University, and Watt, eager finally to meet his labelmate, put out an announcement over the university's paging system asking to meet Thorn in reception. A lasting romantic and professional partnership was immediately formed.

12 Former **Traffic** percussionist **Reebop Kwaku Baah** dies from a brain hemorrhage in Stockholm. The Nigerian-born musician worked with **Steve Winwood**'s **Traffic** before hooking up with German bands, **Can**, and **Zahara**, and played on albums by the **Rolling Stones** and **Ginger Baker**.

17 Country music enjoys a big night at the 10th American Music Awards, at Los Angeles' Shrine Auditorium. **Kenny Rogers** picks up three trophies, including the Special Award of Merit, and **Willie Nelson** wins a pair. **Alabama** is named Favorite Band, Duo or Group in country music, beginning a 12-year run in that category.

27 In New York, **David Bowie** signs a new five-year contract with EMI America Records, reportedly worth $10 million. His first album out of the box, ***Let's Dance*** – largely co-written and produced with **Chic**'s **Nile Rodgers** – will go platinum in both the UK and the US, and its extracted title track will be his first No. 1 single in both countries. His most enduring set, it will outsell all previous outings and yield three huge global hits: the title cut (featuring 28-year-old Texan **Stevie Ray Vaughan** on guitar), *China Girl* (co-written with **Iggy Pop**), and *Modern Love.*

28 **Billy Fury** dies from heart failure, age 41, having nursed a desperately weak heart – brought on by rheumatic fever when he was six – for most of his life. His 1965 hit, *I'm Lost Without You*, will be played at his funeral.

29 **Men at Work** repeat **Rod Stewart**'s 1971 chart feat, simultaneously topping both the singles (*Down Under*) and album (***Business As Usual***) surveys in both the US and the UK.

29 **Grandmaster Flash and the Furious Five**'s **Melle Mel** performs *The Message* on "Soul Train." A recent US R&B No. 4 success (though it found virtually no domestic crossover appeal), it was a mainstream smash in the UK at No. 8 last October. The radical 12in single – which credits **Duke Bootee** on the label copy – is the first charted rap disc to espouse a strong political/ social message. Its rebellious tone, and repeated ghetto-born refrain, "Don't push me 'coz I'm close to the edge," offers a serious theme that distinguishes it from the dance-party fare that the Sugar Hill label has released so far. It predates an onslaught of angry, street-themed rap that will eventually dominate the genre.

February

1 **Air Supply**'s third album, ***Now And Forever***, is certified platinum by the RIAA. Unfashionable to a fault, the Australian duo of **Russell Hitchcock** and **Graham Russell** have been quietly racking up worldwide hits since ***Lost In Love*** in 1980. Signed to Clive Davis's Arista label, their richly harmonic adult contemporary ballad fare has found its biggest success in the US, where they have logged up seven consecutive top five hits since 1980, including the 1981 chart-topper, *The One That You Love.* Their final smash will be the typically melodramatic Jim Steinman-penned *Making Love Out Of Nothing At All*, which will reach US No. 2 in October.

4 After a long battle with anorexia and bulimia nervosa, **Karen Carpenter** is found unconscious at her parents' home in Downey, California. A frail, almost skeletal, figure, she is rushed to the Downey Community Hospital where she dies, age 32, at 9:51 am. An angelic singer who scored 29 US hits in 12 years with her brother **Richard**, Carpenter will be buried next to her father at the Forest Lawn Memorial Park in Cypress, California.

5 Having established themselves over two years as Boston talent show champs, and with several lip-synching gigs in the northeastern states under their belt, R&B teen group **New Edition** makes its residency debut at New York's Copacabana Club. **Ricky Bell**, **Ralph Tresvant**, **Michael Bivins**, **Ronald DeVoe**, and **Bobby Brown** (all aged between 13 and 15) are under the wing of pop entrepreneur, manager, and producer Maurice Starr, who has already secured a recording deal with the local independent Streetwise label.

8 **Dexy's Midnight Runners**' *Come On Eileen* is named Best British Single, and **Barbra Streisand**'s ***Love Songs*** is Best Album, at the second BPI awards. **Paul McCartney** wins Best British Male Solo Artist, and **Kim Wilde** is named Best British Female Solo Artist, while **Dire Straits** are Best British Group. **Yazoo** – the new duo formed by **Vince Clarke** and **Alison Moyet**, who broke through with the synth-pop classic, *Only You*, last year – receive the award for Best British Newcomer. The **Beatles** are honored for their Outstanding Contribution to British Music.

9 **Frank Zappa** conducts the San Francisco Contemporary Music Players at the Edgar Varèse Memorial Concert, to celebrate the 100th anniversary of the composer's birth. **Grace Slick** acts as Master of Ceremonies at the event, held at San Francisco's War Memorial Opera House.

11 **Bob Seger & the Silver Bullet Band** receive their seventh consecutive US platinum award for ***The Distance***. Seger's no-nonsense brand of straightahead, melodic rock has seen domestic album sales exceed 25 million to date.

23 **Toto** – an aggregation of top Los Angeles session musicians – win Album of the Year for ***Toto IV***, and Record of the Year for *Rosanna*, at the 25th Grammys, along with three more statuettes from 11 nominations. Their lead guitarist, **Steve Lukather**, picks up another Grammy as co-writer of the Best Rhythm & Blues Song, *Turn Your Love Around.* John Christopher, Mark James, and Wayne Carson Thompson's *Always On My Mind* – a hit for **Willie Nelson** – becomes the first country song to win Song of the Year since *Little Green Apples* in 1968. **Marvin Gaye** wins his first Grammys, Best R&B Vocal Performance, Male, and Best R&B Instrumental Performance for *Sexual Healing*, while **Jennifer Holiday**'s astonishing performance on *And I Am Telling You I'm Not Going* wins her Best R&B Vocal Performance, Female.

28 With *Love On Your Side* peaking at UK No. 9, the **Thompson Twins** appear at the Hammersmith Palais, London, with **Kissing the Pink** in support. Formed in 1977 as a sextet by aspiring classical pianist **Tom Bailey**, the Thompson Twins have been trimmed down to a

Michael Jackson's performance on NBC-TV's "Motown 25: Yesterday, Today, Forever" created a defining moment in American pop culture.

Thompson Twins

Wham!

Toto came together when they backed Boz Scaggs on his *Silk Degrees* album... The Thompson Twins took their name from a pair of identical detectives in Hergé's cartoon creation Tintin... Dick Clark mistook Wham! for a duo from Detroit when they debuted on "American Bandstand."

trio, with co-singer/saxophonist **Alannah Currie** (Bailey's New Zealander girlfriend), and percussionist **Joe Leeway**. They take their name from a pair of identical detectives in Hergé's cartoon creation, Tintin. They have been gigging constantly in pubs and clubs for the past three years, with the pledge that they can play anywhere, anytime.

March

3 Appearing before a Senate Judiciary panel, "Chuck," a former member of the Oakland unit of the Hell's Angels, reveals that the California chapter of the motorcycle gang has held a grudge against **Rolling Stone Mick Jagger** since the Altamont concert in 1969. The Angels have reportedly had a contract out on the singer and failed at two assassination attempts.

5 The **Michael Jackson**-penned, irresistible pop/dance radio smash *Billie Jean* tops the US chart. It will stay there for seven weeks, coinciding for one week with its UK No. 1 position. Having entered the US list in January, it is transforming the fortunes of ***Thriller***, Jackson's career, the financial status of Epic Records, and the fabric of modern music itself. Only when it hits US No. 1 does MTV, previously reluctant to air "black videos," show the *Billie Jean* clip (relenting only after a threatened service boycott by Epic/Columbia). Featuring pioneering self-choreographed dance steps, the visuals combine with audio innovation to provide what many critics regard as the perfect modern-single project. In contrast to his future recordings, Jackson's vocals for *Billie Jean* were made in one take, and feature an uncredited lyric on solo by **Tom Scott**.

5 **Wham!** make their US television debut, appearing on "American Bandstand," performing the dance/pop nuggets *Wham Rap!* and *Young Guns (Go For It)*.

7 **Stevie Wonder**'s two children, Aisha and Keita, accept their father's induction award to the Songwriters Hall of Fame at the 14th annual ceremony, held at the Waldorf Astoria Ballroom in New York. **Neil Sedaka** is also inducted, performing a selection of past hits. **Willie Nelson** receives a Lifetime Achievement award.

"If everyone they've met in a studio during the last few years votes for them, it'll be a runaway."

Robert Hilburn on Toto's Grammy chances, **Los Angeles Times**, February 1983

25 Tamla Motown Records celebrates its 25th anniversary with a spectacular concert. **Stevie Wonder**, the **Supremes**, the **Four Tops**, the **Temptations**, the **Commodores**, **Lionel Richie**, **Jr. Walker & the All Stars**, **Martha Reeves** without the **Vandellas**, **Michael Jackson**, the **Jackson 5**, **Marvin Gaye**, and **Smokey Robinson** perform at the Civic Auditorium in Pasadena. Highlights of a memorable evening are a "Battle of the Bands" contest between the Four Tops and the Temptations (which will lead the two veteran soul groups to tour together later in the year), **Linda Ronstadt** joining Smokey Robinson on *Ooh Baby*, but above all a performance by Michael Jackson of *Billie Jean*, featuring his celebrated "moonwalk" dance style. When the show airs on NBC as "Motown 25: Yesterday, Today, Forever" on May 16, Jackson's groundbreaking choreography and his toe-tipping, hat-tossing performance will create a defining moment in American pop culture.

31 The all-white MTV adds **Michael Jackson**'s *Beat It* to the mix, and another hot video for the cut, directed by Bob Giraldi, keeps the song in heavy rotation. It features two rival gangs who perform perfectly synchronized dance steps, led and choreographed by Jackson with assistant choreographer Michael Peters; its innovative dance sequences will be much copied over the next ten years (notably by Jackson's younger sister, **Janet**).

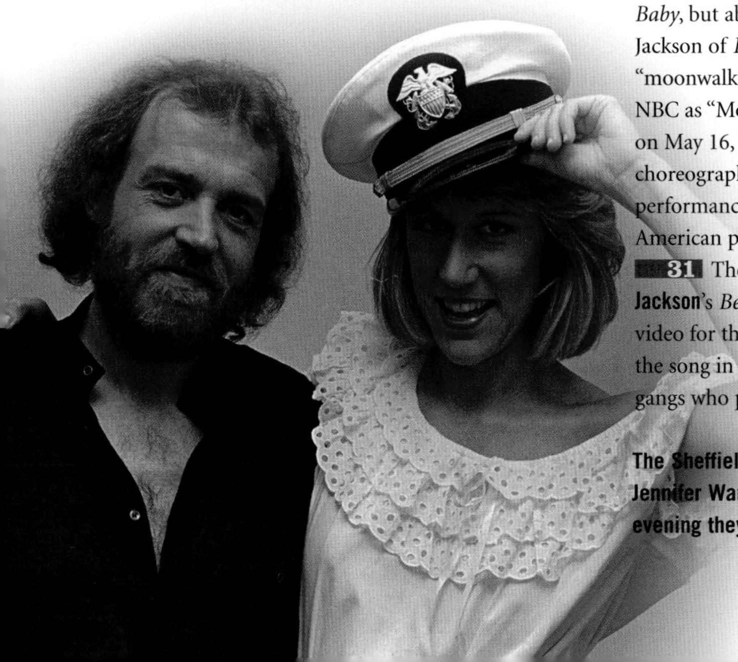

The Sheffield-born Joe Cocker and Californian Jennifer Warnes met for the first time on the evening they recorded *Up Where We Belong*.

April

2 **Pink Floyd**'s ***The Final Cut*** becomes their third UK chart-topper, and will hit US No. 6. The album, which has an anti-war theme and is co-produced with Michael Kamen, is almost entirely the work of **Roger Waters**. (With animosity between him and **David Gilmour** at an all-time high, it will prove to be his final work with the group.) The disc utilizes a novel recording technique (already used by **Genesis P. Orridge**'s band **Psychic TV**): a 3D sound effect called Holophonics, designed by Argentinian-Italian scientist Hugo Zuccarelli.

5 **Danny Rapp**, lead singer of 1950s rock 'n' roll act, **Danny & the Juniors**, is found dead in Parker, Arizona, having apparently shot himself. The *At The Hop* hitmaker, dead at the age of 41, will be buried in St. Mary's Cemetery, Bellmawr, New Jersey.

5 US Interior Secretary James Watt announces that the **Beach Boys** and the **Grass Roots** are being banned from performing at the annual Fourth of July celebration in Washington, D.C., because they attract "the wrong element of people." New York Democratic State Senator Daniel P. Moynihan says: "If I understand correctly, the **Monkees**, the **Turtles**, the **Beatles** – indeed the **Animals** – are already extinct without any assistance from Mr. Watt." Watt's choice to replace the Beach Boys? **Wayne Newton**.

11 **Joe Cocker** and veteran 36-year-old singer **Jennifer Warnes** perform their US chart-topper *Up Where We Belong* (from the 1982 film soundtrack for "An Officer and a Gentleman") at the Academy Awards, held at the Dorothy Chandler Pavilion in Los Angeles. It is also named Best Music, Song, for its co-writers Jack Nitzsche, Buffy Sainte-Marie, and Will Jennings.

Apr # 1983

Muddy Waters dies... Run-D.M.C... The Smiths on "The John Peel Show"...

14 The **Pretenders' Pete Farndon**, who was thrown out of the band last year (two days before **James Honeyman-Scott**'s drug-related death) and has recently been setting up a group with **Rob Stoner** and ex-**Clash** drummer **"Topper" Headon**, is found dead in his bathtub. The 30-year-old bassist has overdosed on heroin.

17 Gail Pappalardi, wife of record producer and former **Mountain** bassist **Felix Pappalardi**, makes a 911 call at 6:00 am. When police arrive at the couple's Waterside Plaza apartment on New York City's East Side, they find Pappalardi dead from a gunshot in the neck. A .38-caliber Derringer is recovered, and Mrs. Pappalardi is charged with second-degree murder and criminal possession of a weapon. The 41-year-old Pappalardi was born in the Bronx, and began his career as a folk artist in Greenwich Village in the 1960s, working with **Joan Baez**, the **Lovin' Spoonful**, and the **Youngbloods**, before making his name as the producer of rock trio **Cream**.

30 One month after his 68th birthday, blues legend **Muddy Waters** suffers a heart attack in his sleep, and dies at home in suburban Westmont, Illinois. Born in Rolling Fork, Mississippi, Waters followed in the great tradition of Delta bluesmen, such as **Charley Patton**, **Son House**, and **Robert Johnson**, mastering the "bottleneck" guitar-style. He moved to Chicago in 1943, initially cutting sides for Columbia, before recording for Chess and its precursor, Aristocrat. A series of seminal blues cuts followed, including *Rollin' Stone, Rollin' And Tumblin', I Just Want To Make Love To You, Hoochie Coochie Man, Just To Be With You*, and *Got My Mojo Working*. A paragon for the British blues movement of the early 1960s – he particularly influenced **Eric Clapton** and the **Rolling Stones**, who took their name from his *Rollin' Stone* as well as recording several of his songs early in their career – Waters continued to play his music to fans until his death.

30 **Michael Jackson** hits US No. 1 with *Beat It*, failing to replace his own *Billie Jean* at the top spot by only one week – the shortest gap registered since the **Beatles**' achievement in 1964. The self-penned smash is highlighted by searing guitar work by **Eddie Van Halen** – a genre-mixing idea conceived by producer Quincy Jones – which Van Halen agreed to do as a favor without being paid.

May

1 **Paul Weller**'s new musical venture, the **Style Council**, plays its first live gig, as part of the May Day Show for Peace and Jobs benefit for the Merseyside Trade Union Community and Unemployed Resource Centre, at the Empire Theatre, Liverpool. They headline a bill that also features new Liverpool-based rock combo the **Farm**, the **High Five**, writer Alan Bleasdale, the Everyman Youth Theatre, and characters from the TV series "The Boys from the Blackstuff."

5 In one of the most diverse Ivor Novello award presentations in its history, **Madness** win the Best Pop Song for *Our House*, while **Dexy's Midnight Runners** pick up the Best Selling A-side honor for *Come On Eileen*. The **Stranglers**' entirely non-punk *Golden Brown* is named Most Performed Work of 1982, Gaelic band **Clannad** win Best Theme from a Television or Radio Production for their haunting *Theme From Harry's Game*, and the **Mark Knopfler**-penned *Private Investigations* wins the Outstanding British Lyric. **Peter Gabriel** and **Genesis** are honored for their Outstanding Contribution to British Music, and the **Shadows** receive the Special Award for 25 Years in the Music Business.

10 Heavy-metal quartet **Metallica** begin recording their first album, with producer Paul Curcio, at the Music America Studios in Rochester. Costing $15,000, the sessions will end on the 27th. The band has recently undergone a critical line-up change, with ex-**Exodus** guitarist **Kirk Hammett** replacing **Dave Mustaine**, who departed on April 1 (and will soon form **Megadeth**). Pioneering a blistering brand of thrash metal, Metallica was formed in 1981 by Danish emigré and ex-**Diamond Head** drummer **Lars Ulrich**, who recruited Los Angeles-born singer/guitarist **James Hetfield**; they were joined by ex-**Trauma** bassist **Cliff Burton**. The group, now based in New Jersey, signed last year to US metal label Megaforce – who will license their debut album, ***Kill 'Em All***, to UK metal specialist indie label, Music for Nations.

Already a major presence in Australia, INXS broke into the US market in 1983 with their third album, *Shabooh Shoobah*.

21 *It's Like That* enters the US R&B chart for **Run-D.M.C.**, set to hit No. 15. A spare but powerful rap outing, with hard beats and overlapping vocals, it is produced by Larry Smith (the unheralded king of new urban rap), mixed by **Kurtis Blow**, and overseen by Blow and Run-D.M.C.'s manager, Russell Simmons, who recently formed the hip-hop management company Rush Productions. The group – founded last year in the middle-class Hollis neighborhood of Queens, New York – comprises **Joseph Simmons** (Russell's brother, aka **Run**), **Darryl McDaniels** (**D.M.C.**), and DJ **Jason Mizell** (**Jam Master Jay**). They are pioneering a new breed of hardcore, street-based, roots hip-hop, with an accompanying image of baggy leather jackets and Adidas trainers. Russell Simmons has negotiated a $2,500 advance deal for the group with Priority Records, who will also promote the single's B-side, *Sucker M.C.'s*, which brings both "Sucker" and "M.C.'s" into the rap vernacular. Both sides will set the tone for much to come.

28 Steven Wozniak decides to lose some more money by staging a second US Festival at the Glen Helen Regional Park in San Bernadino. The **Clash** (giving their last performance with guitarist **Mick Jones**), the **Cars**, **Men At Work**, rockabilly revivalists the **Stray Cats**, the (**English**) **Beat**, **A Flock of Seagulls**, and a trio of in-vogue new wave bands – **Oingo Boingo**, **Wall of Voodoo**, and the **Divinyls** – play on the first of the three days. A Flock of Seagulls and the Beat have a spat over who should go on first. Today's line-up also marks the American festival debut of hard-working Australian rockers **INXS**. Formed in Sydney in 1977 as the Farriss Brothers, the sextet is led by telegenic frontman, singer **Michael Hutchence**.

29 "Heavy Metal Sunday" at the US Festival sees **Van Halen** headline a bill featuring the **Scorpions**, Canadian hard-rock trio **Triumph**,

> **"A lot of bands forget what they are, that they're a product, another supermarket... and your product has to be as good as the next."**
>
> Boy George, **Record Mirror**, April 9, 1983

THE SMITHS

May 18 The Smiths record their first BBC session, for "The John Peel Show" on Radio 1, taping *Miserable Lie, Reel Around The Fountain, Handsome Devil*, and *What Difference Does It Make.* The show will air on June 1. Most of the group's current live shows feature Morrissey paying tribute to his various influences/obsessions: a bunch of gladioli, often tucked into the seat of his pants, represents Oscar Wilde, and he wears a hearing aid in tribute to early 1950s vocalist Johnnie Ray. He also styles much of his appearance – including his hairstyle – on his favorite vocalist, the recently deceased Billy Fury.

The Smiths signed a deal with Rough Trade that saw their debut single, *Hand In Glove*, top the UK Independent chart.

Judas Priest, **Ozzy Osbourne** (whose first three solo albums have all found platinum success in the US), **Mötley Crüe**, and **Quiet Riot**, a raucous Los Angeles-based quartet whose ***Metal Health*** entered the US chart last month on its way to No. 1, courtesy of its breakout smash, a cover of **Slade**'s *Cum On Feel The Noize.*

30 **David Bowie** tops the bill on the third day of the US Festival, receiving a record fee of $1 million. **Stevie Nicks**, **Joe Walsh**, the **Pretenders**, American new wave quintet **Missing Persons**, **U2** (currently touring in support of ***War***), Oregon-based rock unit **Quarterflash**, electropop/rock combo **Berlin**, and **Little Steven & the Disciples of Soul** (led by **Bruce Springsteen**'s sideman guitarist, **Miami Steve Van Zandt**) also perform. With some 800,000 attendees needed to break even, 300,000 show up, leaving Wozniak with a further loss of $8 million.

June

3 Renowned session drummer **Jim Gordon** drives to his mother's North Hollywood apartment at about 11:30 pm, attacking her with a hammer before stabbing her. He will be found guilty of second-degree murder. Gordon was one of an elite group of drummers, along with **Hal Blaine**, **Earl Palmer**, and **Jim Keltner**, who laid the musical soundtrack of the 1960s and 1970s. He drummed for **John Lennon**, **George Harrison**, the **Beach Boys**, the **Everly Brothers**, **Carly Simon**, **Jackson Browne**, **Frank Zappa**, **Joe Cocker**, **Traffic**, and countless others, as well as founding **Derek & the Dominos** with **Eric Clapton**. (The piano coda in *Layla* is Gordon's work.) But over the past three years, his acute paranoid schizophrenia has taken hold. Hearing voices and at odds with his mother – who is weeks away from moving to Seattle because of her fear that he will carry out his promise to kill her – Gordon, in a downward spiral of insanity, makes good on the promise. His attorney will describe his plight as "the most tragic case of my career."

5 Wisely filmed for posterity, **U2**'s open-air gig at the Red Rocks Amphitheater in Colorado includes a rousing version of their increasingly popular anthem *Sunday, Bloody Sunday.* In driving rain and fog, with torches burning around the venue, **Bono** emotively belts out the number, marching back and forth waving a large white flag, and climbing up the sound system rigging. The group's rhythm section, on pounding form, is led by the song's striking guitar chords courtesy of **The Edge.** Some of today's concert will be added to recorded performances in Germany and Boston, for release in December as the EP, ***Under A Blood Red Sky***, and an equally popular video cassette under the same title: both will help elevate the group from cult college favorites to A-league rock stardom.

"The morning of the show, we were told the weather had turned bad and it was going to be canceled. People came anyway. So we literally performed in a cloud, which, in hindsight, made the event all the more visually spectacular." The Edge on U2's Red Rocks concert, June 5, 1983

17 With the band's signature hit *Blue Monday* in the middle of a 34-week chart run in the UK, **New Order** begin a US tour at Club 688 in Atlanta. Someone in the audience yells "Where's Ian?" – referring to **Joy Division**'s late frontman, **Ian Curtis**. (By 1987, the UK 12in-only *Blue Monday* classic will have sold over 600,000 copies, to become Britain's biggest-selling 12in single ever, with a global tally of over three million.)

19 England's three-day Glastonbury Festival closes. This year, as a result of new legislation, organizer Michael Eavis has had to obtain a Public Entertainments License from Mendip District Council, which set a crowd limit of 30,000, as well as stipulating adequate access roads, water supplies, and hygiene facilities. The festival – which sees the introduction of its own radio station, Radio Avalon – includes performances by **UB40** (who recently recorded their upcoming first UK chart-topper, a cover of **Neil Diamond**'s *Red Red Wine*), the **Fun Boy Three**, the (**English**) **Beat**, progessive British rockers **Marillion** (who are led by Scottish vocalist **Fish**), R&B legend **Curtis Mayfield**, and popular Nigerian juju guitarist **King Sunny Ade**. £45,000 ($67,500) is raised for the Campaign for Nuclear Disarmament and local charities.

25 For the first time ever, the US Hot 100 contains more foreign records than American ones. Although New Yorker **Irene Cara** heads the list, artists from England, Guyana, Brazil, and Australia occupy seven of the top 10 spots. Canada has one its healthiest showings, with **Bryan Adams**, **Loverboy**, **Paul Anka**, and **Sheriff** on the survey.

June 1983

Every Breath You Take... The Clash go their separate ways... KISS expose themselves...

30 After ten years of estrangement, the **Everly Brothers**' differences are finally settled, and they announce plans for a reunion concert in September. Phil is quoted as saying, "We settled it in a family kind of way – a big hug did it!"

July

1 New Jersey-based hard rock quintet **Bon Jovi** sign to Phonogram's Mercury label in New York. Lead singer, 21-year-old **Jon Bon Jovi**, and keyboardist **David Bryan** formed the band earlier this year, and recruited guitarist **Richie Sambora**, bassist **Alec John Such**, and drummer **Tico Torres**, assembling a solid line-up that will endure well into the next decade. Recording for the self-titled debut album will begin in the fall.

6 **Jean Michel Jarre**'s album ***Musique Pour Supermarché*** is auctioned at the Hôtel Drouot in Paris to an unknown bidder for $15,000. Made expressly by Jarre to voice his distaste and disregard for the music business, only one copy of the album is pressed, although Radio Luxembourg has played it on air. Jarre will destroy the master tapes.

9 **Wham!**'s self-penned, pop/dance-filled debut album, ***Fantastic***, co-produced by George Michael and Steve Brown, enters the UK chart at No. 1, while their fourth single, ***Club Tropicana***, hits UK No. 4. Michael, the main songwriting force, has assumed control of their musical direction, while Andrew Ridgeley concentrates on their visual style, image, and stage presentation.

9 *Every Breath You Take*, Sting's mid-tempo song about obsessive love, hits US No. 1 for the first of eight weeks. It has already topped the British survey for a month, its fortunes spurred by a stylish black and white video – conceived and directed by ex-**10cc** founders, **Kevin Godley** and **Lol Creme** – which is receiving heavy rotation on MTV. The track is taken from the **Police**'s legacy-defining final album, ***Synchronicity***, most of which **Sting** wrote at the former home of James Bond author Ian Fleming in Jamaica. Recorded in Montserrat, and at Le Studio in Quebec, under the direction of magic-touch producer Hugh Padgham, the album entered the UK chart at No. 1 two weeks ago. Two weeks from now it will begin a staggering 17-week ride at US No. 1, confirming guitarist **Andy Summers**'s understated conclusion that, "It's maybe the best album we've made." Sting – long the main creative force behind the group's success, notably in the area of composition – has based ***Synchronicity***'s lyrical direction on works by Arthur Koestler, and its title refers to psychologist Carl Jung's theory of meaningful coincidence.

12 Former **Traffic** flautist and saxophonist **Chris Wood** dies of pneumonia, age 39, at Birmingham's Queen Elizabeth Hospital, following a debilitating ten-year illness brought on by alcholism and drug addiction.

"It would be wrong to pretend we're doing something new becasue we're not. We're just very good at what we do. It's standard but it's still enjoyable."

George Michael, **Record Mirror**, August 20, 1983

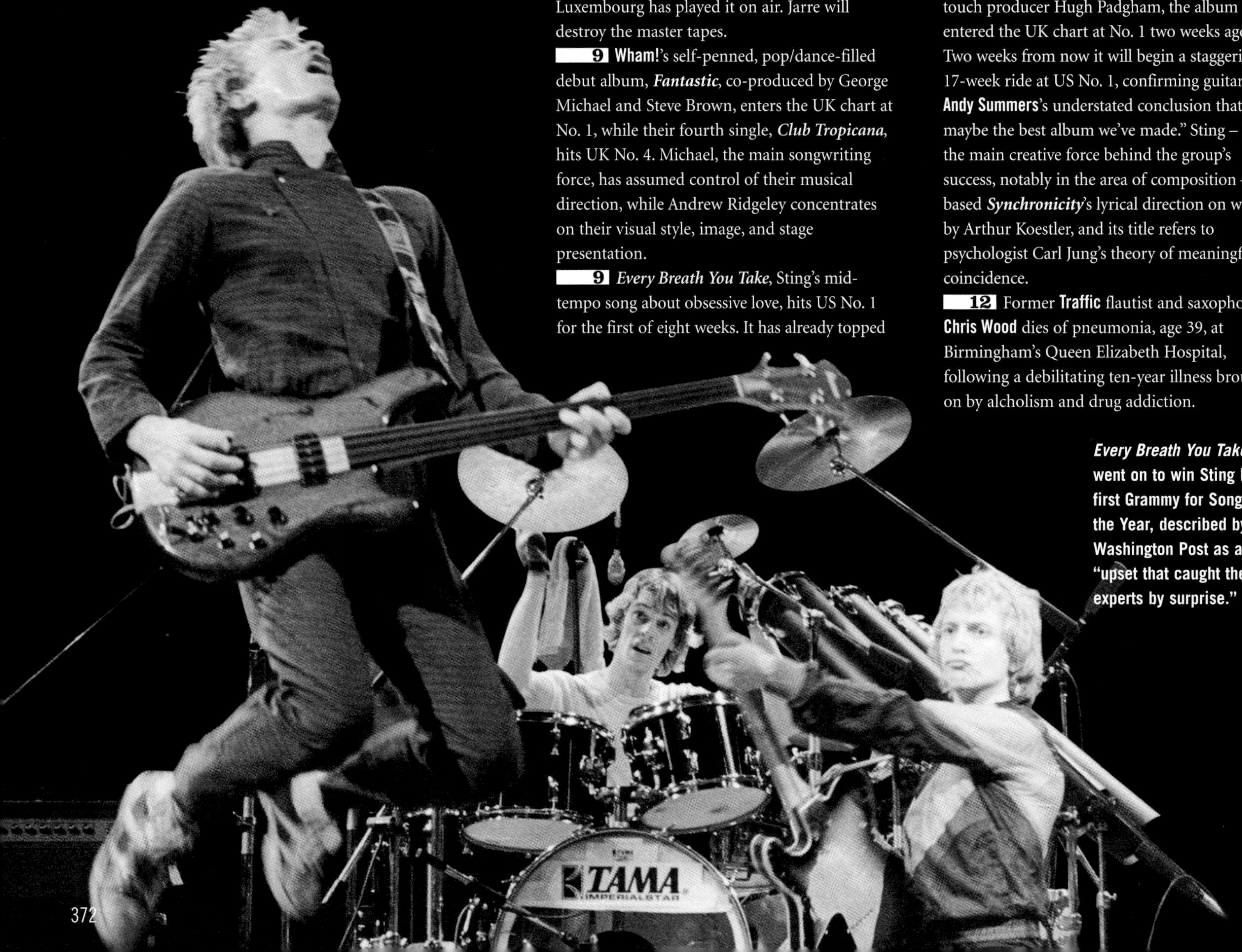

***Every Breath You Take* went on to win Sting his first Grammy for Song of the Year, described by the Washington Post as an "upset that caught the experts by surprise."**

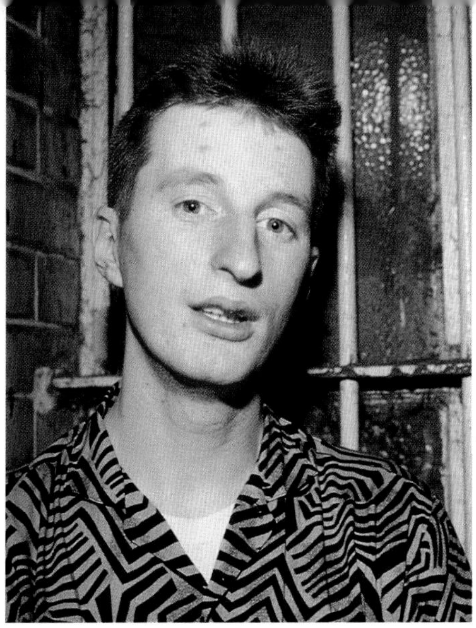

Billy Bragg saw the error of his ways when he bought himself out of the Army after serving 90 days with a tank division.

18 EMI opens Abbey Road Studios to the public, temporarily making it one of London's top tourist attractions.

19 **Simon & Garfunkel** embark on another US reunion tour, at the Rubber Bowl in Akron, Ohio. It will be a major success, and a new album, ***Think Too Much***, will be planned as a follow-up, though the duo will separate once more during its recording, with the revamped album subsequently appearing as Simon's solo effort, ***Hearts And Bones***.

27 **Billy Bragg** makes his UK radio debut on "The John Peel Show." The 25-year-old singer-songwriter from Barking, East London, is promoting his debut release, the two-track-recorded mini-album ***Life's A Riot With Spy Vs. Spy***, which he nailed in three afternoons of studio time, offered to him to record demos for the Chappell music publishing company. The short set showcases Bragg's abrasive Essex vocal style, extreme leftwing political views, and raw guitar technique. It is attracting positive reviews from the alternative UK music press, which will lead to his licensing the LP – originally issued by the Utility label – to Go! Discs, an innovative London indie label set up by Andy McDonald.

August

2 Legendary Motown bassist **James Jamerson** dies in Los Angeles. A native of Charleston, Jamerson moved to Detroit in his teens, and began playing bass in high school. In 1958, he started doing sessions for a number of small Detroit labels, including Anna Gordy's Anna Records. Showing up at 2648 West Grand Boulevard, where the fledgling Motown label was based, Jamerson took over from a player who was having trouble laying down a bass line, and effortlessly played the part. Berry Gordy hired him to go on the road with the Motown package tours. In 1964, he became Motown's resident studio bassist, playing on virtually all its classic hits, many of them in tandem with drummer **Benny Benjamin**. A serious problem with alcohol led him to be hospitalized in the late 1970s, and his condition deteriorated until his death from cirrhosis and heart failure at 45.

3 With his fifth album, ***1999***, having taken six months to peak at US No. 9 (spurred by the crossover hits *Little Red Corvette* and *1999*, the party anthem for the impending end of the millennium), **Prince & the Revolution** premiere six tracks from their forthcoming project, ***Purple Rain***, at a benefit concert at the First Avenue club in Minneapolis. Guitarist **Wendy Melvoin** is playing her first gig with the Revolution.

5 After sleeping through most of the trial, **David Crosby** is convicted in a Dallas court on charges of possessing cocaine and carrying a gun into a bar. He is sentenced by Judge Pat McDowell to five years in the Texas State Penitentiary for cocaine possession and three years for possession of illegal firearms. He will remain free while the sentence is appealed.

14 **U2** headlines the Irish open-air rock festival, A Day at the Races, before a crowd of 20,000 people at Dublin's Phoenix Park. **Bono** dedicates a song to **Red Rockers**' drummer **Jim Reilly**, whose brother Tom was fatally shot by a British soldier in Belfast last week. **Simple Minds**, **Eurythmics**, British reggae combo **Steel Pulse**, and local act **Perfect Crime** also perform – as do **Big Country**, a hot new British rock quartet led by ex-**Skids** guitarist/singer **Stuart Adamson**. They are breaking though with two hits, the anthemic *Fields Of Fire (400 Miles)* and the self-proclaiming *In A Big Country*, both featured on ***The Crossing***, their newly-released debut album produced by Steve Lillywhite.

19 On assignment to interview Sting for British pop magazine **Smash Hits** in New York, 29-year-old journalist and would-be pop star **Neil Tennant** meets his long-time hero, high-energy dance producer Bobby "O" Orlando. Over a cheeseburger and carrot cake at the Applejack restaurant, Orlando offers to produce Tennant's new project, the **Pet Shop Boys** – a work-in-progress duo he formed after meeting keyboardist **Chris Lowe** two years ago today.

21 **Joey Ramone** – the **Ramones**' lead singer – undergoes emergency surgery to remove blood clots from his brain, after a fight outside his East 10th Street apartment with **Seth Micklaw**, a member of punk band **Sub Zero Construction**. Violence flared when Ramone saw his girlfriend, Cynthia "Roxy" Whitney, with Micklaw, and a brief fist fight led to Micklaw knocking Ramone down and kicking him with his steel toe-capped boots.

24 Shawn Michelle Stevens, the 25-year-old fifth wife of **Jerry Lee Lewis** (they married on June 7), is found dead at the singer's Mississippi home. An autopsy will confirm the cause of death to be a methadone overdose, with a grand jury finding no reason to suspect foul play. A subsequent **Rolling Stone** article by Pulitzer Prize winner Richard Ben Cramer will point to disturbing circumstantial evidence surrounding her death: broken glass on the floor, a sack of bloodstained clothes in the room where she died, and blood and bruises on her body. Her mother claimed Shawn had called her the day before her death and said she was going to leave Lewis following a series of physical fights. "The Killer" survives the scandal.

25 **Mick Jagger** and **Keith Richard** reach agreement with Columbia Records head Walter Yetnikoff to sign with the label, at 3:00 am in the Ritz Hotel in Paris. Reportedly worth $28 million, the deal calls for four **Stones** albums.

27 A Stateside-only release, **Culture Club**'s *I'll Tumble 4 Ya* hits US No. 9. *Do You Really Want To Hurt Me* got to US No. 2 in March, the same position reached by *Time (Clock Of The Heart)* in June.

With drummer Benny Benjamin, James Jamerson was responsible for the rhythm sound of countless Tamla Motown classics throughout the 1960s.

Sept

1983

Now That's What I Call Music!... Beach Boy Dennis Wilson drowns...

September

10 A CBS Records "**Clash** Communiqué" reads: "**Joe Strummer** and **Paul Simonon** have decided that **Mick Jones** should leave the group. It is felt that Jones has drifted apart from the original idea of the Clash." Jones will re-emerge with his hitmaking band **Big Audio Dynamite**.

15 Reggae artist **Prince Far I** is shot dead at home in Marie Avenue, St. Catherine's, Jamaica. He and his family are entertaining visitors when, around 9:30 pm, two gunmen enter and order everyone to lie on the floor, before opening fire, killing Far I and injuring his wife Carol. The murder will remain unsolved. Working with Coxsone Dodd and Joe Gibbs, Far I was one of the finest interpretators of "dub" music, most evident on his debut album ***Psalms For I***.

18 **KISS**, appearing on MTV to promote their new album ***Lick It Up***, "expose" themselves, going make-up-free for the first time. (Last month, they had to cancel a three-day tour of Argentina when the extremist Free Fatherland Nationalist Commando movement threatened to stop the tour, even if it had to go "so far as to cost the very lives of that unfortunate band.")

20 A benefit concert is held at London's Royal Albert Hall, in aid of ARMS (Action for Research into Multiple Sclerosis), for former **Face Ronnie Lane**, who was admitted to a Florida hospital in March last year for treatment for the condition (with the **Rolling Stones** reportedly helping with his medical bills). The superstar line-up includes **Eric Clapton**, **Jeff Beck**, **Steve Winwood**, **Jimmy Page**, **Paul Rodgers**, and Lane himself. The house band for the night comprises Winwood, **Andy Fairweather-Low** (guitar and vocals), **Chris Stainton** (piano), **Bill Wyman** (bass), **Charlie Watts** and **Kenney Jones** (drums), and **Ray Cooper** (percussion).

24 **Culture Club**'s latest catchy pop smash, the band-penned *Karma Chameleon*, tops the UK chart at the start of a six-week run and million-plus selling sales (the only BPI-certified platinum single of the year), supported by a striking video filmed on a Mississippi steamboat. The group's fourth top three UK hit in 12 months, it is taken from their new album, ***Colour By Numbers*** – once again produced by Steve Levine – which will also head the UK chart for the first of three weeks on October 22 (returning to the top spot for a further two weeks on November 19). With **Boy George** currently the world's biggest and most camp media darling, the album will achieve multiplatinum status in Australia, Canada, Japan, New Zealand, and the US. The singalong cuteness of *Karma Chameleon* will also result in the band's first US No. 1 next February.

24 **ZZ Top**'s seventh album, ***Eliminator***, is certified platinum by the RIAA. Although they have forged an increasingly successful live and album chart career since their 1970 debut, it is with this record that the Texas-based boogie-rock trio – singer/guitarist **Billy Gibbons**, bassist **Dusty Hill**, and drummer **Frank Beard** – will finally score a string of worldwide crossover hits. ***Eliminator*** will hit US No. 9 during a 183-week chart tenure, and UK No. 3 during a 135-week stay. The real Eliminator is a 1933 Ford three-window coupé, much featured in the album's popular promo video clips for *Gimme All Your Lovin'*, *Sharp Dressed Man*, and *Legs*. The mini-films are additionally highlighted by common ZZ Top images, including stocking-clad babes, heroic storylines, and the striking ZZ Top car and keyring – not to mention the distinctive long beards worn by both Gibbons and Hill, who stopped shaving in 1979.

October

15 ***Genesis***, co-produced with Hugh Padgham, tops the UK chart. Recorded at the Farm in Surrey, England, it is an entirely self-contained effort and marks the group's transition from its grand, theatrical, progressive-rock stance of the 1970s to an even more popular, relaxed, stripped-down, melody-based, contemporary rock style, not entirely dissimilar to **Phil Collins**'s increasingly successful solo work.

24 The sexually explicit *Relax* by **Frankie Goes to Hollywood**, fronted by lead singer **Holly Johnson**, is released in the UK as the second single on the Zang Tumb Tumm label, produced by company co-owner Trevor Horn. The B-side is a cover of fellow Merseysiders **Gerry & the Pacemakers**' *Ferry Cross The Mersey*. The thumping dance/pop anthem – first aired on last year's "The Tube" – will be promoted with "Relax" and "Frankie Says..." T-shirts: an idea dreamed up by journalist and Zang Tumb Tumm executive Paul Morley. The risqué promotion video will be banned by British television, requiring the substitution of a tamer version.

29 **Pink Floyd**'s ***The Dark Side Of The Moon*** racks up its 491st week aboard the US album chart, breaking **Johnny Mathis**'s record of 490 weeks with ***Johnny's Greatest Hits***, held since 1968.

> **"We're R.E.M. Actually we're not. They couldn't make it so we're here in their place, playing all the hits of the day."**
>
> R.E.M.'s Michael Stipe at the Marquee, November 22, 1983

For their Worldwide Texas tour in the mid-1970s, ZZ Top transported buffalo, steers, and snakes (among $140,000 worth of Texas livestock), as well as a stage in the shape of Texas.

MADONNA

Sept 24 Madonna performs *Holiday, Physical Attraction, Everybody,* and *Burning Up* at Uncle Sam's Club in Levittown, New York. The 25-year-old singer-songwriter/dancer from Bay City, Michigan, has a varied resumé to date. She performed in the Patrick Hernandez Revue in Paris in 1979, before singing in her first band, the Breakfast Club, later that year. Landing a part in Stephen Jon Lewicki's low-budget 60-minute movie thriller, "A Certain Sacrifice," in 1980, she then signed to rock manager Adam Atler's Gotham Productions, taking a series of odd jobs to pay her way, including part-time nude modeling for photographers and art students. She cut demos at home and in recording studios around New York, and her break came at the Danceteria club last year, when she gave DJ/producer Mark Kamins a tape of the dance material she had been recording with a friend, Steve Bray. Kamins introduced her to Sire Records' executive Michael Rosenblatt and label head Seymour Stein, who signed her up. Her first single, *Everybody,* was released in the US last October, while her pop/dance mix *Holiday* is currently at No. 1 on the US Hot Dance Music/Club Play chart, and is set to become her first Hot 100 chart entry next month. Her maiden set, *Madonna,* produced by Reggie Lucas, entered the US chart three weeks ago. With several tracks becoming huge club hits, it will eventually hit No. 8 during a 168-week residence.

November

22 Having made their first ever television appearance on "The Tube" on Friday, **R.E.M.** play their second gig in London at the Marquee.

23 Eight years after **Pete Ham** hanged himself, his co-writer and fellow **Badfinger** member, **Tom Evans**, commits suicide in the same manner at his Surrey home. Evans has been fighting a continuing battle to receive a fair royalty deal for his songs, especially for the multimillion-selling *Without You.* He is 36.

26 *Thriller*, the title track to **Michael Jackson**'s new album, hits UK No. 10, six months ahead of its US release. Written by **Rod Temperton**, it features a ghostly rap from horror-movie veteran Vincent Price (though he does not appear in the Jon Landis-directed mini-epic video, the peak of Jackson's video triumphs).

30 A press conference is called by boxing promoter Don King at the Tavern on the Green in New York City, to announce an 18-city, 40-date US tour by the **Jacksons** (six-strong, with **Jermaine** rejoining his brothers after leaving Motown), commencing next summer.

December

16 The **Who**'s Pete Townshend issues a statement: "I will not be making any more records with the Who... I will not perform live again anywhere in the world with the Who." **Roger Daltrey** says the announcement is a "wonderful Christmas present."

17 In the second of 50 weeks on the survey, ***Now That's What I Call Music!*** tops the UK chart. A co-operative venture by EMI and Virgin Records, it is a collection of recent hit singles by different artists on different labels, and begins a phenomenally successful series of compilations. ***Now That's What I Call Music! 2*** will arrive next spring, with subsequent volumes being issued at the average rate of two per year. Generic "***Now***" collections such as ***Now – The Christmas Album*** and ***Now – The Summer Album*** will also find retail appeal, prompting CBS and WEA to launch their own "***Hits***" series. By the end of the 1980s all the major companies will combine in either the "***Now***" or "***Hits***" camps, though despite their sales success in Britain, the US market will wait until 1998 to follow suit.

23 While **Frankie Goes to Hollywood**'s *Relax* languishes near the bottom of the UK chart, the band is featured on the Christmas edition of "The Tube." Their appearance will move the record into the Top 40, resulting in a "Top Of The Pops" showing.

28 **Beach Boys** drummer **Dennis Wilson**'s body is pulled from 13ft of murky water in Marina del Rey, California. A few days ago, 39-year-old Wilson checked into the detox unit at Santa Monica's St. John's Hospital, but left on Christmas Day. He then checked into the Daniel Freeman Marina Hospital two days ago, before leaving yesterday. Today, after a bout of heavy drinking starting at 9:00 am, Wilson has been diving off Bill Oster's yacht, *Emerald,* dressed only in cut-off jeans, collecting mementoes. At about 4:15 pm, he comes up for the last time, and his body is found just over an hour later. Special dispensation will be granted, with the help of President Reagan – who sends his condolences to the Wilson family – for a burial at sea (normally reserved for naval personnel) for the only genuine surfer in the Beach Boys.

ROOTS During this year: Adelphi University students Chuck D and Hank Shocklee spin a three-hour "Super Special Mix Show" for the college's WBAU radio station, at the invitation of program director Bill Stephney. This will lead to their recording their own basement tapes and forming Public Enemy... hi-fi manufacturer Linn invites Scottish band Blue Nile to record material to test the company's record-cutting technology; impressed with what they hear, they will form their own Linn Records offshoot specifically for the group... Liverpool band the Excitements changes its name to the Farm... Harlem singer Freddie Jackson moves to Los Angeles and joins R&B outfit Mystic Merlin... Canadian songstress k.d. lang releases her debut album, *A Truly Western Experience*, in her native country... formed three years ago by Ian Brown and John Squire, who grew up two doors apart in Sale, Lancashire, England, Patrol changes its name to English Rose... Henry Rollins, already a member of the successful Black Flag group, begins touring as a spoken-word artist...

Dec 2 MTV airs the seminal, full-length, 14-minute "Thriller" video for the first time. Jackson's disclaimer at the beginning of the film, "Due to my strong personal convictions, I wish to stress that this film in no way endorses a belief in the occult," has been added after church elders of the Encino Kingdom Hall threatened him with expulsion because of its subject matter.

Thriller **was certified gold and platinum on January 31, 1983. On October 30, 1984, it received its next certification – for 20 million sales. Throughout the 1990s it continued selling, reaching 26 million in 2000. It remains the second biggest-selling album of all time in the US, behind the Eagles' *Their Greatest Hits 1971–1975* at 28 million.**

Do They Know It's Christmas?

1984

No.1 US SINGLES

- **Jan 7** Say Say Say **Paul McCartney & Michael Jackson**
- **Jan 21** Owner Of A Lonely Heart **Yes**
- **Feb 4** Karma Chameleon **Culture Club**
- **Feb 25** Jump **Van Halen**
- **Mar 31** Footloose **Kenny Loggins**
- **Apr 21** Against All Odds (Take A Look At Me Now) **Phil Collins**
- **May 12** Hello **Lionel Richie**
- **May 26** Let's Hear It For The Boy **Deniece Williams**
- **June 9** Time After Time **Cyndi Lauper**
- **June 23** The Reflex **Duran Duran**
- **July 7** When Doves Cry **Prince**
- **Aug 11** Ghostbusters **Ray Parker Jr.**
- **Sept 1** What's Love Got To Do With It **Tina Turner**
- **Sept 22** Missing You **John Waite**
- **Sept 29** Let's Go Crazy **Prince & the Revolution**
- **Oct 13** I Just Called To Say I Love You **Stevie Wonder**
- **Nov 3** Caribbean Queen (No More Love On The Run) **Billy Ocean**
- **Nov 17** Wake Me Up Before You Go-Go **Wham!**
- **Dec 8** Out Of Touch **Daryl Hall & John Oates**
- **Dec 22** Like A Virgin **Madonna**

No.1 UK SINGLES

- **Jan 7** Only You **Flying Pickets**
- **Jan 14** Pipes Of Peace **Paul McCartney**
- **Jan 28** Relax **Frankie Goes to Hollywood**
- **Mar 3** 99 Red Balloons **Nena**
- **Mar 24** Hello **Lionel Richie**
- **May 5** The Reflex **Duran Duran**
- **June 2** Wake Me Up Before You Go-Go **Wham!**
- **June 16** Two Tribes **Frankie Goes to Hollywood**
- **Aug 18** Careless Whisper **George Michael**
- **Sept 8** I Just Called To Say I Love You **Stevie Wonder**
- **Oct 20** Freedom **Wham!**
- **Nov 10** I Feel For You **Chaka Khan**
- **Dec 1** I Should Have Known Better **Jim Diamond**
- **Dec 8** The Power Of Love **Frankie Goes To Hollywood**
- **Dec 15** Do They Know It's Christmas? **Band Aid**

R.E.M.

Bruce Springsteen

During their 1984 tour, R.E.M. were joined onstage by Roger McGuinn in a performance of *So You Want To Be A Rock 'n' Roll Star*... Bruce Springsteen had tallied just four gold and two platinum discs in almost a decade of recording. By the end of 1984, *Born In The USA* had sold three million copies.

While music and a message have always been a natural union, not since George Harrison's Bangla Desh bash had one musician's concern for human suffering spurred such a collective effort as when **Bob Geldof** began his "Band Aid" crusade. Suffering at an individual level – **Marvin Gaye**'s alienation and paranoia – put a premature end to one of R&B's greatest talents. Meanwhile, the year's most significant comeback belonged to **Tina Turner**.

Hook-filled pop still dominated the airwaves, joined by the raunchy **Madonna** and the mischievous postpunk of **Cyndi Lauper**. At his creative zenith, **Prince** followed up the range of *1999* with the hot-selling ***Purple Rain***. Poppy electro-funk, streaked through with exuberance and supplicant vocals, it yielded one classic track after another. In a very different category, but with a similar impact, **U2**'s ***The Unforgettable Fire*** brought the band together with producers **Brian Eno** and **Daniel Lanois**, who helped them show off their range.

Years of playing student gigs and pizza parlors had turned **R.E.M.** into a tight outfit, with the edgy and enigmatic lyrics of **Michael Stipe** complementing **Peter Buck**'s jangly guitar and **Mike Mills**'s bass lines. Theirs was a unique variant of postpunk rock (they had covered the **Sex Pistols** in early gigs), mercifully free of synthesizers and relying on pure musicianship. They produced their best album to date with *Reckoning*, which broke into the Top 30, and were rapidly becoming a cult item on campuses in both the US and Europe.

Bruce Springsteen returned with more blue-collar rock on ***Born In The USA***. The album would go multiplatinum and usher in his most successful attack on the singles charts. The lyrics might at times be equally suited to a blues set, dreaming of escape from hard times and small towns, and there was real depth in songs like *My Hometown*, but Springsteen could also combine poignant sentiments with a rollicking rock tempo better suited to cruising down the freeway.

Marching to an entirely different beat, hip-hop continued its ascent, helped by the formation of Def Jam Records by **Russell Simmons** and **Rick Rubin**, operating out of a New York City bedroom. The label would go on to sign the **Beastie Boys** and become the genre's marque.

It was a good year for causes. The antinuclear movement was at its most vocal, and was a financial beneficiary of festivals such as England's Glastonbury. In November, **Bob Geldof** turned on the TV and saw a harrowing report about famine in Ethiopia. He started dialing other musicians, and "**Band Aid**" was born. Weeks later, the cream of British pop were all at No. 1 with the benefit single *Do They Know It's Christmas?* – the least Orwellian moment of 1984 (next to **Wham!**'s *Wake Me Up Before You Go-Go*.)

"What you've heard about me is true. I change the rules to do what *I* wanna do."

Tina Turner, **Rolling Stone**, October 11, 1984

Jan 1984

The BBC bans *Relax*... Jackson at the Grammys... Marvin Gaye is shot...

Michael Jackson

Dressed as if he had stepped off the sleeve of *Sgt. Pepper's Lonely Hearts Club Band*, the Gloved One dominated the 26th Grammys, winning eight awards... Huey Lewis's *Sports* sold five million copies in the US alone in just over a year... Cyndi Lauper had four consecutive US top five hits.

January

1 Influential bluesman **Alexis Korner** dies in London. A perpetual smoker, he has succumbed to cancer at 55. Born in Paris, France, Korner was a father figure in the British R&B movement of the early 1960s. With **Cyril Davies**, he converted the London Skiffle Club into the London Blues and Barrelhouse Club, where they introduced many US bluesmen to British audiences. They formed the seminal **Blues Incorporated** in 1961, and soon established the Ealing Rhythm and Blues Club in the basement of a movie theater, with Blues Incorporated in residency. A generation of aspiring musicians passed through the band, including **Charlie Watts**, **Jack Bruce**, **Graham Bond**, **Ginger Baker**, **Art Wood**, **Mick Jagger**, **Paul Jones**, and **Long John Baldry**. A decade later, Korner had his only commercial success with **CCS**, a pop-based big band that scored hits with *Whole Lotta Love* – which became the theme of "Top Of The Pops" – *Walkin'*, and *Tap Turns On The Water.* He pursued a second career with his own distinctive show on BBC Radio 1.

13 Radio 1 bans **Frankie Goes To Hollywood**'s *Relax*, following a one-man campaign by DJ Mike Read, who calls it "overtly obscene," despite having played it several times. A ban by BBC-TV follows. By the end of the month the record will top the UK chart for the first of five weeks.

21 **Jackie Wilson** dies in Mount Holley, New Jersey, age 49, having been in permanent care since his heart attack in 1975. His funeral will be held at Chrysler Drive Baptist Church in Detroit, Michigan, where he once sang gospel music. The **Four Tops**, the **Spinners**, and **Berry Gordy, Jr.**, all pay their respects to the R&B legend.

27 **Michael Jackson** is hospitalized at the Cedars-Sinai Medical Center, Los Angeles, with "second-degree burns on his skull," following an accident on the set of a Pepsi commercial shoot directed by Bob Giraldi. A spark ignites Jackson's hair on the sixth take (Marlon Brando's son Miko, working as a bodyguard for the **Jacksons**, is the first to douse the flames). The singed star will receive a letter from President Reagan, written February 1, reading, "I was pleased to learn that you were not seriously hurt in your recent accident. I know from experience that these things can happen on the set, no matter how much caution is exercised." Pepsi will pay compensation of $1.5 million, which Jackson will donate to the Brotman Memorial Hospital in Culver City, where he is treated. The Michael Jackson Burns Center will open, but close in October 1987 due to financial difficulties.

28 With South African guitarist **Trevor Rabin** new to the line-up, **Yes** make a surprise comeback, spending a second week at US No. 1 with *Owner Of A Lonely Heart*, written by the group but benefiting from the high-gloss production style of producer and ex-Yes man **Trevor Horn**. With *Relax*, also his production, at UK No. 1, Horn is having a spectacular week. The 34-year-old studio whizz/keyboardist, born in Durham, England, worked his way up from playing in disco singer **Tina Charles**'s backing band, forming the **Camera Club** with **Thomas Dolby** in 1978, and **Buggles** in 1979. Having produced hits for UK pop duo **Dollar**, **Malcolm McLaren**, and the debut album for **ABC**, last year Horn co-founded ZTT Records, to which **Frankie Goes To Hollywood** is signed.

Producer Trevor Horn would have to wait another 11 years before his second chart-topper – Seal's *Kiss From A Rose* – in 1995.

February

7 **Michael Jackson** is inducted into **The Guinness Book of Records** at the American Museum of Natural History in New York, as global sales of ***Thriller*** shoot past 25 million.

21 **Culture Club** are named Best British Group, and *Karma Chameleon* Best British Single, at the third BPI awards at London's Grosvenor House Hotel. **David Bowie** and **Annie Lennox** (who is finding huge success as one half of **Eurythmics**) win the trophies for Best British Male Solo Artist and Best British Female Solo Artist. **Paul Young** is Best British Newcomer, and **Michael Jackson**'s ***Thriller*** is Best Album. Producer **George Martin** receives the award for Outstanding Contribution to British Music.

28 At the 26th Grammys, **Michael Jackson**'s masterpiece, ***Thriller***, wins eight awards, including Album of the Year and Best Engineered Recording (Non-Classical) for Bruce Swedien, while the extracted *Beat It* is named Record of the Year, and wins Jackson Best Rock Vocal Performance, Male. *Billie Jean* is named Best New Rhythm & Blues Song, and wins him Best R&B Vocal Performance, Male, while *Thriller* is named Best Pop Vocal Performance, Male. Jackson and **Quincy Jones** are both hailed Producer of the Year. In the shadow of this dominance, **Sting**'s *Every Breath You Take* takes the prize for Song of the Year, while the Best Pop Performance by a Duo or Group with Vocal goes to the **Police**. The trio's ***Synchronicity*** is named Best Rock Performance by a Duo or Group with Vocal, and Sting's solo *Brimstone And Treacle* wins Best Rock Instrumental Performance.

29 **Huey Lewis & the News**' ***Sports*** is certified platinum by the RIAA. Studiously avoiding music trends, 33-year-old New Yorker and ex-**Clover** singer/harmonica player Lewis is gradually building a fervent following with his self-penned brand of hip-to-be-square melodic pop-rock. Among many avid listeners to his current fast-rising ***Sports*** extract, *I Want A New Drug*, is **Ray Parker, Jr.** (who will hear from Lewis's attorneys later in the year). The chart-topping ***Sports*** will yield several other signature hits, including *The Heart Of Rock 'n' Roll* and *If This Is It*, and will eventually sell more than seven million copies in the US alone.

March

1 **Frankie Goes To Hollywood**'s *Relax* is certified platinum by the BPI. Its success has been spurred by the broadcast ban and a myriad of release formats, including seven remixes of the single on 7in, 12in, picture disc, and "cassingle." With eventual global sales topping 12 million, the song's 48-consecutive-week UK chart run will be the longest since **Engelbert Humperdinck**'s *Release Me* in 1967–68.

Huey Lewis & the News

Cyndi Lauper

1 With her debut chart single, *Girls Just Want To Have Fun*, at US No. 3, one week away from its No. 2 peak, **Cyndi Lauper** makes her US network television bow on "The Tonight Show With Johnny Carson." The 30-year-old New Yorker began her music career in 1974, when she joined Long Island band **Doc West** as lead singer. She lost her voice in 1977 – and was told that she wouldn't sing again – but recovered and emerged in 1978 as lead singer with **Blue Angel**, who cut a self-titled album in 1980. Managed since 1981 by her beau David Wolff, Lauper was declared bankrupt last March, but her fortunes have improved since signing to Columbia imprint, Portrait Records, for whom she cut her maiden solo effort, ***She's So Unusual***, paired with songwriters **Eric Bazilian** and **Rob Hyman** of Philadelphia band the **Hooters**. With a colorful postpunk image, and a quirky high-pitched vocal style, Lauper's mix of uptempo nuggets and pop ballad gems will make ***She's So Unusual*** the first female debut album in rock history to yield four consecutive US top five hits: *Girls Just Want To Have Fun*, *Time After Time*, *She Bop*, and *All Through The Night*.

3 ***Thriller*** becomes the first album to spin off seven US Top 10 hits, with its title track finally peaking at US No. 4. (**Michael Jackson** has actually scored eight Top 10 smashes during his thrilling reign: *Say Say Say* – his second success with **Paul McCartney** – topped the US survey last November, but was included only on Macca's ***Pipes Of Peace*** album.)

17 Despite the BPI imposing a £6,000 ($7,200) fine on Warner Bros. Records in Britain for hyping the single, **Van Halen**'s *Jump* hits UK No. 7. It is having more legitimate success in the US, where it is in its fourth week at No. 1, set to become their signature smash. Lead singer **David Lee Roth** wrote the lyrics to **Eddie Van Halen**'s original guitar track while cruising in the back of a 1951 Mercury Lowrider.

22 In an unlikely pairing of guests, **Bob Dylan** and **Liberace** appear on "Late Night With David Letterman." Dylan plays three songs, backed by young rock band the **Plugz**.

April

19 The 29th Ivor Novello awards distinguish themselves once again as perhaps the most credible. **Sting** nabs the Best Song Musically and Lyrically and Most Performed Work trophies for writing the **Police** career highlight, *Every Breath You Take*, and **David Bowie**'s *Let's Dance* is named International Hit of the Year. **Annie Lennox** and **Dave Stewart** are named Songwriters of the Year, and **Mark Knopfler**'s plaintive instrumental, *Going Home*, wins Best Film Theme or Song.

21 During a big year for film soundtrack sales, ***Footloose*** – featuring songs cut for the smash movie starring Kevin Bacon and Lori Singer – begins a ten-week dance topping the US album chart. As well as two Hot 100 chart-toppers (the title track by **Kenny Loggins**, and *Let's Hear It For The Boy* by 32-year-old R&B singer **Deniece Williams**) the album includes the US No. 7 hit ballad *Almost Paradise* – a duet by Loverboy lead singer **Mike Reno** and Heart's **Ann Wilson** – and *Dancing In The Sheets* by **Shalamar** (No. 17).

27 Philadelphia radio station WWSH begins a "No **Michael Jackson**" weekend in protest to his airwave saturation of the past year.

"The Sun Say Frankie Stink! They throw popcorn at me. They insult Gene Kelly. They swear on the radio." Martin Dunn, **The Sun**, January 13, 1984

May

19 Midway through his current European Express Tour, **Elton John** flies from Copenhagen, Denmark, to see his beloved Watford Football Club play in their first FA Cup final at London's Wembley. They lose to Everton, 2–0.

28 ***Legend***, the retrospective collection by **Bob Marley & the Wailers**, is certified double-platinum by the BPI. More popular (in terms of record sales) dead than alive, Marley's legacy will continue to grow, as ***Legend*** becomes one of the most enduring catalog items of the next 15 years. Although he scored only one US Hot 100 placing while fronting the Wailers (*Roots, Rock, Reggae* peaked at No. 56), the anthology album will spend more than two years on the US chart, eventually racking up more than ten million US sales.

MARVIN GAYE

Apr 1 **Following an argument last night "over some insurance dealings," a shoving match breaks out at the home of Marvin (senior) and Alberta Gay at 2101 South Grammercy in Los Angeles, where their son Marvin Gaye has been staying. Gay fetches a .38-caliber handgun, enters Gaye's bedroom, and fires two shots into his son's chest, in full view of Alberta. He walks downstairs and throws the gun on to the front lawn before sitting down to wait for the authorities to arrive. Alberta runs next door to the home of her son Frank, who calls the police. Gaye – who would have been 45 tomorrow – is pronounced dead at 1:01 pm at the California Hospital Medical Center. He had become an increasingly erratic and paranoid figure, addicted to cocaine, in debt to the I.R.S., and a virtual recluse at his parents' home, where he had spent the past few days dressed only in a maroon bathrobe with a gun in the pocket, convinced that his life was in danger from assassins.**

Smokey Robinson read the 23rd Psalm and Stevie Wonder sang *Lighting Up The Candle* at Gaye's funeral.

June 1984

Born In The USA... Tina Turner's comeback... The first MTV Awards...

Frankie Goes To Hollywood

The Jacksons

June

9 Having moved into a Fulham studio apartment, the **Jesus & Mary Chain** play at Alan McGee's Living Room club, above the Roebuck pub in London's Tottenham Court Road. Singer/guitarist **William Reid** and his younger brother **Jim** formed the band last year with bassist **Douglas Hart**, after writing and recording songs at home on a Portastudio (bought by their father with his severance pay), and sending out their demos as the **Poppy Seeds**. They recently moved from Scotland to London, where they met McGee, owner of the independent Creation label, who signed them and became their manager.

16 Following a bitter and permanent split from his former bandmates in **Pink Floyd**, **Roger Waters** embarks on a solo world tour, The Pros and Cons of Hitch Hiking, at the Isstadion in Stockholm, Sweden. With sets designed by Gerald Scarfe, visuals by film director Nicholas Roeg, and a large backing band that includes **Eric Clapton**, **Chris Stainton**, **Andy Newmark**, **Michael Kamen**, and **Tim Renwick**, Waters plays one set of self-penned Pink Floyd standards, and a second half of solo material. The tour will visit seven countries, playing 19 dates. Without the Pink Floyd brand name, however, ***The Pros And Cons Of Hitch Hiking*** album has already stalled at UK No. 13 and US No. 31.

16 With BBC Radio 1 given the airplay premiere of the single, and accompanied by much media ballyhoo, the Trevor Horn-produced **Frankie Goes To Hollywood** follow-up, *Two Tribes*, enters the UK chart at No. 1. It will go silver in two days and gold in seven, the first such achievement for a group's second release. The record's intro includes an impersonation of Ronald Reagan by British mimic Chris Barrie, and its accompanying video, directed by **Godley & Creme**, features Reagan and Konstantin Chernenko look-alikes, wrestling. The single will stay at No. 1 for nine weeks and sell over one million copies in the UK. *Relax* will also return to the chart, eventually re-hitting UK No. 2, held off the top by *Two Tribes*.

22 England's three-day Glastonbury Festival kicks off at Michael Eavis's farm in Pilton, with **Joan Baez**, **Billy Bragg**, **Dr. John**, and **Ian Dury** among today's acts. In January, Eavis successfully defended five prosecutions brought against him by Mendip District Council, alleging contravention of last year's license conditions.

24 The Glastonbury Festival, which has been attended by 35,000 people, closes with performances by folkies **John Martyn**, **Fairport Convention**, and **Christy Moore**. £60,000 ($72,000) is raised for CND and other charities. Yesterday's acts included **Elvis Costello**, the **Smiths**, Irish singer-songwriter **Paul Brady**, and the **Waterboys**, a new Celtic-tinged rock band formed by Scottish singer-songwriter/guitarist **Mike Scott** (whose line-up includes keyboardist **Karl Wallinger**, who will move on next year to form **World Party**).

29 **Bruce Springsteen**'s Born in the USA tour debuts at the Civic Center in St. Paul, Minnesota. **Nils Lofgren** has replaced **Stevie Van Zandt** on guitar in the **E Street Band**, whose lineup also features his first female backing singer, **Patti Scialfa**. It is Springsteen's first live work since the River tour and will take in Europe, Australia, North America, and Japan. Last night he filmed the video for *Dancing In The Dark* at the same venue, with young actress Courteney Cox plucked out of the audience to dance with the Boss. Previously shy of the promotional tool, it is his first official video, and has been directed by Brian De Palma. Both the video and the tour are promoting his first album in two years, ***Born In The USA***, which was released two weeks ago and will become his most successful multiplatinum album, establishing him as one of the dominant forces in 1980s rock music. It will begin a seven-week tenure at US No. 1 next week, during a 139-week album chart stay, and spawn seven Top 10 hits (equaling the record recently set by **Michael Jackson**). Springsteen's ability to match blue collar themes and songs of romance with radio-ready melodies, coupled with his hard-working, blistering live performances, are finally validating the hype that accompanied his earlier work.

> **"The President was mentioning my name the other day and I kinda got to wondering what his favorite album must have been. I don't think it was the *Nebraska* album."**
>
> Bruce Springsteen, September 19, 1984

Sade took their name from their cool, stylish lead singer and songwriter, 25-year-old Helen Folasade Adu, born in Ibadan, Nigeria.

July

5 At a press conference on the eve of the **Jacksons**' Victory tour, **Michael Jackson** refutes claims of greed (with regard to the exorbitant ticket prices), and announces that his entire earnings for the tour will go to three charities: the Michael Jackson Scholarship Fund, established by the United Negro College Fund, Camp Good Times for terminally ill children, and the T.J. Martell Foundation for Leukemia and Cancer Research.

6 The **Jacksons**' 40-date Victory tour opens at Arrowhead Stadium in Kansas City. It is the first time in eight years that all six brothers have performed together live. Don King announces that "anybody who sees this show will be a better person for years to come."

AC/DC

Frankie Goes To Hollywood became the only act to garner UK platinum singles with their first two releases... The six Jackson brothers performed together live for the first time in eight years... AC/DC headlined at August's Monsters of Rock festival... Prince's movie "Purple Rain" loosely depicted his romantic past and his rise in the Minneapolis scene.

Prince

(Presumably, the tour's main financial backer, Chuck Sullivan, won't see it. His losses will be directly responsible for his family losing control of the New England Patriots football team, and its home stadium in Foxborough.)

8 In an encounter from different ends of the cultural spectrum, gender-bending **Boy George** guests on CBS's "Face the Nation" show with tele-evangelist Jerry Falwell.

14 In their first major continental European concert, British soul/pop quartet **Sade** perform at the Montreux Jazz Festival. It is an ideal event for the London-based band to showcase their unique jazz-laced fusion style. **Sade Adu** formed the group last year, with guitarist/saxophonist **Stuart Matthewman**, keyboardist **Andrew Hale**, and bassist **Paul Denman**, from the ashes of their earlier combo, the funk-based **Pride**. At tonight's gig, they perform their recent UK No. 6 breakthrough hit, the sultry *Your Love Is King*, with other cuts from their sterling maiden album, ***Diamond Life*** (including *Why Can't We Live Together, Hang On To Your Love*, the follow-up hit *When Am I Going To Make A Living, Frankie's First Affair*, and the next single, *Smooth Operator*). The album will will be released by Epic Records on the 28th, set for multiplatinum worldwide success, establishing Sade as one of the most beguiling and stylish talents of the decade.

25 Blues singer and songwriter **"Big Mama" Thornton** dies of a heart attack in Los Angeles at the age of 57, having been inducted into the Blues Foundation Hall of Fame earlier this year.

26 A premiere party is held at Graumann's Chinese Theatre in Hollywood to launch **Prince**'s semi-autobiographical "Purple Rain." Its accompanying soundtrack – credited to **Prince & the Revolution** – will elevate his career into the A-league, beginning a recordbreaking 24 consecutive weeks at US No. 1. Largely recorded at Sunset Sound Studio in Los Angeles, the self-penned, self-arranged, self-produced set includes *When Doves Cry*, his first chart-topper and the biggest-selling single of 1984, currently enjoying its fourth week at US No. 1. The album – which will eventually sell over ten million domestic copies – also includes subsequent hits, *Let's Go Crazy* and the title ballad cut, both recorded and filmed "live" at the First Avenue nightclub in Prince's beloved Minneapolis.

August

11 **Ray Parker, Jr.** – now billed without his backing group **Raydio** – tops the US chart with his allegedly self-penned *Ghostbusters*, the title theme to the hit comedy movie. (**Huey Lewis** will sue Parker for plagiarizing his March hit, *I Want A New Drug*; the case will be settled out of court in Lewis's favor.)

15 **Norman Petty**, the songwriter, performer, and producer remembered as the man behind **Buddy Holly**, dies of leukemia, age 54.

18 **AC/DC** headlines the Monsters of Rock festival at Castle Donington for the second time, before a crowd of 65,000. **Mötley Crüe** are making their UK debut at the event, which also features **Van Halen**, **Ozzy Osbourne**, **Gary Moore**, and hard rock combos **Y&T** and **Accept**. The caravan will play a further six "monster" dates in Sweden, Switzerland, Germany, and Italy, and the Crüe will stay on in Europe until mid-November. During a spare moment in Basel, **Tommy Lee** and **Nikki Sixx** will use flare guns to set fire to a mattress in their hotel room, smash mirrors in the elevators, and will be ejected from the hotel.

21 **Tina Turner**'s comeback album, ***Private Dancer***, is certified platinum by the RIAA. Its breakout smash single, the still-climbing *What's Love Got To Do With It* is simultaneously confirmed gold. Having endured years of abuse and blatant infidelity by her husband **Ike**, Tina left him in 1976, with 36¢ and a Mobil gas card as her only material assets, running away from a final beating at the Dallas Hilton. Taking nothing from their 1978 divorce, and continuing to raise her four children, Turner has rebuilt her life, and her solo career has blossomed since teaming up with young Australian promoter Roger Davies in 1980. Initially recording with **Heaven 17** founders/producers **Ian Craig Marsh** and **Martyn Ware** in 1981, their collective update of **Al Green**'s *Let's Stay Together* returned Turner to the spotlight in Europe, hitting UK No. 6 last December. She then signed to Capitol Records. The R&B/rock/pop-fused ***Private Dancer***, recorded in Europe in less than a month, features top writers (such as **David Bowie**, Mike Chapman, Nicky Chinn, **Graham Lyle**, Terry Britten, **Paul Brady**, and **Mark Knopfler**) and guests (including **Jeff Beck** and the **Crusaders**). It has already hit UK No. 2 and US No. 3 at the beginning of lengthy chart stays.

September

1 At the end of her current US tour, opening for **Lionel Richie**, **Tina Turner**'s *What's Love Got To Do With It* tops the US chart for the first of three weeks. It is her first No. 1 hit, and sets a new record for the length of time between an act's first US top 100 entry and first No. 1 record: 24 years.

14 The inaugural MTV Video Music Awards take place at Radio City Music Hall in New York City. **Michael Jackson**'s ***Thriller*** picks up nods for Best Choreography, Best Overall Performance in a Video, and the Viewers' Choice. The **Cars**, **Cyndi Lauper**, **Eurythmics**, the **Police**, **Van Halen** and **ZZ Top** also triumph, but the big winner is jazz-fusion keyboardist **Herbie Hancock**, who wins five awards for his groundbreaking, hi-tech *Rockit* video, directed by pioneering directors **Godley & Creme**. The **Beatles**, **David Bowie**, and film director Richard Lester all receive the Video Vanguard award. It is **Madonna**, however, who steals the limelight, premiering her show-stopping new single *Like A Virgin*, wearing a white wedding dress, lifting up her skirt to reveal white stockings, and sitting on a wedding cake. (After initially being ignored by the music industry, MTV is on a roll, becoming *the* promotional platform for both established and breaking artists. Few acts can afford not to make videos to accompany singles, as the hip network begins to exert enormous influence as the industry tastemaker.)

20 **Steve Goodman**, age 36, dies in Seattle after a bone-marrow transplant to treat leukemia. At heart a folk singer, Goodman demonstrated his musical talent on nearly a dozen albums during a 14-year recording career, traversing blues, bluegrass, country, folk, and rock 'n' roll. He signed with Buddah Records after opening for **Kris Kristofferson** at the Quiet Knight in Chicago, and soon had his first success as a writer, when **Arlo Guthrie** took *The City Of New Orleans* – which Goodman wrote on board the train of the same name – into the Top 20.

22 In the midst of their European tour, The Works, **Queen** lead singer **Freddie Mercury** falls down some stairs during a concert at the Europhalle in Hanover, Germany, while singing *Hammer To Fall*. Despite a badly injured knee, he continues, singing *Bohemian Rhapsody, We Will Rock You*, and *We Are The Champions*.

Sept 1984

Def Jam is launched... Chaka Khan's *I Feel For You*... Band Aid...

U2

Run-D.M.C.

26 Def Jam – a new label formed by New York-based rap impresario/manager/promoter/producer **Russell Simmons**, and New York University senior and part-time turntable DJ, **Rick Rubin** – releases its first single, *I Need A Beat* by solo rapper **LL Cool J**. This is 16-year-old James Todd Smith, who started creating hip-hop demos on DJ equipment at home in Queens three years ago, and sent one to an impressed Rubin. (Another Def Jam creation, **T La Rock** and **Jazzy Jay**'s *It's Yours*, was licensed earlier in the year to Arthur Baker's Streetwise indie label.) Initially run out of Rubin's NYU dormitory, Def Jam will concentrate on rap/hip-hop material, signing a distribution agreement early next year with Columbia Records. While Simmons (who has been instrumental in the launch of gritty, urban hip-hop via his management of **Run D.M.C.**) will focus on black rap, Rubin will widen their roster, signing white thrash metal band **Slayer** next year. Next month, the company's second addition will be the New York-based middle-class teenage trio of **King Ad-Rock** (**Adam Horovitz**) and **MCA** (**Adam Yauch**) on vocals, and **Mike D** (**Michael Diamond**), who perform a punk-rap hybrid as the **Beastie Boys**.

28 Writing about 25-year-old singer-songwriter **Suzanne Vega**, **The New York Times** reviewer Stephen Holden describes her as: "The freshest and clearest new voice on the New York folk music scene." The glowing review will be partly responsible for her signing with A&M in November. Vega grew up in a Hispanic neighborhood, and attended the New York High School of Performing Arts, where she studied dance and began composing songs in 1975. She performed her compositions on the Greenwich Village folk circuit, including gigs at Folk City, the Speakeasy, and the Bottom Line.

October

11 **Bobby Gillespie** – a 20-year-old Scottish drummer/singer who also fronts his own recently formed band, **Primal Scream** – makes his debut behind the drumkit with the **Jesus & Mary Chain** at Glasgow's Venue.

Although *Unforgettable Fire* went platinum in the US, U2 would have to wait until 1987 to have their first chart-topper... In December, Run-D.M.C.'s debut set became the first rap album to be certified gold.

13 Now produced by ex-**Roxy Music** keyboardist and ambient music pioneer **Brian Eno**, and French-Canadian perfectionist **Daniel Lanois**, who are refining the band's innate rawness, **U2**'s new album, ***Unforgettable Fire***, recorded in the ballroom at Slane Castle in Ireland, debuts at UK No. 1. Meanwhile, the group – just back from the Under Australian Skies tour – prepares for a 21-date European tour.

24 The Cable Music Channel, a new 24-hour music television network created by media visionary and CNN founder Ted Turner to rival MTV, begins broadcasting in the US, claiming an initial 2.3 million subscribers. However, by the end of next month, MTV will buy out the start-up operation for $1 million, receiving the Cable Music Channel name and a list of its subscribers, and will close it down. It will not be the last time MTV defends its market position.

November

3 Making her first appearance on "Saturday Night Live," **Chaka Khan** performs her current hit, *I Feel For You*. An electrifying update of a **Prince** song (included on his 1979 ***Prince*** album), it features a personalized "Chaka Khan" rap intro by **Grandmaster Melle Mel** and harmonica fills by **Stevie Wonder**.

Chaka Khan's *I Feel For You* spent three weeks at UK No. 1 before peaking at US No. 3 and earning an RIAA gold disc.

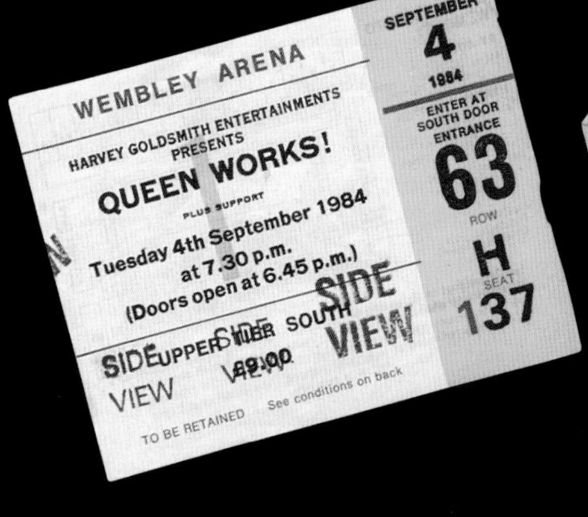

WEMBLEY ARENA
HARVEY GOLDSMITH ENTERTAINMENTS PRESENTS
QUEEN WORKS!
PLUS SUPPORT
Tuesday 4th September 1984
at 7.30 p.m.
(Doors open at 6.45 p.m.)
UPPER TIER SOUTH
£9.00
SIDE VIEW
TO BE RETAINED
See conditions on back
SEPTEMBER
4
1984
ENTER AT SOUTH DOOR ENTRANCE
63
ROW
H
SEAT
137

Queen followed their European tour with a controversial seven-show visit to the Super Bowl in Sun City, Bophuthatswana, South Africa, putting them on the UN's cultural blacklist... Five years since their last hit record, Dr. Feelgood were still a popular live draw.

4 **Prince**'s Purple Rain tour, a 96-date North American trek, begins at the Joe Louis Arena in Detroit, breaking **Neil Diamond**'s record for sellout performances at the 20,000-seat venue. (By the time the tour ends in Miami in April 1985, over 1,692,000 tickets will have been sold; throughout, Prince will play unpublicized free concerts for disabled children.)

11 The **Boomtown Rats**' lead singer, **Bob Geldof**, sees a graphic BBC1 television report on the famine in Ethiopia, and determines to raise awareness and funds. With **Ultravox**'s **Midge Ure**, he will write a song and produce an all-star benefit record from which nobody (from artists to record shops) will take any profit. It is the beginning of the Band Aid relief project, to which Geldof will intermittently devote his not inconsiderable energies over the next five years. He temporarily sets aside his musical career, and the Boomtown Rats effectively cease to be.

25 At **Bob Geldof**'s behest, 36 artists gather at the SARM Studio, St. Luke's Mews in Notting Hill, London, to record *Do They Know It's Christmas?*, written by and featuring Geldof and **Midge Ure**. The largest collection of pop stars ever assembled for one recording features the current cream of British music celebrities (and some visiting American artists): **Bananarama**, the **Boomtown Rats**, **Phil Collins**, **Culture Club** (**Boy George** and **Jon Moss**), **Duran Duran**, **Frankie Goes To Hollywood**, **Heaven 17** (**Glenn Gregory** and **Martyn Ware**), **Kool & the Gang** (**Robert Bell**, **James "J.T." Taylor**, and **Dennis Thomas**), **Annie Lennox**, **Marilyn**, **George Michael**, **Spandau Ballet**, **Status Quo** (**Rick Parfitt** and **Francis Rossi**), **Sting**, **U2** (**Bono** and **Adam Clayton**), **Ultravox**, **Shalamar**'s **Jody Watley**, **Paul Weller**, and **Paul Young**. The historic recording is produced by Ure and filmed for a promotional video. With a lightning turnaround, and great logistical support from Mercury/Polygram and British retailers, the single will be launched with an Ethiopia Benefit concert on December 7 at London's Royal Albert Hall, organized by the Save the Children Fund. All proceeds will go towards famine relief in Ethiopia.

December

1 As head of the Nuclear Disarmament Party, **Peter Garrett** – lead singer with **Midnight Oil**, one of Australia's most popular rock combos – runs for a seat in the Australian Senate. A long-time environmental activist, Garrett will receive nine percent of the vote.

6 The **Clash** perform the first of two benefit shows at London's Brixton Academy, to raise money to help Britain's striking miners.

8 **Mötley Crüe**'s **Vince Neil**, driving a 1972 Ford Pantera sports car with **Hanoi Rocks** drummer **Nick "Razzle" Dingley** as his passenger, is heading back from a liquor store where they bought more booze for a party Neil is throwing in Redondo Beach, California. Speeding and inebriated, he skids across the road and the car slams sideways into the front of another vehicle, seriously injuring the two people in it and killing Dingley. Neil, with minor cuts and bruises, is arrested and released on $2,500 bail. He will appear in court next September.

8 Patrick Cavanaugh, former manager of the **Coasters**, is convicted of first degree murder of band member, bass singer **Nathaniel "Buster" Wilson**. Wilson's dismembered body was found near the Hoover Dam and in a canyon near Modesto, California, more than two years after he disappeared in April 1980. He had been shot and mutilated. Cavanaugh is sentenced to death.

8 **Frankie Goes to Hollywood**'s third single, the festive ballad *The Power Of Love*, hits UK No. 1, with the help of a **Godley & Creme** nativity video. The group becomes the first since **Gerry & the Pacemakers** to have UK No. 1s with its first three singles. On November 10, the group's double album debut, ***Welcome To The Pleasure Dome***, entered the UK chart at No. 1, its one million-plus orders amounting to the country's biggest album ship-out to date.

9 At the end of the **Jacksons**' Victory tour, at Dodger Stadium in Los Angeles, **Michael** announces it will be his last tour with his brothers. Over two million attended the 55 concerts, which grossed a record $75 million. Michael donates $5 million to the charities, as promised. Through its promotion of the tour, Pepsi-Cola for the first time achieves a larger market share than Coca-Cola.

15 *Do They Know It's Christmas?*, released on the Mercury label, enters the UK chart at No. 1, where it will remain for five weeks, selling more than three million copies to become Britain's biggest-selling single ever. With similar non-profit distribution arrangements quickly made in other countries around the world, it will be certified gold for one million US sales by the RIAA on December 19. The official Band Aid Trust will be established as a permanent charity, to ensure the swift collection of funds and distribution of aid to Africa.

31 Driving with his girlfriend from Sheffield, England, to a New Year's Eve party at his parents' home in nearby Dronfield **Def Leppard**'s drummer **Rick Allen** crashes his Corvette Stingray, while racing another driver in an Alfa Romeo down a stretch of the A57. The impact tears off his left arm and badly damages his right. He is taken to the Royal Hallamshire Hospital, where micro-surgeons perform two operations, re-attaching his arm. However, a severe infection will develop and doctors will be left with no alternative but to amputate the arm. A spokesman for the group says: "We're just glad he's alive."

> **"*The Power Of Love* – Frankie Goes To Hollywood's third number one."**
>
> The ZZT label's pre-release publicity for *The Power Of Love*, December 1984

Watching a BBC-TV report on the Ethiopian famine, Bob Geldof conceived "Band Aid."

ROOTS **During this year: Kim Thayil is recruited by roommates Chris Cornell and Hiro Yamamoto, to join Soundgarden, named after a sculpture in a Seattle park... ex-Laker Girls basketball team cheerleader dance coach Paula Abdul wins the Best Choreography trophy at the fourth annual MTV Video Music Awards for her work on Janet Jackson's "Nasty"... 10-year-old singer/actress Alanis Morissette appears on the US cable TV network Nickelodeon's "You Can't Do That On Television" before taking a film acting role opposite future "Friends" star, Matt LeBlanc... looking for a "white New Edition," Maurice Starr discovers Donnie Wahlberg at Copley Square High School, Boston; Wahlberg recommends former classmates from the William M. Trotter Elementary School to create Nynuk, and after a year of molding by Starr they sign with Columbia Records, who insist on a name change to New Kids On The Block... after initially being rejected, 12-year-old Ricky Martin joins the roster-revolving Puerto Rican boy band, Menudo... Fred Durst, attending Hunter Huss High School in Gastonia, North Carolina, writes his first lyrics... and teenage fiddle virtuoso Alison Krauss joins John Pennell's group Silver Rail...**

Everybody Wants To Rule The World

1985

No.1 US SINGLES

Jan 5	Like A Virgin **Madonna**
Feb 2	I Want To Know What Love Is **Foreigner**
Feb 16	Careless Whisper **Wham! featuring George Michael**
Mar 9	Can't Fight This Feeling **REO Speedwagon**
Mar 30	One More Night **Phil Collins**
Apr 13	We Are The World **USA For Africa**
May 11	Crazy For You **Madonna**
May 18	Don't You (Forget About Me) **Simple Minds**
May 25	Everything She Wants **Wham!**
June 8	Everybody Wants To Rule The World **Tears For Fears**
June 22	Heaven **Bryan Adams**
July 6	Sussudio **Phil Collins**
July 13	A View To A Kill **Duran Duran**
July 27	Everytime You Go Away **Paul Young**
Aug 3	Shout **Tears For Fears**
Aug 24	The Power Of Love **Huey Lewis & the News**
Sept 7	St. Elmo's Fire (Man In Motion) **John Parr**
Sept 21	Money For Nothing **Dire Straits**
Oct 12	Oh Sheila **Ready For The World**
Oct 19	Take On Me **a-ha**
Oct 26	Saving All My Love For You **Whitney Houston**
Nov 2	Part-Time Lover **Stevie Wonder**
Nov 9	Miami Vice Theme **Jan Hammer**
Nov 16	We Built This City **Starship**
Nov 30	Separate Lives **Phil Collins & Marilyn Martin**
Dec 7	Broken Wings **Mr. Mister**
Dec 21	Say You, Say Me **Lionel Richie**

No.1 UK SINGLES

Jan 5	Do They Know It's Christmas? **Band Aid**
Jan 19	I Want To Know What Love Is **Foreigner**
Feb 9	I Know Him So Well **Elaine Paige & Barbara Dickson**
Mar 9	You Spin Me Round (Like A Record) **Dead Or Alive**
Mar 23	Easy Lover **Philip Bailey (duet with Phil Collins)**
Apr 20	We Are The World **USA For Africa**
May 4	Move Closer **Phyllis Nelson**
May 11	19 **Paul Hardcastle**
June 15	You'll Never Walk Alone **Crowd**
June 29	Frankie **Sister Sledge**
July 27	There Must Be An Angel (Playing With My Heart) **Eurythmics**

Tears For Fears

Frankie Goes To Hollywood

Tears For Fears took their name from a chapter heading in Arthur Janov's Prisoners Of Pain, concerned with Primal Therapy... While Frankie Goes To Hollywood's name was inspired by a headline about 1950s singer Frankie Vaughan's attempt to launch a career in Hollywood.

Rock devoted much of 1985 to good causes, from famine relief to fighting apartheid, helping America's beleaguered farmers and Britain's legion of unemployed. Inspired by **Bob Geldof**'s **Band Aid**, a galaxy of American talent gathered in January to record *We Are The World*, penned at lightning speed by **Michael Jackson** and **Lionel Richie**. The album ***USA For Africa*** also featured an array of artists, including **Bruce Springsteen** and **Prince**. It was followed by two of the most ambitious concerts in rock history, staged simultaneously in London and Philadelphia, and watched by a television audience estimated at two billion. Inspired by the concept, **Bob Dylan** and others performed at the first Farm Aid later in the year, in aid of struggling American farmers.

Making a huge impression at Live Aid, **Madonna** was certainly making her way in the world. She brought a provocative and pouting sexuality to pop music – an image that would become her trademark in lyrics and on video. Quick to appreciate that sex sells and the media are suckers for it, Madonna was the street punk, the provocative, cynical, funky soul that she played in the movie "Desperately Seeking Susan." What she may have lacked in vocal quality, she more than made up for in marketing savvy. She was nurtured by one of the great label executives, **Seymour Stein**. Another legendary pair of ears, Arista's **Clive Davis**, was playing a similar role for **Whitney Houston**, so successfully that ***Whitney Houston***, elevated by her 64-carat voice, would eventually sell more than 20 million copies worldwide, becoming the most successful debut album to date.

Britain supplied the biggest-selling duos of the year. **Wham!** continued their remarkable run, taking the act to China, and selling more records in Japan than any other overseas act since the **Beatles**. But they were about to separate. Asked about the split, **George Michael** said: "Well, obviously it's not going to damage my musical output." He featured on no less than four records in the UK Top 20 in December. A more serious English pair, **Tears For Fears** began the year at modest English venues and ended it with two global No. 1 singles. Occasionally melodramatic, the duo's keyboard-driven pop boasted sparkling production (from **Chris Hughes**) and texture rich enough to send ***Songs From The Big Chair*** to multiplatinum success.

By dint of exhaustive touring, **Dire Straits** also notched up the No. 1 position in both the UK and US for ***Brothers In Arms***. Its baby-boomer appeal and clean production made it ideal for the CD format. At times orchestral and atmospheric, no fewer than 13 keyboards supported **Mark Knopfler**'s dazzling guitar. The album also included the stab at rock fame, *Money For Nothing* – surely the first time MTV had figured in a song – effortlessly sung by guest vocalist **Sting**.

Aug 3 Into The Groove **Madonna**
Aug 31 I Got You Babe **UB40, guest vocals by Chrissie Hynde**
Sept 7 Dancing In The Street **David Bowie & Mick Jagger**
Oct 5 If I Was **Midge Ure**
Oct 12 The Power Of Love **Jennifer Rush**
Nov 16 A Good Heart **Feargal Sharkey**
Nov 30 I'm Your Man **Wham!**
Dec 14 Saving All My Love For You **Whitney Houston**
Dec 28 Merry Christmas Everyone **Shakin' Stevens**

"The song is the main thing – everything else should be subservient to it."

Mark Knopfler, **Musician**, September 1983

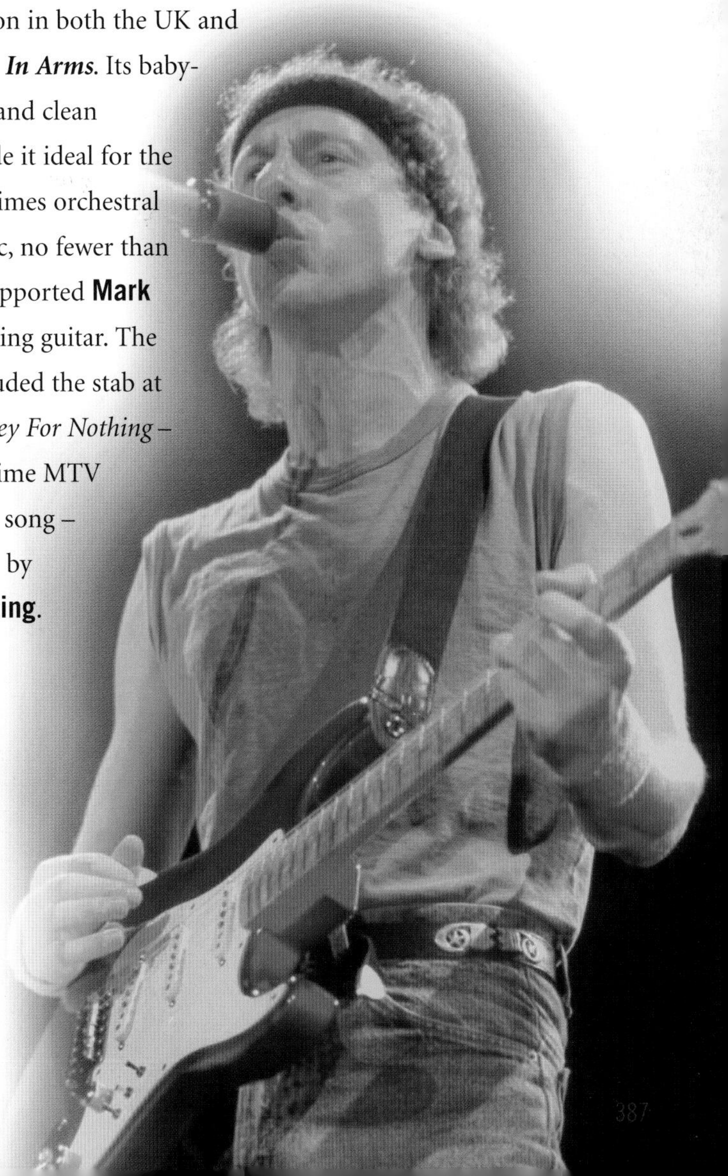

January

1 VH1, a new 24-hour music cable television network, begins round-the-clock broadcasting in the US. The sister network to the revolutionary MTV, and overseen by MTV Networks CEO, Bob Pittman, VH1 (standing for Video Hits One) has been created to fill the adult contemporary music video void, hoping to attract an ageing baby-boomer audience and allow MTV to focus exclusively on the teen market. Its first clip is **Marvin Gaye**'s version of *The Star-Spangled Banner*.

8 The US Postal Service issues a first day cover of **Elvis Presley**, to honor what would have been the legend's 50th birthday. A record-breaking 500 million Elvis stamps will be sold during the promotion.

10 One of the most ambitious festivals ever staged, the 11-day Rock in Rio gets under way at the Barra da Tijua in Rio de Janeiro, with **Ney Matogrosso** singing *South America*. It will feature **James Taylor**, **George Benson**, **AC/DC**, **Al Jarreau**, the **B-52's**, **Iron Maiden**, **Ozzy Osbourne & The Blizzard of Ozz**, the **Scorpions**, **Rod Stewart**, **Tina Turner**, German singer **Nina Hagen**, **Whitesnake**, **Yes**, the **Go-Go's**, **Queen** (who perform despite local clergy issuing a statement that their performance will corrupt the nation's youth), and several Brazilian acts, including **Gilberto Gil**, **Ivan Lins**, and **Moraes Moreira**. Several of the artists will take the stage more than once. The Go-Go's will perform for the first (and last) time with **Jane Wiedlin**'s replacement, **Paula Jean Brown**. Some estimates of crowd attendance will be as high as 1.4 million – a huge turnout, despite constant rain during the second half of the festival, which also coincides with the election of Brazil's first civilian president in more than two decades.

28 Following this year's American Music Awards in Los Angeles, at 10:00 pm, 46 top recording artists arrive at the A&M Studios in Hollywood, to be greeted by a warning notice from producer **Quincy Jones** to "check your egos at the door." They are there at the behest of Jones, **Harry Belafonte** (who has been inspired by **Bob Geldof**'s **Band Aid** single), and Ken Kragen (Kenny Rogers' manager). The song to be recorded, *We Are The World*, was written by **Michael Jackson** and **Lionel Richie** in just two hours, following three days of preparation. It is arranged, produced, and engineered by Jones, Tom Bahler, and Humberto Gatica, and the instrumental tracks have already been recorded by Jones. In the studio, a strip of named tape for each performer has been stuck on the floor, forming a semi-circular ensemble. (Bob Geldof sings as part of the chorus, with a host of stars.) Those chosen for lead vocals will later be grouped close to one of six microphones, as their efforts will be recorded after the choruses. The end result features 21 solo vocal segments which are, in order of appearance: Lionel Richie, **Stevie Wonder**, **Paul Simon**, **Kenny Rogers**, **James Ingram**, **Tina Turner**, **Billy Joel**, **Michael Jackson**, **Diana Ross**, **Dionne Warwick**, **Willie Nelson**, **Al Jarreau**, **Bruce Springsteen**, **Kenny Loggins**, **Steve Perry**, **Daryl Hall**, **Huey Lewis**, **Cyndi Lauper**, **Kim Carnes**, **Bob Dylan**, and **Ray Charles**. **Prince** was invited, but has failed to show (he will contribute a song to the subsequent album). A video team from MTV covers the historic event, resulting in 75 hours of footage, which will be edited to promote the song. After ten hours, only Richie and Jones remain, putting the final touches to an extraordinary recording that will be released under the fundraising banner, **USA For Africa**.

We Are The World was recorded at A&M Studios in Hollywood. All arrived in separate limousines, except Bruce Springsteen, who came by truck.

John Fogerty

Sting

John Fogerty was sued by Fantasy Records, which claimed his *The Old Man Down The Road* infringed his own *Run Through The Jungle*'s copyright... Backed by a group of stellar jazz musicians, Sting made his solo debut at New York City's Ritz Club...

31 **John Fogerty** makes his first live appearance in years, playing on the Chaplin stage at the A&M Soundstage in Hollywood, for a proposed television special. Most of the audience is employed by Warner Bros., for whom he has recorded ***Centerfield***, his first solo album in a decade. With **Albert Lee** (guitar), **Booker T. Jones** (keyboards), **Donald "Duck" Dunn** (bass), **Prairie Prince** (drums), and **Steve Douglas** (sax) backing him, he runs through a selection of R&B covers, none of which will appear on the chart-topping new album.

"I'm very difficult to work with because I demand perfection."

Boy George, **The Record**, February 1985

February

9 **Madonna**'s ***Like A Virgin*** begins a three-week ride at US No. 1, and will become her most successful album, staying on the chart for over two years and selling over ten million domestic copies, though it will have to wait until September to top the UK list. Yielding four top five US hits, its worldwide success – spurred by a marketing campaign built around the image of Madonna as a coy but lacily-trussed "virgin" – will transform her career, put her face on the cover of **Time** magazine, inspire Madonnaland, a clothing concession in Macy's US stores, and influence the style and tastes of an entire generation of young females. With increasingly provocative videos and image changes which accompany each subsequent release, Madonna will rely as much on an outrageous expression of sexual freedom and skillful manipulation of the media, as she does on her singing/dancing talent, to keep her profile the highest of any performer for the next 15 years.

11 **Frankie Goes To Hollywood**'s astounding worldwide success leads them to win big at the fourth BPI awards, held at London's Grosvenor House Hotel. They pick up the Best British Newcomer award, *Relax* wins Best British Single, and **Trevor Horn** is named Best British Producer. **Wham!** win the Best British Group category, with **Duran Duran**'s "Wild Boys" nabbing Best British Music Video. **Sade**'s ***Diamond Life*** is named Best British Album. **Paul Young** and **Alison Moyet** win the Best British Male Artist and Best British Female Artist categories. **Prince** is named Best International Solo Artist, and ***Purple Rain*** wins the Best Film Soundtrack category. With **Sting** about to embark on a solo career – effectively marking the end of the group's activities – the **Police** are honored with the Outstanding Contribution to British Music.

14 On Valentine's Day, Arista Records releases the maiden album from 21-year-old R&B singer **Whitney Houston**. Like her mother **Cissy** and her cousin **Dionne Warwick**, Newark-born Houston began her singing career in a gospel setting, performing *Guide Me, O Thou Great Jehovah* at the age of eight, as a member of the New Hope Baptist Junior Choir. Label boss Clive Davis has personally nurtured the ex-model, signing her to a worldwide contract following a showcase in Manhattan in 1983, and surrounding her with A-list songwriting and production talent. Houston's pop/R&B-filled debut, ***Whitney Houston***, will get off to a slow start, but is set to explode following the August release of the Michael Masser/Gerry Goffin ballad smash, *Saving All My Love For You*. With drop-dead gorgeous looks and a voice like an angel flying low, a major new career is launched.

25 **Sting** makes his solo debut at the Ritz Club in New York City, backed by a stellar group of jazz musicians. He premieres five new songs, along with **Police** favorites. Following a week in May at the Theatre Mogador in Paris, he will return to the US in August, playing a three-month tour promoting his jazz-laced solo debut album, ***The Dream Of The Blue Turtles***.

26 After a series of sweeps over the past few years at the Grammys, at the 27th awards the spoils are shared across the board, highlighted by **Tina Turner**'s comeback. Thanking a hushed crowd at the Shrine Auditorium in Los Angeles, an ebullient Turner simply says: "I've been waiting so long for this." She wins Record of the Year and Best Pop Vocal Performance, Female for *What's Love Got To Do With It*, which also gives its writers **Graham Lyle** and Terry Britten the coveted Song of the Year prize. **Lionel Richie**'s ***Can't Slow Down*** is named Album of the Year. **Prince** picks up his first Grammy for Best Rock Performance by a Duo or Group with Vocal for *Purple Rain*, and R&B Song of the Year for *I Feel For You*, a hit for **Chaka Khan**. **Billy Ocean** wins Best R&B Vocal Performance, Male category for the dance/pop chart-topper *Caribbean Queen*, which gave the 35-year-old Trinidad-born singer-songwriter his global breakthrough last year. **Bruce Springsteen** also wins for the first time, picking up the Best Rock Vocal Performance, Male trophy for *Dancing In The Dark*. Classic-rock stalwarts **Yes** nab their first Grammy: Best Rock Instrumental Performance for *Cinema*. Performance highlights include Prince's eight-and-a-half minute version of *Baby, I'm A Star* and **Stevie Wonder**'s synthesizer medley with **Herbie Hancock** and **Thomas Dolby**.

Whitney Houston had already pursued a career as a model, featuring in Glamour and Seventeen, and as an actress, appearing in TV shows such as "Silver Spoons" and "Gimme A Break", before she embarked on a singing career.

Randy Travis at the Grand Ole Opry... Wham! in China... Dire Straits' *Brothers In Arms*...

Bryan Adams, who attended military schools in Israel, Austria, Portugal, and France, got his break when he replaced Nick Gilder as lead singer of the Canadian rock outfit Sweeney Todd.

March

7 Country singer **Randy Travis** makes his debut on the legendary "Grand Ole Opry" radio showcase at Opryland in Nashville. Travis is already a country music veteran, having formed a duo with his brother Ricky at the age of ten, and won a talent contest at the Country City USA club in Charlotte, North Carolina. He made his recording debut for the local Paula Records, cutting *Dreamin'* and *She's My Woman*. Relocating to Nashville at the beginning of the decade, he concentrated on songwriting, initially earning a living as a cook and dishwasher. Over the next four years he became a seasoned country performer, signing to Warner Bros. Records in January, and making his label debut recording *Prairie Rose* for inclusion on the movie soundtrack album, ***Rustler's Rhapsody***.

Wham! became the first western rock act to play live in China, when they gave two concerts, in Beijing and Peking.

13 Following their success at the BPI awards last month, **Frankie Goes To Hollywood** win again, this time at the 30th Ivor Novello Awards luncheon in London with *Two Tribes* picking up the Best Contemporary Song honor. Once again showing that these are the most respected awards within the industry, **Elton John** presents **George Michael** with the Songwriter of the Year trophy, proclaiming him to be a "major songwriter in the tradition of **Paul McCartney** and **Barry Gibb**." Michael accepts the award with great emotion, becoming its youngest ever recipient. Not surprisingly, **Bob Geldof** and **Midge Ure** receive the Best Selling A-Side award for *Do They Know It's Christmas?* **Duran Duran**'s *The Reflex* is named International Hit of the Year, while veterans Paul McCartney and **Phil Collins** win Best Film Theme or Song for *We All Stand Together*, and Best Song Musically And Lyrically for *Against All Odds (Take A Look At Me Now)* respectively. George Michael is on a roll: *Careless Whisper* – which is named Most Performed Work – has topped charts around the world, including a three-week run in the US last month. **Wham!**'s follow-up album, ***Make It Big***, already a UK chart-topper and arranged, written and produced by Michael, is currently heading the US survey, with another extract, *Everything She Wants*, also on its way to US No. 1.

14 During his second UK tour, supporting **Tina Turner** on her Private Dancer trek, **Bryan Adams** performs at London's Wembley Arena. The 25-year-old rock singer-songwriter/guitarist from Kingston, Canada, has been composing and performing an increasingly popular mix of straight-ahead, fiery rock numbers, and melodic ballads since teaming with co-writer Jim Vallance in 1977, and signing with A&M Records in 1979. His latest, *Run To You*, recently became his first US Top 10 hit, and also opened his UK chart account last month at No. 11.

25 History is created at the 57th Academy Awards, when the best Original Song and Original Song Score Oscars are awarded to two African-American artists for the first time. **Stevie Wonder**'s *I Just Called To Say I Love You* (from "The Woman in Red" soundtrack) triumphs in the Original Song category, while **Prince** nabs Original Song Score for "Purple Rain." Wonder dedicates his win to imprisoned South African ANC leader Nelson Mandela.

26 South African radio stations ban the playing of all **Stevie Wonder**'s records, in response to his Mandela tribute last night.

26 **Tears For Fears** begin a 25-date headlining British tour at the modest Golddiggers nightclub in Chippenham, England to promote their second album, ***Songs From The Big Chair***. Little do co-founders **Roland Orzabal** (guitar/keyboards/vocals) and **Curt Smith** (bass vocals) know that by the end of this year they will be second only to **Wham!** as the biggest-selling duo in the world: the anthemic *Shout* will hit UK No. 4 and US No. 1, and its follow-up, *Everybody Wants To Rule The World*, will make UK No. 2 and US No. 1. (The latter will become the band's most popular cut on US radio, and will be cited by BMI in October 1994 for two million broadcast performances.) The English-born pair – creatively led by Orzabal – originally played together in pop/ska combo **Graduate** before forming Tears for Fears in 1981. Their name is taken from the title of a chapter on primal therapy in Arthur Janov's book, **Prisoners of Pain**.

April

1 With his four-track solo EP, ***Crazy From The Heat***, currently sitting at its US No. 15 peak, **David Lee Roth** officially quits **Van Halen** to pursue a solo career. Although his first two albums, ***Eat 'Em And Smile*** and ***Skyscraper***, will both go platinum, Roth's career will then stall, while Van Halen – with ex-**Montrose** lead singer **Sammy Hagar** as their new frontman – will score three consecutive US chart-topping albums.

1 In New York, **U2** – who were featured on the front cover of **Rolling Stone** on March 14 with the caption "Our Choice: Band Of The '80s" – appear at Madison Square Garden for the first time, playing to a sellout crowd.

4 Columbia ships 2.7 million copies of the rush-released ***We Are The World*** in the US. Donated cuts are from **Bruce Springsteen**, **Prince**, **Huey Lewis & the News**, **Chicago**, **Tina Turner**, the **Pointer Sisters**, **Kenny Rogers**, **Steve Perry**, **USA For**

Africa, and **Northern Lights** (the all-Canadian contribution). The track *Tears Are Not Enough*, produced by hitmeister David Foster, features **Bryan Adams**, John Candy, **Burton Cummings**, **Corey Hart**, **Dan Hill**, **Gordon Lightfoot**, **Joni Mitchell**, **Anne Murray**, and **Neil Young**, among others.

5 At 3:50 pm GMT, over 5,000 radio stations worldwide unite for 7:02 minutes, as *We Are The World* is aired.

5 Having signed with Parlophone last month, **Neil Tennant** leaves his job at **Smash Hits**. The magazine's next issue will feature a faux obituary, predicting that Tennant will come "crawling back on bended knees" when the **Pet Shop Boys** fail. Tennant tells of phoning his mother to tell her the news: "I spoke to my mum on the telephone and said how we'd signed with EMI and she said, 'But you're not going to give up your job, are you?' I said actually I did last week." They will release their first Parlophone single, *Opportunities*, in July, before playing live for the first time at the ICA Rock Week in London in August. By January 1986, they will be celebrating their first No. 1, with *West End Girls*.

7 **Wham!** perform at the 10,000-seater Workers' Gymnasium in Beijing, becoming the first western rock act to play live in China. Today's and tomorrow's concerts have followed lengthy negotiations between the duo's manager, Simon Napier-Bell, and the Chinese government.

12 **Madonna** embarks on her first full series of concert dates, the Virgin Tour, at the Paramount Theater in Seattle. Some 355,000 fans in 28 cities will pay to see both the Material Girl and her up-and-coming opening act, rap pack the **Beastie Boys**, who sport the street fashion of baggy jeans, reversed baseball caps, Adidas trainers, chunky gold chains, and hooded sweat shirts. On the final date – at New York City's Madison Square Garden – Madonna will be carried off stage by her father, Tony.

"My solo career was the direct result of being thoroughly miserable."

Phil Collins, **Melody Maker**, March 30, 1985

13 Already certified for four million US sales, *We Are The World* – distributed by Columbia Records – hits US No. 1, where it will stay for four weeks. It will top the charts in most western territories, beginning a two-week stay at UK No. 1 next week. Meanwhile, the USA for Africa Foundation's legal counsel, Jay Cooper, claims that bootleg merchandise, particularly T-shirts, is appearing in many US cities. Authorized merchandisers, Winterland, take measures to clamp down on the pirates.

23 New York Federal Court Justice Vincent L. Broderick dismisses Columbia Records' lawsuit against **Boston**'s **Tom Scholz**. Scholz, a notoriously slow worker in the studio, and his attorney, Don Engel, worked out an agreement with MCA Records last August to release the band's new album, ***Third Stage***. Hearing of the deal, Columbia demanded $900,000 from MCA, before allowing Boston to join the label. Broderick states that Columbia failed to prove that it would suffer "irreparable harm" if it could not release the album, and that by demanding payment from MCA, it killed any negotiations. "That, so far as I'm concerned, destroyed any argument of irreparable damage here. Before this litigation really got under way, Columbia had already fixed its price." Boston's first two albums have, together, sold 22 milion copies in the US.

May

16 An initial check for $6.5 million in royalties for sales of the **USA For Africa** song and album is handed to Ken Kragen by Columbia executive, Al Teller. Receipts from records and merchandise will ultimately exceed $50 million.

18 Already a chart fixture in their native UK, **Simple Minds** achieve a major breakthrough in the US, as *Don't You (Forget About Me)* – from the soundtrack to the "brat-pack" movie, "The Breakfast Club" – tops the chart. Their first release that is not self-penned, the song was written by Keith Forsey and Steve Chiff, and rejected by both **Billy Idol** and **Bryan Ferry**. It will also hit UK No. 7, spending more than six months on the survey.

DIRE STRAITS

Apr 25 **Dire Straits' Brothers in Arms tour opens at the Soccer Stadium in Split, Yugoslavia. This lengthy outing will take the group to a new level, performing 248 shows in 117 cities and 23 countries, attended by some three million people. Finishing a year from tomorrow in Sydney, Australia, they will play 23 consecutive nights in London in December, as well as appear at Live Aid at London's Wembley Stadium. The attendant album, *Brothers In Arms* – a career highlight that hits all the right notes with baby-boomers – will reach UK No. 1 next month, before going on to be the group's only US chart-topper (for nine weeks) in August, as well as finding pole position in another 22 countries. The extracted title track will become the first single released in Britain as a commercially available CD single, with a limited pressing of 400 copies. *Money For Nothing*, featuring co-writer Sting as guest vocalist, also gives the group its first US chart-topping single – one of five hits taken from the album. A triumph for headband-wearing lead singer, songwriter, and lead guitarist, Mark Knopfler, *Brothers In Arms* will also become the album that transforms record-buying habits from the LP to the new kid on the block, the compact disc, becoming the biggest-selling CD of the decade.**

Hall & Oates at the Apollo... Live Aid... Michael Jackson buys the Beatles...

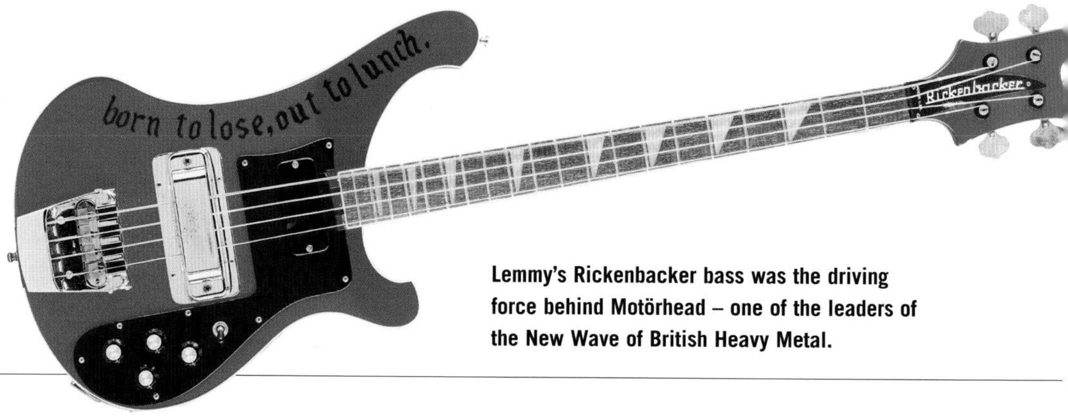

Lemmy's Rickenbacker bass was the driving force behind Motörhead – one of the leaders of the New Wave of British Heavy Metal.

20 **Daryl Hall & John Oates**, paying tribute to the soul music that inspired them in their youth, perform at the re-opening of the legendary Apollo Theater in Harlem, joined, at their invitation, by **David Ruffin** and **Eddie Kendricks** of the **Temptations**. The event – recorded for a live Hall & Oates album release in September – benefits the United Negro College Fund.

20 With charity records all the rage, the **Crowd** – an aggregation of artists, including **Paul McCartney**, **John Entwistle**, **Phil Lynott**, **Kiki Dee**, **Denny Laine**, **Motörhead**, and others – record *You'll Never Walk Alone*, in an arrangement by **10cc**'s **Graham Gouldman**, to raise money for the families of the victims of England's Bradford City Football Club fire, which killed 56 spectators the week before last. **Gerry Marsden** – whose version of the song topped the charts in 1963 – takes the lead vocal in the hymnal style of his original recording. When the record tops the UK chart next month, Marsden will become the first act to hit No. 1 with two different versions of the same song.

21 Following the demise of quirky Australasian outfit **Split Enz**, the trio of **Neil Finn**, recent Split Enz alumnus **Paul Hester**, and **Nick Seymour** begin their Coaster to Coaster tour of Australia as the **Mullanes**, at the Arts Factory in Byron, New South Wales. With Finn offered a contract by Capitol Records in Los Angeles, the trio will relocate there next month, initially augmented by guitarist **Craig Hooper**. They will play acoustic local club shows billed as the Largest Living Things, before settling on the name **Crowded House** (a reference to their cramped living conditions in their rented house off Sunset Boulevard).

June

14 With the first airlift of supplies flown to Africa on June 10, and various local fundraising efforts still gathering momentum, video distributor RCA/Columbia ships "We Are The World – The Video Event," to swell **USA For Africa** funds.

21 With the Glastonbury Festival gaining annual momentum as the best music festival in the UK, organizer Michael Eavis – having outgrown his own Worthy Farm – has bought the adjacent Cockmill Farm to enlarge the site

The Bangles came together through an ad placed in The Recycler – "Band members wanted: Into the Beatles, Byrds and Buffalo Springfield."

David Bowie & Mick Jagger

The Housemartins

David Bowie's chart-topper with Mick Jagger was his second with another artist. He made No. 1 with Queen in 1981... The Housemartins sardonically described themselves as "the fourth best band in Hull."

by 100 acres. **Echo & the Bunnymen**, **Joe Cocker**, the **Style Council**, the **Boomtown Rats**, and **Aswad** are among the acts who will perform over the next three days, mainly in appalling weather. Tractors are the only possible means of towing vehicles stuck in the mud, prompting Eavis to say: "We have had the mud bath and proved we can still cope with the conditions."

22 The bad weather is also affecting an all-day festival at England's Knebworth Park. Home in the UK after four dates in Stockholm earlier this week, **Deep Purple** headline the event, before an estimated 70,000 people, supported by other hard rock acts **Alaska**, **Blackfoot**, **Mama's Boys**, **Meat Loaf**, **Mountain**, the **Scorpions**, and **U.F.O.** Some 300 rain-sodden fans are treated for hypothermia and various injuries: ten are taken to Lister Hospital in Stevenage, some with burns from fires lit in a bid to keep warm. Meanwhile, 50,000 people attend the Longest Day concert at the Milton Keynes Bowl, with a bill headlined by **U2**, and featuring the **Ramones**, **Billy Bragg**, **R.E.M.**, **Spear of Destiny**, and the **Faith Brothers**.

29 Two weeks before an appearance at Live Aid, **Mick Jagger** and **David Bowie** convene at Westside Studios in London, under the watchful eyes of producers Clive Langer and Alan Winstanley. They record a new version of the Motown classic, *Dancing In The Street*, adding subsequent mixes from Bob Clearmountain and Steve Thompson, as well as a dub version. It will go gold and top the UK chart in September.

29 **John Lennon**'s Rolls-Royce Phantom V is auctioned at Sotheby's in New York. It is owned by the Cooper-Hewitt Museum – to whom Lennon donated the vehicle in 1977. The psychedelia-painted car, bought in 1965, to which he added the WEYBRIDGE 46676 license plate, is expected to fetch $250,000 – but sets a new record as the most expensive car ever sold when Ripley's Believe It or Not museum owner, Jim Pattison of South Carolina, makes his final bid: $2,299,000.

July

8 **Playboy** beats **Penthouse** to the newsstands with its nude pictorial of **Madonna**, featuring revealing snaps of the singer taken in 1977. Her response to the scoop? "So what? I'm not ashamed." Just six weeks ago, **Time** magazine featured Madonna on its front cover with the headline "Why She's Hot."

21 The **Housemartins**, a quirky pop-rock quartet proudly based in Hull in the north of England, make their radio debut performing *Drop Down Dead* and other tracks on "The John Peel Show" on Radio 1. Comprising lead singers **Paul Heaton** and **Norman Cook**, bassist **Stan Cullimore**, and drummer **Hugh Whitaker**, their acerbic lyrical bent and accent on simple melodies will secure a record deal with the hip Go! Discs label in October.

August

11 Four weeks after **Duran Duran**'s James Bond theme song, *A View To A Kill*, hits US No. 1, sailing fanatic **Simon Le Bon**'s 77ft yacht *Drum of England* overturns, 3 miles off Falmouth in Cornwall, England, when its keel sheers off during the Fastnet race. Le Bon and five other members of his 24-strong crew are trapped under the boat for 40 minutes, surviving in an air pocket. The yacht sinks soon after they are rescued by the Royal Navy.

14 Much to **Paul McCartney**'s chagrin, **Michael Jackson**, formerly his friend and music collaborator, outbids the ex-**Beatle** in the acquisition of the ATV music publishing catalog – which includes a large portion of the **Lennon** and McCartney songbook – paying $47.5 million for the company. Jackson can afford it: he reportedly received a $58 million royalty check from Epic Records in May. McCartney sees it as an act of betrayal, and their relationship is permanently soured.

16 On her 27th birthday, **Madonna** marries actor Sean Penn in Malibu. While the coastal cliffside wedding takes place, news crews buzz overhead in a fleet of helicopters. Following their honeymoon at the Highlands Inn in Carmel, Madonna will begin work on her third album.

31 Re-promoted in the UK following its dramatic use during Live Aid (providing mood backing for footage of the African famine), the **Cars**' *Drive*, a million-seller in the US last year, re-hits No. 4. Writer **Ric Ocasek** will donate all subsequent *Drive* royalties to the Band Aid Trust.

> **"We're just a bunch of honest guys trying to make an honest buck doing what we want to do."**
>
> Foreigner's Mick Jones, **Creem**, June 1985

September

13 Not unexpectedly, "We Are The World" wins the Best Group Video and Viewers' Choice categories, at the second MTV Video Music Awards, held at Radio City Music Hall in New York, and **Bob Geldof** is honored with a one-time Special Recognition award. Ex-**Eagle Don Henley**'s stylish monochrome clip "The Boys Of Summer" receives four awards: Best Video, Best Direction in a Video (John Baptiste Mondino), Best Art Direction in a Video (Bryan Jones), and Best Cinematography in a Video (Pascal Lebeque). **Art of Noise**'s "Close To The Edit" picks up two awards: Best Editing in a Video and Most Experimental, both for director Zbigniew Rybczynski. **Bruce Springsteen** ("I'm On Fire") and **Tina Turner** ("What's Love Got To Do With It") win Best Male Video and Best Female Video respectively. Springsteen also nabs Best Stage Performance in a Video for "Dancing in the Dark."

14 Summer sessions for ***Different Light***, the second album by the **Bangles**, end at the Sunset Sound studios in Hollywood, with producer David Kahne. The all-female Los Angeles-based pop-rock quartet, managed by Miles Copeland and comprising singer/guitarist **Susanna Hoffs**, guitarist/vocalist **Vicki Peterson**, bassist/vocalist **Michael Steele**, and drummer/vocalist **Debbi Peterson**, will deliver the recordings to Columbia Records on Monday. They include the album's first single, *Manic Monday* (written by **Prince**, under the pseudonym Christopher).

July 13 At 12:01 pm, **Status Quo** begin the Live Aid benefit concert extravaganza, organized by **Bob Geldof** and **Midge Ure** with help from legendary rock promoters Harvey Goldsmith and Bill Graham, as a follow-up to the **Band Aid** project. The world's biggest rock acts participate in the global fundraising event, which switches between joint venues: Wembley Stadium in London, in the presence of the Prince and Princess of Wales, and the JFK Stadium in Philadelphia. The 16-hour mega-concert includes appearances by **Paul Weller**, Bob Geldof and the **Boomtown Rats**, **Adam Ant**, **INXS**, **Ultravox**, **Spandau Ballet**, **Elvis Costello**, currently in-vogue British pop singers **Nik Kershaw** and **Howard Jones**, **B.B. King**, **Sade**, **Sting**, **Bryan Ferry**, **Paul Young**, **Alison Moyet**, **Bryan Adams**, **U2**, the **Beach Boys**, **Dire Straits**, **Queen**, **Simple Minds**, **David Bowie**, the **Pretenders**, the **Who**,

"If there's a problem, you have to...

Santana, jazz fusion guitarist **Pat Metheny**, **Elton John**, **George Michael**, **Madonna**, the **Thompson Twins**, **Paul McCartney**, **Tom Petty**, **Neil Young**, **Power Station**, **Led Zeppelin** (re-forming just for today, with **Phil Collins** helping out on drums), **Duran Duran**, **Cliff Richard**, **Daryl Hall & John Oates**, **Tina Turner**, **Bob Dylan**, the **Rolling Stones' Mick Jagger**, **Keith Richard**, and **Ron Wood**, **Lionel Richie**, **Harry Belafonte**, and **Patti LaBelle.** Collins makes transatlantic rock history by first performing at Wembley, then flying immediately to Philadelphia to play a second set later in the day.

Watched by a television audience estimated at two billion, with telethons in 22 countries, Live Aid raised some $70 million, becoming a defining co-operative moment in the rock era.

go out and solve it." Bob Geldof, June 13, 1985

Sept

1985

Farm Aid... Artists United Against Apartheid... Rick Nelson is killed...

Dee Snider

Russell Simmons

Twisted Sister's Dee Snider gave testimony at a Senate Committee discussing the "contents of music and the lyrics of records"... Russell Simmons was perhaps the most important minority industry figure to emerge since Berry Gordy.

19 A Senate Committee on Commerce, Science & Transportation convenes to discuss the "contents of music and the lyrics of records," following serious lobbying from the Parents' Music Resource Center. Chaired by Missouri Republican John C. Danforth, and including senators Al Gore, John D. Rockefeller, Barry Goldwater, and Bob Packwood, the 17-member panel listens to testimony from PMRC's vice-president and views a segment of **Twisted Sister**'s "We're Not Going To Take It" video. **John Denver**, testifying to his opposition to any form of rating system, says: "The suppression of the people of a society begins in my mind with the censorship of the written or spoken word. It was so in Nazi Germany." Twisted Sister's **Dee Snider** is called next, taking particular umbrage at Al Gore's wife Tipper's objection to the band. After his testimony, Snider says: "They had no idea I spoke English fluently, which threw them for a loop. I kicked ass in there." Finally **Frank Zappa** is called, and immediately quotes the First Amendment to the Constitution: "Congress shall make no law respecting an establishment of religion or prohibiting the free exercise thereof, or abridging the freedom of speech or of the press or the right of the people peaceably to assemble and to petition the government for a redress of grievances." Despite the eloquence of Denver, Snider, and Zappa, the recording industry will eventually agree to institute a parental-advisory sticker on certain records.

20 **Mötley Crüe**'s **Vince Neil** pleads guilty to a vehicular manslaughter charge, stemming from last December's car crash, in which **Hanoi Rocks**' **Nick "Razzle" Dingley** died. Neil is sentenced to 30 days in jail, to be served next year at the end of the band's current tour, plus 200 hours of community service. He is also ordered to pay $2.6 million in restitution to Dingley's family. His lawyer argues that since most of those at the party prior to the crash were members of Mötley Crüe and Hanoi Rocks, it can be interpreted as a business meeting, allowing the band's limited liability insurance to cover the payment of much higher damages to the victims than if Neil were to have to pay them himself. Newspapers respond to the light sentence with such headlines as: "Drunk Killer Vince Neil Sentenced To Touring World With Rock Band."

21 Aided by an innovative, animated promo video, directed by Steve Barron, which is receiving heavy MTV rotation, **Dire Straits**' *Money For Nothing* tops the US chart for the first of three weeks, becoming the band's biggest US hit and its first million-selling single.

22 Inspired by **Bob Dylan**'s comment at Live Aid ("Wouldn't it be great if we did something for our own farmers right here in America?"), Farm Aid is held at the University of Illinois' Memorial Stadium in Champaign. The all-day festival raises $1,450,000, plus a further estimated $6 million in donations. Bob Dylan, backed by **Tom Petty & the Heartbreakers** (who also play their own set), **Willie Nelson**, **John Mellencamp**, **Neil Young**, **B.B. King**, **Roy Orbison**, the queen of country **Loretta Lynn**, up-and-coming New Jersey rockers **Bon Jovi**, **Foreigner**, who perform *I Want To Know What Love Is* accompanied by a 30-strong choir, **Billy Joel**, and **Randy Newman** (who perform *Sail Away*, *Political Science*, *Only The Good Die Young*, and *Stagger Lee* together) are among 60 artists taking part. The event – chiefly organized by Nelson, Mellencamp, and Young – will become an annual festival into the 1990s.

> **"If you write a song with a political message, then you're guilty of politics. You are guilty of trying to sway people and, therefore, you are guilty of propaganda, of trying to influence, pervert, subvert."**
>
> Sting, **Playboy**, November 1985

October

12 Three days after his sister **Cindy** discovered he has AIDS, the **B-52's** guitarist and founding member **Ricky Wilson** dies at the age of 32 at New York City's Memorial Sloan Kettering Hospital, the first notable musician to succumb to the disease.

21 At Limehouse Studios, London, a television special is taped to mark the 30th anniversary of the release of *Blue Suede Shoes*. It consists of a performance by "Carl Perkins And Friends", who include **George Harrison**, **Ringo Starr**, **Eric Clapton**, **Dave Edmunds** (who coordinates the band and music), and the **Stray Cats**' **Lee Rocker** and **Slim Jim Phantom**.

26 The soundtrack to the first rap movie, "Krush Groove," enters the US album chart. Based on the life of **Russell Simmons** – depicted as Russell Walker, played by Blair Underwood – both the film and its album feature some of the hottest acts on the hip-hop and R&B scene, including **Run-D.M.C.**, the **Fat Boys**, the **Beastie Boys**, **Sheila E.**, **Kurtis Blow**, **New Edition**, Russell Simmons (as Crocket), **Rick Rubin**, and **LL Cool J**.

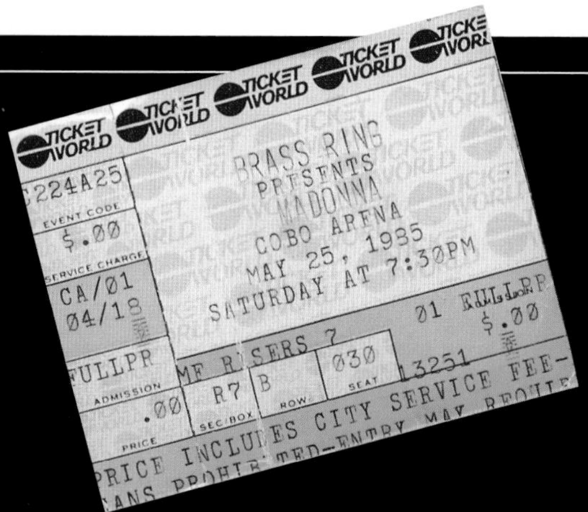

Bette Midler introduced Madonna at Live Aid in Philadelphia with the words, "a woman who pulled herself up by her bra-straps"... Highlights of Farm Aid included Billy Joel and Randy Newman performing together, as well as John Fogerty's first solo appearance.

Farm Aid

George Michael sang ***Don't Let The Sun Go Down On Me*** with Elton John at Live Aid in July, pre-dating a 1991 recording of the song.

PHIL COLLINS

Nov 30 **Phil Collins celebrates his third US chart-topper of the year, as the Stephen Bishop-penned *Separate Lives* hits No. 1. A duet with Marilyn Martin, recorded as the love theme for the Mikhail Baryshnikov/ Gregory Hines movie "White Nights," it is his fifth million-selling single from his last six releases. It has been a triumphant and busy year for the Genesis drummer/singer. *Easy Lover*, an uptempo dance number jointly credited with Earth, Wind & Fire's Philip Bailey, hit US No. 2 and spent four weeks at UK No. 1. At the 27th Grammy Awards in February he won the Best Pop Vocal Performance, Male category for *Against All Odds*, a self-penned composition that was also named Best Song Musically and Lyrically at the 30th Ivor Novello Awards. The Eric Clapton album *Behind The Sun*, produced by Collins, was another success, while his own *No Jacket Required* spent more than a month astride both the UK and US album charts. He also played twice at Live Aid.**

November

17 **Prince** – who rarely grants media interviews – gives his second of the year. Following an unrevealing chat with Neal Karlen in **Rolling Stone** in April, his Purple Highness now appears on MTV.

December

6 At a **John Mellencamp** concert at New York's Madison Square Garden, the sound system breaks down twice. Mellencamp waits patiently for the problem to be resolved, then plays for two hours and tells the audience that anyone with a ticket stub can get their money back if they wish.

7 **Mr. Mister** make their network television debut on "Saturday Night Live," performing their recent US No. 1 smash *Broken Wings*, and their just-released follow-up, *Kyrie* (which will also head to the top). The pop/rock quartet, and current FM radio favorites, arose two years ago in Los Angeles from the ashes of earlier combo the **Pages** – both fronted by lead singer and bassist **Richard Page**.

12 Known as the "sixth **Rolling Stone**," keyboardist **Ian Stewart** – having played as part of **Rocket 88** at the Old Vic Tavern in Nottingham, England, last night – dies of a heart attack in his doctor's Harley Street reception room while waiting to see him. All the Stones will attend his funeral in Leatherhead on December 20.

14 At the end of a banner year, **George Michael** features on four Top 40 records in the UK Christmas chart: **Wham!**'s *I'm Your Man* (No. 2), **Band Aid**'s re-charted *Do They Know It's Christmas?* (No. 6), **Elton John**'s *Nikita* (No. 18) – as backing vocalist – and the re-entered Wham! seasonal treat, *Last Christmas* (No. 32).

14 Capping a year that has seen an unprecedented number of fundraising ventures, **Artists United Against Apartheid** make US No. 38 and UK No. 21 with *Sun City*. The music collective, organized by **Little Steven** and producer **Arthur Baker**, comprises 49 artists, including **Peter Gabriel**, **Bono**, **Bob Dylan**, **Lou Reed**, **Bonnie Raitt**, **Jackson Browne**, **Pat Benatar**, **Bruce Springsteen**, **Bob Geldof**, **Herbie Hancock**, **Miles Davis**, **Pete Townshend**, **Gil Scott-Heron**, **Rubén Blades**, **Peter Garrett**, and **Afrika Bambaataa**.

21 **Madness**, **Ian Dury**, **Marc Almond**, and others participate in the Christmas Party for the Unemployed, organized by the Greater London Council at Finsbury Park.

21 *Do They Know It's Christmas?*, re-charting in the UK, hits No. 3. Special Christmas messages by artists including **David Bowie** and **Paul McCartney** are now collected on the B-side. It will continue to be seasonally re-issued.

23 Raymond Belknap, age 18, and James Vance, 20, having apparently spent several hours drinking beer, smoking marijuana, and listening to **Judas Priest**'s ***Stained Class*** album, make a suicide pact. They go to a church schoolyard in Sparks, Nevada, to carry out their plan. Belknap holds a sawn-off shotgun under his chin, fires, and dies instantly, but Vance survives, seriously wounded. Their families will file a $6.2 million lawsuit against the band and Columbia Records.

31 One of the first teen idols of the rock 'n' roll era, **Rick Nelson** is killed at the age of 45, when a chartered DC3 carrying him between concert dates in Guntersville, Alabama, and Dallas catches fire and crashes near De Kalb, Texas. Rumors will persist that the fire was caused by the plane's occupants freebasing cocaine, but the allegation will prove to be without foundation.

ROOTS During this year: Brett Anderson, the son of an ice-cream vendor in Haywards Heath, England, forms Geoff with schoolfriends Mat Osman, Gareth Perry, and Danny Wilder... comic-book collector Rob Zombie meets female bassist Sean Yseult at New York's CBGB club... Nellee Hooper, a member of the Bristol-based Massive Attack, meets Jazzie B, a member of Soul II Soul, when he rents the band's equipment for a London gig... having left home at the age of 18 and headed to Florida, Chicagoan Billy Corgan forms goth-rock band Marked... Hurby Azor, who is working on a class project at New York's Center for Media Arts, invites friends Cheryl James and Sandra Denton to rap on *The Show Stoppa*; following the success of the track, which becomes an R&B hit, the duo, still under Azor's direction, become Salt-N-Pepa... Kevin Wasserman joins Manic Subsidal, formed last year by Bryan Holland, as they now become Offspring... after a series of part-time jobs, including one as a kiss-o-gram French maid, Sinéad O'Connor begins performing solo in Dublin pubs... and working at the Pi Corporation retail synthesizer store in Cleveland, Ohio, Trent Reznor joins local band Exotic Birds...

(You Gotta) Fight For Your Right (To Party!)

1986

No.1 US SINGLES

Jan 4 Say You, Say Me **Lionel Richie**
Jan 18 That's What Friends Are For **Dionne & Friends**
Feb 15 How Will I Know **Whitney Houston**
Mar 1 Kyrie **Mr. Mister**
Mar 15 Sara **Starship**
Mar 22 These Dreams **Heart**
Mar 29 Rock Me Amadeus **Falco**
Apr 19 Kiss **Prince & the Revolution**
May 3 Addicted To Love **Robert Palmer**
May 10 West End Girls **Pet Shop Boys**
May 17 Greatest Love Of All **Whitney Houston**
June 7 Live To Tell **Madonna**
June 14 On My Own **Patti LaBelle & Michael McDonald**
July 5 There'll Be Sad Songs (To Make You Cry) **Billy Ocean**
July 12 Holding Back The Years **Simply Red**
July 19 Invisible Touch **Genesis**
July 26 Sledgehammer **Peter Gabriel**
Aug 2 Glory Of Love **Peter Cetera**
Aug 16 Papa Don't Preach **Madonna**
Aug 30 Higher Love **Steve Winwood**
Sept 6 Venus **Bananarama**
Sept 13 Take My Breath Away **Berlin**
Sept 20 Stuck With You **Huey Lewis & the News**
Oct 11 When I Think Of You **Janet Jackson**
Oct 25 True Colors **Cyndi Lauper**
Nov 8 Amanda **Boston**
Nov 22 Human **Human League**
Nov 29 You Give Love A Bad Name **Bon Jovi**
Dec 6 The Next Time I Fall **Peter Cetera with Amy Grant**
Dec 13 The Way It Is **Bruce Hornsby & the Range**
Dec 20 Walk Like An Egyptian **Bangles**

No.1 UK SINGLES

Jan 4 Merry Christmas Everyone **Shakin' Stevens**
Jan 11 West End Girls **Pet Shop Boys**
Jan 25 The Sun Always Shines On T.V. **a-ha**
Feb 8 When The Going Gets Tough The Tough Get Going **Billy Ocean**
Mar 8 Chain Reaction **Diana Ross**
Mar 29 Living Doll **Cliff Richard & the Young Ones featuring Hank Marvin**
Apr 19 A Different Corner **George Michael**
May 10 Rock Me Amadeus **Falco**

Pet Shop Boys

Janet Jackson

The Pet Shop Boys came together when Neil Tennant, the assistant editor of British pop magazine Smash Hits, met architecture student Chris Lowe in a hi-fi shop in London's King's Road... Janet Jackson appeared with her brothers' stage show at the MGM Grand Hotel in Las Vegas when she was seven years old.

In a year of cross-currents, with no dominant genre, synth-driven pop-dance was perenially popular, while hip-hop, the re-emergence of country, and "world music" made for a more diversified palate, and the fashion for benefit concerts persisted.

Janet Jackson shot to prominence, though not – like **Whitney Houston** the year before – with her debut album. ***Control*** was a much funkier offering than Whitney's, thanks largely to producers **Jimmy Jam** and **Terry Lewis**. It went to US No.1, beginning a long and profitable partnership that would yield many of the most danceable tracks of the times.

In November, female artists claimed the top three positions on the **Billboard** US singles chart for the first time. Janet was one, **Tina Turner** was another, and the third was the idiosyncratic (OK eccentric) **Cyndi Lauper**, whose album ***True Colors*** generated a No.1 single. **Madonna**'s album ***True Blue*** revealed a maturing talent.

Elbowing aside Madonna and other established stars were the first Norse invaders since **Abba**. The pretty boys of **a-ha** swept aside rivals at the MTV awards, and conquered the charts with ***Take On Me*** and ***The Sun Always Shines On T.V.*** A more enduring electronic/pop unit would be the **Pet Shop Boys**. Their lush melodies, irreverent lyrics, and ability to navigate changing styles would guarantee a string of hits, the first being the coolly elegant *West End Girls.*

White American adolescent males continued to patronize hard rock acts, the latest to break through being New Jersey's **Bon Jovi**. **Jon Bon Jovi**'s husky vocals and **Richie Sambora**'s guitar powered their album ***Slippery When Wet*** all the way to the top. Rock veterans **Steven Tyler** and **Joe Perry** of **Aerosmith** became part of the most unusual double act of the year, combining with hip-hop champions **Run-D.M.C.** on *Walk This Way.* Both parties had to be prodded by Def Jam's **Rick Rubin**, but the song was eventually recorded and rocketed hip-hop out of the inner cities to the white suburbs of America.

Perhaps the most original and daring work of the year was **Paul Simon**'s ***Graceland*** – and his embrace of world music and especially South African harmonies. In a set of gems, Simon's collaboration with vocal group **Ladysmith Black Mambazo** was captivating. The album was instrumental in building interest in world music.

Thirty years after **Elvis** and company kick-started rock 'n' roll, they received official recognition with the creation of the Rock and Roll Hall of Fame. **Sam Cooke**, **Chuck Berry**, and **James Brown** were also among the first inductees. So was the man whose Sun Records incubated so much early rock – **Sam Phillips**. Not a moment too soon, as some of the originals were passing on.

"We're more rock 'n' roll than Def Leppard."

a-ha's Pal Waaktaar, 1987

- **May 17** The Chicken Song **Spitting Image**
- **June 17** Spirit In The Sky **Dr. & the Medics**
- **June 28** The Edge Of Heaven **Wham!**
- **July 12** Papa Don't Preach **Madonna**
- **Aug 2** The Lady In Red **Chris De Burgh**
- **Aug 23** I Want To Wake Up With You **Boris Gardiner**
- **Sept 13** Don't Leave Me This Way **Communards**
- **Oct 11** True Blue **Madonna**
- **Oct 18** Every Loser Wins **Nick Berry**
- **Nov 8** Take My Breath Away (Love Theme From "Top Gun") **Berlin**
- **Dec 6** The Final Countdown **Europe**
- **Dec 20** Caravan Of Love **Housemartins**
- **Dec 27** Reet Petite (The Sweetest Girl In Town) **Jackie Wilson**

Jan 1986

The first Rock and Roll Hall of Fame inductees... Geffen signs Guns N' Roses...

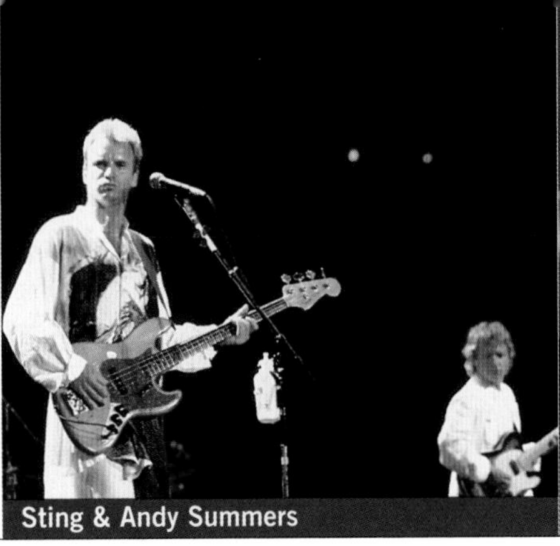

Sting & Andy Summers

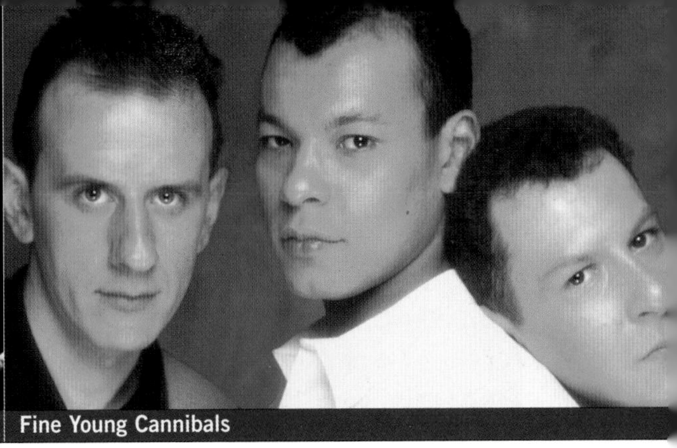

Fine Young Cannibals

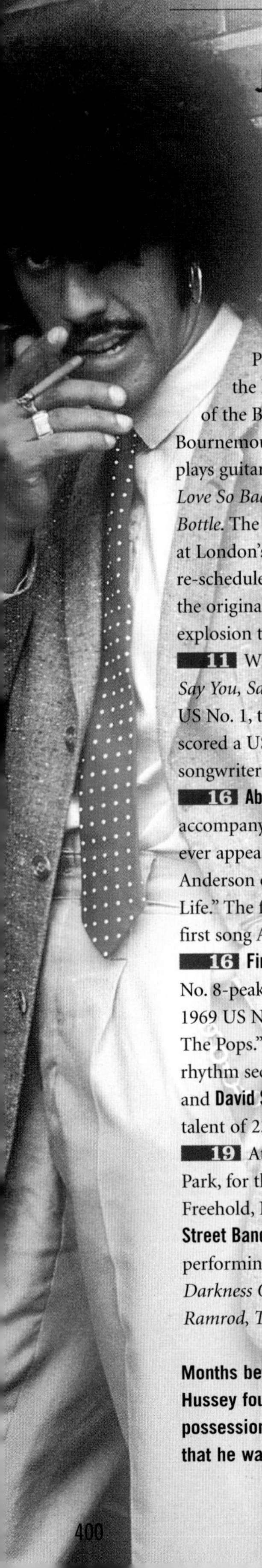

January

4 A long-time heroin addict, former **Thin Lizzy** frontman **Phil Lynott** dies, age 36, in Salisbury General Infirmary, with his wife Caroline and father-in-law, Leslie Crowther, at his bedside. He will be buried in St. Fintan's cemetery, Howth, overlooking Dublin Bay.

4 **Andy Summers** joins former Police man, **Sting**, at the beginning of the latter's 19-date UK leg of the Dream of the Blue Turtles World Tour, at the Bournemouth International Centre. Summers plays guitar on *Every Breath You Take, Need Your Love So Bad, Demolition Man,* and *Message In A Bottle.* The tour, which will include six nights at London's Royal Albert Hall, will end with a re-scheduled date at Newcastle's City Hall, after the original concert is canceled when an explosion takes out the power supply.

11 With **Lionel Richie**'s latest ballad smash *Say You, Say Me* spending its final week at US No. 1, the popular tunesmith has now scored a US chart-topper – either as singer or songwriter – every year for the past nine years.

16 **Abba**, with **Benny Andersson** accompanying on accordian, reunites for a last ever appearance to honor manager Stig Anderson on Swedish television's "This Is Your Life." The foursome perform *Tivedshambo,* the first song Anderson wrote, in 1947.

16 **Fine Young Cannibals** perform their UK No. 8-peaking cover version of **Elvis Presley**'s 1969 US No. 1 hit, *Suspicious Minds,* on "Top Of The Pops." The emerging trio combines the tight rhythm section of ex-**Beat** members **Andy Cox** and **David Steele** with the distinctive vocal talent of 23-year-old frontman, **Roland Gift**.

19 At a benefit at the Stone Pony, Asbury Park, for the laid-off workers of the 3M plant at Freehold, New Jersey, **Bruce Springsteen & the E Street Band** make a surprise appearance, performing *The Promised Land, Badlands, Darkness On The Edge Of Town, Stand On It, Ramrod, Twist And Shout,* and *My Hometown,* which the workers have adopted as their anthem. Next month Chrysler Corporation head, Lee Iacocca, will reportedly offer Springsteen $12 million to license *Born In The USA* for a series of Chrysler car commercials. The Boss will reject the boss's offer.

20 The first Martin Luther King Day is celebrated with concerts in Atlanta, New York City, and the John F. Kennedy Performing Arts Center in Washington, where **Bob Dylan** performs *I Shall Be Released, Blowin' In The Wind,* backed by **Peter, Paul & Mary** and **Stevie Wonder**, and a duet with Wonder on *The Bells Of Freedom.* The concert is highlighted by all the participants – backed by an orchestra conducted by **Quincy Jones** – singing Wonder's *Happy Birthday.*

Months before his death, Dublin Judge Gillian Hussey found Phil Lynott guilty of narcotics possession, prophetically saying of the singer that he was "only destroying himself."

Although the Police effectively disbanded in 1985, Andy Summers joined Sting during the latter's solo The Dream Of The Blue Turtles World Tour... Former members of the (English) Beat, Andy Cox and David Steele, invited Roland Gift, an actor with the Hull Community Theatre Workshop, to form Fine Young Cannibals.

"It's hard for me to induct Chuck Berry, because I lifted every lick he ever played!"

Keith Richards at the inaugural Rock and Roll Hall of Fame induction ceremonies, January 23, 1986

23 The first class of inductees enters the Rock and Roll Hall of Fame: **Chuck Berry**, **James Brown**, **Ray Charles**, **Sam Cooke**, **Fats Domino**, the **Everly Brothers**, **Buddy Holly**, **Jerry Lee Lewis**, **Elvis Presley**, and **Little Richard**. **Robert Johnson**, **Jimmie Rodgers**, and **Jimmy Yancey** make it in the Early Influence category. The Lifetime Achievement honor is bestowed on **John Hammond**, while **Alan Freed** and **Sam Phillips** are the two Non-Performers inductees. The inaugural induction dinner ends with an all-star jam – a tradition that will continue through the years – featuring Chuck Berry, Jerry Lee Lewis, **Chubby Checker**, **Keith Richards**, **Ron Wood**, **John Fogerty**, **Billy Joel**, **Julian Lennon**, and **Steve Winwood**, backed by a band led by **Paul Shaffer**. The Rock and Roll Hall of Fame Foundation was established in 1983 by leaders of the music industry to "recognize the contributions of those who have had a significant impact on the evolution, development, and perpetuation of rock and roll by inducting them into the Hall of Fame." In future years, the number of inductees in the main Performer category will be limited to between five and seven acts, selected from a longer list initially assembled by the Foundation's nominating committee, and voted upon by "an international voting body of about 1,000 rock experts."

February

10 **Phil Collins** is named Best British *Male* Solo Artist, and his bestseller ***No Jacket Required*** is hailed Best Album at the fifth BPI Awards in London. UK pop duo **Go West** (**Richard Drummie** and **Peter Cox**) win both Best British Newcomer and Best British Group – the first time these awards have gone to one act. Ironically, their biggest hit is already behind them: last year's UK No. 5, *We Close Our Eyes.* **Annie Lennox** wins her second Best British Female Solo Artist award, **Huey Lewis & the News** are named Best International Group, and **Paul Young** wins the Best British Video award for "Every Time You Go Away" – which gave the 30-year-old pop singer his first US chart-topper last year. **Tears for Fears**' *Everybody Wants To Rule The World* is named Best British Single, and **Elton John** and **Wham!** share the award for Outstanding Contribution to British Music.

13 **Rolling Stone** publishes the only known photograph of blues legend **Robert Johnson** – smoking a cigarette and with his fingers caressing the neck of an acoustic guitar – taken in a coin-operated photo booth in the early 1930s.

25 *We Are The World,* the most successful single in US history, receives four awards at the 28th Grammys: Record of the Year, Song of the Year, Best Group Pop Vocal Performance, and Best Short Form Music Video. Producer **Quincy Jones**, accepting the Record of the Year trophy, thanks "the generation that changed 'I, Me, My' to 'We, You, Us'." In a category that included three English acts, **Phil Collins**'s ***No Jacket Required*** wins Album of the Year – his third award of the night.

March

4 After playing two sets at the Cheek to Cheek Lounge in Winter Park, Florida, during a reunion tour with the **Band** (sans **Robbie Robertson**), 42-year-old **Richard Manuel**, apparently in a fit of depression, hangs himself in his motel room at the Quality Inn next door.

8 One year after its release, ***Whitney Houston*** finally tops the US chart, having peaked at UK No. 2 in December. Featuring three US No. 1 singles, its worldwide sales will eventually exceed 22 million, making it the highest-selling debut album by a female artist to date.

20 The **Housemartins** perform at the Clarendon Hotel Ballroom in Hammersmith, during their Twisted Roadshow tour. Claiming poverty, they help pay for National Travel bus passes by collecting Mars bar wrappers with promotional coupons, and introduce "Adopt-a-Housemartin": wherever they are playing, members of the audience are requested to invite group members to stay for the night to save hotel bills.

24 Parlophone/EMI releases ***Please*** in the UK, the debut album by the **Pet Shop Boys**, which includes their recent UK No. 1 smash *West End Girls*, also headed to US No. 1 on May 10. It marks the beginning of one of the most enduring careers for a British synth-pop group: media-friendly Neil Tennant and media-shy partner Chris Lowe will enjoy long-term success into the next century, with a commercially appealing formula of melody-driven, dance/pop confections topped with clever lyrical themes and groundbreaking videos.

25 Following intensive live work in California and record label competition, **Guns N' Roses** are signed worldwide to Geffen Records by A&R heads Tom Zutaut and Teresa Ensenat. The Los Angeles-based hard-rock quintet with a hedonistic bent comprises ex-**L.A. Guns** members, lead singer **Axl Rose** and guitarist **Izzy Stradlin**, lead guitarist **Slash**, bassist **Duff McKagan**, and drummer **Steven Adler**. Recording sessions will be completed by December at Rumbo Studios for its debut album, which will emerge next year entitled ***Appetite For Destruction***.

29 **Cliff Richard** has his 11th UK No. 1 (his first since 1979) with a spoof revival of his own former chart-topper *Living Doll*, recorded with anarchic television comedy team the **Young Ones**. With long-time cohort **Hank Marvin** guesting on guitar, all proceeds from the hit are benefiting the Comic Relief charity.

31 **O'Kelly Isley** – eldest of the three legendary **Isley Brothers** – dies of a heart attack, age 48, at his home in Alpine, New Jersey.

April

4 **Cliff Richard**, **Kate Bush**, **Howard Jones**, **Bob Geldof**, and **Midge Ure** provide the music for the Utterly Utterly Live Comic Relief concert (the first of three) at the Shaftesbury Theatre in London. **Billy Connolly**, Lenny Henry, Ben Elton, Rowan Atkinson, and French & Saunders provide the comedy. Bush sings *Do Bears...* with Atkinson, Richard joins the **Young Ones** on *Living Doll*, and Geldof and Ure perform *Feed The World*.

4 The movie musical "Absolute Beginners" receives its Royal Charity Premiere at the Odeon Cinema, Leicester Square, London, attended by Princess Anne. Directed by Julien Temple, it is based on Colin MacInnes's 1950s beat novel, and stars **Patsy Kensit** – emerging starlet and lead singer with UK synth-pop outfit, **Eighth Wonder** – **David Bowie**, **Ray Davies**, **Sade**, punkabilly singer **Tenpole Tudor**, reggae artist **Smiley Culture**, **Sandie Shaw**, and **Zoot Money**. It opens to mixed reviews, but the soundtrack – mixing material from Bowie and Davies with jazz great, **Gil Evans** – will do better, yielding a UK No. 2 hit for Bowie's title track.

7 In a ceremony honoring the best in British songwriting, veterans hold sway at the 31st Ivor Novello Awards. **Elton John** is recognized for his Outstanding Contribution to British Music, as well as nabbing the Best Song Musically and Lyrically for *Nikita*. **Eric Clapton** wins the Best Theme for a TV or Radio Production for the BBC television thriller "Edge Of Darkness." **Phil Collins**'s *Easy Lover* is named the Most Performed Work, and **Elaine Paige & Barbara Dickson**'s duet *I Know Him So Well*, from the musical "Chess," is the Best Selling A-Side of 1985. Relative newcomer **Roland Orzabal** is named Songwriter of the Year, for his hits with **Tears For Fears**.

9 The musical "Time" – devised, co-written, and produced by drummer **Dave Clark** (who eschews all offers to re-form the **Dave Clark Five**) – premieres at London's Dominion Theatre. **Cliff Richard**, in the leading role, is described by the **Evening Standard**'s Milton Shulman as "wearing the worried look of a man trying to be good and eternally young forever." Despite Shulman's less-than-glowing review – "It has been a long time since I have seen so much expensive technological ingenuity squandered on such an infantile project" – the show will have a run long enough to allow **David Cassidy** to take over Richard's role next April.

BON JOVI

Feb 20 Sessions begin for Bon Jovi's third album at Little Mountain Studios, Vancouver (owned by producer Bruce Fairbairn). The group's main writers, Jon Bon Jovi and Richie Sambora, have enlisted the help of songwriter Desmond Child, with whom they fashion four of the ten songs. The result, *Slippery When Wet* – a sturdy mix of driving rockers and power ballads – will propel them to the forefront of American hard rock in the late 1980s. It will begin an eight-week stay at US No. 1 on October 25, and will become one of the biggest-selling rock albums of the decade, eventually shifting more than ten million domestic copies. It includes a pair of US chart-toppers – *You Give Love A Bad Name*, which will hit No. 1 on November 29, becoming their first million-selling single worldwide, and *Livin' On A Prayer*, written in similar style by Bon Jovi/Sambora/Child – and the US No. 7-peaking *Wanted Dead Or Alive*. With their videos receiving saturation rotation on MTV, the New Jersey rockers will also embark on a headlining world tour in October that will keep them busy for two years.

Rockers Bon Jovi are led by the former John Francis Bongiovi Jr

May 1986

Bob Geldof and Paula Yates

Conspiracy of Hope concerts... "Sir Bob"... Wham!'s Final Concert...

Bob Geldof, accompanied by his then wife Paula Yates, received his honorary knighthood in a ceremony at Buckingham Palace... George Michael said goodbye to shuttlecocks three days after his 23rd birthday.

May

3 **Robert Palmer**'s *Addicted To Love*, with vocal arrangements by **Chaka Khan**, hits US No. 1, set to become his first worldwide million-selling single. Its chances of success are dramatically improved by a striking testosterone-inducing video, filmed by photographer Terence Donovan and featuring emotionless black-mini-skirted models strumming instruments behind an ever-dapper, besuited Palmer. Hotly rotated on MTV, it will be one of the decade's most enduring clips.

6 **Michael Jackson**'s manager Frank DiLeo, business affairs adviser John Branca, and Pepsi president Roger Enrico complete Jackson's second contract for the soft drinks giant. This time for $15 million, it will include two further ads and sponsorship of a solo world tour.

> "We don't care about no boy who wears tight pants and struts around like a woman."
>
> Dugan Wragge, rancher, on Prince, July 1, 1986

13 **Ted Nugent**, appearing on sex therapist Dr. Ruth Westheimer's TV show, says, "Life is one big female safari and Dr. Ruth is my guide." Last month while on a US tour, Nugent allegedly stripped a 19-year-old fan down to her underwear: "I did such a good job, they didn't have the heart to arrest me."

14 **Prince** makes a guest appearance with the **Bangles**, at San Francisco's Warfield Theater, performing the self-penned *Manic Monday* (which peaked at US No. 2 last month) and the **Jerry Lee Lewis** classic, *Whole Lotta Shakin' Going On*.

17 Around 30,000 fans attend Self-Aid – Make It Work, a post Live Aid effort to raise funds for the unemployed in Eire (some 250,000 of the nation's 3.5 million are currently without a job), at the R.D.S. Jumping Arena in Dublin. The 27-act bill, headlined by **U2** and featuring **Van Morrison**, **Elvis Costello & the Attractions**, the **Boomtown Rats**, *Lady In Red* tunesmith **Chris de Burgh** (who was actually born in Argentina), and the **Pogues**, lasts for 14 hours. The performances are shown live on Irish television, reportedly attracting the country's largest ever TV audience.

31 **Mark Knopfler**, recuperating after a year-long worldwide tour with **Dire Straits**, teams up with **Steve Phillips** and **Brendan Croker** to play a one-time only gig at the Grove pub in the Leeds suburb of Holbeck, England. (Knopfler and Phillips first met in 1968, when both were writing for the **Yorkshire Evening Post**.) Billed as the **Notting Hillbillies**, they receive the princely sum of £66 ($99). A good time is had by all at the gig, which will lead to recording sessions and a tour, with Dire Straits manager Ed Bicknell recruited as drummer, **Guy Fletcher** (keyboards), **Paul Franklin** (pedal steel), and **Marcus Cliff** (bass). The recordings will be released as ***Missing... Presumed Having A Good Time***, a tribute to American bluegrass and country music.

June

4 The first of six Conspiracy of Hope benefit concerts takes place at the Cow Palace in San Francisco. Celebrating the 25th anniversary of the founding of human rights organization Amnesty International, **Sting** – who will be joined by **Stewart Copeland** and **Andy Summers** for the last three dates of the tour – **Bono**, **Peter Gabriel**, **Bryan Adams**, **Lou Reed**, **Jackson Browne**, the **Neville Brothers**, and **Joan Baez** perform solo sets before joining together at the end to sing *I Shall Be Released*. The caravan will also visit Los Angeles, Denver, Atlanta, and Chicago, before coming to an end in East Rutherford, New Jersey, where the 12-hour show – attended by 50,207 fans – will be simulcast on MTV and the Westwood One radio network. **Whitney Houston**, **Jeff Beck**, **Pete Townshend**, **Carlos Santana**, **Third World**, **ZZ Top**, **Run-D.M.C.**, and **Miles Davis** are among many artists who will take part in the final event. More than 116,000 people will see the concerts, doubling Amnesty International's membership over the next weeks.

14 **Bob Geldof** is named in the Queen's Birthday Honours List, receiving an honorary knighthood in recognition of his humanitarian activities. Being Irish, he cannot be knighted, but Bob Geldof K.B.E. is affectionately nicknamed "Sir Bob" by the UK press.

15 **Mötley Crüe**'s **Vince Neil** enters Gardena City Jail, to begin his 30-day sentence. As a trustee, he will clean cells, wash police cars, and deliver food to inmates in order to earn a reduction in his sentence. He shares his cell with a prisoner serving time for stealing expensive cars. His celebrity will earn him privileges of burgers and beer, in part due to having his photo taken with prison guards. He will be released after 18 days as a result of his good behavior – perhaps the only time that the words "Vince Neil" and "good behavior" have ever been used in the same sentence.

20 The Prince's Trust tenth Anniversary Birthday Party concert, in the presence of Prince Charles and Princess Diana – now a top-drawer annual fundraiser – boasts an all-star bill, with **Eric Clapton**, **Phil Collins**, **Elton John**, **Paul McCartney**, **George Michael**, **Rod Stewart**, **Tina Turner**, **Bryan Adams**, **David Bowie** and **Mick Jagger**, and others, at Wembley Arena, London. John plays piano on McCartney's *Get Back* and *I Saw Her Standing There*, while **Sting** joins the all-star band on *Money For Nothing*.

20 The Glastonbury Festival takes place at its traditional Worthy Farm location in Pilton, Somerset, England, continuing its expansion to stake its claim as the most important event on the UK's festival calendar. The Theatre and Children's Areas move to new locations, and for the first time a classical music tent is introduced. The 60,000 attendees help to raise £130,000 ($195,000) for CND and local charities. This year's acts, appearing over the next three days, include the **Cure** (who is currently crossing over to become the darlings of the emerging modern rock radio scene in the US), **Madness**, the **Pogues**, the **Waterboys**, and the **Housemartins**. Also on the bill are two hot UK acts who are breaking internationally: **Level 42**, whose pop/funk mix is

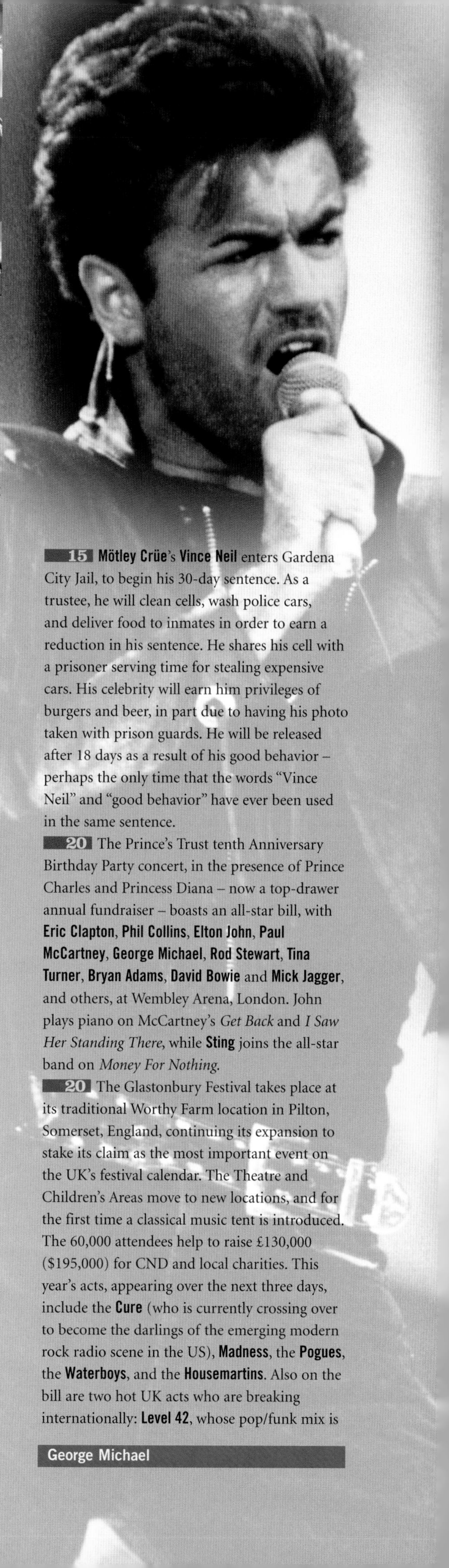
George Michael

dominated by thumb-thumping bassist/vocalist **Mark King**, and whose album ***World Machine*** hit US No. 18 last month; and **Simply Red**, a Manchester group that revolves around the songwriting and singing talent of 26-year-old, red-haired frontman **Mick Hucknall**. Their soul/pop-fused gem, *Holding Back The Years* is about to peak at UK No. 2 and US No. 1.

28 With their final single – a four-track EP, featuring the double-A billed *The Edge Of Heaven/Where Did Your Heart Go* – topping the UK chart, **Wham!**'s glittering four-year career, during which they have scored ten Top 10 hits in the UK and three No. 1s in the US, comes to an end before 72,000 delirious fans at the Final Concert at Wembley Stadium, London. Opening the event, **Gary Glitter** makes his first appearance at the venue in 14 years, followed by ex-**Haircut 100** lead singer, the now solo member **Nick Heyward**, before Michael dances on stage to the strains of *Everything She Wants*. As the duo get set to perform an evening of their greatest hits, Michael tells the crowd: "This is obviously the most important gig we have ever played. We've got four years of thank yous to say this evening and I know we are going to enjoy saying them, so let's get started." **Elton John** comes on stage in the guise of Ronald McDonald to back Michael on *Candle In The Wind*, later returning in a grape-colored jacket, topped with a pink Mohican wig, before **Simon Le Bon** joins in the duo's finale, *I'm Your Man*.

28 **Boy George** makes a brief appearance at an anti-apartheid concert featuring **Sting**, **Peter Gabriel**, **Sade**, and others on London's Clapham Common. Inexplicably covered in flour, he introduces himself as "your favorite junkie." Within a week, his brother, fearing for George's life, will leak the story of the singer's heroin addiction to the press. The star, who has publicly denounced drugs, is now himself an addict, although denying persistent rumors that his weight loss is caused by AIDS. He will soon enter a drug treatment facility for heroin addiction.

July

1 **Prince** attends the premiere of his new movie, "Under the Cherry Moon," at the Centennial Twin theater in the small town of Sheridan, Wyoming, with local motel chambermaid Lisa Barber as his date. A veteran contest entrant, Barber was the 10,000th caller to an MTV contest number to win the date. Following the premiere, Prince performs a 45-minute set at the nearby Holiday Inn.

4 Following the enormous success of last year's inaugural Farm Aid benefit concert, another is held at Manor Downs in Austin, Texas, featuring more than 60 acts. The event's movers and shakers – **Willie Nelson**, **John Mellencamp**, and **Neil Young** – once again perform. Latin crooner **Julio Iglesias** charters a private jet from Las Vegas, Nevada, where he is performing at Harrah's, to sing *To All The Girls I've Loved Before* with Nelson. **Bon Jovi**, **Bob Dylan**, **Tom Petty & the Heartbreakers**, **Alabama**, **Bonnie Raitt**, and "New Country" pioneer **Dwight Yoakam** also perform.

5 Fifty days after her 20th birthday, **Janet Jackson** tops the US chart with ***Control***, and becomes the youngest artist, since 13-year-old **Little Stevie Wonder** in 1963, to top the album survey. The album includes her breakthrough smash, the crisp, funk-dance number, *What Have You Done For Me Lately* – which has already topped the US R&B chart – and marks a major change of direction. Moving away from the bland pop/soul mix of her 1984 debut effort ***Dream Street*** – which even included a duet with **Cliff Richard** – Jackson has teamed up with red-hot Minneapolis songwriters/producers Jimmy Jam and Terry Lewis, who will provide the music backbone for all her material to the end of the century. Graduating from their early 1980s R&B combo **Time**, Jam and Lewis are the fast-rising hitmakers behind a slew of recent R&B hits, including those by the **S.O.S. Band**, **Patti Austin**, **Cherrelle**, **Alexander O'Neal**, and **Force M.D.'s**. Their slick, urbane mix of highly polished uptempo dance grooves and smooth ballads has also been put to good use in a recent collaboration with the **Human League**, who began four months of sessions with them in February. Their first release, the Jam and Lewis-penned *Human*, will hit US No. 1 on November 22.

12 No sooner have the headlines slipped off the front pages – police have arrested **Boy George**, his friend **Marilyn**, and several others for drug possession – than New York keyboardist **Michael Rudetski**, who played on the final **Culture Club** album and was signed up for another, dies of a heroin overdose in George's London home. Subsequently appearing at Marylebone Magistrates' Court on the drugs charge, George confirms that he will undertake Dr. Meg Patterson's electronic "black box" treatment to cure his addiction.

19 In the first major hip-hop festival in the UK, **Grandmaster Flash** and **Afrika Bambaataa** headline UK Fresh, a rap segment of the Capital Music Festival held at London's Wembley Arena.

27 Concertgoer Jon Moreland, having been jilted by his girlfriend, clambers on stage at a **Cure** concert in Los Angeles, California, and stabs himself repeatedly with a hunting knife. The 18,000 crowd cheers enthusiastically, thinking it is part of the show.

30 RCA Records drops **John Denver** from his contract. Industry insiders speculate that RCA's new owner, General Electric (a top military contractor), has taken exception to his new track *Let Us Begin (What Are We Making Weapons For?)*, which he recently recorded with top Soviet singer, **Alexandre Gradsky**, in Moscow's Melodiya studio.

August

1 **U2** begin seven months of intermittent recording sessions for their next album at the Windmill Lane Studios in Dublin, Ireland, with Brian Eno and Daniel Lanois producing. The results will yield next year's ***The Joshua Tree***.

4 **Michael Jackson** and co-producer **Quincy Jones** move into Studio D at Westlake Studios to begin recordings for their follow-up to ***Thriller***. Jackson has already written 62 songs for consideration, and Jones invites outsiders to offer more. (The Beatles' *Come Together* is recorded, but rejected.) Jackson insists that his snake, Crusher, and constant companion, Bubbles the chimp, be present at recording sessions. (Bubbles will enjoy studio rides on the back of engineer Bruce Swedien's Great Dane.)

9 **Queen**, returning from three gigs in Spain – part of a 25-date European tour that included a concert in Hungary, where they were the first western act to perform since Louis Armstrong in 1964 – top the bill at this year's Knebworth Park festival in the UK. Their 658th gig, it will also be their last. **Status Quo** and **Big Country** are among the supporting acts, playing in front of a crowd of 200,000.

9 **Randy Travis**'s debut album for Warner Bros., ***Storms Of Life***, which has cost $65,000 to produce and will ultimately earn the label $5.2 million, tops the US Country chart, on its way to US No. 85 and multiplatinum sales status. It is hailed as one of the pioneering releases for the "New Country" movement, alongside **Dwight Yoakam**'s first album, the recently released ***Guitars, Cadillacs, Etc., Etc.*** Although its roots lie in traditional country music, "New Country" is moving away from the staid sugary fare that has dominated a stagnant country scene for years.

Boy George confirmed his rehabilitation from drug addiction and the demise of Culture Club in early 1987 in an appearance on BBC1-TV's "Wogan" chat show.

May 10 **Paul Simon** and and veteran South African vocal ensemble, **Ladysmith Black Mambazo**, perform publicly for the first time together on “Saturday Night Live.” It is the first look into Simon’s upcoming new album, ***Graceland***, a groundbreaking work that fuses his deft songwriting skills with world music flavors, notably from South Africa. Simon was there last year, recording for nine days at the Ovation Studio with an ensemble of legendary indigenous musicians. He was inspired to recruit Ladysmith after seeing them perform on the BBC-TV documentary “Rhythm Of Resistance: The Music Of South Africa,” and subsequently recorded the haunting *Homeless* with them at

“Even if the album isn’t a hit....

London's Abbey Road Studios, a stunning performance showcasing the rich vocal talent of the group's leader, **Joseph Shabalala**. Although the album's South African bent will receive most notice, ***Graceland*** also includes the Cajun zydeco of **Rockin' Dopsie & the Twisters**, and the Chicano Latin rock of **Los Lobos**, while the title cut features the timeless backing harmonies of the **Everly Brothers**. With the album's release in September, Simon will score his biggest-selling solo work, and will be credited with opening the door to the first wave of ethnic "World Music."

Paul Simon followed *Graceland* – at five million US sales by far his most successful solo recording – by turning to South American music for his followup, *The Rhythm Of The Saints*, after meeting legendary Brazilian musician Milton Nascimento in a Los Angeles parking lot.

I don't plan to modify anything."

Paul Simon, **The New York Times**, August 24, 1986

Aug

1986

MTV airs *Walk This Way*... The first Bridge School Benefit...

Run-D.M.C.

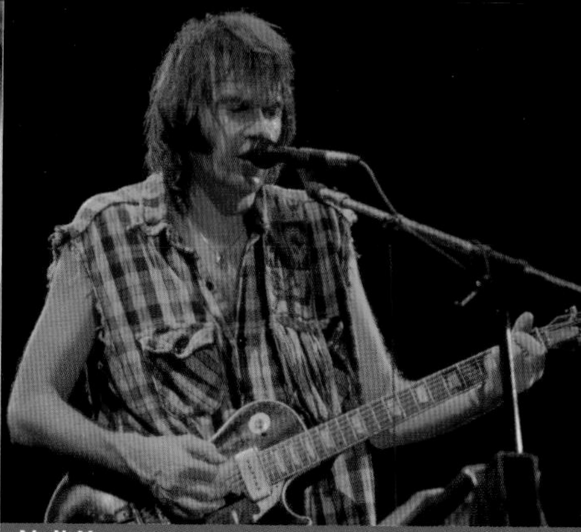
Neil Young

16 MTV begins airing the new **Run-D.M.C.** video, "Walk This Way." A groundbreaking recording, the hit single – currently on its way to US No. 4 – is a daring collaboration between the pioneering rap trio and **Aerosmith** frontmen **Steven Tyler** and **Joe Perry**. A rap/metal hybrid that updates Aerosmith's 1977 US No. 10 original, the union of rock's past with rap's future is the idea of Def Jam label co-owner Rick Rubin. With instant crossover appeal, *Walk This Way* and its attendant double-act video will bring rap to the attention of white youth. It will also recharge Aerosmith's career, sidelined – mostly through drug and alcohol abuse – since 1980. As Run-D.M.C. becomes the first hardcore rap act to hit the Top 10, their current ***Raising Hell*** is the first rap album to be certified platinum in the US.

17 Following five US gigs featuring **Run-D.M.C.** and the **Beastie Boys** (Pittsburgh, Cleveland, Atlanta, Cincinnati, and New York), where crowd trouble has been prevalent, a full-scale riot erupts between rival Los Angeles gangs – the Crips and the Bloods – at a Long Beach concert, resulting in 42 serious injuries. The incident will spark further outbursts and future bans from many other US venues.

"Michael Jackson's Bizarre Plan To Live To 150."

The National Enquirer, September 21, 1986

September

11 The third annual MTV Awards, held transcontinentally at the Universal Amphitheater in Universal City, California, and the Palladium in New York City, with a performance from **Van Halen** live from New Haven, Connecticut, are swept by the unlikeliest of bands – a telegenic trio from Norway, by the name of **a-ha**. Their two singles, *Take On Me* (with a pioneering film/animation hybrid directed by Steve Barron, with animations by Michael Patterson) and *The Sun Always Shines On T.V.*, win seven awards between them, with an eighth going to the band as the Viewers' Choice. **Dire Straits** pick up a pair of awards for the animated "Money For Nothing" clip, with **Whitney Houston**, **Robert Palmer**, **Prince & the Revolution**, **ZZ Top**, **David Bowie** and **Mick Jagger**, **Bryan Adams**, and **Tina Turner** sharing the remaining spoils.

20 **Cameo** – a ten-year-old soul/funk trio based in New York and led by singer/drummer **Larry Blackmon** – performs at London's Town & Country club during BBC2's live "Rock Around the Clock" all-night broadcast. They play *Word Up*, an international breakthrough smash that is climbing to UK No. 3 and No. 1 on the US R&B chart. It is taken from ***Word Up!***, the group's 12th and most successful album, which will hit UK No. 7 and US No. 8.

21 The **National Enquirer** magazine features a cover picture of **Michael Jackson** in what it claims is an oxygen chamber, with the headline: "Michael Jackson's Bizarre Plan to Live to 150." (During a 1993 TV chat with Oprah Winfrey, Jackson will strongly refute this story, claiming that it was merely a picture of him lying in a burn victims' machine he paid for and donated to the Michael Jackson Burns Center at the Brotman Memorial Hospital.)

27 Traveling between concert dates in Stockholm and Copenhagen on a Scandinavian tour to promote their latest release, ***Master Of Puppets***, **Metallica**'s tour bus skids off the road near Ljungby in southern Sweden. Bassist **Cliff Burton** is thrown out of a window, and the bus falls on top of him. He is killed instantly. No one else is seriously injured. The band will return to California to attend Burton's funeral in San Francisco, where his ashes will be scattered in the Bay.

October

13 Organized by **Neil Young** and his wife Pegi, the first Bridge School Benefit concert takes place at the Shoreline Amphitheater in Mountain View, California. Lending their time and talent alongside Young: **David Crosby**, **Stephen Stills**, **Graham Nash**, **Bruce Springsteen**, **Tom Petty**, **Nils Lofgren**, **Don Henley**, and comedian Robin Williams. The event will become an annual highlight on the Bay Area's fall music schedule (though it will skip a year in 1987), providing funds for the Bridge School programs, which are designed to "enable physically challenged, severely speech-impaired children to cross the threshold to achieving their full educational and social potential."

16 Following a full dress rehearsal yesterday, a special concert at the Fox Theater in St. Louis, Missouri, organized by the **Rolling Stones' Keith Richard**, is held to celebrate **Chuck Berry**'s 60th birthday, and to form the basis of a documentary film. Richard leads the backing band – which includes **Eric Clapton**, **Julian Lennon**, **Linda Ronstadt**, **Joe Walsh**, young trad/blues rock guitarist **Robert Cray**, and **Etta James** – and the date follows a week of rehearsals at Berry's farm

Metallica

Metallica spent much of 1986 on the road with the Master of Puppets world tour.

Def Leppard's Rick Allen

The City of Los Angeles rescinded an invitation for Run-D.M.C. to take part in the Los Angeles Street Scene Festival because of troubles at several band gigs... Neil Young organized the first Bridge School Benefit concert in October... Playing a customized drum kit, Def Leppard's Rick Allen made his first UK public apppearance since losing his arm in a car crash.

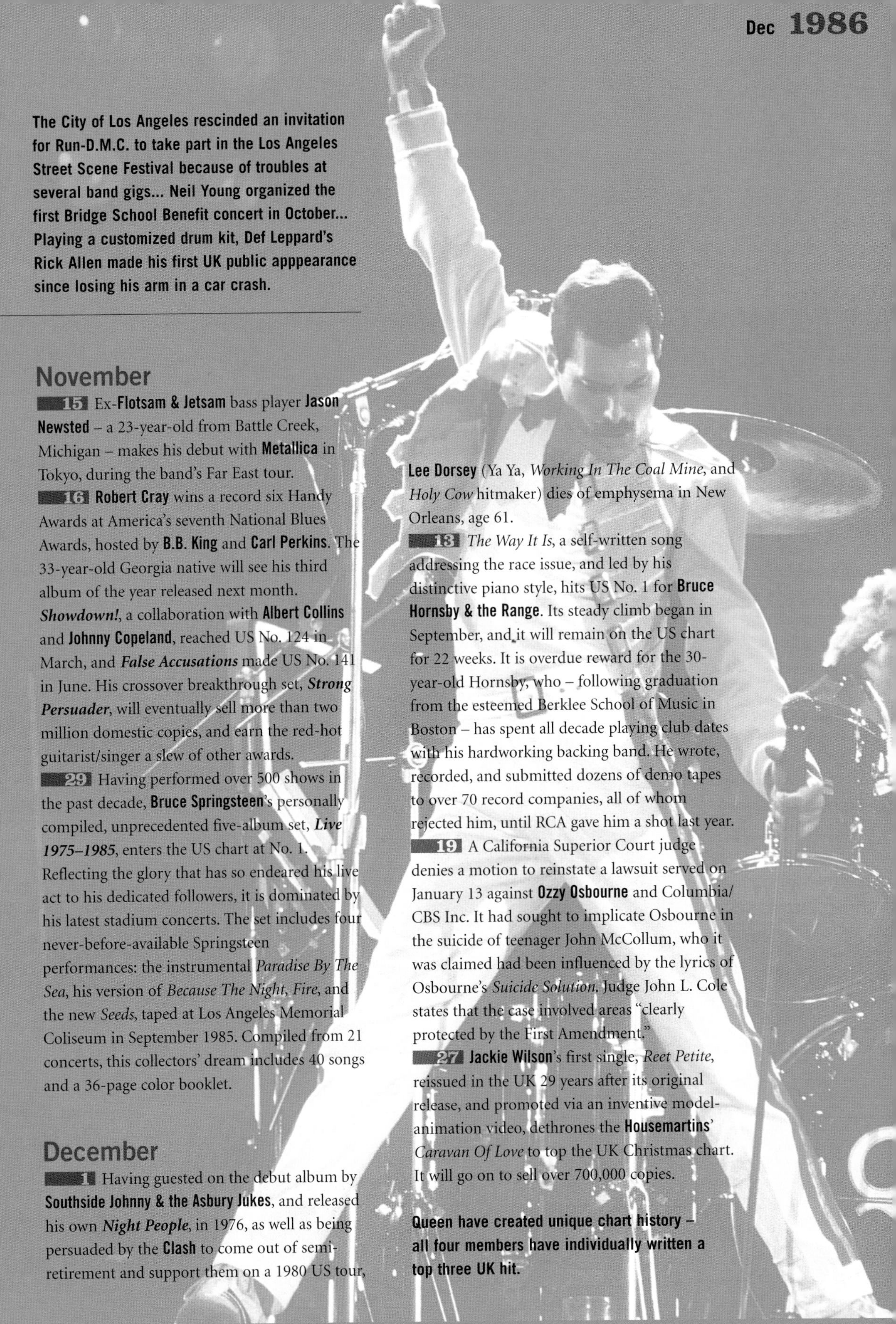

in Wentzville. Despite a public feud (caused by TV film crew delays), Richard and Berry finish the sequence, with Richard later reporting, "I could have killed him."

25 Newly signed to MCA Records at the instigation of notable Nashville shaker **Emory Gordy, Jr.**, 31-year-old singer-songwriter/guitarist **Steve Earle** releases his label debut. The rocking, outlaw country-styled ***Guitar Town***, co-produced by Gordy, Jr., and Tony Brown, is set to hit No. 1 on the US Country chart during a 66-week stay. Following its critical and commercial success, and sellout dates throughout the US, Earle will be voted Top Country Artist in **Rolling Stone** magazine. Alongside **Randy Travis** and **Dwight Yoakam**, he will be heralded as a pioneer of "new country" at country music award shows.

25 For the first time in US chart history, three female artists occupy the top three positions on the Hot 100: **Cyndi Lauper** is at No. 1 with the ballad *True Colors*, **Tina Turner** is runner-up with *Typical Male*, and **Janet Jackson** falls off the top spot to No. 3 with her first chart-topper, *When I Think Of You*.

31 **Roger Waters** files suit in the High Court in London to dissolve the **Pink Floyd** partnership and, as band leader and creator of their most successful recordings, to block **David Gilmour** and **Nick Mason** from using the name for future recording and touring. Gilmour, Mason, and **Rick Wright** (now a salaried employee) will fire back on November 11, with a press release saying the group has no intention of disbanding, and that a new album is on the way. They decide their project should be under the Pink Floyd name, which Waters will claim they have no right to use. They will win temporary rights to use the much coveted name, which will turn into a longterm victory.

November

15 Ex-**Flotsam & Jetsam** bass player **Jason Newsted** – a 23-year-old from Battle Creek, Michigan – makes his debut with **Metallica** in Tokyo, during the band's Far East tour.

16 **Robert Cray** wins a record six Handy Awards at America's seventh National Blues Awards, hosted by **B.B. King** and **Carl Perkins**. The 33-year-old Georgia native will see his third album of the year released next month. ***Showdown!***, a collaboration with **Albert Collins** and **Johnny Copeland**, reached US No. 124 in March, and ***False Accusations*** made US No. 141 in June. His crossover breakthrough set, ***Strong Persuader***, will eventually sell more than two million domestic copies, and earn the red-hot guitarist/singer a slew of other awards.

29 Having performed over 500 shows in the past decade, **Bruce Springsteen**'s personally compiled, unprecedented five-album set, ***Live 1975–1985***, enters the US chart at No. 1. Reflecting the glory that has so endeared his live act to his dedicated followers, it is dominated by his latest stadium concerts. The set includes four never-before-available Springsteen performances: the instrumental *Paradise By The Sea*, his version of *Because The Night*, *Fire*, and the new *Seeds*, taped at Los Angeles Memorial Coliseum in September 1985. Compiled from 21 concerts, this collectors' dream includes 40 songs and a 36-page color booklet.

December

1 Having guested on the debut album by **Southside Johnny & the Asbury Jukes**, and released his own ***Night People***, in 1976, as well as being persuaded by the **Clash** to come out of semi-retirement and support them on a 1980 US tour, **Lee Dorsey** (Ya Ya, *Working In The Coal Mine*, and *Holy Cow* hitmaker) dies of emphysema in New Orleans, age 61.

13 *The Way It Is*, a self-written song addressing the race issue, and led by his distinctive piano style, hits US No. 1 for **Bruce Hornsby & the Range**. Its steady climb began in September, and it will remain on the US chart for 22 weeks. It is overdue reward for the 30-year-old Hornsby, who – following graduation from the esteemed Berklee School of Music in Boston – has spent all decade playing club dates with his hardworking backing band. He wrote, recorded, and submitted dozens of demo tapes to over 70 record companies, all of whom rejected him, until RCA gave him a shot last year.

19 A California Superior Court judge denies a motion to reinstate a lawsuit served on January 13 against **Ozzy Osbourne** and Columbia/CBS Inc. It had sought to implicate Osbourne in the suicide of teenager John McCollum, who it was claimed had been influenced by the lyrics of Osbourne's *Suicide Solution*. Judge John L. Cole states that the case involved areas "clearly protected by the First Amendment."

27 **Jackie Wilson**'s first single, *Reet Petite*, reissued in the UK 29 years after its original release, and promoted via an inventive model-animation video, dethrones the **Housemartins**' *Caravan Of Love* to top the UK Christmas chart. It will go on to sell over 700,000 copies.

Queen have created unique chart history – all four members have individually written a top three UK hit.

ROOTS **During this year: nascent rapper Erica Wright (Erykah Badu) guests on her local Dallas radio station, KNON-FM... former Altered Images and Hipsway bassist Johnny McElhone recruits Sharleen Spiteri to become lead singer of his new venture, Texas... the Shamen, founded by part-time psychiatric nurse Colin Angus, sign a deal with indie label Moshka, which releases the first of two singles by the band... Swedish music veterans, Marie Fredriksson and Per Gessle, form the duo Roxette... Kim Deal is the only respondent to an ad – "into Hüsker Dü and Peter, Paul and Mary" – placed by Black Francis, who is looking to form a band in Boston; a flick through a dictionary gives them the name the Pixies... partly to avoid compulsory military service in his native South Africa, Dave Matthews settles in Charlottesville, Virginia, where he will meet like-minded musicians, forming their first band in 1990... Mick Jagger sees the band Living Colour perform at CBGBs in New York, and invites them to play on his forthcoming solo album, *Primitive Cool*... and graduating from Commonwealth School in Boston, Evan Dando, Ben Deily, and Jesse Peretz record four tracks for $100, releasing 1,000 7in EPs under the title *Laughing All The Way To The Cleaners*...**

Pump Up The Volume

1987

No.1 US SINGLES

Jan 3 Walk Like An Egyptian **Bangles**
Jan 17 Shake You Down **Gregory Abbott**
Jan 24 At This Moment **Billy Vera & the Beaters**
Feb 7 Open Your Heart **Madonna**
Feb 14 Livin' On A Prayer **Bon Jovi**
Mar 14 Jacob's Ladder **Huey Lewis & the News**
Mar 21 Lean On Me **Club Nouveau**
Apr 4 Nothing's Gonna Stop Us Now **Starship**
Apr 18 I Knew You Were Waiting (For Me) **Aretha Franklin & George Michael**
May 2 (I Just) Died In Your Arms **Cutting Crew**
May 16 With Or Without You **U2**
June 6 You Keep Me Hangin' On **Kim Wilde**
June 13 Always **Atlantic Starr**
June 20 Head To Toe **Lisa Lisa & Cult Jam**
June 27 I Wanna Dance With Somebody (Who Loves Me) **Whitney Houston**
July 11 Alone **Heart**
Aug 1 Shakedown **Bob Seger**
Aug 8 I Still Haven't Found What I'm Looking For **U2**
Aug 22 Who's That Girl **Madonna**
Aug 29 La Bamba **Los Lobos**
Sept 19 I Just Can't Stop Loving You **Michael Jackson**
Sept 26 Didn't We Almost Have It All **Whitney Houston**
Oct 10 Here I Go Again **Whitesnake**
Oct 17 Lost In Emotion **Lisa Lisa & Cult Jam**
Oct 24 Bad **Michael Jackson**
Nov 7 I Think We're Alone Now **Tiffany**
Nov 21 Mony Mony "Live" **Billy Idol**
Nov 28 (I've Had) The Time Of My Life **Bill Medley & Jennifer Warnes**
Dec 5 Heaven Is A Place On Earth **Belinda Carlisle**
Dec 12 Faith **George Michael**

No.1 UK SINGLES

Jan 3 Reet Petite (The Sweetest Girl In Town) **Jackie Wilson**
Jan 24 Jack Your Body **Steve "Silk" Hurley**
Feb 7 I Knew You Were Waiting (For Me) **Aretha Franklin & George Michael**
Feb 21 Stand By Me **Ben E. King**
Mar 14 Everything I Own **Boy George**
Mar 28 Respectable **Mel & Kim**
Apr 4 Let It Be **Ferry Aid**
Apr 25 La Isla Bonita **Madonna**
May 9 Nothing's Gonna Stop Us Now **Starship**

U2

Run-D.M.C.

U2 made the cover of Time in May with the headline: "U2 – Rock's Hottest Ticket" during their 110-date arena world tour... Run-D.M.C.'s performance of *Walk This Way* with Aerosmith at the MTV Music Awards was a defining moment in rap history.

From Michigan to Manchester, clubs thudded to a new hybrid, quickly dubbed house music, that showed the growing influence of rap and electronica. An expanding rap roster included the **Beastie Boys** and **Public Enemy**, while more mature audiences sought refuge in **U2**, **Dire Straits**, **Sting**, or **Whitney Houston**. Even the **Bee Gees** enjoyed a return to chart success.

Like punk, house music gave young fans an identity and a similar (if more stylish) sense of rebellion. It started in Chicago, but crossed over more quickly in Britain, where it dominated the clubs in more racially integrated cities, and inspired a culture of underground dance events soon known as raves. The Beastie Boys had supported **Run-D.M.C.** on tour, and their album ***License To Ill*** showed that rap had crossed the racial divide. Other rap acts attracted more notoriety. Rap's emphasis on violence, drinking, drugs, and sex was beginning to cause a backlash. The city of Jacksonville, Florida, tried to enforce a "mature audiences only" warning on the Beastie Boys' concert tickets, and many stores pulled **2 Live Crew**'s album, rather than face prosecution for selling it to minors.

George Michael certainly wasn't rap, but his funky single *I Want Your Sex* also ran into trouble. It was banned by the BBC and some US radio stations, and the video was recut by MTV.

"I don't look like a singer with a deep soulful voice... I look like a young lad." Rick Astley, **New Musical Express**, August 15, 1987

As a result, the single raced to the top on both sides of the Atlantic. Three British producers, **Mike Stock**, **Matt Aiken**, and **Pete Waterman**, devised a highly successful "manufactured pop" formula for impossibly catchy (and sometimes thoroughly annoying) hits. **Rick Astley**'s *Never Gonna Give You Up* became the biggest single of the year in Britain (and a No. 1 in 16 other countries), and the production trio would conjure a dozen more No. 1s in succeeding years. It's said they wrote **Kylie Minogue**'s breakout smash, *I Should Be So Lucky*, in ten minutes. Others should be so lucky.

U2 went from strength to strength, releasing the seminal ***The Joshua Tree***, which would eventually sell more than 20 million copies worldwide. The same soaring vocals from **Bono**, the same jagged guitar from **The Edge**, and the same polished production of **Daniel Lanois** and **Brian Eno**, but lyrically a journey of yearning and desperation. The album's superbly addictive melodies softened its dark tone, and the whole made the band the biggest rock group in the world.

As MTV exported its success to Europe, the year's most popular music video came not from a rap band nor a slick pop act, but from rock veteran **Peter Gabriel** with "Sledgehammer," a tour de force of claymation that set the standard for this burgeoning industry.

- **June 6** I Wanna Dance With Somebody (Who Loves Me) **Whitney Houston**
- **June 20** Star Trekkin' **Firm**
- **July 4** It's A Sin **Pet Shop Boys**
- **July 25** Who's That Girl **Madonna**
- **Aug 1** La Bamba **Los Lobos**
- **Aug 15** I Just Can't Stop Loving You **Michael Jackson**
- **Aug 29** Never Gonna Give You Up **Rick Astley**
- **Oct 3** Pump Up The Volume/Antina (The First Time I See She Dances) **M/A/R/R/S**
- **Oct 17** You Win Again **Bee Gees**
- **Nov 14** China In Your Hand **T'Pau**
- **Dec 19** Always On My Mind **Pet Shop Boys**

Jan

1987

The "house" scene... Paul Simon's Graceland tour... The Beatles on CD...

The Beastie Boys signed to Rick Rubin's fledgling Def Jam label in 1984, soon after supporting Madonna on her US tour.

January

1 In Sydney, **Elton John** announces he is canceling the rest of his tour to undergo surgery on a non-malignant lesion in his throat. He will not be able to perform again until April.

6 **Eric Clapton** begins a series of six concerts (which will become a popular annual event) at London's Royal Albert Hall. His top-drawer band features **Mark Knopfler** (guitar), **Nathan East** (bass), **Greg Phillinganes** (keyboards), and **Steve Ferrone** (drums). On the 8th he will be joined by **Sting** and **Steve Winwood** on encores of *Money For Nothing* and *Sunshine Of Your Love*, while **Phil Collins** will play drums for the performance on the 12th.

21 The second Rock and Roll Hall of Fame induction dinner takes place at the Waldorf Astoria Hotel in New York City, honoring **Bill Haley**, **Eddie Cochran**, **Rick Nelson**, **Bo Diddley**, **B.B. King**, **Clyde McPhatter**, **Aretha Franklin**, the **Coasters**, **Marvin Gaye**, **Roy Orbison**, **Carl Perkins**, **Smokey Robinson**, **Big Joe Turner**, and **Jackie Wilson** – inducted three years to the day since his death. **Louis Jordan**, **T-Bone Walker**, and **Hank Williams** enter as Early Influences. **Brian Wilson** inducts songwriters **Leiber and Stoller** as Non-Performers (after which Sire Records boss Seymour Stein approaches him to record a solo album).

24 The nascent "house" scene breaks big-time, when **Steve "Silk" Hurley**'s *Jack Your Body* becomes its first international success, hitting UK No. 1. The genre has been bubbling in Chicago for the past two years, having been born at the Warehouse, owned by the godfather of house, DJ Frankie Knuckles. Chicago DJ Hurley is pioneering the hybrid dance movement, which combines electro, rap, gospel, disco, and soul with a steady drum machine backbeat. His nickname refers to his smooth, seamless method of sampling and mixing different musical elements. House is exploding on the hip UK club scene, notably at the Hacienda in Manchester and the Garage in Nottingham – the first to pick up on another Chicago house innovator, **Farley Jackmaster Funk**, who hit UK No. 10 last September with *Love Can't Turn Around*.

February

1 After a press conference in London two days ago, at which he stated that both the African National Congress and the UN have removed him from their blacklists – the bans were imposed after he broke the boycott on recording in South Africa – **Paul Simon** embarks on his Graceland tour of Europe at the Ahoy in Rotterdam. He will be supported by **Ladysmith Black Mambazo**, and South African music legends **Hugh Masekela** and **Miriam Makeba**. His April concerts at the Royal Albert Hall will be picketed by anti-apartheid protesters.

9 **Eric Clapton** is honored with the Outstanding Contribution to British Music, and **Dire Straits**' ***Brothers In Arms*** is named Best British Album, at the sixth BPI Awards, held at London's Grosvenor House Hotel. The **Pet Shop Boys**' *West End Girls* is named Best British Single, and **Peter Gabriel** and **Kate Bush**, who have recently shared a Top 10 hit with *Don't Give Up*, win the Best British Male Solo Artist and Best British Female Solo Artist awards respectively. (Bush somehow manages to win despite not having released a solo record in the past year.) Gabriel also wins Best British Video, for his groundbreaking "Sledgehammer" claymation video. Young UK R&B family combo **Five Star** – with their latest single *Stay Out Of My Life* heading toward the Top 10 on the heels of four consecutive hits last year – are named Best British Group. Their fall will be rapid however, following a final Top 10 showing with *The Slightest Touch* in May. On the other hand, Best International Group winners, the **Bangles** – picked on the strength of last year's No. 2 *Manic Monday* and No. 3 *Walk Like An Egyptian* – are yet to have their biggest hit: the May 1989 chart-topper *Eternal Flame*. The **Housemartins** are named Best British Newcomer.

24 AIDS and apartheid dominate the 29th Grammy Awards at Los Angeles' Shrine Auditorium, as the charity single, *That's What Friends Are For*, is named Song of the Year, and **Paul Simon**'s ***Graceland*** picks up the coveted Album of the Year award. Simon opens the proceedings backed by **Ladysmith Black Mambazo** on *Diamonds On The Soles Of Her Shoes*, before double winner **Anita Baker** sings a stirring rendition of *God Bless America*. Baker – the 29-year-old former lead singer of **Chapter 8**, and soul music's fastest-rising star – takes home trophies for Best R&B Vocal Performance, Female (for ***Rapture***), and Best R&B Song (for its smash extract *Sweet Love*). **Steve Winwood** wins Record of the Year and Best Pop Vocal Performance, Male (both for *Higher Love*) with his first nominations in a 20-year career. **Tina Turner** receives her third straight Best Rock Vocal Performance, Female award, while **Bruce Hornsby & the Range**'s Best New Artist win is as popular as it is artistic. The **Art of Noise**'s *Peter Gunn*, with a guest appearance

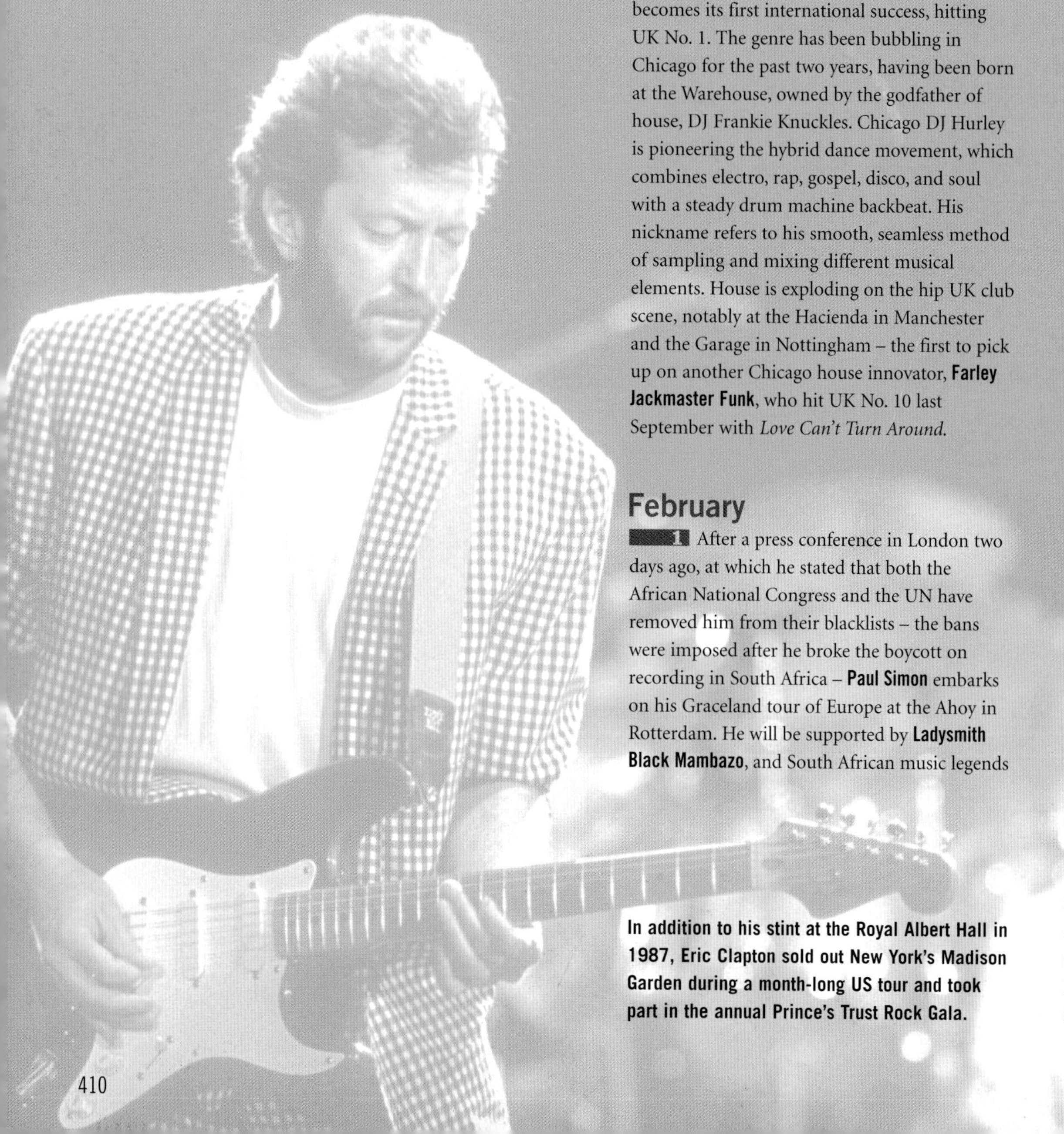

In addition to his stint at the Royal Albert Hall in 1987, Eric Clapton sold out New York's Madison Garden during a month-long US tour and took part in the annual Prince's Trust Rock Gala.

from twang guitar giant **Duane Eddy**, is named Best Rock Instrumental Performance. (**Henry Mancini**'s song, from his double Grammy-winning album *The Music From Peter Gunn*, featured in the first awards ceremony 28 years ago.) During the televised ceremony, Pepsi-Cola airs the new Michael Jackson teaser commercial: "This Spring… The Magic Returns."

25 London's **The Sun** prints the first in a series of lurid front-page stories alleging that **Elton John** has engaged in homosexual sex-and-drug orgies. Today's headline reads: "Elton In Vice Boys Scandal." The reports are strenuously denied by the star, who immediately begins libel proceedings. Tomorrow's headline will be "Elton's Kinky Kinks," followed by "Elton's Drug Capers," and "Elton's Pink Tutu Party." The source is an alleged rent boy called Stephen Hardy, who appears in the paper as Mr. Graham X. **The Sun** has paid him a £2,000 ($3,800) advance and a retainer of £250 ($475) a week. Hardy, in an article published in **The Independent** magazine, will reveal: "97 percent of it was untrue. I would give **The Sun** a line and they would write it all up. It was a manufactured story." When John's lawyers seek a retraction, **The Sun** leads with "You're A Liar Elton," even though it knows the stories to be untrue. It will have to pay the artist £1 ($1.9) million in damages and print an apology, which, in typical Sun fashion, will read: "Sorry, Elton."

28 This week's NME cover features 24-year-old newcomer, **Terence Trent D'Arby**, with the headline: "The New Prince of Pop." The New York-born performer, an outspoken singer-songwriter with an impressive rock/R&B vocal range, is a former Golden Gloves boxing champ and US Army recruit, who was posted to the Third Armored Division (Elvis Presley's unit), near Frankfurt, Germany. Since 1984 he has lived in London, where he was signed by CBS Records last year on the strength of a demo tape. He has just completed his debut album, *Introducing The Hardline According To Terence Trent D'Arby*, which will top the UK chart in July after strong critical notices and two Top 10 UK hits, *If You Let Me Stay* and *Wishing Well.*

March

7 With the **Beatles**' back catalog being systematically released on CD, the group's timeless popularity is underlined as they return to the UK charts: *Please Please Me* is at No. 32, *With The Beatles* at No. 40, *A Hard Day's Night* at No. 30, and *Beatles For Sale* at No. 45. Nine other reissues will make the chart this year.

7 The **Beastie Boys**' debut album, *Licensed To Ill* becomes the first rap album to top the US chart, beginning seven weeks at the top. Co-produced and written by the trio with Def Jam co-head Rick Rubin, it features samples ranging from **Led Zeppelin** to the television series "Mr. Ed." Meanwhile, the extracted single, the raucous brat-rant *(You Gotta) Fight For Your Right (To Party)* hits US No. 7. Their in-your-face brand of white-bread hardcore punk/rap is rapidly catching on internationally: the single will peak at UK No. 11 in two weeks, despite a BBC ban on the accompanying video. Their confrontational stage act and rebellious offstage antics invite a love/hate relationship with the press, particularly in Europe – where fans delight in making their own Beastie Boys neckwear using Volkswagen car badges (which they rip off cars) as pendants.

9 Island Records releases *The Joshua Tree*, **U2**'s fifth studio album. The group appears at midnight at Tower Records in Belfast to sign autographs. Meanwhile in London, more than 1,000 U2 devotees – reportedly including **Elvis Costello** – have lined up outside another Tower store to buy the record. It will sell 235,000 copies in Britain in its first week, having gone platinum in 48 hours: the fastest-selling album in UK chart history to date. Regarded as a career highlight, the **Daniel Lanois/Brian Eno**-helmed set will confirm U2 as the world's biggest-retailing rock act. It will yield three major global hits: *With Or Without You* which will hit UK No. 4 on the 28th, before becoming their first US chart-topper on May 16, *I Still Haven't Found What I'm Looking For* which will also hit the top in the US, and *Where The Streets Have No Name.* The album is dedicated to the group's personal assistant, Greg Carroll, who was killed in a motorcycle accident in Dublin in July last year.

16 Legendary Irish folk group the **Dubliners** celebrate their 25th anniversary with a special edition of "The Late Late Show" on Irish television, bringing the show its highest-ever ratings. They are joined by **U2**, the **Pogues** (who perform with the group on their signature *The Irish Rover*), the **Fureys & Davey Arthur**, and other guests. All join together at the end of the show for a rousing rendition of *The Auld Triangle.*

16 MTV's first foreign channel debuts in Australia, created via a licensing deal with the Nine Network.

"Success means more to me than hip. Success means selling 20 million albums, filling 20,000-seat coliseums. I want as many people to hear my music as possible." Lionel Richie, **Playboy**, March 1987

23 The inaugural Soul Train Music Awards take place at the Santa Monica Civic Auditorium. **Gregory Abbott** wins Best Single, Male for his US No. 1 *Shake You Down* and is named Best New Artist (though he will never return to the Top 50). **Cameo** win Album of the Year, Group/Band (*Word Up*) and Best Single, Group/Band (*Word Up*). **Run-D.M.C.** win the Best Rap Single (*Walk This Way*) and Album (*Raising Hell*) categories. **Janet Jackson**'s *Control* is named Album of the Year, Female, with "What Have You Done For Me Lately" named Best Music Video. Co-host **Luther Vandross** wins Album of the Year, Male for *Give Me A Reason.* **Stevie Wonder** receives the first Heritage Award, for outstanding career achievements in entertainment.

Terence Trent D'Arby told the NME in 1987 that he was "a genius. Point f*ing blank." In 2003 he was "excited as ever [to bring] his uncompromising inspiration to the public."**

2 Live Crew... Tom Jones's comeback... Tiffany goes shopping...

U2

Tiffany

U2's *The Joshua Tree* was the fastest-selling album in UK history, selling 235,000 in its first week of release... At the age of 30, Tiffany – with her chart career more than a decade behind her – posed nude in Playboy.

27 **U2** film the video for their single, *Where The Streets Have No Name*, on the Republic Liquor store roof at the intersection of 7th and Main in downtown Los Angeles, drawing a crowd of thousands. Police eventually break up the proceedings, with their intervention neatly captured for rock 'n' roll posterity.

April

2 With ***The Joshua Tree*** bowing this week at No. 7 in the US – the highest new entry on the album chart in seven years – **U2** begin the 114-date Joshua Tree tour at Arizona State University in Tempe. The state recently stopped honoring a public holiday for Martin Luther King, prompting the band to open the tour here in protest.

15 **Queen** is honored with the trophy for Outstanding Contribution to British Music at the 32nd annual Ivor Novello Awards, held at London's Grosvenor House Hotel. **Eurythmics' Annie Lennox** and **Dave Stewart** are named Songwriters of the Year, with their composition *It's Alright (Baby's Coming Back)* winning the Best Contemporary Song category. The **Pet Shop Boys'** *West End Girls* wins the award for International Hit of the Year, and the American-recorded but British-written *Sweet Freedom* (recorded by **Michael McDonald** but written by **Rod Temperton**) and *Chain Reaction* (recorded by **Diana Ross** but written by the **Bee Gees**) are named Best Film Theme or Song and Most Performed Work respectively. **Peter Gabriel**'s *Don't Give Up* is named Best Song Musically and Lyrically.

"A rock band even nastier than the Beastie Boys."

The **Daily Star** commenting on Guns 'N Roses, June, 1987

17 Former Wailer **Carlton Barrett** is shot and killed outside his Manning Hills home in Kingston, Jamaica. His wife, Albertine, her lover, Glenroy Carter, and accomplice, Junior Man, will be found guilty of conspiracy to murder.

20 A part-time record store clerk is arrested in Callaway, Florida, for selling a minor a cassette of controversial rap act **2 Live Crew**'s ***2 Live Is What We Are***. The shop is closed, while other stores pull the album from the shelves. The clerk will be cleared. The group is fronted by Miami-based rap entrepreneur and label owner **Luther Campbell** (aka Luke Skyywalker) who will push the boundaries of obscenity with each new release, delighting in misogynistic and pornographic lyrics and videos. He will be the first rap artist to issue "clean" and "dirty" versions of the same album, beginning with the group's follow-up, ***Move Somethin'***.

25 **Madonna** becomes the first female artist to score four UK No. 1s, as *La Isla Bonita* tops the chart.

May

1 Following the recent release of *The Boy From Nowhere*, his first single in a decade, **Tom Jones** appears on Channel 4's "The Last Resort With Jonathan Ross," performing a dynamic version of **Prince**'s *Kiss*. This memorable appearance will lead to an unlikely collaboration with the **Art of Noise**, resulting in a UK No. 5 hit in November, and rejuvenating his career.

4 After a lengthy recording silence, broken last year with the US release of ***The Legendary Paul Butterfield Rides Again*** on Amherst Records, Chicago bluesman **Paul Butterfield**, 44 –

The British hard-rock band Whitesnake, led by David Coverdale, was finding global favor with the recently released Whitesnake 1987.

DEF LEPPARD

June 24 Def Leppard's 16-month Hysteria world tour begins at the Nooderligt in Tilburg, Holland. With September taken up with UK dates, the five-month North American leg will begin on October 1, at the Civic Center in Glens Falls, New York. The accompanying album, due for release on August 29, has been three years in the making, sidelined by drummer Rick Allen's serious accident, and delayed yet further when producer Robert John "Mutt" Lange was involved in his own car accident last November, and singer Joe Elliott contracted mumps in December. Def Leppard cut the final versions of *Hysteria* – which cost more than $1 million to record – in February. Spurred by magic-touch producer Lange's innate talent for combining tasty guitar licks with solid melodic harmonies, the album will sell 18 million copies worldwide and spin off seven US chart singles, including the anthemic chart-topper *Love Bites*, the No. 2-peaking *Pour Some Sugar On Me*, and the No. 3 smash, *Armageddon It*. Together with Whitesnake, Def Leppard will prove to be the most successful UK heavy metal band of the decade.

perhaps the finest harmonica player of his generation – is found dead in his North Hollywood apartment. An autopsy will reveal that he died from a drug overdose.

18 **Bill Drummond** – a Liverpool-based, South African-born music industry rebel – and guitarist **Jimmy Cauty**, in the guise of the **Justified Ancients of Mu Mu**, release *All You Need Is Love*. This attack on the media's coverage of the AIDS health crisis includes samples of **Beatles** records, BBC broadcasts, and topless model **Samantha Fox**. The Justified Ancients of Mu Mu will come under the umbrella of KLF Communications, an anarchic organization bent on guerilla warfare against the traditional music business, which will provide Drummond and Cauty with both a media voice and a label outlet for a number of music projects, including the duo's various incarnations: **JAMs**, **Disco 2000**, the **Timelords**, and **KLF**.

30 During the band's Together Forever European tour with **Run-D.M.C.**, **Beastie Boy Adam Horovitz** is arrested and charged in Liverpool, when he allegedly hits fan Jo-Anne Clarke with a beer can during a disturbance ten minutes into the band's concert at the Royal Court Theatre. (He will be acquitted in November.)

June

1 ITV airs "It Was Twenty Years Ago Today," a documentary on the making of ***Sgt. Pepper's Lonely Hearts Club Band*** and its cultural significance. The album – still widely regarded as the most important record of the rock era – is now released on CD and will hit UK No. 3 next week.

3 **Smash Hits** includes an interview with **George Michael**, reacting to the BBC's recent ban of his new single, *I Want Your Sex*. Michael insists that the lyrics promote monogamous relationships and (literally) spells this out on the accompanying video, which stars his current "girlfriend," US make-up artist Kathy Jueng. His first post-**Wham!** single, the funky cut is released ahead of his debut album, but is included on the soundtrack album ***Beverly Hills Cop II***, causing a storm on both sides of the Atlantic. Radio 1 will subsequently relent, but will air the cut only after 9:00 pm. US MTV re-edits the provocative video three times before it is deemed acceptable. Despite (or because of) the media censorship, *I Want Your Sex* will hit UK No. 3 and US No. 2.

5 The fifth annual Prince's Trust Rock Gala, at Wembley Arena in London, boasts its best line-up yet in concerts today and tomorrow. **George Harrison** is joined by **Eric Clapton** on *While My Guitar Gently Weeps* and by **Jeff Lynne** on *Here Comes The Sun*, and backs **Ringo Starr** on *With A Little Help From My Friends*. **Phil Collins** and **Paul Young** duet on *Reach Out I'll Be There*, while **Elton John** sings *Saturday Night (Is Alright For Fighting)*. Other performances include **Bryan Adams** (*Run To You*), **Ben E. King** (*Stand By Me*, which hit UK No. 1 in February as a reissue tied to a Levi's 501 jeans commercial), **Level 42**'s **Mark King** (*Running In The Family*), **Alison Moyet** (*Invisible*), and **Midge Ure** (*If I Was*).

23 **Tiffany**, a 15-year-old pop singer from Norwalk, California, begins The Beautiful You: Celebrating the Good Life Shopping Mall Tour '87 at the Bergen Mall in Paramus, New Jersey. Set up by the Shopping Center Network and sponsored by Toyota, Clairol, and Adidas, the tour will visit ten malls during Tiffany's school vacation, involving three shows each weekend. She performs free for passing consumers: an innovative idea that generates enormous media interest. Tiffany's career is being steered by producer/manager George Tobin, whom she impressed by performing country songs in 1984. She signed to his company before securing a worldwide recording contract with MCA Records last year.

27 *I Wanna Dance With Somebody (Who Loves Me)* by **Whitney Houston** tops the US chart, while ***Whitney*** simultaneously becomes the first album by a female singer to debut on the **Billboard** chart at No. 1, where it will remain for 11 weeks (it reached UK No. 1 two weeks ago). The single was written by **George Merrill** and **Shannon Rubicam** (who will later find success as **Boy Meets Girl**) and produced by dance/pop producer du jour Narada Michael Walden (who reignited **Aretha Franklin**'s career in 1985 with her first Top 10 hits in 12 years). The album continues a familiar mix of sassy dance-pop numbers (the current smash and *So Emotional*) and ballads (*Didn't We Almost Have It All* and *The Greatest Love Of All*) and includes a duet with Whitney's mother **Cissy**, covering *I Know Him So Well* from the musical "Chess." Next month, Arista will sign a two-year development deal with Tri-Star Pictures to find a film vehicle for its leading female vocalist.

July

6 **Kris Kristofferson** makes a public apology after a memorial plaque given to him by Veterans at the Welcome Home benefit (which took place two days ago in Washington, D.C., and also starred **Stevie Wonder**, **Neil Diamond**, **John Fogerty**, **Bonnie Raitt**, and **James Ingram**) is found in a trash can. He will donate $1,000 to the Vietnamese Veterans Association.

13 Fifty of America's biggest record retail heads are invited to **Michael Jackson**'s Encino home to preview his new album, ***Bad***. Hosted mainly by **LaToya** and Joe Jackson, dinner and a tour of the mansion are included, with the notoriously shy Michael appearing only briefly to pose for photos.

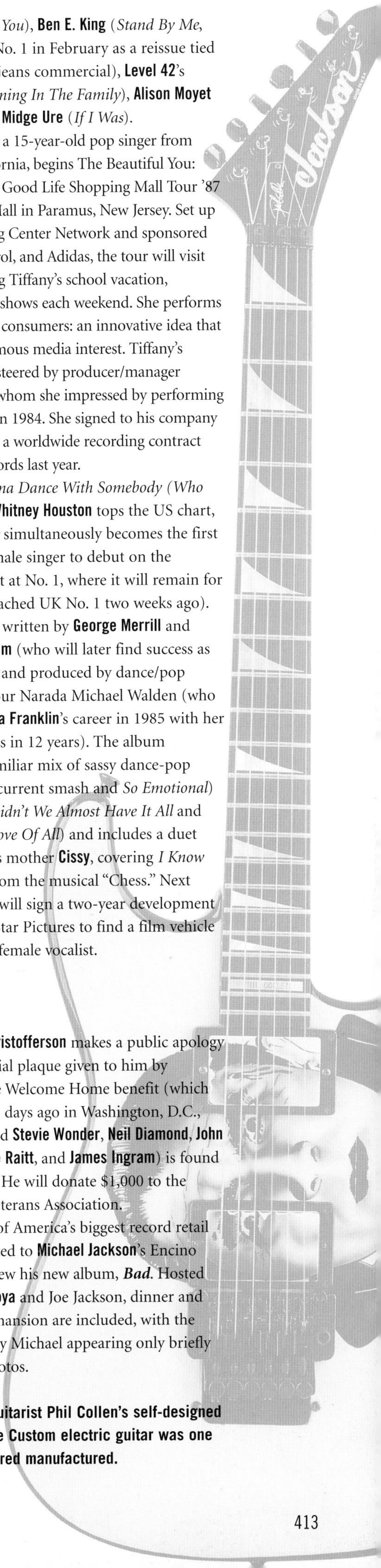

Def Leppard guitarist Phil Collen's self-designed Players Choice Custom electric guitar was one of only a hundred manufactured.

MTV Europe is launched... Michael Jackson's *Bad*... A Black and White Night...

Stock Aitken Waterman

Pete Waterman's chart career started out inauspiciously as co-writer and producer of Susan Cadogan's innocuous Northern Soul hit *Love Me Baby* and as the artist 14/18 with *Good-bye-ee*, a popular song during the First World War... Peter Gabriel's "Sledgehammer" redefined the art of video-making.

17 Promoting his latest album, ***Tribute*** (dedicated to the late **Randy Rhoads**), **Ozzy Osbourne** breaks in his new guitarist, **Zakk Wylde**, embarking on a six-week tour of UK prisons highlighted by a heavy metal version of *Jailhouse Rock*.

27 Following 18 months of rehearsal, grooming, and styling at the PWL Studios in London – owned by the British hitmaking trio of **Mike Stock**, **Matt Aitken**, and **Pete Waterman** – 21-year-old blue-eyed soul/pop singer **Rick Astley** is launched in Britain via a PWL worldwide licensing deal with RCA Records. His first single, the instantly catchy *Never Gonna Give You Up*, is released today. It will immediately take off, entering the UK chart next week at No. 32, vaulting to the top for five weeks, and becoming the biggest-selling single of the year. Brought up in Newton-le-Willows, England, Astley was spotted singing at the Monks Sports and Social Club in Warrington by Waterman, who initially employed him as a tape operator at PWL. Waterman linked with Stock and Aitken in 1984, when the songwriting/production trio issued their first collaboration, the non-charting **Andy Paul** single *Anna-Marie Elena*. Later that year SAW scored their first UK No. 1 with *You Spin Me Round (Like A Record)* by **Dead or Alive**. Prodigiously writing and helming an infectious stream of often indistinguishable dance/pop ditties, SAW has already created hits for the likes of **Hazell Dean**, **Princess**, **Brilliant**, **Phil Fearon**, and **Bananarama**. They nabbed their second UK chart-topper in March, with pop duo **Mel & Kim**'s *Respectable*, and their third with **Ferry Aid**'s *Let It Be*. Forging a veritable production line at their self-proclaimed Hit Factory, SAW will dominate the UK singles chart for the rest of the decade, amassing an astonishing and record-breaking 13 UK No. 1s and 11 separate UK No. 2s, before their chart-topping run ends in 1990.

27 Mushroom Records in Australia releases *The Loco-motion*, the first single by television soap actress **Kylie Minogue**. The perky 19-year-old secured her first acting role, as a Dutch girl, in the Australian soap opera "The Sullivans" in March 1979. She went on to star in a succession of popular series, climaxing in her Logie Award-winning role as Charlene Mitchell in the top-rated soap "Neighbours" (in which she co-stars with another would-be pop singer, **Jason Donovan**). In April, Minogue was invited to sing at an Australian Rules Football game in Melbourne, and performed her version of **Little Eva**'s 1962 hit *The Loco-motion*, which led to her signing with Mushroom. Becoming the biggest-selling single of the year in Australia, where it will spend eight weeks at No. 1, the record will go on to hit UK No. 1 and US No. 3. It has been produced by engineer Mike Duffy, who will bring Minogue to the attention of **Pete Waterman** in London. Beginning a ten-day recording session at PWL studios in September, she will effectively relocate to England, and SAW will write and produce an extraordinary run of hits until 1990 (doing the same for Donovan).

29 Named after the **Grateful Dead** frontman, Ben & Jerry's "Cherry Garcia" ice cream goes on sale in the US. Under the agreement between **Jerry Garcia** and the company, half the royalties will go to the guitarist's Rex Foundation.

> **"I've been wearing Lenny Bruce's shoes for over a year, and I don't think they fit very well."**
>
> The Dead Kennedys' Jello Biafra after being cleared of "distributing harmful matter to a minor," August 27, 1987

Kylie Minogue began her UK chart career with 13 consecutive Top 10 hits, eclipsing Madonna's astonishing chart successes.

August

1 **Los Lobos**' version of *La Bamba* – which is on its way to the top in the US – hits UK No. 1, becoming the first Spanish-language recording to so do.

1 **Elton John** launches MTV Europe to 1.6 million households from the Roxy in Amsterdam at 12:01 pm. The continent's first 24-hour music video network, it begins with the **Sting**-sung refrain, "I want my MTV." The first video clip is **Dire Straits**' "Money for Nothing."

6 The **Beastie Boys** sue the city of Jacksonville, Florida, when a disclaimer, stating "For mature audiences only," is printed on concert tickets, ads, and posters. The group will be awarded a temporary restraining order and the disclaimer removed.

7 **Madonna**, interviewed by Jane Pauley on NBC-TV's "Today" show, calls her hometown of Bay City a "smelly little town," much to the consternation of those who live there. In two weeks, the Material Girl will score her sixth US No. 1 in less than three years, with *Who's That Girl*, the title cut from her latest movie, for which she has received reviews similar to her opinion of her birthplace.

14 **Roger Waters**, with his **Bleeding Heart Band**, opens the US leg of his Radio KAOS world tour at the Civic Center in Providence, Rhode Island. Throughout the tour, Waters will install temporary phone booths in concert halls,

Peter Gabriel

enabling fans to call him on stage with their song requests. Each concert, often playing in direct competition with **Pink Floyd**'s current tour, A Momentary Lapse of Reason, is previewed by a video of Pink Floyd's 1967 standard, *Arnold Layne.*

15 **Freddie Jackson**'s *Jam Tonight* tops the US R&B survey, making Jackson – a 28-year-old soul singer-songwriter from New York, who started as a backing vocalist for **Melba Moore** and **Evelyn King** – the only artist to score six R&B No. 1s in the 1980s.

25 "Dirty Dancing" receives its world premiere in Los Angeles, attended by its stars Patrick Swayze and Jennifer Grey. While box office receipts will be reasonable, its soundtrack album will prove a major success, entering the US chart on September 19 for a run of 143 weeks. Swarming US radio, it will yield the No. 1 hit duet *(I've Had) The Time Of My Life* by **Jennifer Warnes** and ex-**Righteous Brother Bill Medley**, *Hungry Eyes* by **Eric Carmen**, peaking at US No. 4, and *She's Like The Wind*, a No. 3 hit ballad by the lead actor.

27 Four days ahead of its release, **Michael Jackson**'s new album ***Bad*** is previewed on a Los Angeles radio station. It has received the largest advance order – 2.2 million copies – in US history.

September

11 **Peter Gabriel**'s"Sledgehammer" video conquers the fourth MTV Video Music Awards at the Universal Amphitheater, winning a record-breaking nine statuettes: Best Male Video, Best Overall Performance in a Video, Best Art Direction (Stephen Johnson, Stephen Quay, and Tim Quay), Best Concept Video (Gabriel and Johnson), Best Direction in a Video (Johnson), Best Editing (Johnson and Colin Green), Best Special Effects (Johnson and Peter Lord), Most Experimental (Johnson and Gabriel), and for good measure Gabriel is also honored with the Video Vanguard award. Picking up the leftovers are **Madonna** (Best Female Video for "Papa Don't Preach"), **Janet Jackson** (Best Choreography in a Video for "Nasty," choreographed by 25-year-old **Paula Abdul**, who is preparing to launch her own singing career next year), **Talking Heads** (Best Group Video for "Wild Wild Life"), **Robbie Nevil** (Best Cinematography for "C'Est La Vie"), **Bon Jovi** (Best Stage Performance in a Video for "Livin' On A Prayer"), **Crowded House** (Best New Artist in a Video for "Don't Dream It's Over"), and **U2** (Viewers' Choice for "With Or Without You").

11 **Level 42**'s *It's Over* becomes the first CD video single to go on sale in Britain, though the video will remain unseen until CDV players become available.

11 Five months after fellow **Wailer Carlton Barrett** was fatally shot, reggae star **Peter Tosh** is murdered in his Barbican home in Kingston, Jamaica. His friend Dennis Lobban, who had been staying with him but left after an argument with Tosh's girlfriend, Marlene Brown, returns with two gunmen and demands money. Tosh and the six other people in the house are shot in the head. DJ Jeff "Free I" Dixon, Wilton "Doc" Brown, and Tosh are killed, but four – including Marlene Brown – miraculously survive. Lobban will be sentenced to death.

12 With ***Bad*** debuting at UK No. 1 this week (it will repeat the feat in the US in two weeks' time), **Michael Jackson** begins his first solo tour with the first of 14 sellout dates at the Korakuen Stadium in Yokohama, Japan. He will break a world record when 504,000 people, attending seven shows, see him at Wembley Stadium in London. The 123rd and final show will take place at the Sports Arena in Los Angeles on January 24, 1989. With a total audience of 4.4 million, the tour will gross over $125 million – the most ever by an entertainer. Jackson's 250-strong personal entourage includes manager Frank DiLeo, who will handle all interviews, and his two current business managers, **Jimmy Osmond** (ex-**Osmonds**) and Miko Brando (son of Marlon).

14 "American Bandstand" enters the record books as the longest-running US entertainment show on television.

19 The third annual Farm Aid benefit takes place at the University of Nebraska's Memorial Stadium in Lincoln. **John Mellencamp**, **Willie Nelson**, and **Neil Young** once again take part. They are joined this year by **Steve Earle**, ex-**Pure Prairie League** vocalist and now solo **Vince Gill**, the **Grateful Dead**, **Kris Kristofferson**, literate singer-songwriters **Delbert McClinton** and **John Prine**, **Emmylou Harris**, **Lou Reed**, and, making his major concert debut, **Lyle Lovett** – a 29-year-old singer/guitarist from Texas whose off-beat, rootsy country/folk/blues/swing blend was introduced on last year's well-received ***Lyle Lovett*** debut.

27 Paradise Garage at 84 King Street in New York City, the original "garage" club, closes down. A seminal underground dance venue since 1977, it was the home base for legendary DJ/producer Larry Levan, who pioneered a succession of club culture genres, most recently "house" and "garage" – the latter some ten years before it will gain widespread appeal in Europe.

30 A Black and White Night, a club concert at the Coconut Grove in the Ambassador Hotel in Los Angeles, pays tribute to its star, **Roy Orbison**. **Jackson Browne**, **T-Bone Burnette**, **Elvis Costello**, Canadian alt-country chanteuse **k.d. lang**, **Bonnie Raitt**, ex-**Alpha Band** singer/guitarist **Steven Soles**, West Coast singer-songwriter **J.D. Souther**, **Bruce Springsteen**, **Tom Waits**, **Jennifer Warnes**, and a band featuring **James Burton** (guitar), **Glen D. Hardin** (piano), **Ron Tutt** (drums), **Jerry Scheff** (bass), **Alex Acuna** (percussion), and **Mike Utley** (keyboards) take part in an evening of unadulterated hero worship.

***Bad* sold four million copies in the US alone within three months of its release – well short of *Thriller*, which had sold 20 million copies in just two years.**

1987 Oct

Pump Up The Volume... Dire Straits with the biggest-selling UK album...

Michael Timmins and Alan Anton came together as Hunger Project, playing music mainly influenced by the Velvet Underground and Siouxsie & the Banshees... Public Enemy's beginnings were at college radio station WBAU, where Chuck D and Hank Schocklee presented the "Super Special Mix Show."

Cowboy Junkies

October

3 **M/A/R/R/S**' *Pump Up The Volume* hits UK No. 1. The landmark recording is a breakthrough acid house anthem, conceived by 4AD label owner Ivo Watts-Russell. It combines four separate talents: **Martyn** and **Steve Young** from innovative dub fusion/industrial combo **Colourbox**, ambient trip-hop pioneers **A.R. Kane** (**Alex Ayuli** and **Rudi Tambala**), red-hot dance remixer **Chris "C.J." Mackintosh**, and London-based DJ **Dave Dorrell**. Using state-of-the-art electronics, classic soul cuts, turntable scratching, and house rhythms, topped off with a title rap sample from hip-hop pioneers **Eric B. & Rakim**, *Pump Up The Volume* sets a new standard for hybrid dance records that will influence a whole generation of remixers, DJs, and dance producers. The UK house scene – together with the current hallucinogenic drug of choice, ecstasy – is being popularized by an increasing number of illegal dance gatherings known as raves, held at secret locations revealed only by word of mouth and underground flyers.

8 **Chuck Berry** is awarded his star on the Hollywood Walk of Fame, at 1777 North Vine Street, as the bio-movie about the rock legend, "Hail! Hail! Rock 'n' Roll," premieres in the US.

10 **ZZ Top** announce that they have booked seats for the first passenger flight to the Moon.

17 Frozen out of the Top 10 since 1979 (and branded with the stigma of disco), the **Bee Gees** triumphantly return to the UK chart. Hitting No. 1 with the anthemic *You Win Again*, they become the only band to top the British charts in each of the last three decades.

At age 14, Sinéad O'Connor was asked to sing at the wedding of a teacher at the Mayfield College in Drumcondra, Dublin, Ireland.

November

1 Benefiting from the advent of compact discs, three-million UK sales of **Dire Straits**' ***Brothers In Arms*** are officially certified, making it Britain's all-time best-selling album and its second biggest-selling recording of any kind. (Only **Band Aid**'s *Do They Know It's Christmas?* has a higher UK sales total.)

10 **Terence Trent D'Arby** cancels a concert in Vienna, in protest over Kurt Waldheim's confirmation as the new President of Austria. Waldheim was recently accused of being a Nazi sympathizer during World War II.

13 **Sonny & Cher** sing *I Got You Babe*, for the first time in ten years, on "Late Night With David Letterman."

13 Just two weeks after a crash on the stock market, **U2** play a Save the Yuppies concert at the Justine Hermine Plaza, and bring chaos to the San Francisco business district. One hour after a local radio station announces the show, 20,000 fans turn up. **Bono** says: "The business community is a bit short this week. That's why I'm wearing this hat, we'll be passing it round later." At two Los Angeles Coliseum concerts next week, an audience member will be pulled on stage to sing *People Get Ready* (the ever-alert wannabe punter hands them a demo tape), and the band will open for themselves in the guise of country/rock outfit, the Dalton Brothers – Alton (Bono), Luke (**The Edge**), Betty (**Adam Clayton**), and Duke (**Larry Mullen Jr.**).

18 Irish singer-songwriter **Sinéad O'Connor**'s first UK radio session is broadcast on the Simon Mayo show on Radio 1. She is accompanied by ex-**Adam & the Ants** alumni **Marco Pirroni** on drums and **Kevin Mooney** on guitar. She began performing two years ago at the age of 18, and was featured on **The Edge**'s soundtrack album to

Mayhem ensued at Billy Joel's concert in Leningrad in August when fans went wild and broke more than 200 chairs by dancing on them... The Run-D.M.C. and Beastie Boys tour brought rap music to the masses.

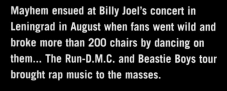

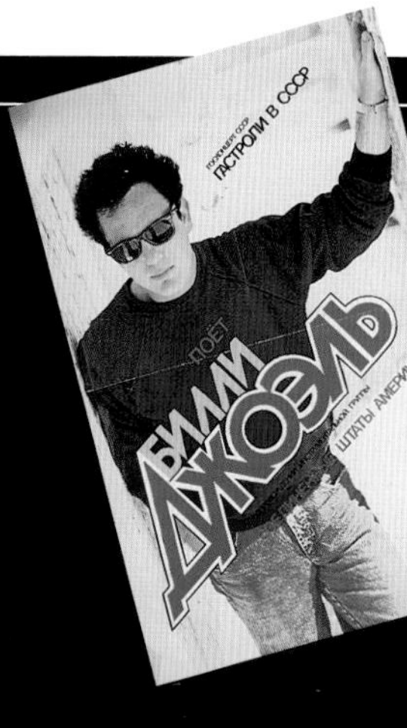

Public Enemy

"Merely the greatest piece of rock and roll released in 1987."

Robert Christgau reviewing Public Enemy's *Bring the Noise* single, 1987

the film "Captive." Spotted singing with Irish band **Ton Ton Macoute**, she was signed to Ensign Records last year by Nigel Grainge and Chris Hill, and has recently completed her maiden album, ***The Lion And The Cobra***. Tonight's session includes her single, *Jump In The River*.

27 Splashing out $162, Canadian quartet **Cowboy Junkies** record their second album, ***The Trinity Session***, in one day at the Church of the Holy Trinity, Toronto. The three **Timmins** siblings (singer **Margo**, guitarist **Michael**, and drummer **Peter**), augmented by bassist **Alan Anton**, write and perform in a sparse, hushed style. The album, initially released on the Latent indie label, will eventually secure the group a contract with RCA Records and – although taking two years to break through – will ultimately accumulate over one million worldwide sales.

December

1 The US Supreme Court rejects an appeal by a Kentucky schoolteacher, who was fired for showing the movie "Pink Floyd – The Wall" to students in grades 9 to 11 on the last day of school.

3 As **R.E.M.**'s ***Document*** becomes their first US Top 10 album, the group appears on the cover of **Rolling Stone**, hailed as "America's Best Rock & Roll Band." **NME** readers have also voted four R.E.M. albums into the all-time Top 100 appearing in its year-end issue.

5 **Jesus & Mary Chain** are banned from appearing on the shortlived US version of "Top Of The Pops," having refused to be billed as JAMC at the request of CBS-TV, who consider the group's name "blasphemous." It has been a bad month for the group: they were thrown off ITV's "The Roxy" for not bothering to mime during a rehearsal of *Darklands*, and during their current North American tour, **Jim Reid** was arrested after a gig at the RPM club in Toronto, for allegedly hitting troublesome fans with a microphone stand. He will later be acquitted.

7 **Prince**'s ***The Black Album*** – scheduled for release by Warner Bros. today, and issued in a plain black sleeve with no recording or artist credits – fails to reach stores. Several thousand copies have been pressed in Europe and, when the recall notice comes (reportedly at the behest of the artist), 100 copies slip out of WEA Records' German plant. These (directly or via a German radio broadcast), together with advance promo cassettes, will become the sources for a flood of ***Black Album*** bootlegs, comprising eight tracks of hardcore erotic funk out-takes: *Le Grind, Cindy C, Dead On It, When 2 R In Love, Bob George, Supercalifragisexi, 2 Nigs United 4 West Compton*, and *Hard Rock In A Funky Place*.

13 **Paul Simon**, **Bruce Springsteen**, **Billy Joel**, **James Taylor**, and **Lou Reed** are among an all-star cast performing at the Madison Square Garden, to benefit the New York Children's Health Project. Springsteen, Simon, and Joel sing *Glory Days* together, while rock 'n' roll veteran **Dion** performs his classic *Teenager In Love*, backed up by Springsteen, Joel, Taylor, Simon, Reed, and **Rubén Blades**. Fellow performers, including **Laurie Anderson**, **Ladysmith Black Mambazo**, stylish Jamaican club queen **Grace Jones**, **Debbie Harry**, **Chaka Khan**, and **Bill Cosby**, end the show with an ensemble rendition of **Chuck Berry**'s *Rock And Roll Music*.

19 At a **Public Enemy** gig in Nashville, two girls are crushed to death when fans rush out of the auditorium after reports of gunfire. The hardcore rap quartet, comprising vocalists **Chuck D** and **Flavor Flav**, DJ scratcher **Terminator X**, and Minister of Information **Professor Griff**, is quickly building a reputation as the genre's most militant protagonists. Signed to Def Jam, the group is managed and produced by two former classmates from Adelphi University of Long Island, New York: Hank Shocklee and Bill Stephney (who describes them as "the Black Panthers of rap"). Their innovative, aggressive, urban rap has already been trademarked with the release in May of their debut album, ***Yo! Bum Rush The Show***, hailed in this week's issue of the **NME** as the number one album of the year. American rock critic Robert Christgau has also cited the group's current single, *Bring The Noise* – which features samples from **James Brown** (*Funky Drummer*), **Funkadelic** (*Let's Take It To The Stage* and *Get Off Your Ass And Jam*), and **Marva Whitney** (*It's My Thing*) – as "merely the greatest piece of rock and roll released in 1987."

22 Just back from a tour of the Far East, Mötley Crüe's **Nikki Sixx** embarks on a drugs and alcohol binge that sees him pronounced DOA in an ambulance. Two needles of adrenalin are inserted into his chest to get his heart beating again, and when he wakes up in Cedar-Sinai Hospital, a police officer is shining a flashlight in his eyes, asking him where he got the drugs. Against medical advice, Sixx removes the IV from his arm and signs himself out of hospital wearing only his leather pants. Once home, he changes his answering machine to say, "Hey, it's Nikki. I'm not home because I'm dead," before taking some more heroin and passing out again.

31 Coming on stage just before midnight, **Prince** performs at a benefit concert for the Minnesota Coalition for the Homeless at his Paisley Park Studios in Chanhassen. Highlighting a greatest hits set, the sixth number played is *Auld Lang Syne*.

ROOTS **During this year: 16-year-old DJ Liam Howlett joins hip-hop combo Cut To Kill, after buying a pair of turntables with money saved from summer jobs... to earn money to raise her three younger siblings after their parents have been killed, Eilleen Twain performs at the Deerhurst Resort in Huntsville, Ontario, Canada, in a Las Vegas-style revue... Scott Weiland and Robert DeLeo meet at a Black Flag concert in Long Beach, California, and immediately form Mighty Joe Young in their hometown, San Diego, changing their name to Shirley Temple's Pussy before settling on the Stone Temple Pilots in 1990... Kurt Cobain, currently living with his mother in an Aberdeen trailer park, and Krist Novoselic, the son of Croatian immigrants, form covers band Skid Row in Seattle... Halifax, Nova Scotia, native Sarah McLachlan begins performing on the Canadian folk circuit... and graduating from high school in South Florida, Brian Warner takes part in poetry readings at the Squeeze Club in Fort Lauderdale; inspired by heavy metal, gothic, and satanic themes, he will change his name to Marilyn Manson in 1989, when he forms his first group...**

Don't Worry, Be Happy

1988

No.1 US SINGLES

Jan 2 Faith **George Michael**
Jan 9 So Emotional **Whitney Houston**
Jan 16 Got My Mind Set On You **George Harrison**
Jan 23 The Way You Make Me Feel **Michael Jackson**
Jan 30 Need You Tonight **INXS**
Feb 6 Could've Been **Tiffany**
Feb 20 Seasons Change **Exposé**
Feb 27 Father Figure **George Michael**
Mar 12 Never Gonna Give You Up **Rick Astley**
Mar 26 Man In The Mirror **Michael Jackson**
Apr 9 Get Outta My Dreams (Get Into My Car) **Billy Ocean**
Apr 23 Where Do Broken Hearts Go **Whitney Houston**
May 7 Wishing Well **Terence Trent D'Arby**
May 14 Anything For You **Gloria Estefan & Miami Sound Machine**
May 28 One More Try **George Michael**
June 18 Together Forever **Rick Astley**
June 25 Foolish Beat **Debbie Gibson**
July 2 Dirty Diana **Michael Jackson**
July 9 The Flame **Cheap Trick**
July 23 Hold On To The Nights **Richard Marx**
July 30 Roll With It **Steve Winwood**
Aug 27 Monkey **George Michael**
Sept 10 Sweet Child O' Mine **Guns N' Roses**
Sept 24 Don't Worry Be Happy **Bobby McFerrin**
Oct 8 Love Bites **Def Leppard**
Oct 15 Red Red Wine **UB40**
Oct 22 Groovy Kind Of Love **Phil Collins**
Nov 5 Kokomo **Beach Boys**
Nov 12 Wild, Wild West **Escape Club**
Nov 19 Bad Medicine **Bon Jovi**
Dec 3 Baby, I Love Your Way/Freebird Medley (Free Baby) **Will To Power**
Dec 10 Look Away **Chicago**
Dec 24 Every Rose Has Its Thorn **Poison**

No.1 UK SINGLES

Jan 2 Always On My Mind **Pet Shop Boys**
Jan 16 Heaven Is A Place On Earth **Belinda Carlisle**
Jan 30 I Think We're Alone Now **Tiffany**
Feb 20 I Should Be So Lucky **Kylie Minogue**
Mar 26 Don't Turn Around **Aswad**
Apr 9 Heart **Pet Shop Boys**
Apr 30 Theme From S-Express **S-Express**

Sting

INXS

Sting, after winning a BRIT and a Grammy in the space of a month, performed at the Nelson Mandela tribute concert and on the Amnesty International tour... INXS's first US chart-topper, *Need You Tonight*, preceded a further five Top 10 hits.

The music business, worth billions of dollars worldwide, was beginning to agglomerate in a series of mergers and acquisitions. Acid, house, and a surfeit of sub-genres emerged from the underground, **INXS** emerged from down under, and the **Pixies** became heroes of college rock.

Sony's acquisition of CBS/Columbia was the latest example of consolidation, which would affect creativity as well as financing. Increasingly, corporations would look for short-term return, shunning the risk of developing artists' careers. Motown's takeover by MCA was a further step in the process, though **Berry Gordy** astutely retained the highly profitable publishing arm.

Nothing could be less corporate than the hedonistic explosion of acid music in British clubs, and "hothouse" music on the Mediterranean island of Ibiza, which drew 20-somethings from all over Europe. DJs became bona fide performers, remixing, adding basslines and repetitive techno motifs.

Meanwhile, adult audiences were looking to **George Michael**, **Sting**, **U2**, and even **George Harrison**, who reappeared with a cover of the Rudy Clark-penned *I Got My Mind Set On You*. Harrison then joined **Tom Petty**, **Bob Dylan**, and **Roy Orbison** to form perhaps the least likely supergroup, the **Traveling Wilburys**, and record a cheerful, laid-back album.

The year also saw a diverse flowering of female singer-songwriters. **Enya**'s sound was unique and would become instantly recognizable for its multilayered vocals and fusion of Celtic and New Age music. Also from Ireland, **Sinéad O'Connor** released her debut album ***The Lion And The Cobra***. Her angular and often tortured voice was complemented by precocious songwriting. Diametrically opposite was **Tracy Chapman**, whose urban-folk odyssey *Fast Car* became a breakthrough hit.

Chapman was on hand at a 70th birthday tribute to the still-jailed Nelson Mandela. The anti-apartheid cause had received earlier musical support from **Peter Gabriel** (with *Biko*) and most famously from the **Specials**, with *Nelson Mandela*. This concert was broadcast internationally (though not to South Africa), and also featured **Stevie Wonder**, **Dire Straits**, and **Whitney Houston**.

Backed by the cream of session musicians, **Sting** packed them in for the US follow-up tour to his album ***Nothing Like The Sun***. Proving himself the complete musician, he was at home with jazz, dance, and rock – even if the lyrical content of his songs extended to the political and even tender. **George Michael** garnered yet another US No. 1 with *Monkey* – aided by the brains behind **Janet Jackson**'s success, Jimmy Jam and Terry Lewis. It was yet another track from the phenomenally successful ***Faith***, which won a Grammy as Album of the Year.

"I don't see myself making black or white music."

Tracy Chapman, **Q**, June 1988

May 14 Perfect **Fairground Attraction**
May 21 With A Little Help From My Friends/ She's Leaving Home **Wet Wet Wet/ Billy Bragg with Cara Tivey**
June 18 Doctorin' The Tardis **Timelords**
June 25 I Owe You Nothing **Bros**
July 9 Nothing's Gonna Change My Love For You **Glenn Medeiros**
Aug 6 The Only Way Is Up **Yazz & the Plastic Population**
Sept 10 Groovy Kind Of Love **Phil Collins**
Sept 24 He Ain't Heavy He's My Brother **Hollies**
Oct 8 Desire **U2**
Oct 15 One Moment In Time **Whitney Houston**
Oct 29 Orinoco Flow (Sail Away) **Enya**
Nov 19 The First Time **Robin Beck**
Dec 10 Mistletoe And Wine **Cliff Richard**

George Harrison's comeback... Nirvana's demo... the Grammy-winning *Graceland*...

Paul McCartney was noticably absent when the Beatles were indicted into the Rock and Roll Hall of Fame, citing business differences with the rest of the group.

January

16 In one of the more significant comebacks in rock history, **George Harrison** tops the US chart with *Got My Mind Set On You* (a revival of **James Ray**'s 1962 original), which hit UK No. 2 last month. It is nearly 24 years since he first topped the US chart with the **Beatles**' *I Want To Hold Your Hand*, and 13 years since he last topped it as a solo artist, with *Give Me Love (Give Me Peace On Earth)*.

20 With many of the founders of rock 'n' roll already members of the Rock and Roll Hall of Fame, their heirs – the **Beatles**, the **Beach Boys**, and **Bob Dylan** – are among those inducted at the third annual dinner at the Waldorf Astoria Hotel in New York. The Beatles, inducted by **Mick Jagger**, are represented by **George Harrison**, **Ringo Starr**, and **Yoko Ono**. **McCartney** cites his business differences with the rest of the group as the reason for his absence. In his speech Harrison says: "I don't have much to say 'cause I'm the quiet Beatle." **Bruce Springsteen** inducts **Bob Dylan**, and **Elton John** inducts the Beach Boys, whose **Mike Love** gives a rambling and largely nonsensical acceptance speech. The **Drifters** and the **Supremes** are also inducted. (At least 40 people can legitimately claim to have been bona fide Drifters over the group's 35-year history, and most of them have also masqueraded in several bogus groups of touring "Drifters.") The Early Influences are **Woody Guthrie**, **Leadbelly**, and guitar innovator **Les Paul**, who is inducted by **Jeff Beck**. The Non-Performer honor goes to Berry Gordy Jr., founder of the Motown empire.

22 Dutch electronics giant Philips having bought Polygram last year, the Japanese Sony Corporation now acquires CBS/Columbia Records and its label affiliates for $2 billion. The industry will continue to shrink through corporate takeovers: next year Polygram will swallow both A&M and Island.

23 Seattle-based trio **Nirvana** records a ten-song demo tape with local alt-rock producer Jack Endino. The group was formed last year by drummer/singer **Kurt Cobain** (born in 1967 in Hoquiam, Washington, and currently living with his cocktail waitress mother in an Aberdeen trailer park) and guitarist **Krist Novoselic**. Cobain quickly switched to guitar with the addition of **Melvins**' drummer **Dale Crover**, before they played their first gig in Raymond last spring. They will spend much of the year building a reputation as one of Seattle's most explosive new alternative acts.

> **"Great things rise to the top... We don't need record-company people standing around going 'C'mon, guys, write a hit.' It's in the band already."**
> INXS's Michael Hutchence, **Rolling Stone**, January 14, 1988

February

8 To celebrate receiving the Outstanding Contribution to British Music, the **Who** reform for a single appearance at the seventh BPI Awards, at the Royal Albert Hall, London, broadcast live on BBC1. Unfortunately, not all goes to plan. Their three-song set – *My Generation*, *Substitute*, and *Who Are You* – overruns its allotted time, preventing Best British Single winner **Rick Astley** from receiving his award, and being faded out mid-song when the "Nine O'Clock News" comes on air on the hour. **Alison Moyet**, who won Best British Single last year, wins her second Best British Female Solo Artist award, and the **Pet Shop Boys** receive the Best British Group trophy. **George Michael** is named Best British Male Solo Artist, **Sting**'s ***Nothing Like The Sun*** is Best Album, and **U2** pick up the Best International Group award. **New Order**'s innovative "True Faith," directed by Jean Baptiste Mondino, is named Best British Video, and **Wet Wet Wet** and **Terence Trent D'Arby** are Best British and Best International Newcomer respectively. The Pet Shop Boys and **Dusty Springfield** mime to their UK No. 2 collaborative confection, *What Have I Done To Deserve This?*, causing Tennant to comment: "It's kind of macho nowadays to prove you can cut it live. I quite like proving that we can't cut it live. We're a pop group, not a rock 'n' roll group." (The award-winning Pet Shop Boys and New Order hits were produced by Stephen Hague.)

11 **Run D.M.C.** give two 30-minute concerts at Eastside High School in Paterson, New Jersey, in support of maverick school principal, Joe

Fronted by singer Marti Pellow, Scottish pop/rock quintet Wet Wet Wet broke through in 1987 with their debut album *Popped In Souled Out*.

THE TRAVELING WILBURYS

Apr 3 **The Traveling Wilburys, an ad hoc quintet comprising Lucky Wilbury (Bob Dylan), Otis Wilbury (Jeff Lynne), Nelson Wilbury (George Harrison), Charlie T., Jnr. (Tom Petty), and Lefty Wilbury (Roy Orbison), begin recording *Handle With Care* at Lucky's garage studio in Malibu. They will finish recording sessions for a complete album at Eurythmic Dave Stewart's home studio in Los Angeles during May. Produced by Otis and Nelson, *The Traveling Wilburys – Volume One* will be released by the Wilbury Record Company on October 18, set for glowing reviews and triple-platinum US sales. Offering some insight into the Wilburys' evolution, the album's liner notes will state: "A remarkable sophisticated musical culture developed, considering there were no managers or agents... they found themselves the object of interest among many less-developed species – nightclub owners, tour operators, and recording executives."**

The band's followup album, *Vol. 3*, featured Muddy, Boo, Clayton, and Spike Wilbury.

Clark, who is under fire for his get-tough policy. At a news conference, **Russell Simmons** states: "Our principal wasn't as strict as Joe Clark, and we needed somebody like that."

12 Developing **Guns N' Roses**' reputation as a turbulent and volatile group, their lead singer **Axl Rose** walks off stage at the end of *Nightrain*, during a performance at the Celebrity Theater in Phoenix, Arizona. A series of dates supporting **David Lee Roth** will subsequently be canceled when Rose loses his voice, although some will claim he has been fired from the band.

15 **Def Leppard** cancel a show in El Paso after receiving threats to disrupt the concert. This follows a gig in Tucson on September 7, 1983, when lead singer **Joe Elliott** allegedly referred to El Paso as "the place with all those greasy Mexicans."

"It's difficult to stand in the same room and be civil to people who are trying to wreck my career."

George Michael to the press in Rotterdam, April 12, 1988

March

2 The 30th Grammy Awards spring several surprises, not least **Michael Jackson** – nominated four times for ***Bad*** – coming away empty-handed, causing the **Los Angeles Times** to write that he "couldn't have looked any more heartbroken if someone had just run away with his pet chimp." **Paul Simon**'s *Graceland* is named Record of the Year, despite peaking at No. 81 – the first time the winning record has not made the Top 40. **Sting**'s *Bring On The Night*, despite not charting at all, wins Best Pop Vocal Performance, Male. **George Michael** and **Aretha Franklin** win Best R&B Performance by a Duo or Group for the smash duet *I Knew You Were Waiting (For Me)*. Astonishingly, **Smokey Robinson**, **Bill Medley**, **Barry Mann**, and Cynthia Weil all receive their first Grammys. **U2** takes home two trophies for ***The Joshua Tree***: Album of the Year and Best Rock Performance by a Duo or Group with Vocal. **The Edge**, in his acceptance speech for Album of the Year, thanks "Jack Healy and Amnesty International for all their work, Desmond Tutu for his courage, Martin Luther King. I'd like to thank, uh, **Bob Dylan** for *Tangled Up In Blue*, Flannery O'Connor, **Jimi Hendrix**, Walt Disney, John the Baptist, Georgie Best, Gregory Peck, James T. Kirk, Morris Pratt, Dr. Ruth, Fawn Hall, Batman and Robin, Lucky the Dog, Pee Wee Herman, the YMCA, Eddie the Eagle, sumo wrestlers around the world, and, of course, Ronald Reagan." Not to be upstaged, **Little Richard**, announcing the winner of the Best New Artist prize, says: "And the winner is me! I have never received nuthin'! You never gave me no Grammys and I've been singing for years... I am the architect of rock 'n' roll. I am the originator." Obviously the audience agrees, giving him a standing ovation. **Frank Zappa**, receiving his first Grammy, for Best Rock Instrumental Performance (Orchestra, Group or Soloist), says: "I find it difficult to believe that **Whitney Houston** is the answer to all of America's music needs." As her ***Aretha*** album receives the Best Rhythm & Blues Vocal Performance, Female, **Aretha Franklin** becomes the leading female artist Grammy winner, with her 14th nod, surpassing Leontyne Price. In the country genre, 45-year-old **K.T. Oslin**, described by the **Washington Post** as a "veteran newcomer," wins Best Country Vocal Performance, Female. **Ray Charles** is honored with a Lifetime Achievement Award, with the Academy noting that he is "the father of soul, whose unique and effervescent singing and piano-playing have personified the true essence of soul music in all his recorded and personal performances of basic blues, pop ballads, jazz tunes and even country music."

6 German DJ Ruth Rockenschaub plays **Prince**'s ***The Black Album*** (withdrawn last December) on her radio program, broadcast throughout Germany and parts of Austria and Switzerland. She will play it again on the 9th, before receiving a telex next day from WEA telling her to desist or risk a $6,300 (£3,500) fine.

10 **Andy Gibb**, admitted to the John Radcliffe Hospital in Oxford, England, with severe stomach pains three days ago, dies from myocarditis five days before his 30th birthday, following a long battle with cocaine addiction. He was working on a new album while living on his brother **Robin**'s country estate.

20 American singers **Tracy Chapman** and **Natalie Merchant** perform solo showcases at London's Donmar Warehouse. The 23-year-old Chapman, from Cleveland, signed to Elektra Records last year. Together with New York-based **Suzanne Vega** (who broke through with last year's *Luka*) she is spearheading a new wave of female folk/pop singer-songwriters. Her self-titled debut album will explode in the summer, thanks to the out-of-the box smash single, *Fast Car*. Meanwhile, 24-year-old New York State native Merchant successfully fronts college folk/rock favorites **10,000 Maniacs** (also signed to Elektra) whose ***Blind Man Zoo*** album became their first charted album last year.

Nelson Mandela birthday concert... MCA buys Motown Records...

The Pixies

Whitney Houston

April

8 American college rock darlings the **Pixies** open a seven-date sellout tour of England at the Mean Fiddler in London, embarking on a European tour supporting fellow 4AD labelmates **Throwing Muses**. The Boston-based alt-rock quartet, comprising lead singer/guitarist **Black Francis**, lead guitarist **Joey Santiago**, bassist **Kim Deal**, and drummer **David Lovering**, are touring in support of their second album, ***Surfer Rosa***. Produced by Steve Albini, it has already been hailed as an underground classic. One critic describes the two bands as the finest double act since "the Romans decided to put the Christians and the lions on the same bill!" During a second trip to the UK in October, the Pixies will meet producer Gil Norton, who will record them in Boston during the last six weeks of the year.

9 On discovering that the **Shamen**'s *Happy Days* – which the group offered to McEwans for its £1 ($1.8) million television beer ad campaign – is a veiled attack on the Thatcher government, the company withdraws the commercial. McEwans was made aware of the song's content by the **Glasgow Evening Times**, who ran such headlines as "Shame Of The Shamen" and "McEwans Bosses In A Froth." The band's **Will Sinnott** will comment: "We couldn't believe they'd wanted to deal with us in the first place, and when they accepted the song, that came as something of a surprise as well." Keyboardist Sinott (aka **Will Sin**) joined with singer/bassist founder **Colin Angus** last year, and is steering the group in a pioneering techno-dance direction that will bear full fruit in 1992.

9 Soul music suffers a double blow: **Brook Benton** succumbs at 56 to spinal meningitis-related pneumonia in New York City, and 50-year-old **Dave Prater**, of **Sam & Dave**, is killed when his car hits a tree in Ocilla, Georgia. Benton racked up 50 US chart hits, spanning almost 23 years between his first entry in 1958, *A Million Miles From Nowhere*, and his last in 1971, *Shoes*. His one gold record was his definitive reading of **Tony Joe White**'s *Rainy Night In Georgia*. Prater, for some years at odds with his soulmate **Sam Moore**, was best known for the duo's two gold singles, the classic *Soul Man* and *I Thank You*.

15 **Shawn Colvin**, a 30-year-old folk singer-songwriter/guitarist from South Dakota, performs at the Somerville Theater in Massachusetts. An itinerant performer, she records the concert to sell on cassette at future gigs. Colvin's tape will be broadcast on Boston's WERS-FM, leading to the first headlining concert of her career at Harvard's Paine Hall in September and, after a lengthy wait on the sidelines, to her signing with Columbia Records. Colvin worked on backing vocals for **Suzanne Vega**'s recent transatlantic hit *Luka*.

23 **Whitney Houston** equals **Michael Jackson**'s record, created just two weeks ago, of four chart-topping hits taken from the same album, as her latest ballad, *Where Do Broken Hearts Go* hits US No. 1, displacing Billy Ocean's *Get Outta My Dreams (Get Into My Car)*. She also breaks the record for consecutive US chart-toppers, with seven, overtaking the previous record of six achieved by both the **Beatles** and the **Bee Gees**.

30 Switzerland wins its first ever Eurovision Song Contest – the 33rd – held at the Royal Dublin Society, with the song *Ne Partez Pas Sans Moi* winning handily over Luxembourg's entry. The singer is 20-year-old French Canadian **Celine Dion**. The youngest of 14 children in a musical family, Dion gave her first public performance at the age of 5. At 12, she recorded a demo tape which her brother Michael sent to an address on the back of an album by her idol, French singer **Ginette Reno**. The address was that of Reno's manager, Quebec-based entrepreneur René

The Pixies came together when Black Francis placed an ad for a bassist "into Husker Du and Peter, Paul and Mary"... Whitney Houston's first two albums have sold 22 million copies in the US.

"I'm horrified by this man's behavior – it goes beyond the bounds of entertainment... It's an indication of the sick society we're moving into..."

Sheffield's Labour Member of Parliament David Blunkett after hearing about an Alice Cooper concert, April 5, 1988

Atlantic Records celebrates its 40th anniversary with an all-star concert at Madison Square Gardens in New York.

Angelil. Taking her under his wing, Angelil steered the young singer's career, remortgaging his house to finance the recording of her maiden album, 1981's ***La Voix Du Bon Dieu***. Possessing a dramatic and powerful vocal style, Dion recorded nine more French-speaking albums during the decade, four of which have been certified platinum in Canada. Her international recognition began when she won the Gold Medal at the 1982 Yamaha World Song Festival in Tokyo, followed by her becoming the first Canadian to receive a gold disc in France in 1983 (for the 700,000-selling ***D'Amour Ou D'Amité***).

May

5 **Michael Jackson** becomes the first non-Soviet to be featured advertising a product on Russian television, when Pepsi-Cola runs its first paid commercial during "Pozner in America," a joint US-Soviet production.

14 Atlantic Records celebrates its 40th anniversary with a 13-hour marathon all-star concert at Madison Square Garden in New York. Many of the label's top acts perform, including the **Bee Gees**, **Yes**, **Crosby Stills & Nash**, **Genesis**, **Iron Butterfly**, the **Rascals**, **Foreigner**, **Paul Rodgers**, **Bob Geldof**, **Booker T. Jones**, the **Average White Band**, **Wilson Pickett**, the **Coasters**, the **Spinners**, **Roberta Flack**, **Manhattan Transfer**, **Debbie Gibson** (the label's current 17-year-old singer-songwriting ingenue), R&B veterans **Ruth Brown**, **LaVern Baker**, and **Ben E. King**, and **Vanilla Fudge**. The evening ends with the ever-dapper Ahmet Ertegun introducing **Led Zeppelin**, with **Jimmy Page**, **Robert Plant**, and **John Paul Jones** joined by **John Bonham**'s son **Jason**.

19 The House of Lords rejects a case brought by the British Phonographic Industry against electronics company Amstrad, seeking to prevent it from selling a high-speed twin cassette deck, on the grounds that it violates the Copyright Act of 1956 in allowing consumers to make unauthorized copies of copyrighted works. The Lords admits that even though this may be the case, Amstrad includes printed warnings about copyright infringement with the decks; the company is not inciting people to break the law.

June

7 Weeks after Atlantic Records celebrated its 40th anniversary, the company agrees to recalculate the royalty rate for some of its earliest recording artists, and sets up a $1.5 million trust fund to provide tax-free grants to those in need.

11 Nelson Mandela's 70th Birthday Tribute, honoring the political prisoner who is in the 24th year of his sentence, takes place at Wembley Stadium in London. It is televised live on BBC2 and broadcast to 40 countries around the world, with an estimated audience of one billion. **Phil Collins**, **Whitney Houston**, **Tracy Chapman**, **Dire Straits**, **George Michael**, **Peter Gabriel**, the **Bee Gees**, **Eurythmics**, **Al Green**, **Harry Belafonte**, **Stevie Wonder**, and **Aswad** are among a galaxy of stars performing throughout the day and evening. The issue of apartheid and Mandela's incarceration have become a cause célèbre among the rock fraternity, with several artists cutting protest songs, including **Simple Minds**, Peter Gabriel, and the **Specials** – whose 1984 hit *Nelson Mandela* provides the event's multistar show-closing anthem. The group's founder, **Jerry Dammers**, has been a prime mover in organizing today's tribute. Three years after Live Aid the power of the people remains as strong as ever, and within two years Mandela will walk free.

18 Mixing an original **Jimmy Cauty** rhythm track with the theme to the BBC television series "Dr. Who," and **Gary Glitter**'s *I'm The Leader Of The Gang*, KLF Communications offshoot, the **Timelords**, hit UK No. 1 for a week with *Doctorin' The Tardis*. The recording is a deliberate attempt by KLF's Cauty and **Bill Drummond** to create a chart-topping single using, in Drummond's words, "the lowest common denominator in every aspect." Glitter himself has been recruited for a 12in remix, *Gary In The Tardis*. Under the guise of the Timelords, the pair will publish **The Manual** in September, a £5.99 ($11) instruction book on how to secure a No. 1 record. (It includes a tribute to UK DJ Steve Wright: "You don't even have to like him to be awed by him. The man is a genius, he is the most popular DJ in the country and has been the heartbeat of the British psyche since 1985.")

25 **Debbie Gibson**'s *Foolish Beat* tops the US chart, making her the youngest artist ever to write, produce, and perform a US No. 1 single. Tomorrow, Gibson will graduate with honors from Calhoun High School, Merrick, New Jersey.

27 Motown Records is bought by MCA Inc. and Boston Ventures (an investment banking firm), for $61 million. Motown spokeswoman Rosalind Stevenson says MCA will get the Motown record label, while Gordy retains the company's lucrative publishing arm, Jobete Music Corp., and its film business, which will be known as Gordy Co. MCA will put up 20 percent of the purchase price and Boston Ventures will supply the remainder. The deal calls for MCA to buy out Boston Ventures' share "down the road." Gordy tells **Variety**: "In today's economy, the big get bigger and the small get extinct. In order to prevent that from happening, and to ensure the perpetuation of Motown and its heritage, I decided to clasp hands with one of the most formidable giants in our business, MCA." (In 1996 EMI will buy 50 percent of Jobete from Gordy for $132 million.)

Simple Minds' Jim Kerr was decribed by fellow Scot, MP Nicholas Fairburn, as "left-wing scum" for appearing at the Nelson Mandela 70th Birthday Tribute concert.

Acid house... MTV's first hip hot/rap shop... Amnesty tour...

The Hacienda Club was founded by New Order and opened in 1982 with a performance by comedian Bernard Manning. The club closed in 1997 and was torn down and auctioned off.

July

13 The Hacienda club in Manchester, England – already a seminal nightspot – inaugurates its new specialist "house" night, dubbed "Hot." To transform the venue into a beach-like setting reminiscent of dance raves in Ibiza, Spain (which have become extremely popular with European teenagers over the past year), podiums have been added to the dancefloor, along with a swimming pool, beach balls, and ice pops. Throughout what will become known as Britain's own "Summer of Love," Hot Nights each Wednesday will see 2,500 young people dancing to the city's leading DJs, spinning a mesmerizing, trance-inducing mix of the latest "acid house" recordings. The sub-genre fuses elements of traditional Chicago house with techno sounds and deep basslines (often made using the Roland TB-303 synthesizer). Pioneering club DJs **Paul Oakenfold** and Danny Rampling have also brought the Balearic Ibiza/acid house sound to London clubs: Spectrum, Future, Heaven, and Shoom are all hosting similar weekly rituals, at which ecstasy is in plentiful supply. With illegal raves now attracting up to 10,000 spaced-out youths, the UK charts are about to host a succession of DJ/producer-led acid house hits, following the genre's first major success, *Theme From S'Express* by **S'Express**.

> **"If John [Lennon] were gay, you'd think he'd have made a pass at me at least once in 20 years."** Paul McCartney refuting Albert Goldman's assertion in his book, **The Lives of John Lennon**, August 7, 1989

15 MTV bans **Neil Young**'s "This Note's For You" video, in which a **Michael Jackson** look-alike's hair catches fire while performing a Pepsi-like commercial, only for a **Whitney Houston** double to extinguish it with a can of Coca-Cola. The censorship of the star-mimicking, corporate sponsorship-attacking clip will be called "senseless" by Young.

17 In the middle of an unbroken 14-month touring period, **Guns N' Roses** begins a concert series at major US venues, behind newly popular veterans **Aerosmith** (who are enjoying their biggest success in years with ***Permanent Vacation***), at the Poplar Creek Music Theater in Hoffman Estates, Illinois. Aerosmith, whose members now reject the chemical and substance abuse of their earlier days, has insisted on a rider in their contract requesting that hard-partying Guns N' Roses members confine their drug and alcohol activities to their own dressing room. By mid-tour, the red-hot Roses will be the main attraction, with their slow-rising debut album ***Appetite For Destruction*** – released last August – finally set to hit US No. 1 in three weeks. Produced by Mike Clink and written and arranged by the group, it will sell six million US copies by the end of the year. It will also yield four huge crossover hits: *Sweet Child O' Mine* – written about Axl's girlfriend Erin Everly (**Don**'s daughter) – which will top the US chart in September, the Los Angeles urban anthem *Welcome To The Jungle* (featured in the latest Dirty Harry movie, "Dead Pool," in which the group has a cameo spot), *Paradise City*, and *Patience*. Painstakingly building a reputation as rock's latest bad-ass group, the band's image revolves around bandana-wearing lead singer **Axl Rose**, and black top hat-toting guitarist **Slash**.

Two festival-goers die in a slamdancing crowd at Guns N' Roses' performance at the Monsters of Rock festival at Castle Donington, England.

23 With his self-penned rock ballad, *Hold On To The Nights*, topping the US chart, Chicago-born pop/rock singer-songwriter **Richard Marx** becomes the first male singer to notch up four top three hits from a debut album, ***Richard Marx*** (edging out **George Michael** by a month). As his solo career soars, the ex-jingles tunesmith continues to write and produce projects with other artists, including **Randy Meisner** (ex-**Eagles**), **Fee Waybill** (ex-**Tubes**), and new all-girl rock group **Vixen**.

August

6 "Yo! MTV Raps," the network's first hip-hop/rap show – co-conceived by Ted Demme – begins airing, initially hosted by Fab 5 Freddy.

14 Blues guitarist **Roy Buchanan**, age 48, hangs himself with his own shirt in a cell in Fairfax, Virginia, following an arrest for a minor alcohol-related incident. A sorely underrated talent – the subject of the 1971 documentary "The Best Unknown Guitarist in the World" – he was seemingly only at peace with his trademark battered Fender Telecaster guitar, and had made several unsuccessful suicide attempts.

27 *Monkey* – remixed by Jimmy Jam and Terry Lewis – becomes **George Michael**'s fourth straight US No. 1, and the last from his debut solo album, ***Faith***. Including his hits with **Wham!**, it is Michael's eighth US No. 1 of the 1980s, a tally beaten only by **Michael Jackson**'s nine. ***Faith*** was written, arranged, and produced by Michael, and features him on most instruments (though ex-Wham! bassist **Deon Estus** remains as a regular sideman). It has already topped the UK chart (during a 72-week run) and spent 12 weeks

"Of course we write songs. What happens is you get a drum beat going and you get the bass in and you sing what you want and that's it."

Bananarama's Keren Woodward, **Q**, September 1988

astride the American survey during an 87-week residence, yielding the title cut hit followed by *Father Figure* and the ballad *One More Try*. Recovered from a minor operation in June to remove a benign vocal chord cyst, Michael – currently midway through the second North American leg of an extensive world tour that began in Japan on February 19 – is the most popular British performer of the moment, with his videos on hot rotation on MTV, and his concerts receiving A-list reviews.

28 The highlight of the annual Reading Rock Festival – this year featuring, among others, the **Ramones**, **Iggy Pop**, the Birmingham-based **Wonder Stuff**, Irish critics' faves **Hothouse Flowers**, **Runrig**, Scottish pop/rock combo **Deacon Blue**, and soul newcomer **Roachford** – is **Meat Loaf**'s appearance. Receiving a hail of plastic bottles near the beginning of his set, he asks the audience: "Do you wanna hear some music or do you wanna be stupid and throw things?" (Some report the altercation as follows: "Do you wanna rock 'n' roll or do you wanna throw shit?" The crowd responds, "Throw shit!") Engulfed by more bottles, he promptly leaves the stage. Returning to sing *Bat Out Of Hell*, he is again assailed by a hail of bottles, and this time gives up permanently. When security staff are sent on stage to clear up, they meet a similar fate.

September

7 Australian band **INXS** dominate the fifth MTV Video Music Awards at the Universal Amphitheater in Universal City, scooping up five trophies. They win Best Video, Best Group, Breakthrough Video, Best Editing, and the Viewers Choice award, all for the video to their US No. 1 smash, *Need You Tonight*. (They are in the middle of a phenomenal year, with their most recent album, ***Kick***, on its way to ten million worldwide sales, yielding three Top 10 US hits.) Brit group **Squeeze**, who re-formed in 1985, pick up two awards (Best Art Direction and Best Special Effects) for their "Hourglass" clip. **Michael Jackson** receives the Video Vanguard award. Among the performances are **Guns N' Roses** – winners of Best New Artist in a Video ("Welcome To The Jungle") – **Crowded House**, **Aerosmith**, **Cher**, **Depeche Mode**, **Rod Stewart**, and rap trio the **Fat Boys**. **Pink Floyd** win their first award for Best Concept Video ("Learning To Fly"), and **Prince** wins his second and third trophies for Best Male Video and Best Stage Performance in a Video, both for "U Got the Look" (featuring guest vocalist **Sheena Easton**).

23 **The Complete Beatles Recording Sessions**, by acknowledged Beatles authority Mark Lewisohn, is published in the UK. A day-by-day account of the group's studio activity, it is a companion study to his exhaustive **The Beatles Live**, first published in 1986, which detailed every live performance by the group.

AMNESTY TOUR

Sept 2 Celebrating the 40th anniversary of the Universal Declaration of Human Rights – adopted by the UN General Assembly in December 1948 – the Amnesty International Human Rights Now! tour opens at London's Wembley Stadium. The bill, comprising Bruce Springsteen & the E Street Band, Sting, Peter Gabriel, Tracy Chapman, and Youssou N'Dour, will play 20 dates in 15 countries, including Costa Rica, Hungary, India, Japan, the Ivory Coast, and Zimbabwe. The tour will end on October 15 at the Estadio River Plate in Buenos Aires.

The artists covered 35,000 miles in five continents.

1988

Nirvana's first single... Roy Orbison dies... The Smiths go their separate ways...

Enya

The Beach Boys in Times Square

October

8 **Freddie Mercury** and opera star Montserrat Caballé highlight a star-studded show to launch Barcelona's bid to stage the 1992 Olympic Games, at the Avinguda De Maria Cristina stadium.

16 **U2**, Scottish alt-rock favorites **Aztec Camera** (led by literate singer-songwriter/guitarist **Roddy Frame**), **Joan Armatrading**, **Eddy Grant**, **Keith Richard**, and **Ziggy Marley & the Melody Makers** take part in Smile Jamaica, a benefit concert at London's Dominion Theatre, to raise money to aid Jamaica's recovery after Hurricane Gilbert. Richard joins U2 on *When Love Comes To Town* and *Love Rescue Me*.

23 **Michael Jackson** tours the house on West Grand Boulevard where Berry Gordy, Jr. launched Motown Records in 1959. Jackson donates $125,000, a stage uniform from 1972, a rhinestone-studded glove, and a hat to the Motown Museum, as he prepares for his sellout concerts on the 25th and 26th at the nearby Palace of Auburn Hills. A man of few words, he says: "I'm very happy and proud to be back to the soil from which I came. Berry Gordy is the man that made it all possible for me. I want to say thank you, Berry, and I love you."

27 Four days before its UK opening, the **U2** documentary "Rattle and Hum" receives its world premiere at the Savoy Cinema in Dublin. The group performs a short acoustic set prior to the screening. The movie mostly features live footage filmed on December 19 and 20 last year at the Sun Devil Stadium in Tempe, Arizona, and the accompanying double album – produced by Jimmy Iovine – also includes nine new studio cuts.

29 Eithne Ní Bhraonáin – known simply as **Enya** – scores her breakthrough hit with *Orinoco Flow*, which reaches UK No. 1. The 27-year-old Irish singer-songwriter/pianist, one of a family of nine, studied classical music as a child. She joined two of her brothers, a sister, and two uncles to perform in the Celtic folk band **Clannad** in 1980, appearing on two of their albums, ***Crann Ull*** and ***Fuaim***. Subsequently concentrating on a solo career, Enya received two commissions: one from director David Putnam to score his 1984 film "The Frog Prince," the other from the BBC to compose music for "The Celts," a TV documentary aired last year. Signed to WEA Records by label boss Rob Dickins, her first single (named after Venezuela's Orinoco River and including a lyrical reference to Dickins) showcases her unique style: a meticulously crafted, multilayered, ethereal vocal form bathed in an oceanic synthesized sound. It is taken from the equally innovative album ***Watermark***, which will hit UK No. 5 next week during a 63-week chart tenure. Produced by her friend, ex-Clannad engineer Nicky Ryan (with lyrics by his wife Roma), the part-English, part-Gaelic set, composed by Enya, is the result of hundreds of hours in the Ryans' home studio, overdubbing scores of vocal tracks to produce a symphonic cathedral of sound.

> **"The reality is that the standard American recording contract is a greater work of art than the standard pop song."**
>
> Midnight Oil's Peter Garrett, **Spin**, November 1988

Enya released just five albums in 15 years, but total US sales of those albums have amounted to 18 million... The Beach Boys preceded their *Kokomo* chart-topper with *Wipeout* – an ill-advised teaming with the Fat Boys.

November

1 Sub Pop Records issues 1,000 copies of *Love Buzz/Big Cheese* (SP23), the first release by **Nirvana**. (The A-side is a cover of an original by 1970s Dutch rock band **Shocking Blue**.) The Seattle-based independent underground label – which sprang from a local music column called "Sub/Pop," started in 1983 by Bruce Pavitt for **Rocket** magazine – is building a strong roster of local bands, including **Green River** (one of Pavitt's earliest signings in 1986, which has recently regrouped as **Mudhoney**), and Nirvana. Sub Pop also issued *Hunted* and ***Screaming Life EP*** last year, the first two releases by **Soundgarden**, a quartet led by wailing frontman **Chris Cornell**. They have recently signed to another indie label, SST Records, for the issue of their groundbreaking debut album, ***Ultramega OK***, which is attracting rave reviews from alt-rock critics. With each group quickly building a loyal local following, they are collectively creating their own pioneering "grunge" sound – a new brand of rock unique to Seattle. The burgeoning genre mixes the muscular thickness of heavy metal with the ferocity and rebellious lyrical aesthetic of punk.

5 Following the example set by **George Harrison** in February, the venerable **Beach Boys** make a remarkable comeback, hitting US No. 1 with *Kokomo* – more than 24 years after *I Get Around* became their first chart-topper. Featured in the hit movie "Cocktail," it is, ironically, their

Michael Jackson took to wearing one glove – for the right hand – on his 1984 tour... Slash's black leather jacket featured a skull with the guitarist's familiar black

ROY ORBISON

Dec 6 Following a day spent shopping for parts for remote-controlled model airplanes with his bus driver and friend Benny Birchfield, Roy Orbison has dinner with Birchfield and his wife, country singer Jean Shepard, then visits his mother's house to see his son, Wesley. At about 11:00 pm, Orbison having gone to the bathroom and not come out, Wesley forces the door and finds his father's lifeless body. Orbison is rushed to Hendersonville Hospital, where he is pronounced dead of a heart attack at 11:54. Once described by Elvis Presley as "the greatest singer in the world," he is dead at the age of 52. Ironically, he has recently wrapped up his most creative year of the decade, recording the now-charting *Traveling Wilburys* album in the spring, followed by his own comeback set, *Mystery Girl*, which is due for release by Virgin in January. Having spent the past few years living with his wife Barbara in Malibu, Orbison will be buried in an unmarked grave at Westwood Memorial Park in Los Angeles. While his body is flown to Santa Monica, December 9 will be declared "Roy Orbison Day" by Mayor Maxie Watts in his home town of Wink, Texas.

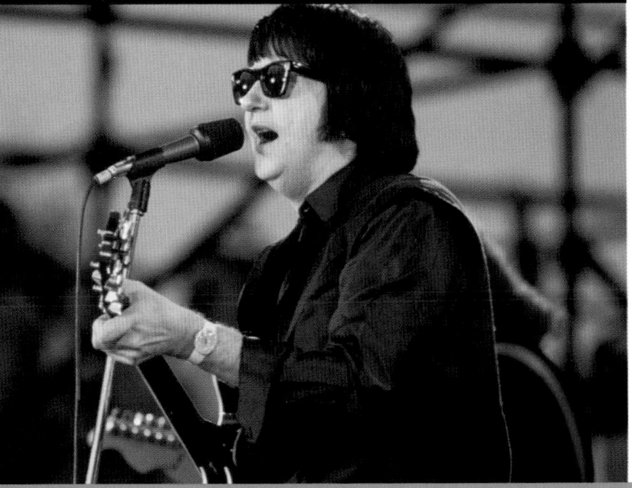

LL Cool J's grandfather gave him some DJ equipment and his mother bought him a drum machine when he was nine.

only major hit not penned by **Brian Wilson**. Wilson is currently under the "care" of controversial therapist Dr. Eugene Landy (who will be stripped of his license to practice next April). During a UK promotion visit last month, Wilson unexpectedly showed up at the tenth annual British Beach Boys Convention, held at the Parish Centre in Greenford, west London.

25 **Pink Floyd**'s **David Gilmour** and **Nick Mason** watch the launch of the Soviet-French Soyuz 7 space mission. On board is a cassette of the group's forthcoming album, ***Delicate Sound Of Thunder*** – the first rock record to be played in outer space.

30 **LL Cool J** plays the first rap concert in Africa, in the Ivory Coast's capital, Abidjan. Halfway through the concert, people faint, fights break out, the stage is stormed, and the show ends abruptly. Nevertheless, Cool will help establish a local hospital, which will lead the village elders of Grand Bassan to crown him Chief Kwasi Achi-Brou.

December

10 **Cliff Richard**'s 100th single, the seasonal *Mistletoe And Wine*, tops the UK chart, becoming the biggest-selling UK single of the year. Of his singles this century, 12 have been UK No. 1s, 55 have hit the Top 10, and only nine have failed to make the Top 40. Since his chart debut in 1958, Richard has had only two blank years – 1975 and 1978. And he's not finished yet...

15 At the end of perhaps his busiest year – hardly any of which had anything to do with music – **James Brown** is sentenced to a six-year jail term, following a series of run-ins with the law. He has been arrested five times over the past 12 months, resulting in charges of assault with intent to murder, aggravated assault and battery, possession of drugs and illegal weapons, and resisting arrest. He also announced that, despite loving his wife Adrienne, he was divorcing her. Things haven't been much better for her. She was arrested twice for the possession of drugs, and while fighting charges of air ticket violations in court, claimed diplomatic immunity because she was the wife of the "official Ambassador of Soul." She also pled innocent to setting fire to a hotel room and announced that she was filing for a legal separation from her husband.

16 **Sylvester**, a pioneer of the gay disco scene, who scored hits with *Dance (Disco Heat)*, *You Make Me Feel (Mighty Real)*, *I (Who Have Nothing)*, and *Do Ya Wanna Funk*, dies from AIDS in San Francisco. Along with mixer and producer Patrick Cowley – who succumbed to the disease in 1982 – Sylvester set the table for the burgeoning hi-NRG and house styles, which have dominated the club scene of the 1980s.

18 **Enya** is interviewed by Gloria Hunniford on ITV's "Sunday Sunday" show, and performs a Gaelic version of *Silent Night*. She made her very first television appearance on another Gloria Hunniford show in Northern Ireland in 1980.

22 With his solo career in full swing following the dissolution of the group earlier in the year, **Morrissey** performs a last-gasp farewell **Smiths** gig with colleagues **Andy Rourke** and **Mike Joyce** at England's Wolverhampton Civic Hall. **Craig Gannon** plays in place of the noticeably absent **Johnny Marr**. The first 1,700 fans wearing either Smiths or Morrissey T-shirts get in free. The concert is filmed for a promotional video for Morrissey's new solo single, *The Last Of The International Playboys*, a song about legendary gangsters Ronnie and Reggie Kray.

ROOTS During this year: 13-year-old Lauryn Hill makes her stage debut on "Amateur Night" at the Apollo Theater in Harlem, New York City, singing Smokey Robinson's *Who's Loving You*... student songwriters Steven Page and Ed Robertson form Barenaked Ladies in Scarborough, Toronto... hard-core punk revivalist band Blue Generation is founded in Blackwood, Wales, by James Dean Bradfield and his cousin, Sean Moore; following the recruitment next year of Richey Edwards and Nicky Wire, they will release a self-financed single, *Suicide Alley*... having formed the short-lived Polekats trio, Polly Jean Harvey joins John Parish's band Automatic Dlamini... with Mellow Man electing for a solo career, DVX – now a trio – becomes Cypress Hill, after a Southgate, Los Angeles, neighborhood... Mariah Carey successfully auditions to be a backup singer for Brenda K. Starr, who passes her demo tape to Columbia Records' president, Tommy Mottola... Boyz II Men come together at Philadelphia's High School of Creative and Performing Arts... and spotted by the label's Len Scholds at Nashville's Bluebird Café, Garth Brooks signs with Capitol Records...

Another Day In Paradise

1989

No.1 US SINGLES

Jan 7 Every Rose Has Its Thorn **Poison**
Jan 14 My Prerogative **Bobby Brown**
Jan 21 Two Hearts **Phil Collins**
Feb 4 When I'm With You **Sheriff**
Feb 11 Straight Up **Paula Abdul**
Mar 4 Lost In Your Eyes **Debbie Gibson**
Mar 25 The Living Years **Mike & the Mechanics**
Apr 1 Eternal Flame **Bangles**
Apr 8 The Look **Roxette**
Apr 15 She Drives Me Crazy **Fine Young Cannibals**
Apr 22 Like A Prayer **Madonna**
May 13 I'll Be There For You **Bon Jovi**
May 20 Forever Your Girl **Paula Abdul**
June 3 Rock On **Michael Damian**
June 10 Wind Beneath My Wings **Bette Midler**
June 17 I'll Be Loving You (Forever) **New Kids On The Block**
June 24 Satisfied **Richard Marx**
July 1 Baby Don't Forget My Number **Milli Vanilli**
July 8 Good Thing **Fine Young Cannibals**
July 15 If You Don't Know Me By Now **Simply Red**
July 22 Toy Soldiers **Martika**
Aug 5 Batdance **Prince**
Aug 12 Right Here Waiting **Richard Marx**
Sept 2 Cold Hearted **Paula Abdul**
Sept 9 Hangin' Tough **New Kids On The Block**
Sept 16 Don't Wanna Lose You **Gloria Estefan**
Sept 23 Girl I'm Gonna Miss You **Milli Vanilli**
Oct 7 Miss You Much **Janet Jackson**
Nov 4 Listen To Your Heart **Roxette**
Nov 11 When I See You Smile **Bad English**
Nov 25 Blame It On The Rain **Milli Vanilli**
Dec 9 We Didn't Start The Fire **Billy Joel**
Dec 23 Another Day In Paradise **Phil Collins**

No.1 UK SINGLES

Jan 7 Especially For You **Kylie Minogue & Jason Donovan**
Jan 28 Something's Gotten Hold Of My Heart **Marc Almond featuring Gene Pitney**
Feb 25 Belfast Child **Simple Minds**
Mar 11 Too Many Broken Hearts **Jason Donovan**
Mar 25 Like A Prayer **Madonna**
Apr 15 Eternal Flame **Bangles**
May 13 Hand On Your Heart **Kylie Minogue**
May 20 Ferry 'Cross The Mersey **Christians, Holly Johnson, Paul McCartney, Gerry Marsden, & Stock Aitken Waterman**

Don Henley

Madonna

Don Henley released his third, and most ambitious, solo album, *The End Of The Innocence*... Madonna's $5 million sponsorship deal with Pepsi-Cola was withdrawn after widespread complaints about the singer's "Like A Prayer."

The Berlin Wall fell; China's democratic movement was crushed; Ayatollah Khomeini died. And the wet industrial city of Manchester boasted of being the center of musical gravity. It had already delivered the influential **Smiths**. Now, the Hacienda club was at the heart of the city's music scene, hosting "house" nights with Europe's most innovative DJs, and presenting bands like **Stone Roses** and the **Happy Mondays**. To the south, Londoners **Soul II Soul** combined reggae, hip-hop, and R&B in mellow, stylish fashion. Led by producer/composer DJ **Jazzie B** and **Nellee Hooper** (ex-**Massive Attack**), their debut album drew on influences as diverse as **Chic** and African rhythms, and delivered cool harmonies over silky electronic grooves.

The **Fine Young Cannibals** were riding the success of their second album ***The Raw And The Cooked.*** Featuring two former members of the (**English**) **Beat** (whose sound is echoed on this album) it boasted several outstanding tracks, with *She Drives Me Crazy* vaulting to the top of the US chart shortly before the album did the same. **Roland Gift**'s distinct if somewhat melodramatic vocals well suited infectious pop songs like *Good Thing.*

In the US, **Gloria Estefan & the Miami Sound Machine** showed the growing significance of the Hispanic community, and brought Latin dance and ballads into the charts. Choreographer **Paula Abdul** had worked with **Janet Jackson** on *Nasty*, as well as **George Michael** and **Duran Duran**. In 1989 she stepped out of the shadows, styling herself very much in the Ms. Jackson mold, and came up with three No. 1 US hits.

Madonna continued to produce irresistible songs while courting controversy. *Like A Prayer* offended the Catholic hierarchy; and Pepsi quickly dropped the commercial that featured it. But the album of the same name was evidence of a mature singer-songwriter, less reliant on dance numbers and stronger on melody. *Express Yourself* reaffirmed Madonna's status as confident sex icon, and *Till Death Us Do Part* was another top-drawer ballad.

R.E.M. embarked on a major tour in support of ***Green,*** released late in 1988. The album was more upbeat than some of their previous work, and confirmed the band's metamorphosis from college cult to rock stars in the US (though in Europe they continued to play clubs rather than arenas). The lyrics were less obscure; the hooks more obvious and the result a major success – though the tour took its toll.

"[Gloria] Estefan is Anne Murray with a dollop of salsa." **Los Angeles Times**, July 23, 1989

June 10 Sealed With A Kiss **Jason Donovan**
June 24 Back To Life (However Do You Want Me) **Soul II Soul**
July 22 You'll Never Stop Me Loving You **Sonia**
Aug 5 Swing The Mood **Jive Bunny & the Mastermixers**
Sept 9 Ride On Time **Black Box**
Oct 21 That's What I Like **Jive Bunny & the Mastermixers**
Nov 11 All Around The World **Lisa Stansfield**
Nov 25 You Got It (The Right Stuff) **New Kids On The Block**
Dec 16 Let's Party **Jive Bunny & the Mastermixers**
Dec 23 Do They Know It's Christmas? **Band Aid II**

Jan

1989

Bobby McFerrin wins at the Grammys... *Like A Prayer...*

Dreadlocked hair, muscular bodies, tight clothing, and sexy dance routines made Europop/dance duo Milli Vanilli the pop media darlings.

January

18 At the age of 38, **Stevie Wonder** becomes the youngest living inductee into the Rock and Roll Hall of Fame. At the fourth annual dinner, held at New York's Waldorf Astoria Hotel, the other performers inducted are **Dion**, **Otis Redding**, **the Rolling Stones**, and **the Temptations**. The Early Influences are the **Inkspots**, **Bessie Smith**, and the **Soul Stirrers**. The only Non-Performer inducted this year is **Phil Spector**. At the perfunctory post-induction jam, **Mick Jagger** duets with **Tina Turner**, who did the honors for Spector, on *Honky Tonk Women*, and with **Little Richard**, who inducted Redding, on *I Can't Turn You Loose*.

25 While wowing fans with his provocative dance antics, ex-**New Edition** singer **Bobby Brown** is arrested at Municipal Auditorium in Columbia, Georgia, and fined $652 under the Anti-Lewdness Ordinance for giving a "sexually explicit performance harmful to minors on city property, whether the performers are clothed or not." The 19-year-old R&B star hit US No. 1 two weeks ago with *My Prerogative*, and his second album, *Don't Be Cruel*, begins a six-week run in the US top slot this week.

30 Tonight's **Stone Roses** gig at the Hacienda is filmed for BBC2's "Snub TV" series. The Manchester-based quartet, led by singer **Ian Brown** and guitarist **John Squire**, with bassist **Gary "Mani" Mounfield** and drummer **Alan "Reni" Wren**, is emerging as one of the city's most innovative rock/dance groups and the latest alt-rock music media darlings. The band cut indie favorite *Elephant Stone* (produced by **New Order's Peter Hook**) for the Silvertone label in 1987, and their new offering *Made Of Stone* will be selected as Single of the Week by the NME in its March 11 edition ("Proof that everything's coming up Stone Roses"). Their debut album, *Stone Roses*, will receive similar praise when released on May 2, including "This is a masterpiece" in Sounds.

30 **George Michael** and **Randy Travis** win three awards each at the 16th American Music Awards, held at the Shrine Auditorium. Michael wins the Favorite Album Soul/Rhythm & Blues category for *Faith*, and Favorite Male Artist in both the Pop/Rock and Soul/Rhythm & Blues fields. Travis clears the table in the Country categories for the second year running, winning Favorite Single, Favorite Album, and Favorite Male Artist. **Def Leppard**, **DJ Jazzy Jeff & the Fresh Prince** (a Philadelphia-based mainstream rap duo with DJ **Jeff Townes** and 20-year-old actor/rapper **Will Smith**), and **Whitney Houston** each win a slew of awards. **Willie Nelson** is given the Special Award of Merit, and **Michael Jackson** receives the Award of Achievement, a tribute specifically created for the occasion. Winning their first major award, **Gloria Estefan & the Miami Sound Machine** are named Favorite Band, Duo or Group, Pop/Rock. A Miami-based Cuban combo formed in 1974 by Gloria's boyfriend (now her husband), songwriter/producer **Emilio Estefan**, the group has been the springboard for a glittering solo career for Gloria. Her solo-credited album, *Cuts Both Ways*, will begin a multiplatinum rise up the US chart in July. Their infectious mix of Spanish and English language ballads and pop-dance numbers makes the Estefans the most successful crossover Latin act since **Ritchie Valens**.

February

2 **George Michael** accepts undisclosed damages in excess of £100,000 ($160,000) from The Sun newspaper, following a libel action over articles printed on October 13 and 15, 1986. They claimed the singer had gatecrashed a party hosted by Andrew Lloyd Webber, and was drunk and abusive.

13 Known for seven years as the BPI Awards, the newly renamed BRITS couldn't have a more embarrassing beginning than the eighth ceremony. Following the bizarre decision to pair topless model and pop singer **Samantha Fox** with drummer **Mick Fleetwood** as co-presenters, whatever can go wrong does go wrong. When the hosts introduce the **Four Tops**,

The Stone Roses, along with the Happy Mondays, were pioneers of the brief Madchester scene.

The German leg of R.E.M.'s Green World Tour came to an abrupt end when drummer Bill Berry came down with Rocky Mountain Spotted fever.

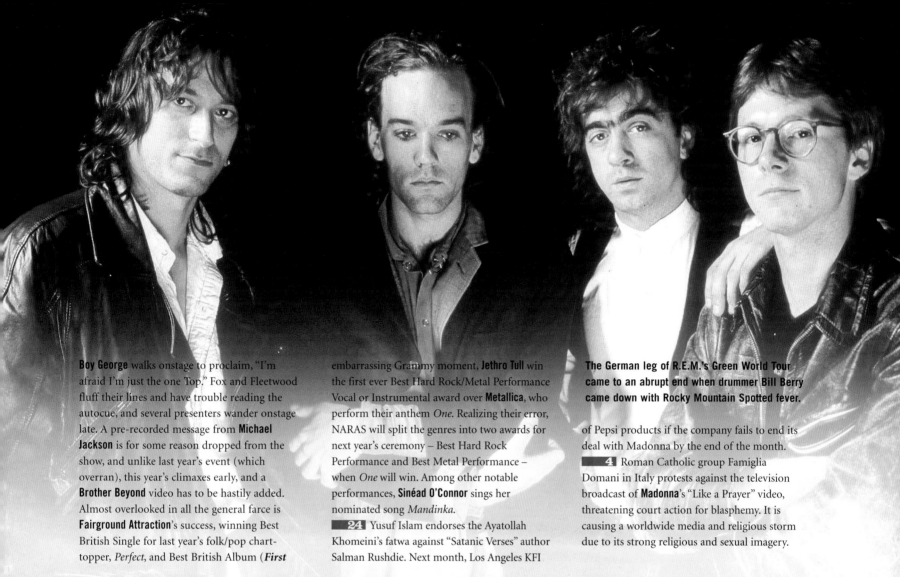

Boy George walks onstage to proclaim, "I'm afraid I'm just the one Top." Fox and Fleetwood fluff their lines and have trouble reading the autocue, and several presenters wander onstage late. A pre-recorded message from **Michael Jackson** is for some reason dropped from the show, and unlike last year's event (which overran), this year's climaxes early, and a **Brother Beyond** video has to be hastily added. Almost overlooked in all the general farce is **Fairground Attraction**'s success, winning Best British Single for last year's folk/pop chart-topper, *Perfect*, and Best British Album (***First Of A Million Kisses***): the first time an act has walked off with both awards. **Annie Lennox** accepts her third Best British Female Artist trophy, and **Phil Collins** wins his second Best British Male Solo Artist award, and picks up the Best Soundtrack/Cast Recording for "Buster." **Cliff Richard** is honored for his Outstanding Contribution to British Music.

22 In one of the more surprising Grammy Awards ceremonies, jazz-lite virtuoso vocalist **Bobby McFerrin** comes from nowhere to scoop four awards, including the coveted Record and Song of the Year for *Don't Worry, Be Happy*, which was featured in the Tom Cruise movie "Cocktail." The hit is also named Best Pop Vocal Performance, Male. **Tracy Chapman** is named Best New Artist, Best Pop Vocal Performance, Female for *Fast Car*, and Best Traditional Folk Recording for ***Tracy Chapman***. **Robert Palmer** – in a strong field including **Eric Clapton**, **Joe Cocker**, **Robbie Robertson**, and **Rod Stewart** – wins the Best Rock Vocal Performance, Male trophy for *Simply Irresistible*. **Tina Turner** nabs her fourth Best Rock Vocal Performance, Female statuette for ***Tina Live In Europe***. **George Michael** becomes only the second British solo artist (after **Phil Collins**) to win the Album of the Year. In a predictably embarrassing Grammy moment, **Jethro Tull** win the first ever Best Hard Rock/Metal Performance Vocal or Instrumental award over **Metallica**, who perform their anthem *One*. Realizing their error, NARAS will split the genres into two awards for next year's ceremony – Best Hard Rock Performance and Best Metal Performance – when *One* will win. Among other notable performances, **Sinéad O'Connor** sings her nominated song *Mandinka*.

24 Yusuf Islam endorses the Ayatollah Khomeini's fatwa against "Satanic Verses" author Salman Rushdie. Next month, Los Angeles KFI radio personality Tom Leykis will drive a steamroller over all of **Cat Stevens**'s records, beginning a more serious boycott of the singer's work by a large number of US radio stations.

"I play with my voice because a voice, when it's good, is when you are coming through." Fine Young Cannibals' Roland Gift, **Melody Maker**, April 4, 1989

March

1 Following the opening segment of their Green world tour in Japan, Australia, and New Zealand, **R.E.M.** begin the North American leg at the City Gardens in Louisville, Kentucky. They are supported initially by alt-rock critics' fave, **Robyn Hitchcock** (promoting ***Queen Elvis***), and latterly by Georgia-based folk rock duo **Indigo Girls** (with singer-songwriter/guitarists **Amy Ray** and **Emily Saliers**). The pair were signed last year to Epic Records, which has just released their second album, ***Indigo Girls***.

2 The gospel-tinged *Like A Prayer* airs during NBC-TV's "The Cosby Show," as Pepsi-Cola begins a $5 million sponsorship deal with **Madonna**. It is the first time a song by a major star has been used for a television commercial ahead of its retail release. Controversy swirls around the record's provocatively religious theme. Evangelist Donald Wildmon, of the American Family Association, threatens a one-year boycott of Pepsi products if the company fails to end its deal with Madonna by the end of the month.

4 Roman Catholic group Famiglia Domani in Italy protests against the television broadcast of **Madonna**'s "Like a Prayer" video, threatening court action for blasphemy. It is causing a worldwide media and religious storm due to its strong religious and sexual imagery.

April

4 Pressure from religious groups around the world leads Pepsi-Cola to ban all broadcasts of **Madonna**'s *Like A Prayer* commercial in the US, and cancel her one-year contract and sponsorship of her world tour. (Tomorrow, Pepsi-Cola in Canada will announce that it will continue broadcasting the video.)

8 *She Drives Me Crazy* by **Fine Young Cannibals** is the first song to be featured on the USA Network's broadcast of a revamped "American Bandstand," with new host David Hirsh. Taken from the trio's recently released second album ***The Raw And The Cooked*** – a cunning mix of mostly self-written and produced pop, dance, and soul – *She Drives Me Crazy* will hit US No. 1 next week, as will its follow-up, *Good Thing*, on July 8. It topped the UK chart two months ago and the US chart on June 3, the start of a seven-week reign.

8 Europop/dance duo **Milli Vanilli** make their major US television debut on "Soul Train," lip-synching to their recent breakthrough US No. 2 smash, *Girl You Know It's True*, and their new single, *Baby Don't Forget My Number*. Both confections are the work of German hitmeister, songwriter/producer **Frank Farian** (the man behind **Boney M** and **Far Corporation**, among others), who selected Frenchman **Fabrice Morvan** and German dancer **Rob Pilatus** to front the project visually. With their muscular build, long,

New Kids On The Block... Public Enemy embroiled in controversy ...

mildly dreadlocked hair, tight black leggings, and hot dance routines, the pair will become pop media darlings. **Milli Vanilli** records will dominate the pop charts worldwide for the rest of the year, scoring three US chart-toppers by November.

21 **Soul II Soul**'s debut album, ***Club Classics Volume One***, combining a hybrid soundscape of dance, reggae, hip-hop, and soul, is released in the UK by 10 Records/Virgin, and set to hit UK No. 1 on July 15. The innovative London band is a soul collective formed around frontman **Jazzie B**, which includes pioneering arranger/producer **Nellee Hooper** (also a member of another groundbreaking trip-hop/R&B ensemble, **Massive Attack**) and DJ **Daddae Harvey**. Featuring dozens of permanent and temporary Soul II Soul collective members, ***Club Classics Volume One*** will bring mainstream success for Jazzie B's trademark rhythms. Its breakthrough single, *Keep On Movin'*, currently at UK No. 5, features Soul II Soul fixture **Caron Wheeler** on lead vocals. The single mixes a spacious reggae feel with a hallmarking dance shuffle percussive rhythm. It will spawn dozens of imitations over the next two years, and itself provide the distinctive backbeat to Soul II Soul's next two hits. The album will finally reach UK No. 1 on July 15. Increasingly in demand as producers and arrangers, Jazzie B and Hooper will soon begin work with **Sinéad O'Connor**, covering an old **Prince** composition, *Nothing Compares 2 U.*

May

4 Not to be upstaged by fellow **Happy Mondays** member, **Mark "Bez" Berry**, fined £700 ($1,120) last week after pleading guilty to a charge of possessing cannabis, the group's lead singer **Shaun Ryder** is arrested in Jersey and charged with possession of cocaine. He will be released on £5,000 ($8,000) bail. Signed to Tony Wilson's Factory Records, the Mondays are emerging as leaders of the current Manchester-based "baggy" craze sweeping the UK's acid house dance rave scene. Their latest single, *Lazyitis (One Armed Boxer)*, which teams Ryder with 1960s yodeler **Karl Denver**, is finding dancefloor favor via a retooling by mixmaster **Paul Oakenfold.**

7 **Elvis Costello** plays the first of four concerts, titled A Month of Sundays, at the London Palladium, at the start of a month-long

NEW KIDS ON THE BLOCK

Apr 24 **Massachusetts Governor Michael Dukakis designates today "New Kids On The Block Day" (the Kids will also perform at a Dukakis-formed Alliance Against Drugs benefit later in the year). The members of the red-hot Boston boy band – singer-dancers Donnie Wahlberg, Danny Wood, Jordan Knight, Jonathan Knight, and Joey McIntyre – were recruited by ex-Johnson Brothers music veteran and entrepreneur Maurice Starr and his brother Michael Jonzun, following their earlier success with New Edition. Starr has molded and trained the group since 1984 (when they were initially known as Nynuk) and secured a record deal in 1986 with CBS. Tomorrow, at the Boston Music Awards, the Beantown boys will win the Outstanding R&B Single and Outstanding Music Video categories, while Starr will be named Producer of the Year. During a half-year chart residence, the pop/rap smash *You Got It (The Right Stuff)* hit US No. 3 on March 11. With New Kids teen-throb mania exploding across North America, their second album *Hangin' Tough*, helmed by Starr, hit US No. 4 last month, and will remain charted for over two years, accumulating eight RIAA platinum certifications, and launching the hottest US teen-idol group phenomenon of the decade. Currently on a lengthy US jaunt with bubblegum diva Tiffany, their ballad, *I'll Be Loving You (Forever)*, will hit US No. 1 on June 17, while their first album, *New Kids On The Block*, which initially sold just 5,000 copies when released last spring, is on its way to US No. 25 and three million domestic sales. *You Got It (The Right Stuff)* will also become a global fixture by the end of 1989, topping the UK survey in November prior to the release of their third US charted album of the year, *Merry, Merry Christmas.***

Three of the New Kids' videos sold more than 1 million copies each in the US

Elvis Costello

Soul II Soul

Elvis Costello played four concerts under the banner "A Month of Sundays" at the London Palladium in May... Soul II Soul's Jazzie B lived by his oft-quoted ethos: "A smiling face, a thumping bass for a happy race."

UK tour with **Nick Lowe**, which will include three consecutive nights at the Royal Albert Hall. During the summer, he will do the rounds of the European festivals, appearing at Glastonbury, Le Ballon, Monza Rock, Roskilde, Torhout, Werchter, and Montreux. His Warner Bros. debut album, *Spike*, was released in February and featured the hit single, *Veronica*, written with **Paul McCartney**. The pair have also collaborated on Macca's latest outing, ***Flowers In The Dirt***, an experience the ex-**Beatle** likens to working with **John Lennon**.

9 Emerging country star **Keith Whitley** is found dead from alcohol poisoning in his Nashville home. He is 34. The Kentuckian joined **Ralph Stanley**'s group, **Clinch Mountain Boys**, with **Ricky Skaggs** in 1970. Signing with RCA, he released his debut album, ***Hard Act***, in 1984, but teaming up with producer Garth Fundis brought him acclaim for last year's ***Don't Close Your Eyes*** album, which spawned three country No. 1s. He leaves a widow, country singer **Lorrie Morgan**.

9 **R.E.M.** cancel the first of four German dates on their Green tour after **Bill Berry** collapses in Munich from a bronchial infection (reported as Rocky Mountain Spotted Fever), having been bitten by a tick while tending his garden.

20 A collaboration by **Gerry Marsden** and **Paul McCartney**, with fellow Liverpudlian acts the **Christians** and **Holly Johnson**, enters the UK chart at No. 1 with their update of Marsden's *Ferry 'Cross The Mersey*. Produced by the ubiquitous **Stock Aitken Waterman** tandem, it is released to raise money for the Hillsborough Football disaster fund, after 96 Liverpool fans were crushed to death at the F.A. Cup semi-final in April.

24 **Madonna** takes part in Don't Bungle the Jungle, a benefit to raise awareness of rain forest destruction, at the Brooklyn Academy of Music. She duets with gal pal Sandra Bernhard on **Sonny & Cher**'s *I Got You Babe*. The **B-52's** and the **Grateful Dead**'s **Bob Weir** also appear.

31 The first International Rock Awards take place at the Lexington Avenue Armory in New York City. **Keith Richard** is inducted as a Living Legend, receiving his Elvis statuette from **Eric Clapton**, who is awarded the Best Guitarist prize. **David Bowie**'s new band, **Tin Machine**, make their live debut at the event, playing *Heaven's In Here*.

"Offensive remarks by Professor Griff are not in line with Public Enemy's program... We apologize to anyone who might have been offended... We're offended too."

Public Enemy's Chuck D, June 21, 1989

June

3 Our Common Future, a five-hour ecological-awareness world-satellite concert, is broadcast in over 100 countries. It features performers from around the globe, including **Sting**, **Stevie Wonder**, **Tom Jones**, **Elton John**, **Melissa Manchester**, **Manu Dibango**, **R.E.M.**, **Kenny Loggins**, **Maureen McGovern**, **John Denver**, the **Gipsy Kings**, and **Diana Ross**. Among many others taking part is relative unknown **Lenny Kravitz**, a 25-year-old rock/R&B singer-songwriter/multi-intrumentalist, recently signed to Virgin Records.

9 Three days after **Chrissie Hynde** was quoted as saying at a Greenpeace press conference in London that her contribution to the environment would be "firebombing McDonald's restaurants," a McDonald's in Milton Keynes is firebombed. The corporation threatens legal action against Hynde, and asks her to sign a written document agreeing not to repeat her statement. She signs.

12 The Graceland estate opens the **Elvis** automobile museum in Memphis. Ironically, WHBQ radio, the first station to have played the King's records, suspends all playing of his songs.

14 On his way to a rehearsal as part of the newly regrouped **Echo & the Bunnymen** (sans **Ian McCulloch**, who is starting a solo career), 27-year-old drummer **Pete de Freitas** is killed when his motorcycle collides with a car in Rugley, England.

16 To celebrate his 30th year in the music business, and more than 100 singles releases, **Cliff Richard** performs the first of two sellout concerts to an audience of 72,000, at London's Wembley Stadium. Cliff Richard – The Event features his handpicked support acts, including **Aswad** (with whom he duets on *Share A Dream With Me*), **Gerry & the Pacemakers**, the **Searchers**, the **Kalin Twins** (with whom he toured as support in 1958), and the **Shadows**. Richard also performs his forthcoming Stock Aitken Waterman-helmed single, *I Just Don't Have The Heart*.

21 The **Who** start their The Kids Are Alright Tour: 1964–1989 – their 25th anniversary reunion tour – at the Glen Falls Civic Center in New York state. **Pete Townshend** spares his rapidly failing hearing by playing an acoustic guitar, with additional musicians **Steve "Boltz" Bolton** (lead guitar), **John "Rabbit" Bundrick** (keyboards), and **Simon Phillips** (drums) on board. The 40-city soldout North American tour features material from **Townshend**'s ***The Iron Man*** (based on the children's story by Ted Hughes) and **Who** classics.

21 **Chuck D** announces the dismissal from **Public Enemy** of **Professor Griff**, after a May 22 interview with **Washington Post** reporter David Mills (reprinted on June 14 in **The Village Voice**), in which he allegedly made anti-Semitic statements, including: "Jews are responsible for the majority of wickedness that goes on across the globe." Tomorrow he will again prematurely announce the breakup of the band on New York

Although record sales had diminished, the Who were still a major act, as witnessed by the hugely successful The Kids Are Alright tour.

Club MTV Live... Izzy Stradlin causes a disturbance...

Paula Abdul

Living Colour

Paula Abdul and Living Colour shared the honors with Madonna at the MTV Video Music Awards.

radio station WLIB. In a subsequent MTV interview, he will guardedly retract the statement. The group's latest single, the typically provocative and career-defining *Fight The Power*, is featured as the repetitive central theme in Spike Lee's hit urban-uprising movie, "Do The Right Thing."

24 *Voodoo Ray* by **A Guy Called Gerald** re-enters the UK chart after a fleeting stay in April, set to reach No. 12. Subsequently regarded as a seminal track in the Manchester-led acid house scene, it was created by ex-**808 State** member **Gerald Simpson**. The group – named after the Roland 808 drum machine it uses – was formed last year by record shop owner **Martin Price**, **Graham Massey**, and Simpson. With DJs **Andrew Barker** and **Darren Partington** (the **Spinmasters**) replacing the now solo Simpson, **808 State** recently released the equally pioneering ***Quadrastate EP***, which includes the club smash *Pacific*. Trevor Horn will shortly sign the group to his ZTT label, recutting *Pacific*. Together, it and *Voodoo Ray* will become the most influential Mancunian acid house crossover hits of the year.

29 The **Pet Shop Boys** embark on their first world tour at the Coliseum in Hong Kong, also taking in Japan and the UK – 13 dates in all. They are admittedly nervous about the venture, but their performances, prominently featuring a number of visual art enhancements, are well received. At the post-show party, **Neil Tennant** says: "And they said it would never happen." They have recently finished writing and recording a new album for **Liza Minnelli**.

30 Taking the network's popular show on the road, "Club MTV: Live," hosted by VJ Downtown Julie Brown and the Club MTV Dancers, arrives at the Miami Arena. On the bill are deep-voiced rapper **Tone Lōc** (whose huge smash *Wild Thing* has just been confirmed double platinum in the US), **Was Not Was** (a Detroit-based R&B/funk ensemble headed by producer brothers **David** and **Don Was**), **Lisa Lisa** (a Harlem-based dance/pop trio fronted by **Lisa Valez**, who scored two US No. 1s in 1987), techno dance/pop quartet **Information Society**, and **Milli Vanilli**. The standout attraction is singer **Paula Abdul**. The 26-year-old award-winning choreographer and ex-Lakers cheerleader was snapped up last year by Virgin America. Her debut album, the pop/dance-fused ***Forever Your Girl***, is midway through a lengthy climb to US No. 1, yielding an astonishing four chart-topping singles.

July

11 A press conference is held beside Track 42 in New York's Grand Central Station to announce the **Rolling Stones**' forthcoming tour. The group steps off a Metro North train boarded at 125th Street to announce full details of the tour and album release. **Mick Jagger** previews the album, ***Steel Wheels***, on a boombox in front of 500 assembled journalists.

11 A Bo Jackson Nike television commercial, featuring **Bo Diddley** saying, "Bo, you don't know Diddley," airs for the first time in the US during

While on the Rolling Stones' "Steel Wheels" tour, Mick Jagger joined fans in the parking lot of the Foxboro Stadium in Massachusetts for a few verses of *You Can't Always Get What You Want.*

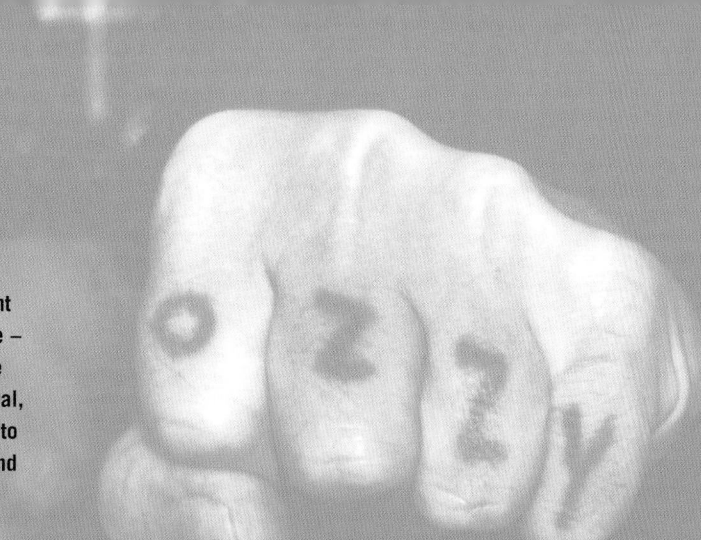

One month before an incident with his wife, Ozzy Osbourne – ironically – performed at the Moscow Music Peace Festival, the proceeds of which went to programs that fought drug and alcohol abuse.

Major League Baseball's All-Star game. (It will cause Diddley to remark: "You work your buns off all these years... Then I make a commercial with Bo Jackson and all I say is 'Bo, you don't know Diddley.' All of a sudden I'm back up at the top again. I ain't figured it out yet.")

22 **De La Soul**'s *Say No Go* peaks at UK No. 18, while *Me Myself And I* makes US No. 34. Both are featured on their critically revered, mellow psychedelic/hip-hop-fused debut album ***3 Feet High And Rising***, which samples diverse snippets ranging from TV show soundtracks to the music of **Steely Dan** and **Curiosity Killed The Cat**. The pioneering set is, however, getting the trio – **Kelvin Mercer** (aka **Posdnuos**), **Vincent Mason** (**Mase**), and **David Jolicoeur** (**Trugoy**) – into legal trouble. Ex-**Turtles** members and songwriters, **Mark Volman** and **Howard Kaylan**, are suing them for $1.7 million, for the unauthorized sampling of part of their *You Showed Me*. As illegal sampling becomes a hot-button issue in the music industry, the case will be settled out of court.

24 In a Newsweek interview, **Mick Jagger** responds to the allegation that the **Stones** only tour for money, saying: "No, that's the **Who**."

27 **Paul McCartney** announces an upcoming world tour at a press conference at London's Playhouse Theatre, and treats 400 fan club members to a 90-minute set, including several **Beatles**' tracks, previewing the live show.

30 **Eric Clapton** finishes a month-long tour visiting Holland, Switzerland, Israel, Swaziland, Zimbabwe, and Botswana with a free concert in front of 102,000 fans, for the King's Trust (established in 1988 by King Mswati III), at the Estadio da Machava in Maputo, Mozambique.

August

5 *Batdance* hits US No. 1, becoming **Prince**'s third US chart-topper as a performer. It is the first cut from the Prince-composed and produced soundtrack for the summer's hottest movie, "Batman," the focus of a massive multi-entertainment project by Warner Bros.

6 **U2**'s **Adam Clayton** is arrested in the parking lot of the Blue Light Inn in Dublin, charged with possession of marijuana and intent to supply the drug to another person.

17 **Pete Townshend** injures his right hand during a **Who** concert at the Tacoma Dome, while executing a trademark windmill guitar riff during *Won't Get Fooled Again*.

21 **Don Henley** makes a statement to the press regarding "the phony version of *Life In The Fast Lane*" that **Joe Walsh** is performing while touring with **Ringo Starr**. Hensley says, "Walsh wrote the little guitar riff in the intro and that's all." Henley's third solo album, ***The End Of The Innocence***, featuring a hit title cut co-written and performed with **Bruce Hornsby**, was released last month, and is set to become his most successful solo disc: it will eventually sell more than five million domestic copies.

30 **Guns N' Roses' Izzy Stradlin** is arrested at Phoenix Airport for making a public disturbance after urinating on the floor, verbally abusing a flight attendant, and smoking in the non-smoking section, on a US Air flight from Los Angeles to Indianapolis. Stradlin was apparently angry at having to wait to use the restroom. A publicist will say it was just Izzy's "way of expressing himself." Stradlin will plead guilty in October. The court will sentence him to six months probation, during which he must receive counseling, and order him to pay a $2,000 fine and $1,000 cleaning costs.

31 The **Rolling Stones**' Steel Wheels North American Tour 1989 kicks off at Veterans Stadium in Philadelphia, before a sellout crowd of 55,000. The live lineup includes **Bobby Keyes** (sax), **Chuck Leavell** and **Matt Clifford** (keyboards), **Cindy Mizelle**, **Bernard Fowler**, and **Lisa Fischer** (backing vocals). Hotly touted US black rock band **Living Colour** – fronted by guitarist **Vernon Reid** and singer **Corey Glover** – is the supporting act.

September

1 **U2**'s **Adam Clayton**'s marijuana conviction is waived in exchange for paying £25,000 ($40,000) to the Dublin Women's Aid & Refuge Centre. (Devoted fan Paul Matthews, a member of U2 tribute band the **Joshua Trio**, will set free 25,000 white butterflies as a parallel gesture.) Clayton will reflect on the episode: "It was my own fault. And I'm sure I was out of my head – emotionally apart from anything else. But it is serious because it is illegal."

2 **Ozzy Osbourne** – who recently scored his biggest hit single, *Close My Eyes Forever*, a duet with ex-**Runaway Lita Ford** – is arrested and charged with threatening to kill his wife and manager Sharon, following a drinking binge during which he consumed four bottles of vodka. He is released on bail on condition that he immediately goes into detox for three months, and stays away from her. The case will be dropped when the couple decide to reconcile.

6 **Madonna**, **Paula Abdul**, and **Living Colour** share 11 of the awards up for grabs at the sixth MTV Video Music Awards, at the Universal Amphitheatre in Universal City. Madonna's feminist-themed "Express Yourself" wins Best Art Direction in a Video, Best Cinematography, and Best Direction in a Video. "Like A Prayer" is the Viewers' Choice winner. Abdul also wins four awards, all for "Straight Up" – Best Dance Video, Best Editing, Best Female Video, and Best Choreography in a Video (no surprise there). Living Colour's "Cult Of Personality" wins three trophies: Best Group Video, Best Stage Performance in a Video, and Best New Artist in a Video. *Buffalo Stance* hitmaker, 24-year-old Swedish-born singer-songwriter **Neneh Cherry**, who is a fellow nominee in the last category, fares less well, reportedly collapsing in her dressing room during the ceremony. (Lyme disease is suspected but never conclusively diagnosed. She will pull out of a major US tour

A TV commercial for De La Soul's *3 Ft High And Rising* was banned in the UK in December for its use of the CND peace logo.

Sept 1989

McCartney's first world tour... A&M is sold to PolyGram... Madchester...

as the supporting act to **Fine Young Cannibals**.) **Neil Young**'s "This Note's For You" – banned last year by MTV – triumphantly wins the Best Video award, and Puerto Rican pop star **Chayanne** receives the first International Video award, winning for "Este Ritmo Se Baila Asi."

13 **Bruce Springsteen** records *Viva Las Vegas* at the One on One Studio in North Hollywood, for ***The Last Temptation Of Elvis***, a benefit album comprising cover versions of **Elvis Presley** hits. Organized by **Roy Carr** of the **New Musical Express** to raise funds for the Nordoff-Robbins Music Therapy charity, other contributions to the album will include: **Paul McCartney** (*It's Now Or Never*), **Robert Plant** (*Let's Have A Party*), the **Jesus & Mary Chain** (*Guitar Man*), and the **Pogues** (*Got A Lot O' Livin' To Do*.)

25 The trial commences in **Bette Midler**'s $10 million lawsuit against the Ford Motor Co. and the Young & Rubicam advertising agency, for using a soundalike (earlier Midler backing singer **Ula Hedwig**) to impersonate her singing *Do You Want To Dance* in a 1985 Mercury Sable commercial. Midler, who declined to do the ad herself, will win the case, and be awarded $400,000. Meanwhile, **Billy Joel** files a $90 million lawsuit against former manager Frank Weber in New York, charging him with fraud and breach of fiduciary duty. Joel will be awarded $2 million.

24 **Bob Dylan** participates in the "L'Chaim – To Life!" telethon on Chabad TV with **Peter Himmelman** (husband of Dylan's daughter Maria) and actor Harry Dean Stanton on guitars. Named **Chopped Liver**, they perform three songs, including *Hava Nagila*, with Dylan on flute and recorder.

26 **Paul McCartney** begins his first world tour for 13 years at the Drammenshallen in Drammen, Norway. In a 32-song set, he mixes the old with the new, with more than half of the songs from his **Beatles** days in homage to that era. The 103-date tour will come to an end next July at Soldier Field in Chicago.

29 **Bruce Springsteen**, traveling from Los Angeles on his motorcycle, drops in at Matt's Saloon in Prescott, Arizona, and jams with the house combo Mile High Band, singing *Sweet Little Sixteen*, *Don't Be Cruel*, *Route 66*, and *I'm On Fire*. In a few weeks, he will send Matt's barmaid Brenda Pechanec $100,000 to pay her hospital bills.

29 While the prospect of a fully fledged **Eagles** reunion remains unfulfilled, despite reported studio tryouts, **Glenn Frey** finally joins **Don Henley** on stage for the first time since the group broke up, at a concert in Los Angeles. The pair will perform with **Timothy B. Schmit** next year, during Henley's April 24–25 Walden Woods benefit festival in Worcester, Massachusetts.

October

8 Two days after the **Who** begin a 25th anniversary UK tour, **Pete Townshend** replies to **Ron Wood**'s comment that the Who is touring for the money, saying, "Mick [Jagger] needs a lot more than I do. His last album was a flop."

11 **Michael Jackson** attends a ceremony at his former Gardner Street Elementary School, inaugurating the Michael Jackson Auditorium. His typically succinct speech goes: "This is the happiest day of my life. I love you all." Jackson has pledged to pay the annual salary of the school's music teacher.

19 Following yesterday's outburst at a Los Angeles' Memorial Coliseum gig, opening for the **Rolling Stones**, **Guns N' Roses' Axl Rose** delivers a five-minute anti-drug oration and apologizes for saying he would quit. He had said: "I hate to do

NIRVANA

Oct 23 **With Melody Maker having recently run a series of articles on the burgeoning Seattle grunge scene, Nirvana make their UK debut at the Riverside in Newcastle, England – the first date of a week-long Sub Pop label tour, part of a larger six-week European visit. Their first album, *Bleach*, was issued by the label in June. Recorded on eight-track in three days for $606.17, it was produced by Jack Endino, and features temporary second guitarist, Mindfunk's Jason Everman. The album is proving popular on college radio, not least on KCMU, the 401 watt University of Washington radio station, which was also the first to air cuts by Soundgarden and Mudhoney.**

After 116 days in the High Court, ten in the Appeal Court, and one at the European Commission – at an estimated total cost of £7 million ($11.2 million) – all outstanding lawsuits between Paul McCartney, George Harrison, Ringo Starr, Yoko Ono, Apple, and EMI/Capitol were resolved in November.

Roxette

Aerosmith

Roxette's Per Gessle wrote a song for Abba's Frida Lyngstad's 1982 album *Something's Going On...* As part of a promotion for Aerosmith's saucy *Love In An Elevator* single, a couple got married in an elevator during a show.

this on stage. But I tried every other f***ing way. And unless certain people in this band get their shit together, these will be the last Guns N' Roses shows you'll f***ing ever see. Cause I'm tired of too many people in this organization dancing with Mr. Goddamn Brownstone." By contrast, ex-addict but true gentleman **Eric Clapton** joins the Rolling Stones on stage, playing lead guitar on *Little Red Rooster*.

21 After 27 years of hits, **Herb Alpert** and Jerry Moss sell A&M Records to Polygram for a reported $500 million – having initially invested $200. They will retain their Almo/Irving/Rondor music publishing companies. The sale follows Polygram's acquisition of Chris Blackwell's Island Records in August for £300 ($480) million. In an ever-shrinking music and media universe, with previously independently owned labels being swallowed whole, Time-Life is currently negotiating to buy Warner Communications (which includes the entire Warner music group). Next January, the $14 (£8.75) billion deal will create the world's largest entertainment concern.

25 Guitar virtuosos **Jeff Beck** and **Stevie Ray Vaughan** embark on a US arena tour dubbed The Fire and the Fury, which begins at the Northrop Memorial Auditorium in Minneapolis, Minnesota. The only time they have previously met was at a Columbia Records convention in Hawaii in 1984.

November

4 Already the most popular Swedish export since **Abba**, **Roxette** – singer/songwriters **Per Gessle** and **Marie Fredriksson** – score a second US No. 1 of the year with the power ballad, *Listen To Your Heart*. It is notable as the first chart-topper available in cassette form only.

5 **Sting** opens in a revival of Bertolt Brecht and Kurt Weill's "Threepenny Opera" at the Lunt-Fontanne Theater in New York, following the premiere at Washington's National Theater. **The New York Times**' Frank Rich says of Sting's performance as Macheath: "[He] is a stiff on-stage. He seems to hope that a large cane and a smug, insistent pout will somehow convey the menace of a character who is a murderer, rapist, thief and arsonist."

7 MTV Europe broadcasts live in East Berlin for the first time – two days before the Berlin Wall falls. On the 11th, **Joe Cocker** and 28-year-old blues rocker **Melissa Etheridge** will perform free acoustic shows at the Wall.

23 The **Happy Mondays** and the **Stone Roses**, regarded as pioneers of the new movement bursting from Manchester's rock dance scene – dubbed "Madchester" – make their "Top Of The Pops" debuts. The Stone Roses' appearance goes off without a hitch, unlike their debut on BBC2's "The Late Show" two days ago, when the power in the studio failed 45 seconds into *Made Of Stone*. After several awkward moments, presenter Tracey MacLeod apologized while the producer hastily inserted their "One Love" video. **Ian Brown** blamed the studio technicians, commenting, "You're wasting our time, lads," before starting up a chant of "Amateurs," but a "Late Show" staffer reported: "What happened was that power circuits blew because they were playing too loud. My own notes say 'too many decibels here.'"

December

16 **Jive Bunny & the Mastermixers** score their third UK No. 1 of the year with *Let's Party*, following the success of *Swing The Mood* and *That's What I Like*. They become only the third act in UK chart history (succeeding **Gerry & the Pacemakers** and **Frankie Goes to Hollywood**) to nab three No. 1s with their first three releases. Each single is acollection of segments from pop oldies, set to a dancefloor beat: a popular megamix idea created by producers **Ian Morgan** and **John Pickles**.

19 Four days after finishing the North American leg of his world tour, with four sellout shows at New York's Madison Square Garden before 62,351 customers, **Paul McCartney** is honored by the Performing Rights Society for his "unique achievement in popular music" at a luncheon at Claridge's Hotel, London.

21 As part of a promotion for **Aerosmith**'s saucy *Love In An Elevator* single, a couple get married in a elevator at the Scope Arena in Norfolk, Virginia, during the band's show.

23 A **Stock Aitken Waterman**-conceived re-recording of *Do They Know It's Christmas?*, credited to Band Aid II, enters the UK chart at No. 1. It features **Kylie Minogue, Jason Donovan** (the SAW prodigy who has scored three UK No. 1s this year), **Chris Rea, Matt Goss** (of **Bros**), **Wet Wet Wet**'s **Marti Pellow, Cliff Richard, Sonia** (another SAW find), and blue-eyed soul newcomer **Lisa Stansfield** (who topped the UK chart with *All Around The World* last month).

27 The **Grateful Dead** play their final dates of 1989 – four shows at the Oakland-Alameda County Coliseum – with support act **Bonnie Raitt**. **Forbes**' annual year-end list of the 40 highest-paid entertainers in the world will rank the Grateful Dead at No. 29, with an estimated annual income of $12.5 million.

ROOTS

During this year: Mancunian Noel Gallagher sets his heart on a career in music after attending a gig by Stone Roses... Following the dissolution of Suave & Elegant, Brett Anderson and Mat Osman place an ad in the NME for a "non-muso" guitarist... former Bag O' Bones members Stephen Malkmus and Scott Kannberg form a part-time garage band in their hometown of Stockton, California... brothers Attrell and Jarrett Cordes, going by the names Prince Be and DJ Minutemix, record their first song *Check The Logic* at a Long Island studio... recently relocated to Los Angeles, San Franciscan Courtney Love places an ad in the Recycler: "I want to start a band. My influences are Big Black, Sonic Youth, and Fleetwood Mac"... Billie Joe Armstrong and Mike Dirnt, pals who hung out at the Gilman Street Project club in Oakland, California, change the name of their band from Sweet Children to Green Day... the Gin Blossoms, a Byrds-influenced country-rock/roots quintet, forms in Tempe, Arizona, within 12 months releasing their self-financed debut album, *Dusted*... and Beck Hansen takes a cross-country bus to New York, where he immerses himself in the lock punk-folk scene, playing at venues on the Lower East Side...

"The 1990s proved to be one of the more versatile times in music history. We saw the birth of grunge, the resurgence of pop, and in particular the movement of hip-hop into the mainstream." Sean "P. Diddy" Combs, 2003

"I would describe 1990s music as 'eclectic.' It was not unusual to hear people blasting their mixed CDs of Vanilla Ice, Nirvana, Jay Z, 2Pac, Ricky Martin, and Britney Spears. You gotta love the 1990s!!" Lance Bass, 2003

"During the 1990s, people were listening to a lot of different music. There was Nirvana in the early '90s, who started the whole grunge revolution, then hip-hop and R&B was at the top of the charts, and then later in the decade pop music really took off." Britney Spears, 2003

THE NINETIES

1990

The Humpty Dance

1990

No.1 US SINGLES

Jan 6 Another Day In Paradise **Phil Collins**
Jan 20 How Am I Supposed To Live Without You **Michael Bolton**
Feb 10 Opposites Attract **Paula Abdul**
Mar 3 Escapade **Janet Jackson**
Mar 24 Black Velvet **Alannah Myles**
Apr 7 Love Will Lead You Back **Taylor Dayne**
Apr 14 I'll Be Your Everything **Tommy Page**
Apr 21 Nothing Compares 2 U **Sinéad O'Connor**
May 19 Vogue **Madonna**
June 9 Hold On **Wilson Phillips**
June 16 It Must Have Been Love **Roxette**
June 30 Step By Step **New Kids On The Block**
July 21 She Ain't Worth It **Glenn Medeiros**
Aug 4 Vision Of Love **Mariah Carey**
Sept 1 If Wishes Came True **Sweet Sensation**
Sept 8 Blaze Of Glory **Jon Bon Jovi**
Sept 15 Release Me **Wilson Phillips**
Sept 29 (Can't Live Without Your) Love And Affection **Nelson**
Oct 6 Close To You **Maxi Priest**
Oct 13 Praying For Time **George Michael**
Oct 20 I Don't Have The Heart **James Ingram**
Oct 27 Black Cat **Janet Jackson**
Nov 3 Ice Ice Baby **Vanilla Ice**
Nov 10 Love Takes Time **Mariah Carey**
Dec 1 I'm Your Baby Tonight **Whitney Houston**
Dec 8 Because I Love You (The Postman Song) **Stevie B**

No.1 UK SINGLES

Jan 6 Do They Know It's Christmas? **Band Aid II**
Jan 13 Hangin' Tough **New Kids On The Block**
Jan 27 Tears On My Pillow **Kylie Minogue**
Feb 3 Nothing Compares 2 U **Sinéad O'Connor**
Mar 3 Dub Be Good To Me **Beats International featuring Linda Layton**
Mar 31 The Power **Snap!**
Apr 14 Vogue **Madonna**
May 12 Killer **Adamski**

Billy Joel

Mariah Carey

In June 1990 Billy Joel became the first rock act to perform at the Yankee Stadium in New York, playing before two sellout crowds of over 100,000... Columbia Records launched its new signing Mariah Carey, with an invitation-only soirée, at which she sang three song accompanied by Richard Tee on the piano.

Following last year's acquisition by Polygram of A&M for $500 million, the new decade began with further corporate takeovers. MCA snapped up Geffen, EMI swallowed Chrysalis and the world's largest all-media company was created when Time Life bought Warner Bros. With the number of major/large independent companies shrinking annually – much to the concern of many artists – it was small wonder that an adventurous new label in Seattle would be responsible for kick-starting the first significant new music genre since punk – and use do-it-yourself punk ethics as its creed. Sub Pop signed and promoted a number of little known but locally popular post-punk/hard-rocking apprentice groups like **Mudhoney**, **Soundgarden**, **Mother Love Bone**, and **Nirvana**. They collectively created the vibrant "grunge" sound – a movement that would reignite rock music for restless Gen-Xers during the first half of the decade.

Rap continued to go mainstream with baggy pants pioneer **M.C. Hammer**'s *U Can't Touch This* and **Vanilla Ice**'s *Ice Ice Baby* racking up monstrous sales for their parent albums. Both borrowed heavily from well-known prior hits, respectively **Rick James**' *Super Freak (Part 1)* and **Queen/Bowie**'s *Under Pressure.* Both became global multi-platinum staples and both were signature hits for each artist. The artists' mutual demise – Hammer will dwindle a vast fortune while Vanilla Ice will never recover from the novelty of scoring the first ever solo "white" rap hit – will prove to be as rapid as their ascent.

While grunge was percolating in the US, the British music scene became even more focused on dance music. In the British music media's tireless pursuit of new sub-genres, the dance scene was fracturing into several acid-house off-shoots, including acid jazz, ambient house (pioneered by **808 State**) and jungle – a meld of house, techno, and hip-hop introduced by the underground combo, **Meat Beat Manifesto**. Jungle would in turn yield its popular cousin, the stripped-down drum 'n' bass sound.

The biggest scandal of the year was created by the ineptitude of the Grammy organization, NARAS – and the group to whom they gave the Best New Artist Award, **Milli Vanilli**. Failing to realize that the duo – unlike their fellow nominees **Neneh Cherry**, **Indigo Girls**, **Soul II Soul**, and **Tone Lōc** – didn't actually sing on their records, NARAS set a new standard in a long list of Grammy fumbles. The hapless Milli boys were asked to hand back their trophy in November – for the first time in the Awards' history.

June 9 World In Motion **Englandneworder**
June 23 Sacrifice/Healing Hands **Elton John**
July 28 Turtle Power **Partners in Kryme**
Aug 25 Itsy Bitsy Teeny Weeny Yellow Polka Dot Bikini **Bombalurina**
Sept 15 The Joker **Steve Miller Band**
Sept 29 Show Me Heaven **Maria McKee**
Oct 27 A Little Time **Beautiful South**
Nov 3 Unchained Melody **Righteous Brothers**
Dec 1 Ice Ice Baby **Vanilla Ice**
Dec 29 Saviour's Day **Cliff Richard**

"I present to America a very exciting package as an entertainer. My show crosses all barriers and boundaries."

M.C. Hammer, **People Weekly**, August 6,1990

Jan 1990

MTV Unplugged premieres... Rainforest Foundation benefit... Grammy win by Bonnie Raitt...

Sting's first Rainforest Foundation benefit took place at a Beverly Hills mansion.

January

8 Previewing her second album, **Sinéad O'Connor**'s *Nothing Compares 2 U* is released in the UK by Ensign Records. It is a stunning cover version of a song by **Prince**, which she heard three years ago on a 1985 self-titled album by Paisley Park act the **Family**. With an arrangement by **Soul II Soul**'s **Jazzie B** and **Nellee Hooper**, and produced by O'Connor with Hooper, the melancholic ballad of lost love showcases the Irish singer's emotive vocal style. It will become one of the fastest-selling singles in world chart history, spurred by a strikingly uncomplicated video directed by John Maybury. It will top the charts in 17 countries, including Ireland, the UK (for five weeks), and the US (for four), and underpin the multiplatinum success of the upcoming ***I Do Not Want What I Haven't Got***. O'Connor will use her resulting global celebrity as a platform from which to expound her many outspoken views.

17 The **Platters**, **Hank Ballard**, **Bobby Darin**, the **Four Seasons**, the **Four Tops**, the **Who**, the **Kinks**, and **Simon & Garfunkel** are inducted into the Rock and Roll Hall of Fame at the Waldorf Astoria Hotel in New York City. During his induction speech, Ballard breaks down as he pays tribute to his wife and manager, Theresa McNeil, who was killed by a hit-and-run driver in New York three months ago. His status as an influential R&B innovator – he created *The Twist* – is finally secured. It will be reiterated on February 26, 1992, when the Rhythm & Blues Foundation in New York (a nonprofitmaking organization) will make a financial award to Ballard, in honor of his contribution to the wider recognition of the genre. The original **Kinks** line-up is together for the first time in years, including bassist **Pete Quaife**, who is now an airbrush artist living in Ontario, Canada. In the Early Influences category, **Rickie Lee Jones** inducts **Louis Armstrong**; **George Benson**, and **Living Colour**'s **Vernon Reid** do the same for electric guitarist pioneer, the late **Charlie Christian**; **Ma Rainey** is inducted by **Bonnie Raitt**. The Non-Performers category is swelled by the induction of songwriters **Gerry Goffin** and **Carole King** (inducted by **Ben E. King**), and Motown's hit writers **Brian Holland**, **Lamont Dozier**, and **Eddie Holland** (inducted by **Diana Ross**). The high point of the traditional after-dinner jam is **Simon & Garfunkel** performing together again, singing *Bridge Over Troubled Water* and *The Boxer*.

21 MTV premieres "MTV Unplugged," a series of mostly acoustic performances. Tonight's show, taped last October at the National Video Center in New York City, features **Squeeze**, the **Cars' Elliot Easton**, and **Syd Straw**. Subsequent performers in this first season will include the **Smithereens**, **Graham Parker**, **10,000 Maniacs**, **Michael Penn**, the **Alarm**, **Joe Walsh**, **Dr. John**, **Stevie Ray Vaughan**, **Michelle Shocked**, **Indigo Girls**, **Sinéad O'Connor**, **Don Henley**, **Crowded House**, **Daryl Hall & John Oates**, **Elton John**, **Aerosmith**, **Crosby, Stills & Nash**, the **Black Crowes**, the **Allman Brothers Band**, and **Poison**.

26 CBS Records issues cassettes of **Billy Joel**'s recent US chart-topper *We Didn't Start The Fire*, featuring a ten-minute talk by the singer. They are distributed to 40,000 students with **Junior Scholastic** and **Update** magazines, after the fifth grade class at the Banta Elementary School in Menasha, Wisconsin, used the song's lyrics to select topics for history reports.

30 In Paris during a four-day stint at the Rex Theater, **Bob Dylan** is awarded France's highest cultural honor, Commandeur dans l'Ordre des Arts et des Lettres, by Minister of Culture Jack Lang, in a ceremony held at the Palais Royal.

"The music we make may not be for everybody... We think of ourselves as comics." 2 Live Crew's Luke Skyywalker, **Los Angeles Times**, March 25, 1990

30 The **Stone Roses**, incensed over the video accompanying the reissue of *Sally Cinnamon*, visit the offices of their former record company in Goldthorn Hill, Wolverhampton, England. They pour paint over managing director Paul Birch and his girlfriend, before starting on the walls. On their way out, **Ian Brown** puts a brick through the windshield of Birch's Mercedes. They will be arrested tomorrow, and granted conditional bail by Wolverhampton magistrates. Brown will explain that the video is "insulting. Blokes selling fruit, a few pigeons, some black woman holding a baby, a picture of me on the front of **The Face**, a few people in flares... So we went and painted him."

Sinéad O'Connor's video of *Nothing Compares 2 U*, in which the singer cried on camera, was MTV's most requested video of 1990.

February

6 For the first time in UK chart history, the top three singles feature neither British nor American acts: Ireland's **Sinéad O'Connor** is at No. 1, Australia's **Kylie Minogue** is at No. 2, and Belgium's **Technotronic** is at No. 3.

8 *Runaway* legend **Del Shannon** dies from a self-inflicted gunshot wound from a .22 caliber rifle, at his home in Santa Clarita Valley, California. He is 55. He had been prescribed the controversial antidepressant Prozac, and his widow will begin litigation against the drug's makers next year. Shannon performed at the annual **Buddy Holly** memorial concert in Fargo, North Dakota, last weekend.

12 Evening in Brazil, hosted by producer Ted Field and his wife Susie at their Beverly Hills mansion, raises more than $1 million for the Environmental Media Association and **Sting**'s Rainforest Foundation. The all-star cast includes Sting, **Bruce Springsteen**, **Don Henley**, **Paul Simon**, **Jackson Browne**, **Bruce Hornsby**, **Branford Marsalis**, and **Herbie Hancock**. Henley tells the audience: "Sting and I were in the coatroom and saw about a quarter of a million dollars' worth of dead animals down there. Sting said we should burn them. The security guard must have heard us because we went back and they had moved them. So your coats are safe." After the show, Springsteen repairs to the China Club, where he joins Hornsby, Henley, Sting, and Marsalis for a 45-minute impromptu set.

17 **Aerosmith**, music guests on "Saturday Night Live," takes part in a "Wayne's World" skit with "not worthy" Mike Myers and Dana Carvey. Their version of the home-cable spoof's title song becomes an in-demand bootleg item.

21 The 32nd Grammys are perhaps the most interesting in the history of the awards – both good and bad. The good is the surprise multi-award win by **Bonnie Raitt**, whose ***Nick Of Time***, impeccably produced by Don Was, wins Album of the Year and Best Rock Vocal Performance, Female, while its title track gives Raitt the Best Pop Vocal Performance, Female award. She also wins Best Traditional Blues Recording for *I'm In The Mood*, from **John Lee Hooker**'s ***The Healer***. Raitt, the daughter of Broadway musical star John Raitt (the original Billy Bigelow in "Carousel"), has, in a two-decade career, scored only two gold albums before ***Nick Of Time***. The ultimate musician's musician, Raitt finally gets her reward. The bad news is the Best New Artist honor bestowed on **Milli Vanilli** – the NARAS voters are apparently the only people still unaware that the dreadlocked duo's talents do not include singing. (Milli Vanilli producer Frank Farian will finally come clean in November.) At least the voters correct last year's aberration, by giving **Metallica** – who lost to **Jethro Tull** in 1989 – the award for Best Metal Performance, Vocal or Instrumental.

26 **Frank Zappa** hosts the first of three "Frank Zappa's Wild Wild East" talk shows in the cable-TV Financial News Network's "Focus" series. He interviews Czech president, Vaclav Havel – who recently appointed him Trade & Cultural Emissary – for the program, and subsequently reports: "He told me he liked my records, especially ***Bongo Fury***."

March

1 With her latest single, *Escapade*, at US No. 1, **Janet Jackson** begins her first world tour at the Miami Arena, with **Chuckii Booker** as musical director for her opening act. The appropriately named Rhythm Nation World Tour will last nine months, and she will make her overseas debut in Japan in May. ***Janet Jackson's Rhythm Nation 1814*** (1814 was the year that the US national anthem was composed) spent four weeks at US No. 1 last fall. It was produced by Jimmy Jam and Terry Lewis, who also wrote or co-wrote all the songs, except the Jackson-penned *Black Cat* (which features **Living Colour**'s **Vernon Reid** on guitar), which also hits US No. 1. *Rhythm Nation* hit US No. 2 in January, with a video clip featuring Jackson's now trademark dance army, mostly clad in black, performing synchronized set pieces.

10 **Billboard** magazine reports that the **New Kids On The Block** 1-900 telephone number currently receives 125,000 calls a day.

17 The artists in the Arista Records stable take part in the company's That's What Friends Are For 15th anniversary concert at New York's Radio City Music Hall, raising more than $2 million for Gay Men's Health Crisis and other AIDS organizations. Participating are **Whitney Houston**, **Dionne Warwick**, **Daryl Hall & John Oates**, **Barry Manilow**, **Lisa Stansfield**, **Jermaine Jackson**, **Melissa Manchester**, **Anderson Bruford Wakeman & Howe**, R&B singer **Jeffrey Osborne**, female dance/pop trio **Exposé**, Canadian-based blues-rock trio the **Jeff Healey Band**, ex-"Dreamgirls" soul belter **Jennifer Holliday**, **Burt Bacharach**, multiplatinum saxophonist **Kenny G**, **Milli Vanilli**, **Eric Carmen**, **Air Supply**, **Patti Smith** (and husband Fred), **Bob Weir**, and **Rob Wasserman**, and rising country star, singer/guitarist **Alan Jackson**.

Janet Jackson picked up three Soul Train music awards in March 1990, doubling her total from the three previous years.

19 MCA Records announces it has acquired Geffen Records, giving founder David Geffen a reported 10 million shares of MCA stock, valued at $550 million; it will rise to $710 million in eight months, when MCA is sold to Matsushita. It is wonderboy Geffen's second successful label deal, following the sale of Asylum Records to Warner Bros. In a shrinking corporate market, Thorn EMI is currently negotiating to feast on its remaining 50 percent share of Chrysalis Records.

Earth Day concerts... The Beatles reach for the stars... Mariah Carey's TV debut...

Elton John created the Elton John AIDS Foundation in 1991 after befriending Ryan White shortly before the teenager's death.

20 CBS loses its $20 million lawsuit against **Boston**'s **Tom Scholz**. The five-week trial in US Federal Court in White Plains, New York, has heard how CBS claimed that Scholz reneged on a contract that reportedly required the delivery of ten albums in five years. Scholz countersued, claiming millions in unpaid royalties.

April

7 **Elton John** makes a surprise appearance at Farm Aid IV in the Hoosier Dome in Indianapolis, at which he dedicates *Candle In The Wind* to 18-year-old AIDS victim Ryan White, for whom John has been maintaining a bedside vigil. White will die hours later. **Crosby, Stills & Nash** are joined by occasional bandmate, **Neil Young**, **Bonnie Raitt** performs with **Jackson Browne**, and **Bruce Hornsby** with **Don Henley**. Among the many regular Farm Aid performers is up-and-coming country singer, 28-year-old **Garth Brooks** (who scored his first US Country No. 1 last year with *If Tomorrow Never Comes*).

11 **Elton John** sings *Skyline Pigeon* and acts as a pallbearer at Ryan White's funeral in the Second Presbyterian Church in Indianapolis.

12 Asteroids 4147–4150, discovered in 1983 and 1984 by Brian A. Skiff and Dr. Edward Bowell of the Lowell Observatory in Flagstaff, Arizona, are now named **Lennon**, **McCartney**, **Harrison**, and **Starr**. The announcement is made by the International Astronomical Union's minor planet center in Cambridge, Massachusetts.

22 **R.E.M.**'s **Michael Stipe** and **Peter Buck**, **10,000 Maniacs**, **Indigo Girls**, and **Billy Bragg** take part in A Performance for the Planet, to celebrate Earth Day, at the Merriweather Post Pavilion in Columbia, Maryland. A parallel concert takes place in Central Park, New York, with the **Cars**' **Ric Ocasek**, the **B-52's**, **Daryl Hall & John Oates**, singer-songwriter **Edie Brickell**, and alt-folk vocal trio the **Roches**.

With his enormous entourage and equally large trademark pants, Hammer was becoming a hot commodity: his own "Hammerman" series would premiere on US television in September.

May

5 **Robert Plant**, **Jimmy Page**, and **John Paul Jones** join **Jason Bonham**, who is continuing his own career fronting **Bonham**, for a five-song set at the Heath Hotel in Bewdley, near Kidderminster, England. The occasion is the reception following Bonham's wedding to his childhood sweetheart, Jan Charteris.

5 The John Lennon Tribute Concert is held at the Pier Head Arena in Merseyside, celebrating the artist's songs. Acts taking part, either live or on video, include **Al Green**, the **Christians**, **Joe Cocker**, **Lenny Kravitz**, **Kylie Minogue**, **Natalie Cole**, **Wet Wet Wet**, **Ringo Starr**, **Jim Keltner**, **Jeff Lynne**, **Tom Petty**, **Joe Walsh**, the **Moody Blues**, **Lou Reed**, **Terence Trent D'Arby**, **Randy Travis**, **Cyndi Lauper**, **Deacon Blue**, **Lou Gramm**, **Dave Stewart**, **Ray Charles**, **Dave Edmunds**, **Daryl Hall & John Oates**, and **Roberta Flack**. Proceeds from the event will go to the Spirit Foundation established by **John** and **Yoko**.

10 **Adamski** (Adam Tinley) performs this week's UK No. 1, his acid house kicking *Killer*, on "Top Of The Pops." The song's featured vocalist, **Seal**, is suddenly a hot property after ten years of trying to break through. The 27-year-old singer-songwriter (who co-penned *Killer*) will shortly agree to a publishing deal with Trevor Horn's Beethoven Street company, also signing to the producer's ZTT label.

27 The week-long 19th Tokyo Song Festival begins, with American pop vocal trio **Wilson Phillips** winning the event's Grand Prize with *Hold On*. Combining the genetic talents of **Brian Wilson**'s daughters **Carnie** and **Wendy** with **Chynna Phillips** (daughter of **John** and **Michelle Phillips** of the **Mamas & the Papas**), the harmonious act will hit US No. 1 with the song on June 9 – 25 years to the day after the **Beach Boys** were at No. 1 with *Help Me Rhonda*.

30 In New York for a performance at Radio City Music Hall to promote their current release, the politically charged *Blue Sky Mining*, **Midnight Oil** plays a noontime concert in front of the Exxon Building in Manhattan. It is in protest at the company's global pollution activities, not least the *Exxon Valdez* oil spill in Alaska. Some 10,000 people attend the free agit-pop event, which features a large backdrop reading "Midnight Oil Makes You Dance... Exxon Oil Makes Us Sick."

June

1 **Mariah Carey** makes her national television debut performing *Vision Of Love* on "The Arsenio Hall Show." The 20-year-old Venezuelan-American singer-songwriter – blessed, according to her publicists, with a seven-octave vocal range – was working as a waitress in New York in 1988, when she won an audition to be backup singer for **Brenda K. Starr**. Starr passed Carey's demo tape to CBS Records president, Tommy Mottola, who signed her. Her show-stopping debut tonight, followed by a heart-stopping rendition of the national anthem at an NBA Finals game, will shoot Carey to overnight success. *Vision Of Love* will top the US chart in August, followed by the release of her multiplatinum, chart-topping debut album, *Mariah Carey*. A second extract, the ballad *Love Takes Time*, will begin a three-week gold hold at US No. 1 in November, with two further chart-toppers following next year, all from the same set. With global success around the corner, a pop/R&B star to rival **Whitney** has arrived.

2 **Billy Bragg**, the **Associates**, **Wet Wet Wet**, **Aswad**, the **Average White Band**, **Big Country**, **Deacon Blue**, **Sheena Easton**, **Nanci Griffith**, the **Hothouse Flowers**, and **John Martyn** perform at the Big Day, Scotland's largest-ever free open-air festival. It is attended by 250,000 at various locations in Glasgow, and airs live on Channel 4 television. **Michael Stipe** and **Natalie Merchant** join Bragg in singing **John Prine**'s *Hello In There*.

15 The original **Velvet Underground** members play together for the first time since 1969, performing *Heroin*, when they attend the opening of the Cartier Foundation's Andy Warhol retrospective at Jouy-en-Josas, outside Paris, France.

16 **R.E.M.** begin five days of sessions at John Keane's Studio in Athens, Georgia, writing and rehearsing songs for their next album. The new material includes *It's A Free World Baby*, *Radio Song*, *Shiny Happy People*, and *Losing My Religion*. The group will return to cut more demos throughout August, recording final versions of what will emerge as *Out Of Time* in September, at Bearsville Studios, Woodstock, New York. The final album, produced by Scott Litt and mixed at Prince's Paisley Park Studios in Minneapolis, Minnesota, in November, will be issued next March. It will include guest appearances by the **B-52's' Kate Pierson** and rapper **KRS-One**, though it will be the strings-laden, mandolin-led pop/rock anthem *Losing My Religion* that will become a career-defining hit, transforming the group from American college rock favorites to international rock stars.

20 **Run-D.M.C.** joins fellow rappers **KRS-One**, **Public Enemy**'s **Chuck D**, female hip-hop pioneer **Queen Latifah**, **MC Lyte**, **LL Cool J**, **Big Daddy Kane**, **Rebel MC**, and **Ziggy Marley** to record *H.E.A.L.*, for KRS-One's HEAL (Human Education Against Lies) campaign at Power Play Studios in Long Island, New York.

23 Having already peaked at No. 8 on the Hot 100 last week, **MC Hammer**'s *U Can't Touch This* hits US R&B No. 1, becoming the first major rap hit to sample an entire previous recording – namely **Rick James**'s 1981 smash, *Super Freak (Part 1)*. While most of today's rap/

The environmentally conscious Midnight Oil ensured that the "long box" CD display rack for their album *Blue Sky Mining* was made of recycled paper

"In the night sky of the American imagination Madonna looms."

New Republic, August 1990

July 2 The Italian Bishop's Conference campaigns to ban **Madonna** from playing three dates in Italy, issuing the statement: "Her new show, with the symbols it uses and the values it expresses, is an offense to good taste." When she arrives next week, Madonna will hold a press conference at Rome Airport, defending her concert and voicing her opinions on artistic expression and freedom of speech.

The "Madonna – Live! Blonde Ambition World Tour '90" concert aired on HBO TV in August 1990 and became the most watched show in the station's 18-year history.

Silver Clef concert at Knebworth... Sinéad O'Connor creates controversies... Stevie Ray Vaughn is killed...

hip-hop is reliant upon sampled snippets, the most overused being **James Brown**'s 1970 single *Funky Drummer (Part 1)*, Hammer has gone all the way. The song is featured on his third album, ***Please Hammer Don't Hurt 'Em***, currently in the third of its 21 weeks at US No. 1: by December it will have logged the longest uninterrupted residence at either No. 1 or No. 2 since separate mono/stereo album listings began in 1963. It will sell over ten million domestic copies alone, and the rapper will be presented with a Ferrari Testarossa by Capitol Records, after betting the label that ***Please Hammer*** would be the biggest-selling rap album ever.

30 After a four-year break, Knebworth House hosts the Silver Clef Award Winners, a day-long rock concert featuring most of the 15 previous Silver Clef winners: **Pink Floyd**, **Eric Clapton**, **Phil Collins**, **Genesis**, **Robert Plant**, and **Jimmy Page**, **Paul McCartney**, **Cliff Richard** and the **Shadows**, **Status Quo**, **Mark Knopfler**, and **Tears For Fears**. The concert is in aid of the Nordoff-Robbins Music Therapy Centre and the BRIT School for the Performing Arts. Also appearing is **Elton John**, who is currently at UK No. 1 with *Sacrifice/Healing Hands*: astonishingly, this is his first solo UK chart-topping single (not including his duet with **Kiki Dee**).

> **"You make records for other people... That's what it's about. I'm making it for the marketplace."**
>
> Van Morrison, **Rolling Stone**, August 9, 1990

July

18 Dogged by the UK gutter press, **Madonna** – in London for three dates at Wembley Stadium – goes jogging in Hyde Park, causing criticism in the media following claims that she had previously agreed to help launch the fundraising ***Nobody's Child*** album to benefit Romanian orphans.

29 Following years of self-abuse, **Elton John** listens to the urgings of a close friend to get help and avoid self-destruction. He duly embarks on six weeks of "recovery" at the Parkside Lutheran Hospital in Chicago, a rehabilitation clinic, to address his bulimia and addiction to drugs and alcohol. After this, he will take a year off from recording and touring.

August

13 Soul legend **Curtis Mayfield** is crushed when a strong gust of wind brings down a lighting rig during an outdoor concert at Wingate High School Football Field in Flatbush, Brooklyn, New York. Paralyzed from the neck

Curtis Mayfield was rightly honored with a slew of honors in the 1990s, including induction into the Rock and Roll Hall of Fame and the NAACP Hall of Fame.

ROBERT JOHNSON

Aug 28 **CBS releases *The Complete Recordings*, representing the entire recording legacy of blues great Robert Johnson. Diligently assembled by the label's Lawrence Cohn and expert researcher Steve LaVere (who has also endeavored to rescue Johnson's compositions from the public domain to remunerate the artist's heirs), it includes a 48-page booklet with essays by Eric Clapton and Keith Richard. The collection will enjoy a 31-week chart ride and earn platinum certification. It will also receive a Grammy Award next year, named Best Historical Recording. A journeyman blues singer who died in 1938, Johnson pioneered a unique and unconventional guitar technique (underpinned by walking bass lines) which greatly influenced successive generations of blues and rock guitarists. The Rock and Roll Hall of Fame will honor him in a week-long American Music Masters Series tribute in 1998.**

A month before his death, Stevie Ray Vaughan completed work on *Family Style*, an album recorded with his brother Jimmie.

down, he will be transferred next week from King's County Hospital to Shepherd Spinal Center, near his Atlanta, Georgia, home. Doctors fear he will remain paralyzed.

18 **Soul II Soul**'s **Jazzie B** suffers back injuries in a seven-car pile-up on Interstate 290 as the group travels from Detroit, Michigan, to Chicago, Illinois, for a Poplar Creek Music Theater concert. The accident sends 31 people to hospital and causes the cancellation of the group's North American tour.

24 At New Jersey's Garden State Arts Center in Holmdel, **Sinéad O'Connor** refuses to perform her scheduled gig if the American national anthem is played. Her protest is initially aimed at US patriotism, and subsequently at the current wave of music censorship prevailing in the US. The incident will become a major international news story.

27 Following a concert at the Alpine Valley Music Theater in East Troy, Wisconsin, 35-year-old **Stevie Ray Vaughan** is killed when the helicopter in which he is traveling to Chicago crashes in thick fog. (The pilot and three members of **Eric Clapton**'s entourage are also killed.) Vaughan's appearance on stage, earlier tonight, ended with a jam featuring his brother **Jimmie**, Clapton, **Robert Cray**, **Buddy Guy**, and **Phil Palmer**. Vaughan has scored five consecutive platinum albums and gained a sterling reputation as one of blues-rock's most gifted guitar players.

31 **Stevie Wonder**, **Bonnie Raitt**, and **Jackson Browne** sing *Amazing Grace* at the memorial service for **Stevie Ray Vaughan**, held at the Laurel Land Memorial Park in Oak Cliff, Dallas, Texas.

September

1 The **Cure** broadcasts a four-hour pirate radio show from a secret London location – a transmitter on the roof of their manager's office in Maida Vale – to premiere their new album of remixes, ***Mixed Up***. The show, "Cure FM," starts at 2:00 am, and features interviews, unreleased recordings, news, weather, traffic reports, and commercials, all presented in unpredictable Cure style.

7 As **Madonna** gives a period-costumed, dress-lifting live performance of the song, her "Vogue" video scoops the Best Editing, Best Cinematography, and Best Direction trophies at the seventh MTV Video Music Awards at the Universal Amphitheater, Universal City. The equally controversial **Sinéad O'Connor** also wins three awards for "Nothing Compares 2 U" – Best Video, Best Female Video, and Best Post Modern Video. The heady success of the night leads a drunken O'Connor to ask **Living Colour**'s **Vernon Reid** to marry her and have her love child. **MC Hammer** wins Best Dance and Rap Videos for "U Can't Touch This," and the **B-52's** pick up Best Group Video and Best Art Direction for "Love Shack." **Tears For Fears**' "Sowing The Seeds Of Love" wins Breakthrough Video and Best Special Effects. **Aerosmith**'s controversial "Janie's Got A Gun" wins Best Metal/Hard Rock Video and Viewers' Choice, and **Janet Jackson** – the recipient of the Video Vanguard Award – also wins Best Choreography in a Video for "Rhythm Nation."

15 **Steve Miller**'s 1974 US chart-topper, *The Joker*, finally achieves the same success across the Atlantic, having been chosen to underscore a Levi jeans television commercial.

October

1 **Forbes** magazine lists the **New Kids On The Block** as the fifth richest entertainers in the US, with pre-tax income of $78 million.

4 Two cases are filed in Macon, Georgia, against **Ozzy Osbourne** and CBS Records, by the parents of teenagers Michael Waller and Harold Hamilton, who shot themselves in the head – Waller in May 1986 and Hamilton in March 1988 – apparently after listening to Osbourne's *Suicide Solution*. Ozzy will tell the Foundation Forum censorship panel: "If I wrote music for people who shot themselves after listening to my music, I wouldn't have much of a following."

11 After **Mudhoney**'s **Dan Peters** temporarily filled in on drums for **Nirvana** last month, permanent replacement drummer **Dave Grohl** – previously of **Scream** – performs his first gig with the band at the North Shore Surf Club in Olympia, Washington.

13 **Bob Dylan** performs for 4,000 cadets in the Dwight D. Eisenhower Hall at the US Military Academy in West Point, New York. Hundreds of cadets join him in singing *Blowin' In The Wind*.

Madonna appeared in a Rock The Vote TV ad draped in nothing more than an American flag.

Oct # 1990

2 Live Crew on obscenities charges... Vanilla Ice... The truth about Milli Vanilli...

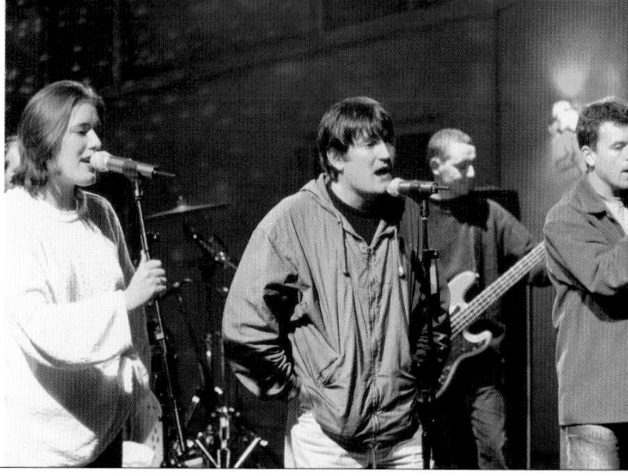

The Beautiful South's council-house, leatherette-sofa humor was lost in the translation when they toured the US.

Dave Grohl played his first gig with Nirvana at the North Shore Surf Club in Olympia, Washington, in October 1990.

20 Three members of **2 Live Crew** are acquitted of obscenity charges at Broward County Courtroom, Hollywood, Florida, following a nightclub gig on June 10 at the city's Club Futura. Mayor Sal Oliveri had warned club owner, Ken Geringer, not to let the show go ahead: "Mr. Geringer, I think you see the handwriting on the wall. There are devices and many means a city can use to discourage a merchant from continuing business in a city... I hope that we don't have to resort to that." After the gig, they did. Police harassed his patrons. City officials ignored fire code violations, allowing burglars to vandalize the club. Geringer's attorney, Stewart Karlin, says: "It's outrageous... The City of Hollywood, from the moment of the 2 Live Crew concert, carried out a vendetta against my client. Unfortunately, they were successful."

20 MTV Brasil is launched in Brazil, following a licensing deal with magazine publisher, the Abril Group.

22 After meeting for the first time last week, singer **Eddie Vedder**, bassist **Jeff Ament**, guitarists **Stone Gossard** and **Mike McCready**, and drummer **Dave Krusen** debut at Seattle, Washington's Off Ramp Café. They call themselves **Mookie Blaylock**, after the New Jersey Nets point guard, whose sports card they found in a box with their demo tape. Following the death on March 19 of **Mother Love Bone**'s lead vocalist **Andrew Wood** (of a heroin overdose), Ament and Gossard, both also ex-**Green River**, were joined by local veteran musician McCready. In search of a lead singer, their three-track demo tape reached San Diego, California-based **Vedder**, via **Red Hot Chili Peppers' Jack Irons**. After writing lyrics and completing the vocal to the demos, Vedder was asked to complete the line-up. The combo, temporarily augmented by **Soundgarden**'s **Matt Cameron** and **Chris Cornell**, will be given a new name by Vedder: **Pearl Jam**. The name comes from his grandmother, Pearl, and her homemade preserves – believed to be of a hallucinogenic nature.

27 **Beautiful South** – the acerbic, dry-witted, British pop combo fronted by **Paul Heaton** and **Dave Hemmingway** – is at UK No. 1 with *A Little Time*, the second chart-topper of year for an act related to the **Housemartins**. Their ex-colleague **Norman Cook** has taken off in a club direction with **Beats International**, which also hit the top spot in March with *Dub Be Good To Me*, an update of the **S.O.S. Band**'s *Just Be Good To Me*.

November

3 **Vanilla Ice** becomes the first solo white rapper to hit US No. 1, with his breakout smash, *Ice Ice Baby*. Built on the catchy bass riff sample from **Queen** and **David Bowie**'s 1981 hit *Under Pressure*, it is also becoming a global success, set to begin four weeks at UK No. 1 on December 1. **Ice** (22-year-old Dallas-based Robert Van Winkle) was introduced to SBK/Capitol Records by **Public Enemy**'s **Chuck D**. His platinum success will be shortlived: within 12 months his career will be as cold as it is now hot, although not before he has sold more than seven million copies of his debut album, ***To The Extreme***.

For David Bowie's world tour in 1990, the singer invited audiences to decide on a "greatest hits" running order for each show... Perhaps his lack of sartorial elegance led to Vanilla Ice's rapid demise.

"I will not go on stage after the national anthem of a country which imposes consorship on its artists."

Sinéad O'Connor, **Q**, December 1990

14 At a press conference, Frank Farian reveals that the long-standing rumors about **Milli Vanilli** not singing on their debut album are true: "I've never heard such a bad singer. They wanted to sing. They wanted to write songs. It never happened. They went instead to discos till 4:00 am and slept all day." He goes on to say that he doesn't understand the fuss. "What was the betrayal? Did anyone in America believe that the Village People or the Monkees really sang themselves? The Archies? Please. Everyone's been doing it for 25 years." Rob Pilatus tells the **Los Angeles Times**: "I feel like a mosquito being squeezed. The last two years of our lives have been a total nightmare. We've had to lie to everybody. We are true singers, but that maniac Frank Farian would never allow us to express ourselves." The actual singers were less photogenic, 40-ish Brad Howell and John Davis. On November 19, NARAS will rescind the Best New Artist Grammy won by the duo – the first time in the 33-year history of the Grammys that an award has been withdrawn.

26 **Janet Jackson** is the big winner at the inaugural **Billboard** Music Awards, staged in Santa Monica. She triumphs in the Hot 100 Singles Artist, Top Pop Album, Hot R&B Singles Artist, Top R&B Albums Artist, Top R&B Album, Top R&B Artist, Top Dance Club Play Artist, and Top Dance 12in Singles Sales Artist categories.

December

3 ABC airs in full **Madonna**'s latest erotic offering, the "Justify My Love" video – which has been banned by most other media – on its "Nightline" telecast. Anchorman Forrest Sawyer quizzes the singer on the steamy black and white clip, shot in a hotel bedroom and co-starring her current beau, Tony Ward. The song, co-written by Madonna and **Lenny Kravitz** and produced by Kravitz, will hit US No. 1 in January.

11 The RIAA certifies multiplatinum sales of four **Led Zeppelin** albums: ***Presence*** (two million), ***Led Zeppelin*** (four million), ***In Through The Out Door*** (five million), and ***Physical Graffiti*** (four million).

12 **Q** magazine holds its first awards at Ronnie Scott's club in London. Eight trophies are handed out, including Best Album (**World Party**'s ***Goodbye Jumbo***), Best Songwriter (**Prince**), Best Producer (**Paul Oakenfold** and Steve Osborne), Best New Act (**They Might Be Giants**), Best Live Act (the **Rolling Stones**), Best Act in the World Today (**U2**), Recorded Music (the **Beach Boys**' ***Pet Sounds*** CD), and the **Q** Merit Award (**Paul McCartney**). In his acceptance speech, McCartney thanks his band, **Harry Secombe**, Jeffrey Archer, Edwina Currie, and **Vic Reeves**. **Bill Wyman**, representing the Rolling Stones, says: "On behalf of my backing group, **Mick**, **Keith**, **Charlie**, and the new one... what's his name... **Ronnie Wood**, I'd like to say thank you to everyone. It's very nice."

19 **R.E.M.** performs *Losing My Religion* live for the first time, during a one-night gig at the 40 Watt Club in Athens, Georgia.

21 The first of two **John Lennon** tribute concerts takes place at the Tokyo Dome in Japan, with **Miles Davis** (performing *Strawberry Fields Forever*), **Natalie Cole & Toshinobu Kubota** (*Ticket To Ride*), **Linda Ronstadt** (*Good Night*), **Daryl Hall & John Oates** (*Julia* and *Don't Let Me Down*), and **Sean Lennon** (*You've Got To Hide Your Love Away*).

Vanilla Ice's debut album *To The Extreme* sold seven million copies in the US. His followup, *Extremely Live*, sold 500,000.

ROOTS **During this year: 15-year old Canadian pop/dance singer Alanis Morissette's first album, *Alanis*, is released by MCA Records Canada, and sells more than 100,000 copies... Bob Dylan's son Jakob forms his first band, the Apples, after briefly attending Parson's Art School in New York City... Chicago R&B combo MGM, including R. Kelly, win the syndicated television talent show "Big Break"... two pairs of brothers – Joel and Cedric Hailey and Donald and Dalvin DeGrate – come together in Tiny Grove, North Carolina, as Jodeci... 16-year-old Jewel Kilcher wins a voice scholarship to the Interlochen Fine Arts Academy in Michigan... Dolores O'Riordan successfully auditions for Limerick, Ireland-based band the Cranberries, making her debut at Ruby's, a club in the basement of a Limerick hotel... Adam Duritz and David Bryson begin gigging in the San Francisco Bay area as Sordid Humor, a folk/roots duo... and sibling quartet the Corrs forms in its native Dundalk, Ireland, and the youngest – Andrea – wins a small part in Alan Parker's movie "The Commitments"...**

Smells Like Teen Spirit

1991

No.1 US SINGLES

Jan 5	Justify My Love **Madonna**
Jan 19	Love Will Never Do (Without You) **Janet Jackson**
Jan 26	The First Time **Surface**
Feb 9	Gonna Make You Sweat (Everybody Dance Now) **C&C Music Factory featuring Freedom Williams**
Feb 23	All The Man That I Need **Whitney Houston**
Mar 9	Someday **Mariah Carey**
Mar 23	One More Try **Timmy -T-**
Mar 30	Coming Out Of The Dark **Gloria Estefan**
Apr 13	I've Been Thinking About You **Londonbeat**
Apr 20	You're In Love **Wilson Phillips**
Apr 27	Baby Baby **Amy Grant**
May 11	Joyride **Roxette**
May 18	I Like The Way (The Kissing Game) **Hi-Five**
May 25	I Don't Wanna Cry **Mariah Carey**
June 8	More Than Words **Extreme**
June 15	Rush, Rush **Paula Abdul**
July 20	Unbelievable **EMF**
July 27	(Everything I Do) I Do It For You **Bryan Adams**
Sept 14	The Promise Of A New Day **Paula Abdul**
Sept 21	I Adore Mi Amor **Color Me Badd**
Oct 5	Good Vibrations **Marky Mark & the Funky Bunch featuring Loleatta Holloway**
Oct 12	Emotions **Mariah Carey**
Nov 2	Romantic **Karyn White**
Nov 9	Cream **Prince & the N.P.G.**
Nov 23	When A Man Loves A Woman **Michael Bolton**
Nov 30	Set Adrift On Memory Bliss **P.M. Dawn**
Dec 7	Black Or White **Michael Jackson**

No.1 UK SINGLES

Jan 5	Bring Your Daughter... To The Slaughter **Iron Maiden**
Jan 19	Sadeness Part 1 **Enigma**
Jan 26	Innuendo **Queen**
Feb 2	3 A.M. Eternal **KLF featuring Children of the Revolution**
Feb 16	Do The Bartman **Simpsons**
Mar 9	Should I Stay Or Should I Go **Clash**
Mar 23	The Stonk **Hale & Pace & the Stonkers**
Mar 30	The One And Only **Chesney Hawkes**

The Smashing Pumpkins

Nirvana

Smashing Pumpkins, fronted by goth-rocker Billy Corgan, released their first alt-rock album, *Gish*, produced by Corgan and Butch Vig... "All in all, we sound like the Knack and the Bay City Rollers being molested by Black Flag and Black Sabbath" was how Nirvana described themselves in their band biography.

The rock landscape would be changed forever by the birth of a new wave of alternative rock. Led by **Billy Corgan**, Chicago-based **Smashing Pumpkins** had paid their dues in some of Illinois's less salubrious haunts. Clearly, they were destined for success, but **Nirvana**'s punk had the more dramatic impact on America's alienated youth. Their single *Smells Like Teen Spirit* was an instant hit on MTV, and a small scent of the nihilistic alt-rock fusion of punk and metal that comprised the band's 1991 opus ***Nevermind***, with which alternative ambushed the mainstream. The band would soon become rock's leading anti-heroes, but not before blazing a trail for such groups as **Soundgarden** and **Pearl Jam**, and establishing the hitherto staid city of Seattle, Washington, as the home of grunge.

Guns N' Roses had an eventful year, which started in front of 120,000 people at the second Rock in Rio festival. A US tour included a riot in Missouri, provoked by **Axl Rose**'s fury at a fan with a camera. The albums ***Use Your Illusion I*** and ***Use Your Illusion II*** – released simultaneously – were once again a platform for Rose's snarling, screeching vocals and **Slash**'s accomplished guitar chops. Reinforcing each other's success, Guns N' Roses toured with **Metallica**, whose self-titled album captured the No. 1 positions in both Britain and the US.

Country music continued its relentless surge with the success of **Garth Brooks**. He cleverly tied country instincts with pop sensibilities, and offered sincere and nostalgic fare to an increasingly cynical urban world, forging a reputation as the boy-next-door with the common touch. The year was not without controversy for him. The video for his song *The Thunder Rolls* was pulled by the Nashville Network for its depiction of a wife-abuser gunned down by his spouse.

Janet and **Michael Jackson** both nabbed huge new record deals, with Virgin and Sony respectively. The "King of Pop's" ***Dangerous*** sold bucket-loads, though the reviews were not entirely favorable. Matching Janet Jackson hit for hit, **Mariah Carey** registered her fifth consecutive US No.1 with *Emotions*.

The music scene in Britain may not have been as varied as that in the US, but **Simply Red**, **Seal**, and **Massive Attack** were evidence of its buoyancy. Trip-hop pioneers Massive Attack conjured hypnotic and darkly sensual grooves that would be influential way beyond the group's selling power. Simply Red enjoyed a stellar year with the pop-soul classic set, ***Stars*** – the biggest-selling CD in Europe.

Two very different giants of popular music passed away in 1991. **Miles Davis** died in September. His influence on postwar jazz was inestimable; his influence on rock was also highly significant. Several weeks later, **Freddie Mercury** of **Queen** succumbed to complications from AIDS – and Britain lost its most dashing champion of glam rock, and one of the most distinctive vocalists of his generation. Queen would never be the same again.

May 4 The Shoop Shoop Song (It's In His Kiss) **Cher**
June 8 I Wanna Sex You Up **Color Me Badd**
June 29 Any Dream Will Do **Jason Donovan**
July 13 (Everything I Do) I Do It For You **Bryan Adams**
Nov 2 The Fly **U2**
Nov 9 Dizzy **Vic Reeves & the Wonder Stuff**
Nov 23 Black Or White **Michael Jackson**
Dec 7 Don't Let The Sun Go Down On Me **George Michael & Elton John**
Dec 21 Bohemian Rhapsody/These Are The Days Of Our Lives **Queen**

"I'm thankful for the success, but I have no idea why it's happening."

Garth Brooks, **The New York Times**, September 18, 1991

Janet and Michael Jackson both sign massive recording deals...

Def Leppard's Steve Clark

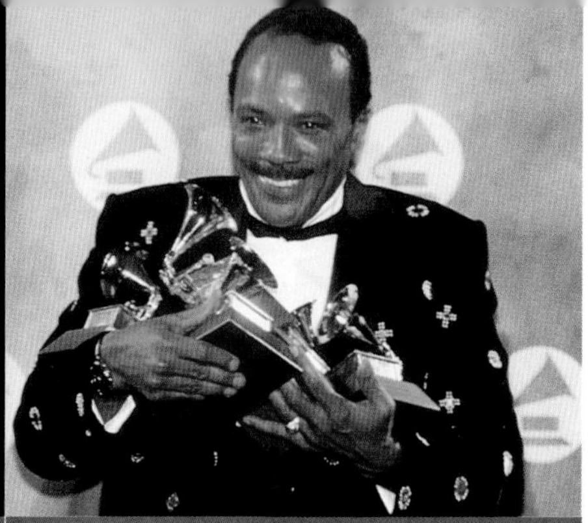

Quincy Jones

Flavor Flav was arrested in February after a quarrel with girlfriend Karen Ross, and pled guilty to third degree assault and served 30 days in jail. Ross was granted a permanent order of protection against her Public Enemy No. 1.

Def Leppard suffered their second major career setback with the death of guitarist Steve Clark... Quincy Jones won the first of his 25 Grammys in 1964 for Best Musical Arrangement.

January

8 **Def Leppard** guitarist **Steve Clark** is found dead by his girlfriend. The autopsy will confirm the cause as respiratory failure due to a compression of the brain stem, resulting from excess alcohol mixed with antidepressants and painkillers. Dead at the age of 30, the guitarist had been in rehab six times.

8 On what would have been **Elvis Presley**'s 56th birthday, the Hard Rock Café in Orlando, Florida, serves a memorial meal, supposedly his favorite: a 6lb beef roast, creamed potatoes with butter, mixed vegetables with butter, peas with salt pork, cornbread, and banana pudding.

> "I think Steely Dan as a concept is really a part of its time and we wouldn't want to revive it."
>
> Donald Fagen, **Vox**, January 1991

16 **David Crosby**, in his induction speech into the Rock and Roll Hall of Fame as a member of the **Byrds**, announces: "An airstrike has just started on Baghdad," heralding the onset of the Gulf War. During the sixth awards dinner, held at the Waldorf Astoria Hotel in New York, **Bonnie Raitt** inducts **John Lee Hooker**, **Tracy Chapman** welcomes the **Impressions**, and **Bobby Brown** honors **Wilson Pickett**. Blues great **Jimmy Reed** is posthumously inducted, and **Phil Spector** accepts **Ike & Tina Turner**'s induction on their behalf. **LaVern Baker** is also honored, and in the Early Influences category, **Howlin' Wolf** receives his due. **Nesuhi Ertegun** receives the Lifetime Achievement award. The Non-Performers are **Dave Bartholomew** and **Ralph Bass**.

19 The Jimmy Jam and Terry Lewis-penned *Love Will Never Do (Without You)* gives **Janet Jackson** her fifth US chart-topper, making her the first artist to score seven top five hits from the same album.

22 ***Elvis' Golden Records*** is released in China, on cassette, selling for nine yuan ($1.73).

25 **Paul McCartney** records an acoustic set before a small audience at London's Limehouse Studios, for the premiere worldwide broadcast of the "MTV Unplugged" series (which has already gained success domestically in the US) on April 3. Backed by **Paul "Wix" Wickens**, **Blair Cunningham**, **Robbie McIntosh**, **Hamish Stuart** and **Linda McCartney**, he rips through a 22-song set, including the first song he ever wrote, at the age of 14: *I Lost My Little Girl*. He also performs a mix of rock 'n' roll classics, and several **Beatles** tunes. For his final number – a cover of **Bill Withers**'s *Ain't No Sunshine* – McCartney takes over on drums, with Stuart singing the lead vocal.

27 With patriotism at an all-time high during the Gulf War crisis, **Whitney Houston** captures America's heart by singing *The Star Spangled Banner* prior to Super Bowl XXV at Joe Robbie Stadium in Miami, Florida. Reaction to her performance will result in a rush-released single and video. **New Kids On The Block** provides the half-time entertainment, performing "A Small World Salute to 25 Years of the Super Bowl" with 2,000 children.

29 **Pearl Jam** records *Alive*, *I've Got a Feeling*, and *Wash* at London Bridge Studios in Seattle, Washington, which will help them secure a recording contract with Epic Records.

February

1 Having already announced that she is pulling out of the forthcoming BRIT Awards, **Sinéad O'Connor** tells NARAS that she will not attend the Grammy Awards because she does not like the music industry's values: "I signed my record deal when I was 17 and it has taken me this time to gather enough information and mull it over and reach a conclusion. We are allowing ourselves to be portrayed as being in some way more important, more special than the very people we are supposed to be helping – by the way we dress, by the cars we travel in, by the 'otherworldliness' of our shows and by a lot of what we say in our music." (NARAS president Michael Greene will respond caustically in future interviews, questioning O'Connor's motives, and noting that she did not have any problem attending the MTV and American Music Awards.)

5 Anarchic pop unit **KLF** is arrested in Battersea, London, for defacing a **Sunday Times** billboard by amending "Gulf" to "KLF." The group is let off with a warning, but is required to pay £500 ($950) compensation for vandalizing the hoarding. Their anthemic electronic dance smash, *3 AM Eternal*, is in its second week at UK No. 1.

20 **Bette Midler** opens the 33rd Grammy Awards at Radio City Music Hall, New York, with a live version of the patriotic *From A Distance*, which also wins Song of the Year for its writer Julie Gold. However, the night belongs to veteran composer/arranger/producer **Quincy Jones**, whose six Grammys take his career total to 25, surpassing **Henry Mancini** in the non-classical field. Jones's ***Back On The Block*** is named Album of the Year, as well as winning Best Rap Performance by a Duo or Group, Best Jazz Fusion Performance, Best Arrangement of an Instrumental, and Best Instrumental Arrangement Accompanying Vocals. He also wins his third Producer of the Year award. **Phil Collins**'s *Another Day In Paradise* – he performs the song tonight, with **David Crosby** providing harmony vocal – beats out *From A Distance* for Record of the Year. **Mariah Carey** is named Best New Artist, and also wins Best Pop Vocal Performance, Female for *Vision Of Love*. **Living Colour** pick up the Best Hard Rock Performance prize, and **Angelo Badalamenti**'s haunting *Twin Peaks Theme* is named Best Pop Instrumental Performance. Veterans **Linda Ronstadt**, **Aaron Neville**, **Eric Clapton**, and **Ray Charles** are all winners, with a posthumous award going to **Roy Orbison**, whose *Oh Pretty Woman* is named Best Pop Vocal Performance, Male. **Bob Dylan** is honored with a Lifetime Achievement Award. In a typically obtuse speech, Dylan says that his father told him: "It's possible to be so defiled in this world that even your mother and father won't know you. But God will always believe in your own ability to mend your own ways."

March

1 Launched on Leningrad's cable TV channel, MTV becomes the only non-Soviet television network to be broadcast round the clock in Russia.

11 Stocking up on superstar names prior to a much-rumored sale of the company, Virgin Records signs a $50 million deal with **Janet Jackson**, reportedly for a mere two albums. The deal has been personally supervised by high-flying label supremo Richard Branson, who says: "A Rembrandt rarely becomes available. When it does, there are many people determined to get it. I was determined."

16 Following a private concert for IBM executives near San Diego, California, seven members of country superstar **Reba McEntire**'s backing band – **Chris Austin**, **Kirk Cappello**, **Joey Cigainero**, **Paula Kaye Evans**, **Terry Jackson**, **Tony Saputo**, **Michael Thomas**, and her road manager, Jim Hammon – are killed in a plane crash on their way to Fort Wayne, Indiana. McEntire and her husband, Narvel Blackstock, traveling on another plane, learn of the tragedy during a refueling stop in Memphis, Tennessee.

18 **U2** pay a fine of £500 ($895) imposed on the Irish Family Planning Association, which has been found guilty of selling condoms illegally at the Virgin Megastore in Dublin, Ireland.

20 One week after Virgin announced the most lucrative record deal in pop history with **Janet Jackson**, her brother **Michael**'s new contract with Sony makes hers look like lunch money. Heralded as the first billion-dollar entertainer contract, it includes an $18 million cash advance for his forthcoming ***Dangerous*** album release alone. Jackson is made CEO of his own newly formed Nation Records (to be renamed MJJ), a subsidiary of the Jackson Entertainment Complex, which will also include television, video, and film divisions. His royalty rate is an unprecedented $2.08 per album, with guarantees of post-***Dangerous*** advances of $5 million per project. It is also announced that David Lynch, Tim Burton, Chris Columbus, and Sir Richard Attenborough are already lined up to direct forthcoming promo film clips to accompany the ***Dangerous*** singles.

21 Chicago-based alt-rock combo **Smashing Pumpkins**, steadily building a reputation throughout Illinois, sign a seven-album deal with Caroline Records/Virgin in the US. Their frontman, singer/guitarist **Billy Corgan**, the son of a jazz guitarist, left home at the age of 18 and headed to Florida, where he formed the shortlived, goth-rock band **Marked**. He put together Smashing Pumpkins in 1988, initially as a duo with bassist **D'Arcy** (**Wretzky-Brown**), and they made their live debut at the local Avalon club, with an audience estimated at 50 people. The group now includes guitarist **James Iha** and drummer **Jimmy Chamberlin**.

23 During the second of **George Michael**'s two Cover to Cover concerts at London's Wembley Arena, **Elton John** joins him in a spirited duet on *Don't Let The Sun Go Down On Me*. The song is recorded and will top charts around the world, beginning in the UK in December.

"When I'm at home I listen to the Carpenters."

Motörhead's Lemmy, **New Musical Express**, February 2, 1991

Whitney Houston captured patriotic fever with a stellar, if pre-taped, version of *The Star Spangled Banner*, sung at Super Bowl XXV.

Garth Brooks at the CMAs...
The Simple Truth concerts...
(Everything I Do) I Do It For You...

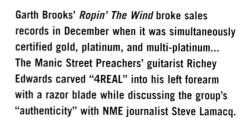

Garth Brooks

The Manic Street Preachers

Garth Brooks' *Ropin' The Wind* broke sales records in December when it was simultaneously certified gold, platinum, and multi-platinum... The Manic Street Preachers' guitarist Richey Edwards carved "4REAL" into his left forearm with a razor blade while discussing the group's "authenticity" with NME journalist Steve Lamacq.

April

5 By the end of a three-day set of **Grateful Dead** concerts at the Omni in Atlanta, Georgia, 57 people have been arrested. The total drug haul from the arrests is 4,856 "tabs" of LSD, 29 bags of "mushrooms," 24 "lids" of marijuana, one vial of crack cocaine, and 18 cylinders of nitrous oxide.

17 **Nirvana** perform a new song called *Smells Like Teen Spirit* for the first time at a concert at the OK Hotel in Seattle, Washington. It has been written by band members **Kurt Cobain**, **Dave Grohl**, and **Krist Novoselic**.

20 England's Bristol-based R&B trio **Massive Attack**'s critically revered debut set, ***Blue Lines***, show-casing soulful, urban-themed, slick beat grooves, makes UK No. 13 in its week of entry. Pioneering the new "trip-hop" genre, and featuring guest vocalists – reggae singer **Horace Andy**, rapper **Tricky**, and soul vocalist **Shara Nelson** (on the groundbreaking masterpiece *Unfinished Sympathy*) – it will be nominated for a BRIT Award and named as Album of the Year by England's celebrity magazine, **The Face**. Pop newspaper the **New Musical Express** (**NME**) has already given the set a perfect 10/10 review. The group's nucleus is the trio of graffiti artist **3-D** (**Robert Del Naja**), songwriter **Daddy G** (**Grant Marshall**), and singer **Mushroom** (**Andrew Vowles**).

24 **Garth Brooks** picks up six trophies at the 26th Academy of Country Music Awards in Los Angeles, including the big one: Entertainer of the Year – a category he will win six times during the 1990s. He also wins Top Male Vocalist, Album of the Year (the Allen Reynolds-produced ***No Fences***), Video of the Year (his groundbreaking "The Dance"), Song of the Year (*The Dance*, written by Tony Arata), and Single of the Year (*Friends In Low Places*). The son of **Colleen Carroll**, a successful country singer in the 1950s, the Tulsa, Oklahoma-born Brooks played in a bluegrass band while a student working as a bouncer at a Stillwater, Oklahoma, club called Tumbleweeds, where he met Sandy Mahl, whom he married in 1986. They moved to Nashville, Tennessee, the following year, where Brooks honed his style in local clubs. He was picked up by Capitol Records three years ago. Knocking down the "New Country" door opened by **Randy Travis** and **Dwight Yoakam**, Brooks is on a meteoric rise. ***No Fences***, which mixes honky-tonk styled uptempo numbers with sensitive folk-inflected ballads, is on its way to a staggering 16 million US sales. His follow-up album, ***Ropin' The Wind***, will spend 18 non-consecutive weeks topping the US survey from September. With a high-octane concert style – which will soon fill arena-sized venues – Brooks will transform country music and become the first such act to reach a previously untapped mass audience.

30 Introduced to label A&R executive Mark Kates by **Sonic Youth** bassist **Kim Gordon** – and recently courted by Capitol and CBS Records, among others – **Nirvana** sign to Geffen Records imprint DGC, for a debut album advance of $287,000.

Following lead singer Chris Robinson's repeated derogatory comments about tour sponsorship, at the top of their live set while opening for ZZ Top, the Black Crowes are dropped from the Recycler tour after the second of three shows at the Omni in Atlanta.

May

2 The **Rolling Stones** are honored with the Outstanding Contribution to British Music award at the 36th Ivor Novello Awards, even though **Jagger** and **Richards** have never previously been recognized by the British Academy of Songwriters, Composers and Authors. **Phil Collins** is hailed Songwriter of the Year, while **Elton John**'s *Sacrifice* wins the Best Selling A-Side and Best Song Musically and Lyrically categories. **Lisa Stansfield**'s All Around The World is named International Hit of the Year, and **Erasure**'s Blue Savannah is named the Most Performed Work of 1990. **Seal** wins his first Ivor as co-author of Killer, which is named Best Contemporary Song. His first solo cut, the career-defining Crazy – spurred by Trevor Horn's production gloss and an innovative special-effects promo clip – recently hit UK No. 2. It is featured on his upcoming soul/rock-fused first album, *Seal*.

4 The **Manic Street Preachers** storm off stage midway through a set at the Downing College May Ball at Cambridge University, England, smashing amplifiers and their drumkit, after the PA company, Criterion, pulls the plug on **Nicky Wire** when he kicks a mike stand around the stage. The controversial hardcore punk revivalist quartet was formed two years ago in Wales by singer/guitarist **James Dean Bradfield**, his cousin, drummer **Sean Moore**, guitarist **Richey Edwards**, and bassist Wire. This month they will sign a reported £250,000 ($475,000) deal with Sony Records. Wire, talking to the NME, will say: "You don't have a dream so you can cut off little faded pieces from fanzines all your life. Signing to a major record company is the price of an education, we don't care what they do to us. The credibility of indie labels is shit."

12 More than 50 million people around the globe tune in to "The Simple Truth – A Concert for Kurdish Refugees" from London's Wembley Arena. It includes contributions via satellite – recorded last week in the Hague, The Netherlands – with **Peter Gabriel**, **Sting**, and **Sinéad O'Connor** singing *Games Without Frontiers* with Sting's band. **Paul Simon** appears from the G-Mex in Manchester, England, and **New Kids On The Block**'s contribution comes from the Ahoy in Rotterdam, Holland, and that of **INXS** from Melbourne, Australia. **Whitney Houston**, **Gloria Estefan**, **Daryl Hall & John Oates**, **Rod Stewart**, and **Yes** also appear via satellite, while **Lisa Stansfield**, **Alison Moyet**, **MC Hammer**, and **Alexander O'Neal** perform live at Wembley.

20 High Court Judge John Humphries frees the **Stone Roses** from their contract with Silvertone Records, citing it as an "unfair, unjustified and unjustifiable restraint of trade." They will shortly sign a reported $4 million deal with Geffen Records.

24 **Guns N' Roses'** Get in the Ring tour opens with the first of two gigs at Alpine Valley Music Theater in East Troy, Wisconsin, with heavy-metal band **Skid Row** as opening act. Before the concert, **Axl Rose** visits the Milwaukee County Medical Complex, having torn ligaments in his left foot after jumping off a speaker at last week's Ritz gig.

Police tore up a traffic ticket issued to Guns N' Roses' Axl Rose before a July concert in Los Angeles. Captain James Seymour said, "We don't need 19,000 people at the Forum rioting over a traffic ticket."

June

1 Former **Temptation**, 50-year-old **David Ruffin** dies of a drug overdose at the Hospital of the University of Pennsylvania at 3:55 am. He has been brought to the emergency room in a limousine, though the driver does not identify the singer. An FBI check of his fingerprints confirms that it is indeed the one-time Temptation.

2 "Liquid Television," the network's first animated series, debuts on MTV. It includes what will become a regular feature – Mike Judge's deadpan characters, "Beavis and Butt-head." Their popular antisocial antics and love of heavy metal will propel the cartoon morons from cult status to cultural icons, as stars of their own spinoff series – a fitting indictment of MTV's core audience.

22 Dominated by **Eazy-E**'s extremely provocative lyrics, and the increasingly deft production skills of **Dr. Dre**, **N.W.A.**'s *Efil4zaggin* becomes the first gangsta rap album to top the US chart.

July

2 **Axl Rose** sparks an hour-long riot during a concert at the Riverport Amphitheater in Maryland Heights, Missouri, by yelling at security guards to remove a camera from a fan, before leaping into the crowd to enact his own style of security. More than 50 people, including 15 police officers, are injured in the ensuing brouhaha, and the damage to the newly opened theater is so severe that a July 4 concert has to be canceled. **Guns N' Roses** gigs in Chicago and Bonner Springs, Kansas, will also be axed.

13 **Bryan Adams**'s *(Everything I Do) I Do It For You* tops the UK chart, where it will remain for 16 weeks – the longest consecutive stay at No. 1 in chart history. An instant classic, the ballad was co-written by composer/arranger

July 1991

Lollapalooza... Miles Davis dies... *Smells Like Teen Spirit...*

Bryan Adams was honored with the Order of Canada and the Order of British Columbia after he scored a record-breaking, career-defining hit with the ballad *(Everything I Do) I Do It For You.*

Bryan Adams

Michael Kamen, Adams, and producer Robert "Mutt" Lange, as the theme to the current movie, "Robin Hood: Prince Of Thieves," starring Kevin Costner. Kamen sent Adams an aural impression of harpsichord and lute sounds, based on a tune he had written in the 1960s. Adams co-penned the lyrics with Lange, and fleshed out the instrumentation to complete the song, which was recorded in London. (Kamen's original melody had been offered to **Kate Bush** and **Annie Lennox**, who both turned it down, and **Lisa Stansfield** – whose enthusiasm to record it was reportedly overruled by Clive Davis.) The global hit will begin seven weeks at US No. 1 in two weeks, becoming the biggest-selling US single since *We Are The World.*

18 Conceived by **Perry Farrell**, frontman of **Jane's Addiction**, the alt-rock stuffed Lollapalooza package tour opens at Compton Terrace in Phoenix, Arizona, featuring Jane's Addiction, **Living Colour**, **Siouxsie & the Banshees**, post-punk poet **Henry Rollins**, and sleazy, hardcore, underground favorites **Butthole Surfers**. Farrell is fast becoming a seminal alt-rock figure: Jane's Addiction's last two albums, ***Nothing's Shocking*** and ***Ritual De Lo Habitual***, have both gone platinum in the US, profoundly influencing a new wave of modern-rock bands. His savvy Lollapalooza concept will grow to become the most successful annual alternative rock caravan of the decade. Making a big impression on this year's bill are **Nine Inch Nails**, an uncompromising industrial-rock combo formed by frontman, 26-year-old multi-instrumentalist **Trent Reznor**, who signed with TVT Records three years ago.

August

3 Elektra Entertainment invites fans to the world premiere listening party at Madison Square Garden, New York, for **Metallica**'s new self-titled album, giving away 19,000 free tickets. ***Metallica*** will enter both US and UK charts at No. 1 by the end of the month, and will sell more than 12 million US copies by the end of the 1990s – making it the decade's biggest-selling heavy-metal record. Having pioneered the new wave of heavy metal in the late 1970s, Metallica is at the forefront of mainstream metal. The album's focus cut, *Enter Sandman*, will be certified gold by the RIAA next month.

16 Still signed to Geffen, **Aerosmith** ink a four-album deal with Sony Music, which will come into effect in 1995. It reportedly involves a $10 million advance per album and 22 percent royalties. The average age of the band members will be over 45 when the deal kicks in.

17 Unable to oust **Bryan Adams** from the top spot, **Right Said Fred** hit UK No. 2 with *I'm Too Sexy*, which will become the fourth best-selling single of the year in Britain – behind Adams, **Queen**'s *Bohemian Rhapsody*, and **Cher**'s *The Shoop Shoop Song (It's In His Kiss)* – and the anthem for the British phenomenon known as Essex Girls, who delight in the song's saucy, monotonous lyrics. The trio, brothers **Richard** and **Fred Fairbrass** with **Rob Manzoli**, made the record for £1,500 ($2,850), and will make it to the top spot in the US with *Sexy*, reaching pole position in the UK next year with *Deeply Dippy*.

18 Unimpressed by their first performance tonight at Manchester's Boardwalk club, audience member **Noel Gallagher** – who has been touring with **Inspiral Carpets** as their guitar technician and roadie – offers to join Manchester-based band **Oasis** on the condition that they perform only his songs and that he retains complete control over their progress. They eagerly agree after hearing his self-performed demo of *Live Forever*. The group (named after the Swindon Oasis venue) comprises Noel's brother **Liam Gallagher** (lead vocals), **Paul Arthurs** (guitar), **Paul McGuigan** (bass), and **Tony McCarroll** (drums).

Jane's Addiction frontman Perry Farrell, who was behind the alt-rock Lollapalooza palava, celebrated the end of his band by performing the second half of their farewell gig in Honolulu stark naked.

September

5 The night belongs to **R.E.M.** at the eighth MTV Video Music Awards, as they collect six awards for "Losing My Religion" – Best Art Direction, Best Direction in a Video, Best Editing, Best Group Video, Best Video, and Breakthrough Video. **Chris Isaak** wins three awards for "Wicked Game" – Best Male Video, Best Cinematography, and Best Video from a Film. **C&C Music Factory**, a dance duo led by writer/producers **Robert Clivillés** and **David Cole**, who already have three top five hits this year, win two awards for "Gonna Make You Sweat (Everybody Dance Now)" – Best Dance Video and Best Choreography in a Video. **LL Cool J**, currently featured in a five-page fashion spread in **Rolling Stone**, wins Best Rap Video for "Mama Said Knock You Out," and performs *Don't Call It A Comeback*. **Prince** performs *Gett Off*, before adjourning to a post-show gig at the 20/20 Club. **Don Henley** sings *The Heart Of The Matter* at an otherwise rap and metal-crowded ceremony. British pop quintet **EMF** perform the transatlantic chart-topper, the anthemic, hook-laden pop-rock gem, *Unbelievable*, live via satellite from London's Town & Country Club. With **Jon Bon Jovi** nominated in two categories for "Blaze Of Glory," his band is presented with the Michael Jackson Video Vanguard trophy.

15 Initially receivable in 30 countries on the Star-TV system, MTV Asia is launched, as a joint venture between its parent company Viacom and Hutchvision.

17 At 12:01 am, 4.2 million copies (the largest shipment in pop history) of **Guns N' Roses**' ***Use Your Illusion I*** and ***Use Your Illusion II*** are simultaneously released for sale in the US.

19 "Ray Charles: 50 Years in Music, Uh-Huh!" – a musical tribute featuring the soul legend in duet with **Stevie Wonder**, **Willie Nelson**, **Michael Bolton**, **Randy Travis**, **James Ingram**, and **Michael McDonald** – takes place in Pasadena, California. The concert is a benefit for the Starlight & Starlight Pavilion Foundations, and will air on the Fox network on October 6.

28 **Garth Brooks** achieves another first, becoming the only country artist to enter the **Billboard** Top 200 album chart at No. 1. Only the ninth record of any genre to do so, ***Ropin' The Wind*** also becomes the first album to debut simultaneously at the top of **Billboard**'s pop and country listings. However, since the advent of new chart-compiling company SoundScan in May – which has introduced a more accurate method of compiling charts – there have been several No. 1 debuts on the **Billboard** surveys.

28 Two months after a frail **Miles Davis** played a final gig at the Royal Festival Hall in London, the "birth of the cool" jazz legend dies at the age of 65 in Santa Monica Hospital, of pneumonia, respiratory failure, and stroke. The trumpeter, composer, and bandleader, whose musical collaborators have ranged from **Charlie Parker** to **Prince**, recently said: "I want to keep creating and changing. Music isn't about standing still and becoming safe." On his last European trip, Davis performed at France's Montreux Jazz Festival, backed by a 50-piece orchestra led by **Quincy Jones**, paying tribute to his one-time collaborator, **Gil Evans**. He also received the title Commandeur dans l'Ordre des Arts et des Lettres from the Ministry of Culture in Paris, where he played a reunion gig with former sidemen **Wayne Shorter** and **Dave Holland**.

29 MTV broadcasts the video of **Nirvana**'s new single, *Smells Like Teen Spirit*. Capturing the emotion of which its title speaks (although it is named after a deodorant) – the angst and fury of Generation X – the song and its explosive, high school gym-located, promo clip will become a defining musical icon of the new decade, and its reverberations will be felt for years to come. Their record label, DGC, obviously unaware of the impact the song will have, ships only 50,000 copies of the parent album ***Nevermind***, featuring four-month-old Spencer Elden on its cover. Produced by **Butch Vig**, the punk/metal-fused, grunge-pioneering set will hit US No. 1 in January, rack up 10 million US sales by the end of the decade, and become an equally popular alt-rock mainstay around the world. Regarded as a seminal alternative rock classic, the album's success inaugurates the 1990s Seattle "grunge" rock wave, and opens the door for **Pearl Jam**, **Mudhoney**, and **Soundgarden**. (The CD format of ***Nevermind*** features an additional track: after ten minutes of silence, a 13th song, *Endless, Nameless*, magically appears.)

"If I had been born white there never would have been an Elvis Presley."

Little Richard, **USA Today**, July 17, 1991

October

3 **Simply Red**'s **Mick Hucknall** is honored by the American Society of Composers, Authors, and Publishers at its 11th awards ceremony, held at Claridges in London, for the broadcast success of the chart-topping *Holding Back The Years*. Next week, the Hucknall-penned ***Stars***, produced by Steve Levine, will enter the UK chart at No. 1. It will become the biggest-selling album of the next two years in Britain, making five trips to the summit, and achieving platinum sales nine times over, including the sale of 1.32 million units in its first 14 weeks at retail. Worldwide sales will top nine million. Curiously, despite its smooth production, radio-friendly pop gems, and Hucknall's impeccable blue-eyed soul delivery, ***Stars*** will stall at US No. 79 – the only major territory where it will not make a significant impression.

11 Apple Computers and Apple Corps. – battling over the "Apple" trademark – finally reach an amicable settlement. The case spent 116 days in the High Court, ten in the Court of Appeal and one at the European Commission, at a cost of £7 million ($13.3 million).

12 *Emotions* hits the top spot, giving **Mariah Carey** five US No. 1s with her first five single releases. She becomes the first act to

Metallica

After winning their second consecutive Grammy in February, Metallica went on the road with Mötley Crüe, the Black Crowes, and Queensryche for the Monsters of Rock tour.

A one-time student at the Juillard School of Music, Miles Davis once said "I always listen to what I can leave out."

Concert for Walden Woods... Bill Graham is killed... Freddie Mercury dies...

Simply Red's Mick Hucknall

Mariah Carey

achieve this, breaking the **Jackson 5**'s record of four, set in 1970. Carey co-produced the track – the title cut from her second album – with **Robert Clivillés** and **David Cole** of the red-hot **C&C Music Factory**.

24 The last of three benefits organized by **Don Henley**, under the banner The Concert for Walden Woods – A Musical Event to Protect and Preserve a National Treasure, takes place before a sellout Madison Square Garden, New York, crowd. It features Henley, **Bonnie Raitt**, and **Jimmy Buffett**. The first two concerts, earlier this week, featured **Sting** and **Billy Joel** performing with Henley. Massachusetts' historic Walden Woods, the retreat of 19th-century author and philosopher Henry Thoreau, is under threat from developers who want to build an office building and condominium complex there. The project has become a personal crusade of Henley's, and $2,903,800 is raised to help preserve the land.

26 Flying home after attending a **Huey Lewis & the News** gig at the Pavilion in Concord, California, legendary American promoter **Bill Graham** is killed (together with his companion, Melissa Gold, and the pilot), when his helicopter, in high winds and heavy rain, crashes into a power transmission tower near the Sears Point Raceway, northwest of Vallejo, California.

November

3 Demonstrating the regard in which **Bill Graham** was held, an all-star cast of musicians perform at the memorial concert, Laughter, Love and Music: To Celebrate the Lives of Bill, Steve and Melissa, at San Francisco's Golden Gate Park Polo Field. Before a crowd of 350,000, **Crosby, Stills, Nash & Young** sing *Teach Your Children*, *Love The One You're With*, *Long May You Run*, *Long Time Gone*, *Southern Cross*, *Only Love Can Break Your Heart*, *Wooden Ships*, and *Ohio*. **Journey**'s **Steve Perry**, **Neal Schon**, and **Jonathan Cain** reunite for the day, **Jackson Browne** performs *For A Dancer*, and **John Fogerty** sings *Born On The Bayou*; *Green River*; *Bad Moon Rising*; and *Proud Mary*. He is backed by the **Grateful Dead**, who also perform **Bob Dylan**'s *Forever Young* with **Neil Young**. **Santana**, **Aaron Neville**, **Los Lobos**, and **Tracy Chapman** also take part, and the event closes with **Joan Baez**, **Kris Kristofferson**, and **Graham Nash** performing *Amazing Grace*.

7 **Frank Zappa**'s children, **Moon** and **Dweezil**, announce that their father is battling prostate cancer, and is canceling a four-night tribute (Zappa's Universe) to honor his 51st birthday, as well as today's scheduled interview on CNN's "Showbiz Today."

Simply Red's *Stars* album sold 1.32 million copies in the UK in just 14 weeks before Christmas... Mariah Carey's single *Emotions* was certified gold and her first two albums multi-platinum in the space of two months.

30 Following changes in the albums list in May, **Billboard** introduces a new methodology for its Hot 100 singles ranking, combining point-of-sale retail scans from SoundScan with accurate "fingerprint" airplay monitoring from Broadcast Data Systems. The chart's first No. 1 is *Set Adrift On Memory Bliss*, a pop/hip-hop pearl by **P.M. Dawn**: **Prince Be** and **DJ Minutemix** (brothers **Attrel** and **Jarrett Cordes**) have added their melodious "daisy-age rap" to a sample of the memorable 1983 **Spandau Ballet** smash, *True*.

> **"Opera and ballet did not cut the ice in the Cold War years. They used to exchange opera and ballet companies and circuses, but it takes rock 'n' roll to make no more Cold War."**
>
> AC/DC's Brian Johnson, performing before an crowd of 500,000 in Moscow, September 28, 1991

9 As **Bill Drummond** and **Jimmy Cauty**'s current incarnation, the **Justified Ancients of Mu Mu**, enters the UK Top 40 with *It's Grim Up North*, graffitti bearing the legend has appeared at the junction of the M1 and M25 motorways. Earlier this week Joe Ashton, Labour MP for Bassetlaw, expressed concern in the House of Commons over its appearance, asking that it be replaced in the interests of "restoring regional balance." Ashton's alternative suggestions include: "It's gruesome in the Midlands," or "There's nowt but folk living in cardboard boxes in London."

December

9 Jamaican Supreme Court Justice Clarence Walker, ending a decade of legal wrangles, directs that **Bob Marley**'s assets be sold for $11.5 million to his widow, children, and Chris Blackwell's Island Logic Ltd., despite MCA's higher offer. **Ziggy Marley** names his daughter, born today, Justice.

14 Besieged Soviet Union president Mikhail Gorbachev, impressed by the "Cold War end" theme of the **Scorpions**' worldwide hit rock anthem, *Wind Of Change*, invites them to meet him at the Kremlin.

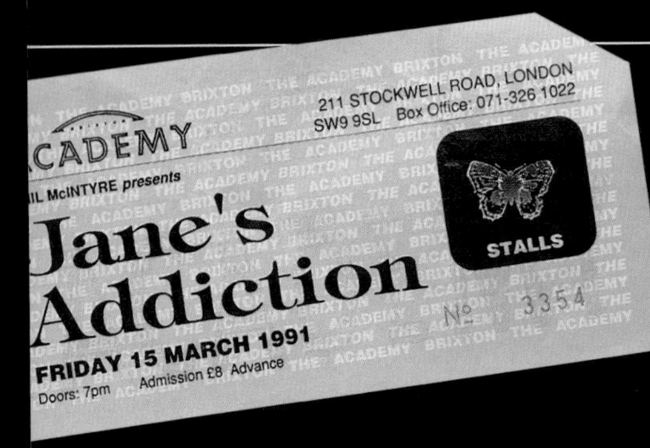

After Jane's Addiction played their last gig in September, Perry Farrell was arrested and charged with being under the influence of a controlled substance... Alice Cooper's 1991 album *Hey Stoopid* featured the track *Snakebite*.

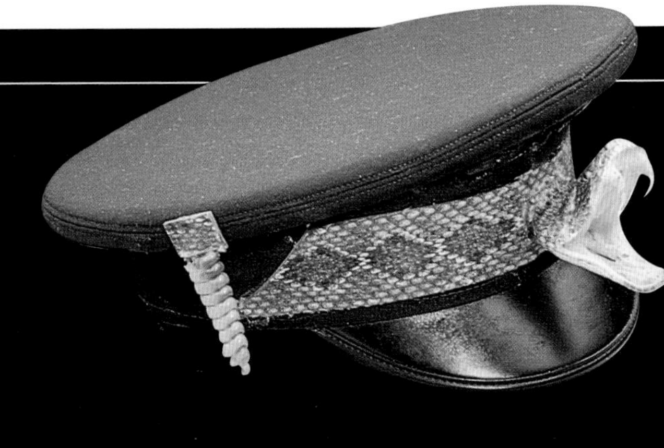

18 In a historic case, 1970s hitmaker **Gilbert O'Sullivan** is granted an injunction in Manhattan Federal Court to prevent rap star **Biz Markie** from sampling his *Alone Again (Naturally)* for his single, *Alone Again*. The lawsuit will be settled in O'Sullivan's favor on the 31st.

20 In a **USA Weekend** interview, **Natalie Cole**'s mother, Maria, says that she can't bear to listen to ***Unforgettable...With Love*** (a tribute to Natalie's father, **Nat**, which topped the US chart in July) or attend any of her daughter's concerts. She adds: "I just feel that everything belonged to Nat – it evokes such memories for me."

21 On a Saturday, recently formed Oxford-based rock group **On A Friday** signs to Parlophone Records, following a label showcase at Oxford's Jericho Tavern in November, which was attended by 25 A&R reps. Next March, the group – comprising singer/guitarist/pianist **Thom Yorke**, guitarists **Ed O'Brien** and **Jonny Greenwood**, his brother, bassist **Colin Greenwood**, and drummer **Phil Selway** – will change their name to **Radiohead**, taken from a **Talking Heads** track on ***True Stories***.

28 A rap celebrity basketball game, promoted by music impresario **Sean Combs** at the Nat Holman Gym at City College in Manhattan, turns deadly, when too many spectators show up. Scheduled to start at 6:00 pm, crowds begin arriving at 2:00 pm. At 3:45 pm, Combs shows up and starts making arrangements for the collection and sale of tickets. By 4:00 pm, 1,500 people are waiting in line. As the crowd gets out of control, barricades are broken and glass doors smashed. With too few police on the scene, trouble inside the building gets worse when there is a call for a "bum rush" (hip-hop code for storming clubs that bar rap fans because of their race). A crowd stampedes down a staircase to closed doors, where about 50 people are already waiting to get in. Within minutes, nine people lie dead, with 29 injured. Despite this incident, Combs is on the fast-track to music industry success. Head of A&R at Motown imprint, Uptown Records, at the age of 18, he is currently steering the careers of new signings **Father MC** and 20-year-old hip-hop discovery **Mary J. Blige**.

31 Radio Luxembourg closes down, with DJ Mike Hollis saying goodbye on behalf of Europe's oldest commercial radio station – which began broadcasting, in German, in 1929.

FREDDIE MERCURY

Nov 24 Freddie Mercury dies of pneumonia-related complications from AIDS at his home in Holland Park, London. He is 45. A statement is issued by the group and Jim Beach: "We have lost the greatest and most beloved member of our family. We feel overwhelming grief that he has gone, sadness that he should be cut down at the height of his creativity, but above all great pride in the courageous way he lived and died. It has been a privilege for us to have shared such magical times. As soon as we are able we would like to celebrate his life in the style to which he was accustomed." His body will be cremated at Kensal Green Cemetery in west London, and his ashes scattered on the shore of Lake Geneva. The group's publicist, Roxy Meade, requests that donations be sent to the Terrence Higgins Trust.

Zanzibar-born Mercury – real name Farrokh Bulsara – was the flamboyant frontman and main songwriter for Queen for two decades.

ROOTS During this year: nine-year-old Britney Spears wins a place at New York's Professional Performing Arts School... Tionne Watkins and Lisa Lopes, of teen duo Second Nature, sign a management deal with Pettibone Productions... Gaz Coombes, still a student at Wheatley Park Comprehensive School in Oxford, England, Andy Davies, and brothers Danny and Nick Goffey form the Jennifers... former Lock Up group members Tom Morello and Brad Wilk recruit Zack de la Rocha and Timmy C to create Rage Against The Machine... 6-year-old Zac Hanson joins his two old brothers, Isaac and Taylor Hanson, playing their first gig as a trio at a local "Mayfest" gathering in Tulsa, Oklahoma... Mary J. Blige comes to the attention of Uptown Records' Andre Harrell, who hears a demo of hers cut in a shopping mall karaoke studio in Yonkers... and rehearsing at a Gothenburg warehouse/studio, which they share with car mechanics, among others, Ace of Base cut their first demo, which is rejected by Polar Records...

Rhythm Is A Dancer

1992

No.1 US SINGLES

- **Jan 4** Black Or White **Michael Jackson**
- **Jan 25** All 4 Love **Color Me Badd**
- **Feb 1** Don't Let The Sun Go Down On Me **George Michael & Elton John**
- **Feb 8** I'm Too Sexy **R*S*F* (Right Said Fred)**
- **Feb 29** To Be With You **Mr. Big**
- **Mar 21** Save The Best For Last **Vanessa Williams**
- **Apr 25** Jump **Kris Kross**
- **June 20** I'll Be There **Mariah Carey**
- **July 4** Baby Got Back **Sir Mix-A-Lot**
- **Aug 8** This Used To Be My Playground **Madonna**
- **Aug 15** End Of The Road **Boyz II Men**
- **Nov 14** How Do You Talk To An Angel **Heights**
- **Nov 28** I Will Always Love You **Whitney Houston**

No.1 UK SINGLES

- **Jan 4** Bohemian Rhapsody/These Are The Days Of Our Lives **Queen**
- **Jan 25** Goodnight Girl **Wet Wet Wet**
- **Feb 22** Stay **Shakespear's Sister**
- **Apr 18** Deeply Dippy **Right Said Fred**
- **May 9** Please Don't Go/Game Boy **KWS**
- **June 13** Abba-Esque (EP) **Erasure**
- **July 18** Ain't No Doubt **Jimmy Nail**
- **Aug 8** Rhythm Is A Dancer **Snap!**
- **Sept 19** Ebeneezer Goode **Shamen**
- **Oct 17** Sleeping Satellite **Tasmin Archer**
- **Oct 31** End Of The Road **Boyz II Men**
- **Nov 21** Would I Lie To You **Charles & Eddie**
- **Dec 5** I Will Always Love You **Whitney Houston**

Pearl Jam

Eric Clapton

Fronted by Eddie Vedder, Pearl Jam joined Nirvana as the leading torch-bearers of grunge... One of the more enduring moments of 1992 was Eric Clapton's performance of *Tears In Heaven* on "MTV Unplugged", ten months after his son Conor's tragic death.

In an unchallenging year, **Boyz II Men** became the biggest R&B group on the planet, **Garth Brooks** sold truckloads of records to a strictly North American audience, and both **Madonna** and **Sinéad O'Connor** shocked and provoked more than ever. Boyz II Men spent a record 13 weeks astride the US Hot 100, becoming Motown's biggest-selling act since **Lionel Richie**. Their main producers, **L.A. Reid** and **Babyface**, were becoming the hottest production team: in addition to their Boyz work, the duo oversaw projects by **TLC**, **Whitney Houston**'s outing of the previous year, the multiplatinum ***Boomerang*** soundtrack, and **Bobby Brown**'s red-hot career. They also introduced the latest signing to their own LaFace label, **Toni Braxton**.

MTV's ingenious "Unplugged" series hit two home runs, and became a must-see musical brand. **Eric Clapton** and **Mariah Carey** recorded memorable sets – so strong on emotion and naked talent that they spawned multiplatinum ***Unplugged*** albums and a stream of hit singles and awards. On the rock front, funk/thrash pioneers **Red Hot Chili Peppers**' ***Blood Sugar Sex Magik*** dominated the alt-rock US scene, while their videos nabbed three trophies at the MTV Video Music Awards.

The biggest star in the US – in any genre – was Garth Brooks. Unfashionable to a fault, he was building a sales sheet that would amass more than 100 million records by the decade's end. Although not the founder of New Country, he became its indisputable king, with a cunning mix of tender ballads and emotion-driven pop/rock/country numbers. Topped off with a six-gallon black hat, a fondness for wearing jockey shirts, and way-too-tight black jeans, his live prowess was as impressive as his record sales: somehow he became a sex symbol to many in the South, perhaps excited by his galloping around the stage like a horse on steroids.

A major new talent on the British front was **Seal** – the first artist to win three BRIT Awards in one night. He also appeared at A Concert for Life – a notable event at which A-list stars paid homage to **Freddie Mercury**. Seal's debut album success owed a debt to producer **Trevor Horn**, the man behind a slew of successful British talent over the previous decade, who was still creating slick pop magic.

Although litigation had become as much a part of the record business as CD reissues, two 1992 lawsuits hinted at things to come: soul icon **Luther Vandross** invoked California Labor Code section 2855 – which states that personal service contracts cannot exceed seven years – to free himself from what he considered a highly restrictive contract with Sony Entertainment. Sony also bore the brunt of a similar freedom chant by **George Michael**, who used a restraint of trade accusation in a (subsequently) failed attempt to leave the company. Both moves were prophetic, with a growing number of top artists prepared to take on the increasingly complacent and greedy majors.

"We were singing in the bathroom one day... We were harmonizing... And we were like, 'Yo! That sounds good'."

Boyz II Men's Shawn Stockman, **Spin**, July 1992

Jan 1992

Paul Simon performs in South Africa... Eric Clapton on MTV's "Unplugged"... Wayne's World...

January

3 **Luther Vandross** files suit in Los Angeles Superior Court in Santa Monica, against Sony Entertainment (his record label Epic's parent company), citing the California Labor Code section 2855, which prevents any personal service contract exceeding seven years – thereby negating the term of his multi-album deal. (It is the first salvo in a long battle between top artists, seeking freedom from restrictive long-term contracts, and record companies wanting to milk their stars indefinitely.)

7 US Postmaster General Anthony M. Frank announces on CNN's "Larry King Live" that a commemorative **Elvis Presley** stamp will be issued on the King's birthday next year.

7 With the approval of the African National Congress and Nelson Mandela, **Paul Simon** arrives in South Africa, at the invitation of the multiracial South African Musicians' Alliance, to give five shows. The first date, at Ellis Park Stadium in Johannesburg, will be the 151st concert of his 27-country Born at the Right Time tour. The radical Azanian People's Organization (AZAPO) objects, and the Azanian National Liberation Army claims responsibility for a bomb that goes off at Network Productions in Johannesburg, the promoter of the series. The opening concerts suffer from low attendance following other threats of violence from black nationalist groups – notably the Azanian Youth Organization (AZAYO), whose leader is arrested. Simon will spend much of January 9 in meetings with the organization, to defuse threats against his show scheduled for the 11th.

12 Having lost none of his confrontational zeal, **Bob Geldof** is arrested after a disturbance on a Boeing 727 plane, and grounded for five hours on the tarmac at Stansted Airport, in England. More constructively, as the Band Aid Trust closes down, Geldof confirms that a total of $144,124,694 has been raised. He will shortly issue the following statement: "It seems so long ago that we asked for your help. Seven years. It was only meant to last seven weeks, but I hadn't counted on the fact that hundreds of millions of people would respond and I hadn't reckoned on over $100 million. Seven years. You can count them now in trees and dams and fields and cows and camels and trucks and schools and health clinics, medicines, tents, blankets, clothes, toys, ships, planes, tools, wheat, sorghum, beans, research grants, workshops. Seven years ago I said I did not want to create an institution, but I did not want the idea of Band Aid to die. I did not want the potential of it to cease. There were a few dozen aid agencies and they do great work, but that was not our function. Our idea was to open the avenues of possibility. The possibilities of ending hunger in Africa are there. There can be other Band Aids; there must be others, in new times, in different ways. I once said that we would be more powerful in memory than in reality. Now we are that memory."

15 As the cornerstone of the Memphis soul sound of the 1960s, **Booker T. & the MG's** are inducted into the Rock and Roll Hall of Fame, along with the **Jimi Hendrix Experience** (inducted by **Neil Young**), **Bobby "Blue" Bland** (**B.B. King**) and **Johnny Cash** (**Lyle Lovett**). Attending the seventh ceremony, at New York's Waldorf Astoria Hotel, as a member of the inducted **Yardbirds**, **Jeff Beck** says of the legendary group: "We paved the way for barbarism – and we set fire to things." **Billy Joel** inducts **Sam & Dave**, whose **Sam Moore** sings *When Something Is Wrong With My Baby* at the post-dinner jam. **Little Richard** inducts the **Isley Brothers**, joining with them on *Shout*. When the **Neville Brothers** induct the late **Professor Longhair** as an Early Influence, **Aaron Neville** calls the legendary piano player "the grandfather of rock 'n' roll. Where did rock 'n' roll come from? It's the baby of R&B." **Robbie Robertson** welcomes **Elmore James**. **Keith Richards** inducts Non-Performer **Leo Fender**, while **John**

Paul Simon met Nelson Mandela during his concerts in South Africa. In May 1994, Mandela became the country's first black President.

ERIC CLAPTON

Jan 16 **Eric Clapton tapes an all-acoustic set, for MTV's "Unplugged" show, at Bray Studios, England. Among several chestnuts, including a stripped-down *Layla*, he sings new material inspired by the death of his four-year-old son Conor, not least *The Circus Left Town* and the deeply moving *Tears In Heaven*. (Conor died last March, falling from the open window of a 53rd-floor apartment in Manhattan, where his mother, Lori Del Santo, was staying.)**

Yet another highlight in a richly diverse and unique career, the massive commercial success of Clapton's *Unplugged* album raised the profile of MTV and inaugurated a successful series of other A-list "Unplugged" showcases.

Michael Jackson

Seal

Michael Jackson, anointed the "King of Pop" by his close friend, Elizabeth Taylor, was made "King of the Sanwis" during a February visit to the Ivory Coast... 1995 was a career year for Seal, but in 1992 he won three awards at the BRITS, as well as a brace at the Ivor Novello Awards.

Fogerty inducts the late rock promoter **Bill Graham**, for whom **Carlos Santana** performs *I Love You Much Too Much* as a musical tribute to the man who taught him the song. Legendary songwriter **Doc Pomus**, who died last March from lung cancer, is also inducted.

February

3 **Michael Jackson** holds a press conference at New York City's Radio City Music Hall to announce a forthcoming world tour, to be sponsored by Pepsi in the largest promotion deal ever. Proceeds will go to his recently formed Heal the World foundation, devoted to helping the world's children. This evening, a video clip of the second cut from ***Dangerous***, the jack-swing *Remember The Time*, premieres on multiple US cable channels. It features **Eddie Murphy**, model Iman (with whom Jackson shares his first screen kiss), and Earvin "Magic" Johnson, in an Egyptian tale directed by John Singleton.

12 At the 11th BRIT Awards, at London's Hammersmith Odeon, **Seal** becomes the first artist to win three BRITs at the same ceremony: he is named Best British Male Solo Artist, "Killer" is named Best British Video, and ***Seal*** is Best Album. **Queen**'s *These Are The Days Of Our Lives* receives the award for Best British Single, and the much missed **Freddie Mercury** is honored with the Outstanding Contribution to British Music. **U2** win their fourth Best International Group trophy in five years. The evening's controversy is courtesy of the ever-creative **KLF**: sharing the Best British Group honor (with **Simply Red**), they have already left the event when the trophy is presented. Earlier, joined by **Extreme Noise Terror**, they performed a thrash-metal version of *3 A.M. Eternal*, immediately followed by **Bill Drummond** firing machine-gun blanks into the music industry audience, and an announcement over the PA system: "Ladies and gentlemen, the KLF have now left the music business." Earlier, Drummond and **Jimmy Cauty** collected a freshly killed sheep from a slaughterhouse and – persuaded not to disembowel the animal on stage as planned – dumped it outside the Royal Lancaster Hotel, venue for the post-Awards party, with a note attached: "I died for you. Bon appetit!"

14 **Mötley Crüe**'s record label, Elektra, issues a press release: "Race car driving has become a priority in [**Vince**] **Neil**'s life, and he's dedicated much of his time and energy to it. The Crüe's relationship with Vince began to deteriorate because his bandmates felt he didn't share their determination and passion for music. Vince was the only Crüe member who didn't regularly participate in the songwriting process." He initially failed to show up for rehearsals at the beginning of the week, having been involved in a brawl at the Roxy club at the weekend.

14 "Wayne's World" – a full-length movie offshoot of the popular "Saturday Night Live" sketch, featuring Mike Myers and Dana Carvey – premieres in US movie theaters. The soundtrack album, with classic rock cuts by the likes of **Jimi Hendrix**, **Eric Clapton**, and the **Red Hot Chili Peppers**, will hit US No. 1 in April. The inclusion of **Queen**'s *Bohemian Rhapsody* will reignite the epic song's US fortunes, improving its original 1976 chart showing by seven positions when it hits US No. 2.

Although Wayne Campbell and Garth Algar thought they were not worthy, "Wayne's World" grossed more than $121 million in the US.

Feb 1992

EMI buys Virgin... A Concert for Life... Madonna's Maverick Corporation...

INXS

Madonna

22 **Madonna** makes a surprise guest appearance on the "Coffee Talk" segment of "Saturday Night Live," as Liz Rosenberg (coincidentally the name of Warner Bros. Records' New York Vice President of Publicity), in a sketch with Mike Myers playing regular hostess, Linda Richman. The tables are turned however, when **Barbra Streisand** makes an unannounced appearance in the spot, leaving both Madonna and Myers a little *verklempt*!

25 Controversy surrounds **Michael Bolton** as he collects the Best Pop Vocal Performance, Male for *When A Man Loves A Woman* at the 34th Grammy Awards at Radio City Music Hall, New York. Earlier today, he was named in a lawsuit filed on behalf of the **Isley Brothers** by Three Boys Music Corp., charging that their 1966 song, *Love Is A Wonderful Thing*, was copied for Bolton's 1991 hit single of the same title. Things don't get much better when, in his acceptance speech, veteran songwriter Irving Gordon (whose *Unforgettable* is named Song of the Year) aims his comments at Bolton: "It's nice to have a song accepted that you don't get a hernia when you sing it." Backstage, he continues: "I did it in front of Michael Bolton. That's how I feel – it's not necessary to scream your head off to say I love you." The Bolton brouhaha cannot prevent it being an unforgettable night for **Natalie Cole**, who wins Album of the Year, Record of the Year, Best Traditional Pop Performance for her tribute to her late father, **Nat King Cole** – a 22-track collection of his classic hits. **Bonnie Raitt** follows her four Grammy wins from two years ago with another this year. **Metallica**, winning their third Best Metal Performance in a row, echo **Paul Simon** in 1976, by thanking "Jethro Tull for not putting out an album this year." **Boyz II Men** – a sweet-voiced, R&B vocal harmony quartet from Philadelphia – win the Best R&B Performance by a Duo or Group with Vocal category for their first effort, ***Cooleyhighharmony***. The group also perform during the ceremony, in their trademark matching 1950s high-school garb.

INXS performed in March at the Concert for Life in Sydney – billed as the largest single community event in Australian history... Madonna made the annual list of the Top 100 art collectors in Art & Antiques magazine.

March

20 Thorn EMI buys Virgin Music Group for £560 million ($840 million) from Richard Branson and his business partner, Fujisankei. The British entrepreneur will plow the money into his fledgling Virgin Airlines (and re-emerge with a new label, V2, later in the decade).

27 During **U2**'s Zoo TV tour concert at the Palace of Auburn Hills in Michigan, **Bono** orders 10,000 pizzas to go from Speedy Pizza. An hour later, 100 pepperoni pizzas arrive with three delivery men, who each receive a $50 tip.

28 Billed as the largest single community event in Australian history, the Concert for Life, headlined by **INXS** and also starring **Crowded House**, takes place in Centennial Park, Sydney, Australia. The $1.5 million-grossing fundraiser will benefit the Victor Chang Cardiac Research Centre and the AIDS Patient Services and Research Centre at St. Vincent Hospital, Sydney.

April

1 Still climbing the US survey, ***Blood Sugar Sex Magik*** becomes **Red Hot Chili Peppers**' first RIAA certified platinum disc. The band signed to Warner Bros. last year, and the album has been overseen by golden-touch producer Rick Rubin. It reflects a major breakthrough for the group's pioneering funk/thrash meld, yielding mainstream hits *Under The Bridge* and *Give It Away*.

9 In Fort Smith, Arkansas, 19-year-old Sean Pierce is arrested while walking home, charged with "violating a statute against wearing a smutty shirt." He bought a For Unlawful Carnal Knowledge T-shirt at **Van Halen**'s concert yesterday. The band will phone Pierce and offer to pay his fine should he be convicted.

U2's Zoo TV/Zooropa tour began in Lakeland, Florida, in February and came to a close in Tokyo, Japan, in December 1993.

20 **Freddie Mercury**'s life and work are celebrated with the all-star benefit, "A Concert for Life," broadcast from Wembley Stadium, London, to 70 countries. The event features an AIDS awareness plea by Elizabeth Taylor, and performances by **Metallica**, **Extreme**, **Bob Geldof**, **Spinal Tap**, **Def Leppard**, **Guns N' Roses**, and **U2** (via satellite from Sacramento). There is a first-ever live concert link with South Africa, and versions of **Queen**-backed songs by **George Michael**, **David Bowie** (who also recites the Lord's Prayer), **Annie Lennox**, **Seal**, **Paul Young**, **Robert Plant**, and **Roger Daltrey**. **Elton John** performs *Bohemian Rhapsody* – with help from **Axl Rose** – and *The Show Must Go On*, a Mercury song that Queen was never able to play live. **Liza Minnelli** leads the all-star choral finale of *We Are The Champions*, and **Brian May** closes an emotional night by providing the guitar part to *God Save The Queen*. (**Spinal Tap** members, resplendent in regal outfits, introduce their performance by declaring that they will cut short their set by 35 songs, "because we know Freddie would have wanted it this way.")

May

8 City officials in Rolling Fork, Mississippi, dedicate a monument with the inscription: "**Muddy Waters**, master of the blues, was born McKinley Morganfield in 1915, near Rolling Fork. His special technique and interpretation powerfully influenced the development of Delta blues music."

9 After giving a private performance during the week at New York's Bottom Line for Columbia Records staff and executives, **Bruce Springsteen** makes his US network television debut – 17 years after first charting – performing *Lucky Town*, *57 Channels*, and *Living Proof* on "Saturday Night Live," hosted by Tom Hanks.

9 **Kris Kross** perform their current US No. 1, *Jump*, on "Soul Train." Lodging at the top for eight weeks, the double-platinum single is taken from the Atlanta-based teenage rap duo's debut album, ***Totally Krossed Out***. It will top the US chart in two weeks. With hip-hop fully integrated into mainstream pop, another equally catchy – though more risqué – rap smash, *Baby Got Back*, by genre veteran **Sir Mix-A-Lot** (Seattle-born **Anthony Ray**), will begin a five-week reign in July. It will be the summer's biggest US party anthem, and the first US No. 1 single for Rick Rubin's label, Def American.

"My mother likes our music, so if I can please her, that means we're doing something right."

Kurt Cobain, **Q**, April 1992

20 Time Warner Inc. announces a new seven-year cross-media contract with **Madonna**'s newly formed Maverick group of companies, which includes record label, publishing company, book, television, merchandizing, and motion picture subsidiaries. (The name is derived from the first two letters of her names, Madonna Veronica, and the last three of her manager's, Frederick DeMann.) Although each of her last five albums has sold less than the previous one (in the US), media estimates suggesting that the deal is worth $60 million to the industry's latest mogul are described by DeMann as "low." Early Maverick projects include Madonna's ninth solo album, the signing of new acts, her production of the debut set by **Jose & Luis**, a coffee table sex-photo book by photographer Steven Meisel, an HBO cable television biography of Mexican artist Frida Kahlo, and the Maverick Picture Co. debut film, and the $10 million project "Snake Eyes," directed by Abel Ferrara, with the diva starring.

25 Having signed a two-single deal with the independent Nude Records in March, at the instigation of label boss Saul Galpern, hotly tipped newcomers **Suede** achieve the rare distinction of making the front cover of **Melody Maker** without having released any material. The British glam-rock inspired, alt-rock quartet is centered around singer **Brett Anderson** and guitarist **Bernard Butler**. Anderson's girlfriend, second guitarist **Justine Frischman**, left the band last month, and will re-emerge in the equally touted **Elastica**.

16 A full-page ad, taken out by the gloriously original **KLF Communications** (who scored four top five UK hits in the past year alone) on the back of this week's **NME**, states: "We have been following a wild and wounded, glum and glorious, shit but shining path these past five years; the past two of which have led us up onto the commercial highground. We are at a point now where the path is about to take a sharp turn from these sunny uplands down into a netherworld of we-know-not-what. For the forseeable future there will be no further record releases from the **Justified Ancients of Mu Mu**, the **JAMs**, the **Timelords**, the **KLF** and any past, present or future name attached to our activities." Confirming that all KLF-label record releases are now deleted, it ends: "There is no further information." An answering machine at KLF Communications' office states: "This is a recorded announcement... **Bill Drummond** and **Jimmy Cauty** have now left the music business." Distraught UK DJ Steve Wright will say: "We were all devastated when we heard about it. We thought they were the most exciting and original group around. It's definitely the worst news since **Cliff Richard** split with the **Shadows**."

27 With its ***Southern Harmony And Musical Companion*** at US No. 1, the **Black Crowes** make their first appearance on NBC-TV's "The Tonight Show With Jay Leno."

In April, George Michael donated $500,000 royalties from the sale of *Don't Let The Sun Go Down On Me* to various British and American AIDS and children's educational charities.

June 1992

Michael Bolton is sued... U2 meet Abba... *End Of The Road...*

Boyz II Men

June

6 **Aerosmith**'s **Steven Tyler** and **Joe Perry**, **Soundgarden**, **Lenny Kravitz** (who broke through with last year's retro soul-pop hit, *It Ain't Over 'Til It's Over*), and guitar hero **Jeff Beck** guest on "Guns N' Roses Invade Paris!" The US cable pay-per-view extravanganza is broadcast live from the Hippodrome de Vincennes Stadium, Paris.

8 While the court case against **Michael Bolton** continues, **Ronald Isley** issues a statement insisting: "There is no doubt in my mind that Michael used my song. It's humiliating that he is being honored while the original writers are ignored." (Bolton has received two awards for *Love Is A Wonderful Thing* in the past three weeks.) "We want him to give back the awards he won. The song he claims is his has the same hook, the same chorus, the same everything as ours. It's not fair." Isley also says he is insulted by a "settlement offer" proposed by a third party, suggesting the group could write and record a new song with Bolton.

Synth-duo Erasure played sellout dates in Europe and the US during their "Phantasmagorical Entertainment" tour.

11 During the European leg of its Zoo TV tour, **U2** are joined on stage at the Globe in Stockholm, Sweden, by **Abba**'s **Benny Andersson** and **Björn Ulvaeus**, for a rendition of *Dancing Queen*. Other guests on the tour include **Axl Rose** in Vienna, Austria, and **Aerosmith**'s **Steven Tyler** and **Joe Perry** in Paris, France. The European leg closes on the 19th, with the Greenpeace Stop Sellafield (nuclear plant) campaign concert at Manchester's G-Mex Centre in England, with **Public Enemy**, **Big Audio Dynamite II**, and **Kraftwerk**.

13 Heralding a substantial revival of interest in **Abba**, **Erasure**'s homage EP *Abba-esque* enters the UK chart at No. 1, where it will lodge for five weeks. Its success will prompt the UK No. 1 reissue of an Abba's greatest hits collection, and will spawn the novelty act, **Björn Again**. After an unbroken six-year run of 18 Top 30 UK singles successes, Erasure's ***Pop! – The First 20 Hits***, will enter the UK chart at No. 1 in November. Spotlight-shy Erasure founder **Vince Clarke** has been quietly racking up some of the most infectious and popular Euro-synth hits of the past 11 years (all for Daniel Miller's seminal indie label, Mute). Beginning as keyboard player and chief songwriter with **Depeche Mode**, Clarke teamed with **Alison Moyet** in **Yazoo** (named **Yaz** in the US), and hit UK No. 4 in 1983 with his ad-hoc collaborative project, **Assembly** (with ex-**Undertones** frontman **Feargel Sharkey**). He has found even greater success with Erasure, in partnership with singer **Andy Bell**.

22 As ticket demand for **Garth Brooks**'s July 19 concert reaches fever pitch, 198,000 calls jam telephone lines in Phoenix, Arizona.

22 California history professor Jonathan Wiener wins the latest round in a nine-year legal battle with the FBI, paving the way to open the agency's files on **John Lennon**, which began at the instigation of the CIA in 1967.

July

18 **Whitney Houston** marries **Bobby Brown** at her New Jersey estate in Mendham. **Anita Baker**, **Aretha Franklin**, **Freddie Jackson**, **Gloria Estefan**, **Luther Vandross**, **Natalie Cole**, **Patti LaBelle**, and **Stevie Wonder** are among the celebrities who attend.

18 Following the enormous success of last year's Lollapalooza alt-rock caravan, a second, more adventurous, tour takes off at the Shoreline Amphitheater in Mountain View, California. The trek will feature the **Red Hot Chili Peppers**, the red-hot **Pearl Jam**, the **Jesus & Mary Chain**, **Soundgarden**, industrial rock pioneers **Ministry**, ex-**N.W.A.** founder **Ice Cube**, dreamy British shoegazers **Lush**, and various guests. It will end on September 13 at the Irvine Meadows Amphitheater in Laguna Hills, after 37 dates before crowds totaling close to 750,000, grossing over $19 million.

August

5 **Toto**'s drummer **Jeff Porcaro** dies of a heart attack at home in Hidden Hills, Los Angeles. At tomorrow's Meadowlands gig in East Rutherford, **Bruce Springsteen** will dedicate *Human Touch* to musicians' musician Porcaro. **Don Henley**, **Donald Fagen**, **Boz Scaggs**, **Michael McDonald**, and **Eddie Van Halen** will take part in a memorial concert on December 14, creating an educational trust for Porcaro's sons. Toto, an assembly of six Los Angeles session musicians, racked up a slew of adult contemporary hits between 1978 and 1988, including the award-winning *Rosanna* and *Africa*.

9 Under the banner Madstock!, **Madness** play the second of two open-air concerts at Finsbury Park, London, with guests **Ian Dury & the Blockheads**, and **Flowered Up**. **Prince Buster** joins the band for *One Step Beyond* and *Madness*, while **John Lydon** joins Dury on stage, playing guitar on *Sex And Drugs And Rock 'n' Roll*. (Madness guitarist **"Chrissie Boy" Foreman** announced: "We will re-form at 9:30 pm on August 8 and plan to split up again an hour-and-a-half later and then at midnight we'll turn back into pumpkins. And it's my birthday that day so if anyone wants to buy me a drink please form an orderly queue after the show.") Things go less well for **Morrissey**, who was pelted by missiles last night while singing *Glamorous Glue* draped with a Union Jack. He fails to show, and Madness singer **Suggs** comments: "A fag paper blew on stage last night and nearly took one of his ears off."

Primal Scream

Boyz II Men's cool, high harmonies struck a popular chord as their single *End Of The Road* spent more than six months on the Hot 100, including 13 weeks at the top... Uncompromising British alt-rock pioneers, Primal Scream, fused funk with psychedelia for *Screamadelica* to scoop the inaugural Mercury Music Prize. Legendary producer George Martin presented them with the award.

15 **Boyz II Men**'s mournful ballad *End Of The Road* – featured in the Eddie Murphy movie "Boomerang" – in just its fifth week on the survey, hits US No. 1, where it will remain for a record 13 weeks (also hitting UK No. 1 in October). The Grammy-winning parent album ***Cooleyhighharmony***, is already the biggest-selling record by an R&B group in pop history, with US sales of four million confirmed in April. With its chart-busting single, it marks the beginning of an extremely fruitful relationship with producers **Babyface** and **L.A. Reid**, who are emerging as America's leading R&B songwriting/production team alongside **Jimmy Jam** and **Terry Lewis**. (The single also features a third writer, burgeoning composer/producer talent Daryll Simmons.) Babyface and Reid are enjoying a remarkable run: **TLC**'s *Baby-Baby-Baby*, released on the duo's own LaFace label (and once again penned and produced by the Reid/Babyface/Simmons trio), hits US No. 2 this week behind Boyz II Men. It is the second smash for spunky, all-girl, Atlanta-based R&B/pop threesome TLC, comprising **Tionne "T-Boz" Watkins**, **Rozonda "Chilli" Thomas**, and **Lisa "Left Eye" Lopes**. Their brassy debut album, naturally overseen by Babyface/Reid, ***Ooooooohhh... On The TLC Tip***, is on its way to four million-plus US sales. Babyface and Reid produced last year's hit album for **Whitney Houston**, and helped out on next month's ***Bobby*** release for her husband **Bobby Brown**. Their next project is overseeing the debut album by 23-year-old R&B newcomer **Toni Braxton**, who LaFace is currently introducing via her duet with Babyface on *Give You My Heart*, also featured on the label's triple-platinum ***Boomerang*** soundtrack.

September

8 Amid chaotic scenes, **Primal Scream** receive the Mercury Music Prize for ***Screamadelica*** from George Martin, at the inaugural dinner at London's Savoy Hotel. Uniquely pitching mainstream releases against more obscure fare, the prize is given to the "best contemporary album made by a British act." Melding acid-house dance grooves with late 1960s psychedelic rock, Primal Scream's seminal set will be hailed by **Q** magazine as the second best album released between 1986–2001.

9 After several years that have been dominated by a single video, no one wins more than three statuettes at the ninth MTV Video Music Awards. The **Red Hot Chili Peppers** win Breakthrough Video and Best Art Direction for "Give It Away," and the Viewers Choice award. **Van Halen** pick up three awards for "Right Now," including Video of the Year. Presenting the trophy, **Mick Jagger** thanks Woody Allen and Mia Farrow for "making our rock 'n' roll marriages seem so blissful." **Queen**'s **Brian May** and **Roger Taylor**, on hand to receive the Best Video from a Film for "Bohemian Rhapsody," give a check for $300,000 to Magic Johnson for the Magic Johnson Foundation for AIDS Research. **Pearl Jam** perform their breakthrough signature song, *Jeremy*, and **Michael Jackson**'s live performance of *Black And White* is broadcast via satellite from London's Wembley Stadium.

20 **Pearl Jam** give a free Drop in the Park concert at Magnuson Park in Seattle, Washington, with 20,000 tickets given away in two hours, and 3,000 Rock the Vote registrations collected. In a disturbing music industry trend, Epic has held back the US commercial release of the group's standout cut, *Jeremy*, to boost sales of its parent album, the career-defining ***Ten***, which hit US No. 2 on August 22, on its way to a phenomenal ten million-plus US sales tally. *Breath* and *State Of Love And Trust* are also featured on the current US No. 5-peaking ***Singles*** soundtrack, and the band appears in the Seattle-based Gen-X movie, as star Matt Dillon's backing band, Citizen Dick. Meanwhile, local label Stardog Records has recently released (via A&M) ***Temple Of The Dog***, a collaborative tribute album recorded two years ago by members of **Soundgarden** and Pearl Jam for **Andrew Wood**, the former lead singer of seminal grunge pioneers **Mother Love Bone**, who died following a heroin overdose in 1990. The album will hit US No. 5, earning a platinum disc.

22 Vice-President Dan Quayle blames **2Pac**'s ***2Pacalypse Now*** album for the fatal shooting of a Texas state trooper in Hempstead. The shooter, 19-year-old Ronald Ray Howard, had been listening to the album. Quayle says the record "has no place in our society." Fans of

Alt-rock quintet Pearl Jam swarmed both modern rock and adult rock FM radio, at the forefront, with Nirvana, of Seattle's grunge explosion.

Sinéad O'Connor on "Saturday Night Live"... Bob Dylan's 30th Anniversary...

Bob Dylan's anniversary concert

The Bodyguard

gangsta rap disagree. Briefly a member of seminal rap-funk combo **Digital Underground** last year, provocative 21-year-old rapper/actor 2Pac's debut solo set – released by über-producer Jimmy Iovine's new Interscope label – has already notched up glowing reviews and a gold disc in the US.

October

3 **Sinéad O'Connor** guests on "Saturday Night Live," singing *Success Has Made A Failure Of Our Home*, and a passionate a cappella version of **Bob Marley**'s *War*. At the end of the song she tears up a picture of the Pope and proclaims "Fight the real enemy" to a reaction of stunned audience silence. The gesture will cause uproar in the Catholic community and result in her receiving a lifetime ban from the program.

8 "Later With Jools Holland," a new weekly music television series featuring in-studio performances from diverse acts, hosted by the ex-**Squeeze** keyboardist, premieres on BBC2. On tonight's opener are **Paul Weller**, the **Christians**, **D-Influence**, and the **Neville Brothers**.

10 Having spent the summer touring the US on the Horizon Rock Developing Everywhere trek, with a trio of **Grateful Dead**-inspired bands – **Blues Traveler** (led by vocalist/harmonica player extraordinaire **John Popper**), jam-obsessed, neo-hippie quartet **Phish**, and rootsy southern rockers **Widespread Panic** – the **Spin Doctors** guest on "Saturday Night Live." The group's breakthrough performance spurs sales of its debut studio album, ***Pocket Full Of Kryptonite***. The four-piece rock combo was formed when **Chris Barron**, **Eric Schenkman**, and **Aaron Comess**, students at New York City's New School, came together and began rehearsing for a gig at a Columbia University fraternity house, with bassist **Mark White** the last to join. The group adopted its name during the 1988 Presidential election, at the suggestion of one of Schenkman's tutors. ***Kryptonite***, currently standing at US No. 38 after being certified gold ten days ago, is on its way to five million sales, spurred by the pop/blues-laced, *Little Miss Can't Be Wrong*.

10 With his prematurely released seasonal set, ***Beyond The Season***, already at US No. 2, **Garth Brooks**'s fifth album, ***The Chase***, debuts at US No. 1. It will be certified for five million US sales in just eight weeks. Brooks was recently quoted in a press release from rock legends **KISS**, saying, "My biggest influence through junior high was KISS. That was my thing." He is currently the biggest solo star in any genre in the US (though virtually unknown abroad), and appeared on the front cover of **Time** in March. He will shortly sign a 20-year deal with Liberty Records/Capitol.

15 **Madonna**'s Sex party is held at Manhattan's Industria Superstudio, for 800 guests, to promote her forthcoming album and book. The latter, also titled **Sex**, is a metal-covered collection of provocative auto-erotic photographs. It will reportedly sell 500,000 copies in its first week. Ever the media chameleon, Madonna arrives carrying a toy lamb and dressed as Little Bo Peep.

16 The **Bob Dylan** 30th Anniversary Concert Celebration, held at New York City's Madison Square Garden, features an all-star cast led off by **Booker T. & the MG's**, **Eric Clapton**, **George Harrison**, **Roger McGuinn**, **Tom Petty**, and **John Mellencamp**. Other performers include the **Band** (sans **Robbie Robertson**), **Johnny Cash** and **June Carter**, **Johnny Winter**, **Nanci Griffith** and **Carolyn Hester**, **Neil Young**, the **O'Jays**, **Pearl Jam**'s **Eddie Vedder** and **Mike McCready**, **Chrissie Hynde**, **Lou Reed**, **Ron Wood**, **Stevie Wonder**, **Richie Havens**, **Tracy Chapman**, **Willie Nelson**, and **Kris Kristofferson**. Scheduled to sing *I Believe In You*, **Sinéad O'Connor** is booed by the audience, so defiantly sings *War*, eventually exiting in tears. Dylan performs *My Back Pages*, backed by Clapton, Harrison, McGuinn, and Petty, and the entire ensemble close the show with *Knockin' On Heaven's Door*.

Johnny Cash described Bob Dylan as "our greatest American folk songwriter" at the 30th anniversary concert... The suggestion for Whitney Houston to record *I Will Always Love You* came from her "bodyguard", fellow actor Kevin Costner.

25 *King Of The Road* hitmaker **Roger Miller** dies of throat cancer in Century City Hospital, Los Angeles, California. After serving in Korea, Miller tried his luck in Nashville, Tennessee, where he worked as a bellhop before becoming a songwriter – subsequently penning over 800 compositions. He won 11 Grammy awards in 1965 and 1966, and "Big River," an adaptation of **The Adventures of Huckleberry Finn** and his first attempt at a musical, won seven Tony awards in 1986. Miller hits the road at 56.

30 **George Michael**'s lawyer Tony Russell files a High Court writ, claiming that the singer's deal with Sony Entertainment (the parent of Epic Records) is weighted heavily in favor of Sony, and effectively amounts to restraint of trade. Disputing both the creative and marketing abilities of Epic, Russell claims that Michael is not bound by his contract and owns his masters, beginning a lengthy court case between artist and label. Next month, Michael will issue the following

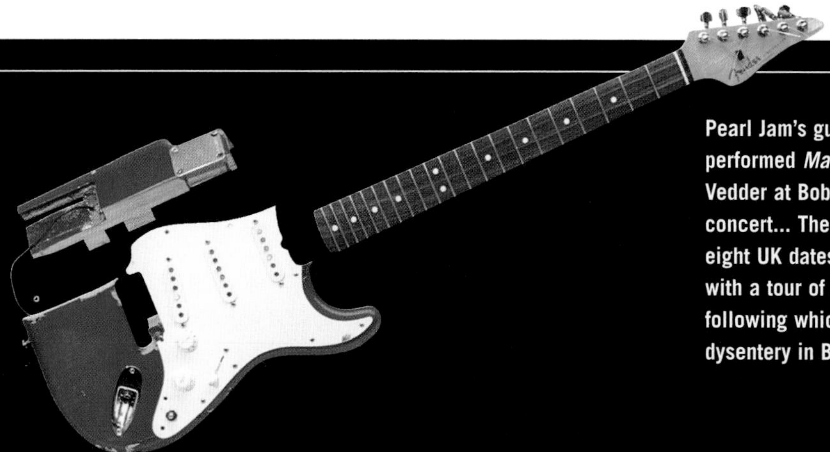

Pearl Jam's guitarist Mike McCready performed *Masters Of War* with Eddie Vedder at Bob Dylan's 30th anniversary concert... The Red Hot Chili Peppers played eight UK dates in March and ended the year with a tour of Australia and New Zealand, following which Anthony Kiedis contracted dysentery in Borneo.

Spunky British pop quintet Take That spearheaded a new "boy band" cycle in Europe, which continued with Boyzone and Westlife.

statement: "Since Sony Corporation bought my contract, along with everything and everyone else at CBS, I have seen the great American company that I proudly signed to as a teenager become a small part of the production line for a giant electronics corporation which, quite frankly, has no understanding of the creative process. Sony appears to see artists as little more than software."

25 "The Bodyguard," in which **Whitney Houston** makes her major motion-picture debut opposite Kevin Costner (who personally campaigned to have her co-star), opens nationwide in the US – to poor reviews but sensational box-office returns. The movie was written some 20 years ago by Lawrence Kasdan, with Ryan O'Neal and **Diana Ross** in mind. The extracted single, *I Will Always Love You*, is a decade-old song written by **Dolly Parton**. Recorded at the suggestion of Costner, and produced by David Foster, it begins a record-breaking 14-week stay at US No. 1 this week, and a ten-week run at UK No. 1 next week. Next month, SoundScan will report one-week US sales of the single at 399,000, topping **Bryan Adams**'s 392,000 last year. ***The Bodyguard*** will top the US survey on December 12. It contains other Whitney cuts, plus a **Kenny G & Aaron Neville** duet, and songs by **Lisa Stansfield**, **Joe Cocker**, and others.

"Being a Beatle was no hindrance on my career."

George Harrison, December 9, 1992

November

13 **Sting** receives an honorary doctorate of music from the University of Northumbria in Newcastle-upon-Tyne, England, from Vice Chancellor Lord Glenamara in recognition of his contribution to the arts and his campaigning on ecological issues.

15 Billed as his last-ever live performance, **Ozzy Osbourne**'s final US date on his current tour, at the Pacific Amphitheater in Costa Mesa, California, ends with an original **Black Sabbath** reunion (the first of many). The 30-minute Sabbath set features Osbourne, **Tommy Iommi**, **Geezer Butler**, and drummer **Vinny Appice**. Earlier today, Ozzy was honored with a star on the Rock Walk on Hollywood's Sunset Boulevard. (Talking of retirement, Osbourne will subsequently say: "Who wants to be touring at 46? I screwed all the groupies when it was safe... It's time to go home.")

December

6 With their debut album ***Take That And Party*** having debuted at its initial UK No. 5 peak in September, rising British boy-band **Take That** nab seven trophies at the **Smash Hits** Readers Poll Party Awards, held at London's Olympia, at which the group also performs. The telegenic, all-vocal quintet was hand-picked last year by its manager Nigel Martin-Smith, who was determined to assemble a teen-based dance/pop quintet in the mold of **New Kids On The Block**. The five plucky singers chosen were all Manchester-based: ex-**Cutest Rush** member **Gary Barlow**, the group's main songwriter, with producer Ray Hedges, and featured vocalist; cheeky ex-double-glazing salesman **Robbie Williams**; former bank clerk **Mark Owen**; ex-car mechanic **Howard Donald**; and **Jason Orange**, formerly a member of a break-dancing act **Street Beat**.

9 **Tom Petty** presents **Billboard**'s first Century Award to **George Harrison** at the third **Billboard** Music Awards, held at the Universal Amphitheater in Universal City, California.

11 At a concert at London's Kilburn National, the **Manic Street Preachers**' bassist **Nicky Wire** – who this year has attacked a Japanese cameraman, and sent a security guard to hospital after whacking him with his bass – tells the audience that he "hopes **Michael Stipe** goes the same way as **Freddie Mercury** pretty soon."

ROOTS **During this year: Geoff Barrow and Beth Gibbons, having met while both on the government-run Enterprise Allowance job creation program, are invited to spend time with Neneh Cherry and husband Cameron McVey in their home-based studio... both returning to their native Seattle, after graduating from East Coast universities, Chris Ballew and Dave Dederer form their first band, Go!... Gavin Rossdale forms Bush with three painters – Nigel Pulsford, Dave Parsons, and Robin Goodridge; they play their first gig together in an outdoor parking lot... David Gray records his first album, *A Century Ends*, to universal disregard... Joan Osborne releases her debut album, *Soul Show*, on the Womanly Hips label... soul/folk singer-songwriter/guitarist Ben Harper is snapped up by Virgin Records... M People, a solo production project put together by Mike Pickering with various guest vocalists and musicians, release their debut album *Northern Soul*... singer-songwriter Duncan Sheik graduates in Semiotics from Brown University in Rhode Island; during his time there, he teamed with singer/songwriter Lisa Loeb as the duo Liz & Liza... Maxwell, having already recorded several demos, begins playing the New York club scene... and Morphine, led by Mark Sandman, release their first album, *Good*, on the indie label Accurate...**

Livin' On The Edge

1993

No.1 US SINGLES

Jan 2 I Will Always Love You **Whitney Houston**
Mar 6 A Whole New World (Aladdin's Theme) **Peabo Bryson & Regina Belle**
Mar 13 Informer **Snow**
May 1 Freak Me **Silk**
May 15 That's The Way Love Goes **Janet Jackson**
July 10 Weak **SWV (Sisters With Voices)**
July 24 Can't Help Falling In Love **UB40**
Sept 11 Dreamlover **Mariah Carey**
Nov 6 I'd Do Anything For Love (But I Won't Do That) **Meat Loaf**
Dec 11 Again **Janet Jackson**
Dec 25 Hero **Mariah Carey**

No.1 UK SINGLES

Jan 2 I Will Always Love You **Whitney Houston**
Feb 13 No Limit **2 Unlimited**
Mar 20 Oh Carolina **Shaggy**
Apr 3 Young At Heart **Bluebells**
May 1 Five Live (EP) **George Michael & Queen with Lisa Stansfield**
May 22 All That She Wants **Ace of Base**
June 12 (I Can't Help) Falling In Love With You **UB40**
June 26 Dreams **Gabrielle**
July 17 Pray **Take That**
Aug 14 Living On My Own **Freddie Mercury**
Aug 28 Mr. Vain **Culture Beat**
Sept 25 Boom! Shake The Room **Jazzy Jeff & the Fresh Prince**
Oct 9 Relight My Fire **Take That featuring Lulu**
Oct 23 I'd Do Anything For Love (But I Won't Do That) **Meat Loaf**
Dec 11 Mr. Blobby **Mr. Blobby**
Dec 18 Babe **Take That**

Radiohead

Beck

Radiohead began 1993 on the road with their month-long Anyone Can Play Guitar UK tour, but come summer they found themselves the darlings of the US college scene... Beck hopped on a Greyhound bus bound for New York when he was 18, citing Los Angeles as a "cultural void."

Despite diverse musical offerings, it was not a happy year. Allegations arose about **Michael Jackson**'s propensity for sharing his bedroom with young boys, **Kurt Cobain** suffered several drug overdoses, rap music lurched toward gang violence, and censorship reared its ugly head. While the King of Pop saw his career derailed, the Queen of Pop was indisputably **Whitney Houston**, whose extraordinary vocals were rarely put to better effect than on her cover of **Dolly Parton**'s *I Will Always Love You*. The reward was a record-breaking 14-week run at US No. 1, as well as pole position everywhere from Austria to Australia. The same success greeted ***The Bodyguard***, the soundtrack to her debut movie.

Nirvana were the shooting stars of 1990s alt-rock. The third and final studio album of their short but explosive career, ***In Utero***, was both abrasive and melancholy. This was unfiltered, raw, and deeply emotional music – reflecting the state of mind of Kurt Cobain.

Dr. Dre changed the face of rap with his debut album ***The Chronic***, featuring protégé **Snoop Doggy Dog**. Dr. Dre's hard urban gangsta themes put the West Coast on the rap map, and blew speakers far into the white suburbs, even though the subject matter was strictly from the 'hood. Released on Dre's Death Row Records (formed with the notorious **"Suge" Knight**), the album introduced West Coast rappers like **Nate Dogg**, **Tha Dogg Pound**, and **Warren G**. Snoop followed with his own ***Doggystyle***, featuring the same G-funk production style and his own inimitable stoned-gangsta charisma. Adding to the growing rap stable, **Arrested Development**'s hybrid of roots and rap picked up two Grammys. But rap was bedeviled by guns and drugs, with **Tupac Shakur** and **Public Enemy**'s **Flavor Flav** both facing serious criminal charges.

Soon to become one of the most influential bands of the decade, and ranging across a variety of styles, **Radiohead** released their debut album ***Pablo Honey***. Another standard-bearer of alt-rock, **Beck**, was also about to break through, thanks to the more imaginative radio stations on the West Coast playing *Loser*. Alternative to the point of being avant-garde, ex-**Sugarcube** and Icelandic pixie **Björk** was also finding favor with her debut album in Britain.

Sting reconfirmed his status as a leading songwriter with the release of ***Ten Summoner's Tales*** – a magnificently produced set of ballads, gentle rock, and jazz-tinged pop, with more hooks than a well-equipped cloakroom. His long tour in support of the album included appearances with the **Grateful Dead** – a combination almost as strange as Whitney Houston and Kevin Costner. **Eric Clapton** showed his remarkable staying power, nabbing six Grammy trophies for 1992's ***Unplugged*** classic.

"Onstage, Nirvana is unstoppable."

The New York Times, July 26, 1993

Jan 1993

Stevie Wonder ends his Arizona boycott... Michael Jackson on "Oprah"...

Fleetwood Mac reformed for the 52nd Presidential Gala in January after Bill Clinton had used *Don't Stop* as his theme tune during campaigning.

January

2 **Elton John** breaks **Elvis Presley**'s record for the most consecutive years (23) with a Top 40 hit on the US Hot 100: *The Last Song* is at No. 24.

12 Momentarily overcoming the lingering bitterness between **Ginger Baker** and his former colleagues, **Eric Clapton** and **Jack Bruce**, **Cream** reunite for the first time in nearly 25 years to perform at the eighth Rock and Roll Hall of Fame awards dinner, where they are inducted by **ZZ Top**. After **Creedence Clearwater Revival** have been inducted by **Bruce Springsteen**, **John Fogerty** refuses to allow **Doug Clifford** or **Stu Cook** on stage for his ceremony-ending jam of Creedence hits. Inducting the **Doors**, **Pearl Jam**'s **Eddie Vedder** – now compared to **Jim Morrison** himself, and asked to perform with the remaining members – states, "I figured it was either me or William Shatner." **Stevie Wonder** inducts **Frankie Lymon & the Teenagers**, and **Sly & the Family Stone** receive their honor from **George Clinton**. The elusive and enigmatic **Van Morrison** fails to show, becoming the first living inductee to miss the event. The honor is accepted on his behalf by **Robbie Robertson**. Giants in the soul/R&B blues/jazz genres – **Ruth Brown**, **Etta James**, and Early Influence **Dinah Washington** – rightfully take their place in the Hall.

> **"A lot of people don't agree with some of the things I say, but hell, you can only live once... at a time anyway."** Neil Young, **Q**, January 1993

Led by the hat-loving Jason Kay, Jamiroquai's particular brand of British acid-jazz fusion peaked in 1997, with the award-winning single *Virtual Insanity*.

13 **Jamiroquai** play a sellout showcase date at the Town & Country in Leeds, England. The London-based band is led by 22-year-old singer **Jason Kay**, whose trademark is a large furry hat, described by **The Independent**'s Ben Thompson as "two bearskins caught in the act of reproduction." The son of 1970s nightclub jazz singer, Karen Kay, he bought a synthesizer and recorded solo demos in the late 1980s, taking one track, *When You Gonna Learn?* to the London-based R&B radio station, KISS FM. It played the cut, and also brought it to the attention of the Acid Jazz indie label. Interested in pioneering an acid-jazz fusion, combining soul, jazz, hip-hop, funk, and pop, Kay has assembled an initially fluid aggregation of young, like-minded musicians for his Jamiroquai collective (the name is taken from the Native American Iroquois tribe). On the strength of the one single, Kay recently signed a publishing deal, and a lucrative eight-album recording contract, with Sony Music's Soho Square label.

14 **Radiohead** play a low-key free gig at the University of London Union, prompting **Melody Maker** to write: "To watch Radiohead perform in 1993 is to watch a rare and magical thing." Their critically lauded debut album, ***Pablo Honey***, will be released next month.

15 **Stevie Wonder** ends his boycott of Arizona, appearing at a rally and performing before 17,000 people at the America West Arena in Phoenix, to mark the state's first official observance of the Martin Luther King Jr. holiday on January 18.

19 An American Reunion: The 52nd Presidential Gala, an inaugural concert to honor President-elect Bill Clinton, takes place at the Capital Center, Landover, Maryland. **Michael Jackson** performs *Gone Too Soon*, a tribute to Ryan White, and *Heal The World*. **Aretha Franklin** sings *I Have A Dream*, **Judy Collins** contributes her signature tune, *Amazing Grace*, and **Michael Bolton** – the son of a Democrat Party official – sings *Lean On Me*. Rock 'n' roll legends **Chuck Berry** and **Little Richard** perform *Reelin' & Rockin'* and *Good Golly Miss Molly* with an all-star band comprising **Stephen Stills**, **David Pack**, **Max Weinberg**, **Nathan East**, **Greg Phillinganes**, and **Ingrid Berry**. In a much-ballyhooed return, **Fleetwood Mac** reform their most popular line-up, of mainstay **Mick Fleetwood**, **Lindsey Buckingham**, the **McVies**, and **Stevie Nicks**, for a one-off performance of *Don't Stop*, which Clinton had used as his theme tune while campaigning.

28 Geffen Records files a breach-of-contract suit against **Don Henley** in the Los Angeles Superior Court, seeking at least $30 million in damages and an injunction barring him from recording for another label. Geffen claims that he has failed to deliver the number of albums agreed under the terms of his 1988 renegotiated contract. Henley is becoming an increasingly outspoken guardian of artists' rights in the face of corporate bullying.

February

5 Reunited for the occasion with **Ron Wood**, **Rod Stewart** tapes "MTV Unplugged" at California's Universal Studios, to be broadcast on May 5. He includes an emotional reading of **Van Morrison**'s ballad *Have I Told You Lately* – which will become his first gold US hit in 15 years. The resultant ***Unplugged... And Seated*** will sell over five million copies worldwide.

6 During a **Van Morrison** gig at The Point in Dublin, Ireland, the mercurial Irishman is joined on *It's All Over Now Baby Blue* by **Bono**, **Bob Dylan** (providing harmonica to his own song), **Elvis Costello**, **Steve Winwood**, **Chrissie Hynde**, and **Kris Kristofferson**. Bono also helps out on a medley of *Gloria* and *Shakin' All Over*.

DR. DRE

Feb 13 ***The Chronic*** **– the debut album by ex-N.W.A. member/producer, Dr. Dre – hits US No. 3. (Its title is slang for marijuana.) It is hailed as redefining the rap genre, with Dre's tight, innovative production techniques, clever archival sample choices, hedonistic urban gangsta themes, and the dope-strained rapping by his protégé: ex-convict and Crips gang member, 21-year-old Calvin Broadus, aka Snoop Doggy Dogg. The album is released on Dre's own Death Row Records (co-founded with Suge Knight), which he wants to be "the Motown of the '90s." Over the next few years (until the label's controversial collapse in 1996), Dre's "G-Funk" production style will hallmark a succession of multiplatinum rap releases, by the likes of Dogg (including this year's US No. 1** ***Doggystyle*** **debut), BLACKstreet, Tha Dogg Pound, and Warren G (Dre's stepbrother).** ***The Chronic*** **will reach triple-platinum status in the US by November.**

10 **Michael Jackson** conducts his first television interview in 14 years on a special edition of "Oprah Winfrey," broadcast live from his Neverland Valley Ranch in California's Santa Ynez Valley. During the candid conversation, Jackson admits to "cry[ing] through loneliness at age eight. I didn't have any friends growing up. I'd wash my face in the dark and my father would tease me. He was very strict." On the subject of his much-changed skin color, he states: "I have a skin disorder which destroys the pigment of my skin. It's in my family. We're trying to control it. I am a black American." Asked about his notorious crotch-grabbing, he responds: "I'm a slave to the rhythm." On his personal life, Jackson says that he is dating Brooke Shields, and that "I have been in love two times." When probed on the question of virginity, he quietly responds: "I'm a gentleman. Call me old-fashioned." At the end of the interview, which has taken place in his house, funfair, and private movie theater (in which he has erected beds in private booths so that terminally sick kids can watch films), he introduces the world premiere of *Give In To Me*, in a concert video clip featuring **Slash**.

15 Reacting to news that he will receive a Lifetime Achievement Award at a dinner the night before the Grammys and not at the ceremony itself, an angry **Little Richard** says, "This is the crowning achievement of my career and they want to give it to me secretly. It's like I'm in the kitchen doing all the cooking and the waiters get all the credit. I cried [when I heard] – I've been waiting so long." NARAS president, Michael Greene, replies: "Everybody is always mad at us. We have over 400 nominees and just X amount of real estate."

16 The BRIT Awards come of age, with a ceremony – staged for the first time at London's cavernous Alexandra Palace – that sees **Peter Gabriel**, **Prince**, **Nirvana**, **R.E.M.**, **Simply Red**, and **Annie Lennox** among the winners. Lennox wins her fifth and sixth BRITs – for Best British Female Solo Artist and Best British Album for ***Diva***. Simply Red – with ***Stars'*** worldwide sales currently standing at eight million – pick up the award for Best British Group, and their lead singer, **Mick Hucknall**, wins Best British Male Solo Artist. Up-and-comers **Take That** are presented with the award for Best British Single, for *Could It Be Magic*. One-time **Steam Packet** colleague **Long John Baldry** presents **Rod Stewart** with the award for Outstanding Contribution. Stewart reunites with the **Faces** (minus **Ronnie Lane**, whom he fails to thank in his acceptance speech), and **Rolling Stone Bill Wyman** on bass for a one-off performance, singing *Ruby Tuesday* and *Stay With Me*.

20 Confirming **Buddy Holly**'s timeless appeal – all the more extraordinary given the brief two-year timespan of his original hit chapter in the late 1950s – yet another UK retrospective collection, ***Words Of Love***, bows at UK No. 1. Holly has now hit the Top 10 of the UK album chart in each decade.

24 **Peter Gabriel** opens the 35th Grammy proceedings at the Shrine Auditorium, Los Angeles, with a performance of *Steam* featuring the Cirque du Soleil, and later takes home the Best Short Form Video trophy for "Digging In The Dirt." His compatriot, **Eric Clapton** – interrupting his latest string of London concerts – collects six trophies: Record of the Year for *Tears In Heaven* (which he also performs), Song of the Year (with co-writer

Following the release of their debut album ***Walthamstow*** **(reviewed by Vox as "lad-pop"), East 17 attended a reception at Walthamstow Town Hall in the presence of the Mayoress of Waltham Forest and 3,000 screaming girl fans.**

I Will Always Love You... Ace of Base... Prince celebrates symbolic birthday...

With two US No. 1 hit singles and four UK No. 1s, Shaggy has had more chart-toppers than any other Caribbean artist... Ace of Base's Jonas Berggren formed a band with equipment acquired through a Swedish government program subsidizing would-be musicians.

Shaggy

Will Jennings), and Best Pop Vocal, Male; Album of the Year and Best Rock Album, Male, for ***Unplugged***, and Best Rock Song for extract *Layla*. Accepting his final award for Record of the Year from **Tina Turner**, Clapton says: "There are a lot of people I would like to thank, but most of all I want to thank my son, for his love and for this song." As ***Dangerous*** continues its climb back up the US chart (hitting No. 10 next week), **Michael Jackson** continues his current unexpected rush of participatory media promotion, and receives the Grammy Legend Award from his sister **Janet**, who delivers an interminable eulogy. Beginning his longest-ever acceptance speech, he says: "In the last few weeks I've gone from 'Where is he?' to 'Here he is again.'" Newcomers **Arrested Development**, increasingly revered for their roots/rap hybrid, collect the Best New Artist and Best Rap Duo or Group trophies from presenters **LL Cool J** and basketball star Magic Johnson. **L.A. Reid** and **Babyface** share the Producer of the Year award with U2 helmers, **Daniel Lanois** and **Brian Eno**. NARAS President Michael Greene, who told **Little Richard** that there would not be time in the live telecast for him to thank his peers for his Lifetime Achievement Award, makes a rambling ten-minute speech. In a musical melange, awards also go to **Dr. John**, **Linda Ronstadt**, **Melissa Etheridge**, **Tom Waits** (his first), **Stevie Ray Vaughan** (his brother **Jimmie** collecting), **Alison Krauss**, dancehall reggae pioneer **Shabba Ranks**, **Enya**, **Nine Inch Nails**, the **Chieftains**, and **U2**. The **Red Hot Chili Peppers**, winners of the Best Hard Rock Song trophy for *Give It Away*, perform it with **George Clinton's P-Funk All-Stars**. **Natalie Cole** and **Tony Bennett** perform *The Lady Is A Tramp*.

27 In its 14th week at US No. 1, **Whitney Houston**'s *I Will Always Love You* becomes the longest-ever US chart-topper, taking over from **Boyz II Men**'s 1992 hit, *End Of The Road* (which falls off the survey this week after a 32-week run). Already certified quadruple platinum, with four million US sales, the disc is also the second biggest-selling US single of all time, behind **USA For Africa**'s *We Are The World*. *I Will Always Love You* is also still No. 1 in Austria, Australia, Belgium, Canada, Denmark, Germany, Holland, Norway, Sweden, and Switzerland, and has spent ten weeks topping the UK survey. Meanwhile, ***The Bodyguard*** continues its stranglehold at US No. 1 for the 12th straight week (also topping the UK compilation album chart), having sold over seven million copies in the US (it will eventually spend 20 weeks at the top).

"The definition of music my grandmother told me was anything pleasing to the ear... If I hear something that's pleasing to the ear then it's music, that's all I need to know."

Willie Nelson, **New Musical Express**, May 15, 1993

March

2 Scheduled to appear tomorrow on NBC-TV's "The Tonight Show," 27-year-old Jamaican reggae star **Shabba Ranks** is axed from the program, following complaints by GLAAD (Gay and Lesbian Alliance Against Defamation) over his latest comments on homosexuality. He comments: "Everybody has their own beliefs in life. If they say Shabba is anti-gay, that's their belief. If they say Shabba is gay, that's their belief. Each to his own." Ranks caused controversy last December, when he remarked on the UK's Channel 4's "The Word" that "Gays deserve crucifixion."

3 After a return appearance on "Saturday Night Live" last month, and playing three shows last week supporting the **Grateful Dead**, as warm-up dates for his world tour – he says: "I want to see this Deadhead phenomenon. I want to see it first-hand" – **Sting** hosts his annual Rainforest benefit concert at New York's Carnegie Hall. The guests, **Don Henley**, **Bryan Adams**, **George Michael**, **James Taylor**, **Tom Jones**, and **Tina Turner**, close the show with an ensemble version of *River Deep, Mountain High*. Sting's fourth album, ***Ten Summoner's Tales***, will be released in two weeks, set to hit US and UK No. 2; it will mark the greatly respected singer-songwriter's solo commercial peak. Once again co-produced with regular helmsman Hugh Padgham, it effortlessly combines his alternately sophisticated offbeat, jazz-laced stylings with moments of pure, literate, pop/rock sweetness. It includes the global smash, *If I Ever Lose My Faith In You*, and the stunning, timeless ballad highlight, *Fields Of Gold*. Sting remains universally popular with critics and fans, young and old, black and white.

20 Jamaican-born, Brooklyn-based dancehall reggae singer Orville Burrell – going by the name **Shaggy** – performs this

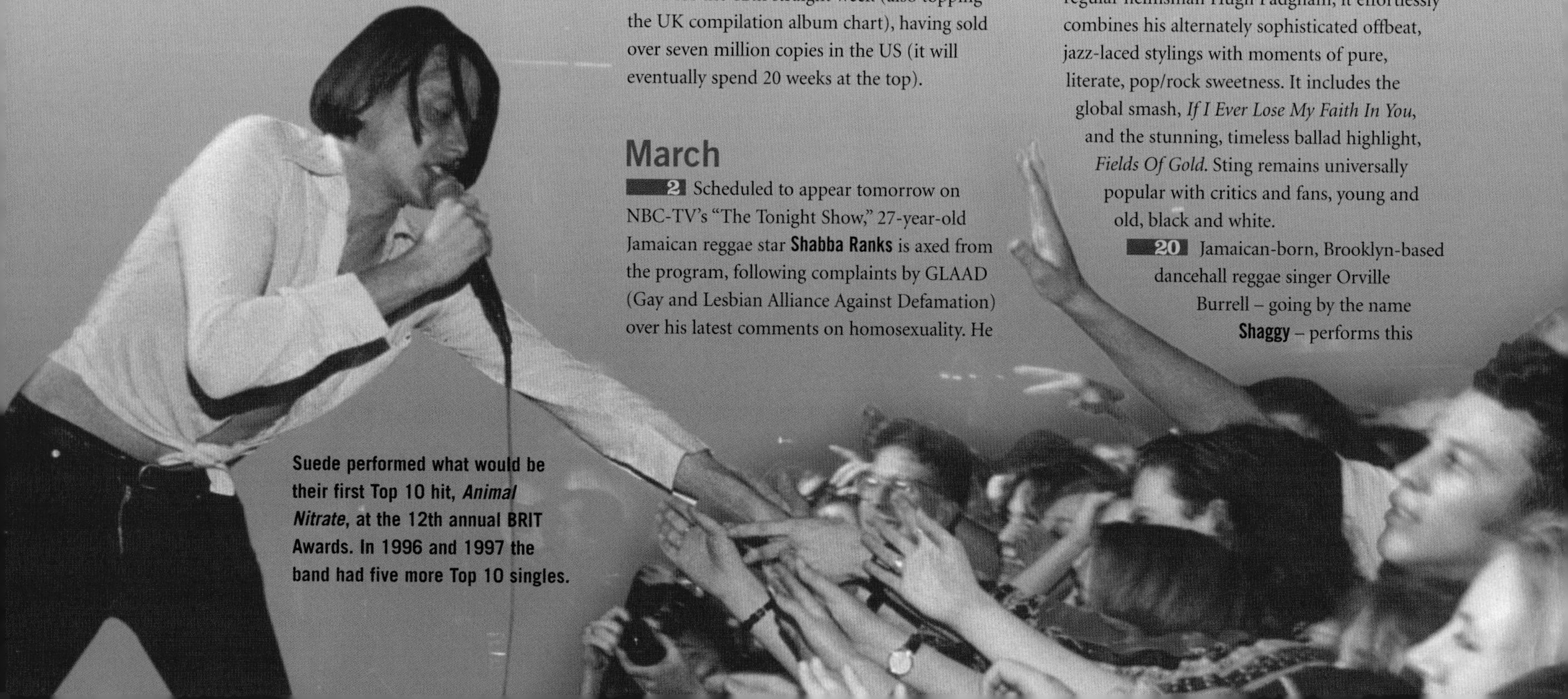

Suede performed what would be their first Top 10 hit, *Animal Nitrate*, at the 12th annual BRIT Awards. In 1996 and 1997 the band had five more Top 10 singles.

Ace of Base

On his 35th birthday, Prince announced he was changing his name to ♱, leaving the media to refer to him as the Artist Formerly Known As Prince.

week's chart-topper, *Oh Carolina*, on "Top Of The Pops." Signed to Virgin, Shaggy recorded the single – his clever cover of the 1960s reggae original by the **Folkes Brothers** – while still serving in the US Army at Camp Le Jeune, North Carolina. He is determined not to become a one-hit wonder (as the novelty hit suggests he might), and will score a major breakthrough in the US in 1995 with the platinum-selling *Boombastic*.

27 **Suede** begin a tour of the UK and Ireland at the Tivoli Club in Dublin, Ireland, in support of their glam-rock-inspired debut album ***Suede***, to be released next week. Lyrically directed by lead singer **Brett Anderson**'s writing, it will enter the UK chart at No. 1, achieving the biggest one-week sales by a debut act since **Frankie Goes To Hollywood**'s ***Welcome To The Pleasuredome***.

April

9 **Nirvana** play their first gig since the Hollywood Rock Festival in Rio de Janeiro in January – at San Francisco's Cow Palace, in aid of the Tresnjevka Women's Group in Zagreb, Croatia. They are joined by a trio of alt-rock acts: **L7**, the **Breeders**, and the **Disposable Heroes of Hiphoprisy**. The benefit was instigated by **Krist Novoselic** (whose parents are Croatian emigrés): "I was really pissed off by everything I'd been reading and nobody was doing anything about it."

29 **Mick Ronson**, the one-time **Mott the Hoople** guitarist and long-time associate of **David Bowie**, dies of liver cancer in London at the age of 46. Bowie issues a short statement: "I miss him terribly," and Leppard's **Joe Elliott** says, "If there's a God up there why does he do this? It can only be because he's trying to put together the ultimate band."

30 **Orchestral Manœuvres' Andy McCluskey**, underrated singer-songwriter **Kirsty MacColl**, **World Party**, **Richard Thompson**, and **Tim Finn** perform at Virgin Radio's launch-day bash, at London's Piccadilly Theatre. Richard Branson's latest enterprise, devoted to giving its audience "classic album tracks and today's best music," launches at 12:15 pm at the Virgin Megastore in Manchester. The first record is **INXS**' specially recorded *Born To Be Wild*, and the second is the **Cure**'s version of *Purple Haze*, although DJ Richard Skinner announces it as *Hey Joe*.

May

9 A police report states that **Nirvana**'s **Kurt Cobain** injected himself with $30–40 worth of heroin, and that his wife, **Courtney Love**, injected him with buprenorphine at a party. He is taken to Seattle, Washington's Harborview Medical Center, before voluntarily checking into a California rehab facility. Love is still trying to achieve success with her all-female band, **Hole**.

22 Already a chart-topper in Germany, **Ace of Base**'s *All That She Wants*, an instantly infectious pop-reggae smash, hits UK No. 1. Sub-licensed by Danish label Mega Records, which reportedly signed the group to London Records for a down-payment of £2,900 ($4,350), it is featured on their upcoming debut album (released only in Europe), ***Happy Nation***.

31 Attending a gig at the King Tut's Wah Wah Club in Glasgow, Scotland, to see **18 Wheeler**, Creation Records boss Alan McGee is impressed by the five-song performance by **Oasis**. He immediately offers to sign the band, convinced he has found a hybrid of the **Sex Pistols** and the **Beatles**. (The band, who were not officially asked to perform, reportedly threatened to trash the club if not offered a chance to play.)

June

2 Polygram Holding Inc., Island's parent company, announces it is signing **U2** to a new longterm deal. The New York Post reports it is worth $200 million, although it is believed to be more like $50 million.

6 The stage version of **Pete Townshend**'s "Tommy" wins five Tonys at the annual

Beck's *Loser*...
Björk's solo debut...
Pearl Jam win big at the MTV Awards...

theatrical awards ceremony in New York City, picking up honors in the Direction of a Musical, Scenic Design, Lighting Design, Choreography and Best Score categories. The adaptation originated at La Jolla Playhouse, before transferring to Broadway. It will close in June 1995, after a run of 899 performances.

7 **Chuck Berry**, the **Coasters**' **Carl Gardner**, the **Drifters**' **Bill Pinkney**, **Sam & Dave**'s **Sam Moore**, **Pete Townshend**, and **Billy Joel** are among many rock celebrities present at the ground-breaking ceremony of the Rock and Roll Hall of Fame and Museum in Cleveland, Ohio.

12 Having racked up 36 UK chart hits, **UB40** score their third UK No. 1 with *Can't Help Falling In Love*, a cover of the **Elvis Presley** classic (the others were also cover versions: *Red Red Wine* and *I Got You Babe*). The single is featured in the Sharon Stone/William Baldwin movie, "Sliver." ***The Best Of UB40 Volume 1*** went over the million mark in the UK in March, and the single will top the US chart on July 24.

13 **Neil** and **Tim Finn** receive OBEs for their contribution to New Zealand music.

July

12 On his "Morning Becomes Eclectic" show, Chris Douridas, music director at Los Angeles public radio station KCRW, plays a 12in vinyl single from 23-year-old alt-rock/folk newcomer **Beck**, delivered to the station by Bong Load Records. The single, *Loser*, consisting of a sample of **Dr. John**'s *I Walk On Gilded Splinters* and the lyric, "I'm a loser, baby, so why don't you kill me," will soon get play on Seattle's KNDD and Los Angeles' KROQ. Within weeks, the singer-songwriter's club shows around town will become standing-room-only affairs, and a bidding war will break out between Capitol,

Rage Against The Machine, led by singer Zach de la Rocha and founding guitarist Tom Morello, were formed in 1991.

BJÖRK

Aug 19 **Björk makes her solo debut at the Kentish Town Forum in London, promoting her *Debut* album, which peaked at No. 3 on July 17. The Guardian writes that the Icelandic artist's performance "deserves every superlative in the thesaurus." Signed to One Little Indian in the UK, and Elektra in the US, the singer-songwriter's avant-garde album is produced by Nellee Hooper. Intent on a solo career, Björk disbanded adventurous alt-rock combo the Sugarcubes last September and relocated to London.**

Björk scored a native hit as an 11-year-old child-prodigy pop singer with her version of Tina Charles's 1976 hit *I Love To Love*.

Depeche Mode embarked on the US leg of their world tour in September. Under the guidance of producer Flood, their hard-edged rock-fueled, *Songs Of Faith And Devotion*, penned as ever by Martin Gore and led by Dave Gahan's distinctive vocal style, entered both the UK and US album charts at No. 1 in April.

Geffen, and Warner Bros. Records, among others. Beck will sign to Geffen's DGC imprint after a personal intervention by David Geffen.

18 Appearing completely nude at a Lollapalooza gig in Philadelphia, Pennsylvania, **Rage Against the Machine** refuse to play a note, and spend 25 minutes in silent protest: they wear duct tape across their mouths and the initials P-M-R-C (for Parents' Music Resource Center, the pro-censorship pressure group) scrawled across their chests – one letter on each chest. The confrontational West Coast-based quartet was eagerly snapped up by Epic Records (after rejecting overtures from, among others, **Madonna**'s Maverick label) on the strength of raucous early live shows and 5,000 12-cut cassette tapes sold at gigs. Their venomous and uncompromising debut album, ***Rage Against The Machine***, spurred by glowing reviews from the alternative music media, has already broken through in the UK, hitting No. 17 in March. One of the first popular albums to combine hardcore heavy metal with funk and rap, it entered the US chart on May 1, but will take nearly a year to peak.

August

3 During current US dates, the **Stone Temple Pilots** – an aggressive modern-rock quartet fronted by 25-year-old singer **Scott Weiland** – play the first of two sellout gigs at New York City's Roseland Ballroom, in the guise of their teen heroes, **KISS**. Their 1970s rock-influenced debut album, ***Core***, produced by Brendan O'Brien and released a year ago, finally hit US No. 3 last month.

7 **Cypress Hill**'s ***Black Sunday*** tops the US album chart. The hardcore Latino trio, led by Cuban-born rapper **Sen Dog** (Senen Reyes), complemented by **B-Real** and House of Pain producer/DJ **Muggs**, signed to pioneering rap label, Ruffhouse, in 1991. They are finding multiplatinum success with their unique stoned-funk hip-hop (frequently laced with a pro-marijuana message).

11 On the first of four nights at London's Wembley Stadium during **U2**'s continuing Zooropa world tour, controversial author Salman Rushdie – whose whereabouts have been unknown since the Ayatollah Khomeini imposed a *fatwa* on him – wanders onstage and says to **Bono** (who is in his Macphisto persona): "I'm not afraid of men who wear horns. I know who the real devils are." When Rushdie told his son of his plans to make the appearance, the 14-year-old said: "Just don't sing, Dad. If you sing, I'll have to kill myself."

24 One day after the Los Angeles Police Department announced that **Michael Jackson** is under criminal investigation, confidential documents leaked from the Los Angeles County Department of Children's Services reveal that Dr. Evan Chandler, a Beverly Hills dentist, claims that his 13-year-old son has been sexually abused by Jackson. Jackson's private investigator, Anthony Pellicano, will state that Chandler has tried to extort $20 million from the singer and, having failed to do so, has made the accusation.

25 Philip Woldemariam, a 20-year-old Ethiopian immigrant, and a member of the By Yerself Hustlers gang, is shot dead by **Snoop Doggy Dogg**'s bodyguard, McKinley Lee, in front of Snoop's new home in Woodbine Park, Los Angeles. Already on $10,000 bail for a gun possession charge, Snoop will be charged as an accessory to murder. He will hand himself in to police after appearing at the MTV Awards show of September 2, with bail set at $1 million.

September

2 **Pearl Jam**'s "Jeremy" wins four moonmen: Best Video of the Year, Best Group Video, Best Metal Hard Rock Video, and Best Director, at the tenth MTV Awards, at which the band perform *Rockin' In The Free World* with **Neil Young** (who they regard as their grunge mentor). Sassy R&B ***Funky Divas*** quartet **En Vogue** wins the Best R&B Video, Best Dance Video, and Best Choreography categories for "Free Your Mind." **Arrested Development** win Best Rap Video (for "People Everyday") for the second year running. **Lenny Kravitz** and **k.d. lang** win the Best Male ("Are You Gonna Go My Way") and Best Female ("Constant Craving") Video categories. **Madonna** opens the show with *Bye Bye Baby*, before performances by **Janet Jackson** (whose ***janet*** recently spent six weeks at

Pearl Jam's Eddie Vedder told Meat magazine in 1991 that the group was "letting the music take us where it may."

993

July 23 **Kurt Cobain** overdoses on heroin in the bathroom of his New York hotel, before performing at the city's New Music Seminar at the Roseland Ballroom, where **Nirvana** premiere much of ***In Utero***, due for release in September. **Courtney Love**, whose 911 call last month after an argument with Cobain resulted in his arrest for domestic assault, allegedly revives him with an illegal drug.

"We are one of the biggest rock 'n' roll bands in history."

Kurt Cobain, July 23, 1993

MEN DON T
PROTECT YOU
ANYMORE

Take That... Frank Zappa dies... Snoop Doggy Dogg on top...

US No. 1), **R.E.M.**, **Sting**, modern rock combo **Soul Asylum**, the **Spin Doctors**, and **Aerosmith**, who perform their Viewers Choice Award winner, *Livin' On The Edge*.

8 **Suede** win the Mercury Music Prize, with their self-titled album, at the second annual ceremony in London. (It will go on to amass more than 100,000 sales in the UK, 69,000 in Japan, 42,000 in Germany, 39,000 in Sweden and 37,000 in France, but will make little impression in the US.) Lead singer **Brett Anderson** graciously says of the win: "The point of the prize is not the money at all; it's the honour of being nominated," as the band decides to donate its £25,000 prize to Cancer Research.

28 Hundreds of screaming fans greet **Take That** as they arrive at **The Sun**'s Wapping headquarters in London, to pen tomorrow's "Bizarre" column. With their debut album ***Take That And Party*** racking up its 56th consecutive week on the UK album chart, they are taking on the mantle of *the* teen band of the era, with their catchy pop fare picking up chart success around the world (except in the Americas). Pre-dating a slew of similar-sounding boy band acts, which will dominate the pop market at the end of the decade, Take That will notch up five top three UK hits during the year, including three chart-toppers: *Pray*, next month's *Relight My Fire* (an inspired duet with perennially perky Scottish lass **Lulu**), and December's *Babe*. Dominated by compositions by **Gary Barlow**, who is emerging as a top drawer pop writer, their next album ***Everything Changes*** will also debut at UK No. 1 next month, and will be nominated for the third Mercury Music Prize next year (a surprising nod for such an overtly commercial act). With Take That mania swarming around Europe, the album will quickly garner three million sales.

FRANK ZAPPA

Dec 4 **Frank Zappa succumbs to complications resulting from prostate cancer at his Los Angeles home, after a two-year battle with the disease. In its obituary on the 7th, The Independent will say: "A renegade spirit even by the nonconformist standards of the late Sixties counter-culture, Frank Zappa was a largely self-taught musician and composer whose prolific output ranged from highly complex modern orchestral pieces to doowop vocal group arrangements. Staunchly libertarian in both economic and social matters, he also became one of the most articulate anti-censorship campaigners in the United States throughout the Seventies and Eighties." A creatively restless and pioneering musical soul, one of the great originals in rock history is dead at the age of 52. He will be buried at Westwood Memorial Park in Los Angeles.**

"No singer ever had a bigger impact on my musical life than Ray Charles."

President Bill Clinton, October 7, 1993

October

16 In London, **Bryan Adams** and **Sting** record their vocal parts for *All For Love*, written by Adams with regular cohorts Michael Kamen and producer Robert John "Mutt" Lange. It is the main ballad theme (and transatlantic smash) for the forthcoming movie "The Three Musketeers." The final vocal contribution – from **Rod Stewart** – will be recorded (with Adams present) in Los Angeles in two days time.

23 Almost 12 years since he had his only previous Top 10 UK hit, **Meat Loaf** tops the chart with *I'd Do Anything For Love (But I Won't Do That)*, and will hit US No. 1 in two weeks. The track is from his Virgin debut, ***Bat Out Of Hell II – Back Into Hell***, which entered at the summit in September, and will hit the top spot in the US next week. Not coincidentally, Meat Loaf's comeback coincides with his reunion with "Bat" collaborator and composer, Jim Steinman.

November

1 **Public Enemy**'s **Flavor Flav** is arrested in the Bronx and charged with unlawfully possessing a gun, after allegedly shooting at his neighbor. Flav will book himself into the Betty Ford Clinic to overcome a cocaine addiction.

4 Sony A&R executive Dave Massey sees **Oasis** play their first London gig at the Powerhaus club, and agrees with Alan McGee's enthusiasm (Creation is now licensed via Sony). He signs Oasis to Sony for the rest of the world.

18 **Pearl Jam**'s **Eddie Vedder** is arrested in New Orleans, Louisiana – the band is in town for three concerts at the UNO Lakefront Arena – after a fight in a French Quarter bar. ***Ten***, still on the album chart after almost two years, will pass six-million sales on December 1. Its follow-up

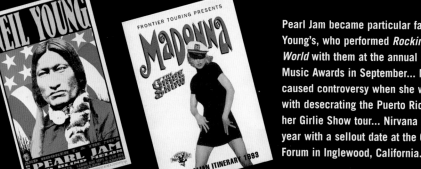

Pearl Jam became particular favorites of Neil Young's, who performed *Rockin' In The Free World* with them at the annual MTV Video Music Awards in September... Madonna caused controversy when she was charged with desecrating the Puerto Rican flag during her Girlie Show tour... Nirvana closed out the year with a sellout date at the Great Western Forum in Inglewood, California.

set, *Vs.*, entered the US chart at No. 1 two weeks ago, recording the highest-selling one-week total in history, with 950,378 copies.

18 **Nirvana** record an acoustic set at Sony Studios in New York City for the "Unplugged" series. The resultant album, *MTV Unplugged In New York*, will top both the UK and US charts next year, amassing five million domestic sales alone.

23 **Tupac** is indicted by a grand jury in Manhattan, New York City, on two counts of sodomy in the first degree, one count of attempted sexual abuse, three counts of sexual abuse, one count of criminal possession of a weapon in the third degree, and two counts of criminal possession of a weapon in fourth. He is accused of molesting a 19-year-old woman in his suite at the Parker Meridien Hotel last week.

30 The day after **Michael Jackson**'s former security guards told syndicated TV's "Hard Copy" that he frequently had children staying overnight in his room, his chauffeur makes a sworn statement that his employer slept at least 30 straight nights at the home of the 13-year-old boy he is alleged to have sexually abused.

December

5 The body of the **Gin Blossoms**' former lead guitarist, **Doug Hopkins**, is found in his Tempe, Arizona, apartment. He shot himself in the mouth with a .38-caliber pistol some time after leaving a detoxification center in Phoenix two days ago. His sister Sara says it was his sixth suicide attempt in the past decade – the last being two weeks ago. When she saw him three nights ago, she noticed the Yellow Pages open at gun-shop ads. "I knew I'd never see him again. I just said 'Goodbye, Doug,' and my mother did the same a few nights before." Hopkins was fired from the band last year because of his problem with alcohol. Ironically, the rootsy, jangly, pop/rock combo, formed in 1987 in Tempe, are currently scoring their first hit with the Hopkins-penned *Hey Jealousy*, from their breakthrough multi-platinum set, the college rock classic, ***New Miserable Experience.***

6 Fueling industry rumors of a comeback, a quasi-**Eagles** reunion takes place, on the Hollywood set of country singer **Travis Tritt**'s video for his cover version of *Take It Easy*. **Don Henley**, **Glenn Frey**, **Don Felder**, **Joe Walsh**, and **Timothy B. Schmit** are all present.

10 Following an anonymous request (possibly by ex-flame Kathy Etchingham), Scotland Yard re-opens the investigation into the circumstances of **Jimi Hendrix**'s death.

11 **Snoop Doggy Dogg**'s *Doggystyle*, produced by and featuring **Dr. Dre**, and recorded with his Death Row backing rap aggregate **Tha Dogg Pound**, simultaneously enters at its US No. 1 and UK No. 38 peaks. It is the first time a debut artist's album has reached US No. 1 in its first week of release, selling 800,000 copies in seven days. It will eventually sell over four million copies in the US and 140,000 in the UK.

16 At the end of **Michael Jackson**'s annus horribilis, KEZK station manager Joe Cariffe says in an on-air editorial that the St. Louis station will no longer play the singer's records.

22 **Michael Jackson** responds publicly for the first time to the furor surrounding child sex-abuse allegations, in a four-minute live satellite broadcast from Neverland Valley. He denies everything: "I ask all of you to wait to hear the truth before you label or condemn me. Don't treat me like a criminal because I am innocent." Commenting on a body search by police this week, he says: "They served a search warrant on me which allowed them to view and photograph my body, including my penis, my buttocks, my lower torso, thighs and any other areas that they wanted... It was the most humiliating ordeal of my life..." Although humiliated, the "King of Pop" will be seen at the Treasure Island Resort in Las Vegas, Nevada, next week, with the "King of Junk Bonds" parolee Michael Milken.

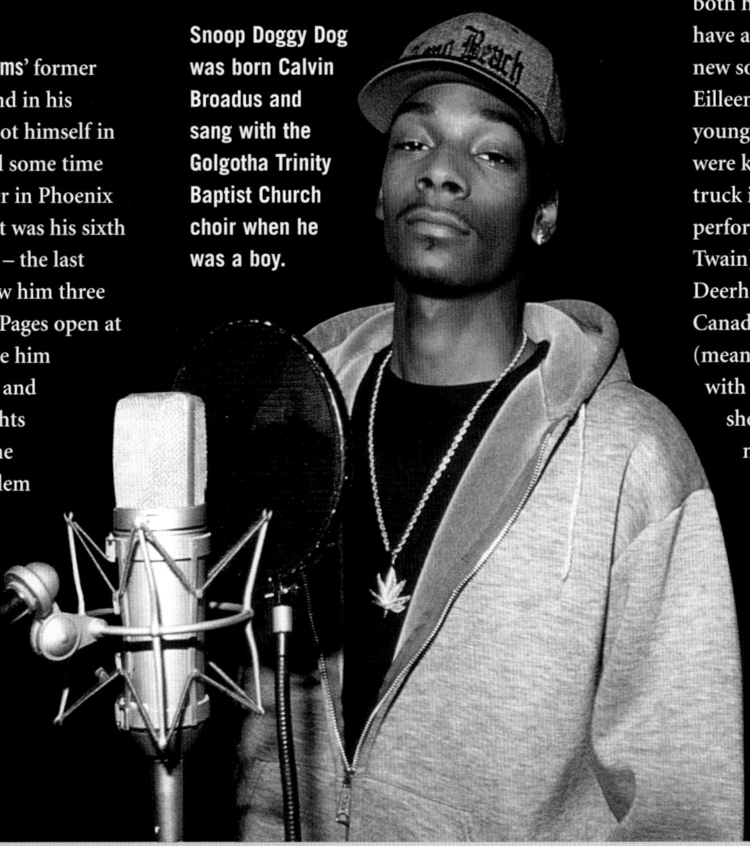

Snoop Doggy Dog was born Calvin Broadus and sang with the Golgotha Trinity Baptist Church choir when he was a boy.

25 In an all-time low for both UK novelty hits and Christmas chart-toppers, television character **Mr. Blobby** scores his second No. 1 of the year with the truly dreadful *Mr. Blobby*.

28 Having first communicated by phone for some months, and then met backstage at a Nashville Fan Fair earlier in the year, 28-year-old country singer **Shania Twain** marries Robert John "Mutt" Lange, famed rock producer for acts such as the **Cars**, **Foreigner**, **Def Leppard**, and **Bryan Adams**. The event will dramatically change both her personal and professional life (they have already begun collaborating on a batch of new songs). Canadian-born Twain (real name Eilleen Regina Edwards), had to raise her three younger siblings on her own, after her parents were killed in a head-on collision with a logging truck in 1987. She made ends meet by performing (under her adopted name Eileen Twain) in a Las Vegas-style revue at the Deerhurst Resort in Huntsville, Ontario, Canada. Adopting the Ojibway name, Shania (meaning "I'm on my way") in 1990, and armed with a clutch of mostly self-penned demos, she headed for Nashville, Tennessee, meeting up with local attorney Dick Frank. This led to formal demo sessions with songwriter Norro Wilson and Mercury Records' A&R executive Buddy Cannon, who signed her to the label's Nashville imprint last year. Her first two singles both peaked at No. 55 in the Country Singles chart earlier in the year, while her debut album, *Shania Twain*, spent a scant four weeks in the Country Album chart.

ROOTS During this year: having dropped out of high school to drift around the southeast US while learning his trade as a singer and writer, Rob Thomas puts together his first band, Tabitha's Secret... while attending local acting auditions in Orlando, Florida, high-school students Howie D., Nicholas Carter, and A.J. McLean become friends and decide to form a pop vocal group, recruiting Brian Littrell and his cousin Kevin Richardson; they begin performing at high school and graduation dances... 11-year-old Britney Spears becomes a mouseketeer on the "Mickey Mouse Club" TV show, along with Christina Aguilera, Justin Timberlake, and J.C. Chasez... schoolfriends Brian Welch and James Shaffer see Jonathan Davis perform with the hard-rock combo Sexart in a Bakersfield bar; hooking up with David Silveria and Reggie Arvizu, they will become KoRn next year... Louis Welch holds auditions in Dublin, Ireland, with the intention of molding an Irish "boy band"; selecting five from more than 300 hopefuls, he creates Boyzone... All Saints – comprising Melanie Blatt, Shaznay Lewis, and Simone Rainford – sign with ZTT Records... and LeToya Luckett joins Beyoncé Knowles, LaTavia Roberson, and Kelly Rowland – the quartet adopt their name, Destiny's Child, from the Book of Isaiah...

Can You Feel The Love Tonight

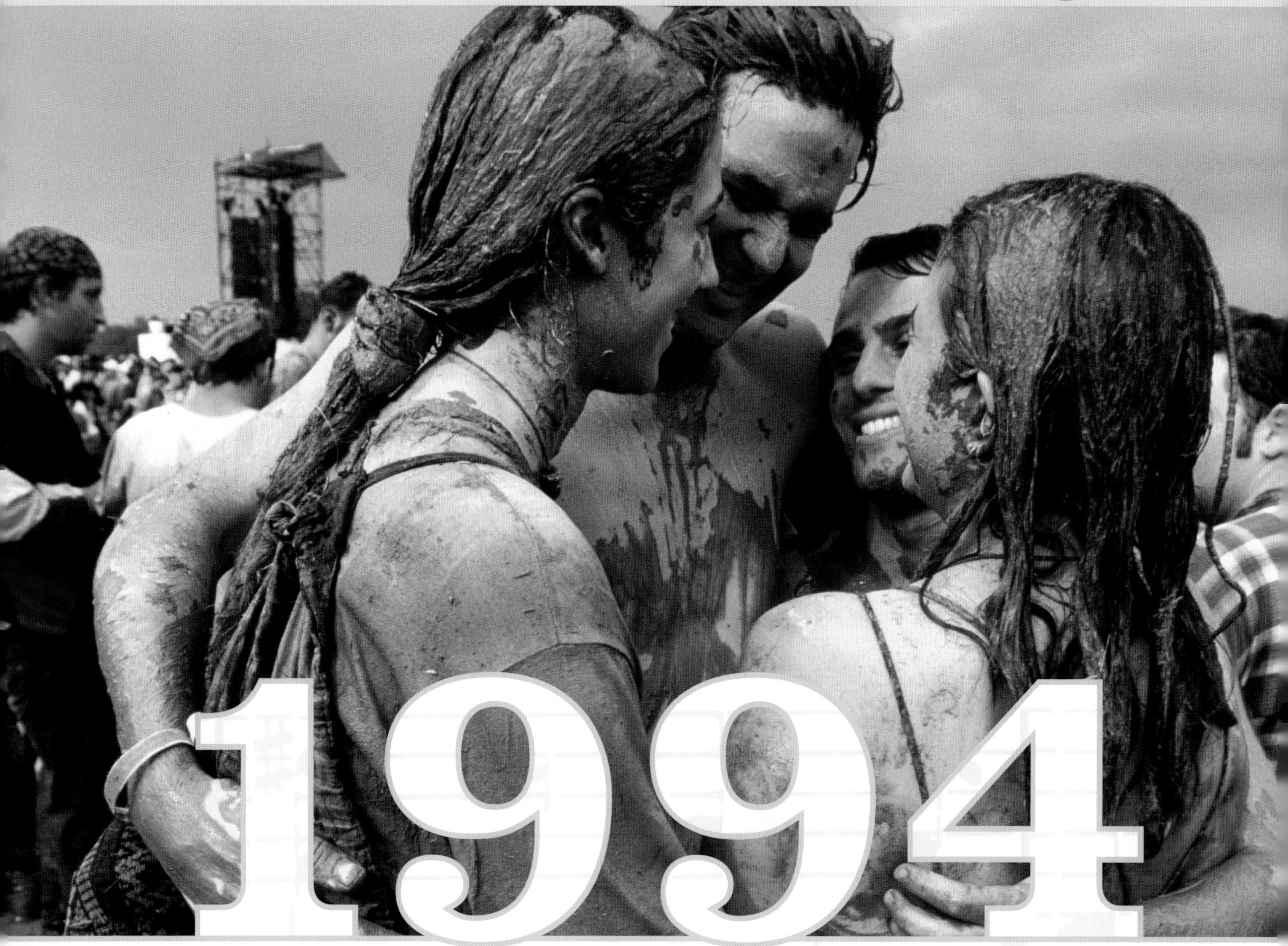

1994

No.1 US SINGLES

Jan 1	Hero	**Mariah Carey**
Jan 22	All For Love	**Bryan Adams/Rod Stewart/Sting**
Feb 12	The Power Of Love	**Celine Dion**
Mar 12	The Sign	**Ace of Base**
Apr 9	Bump N' Grind	**R. Kelly**
May 7	The Sign	**Ace of Base**
May 21	I Swear	**All-4-One**
Aug 6	Stay (I Missed You)	**Lisa Loeb & Nine Stories**
Aug 27	I'll Make Love To You	**Boyz II Men**
Dec 3	On Bended Knee	**Boyz II Men**
Dec 17	Here Comes The Hotstepper	**Ini Kamoze**
Dec 31	On Bended Knee	**Boyz II Men**

No.1 UK SINGLES

Jan 1	Mr. Blobby	**Mr. Blobby**
Jan 8	Twist And Shout	**Chaka Demus & Pliers with Jack Radics & Taxi Gang**
Jan 22	Things Can Only Get Better	**D:Ream**
Feb 19	Without You	**Mariah Carey**
Mar 19	Doop	**Doop**
Apr 9	Everything Changes	**Take That**
Apr 23	The Most Beautiful Girl In The World	
May 7	The Real Thing	**Tony Di Bart**
May 14	Inside	**Stiltskin**
May 21	Come On You Reds	**Manchester United Football Squad**
June 4	Love Is All Around	**Wet Wet Wet**
Sept 17	Saturday Night	**Whigfield**
Oct 15	Sure	**Take That**
Oct 29	Baby Come Back	**Pato Banton**
Nov 26	Let Me Be Your Fantasy	**Baby D**
Dec 10	Stay Another Day	**East 17**

Oasis

Alice In Chains

Leading the vibrant BritPop charge, Oasis were fronted by the controversial, booze-swilling Gallagher brothers... Alice In Chains's Layne Staley described the band's music as "an acquired taste."

Regrettably, like the previous year, 1994 saw too much death, drug addiction, battles about "offensive" lyrics, and legal wrangling. And the music? **Oasis**, the **Cranberries**, **Celine Dion**, and **Sheryl Crow** broke through – and **Boyz II Men** smashed records.

Kurt Cobain – a heroin addict unable to deal with the profile thrust upon him – committed suicide. He had had a meteoric rise to fame and had become an idol of alienated teens – even though he was the definition of anti-hero. His influence could be heard most immediately on **Alice In Chains**' highly successful EP *Jars Of Flies*. Alice was more metallic than **Nirvana**, but shared its nihilism and self-loathing. Even so, **Layne Staley**'s voice had something of the blues-rock tradition, and **Jerry Cantrell**'s guitar licks could be highly finessed.

In other episodes in a disturbed year, **Lisa "Left-Eye" Lopes** of **TLC** burned her boyfriend's mansion to the ground, and rapper **Tupac Shakur** was gunned down by unknown assailants (he survived). In Britain, aggravation took on a more pugilistic form, and usually involved **Oasis**. Repeated punch-ups only served to heighten the band's appeal; their debut album ***Definitely Maybe*** entered the British chart at No. 1. This was gutsy rock 'n' roll, with nods to **T. Rex** and the **Smiths**, written by **Noel Gallagher** and delivered with the distinctive wail of **Liam Gallagher**'s vocals, heavy drums and fast-paced lead guitar. Comparisons with the **Beatles** may have been absurd but, whatever their bad-boy antics, the guys could make music.

Michael Jackson and **George Michael** both signed large checks, one to end accusations of child molestation – even if he failed to quash the rumors – the other to get out of a record contract. A dispute over artistic freedom, the long legal battle between George Michael and his record label, Sony, foreshadowed a growing divergence between artists and labels.

The year's biggest pop act was the R&B combo **Boyz II Men**. Assisted by the cream of producing talent (including **Babyface**, and **Jimmy Jam** and **Terry Lewis**), their album ***II*** went straight to US No. 1. Their lush ballads might have been corny, but the boy meets girl, boy loves girl, boy loses girl or gets girl back formula worked time and time again, and the album included a daring a capella version of the **Beatles**' *Yesterday*.

The godfathers of rock were not forgotten in 1994. **John Lennon** and **Bob Marley** were posthumously inducted into the Rock and Roll Hall of Fame, while **Axl Rose** graciously inducted **Elton John**. After a 14-year gap, the **Eagles** re-formed for a highly lucrative tour. **Aerosmith** were among the first to harness the opportunites presented by cyberspace – releasing the unissued *Head First* via the internet. It took an hour to download, but the precedent was set. The **Rolling Stones** made available 20 minutes of their Dallas concert live via the web. The future had arrived, and rock would begin to undergo technological change of tectonic proportions.

"At the end of the day, we just play music that we like, and if anyone else likes it that's a bonus."

The Cranberries' Noel Hogan, **Vox**, November 1994

McCartney inducts Lennon... Auditions held for Spice Girls...

Green Day's rapid-fire, hardcore punk delivery was styled after the UK punk pioneers of the mid-1970s, particularly the Buzzcocks and the Sex Pistols.

Sub Pop, the grunge label that launched the Seattle sound, had chart success with Nirvana, Afghan Whigs, Mudhoney, and Sebadoh.

January

19 At a particularly poignant Rock and Roll Hall of Fame induction dinner in New York, **Paul McCartney** inducts **John Lennon**. He says: "The thing you must remember is that I'm the number one John Lennon fan. I love him to this day and I always did love him. All these people assembled to thank you for everything that you mean to all of us. Tonight you're in the Rock and Roll Hall of Fame. God bless you." **Bono** inducts the late **Bob Marley** in a memorable and impassioned speech: "I know claiming Bob Marley as Irish might be a little difficult, but bear with me. Jamaica and Ireland have lots in common. Chris Blackwell, weeds, lots of green weeds. Religion. The philosophy of procrastination (don't put off till tomorrow what you can put off till the day after), unless of course it's freedom... He wanted everything at the same time and was everything at the same time: prophet, sole rebel, Rastaman, herbsman, wild man, a natural mystic man, ladies' man, island man, family man, Rita's man, soccer man, showman, shaman, human, Jamaican!" Unable to attend because of an earthquake in Los Angeles on Monday, **Rod Stewart** is inducted by **Jeff Beck**, who says of their love-hate relationship: "He loves me and I hate him." Having recently released ***Jericho***, their first new album in 17 years, the **Band** are inducted by **Eric Clapton**. For their subsequent jam on *The Weight*, **Robbie Robertson** is reunited with the group for the first time in 15 years, although **Levon Helm** is absent from tonight's proceedings. **Bruce Hornsby** inducts the **Grateful Dead** – absentee **Jerry Garcia** is represented by a life-size cardboard cutout. The **Animals** and **Duane Eddy** are also inducted, along with **Willie Dixon** (Early Influence), and **Johnny Otis** (Non-Performer). **Bruce Springsteen**, making his annual appearance at the post-dinner jam, sings *Come Together* with **Axl Rose**.

25 **Michael Jackson** makes a multimillion-dollar payment to the boy who accused him of molestation in settlement of his civil suit. Jackson's lawyer insists that the decision to avoid a court case is "in no way an admission of guilt."

February

8 **Oasis**'s planned live debut outside the UK, opening for rising British indie-rock quartet the **Verve** at the Sleepin Arena in Amsterdam, Holland, is scrapped following a melée on the ferry from Harwich, England. **Liam Gallagher** and **Paul "Guigsy" Arthurs**, having imbibed a little too much champagne and Jack Daniel's, trash various fixtures and fittings on board, resulting in their immediate return to Britain.

10 **Snoop Doggy Dogg** – promoting his new album ***Gin And Juice*** – makes his live UK debut at Leicester Square's Equinox in London, though the visit is marred when he is ordered out of the Milestone Hotel in Kensington when management is made aware of his murder charge. He checks into the Halcyon Hotel in Holland Park. The **Daily Star** runs a front-page story headlined "Kick This Evil Bastard Out!" His UK promotion includes a justified physical attack on Rod Hull's Emu puppet on "The Word."

12 Entering at No. 1, **Alice In Chains**' ***Jar Of Flies*** becomes the first EP ever to top **Billboard**'s album survey. Formed in 1987 by frontman **Layne Staley** and guitarist **Jerry Cantrell**, the group graduated through the Seattle grunge scene as one of its darker proponents.

19 **Green Day**'s third album, ***Dookie***, produced by Rob Cavallo, enters the US survey, where it will stay for over two years, peaking at No. 2. The California-based trio's punk influences dictate their anti-establishment behavior. Accused of selling out by fans and alt-music media alike for signing to a major label (Reprise/WEA), they do so in grand style: the album will sell 12 million copies worldwide, ten million of them in the US, becoming the best-selling "punk" album of all time.

> **"For myself, no one has been more of an inspiration than Elton John. When I first heard *Bennie And The Jets*, I knew I had to be a performer."** Axl Rose inducting Elton John into the Rock and Roll Hall of Fame, January 19, 1994

SHERYL CROW

Mar 19 ***Tuesday Night Music Club*** **– the maiden offering from singer-songwriter/guitarist Sheryl Crow – enters the US album chart. It will be exactly a year before it peaks at No. 3 – time for US FM radio to embrace a trio of well-crafted, melodic pop/rock gems:** ***Leaving Las Vegas*****, the breakthrough US No. 2 smash** ***All I Wanna Do*** **(which strongly recalls Stealers Wheel's 1973 hit** ***Stuck In The Middle With You*****), and** ***Strong Enough*****. Crow began writing songs at 13, before graduating with a music degree from the University of Missouri in 1984. She landed her first major assignment as a backing singer on Michael Jackson's 1987 Bad world tour, and signed a songwriting deal with Warner/Chappell. Encouraged by her friend Don Henley, she secured covers by Eric Clapton, Celine Dion, and Wynonna Judd, while also singing backup on a number of major albums (including Henley's** ***The End Of The Innocence*****) and tours (for the likes of Rod Stewart, Joe Cocker, and George Harrison). Signed to A&M, her first sessions with Hugh Padgham were shelved prior to completing her multiplatinum debut with Bill Bottrell. At Bottrell's Los Angeles home, she attended informal jamming sessions known as the "Tuesday Night Music Club," begun by her songwriter boyfriend Kevin Gilbert.**

23 A Judiciary Juvenile Justice Subcommittee hearing in Washington, DC, discusses "gangsta rap." Senator Carol Moseley-Braun, Democrat for Illinois, presiding, says: "At issue is whether the music industry that makes so much money from these lyrics has any responsibility for the type of music it disseminates." Among the 17 witnesses called, singer **Dionne Warwick** calls it pornography, while Rock the Vote executive Nicholas Butterworth says it is poetry. Others talk of youthful alienation, and whether music or society in general is responsible.

24 **Tag Team**'s novelty smash *Whoomp! (There It Is)*, despite not making it to No. 1 in the US chart last year, is certified four times platinum – becoming one of the ten biggest-selling singles of all time for the Atlanta-based hip-hop duo of **Cecil Glenn** and **Steve Gibson**.

March

1 **Whitney Houston** delivers a show-stopping performance of *I Will Always Love You* at the 36th Grammy Awards at New York City's Radio City Music Hall, as she picks up three more Grammys – Record of the Year and Best Pop Vocal Performance, Female (for *I Will Always Love You*), and Album of the Year (for ***The Bodyguard***.) Winning Best Alternative Music Album (for ***Zooropa***), **U2**'s **Bono** states: "We shall continue to abuse our position and f**k up the mainstream." He presents **Frank Sinatra** with his Living Legend honor, with a typically fascinating diatribe (the Chairman of the Board's acceptance speech will be rudely cut short by the show's producers). **Bruce Springsteen**, **Steve Winwood**, **Bonnie Raitt**, **B.B. King**, **Steve Cropper**, **Don Was**, and R&B trio **Tony! Toni! Tone!** perform a tribute to **Curtis Mayfield**, who receives a Grammy Legend Award. Building a bridge between rock and the burgeoning world music genre, **Ry Cooder** becomes a two-time Best World Music Album winner for ***A Meeting By The River*** with Indian mohan vina musician **Vishwa Mohan Bhatt**. **Meat Loaf**, nabbing Best Rock Solo Performance, Male with *I'd Do Anything For Love (But I Won't Do That)* and **Ozzy Osbourne** (with *I Don't Want To Change The World* picking up Best Metal Performance), collect their first ever Grammys. **Ray Charles** wins his 13th trophy, for Best Male R&B Performance.

3 Despite having the week's highest new chart entry, the **Smashing Pumpkins** – fast becoming one of alt-rock's most popular combos – are banned from appearing on "Top Of The Pops," because of objections to the lyrics of *Disarm*. It is taken from the melodic grunge, rock-based breakthrough set, ***Siamese Dream***, which will be certified triple platinum in the US in August. It is helmed by producer du jour, **Butch Vig**, who also produces **Nirvana** and alt-rock media faves, **Sonic Youth**. Later this month, he will see Scottish rock singer **Shirley Manson**, ex-**Goodbye Mr. MacKenzie**, perform *Suffocate Me* on MTV's "120 Minutes," with her latest band, **Angelfish** – and will invite her to join his new group, **Garbage**. With a substantial pedigree and impeccable credentials (the quartet is completed by veterans, guitarist/bassist **Steve Marker** and guitarist/keyboardist **Duke Erikson**, with Vig on drums), the pop/rock quartet will sign to Almo Sounds by the end of this year.

4 Having searched dance and drama schools in London and southeast England with a view to forming a female version of the hugely popular British teen-pop act **Take That**, Chris Herbert and his father Bob, who run the management company Heart, have placed an advertisement in **The Stage**: "R.U. 18–23 with the ability to sing/dance. R.U. streetwise, outgoing, ambitious and dedicated?" In response, 400 girls show up at the Danceworks Studio in London. Each is given 30 seconds to perform, and given marks out of ten for singing, dancing, looks, and personality. The final ten include two **Melanies** (**Brown** and **Chisholm**), **Michelle Stephenson** (who gets the highest score), and ex-**Persuasion** singer, **Victoria Adams**. **Geri Halliwell**, who recently appeared as a hostess on Turkish TV game show "Secbakalim," auditions on April 28 because she could not make today's date. Stephenson will leave the line-up in July, replaced by **Emma Bunton** (who is training with the group's singing teacher) as they start to rehearse under the name **Touch** (and then **Spice**).

The Smashing Pumpkins – led by Billy Corgan – became the darlings of the summer's Lollapalooza trek.

Apr 1994

Kurt Cobain's suicide... George Michael sues Sony Music... Woodstock '94...

Michael and Lisa Marie Jackson

The Cranberries

Michael Jackson and Lisa Marie Presley married in La Vega, Dominican Republic, in May – an event they denied took place for more than two months... The enchanting *Linger* brought Irish group the Cranberries its only US gold single.

April

1 **Kurt Cobain**, who yesterday checked into the Exodus Recovery Center of the Daniel Freeman Marina Hospital in Marina del Rey, California (**Dave Grohl** and **Krist Novoselic** have threatened to disband **Nirvana** if he doesn't enter a rehab facility), tells **Courtney Love** over the phone: "Courtney, no matter what happens, I want you to know that you made a really good record. Just remember, no matter what, I love you." At 7:25 pm, he leaves the center by scaling the 6ft wall surrounding its patio and heads back to Seattle, Washington, arriving in the early hours of tomorrow.

2 *The Sign*, a re-packaging of **Ace Of Base**'s European release *Happy Nation*, augmented by four newly recorded tracks for the North American market, hits US No. 1 for one week (and will return to the summit for a further week on June 11). Its title track also holds the top spot on the Hot 100. Ace Of Base becomes the first Swedish act to top the US album chart, a feat not even achieved by their pop forefathers, **Abba**.

8 Three days after the suicide of **Kurt Cobain**, who was seemingly unable to cope with his sudden rise to fame and wealth, Gary Smith, a 50-year-old electrician contracted to install a burglar alarm, finds the singer's body at approximately 8:40 am, lying on the floor with a gun on his chest. Nearby is a suicide note, which quotes **Neil Young**'s *My My, Hey Hey (Out Of The Blue)*: "It's better to burn out than fade away." He was revered by Gen X-ers in Seattle, with a hero-worship that he failed to live up to, and public mourning will be overwhelming, with Lennon-like candlelit vigils outside his home. The coroner's report will reveal high levels of heroin and traces of Valium in Cobain's bloodstream. A private funeral will be held at the Unity Church of Seattle on April 10, following a public memorial service.

9 With *Everything Changes* bowing at UK No. 1, **Take That** become the first group to enter the chart at the top spot four times.

10 At the public memorial service for **Kurt Cobain** at Seattle Center's Flag Pavilion, **Nirvana** fan Daniel Kaspar – allegedly overcome by the singer's death – kills himself.

13 **George Michael**'s lawsuit against Sony Music – heard in the High Court in London – ends after 74 days. Disputing both the creative and marketing abilities of Sony imprint, Epic Records, Michael's lawyer, Tony Russell, has insisted that Michael is not bound by his contract, and owns his own master recordings. Michael has claimed: "Since Sony Corporation bought my contract, along with everything and everyone else at CBS, I have seen the great American company that I proudly signed to as a teenager become a small part of the production line for a giant electronics corporation which, quite frankly, has no understanding of the creative process. Sony appears to see artists as little more than software."

13 *Whatta Man*, by rap threesome **Salt-N-Pepa** is certified platinum. **Salt** (**Cheryl James**) and **Pepa** (**Sandy Denton**), with DJ **Dee Dee "Spinderella"** (**Deirdre Roper**), sing the smash hit with R&B divettes **En Vogue**. This combines the talents of the leading female R&B trios of the past five years.

23 After 40 previous chart showings on the UK singles chart, ♀ finally nabs No. 1 with *The Most Beautiful Girl In The World.*

KURT COBAIN

Apr 5 **Kurt Cobain, who turned 27 in February, barricades himself into the room above the garage of the Seattle home he shares with Courtney Love (who is not in town) and fatally shoots himself with a Remington 20-gauge shotgun. He recently bought the weapon (with his long-time friend Dylan Carlson) from Stan Baker Sports in Seattle, ostensibly because he was concerned about the number of trespassers around his property.**

Cobain's premature demise placed him firmly in the annals of rock history as the leading pioneer of grunge rock.

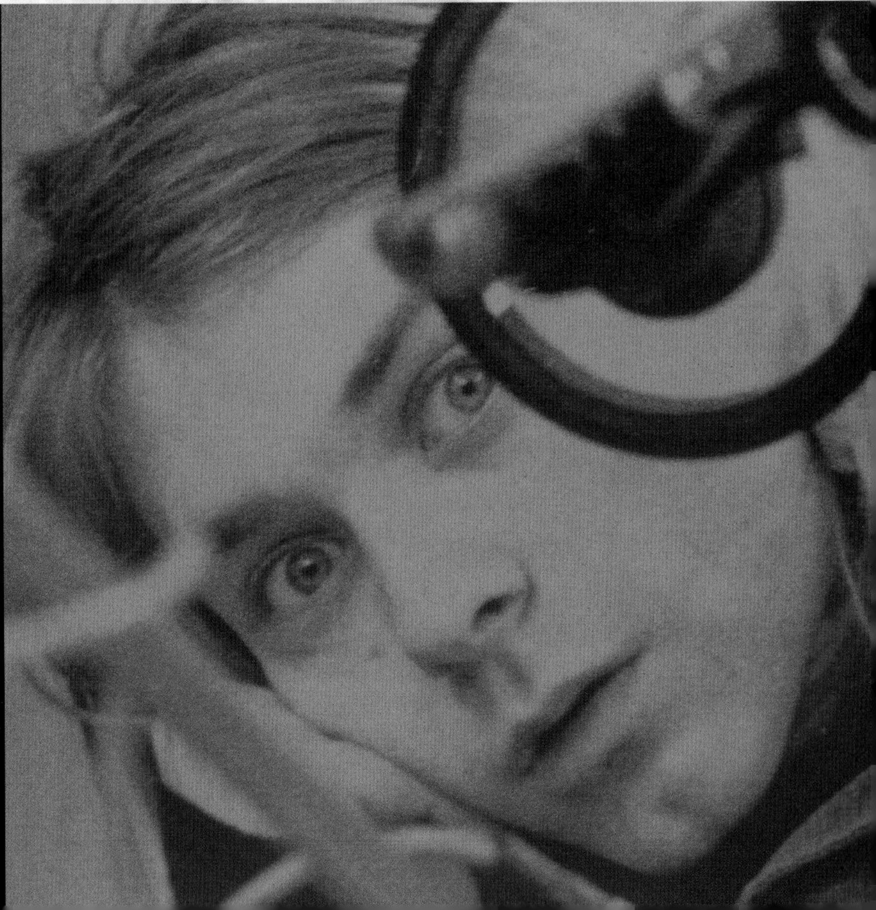

25 Following a joint performance by **Don Henley**, **Glenn Frey**, and **Joe Walsh** before a packed audience at the Double Diamond Club in Aspen, Colorado, on February 13, a full-blown **Eagles** reunion finally takes place, with the first of two televised performances before an invited audience at the Warner Burbank Studios. **Don Henley**, **Glenn Frey**, **Joe Walsh**, **Don Felder**, and **Timothy B. Schmit** give note-perfect renditions of past glories and new compositions. Their first gig in 14 years, it will be watched by more than two million viewers when first broadcast by MTV on October 26. Their motivation has partly come from the multiplatinum success of ***Common Thread: The Songs Of The Eagles***, featuring cover versions by top country stars, which was released last October and was named Album of the Year by the Country Music Association.

"There are always going to be two opposing sides – the artist side and the record company side... They think we're brats. We think they're expensive, stinky-cheese schmoozers."

Tori Amos on George Michael's legal battle with Sony, 1994

May

21 **All-4-One**'s *I Swear* begins an 11-week ride at US No. 1, the longest residence of the year. Written five years ago by country songwriters Gary Baker and Frank J. Myers, it has already been a country No. 1 for **John Michael Montgomery** in February. Atlantic Records head, Doug Morris, suggested to the California-based All-4-One, a multiracial, all-boy vocal quartet, that they cut a pop version – which they did, under the production gloss of veteran hitmaker, David Foster.

27 The **Eagles**' 50-date Hell Freezes Over US tour (a reference to a **Don Henley** quote about the prospects of an Eagles reunion), opens with sellout dates at Irvine Meadows Amphitheater in California. It will yield the US No. 1 album, ***Hell Freezes Over***, which will incorporate four new compositions, including the singles *Get Over It* (US) and *Love Will Keep Us Alive* (UK). Commenting on their reunion tour, **Glenn Frey** says: "We never broke up, we took a 14-year vacation."

June

11 The **Cranberries** perform on "Later With Jools Holland." Brothers **Noel** and **Mike Hogan**, with drummer **Feargal Lawler**, formed the band in Limerick, Ireland, in 1989, and recruited lead singer **Dolores O'Riordan** the following year. Signed to Island Records in 1991, and teamed with **Morrissey**'s producer, Stephen Street, their pop/rock debut ***Everybody Else Is Doing It, So Why Can't We?*** has global appeal. Having reached US No. 18 last November, it will top the UK chart in two weeks, spurred by the memorable, strings-laden modern rock nugget, *Linger*.

21 Justice Jonathan Parker delivers a 273-page ruling, in favor of Sony, in the case brought against the corporation by **George Michael**. After the verdict, Michael's answering machine message is changed to, "I'm never going to sing again. Bastards! Bastards!" to the tune of *Careless Whisper*. Appearing on BBC2-TV's "Newsnight," **Billy Bragg** says that Michael "would have got a better result if he'd sued his hairdresser." Michael will be ordered to pay both sides' costs, estimated at £3 million ($4.8 million).

24 "The Lion King," the latest animated feature film from the Walt Disney Studio, opens in US theaters. Its soundtrack marks a new direction for **Elton John**. Teamed with lyricist **Tim Rice**, the pair have created a wildly popular collection of songs, including John's first solo US top five hit in six years, the anthemic ballad, *Can You Feel The Love Tonight*. The soundtrack album will spend ten summer weeks at US No. 1.

27 CompuServe begins a week-long promotion, during which fans can download **Aerosmith** music via the internet. A major event in the history of music delivery, it is the first time a major-label band has released an entire song via a computer network. Geffen Records insists that the recording – the previously unissued *Head First*, which takes fans over an hour to download – will never be made commercially available in any other medium (and will only be available online for seven days). Both Geffen and CompuServe waive fees for this unique experiment.

Gen-Xers mourned the death of Kurt Colbain, their reluctant spokesman – one fan going so far as to emulate his hero and commit suicide.

July

21 **Oasis** make their US debut with a performance at the New Music Seminar held in New York City, going on stage at the Wetlands club at midnight. This once-only gig precedes their first tour, which will begin at Moe's in Seattle, Washington, on September 23.

25 **Alice In Chains** pull out of the opening slot for **Metallica**'s 20-date US Shit in the Sheds tour, one day prior to its opening at the Velodrome Field, Cal State Dominguez Hills in Carson, California, amid rumors of singer **Layne Staley**'s heroin addiction. The group's management company denies the allegations, stating that Staley is in good health, but the band had to "resolve the situation in privacy."

25 **Lisa Loeb** makes her US television network debut, performing her rising hit *(Stay) I Miss You* on CBS-TV's "Late Show With David Letterman." Next week, the New York-based singer-songwriter – together with her **Nine Stories** backing band – will become the first unsigned act in pop history to top the chart. *(Stay) I Miss You* has been included as a single on the soundtrack of the movie "Reality Bites," at the personal request of actor Ethan Hawke. Loeb has been unable to secure a label deal since her live debut in 1990, but a hasty bidding war is now under way, to be won by Geffen Records.

30 With guitarist **Richey Edwards** recently booking himself into a psychiatric hospital in Cardiff, Wales, to be treated for "nervous exhaustion" and anorexia (he apparently weighs a mere 90lb), a three-piece **Manic Street Preachers** perform at the inaugural T In The Park festival in Motherwell, Scotland. Fans not only have to do without Edwards, but are kept waiting for an hour by a tardy **Cypress Hill**. All is forgiven, however, when emerging, mod-influenced, BritPop band **Blur**, a pioneering rock quartet led by singer **Damon Albarn** and guitarist **Graham Coxon**, delivers a sublime set at the end of the day. Those who wait around for tomorrow's line-up will be treated to what **Noel Gallagher** will describe as **Oasis**'s best gig ever.

August

9 On the first date of **Oasis**'s European tour, at the Riverside in Newcastle, England, mayhem breaks out when an unnamed assailant storms the stage in the middle of *Bring It On Down*, and punches **Noel Gallagher** in the face. Only five songs into their set, the enthusiastic Gallagher brothers jump into the crowd in pursuit of the attacker. The gig is canceled and Noel is taken to the Royal Victoria Hospital. In response to the cancellation, the crowd shows its appreciation by smashing the windows of the band's van. (Not to be outdone, Noel's brother **Liam** will break his foot after leaping off a moving tour bus after a gig at the end of the week at the Hultsfred Festival in Sweden.)

14 The three-day Woodstock '94 festival, at Winston Farm in Saugerties, New York, comes to an end in a sea of mud, with the words of co-organizer Michael Lang still echoing: "We want to stay true to the spirit born at Woodstock and hope that this generation will take that spirit and make this festival uniquely its own. Woodstock '94 will focus on the ideals and music of today. That should result in a great rock festival that will endure as long as the first one." Friday opened with rock quartet **Candlebox**, Georgia-based melodic rockers **Collective Soul** (led by brothers **Ed** and **Dean Roland**), **Sheryl Crow**,

Aug

1994

Jimmy Page and Robert Plant back together... Bad Boy Records... *Love Is All Around...*

veteran quartet **Live**, popular punk-folk hybrid trio the **Violent Femmes**, and others. Yesterday's sets came from the **Cranberries**, Italian singer **Zucchero**, Senegal-born world music pioneer **Youssou N'Dour**, the **Band**, **Salt-N-Pepa** (one of just a half-dozen black acts among the 30-plus artists), **Blind Melon** (a Los Angeles rock band led by singer **Shannon Hoon**), the **Henry Rollins Band**, **Melissa Etheridge** (whose career-defining album, ***Yes I Am*** is racking up six million US sales), **Nine Inch Nails**, **Metallica**, **Aerosmith**, and two veterans of the original festival: **Joe Cocker** and **Crosby, Stills & Nash**. Having shunned the original Woodstock, **Bob Dylan** performs on the final day, along with the **Neville Brothers**, **Santana**, **Arrested Development**, the **Allman Brothers Band**, **Traffic**, the **Spin Doctors**, **Porno For Pyros** (**Perry Farrell**'s new alt-rock combo), the **Red Hot Chili Peppers**, **Peter Gabriel**, and **Green Day**, whom many regard as the highlight of the festival. An estimated 235,000–350,000 attend, and as before, many get in without paying. Otherwise far removed from the original Woodstock, this festival – at $135 a ticket and with an exclusive beverage deal with Pepsi – demonstrates the quantum leap from the socially and politically active youth of 1969, to a largely hedonistic Gen-X crowd. Meanwhile 15,000 attend an alternative Woodstock at the original Bethel site, with **Country Joe McDonald**, **Arlo Guthrie**, **Melanie**, **Sha Na Na**, **Richie Havens**, **Ten Years After**, **Canned Heat**, and the **Rascals**.

21 At a concert at the Arrowhead Pond of Anaheim, California, during her current US tour, **Whitney Houston** asks for a spotlight to be turned on Sydney and Justin Simpson, whose father O.J. Simpson is currently on trial for the murder of their mother, Nicole Brown.

25 **Jimmy Page** and **Robert Plant** reunite at LWT Studios in London, to perform a set for MTV's "Unplugged" series, titled "Unledded." It will receive the series' highest ever rating when broadcast on October 12. (Not invited to the reunion, **John Paul Jones** continues a well-respected production career, currently for **Heart** and **Diamanda Galas**.)

Robert Plant and Jimmy Page's "Unledded" show for MTV featured acoustic versions of Led Zeppelin classics as well as new material penned by the pair.

Salt-N-Pepa picked up three moonmen at the MTV Video Music Awards for *Whatta Man*, which sampled Linda Lyndell's 1968 R&B hit *What A Man.*

> **"On a scale of 1 to 10, I give him a 2, because it took so bloody long. The Who could've done the job in one minute."**
>
> Roger Daltrey on Johnny Depp trashing his hotel room, September 13, 1994

31 Chicago native, R&B singer-songwriter/producer **R. Kelly** marries Detroit-born **Aaliyah** (née Aaliyah Haughton) in Rosemont, Illinois, even though the bride is only 15 years old, one year under the state's legal age (the marriage will be annuled for that reason). Last month, *Back & Forth*, written and produced for Aaliyah by 25-year-old Kelly, and taken from her debut album, ***Age Ain't Nothing But A Number***, hit US No. 5. Kelly's own career – which took off with 1992's ***Born Into The '90s*** – is also soaring, with his multiplatinum, overtly sex-themed set ***12 Play*** hitting US No. 2 in March, spurred by the US No. 1 smash, *Bump N' Grind.* Much in demand as a songwriter and producer, Kelly's current successes include projects for **Toni Braxton**, **Lisa Stansfield**, **Janet Jackson**, **Ex-Girlfriend**, **Gladys Knight**, **David Peaston**, the **Winans**, and **N-Phase**.

September

8 Newly-weds **Michael** and **Lisa Marie Jackson** kiss passionately at the 11th MTV Video Music Awards at New York City's Radio City Music Hall. An equally unlikely couple, talk-show king David Letterman and **Madonna** present **Aerosmith** with the Best Video for *Cryin'*, which also wins Best Group Video. A shaven-headed **Michael Stipe** is on hand to collect four awards for **R.E.M.**'s *Everybody Hurts.* **Nirvana** pick up a pair of moonmen for Best Alternative Video and Best Art Direction, while **Soundgarden** and the **Stone Temple Pilots** – both of whom have scored their first US chart-topping albums this year –

HOOTIE & THE BLOWFISH

Sept 2 Personally picked by the host after he heard the band on New York radio station WNEW-FM, Hootie & the Blowfish make their network debut on CBS-TV's "Late Show With David Letterman." The group's self-penned Atlantic debut, *Cracked Rear View*, produced by Don Gehman, is an exuberant, no-nonsense melodic rock set, highlighted by Darius Rucker's powerful rock/soul vocal style. Lead singer Rucker and guitarist Mark Bryan formed the band while attending the University of South Carolina, with Dean Felber, a fellow student, soon recruited along with drummer Brantley Smith. In 1989, Smith was replaced by Jim Sonefeld. The self-financed, six-song EP *Kootchypop* was issued in July last year, recorded with the help of R.E.M. producer Don Dixon. Atlantic A&R scout Tim Sommer, impressed by *Kootchypop*, signed the band last October.

Cracked Rear View topped the US chart in May 1995 and became the biggest-selling debut set in US history.

also receive awards. The Best New Artist Video category is won by **Counting Crows**, for "Mr. Jones." Recently opening US dates for the **Rolling Stones**, the red-hot modern rock sextet, fronted by dreadlocked UCLA dropout, **Adam Duritz**, made their first big-time engagement at last year's Rock and Roll Hall of Fame induction dinner, filling in live for no-show **Van Morrison**.

13 Actor Johnny Depp is arrested on charges of criminal mischief after trashing his room at New York City's Mark Hotel. His blitzkrieg wakes next-door guest **Roger Daltrey**.

13 Bad Boy Records releases its first album, **Notorious B.I.G.**'s (prophetic) *Ready To Die*, (No. 73002) one week ahead of (No. 73001) (*Project: Funk Da World* by **Craig Mack**). The new label, formed by **Sean Combs** (who records and produces under the name **Puff Daddy**), with a strong roster of talented, New York-based R&B and hip-hop artists, is setting the tone and scene for the exploding East Coast rap movement. With the company currently nabbing its first platinum single (Mack's *Flava In Yer Ear*), it will be the Notorious B.I.G. (rapper **Christopher Wallace**) who will become Bad Boys' biggest early success, scoring two platinum US singles next year.

15 At Sotheby's, EMI Records pays £78,500 ($125,600) for a reel-to-reel tape sold by 53-year-old retired policeman Bob Molyneux, of the **Quarry Men**'s gig at St. Peter's Parish Church Garden party in Woolton on July 6, 1957, featuring *Puttin' On The Style* and *Baby Let's Play House*.

15 As **Wet Wet Wet**'s *Love Is All Around* drops off the top spot – after 15 weeks, one week shy of **Bryan Adams**' record-breaking *(Everything I Do) I Do It For You* – the group's manager, Elliot Davis, phones Phonogram managing director Howard Berman to ask the label to delete the record. The summer record of 1994, the band's revival of the **Troggs**' original 1967 UK No. 5 has been featured in the top movie of the year, "Four Weddings And A Funeral."

17 Recorded at Granny's House studio in Reno, Nevada, **Boyz II Men**'s album *II* debuts at US No. 1, the first Motown album to do so since **Stevie Wonder**'s *Songs In The Key Of Life*. Variously produced by **Babyface**, Dallas Austin, Tim Kelly and Bob Robinson, and **Jimmy Jam** and **Terry Lewis**, it will sell six million copies in the US by the end of 1994 – which will prove to be the Boyz' signature year. The album includes a version of *Yesterday*, which **Michael McCary** and **Nathan Morris** used to sing in their school choir, and their current 14-week US chart-topping ballad, *I'll Make Love To You*. Its successor in the top spot will be the six-week holding *On Bended Knee*, written and helmed by Jam and Lewis – making Boyz II Men only the third act in chart history to replace themselves at US No. 1, following **Elvis Presley** and the **Beatles**.

With the band already hailed as leading pioneers of BritPop, Oasis's debut album *Definitely Maybe*, produced with Mark Coyle, entered the UK chart at No. 1 in September

1994

Nov 18 The **Rolling Stones** become the first major band to have a segment of a gig broadcast live on the internet, when 20 minutes of tonight's Cotton Bowl show in Fair Park, Dallas, Texas, are made available by multimedia company Thinking Pictures.

"We sensed that people were coming to see if we could still make it for two hours."

Keith Richards, on why people were going to their Voodoo Lounge concerts, **Mojo**, November 1997

At the start of the Rolling Stones' Voodoo Lounge tour, the National Affinity Cards and the Maryland Chevy Chase Savings Bank introduced the band's Mastercard and Visa card, complete with the Stones' famous red tongue logo, available at 1-800 615 ROCK.

Oct 1994

Elvis Presley tribute concert... Inaugural MTV European Music Awards...

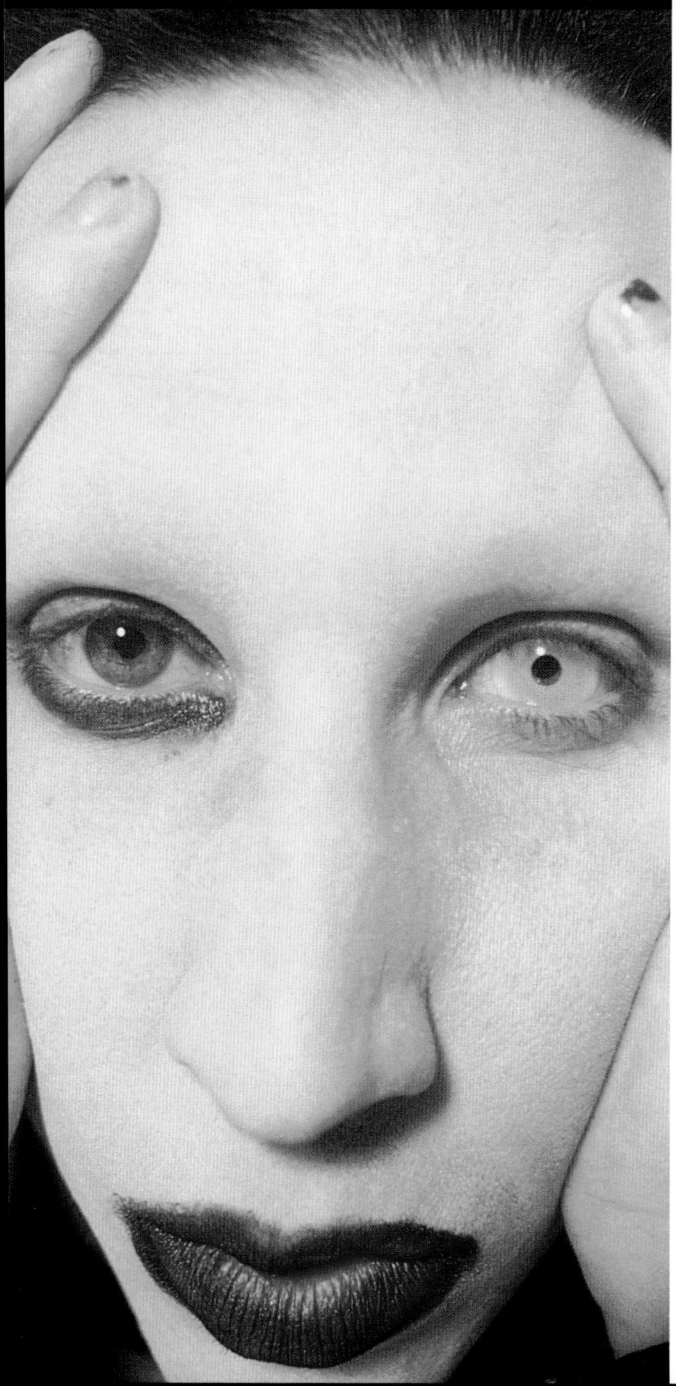

October

1 The **Daily Mirror** prints a color photo of Michael Jackson in scoutmaster's uniform with five other Boy Scouts. When word reaches the Boy Scouts of America, they express their displeasure in a statement: "Michael Jackson is not and has not been a registered leader or member of the Boy Scouts of America. Our Approval for publication was not sought, and the publisher has not returned our phone calls."

8 "Elvis Aaron Presley: The Tribute," staged at the Pyramid Arena in Memphis, is broadcast live on US pay-per-view TV, with the King's daughter, **Lisa Marie**, in attendance with her husband, **Michael Jackson**, and his sister **Janet**. Narrated by **Kris Kristofferson**, the tribute features performances from **Bryan Adams**, **Jeff Beck**, **Michael Bolton**, **John Cale**, **Cheap Trick**, **Cher** (who has just launched her gothic mail order catalog Sanctuary), **Sheryl Crow**, **Melissa Etheridge**, **Marianne Faithfull**, **Sammy Hagar**, **Michael Hutchence**, **Chris Isaak**, **Alan Jackson**, **Sam Moore**, **Aaron Neville**, **Iggy Pop**, **Paul Rodgers**, the **Scorpions**, **U2**, **Wet Wet Wet**, **Heart**'s **Ann Wilson**, and **Dwight Yoakam**. Top producer **Don Was** is the musical director, while **Scotty Moore** and the **Jordanaires** provide house backing. Presley contemporaries **Fats Domino**, **Jerry Lee Lewis**, and **Carl Perkins** also take part.

12 A 15-date stint of **Pink Floyd**'s Division Bell tour at London's Earls Court – the band's first UK dates in seven years – opens disastrously, when a section of seating collapses a minute into the band's opening number, and 1,000 people plunge to the floor. The tour is benefiting various charities, including Amnesty International and Greenpeace. ***The Division Bell*** spent four weeks at US No. 1 in the spring.

18 As their controversial stage act draws increasing media attention, the Delta Center in Salt Lake City, Utah, bans **Marilyn Manson** from tonight's performance, opening for **Nine Inch Nails**. Androgynous lead singer, 25-year-old Marilyn Manson (**Brian Warner**), is invited on stage by NIN's lead singer, **Trent Reznor** (who has signed them to his Nothing label), and explains why they aren't playing tonight, before shredding a copy of the **Book of Mormon** and throwing it into the audience. He then heads backstage to trash the venue's dressing rooms.

23 The first Stonewall Equality benefit, a fundraiser for gay and lesbian rights, takes place at London's Royal Albert Hall. Headlined by **Elton John** and **Sting**, the bill also includes the **Pet Shop Boys**, **Alison Moyet**, and **Melissa Etheridge**.

> **"Politicians don't work for the people; the system works for the politicians... Politicians are one step below used-car salesmen."**
>
> Cher responding to her ex-husband's congressional win, **Washington Post**, November 11, 1994

Marilyn Manson was made Priest of the Church of Satan by its founder, Dr. Anton Szandor LaVey, in October. He will call himself Reverend Manson.

November

8 Having shunned music for a career in politics, ex-Palm Springs Mayor **Sonny Bono** wins California's 44th district congressional seat in the House of Representatives.

24 The inaugural MTV European Music Awards, hosted by the suddenly hip **Tom Jones**, is broadcast live against the backdrop of the Brandenburg Gate in Berlin, Germany. In a refreshingly diverse list of winners, **Bryan Adams** and **Mariah Carey** win the Best Male and Best Female categories, and quirky Canadian quintet **Crash Test Dummies**, led by the distinctive deep baritone of **Brad Roberts**, is named Breakthrough Artist. It recently scored a major transatlantic hit with *Mmm, Mmm, Mmm, Mmm*. **Aerosmith** – the only double winners of the evening – pick up Best Rock Band and Best Rock Act. **Neneh Cherry**'s duet with **Youssou N'Dour**, *7 Seconds*, is named Best Song, and **Take That** and **Prodigy** take home Best Group and Best Dance Act respectively. Best UK Group honors go to **Oasis**, who are also chosen by British viewers as top "local heroes." Best Dance Act goes to British techno/electronica/punk combo **Prodigy**, led by DJ/keyboardist **Liam Howlett**; their breakthrough album, the provocative ***Music For The Jilted Generation***, hit UK No. 1 in July.

30 While on trial for sex and weapons charges, rapper **Tupac Shakur** heads to Times Square's Quad Recording Studio in New York

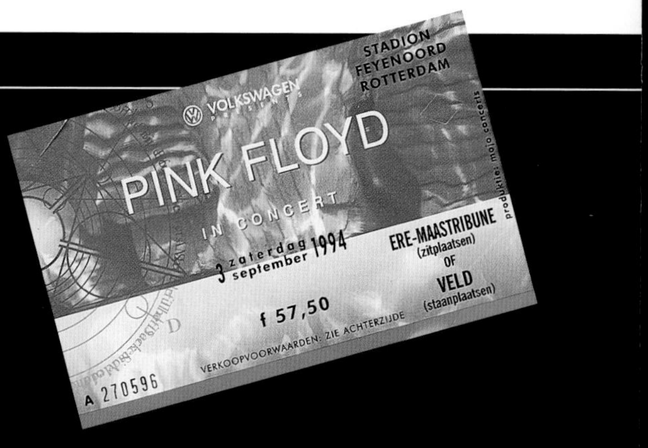

Pillowcases, a music box and a wall clock were among ungrunge-like Alice In Chains (shown as dolls here) merchandise... Pink Floyd's *The Division Bell*, which topped the US chart for four weeks in the spring, took its title from the bell that is rung in Britain's House of Commons when a vote is cast.

Signed to alt-rock label Epitaph, Offspring rocketed to mainstream Gen-X success, joining Green Day as genre-stealing pioneers of the American version of the UK punk scene, circa 1976.

City to record a track with **Little Shawn**, knowing that it may be his last recording session for some time. As he enters the studio with his three-man entourage, three unknown men – thought by Tupac to be security – follow them to an elevator, where they pull out guns and tell everyone to "Give up the jewelry, and get on the floor!" Tupac pulls his gun, and is immediately shot five times, twice in the head. The robbers get away with $45,000 worth of jewelry, including Tupac's $30,000 diamond ring, and the severely wounded rapper is taken up to the eighth-floor studio, where producer/impresario **Sean "Puffy" Combs** and his protegé **Biggie Smalls** are working. Three of the policemen who arrive on the scene turn out to be the arresting officers from Tupac's current court case. He is rushed to Bellevue Hospital, and has surgery on a damaged blood vessel in his right leg, but less than three hours after the operation, and against the vociferous pleas of his doctors, he checks himself out, still in fear of his life.

Tupac Shakur was found guilty on three counts of first-degree sex abuse.

December

1 Having secretly checked into the Metropolitan Hospital Center under the name of Bob Day after the court's morning session, Tupac is acquitted of sodomy and weapons charges, but found guilty on three counts of first-degree sex abuse of a 19-year-old fan last November. He remains free, on bail set at $25,000, while awaiting sentence.

6 Some 200 fans begin queuing outside Tower Records in London's Piccadilly Circus to be the first to purchase ***Live At The BBC***, the first "new" **Beatles** album since ***The Beatles At The Hollywood Bowl*** in 1977. A double album comprising 69 tracks, it includes material recorded for BBC radio shows, such as "Easy Beat," "Saturday Club," "Top Gear," and "Pop Go The Beatles," between March 1962 and June 1965. Showing once again that the group has no peers, it will top the UK chart immediately, selling 600,000 copies by January 1, and a further two million in the US by the beginning of February.

7 With the California-based US punk scene at full throttle, one of its most popular proponents, **Offspring**, perform *Bad Habit* to open the fifth **Billboard** Music Awards held at the Universal Amphitheater, Universal City. Their breakthrough album, the rock/ska/punk-fused ***Smash***, hit US No. 4 in October, and will rack up five million US sales.

16 Having taped a performance on "Later With Jools Holland" on the 13th, and presented "Top Of The Pops" last night, **Blur** play a secret gig for 400 students at Colchester Sixth Form College in England, following an appeal from **Damon Albarn** and **Graham Coxon**'s former music teacher, Nigel Hildreth. The school's 17-piece orchestra plays Hildreth's arrangements of *Parklife*, *End Of A Century*, and *Girls And Boys* at the concert, which raises £3,000 ($4,800) for an orphanage in India. Albarn will later say, "We wouldn't let the **Colchester Evening Gazette** in, because they were always giving us bad reviews. They'd always been very bitter."

17 Having already notched up the US chart longevity record for any act (38 years and 7 months), when an unnecessarily remixed version of *December, 1963 (Oh, What A Night)* re-entered the Hot 100 on August 13, the **Four Seasons**' disc now becomes the longest ever Hot 100 resident, with 46 accumulated weeks.

24 **Pearl Jam**'s ***Vitalogy*** tops the US chart, having sold 877,001 copies on CD and cassette in its first week, the second biggest debut-week sales total ever, behind their own ***Vs.*** (950,378). The vinyl format was issued two weeks ago, prompting an initial, and rare, vinyl-only US chart peak of No. 55. The album contains the group's first ever US 45, *Spin The Black Circle.*

27 Fresh off a protracted US tour with **Nine Inch Nails**, **Marilyn Manson** plays at Club 5 in Jacksonville, Florida, at the start of their American Family Tour. Performing some of the set naked, Manson is arrested by undercover vice cops and charged with violating the Adult Entertainment Code. He spends 16 hours in jail.

ROOTS **During this year:The quirkily named trio Ben Folds Five forms in Chapel Hill, North Carolina... Erykah Badu and Robert "Free" Bradford begin performing around Dallas as Erykah Free... Andy Slater, boss of Clean Slate Records, signs 16-year-old Fiona Apple to his label, initially nurturing her talent before releasing any material... Swedish quintet the Hives begin gigging in and around Fagersta... having played their first gig on Halloween night last year, the Bluetones are seen at the Bull & Gate pub in London by Neil Burrow, who becomes their enthusiastic manager... North Carolinian Ryan Adams, already a member of high school punk band Patty Duke Syndrome, forms Whiskeytown... Darren Hayes and Englishman Daniel Jones meet while playing in bar bands in Queensland, Australia; almost immediately signing a management and recording contract with JDM, they become Savage Garden... and teenage rapper Lil' Kim joins Notorious B.I.G.'s rap collective Junior M.A.F.I.A., making her recording debut on the band's *Conspiracy* album...**

You Are Not Alone

1995

No.1 US SINGLES

Jan 7	On Bended Knee **Boyz II Men**
Jan 28	Creep **TLC**
Feb 25	Take A Bow **Madonna**
Apr 15	This Is How We Do It **Montell Jordan**
June 3	Have You Ever Really Loved A Woman? **Bryan Adams**
July 8	Waterfalls **TLC**
Aug 26	Kiss From A Rose **Seal**
Sept 2	You Are Not Alone **Michael Jackson**
Sept 9	Gangsta's Paradise **Coolio featuring LV**
Sept 30	Fantasy **Mariah Carey**
Nov 25	Exhale (Shoop Shoop) **Whitney Houston**
Dec 2	One Sweet Day **Mariah Carey & Boyz II Men**

No.1 UK SINGLES

Jan 7	Stay Another Day **East 17**
Jan 14	Cotton Eye Joe **Rednex**
Feb 4	Think Twice **Celine Dion**
Mar 25	Love Can Build A Bridge **Cher, Chrissie Hynde & Neneh Cherry with Eric Clapton**
Apr 1	Don't Stop (Wiggle Wiggle) **Outhere Brothers**
Apr 8	Back For Good **Take That**
May 6	Some Might Say **Oasis**
May 13	Dreamer **Livin' Joy**
May 20	Unchained Melody/White Cliffs Of Dover **Robson & Jerome**
July 8	Boom Boom Boom **Outhere Brothers**
Aug 5	Never Forget **Take That**
Aug 26	Country House **Blur**
Sept 9	You Are Not Alone **Michael Jackson**
Sept 23	Boombastic **Shaggy**
Sept 30	Fairground **Simply Red**
Oct 28	Gangsta's Paradise **Coolio featuring LV**
Nov 11	I Believe/Up On The Roof **Robson Green & Jerome Flynn**
Dec 9	Earth Song **Michael Jackson**

Radiohead

Alanis Morissette with backing band

By the end of 1995, Radiohead's *The Bends* will appear in a host of magazine Top 10 year's best lists, including People Weekly, Entertainment Weekly, Billboard, Musician, Melody Maker and the New Musical Express... When Alanis Morissette's *Jagged Little Pill* hit the top in the US in October, she became the first Canadian female artist to top the American chart Rock and Roll Hall of Fame and Museum.

While the American rock scene was still dominated by grunge and college rock, British music was going through a renaissance, and rock history finally had a home it could call its own: the Rock and Roll Hall of Fame and Museum opened in Cleveland, Ohio. To inaugurate the site, a seven-hour all-star concert on September 2 celebrated nearly half a century of rock 'n' roll. Rounding out the year – and 25 years after they broke up – the **Beatles** registered yet another US No. 1 album, shifting nearly a million copies of ***Anthology Volume 1*** in its first week.

Spearheading a diverse mix of top new British talent, **Oasis** and **Blur** were locked in mortal combat for the title of best of BritPop, with Oasis leading the gritty northern rockers camp and Blur the southern, artschool brigade. Blur's ***Parklife*** picked up a record number of BRIT Awards, while to great expectations Oasis released ***(What's The Story) Morning Glory?***, which reflected the tensions between the brothers **Gallagher** (and was probably better for them). Another British band winning fans across the Atlantic was **Radiohead**, whose ***The Bends*** was hailed by many as one of the era's seminal albums. Soaring vocals from **Thom Yorke**, a swirl of guitar, and clever (sometimes too clever) lyrics made it clear that Radiohead would be more than *Creep*.

Portishead became the foremost exponents of British trip-hop. Mixing hip-hop, soul, and bluesy vocals from **Beth Gibbons**, the band's debut album followed in the footsteps of **Massive Attack**, and was, for one critic, the "perfect distillation of the emotion called longing," with its melancholy melodies and spacey sound effects. The **Chemical Brothers**' ***Exit Planet Dust*** fused techno and rock, synthesized bass, samplers, and computers for an "electro-gliding" effect: a dazzling hybrid that put electronica in the mainstream.

While **Pearl Jam**'s dark and powerful multiplatinum ***Vitalogy*** kept the grunge flame lit in the US, the **Smashing Pumpkins** launched their ambitiously titled double opus ***Mellon Collie And The Infinite Sadness*** – seemingly an attempt to encapsulate the modern history of rock. Their crunching metal sound was there, but so was a delicate piano, and classical, pop, and rock influences. Adding to an increasingly crowded scene of female singer-songwriters, **Alanis Morissette** prescribed her ***Jagged Little Pill***, on which she sounded by turns vulnerable, venomous, introspective, and defiant – but always preoccupied with relationships and sex.

The most notable rock legend to expire in 1995 was **Jerry Garcia**. He'd toured until the very end, and there were few more loyal fans than those of the Dead. He had said: "Certainly one of the things that makes the **Grateful Dead** interesting, from my point of view, is that it's a group of people. The dynamics of the group is the part that I trust." Without him, there seemed no point in continuing, and the band called it quits.

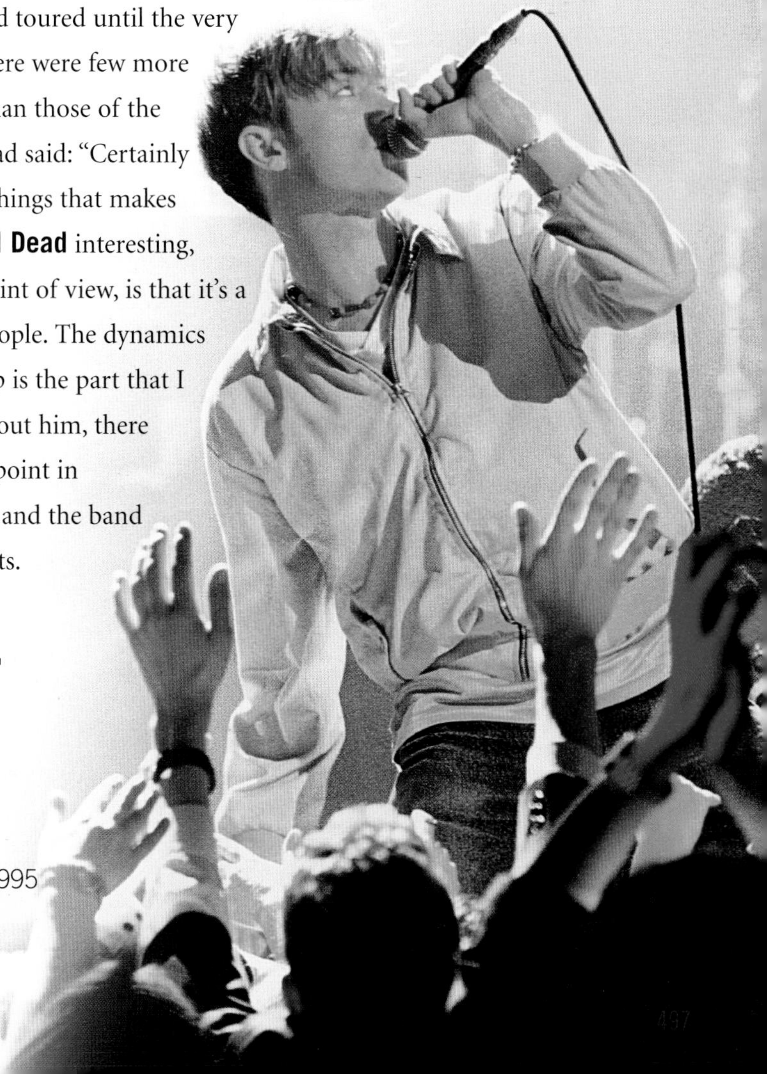

"British music has started to re-establish itself. There's a lot of great music being made in Britain. It's time kids stopped listening to American rubbish." Damon Albarn at the BRITS, February 20, 1995

1995

Led Zeppelin inducted into the Hall of Fame... Tejano superstar Selena murdered...

Steve Winwood sang at the memorial service of his close friend Vivian Stanshall, who had written lyrics for several Winwood songs... Having gone 25 years between appearances on NBC-TV's "The Tonight Show", Joni Mitchell made a return visit just 10 months later.

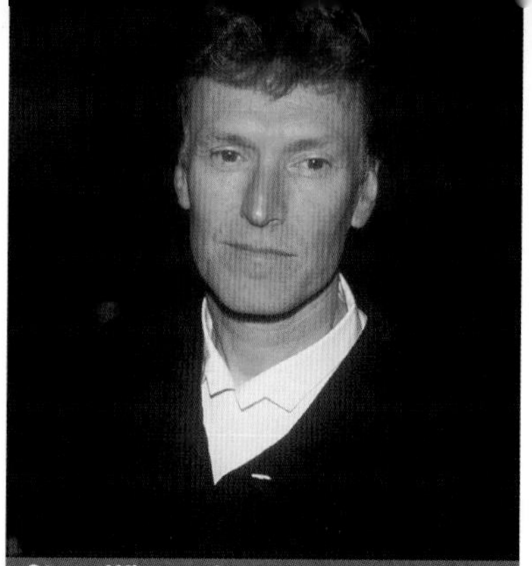

Steve Winwood

January

8 Pearl Jam's Eddie Vedder plays DJ on over four hours of late-night radio, broadcast as "Self Pollution Radio" from his dilapidated house in Seattle, Washington, where the band rehearses. Pearl Jam sings ten songs in an adjacent bedroom, as do Soundgarden, Mudhoney, the Fastbacks, and Mad Season (a collaboration between Pearl Jam's Mike McCready and Alice In Chains' Layne Staley). As an added bonus, there are tracks from Nirvana drummer Dave Grohl's forthcoming solo album, and a spoken-word piece from bandmate Krist Novoselic.

12 Led Zeppelin's Jimmy Page, Robert Plant, and John Paul Jones jam with Aerosmith's Steven Tyler and Joe Perry, after their induction by the Toxic Twins into the Rock and Roll Hall of Fame at the tenth ceremony. Eddie Vedder inducts Neil Young (Young and Pearl Jam will join forces this weekend for two benefit concerts for Voters for Choice, at the DAR Constitution Hall in Washington D.C.). Willie Nelson inducts the Allman Brothers Band, singing *Funny How Time Slips Away* with inductee Al Green, who is welcomed into the Hall of Fame by Natalie Cole. Melissa Etheridge inducts Janis Joplin, honoring the late singer by performing *Piece Of My Heart*. Lou Reed inducts Frank Zappa, and the B-52's Kate Pierson and Fred Schneider induct Martha & the Vandellas. R&B pioneers the Orioles are inducted as the only Early Influence, and journalist and historian Paul Ackerman is the only Non-Performer.

21 During Hole dates in Australia, Courtney Love, currently hailed as the queen of the media-invented Riot Grrrl movement, is arrested for offensive behavior on a plane flying from Brisbane to Melbourne. She had put her feet up on the first class bulkhead, and refused to remove them; on being told she would be reported for offensive behavior, she replied, "Go the f**k ahead."

24 Portishead is named Best Dance Act at the NME's BRAT Awards in London (the magazine's alternative to the industry's BRITs). Their full-length debut album ***Dummy*** was recently hailed album of the year (for 1994) by The Face, Melody Maker, Mix Mag, ID, and The Daily Telegraph, among others. Mixing retro-sounding cinematic themes with hip-hop, soul, jazz, and blues flavors and showcasing lead singer Beth Gibbons's powerful blues vocal chops, the album is regarded as a pioneering release in the burgeoning trip-hop genre. The innovative quartet, rounded out by Geoff Barrow, Adrian Utley, and Dave McDonald, has emerged from Bristol's highly creative dance/R&B scene, which has also given rise to hot production team Smith & Mighty, and Massive Attack.

26 The Fraunhofer Institute for Integrated Circuits in Germany applies for a US patent (which will be granted next year) for its MPEG-3 technology, which allows for the compression of digitally recorded music files without compromising sound quality. Work on the pioneering format began in 1987, and the first version, MPEG-1, was adopted as an industry standard in 1992. MP3 will revolutionize the way music is distributed, stored, and played. As the popularity of the internet gathers steam, it will become the accepted method of transferring music around the worldwide web.

February

3 Following an appearance on January 26 at the Wells Fargo Theater in the Gene Autry Museum, Los Angeles, to promote her new album, ***Turbulent Indigo*** (featuring Seal, among others), Joni Mitchell appears on "The Tonight Show," hosted by Jay Leno. By her recollection, it is her first television appearance since the "Johnny Cash Show" in 1970.

17 Manic Street Preachers guitarist Richey Edwards's car is found abandoned on the English side of the Severn Bridge. He was last seen leaving the Embassy Hotel in Bayswater, London, on February 1, heading for his apartment in Cardiff, Wales, where he has left his passport, Prozac prescription, credit cards, and a folder of lyrics and poems.

17 With Garth Brooks's first compilation, ***Hits***, at US No. 1 this week, the RIAA certifies multiplatinum sales for ***The Chase*** (six million), ***Ropin' The Wind*** (11 million), and ***No Fences*** (13 million), confirming him as the biggest-selling country artist of all time. His sales outside the US are minuscule by comparison.

20 BritPoppers Blur celebrate the biggest single-night win in the history of the BRIT Awards, at the 14th ceremony held at London's Alexandra Palace. They win trophies for the Best British Single (*Parklife*), Best British Video ("Parklife"), Best British Album (***Parklife***), and Best British Group. Rivals Oasis pick up the Best British Newcomer award, with Paul Weller and ex-Fairground Attraction singer-songwriter Eddi Reader winning the Best British Male and Female Solo Artist trophies. After performing an unlikely duet with Best British Dance Act winners, M People, Sting presents Elton John with the Outstanding Contribution. Other winners include R.E.M. (Best International Act – their second), ⚥ (Best International Male

After an airborne fracas, Courtney Love pled guilty to abusing a flight attendant, was required to be on "good behavior" for one month, and fined $500.

Joni Mitchell

Artist), **k.d. lang** (Best International Female Artist), and **Lisa Loeb** (Best International Newcomer). **Madonna** opens the ceremony singing *Unconscious*, no doubt happy that her *Bedtime Stories* album brings its producer, **Nellee Hooper**, the Best British Producer nod.

25 **Elton John** gives a soul-searching interview to the **NME**, in which he reveals that in the past five years he has attended over 1,350 counseling sessions. Of his cocaine habit, he says: "Sting said it was God's way of telling me that I had too much money."

Bruce Springsteen's stirring *Streets Of Philadelphia* won three Grammys, including Song of the Year, and an Oscar.

26 **Neil Young** and **Pearl Jam** perform together at the Moore Theater in Seattle, billed as the **Piss Bottle Men.**

March

1 **Bruce Springsteen** opens the 37th Grammy Awards, at the Shrine Auditorium in Los Angeles, with a performance of *Streets Of Philadelphia* (for which he won last year's Oscar for Best Music, Song). It goes on to win the Song of the Year, Best Male Rock Vocal Performance, and Best Rock Song Written Specifically for Motion Picture or Television. Having been presented with a Lifetime Achievement Award in 1987, the **Rolling Stones** receive their first Grammys: Best Rock Album (*Voodoo Lounge*) and Best Music Video Shortform ("Love Is Strong"). **Bob Dylan** – previously a winner in a rock category – wins the Best Traditional Folk Album award for *World Gone Wrong*. **Eric Clapton** picks up his ninth Grammy, winning the Best Traditional Blues Album category for *From The Cradle*. **Sheryl Crow** wins Record of the Year and Best Pop Vocal Performance, Female for *All I Wanna Do*, also picking up Best New Artist award. *The Rhythm Country & Blues* album, a collaboration between the best in R&B and country, wins two awards – Best Country Vocal Collaboration for **Aaron Neville** and **Trisha Yearwood**'s *I Fall To Pieces*, and Best Pop Vocal Collaboration for **Al Green** and **Lyle Lovett**'s *Funny How Time Slips Away*. **Tony Bennett**, after a fallow period (he won twice in 1963), picks up his third consecutive Best Traditional Pop Vocal Performance and, in perhaps the most popular decision of the evening, wins Album of the Year for his ultra-hip *MTV Unplugged* album.

15 **Madonna** is signed to star as Eva Peron in the film version of the **Andrew Lloyd Webber/Tim Rice** hit musical "Evita" – a role she has coveted for many years. She is currently midway through a seven-week stretch at US No. 1 with *Take A Bow*, co-written and performed with **Babyface.**

18 **Annie Lennox** guests on "Saturday Night Live," promoting *Medusa*, the follow-up to her six-million-selling debut, *Diva*. A covers album produced by Stephen Lipson, and featuring **Procol Harum**'s *A Whiter Shade Of Pale* (the first record she ever bought at age 14), **Al Green**'s *Take Me To The River*, **Bob Marley**'s *Waiting In Vain*, **Blue Nile**'s *Downtown Lights*, plus songs originally performed by the **Temptations**, **Neil Young**, the **Clash**, the **Persuaders**, and **Paul Simon**, it entered the UK chart at No. 1 this week.

21 **Steve Winwood** sings *Arc Of A Diver* at the memorial service for the **Bonzo Dog Doo Dah Band**'s **Vivian Stanshall** – on what would have been his 52nd birthday – at St. Patrick's Church in London's Soho Square. The eccentric Stanshall, having recently returned to public view in Ruddles Ale TV commercials, died in a fire in his London flat on March 5. Yesterday, Island released a four-CD retrospective, *The Finer Things*, chronicling Winwood's career from the **Spencer Davis Group** through **Blind Faith**, **Traffic**, fusion experiments with **Stomu Yamashta**'s **Go**, **Winwood/Kanaka/Amao**, and subsequent solo highlights with both Island and Virgin.

31 The 23-year-old Grammy award-winning singer and Tejano superstar, **Selena**, is shot to death at the Days Inn motel in Corpus Christi, Texas. Her killer, 32-year-old Yolanda Saldivar, described as a former fan club president and ex-employee, is arrested following a nine-hour standoff with police, during which she threatens to kill herself.

April

8 **Take That**'s *Back For Good* debuts at UK No. 1, having sold more than 300,000 copies in a week, the highest opening tally for ten years.

16 **George Michael** raises £70,000 ($112,000) – and Sony's ire – by giving his new single *Jesus For A Child* a one-shot airing on Capital Radio's "Help a London Child" charity broadcast.

20 Increasingly at odds with his notoriously antagonistic bandmates, **Oasis** drummer **Tony McCarroll** is involved in a fracas with the **Gallagher** brothers after a gig at the Bataclan in Paris, France. Next weekend, after the group's appearance on "Top Of The Pops," he will find himself out of work. (The band will strenuously deny he was fired, saying he left by mutual consent.)

23 **The Sunday Times** reports that welder Peter Hodgson, while clearing out his attic, has found a 1959 recording of 16 songs by the **Quarry Men** on a Grundig reel-to-reel tape recorder lent by his father to **Paul McCartney**.

The Eagles

***Jagged Little Pill* is released... Wolfman Jack dies... The Ramones' farewell tour...**

May

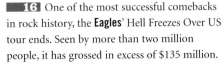

15 **Jewel**, a 20-year-old folk/pop singer-songwriter born in Utah but raised in Anchorage, Alaska, makes her network television debut on NBC-TV's "Conan O'Brien Show." Her maiden set, the fragile, mostly self-penned, Starbucks-aimed ***Pieces Of You***, was released in the US by Atlantic on February 17. It includes her first single, *Who Will Save Your Soul*, which initially flops, as will a remixed version of *You Were Meant For Me* with electric guitar added.

15 Having scrapped two weeks of recording sessions in February, **Stone Temple Pilots' Scott Weiland** is arrested for heroin and cocaine possession in Pasadena, California.

16 One of the most successful comebacks in rock history, the **Eagles**' Hell Freezes Over US tour ends. Seen by more than two million people, it has grossed in excess of $135 million.

20 With an unnecessary cover version of the standard by British television actors **Robson Green and Jerome Flynn**, *Unchained Melody* becomes the first song to hit UK No. 1 three times by different artists. The other two were **Jimmy Young** in 1955 (the year the song was written by Alex North and Hy Zaret), and the definitive version by the **Righteous Brothers** (which recharted at No. 1 in 1990).

23 **Troggs** member **Reg Presley** collects the Best Selling Song, the PRS Most Performed Work, and International Hit of the Year trophies (all for *Love Is All Around*) at the 40th Ivor Novello Awards at London's Grosvenor House Hotel. **Georgie Fame** presents the Lifetime Achievement Award to **Van Morrison**, who in turn does the honors for **Lonnie Donegan**, recipient of the Outstanding Contribution to British Music Award. Ambient pioneer and A-list producer **Brian Eno** is presented with the Radio 1 Award for Continuing Innovation in Music. **Elvis Costello** wins the Outstanding Contemporary Song Collection, and **Elton John** and **Tim Rice**'s *Circle Of Life* is named Best Song Included in a Film. **Celine Dion**'s *Think Twice*, written by **Andy Hill** and **Pete Sinfield**, wins the Best Song Musically and Lyrically category. **East 17**'s **Tony Mortimer** is named Songwriter of the Year, while R&B newcomer, London-born **Des'ree**'s infectious *You Gotta Be* receives the Best Contemporary Song award.

25 The earliest known recording by **Mick Jagger** and **Keith Richards**, on a reel-to-reel tape from 1961, is auctioned at Christie's in London. The line-up on the 30-minute recording is believed also to feature **Dick Taylor**, **Bob Beckwith**, and **Allen Etherington**. The anonymous winning bid is made by Jagger.

In an unlikely career move, Jewel played Dorothy in an all-star cast concert version of "The Wizard Of Oz" in 1995 at New York's Avery Fisher Hall.

27 **Paul Weller**'s third solo album, ***Stanley Road***, enters the UK chart at No. 1. The album, named after his childhood home in Woking, England, has a sleeve design by Peter Blake, and features **Steve Winwood**, **Noel Gallagher**, **Carleen Anderson**, and former **Style Council** member **Mick Talbot** among its guests.

June

7 Eight dates into the band's North American tour, during a performance at Peabody's Down Under in Cleveland, **Radiohead**'s **Jonny Greenwood** almost collapses on stage when his ear leaks blood. The diagnosis is an arm problem, caused by repetitive guitar playing. The group is touring to promote the vibrant, critically revered ***The Bends***, which will appear in a host of magazine top tens of the year lists, including those in **People**, **Melody Maker**, **NME**, **Musician**, **Billboard**, and **Options**.

13 **Alanis Morissette**'s critically acclaimed debut album for **Madonna**'s Maverick label, ***Jagged Little Pill***, is released in the US. Its lead-off single *You Oughta Know* – featuring the **Red Hot Chili Peppers' Flea** and **Dave Navarro** – will be her first hit in the UK in August, but will remain a No. 1 Modern Rock chart radio-only cut in the US, as will its follow-ups, *Hand In My Pocket* and *All I Really Want*. The set's first Hot 100 hit will be *Ironic* at US No. 4 next year. The 21-year-old singer-songwriter from Ottawa is no newcomer to the world of entertainment. She wrote her first tunes when she was nine and appeared in the Nickelodeon show "You Can't Do That On Television" for two years from the age of 10. Her first self-released single led her to sign with MCA Records in Canada, where her debut album, the dance-based ***Alanis***, sold over 100,000 copies, and won her a domestic Juno Award as Canada's Most Promising Female Artist. Following the pop/soul-fused ***Now Is The Time*** in 1992, Morissette relocated to Los Angeles, where she secured an acting role opposite Corey Haim in Fox-TV's shortlived sitcom "Just One Of The Girls." Set on a new

"When you get to 50 you know darn well it's going to be over one day. The party can't go on forever." Rod Stewart, **Mojo**, May 1995

The Chemical Brothers

The RIAA announced the total sales of Eagles records in the US had reached 56 million... The Chemical Brothers' Tom Rowlands and Ed Simons met while studying history at Manchester University in 1989. They attended the same Chaucer and Russian classes.

direction as a serious singer-songwriter, but without a new label deal, she teamed with rock/pop producer Glen Ballard, to whom she was introduced through MCA publishing executive Kurt Denny. They wrote and recorded ***Jagged Little Pill*** at his home studio in San Fernando Valley, and it impressed 21-year-old Guy Oseary, an A&R scout for Maverick.

14 Irish blues/rock guitarist **Rory Gallagher** dies, age 46, following a liver transplant. First finding fame as a member of **Taste** in the late 1960s, Gallagher uncomprisingly stuck to his musical roots, eschewing commercial success. In its obituary, **The Times** will describe him as "a courageously honest performer [who wrote] his own material, and considered the blues to be the most personal form of musical expression."

15 The day after **Michael Jackson**, with Lisa Marie by his side, is interviewed by Diane Sawyer on ABC-TV's "Primetime Live," a 33ft statue of Jackson sails under London's Tower Bridge, as the worldwide hype over the double set ***HIStory: Past, Present And Future Book 1*** increases to fever pitch. Part hits and part new material, the album features new productions by Jam and Lewis, David Foster, **R. Kelly**, and Dallas Austin.

23 The **Chemical Brothers**' ***Exit Planet Dust*** is released in the UK. Receiving high critical praise as a groundbreaking dance album, its deep beats, innovative samples, and anthemic soundscapes, fusing techno and rock, introduce the new "big beat" genre that is moving from the clubs and into the charts. Having perfected their dancefloor chops as live DJs during the Madchester scene at the beginning of the decade, **Tom Rowlands** and **Ed Simons** are currently the hottest UK club DJs, with a residency at London's Heavenly Sunday Social.

30 **Garth Brooks** buries the master of ***The Hits*** beneath his Hollywood Walk of Fame star, in front of Capitol's offices on the corner of Sunset and Vine. The album was limited to a mere ten million copies, and was deleted on June 1.

July

1 Legendary American DJ **Wolfman Jack** dies from a heart attack at home in Belvidere, North Carolina. Blessed with one of the most distinctive voices on air, the Brooklyn-born Robert Smith broke through in the golden age of Top 40 radio. A self-styled public enigma before receiving wide attention in the 1973 rock 'n' roll movie, "American Graffiti," he made a final syndicated broadcast from the Planet Hollywood restaurant in Washington, D.C. last night.

4 Lollapalooza '95 opens at the Gorge in George, Washington, boasting **Sonic Youth**, **Hole**, **Cypress Hill**, **Pavement**, **Sinéad O'Connor**, **Beck** (who broke last year with his signature hit *Loser*, an anthem for disaffected American Gen-X youth), underground industrial rock unit **Jesus Lizard**, and the ska/rock-fusing **Mighty Mighty Bosstones**. O'Connor will leave eight dates into the six-week trek, because of her pregnancy. **Elastica**, cross-genre, techno-electronic pioneer **Moby**, and obsessively independent alt-rockers **Superchunk** will join the tour on some dates.

13 Sony announces that **George Michael** has won his freedom from the company, enabling him to sign as the first music act to Dreamworks SKG in the US, and Virgin Records for the rest of the world, in a two-album deal. Sony will receive an estimated $40 million, plus 3 percent of retail sales of his next two albums, his back catalog, and a greatest hits album.

22 In the latest incident in **R.E.M.**'s troubled world trek, two teenagers drown in the Boyne River during the group's concert at Slane Castle in County Meath, Ireland. **Oasis**, American alt-pop/rock quartet **Belly** (led by ex-**Throwing Muses** and ex-**Breeders** singer, **Tanya Donelly**), Irish-born folk stylist **Luka Bloom**, fellow Irish native, accordionist/fiddle player **Sharon Shannon**, and funk-rappers **Spearhead** (led by **Michael Franti**) appear before the 100,000-strong crowd.

August

2 The **Ramones**' Adios Amigos farewell tour opens at the Strand Theater in Providence, Rhode Island, set to close in the US on September 17 at the Ted Gormley Stadium in New Orleans, before a five-date jaunt in Buenos Aires.

2 Reunited with the **Attractions**, **Elvis Costello** begins five nights at New York's Beacon Theater. His sets include songs written for others, including *Complicated Shadows*, *You Bow Down*, and *God Give Me Strength*, written with **Burt Bacharach** (via fax and phone) for the Allison Anders movie "Grace of the Heart," about the legendary Brill Building.

Robbie Williams made his solo debut at Capital Radio's "Music Jam."

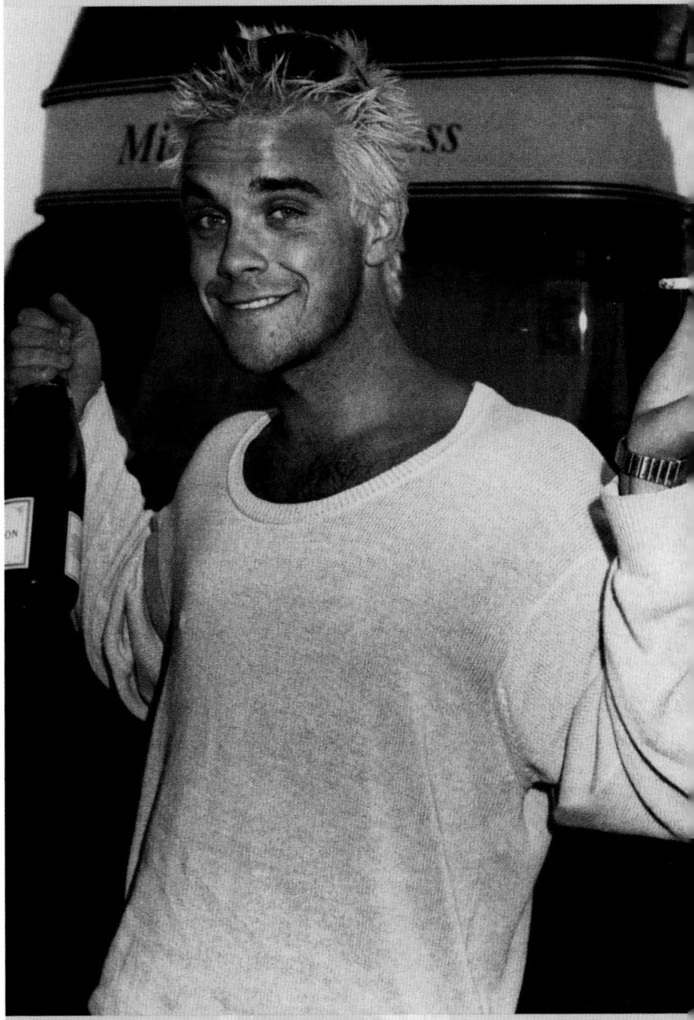

ROBBIE WILIIAMS

July 17 **A statement is issued by Take That: "Robbie Williams is to leave chart-topping group Take That. He has left the group as he was no longer able to give Take That the long-term commitment they needed." The increasingly erratic Williams appeared with the band at the Glastonbury Festival last month sporting a newly spiked blond hairstyle, and in an inebriated state. He had announced his intention to leave at the end of their forthcoming tour, but is ousted with immediate effect, resulting in bitter legal action with manager Nigel Martin-Smith and much lingering acrimony with his ex-colleagues.**

The inaugural Soul Train awards... Jerry Garcia dies... The Rock and Roll Hall of Fame and Museum opens...

6 The inaugural Lady Soul Train Awards ceremony takes place at the Civic Auditorium in Santa Monica. **Brandy**, a 16-year-old newcomer, is the night's big winner, picking up three awards (Best R&B/Soul Single Solo, R&B/Soul Song of the Year and Best R&B/Soul New Artist) for *I Wanna Be Down*, and one for R&B/Soul Album of the Year, Solo (***Brandy***). **TLC** wins Best R&B/Soul Single, Group, Band or Duo for this year's chart-topping *Creep*, and R&B/Soul Album of the Year, Group, Band or Duo for ***CrazySexyCool***. **Salt-N-Pepa** receives the 1995 Aretha Franklin Award as Entertainer of the Year.

11 **Jerry Garcia**'s funeral is held at St. Stephen's Episcopal Church in Belvedere, California, with the deceased reportedly laid to rest in a black T-shirt and sweatpants. "An Elegy for Jerry" is read by **Robert Hunter**. A public memorial hosted by the City of San Francisco and the **Grateful Dead** will take place in two days' time at the Polo Field, Golden Gate Park.

15 One of the hardest working groups currently playing in the US, the **Dave Matthews Band** perform at the dramatic Red Rocks Amphitheater in Denver, and the concert is recorded for a subsequent live double-CD release in 1997. The roots rock quintet, formed by South African-born singer-songwriter/guitarist Matthews in 1991 in Charlottesville, is building a devoted fan following in the US, particularly with college kids. Their near constant gigging is this year in support of their triple-platinum second set, ***Under The Table And Dreaming***.

24 Microsoft's TV commercial for its Windows '95 software launch premieres simultaneously in the US, UK, Australia, and Canada, using the **Rolling Stones**' *Start Me Up* as its background theme. Bill Gates's company has reportedly paid $12 million for the privilege.

26 At the height of a bitter media-fed feud between BritPop champs **Blur** and **Oasis** (both of whom have scored recent UK No. 1 hits) Blur's *Country House* enters the UK chart at No. 1, selling 274,000 copies in its first week and outsmarting Oasis's *Roll With It* (at sales of 216,000), which enters at No. 2.

30 The day after his 53rd birthday, founding **Velvet Underground** member **Sterling Morrison** dies in Poughkeepsie, New York, after a lengthy battle with non-Hodgkins lymphoma. In his post-Velvets life, Morrison worked as a tugboat captain in Houston, Texas, as an English professor, and as a featured performer with the Hudson Valley Philharmonic.

September

2 The Rock and Roll Hall of Fame and Museum in Cleveland celebrates its opening with the all-star sellout Concert for the Hall of Fame at Cleveland Stadium. It includes contributions from **Al Green**, **Aretha Franklin**, **Booker T. & the MG's**, **Bob Dylan**, **Dr. John**, **George Clinton**, **Bon Jovi**, **Chuck Berry**, **Bruce Springsteen**, **Heart**, **Iggy Pop**, **Jackson Browne**, **Jerry Lee Lewis**, **John Mellencamp**, **Johnny Cash**, **Little Richard**, **Melissa Etheridge**, **Natalie Merchant**, the **Pretenders**, **Sam Moore**, **Sheryl Crow**, **Soul Asylum**, the **Allman Brothers Band**, **Boz Scaggs**, **John Fogerty**, **Gin Blossoms**, **Robbie Robertson**, **James Brown**, **Ray Davies**, **Lou Reed**, **Bruce Hornsby**, and **Martha Reeves**. The concert is part of a Labor Day weekend bash, which began yesterday morning with the Rockin' in the Streets Parade, followed by a ribbon-cutting ceremony to open the $92 million museum, sitting on the banks of Lake Erie and designed by I.M. Pei.

7 **Janet** and **Michael Jackson** collect their Best Dance Video, Best Choreography, and Best Art Direction trophies for their monochromatic duet, "Scream," at the 12th MTV Video Music Awards at New York's Radio City Music Hall. In between presentation duties, **Seal** nabs Best

JERRY GARCIA

Aug 9 **Jerry Garcia is found dead in his sleep at the Serenity Knolls drug treatment center in Forest Knolls, California. The coroner's report cites the official cause of death as a heart attack caused by hardening of the arteries, but indicates that the 53-year-old Garcia probably used heroin the day before he died (the guitarist was a long-term user). San Francisco Mayor Frank Jordan orders city flags to be lowered to half-mast, and a tie-dyed Dead flag to be temporarily placed on the City Hall flagpole. Bob Dylan is quoted as saying: "There's no way to convey the loss. It just digs down really deep."**

Hall of Fame Concert

Portishead

Ahmet Ertegun described the Rock and Roll Hall of Fame and Museum as "an endeavor to recognize the people who were responsible for what became the most popular music in the world, of all time"... Portishead's Geoff Barrow told a reporter from the Washington Post that the band wanted to just "put out lots of records."

Video from a Film for "Kiss From A Rose" – taken from "Batman Forever," the song topped the US chart last month. **Dr. Dre**'s "Keep Their Heads Ringin'" is named Best Rap Video, and **Hootie & the Blowfish** collect the award for Best New Artist Video for "Hold My Hand". **Madonna**'s "Take A Bow" wins the Best Female Video category, and **TLC**'s "Waterfalls" picks up Best Video, Best Group Video, Best R&B Video, and the People's Choice of the Year. **Tom Petty** wins the Best Male Video category for "You Don't Know How It Feels." The **Rolling Stones**' "Love Is Strong" wins the Best Cinematography field. Unconventional alt-pop newcomer **Weezer** receives the trophy for Best Alternative Video, Best Direction (Spike Jonze), Best Editing (Eric Zumbrunnen), and Breakthrough Video, for the quirky and popular clip "Buddy Holly." **Black Sabbath**-influenced hard-rock combo **White Zombie** – led by avid comic-book collector frontman **Rob Zombie** – performs *More Human Than Human*, for which the group collects the Best Hard Rock Video trophy. **R.E.M.** collects the lifetime achievement Video Vanguard honor.

8 **Annie Lennox** performs a free concert in Central Park: her first New York concert since 1988 and her only scheduled US appearance of the year. The 6,000 tickets, given away in two New York stores, were snapped up in 15 minutes. The performance is recorded for a limited edition eight-track live album, ***Live In Central Park***, which will be paired with copies of ***Medusa*** worldwide, though it will not emerge in the US until the following spring.

12 **Portishead**'s *Dummy* wins this year's hotly contested Mercury Music Prize at London's Savoy Hotel. The eclectic and diverse runners-up are: **Guy Barker** (***Into The Blue***), **Elastica** (for its highly-praised debut album, ***Elastica***), **P.J. Harvey**'s first solo set, ***To Bring You My Love***, house music revivalist production/remixing duo, **Leftfield** (***Leftism***), **James MacMillan** (***Seven Last Words From The Cross***), **Van Morrison** (***Days Like This***), **Oasis** (***Definitely Maybe***), Oxford-based newcomer **Supergrass** (for their rapid-fire, quirky debut album, ***I Should Coco***), and ***Maxinquaye*** by **Tricky**, a fresh, outspoken Brit trip-hop provocateur, who has emerged from Bristol's **Massive Attack**/**Portishead** ranks.

12 The RIAA confirms that **TLC** is now the all-time biggest-selling female recording act in the US, having sold 19 million singles and albums (though the **Supremes**' massive tally in the 1960s has yet to be ratified). The trio's ***CrazySexyCool*** has now sold six million domestic copies (it will eventually top ten million). This follows three million sales of ***Ooooooohhh...On The TLC Tip***, and a slew of gold and platinum singles, including their recent US No. 1s, *Creep* (produced by Dallas Austin) and *Waterfalls*, the closely harmonized, radio-catchy smash produced by the Organized Noize.

"I don't believe that the ten albums of the year should be judged anyway. How can you really say that there is just one winner?"

Portishead's Geoff Barrow, after winning the Mercury Music Prize, September 12, 1995

14 **Paul McCartney**'s hand-written lyrics for *Getting Better* sell for $249,200 at a Sotheby's auction in London, setting a new world record for a **Beatles** composition.

19 Go Discs! releases ***Help!*** in the UK, a various artists album to benefit the War Child charity, recorded just five days earlier under the direction of prime movers **Brian Eno** and **Radiohead**'s **Thom Yorke**. Controversially excluded from the main UK album chart (which does not currently include various artists projects), it will immediately head to No. 1 on the compilations survey.

25 **Courtney Love** pleads guilty to a charge of fourth-degree assault on **Bikini Kill**'s **Kathleen Hanna**, during a Lollapalooza gig on July 4. She is given a one-year suspended sentence, on condition that she refrain from violence for two years and enroll in anger management classes. Judge Richard Fitterer tells her: "You need to get a grip on some issues – fame and money, rumored substance abuse, grief. Your fame is a responsibility."

TLC were confirmed as the all-time biggest-selling female recording act in US history with 19 million sales.

Sir Cliff... Soul Train celebrates its 25th anniversary... "The Beatles Anthology"...

October

7 ***Jagged Little Pill*** tops the US chart, making **Alanis Morissette** the first Canadian female artist to achieve this. As both the artist and the album become global phenomena over the next two years, ***Jagged Little Pill*** will eventually sell more than 16 million copies in the US alone – the biggest-selling debut by a female artist. With its perceived male-bashing lyrics and generally angst-ridden tone, it reveals a frank, rebellious, and impulsive style that immediately connects with Generation X-ers – particularly women. It will be confirmed nine times platinum by the BPI in the UK, and will garner top awards over the next year. Its success will keep Morissette, who is midway through a US tour, on the road until next October.

21 **Blind Melon**'s sound engineer finds lead singer **Shannon Hoon** dead on the group's tour bus, when he tries to wake him for a sound check before tonight's gig at Tipitina's nightclub in New Orleans. The 28-year-old is believed to have died from a cocaine overdose. He will be buried at the Dayton Cemetery in Tippecanoe County, Indiana.

23 On what is designated **Def Leppard** Day, the group performs three concerts on three continents on the same day: they begin at the Cave of Hercules in Tangiers at 5:00 am, perform at Bottom Line in London's Shepherd's Bush at midday, and at the Commodore in Vancouver at 9:00 pm.

25 **Cliff Richard** receives a knighthood, the first pop star to achieve the honor. After the ceremony, he goes to St. Martins-in-the-Fields Church, London, to attend the memorial service of **Jerry Lordan**, who penned several hits for Cliff and, particularly, the **Shadows** – most notably *Apache*, *Wonderful Land*, and *Atlantis*.

November

2 "Soul Train" celebrates its 25th anniversary at the Shrine Auditorium, inducting ten soul legends (and rapper **Hammer**) into the newly-founded Hall of Fame. Several inductees also perform at the ceremonies, which will air on CBS-TV on the 22nd, including **Al Green**, **Bill Withers**, **Diana Ross**, **Patti LaBelle**, and **Stevie Wonder**. The other inductees are **Michael Jackson**, **Whitney Houston**, **Curtis Mayfield**, and **Barry White**, who is unable to attend after being admitted to a Las Vegas hospital suffering from exhaustion. **Marvin Gaye** is posthumously inducted.

7 Following two soldout nights at Earl's Court yesterday and the day before, **Oasis** is named Best Live Act at the **Q** Awards at the Park Lane Hotel in London. A typically disgruntled **Noel Gallagher** graciously comments on their win: "I'll accept this award on behalf of a crap album with crap lyrics." Their second set, ***(What's The Story) Morning Glory?*** with Noel's **Beatles**-inspired compositions and **Liam**'s top-gear vocals in full flow, debuted at UK No. 1 three weeks ago. The extracted sweeping rock anthem *Wonderwall* is at UK No. 2. Currently Britain's most popular and critically revered band, the group's offstage rock star antics – often fueled by drugs and booze – are popular tabloid fodder. The Gallagher brothers' confrontational position on virtually everything can be summed up by Noel's explanation (reported in **Billboard**) for their reluctance to tour in Australia, despite being huge there: "We don't f**kin' wanna fly to the other f**kin' end of the world and play like f**kin' shit."

7 Admitting he is "mellowing out with age," **Eric Clapton** receives his OBE from the Prince of Wales at Buckingham Palace, then goes to the Park Lane Hotel to receive **Q** magazine's Merit Award. **David Bowie** and **Brian Eno** are presented with the **Q** Inspiration Award by **Jarvis Cocker**, who says: "Some people would say they are the Morecambe & Wise of conceptual music which – listen don't laugh – is better than being the Cannon & Ball of conceptual music." Eno comments, "We were sort of expecting Best New Act actually."

8 **Paul McCartney** becomes the first pop musician to be made a Fellow of the Royal College of Music.

11 **Smashing Pumpkins** perform on "Saturday Night Live." Having entered at its UK No. 4 high last week, the Virgin Records-released double-CD ***Mellon Collie And The Infinite Sadness*** debuted at US No. 1 this week. Co-produced by Flood, Alan Moulder, and **Billy Corgan**, its phenomenal success (more than five million worldwide sales) will be spurred by a pair of US gold singles, *Bullet With Butterfly Wings* and the modern rock classic, *1979*.

19 The first part of "The Beatles Anthology" airs on ABC-TV. (Parts two and three will be shown on the 22nd and 23rd.) Including extensive new interviews with the remaining trio, edited in with old **John Lennon** interviews, personal anecdotes and observations, it attempts to build a definitive archival documentary of the **Beatles**' early years. The first program ends with the television premiere of the

To promote her dance-based debut album, *Alanis*, Alanis Morissette served as an opening act for Vanilla Ice.

Oasis

Oasis played a 40-minute acoustic set at midnight at the Virgin Megastore before a crowd of about 500, waiting in line to buy the band's new album... Alanis Morissette made her UK debut at a showcase to promote *Jagged Little Pill* at the Hanover Grand in London in June.

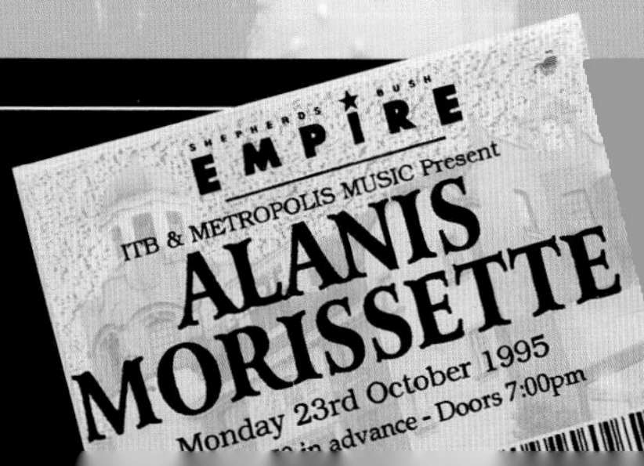

A radio station in Sydney, Australia, held a contest to decide upon a new name for ♀. Listeners chose "Davo."

Beatles' first "new" recording since their split: *Free As A Bird*. It was assembled around a previously unissued Lennon demo that **Yoko Ono** passed to **Paul McCartney** (along with another track, *Real Love*), to which the remaining members added a relevant rhythm section and harmony vocal parts, under the guidance of co-producer **Jeff Lynne**. The television series, broadcast in six one-hour programs in the UK, is the first salvo in a period of renewed Beatles activity. It will see the staggered release of three double-CD anthologies, diligently researched and assembled by the surviving Beatles with producer **George Martin**. Released as a chronological series, each one will include previously unreleased material, out-takes, alternate takes, rehearsals, rare B-sides, studio banter, and past hits.

> **"What a city. What a night. What a bomb. What a mistake. What a wanker you have for president."**
>
> Bono on French President Jacques Chirac's nuclear policy, MTV Europe Awards, November 23, 1995

20 A DJ at a post-Australian Grand Prix party at the Hilton Hotel in Adelaide becomes the first person to broadcast the new **Beatles** single *Free As A Bird*. **George Harrison**, attending the party, has a copy with him and gives it to the DJ 24 hours before it is broadcast anywhere else in the world.

21 Elektra Records US releases its first E-CD, **Natalie Merchant**'s multimedia-enhanced single *Wonder*, taken from her recently released, hotly rated maiden solo album, ***Tigerlily***. Hailed by the **Wall Street Journal** as "A gem...***Tigerlily*** has the presence of a timeless classic," the album will eventually sell more than four million copies in the US alone.

21 Toward the end of their US trek, **Green Day**'s **Billie Joe** is arrested after mooning the audience during a show at the Milwaukee Arena.

23 Having received the Pioneer Award at the sixth Rhythm and Blues Foundation ceremony at the Hollywood Palladium in March, sax-playing Motown legend **Jr. Walker** dies of cancer, age 64, in Battle Creek, Michigan.

23 **George Michael** and **Bono** politicize the second MTV Europe Awards staged at Le Zenith in Paris, with comments about France's nuclear policy. Presenting the Free Your Mind Award to Greenpeace, Michael criticizes Prime Minister John Major for his support of Jacques Chirac's French nuclear policy, saying: "If business means looking the other way while your partners endanger the planet, we are better off on our own." **U2** take home the Best Group Award. Other winners include **Michael Jackson** (Best Male Artist), **Take That** (Best Live Act), **Björk** (Best Female Artist), and **East 17** (Best Dance Group).

26 **Bruce Springsteen** begins his first solo acoustic tour, promoting the dark, mainly acoustic set, ***The Ghost Of Tom Joad***, at the Wiltern Theater in Los Angeles.

December

6 Currently enjoying his second UK No. 1 of the year with *Earth Song*, **Michael Jackson** collapses on stage while rehearsing for his upcoming HBO special "Michael Jackson: One Night Only" at New York's Beacon Theater. He is treated for apparent dehydration.

6 **Stevie Wonder** performs *Pastime Paradise* with **Coolio** at the sixth **Billboard** Music Awards, held at New York's Coliseum. Rap star Coolio recently hit US No. 1 with *Gangster's Paradise*, a hip-hop rendition of the Wonder original. The update is named Single of the Year. Veteran alt-rock trio **Goo Goo Dolls** – formed by lead singer/guitarist **Johnny Rzeznik**, bassist **Robby Takac**, and drummer **Mike Mallinin** ten years ago in Buffalo, New York, and finally breaking through with their No. 1 Modern Rock chart hit, *Name* – perform the ballad live before accepting an award on behalf of the hospitalized **Michael Jackson**.

8 With **Michael Jackson** in intensive care, being treated for inflammation of the stomach, dehydration, and kidney and liver irregularities (and surrounded by framed posters of Shirley Temple, Mickey Mouse, and Topo Gigio), it is revealed that he is suffering from a viral infection and had been ill for at least a week before collapsing.

9 Having sold 855,000 copies in its week of release, the **Beatles**' ***Anthology Volume 1*** debuts at US No. 1, becoming the group's 16th chart-topping US album. It extends their lead over **Elvis Presley** and the **Rolling Stones**, who have nine each. The album also sets a new chart longevity record, for the longest span – 31 years and 10 months – between an act's first and last No. 1 albums. The 60-track first-phase retrospective encompasses the group's 1958 recordings at the Phillips Sound Recording Service in Liverpool, through to 1964. It is led off by the "new" track, *Free As A Bird*. A global triumph underscoring their unique position in rock history, the album will reach the three-million mark in the US by next April.

16 The **Beatles**' *Free As A Bird* peaks at UK No. 2, behind **Michael Jackson**'s *Earth Song*. **Paul McCartney** says of the recording: "We took the attitude that **John** had gone on holiday, saying, 'I finished all the tracks except this one, but I leave it to you guys to finish it off.'"

26 ♀, citing "irreconcilable differences" and the "unstable and ever-changing management structure" of the record company, announces that he has "officially given notice to Warner Bros. Records of his desire to terminate his recording agreement."

28 **Noel Gallagher** tells Radio 1 listeners that he cried on hearing Manchester City soccer club supporters singing *Wonderwall* on the terraces.

29 The **Manic Street Preachers** play their first gig since **Richey Edwards** disappeared, performing as a trio at London's Wembley Arena, supporting the **Stone Roses**. Edwards's sister Rachel made an appeal for her missing brother on ITV's "Missing At Christmas" show last Saturday.

ROOTS **During this year: singer/pianist Norah Jones makes her live debut on her 16th birthday, at an open mic night at a Dallas coffeehouse... 14-year-old Ashanti Douglas lands a recording contract with Jive Records... DJ Lyfe sees Incubus play live and asks whether they would be interested in using some of his hip-hop tracks; he joins full-time after one rehearsal... Iowa band Slipknot form, soon recording a self-released album, *Mate, Feed, Kill, Repeat...* 14-year-old Alicia Keys begins writing and demoing material which will result in her being signed by Clive Davis at the age of 18... with the encouragement of a teacher who hears her singing in a hallway, Kelly Clarkson joins the school choir at the Pauline Hughes Middle School in Burleson, Texas... Mike Mushok and Aaron Lewis, who met at a Christmas party in Springfield, Massachusetts, in 1993, form Staind, playing their first gig in February... and Ja Rule commits to disc for the first time, with a guest appearance on *Time To Build*, a Mic Geronimo B-side ...**

You Must Love Me

1996

No.1 US SINGLES

Jan 6 One Sweet Day **Mariah Carey & Boyz II Men**
Mar 23 Because You Loved Me **Celine Dion**
May 4 Always Be My Baby **Mariah Carey**
May 18 Tha Crossroads **Bone Thugs-N-Harmony**
July 13 How Do U Want It **2Pac (featuring K-Ci & JoJo)**
July 27 You're Makin' Me High **Toni Braxton**
Aug 3 Macarena (Bayside Boys Mix) **Los Del Rio**
Nov 9 No Diggity **Blackstreet (featuring Dr. Dre)**
Dec 7 Un-break My Heart **Toni Braxton**

No.1 UK SINGLES

Jan 6 Earth Song **Michael Jackson**
Jan 20 Jesus To A Child **George Michael**
Jan 27 Spaceman **Babylon Zoo**
Mar 2 Don't Look Back In Anger **Oasis**
Mar 9 How Deep Is Your Love **Take That**
Mar 30 Firestarter **Prodigy**
Apr 20 Return Of The Mack **Mark Morrison**
May 4 Fast Love **George Michael**
May 25 Ooh Aah ... Just A Little Bit **Gina G**
June 1 Three Lions (The Official Song Of The England Football Team) **Baddiel and Skinner and the Lightning Seeds**
June 8 Killing Me Softly **Fugees**
July 20 Forever Love **Gary Barlow**
July 27 Wannabe **Spice Girls**
Sept 14 Flava **Peter André**
Sept 21 Ready Or Not **Fugees**
Oct 5 Breakfast At Tiffany's **Deep Blue Something**
Oct 12 Setting Sun **Chemical Brothers**
Oct 19 Words **Boyzone**
Oct 26 Say You'll Be There **Spice Girls**
Nov 9 What Becomes Of The Broken Hearts/ Saturday Night At The Movies/You'll Never Walk Alone **Robson & Jerome**
Nov 23 Breathe **Prodigy**
Dec 7 I Feel You **Peter André**
Dec 14 A Different Beat **Boyzone**
Dec 21 Knockin' On Heaven's Door/ Throw These Guns Away **Dunblane**
Dec 28 2 Become 1 **Spice Girls**

2Pac

Mick Hucknall with the Fugees

Like many before him, 2Pac had greater sales success in death than when he was alive – accruing three multi-platinum albums in the US between 1999 and 2003... The Fugees' Lauryn Hill and Wyclef Jean celebrated their MTV Video Music Award for "Killing Me Softly" with Simply Red's Mick Hucknall.

Rap had already gained a reputation for gang-related violence – and not just in its lyrics. **Tupac Shakur** was the victim of an almost moblike attack in Las Vegas. His death fueled an already serious East/West Coast rap rivalry, with gangs such as the Southside Crips becoming associated with rap figures. Theories swirled about the murder, which would remain unsolved despite rumors of the involvement of rap rival, **Notorious B.I.G.** (who would be slain next year).

Michael Jackson continued to be dogged by controversy of a different nature. His new material was not setting the world on fire, and the sobriquet "Wacko Jacko" had stuck in Britain. In any case, R&B had moved on. **Mary J. Blige** was establishing herself as the Queen of Hip-Hop, and a more soulful R&B came from **Toni Braxton**, whose album ***Secrets*** covered the gamut of love, longing, and a little lust. Slinky, midtempo, with unfussy arrangements courtesy of **Babyface** – it was manna from heaven for radio. **Boyz II Men** held another license to print money (for one more year at least): *One Sweet Day*, their duet with **Mariah Carey**, became the longest running No. 1 single in US chart history.

While America's most successful bar band, **Hootie & the Blowfish**, rode a phenomenal wave, perhaps the freshest rock sound came from California band **No Doubt** – fronted by the sex-bomb platinum blonde **Gwen Stefani**. Having plugged away on the California club circuit for nearly ten years, they finally broke through with the ska-beat laced ***Tragic Kingdom***, which went five times platinum. The antidote to grunge, **No Doubt** mixed up ska, punk, and **Blondie**-style pop.

"Best act today. Tomorrow. The day after that. And the day after that."

Noel Gallagher at the **Q** Awards, November 8, 1996

The musical landscape in Britain was dominated by **Oasis** and the emergence of pop acts aimed at the teenage market. Oasis scored four gold singles, and their albums ***(What's The Story) Morning Glory?*** and ***Definitely Maybe*** sold nearly six million between them – roughly one copy per ten UK citizens. The brothers **Gallagher** were seldom out of the tabloid press, with reports of fights and "laddish" behavior, drinking binges, and rumors of the band's breakup. Even so, few rock groups have created such an adored body of work in such a short time.

For younger fans there was a new batch of boy bands to adore. Even as **Take That** broke up, Irish quintet **Boyzone** topped the UK chart with their second album ***A Different Beat***. The music may have been bland and there were plenty of covers rather than original songs, but the harmonies and the boys' good looks helped sell more than two million copies worldwide. As Europe seemed more receptive to such groups, Jive Records launched the Florida-based **Backstreet Boys** there before trying to sell them to an American audience – a canny move.

In Britain, producers Stannard and Rowe were doing much the same for the **Spice Girls**, whose first three singles topped the UK chart. The girls' catchy, "cheeky" pop, danceable beats, and novel "girl power" philosophy worked for millions of teenage girls (and not a few boys) and propeled their debut album ***Spice*** straight to UK No. 1, before phenomenal worldwide success in 1997.

Jan

1996

Take That split... Michael Jackson vs. Jarvis Cocker...

Coolio was named Favorite Rap/Hip Hop Artist at the American Music Awards... The Buena Vista Social Club's highly original roots set – showcasing the previously unheralded quality of Cuba's indigenous musicians – became a rare word-of-mouth world music platinum success.

Coolio

January

6 O.J. Simpson calls a Los Angeles radio station and requests **Mariah Carey & Boyz II Men**'s *One Sweet Day*, dedicating the current hit to his murdered wife, Nicole.

17 Describing them as the "ultimate rock and roll anomaly," the **Smashing Pumpkins**' **Billy Corgan** inducts **Pink Floyd** (sans **Roger Waters**) into the Rock and Roll Hall of Fame, at the 11th awards dinner at the Waldorf Astoria in New York. Fellow Brit **David Bowie** is introduced into the Hall by **David Byrne**. With **Grace Slick** a no-show – reportedly suffering from a foot ailment – the **Grateful Dead**'s **Phil Lesh** and **Mickey Hart** induct **Jefferson Airplane**. **Mariah Carey** inducts **Gladys Knight & the Pips**, who have not sung together since 1990. **Patti Smith** inducts the **Velvet Underground**: they perform in the US for the first time in 25 years, singing *Pale Blue Eyes* and *Last Night I Said Goodbye To My Friend*, written a few days ago and dedicated to **Sterling Morrison**, who died in August. Already honored at the fifth Rhythm and Blues Foundation Pioneer Awards show in May 1994, the **Shirelles** are welcomed into the Hall of Fame by **Marianne Faithfull**. **Stevie Wonder** inducts **Little Willie John**, and duets on *Fever* with the blues great's son, **Keith**, and in honor of **Gladys Knight & the Pips**, sings *I Heard It Through The Grapevine* with **Joan Osborne**. **Harry Belafonte** and **Arlo Guthrie** induct folk legend **Pete Seeger** as an Early Influence, while Elektra Records founder **Bob Krasnow** inducts the legendary San Francisco DJ Tom Donahue as a Non-Performer.

"With all due respect to the people who voted, I'm gonna leave this right here." Garth Brooks on winning the Favorite Artist of the Year trophy at the American Music Awards, a prize he felt should have gone to Hootie & The Blowfish, January 29, 1996

February

13 After achieving seven No. 1 singles and two No. 1 albums, members of **Take That** announce their intention to split. The 24-hour helplines, Childline and the Samaritans, report they are deluged with calls from distraught fans.

14 On Valentine's Day, long-time bachelor ♀ marries belly dancer, singer, and songwriter **Mayte Garcia**, at the Park Avenue United Methodist Church in Minneapolis (not in Paris as originally planned). *Friend, Lover, Sister, Mother/Wife*, penned by the bridegroom for his bride, is played as the couple take to the dance floor at the wedding reception.

19 **Michael Jackson**'s performance of *Earth Song* at the 15th BRIT Awards at London's Earl's Court, at which he also picks up the Artist of a Generation award, is interrupted when **Pulp**'s **Jarvis Cocker** walks on stage. During the ensuing melée it is claimed that some of the children sharing the stage with Jackson are injured. Cocker will claim that his behavior, for which he will be arrested but not charged, was "a form of protest at the way Michael Jackson sees himself as some Christlike figure with the power of healing." Cocker's performance upstages a surly acceptance speech by **Oasis**, referring to record industry types as "corporate pigs." Oasis take home the Best Video (for "Wonderwall"), Best Group, and Best Album (***(What's The Story) Morning Glory?***) trophies. Prime Minister Tony Blair presents **David Bowie** with the Outstanding Contribution to British Music honor. **Annie Lennox** wins a record sixth Best British Female Artist award, and **Björk** is named Best International Female Artist. Taking a break from her current tour, **Alanis Morissette** receives the Best International Newcomer award. **Take That** win the Best Single trophy for *Back For Good*. **Roger Taylor** presents the **Freddie Mercury** Award to the War Child charity established by **Brian Eno** – who wins Best Producer again – and **Radiohead**'s **Thom Yorke**.

Lisa Marie filed for divorce from her husband Michael Jackson in a Los Angeles court, citing "irreconcilable differences."

March

2 With record company consolidation continuing unabated, **Billboard** reports that MCA (itself now part of Seagram's takeover of Universal) is buying 50 percent of Interscope, the red-hot, mostly rap/metal-rostered label started by veteran producer Jimmy Iovine.

2 Released by Suge Knight's Death Row label, **2Pac**'s ***All Eyez On Me*** enters the US chart at No. 1, on its way to five million US sales. A tour de force of West Coast gangsta rap, it is the first double-CD hip-hop album to reach the top. It includes the forthcoming US No. 1 single, *How Do U Want It*, featuring ex-**Jodeci** vocalists, **K-Ci** and **JoJo**, and samples **Quincy Jones**'s *Body Heat*. (Knight allegedly posted a $1.5 million appellate

Buena Vista Social Club

bond to free **Tupac Shakur** on appeal following his December 1994 conviction – in exchange for Shakur signing to Death Row.)

4 **Garth Brooks** sends a letter (which will appear in a full-page ad in **Billboard** on the 23rd) asking US radio stations to synchronize a music tribute to commemorate the one-year anniversary of the Oklahoma City bombing on April 19.

9 A week after performing the ballad at the Grammy Awards, **Boyz II Men** break their own record (14 weeks, previously shared with **Whitney Houston**) as the *One Sweet Day* duet with **Mariah Carey** – co-written with producer Walter Afanasieff – logs its 15th consecutive week at US No. 1 (it will hold on for one more week).

10 Amid strong local protest, **Madonna**, in her role as Eva Peron, lip-synchs to *Don't Cry For Me Argentina* on the balcony of the presidential palace in Buenos Aires, where the first lady of Argentina told a crowd she was dying in 1951. Madonna has personally convinced President Carlos Menem to grant permission to film the scene from "Evita" at the historic site – he was earlier quoted condemning it as, "A total and utter disgrace. Pornographic and blasphemous – an insult to Argentine women."

12 **Ry Cooder** begins recording sessions, with a host of local talent, at the state-run Egrem studio in Havana, which will yield the critically lauded ***Buena Vista Social Club***, released in June 1997. Cooder's warm musical assembly includes vocalist **Ibrahim Ferrer**, legendary octogenerian singer **Compay Segundo**, and piano maestro **Rubén González**. The unique sessions have been co-organized with World Circuit's Nick Gold (who heads the label in London and will license the results in the US to Nonesuch Records).

18 At a press conference at the 100 Club in London, **John Lydon** – once again known as **Johnny Rotten** – says: "We have found a common cause, and it's your money." The **Sex Pistols** make their comeback tour, 20 years after splitting up.

29 The highlight of the 10th Soul Train Music Awards, at the Shrine Auditorium in Los Angeles, is a show-stopping performance by **Mary J. Blige** (who is being labeled the "Queen Of Hip-Hop") of her recent US No. 2 smash, *Not Gon' Cry*. Featured on the multiplatinum soundtrack, produced by **Babyface**, of the film "Waiting To Exhale," it is her biggest hit to date. It is a maturing moment for the Bronx-born R&B singer, who turned 25 in January and first broke through with 1992's ***What's The 411?*** under the guidance of **Sean "Puffy" Combs**.

30 The **Beatles**' 45-track ***Anthology Volume 2***, covering the period 1965–68, once again mixing alternate takes and previously unreleased live material, hits UK No. 1. It will do the same in the US next week.

May

11 Bernadette O'Brien, a 17-year-old student from County Cork, Ireland, is among seven people injured when part of the crowd begin "body-surfing" in a mosh pit at the **Smashing Pumpkins**' gig at The Point in Dublin. Told of her injuries, **Billy Corgan** says: "I'm sorry we can't play on. The gig's over. There's a girl out there who's nearly dying. We as human beings cannot play up here while people are getting seriously hurt down there." Tomorrow, the teenager will be taken off life-support at the Mater Hospital, dying of massive internal injuries.

> **"When you come to our gigs, you'll see a bunch of 40-year-olds playing their arses off a lot better than the dullard shite I've had to tolerate for the past ten years."**
>
> Johnny Rotten, March 18, 1996

April

13 **Rage Against the Machine**'s US network television debut on "Saturday Night Live" causes controversy when the group hangs US flags upside down on its amplifiers during a rendition of *Bulls On Parade*. The protest is directed at host Steve Forbes (proprietor of **Forbes** magazine) and General Electric, which owns NBC. The band is not allowed to perform another number, or join the end-of-show line-up.

16 After stunning the Grammy audience by walking on stage in full make-up and costume, **KISS** announce a reunion tour. Opening at Tiger Stadium in Detroit on June 28, it will be the first time all four members have played together in 15 years, and the first time they have worn their trademark make-up in 13 years.

18 Former **Chic** bassist extraordinaire, 43-year-old **Bernard Edwards** – having performed earlier today during the J.T. Super Producers '96 concert series in Tokyo, alongside **Steve Winwood**, **Slash**, **Sister Sledge**, **Simon Le Bon**, and Chic co-founder **Nile Rodgers** – is found dead in his hotel room by Rodgers. The cause of death will be confirmed as pneumonia.

17 The **Fugees**' album, ***The Score***, is certified triple platinum by the RIAA, while still making its way up the US survey. The hip-hop trio boasts the combined talents of Haitian natives **Wyclef Jean** (rap vocal, guitar, producer) and **Pras Michel** (rapper/producer), with lead chanteuse, New Jersey-born, 20-year-old singer/actress **Lauryn Hill**. The fortunes of their second album are inextricably linked to the global breakout success of the hot radio choice *Killing Me Softly*. The abbreviated, smooth, hip-hop-phrased update of **Roberta Flack**'s 1973 soul pearl, *Killing Me Softly With His Song*, will top the UK chart in three weeks (the only million-selling UK single of 1996). Garnering a slew of awards over the next two years, the album will become the highest certified rap set by a group, and one of the five best-selling rap/hip-hop albums ever.

21 Entirely written by **Jakob Dylan** (son of **Bob**), the **Wallflowers**' second album, the solid melodic rock/blues-fused ***Bringing Down The***

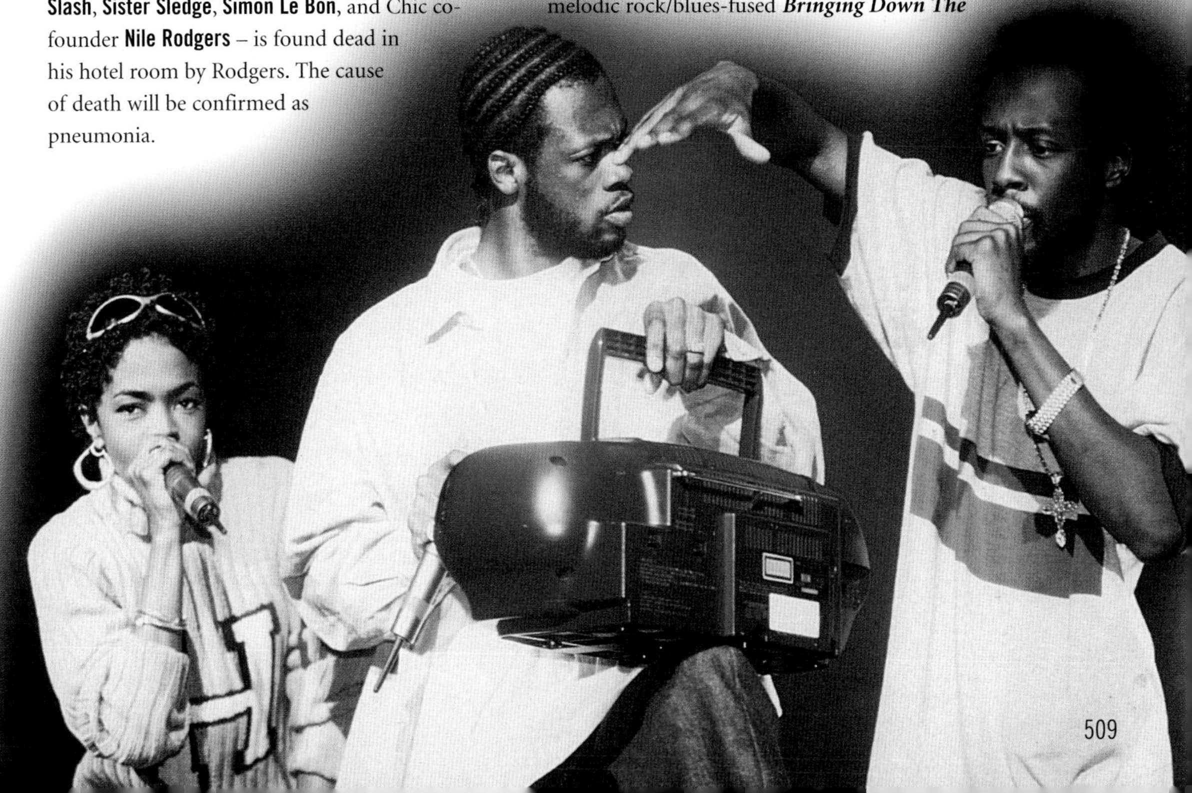

The phenomenal success of the Fugees' *The Score* meant it was the trio's last album of the decade, as it led to solo projects for each member and non-stop production requests for Wyclef Jean.

June 1996

The Tibetan Freedom concerts... The Macarena... Ozz Fest...

1996 was a troubled year for the Smashing Pumpkins, but they did appear in the season finale of "The Simpsons" in the episode titled "Homerpalooza."

Horse, is released by Interscope in the US. Produced by T-Bone Burnette, its musical guests include singer-songwriter **Sam Phillips**, **Counting Crows**' **Adam Duritz**, the **Jayhawks**'s **Gary Louris**, keyboardist **Mike Campbell**, and singer-songwriter **Michael Penn**. It won't even chart for another two months, but will begin the climb to its US No. 4 peak next May, selling three million copies in six months next year.

28 **Depeche Mode**'s **Dave Gahan** is found unconscious at Los Angeles' Sunset Marquis hotel, and rushed to Cedars-Sinai Medical Center Hospital, where he is treated for an apparent drug overdose. He is arrested on suspicion of cocaine and heroin possession. Released on bail, he will reportedly go into the Exodus detox unit, after an official band statement denies that he previously slashed his wrists in a suicide attempt.

June

1 With Britain swept up in the fervor of the European Championship soccer tournament being held there, *Three Lions (The Official Song Of The England Football Team)*, credited to **Baddiel and Skinner and the Lightning Seeds**, enters the UK chart at No. 1. Sole Lightning Seeds member, **Ian Broudie**, has been quietly logging up a substantial modern pop canon in the UK, both as a golden-touch producer (**Echo & the Bunnymen**, **Icicle Works**, **Wah!**, the **Fall**, the **Primitives**, **Terry Hall**, and **Northside**) and as a hook-blessed singer-songwriter in his own right.

3 One-time rapper **Hammer**, who filed for bankruptcy two months ago, tells an Oakland court that he has $9.6 million in assets and $13.7 million in debts. He says that his records "could be selling anywhere out there. [But] as far as being in, like, a regular job, it doesn't work like that." His spectacular financial collapse follows more than 25 million record sales.

10 The Wal-Mart corporation announces that it is no longer going to sell copies of the **Goo Goo Dolls**' thrash-pop album, ***A Boy Named Goo***, after complaints that the baby in the cover photo appears to be smeared with blood. The offending image came from **Carlvision**, a book of photographs of Carl Gellert taken 13 years ago by his father, photographer Vance Gellert. The ban is belated: ***A Boy Named Goo*** was released in March last year, reached its peak in February, and has already sold over 1.5 million copies, more than 50,000 of them through Wal-Mart stores.

15 **Van Morrison** and **George Martin** are named in the Queen's Birthday Honours List: Morrison is awarded an OBE, and the producer becomes Sir George Martin. Morrison celebrates by appearing in concert tonight with **Ray Charles** at Wembley Arena.

15 The **Beastie Boys** host the first of two Tibetan Freedom Concerts at the Polo Fields, Golden Gate Park in San Francisco. **Richie Havens**, **John Lee Hooker**, **Cibo Matto**, **Biz Markie**, **A Tribe Called Quest**, **Pavement**, the **Smashing Pumpkins**, and the Beastie Boys perform today. Day two will feature **Buddy Guy**, **Yoko Ono** and **Ima**, **Beck**, **De La Soul**, the **Skatalites**, the **Fugees**, **Björk**, **Rage Against the Machine**, **Sonic Youth**, and the **Red Hot Chili Peppers**.

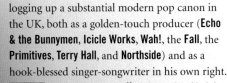

> **"The name of the album is *A Boy Named Goo*. The picture is of a boy covered with goo. What part of this concept are they unclear on?"**
>
> Johnny Rzeznik on Wal-Mart's decision to stop selling the Goo Goo Dolls' album, June 10, 1996

27 With ex-**Take That** singer **Gary Barlow** expected to make the front-running on the solo front, his ex-colleague **Robbie Williams** signs with Chrysalis Records at 12:01 am, when released from RCA. It is a shrewd move by the label: Williams's first solo hit *Freedom* – based on **George Michael**'s *Freedom '90* – will bow at UK No. 2 in August.

27 A man fires a gun during a free rap concert starring the **Fugees**, **KRS-One**, and hardcore rap collective **Wu-Tang Clan**, causing dozens of injuries in the ensuing stampede. The gig, on 125th Street in Harlem, is part of the Hoodshock series, to raise awareness for the Refugee Camp Project.

28 After **Van Halen** announced two days ago that **Sammy Hagar** had left the line-up, Hagar issues a statement saying the split is "a devastating, backstabbing, I-don't-get-it, real big disappointment." The band has invited ex-lead singer **David Lee Roth** to record a new track (*Can't Get This Stuff No More*) for inclusion on a forthcoming greatest hits album, and he is strongly rumored to be Hagar's permanent replacement, though Van Halen confirms that they will hold auditions for their new vocalist.

29 **Eric Clapton** headlines the MasterCard Masters of Music Concert for the Prince's Trust in front of 150,000 fans in London's Hyde Park. (It is the first rock show to be held in the park for 20 years.) **Pete Townshend**, **Roger Daltrey**, and **John Entwistle** perform "Quadrophenia," with help from **Pink Floyd**'s **David Gilmour**, **Gary**

The Beastie Boys held Tibetan Freedom concerts to benefit the Milarepa Fund, an organization working for peace and the freedom of Tibet.

Glitter, **Phil Daniels**, actor Stephen Fry, a 15-piece backing band, and anchorman Trevor McDonald. Daltrey wears an eyepatch over his left eye because Glitter – in the role of Godfather – swung a microphone into his face during yesterday's rehearsals, fracturing his eye socket. Meanwhile, in Manchester, **Madness**, **Simply Red**, **M People**, and **Dodgy** take part in the official Euro '96 concert, "The Crowd are on the Pitch," broadcast on BBC1 from Old Trafford Stadium.

July

3 Sir **Cliff Richard** sings *Summer Holiday*, *The Young Ones*, *Bachelor Boy*, and *All Shook Up*, when rains stops play at the Wimbledon Lawn Tennis Championship, assisted by backing singers Virginia Wade, Martina Navratilova, Conchita Martinez, Pam Shriver, Gigi Fernandez, Hana Mandlikova, and Rosalyn Nideffer. The heavens miraculously clear within 20 minutes, allowing defending champion Pete Sampras to continue his center court match. Tomorrow's **Daily Telegraph** will predict that the event will go down in history as "Cliffstock."

12 After drinking alcohol and injecting heroin, **Smashing Pumpkins**' drummer **Jimmy Chamberlin**, and their road keyboard player, **Jonathan Melvoin**, pass out in their room at the Regency Hotel in New York. When Chamberlin wakes, he is unable to rouse Melvoin, who is declared dead by paramedics. Chamberlin will plead not guilty to a charge of heroin possession.

13 **Chet Atkins**, **Jeff "Skunk" Baxter**, and **Steve Earle** lead 2,000 guitarists in breaking the world record for the largest guitar jam marathon: they play *Heartbreak Hotel* for 75 minutes at Nashville's Riverfront Park. The record was previously held by the City of Vancouver, where **Bachman-Turner Overdrive**'s *Taking Care Of Business* was played for 68 minutes and 40 seconds.

23 The **Charlatans**' **Rob Collins** dies from injuries sustained after crashing his red BMW in Rockfield, near Monmouth, Wales, during recording sessions for the group's fifth album. The group's lead singer, **Tim Burgess**, will issue a statement confirming that the band will stay together despite the tragedy: "The band, their management, and their associates are naturally devastated at the loss of not only an influential member of a brilliant rock 'n' roll band, but also, and more so, a great and loyal friend. The decision has been made to carry on because we have to continue in his memory – it's what he would have wanted."

August

3 Disproving Abraham Lincoln's maxim that you can't fool all of the people all of the time, **Los Del Rio**'s *Macarena (Bayside Boys Mix)* – this year's biggest and most nauseating dance novelty hit – tops the US chart for the first of 14 weeks, on its way to sales of over 3.7 million.

6 Following appearances on the Lollapalooza '96 caravan trek, the **Ramones** play what is believed to be their last farewell gig at the Palace in Hollywood, with cameos by members of **Pearl Jam**, **Soundgarden**, **Motörhead**, and **Rancid**. Needless to say, it won't be.

24 In its 55th week on the **Billboard** chart, **Everything But the Girl**'s *Missing* – radically remixed by Todd Terry as a dance record – breaks the all-time record, besting the **Four Seasons**' split-chart run of 54 weeks with *December, 1963 (Oh, What A Night)*.

September

4 The **Smashing Pumpkins** sweep the 13th MTV Video Music Awards, held at New York's Radio City Music Hall. Winning in all six categories in which they are nominated, they pick up Best Alternative Music Video ("1979"), Best Art Direction in a Video, Best Direction in a Video, Best Cinematography, Best Special Effects in a Video, Best Video, and Breakthrough Video (all for "Tonight Tonight"). Other winners include **Beck**'s "Where It's At" (Best Male Video), **Björk**'s "It's Oh So Quiet" (Best Choreography), the **Foo Fighters**' "Big Me" (Best Group Video), **Coolio**'s "1, 2, 3, 4 (Sumpin' New)" (Best Dance Video) and "Gangsta's Paradise" (Best Rap Video), and **George Michael**'s "Fastlove" (MTV Europe's Viewers Choice). The **Fugees**, who win Best R&B Video, are joined on stage by rapper **Nas**, the red-hot New York-based rapper **Nasir Jones**, who recently scored his first US No. 1 album, ***It Was Written***. In a major surprise, **Van Halen** arrives on stage to present an award with **David Lee Roth** seemingly back in the line-up.

12 **Bone Thugs-N-Harmony** make a cameo appearance in Fox-TV's "New York Undercover" series, in this week's "Tough Love" episode. The Cleveland-based fast-rhyming rap quintet, discovered by **Eazy-E**, recently spent eight weeks topping the US Hot 100 with their crossover smash, *Tha Crossroads*, sampling the **Isley Brothers**' *Make Me Say It Again*.

14 **Ozzy Osbourne**'s first Ozzfest package tour begins at the Merriweather Post Pavilion in Columbia, set to end on October 31 at the

> **"For nine years, we have battled with Jimmy's struggles with the insidious disease of drug and alcohol addiction. It has nearly destroyed everything we are and stand for."**
>
> Smashing Pumpkins' manager Peter Mensch announcing Jimmy Chamberlin's departure, July 17, 1996

TUPAC SHAKUR

Sept 7 **As Tupac Shakur leaves the MGM Grand in Las Vegas, after watching a fight between Mike Tyson and Bruce Seldon, he has an altercation with a man later identified as Southside Crips gang member, Orlando "Baby Lane" Anderson. On the way to Suge Knight's Club 662 in a ten-car Death Row entourage, a white Cadillac draws up alongside Shakur's black BMW, and two men get out and fire 13 rounds into the car. Shakur is hit four times.**

Shakur, dying at the age of 25, left a deep archive of previously unreleased rap recordings that would keep his chart legacy and notoriety alive for years to come.

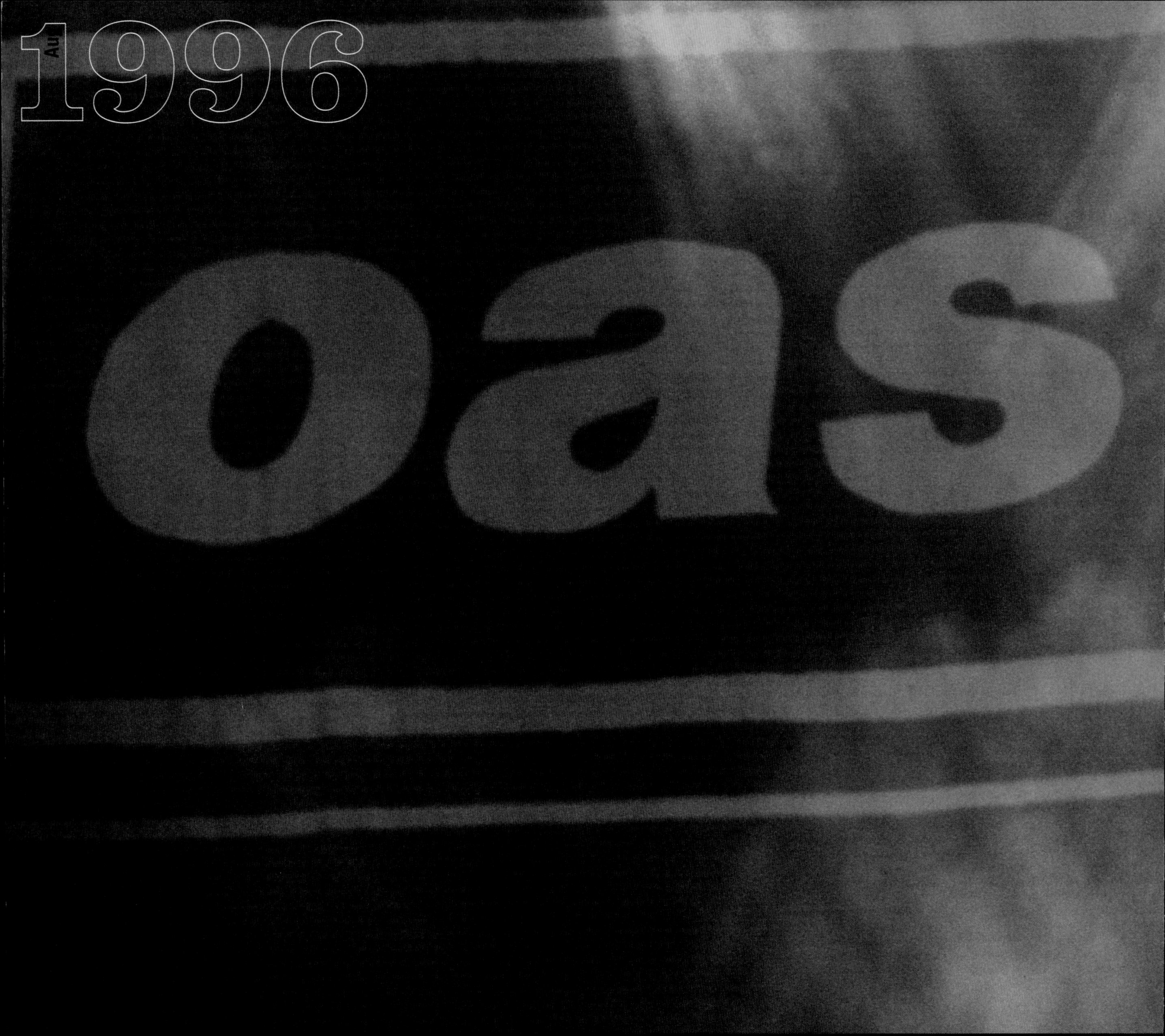

Aug 11 The cream of British rock/dance bands perform tonight and tomorrow evening at Knebworth House in Hertfordshire, England. The 250,000 tickets sold out in two days, with 2.6 million applications. Top acts include **Oasis**, **Prodigy**, BritPop heirs **Ocean Colour Scene**, the re-energized **Manic Street Preachers**, veteran combo the **Charlatans**, **Cast** (formed two years ago by ex-**La**'s bassist **John Power**), the **Chemical Brothers**, and retro-psychedelia, sitar-reviving, rock quartet **Kula Shaker**. (Chemical Brothers' fan **Noel Gallagher** will be featured on their upcoming UK No. 1 smash, *Setting Sun*.)

At their creative and commercial zenith, Oasis had performed two outdoor concerts in front of 80,000 people at Balloch Country Park in Loch Lomond, Scotland, a week before their Knebworth gig.

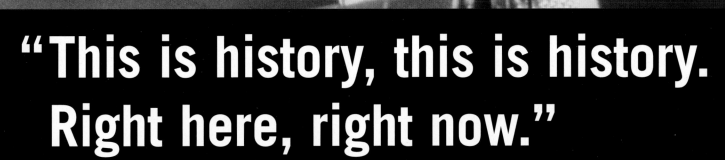

"This is history, this is history. Right here, right now."

Noel Gallagher, August 11, 1996

Sept 1996

Tupac Shakur dies after shooting... The Backstreet Boys emerge... The year of the Spice Girls...

George M. Sullivan Sports Arena in Anchorage, Alaska. It will become a hugely successful annual US caravan, featuring Ozzy headlining a crop of top and emerging metal bands.

17 Scotland Yard's anti-terrorist squad locates a device packed with sulfuric acid at the Tooting mail sorting office in London, addressed by 21-year-old Ricardo Lopez to **Björk**'s Brave Management in England. Lopez was found dead yesterday in his home in Hollywood, Florida. He had committed suicide several days before, with a .38-caliber handgun, videotaping his own death.

18 **John Lennon**'s scribblings of the first one and a half verses of *Being For The Benefit Of Mr. Kite* sell at Sotheby's in London for $103,500, not reaching the $251,000 previously paid for the full handwritten script of **Paul McCartney**'s *Getting Better*. At the same auction, **Julian Lennon** anonymously and successfully bids $39,030 for McCartney's recording notes for *Hey Jude*.

20 **Tupac**, who has remained in the hospital in critical condition since he was shot on September 7, dies of respiratory and heart failure. As the murder remains unsolved, rumors will focus on the violent East Coast/West Coast rivalry that has exploded between gangs and rappers on either side of the States. The **Los Angeles Times** will allege that the Crips gang were hired by **Notorious B.I.G.** to make the hit.

21 **Paul Simon** holds auditions for his new musical "The Capeman" (based on the true tale of Sal Agrón, a Puerto Rican imprisoned for murder in 1960) at New York's Musical Theater Works. The show will be beset with problems from the outset, and will go down in history as one of Broadway's most famous flops. It will, however, showcase the talent of New York-based Latin singer **Marc Anthony**, who will plays the young Agrón.

October

8 **George Michael** records an exclusive one-hour concert for BBC Radio 1, at the Radio Theatre in London, in front of 200 invited guests. In his first full show in five years, he performs ten songs, including *Everything She Wants*, his recent UK chart-topper *Fastlove*, *Praying For Time*, *Freedom*, and *Father Figure*.

"We hate MTV. Even if they want us, we're not going to be there. It's just run by wankers."

Noel Gallagher, **Q** Awards, November 8, 1996

20 British R&B/urban singer **Mark Morrison** is charged with possessing a prohibited weapon (an electric stun gun) and affray, following an incident at a food store in Notting Hill at 4:40 am. He will receive two three-month sentences, to be served concurrently, next year.

28 The **Beatles**' ***Anthology 3*** is issued worldwide. It includes 50 previously unreleased cuts from 1968 (seven "White Album" acoustic demos recorded at **George Harrison**'s home, **Paul McCartney**'s original of *Come And Get It*, *The Long And Winding Road* pre-Phil Spector, a rooftop performance of *Get Back*, and **John Lennon**'s *What's The New Mary Jane*). The album will hit UK No. 4, and top the US chart next month, making the Beatles the first act ever to garner three album chart-toppers in 12 months. Following its release, the remaining Beatles will confirm: "There is no more."

The Backstreet Boys' teen-aimed pop-percolating debut album was mostly written and produced by budding Swedish hitmeister Max Martin at his Cheiron production house in Stockholm.

31 Despite rumors that **Marilyn Manson** is going to commit suicide during his Halloween show at the Convention Hall in Asbury Park, New Jersey, he remains alive at the end of the evening. His latest shock-rock antics are to promote his group's most recent album, ***Antichrist Superstar*** – produced by Trent Reznor – which hit US No. 3 last month.

November

1 Released in Europe in September (but unavailable in their native US until next year), ***Backstreet Boys*** is certified gold by the BPI, having already hit UK No. 12. The **Backstreet Boys** are managed by ex-**New Kids On The Block** road manager Johnny Wright and his wife Donna. Based in Orlando, and named after Backstreet Market, a local open-air shopping area, they began performing at high-school and graduation dances in 1993. A tight, telegenic vocal quintet in the classic boy-band tradition, the members – **Kevin Richardson**, **Nick Carter**, **Brian "B-Rok" Littrell**, **A.J. McLean**, and **Howie D** – the oldest is 24 and the youngest 16 – have varying degrees of teen acting/singing experience. They are signed to Jive Records, and are being launched first in Europe. This is a deliberate move by the Wrights and the label, who feel that the European market, already fizzing with the "boy-group" fever begun by **Take That** and **Boyzone**, will be more receptive to the group's simple, energetic, pop/dance fare.

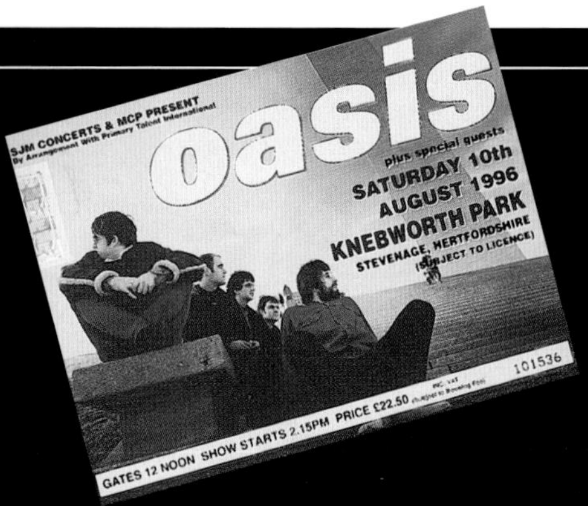

330,000 tickets were sold for Oasis's four concerts at Knebworth Park and Loch Lomond... Although only two of the Spice Girls were vertically challenged, the quintet's platform boots were de rigueur.

At the close of a breakout year for the Spice Girls – and their perky, upbeat "girl power" message – they hosted the Christmas edition of "Top Of The Pops."

8 **Oasis**'s **Noel** and **Liam Gallagher** pick up the Best Act in the World Today at the **Q** Awards, at the Park Lane Hotel. After the ceremony, Liam goes to the St. James club, where he has an altercation with **News of the World** photographer Sean O'Brien. Then he heads for the Groucho Club, where he reportedly has an argument with his girlfriend, actress/singer **Patsy Kensit**, before consuming more alcohol at a hotel bar off Oxford Street. Early tomorrow morning, he will be arrested in Oxford Street on suspicion of possessing cocaine.

9 Helmed by producer Ray Hedges, Irish vocal quintet **Boyzone**'s second album, ***A Different Beat***, tops the UK chart in its week of entry. Now that **Take That** has split, Boyzone – assembled by manager Louis Welch in Dublin in November 1993, and fronted by 19-year-old **Ronan Keating** – are assuming the mantle of Europe's leading boy-band. They will follow last month's UK No. 1 update of the **Bee Gees**' *Words* with the new composition, *A Different Beat*, in December: their second chart-topper and seventh consecutive top five UK smash.

18 The inaugural MOBO (Music Of Black Origin) Awards take place at the New Connaught Rooms in Covent Garden, London, with performances from **Lionel Richie**, **Alexander O'Neal**, and **Chaka Demus & Pliers**. Among the 16 awards handed out, Richie receives the Lifetime Achievement Award, and the **Fugees** pick up trophies for Best International Act, and Best International Single (*Killing Me Softly*). **Baby D** is named Best Dance Act, **Goldie** is Best Jungle Act, and **Mark Morrison** is Best R&B Act. **Gabrielle**'s *Give Me A Little More Time* is named Best Single, and **Soul II Soul**'s **Jazzie B** is honored with the MOBO Choice Contribution Award.

21 ⚥ gives a rare one-hour interview on "Oprah Winfrey" to promote his 36-song, 3-CD set ***Emancipation***, released on his own NPG label. The singer has finally severed all links with Warner Bros. – an acrimonious split that led him to be seen in public with "Slave" written on his face. His new one-time-only alliance is with the EMI-Capitol Music Group.

December

4 **Toni Braxton** performs a heart-stopping rendition of *Un-Break My Heart* at the seventh Billboard Music Awards held at the Aladdin Hotel Theater in Las Vegas. Destined to become her signature hit, the instant soul/pop classic is currently enjoying the first of 11 weeks at US No. 1 (her second of the year) and will help spur US sales of her second album, the soul-dripping, radio-friendly ***Secrets***, to eight million.

5 **Texas** preview ***White On Blonde***, their first album in more than three years, with a concert before friends, family, and the press at the Town House Hotel in Glasgow. In one of the more surprising comebacks, the Scottish band will secure five Top 10 hits from the album, which will sell more than 1.8 million copies by the end of the decade. Texas was originally formed as a quartet in Glasgow in 1986, by ex-**Altered Images** and ex-**Hipsway** bassist **Johnny McElhone**, and vocalist **Sharleen Spiteri**. The group recruited lead guitarist **Ally McErlaine** and drummer **Stuart Kerr**, and were named after the 1985 Wim Wenders movie "Paris, Texas." The group had immediate success with ***Southside*** in 1989 but, after a follow-up failed to catch on, Spiteri took a two-year break in Paris.

5 **No Doubt**, **Shawn Colvin**, **Tracy Chapman**, and **Sheryl Crow** are among an all-star bill performing before a sellout crowd at New York's Madison Square Garden. The California ska/punk quartet, **No Doubt**, led by **Gwen Stefani**, are two weeks away from topping the US album chart with ***Tragic Kingdom***, which will sell 4.4 million by the end of the year – a handsome reward for ten years' work. The success of the album (largely written about the split between Stefani and her boyfriend, bass player **Tony Kanal**) is in part due to the atypical, melodic, radio-friendly track *Don't Speak*, which is receiving saturation airplay but remains unreleased as a single at retail in the US.

28 Spurred by a national fan and media frenzy, reserved for only a handful of pop acts since the 1960s, *2 Become 1* debuts at UK No. 1, making the **Spice Girls** the first female act to have their first three singles top the UK singles chart, all of which are also among the ten best-selling British singles of the year. All are featured on their maiden album, ***Spice***, co-produced by dance/pop specialists Absolute and Stannard & Rowe. It has sold 1.8 million copies in the UK in six weeks.

ROOTS **During this year: Hybrid Theory form in southern California, an alt-metal/hip-hop high-school group which soon changes its name to Linkin Park... Alien Ant Farm play their first gig on Dryden Mitchell's 16th birthday... All Saints record a demo, including the Karl Gordon-originated track *I Know Where It's At*, which reaches John Benson; he promises them a deal in a month – he gets one in ten days... with new bassist Tobin Esperance on board, Papa Roach go into E.S.P. Studios in Pittsburg, California, recording 13 tracks for $700... Australian actress Natalie Imbruglia moves to England, and soon finds herself a recording contract with RCA Records... crack dealer and aspiring rapper Curtis Jackson – aka 50 Cent – is signed by Run-D.M.C.'s Jam Master Jay to his JMJ label; 50 Cent will re-emerge in the next decade on Eminem's Shady Records... childhood friends, singer Brad Arnold, guitarist Matt Roberts, and bassist Todd Harrell form 3 Doors Down in Escatawpa, Mississippi, initially playing covers of Bush and Metallica songs... and 16-year old singer Alecia Moore – aka Pink – is signed to LaFace Records as one-third of all-white R&B vocal trio Choice...**

Quit Playing Games (With My Heart)

1997

No.1 US SINGLES

- **Jan 4** Un-Break My Heart **Toni Braxton**
- **Feb 22** Wannabe **Spice Girls**
- **Mar 22** Can't Nobody Hold Me Down **Puff Daddy featuring Mase**
- **May 3** Hypnotize **Notorious B.I.G.**
- **May 24** MMMBop **Hanson**
- **June 14** I'll Be Missing You **Puff Daddy & Faith Evans (featuring 112)**
- **Aug 30** Mo Money Mo Problems **Notorious B.I.G. featuring Puff Daddy & Mase**
- **Sept 13** Honey **Mariah Carey**
- **Oct 4** 4 Seasons Of Loneliness **Boyz II Men**
- **Oct 11** Candle In The Wind 1997/Something About The Way You Look Tonight **Elton John**

No.1 UK SINGLES

- **Jan 4** 2 Become 1 **Spice Girls**
- **Jan 18** Professional Widow (It's Got To Be Big) **Tori Amos**
- **Jan 25** >Abort, Retry, Fail? (EP) **White Town**
- **Feb 1** Beetlebum **Blur**
- **Feb 8** Ain't Nobody **LL Cool J**
- **Feb 15** Discotheque **U2**
- **Feb 22** Don't Speak **No Doubt**
- **Mar 15** Mama/Who Do You Think You Are **Spice Girls**
- **Apr 5** Block Rockin' Beats **Chemical Brothers**
- **Apr 12** I Believe I Can Fly **R. Kelly**
- **May 3** Blood On The Dance Floor **Michael Jackson**
- **May 10** Love Won't Wait **Gary Barlow**
- **May 17** You're Not Alone **Olive**
- **May 31** I Wanna Be The Only One **Eternal featuring BeBe Winans**
- **June 7** MMMBop **Hanson**
- **June 28** I'll Be Missing You **Puff Daddy & Faith Evans (featuring 112)**
- **July 19** D'You Know What I Mean **Oasis**
- **July 26** I'll Be Missing You **Puff Daddy & Faith Evans (featuring 112)**
- **Aug 16** Men In Black **Will Smith**
- **Sept 13** The Drugs Don't Work **Verve**
- **Sept 20** Candle In The Wind 1997/Something About The Way You Look Tonight **Elton John**
- **Oct 25** Spice Up Your Life **Spice Girls**
- **Nov 1** Barbie Girl **Aqua**
- **Nov 29** Perfect Day **Various Artists**
- **Dec 13** Teletubbies Say Eh-Oh! **Teletubbies**
- **Dec 27** Too Much **Spice Girls**

Puff Daddy

Jewel

One of the musical highlights of the year was Puff Daddy performing *I'll Be Missing You* with Sting at the MTV Video Music Awards... Jewel was voted No. 1 in a CDnow web survey as the female singer with whom men would most like to be stranded on a desert island.

The **Spice Girls** began 1997 as they had ended 1996 – at the summit of charts worldwide, with their "Girl Power" message resonating with adolescent females. *Wannabe* gatecrashed the US chart as the Girls brought their naughty but nice brand of pop to America. They became the first act in nearly ten years to hold pole position simultaneously on both sides of the Atlantic.

While girl power and ongoing boy-band fever may have satiated mass taste in the UK, **Prodigy** became the first British electronica/rave act to cross over into the mainstream, with ***The Fat Of The Land***, an album even the technophobic couldn't ignore. Hardcore, hip-hop-derived breakbeats, layers of unabashed (but creative) sampling, and meaningless shouted lyrics struck a chord beyond the electronic music community. The inclusion of *Firestarter* aided the disc's worldwide success, but it was the ferocity of *Smack My Bitch Up* that caused the most controversy. An overtly misogynistic video clip, and guest **Shahin Bada**'s Indian vocalizations, showed that dance music had come a long way from *Pump Up The Volume*. Leader **Liam Howlett** shored up ten solid songs with bombastic production values, transforming dance music into the art of noise.

Rap was ravaged by further violence: **Notorious B.I.G.** was shot dead in Los Angeles in March. His album, eerily entitled ***Life After Death*** – its cover featuring the rapper standing next to a hearse – was released three weeks after his death and went straight to US No. 1, the latest success for rap impresario and hip-hop tastemaker, **Sean "Puffy" Combs**. Under his recording name, **Puff Daddy**, Combs dedicated his massively successful single *I'll Be Missing You* (sampling the **Police**'s *Every Breath You Take*) to B.I.G. Rap's resilience was confirmed by the success of Puff's multiplatinum ***No Way Out***.

Among veteran acts, **Fleetwood Mac** took their cue from the recently reunited **Eagles**, and recorded a concert for MTV and VH1 that generated a successful live album in ***The Dance***, and an equally lucrative reunion tour. Recovering from severe illness, and apparently seared by the experience, **Bob Dylan** recorded ***Time Out Of Mind***, produced by the ever-versatile and much-in-demand **Daniel Lanois**. Crammed with poetry and neat riffs, it was an instant classic of simple, understated blues. **Sarah McLachlan** emerged with ***Surfacing*** – her most sophisticated album to date, which would generate several hit singles as well as worldwide sales of nearly ten million copies. Arguably the most talented female songstress since **Joni Mitchell**, McLachlan was also instrumental in assembling a superb cast of female performers (including **Sheryl Crow**, **Jewel**, **Shawn Colvin**, and **Tracy Chapman**) for the Lilith Fair tour – a hugely successful project that marked the high point of a solid period of top-drawer female singer-songwriters.

"[Margaret] Thatcher was the first Spice Girl, the pioneer of our ideology – Girl Power."

Geri Halliwell, **The Spectator**, December 1996

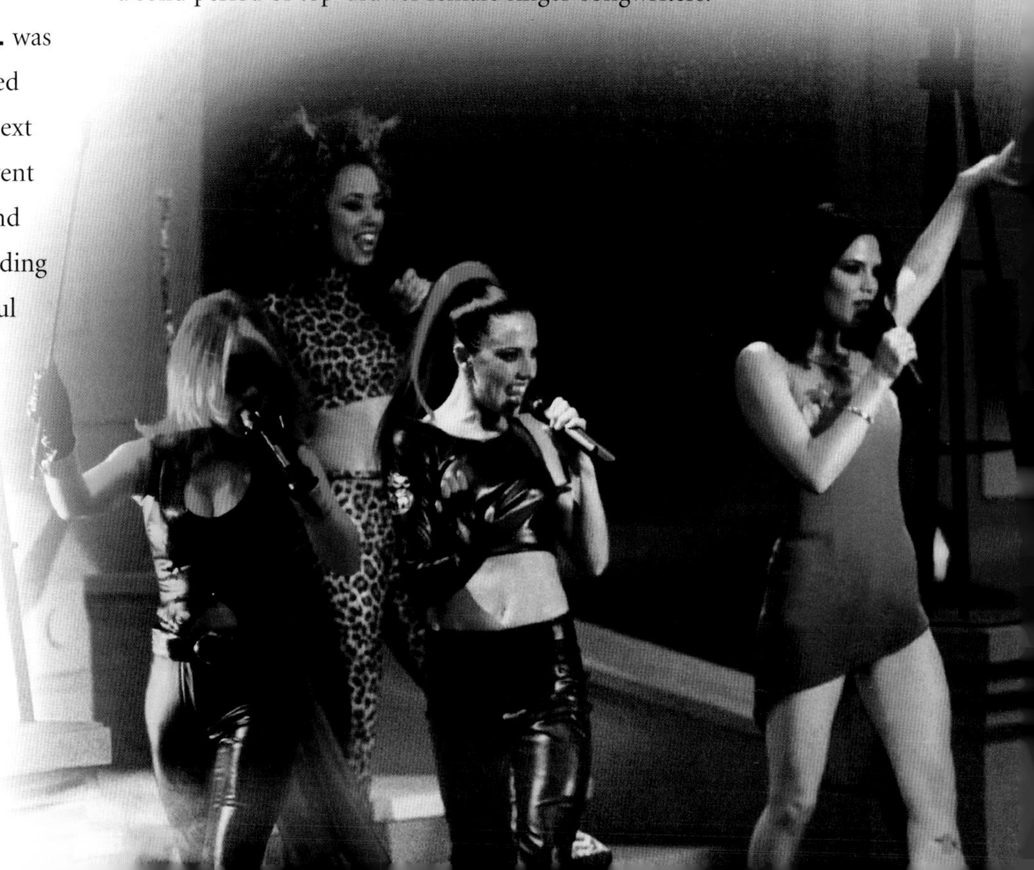

Jan 1997

David Bowie goes public... Notorious B.I.G. killed... Polar Music Prize for Bruce Springsteen...

January

1 Hitless throughout a performing career of nearly 30 years, singer-songwriter/guitarist **Townes Van Zandt** dies from a heart attack, age 52, in Mount Juliet, Tennessee. Despite his lack of commercial success, he is regarded as one of the most literate and soulful contemporary folk/country stylists. His often haunting Americana canon is revered by the likes of **Willie Nelson** and **Merle Haggard** (who scored a US country No. 1 with Van Zandt's *Pancho And Lefty*), **Nanci Griffith**, **Emmylou Harris**, and the **Cowboy Junkies**.

9 **David Bowie** celebrates his birthday (yesterday) with a benefit concert for Save the Children at New York City's Madison Square Garden. Special musical guests include **Lou Reed**, **Robert Smith**, **Frank Black**, **Foo Fighters**, **Sonic Youth**, and alt-rock trio, **Placebo**. The Thin White Duke duets with his guests, and closes the show solo with *Space Oddity*.

23 **Billy Mackenzie**, 39-year-old former lead singer of Scottish art-pop duo the **Associates**, is found dead by his father at home in Auchterhouse, near Dundee, Scotland in the shed where he kept his pet whippets. He was depressed over the recent death of his mother, Lily, and is believed to have taken an overdose of prescription drugs. He leaves a note to his family saying he was sorry. Declared bankrupt in 1995, he signed a new solo record deal with Nude last year.

25 With their "Girl Power" message and popularity spreading like wildfire around the globe, the **Spice Girls** equal **Alanis Morissette**'s record for the highest charting US single by a debut act, as *Wannabe* bows at No. 11.

28 MCA Records holds a press conference at Universal City's Hard Rock Café, confirming a worldwide licensing agreement with **Jimi Hendrix**'s family company, Experience Hendrix, which finally unifies the extensive Hendrix catalog under one label.

David Bowie raised $55 million by floating bonds to private investors, offset against future catalog and publishing royalties.

February

13 Ghanian **Michael Menson** – one half of **Double Trouble**, a British rap/pop duo who teamed with **Rebel MC** for the No. 3 smash *Street Tuff* in 1989 – dies, age 30, 16 days after being found on fire near the North Circular Road in London. Menson, a diagnosed schizophrenic, was initially thought to have immolated himself. It will emerge, however, that it was a racially charged killing, committed by Mario Pereira, Charalambous Constantinou, and Ozgay Cevat, who will all be found guilty in 1999.

25 The **Bee Gees** receive the Outstanding Contribution to British Music honor from Sir Tim Rice at the 16th BRIT Awards at London's Earl's Court Arena, at which they also perform a medley of past hits. Embraced by the mainstream, which they previously so calculatedly despised, the **Manic Street Preachers** receive trophies for Best Group (from Vinnie Jones and Colin Jackson) and Best Album for ***Everything Must Go*** (from DJ Zoë Ball), with **James Dean Bradfield** dedicating the awards to Philip Hall and **Richey Edwards**. The **Spice Girls**' *Wannabe* is named Best Single, and "Say You'll Be There" Best Video. **Elton John** presents the Best Male Vocalist award to an absent **George Michael**. **Prodigy** are named Best Dance Act, sending former BRIT hostess

THE GRAMMY AWARDS

Feb 26 **At the 39th Grammy Awards, Eric Clapton wins the Best Male Pop Vocal Performance category for *Change The World*, which is also named Record of the Year and Song of the Year. *Falling Into You* by Celine Dion (below) receives the coveted Album of the Year Grammy, as well as picking up the Best Pop Album nod. At 14, LeAnn Rimes becomes the first country performer in the event's history to win the Best New Artist honor. She also wins Best Female Country Vocal Performance for her breakthrough smash *Blue*.**

The Beatles won their first Grammys in 29 years – for *Free As A Bird* and "The Beatles Anthology" video.

U2 announced details of their 62-city, 20-country PopMart tour at a press conference in a Kmart store in Manhattan's East Village. Bono serenaded fellow customers as he pushed a shopping cart around the store, and the band played a short set in the lingerie department.

ıamantha Fox to collect the trophy on their ›ehalf, and world heavyweight boxing :hampion Lennox Lewis presents the **Fugees** with the Best International Group award. Among the evening's other performers are **amiroquai** and **Diana Ross**, **Prince**, **Mark Morrison**, ınd red-hot multiracial quartet **Skunk Anansie**.

"Proud to be British, wonderful day and it's a long way from a little :errace [house] in Liverpool."

Paul McCartney on receiving a knighthood, March 11, 1997

28 In Los Angeles Superior Court, Death Row Records owner **Marion "Suge" Knight** receives the maximum nine-year prison sentence for violating probation. He has been arrested eight times since 1987, serving six probations. Knight states he is "closer to God now... I'm needed in the community." The judge responds: "Mr. Knight, you blew it."

March

9 **Notorious B.I.G.** is killed in a drive-by shooting in Los Angeles, following a party sponsored by Vibe magazine at the Petersen Automotive Museum. The Brooklyn-born rapper was the most successful artist on **Sean Combs**'s Bad Boy Entertainment roster, having scored four gold or platinum US singles in the past two years. With the East Coast/West Coast rap war at an all-time high, many in the industry see the killing as copycat retribution for last year's murder of **Tupac Shakur**. (There will be no arrests in either case.) B.I.G. – real name Christopher Wallace – is dead at the age of 24.

10 **LaVern Baker** dies at 67 from diabetes and heart problems (she had her legs amputated last year) at St. Luke's Hospital in New York. She was inducted into the Rock and Roll Hall of Fame in 1991, after being one of the first eight recipients of a Career Achievement Award from the Rhythm & Blues Foundation.

15 With *Mama*, coupled with *Who Do You Think You Are*, entering the UK chart at No. 1 (profits from the double A-side are going to Comic Relief), and *Wannabe* still at No. 1 across the Atlantic, the **Spice Girls** become the first act to top the UK and US charts simultaneously since **Tiffany** in 1988.

April

3 At a Nation of Islam press conference at Louis Farrakhan's Salaam restaurant in Chicago, **Snoop Dogg**, **Public Enemy**'s **Chuck D**, and **Doug E. Fresh** announce plans for a hip-hop peacemaking US tour and a once-only album, dedicated to murdered rap stars **Tupac Shakur** and **Notorious B.I.G.**, **Sean "Puffy" Combs**, **Ice Cube**, and **Ice-T** are also supporting both ventures, although they are not present at the launch. Ice Cube, with members of the **Boo-Ya Tribe** and members of the rival Bloods and Crips street gangs, appeared at a packed Nation of Islam rally on March 23 in south-central Los Angeles, to call for unity in the hip-hop community.

8 **Laura Nyro** dies, age 49, from ovarian cancer in Danbury, Connecticut. A graduate of New York's High School of Music and Art, the highly regarded white soul/gospel-tinged pop singer-songwriter/pianist was steered to Columbia Records in 1968 by manager David Geffen. She cut a series of well-received but modestly selling albums. Her greatest success came from covers by the likes of **Three Dog Night** (*Eli's Comin'*), **Blood Sweat & Tears** (*And When I Die*), and the **5th Dimension** (*Stoned Soul Picnic*).

12 The **Fugees** return to Haiti, homeland of **Wyclef Jean** and **Pras Michel**, to perform before an estimated 60,000 fans at the Coming Home Concert at the Bicentenaire in Port-au-Prince. On the 10th, when thousands of fans showed up at the airport to catch a glimpse of their local heroes, Mayor Manno Charlemagne presented the group with the key to the city. Pras says during the visit: "I was a poor boy, but look where I stand today... I want every Haitian child to follow our example and know that they can be whatever they want to be." With MTV on hand to film the concert, Wyclef says: "This is the chance for people to see that Haiti is a civilized country."

16 **Elton John** is awarded an honorary membership by his alma mater, the Royal Academy of Music, joining 250 so honored, including Franz Liszt, Felix Mendelssohn, and Richard Strauss. (He is perhaps equally honored to become chairman of Watford Football Club once again.)

May

5 About to embark on the European leg of his Ghost of Tom Joad tour, including his first-ever dates in the Czech Republic, Austria, and Poland, **Bruce Springsteen** is honored with the 1997 Polar Music Prize at a ceremony in Stockholm, sharing the honor with Swedish choral conductor Eric Ericson.

Notorious B.I.G., who was killed in March, had said in a Billboard interview that his favorite cut from his new album was *Nobody*, containing the lyric, "You're nobody till somebody kills you."

The Rock and Roll Hall of Fame and Museum opens in Cleveland...

On signing with Mercury Records, Hanson were shipped off to Los Angeles to write and record, paired with veteran songwriters Barry Mann and Cynthia Weil, Mark Hudson, Ellen Shipley, and Desmond Child.

6 Hosted for the first time at the Rock and Roll Hall of Fame and Museum in Cleveland, the 12th induction dinner honors the **Bee Gees**, **Buffalo Springfield**, **Crosby Stills & Nash**, the **Jackson 5**, **Joni Mitchell**, the **Parliament/ Funkadelic** aggregation, and the **Rascals**. The Bee Gees' **Barry Gibb** says, "We are the enigma with a stigma," before thanking **Spinal Tap** "for beautifully filming our life story." Berry Gordy Jr. inducts the Jackson 5, and **James Taylor** sings *Woodstock* as a tribute to an absent Joni Mitchell, who was recently reunited with a daughter she gave up for adoption 32 years ago. Gospel great **Mahalia Jackson**, and **Bill Monroe**, the father of bluegrass, are inducted as Early Influences, and King Records founder **Syd Nathan** is welcomed as a Non-Performer.

The Verve were once described by Oasis's Noel Gallagher as "one of the most important bands in history."

6 Teen trio **Hanson** make their national television debut on "Late Show With David Letterman," performing their infectious pop nugget *MMMBop*, which is three weeks away from topping the US chart, on its way to global fame. Mostly raised in Tulsa, Oklahoma, schooled at home, and encouraged to keep their blond hair long, the photogenic Hanson brothers – 16-year-old Isaac, 14-year-old Taylor, and 11-year-old Zac – formed as a precocious kid trio in February 1991 (when drummer Zac was just six). While attending the South by Southwest Music Conference for unsigned bands in Austin, they gave an impromptu a cappella performance on a street corner for conference attendees Christopher Sabec and Stirling McIlwaine, who became their managers. They recorded two albums that they released on their own independent label, but twelve labels passed on the band between 1992 and 1995, before Sabec sent one of their CDs to Steve Greenberg at Mercury Records in New York.

10 A host of top British acts take part in the Rock the Kop concert at Liverpool Football Club's Anfield stadium. The line-up includes the **Beautiful South**, the **Manic Street Preachers**, the **Lightning Seeds**, the **Bootleg Beatles**, ambient house pioneers **Space** (formed by ex-**Orb** frontman **Dr. Alex Paterson** and ex-KLF co-founder **Jim Cauty**), red-hot Welsh alt-rock trio

FLEETWOOD MAC

May 22 **Having put past conflicts behind them and all now reportedly free from drugs and alcohol problems, the reunited Fleetwood Mac line-up of Lindsey Buckingham, Stevie Nicks, Mick Fleetwood, and Christine and John McVie perform before an invited audience on a Warner Bros. soundstage in Los Angeles. The concert is recorded for an upcoming MTV special. With an impact similar to the Eagles reunion in 1994, the polished comeback will see *The Dance*, a 17-track collection of live material from tonight's show, debut at US No. 1 in September.**

The comeback album sparked the hugely successful Fleetwood Mac reunion tour, The Dance, which opened in September.

Stereophonics (led by singer/guitarist **Kelly Jones**), new Liverpool-based BritPop combo **Smaller**, veteran BritPoppers **Dodgy**, comic song-stylist and all-around oddball **Frank Sidebottom**, and **Holly Johnson**. The concert will benefit the Hillsborough Justice Campaign, set up to find the real causes of the tragedy that saw 96 soccer fans crushed to death before an FA Cup semifinal between Liverpool and Nottingham Forest in 1989.

"I'm just glad to be feeling better. I really thought I'd be seeing Elvis soon."

Bob Dylan leaving hospital, June 2, 1997

June

2 **Bob Dylan** leaves the hospital, where he has been treated for histoplasmosis pericarditis – a fungal infection of the lung. The severe illness will prove a boon to the legend's creativity: his next album, the darkly sparse ***Time Out Of Mind***, produced by Daniel Lanois, will bring some of his best reviews in years.

4 A passenger on board *The American Queen* riverboat spots the body of **Jeff Buckley**, who has been missing since he went for a swim off Mud Island in Memphis on May 29. Crew members pull his body ashore at the foot of Beale Street. Buckley had been appearing at Barrister's every Monday night for the past two months. Son of the late **Tim Buckley**, the 30-year-old singer-songwriter has been a darling of the alt-rock music press since his 1994 debut, ***Grace***.

4 **Ronnie Lane** finally succumbs to multiple sclerosis at his home in Trinidad, Colorado, age 51, having been diagnosed with the disease in 1979. He is the second member of the **Small Faces** to die – **Steve Marriott** died in a house fire in 1991. On hearing that news, Lane apparently said: "I'm jealous."

6 **Iggy Pop** dislocates his shoulder and cuts his head after jumping into a mosh pit and hitting a concrete floor, while singing *Down On The Street* at a concert at the Polaris Theater in Columbus, Ohio, during his R.O.A.R. Tour. Long fond of onstage self-mutilation, Pop is perhaps the most visibly scarred performer in rock history.

7 The first day of the second Tibetan Freedom Concert at Downing Stadium in Randall's Island, New York, is highlighted by tributes paid to **Jeff Buckley** by **Bono** and **Patti Smith**, and a solo set by **Noel Gallagher**. Hip-hop pioneers **A Tribe Called Quest**, earnest pop/rock newcomer **Ben Harper**, **Foo Fighters**, scuzz-blues trio the **Jon Spencer Blues Explosion**, **Porno For Pyros**, rappers **Biz Markie** and **KRS-One**, **Radiohead**, and **Sonic Youth** also perform.

8 **Mike Mills** and **Michael Stipe** appear at the Tibetan Freedom Concert, and are joined on stage by **Eddie Vedder** and **Mike McCready** to sing *The Long Road*. The line-up also includes festival organizers the **Beastie Boys**, **Blur**, the **Mighty Mighty Bosstones**, **Pavement**, pioneering roots-reggae performer/producer **Lee "Scratch" Perry**, **Taj Mahal**, **Björk**, punk revivalists **Rancid**, and **Alanis Morissette**.

14 Dedicated to his slain protégé, **Notorious B.I.G.**, *I'll Be Missing You*, by **Puff Daddy** and **Faith Evans** (featuring **112**) – heavily sampling the **Police**'s *Every Breath You Take* – enters the US chart at No. 1. It will remain at the top for 11 weeks, set to become the second biggest-selling single of the year. While **Sean "Puffy" Combs** is nurturing careers and hit discs for the likes of Evans (B.I.G.'s widow) and **Total** on his own label, he is also much sought after as a producer-for-hire, remixing or working with artists such as **Mariah Carey**, **TLC**, **Aretha Franklin**, **SWV**, **Lil' Kim**, and **Boyz II Men**. Recently named ASCAP's Songwriter of the Year (although much of his solo and production success comes from rather obvious sampling of others' hits), Combs's Bad Boy Entertainment group will be responsible for more than 100 million record sales by the end of the decade. His solo debut album, ***No Way Out***, is also a US chart-topper.

17 Two months before the 20th anniversary of **Elvis Presley**'s death, the festivities begin with RCA's worldwide release of a 100-song, four CD-boxed set ***Platinum – A Life In Music***. It includes the first acetate, 1954's *I'll Never Stand In Your Way*, live tracks, demos, out-takes and home-studio tryouts, 77 of which are previously unreleased. Some of the unissued material was discovered by the compilers, Graceland archivist Greg Howell and Presley researcher Ernst Jorgensen, who discovered over 40 tapes in Presley's father Vernon's filing cabinet.

20 Having become ill on the group's Australian tour in January, **Four Tops** singer **Lawrence Payton** dies from liver cancer, at home in Southfield, Michigan. The quartet received the Rhythm & Blues Foundation's Pioneer Award for Lifetime Achievement in February.

28 The **Verve**'s *Bitter Sweet Symphony*, sampling **Andrew Loog Oldham**'s 1963 orchestral version of the **Rolling Stones**' *The Last Time*, hits UK No. 2. The anthemic single's success soon becomes global and is a bittersweet triumph for the veteran British indie rock act and its rock star-in-waiting frontman, **Richard Ashcroft**. They will have to share a writing credit with **Jagger** and **Richards**, and hand over all the publishing royalties to Allen Klein's company, ABCKO, which controls Stones' copyrights. They will also face legal hassles from Oldham, who claims ownership of the master recording rights.

Lilith Fair... Oasis's *Be Here Now... Candle In The Wind...*

Sarah McLachlan was at the forefront of a new generation of popular female singer-songwriters, having broken through in 1994 with her third album, the highly literate, intimate, and passionate *Fumbling Towards Ecstasy*.

July

5 Conceived by Canadian singer-songwriter **Sarah McLachlan**, the all-female singer-songwriter ensemble tour, Lilith Fair '97, opens at The Gorge in George, Washington, before a sellout crowd of 20,000. The rotating line-up includes **Mary Chapin Carpenter**, **Jewel**, **Indigo Girls**, **Suzanne Vega**, Swedish alt-rock/pop quintet the **Cardigans** (four of whom are male), **Joan Osborne**, **Sheryl Crow**, **Emmylou Harris**, **Tracy Chapman**, **Shawn Colvin**, and **Lisa Loeb**. Defying the skeptics, it will become the most popular summer caravan tour in the US, and $1 from each ticket sold will go to female-oriented charities. The idea came to McLachlan last year, when she was looking at the male-dominated Lollapalooza line-up. She says of this date: "I've been looking forward to this for a really long time... It's a beautiful day and I'm surrounded by beautiful women. Hell, what could be better."

18 **Ricky Martin** performs his new single *La Copa De La Vida* (the official song of the World Cup soccer tournament) before the Cup Final at the Stade de France in Paris. The 26-year old Puerto Rican singer/actor is already a pop phenomenon in Latin markets, having released a succession of multimillion-selling albums since his 1991 debut. Introduced to the US in 1994 as the singing bartender, Miguel Morez, in the television soap opera, "General Hospital," Martin's global success with *La Copa De La Vida* will prepare English-speaking territories for a major chart assault next year.

19 **Prodigy's** ***The Fat Of The Land*** album debuts at No. 1 in 22 countries, including the US, where their ***Music For The Jilted Generation*** peaked at No. 198 in February during a two-week chart stay.

22 **Elton John** and **Sting** sing the 23rd Psalm at a memorial service for fashion designer Gianni Versace at the Duomo Cathedral in Milan. Visibly moved during the service, John is comforted by Diana, Princess of Wales.

24 **Portishead** perform at New York's Roseland Ballroom – their only date of the year – backed by a 30-piece orchestra, warming up for the release of their second album, ***Portishead***. At a press conference tomorrow, **Geoff Barrow** will reveal that the band was "absolutely pooing [itself] most of the way through" the gig.

August

2 Apple Records announces that **George Harrison** has undergone tests for cancer, but is confident that he is free of the disease. He was admitted to a private hospital in Windsor, England, ten days after he found a neck lump.

2 **Fela Kuti** dies from AIDS, age 48, in Lagos, Nigeria. The singer-songwriter/multi-instrumentalist pioneered the hypnotic, horns-driven Afro-beat genre, forming his first band in 1961, and became a musician of enormous popularity and influence in West Africa. More recently discovered by world music enthusiasts in Europe and North America, Kuti's extensive politically charged, roots-infused archive became *the* cultural voice for Nigeria's underclass.

16 **Phish** perform before 65,000 fans at the former Loring Air Force Base near Limestone in northern Maine, at the start of the three-day Great Went festival. Beginning to take on the mantle of the **Grateful Dead**, the band plays a five-hour set, including a keyboard jam in the parking lot.

16 **Nusrat Fateh Ali Khan** dies, age 48, from cardiac arrest in Cromwell Hospital, Kensington, London. With the bulk of his prodigious canon of more than 50 albums released on cassette in his native Pakistan between 1973 and 1993, Khan has been anointed as the "King of Qawwali," an indigenous spiritual genre. Blessed with a rousing, spiritual vocal style, the singer was recently introduced to an international audience via several releases on **Peter Gabriel**'s Real World world music label, and in the past few years he collaborated with the likes of **Alanis Morissette**, **Joan Osborne**, and **Eddie Vedder**. A cultural icon in Pakistan, his body will be flown home for burial.

23 Already certified for 1.5 million sales on pre-orders, the **Oasis** album ***Be Here Now*** sells 696,000 copies in its first two days in Britain, making it the fastest-selling album ever in the UK. It will top the chart next week, and peak at US No. 2 on September 13.

27 Australian pop duo **Savage Garden** receive a record 13 nominations (half of all the categories) for the upcoming 11th Australian Recording Industry Association (ARIA) Awards. They will triumph in ten. Combining the talents of chief songwriter **Darren Hayes** and keyboardist **Daniel Jones**, their melodic debut set, ***Savage Garden*** was released in Australia in April and includes the breakout hits *I Want You*, *To The Moon And Back*, and *Truly Madly Deeply*. With a radio station in Dallas beginning to spin *I Want You* in the US, international success will arrive next year, when ***Savage Garden*** will amass 11 million unfashionable global sales.

Having won two Grammys in February, Beck dominated the MTV Awards in September, picking up five trophies.

ELTON JOHN

Sept 6 **Watched around the world, Elton John sings *Candle In The Wind*, with new lyrics by Bernie Taupin, at the funeral of Princess Diana at Westminster Abbey in London. Following the service he records the song at Townhouse Studios, with Sir George Martin producing. Rush-released on the 13th, it will sell 600,000 copies on its first day in the UK, and 1.5 million in a week, doubling the record for the fastest-selling single ever. The record will be shipped on September 23 in the US, selling 3.4 million copies in its first week and 8.1 million by the end of the year. With proceeds going to the Diana, Princess of Wales Memorial Fund, *Candle In The Wind 1997* will be the last single George Martin produces, and his 30th UK No. 1. In an outpouring of public emotion, its total worldwide sales for 1997 will exceed 35 million, replacing Bing Crosby's *White Christmas* as the all-time global best-seller.**

September

4 **Beck** sweeps the 14th MTV Video Music Awards held at New York's Radio City Music Hall, winning five trophies: Best Male Video, and Best Editing in a Video ("Devil's Haircut"), Best Direction in a Video, Best Art Direction in a Video, and Best Choreography in a Video ("The New Pollution"). **Jamiroquai** are not far behind, with "Virtual Insanity" winning Best Video, Best Cinematography in a Video, Breakthrough Video, and Best Special Effects. Accepting her award for Best New Artist in a Video category (for "Sleep To Dream"), angst-ridden 19-year-old singer-songwriter/pianist du jour **Fiona Apple** breaks out into a rambling diatribe, in which she warns fans not to "model your life about what you think that we think is cool and what we're wearing and we're saying and everything." Much of the evening is a tribute to the recently deceased Princess of Wales. Her close friend, **Elton John**, presenting the Best New Artist award, announces that MTV has donated $100,000 to the Diana, Princess of Wales Memorial Fund. The prize for least classy reference is divided between **Spice Girl Geri Halliwell** – wearing a black armband – who says: "She had a lot of what we're about – girl power," and **Puff Daddy**, who pays homage to Diana along with **Tupac Shakur** and **Notorious B.I.G.**, in his performance of *I'll Be Missing You*. **Marilyn Manson** brings everyone back to earth, performing in an outfit that reveals his buttocks.

12 Former **Abba** manager and co-writer/co-producer of many of their global hits, Stig Anderson dies from a heart attack in Stockholm at the age of 66. He was the prime mover behind the annual Swedish Polar Music Prize.

15 **Paul McCartney**, **Elton John**, **Eric Clapton**, **Phil Collins**, and **Sting** are among a host of stars performing at Music for Montserrat at London's Royal Albert Hall, organized by **George Martin** in aid of the victims of the recent Soufriere Hills volcano. **Carl Perkins**, **Mark Knopfler**, **Jimmy Buffett** – playing his first British gig – **Midge Ure**, and **Arrow** fill out the bill, with everyone joining in on *Hey Jude* to close the concert. (Sky TV will transmit the show on the 18th on pay-per-view – the first such broadcast in the UK.)

October

3 **Garth Brooks** files suit against rapper **Warren G** in Nashville Federal Court, alleging trademark infringement over the singular **"G"** used by both artists in their promotion. G will file his claim against Brooks on October 17. No news from **Kenny G**'s attorney yet.

12 After playing golf at Spyglass Hill in Pebble Beach, **John Denver** is killed when his single-engine Long-EZ experimental plane – bought two days ago – crashes into Monterey Bay, shortly after takeoff. He is 53. On the 18th, over 1,000 family and friends will gather at an amphitheater in Aspen, Colorado, to eulogize Denver, climaxing in the playing of his final recording, *Yellowstone (Coming Home)*. Among the many tributes, **Lyle Lovett** sings *The Texas River Man*, hailing Denver as a formative influence.

21 **John Lydon** tapes an episode of the syndicated TV show, "Judge Judy," on a Hollywood soundstage. Robert Williams is claiming lost wages and civil battery, alleging that Lydon fired him prior to a tour. Lydon claims Williams quit the tour four days before its first date. Judge Judy rules on behalf of Lydon. On leaving, Lydon says: "Now I'm going to get on with my life. We're going after the real killer."

30 During a heated interview with bullish host Clive Anderson, the Brothers Gibb walk off the set of BBC1-TV's "All Talk." When **Barry Gibb** says "Before we became the **Bee Gees** we were Les Tosseurs," Anderson replies: "You'll always be Les Tosseurs to me!"

In typical Phish fashion, the band chose the site of several UFO sightings over the years for the last date of their tour.

Nov 1997

The Wallflowers' Jakob Dylan appeared on stage for the first time with his father, Bob, when his group performed at computer company Applied Materials' 30th anniversary party at the San Jose Civic Arena on November 14.

Shania Twain's *Come On Over*... Michael Hutchence dies... BowieNet...

November

4 Having entered the UK chart at No. 1 in June, **Radiohead**'s third studio set, ***OK Computer*** is named Best Album at the eighth **Q** Awards at the Park Lane Hotel in London. One of the best-reviewed rock albums of the decade, the seminal **Thom Yorke**-led release – regarded as a career highlight – will win a slew of other national and international awards. The group recently ended a soldout US tour, and will return there to appear in concert at the Hammerstein Ballroom in New York City for MTV's "Live From The 10 Spot" on December 19.

4 Capitol Records releases the much-delayed **Beach Boys** project ***The Pet Sounds Sessions (Produced By Brian Wilson)***, featuring backing tracks, prepared by Brian and songwriter/producer **Van Dyke Parks** from the legendary 1967 ***Smile*** sessions.)

6 Raymond Kuntz, of Burlington, North Dakota, testifies before a Senate committee exploring the effects of music on children, following the suicide last December of his 15-year-old son Richard, allegedly after listening to **Marilyn Manson**'s ***Antichrist Superstar***. Kuntz tells the committee: "I failed to recognize that my son was holding a hand grenade and it was live and it was going to go off in his mind."

11 **Green Day** cause havoc at a 40-minute in-store performance at New York City's Tower Records, when lead singer **Billie Joe** spray-paints "Nimrod" (the title of their new album) in black and red on the store walls, and showers beer and water over CD racks. Not content with the mayhem he has caused, he bodysurfs over the crowd to the window, on which he spray-paints "F**k You," and moons the onlookers gathered outside. He tells the fans inside: "You can start a riot. It's your prerogative – you can do anything you want, 'cause you're not at Tower Records, you're at a Green Day concert!" Not surprisingly, a scheduled after-show CD signing is canceled.

15 With ***Spice*** now exceeding 18 million sales worldwide, the **Spice Girls**' next set ***Spiceworld*** enters the UK chart at No. 1. Currently at the peak of their success as the most popular all-girl act of the decade, the ubiquitous quintet was named Best Group at the fourth MTV Europe Music Awards last week, following similar triumphs at the Irish IRMA Awards, the German Echo Awards, and the World Music Awards, with still more honors to come at the **Smash Hits** Awards and the **Billboard** Music Awards. Next month, Media Research Publishing's **Rock Accounts 1998** will estimate that the Spice Girls generated £43 ($70) million during 1997, £12 ($19.2) million more than the second-placed act, the **Rolling Stones**.

18 **Gary Glitter** is questioned by police, following his arrest at the PC World store in Bristol, England, where he took his computer for repair. Store staff allegedly found suspicious material on his computer, prompting the police to search his properties in Somerset and London, where they seized videotapes and photographs. They book him for possession of child pornography. Freed on bail, Glitter denies any wrongdoing and plans to proceed with his forthcoming annual Christmas tour.

22 **Shania Twain**'s unusually long 16-track rock/pop/country-fusing ***Come On Over*** hits US No. 2 in its week of entry, once again helmed and largely co-written by her husband Robert John "Mutt" Lange. It also reaches No. 1 on the Top Country Albums chart, confirming the singer's immense crossover appeal.

22 Back in Sydney, Australia, to rehearse for the band's upcoming 20th anniversary tour, **INXS**'s **Michael Hutchence** fails to show for a performance at local radio station ABC's Gore Hill studios. A housemaid at Sydney's Ritz-Carlton Hotel discovers his body hanging by a leather belt from a door hinge. Police reveal that actress Kim Wilson and her boyfriend Andrew Rayment had been drinking with Hutchence in his hotel room until 4:45 this morning. Hutchence allegedly talked at length of his recent custody and legal battles with **Bob Geldof**, ex-husband of his girlfriend **Paula Yates**. The flamboyant frontman of Australia's most successful rock export since **AC/DC**, Hutchence is dead at 37.

27 **Michael Hutchence**'s funeral, at St. Andrew's Anglican Cathedral in Sydney, is attended by a distraught **Paula Yates**, their 16-

At the Q Awards in November, Phil Spector said, "I was just thinking, are the Spice Girls the anti-Christ?... There's a big difference between a Spice Girls video and a porno film – some porno films have pretty good music."

"We write pop songs. As time has gone on, we've gotten more into pushing our own material as far as it can go. But there was no intention of it being 'art'." Radiohead's Thom Yorke, **Entertainment Weekly**, October 24, 1997

month-old daughter, Heavenly Hiraani Tiger Lily, **Kylie Minogue**, **Diana Ross**, **Tom Jones**, **Nick Cave**, family, friends, and band members. During the service, which is broadcast live on Australian television, a man attempts to jump from a first floor balcony, screaming, "He's dead, he's dead."

28 **Chumbawamba**'s **Danbert Nobacon** is arrested while sightseeing in Florence, Italy. He says: "They saw me in the street and didn't like the fact I was wearing a skirt. They just wanted to have a go at someone who didn't fit their picture of manhood." His bandmates phone around to hospitals and police stations, but are told that no "bald-headed foreigner in a dress" has been seen. He is released after he writes a note explaining who he is, and a police officer recognizes him. The veteran anarchist British group are on tour following the unexpected success of their yob-pop anthem *Tubthumping*, which having hit UK No. 2, now peaks at US No. 6.

29 **Whitney Houston** pulls out of a scheduled $1 million performance at RFK Stadium in Washington, D.C., for the final event of the World Culture & Sports Festival, with a "sudden flulike illness." It seems she was unaware that the event was a mass wedding for 1,300 Moonie couples.

December

5 Wal-Mart and Kmart pull **Prodigy**'s ***The Fat Of The Land*** album from the shelves of 4,400 stores, over objections to the extracted single, *Smack My Bitch Up*. MTV US premieres the controversial single's video clip, directed by Jonas Akerlund, which depicts nudity, drug-taking, and general hedonism. Maverick will alter the titles of two tracks on the new album to *Smack My B**** Up* and *Funky S****, against **Liam Howlett**'s wishes.

9 **Liam Gallagher** rips up a copy of **Paul McCartney**'s biography, **Many Years From Now**, at Glasgow airport, Scotland, before flying to Cardiff, Wales, for a gig at the Indoor Arena tomorrow. Later, in the foyer of Jury's Hotel in Cardiff, he pours lager over ITN journalist Tim Rogers, there to cover a **Gary Glitter** concert.

"This is a long way from Elvis shaking his hips on 'The Ed Sullivan Show.'" Senator Joseph Lieberman on Marilyn Manson's *Antichrist Superstar*, November 6, 1997

17 With today's launch of his subscription-based BowieNet internet site, and the successful Bowiebonds launch in January, **David Bowie**'s reputation as a groundbreaker in music appears to be shifting toward innovation in technology and revenue streams.

27 **Mark Morrison** is arrested after a fight at the Pink Coconut Club in Derby, England. This concludes a year in which the singer has been sentenced in London to 21 days in prison for kicking a parked car and attacking a man who criticized one of his records – and to 14 days (to run concurrently with the previous sentence) for criminal damage to a camera. He was also arrested and charged with carrying an offensive weapon (a truncheon found in his BMW during a routine vehicle check in Notting Hill, London).

Shania Twain was named Best Country Female Vocalist at the American Music Awards in January – an award won by Reba McEntire every year over the previous decade.

ROOTS During this year: after dropping out of high school in ninth grade and performing with Basement Productions, the New Jacks, and D12, rapper Eminem releases his debut album, *Infinite*, on the indie label FBT... 12-year-old Napanee, Ontario, native Avril Lavigne teaches herself the guitar and takes up songwriting... after dreaming of being a professional dancer, studying at the School of American Ballet in New York City, Vanessa Carlton begins writing songs; she wrote her first piece of music as an eight-year-old... Nelly Furtado leaps on stage to sing at a Toronto talent show for mostly black, female performers, and meets her future manager, Chris Smith, who also represents multiplatinum-selling Canadian band the Philosopher Kings; shortly thereafter, the Kings' Gerald Eaton and Brian West produce a demo for the singer... Rick Rubin sees System of a Down at the Viper Room in Hollywood, and makes them his first signing to his American Recordings label... Josh Homme and Alfredo Hernandez, who were in Kyuss together, and Nick Oliveri, who is in the Dwarves, come together as Queens of the Stone Age... the daughter of former "Blue Peter" presenter Janet Ellis, Sophie Ellis Bextor joins theaudience as its lead singer... and minimalist garage rock duo White Stripes perform their first gigs in Detroit...

Gettin' Jiggy Wit It

1998

No.1 US SINGLES

- **Jan 3** Candle In The Wind 1997/Something About The Way You Look Tonight **Elton John**
- **Jan 17** Truly Madly Deeply **Savage Garden**
- **Jan 31** Together Again **Janet Jackson**
- **Feb 14** Nice & Slow **Usher**
- **Feb 28** My Heart Will Go On (Love Theme From "Titanic") **Celine Dion**
- **Mar 14** Gettin' Jiggy Wit It **Will Smith**
- **Apr 4** All My Life **K-Ci & JoJo**
- **Apr 25** Too Close **Next**
- **May 23** My All **Mariah Carey**
- **May 30** Too Close **Next**
- **June 6** The Boy Is Mine **Brandy & Monica**
- **Sept 5** I Don't Want To Miss A Thing **Aerosmith**
- **Oct 3** The First Night **Monica**
- **Oct 17** One Week **Barenaked Ladies**
- **Oct 24** The First Night **Monica**
- **Nov 14** Doo Wop (That Thing) **Lauryn Hill**
- **Nov 28** Lately **Divine**
- **Dec 5** I'm Your Angel **R. Kelly & Celine Dion**

No.1 UK SINGLES

- **Jan 3** Too Much **Spice Girls**
- **Jan 17** Never Ever **All Saints**
- **Jan 24** All Around The World **Oasis**
- **Jan 31** You Make Me Wanna... **Usher**
- **Feb 7** Doctor Jones **Aqua**
- **Feb 21** My Heart Will Go On **Celine Dion**
- **Feb 28** Brimful Of Asha **Cornershop**
- **Mar 7** Frozen **Madonna**
- **Mar 14** My Heart Will Go On **Celine Dion**
- **Mar 21** It's Like That **Run-D.M.C. Vs. Jason Nevins**
- **May 2** All That I Need **Boyzone**
- **May 9** Under The Bridge/Lady Marmalade **All Saints**
- **May 16** Turn Back Time **Aqua**
- **May 23** Under The Bridge/Lady Marmalade **All Saints**
- **May 30** Feel It **Tamperer featuring Maya**
- **June 6** C'est La Vie **B*Witched**
- **June 20** 3 Lions '98 **Baddiel and Skinner and the Lightning Seeds**
- **July 11** Because We Want To **Billie**
- **July 18** Freak Me **Another Level**
- **July 25** Deeper Underground **Jamiroquai**
- **Aug 1** Viva Forever **Spice Girls**
- **Aug 15** No Matter What **Boyzone**

Celine Dion

Boyzone

Celine Dion's *My Heart Will Go On* logged a record 116 million plays in a single week on US radio in February... Boyzone's *No Matter What*, a song from the musical "Whistle Down The Wind," gave writer Andrew Lloyd Webber only his third UK chart-topper.

Percolating in Europe for a couple of years, boy bands – led by **Backstreet Boys** and ***NSync** – began worldwide domination in 1998. Boasting indistinguishable radio-ready ear candy – much of it created by **Max Martin** and **Denniz PoP**, at the Cheiron Studio in Stockholm, Sweden – the two groups between them sold 10.1 million albums in the US alone during 1998. PoP died in September, leaving Martin as chief architect of the teen pop bubble that would shortly produce **Britney Spears**.

In Europe and Asia, Irish boy wonders **Boyzone** were even more popular than their American counterparts. In August, *No Matter What* entered at UK No. 1, making them the first group to debut in the top five with their first 12 singles. Curiously, another Irish band took the honors for the UK's best-selling album this year: the **Corrs**' ***Talk On Corners*** went seven-times platinum in Britain, the only album to outstrip the success of **George Michael**'s career-thus-far anthology ***Ladies & Gentlemen – The Best Of George Michael***. His global popularity was assured everywhere except the increasingly conservative US, where he literally "came out of the closet" in a much publicized episode with a Los Angeles police officer. Overall it was a huge year for pop. **Celine Dion**'s *My Heart Will Go On* sent her record sales into über-diva league. In the country/pop arena, her success was almost matched by **Shania Twain**, whose two albums sold 21 million copies in the US alone during the year.

R&B was dominated by producer/performers/poseurs **Puff Daddy** and **Master P**, while a new crop of talented upstarts emerged, often with singularly fashionable singular names (**Usher, Brandy, Monica**). **Matchbox 20**'s unpretentious fare marked the high tide for the modern rock genre, led by the songwriting skills of lead singer **Rob Thomas**. On the hard side, **KoRn** and **Limp Bizkit** came to the fore, blazing a nu-metal/rap hybrid trail that found great success on the controversial Family Values US caravan tour.

As many artists approached old age pension status, 52-year old **Cher** made another comeback. Leaving behind her previous pop/rock bent, the world's best preserved star bounced back with the dancefloor filler, *Believe* – a huge hit in the dance-dominated European market and the biggest-selling single of the year in Britain. **Madonna** was back on top form with ***Ray Of Light***, her most accomplished album to date, and her first foray into electronica courtesy of ambient/dance production whiz, **William Orbit**. The project yielded two striking videos: one for the title cut, the other for the superb single *Frozen*, and both cleaned up at the US and European MTV Video awards.

Sept 5	If You Tolerate This Your Children Will Be Next **Manic Street Preachers**
Sept 12	Bootie Call **All Saints**
Sept 19	Millennium **Robbie Williams**
Sept 26	I Want You Back **Melanie B featuring Missy "Misdemeanor" Elliott**
Oct 3	Rollercoaster **B*Witched**
Oct 17	Girlfriend **Billie**
Oct 24	Gym And Tonic **Spacedust**
Oct 31	Believe **Cher**
Dec 19	To You I Belong **B*Witched**
Dec 26	Goodbye **Spice Girls**

"I've been on stage my whole life, entertaining people. I'm very, very comfortable with entertaining."

Shania Twain, **Q**, October 1988

Jan

1998

The Eagles enter the Rock and Roll Hall of Fame... Carl Perkins dies...

Chumbawamba

Missy Elliott

January

5 **Sonny Bono** is killed instantly when he skis into a tree next to the Orion trail at the Heavenly Ski Resort in South Lake Tahoe, California. The 62-year old former singer-songwriter had long had a political career.

9 Broadcast live on American television, **Cher** gives an emotional eulogy at her former husband's funeral, held at the St. Theresa Roman Catholic Church in Palm Springs, California. (A biopic of Cher and **Bono**'s life, "And The Beat Goes On," with Renée Faia and Jay Underwood, will air on ABC-TV on February 22 next year. Bono's widow Mary will follow in her late husband's political footsteps.)

12 **Jimmy Buffett** inducts the **Eagles** into the Rock and Roll Hall of Fame at the 13th dinner, held at New York's Waldorf Astoria Hotel. All seven Eagles, including original members **Bernie Leadon** and **Randy Meisner**, uniquely perform together, playing *Take It Easy* and *Hotel California*. **Sheryl Crow** inducts **Fleetwood Mac**, and in a historic moment, the band's reclusive founder, **Peter Green**, plays guitar with fellow inductee **Carlos Santana** on *Black Magic Woman*. **Shania Twain** inducts the **Mamas & the Papas** (**Mama Cass**'s daughter, Owen Kunkel, is there on her mother's behalf). **John Fogerty** inducts **Gene Vincent**: Vincent's daughter, Melody Craddock, accepts the induction, and axemen **Jeff Beck** and **Jonny Lang** perform *Be Bop A Lula*. **Allen Toussaint** is welcomed as a Non-Performer by **Robbie Robertson**, and **Jelly Roll Morton** enters the Hall as an Early Influence. **Nona Hendryx** sings *Son Of A Preacher Man* as a tribute to the cancer-stricken **Dusty Springfield**.

19 Pulled from the Sundance Film Festival in Utah, the movie "Kurt And Courtney" finally gets its premiere screening at Park City, Utah's alternative film fest, Slamdunk. Director Nick Broomfield's documentary explores the unproven allegation that **Courtney Love** was responsible for **Kurt Cobain**'s death. In the film, her estranged father, Hank Harrison, says: "I don't think he killed himself. I think somebody killed him. I'm not saying Courtney did it. I don't really know, but the evidence is so strong." Private investigator Tom Grant, whom Love hired to find Cobain, says in the film: "I think Courtney used Kurt from the beginning and married him for the sole purpose of obtaining wealth and stardom."

Two months before Danbert Nobacon's protest at the BRIT Awards, he had been arrested by police in Florence, supposedly for wearing a short black skirt and panty hose... Missy Elliott was in increasing demand as a featured singer, rapper, producer, and all-around media talent.

19 Following three strokes in two months, rock 'n' roll legend **Carl Perkins** dies, age 65, at the Jackson-Madison County General Hospital, after successfully battling throat cancer in 1993.

23 **George Harrison**, backed by country stars **Garth Brooks**, **Wynonna**, **Billy Ray Cyrus**, and **Ricky Skaggs**, sings *Your True Love* at **Carl Perkins**'s funeral at the R.E. Womack Memorial Chapel of Lambuth University in Jackson, Mississippi.

29 **Eurythmics** reunite to perform at BMG executive John Preston's going away party at London's Cobden Club. They will also take part in a benefit concert at the ICA, London, in May, in honor of **Observer** columnist Ruth Picardie, who died of breast cancer last September, joined by **David Gilmour**, **Kirsty MacColl**, and **Boo Hewerdine**, among others.

Madonna's *Ray of Light* album was laced with techno-ambient soundscaping by co-producer William Orbit.

February

6 **Beach Boy Carl Wilson**, the youngest of the three brothers, dies from lung cancer at 51, at home in Los Angeles.

9 **Chumbawamba**'s **Danbert Nobacon** grabs the headlines at the 17th BRIT Awards, held at the London Arena, when he leaps on to John Prescott's table and douses the Deputy Prime Minister with water. There are disturbances outside the venue as well, when some 200 protesters demonstrate against Polygram allegedly paying CD packers £3 ($5.10) an hour. The night's big non-political winners are the **Verve**, who nab three awards – Best British Group, Best British Album, and Best Album for ***Urban Hymns***. All-girl vocal quartet **All Saints**' recent chart-topper, *Never Ever*, is named Best British Single and Best British Video. **Fleetwood Mac** are honored with the Outstanding Contribution to British Music, **Elton John** wins the Freddie Mercury Award, and the **Spice Girls**

receive a Special Award for their phenomenal worldwide success. Other winners include mellow-soul tripping singer **Finley Quaye** (Best British Male Solo Artist), soul-pop newcomer **Shola Ama** (Best British Female Solo Artist), **Jon Bon Jovi** (Best International Male Solo Artist), **Björk** (Best International Female Solo Artist), **Prodigy** (Best British Dance Act), **Stereophonics** (Best British Newcomer), and **U2** (Best International Group). Surprise winners of the Best International Newcomer are Los Angeles-based alt-rock trio, **eels**, led by singer-songwriter/multi-instrumentalist **E** (Mark Oliver Everett).

14 Red-hot soul rapper **Missy "Misdemeanor" Elliott** makes her network television debut on "Saturday Night Live," performing *Sock It 2 Me*, her gold single from last year with female rapper **Da Brat**, and *Beep Me 911*. The 28-year-old Virginia-born artist (signed to Elektra) teamed with upcoming R&B producer Timbaland to help steer **Aaliyah**'s multiplatinum ***One In A Million*** album in 1996, before recording her own smash maiden set, the stylish, self-penned, platinum ***Supa Dupa Fly***.

14 **Madonna** gives her first club performance in ten years, at the Ice Ball at New York's Roxy dance club. It is the first promotion salvo for her new album, the critically hailed, electronica-based ***Ray Of Light***.

23 During a flight from Hong Kong to Perth for the start of **Oasis**'s Australian tour, **Liam Gallagher**'s behavior results in a ban from Cathay Pacific. Gallagher was recently hailed Dickhead of the Year in the annual NME Premier Awards.

25 Not to be outdone by **Danbert Nobacon** at the recent BRIT Awards, Michael Portnoy rushes on stage during **Bob Dylan**'s performance of *Love Sick* at the 40th Grammy awards, and "dances," bearing the words "Soy Bomb" on his naked chest. The 26-year-old describes himself as a "multigenre mastermind artist." **Wu-Tang Clan**'s **Ol' Dirty Bastard** also takes to the stage, during **Shawn Colvin**'s acceptance speech for Song of the Year (*Sunny Came Home*) – graciously saying to Colvin, "I apologize, my darling" – to proffer the view that his group should have beaten out **Puff Daddy** for Best Rap Album. *Sunny Came Home* is also named Record of the Year – a major triumph for one of America's most literate and underrated singer-songwriting talents, who has finally broken through with the platinum ***A Few Small Repairs***. Dylan wins three awards – Album of the Year and Best Contemporary Folk Album (***Time Out Of Mind***), and Best Rock Vocal Performance, Male (*Cold Irons Bound*). His son **Jakob** wins a pair – Best Rock Song for *One Headlight*, and Best Rock Performance by a Duo or Group with Vocal for the **Wallflowers**.

"The Heart and Voice of an Angel – The World is a Far Lesser Place Without You." Carl Wilson's gravestone at the Westwood Memorial Park, Los Angeles

March

10 ***First Love***, the debut album by New York-born, 15-year-old female singer-songwriting sensation **Hikaru Utada**, is released in Japan by Toshiba. It will become the biggest-selling Japanese record ever, selling seven million copies by May.

17 The **Backstreet Boys** and ***NSync** participate in a benefit concert at the Hard Rock Café at Universal Studios in Orlando, for victims of a recent tornado in Florida. Broadcast live online, the event raises more than $250,000. The Backstreet Boys made their debut on "Saturday Night Live" last weekend, and their ***Backstreet Boys*** is belatedly on its way to being the biggest-selling album of the year (with nine million US sales). Next week will see the US release of ****NSync***, the debut album by Orlando-based vocal quintet comprising the close-harmonizing **Justin Timberlake**, **J.C. Chasez**, **Chris Kirkpatrick**, **Joey Fatone**, and **Lance Bass**. They have spent the past two years touring Europe, Asia, South Africa, and Mexico, building a growing teen following. Both groups are musically directed by Scandinavian pop maestros, Denniz PoP and Max Martin.

17 **Matchbox 20** receive the Best Selling Recording by a New Artist for their debut ***Yourself Or Someone Like You*** at the 1997/1998 Best Seller Awards, organized by the National Association of Recording Merchandisers. Selling 3.2 million copies this year alone in the US, it will spend a total of 118 weeks on the US chart.

23 **Primal Scream**'s **Bobby Gillespie** and pioneering Anglo-Asian combo **Asian Dub Foundation**'s **Chandrasonic** visit Satpal Ram in Hull Prison, England. Ram is serving a sentence for stabbing one of six young men who attacked him in a Bengali restaurant in Birmingham, England, in 1986. He is not being considered for

***NSync initially broke through in Europe, with their first single, in 1997.**

George Michael's arrest... Frank Sinatra dies... U2 perform for peace...

George Michael's attorney

Burt Bacharach and Elvis Costello

parole, because he refuses to admit guilt. The bands play a benefit gig at the Liverpool Lomax in the evening. Ram will finally be released in June 2002, after 13 years in prison.

29 The Not in Our Name – Dead Man Walking benefit concert – aimed at the repeal of the death penalty laws – takes place at the Shrine Auditorium in Los Angeles, California. **Pearl Jam**'s **Eddie Vedder** and **Jeff Ament**, **Steve Earle**, punk folkie **Ani DiFranco** (who releases all her records on her own Righteous Babe indie label), **Lyle Lovett**, feminist alt-folk singer-songwriter/ guitarist **Michelle Shocked**, **Rahat Fateh Ali Khan**, qawwali tabla player **Dildar Hussain**, and (making his first Los Angeles appearance in some years) **Tom Waits** take part. Proceeds will go to the Murder Victims' Families for Reconciliation, and Hope House.

"I am in a relationship with a man right now and I have not been in a relationship with a woman for almost ten years."

George Michael interviewed on CNN, April 10, 1998

April

2 **Joe Walsh**, **Ruth Brown**, **Ike Turner**, **George Clinton**, **Michelle Phillips**, **Eddie Levert**, **Wilson Pickett**, **Peter Wolf**, and **Bo Diddley** attend the grand opening of the Hall of Fame Wing, at the Rock and Roll Hall of Fame and Museum in Cleveland. As ever, **Little Richard** steals the show, arriving late and pronouncing: "You can't do this without the architect [of rock 'n' roll]."

3 Milli Vanilli's **Rob Pilatus**, age 32, is found dead in a Frankfurt, Germany, hotel room. He showed up at Frank Farian's studio yesterday "very intoxicated and shivering all over," according to the producer. He had been taking prescription pills during a drug withdrawal program.

5 **Cozy Powell**, one of Britain's finest rock drummers, is killed when his car hits the central barrier on the M4 highway between London and Bristol, while he is talking to his girlfriend on his cell phone. The 49-year-old Powell had drummed with **Rainbow**, **Whitesnake**, **Black Sabbath**, and the **Michael Schenker Group**.

6 **Wendy O. Williams**, 48-year-old punk iconette, dies from a self-inflicted gunshot wound in the woods behind her house in Storrs, Connecticut. The former lead singer of the **Plasmatics** more recently worked as a licensed wildlife rehabilitator.

7 **George Michael** is arrested in Will Rogers Park in Beverly Hills, California, after allegedly being seen by undercover officer Marcello Rodriquez committing a lewd act in a restroom. He is charged with violating Penal Code 647A, released on $500 bail, and ordered to appear in court on May 5.

Ulster Unionist MP Bob McCartney described Bono's appearance with John Hume and David Trimble as "patronizing, condescending and, to a degree, insulting."

George Michael's attorney Brad Barnholtz reported in December that his client had completed his community service...
Proving himself to be perhaps the coolest septuagenarian on the planet, Burt Bacharach toured with Elvis Costello.

8 The songs of **Burt Bacharach** and **Hal David** are celebrated with a sellout all-star concert, One Amazing Night, at New York City's Hammerstein Ballroom. In a night of many highlights, **Elvis Costello** revs up his increasingly close creative partnership with Bacharach, singing *God Give Me Strength* and *This House Is Empty Now*, accompanied by the maestro on piano. Witty Canadian pop/rock combo **Barenaked Ladies** and the equally eccentric trio **Ben Folds Five** give quirky interpretations of *(They Long To Be) Close To You* and *Raindrops Keep Falling On My Head* respectively. With so many of the pair's finest songs made famous by female singers, the ladies step forward with **Chrissie Hynde** (*Baby It's You* and *Message To Michael*), **Sheryl Crow** (*One Less Bell To Answer*), **Wynonna** (*Anyone Who Had A Heart*) and, naturally, **Dionne Warwick**, who performs the timeless *Walk On By* and *I Say A Little Prayer*.

9 At a memorial service for the First Lady of Country Music, **Tammy Wynette** – who died from a blood clot on the lungs in Nashville, Tennessee, earlier in the week – **Dolly Parton**, **Randy Travis**, and **Wynonna** perform a tribute to the 55-year-old legend at the Ryman Auditorium. At an earlier private service, Parton broke down while singing *Shine On*, and was unable to continue.

10 In an exclusive 15-minute interview with Jim Moret on CNN, **George Michael** acknowledges that he has put himself "in an extremely stupid and vulnerable position" following the incident on the 7th, and says: "I've already kind of done that, haven't I? I've done that in a way I didn't really intend to."

11 **Ry Cooder** and his veteran Cuban collective, the **Buena Vista Social Club**, perform at the Carré Theater in Amsterdam, Holland. Scheduled as a once-only gig, the ongoing success of the ***Buena Vista Social Club*** album will result in a second performance at New York City's Carnegie Hall on July 1 – both filmed by German director Wim Wenders for theatrical release.

MATCHBOX 20

Apr 10 **MTV airs Matchbox 20's "Live From The 10 Spot," taped at New York's Hammerstein Ballroom on March 20. The group was formed in 1993 as Tabitha's Secret, by German-born lead singer/ songwriter Rob Thomas, with bassist Brian Yale and drummer Paul Doucette. In 1995 they changed their name and their line-up, adding guitarists Kyle Cook and Adam Gaynor. Signed with Atlantic's Lava imprint, they are guided by Collective Soul producer, Matt Serletic, and are currently the hottest modern rock band in North America. Their debut album, *Yourself Or Someone Like You*, has found favor on MTV, VH1 and at Modern Rock radio, notably the featured cuts *Push* and *3.a.m.* (neither of which are available as singles).**

The melodic modern rock chops of Matchbox 20's debut album, highlighted by Rob Thomas's passionate and soulful vocal style, positioned him as a major new songwriting talent.

14 **Aretha Franklin**, **Mariah Carey**, **Celine Dion**, **Gloria Estefan**, **Shania Twain**, and **Carole King** perform at the first Divas Live: an Honors Concert for VH1 Save The Music, live from New York City's Beacon Theater. Together with the network's biographical "Behind the Music" series (which began last August), "Divas Live" will become one of VH1's most successful concepts.

17 **Linda McCartney** succumbs to cancer at the age of 56, with **Paul** at her bedside, at the family's farm near Tucson, Arizona. In a later statement, McCartney will reveal: "Finally, I said to her: 'You're up on your beautiful Appaloosa stallion. It's a fine spring day. We're riding through the woods. The bluebells are all out, and the sky is clear blue.' I had barely got to the end of the sentence, when she closed her eyes, and gently slipped away." They have been inseparable throughout their devoted marriage.

29 A planned free concert by the **Indigo Girls**, at Irmo High School in Columbia, Soth Carolina, is canceled after parents complain about the duo's sexuality. Two Tennessee schools, in Germantown and Farragut, will follow suit.

May

11 **Faith Hill** guests on CBS-TV's "Late Show With David Letterman," singing her latest single, the pop-country crossover smash ballad, *This Kiss*, on its way to a No. 7 peak in October. The song's parent album, ***Faith***, currently at its No. 7 peak, is on its way to five million sales. Hill married **Tim McGraw** in October 1996, and both are building highly successful solo careers: 30-year-old neo-traditionalist country singer/ guitarist McGraw broke through in 1994 with his controversial Native American hit *Indian Outlaw*, while his Jackson, Mississippi-born wife – also 30 – is currently second only to **Shania Twain** as country music's hottest crossover diva.

14 **George Michael** pleads no contest to a charge of lewd behavior in California's Beverly Hills Municipal Court. He is fined $810, barred from the Will Rogers Memorial Park, and ordered to undergo psychological counseling and perform 80 hours of community service.

"Today, I think every American would have to smile and say he really did do it his way." President Bill Clinton on the death of Frank Sinatra, May 14, 1998

14 **Frank Sinatra** is pronounced dead from a heart attack at 10:50 pm, at Cedars-Sinai Medical Center in Los Angeles, California. He is 82. New York, in appreciation of Sinatra's career-long homage to the city, will light the top of the Empire State Building in blue for three days.

19 **U2** take part in a free concert to support the upcoming vote on the Peace Agreement at the Waterfront Hall, Belfast, Northern Ireland, backed by fellow Irish group, hot newcomers **Ash. Bono** – who has just been named the 20th most hated person in Ireland – brings SDP leader John Hume and Ulster Unionist leader David Trimble on stage, and in a show of unity, raises their arms aloft.

21 Joseph E. Seagram and Sons, Inc., purchases Polygram Holdings for $10.6 billion. In December, Seagram's Universal Music Group will take control of Polygram, bringing its disparate music divisions under one umbrella. The largest music company in the world will include the combined operations of Polygram, MCA, Geffen, Polydor, Interscope, London, Verve, Mercury, A&M, DG, Island, and Motown – much to the concern of many on the vast roster. Universal will lay off 3,000 employees, and release scores of artists from their contracts.

28 Accepting a special award for *Candle In The Wind 1997* at the 43rd Ivor Novello Awards, **Elton John** says: "This is a bittersweet award to get. I wish the record never had to be made." The recording is also named Best Selling UK Single and International Hit of the Year. **Radiohead** win the Best Contemporary Song (for *Karma Police*), and Best Song Musically and Lyrically (for *Paranoid Android*) categories. Other winners include **Enya**, and **Nicky** and **Roma Ryan** (International Achievement), **Morrissey** (whose solo and **Smiths** archive is recognized for its Outstanding Contribution to British Music), **Puff Daddy**'s *I'll Be Missing You* (based on **Sting**'s *Every Breath You Take* – PRS Most Performed Work) and **Texas** (Best Song Collection).

29 The **New York Post** reports that **Sean "Puffy" Combs** and 27-year-old actress **Jennifer Lopez** are "an item," even though Puffy recently fathered a child with his girlfriend, and Lopez is

Spice Girls tour the US... Family Values Tour...

Limp Bizkit

Natalie Imbruglia

Limp Bizkit was led by energetic and outspoken frontman, 27-year-old Fred Durst... Australian singer Natalie Imbruglia had a worldwide smash on her hands with Torn.

still married to Miami bartender, Ojani Noa. Bronx-born Lopez will shortly sign to Sony Music's Epic imprint at the behest of label head Tommy Mottola, set to begin a highly successful parallel music career.

30 French Culture Minister Catherine Trautmann bestows the Commandeur dans l'Ordre des Arts et des Lettres on **Van Morrison** in Paris, France. Morrison has been touring much of the year, on a hot ticket triple bill with **Bob Dylan** and **Joni Mitchell**.

June

8 A memorial service is held for **Linda McCartney** at St. Martin-in-the-Fields in London, at which the three surviving **Beatles** are seen together in public for the first time in almost 30 years. The service, which begins with *Mull Of Kintyre*, is also attended by **Elton John**, **Peter Gabriel**, **Sting**, and **Pete Townshend**.

13 The first day of the two-day Tibetan Freedom Concert at the Robert F. Kennedy Memorial Stadium in Washington, D.C., is called off during **Herbie Hancock**'s set, when a member of the 50,000-plus crowd is badly injured by a bolt of lightning. **Money Mark**, **Mutabaruka**, **Live**, **Chaksam-Pa**, **KRS-One**, and the **Dave Matthews Band** have already performed. In the evening, **Radiohead** and **Pulp** play at the 9:30 Club to the first 800 of today's ticket holders to show up.

15 The **Spice Girls** open the US leg of their world tour at the Coral Sky Amphitheater in West Palm Beach, Florida, with a rendition of the **Sister Sledge** hit, *We Are Family*. The majority of concertgoers confirm the make-up of the group's core audience: young pre-teen and teenage girls.

27 During a busy weekend of top rock festivals (at Glastonbury and Roskilde), the Princess Diana Memorial Concert is held at Althorp House, England. The mostly British line-up includes **Duran Duran**, hugely popular soul-pop duo **Lighthouse Family** (whose *Ocean Drive* debut has recently been certified four-times platinum in the UK, with their next effort, *Postcards From Heaven* ratified six-times platinum), **Chris De Burgh**, **T'Pau**, **Jimmy Ruffin**, South Africa's unique **Soweto String Quartet**, American actor/singer **David Hasselhoff** (an enormous singing star in Germany), British opera soprano **Lesley Garrett**, and **Sir Cliff Richard**.

July

3 The US leg of the Ozzfest '98 tour, with **Ozzy Osbourne**, **Motörhead**, **Tool**, **Megadeth**, upcoming rap-core rockers **Limp Bizkit**, and others, opens before a sellout crowd at the PNC Bank Arts Center in Holmdel, New Jersey. The Jacksonville, Florida-based Limp Bizkit signed last year to hardcore Interscope subsidiary, Flip Records, following early support by members of **KoRn**. Their debut album, the intense, metal/hip-hop fused, rap-core pioneering *Three Dollar Bill, Y'all$*, which includes a full-throttle cover of **George Michael**'s pop hit *Faith*, is midway through a ten-month US chart-rise.

5 **Boyzone**, **All Saints**, **Natalie Imbruglia** (currently charting around the world with the irresistible *Torn*), UK soul/pop quartet **Eternal**, veteran Scottish pop/rockers **Del Amitri**, **Julian Lennon**, **Shania Twain**, **Gary Barlow**, Irish teen-pop quartet **B*Witched** (who are the youngest group ever to top the UK chart), **Lionel Richie**, ultra-hip country rockers the **Mavericks**, house diva **Ultra Nate** (American-born but succeeding in Europe), and **Des'ree** perform at the Party in the Park charity concert for the Prince's Trust in Hyde Park, London.

14 On the 86th anniversary of **Woody Guthrie**'s birth, **Billy Bragg** performs selections from his latest album *Mermaid Avenue* at the Crystal Theater in Guthrie's birthplace: Okemah, Oklahoma. Guthrie's daughter, Nora, supplied Bragg with the legendary folk singer's unpublished lyrics, which he then set to music in a collaboration with underrated alt-country/folk stylists, **Wilco** – resulting in the critically lauded album.

20 *The Boy Is Mine* – **Brandy**'s pop/soul duet with parallel rising soul starlet **Monica** – is certified double platinum by the RIAA, set to become the top-selling single of the year in the US. It was co-written by Brandy with red-hot

"This album was recorded in our dad's garage. It is ridiculous we are here." Gomez, after winning the Mercury Music Prize, September 16, 1998

Prodigy performed *Smack My Bitch Up* at the Reading Festival, despite a request by the Beastie Boys not to do so. Ad Rock later commented, "From where I'm from, it isn't cool."

Paul McCartney's childhood home at 20 Forthlin Road in Allerton, Liverpool, now the property of the National Trust, opened to the public in July.

R&B producer Rodney Jerkins (and is also the title cut of Monica's forthcoming album. Brandy, steered by the business savvy of her mother, is also currently advertising Candies shoes, and will have her own DC Comics book published in the fall.

August

14 A Day in the Garden, a misnamed three-day festival celebrating the 29th anniversary of Woodstock, begins on its original site in Bethel, New York. Original Woodstock participants, **Melanie**, **Donovan**, **Richie Havens**, and a reformed **Ten Years After** perform, alongside **Lou Reed**, **Joni Mitchell**, **Pete Townshend**, **Stevie Nicks**, **Don Henley**, and others.

17 **Carlos Santana** receives a star on the Hollywood Walk of Fame at 7080 Hollywood Boulevard. He takes the opportunity to launch Cada Cabeza es un Mundo/Each Mind is a World, a national program to prevent Hispanic youth from dropping out of school.

September

4 **Courtney Love** pulls out of an appearance on Channel 4's "TFI Friday" because, according to presenter Chris Evans, the producers were not prepared to accept the terms of a 17-page document received from her lawyers. Love had apparently insisted that no mention be made of, among other topics, **Kurt Cobain**, the Nick Broomfield film, or her father Hank Harrison.

14 "Total Request Live," hosted by Carson Daly, premieres on MTV. Combining existing shows, "Total Request" and "MTV Live," the daily show will emerge as one of MTV's biggest successes, changing its name to "TRL" next March.

16 Described by the judges as "an intriguing blend of swamp blues, bar-room rock and eerie power," **Gomez**'s debut album ***Bring It On*** is a surprise winner at the Mercury Music Prize. The judges reveal that **Asian Dub Foundation**'s *Rafi's Revenge* and **Cornershop**'s *When I Was Born For The 7th Time* came a close second. The other nominees are: **Eliza Carthy** (*Red Rice*), **Catatonia** (*International Velvet*), **4-Hero** (*Two Pages*), **Massive Attack** (*Mezzanine*), **Propellerheads** (*Decksandrumsandrockandroll*), **Pulp** (*This Is Hardcore*), **John Surman** (*Proverbs & Songs*), the **Verve** (*Urban Hymns*), and **Robbie Williams** (*Life Thru A Lens*).

18 In anticipation of their Family Values US tour, with **Limp Bizkit**, **Ice Cube**, German industrial metal combo **Rammstein**, and Los Angeles-based alt-metal quintet **Orgy**, the fiercely anti-establishment **KoRn** invite former US Vice President Dan Quayle to attend one of their concerts. Having established an intensely loyal following without much radio or video play, or mainstream press support, the band's ***Follow The Leader*** entered the US chart at No. 1 two weeks ago. As the first hip-hop/metal caravan, the tour, due to bow on the 22nd, will prove a boon to all the acts, notably Limp Bizkit.

MADONNA

Sept 10 **Three years after she won her last MTV Video Music awards, Madonna is nominated in nine categories, and receives six more moonmen trophies – Best Video of the Year, Best Female Video, Best Choreography in a Video, Best Direction in a Video, Best Editing – all for "Ray Of Light" – and Best Special Effects in a Video for "Frozen." Actor/rapper Will Smith picks up a pair, for Best Rap Video ("Gettin' Jiggy Wit' It") and Best Male Video ("Just The Two Of Us"). Prodigy's controversial "Smack My Bitch Up" is named Best Dance Video and Breakthrough Video. The lackluster ceremony briefly comes to life when Beastie Boy Adam Yauch launches into a tirade about the recent US missile attacks in Afghanistan and the Sudan, condemning Americans for not understanding Muslims.**

Sept 1998

Aerosmith interact... MP3... *NSync and Britney Spears tour together...

Confirming her enduring appeal, Aussie pop kitten Kylie Minogue had her waxwork unveiled at Madame Tussaud's in London in October, updating the original, which went on display nine years earlier.

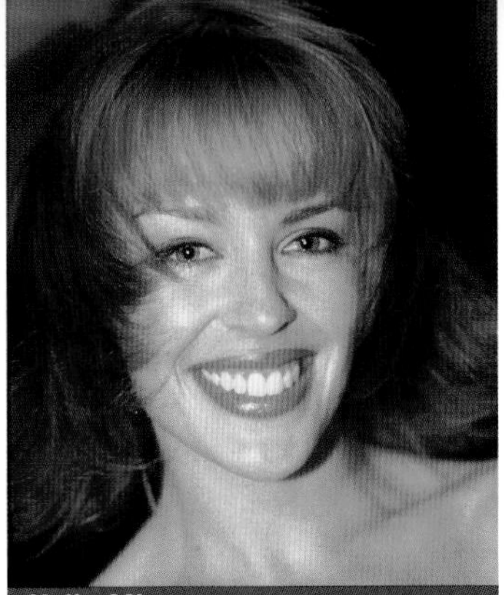

Kylie Minogue

19 Built around the instantly familiar sampled refrain from John Barry's theme for the James Bond movie "You Only Live Twice," **Robbie Williams**'s *Millennium* enters the UK chart at No. 1, spurred by an accompanying video portraying Williams as the hero spy.

October

17 **Aerosmith** give the first truly interactive cybercast from their PNC Bank Arts Center show in Holmdel, New Jersey. Each band member is equipped with microwave cameras which, with three front-of-house cameras, enable viewers to create their own program.

18 **B.B. King**'s tour bus, carrying his beloved guitar, Lucille, gets lost on its way to a gig in Kingston, New York. Mayor T.R. Gallo dispatches police to find the missing bus, and the show starts 45 minutes late.

19 **U2**, sans **Larry Mullen**, kick off an Amnesty International campaign, signing a petition in support of the 50th anniversary of the Universal Declaration of Human Rights. Stopping traffic on Dublin's O'Connell Street Bridge, **Bono** says: "One of the greatest problems in the world is the cynical idea the world can't be changed. But it can. Amnesty International is very simple. You can write a postcard and make a big difference to the life of a prisoner of conscience. And today you can sign your name and be part of one million signatures here."

28 Having met with Secretary General Kofi Annan in New York City last week to announce that she is to become a goodwill ambassador for the United Nations, **Geri Halliwell** sings "Happy Birthday," à la Marilyn Monroe, at a Royal Gala at the Lyceum Theatre in London to celebrate Prince Charles's 50th birthday.

November

12 The fifth MTV Europe Music Awards, held at the Fila Forum in Milan, Italy, continue in controversial vein when Best Video winners **Massive Attack** refuse to shake hands with Sarah, Duchess of York, after she fumbles her introduction of them. They leave the stage with the words: "F**k you very much." **Madonna** wins the Best Female Artist and Best Album categories (for ***Ray Of Light***) and performs her forthcoming single *Power Of Goodbye*. The **Spice Girls** are named Best Pop Act and Best Group, **Prodigy** win the Best Dance Act category for the third straight year, and **George Michael** presents **Robbie Williams** with the Best Male Artist award.

14 **Kylie Minogue** headlines the nine-hour Concert of the Century, at the Melbourne Cricket Ground, to celebrate the 25th anniversary of Australia's most successful record label, Mushroom Records. **INXS** make an emotional return, with **Jimmy Barnes** filling the shoes of **Michael Hutchence**. Mushroom founder Michael Gudinski, who booked the 56 acts for the day, said the concert "reminds me of how it was in the early days, before music became big business. All the artists are just happy to be here and are having a great time."

21 **George Michael**'s 28-track double compilation set ***Ladies And Gentlemen – The Best Of George Michael***, containing a new duet with **Mary J. Blige** on a **Babyface**-produced cover of **Stevie Wonder**'s *As*, debuts at UK No. 1, where it will remain for the rest of the year. *As* will remain unavailable on Epic Records' US pressing of the collection, and become an in-demand import item.

23 Weighing in at 2.4 ounces with a 32 MB Flash Memory, the first portable MP3 player goes on sale in the US. Developed by Diamond Multimedia, the Rio PMP 300 enables users to copy MP3 songs from the internet on to a small portable device similar to a Walkman. Giving considerable momentum to the growing file-swapping MP3 services that are emerging on the web (which are free and bypass most copyright laws), the technology's compression features use about one-twelfth of the space required by an equivalent CD file. Last month the RIAA filed suit against Diamond Multimedia, claiming that it is violating the Audio Home Recording Act, but the judge will rule in favor of Diamond, stating, "The Rio has no digital audio output capability, and therefore is incapable of passing on digital musical files to other Rio devices, or to other manufacturers' devices."

26 Legendary BBC radio personality John Peel receives an OBE. The only original Radio 1 DJ still broadcasting on the station, Peel tells reporters: "My dad always thought I was a bit of a dickhead. I guess he'd be really proud, so it's for him really and my mum and Sheila's [his wife's] mum and dad."

> **"Since we believe it was you who brought the phrase 'family values' to all of our attention, this tour is somewhat of a tribute to you. Listen to what you have created and look what you have wrought. Sincerely, KoRn."** KoRn's invitation to Dan Quayle to attend a concert, September 18, 1998

The world's media worked themselves into a state of frenzy when Geri Halliwell announced she was leaving the Spice Girls in May.

Massive Attack

Trip-hop pioneers Massive Attack began a 24-day upload of their *Mezzanine* album on the internet in anticipation of its release.

26 An alleged "gunshot" interrupts **Snoop Dogg**'s show at the Subterania club in London's Ladbroke Grove. He leaves the stage, but returns later to do four more songs, offering £1,000 ($1,700) to "any motherf**ker who can f**k-up the motherf**cker who f**ked up my show." The club's management deny that there was a gunshot. Snoop recently signed to rap impresario **Master P**'s No Limit stable, and his label debut *Da Game Is To Be Sold, Not to Be Told* was an instant US chart-topper.

December

1 Red-hot teen sensations ***NSync** begin a headlining tour, with fellow teen acts **Britney Spears** and **B*Witched**, at the Veterans Memorial in Columbus, Ohio. Spears – who will turn 17 tomorrow – has recently recorded her maiden set, the pop-dance fused *...Baby One More Time*, initially promoted via a tour of shopping malls. The title cut – spurred by a provocative school-uniform promo clip – entered the US Hot 100 two weeks ago – and is on the fast-track to US No. 1. Born in Kentwood, Louisiana, Spears auditioned for the Disney Channel's "Mickey Mouse Club" in Atlanta at the age of eight, and finally earned her mouse ears as a regular cast member in 1993. A demo tape recorded when she was 15 led to her signing with Jive Records.

2 Universal Records forces **Public Enemy** to remove MP3 files of their new unreleased album from their website. **Chuck D** comments, "It seems like the weasels have stepped into the fire."

3 The RIAA certifies 11 million sales of **Shania Twain**'s 1995 album *The Woman In Me* – the third best-selling album of all time by a female artist, and the best-selling album by a female country artist ever. Her third set, last year's *Come On Over*, is on its way to ten million domestic sales. Its signature cut, the irresistible mid-tempo crossover smash *You're Still The One*, spurred by an insistent refrain and a hot-rotation video clip showcasing the telegenic singer, was certified platinum on May 5, a week after it finally peaked at US No. 2. Both albums were helmed and largely co-written by her husband Robert John "Mutt" Lange, and are the latest musical triumph in a dazzling career for a master songwriter/producer who consistently shuns the spotlight. Twain is currently on a seven-month world tour: its 84 shows will earn over $36 million.

11 Norwegian heart-throb trio **a-ha** perform their first gig in four years at the fifth annual Nobel Peace Prize concert, staged at the Spektrum Stadium in Oslo, in honor of Northern Ireland peacemakers David Trimble and John Hume. **Elton John** performs *Your Song* and *The Way You Look Tonight* and – still busy working for Disney on the soundtrack to his first film score, "Tarzan" – **Phil Collins** sings *Both Sides To The Story* and *Another Day In Paradise*. **Shania Twain**, **Alanis Morissette**, and the **Cranberries** also take part.

24 The **Shamen** "dematerialize" on the 13th anniversary of their first release, following a performance on Channel 5 (UK)-TV's "Melinda Messenger's Big Night In!" They will launch their own website, announcing that they are "departing from the world of 'atoms' in favor of a new existence in the emerging world of 'bits.' All future interactions with the band will be mediated electronically." The first cyber release will come on February 16, with the album *Uv*.

Boyzone's *No Matter What* won the first "Record of the Year" show on ITV, with 238,054 votes – over 100,000 more than second-placed Celine Dion's *My Heart Will Go On*.

ROOTS During this year: Starfish, a band comprising Chris Martin, Guy Berryman, Jonny Buckland, and Will Champion, who met at London's University College, make their live debut at the Laurel Tree in Camden, London; they soon release 500 copies of their first effort, *Safety EP*, on the Fierce Panda indie label as Coldplay... having appeared last year in a production of "Grease" at the Hawk's Well Theatre in Sligo, Ireland, Shane Filan, Kian Egan, and Mark Feehily come together initially as 6 As I and then as IOU, cutting a demo of their own *Together Girl Forever*, which finds its way to Boyzone's manager Louis Walsh; with three new members added, they become Westside and then Westlife... needing a singer to perform at the inauguration ceremony for California governor Gray Davis, producer David Foster enlists unsigned 17-year-old popera vocalist Josh Groban; Foster will recruit Groban again later in the year as a stand-in for Andrea Bocelli at the Grammy Awards in tandem with Celine Dion... studying at Exeter University, Will Young sings in several theatrical productions... and Kerry Katona and Liz McClarnon meet in their home town of Liverpool and decide to form their own band; initially taking the name Automatic Kitten, they will become Atomic Kitten next year when Natasha Hamilton joins...

Livin' La Vida Loca

1999

No.1 US SINGLES

- **Jan 2** I'm Your Angel **R. Kelly & Celine Dion**
- **Jan 16** Have You Ever? **Brandy**
- **Jan 30** ...Baby One More Time **Britney Spears**
- **Feb 13** Angel Of Mine **Monica**
- **Mar 13** Believe **Cher**
- **Apr 10** No Scrubs **TLC**
- **May 8** Livin' La Vida Loca **Ricky Martin**
- **June 12** If You Had My Love **Jennifer Lopez**
- **July 17** Bills, Bills, Bills **Destiny's Child**
- **July 24** Wild Wild West **Will Smith featuring Dru Hill & Kool Mo Dee**
- **July 31** Genie In A Bottle **Christina Aguilera**
- **Sept 4** Bailamos **Enrique Iglesias**
- **Sept 18** Unpretty **TLC**
- **Oct 9** Heartbreaker **Mariah Carey (featuring Jay-Z)**
- **Oct 23** Smooth **Santana featuring Rob Thomas**

No.1 UK SINGLES

- **Jan 2** Chocolate Salty Balls (PS I Love You) **Chef**
- **Jan 9** Heartbeat/Tragedy **Steps**
- **Jan 16** Praise You **Fatboy Slim**
- **Jan 23** A Little Bit More **911**
- **Jan 30** Pretty Fly (For A White Guy) **Offspring**
- **Feb 6** You Don't Know Me **Armand Van Helden featuring Duane Harden**
- **Feb 13** Maria **Blondie**
- **Feb 20** Fly Away **Lenny Kravitz**
- **Feb 27** ...Baby One More Time **Britney Spears**
- **Mar 13** When The Going Gets Tough **Boyzone**
- **Mar 27** Blame It On The Weatherman **B*Witched**
- **Apr 3** Flat Beat **Mr. Oizo**
- **Apr 17** Perfect Moment **Martine McCutcheon**
- **May 1** Swear It Again **Westlife**
- **May 15** I Want It That Way **Backstreet Boys**
- **May 22** You Needed Me **Boyzone**
- **May 29** Sweet Like Chocolate **Shanks & Bigfoot**
- **June 12** Everybody's Free (To Wear Sunscreen) **Baz Luhrmann**
- **June 19** Bring It All Back **S Club 7**
- **June 26** Boom, Boom, Boom, Boom!! **Vengaboys**
- **July 3** (9pm) Till I Come **ATB**
- **July 17** Livin' La Vida Loca **Ricky Martin**
- **Aug 7** When You Say Nothing At All **Ronan Keating**
- **Aug 21** If I Let You Go **Westlife**
- **Aug 28** Mi Chico Latino **Geri Halliwell**

The Corrs

Ricky Martin

In February, the Corrs became the first Irish act to log two albums in the UK top five simultaneously, and in March they opened for the Rolling Stones on several US dates of the No Security tour... Ricky Martin gave a career-changing performance at the Grammys, when he stopped the show with a sizzling, hip-swinging version of *La Copa De La Vida*.

In a vibrant and controversial year, who would have guessed that an 18-year-old college dropout would permanently change the face and the guts of the record industry. **Shawn Fanning**'s ingenious Napster online music service presented the computer-illiterate music business with the greatest challenge to copyright law in recorded music history. While the record labels were appalled and scared, artist reaction was divided: some embraced the internet as a magical new marketing platform, while others sided with their labels. The record companies collectively filed suit in the US to try to shut Napster down, unaware that a door had been opened that would never be closed. The labels had much to lose. By the end of the century, only five majors were left: between them, Universal, Sony, EMI, Warners, and BMG controlled a disturbing 95 percent of albums sold.

The biggest solo artist in Europe was **Robbie Williams**. Having had the foresight to record *Millennium* a year earlier, his ego landed everywhere – except in the US, where rap had become the dominant genre. Black and white suburbia alike couldn't get enough, and were particularly aroused by Marshall Mathers III, aka **Eminem**, aka Slim Shady. With ingenious studio support by gangsta rap pioneer **Dr. Dre**, the brash white rapper exploded on the scene with a previously unheard mix of vulgar, confrontational, witty, in-your-face vitriol: filthy, clever stuff that deliberately pushed every envelope.

On a more musical note, ex-**Fugee Lauryn Hill** scooped just about every awards ceremony with her soulful solo debut, ***The Miseducation Of Lauryn Hill***. She took home trophies for half of her record ten nominations at the Grammys, having already cleaned up at the NAACP Awards. **Cher**'s Euro success with *Believe* finally hit home, setting a new US chart record – 25 years since her last domestic No. 1 – and making her the oldest female to top the Hot 100. At the opposite end of the age scale, **Britney Spears** became the latest tiffany teen phenom, shifting 20 million copies of her debut album: ***...Baby One More Time***.

With the world in party mood, 1999 fittingly greeted a Latin pop explosion. Led by **Ricky Martin**, Latin music burst into the mainstream with a melodic pop sensibility it had previously lacked (**Gloria Estefan** aside). Ironically, it was a veteran who scored the most memorable rock hit: 52-year-old **Carlos Santana** combined with **Matchbox 20**'s **Rob Thomas** for the year's smoothest smash.

One party that went sour was Woodstock '99. A farce from its over-commercialized beginning to its violent end, it was the (ugly) new face of hardcore alt-rock. Although some acts of musical worth performed well, the overall collision of corporate greed (by the organizers) and disturbing talent-challenged bands gave rise to an anarchic display of America's new yob culture.

Sept 4	Mambo No. 5 (A Little Bit Of...) **Lou Bega**
Sept 18	We're Going To Ibiza **Vengaboys**
Sept 25	Blue (Da Ba Dee) **Eiffel 65**
Oct 16	Genie In A Bottle **Christina Aguilera**
Oct 30	Flying Without Wings **Westlife**
Nov 6	Keep On Movin' **Five**
Nov 13	Lift Me Up **Geri Halliwell**
Nov 20	She's The One/It's Only Us **Robbie Williams**
Nov 27	King Of The Castle **Wamdue Project**
Dec 4	The Millennium Prayer **Cliff Richard**
Dec 25	I Have A Dream/Seasons In The Sun **Westlife**

"My audience looks at me like a girlfriend."

Britney Spears, **Entertainment Weekly**, December 24/31 1999

Jan

1999

Robbie Williams wins at the BRITS... Dusty Springfield succumbs to cancer... Cher's *Believe*...

January

1 Still going strong after 35 years in the music business, **Tom Jones** is awarded an OBE. Cancer-stricken **Dusty Springfield** is also so honored, as is **David Essex**, a British showbusiness veteran at 51, for his charity work, particularly with the Voluntary Services Overseas.

2 In a remarkable chart comeback (of sorts), **Isaac Hayes** tops the UK chart with *Chocolate Salty Balls (PS I Love You)*, in the deep-voiced guise of Chef, his character in the wildly popular "South Park" TV series.

11 Making a first US network television appearance in 16 years, **Blondie** perform the title cut from their forthcoming *No Exit* album, with guest rapper **Coolio**, and members of **Wu-Tang Clan** and **Mobb Deep**, at the 26th American Music Awards. ***NSync** win the Favorite Pop/Rock New Artist category, and also sing *You May Be Right* as part of a tribute to Award of Merit recipient, **Billy Joel**. **Whitney Houston** sings *Until You Come Back To Me* and *My Love Is Your Love*, with **Babyface** and **Wyclef Jean**. **Alabama** once again win the Favorite Band, Duo or Group, Country category, and **Garth Brooks** picks up two more awards for Favorite Male Artist, Country, and Favorite Album, Country (for ***Sevens***).

15 The **Corrs**' second album, ***Talk On Corners***, is certified seven times platinum (the best-selling album in Britain last year), by the BPI. Their debut set, ***Forgiven, Not Forgotten***, is certified platinum. Irish sisters **Andrea** (lead vocals/tin whistle), **Caroline** (drums/bodhran/vocals), and **Sharon Corr** (violin/vocals), and their brother **Jim** (guitar/keyboards/vocals), born in Dundalk, Ireland, were snapped up in New York City in 1994, by veteran hitmaking producer David Foster, for his Atlantic imprint, 143. The harmonic, Celtic-tinged pop/rock of their mostly self-penned albums has propelled their fortunes since their breakthrough smash, a cover of **Fleetwood Mac**'s *Dreams*, hit UK No. 6 last May.

The Corrs were discovered by John Hughes, their future manager, who was looking for musicians to appear in Alan Parker's hit film "The Commitments."

In addition to winning five Grammys, Lauryn Hill picked up four trophies at the NAACP Image Awards, four at the Soul Train Music Awards, and a further four at the MTV Video Music Awards.

February

6 Bob Marley – A Tribute to Freedom opens at Universal Studios CityWalk in Orlando. The permanent exhibition includes a re-creation of Marley's Hope Road house in Kingston, Jamaica, with paintings, photos and videos, a gazebo for reggae acts to perform, and a restaurant.

13 Becoming the only group to score a British chart-topper in the 1970s, 1980s, and 1990s, **Blondie**'s comeback is complete when their new single *Maria* hits UK No. 1 in its first week.

16 **Robbie Williams** wins three awards at the 18th BRIT ceremonies: Best British Male Solo Artist, Best British Single (*Millennium*), and Best British Video ("Let Me Entertain You"). Having served his apprenticeship with **Take That**, Williams has emerged as the most popular – and perhaps most unlikely – solo success from the teen act's ranks. Also at the BRITS, a teen collection, comprising current British acts **Billie**, **B*witched**, **Cleopatra**, **Tina Cousins**, and **Steps**, serenade **Björn Ulvaeus** (there to present the **Corrs** with the award for Best International Group) with a medley of **Abba** hits. Having briefly teamed up twice last year – and amid rumors of a full-blown **Eurythmics** reunion – **Annie Lennox** and **Dave Stewart** receive the Outstanding Contribution to British Music honor from **Stevie Wonder**. **U2**'s **Bono** presents Muhammad Ali with the Freddie Mercury Award, for his work with Jubilee 2000, an organization committed to eliminating Third World debt.

23 **Eminem**'s ***The Slim Shady LP***, an extension of his previous demo/indie release ***The Slim Shady EP***, is released in the US. Born Marshall Bruce Mathers III in St. Joseph, Missouri, 26-year-old Eminem moved into the impoverished eastside area of Detroit, Michigan, when he was 12. He began performing – initially

"I'm sorry I can't be here in person tonight, I'm doing panto with Celine Dion in Wolverhampton."

Robbie Williams at the BRIT Awards, February 16, 1999

as M&M – at the Hip-Hop Shop in 1990, and recorded his first album, ***Infinite***, in 1996 (issued only in Detroit), before taking part in the Rap Coalition's 1997 Rap Olympics in Los Angeles. His biting, angst-ridden rap rants, with a cunning lyrical bent, courtesy of his Slim Shady alter ego, caught the ear of Interscope's Jimmy Iovine, who passed him on to **Dr. Dre**. Becoming the rap producer's latest protégé, and signed to his Interscope imprint, Aftermath, Eminem's typically vulgar *I Just Don't Give A F**k* is currently a hit on the rap survey; its follow-up, *My Name Is*, has recently been added to MTV's "Buzz Bin," and will rapidly make the artist the most controversial and successful rapper of his generation. The boldness of his alternately comic and brutal, often misogynistic, lyrical imagery, and the fact that he is a blue-collar white rapper, are pushing the boundaries of the genre, to the delight and disgust of the American public.

24 **Lauryn Hill**, the first woman in Grammy history to be nominated in ten categories, wins five of them, at the 41st awards: Best Female R&B Vocal Performance and Best R&B Song for *Doo Wop (That Thing)*, Best New Artist, Album of the Year, and Best R&B Album (both for her multiplatinum solo debut, ***The Miseducation Of Lauryn Hill***). Nominated in six categories, **Madonna** wins four Grammys: Best Dance Recording (*Ray Of Light*), Best Pop Album (***Ray Of Light***), Best Shortform Music Video ("Ray Of Light"), and Best Package (***Ray Of Light***). **Celine Dion** wins Best Female Pop Vocal Performance, and Best Song Written Specifically for a Motion Picture or Television, for her titanic smash, *My Heart Will Go On*, which is also named Song of the Year and Record of the Year. **Eric Clapton** wins his 14th Grammy – Best Pop Vocal Performance, Male – for *My Father's Eyes*.

March

2 **Dusty Springfield** dies at her home in Henley-on-Thames, England, following a long battle with breast cancer, two weeks before her induction into the Rock and Roll Hall of Fame. Britain's greatest "soul" singer, she is dead at the age of 59.

6 In an astonishing US career rebound, and 25 years since her last domestic No. 1 (a new chart record), **Cher**'s *Believe* hits the top. A significant departure from her late 1980s rock ballad material, *Believe* has been neatly assembled by hot UK production pair Metro, who peppered Cher's vocal with a catchy, distorted, electronic gimmick. The pop-dance smash has already been a major European hit, reaching UK No. 1 last October.

15 **Elton John** inducts the late **Dusty Springfield** into the Rock and Roll Hall of Fame at the 14th induction dinner, held at New York's Waldorf Astoria, describing her as "a songwriter's singer." **Paul McCartney** is inducted as a solo artist by **Neil Young**, and asks his daughter Stella – who sees fit to wear a T-shirt bearing the legend "About f**king time!" – to join him on stage. At his own induction, **Billy Joel**, who is welcomed into the Hall by hero **Ray Charles**, says: "I know I've been referred to as derivative. Well, I'm guilty," adding that if derivative artists were excluded, "there would be no white people here." **U2**'s **Bono** inducts **Bruce Springsteen**, with the words, "It was goodnight Haight Ashbury, hello Asbury Park." **Curtis Mayfield** is inducted by **Sean "Puffy" Combs**, the **Staple Singers** by **Lauryn Hill**, and **Del Shannon** by **Everclear**'s **Art Alexakis**. Early Influences are **Bob Wills & His Texas Playboys** (inducted by **Chris Isaak**), and **Charles Brown** (by **Bonnie Raitt**), while the sole Non-Performer inductee is **Sir George Martin**.

16 The RIAA celebrates the introduction of the prestigious Diamond sales award – for ten million sales of an album – with a diamond-studded line-up at New York City's Roseland Ballroom. In attendance, each having released such an album, are **AC/DC**, **Bon Jovi**, **Boston**, **Boyz II Men**, **Celine Dion**, **Def Leppard**, the **Doobie Brothers**, **Kenny G**, **Guns N' Roses**, **Hammer**, **Billy Joel**, **Elton John**, **Journey**, **Led Zeppelin**, **Metallica**, **Prince**, **Kenny Rogers**, and **ZZ Top**. The **Eagles**, **Garth Brooks**, and **Van Halen** are multiple Diamond recipients. Kenny G proceeds to drop his award, and ZZ Top, receiving theirs for ***Eliminator***, later reveal that a new album should be forthcoming in the fall: "Same three guys, and probably the same three chords."

Robbie Williams arrived in style at the BRIT Awards when he paraglided down to the stage singing *Let Me Entertain You*.

The Diamond awards... Mamma Mia the musical... Napster...

Mary J. Blige

Puff Daddy

17 **Sinéad O'Connor**, **Thomas Dolby**, and **Coldcut** record the first ever single via the internet, as part of the "Megalab 99" television program for "Tomorrow's World." The song, a remake of **Bob Marley**'s *Them Belly Full (But We Hungry)*, is recorded for the War Child charity. O'Connor records her vocals at BBC Television Centre in London, with Dolby playing keyboards in San Francisco.

20 **Sting** and **James Taylor** take part in Shi-Wa, a Tibetan Peace Garden fundraiser at London's new Globe Theatre, singing songs from Shakespeare's plays. Sting also plays Snug the Joiner in a scene from "A Midsummer Night's Dream," in a cast that includes Vinnie Jones as Starveling the Tailor, **Jimmy Nail** as Quince the Joiner, and Ethan Hawke as Flute the Bellowsmender.

April

6 The "All-Star Tribute to Johnny Cash" is recorded at the Hammerstein Ballroom in New York City as part of the TNT Master Series. **Sheryl Crow**, **Emmylou Harris**, **Willie Nelson**, **Lyle Lovett**, **Kris Kristofferson**, **Chris Isaak**, **Trisha Yearwood**, **Dave Matthews**, and **Roseanne Cash** take part, with performances from **Bob Dylan**, **Bruce Springsteen**, and **U2** via satellite. The show ends with the Man in Black himself revealing, "It's been 19 months since I've been on stage. Feels good, feels good." (In recent years, he has been dogged by pneumonia and has developed Parkinson's disease.)

6 "Mamma Mia," a musical featuring 27 **Abba** songs, premieres at London's Prince Edward Theatre 25 years to the day since Abba won the Eurovision Song Contest. It will be a huge international success. Further underlining the group's evergreen appeal, UK Polydor also issues a limited-edition compilation, ***The Singles Collection***, featuring all 28 original A and B sides, including *Waterloo*, in Swedish, German, and French.

10 At London's Royal Albert Hall, the 5,000 attendees of Here, There and Everywhere – A Concert for Linda, commemorating the life of **Linda McCartney**, are treated to a surprise guest, when **Paul McCartney** makes an appearance. He sings *Lonesome Town* and *All My Loving*, before ending the show with *Let It Be*, backed by the show's other performers, **George Michael**, **Elvis Costello**, **Tom Jones**, **Marianne Faithfull**, **Chrissie Hynde**, **Des'ree**, **Neil Finn**, **M People**'s **Heather Small**, **Johnny Marr**, **Ladysmith Black Mambazo**, and **Sinéad O'Connor** (whose off-color remarks indicate that age has yet to mellow her).

Paul McCartney's appearance at the Here, There and Everywhere – A Concert For Linda, was his first after the death of his wife in 1998.

Mary J. Blige took part in the VH1 Divas Live '99 concert in April... Puff Daddy had to undergo anger management counseling in 1999.

11 **Carlos Santana** receives the Special Achievement Award at the annual American Latino Media Arts Awards, held at California's Pasadena Civic Center in honor of both his music and humanitarian accomplishments.

14 "Hate Me Now," the new video by New York City's hottest rap star **Nas**, which features **Sean "Puffy" Combs** in a Christlike crucifixion scene, is aired by MTV in the US – against Combs's wishes. The song is the lead track from Nas's third album, ***I Am...The Autobiography***, which will enter at US No. 1 next week.

15 **Sean "Puffy" Combs** and two accomplices allegedly mete out a severe beating to Interscope executive Steve Stoute, at the latter's New York City office. Combs holds Stoute (who is also **Nas**'s manager) accountable for yesterday's airing of the controversial "Hate Me Now" clip, having requested that his "crucifixion" scene be deleted. Combs will turn himself in tomorrow, and will be ordered to undergo anger management counseling after pleading guilty on September 8. MTV will withdraw the clip tomorrow.

20 **Robbie Williams** introduces himself to the US music industry, playing a five-song set before an invited audience of about 100 at the Phoenix Hotel in Los Angeles. At the end of the evening, he tells the crowd: "Thank you very much. If you've enjoyed me, I'm Robbie Williams. If not, I'm George Michael." (He will embark on his first North American tour, a nine-date swing, on May 1 at the Opera House in Toronto, Canada.)

22 **Sinéad O'Connor** is ordained by Bishop Michael Cox as Mother Bernadette Mary of the Order of Mater Dei, in the dissident Roman Catholic Latin Tridentine church in Lourdes, France. Next week, she will donate $200,000 to the church. Dublin bookmaker Paddy Power opens a book on her becoming the next Pope, quoting odds of 10,000-1.

25 **Paul Simon** sings *Mrs Robinson*, including the lyric "Where have you gone, Joe Di Maggio?" in center field of New York City's Yankee Stadium as a monument is unveiled celebrating the memory of the Yankee Clipper, who died on March 8, at the age of 84.

May

22 With **Mel C** pegged to sing the theme to the new Bond film "The World Is Not Enough," **Emma Bunton** filming "Cinderella" for BBC-TV, **Mel G** and **Victoria Adams** both new mothers, and a new **Spice Girls** single (*My Strongest Suit*) expected, **Geri Halliwell** – amid much hoopla – sees her debut single, *Look At Me*, pipped at the post by **Boyzone**, who reach No. 1 in the UK.

30 In Los Angeles, the **Dixie Chicks** begin recording a cover of the **Supremes**' *You Can't Hurry Love*, with producer Peter Asher, for the film soundtrack to "Runaway Bride." After ten years, the all-blonde country/pop trio, comprising founding members, fiddler **Martie Seidel** and her banjo-player sister **Emily Robison**, with lead singer **Natalie Maines**, have finally broken through in the past 12 months. At the 34th Academy of Country Music Awards earlier this month, they were named Top New Vocal Duo or Group, and Top Vocal Duo or Group, and their quadruple platinum album ***Wide Open Spaces*** was hailed Album of the Year.

31 Having received an honorary Doctorate of Fine Arts from Rutgers University in New Brunswick on the 19th, **Stevie Wonder** receives the Polar Music Prize at a ceremony at the Berwaldhallen in Stockholm, Sweden.

World Arena in Colorado Springs, Colorado. At the opening show, they sing *The Sounds Of Silence*, *I Walk The Line*, *Blue Moon Of Kentucky*, and *Forever Young* together. The 32-date US trek will end on July 31 at the Jones Beach Theatre in Wantagh, New York.

19 **Bono** and **The Edge** join a human chain around the G8 Summit Centre in Cologne, Germany, to draw attention to Jubilee 2000, the organization pledged to get all Third World debts dropped.

25 **Santana**, with **Matchbox 20**'s **Rob Thomas** guesting, perform *Smooth* on "Late Show With David Letterman." The ingenious pairing is the idea of Arista Records boss Clive Davis.

30 **Limp Bizkit**'s **Fred Durst** is appointed Senior Vice President of Interscope Records. Last week the group's Limptropolis tour, fronted by the Bizkit with upcoming labelmates **Staind** (whose signature to Flip Records was instigated by Durst) and **Kid Rock** also on the menu, opened at the Salem Armory in Oregon. Kid Rock (28-year-old Detroit native Bob Ritchie), who has been trying to break through for ten years, is currently riding the hot rap-metal wave with two hits, *Bawitdaba* and *Cowboy*, both featured on his fourth album, the white-trash proud, multiplatinum ***Devil Without A Cause.***

"As always, on occasions like this, I really never know what to do, which is pretty much the way I've handled my career as a musician."

David Bowie, receiving an honorary doctorate from Berklee College of Music in Boston, May 8, 1999

June

1 Created by 18-year-old Northeastern University dropout Shawn Fanning, the Napster music service becomes available on the internet. It allows web users to swap music encoded in the compressed MP3 digital format. Creating a central hub of several hundreds of thousands of songs, music enthusiasts can download virtually any recording made available by other fans – a convenience known as peer-to-peer file sharing. In October, shortsighted major labels, frozen in the headlights of this revolutionary technology, will end negotiations with Napster to distribute music online legally.

5 With boy band/teen-pop at fever pitch, **Backstreet Boys**' ***Millennium*** debuts at US No. 1, having sold 1.13 million copies. (This new opening-week sales record in the US will hold until rivals ***NSync** more than double the number next March.) Once again largely written and produced by Swedish hitmaker, Max Martin, the set is spearheaded by the irresistibly catchy global smash, *I Want It That Way*. In November, the group – currently on a 44-date European tour – will re-sign with Jive Records for a reported $60 million five-album deal.

6 **Bob Dylan** and **Paul Simon**, the premier American singer-songwriters of their generation, tour together for the first time, opening at the

July

1 **Garbage** perform their first ever gig in Edinburgh (lead singer **Shirley Manson**'s home town) at an open-air concert in Princess Street Gardens to celebrate the opening of the Scottish parliament. The RIAA recently certified one million US sales of ***Version 2.0*** and two million of ***Garbage.***

5 **Eurythmics** launch their reunion album and tour with a mini-performance on board Greenpeace's *Rainbow Warrior II*, moored on London's Thames River near Tower Bridge. Performing for the first time in ten years, the duo sing two new songs, *Beautiful Child* and *Peace Is Just A Word*. Proceeds from the tour will benefit Amnesty International and Greenpeace.

8 The 1999 Lilith Fair opens at the UBC Thunderbird Stadium in Vancouver, Canada. Today's line-up includes **Sarah McLachlan**, **Sheryl Crow**, Canadian R&B singer-songwriter **Deborah Cox**, 19-year old R&B newcomer **Mya**, all-girl alt-rockers **Luscious Jackson**, Indian-born alt-pop/rocker **Bif Naked**, organic folk/pop/rock singer-songwriter **Beth Orton**, and alt-Christian quintet **Sixpence None the Richer** (enjoying a global smash with the infectious *Kiss Me*). The 40-date tour will close on August 31 at Canada's Commonwealth Stadium in Edmonton.

RICKY MARTIN

May 29 **Co-produced by Desmond Child and long-time helmsman Robi Rosa, Ricky Martin's first English-speaking album *Ricky Martin* (not to be confused with his 1991 Spanish-language debut) tops the US chart in its week of entry, heralding the arrival of the Latin pop explosion in the States. The album will sell seven million US copies by the end of the year and propel Martin to global pop phenom status.**

Martin opened the crossover door (unlocked by Gloria and Emilio Estefan) for a slew of emerging hot Latin pop/dance acts, including Enrique Iglesias, Christina Aguilera, and Marc Anthony.

July 1999

Eurythmics reunite... Woodstock '99... Eminem is sued by his mom...

Limp Bizkit's Fred Durst, in his role as senior vice-president of Interscope, was responsible for A&R duties, such as signing and marketing bands, producing, remixing, and shooting videos.

Fred Durst was criticized for inciting the crowd to "break stuff" and generally inflaming an already volatile situation at Woodstock '99.

18 **Phish** finish a two-day stint at Oswego County Airport near Volney, New York, before a crowd of 110,000. The jam band's efforts will earn them a place in the **Guinness Book of World Records** for organizing the most participants in a dance – the "meatstick" – breaking the record held for the macarena at Yankee Stadium.

24 As **Will Smith**'s *Wild Wild West*, sampling **Stevie Wonder**'s *I Wish*, tops the Hot 100, Wonder moves into second place among songwriters with the longest span of chart-toppers in the rock era. His co-written *Tears Of A Clown* topped in December 1970, 28 years and 7 months ago. Hugo & Luigi and George David Weiss hold the record, with a gap of 31 years and 7 months between *The Lion Sleeps Tonight* and *Can't Help Falling In Love*.

24 Woodstock '99, held at a disused Air Force base near Rome, New York, is in stark contrast to the "peace and love" of the 1969 original. The organizers temporarily pull the plug midway through **Limp Bizkit**'s set, as chaotic scenes erupt around the rain-soaked event, resulting in several injuries, the tearing down of a broadcast tower, and an alleged mosh-pit rape (one of eight reported during the event). Fires rage on the site, and the emergency medical station and MTV's on-site broadcast booth both have to be closed down. With some 200,000 people paying an inflated $160 each for the three-day festival, three separate stages are hosting acts such as **Rage Against the Machine**, the **Dave Matthews Band**, **Metallica**, **Kid Rock**, **KoRn**, **Alanis Morissette**, **Wyclef Jean & His Refugee Allstars**, and **Counting Crows**. Separate late night raves feature disc spinner **Fatboy Slim** (the most popular incarnation of British music veteran Norman Cook), and electronic pop/rock/techno veteran **Moby** (who has finally broken through with his much praised hybrid album, ***Play***), among others. Criticized as both a corporate ripoff and an ugly indictment of the increasingly mindless culture of American youth, Woodstock '99 is an unqualified disaster. It will be ended tomorrow by swarms of helmeted riot police clearing "fans" from the already demolished site.

August

16 **Mariah Carey**'s video for her new single *Heartbreaker* premieres worldwide on MTV, after the song has debuted exclusively on Microsoft's WindowsMedia website.

21 Irish teen quintet **Westlife** tops the UK chart with *If I Let You Go*, replacing the group's co-manager, **Ronan Keating**, whose solo *When You Say Nothing At All* has spent the past two weeks at No. 1. Westlife thus become the first boy band to nab consecutive No. 1s with their first two singles (following *Flying Without Wings*). Keating says "I couldn't be happier to be knocked off by [them]." Comprising telegenic youngsters **Bryan McFadden**, **Kian Egan**, **Mark Freehily**, **Nicky Byrne**, and **Shane Filan**, Dublin-based Westlife will continue to break chart records, becoming the first act to score four No. 1s in a year.

25 The Gallagher brothers announce that they've "been left holding a shit sandwich here." At a hastily convened press conference at the Water Rats pub in London (where they played their first London gig in January 1994), they reveal that "Guigsy" is leaving **Oasis**, just two weeks after "Bonehead" did the same. When asked what they would look for in replacements, Liam says: "Well they've got to be that taller than me, have nice taste in shoes and a decent haircut, and not Man[chester] United fans."

28 Billed as a "very special guest," former **Dexy's Midnight Runners**' lead singer **Kevin Rowland** makes his first live appearance in 14 years, at the Reading Festival, resplendent in ladies' lingerie and lipstick. Signed to Alan McGee's Creation Records, his album, ***My Beauty***, touted by McGee as one of the albums of the year, will suffer the ignominy of selling only 500 copies.

30 The US postal service unveils a 33¢ Yellow Submarine stamp, part of the Celebrate the Century Program, to mark **Beatles** International Week.

September

17 With ***The Slim Shady LP*** already double platinum, and controversy following his every move, **Eminem**'s mother, Debbie Mathers-Briggs,

Garbage nail polish – manufactured in the same color as the logo on *Version 2.0* – was made available exclusively on the band's website.

files a $10 million slander lawsuit against her son in Michigan State Court, alleging emotional distress and diminished self-esteem as a result of interviews published in **The Source**, **Rolling Stone**, and **Rap Pages**, and an appearance on "The Howard Stern Show" on US radio. Eminem's attorney states: "Eminem's life is reflected in his music. Everything he said can be verified as true – the truth is an absolute defense to a claim of defamation." The rapper was recently named Best New Artist at the MTV Video Music Awards.

18 After attending yesterday's Capitol-hosted listening party at the House of Blues for his ***Run Devil Run*** album, **Paul McCartney** performs at PETA's Party of the Century and Humanitarian Awards in Los Angeles with the **B-52's**, **Sarah McLachlan**, and **Chrissie Hynde**. McLachlan's rendition of her recent hit ballad, *Angel*, apparently reduces McCartney to tears.

22 **Diana Ross** is arrested at London's Heathrow Airport after allegedly assaulting a security officer who touched her when a metal detector went off. Ms. Ross says she was "humiliated" by the experience: "I have been through all the airports of the world and have never been subjected to such an intrusive search. I am a huggy person, I don't mind being touched, but not in this way – it was far too personal." An airport spokesman says: "We are required by law to hand search any passenger who activates the metal detector alarms. Occasionally high-profile celebrities take offence at this procedure."

24 The Family Values 1999 US trek begins at the Bryce Jordan Center, State College, Pennsylvania. It features the cream of current US contemporary alt-rock: **Limp Bizkit**, **Filter**, electronic duo the **Crystal Method**, **Staind**, **Les Claypool**'s alt-metal combo **Primus**, ex-**Wu-Tang Clan** rapper **Method Man**, veteran rapper **Redman**, and emerging modern rockers, **System of a Down**.

October

9 Netaid, a series of three concerts – held in New Jersey, London and Geneva – is broadcast online, with the hope that those watching will donate money via the internet. The bill features **Bryan Adams**, **David Bowie**, **George Michael**, the **Corrs**, **Catatonia**, **Bush**, **Eurythmics**, **Stereophonics**, and **Robbie Williams** from Wembley Stadium, London; **Sting**, **Sheryl Crow**, **Wyclef Jean** and **Bono**, the **Black Crowes**, **Bon Jovi**, **Puff Daddy**, **Jewel**, **Mary J. Blige**, veteran rappper **Busta Rhymes**, **Counting Crows**, world music star **Cheb Mami** (the Algerian-born "Prince of Rai"), Italian singer **Zucchero**, and **Jimmy Page** at the Meadowlands in East Rutherford, New Jersey; and **Bryan Ferry**, **Texas**, **Des'ree**, **Ladysmith Black Mambazo**, and **Michael Kamen** at the Palais des Nations, Geneva. Billed as the largest webcast ever, the event is marred by technical problems and fails to garner substantial donations. Thomas Ritsetter, of consulting firm KPMG, which helped set up the website, says: "Perhaps it may have been a little too ambitious to use internet technology at this point."

15 Confirming her meteoric rise to fame, a collection of six **Britney Spears** dolls is launched in the US by Play Along Toys, whose president

Westlife unprecedently topped the UK chart with their first seven releases, including Against All Odds – a pairing with Mariah Carey.

Bob Geldof described Van Morrison as the "one genius in Irish music."

VAN MORRISON

Sept 1 **Bob Geldof inducts Van Morrison into the Irish Music Hall of Fame. Hall of Fame director Niall Stokes, editor of Hot Press, says: "Van Morrison has been justifiably acknowledged as Ireland's greatest living legend, a multitalented creative force who has created an astonishing body of work of great depth and beauty."**

Net aid... Santana's *Smooth*... Prince performs like it's 1999...

says Spears "represents all the qualities that young girls admire and emulate. She has amazing talent, beauty, and an engaging personality." *...Baby One More Time* will be certified for ten million US sales by the end of this year, and will eventually sell more than double that worldwide. "Spears" is currently the most popular search term on the internet.

23 During a staggering 58-week chart residence, *Smooth*, credited to **Santana (featuring Rob Thomas)**, tops the US Hot 100. Fueling a major comeback for **Carlos Santana**, the Latin-swaying pop nugget is also a major boost for the single's singer Thomas, who is increasingly respected for his songwriting chops (he co-wrote the cut with Itaal Shur). With all things Latin currently in musical vogue, the deeply spiritual Santana is on a roll: his album, *Supernatural*, sees the guitar legend cunningly paired with a host of top-notch talent, including Thomas, **Eric Clapton**, **Lauryn Hill**, **Eagle-Eye Cherry**, **Wyclef Jean**, acoustic hip-hopper and ex-**House of Pain** member **Everlast**, and **Dave Matthews**.

23 **Dr. Dre** and his wildly controversial protégé **Eminem** perform together for the first time on network television, as the musical guests on "Saturday Night Live." The pair have recently completed seven songs for Eminem's next album, due in February.

27 Three of R&B's hottest current acts, **TLC**, **Destiny's Child**, and **Jodeci** spin-off duo **K-Ci & JoJo**, begin a package tour at the Van Andel Arena in Grand Rapids, Michigan, set to close in Phoenix, Arizona, on December 3. Comprising singers **Beyoncé Knowles**, her cousin **Kelly Rowland**, **LaTavia Roberson**, and **LeToya Luckett**, **Destiny's Child** formed in Houston, Texas, in 1990, and has been steered by Knowles's father Matthew.

Santana's *Supernatural* album eventually topped more than 20 million sales worldwide, and garnered a host of A-list awards.

November

9 The Recording Association of America announce its Artists of the Century. Topped by the **Beatles**, with 106 million US album sales, the list names **Garth Brooks** and **Barbra Streisand** as the most successful male and female artists, with 89 million and 62 million sales respectively. **Elvis Presley** has the most gold and platinum singles with 77 (as well as 80 gold and platinum albums), and **Elton John**'s *Candle In The Wind 1997* is named the best-selling single of the century. It is also announced that the **Eagles**' *Their Greatest Hits 1971-1975* has sold 26 million copies, making it the best-selling album of all time, overtaking **Michael Jackson**'s *Thriller*.

11 With a career that has so far produced just three singles and an album, **Britney Spears** is the big winner at the MTV Europe Music Awards, held in Dublin, Ireland. She is named Best Female Act, Best Breakthrough Act, and Best Pop Act, and *...Baby One More Time* is hailed Best Song. **Boyzone** is the only other multiple winner, winning Best Album for *By Request* and Best UK & Ireland Act. Best R&B Act, **Whitney Houston**, performs at the bash, as do **Marilyn Manson**, **Iggy Pop**, and Spears.

12 After being found not guilty at England's Bristol Crown Court of sexually assaulting teenage fan Allison Brown more than 17 years ago, **Gary Glitter** is sentenced to four months in jail after pleading guilty to 43 offenses of downloading child pornography from the internet.

December

7 The RIAA – representing America's most powerful record companies – files suit against Napster, accusing the company of encouraging and facilitating the widespread practice of illegal copying and distribution of copyright music on a massive scale. Citing large-scale copyright infringement, the RIAA is seeking damages of $100,000 per recording copied.

8 **Sarah McLachlan** presents country veteran **Emmylou Harris** with the prestigous Century Award at the Billboard Music Awards, at the MGM Grand Hotel & Casino in Las Vegas, Nevada.

14 With the announcement: "Welcome to the Cavern. It's been a long time and it's great to be back," **Paul McCartney** launches into a set of vintage rock 'n' roll numbers before a crowd of some 300 people inside the legendary Liverpool club, with a further 15,000 watching on a giant video screen in Liverpool's Chavasse Park, and a further three million who log on to the internet. Opening with **Big Joe Turner**'s *Honey Hush*, McCartney – backed by a band featuring **David Gilmour** and **Ian Paice** – performs numbers made famous by **Chuck Berry**, **Little Richard**, **Elvis Presley**, and **Ricky Nelson**. McCartney last played at the hallowed venue (no longer at its original Mathew Street site) on August 3, 1963.

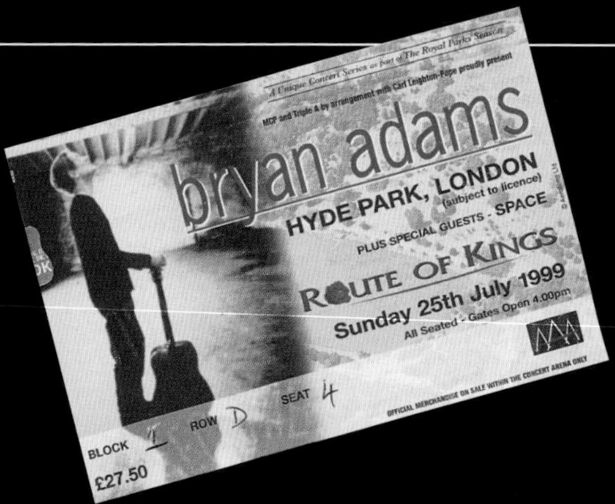

In a busy year which included a date in London's Hyde Park, Bryan Adams opened for the Rolling Stones on the No Security tour and had a hit single with Spice Girl Melanie C.

26 **Curtis Mayfield** dies, age 57, at North Fulton Regional Hospital in Roswell, New Mexico. The "Superfly" R&B legend has suffered from serious health problems since he was paralyzed when a lighting rig fell on him during an outdoor concert in Brooklyn, New York.

27 **Puff Daddy** and current flame **Jennifer Lopez** escape injury in a shooting at New York City's Club New York in Manhattan, in which three people are hurt. The rapper's Lincoln Navigator is later stopped when the driver zooms through a red light, and the police allegedly recover a 9mm handgun from the car. Combs, his driver, and his bodyguard are charged with criminal possession of a weapon and possession of stolen property (the gun). Lopez is released. Jamal Barrow, better known as rapper **Shyne**, is arrested at the club and charged with criminal possession of a weapon.

30 Despite tight security at his Henley-on-Thames estate in England, **George Harrison** and his wife Olivia are attacked by an intruder wielding a knife, and Harrison is stabbed in the chest. He is treated at the Royal Berkshire Hospital in Reading, before being transferred to a special chest unit at Harefield Hospital. His attacker, 33-year-old Liverpudlian Michael Abram, is charged with attempted murder. A spokesman for the Royal Berkshire says Harrison told him that the man wasn't a burglar, but that "he certainly wasn't auditioning for the Traveling Wilburys."

31 As people celebrate the new millennium around the globe, rock 'n' roll gets into the spirit of things, with concerts on every continent: **Björk** in Reykavik, Iceland, **Aerosmith** in Osaka, Japan, **Céline Dion** in Montreal, Canada, the **Chieftains** and **Art Garfunkel** on a cruise heading to the North Pole, and ***NSync** in Honolulu, Hawaii. **Michael Jackson** is at the Sydney Football Stadium, Australia, before flying to Hawaii to perform at the Aloha Stadium in Honolulu. US appearances include the **Eagles**, **Linda Ronstadt** and **Jackson Browne** (Los Angeles), the **B-52's**, **Hootie & the Blowfish**, **Styx** and **Cheap Trick** (Orlando, Florida), **Barenaked Ladies** (Buffalo, New York), the **Bee Gees** (Sunrise, Florida), **Christina Aguilera**, hot modern rockers **Blink 182**, **Bush**, the **Goo Goo Dolls**, **No Doubt** and **Puff Daddy** (New York City), and **ZZ Top** and **Lynyrd Skynyrd** (Houston). In the UK, **Fatboy Slim**, the **Lightning Seeds**, **Orbital**, **Space**, and **Stereophonics** take part in Cream 2000 at Liverpool's Pier Head. Even the **Bay City Rollers** get back together to gig in Edinburgh, Scotland. In New York City, **Sting** closes the year with the Party of the Century concert at the Jacob K. Javits Convention Center and **Billy Joel** performs at Madison Square Garden. **Barbra Streisand** makes a rare live appearance at the MGM Grand Garden in Las Vegas; **Wynonna Judd** reunites with mother **Naomi** at the America West Arena in Phoenix, Arizona. The **Gloria Estefan** Millennium Concert Spectacular opens the American Airlines Arena in Miami, Florida. **Prince** – who has been singing about 1999 for the past 17 years – gives a pay-per-view concert, Rave Un2 the Year 2000, appropriately costing $19.99.

Destiny's Child's destiny did indeed change in early 2000 when original members LaTavia Roberson and Le Toya Luckett left the group.

ROOTS **During this year: the Strokes make their live debut at the Spiral in New York... Berklee School of Music drop-out, singer-songwriter/guitarist John Mayer begins regular gigging around Atlanta, Georgia, notably at the acclaimed acoustic spot Eddie's Attic... fronted by co-founders, singer Amy Lee and guitarist Ben Moody, Evanescence begin performing concerts around the group's home base of Little Rock, Arkansas... a virtual unknown on last year's US Lilith Tour, neo-soul songstress India.Arie is snapped up by Motown Records... north Londoner and Sussex University student Naomi McLean-Daley can be heard DJing on pirate R&B radio stations RAW FM and Freak FM in England; she will emerge next year as clubland star Ms. Dynamite, cutting underground favorite *Booo!* with garage producer Sticky... signed last year to Glen Ballard's Java Records, Lisa Marie Presley begins work on her maiden album (which won't emerge until 2003)... and Good Charlotte support Lit on a series of East Coast dates, which will lead them to sign with Epic Records next year...**

"Hip-hop as a whole is bigger than ever, and it just keeps getting bigger, just when you think it can't... Take this music for what it is." Eminem, 2003

"I have an extreme fear when people tell me that we're the next big thing because I think we're going to be forgotten about in two weeks." Chris Martin, 2000

NEW MILLENNIUM
2000

Oops! ... I Did It Again

No.1 US SINGLES

Jan 1 Smooth **Santana featuring Rob Thomas**
Jan 15 What A Girl Wants **Christina Aguilera**
Jan 29 I Knew I Loved You **Savage Garden**
Feb 19 Thank God I Found You **Mariah with Joe & 98º**
Feb 26 I Knew I Loved You **Savage Garden**
Mar 4 Amazed **Lonestar**
Mar 18 Say My Name **Destiny's Child**
Apr 8 Maria Maria **Santana featuring the Product G&B**
June 17 Try Again **Aaliyah**
June 24 Be With You **Enrique Iglesias**
July 15 Everything You Want **Vertical Horizon**
July 22 Bent **matchbox twenty**
July 29 It's Gonna Be Me ***NSync**
Aug 12 Incomplete **Sisqó**
Aug 26 Doesn't Really Matter **Janet**
Sept 16 Music **Madonna**
Oct 14 Come On Over Baby (All I Want Is You) **Christina Aguilera**
Nov 11 With Arms Wide Open **Creed**
Nov 18 Independent Women Part I **Destiny's Child**

No.1 UK SINGLES

Jan 1 I Have A Dream/Seasons In The Sun **Westlife**
Jan 22 The Masses Against The Classes **Manic Street Preachers**
Jan 29 Born To Make You Happy **Britney Spears**
Feb 5 Rise **Gabrielle**
Feb 19 Go Let It Out **Oasis**
Feb 26 Pure Shores **All Saints**
Mar 11 American Pie **Madonna**
Mar 18 Don't Give Up **Chicane featuring Bryan Adams**
Mar 25 Bag It Up **Geri Halliwell**
Apr 1 Never Be The Same Again **Melanie C/Lisa "Left Eye" Lopes**
Apr 8 Fool Again **Westlife**
Apr 15 Fill Me In **Craig David**
Apr 22 Toca's Miracle **Fragma**
May 6 Bound 4 Da Reload (Casualty) **Oxide & Neutrino**
May 13 Oops! ... I Did It Again **Britney Spears**
May 20 Don't Call Me Baby **Madison Avenue**
May 27 Day & Night **Billie Piper**
June 3 It Feels So Good **Sonique**

*NSync

Limp Bizkit

*NSync began the year with their self-titled album reaching the 10 million mark in the US and finished it with ***No Strings Attached*** doing likewise... Limp Bizkit's Back To Basics free summer tour was sponsored by Napster.

The new millennium began in optimistic mood. With the world's economy on a giddy high – built on the false dreams of internet fortunes – it was fitting that a fantasy-driven teen pop bubble was soaring. It was also fitting that the internet surge was wreaking havoc with copyright law, as the world's computer-savvy youth traded millions of songs on the internet – for free.

Boy bands – led by ***NSync** and the **Backstreet Boys** from America, and **Boyzone** and **Westlife** in Europe – rode a phenomenal wave, while teen siren **Britney Spears** consolidated her position. At the other end of the age spectrum, the biggest selling album of 2000-2001 was the **Beatles'** *1*. **Eric Clapton** became the first artist to be inducted into the Rock and Roll Hall of Fame for a third time, and another virtuoso guitarist, **Carlos Santana**, had his "comeback" confirmed with an astonishing eight Grammys.

Robbie Williams took his cheeky pop chops to success all over the world – except the US – and **Madonna** built on the electronic delights of ***Ray Of Light*** with the equally savvy ***Music***. The Real Slim Shady (aka **Eminem**) was fast becoming the most controversial – and popular – solo artist in the world, spitefully degrading everyone, including himself.

As for misdemeanors, **Whitney Houston** was busted for pot, **Puff Daddy** nervously suited up for a much publicized trial following a New York shooting, and Eminem faced serious weapons charges. Rap's troubled reputation worsened when **Bone Thugs-N-Harmony** rapper **Flesh-N-Bone** was sentenced to 11 years in prison. **Courtney Love** was embroiled in bitter disputes with Geffen/Universal, but perhaps the most wide-reaching lawsuit was a massive assault on naughty file-swapping service Napster, challenged individually by the likes of **Metallica** and **Dr. Dre**, and wholesale by the RIAA.

As if to underline the growing trend of mixing genres, Eminem sampled *Thank You* by an unknown British singer-songwriter, **Dido** Armstrong, for his smash *Stan*, and Dido's star quickly rose on the strength of quality songs and well-produced performance. Her debut album became the year's major success story, alongside another previously unheralded Brit, **David Gray**. Slightly more leftfield, Damon Gough, aka **Badly Drawn Boy**, took home the Mercury Music Prize.

"I am a spoiled rock star. I am overpaid, over-nourished and overdressed."

Bono, November 25, 2000

June 24 You See The Trouble With Me **Black Legend**
July 1 Spinning Around **Kylie Minogue**
July 8 The Real Slim Shady **Eminem**
July 15 Breathless **Corrs**
July 22 Life Is A Rollercoaster **Ronan Keating**
July 29 We Will Rock You **Five & Queen**
Aug 5 7 Days **Craig David**
Aug 12 Rock DJ **Robbie Williams**
Aug 19 I Turn To U **Melanie C**
Aug 26 Groovejet (If This Ain't Love) **Spiller, lead vocals by Sophie Ellis-Bextor**
Sept 2 Music **Madonna**
Sept 9 Take On Me **A1**
Sept 16 Lady (Hear me Tonight) **Modjo**
Sept 30 Against All Odds **Mariah Carey & Westlife**
Oct 14 Black Coffee **All Saints**
Oct 21 Beautiful Day **U2**
Oct 28 Stomp **Steps**
Nov 4 Holler/Let Love Lead The Way **Spice Girls**
Nov 11 My Love **Westlife**
Nov 18 Same Old Brand New You **A1**
Nov 25 Can't Fight The Moonlight **LeAnn Rimes**
Dec 2 Independent Women Part I **Destiny's Child**
Dec 9 Never Had A Dream Come True **S Club 7**
Dec 16 Stan **Eminem**
Dec 23 Can We Fix It **Bob the Builder**

2000 Jan

Puff Daddy indicted... Curtis Mayfield remembered... Clapton is inducted for the third time...

Carlos Santana

The Dave Matthews Band

Supernatural, a sparkling and diverse album guided by Clive Davis, suddenly made the 52-year-old Santana the hottest name in rock... The Dave Matthews Band were the top-grossing touring band in the US in 2000.

January

5 Rapper **Shyne** is indicted for attempted murder in the second degree, among other charges, after last week's shooting at Club New York. **Puff Daddy** and **Jennifer Lopez** testified separately before the grand jury yesterday. Meanwhile on the west coast, **Bone Thugs-N-Harmony** rapper **Flesh-N-Bone** is charged with possession of a firearm by a convicted felon, illegal possession of a shotgun, resisting arrest, and making terrorist threats, after an incident at the Los Angeles home of a relative this week.

11 **Gary Glitter** is smuggled out of Bristol prison, where he has served two months of a four-month sentence for child pornography offenses. He is driven to London, and then to Heathrow Airport, from where he flies to Cuba.

11 Sharon Osbourne resigns as manager of the **Smashing Pumpkins**, because of clashes with the group's frontman, **Billy Corgan**. She releases a statement: "It was with great pride and enthusiasm that I took on management of the Pumpkins back in October. Unfortunately, I must resign today due to medical reasons – Billy Corgan was making me sick!"

13 **Puff Daddy** is indicted on weapons charges, following a grand jury investigation.

17 **Puff Daddy**'s predicament is fodder for comedian Norm MacDonald, hosting the 27th American Music Awards at the Shrine Auditorium in Los Angeles: "Would the owner of a Glock Nine with the inscription 'To Puffy with love' please pick up your gun. It's at the hospitality suite." To celebrate the new millennium, an internet poll chooses Artists of the Decades: **Elvis Presley** (1950s), the **Beatles** (1960s), **Stevie Wonder** (1970s), **Michael Jackson** (1980s), and **Garth Brooks** (1990s). Multiple winners include Brooks (Favorite Country Album – ***Double Live*** – and Favorite Male Country Artist), **Lauryn Hill** (Favorite Soul/R&B Album – ***The Miseducation Of Lauryn Hill*** – and Favorite Female Soul/R&B Artist), and **Shania Twain** (Favorite Female Pop/Rock Artist and Favorite Female Country Artist). **Mariah Carey** receives the Award of Achievement, and actor Andy Garcia presents **Gloria Estefan** with the Award of Merit.

19 Geffen Records files suit in Los Angeles Superior Court, claiming **Hole** owe the label five albums under a 1992 agreement. **Courtney Love** and **Eric Erlandson's** Doll Head Inc. reject the claim. A bitter two-year feud will ensue.

31 Shawn Carter, better known as Grammy-winning rapper **Jay-Z**, is indicted on two assault charges stemming from the December 1 stabbing of record executive Lance "Un" Rivera, during a party for fellow rapper **Q-Tip** at New York's Kit Kat Klub. The **New York Daily News** reports that Rivera is willing to drop the charges in exchange for $1 million in cash, and a production deal with Roc-a-fella Records.

Jay-Z had to wait for his day in court because his attorney was busy defending rapper Shyne.

February

12 **Screamin' Jay Hawkins** dies in Neuilly-sur-Seine, France, following surgery to treat an aneurism. The 70-year-old Hawkins will forever be remembered for his 1956 classic *I Put A Spell On You*.

22 **Curtis Mayfield**'s life is remembered at a memorial service at the First African Methodist Episcopal Church in South Los Angeles, with performances before the 300-strong gathering by **Stevie Wonder**, **Eric Clapton**, **Lauryn Hill**, and the **Impressions**. Wonder sings the Impressions' 1961 classic *Gypsy Woman*, after which Eric Clapton takes to the stage, announcing, "I couldn't sleep last night because I was so excited and nervous. This is one of the greatest privileges I've ever had," before breaking into *Keep On Pushing*, accompanied by the Impressions, for whom it was a Top 10 hit in 1964. Lauryn Hill sings *The Makings Of You*, before an emotional finale of *It's All Right* and *Amen*, with Wonder, Clapton, and Hill joined by the AME Freedom Choir.

23 Continuing his remarkable comeback, 52-year-old **Carlos Santana** wins eight Grammys for ***Supernatural*** at the 42nd Grammy Awards, equaling **Michael Jackson**'s 1983 record. Santana's tally is: Album of the Year and Best Rock Album (***Supernatural***), Record of the Year and Best Pop Collaboration with Vocals (*Smooth* – with **Rob Thomas**), Best Pop Performance by a Duo or Group with Vocal (*Maria Maria*), Best Pop Instrumental Performance (*El Farol*), Best Rock Performance by a Duo or Group with Vocal (*Put Your Lights On* – with **Everlast**), and Best Rock Instrumental Performance (*The Calling* – with **Eric Clapton**). He says: "To live is to dream. To die is to awaken. Please don't wake me up." *Smooth* also wins its writers, Rob Thomas and Itaal Shur, the trophy for Song of the Year. Other multiple winners include **TLC**, who pick up Best R&B Performance and Best R&B Song (*No*

Scrubs), and Best R&B Album (***Fanmail***); **Eminem** receives Best Rap Album and Best Rap Solo Performance, and **Sting** wins his 13th and 14th Grammys for Best Pop Album and Best Pop Vocal Performance, Male. Several veterans are first-time winners, including **Cher** (Best Dance Recording), **Barry White** (Best R&B Performance, Male), and **Black Sabbath** (Best Metal Performance). **Billy Joel**, backed by the **Backstreet Boys**, sings *Philadelphia Freedom* as a tribute to Grammy Legend honoree, **Elton John**. The event will, however, be best remembered for **Jennifer Lopez**'s barely-there dress.

29 While their flawless catalog remains utterly contemporary, ***Two Against Nature***, **Steely Dan**'s first studio album for 20 years, is released by Giant Records in the US. In an interview with **Billboard**, **Walter Becker** says: "After touring as Steely Dan for a couple of seasons, we were hungry to have new songs to play on tour, so the next logical step was to do a new Steely Dan album," to which **Donald Fagen** adds, "And we basically came up with enough songs to fill an album."

Melissa Etheridge inducted Bonnie Raitt into the Rock and Roll Hall of Fame, describing her voice as "sex on a plate."

"For me, it's about the music. I'm just the messenger. I carry a message and I hope to be able to do that as long as I live. If I may, I'll just go over there and play." Eric Clapton, Rock and Roll Hall of Fame, March 6, 2000

March

3 Once again the BRIT Awards are marked by onstage malarkey, described by the BBC as "Brits Behaving Badly," when **Robbie Williams** – winning two awards for *She's The One* (Best British Single and Best British Video) – challenges **Liam Gallagher** to a televised fight. **Rolling Stone Ronnie Wood** is also involved in some unnecessary roughness, when an inebriated club DJ walks on stage and is generally obnoxious until Wood throws a drink at him. Only the intervention of security guards prevents a fistfight. On the plus side, melodic Scottish rock quartet **Travis** pick up awards for Best British Group (having broken through in Britain last year with the six-times platinum triumph, ***The Man Who***) and MasterCard Best British Album for ***The Man Who***, and **Macy Gray** wins Best International Female Solo Artist and Best International Newcomer. The **Spice Girls** – complete unknowns less than four years ago – are presented with the prestigious Outstanding Contribution to British Music honor, and fluffy pop/dance quintet **Steps** receive a special award for Best-Selling British Live Act. The Best British Male Solo and Female Solo awards are given to **Tom Jones** and **Beth Orton** respectively. The **Chemical Brothers** are named Best British Dance Act, **Beck** is Best International Male Solo Artist, and peppy seven-piece group **S Club 7** are named Best British Newcomer.

6 **Eric Clapton** becomes the first artist to be inducted into the Rock and Roll Hall of Fame three times, when he is honored for his solo career at the 15th induction dinner, held at New York's Waldorf Astoria Hotel. Inducted by **Robbie Robertson**, Clapton has already been enshrined as a member of the **Yardbirds** and **Cream**. Soul/funk legends **Earth Wind & Fire** celebrate their induction with the vintage line-up – together for the first time in 20 years – performing *Shining Star* and *That's The Way Of The World*. **Paul Simon** inducts 1950s doo-wop greats the **Moonglows**, **Melissa Etheridge** welcomes **Bonnie Raitt**, and **John Mellencamp** honors the **Lovin' Spoonful**. **Paul McCartney** inducts **James Taylor**. The unsung heroes of rock 'n' roll – the session musicians – are honored for the first time, with the new Sidemen category: **Elvis Presley**'s guitarist **Scotty Moore**, sax great **King Curtis**, Motown bassist **James Jamerson**, and two of the best – if not the best – drummers, **Hal Blaine** and **Earl Palmer**, are all inducted. **Nat King Cole** and **Billie Holiday** make their way into the Hall as Early Influences, as does **Clive Davis** as the Non-Performer.

16 The RIAA confirms seven million sales of the **Dave Matthews Band**'s *Crash*, and six million of ***Under The Table And Dreaming***. Notably popular on college campuses, Dave Matthews's dependably tight backing band comprises **LeRoi Moore** (reeds), **Carter Beauford** (drums), **Boyd Tinsley** (violin), and bassist **Stefan Lessard**. The trend-defying group have quietly amassed a phenomenal following in the US, mostly by word-of-mouth, but their roots-rock fusion – often laced with worldbeat tones – is proving difficult to sell abroad. A fierce opponent of bootlegging, Matthews recently formed his own ATO label (with the band's long-time manager Coran Capshaw). As their first signing, they are licensing the US rights to ***White Ladder***, the fourth album by little-known British singer-songwriter/guitarist, **David Gray** – which will find multiplatinum success around the world over the next year.

18 Some 11,000 fans turn out in Dublin's Smithfield Square to see **U2** and their manager Paul McGuinness made freemen of the city. Nobel Prize laureate Aung Sang Suu Kyi is also honored, with her son Kim Aris accepting on her behalf.

27 **Ian Dury** dies at the age of 57, after a long battle with cancer. Best known for his late 1970s hits with the **Blockheads** – *What A Waste, Hit Me With Your Rhythm Stick*, and *Reasons To Be Cheerful (Pt.3)* – by the late 1980s, he had turned his hand to acting and painting. In the last few years, Dury, who was first diagnosed with cancer in 1996, worked tirelessly for UNICEF. In the BBC-TV special "Ian Dury: On My Life," broadcast last September, he said: "I feel very lucky – almost as if I've had a blessed life. No one's ever been horrible to me."

29 US chart-compilers SoundScan confirm that ***NSync** have broken the record for first-week sales, with their new album ***No Strings Attached*** having sold a staggering 2,416,000 copies. This more than doubles fellow boy band **Backstreet Boys**' tally for ***Millennium***. Having left RCA for Jive Records, also the home of Backstreet Boys and **Britney Spears** (who currently dates *NSync's **Justin Timberlake**), the group's third album is once again a sturdy mix of radio-ready pop/dance numbers and polished ballads, mostly produced by Veit Renn and Rami, with Kristian and Jake Lundin. Its success is initially spurred by its first single, *Bye Bye Bye*, with its hotly rotated, Wayne Isham-directed video. With a major US arena tour beginning in May, *NSync will perform four soldout nights at New York's Madison Square Garden in July. By the end of the year the RIAA will certify US sales of ten million copies of ***No Strings Attached*** (the quintet's second Diamond Award).

Apr 2000

Metallica sue Napster... McCartney becomes a fellow...

Lars Ulrich and Roger McGuinn appeared before a Senate Judiciary Committee hearing on intellectual property issues... LA Reid earned his sobriquet as a teenager when he started wearing a Los Angeles Dodgers T-shirt.

Lars Ulrich and Roger McGuinn

LA Reid

April

1 Opening for **KISS** at the Cynthia Woods Mitchell Pavilion in Houston, **Ted Nugent** launches into a diatribe aimed at Latino immigrants: "If you're not gonna speak English, get the f**k out of America." The venue will ban him from playing a return date on August 22.

2 UK tabloid newspaper the **Sunday People** prints a story claiming that **Motörhead** founder **Lemmy** handcuffed his lover to a bed for a three-day sex and bondage session. Through his lawyers, Lemmy will lodge a complaint about the allegations, claiming: "It was not three days, and she was not handcuffed to the bed. It was seven days and she was hung from the ceiling." The **Sunday People** will respond: "We apologise unreservedly to Mr. Lemmy for any damage to his reputation."

6 Cable network TNT's Master Series features veteran Canadian singer-songwriter **Joni Mitchell**. "An All-Star Tribute to Joni Mitchell," at New York's Hammerstein Ballroom, includes **James Taylor**, **k.d. lang**, **Cyndi Lauper**, **Richard Thompson**, **Wynonna Judd**, and **Bryan Adams**. **Shawn Colvin** and **Mary Chapin Carpenter** sing *Chelsea Morning*, before seguing into *Big Yellow Taxi*, with help from Taylor. **Elton John** performs *Free Man In Paris*, revealing that playing Mitchell's music is more intimidating than playing for the Queen of England. The evening closes with the assembled performers backing Mitchell on *The Circle Game*.

13 **Metallica** state their intention to sue Napster for copyright infringement, claiming that the San Mateo, California-based company is in violation of copyright law by allowing illegal swapping of the band's music. Metallica's **Lars Ulrich** says it is "sickening to know that our art is being traded like a commodity rather than the art that it is. From a business standpoint, this is about piracy – aka taking something that doesn't belong to you – and that is morally and legally wrong." The suit also says that students who use Napster "exhibit the moral fiber of common looters." One of those looting students will respond, hacking into Metallica's official site tomorrow, and leaving the message, "Leave Napster Alone." Next month, Napster will remove over 300,000 members from its service for downloading Metallica songs.

25 Two weeks after the announcement that **Metallica** are suing Napster, **Dr. Dre** joins in the fray, filing his own lawsuit for $10 million against the music sharing site. "Napster has built a business based on large-scale piracy. I don't like people stealing my music." He had given Napster until April 21 to remove his music from their site. Conversely, **Limp Bizkit** announced yesterday that their upcoming Back to Basics tour will be sponsored by Napster.

28 US District Judge Jed S. Rakoff rules that MP3.com is liable for infringing the copyrights of the RIAA. MP3.com's chairman, Michael Robertson, says: "This is not a victory for the record labels – it's a loss. My MP3.com is a system which requires the purchase of CDs in order to function, as opposed to other services like Napster that do not require users to first purchase a CD before accessing music." The RIAA had sued in January, claiming that MP3.com had copied 45,000 CDs into its database without permission.

Smashing Pumpkins' frontman Billy Corgan announced in May that the band were to split.

> **"We believe that the internet and Napster should not be ignored by the music industry... We couldn't care less about the older generation's need to keep doing business as usual. We care more about what our fans want."**
>
> Limp Bizkit's Fred Durst, April 25, 2000

May

2 BMG, the parent company of Arista Records, announces that **Antonio "L.A." Reid** will replace **Clive Davis** as head of the label, when the latter's contract expires at the end of June. Davis founded Arista in 1974 and it has been the home of such acts as **Ace of Base**, **Air Supply**, **Aretha Franklin**, **Kenny G**, **Whitney Houston**, **Barry Manilow**, **Sarah McLachlan**, **Santana**, the **Patti Smith Group**, the **Thompson Twins**, and **Dionne Warwick**. Reid will be taking over as the label has one of its best years ever, posting $425 million in sales during the first nine months of the fiscal year.

16 ♀ makes an announcement at a press conference at the Sports Club/LA in Manhattan: "On December 31, 1999, my publishing contract with Warner/Chappell expired, thus emancipating the name I was given before birth – Prince – from all long-term restrictive documents. I will now go back to using my name instead of the symbol I adopted as a means to free myself from all undesirable relationships." He also announces plans for the week-long Prince: A Celebration, from June 7–13, which will include tours of his Paisley Park recording studios in Chanhassen, a concert at the Northrop Auditorium in Minneapolis, and the release of new music on his website.

EMINEM

May 23 **Promoting today's release of *The Marshall Mathers LP* by Aftermath/ Interscope, Eminem is in New York, signing copies for 500-plus fans at the Virgin Megastore in Times Square. The set includes his current smash, the Christina Aguilera-bashing *The Real Slim Shady* (apparently prompted by comments made about him by Aguilera on MTV). Eminem's barbed wit, cunning use of samples, controversial willingness to address any subject, and unique vocal delivery, is backed by boundary-pushing rhythms and pulses by producer Dr. Dre. The album will sell 1.76 million US copies in its first week, giving Eminem the record for the biggest one-week sales of any solo artist.**

Fast becoming the most popular act – in any genre – in the world, Eminem found mass appeal in black and white suburbia, presenting difficult choices for radio programmers.

23 In an interview on Los Angeles radio station KROQ, **Billy Corgan** says the **Smashing Pumpkins** are splitting. "We're at the end of our road emotionally, spiritually, and musically. We thought that we'd tell people when the album came out, but now that the album's out, it's fine... It's more about completing the circle and leaving things on a positive note. It's just about leaving everybody with a nice kiss, and one more swing." Their current tour will come to a close in Tokyo on July 1.

25 GLAAD (the Gay and Lesbian Alliance Against Defamation) issues an alert against **Eminem**, saying, "***The Marshall Mathers LP*** carries the warning 'Explicit Lyrics.' That is an understatement. Eminem's lyrics are soaked with violence and full of negative comments about many groups, including lesbians and gay men... This is especially negligent when considering the market for this music has been shown to be adolescent males, the very group that statistically commits the most hate crimes."

25 **Paul McCartney** is the first songwriter to be given a fellowship by the British Academy of Composers and Songwriters (BASCA) at the 45th Ivor Novello Awards in London. **Travis**'s **Fran Healy** wins the Best Contemporary Song prize for *Why Does It Always Rain On Me?* as well as being named Songwriter of the Year, and **Robbie Williams** and songwriting partner **Guy Chambers** win Best Song Musically and Lyrically for *Strong*. **Madness** collect the award for Outstanding Song Collection, recognizing nearly 30 hits over the past 20 years, and legendary songwriting duo **Jerry Leiber** and **Mike Stoller** are honored with the Special International Award.

June

3 With her debut album, ***...Baby One More Time*** already over the 12 million mark, **Britney Spears**'s follow-up ***Oops! ... I Did It Again*** hits No. 1 in its week of entry in the US, besting **Mariah Carey**'s one-week sales for a solo female artist. The album will reach nine million sales next March.

4 **Eminem** is arrested outside the Hot Rocks Sports Bar in Warren, Michigan, and charged with disorderly conduct and carrying a concealed weapon. The rapper allegedly pulled a gun on a man whom he had seen kissing his wife Kimberly outside the club.

5 Napster and the **Offspring** come to an agreement to expand the Napster line of merchandise, with profits from the venture going to a charity determined by Napster creator **Shawn Fanning** and the Offspring's **Dexter Holland**. Fanning says: "The Offspring have been great supporters of Napster. We are looking forward to working with them." Holland's only comment? "T-shirts... Good!"

7 After his wife has been arraigned before a Michigan District Court Judge, charged with disturbing the peace, **Eminem** enters a plea of not guilty to assault with a dangerous weapon, and carrying a concealed weapon. He faces up to four years in state prison on the first charge, and up to five years on the second.

8 More weapons charges are brought against **Eminem**, over an alleged incident just hours before the Hot Rocks brawl. He allegedly brandished his gun during an argument with Douglas Dail, a member of **Insane Clown Posse**, outside an electronics store in Royal Oak.

15 After years of legal battles, the Mississippi State Supreme Court rules that Claud Johnson, a 68-year-old retired gravel truck driver from Crystal Springs, Mississippi, is the sole heir to the estate of blues legend **Robert Johnson**. The court accepted Eula Mae Williams's 1998 testimony that she saw Johnson's mother, Virgie Jane Smith, have sex with the bluesman in 1931. The ruling could mean that Johnson will receive more than $1 million in royalties.

23 During **Limp Bizkit**'s set at K-ROQ radio's Dysfunctional Family Picnic in Holmdel, which also features **Stone Temple Pilots**, multiplatinum rocking quartet **Creed**, **Deftones**, Boston-based alt-metal newcomers **Godsmack**, Atlanta-based heavy metal quintet **Sevendust**, and veterans **Black Sabbath**, the outspoken **Fred Durst** launches a verbal volley at Creed frontman **Scott Stapp**: "I want to dedicate this next song to the lead singer of Creed – that guy is an egomaniac. He's a f**king punk and he's backstage right now acting like f**king **Michael Jackson**." On MTV's "Total Request Live" next week, Durst will confirm that Creed have given him an anger management manual following his onstage rant. The RIAA certified six million sales of Limp's ***Significant Other*** on May 31. Creed's unapologetically spiritual and anthemic "emo" rock brand – led by lead singer/songwriter Stapp (the son of a Pentecostal minister) – has also caught fire. Their debut album, the Christian rock-tinged ***My Own Prison***, reached the four million mark in the US last November, while ***Human Clay*** is midway through a staggering ten million domestic haul. Both bands have begun the new century as America's hottest rock acts.

The Experience Music Project... Tragedy at Roskilde... Badly Drawn Boy...

Britney Spears and Christina Aguilera were both Grammy-nominated in the Best New Artist category – Aguilera won.

23 The Experience Music Project, the vision of Microsoft co-founding billionaire Paul Allen, opens its doors in Seattle, Washington with performances by **Metallica**, the **Red Hot Chili Peppers**, **Rickie Lee Jones**, **Joe Jackson**, industrial rockers **Filter**, **Kid Rock** (appropriately promoting his new album ***The History Of Rock***), **Patti Smith**, **Eminem**, **Snoop Dogg**, and **Dr. Dre**. The celebrations will continue over the weekend, with further performances from **Beck**, **Bo Diddley**, **Taj Mahal**, the newly styled **matchbox twenty**, **No Doubt**, **Alanis Morissette**, **Eurythmics**, **James Brown**, and northwest legends the **Kingsmen**, the **Ventures**, and **Paul Revere & the Raiders**. The interactive and user-friendly museum, which has been ten years in the making, is variously described in the press as "Technicolor mushrooms on a soggy lawn" (**Associated Press**), "The $10,000 Italian sofa you'll buy on the day you completely lose your mind" (**Tacoma News Tribune**), and "Crayons in a Cuisinart" and "The wreck of the Partridge Family bus" (**Seattle Times**).

30 During a performance by **Pearl Jam** at the Roskilde festival, near Copenhagen, nine fans are trampled to death near the stage when crowds behind them surge forward. Consistent rain has resulted in muddy conditions, leading those who died to slip and fall. The group, who repeatedly pleaded with the crowd to move back, issue a statement on their official website: "This is so painful... Our lives will never be the same, but we know that is nothing compared to the grief of the families and friends of those involved. It is so tragic... there are no words. Devastated, Pearl Jam."

July

7 **Eminem**'s wife Kimberly tries to commit suicide after attending a party following her husband's performance on the Up In Smoke tour in Detroit. Police, called to the couple's Sterling Heights home after a distress call at 11:30 pm, find her conscious after allegedly slashing her wrists. Eminem is not present. Kim, who is currently suing her husband for $10 million for alluding to killing the mother of his child in the song *Kim*, will file for divorce next month, seeking sole custody of their five-year-old daughter.

11 **Lars Ulrich** takes his crusade to Washington, D.C., testifying before the Senate Judiciary Committee discussing intellectual-property rights on the internet. The **Metallica** drummer tells the committee: "If you're not fortunate enough to own a computer, there's only one way to assemble a music collection the equivalent of a Napster user's: theft. Walk into a record store, grab what you want and walk out. The difference is that the familiar phrase a computer user hears, 'File's done,' is replaced by another familiar phrase – 'You're under arrest.'"

28 The 9th US Circuit Court of Appeals in San Francisco issues a last-minute stay to Napster, allowing it to continue operations until the upcoming case goes to trial. Napster has been ordered by the District Court to stop allowing copyrighted material to appear on its online service by tonight – a move that would essentially shut the service down.

25 **Jack Nitzsche** dies following a bronchial infection in Queen of Angels Hospital, Hollywood. He is 63. Born Bernard Alfred Nitzsche in Chicago, he began his illustrious career after moving to Los Angeles in 1955. Given his start in the music business by **Sonny Bono**, Nitzsche was equally accomplished as an arranger, producer, writer, and musician. He worked with the **Rolling Stones**, **Neil Young**, the **Monkees**, **Ricky Nelson**, **Captain Beefheart**, and the **Tubes**. He co-wrote hit songs such as *Needles And Pins* and *Up Where We Belong*, and penned movie scores such as "One Flew Over the Cuckoo's Nest" and "An Officer and a Gentleman." But his lasting contribution to music was his arrangements for **Phil Spector**: without Nitzsche, there would have been no Wall of Sound.

> **"[This gig is] for all the people who feel left out and excluded by the two major political parties."**
>
> Rage Against the Machine, August 14, 2000

August

14 **Rage Against the Machine** and Latin hip-hop/rock ensemble **Ozomatli** play a free open-air concert in a Los Angeles parking lot opposite the Staples Center, where the Democratic National Convention is taking place. Rage say the gig is "for all the people who feel left out and excluded by the two major political parties. That is the majority of Americans who don't vote because they see no difference between two weak candidates and for those who feel they must settle for the 'lesser of two evils.'"

22 Towards the close of a performance by X-rated rap star **Lil' Kim**, at the second ***Source*** Hip-Hop Music Awards at the Pasadena Civic Auditorium, fighting breaks out, both in the audience and backstage, some two hours into the show. Police bring the event to an end. **Dr. Dre** takes home the most trophies of the evening – five.

September

2 Selling 115,000 copies in its first week, **Madonna**'s *Music* tops the UK chart, and becomes her tenth British No. 1 – a first for a female singer. Spurred by a video directed by Jonas Akerlund, the single will become her 12th US chart-topper in two weeks' time. The album of the same name, a cutting-edge dance-fused collaboration with French producer Mirwais, will also find the top spot in both countries.

7 Music takes a back seat to bad behavior and protests at the 17th MTV Awards, held at Radio City Music Hall. While **Limp Bizkit** accept the award for Best Rock Video, **Rage Against the Machine** bassist **Timmy Commerford** climbs a 10ft stage prop. With the audience shouting "Jump!" he is finally persuaded to come down, before being ushered out of the building and arrested for assault and resisting arrest. **Eminem**, who is greeted on 6th Avenue by protesters from GLAAD, walks in rapping *The Real Slim Shady*, accompanied by a phalanx of Eminem lookalikes. In his acceptance speeches for Video of the Year and Best Male Video for the song, and Best Rap Video with **Dr. Dre** for "Forgot

DIDO

Aug 2 **English singer-songwriter Dido (Armstrong) kicks off her first headlining US tour at the 9:30 Club in Washington, D.C. in support of her maiden album, the electronic pop/acoustic-fused *No Angel*. It was released by Arista in June last year, to strong critical notices, but no support from radio, and minimal sales. Its fortunes are being revived by the use of its lead track *Here With Me* as the theme song to US cable television network WB's popular sci-fi series, "Roswell." It is also about to receive a major boost from the sampling of *Thank You* on Eminem's upcoming single, *Stan*. A latent breakout success, *No Angel* will eventually sell more than 15 million copies worldwide.**

Dido first sang in her brother Rollo's electronic trip-hop band, Faithless – notably on their 1996 multiplatinum outing, *Reverence*.

About Dre," he manages to be an equal-opportunity offender, with a series of pearls of wisdom: "Every time a relative sues me, every time a critic tries to slam me in the press, I sell more records. I really want to thank you people for making my record as big as it was... I'm going to take this home and put it right between my Britney Spears and Christina Aguilera posters... This is the one night where you can fit all the people that I don't like into one room." Napster founder **Shawn Fanning** provides an element of humor, wearing a **Metallica** T-shirt.

12 Damon Gough, the woolly-hatted folk-pop singer-songwriter/multi-instrumentalist **Badly Drawn Boy**, wins the coveted Mercury Music Prize for his debut album, ***The Hour Of Bewilderbeast***. A wistful, irreverent masterpiece, the album has found critical and commercial success in the face of all the pervading genres and marketing ploys, and will even find favor in the modern rock/rap-obsessed US market. The 11 other nominees on the always eclectic albums list are the now solo **Richard Ashcroft** (***Alone With Everybody***), emerging Brit-pop quartet **Coldplay** (the group's ***Parachutes*** has yielded arguably the year's most beautifully simple rock single, *Yellow*), **M.J. Cole** (***Sincere***), **Death In Vegas** (***The Contino Sessions***), the **Delgados** (***The Great Eastern***), **Doves** (***Lost Souls***), **Helicopter Girl** (***How To Steal The World***), **Leftfield** (***Rhythm And Stealth***), **Nicholas Maw** (***Violin Concerto***), **Nitin Sawhney** (***Beyond Skin***), and **Kathryn Williams** (***Little Black Numbers***).

13 **Santana** continue their winning ways with three awards at the inaugural Latin Grammy Awards, held at the Staples Center in Los Angeles. They win Record of the Year and Best Rock Performance by a Duo or Group with Vocal for their collaboration with Latin rock icons **Maná**, *Corazon Espinado*, and Best Pop Instrumental Performance for *El Farol*. **Luis Miguel**'s ***Amarte Es Un Placer*** wins Album of the Year and Best Pop Album, and Colombian-born **Shakira** wins Best Female Pop Vocal Performance for *Ojos Así*, and Best Female Rock Vocal Performance for *Octavo Día*. Co-hosted by **Gloria Estefan**, **Jennifer Lopez**, Andy Garcia, and Jimmy Smits, the show opens with a tribute to mambo king **Tito Puente**, who passed away in June.

13 At a hearing of the Senate Commerce Committee in Washington, D.C., Lynne Cheney – wife of vice-presidential Republican nominee Dick Cheney – says: "I want to focus on one company, Seagram, that is currently marketing **Eminem**, a rap singer who advocates murder and rape. He talks about murdering and raping his mother. He talks about choking women slowly so he can hear their screams for a long time. He talks about using OJ's machete on women, and this is a man who is honored by the recording industry."

22 **Bone Thugs-N-Harmony**'s **Flesh-N-Bone** is sentenced to 11 years in state prison in Van Nuys, California, after being convicted of assault with a deadly weapon and a probation violation.

25 **Ozzy Osbourne** releases a statement, requesting that **Black Sabbath** be removed from the Rock and Roll Hall of Fame nominations: "Just take our name off the list. Save the ink. Forget about us. The nomination is meaningless, because it's not voted on by the fans. It's voted on by the 'supposed' elite of the industry and the media... Let's face it, Black Sabbath have never been media darlings. We're a people's band and that suits us just fine."

October

1 The RIAA introduces guidelines for the present system of Parental Advisory labeling on recordings. RIAA president, Hilary Rosen, says "The program was conceived as a delicate balance – respecting the freedom of expression our recording artists deserve while also respecting the legitimate needs of parents and guardians for a cautionary notice about explicit content."

3 **Benjamin Orr**, co-founder of the **Cars**, dies of pancreatic cancer at his home in Atlanta, age 53. The Cleveland-born Orr played bass and sang with the 1970s new wave band, which he formed with **Ric Ocasek** in Boston in 1976.

14 Having played a sellout gig at the Roseland Ballroom in New York, **Radiohead** make their debut on "Saturday Night Live," singing

On winning the Mercury Music Prize, Badly Drawn Boy (aka Damon Gough) said he would go home the next day and not be able to "write for toffee."

Oct 2000

"It *is* a fight. It is us versus the obvious route... which would be mediocrity, cult sales and living off your past."

Bono, **Q**, November 2000

Oct 19 **U2** play a surprise gig at the Manray in Paris before 150 fans and guests, who thought they were attending a playback of the band's new album, ***All That You Can't Leave Behind***. Meanwhile, the extracted single, the anthemic *Beautiful Day*, tops the UK chart. Their ninth studio album is a mostly solid return to their most popular rock style (following the poorly received experimentation of 1997's ***Pop***) and will top the charts in 31 countries following its release on October 30.

U2 held off a strong bid from Robbie Williams and Kylie Minogue to secure their first UK chart-topper in three years, when *Beautiful Day* hit the top.

2000 Oct

Brooks announces his retirement... The Beatles are No. 1 again...

An estimated 45,000 fans showed up outside the Back Street Boys' hotel in Rio de Janeiro during their whirlwind promotional tour.

The National Anthem and *Idioteque*, as their new album, the electronica-charged ***Kid A***, debuts at No. 1 in the UK. The band will also bow at No. 1 in the US next week – the first British act to do so since **Prodigy**'s ***Fat Of The Land*** in 1997. The album also tops lists in Canada, France, Iceland, Ireland, Israel, and Japan.

24 Fans are notified an hour before **Limp Bizkit**'s concert at the Pepsi Arena in Albany, New York, that the show is canceled because frontman **Fred Durst** is suffering from strained vocal cords. The band are currently on their wryly named Anger Management tour, promoting their new album, ***Chocolate St*rfish And The Hot Dog Flavored Water***, which will sell 1.05 million US copies this week ensuring a No. 1 album chart bow. The album will achieve the sixth-best first-week sales in SoundScan's history, and the fourth this year, moving more than a million copies in its week of release, behind ***NSync**, **Britney Spears**, and **Eminem**.

30 **Elton John** files a £20 ($30) million suit against the Pricewaterhouse Coopers accounting firm and his ex-business manager, Andrew Haydon, charging them with misappropriation of funds and professional negligence. The alleged shortfall was discovered when John split from long-time manager, John Reid.

31 German entertainment giant Bertelsmann announces an alliance with Napster, entailing a subscription service to allow users to swap songs copyrighted by the recording conglomerate. The company will drop its lawsuit against Napster, and loan it an estimated $50 million to develop a legal file-sharing system.

November

15 Michael Abram, a paranoid schizophrenic who attacked **George Harrison** last December, is found not guilty on the grounds of insanity, but is ordered to be held in a psychiatric hospital "without time restriction." Abram's solicitor reveals that his client has written to Harrison begging forgiveness.

15 Capitol Records announces that it has purchased land just north of its building at the corner of Hollywood and Vine, and is planning a museum of memorabilia from Capitol recording artists, from **Frank Sinatra** to the **Beatles**.

15 **Backstreet Boys** announce plans for a Round the World in 100 Hours promotional tour to launch their new album ***Black & Blue***. Following tomorrow night's appearance at the MTV Europe Music Awards, their very expensive whirlwind trip will take in Tokyo, Sydney, Cape Town, Rio de Janeiro, and New York.

16 Host **Wyclef Jean** opens the seventh MTV Europe Music Awards at the Globen Centre in Stockholm, with a rap montage set to Abba's *Dancing Queen*. With **Jennifer Lopez**, **All Saints**, and the **Spice Girls** performing live, it is

Radiohead were voted second, behind David Bowie but ahead of the Beatles, in a survey to determine the biggest influence on the then current generation of musicians.

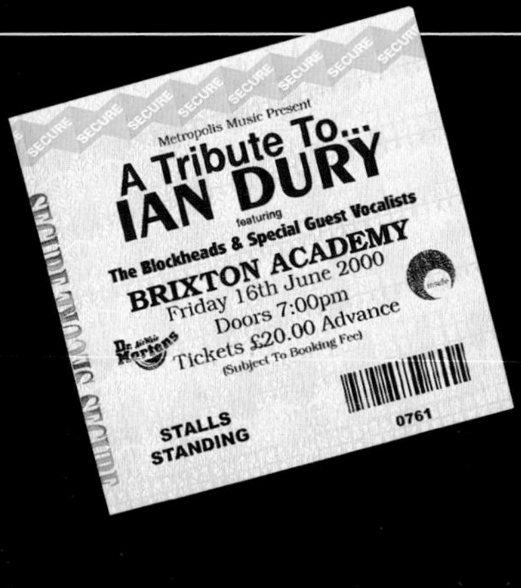

Robbie Williams, Madness, the Clash's Mick Jones, and Kirsty McColl took part in the A Tribute To... Ian Dury concert in June... In October, Garth Brooks announced his retirement at a press conference in Nashville, after which he was honored at a black tie gala for selling more than 100 million albums.

Garth Brooks

veteran **Madonna** (wearing a T-shirt bearing the legend "Kylie Minogue") who steals the show, performing *Music.* Nominated in five categories, **Robbie Williams** picks up just one award – Best Song for *Rock DJ* – but tells the audience: "I am not going to say anything bad about people's choices on this one, but I think it's a terrible song and a silly song."

25 Confirming again that they are without peer, the **Beatles** hit UK No. 1 with ***1***, a 27-track compilation of their UK and US chart-toppers. The album will repeat the feat in the US next week, and in Christmas week will become the fastest-selling album in US history. In all, it will hit No. 1 in 28 countries, selling 12 million copies worldwide in just three weeks (an average rate of six copies per second). Perpetuating the myth that the record never topped the UK chart, *Please Please Me* is a notable omission from the compilation. Meanwhile, the recently published book, **The Beatles Anthology**, telling the group's story in their own words with never-before-seen photographs, also hits bestseller lists.

15 IPC announces that effective the first of the year, **Melody Maker** will close and merge with the **NME**. The venerable UK music weekly, first published in January 1926, has seen its circulation fall by 21 percent in recent months. The paper's famous musicians' section will transfer to the weekly **NME**.

19 Following the shocking death of perennially underrated British singer-songwriter, **Kirsty MacColl**, who was killed yesterday by a speedboat while swimming near Cozumel, Mexico, the music industry also mourns three other prominent musicians: 42-year-old **Rob Buck**, founding member and lead guitarist of **10,000 Maniacs**, who suffers liver failure; legendary jazz bassist **Milt Hinton**, age 90, who played with **Benny Goodman**, **Billie Holiday**, and **Lionel Hampton**; and **Pop Staples**, the patriarch of the **Staple Singers**, who dies in Dolton, Illinois, age 84, following a fall.

"When I was growing up I dreamed of being a pop star and I would like to thank MTV for my three houses, my five cars, and my supermodel girlfriend. Long live the dream." Robbie Williams, November 16, 2000

December

2 The **Smashing Pumpkins** play their final show at Chicago's Cabaret Metro, joined on stage by **Cheap Trick**'s **Rick Nielsen**, **Billy Corgan**'s father Bill Sr., and former drummer **Matt Walker**. Fans, who have endured up to two days in freezing temperatures outside the club, are rewarded with a limited-edition CD of the band's first ever show at the venue on October 5, 1988, and watch a performance lasting almost five hours.

8 Fidel Castro attends the unveiling of a statue of **John Lennon** in Havana's El Vedado Park, coinciding with the 20th anniversary of the singer's murder. Despite denouncing the **Beatles**' music as decadent in the 1960s, the President praises Lennon as a revolutionary.

9 With first-week sales of 1.6 million, **Backstreet Boys**' ***Black & Blue*** debuts at No. 1 on the US album chart, setting two new records – one for being the first artists in the SoundScan era to achieve million-plus first-week sales with back-to-back albums, and another for the highest international first-week sales, with over five million copies sold worldwide.

22 "O Brother, Where Art Thou" opens in US theaters. Directed by Joel Coen and starring George Clooney, John Turturro, and John Goodman, the film's soundtrack has been compiled by producer T-Bone Burnette. With minimal marketing but strong word-of-mouth, the mountain music compilation of old and new traditional bluegrass songs will sell six million albums for Americana label, Lost Highway.

22 Following the christening of their baby son Rocco yesterday at Dornoch Cathedral in Scotland, **Madonna** marries British film director Guy Ritchie at Skibo Castle in Dornoch. Guests at the ceremony, from which the media are excluded, include celebrity pals **Sting**, Gwyneth Paltrow, Rupert Everett, Brad Pitt, George Clooney, and Robin Williams.

Madonna picked up awards for Best Female Artist and Best Dance Act at the MTV Music Awards.

ROOTS **During this year: in London, Islington-based friends Duncan James and Anthony Costa decide to form a boy band while playing pool, subsequently enlisting Lee Ryan and Simon Webbe to create Blue, who are signed to Virgin's Innocent Records imprint by year's end... Madonna's Maverick Records executive Danny Strick spots 16-year-old singer-songwriter Michelle Branch opening for Hanson at the Wilton Theater in Los Angeles – and soon signs her up... southern California-based alt-metal quartet Trapt are signed to Immortal Records following a gig at the Troubadour in Los Angeles; the deal will dissolve after two months but the group will be snapped up by Warner Bros. next year... Surfer magazine names Hawaiian surf champ Jack Johnson's "Thicker Than Water" documentary "Video of the Year;" Johnson is switching gears for a career in music under the guidance of Ben Harper... formed two years ago, the sassy British teen trio of Keisha Buchanan, Siobhan Donaghy, and Mutya Buena sign to London Records as Sugababes... and the Locked On club/dance indie label in England issues *Has It Come To This?*, the first release by aspiring garage/2-step artist, Birmingham native and fast-food restaurant worker Mike Skinner, aka The Streets...**

Because I Got High

No.1 US SINGLES

Jan 6	Independent Women Part I **Destiny's Child**
Feb 3	It Wasn't Me **Shaggy featuring Ricardo "Rikrok" Ducent**
Feb 17	Outkast **Ms. Jackson**
Feb 24	Stutter **Joe**
Mar 24	Butterfly **Crazy Town**
Mar 31	Angel **Shaggy featuring Rayvon**
Apr 7	Butterfly **Crazy Town**
Apr 14	All For You **Janet**
June 2	Lady Marmalade **Christina Aguilera, Lil' Kim, Mya & Pink**
July 7	Remind Me **Usher**
Aug 4	Bootylicious **Destiny's Child**
Aug 18	Fallin' **Alicia Keys**
Sept 8	I'm Real **Jennifer Lopez**
Sept 29	Fallin' **Alicia Keys**
Oct 20	I'm Real **Jennifer Lopez**
Nov 3	Family Affair **Mary J. Blige**
Dec 15	U Got It Bad **Usher**
Dec 22	How You Remind Me **Nickelback**

No.1 UK SINGLES

Jan 6	Can We Fix It **Bob the Builder**
Jan 13	Touch Me **Rui Da Silva featuring Cassandra**
Jan 20	Love Don't Cost A Thing **Jennifer Lopez**
Jan 27	Rollin' **Limp Bizkit**
Feb 10	Whole Again **Atomic Kitten**
Mar 10	It Wasn't Me **Shaggy featuring Ricardo "Rikrok" Ducent**
Mar 17	Uptown Girl **Westlife**
Mar 24	Pure And Simple **Hear'Say**
Apr 14	What Took You So Long **Emma Bunton**
Apr 28	Survivor **Destiny's Child**
May 5	Don't Stop Movin' **S Club 7**
May 12	It's Raining men **Geri Halliwell**
June 2	Do You Really Like It **DJ Pied Piper & the Masters of Ceremonies**
June 9	Angel **Shaggy featuring Rayvon**
June 30	Lady Marmalade **Christina Aguilera, Lil' Kim, Mya & Pink**
July 7	Way To Your Love **Hear'Say**
July 14	Another Chance **Roger Sanchez**
July 21	Eternity/Road To Mandalay **Robbie Williams**

Dido

Craig David

Dido's *No Angel* album has sold 2.4 million copies in the UK and four million in the US... At 18 years, 11 months, and 10 days, Craig David was the youngest male singer to write and sing a UK chart-topper, when *Fill Me In* hit No. 1.

The shocking specter of the World Trade Center towers falling on September 11 changed the perspective of the entire year. As has often been the case with tragic events over the past 40 years, musicians were among the first to respond, helping to heal and raise funds. Several benefit concerts were quickly staged in September and October, and even a previously planned **John Lennon** tribute concert in New York turned into a "Come Together" healing exercise. For many Americans the most poignant musical moment came in November, when country star **Alan Jackson** performed his September 11-inspired *Where Were You (When The World Stopped Turning)* at the Country Music Awards in Nashville.

Following the economic euphoria of the past five years, September 11 also ushered in a new stark reality, which would hit the record industry hard, as sales declined for the first time since the early 1980s. The major labels largely pointed the finger at illegal downloading of tracks on the internet. The courts agreed, and the wildly popular Napster was ceremoniously closed down in the summer (only to be replaced by a crop of even more ingenious file-swapping services).

While sales slipped, singer-songwriter/pianist **Alicia Keys** bucked the trend and gave veteran executive Clive Davis a dreamboat start for his new j records label. Across the Atlantic, another talented young newcomer, **Craig David**, caused equal excitement with his fresh and clever brand of UK soul/rap/pop. He would become a rare example of a British R&B artist making it in the highly competitive US market. **Nelly** arrived on the scene with his infectious hip-hop ditty *Country Grammar*, while Trinidadian native **Shaggy** scored the first ever million-selling reggae hit in the UK with *It Wasn't Me*.

A nauseating new trend emerged with an updated twist on an old television staple – the talent show. Following ABC/MTV's tepid "Making the Band" in 2000, British viewers were subjected to "Popstars," which threw up the hugely popular, manufactured band **Hear'Say**. Its success would unfortunately lead to the even more troubling "Pop Idol" series, its counterpart "American Idol," and a slew of similarly talentless copycats.

Never short on controversy, the Grammy Awards were highlighted by a much-protested performance pairing gay-bashing **Eminem** with gay icon **Elton John**, and an unexpected triple nod for veteran duo **Steely Dan**, whose earlier work from the 1970s still retains a remarkable contemporary edge. While **U2** became the year's top-grossing live act, **Limp Bizkit** conquered charts around the world.

Time was truly marching on: as MTV turned 20, music lost its first **Ramone** (**Joey**) and R&B starlet **Aaliyah** died in a plane crash. Music legends who passed away in 2001 included **Rufus Thomas**, **Chet Atkins** – and **George Harrison**. The **Beatles**, as popular as ever with the still hot-selling ***1***, were down to two.

Aug 4 Eternal Flame **Atomic Kitten**
Aug 18 21 Seconds **So Solid Crew**
Aug 25 Let's Dance **Five**
Sept 8 Too Close **Blue**
Sept 15 Mambo No. 5 **Bob the Builder**
Sept 22 Hey Baby (Uhh Ahh) **DJ Otzi**
Sept 29 Can't Get You Out Of My Head **Kylie Minogue**
Oct 27 Because I Got High **Afroman**
Nov 17 Queen Of My Heart **Westlife**
Nov 24 If You Come Back **Blue**
Dec 1 Have You Ever **S Club 7**
Dec 8 Gotta Get Thru This **Daniel Bedingfield**
Dec 22 Somethin' Stupid **Robbie Williams & Nicole Kidman**

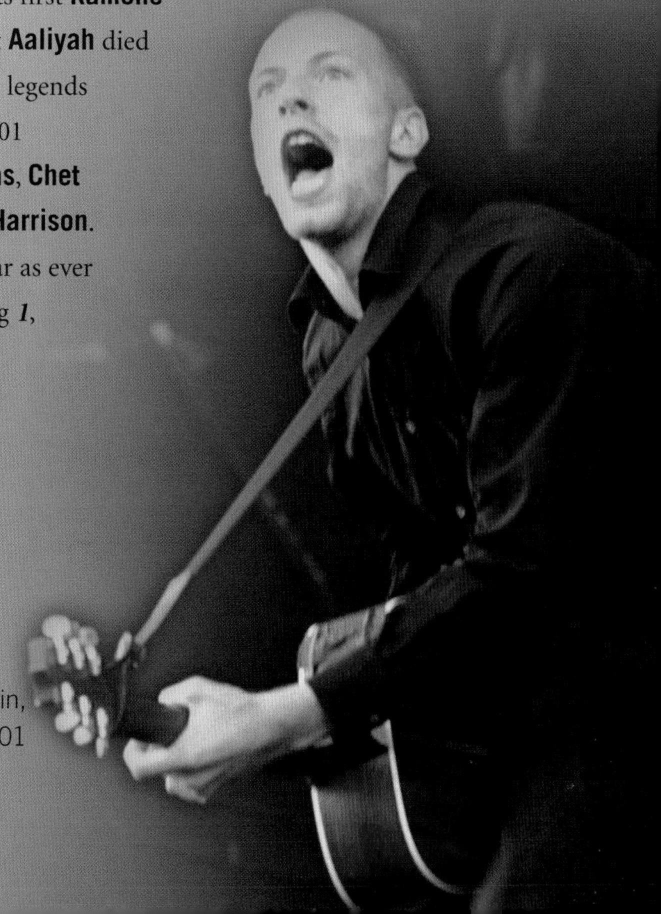

"I have a deep-rooted self-belief."

Coldplay's Chris Martin, **Q**, April 2001

Jan 2001

Tragedy at the Big Day Out... Popstars... The history maker Jennifer Lopez...

After being nominated in 1998, 1999, and 2000, Faith Hill won three American Music Awards in 2001, and then came back in 2002 to win another.

January

8 The country husband-and-wife team of **Faith Hill** and **Tim McGraw** win four awards at the 28th American Music Awards, co-hosted by **Britney Spears** and **LL Cool J**. Hill picks up Favorite Female Artist Pop/Rock, Favorite Female Artist Country, and Favorite Album Country for ***Breathe***, while McGraw is named Favorite Male Artist Country. Rockers **Creed** win Favorite Artist Alternative Music and Favorite Album Pop/Rock for ***Human Clay***, beating albums by teen favorites Britney Spears and ***NSync**, and soulstress **Toni Braxton** wins Favorite Female Artist Soul/R&B and Favorite Album Soul/R&B for ***Heat***.

15 **Sting** is presented with Chile's Gabriela Mistral medal, named after the 1945 Nobel Prize-winning poet, by Foreign Minister Soledad Alvear. Sting has long campaigned for dissidents who disappeared during the 17-year Pinochet regime, writing the Ivor Novello Award-winning song *They Dance Alone* in 1980, as a tribute to the women who lost their husbands.

26 During **Limp Bizkit**'s headlining performance at the Big Day Out festival in Sydney, before a crowd of 45,000, chaotic mosh-pit scenes result in serious injuries, one of which will prove fatal. The group delay their set for 15 minutes, while police and security personnel struggle to control the surging crowd, which is crushing those in front into the barricades. Emergency crews eventually treat more than 60 people for broken limbs and heat exhaustion. Limp Bizkit will abandon their slot on the tour and fly back to the US, blaming their departure on the promoters' inability to implement the safety measures they had suggested. The coroner investigating the death will place most of the blame on the concert promoters, but will also criticize **Fred Durst** for not taking the situation more seriously.

29 Just nominated for a BRIT award (Best British Male), **Badly Drawn Boy** appeals for the return of his woolly hat, stolen in Manchester two days ago. A girl will enter the bar where the theft took place, throw the hat on to the counter and disappear, just in time for the knitted item to be sold at a Kosovan charity auction.

15-year-old Jessica Michalik suffered a fatal heart attack during chaotic mosh-pit scenes at the Big Day Out festival in Sydney, Australia.

February

3 Millions watch the final show of the first "Popstars" UK television series, when – after three weeks of on-air auditions – the judges choose five performers to form a manufactured pop band. They select mother-of-two **Kym Marsh**, puppeteer **Noel Sullivan**, **Cliff Richard** backing singer **Myleene Klass**, actress **Suzanne Shaw**, and trainee primary school teacher **Danny Foster**. Named **Hear'Say**, the group will release their first single, *Pure And Simple*, on March 12, when it will become the third fasting-selling single of all time (behind **Band Aid**'s *Do They Know It's Christmas?* and **Elton John**'s *Candle In the Wind 1997*). Their album, ***Popstars***, will also make No. 1, making them the only act to top both charts with their debuts. Their follow-up single, *The Way To Your Love*, will also top the chart in July, but when their third single, *Everybody*, peaks No. 4 in December, the band will see the writing on the wall and break up.

14 In Macomb County Court in Michigan, **Eminem** pleads guilty to a charge of carrying a concealed weapon. In exchange for the plea, the prosecution drops a felony charge of assault with a deadly weapon. Eminem will be sentenced on April 10, when he will be placed on two years' probation and fined $2,500. He will also be ordered to refrain from excessive alcohol or drug use for two years, and undergo counseling.

17 Fidel Castro is among an audience of 5,000 fans at the Teatro Karl Marx in Havana, who pay the equivalent of 25¢ each to see the **Manic Street Preachers** – the first western act to perform in Cuba in more than 20 years. The group describe their backstage meeting with the 74-year-old President, before the concert, as "the greatest honor" of their lives.

18 The **Los Angeles Times** publishes a letter from a Mrs. Madonna Ritchie, in defence of rapper **Eminem**: "What is the big deal about Eminem? Since when is offensive language a reason for being unpopular? I find the language of George W. Bush much more offensive... I like the fact that Eminem is brash and angry and politically incorrect. At least he has an opinion. He's stirring things up, he's provoking a discussion, he's making people's blood boil, he's reflecting what's going on in society right now. That is what art's supposed to do. And after all he's just a boy."

21 In one of the most musically diverse – and controversial – Grammy Awards ceremonies of recent years, **U2**, **Steely Dan**, **Faith Hill**, and **Eminem** pick up three trophies apiece. (For the first time ever, 100 categories are honored.) After a contentious build-up, gay-bashing Eminem and leading gay icon, **Elton John**, give a memorable duet performance of *Stan*. The rapper wins Best Rap Solo Performance for *The Real Slim Shady*, Best Rap Album for The ***Marshall Mathers LP***, and Best Rap Performance by a Duo or Group, with **Dr. Dre**, for *Forgot About Dre*. Host Jon Stewart attempts to diffuse the brouhaha by saying: "There's a tremendous amount of controversy here tonight. I think we have to deal with it. I met Eminem backstage and he's really gay. About the gayest guy you'd ever meet." **Moby** is less forgiving: "I'm 35 years old and I might be able to appreciate the postmodern irony of his lyrics. But I cannot imagine that an eight-year-old growing up in Idaho can understand that." Against all odds, veteran jazz/rock band **Steely Dan** pick up the Album of the Year, Best Pop Vocal Album, and Best Pop Performance by a Duo or Group with Vocal for ***Two Against Nature***. In a 30-year career, they have never before won a Grammy. **U2** win Song of the Year, Record of the Year, and Best Rock Performance by a Duo or Group with Vocal for *Beautiful Day*. Proving that the NARAS organization is still capable of making bizarre decisions, **Shelby Lynne** is named Best New Artist, despite releasing six albums in the past 13 years.

26 Controversy follows **Eminem** across the Atlantic, as protests accompany his appearance at the 20th BRIT Awards in London, where he receives his Best International Male Artist award from **Elton John**. But perhaps the most controversial part of the evening is the complete

"I loved it! Every time he broke one, he had to buy another one. What a stupid question!" Lifetime Achievement Grammy recipient Les Paul, when asked how he felt when he saw Pete Townshend smash up one of his guitars, February 21, 2001

Lopez revealed on her website that she wanted to record a duet with Craig David.

JENNIFER LOPEZ

Jan 31 **Singer/actress Jennifer Lopez becomes the first artist to top both the US pop and film box office charts in the same week. While SoundScan confirms that her second album, *J. Lo*, with excess sales of 272,000 last week, will debut at No. 1 on the next Billboard Top 200 album chart, dislodging the Beatles' *1*, her latest movie, "The Wedding Planner," reigns at the top of the box office chart, after grossing $14 million in its first week.**

"If there is a better singer in England than Craig David, then I am Margaret Thatcher."

Elton John, February 26, 2001

shutout of 19-year-old R&B sensation **Craig David** who, despite six nominations, walks away without a single award. When *Fill Me In* reached No. 1 last year, David became the youngest British male singer to write and sing a UK chart-topper, while his debut album, ***Born To Do It***, has already exceeded 1.5 million domestic sales. **Robbie Williams** confirms his position as Britain's biggest star, winning Best British Male Artist and Best British Single and Video for *Rock DJ*. **Coldplay** take two of the biggest prizes: Best British Group and Best British Album for ***Parachutes***. Lead singer Chris Martin thanks the teacher who encouraged him to take up music instead of cricket. Receiving the award for Best International Act, **U2**'s **Bono** says: "It's been a great year for pop, hip-hop and R&B – but we feel really great that you're giving this award to a guitar band with lots of soul and attitude." He then dedicates the band's performance of *One* to Craig David, incorporating lyrics from his recent smooth soul/pop hit *Walking Away*. With British acts at an all-time low in the US charts, Craig David and Coldplay, along with **David Gray** and **Dido** (whose 20-month-old ***No Angel*** will hit US No. 4 next week), will be the major British exports across the pond over the next two years.

March

16 **Sean "Puffy" Combs** and his bodyguard Anthony "Wolf" Jones are acquitted of charges stemming from the shooting on December 27, 1999. This month, Combs will change his performing name from **Puff Daddy** to **P. Diddy**.

16 Having recently become a mother for the first time, **Celine Dion** confirms that she will make a full-time concert return in March 2003, with an exclusive three-year engagement at Caesar's Palace in Las Vegas.

The lucky winners of the "Popstars" TV series, assembled as Hear'Say, received £100,000 ($150,000) each.

Mar 2001

Craig David loses then wins... Dylan wins an Oscar... John Lee Hooker dies...

Eva Cassidy's exquisite talent remains largely unknown in her native USA, but in Britain it was a different story, with *Songbird* topping the UK chart and selling close to 2.5 million copies in the process.

18 **John Phillips**, founder of the **Mamas & the Papas**, dies, age 65, at the University of California Medical Center in Los Angeles. Having received a liver transplant in 1992, after years of drug and alcohol abuse, he was admitted to hospital two weeks ago with a shoulder injury, which led to the discovery of a stomach infection. The songwriter behind some of the most memorably harmonious pop hits of the 1960s, he completed a new album, ***Slow Starter***, last year.

19 From the first Latino rock star to the King of Pop himself, eight more performers enter the Rock and Roll Hall of Fame at the 16th dinner, held at the Waldorf Astoria Hotel in New York City. Previous Hall of Famers **Paul Simon** and **Michael Jackson** (supporting himself with a cane after recently breaking his foot) are now welcomed as solo artists. The other inductees are recent Grammy winners **Steely Dan** (inducted by **Moby**), **Aerosmith** (inducted by **Kid Rock**), **Queen** (inducted by the **Foo Fighters**), **Ritchie Valens** (who is inducted by **Ricky Martin**), the **Flamingos** (inducted by **Dion**), and **Solomon Burke** (inducted by **Mary J. Blige**). **Bono** welcomes his label boss **Chris Blackwell** as the Non-Performer, and **Keith Richards** inducts **Johnnie Johnson** and **James Burton** in the Sidemen category.

24 In a remarkable and heartrending musical tale, an unknown American singer who died from cancer, age 33, five years ago, tops the British album chart. **Eva Cassidy**'s ***Songbird*** has had a seven-week climb up the survey, through word of mouth and regular airplay on BBC Radio 2. Comprising her own distinctive and genre-bending versions of classics like *Songbird, Fields Of Gold, People Get Ready, Wade On The Water*, and *Over The Rainbow*, ***Songbird*** – originally released in 1998 – was licensed by Tony Bramwell for his Hot Records label. He introduced Radio 2 producer Paul Walters to its understated treasures, and Walters included her version of *Over The Rainbow* on veteran DJ Terry Wogan's playlist. Cassidy was never signed to a label during her life, and only through the encouragement of her boyfriend, Chris Biondo, did the shy singer ever commit her voice to tape.

25 **Bob Dylan** wins the Oscar for Best Song at the 73rd Academy Awards for *Things Have Changed*, from the movie, "Wonder Boys." The first-time winner performs the song live via satellite from Sydney. As hard as it is to upstage Dylan, **Björk** manages it, performing her nominated song, *I've Seen It All*, sporting a white dress with a stuffed white swan draped around her neck.

> **"Speaking purely for myself, as a high school graduate, this is an upgrade of my educational credentials."** Walter Becker, receiving an honorary doctorate of music with Donald Fagen from the Berklee College of Music in Boston, May 12, 2001

27 The video for **Staind**'s *It's Been A While* – the lead-off single from their upcoming second album ***Break The Cycle*** – bows on MTV in the US, directed by **Limp Bizkit** frontman **Fred Durst**. Comprising lead singer **Aaron Lewis**, guitarist **Mike Mushok**, bassist **Johnny April**, and drummer **Jon Wysocki**, New England-based Staind's emotionally charged alt-rock has resulted in six nominations for the Boston Music Awards. Their new single will become their signature smash, hitting US No. 5, and No. 1 on the Modern Rock list.

Shaggy's UK No. 1 It Wasn't Me became the first reggae single to top the one million sales mark in Britain.

April

2 Former **Crowded House** frontman **Neil Finn** begins a week of concerts at the St. James Theatre in Auckland, where he is joined on stage by **Pearl Jam**'s **Eddie Vedder**, **Radiohead**'s **Ed O'Brien** and **Phil Selway**, the **Smiths' Johnny Marr**, **Soul Coughing**'s **Sebastian Steinberg**, singer-songwriter **Lisa Germano**, and his brother, **Tim**. Finn will embark on a sellout British tour at the end of the month, in support of his second solo album, ***One Nil***, due for release next week.

15 **Joey Ramone** dies from lymphoma, age 50, in New York. As co-founder and lead singer of the **Ramones**, he became the signature voice of American punk. As a tribute at tonight's **U2** gig at the Rose Garden in Portland, Oregon, **Bono** (who reportedly telephoned the ailing punk two days ago) sings *Amazing Grace*, seguing into the Ramones' *I Remember You*.

21 **R.E.M.**'s **Peter Buck** is arrested at the end of a Seattle/Heathrow flight, charged with causing criminal damage to the plane, disobeying an aircraft commander, being drunk on board, and assaulting cabin crew. He is traveling to London to appear with the band to promote their new album, ***Reveal***, and to perform at a South Africa Freedom Day Concert in Trafalgar Square next weekend.

26 VanHalen.com (which recently launched the **Van Halen** internet radio station) posts an official statement from **Eddie Van Halen**, confirming that he has been battling cancer.

May

12 Refuting a fake Reuters email that began circulating widely on May 7, claiming that "Lou Reed was found dead in his apartment last night, apparently from an overdose of the painkiller Demerol," the veteran rocker appears on the Weekend Update egment of "Saturday Night Live." Several radio tations, including Chicago's WXRT, actually roadcast the news, then issued hasty etractions after realizing it was a hoax. The mail included "tributes" from Reed's "close ersonal friends" **David Bowie** and, more izarrely, former US Secretary of State Madeleine Albright.

24 Controversially passed over at the ecent BRITs, **Craig David** gets his just desserts at he Ivor Novello awards in London. His *Seven Days* is named Best Contemporary Song, and he s named Songwriter of the Year (along with Mark Hill). Another fast-rising **David – Gray** – abs Best Song Musically and Lyrically for his deft pop-rock pearl, *Babylon.* Punk pioneers the **Clash** are honored for their Outstanding Contribution to British Music, and **Stevie Wonder** receives a standing ovation when he is given the Special International Award. The Outstanding Song Collection trophy goes o veteran pop wizard, **Roy Wood. Iron Maiden** eceive an International Achievement trophy, and **Pete Townshend** is honored for his Lifetime Achievement as one of the country's foremost ock writers.

une

9 Billed as "an ecstatic celebration of artistry and technology, light and sound, staging and technology from the music world's most visionary star," **Madonna**'s Drowned World Tour (her first in eight years) gets under way at the Palau Saint Jordi arena in Barcelona. The sellout our is set to reach US shores on July 21 at the First Union Center in Philadelphia, and will include five dates at Madison Square Garden.

30 Having battled a brain tumor for several years, legendary guitarist **Chet Atkins** dies at 77, at home in Nashville. During a long and illustrious career, Atkins – the house guitarist at RCA during the dawn of rock 'n' roll (and a subsequent label vice-president) – released more than 100 instrumental albums, which sold over 35 million copies. His distinctive fingerwork can be heard on dozens of iconic recordings, including **Hank Williams**' *Your Cheatin' Heart,* **Elvis Presley**'s *Heartbreak Hotel,* and the **Everly Brothers**' *Wake Up Little Susie.*

July

4 As **Madonna** begins a series of dates at London's Earl's Court arena, BBC1 broadcasts the documentary "There's Only One Madonna." For the UK leg of her Drowned World tour, Madonna has broken several box office records, notably selling all 80,000 tickets in just four hours.

4 With the Napster service down for two weeks while its technical team tries to integrate a foolproof filtering device, US federal judge Marilyn Patel orders it to cease all operations, in a major victory for the record companies.

9 Interrupting their current Black & Blue World Tour, **Backstreet Boys** confirm that band member **A.J. McLean** will tomorrow begin a 30-day rehab program for depression and excessive alcohol abuse: "... AJ is our friend and our brother and we wholeheartedly support him during this difficult time. Fortunately, AJ has realized he can't solve his problems by himself. Because he is unable to be on tour at this time, we are postponing dates and will make them up as soon as we can."

11 With **Moby**'s blues-inflected electronica hybrid, *Play,* having sold more than two million copies in the US (partly thanks to extensive use of every track in television commercials), The Area: One Festival kicks off at the HiFi Buys Amphitheatre in Atlanta, Georgia. A two-stage extravaganza conceived by Moby, it features **Nelly Furtado** (emerging Canadian hip-pop singer-songwriter and *I'm Like A Bird* hitmaker), funk-metal rap combo **Incubus**, gritty southern rap duo **OutKast, New Order,** Pennsylvania's Philadelphia-based "live" rappers **Roots**, and top DJs **Paul Oakenfold, Carl Cox,** and the **Orb**.

David Grey languished without success throughout the early part of the '90s, recording three albums before he struck platinum with *White Ladder.*

JOHN LEE HOOKER

June 21 Blues legend John Lee Hooker dies in his sleep at home near San Francisco. He is 83. "All these years, I ain't done nothin' different," he told The Times during a resurgence in popularity in the 1990s. "I been doing the same things as in my younger days, when I was coming up, and now here I am, an old man, up there in the charts. And I say, well, what happened?" He will be buried at the Chapel of the Chimes Cemetery in Oakland, with the inscription "King of the Boogie" marking his gravestone.

Hooker's intense, primitive blues style hallmarked a peerless canon of more than 100 album releases, which literally helped define the blues.

July 2001

Nelly's *Country Grammar*... Alicia Keys... Aaliyah is killed...

Mariah Carey's deal with Virgin Records and her first movie "Glitter" both turned out to be busts. Carey was admitted to hospital suffering from "extreme exhaustion".

18 Breakout singalong hip-hop star **Nelly**'s debut album, the one-year-old ***Country Grammar***, is certified for seven million US sales, spurred by the success of its three smash singles: *Country Grammar*, *E.I.*, and *Ride With Me*. The album has spent five weeks at US No. 1, thanks to Nelly's accessible, laid-back vocal style and seemingly universal appeal. The street-smart rapper – real name Cornell Haynes Jr. – is also a member of his hometown posse the **St. Lunatics**, formed in 1996, whose debut album, ***Free City***, was released on June 5. Both Nelly and his group are currently touring on MTV's wildly popular "Total Request Live" US caravan, headlined by **Destiny's Child**, and also featuring rapper **Eve** and teen pop newcomer **Jessica Simpson**.

19 Appearing on MTV's "TRL" in New York City, a seemingly unsteady **Mariah Carey** arrives on set wearing a thigh-length T-shirt and shorts, and pushing an ice cream cart. She peels off the shirt (to reveal a smaller one underneath) in front of surprised host Carson Daly, who gasps: "Mariah Carey is stripping on TRL right now," before asking: "What is wrong?" Carey replies: "Every now and then somebody needs a little therapy... And today's that moment for me." Again Daly asks what's wrong, to which Carey responds: "I just wanted one day off when I can go swimming and look at rainbows and, like, eat ice cream." Next week she will check into the Silver Hill Hospital in New Canaan, Connecticut, reportedly suffering from exhaustion.

"I'm desperately trying to get out of this room. And I don't know if that makes any sense to anybody... I'm gonna be taking some time off."

Mariah Carey on her website, July 25, 2001

30 With her j records debut album ***Songs In A Minor*** holding at US No. 1, **Alicia Keys** co-hosts the seventh Soul Train Lady of Soul Awards nominations party at the Paramount Pictures Lot. An accomplished pianist and choir major at Manhattan's Professional Performance Arts School, she wrote most of the album when she was 20. Signed to Arista Records in 1998 and moved sideways to Clive Davis's new j stable, the success of Keys' maiden set has been largely spurred by the soul-drenched smash, *Fallin'*.

31 **Train** – the San Francisco-based pop/rock quintet led by **Patrick Monahan**, who recently scored a global smash with *Drops Of Jupiter* – takes over from pop/rock quartet **Lifehouse** as the opening act for **matchbox twenty**'s current ***Mad Season*** US tour. While **matchbox** is still touring behind the multiplatinum success of ***Mad Season*** (which has gone through the roof since the release of the ballad *If You're Gone*), Lifehouse's breakthrough modern rock hit, *Hanging By A Moment*, will be the most played song of the year on US radio.

August

6 Death Row label boss **Marion "Suge" Knight** is released from a Portland, Oregon, federal prison after serving nearly five years for probation violation. He tells the **Los Angeles Times**: "I want to try to do better things. You know what they say: 'Demonstration is better than conversation.' Watch me. I'm going to the studio tonight." During his absence, both **Dr. Dre** and **Snoop Dogg** have left the label.

25 Nine people, including R&B singer/actress **Aaliyah**, are killed when their plane crashes shortly after take-off from the Caribbean island of Abaco. Aaliyah was in the Bahamas shooting a video for her upcoming single, *Rock The Boat*. Initial reports indicate that the small plane was overloaded with luggage, though it will later emerge that the pilot had traces of alcohol and cocaine in his body. In addition to a successful music career, which included a Grammy nomination earlier this year for Best Female Vocalist, Aaliyah, 22, had appeared in several movies, notably "Romeo Must Die."

25 During Metallibash 2001, in San Francisco, **Metallica** cover-band **Creeping Death** is joined on stage for six songs by none other than **Lars Ulrich** and **Kirk Hammett** – who have been watching the group's set from the audience.

September

7 Ostensibly to celebrate 30 years as a solo artist (though really to prop up interest in his upcoming album ***Invincible***), **Michael Jackson** performs at the first of two self-tribute concerts

Moby, neo-soul/jazz singer Jill Scott, and the anonymous, visually enthralling Blue Man Group gave a dazzling performance at the Grammys.

FATBOY SLIM

Sept 6 **One of the most innovative videos in recent memory, Fatboy Slim's "Weapon of Choice," wins six awards (from nine nominations) at the MTV Music Video Awards. Directed by Spike Jonze, it features besuited actor Christopher Walken dancing and "flying" through a hotel lobby, and wins Best Breakthrough Video, Best Direction in a Video, Best Choreography in a Video, Best Art Direction in a Video, Best Editing in a Video, and Best Cinematography in a Video.**

"The Americans think I'm this hip new kid on the block, whereas in England, I'm this venerable old granddad, the one who always gets pissed at parties and puts a lampshade on his head."

Fatboy Slim, November, 2000

at Madison Square Garden (the second will take place on the 10th). Special guests at the all-star spectaculars include the **Jacksons**, an emaciated **Whitney Houston**, **Britney Spears**, **Monica**, **Al Jarreau**, **Gladys Knight**, **Usher**, **Luther Vandross**, **Dionne Warwick**, **Liza Minnelli**, **Marc Anthony**, ***NSync**, **Shaggy**, **Slash**, and teen country star **Billy Gilman**.

7 Critically lauded, genre-defying, 26-year-old singer-songwriter **Ryan Adams** shoots the video for his upcoming single *New York New York* alongside the Brooklyn Bridge in New York, with the World Trade Center featured in the background. Former frontman of underrated Americana combo **Whiskeytown**, the prolific Adams – who refuses to be lumped in with the burgeoning alt-folk/country genre – recently completed his sterling second effort, ***Gold***.

12 The day after terrorists attacked the World Trade Center, a significant number of US acts currently on tour cancel or postpone tonight's gigs, including **Janet Jackson** (in Tampa, Florida), **Ben Folds** (Washington, D.C.), **Stevie Nicks** (Rochester, New York), **Alison Krauss** (Cincinnati, Ohio), **matchbox twenty** and **Train** (Bossier, Louisiana), **Lifehouse** (Chicago, Illinois), **Weezer** (San Jose, California), **Black Crowes** (Los Angeles), and **Crosby Stills & Nash** (Denver, Colorado). The Latin Grammy Awards are postponed until October 30.

21 A unique commercial-free, multinetwork telethon, "America: A Tribute To Heroes," is broadcast live from New York, Los Angeles, and London, to honor the victims and heroes of the recent 9/11 tragedy. **Bruce Springsteen** opens an emotion-drenched show with his unrecorded homage, *My City Of Ruins*. Other musical tributes are provided by **Billy Joel**, **Paul Simon**, **Neil Young**, **Mariah Carey**, **Sheryl Crow**, **Eddie Vedder**, **Stevie Wonder**, **Jon Bon Jovi**, **Faith Hill**, the **Dixie Chicks**, **Wyclef Jean**, **Celine Dion** with **David Foster**, **Enrique Iglesias**, **Alicia Keys**, **Sting**, **Tom Petty**, and **U2**. **Willie Nelson** closes a somber and patriotic evening with a performance of *America The Beautiful*, backed by an all-star chorus. $150 million is raised in pledges.

23 Anonymously placed by **Yoko Ono** as her response to 9/11, a full-page ad with the words "Imagine all the people living life in peace" appears in today's **The New York Times**.

October

2 "Come Together: A Night for John Lennon's Words and Music" is held at New York's Radio City Music Hall, and is aired live on TNT and the WB. Originally scheduled as a stand-alone **Lennon** tribute, tonight's all-star celebration has taken on additional meaning after the city's recent tragedy, and is being used to raise funds for relief organizations. Among this evening's stellar performers are **Alanis Morissette**, **Stone Temple Pilots**, **Moby**, **Marc Anthony**, ***Natalie Merchant***, and the **Dave**

The Foo Fighters had to cancel the remaining dates of their European tour in August after drummer Taylor Hawkins was hospitalized, apparently due to over-indulgent partying.

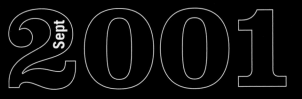

The Concert for New York City... Alan Jackson's patriotic tribute... George Harrison dies...

Matthews Band. The event – organized by TNT with **Yoko Ono** – is hosted by Kevin Spacey, who somehow pulls off a respectable solo version of *Mind Games*, and it climaxes with the whole assembly singing *Give Peace a Chance.*

4 **Usher** wins best R&B Act and Best Album at the sixth annual MOBO Awards held at the London Arena. The 23-year-old throwback R&B stylist from Chattanooga, Tennessee, who auditioned in the office of **LAFace**'s **L.A. Reid** when he was 13, is currently enjoying Top 10 success with his latest effort – *8701* – having already sold six million copies of his sophomore album *My Way.*

20 **David Bowie** opens The Concert for New York City at Madison Square Garden with a version of **Paul Simon**'s *America*, followed by *Heroes*. The five-hour all-star music marathon – broadcast live and commercial-free on VH1 and Westwood One radio, and simulcast on AOL.com – is being staged to benefit the Robin Hood Relief Fund, which is supporting victims of the 9/11 attack, and to honor the Big Apple's fire, police, and rescue workers. Other artists appearing include **Mick Jagger**, **Eric Clapton**, **Billy Joel**, the **Who**, **Elton John**, **Janet Jackson**, the **Backstreet Boys**, **Bon Jovi**, **Bono** and **The Edge** from **U2**, **James Taylor**, **John Mellencamp**, **Destiny's Child**, **Marc Anthony**, **Five for Fighting** (aka singer-songwriter/pianist **John Ondrasik**, whose recent hit, the plaintive ballad *Superman (It's Not Easy)* has become the song perhaps most associated with the 9/11 tragedy), **Macy Gray**, the **Goo Goo Dolls**, **Melissa Etheridge**, and **India.Arie**. **Paul McCartney** closes an alternately sad and triumphant show leading an all-star throng – which includes members of the police, firefighters, and other rescue crews – on *Let It Be.*

21 United We Stand – another 9/11 fundraising concert – is staged at Washington, D.C.'s RFK Stadium, with performances by **P. Diddy**, **O-Town**, **Carole King**, ***NSync**, **Michael Jackson**, the **Backstreet Boys**, **Aerosmith**, **Mariah Carey**, **Rod Stewart**, **Destiny's Child**, **Pink**, the **Goo Goo Dolls**, **Train**, **Bette Midler**, and **America**.

November

7 **Alan Jackson** gives a show-stopping performance of his new song, *Where Were You (When The World Stopped Turning)* – penned in response to the events of 9/11 – at the Country Music Awards in Nashville. He receives a standing ovation. The lyrics include the chorus: "I'm just a singer of simple songs/I'm not a real political man/I watch CNN but I'm not sure I could/Tell you the difference in Iraq and Iran/ But I know Jesus and I talk to God/And I remember this from when I was young/Faith, hope, and love are some good things he gave us/And the greatest is love."

8 Beamed to 139 countries, and highlighted by a performance of **Led Zeppelin**'s *Thank You* by **Fred Durst**, **Jimmy Page**, and **Wes Scantlin** (lead singer with **Puddle of Mudd**, an emerging alt-metal combo and one of the first signings to Durst's new Flawless label), the MTV European Music Awards are held at the Festival Hall Arena, Frankfurt, Germany. **Blur**'s **Damon Albarn** – collecting trophies for Best Song (*Clint Eastwood*) and Best Dance Act (both for his "virtual" dance band, **Gorillaz**, who exist only in animated form) – points to his CND T-shirt and says, in reference to the war in Afghanistan, "See this symbol. This is the Campaign for Nuclear Disarmament. Bombing one of the poorest countries in the world is wrong." Several American artists – including Best Female honoree **Jennifer Lopez** – have elected to stay in the US during these troubling times but Best Pop Act winner **Anastacia**, the American dance/pop singer who has stormed the Euro-dance scene with her debut album *Not That Kind*, comments: "I don't believe in fear. I don't believe in intimidation. I respect the way the other [Americans] feel. I lost half my band because people wouldn't travel. I

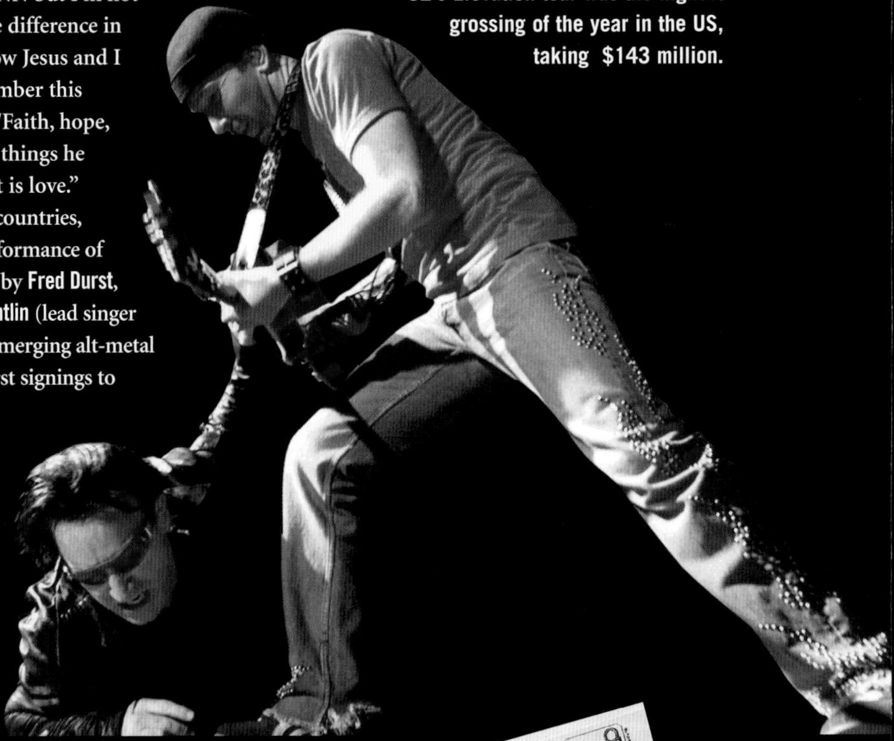

U2's Elevation tour was the highest grossing of the year in the US, taking $143 million.

Madonna broke several box office records for the UK leg of her Drowned World tour, not least selling all 80,000 tickets in just four hours.

Destiny's Child dismissed rumors they were splitting up in a statement published in Billboard in December, although acknowledged solo projects were planned.

had to hire new people. I wanted to be on stage and I wanted to perform." One of the evening's hottest performances – which also include those by Best New Act **Dido**, **U2**, **R.E.M.**, **Depeche Mode**, and **Atomic Kitten** – comes from sex kitten **Kylie Minogue**, performing her recent UK chart-topping sizzler, *Can't Get You Out Of My Head*. **Robbie Williams** is named Best Male Act, **Limp Bizkit** triumph in three categories, **Craig David** picks up two, and **Eminem** is named Best Hip-Hop Act.

21 Former music impresario and hitmaker, 56-year-old **Jonathan King** is given a seven-year prison sentence in a London court. Having consistently denied all allegations and charges, he was found guilty on September 27 of four indecent assaults and two serious sexual offences against boys aged 14 and 15, committed in the 1980s. He will have to sign the sex offenders' register for life, and will be barred from working with children. Character witnesses for King have included former BBC Radio 1 colleague and DJ Simon Bates, lyricist Sir Tim Rice, and "Wheel of Fortune" presenter Jenny Powell.

30 A book of condolence is opened for **George Harrison** at Liverpool Town Hall, where flags fly at half-staff. In London, the Coldstream Guards band play a tribute **Beatles** medley during the Changing of the Guard ceremony at Buckingham Palace. Speaking outside his home in St. John's Wood, **Sir Paul McCartney** says: "I am devastated and very very sad. We knew he'd been ill for a long time. He was a lovely guy and a very brave man and had a wonderful sense of humour. He is really just my baby brother."

December

11 Performing at a show to celebrate the 100th anniversary of the Nobel Peace Prize at the Spektrum Concert Hall in Oslo, Norway, **Sir Paul McCartney** is joined by **Anastacia**, **Wyclef Jean**, and **Youssou N'Dour** on *Let It Be*. He also sings *Your Loving Flame* and *Freedom*, from his latest solo album, and says: "The first one I wrote for my fiancée, Heather [Mills], and the second one I wrote for the American people after September 11, but tonight I'd like to dedicate them both to my friend George."

15 R&B legend **Rufus Thomas** dies at the St. Francis Hospital in Memphis, Tennessee, age 84. His seven-decade music career included a stint in the 1940s as one of the city's most popular DJs on WDIA. One of the foremost pioneers of 1950s R&B, the Official Ambassador of Beale Street recorded for both Sun Records and Stax. He was still performing around the world into his eighties, even appearing at the groundbreaking ceremony for the Stax Museum of American Soul Music on April 20 this year.

19 In Los Angeles, **Dick Clark** files a $10 million lawsuit against beleaguered NARAS president Michael Greene, alleging that he keeps a "blacklist" of artists that prevents them from appearing on the Grammy Awards if they attend the competing American Music Awards (produced by Dick Clark Productions). The allegations specifically cite Greene taking recent action to stop **Michael Jackson** from appearing on the upcoming AMAs on January 9. The Academy denies any wrongdoing. It will, however, soon settle a $650,000 sexual-harassment/battery lawsuit brought against Greene by former NARAS executive Jill Marie Geimer. Greene will resign from NARAS on April 27 next year.

GEORGE HARRISON

Nov 29 George Harrison loses his battle with cancer, dying at approximately 1:30 pm in Los Angeles, at the age of 58. Long-time friend Gavin De Becker says: "He died with one thought in mind – love one another." His wife Olivia and 24-year-old son Dhani are both with him when he passes away. His body will be cremated in a cardboard coffin without a ceremony, in accordance with Harrison's eastern faith, and his ashes will reportedly be scattered on the River Yamuna in India. The family's statement reads: "He left this world as he lived in it, conscious of God, fearless of death, and at peace, surrounded by family and friends. He often said, 'Everything else can wait but the search for God cannot wait, and love one another'."

ROOTS During this year: beating out hundreds of other wannabes in auditions for TV director/producer Ivan Shapovalov, teen-pop duo – and alleged lesbian lovers – 15-year-old Julia Olegovna Volkova and 16-year-old Elena Sergeevna Katina are signed to Universal Music Russia under the name t.A.T.u.... progressive UK dance/electronic trio Dirty Vegas record their first single, *Days Go By* – which will be picked up for a Mitsubishi car commercial next year and become a global smash... New Zealand-born, UK-based dance/pop singer-songwriter Daniel Bedingfield records *Gotta Get Thru This* on a computer in his bedroom, subsequently eliciting universal disinterest from major record labels; the song will eventually emerge on the underground club compilation *Pure Garage 4*... BBC Radio 1 FM DJ Steve Lamacq hails Leeds-based British rock quartet the Music as the "best unsigned band in Britain"... meanwhile, the NME declares unknown Aussie garage rock protagonists the Vines as "the coolest band on the planet"...

A Moment Like This

2002

No.1 US SINGLES

Jan 5	How You Remind Me **Nickelback**
Jan 19	U Got It Bad **Usher**
Feb 23	Always On Time **Ja Rule featuring Ashanti**
Mar 9	Ain't It Funny **Jennifer Lopez featuring Ja Rule**
Apr 20	Foolish **Ashanti**
June 29	Hot In Herre **Nelly**
Aug 17	Dilemma **Nelly featuring Kelly Rowland**
Oct 5	A Moment Like This **Kelly Clarkson**
Oct 19	Dilemma **Nelly featuring Kelly Rowland**
Nov 9	Lose Yourself **Eminem**

No.1 UK SINGLES

Jan 5	Somethin' Stupid **Robbie Williams & Nicole Kidman**
Jan 12	Gotta Get Thru This **Daniel Bedingfield**
Jan 19	More Than A Woman **Aaliyah**
Jan 26	My Sweet Lord **George Harrison**
Feb 2	Hero **Enrique Iglesias**
Mar 2	World Of Our Own **Westlife**
Mar 9	Evergreen/Anything Is Possible **Will Young**
Mar 30	Unchained Melody **Gareth Gates**
Apr 27	The Hindu Times **Oasis**
May 4	Freak Like Me **Sugababes**
May 11	Kiss Kiss **Holly Valance**
May 18	If Tomorrow Never Comes **Ronan Keating**
May 25	Just A Little **Liberty X**
June 1	Without Me **Eminem**
June 8	Light My Fire **Will Young**
June 22	A Little Less Conversation **Elvis Vs. JXL**
July 20	Anyone Of Us (Stupid Mistake) **Gareth Gates**
Aug 10	Colourblind **Darius**
Aug 24	Round Round **Sugababes**
Aug 31	Crossroads **Blazin' Squad**
Sept 7	The Tide Is High (Get The Feeling) **Atomic Kitten**
Sept 28	Just Like A Pill **Pink**
Oct 5	The Long And Winding Road/Suspicious Minds **Will Young/Gareth Gates**
Oct 19	The Ketchup Song (Aserje) **Las Ketchup**
Oct 26	Dilemma **Nelly featuring Kelly Rowland**
Nov 9	Heaven **DJ Sammy & Yanou featuring Do**
Nov 16	Unbreakable **Westlife**
Nov 23	Dirrty **Christina Aguilera featuring Redman**

Norah Jones

Nelly

Norah Jones, daughter of Ravi Shankar, proved that, when all is said and done, it's the songs that count... Nelly became the first artist to replace himself at US No. 1 since the Beatles did it in 1964.

As rock 'n' roll approached its 50th anniversary, style – more than ever – became more important than substance. Music was being mixed into previously unthinkable hybrids. **Limp Bizkit**, **Staind**, and **Puddle of Mudd** led an aggressive armada of hybrid rock/rap/nu-metal groups that plugged into a nu generation of disaffected youth. Rap became the predominant seller, with **Eminem** using the time-honored device of shocking everyone to sell tens of millions of albums. Joining him as one of the world's few new global stars was **Nelly**, with a more mainstream, sex/pop meld.

As profane as Eminem, but immensely more likeable, metal veteran **Ozzy Osbourne** scored a surprise television hit with "The Osbournes," while another cheeky Brit, **Robbie Williams**, signed a jaw-dropping multi-album deal with EMI. **Creed** and **Nickelback** spearheaded the limp but successful "emo" power rock genre in the US, and veteran acts like **Elton John**, **Paul McCartney**, and the **Rolling Stones** received their biggest paychecks from hugely successful tours – even though they were now shut out from Top 40 radio.

The record industry moaned about declining sales, chiefly blaming internet and CD piracy, but while new technology was making life difficult for the mostly cloth-eared accountants and lawyers running the industry, their lack of what **George Martin** once called "good ears" was at the root of the problem. When a label did get it right, no amount of piracy prevented huge sales. The venerable jazz imprint Blue Note Records released an album by **Norah Jones** that defied the slump for one simple reason: it was great music. With intelligent promotion and strong word of mouth, the multi-Grammy winning ***Come Away With Me*** shifted more than 10 million copies worldwide.

The monopolistic consolidation of radio was making good music hard to find. While Europe played catch-up with the stultifying American strategy of strictly formatted, genre-specific radio stations, corporate US radio was making it nearly impossible to hear new music. Meanwhile, the record companies virtually refused to release singles in the US, but why would anyone shell out $20 for an album with only one good song on it? In the absence of the record labels doing their job, it was left to television talent shows to do their A&R for them. The trend, unsurprisingly, threw up a truly average bunch of 15-minute wonders. And they wondered why the industry was in decline...

While the good and great of rock's early and middle years were passing away, the new vanguard of mainstream pop music was mostly a vapid collection of rappers, rockers, and DJs (who aren't musicians). Everything was getting dumbed down. Great music – featuring real musicianship – was still, as always, being created by talented musicians (**Coldplay**) and songwriters (**John Mayer**) – but it was becoming increasingly hard to hear, see, or find.

When **Sam Phillips** set up shop in Memphis, it is doubtful he could have imagined what would follow.

Dec 7 If You're Not The One **Daniel Bedingfield**
Dec 14 Lose Yourself **Eminem**
Dec 21 Sorry Seems To Be The Hardest Word **Blue featuring Elton John**
Dec 28 Sound Of The Underground **Girls Aloud**

"We feel more united, ambitious and stronger than ever."

Hear'Say, following the departure of Kym Marsh. By the end of the year, they were no more. January 24, 2002

Jan 2002

Mariah Carey says goodbye to Virgin... "Pop Idol"... Alicia Keys is the big Grammy winner...

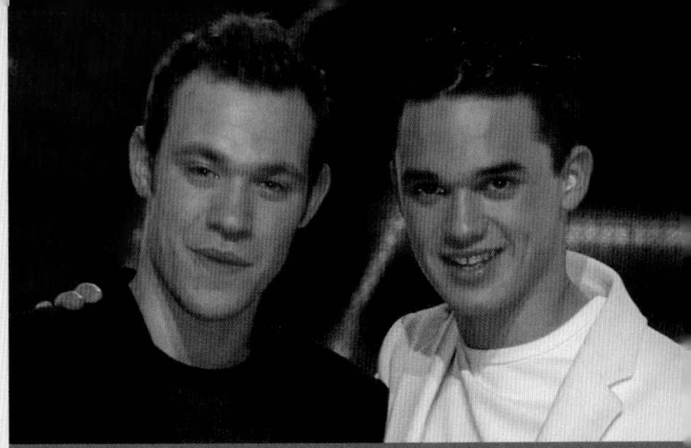
Will Young and Gareth Gates

January

12 **Pink** performs her current smash, *Get The Party Started*, and its follow-up, *Don't Let Me Get Me*, on "Saturday Night Live." Promoting her second album, ***M!ssundaztood***, the sassy 22-year-old pop/R&B singer-songwriter and self-confessed "wild child" is building on the global success of her maiden offering, ***Can't Take Me Home***. Her first headlining US tour begins on May 2 in Phoenix, Arizona.

14 Having been arrested two days ago following a disturbance at the Prince of Wales pub in Kentish Town, north London, **Adam Ant** is arrested again at Camden Lock, after relatives – concerned that he is suicidal – contacted the police. He is taken to the secure ward of the Royal Free Hospital and sectioned under the Mental Health Act. Ant is scheduled to join **Spandau Ballet** and **Toyah** on a 1980s revival UK tour in April.

16 The Official UK Charts Company reveals that it has erred in nominating **Dido** for a Best New Artist BRIT award, as her inclusion in last year's nominations for Best Female Artist makes her ineligible. Singer-songwriter **Tom McRae** replaces her, joining other nominees **Atomic Kitten** (also nominated last year), rising UK boy band **Blue**, guitar-based Mancunian quintet **Elbow**, virtual hip-hoppers **Gorillaz**, British all-female act **Mis-Teeq** (who are pioneering mainstream acceptance of garage/2-Step), equally fresh 2-Step combo **So Solid Crew**, current rock media faves **Starsailor**, alt-folk/pop duo **Turin Brakes**, and red-hot electronica combo **Zero 7**. Dido doesn't seem too concerned. Her debut album, ***No Angel***, was last year's biggest-selling album, and she is nominated in three other BRIT categories: Best Video, Solo Female, and Album. (This is not the first time such an error has occurred. Two years ago, **Wamdue Project**'s *King Of My Castle* was removed from the Best British Single category, when it was discovered that the act was an American called **Chris Brann**.)

Pink, real name Alecia Moore, was signed to L.A. Reid's LaFace label in 1999.

> **"I think my father thought that nothing was going to happen, that I wasn't going to be successful, but not because he doesn't believe in me – he was just being realistic about the music industry."**
>
> Enrique Iglesias, **Sunday Times**, January 13, 2002

23 Just over two weeks after EMI Records denied that she was being dropped by its Virgin subsidiary, **Mariah Carey** receives a $28 million buyout from the company (which is looking to cut costs amid rumored corporate mergings, first with Warner Music, then with BMG), one album into her five-album deal.

February

3 **U2** give a memorable half-time performance at Super Bowl XXXVI in New Orleans. Performing *Beautiful Day*, *MLK*, and *Where The Streets Have No Name*, they pay tribute to those who lost their lives on 9/11, with the names of the victims scrolled on a screen behind them. **Paul McCartney**, who was in New York when the hijacked planes struck the World Trade Center, sings his 9/11-inspired *Freedom*.

9 During the two-hour final between singers **Gareth Gates** and **Will Young**, some nine million ITV viewers vote to decide the winner of the inaugural "Pop Idol" series. Young's win will instantly translate into commercial success, with his double A-side single, *Evergreen/Anything Is Possible*, shooting to UK No. 1 next month, and becoming the fastest-selling debut single in UK history. Loser Gates's own debut – yet another revival of *Unchained Melody* – replaces Young in the top spot. A total of 14 million viewers tune into the "Pop Idol" climax to see Young win. The creation of Simon Fuller, the man behind the **Spice Girls** and **S Club 7**, "Pop Idol" was launched last fall on Thames Television, and will go on to create similar hoopla in the US, when re-versioned as "American Idol" in the summer on Fox TV. The US winner will be **Kelly Clarkson**, whose debut single *A Moment Like This*, will achieve similar success, vaulting from No. 52 to No. 1 in October, breaking the **Beatles**' 38-year-old record (when *Can't Buy Me Love* leapt from No. 27 to No. 1). (Swedish tunesmith **Jorgen Elofsson** is a co-writer on both Young's and Clarkson's hits.) Both the domestic and US versions of the show will make a star out of judge Simon Cowell, a veteran record executive whose no-holds-barred comments cause many an upset. Tamika Bush, a contestant on "American Idol," on being told that she is not a very good singer, responds by calling Cowell an ass, going on to say, "He can kiss my natural-born black ass."

14 In a week that has seen the deaths of veteran folk and blues singer **Dave Van Ronk** and country legend **Waylon Jennings**, **Mick Tucker** (drummer with 1970s glam rockers the **Sweet**) dies from leukemia in Welwyn Garden City, England. Bassist **Steve Priest** says: "He was the best drummer England ever produced and it is a sad loss to the music world." Van Ronk, who succumbed to colon cancer at the New York University Medical Center on the 10th, was a profound influence on such artists as **Bob Dylan**, **Tom Paxton**, and **Peter Yarrow**, as well as a subsequent generation of folk artists, including **Janis Ian**, **Christine Lavin**, and **Suzanne Vega**. Jennings died at home in Chandler, Arizona, yesterday, after a long battle with diabetes. With **Willie Nelson**, he pioneered the "outlaw" country movement in the mid-1970s, and then became a

U2

Fourteen million viewers tuned in to watch the "Pop Idol" final between Will Young and Gareth Gates... After U2's performance, the Super Bowl ended fittingly with the underdog New England Patriots, wearing red, white, and blue, upsetting the heavily favored St. Louis Rams, with Adam Vinatieri's 48-yard field goal as time expired.

member of the **Highwaymen**, with Nelson, **Johnny Cash**, and **Kris Kristofferson**. Never afraid to buck the trend, he even had a Hot 100 hit with a country version of **Jimmy Webb**'s *MacArthur Park*, and made the Country singles charts nearly 100 times, with more than a dozen No. 1s. Despite the impact he made on country music, Jennings is perhaps best remembered for giving up his seat to the **Big Bopper** on the fateful flight that killed **Buddy Holly** in 1959.

20 At a particularly lackluster ceremony, **Dido** and **Kylie Minogue** win a pair of awards each at the 21st BRIT Awards, Dido for Best British Female Solo Artist and Best British Album (***No Angel***), and Kylie for Best International Female Solo Artist and Best International Album (***Fever***). **Robbie Williams**, winning his third Best British Male Solo Artist award in four years, is on typically brash form: "Third time, Best Male Artist – it's amazing, it really is amazing. I'd just like to say to Will from "Popstars" [sic], I'm too strong buddy. You want to come and take my food off my table, stop my kids going through school. **Craig David** couldn't do it – what makes you think you can do it?" Garage-rock revivalists the **Strokes**, a New York band more popular in the UK than at home, pick up the Best International Newcomer award, and **Travis** win their second BRIT, this time for Best British Group.

26 Four Concerts for Artists' Rights take place simultaneously at four venues in the Los Angeles area, to raise funds for the Recording Artists' Coalition. The organization is working, among other things, for the repeal of the section of the California Labor Code that excludes recording artists from the personal service contract, limiting employment to seven years. The four sellout shows feature the **Eagles** – whose **Don Henley** is a prime mover in the coalition – **Sheryl Crow**, **John Fogerty**, **Billy Joel**, and **Stevie Nicks** at the Forum; **No Doubt**, the **Offspring**, and **Weezer** at the Long Beach Arena; the **Dixie Chicks**, folk singer-songwriter **Patty Griffin**, **Emmylou Harris**, country superstar **Trisha Yearwood**, and **Dwight Yoakam** at the Universal Amphitheatre; and **Beck**, **Eddie Vedder**, **Thom Yorke**, and ex-**Social Distortion** frontman, **Mike Ness**, at the Wiltern Theatre. With RAC leading a growing sentiment of artist independence throughout the industry, a reported $2.7 million is raised.

Kylie Minogue was on another career roll, spurred by her sizzling pop/dance smash (and steamy video) *Can't Get You Out Of My Head*, which restored her chart status in the US.

Paul McCartney drives through the US... Norah Jones emerges... Lisa "Left Eye" Lopes is killed...

27 Newcomer **Alicia Keys** picks up five Grammy Awards at the 44th ceremony, including Song of the Year (for *Fallin'*) and Best New Artist. However, the surprise of the evening is the Album of the Year: a bluegrass soundtrack collection, and a triumph for its veteran producer T-Bone Burnette. ***O Brother, Where Art Thou?***, an integral part of the Coen Brothers' 21st-century movie interpretation of Homer's "Odyssey," entered the US chart at No. 192 last January, and this week actually drops from No. 11 to No. 16, before topping the survey next month on the strength of its unexpected honor. It features songs from **Alison Krauss**, **Emmylou Harris**, **Gillian Welch**, bluegrass great **Ralph Stanley**, **John Hartford**, and the **Fairfield Four**. (Only three records have taken longer to top the chart.) The album's success has spawned the equally successful Down from the Mountain tour, featuring Krauss, Harris, Welch, **Patty Loveless**, and others. **U2** have another big night – winning Record of the Year for *Walk On*, Best Rock Album (***All That You Can't Leave Behind***), Best Pop Performance by a Duo or Group (*Stuck In A Moment You Can't Get Out Of*), and Best Rock Performance by a Duo or Group (*Elevation*). The most nominated act of the night, lead singer **Bono** says: "Being Irish, if you get eight nominations and got no awards they wouldn't let you back in the country... so this is a public safety issue." Three-time winners last year, U2's Grammy tally now stands at 14. In what will turn out to be his last Grammys as president of NARAS, Michael Greene delivers a particularly controversial speech on the "insidious virus in our midst... the illegal downloading of music on the net," continuing, "This illegal file sharing and ripping of music files is pervasive, out of control, and oh so criminal."

March

18 **Isaac Hayes**, **Tom Petty & the Heartbreakers**, the **Ramones**, **Talking Heads**, and the long overdue **Brenda Lee** and **Gene Pitney**, take their place in the Rock and Roll Hall of Fame at the 17th ceremony, at New York's Waldorf Astoria Hotel. Lee, feeling "like Cinderella at the ball," is inducted by **Jewel**, and Pitney is welcomed by **Darlene Love**. **Eddie Vedder** inducts the Ramones, with a speech that lasts almost as long as one of their albums; **Jakob Dylan**, who used to watch from the wings as his father performed with the act, inducts Tom Petty & the Heartbreakers, and Hayes is inducted by **Alicia Keys**. Talking Heads (inducted by **Anthony Kiedis**) perform together for the first time for 18 years, singing *Psycho Killer, Burning Down The*

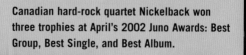

Canadian hard-rock quartet Nickelback won three trophies at April's 2002 Juno Awards: Best Group, Best Single, and Best Album.

THE OSBOURNES

Mar 5 **MTV premieres "The Osbournes," a fly-on-the-wall documentary of life with rocker Ozzy Osbourne and his family – wife Sharon, daughter Kelly, and son Jack – as they move into their new Beverly Hills home. The series will quickly join the echelon of "must-see" and water-cooler topic TV, as the bumbling patriarch struggles with his TV remote control, swears at the not-yet-housetrained dogs, and mediates rows between siblings Kelly and Jack – while stoic matriarch Sharon just tries to keep it all together. The family, who are fond of profanity (and whose favorite word begins with the letter F) have to be bleeped some 60 times in this opening episode. The show will elevate the genial veteran rocker into a media darling.**

"The Osbournes" first episode was MTV's highest-rated premiere, with 3.2 million households tuning in.

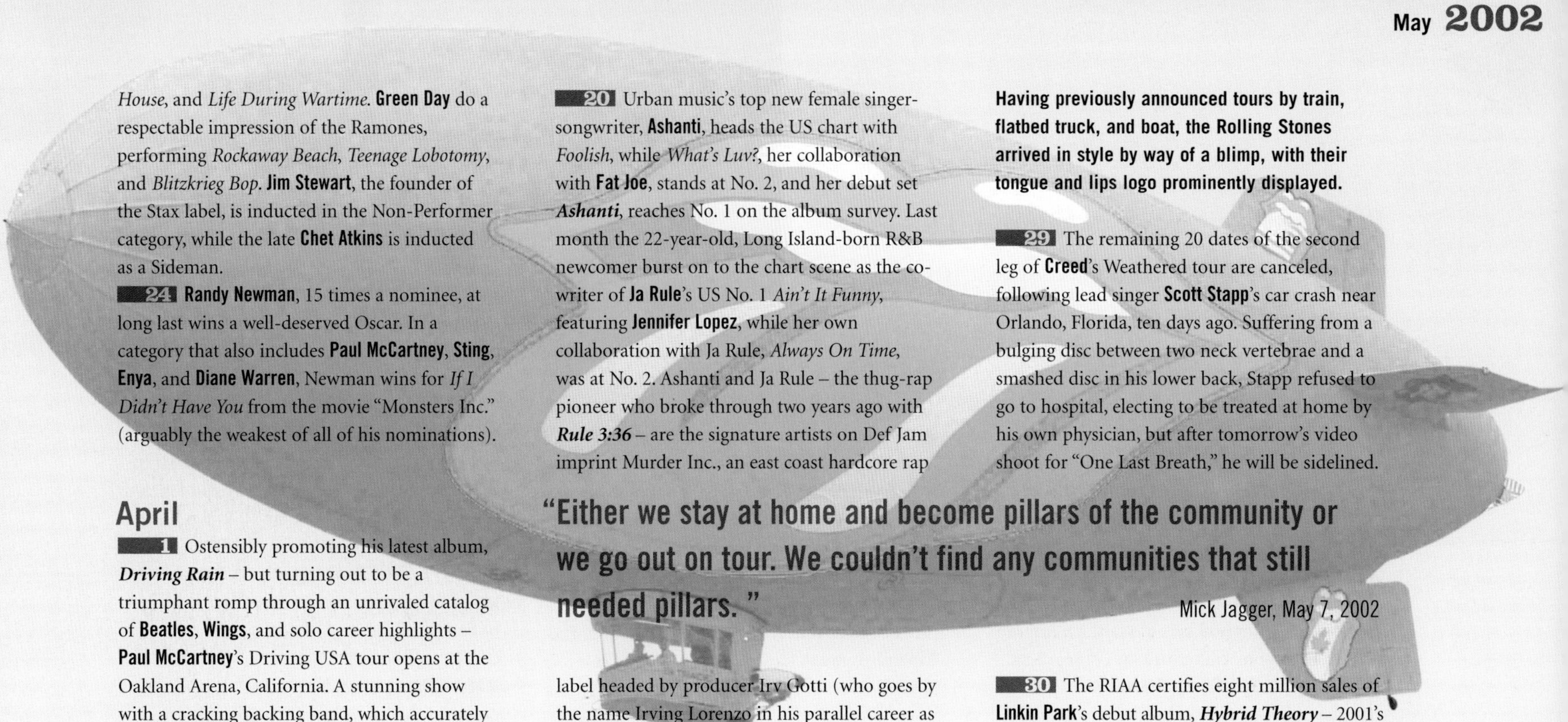

House, and *Life During Wartime*. **Green Day** do a respectable impression of the Ramones, performing *Rockaway Beach*, *Teenage Lobotomy*, and *Blitzkrieg Bop*. **Jim Stewart**, the founder of the Stax label, is inducted in the Non-Performer category, while the late **Chet Atkins** is inducted as a Sideman.

24 **Randy Newman**, 15 times a nominee, at long last wins a well-deserved Oscar. In a category that also includes **Paul McCartney**, **Sting**, **Enya**, and **Diane Warren**, Newman wins for *If I Didn't Have You* from the movie "Monsters Inc." (arguably the weakest of all of his nominations).

April

1 Ostensibly promoting his latest album, ***Driving Rain*** – but turning out to be a triumphant romp through an unrivaled catalog of **Beatles**, **Wings**, and solo career highlights – **Paul McCartney**'s Driving USA tour opens at the Oakland Arena, California. A stunning show with a cracking backing band, which accurately recreates the sound of each era of his career, and including musical tributes to his late wife **Linda**, his bride-to-be Heather Mills, and **George Harrison**, it will become the top-grossing trek of the year, raking in $103.3 million from 53 shows in 43 cities on two North American legs (the second of which is called Back in the U.S.), and further dates in Japan and Mexico.

5 **R.E.M.**'s guitarist **Peter Buck** is cleared of all charges stemming from the incident aboard a British Airways flight last April.

13 Singer-songwriter/pianist **Norah Jones** makes her major TV debut on CNN International's "The Music Room." The New York-born 23-year-old (who is reluctant to discuss the fact that she is a daughter of **Ravi Shankar**) attended the Booker T. Washington School for the Performing and Visual Arts in Dallas, and began performing live at the age of 16. Signed to jazz label Blue Note early last year, her plaintive maiden album, ***Come Away With Me*** – a critically lauded, mellow and sensual collection of jazz/soul/country/folk-laced gems – will gather commercial steam throughout the year, mostly via word of mouth and notably as a stunning musical antidote to just about every popular music genre around.

19 **Alice In Chains**' lead singer **Layne Staley** is found dead in his Seattle home from an apparent heroin overdose at the age of 34. The band – a staple of US alt-rock during the mid-1990s – topped the US album chart twice, but Staley's drug addiction had constantly hindered their progress.

20 Urban music's top new female singer-songwriter, **Ashanti**, heads the US chart with *Foolish*, while *What's Luv?*, her collaboration with **Fat Joe**, stands at No. 2, and her debut set ***Ashanti***, reaches No. 1 on the album survey. Last month the 22-year-old, Long Island-born R&B newcomer burst on to the chart scene as the co-writer of **Ja Rule**'s US No. 1 *Ain't It Funny*, featuring **Jennifer Lopez**, while her own collaboration with Ja Rule, *Always On Time*, was at No. 2. Ashanti and Ja Rule – the thug-rap pioneer who broke through two years ago with ***Rule 3:36*** – are the signature artists on Def Jam imprint Murder Inc., an east coast hardcore rap label headed by producer Irv Gotti (who goes by the name Irving Lorenzo in his parallel career as a hit songwriter).

25 **Lisa "Left Eye" Lopes**, of the R&B trio **TLC**, dies following a car accident near Jutiapa in Honduras. She is driving a rental car, with six passengers on board, which leaves the road. She is the only fatality. Her TLC colleagues, **Rozonda Thomas** and **Tionne Watkins**, issue a statement: "We had all grown up together and were as close as a family. Today we have truly lost our sister." Lopes recently signed a deal with Suge Knight's new Tha Row label, for a solo project under the name NINA (New Identity Not Applicable).

"Either we stay at home and become pillars of the community or we go out on tour. We couldn't find any communities that still needed pillars."

Mick Jagger, May 7, 2002

Having previously announced tours by train, flatbed truck, and boat, the Rolling Stones arrived in style by way of a blimp, with their tongue and lips logo prominently displayed.

29 The remaining 20 dates of the second leg of **Creed**'s Weathered tour are canceled, following lead singer **Scott Stapp**'s car crash near Orlando, Florida, ten days ago. Suffering from a bulging disc between two neck vertebrae and a smashed disc in his lower back, Stapp refused to go to hospital, electing to be treated at home by his own physician, but after tomorrow's video shoot for "One Last Breath," he will be sidelined.

30 The RIAA certifies eight million sales of **Linkin Park**'s debut album, ***Hybrid Theory*** – 2001's best-selling US record. Following in the footsteps of **KoRn** and **Limp Bizkit**, the Los Angeles-based nu-metal sextet, formed in 1996, signed with Warner Bros. in 1999, when lead singer Chester Bennington joined. Last year they took part in the Family Values, Ozzfest, and Projekt Revolution caravans, playing 324 shows in all.

May

6 **Otis Blackwell**, songwriter behind some of the most memorable hits of the 1950s, including *All Shook Up*, *Don't Be Cruel*, *Fever*, and *Great Balls Of Fire*, dies of a heart attack in Nashville, at the age of 70. His career began after he sold a demo tape of six of his songs to a music publisher for $150 in 1955. One of them, *Don't Be Cruel*, caught the ear of **Elvis Presley**, who recorded the song in similar vein to Blackwell's own demo. His renowned versatility led Al Stanton, of the Shalimar publishing company, to challenge him to write a song about a bottle of fizzy drink. His response? *All Shook Up*, a No. 1 smash for Presley in 1957. He wrote several other hits for Presley, including *One Broken Heart For Sale* and *Return To Sender*. Blackwell, credited with penning more than 1,000 songs, once commented, "It makes me feel wonderful for other people to do my songs and have them still be around."

7 The **Rolling Stones** announce their latest tour in New York City's Van Cortlandt Park. The 32-date trek will open at Foxborough's CMGI Field on September 5, celebrating the band's 40th anniversary. After the North American leg, the tour will travel through Europe, Australia, Mexico, and the Far East, where concerts in Hong Kong, Shanghai and, Beijing will be canceled because of the SARS epidemic.

Ashanti's debut album sold more than 500,000 copies in its first week in the stores, going gold, platinum, and multi-platinum inside a month.

2002 May

British rock royalty celebrate the Queen's 50th... Dee Dee Ramone dies... Sir Mick Jagger...

R. Kelly

Alan Lomax

22 **Alien Ant Farm** and six members of their crew are injured, and their driver is killed, when their tour bus crashes near Navalmoral de la Mata in Spain. The Grammy-nominated band – who broke through to the mainstream last year with their alt-rock cover of **Michael Jackson**'s *Smooth Criminal* – were traveling from Luxembourg to Lisbon, at the end of a European tour in support of their platinum-selling album, ***ANThology***. Singer **Dryden Mitchell** is airlifted to hospital in London, while the rest of the band return home.

25 The annual Memorial Day weekend HFStival – sponsored by radio station 99.1 WHFS – gets under way at the RFK Stadium in Washington, D.C., with a headlining performance by **Eminem**, in support of his new album, ***The Eminem Show***, due in stores tomorrow. His set is delayed when two dozen people are injured in a mosh pit close to the stage. Also on hand are the **Strokes**, **N.E.R.D.** – the recording/performing arm of the **Neptunes** (**Chad Hugo** and **Pharrell Williams**, who are the hottest hip-hop production team of the past three years) – alt-metal rockers **Papa Roach**, and much-touted San Francisco-based rock trio, **Black Rebel Motorcycle Club**. An alternative stage features up-and-coming acts, red-hot Australian post-grungers the **Vines**, and indie rockers **Phantom Planet**, while UK DJ **Paul Oakenfold** spins and mixes in the rave tent.

27 Skater-punk/pop newcomer, 17-year-old Ontario-born **Avril Lavigne**'s first "journal" entry appears on her website, with a PS: "my cd comes out in like a week. June 4. all I can really say is... Finally!"

June

3 Celebrating Elizabeth II's 50 years as British monarch, the Party at the Palace all-star rock bash takes place at Buckingham Palace. Opening with **Queen**'s **Brian May** performing *God Save The Queen* from the Palace roof, the varied line-up includes **Elton John**, **Cliff Richard**, **Ozzy Osbourne**, **Will Young**, **Joe Cocker**, **Tom Jones**, **Rod Stewart**, **Annie Lennox**, the **Kinks**' **Ray Davies**, **Steve Winwood**, **Phil Collins**, and **Eric Clapton** performing with **Brian Wilson** and the **Corrs**. The climax features **Paul McCartney** leading a celebrity throng in *Hey Jude* and *All You Need Is Love*, having earlier performed *Her Majesty* (from ***Abbey Road***) which begins, "Her Majesty's a pretty nice girl/But she doesn't have a lot to say."

5 Grammy-winning R&B star **R. Kelly** is arrested in Haines City, Florida, after a grand jury in Chicago indicts him on 21 counts of child pornography. The **Chicago Sun-Times** reported in February that it had received a videotape, purportedly showing the 35-year-old Kelly having sex with a 14-year-old girl, which it handed over to Chicago police. If found guilty, he could face up to 15 years in prison, and have to register as a sex offender.

The breakout success of Avril Lavigne's *Complicated* would help *Let Go* become the biggest-selling debut album of the year worldwide.

R. Kelly had already settled two lawsuits with underage girls out of court before his arrest in June... Alan Lomax's influence was still felt at the time of his death, with the "O Brother, Where Art Thou?" soundtrack.

5 **Dee Dee Ramone** (49-year-old Douglas Colvin), a founding member of the **Ramones**, is found dead at home in Hollywood by his wife, Barbara, 14 months after fellow Ramone, **Joey**, succumbed to cancer, and just 11 weeks after the band was inducted into the Rock and Roll Hall of Fame. Drug paraphernalia is found near his body. In an interview from last year, Dee Dee – whose legacy will remain intact in the shape of his "1-2-3-4" count at the beginning of all Ramones songs – said: "I'm really lucky I'm still around. Everybody expected me to die next... But it was always someone else instead of me."

15 **Mick Jagger** is awarded a knighthood in the Queen's Birthday Honours' List announced today. Nominated by a fan – Prime Minister Tony Blair – he joins **Paul McCartney**, **Cliff Richard**, **George Martin**, and **Elton John** as "Sirs." **Keith Richards** will announce that he will not be calling Jagger "Sir." ***Sgt. Pepper*** sleeve designer Peter Blake is also knighted.

27 Who bassist, 57-year-old **John Entwistle**, is found dead in his room at the Hard Rock Hotel in Las Vegas, on the eve of the band's forthcoming North American tour. The Clark County coroner will reveal the death to be the result of cocaine causing the contraction of coronary arteries already damaged by heart disease. The remaining band members, **Roger Daltrey** and **Pete Townshend**, will go ahead with the tour, with **Pino Palladino** taking Entwistle's place. Canceling the first two concerts, they will open at the Hollywood Bowl on 1 July. It will later be revealed that Entwistle was being entertained by a stripper at the time of his death.

July

16 Earnest singer/songwriter John Mayer kicks off his first major USA tour at The Pier in Baltimore, Maryland. Mayer, who is currently riding high with his platimum-selling debut

NELLY

Aug 17 **Hip-hop star Nelly replaces himself at No. 1 on the US chart, when *Dilemma*, featuring Kelly Rowland from Destiny's Child, hits the top for the first of ten weeks, knocking *Hot In Herre* down to No. 2 after a seven-week stay at the summit. In doing so, he becomes the first artist since the Beatles to achieve this with his first two chart-toppers. At the end of the year, the rapping superstar's current album *Nellyville* will be certified for five million US sales, shortly after eight million domestic sales are confirmed for its predecessor, his debut set *Country Grammar*. Together with Eminem, Nelly is defying a worrying downturn in global record sales, attributed by many industry suits to CD and internet piracy, but by more savvy critics to cloth-eared A&R, corporate centralization, and narrow-casting radio formatting.**

Room For Squares, moved to Atlanta, Georgia, in 1999 following a brief spell at the prestigious Berklee College of Music in Boston. He was signed to Aware Records after his performance at the South by Southwest music conference in 2000 drew the attention of several major labels.

19 Legendary music archivist **Alan Lomax** dies at the age of 87. As a 17-year-old in 1933, Lomax began to accompany his father, folklorist John Lomax, recording traditional blues and folk music in the Deep South, and it was on these trips that they discovered **Leadbelly**, **Jelly Roll Morton**, and **Muddy Waters**. Their recordings formed the Archive of American Folk Song, a collection of 15,000 songs compiled for the Library of American Congress. After his father retired in 1940, Lomax took over as curator of the Archive, recording at CBS Studios, where he had a weekly radio show. One of the first artists to be recorded there was **Woody Guthrie**. Lomax also collected folk music in Italy, Spain, and Britain – where he spent several years in the 1950s – and the Caribbean, when he spent 1962 archiving indigenous music. His influence is still felt today, with **Moby**'s ***Play*** using three of his recordings, and his 1959 recording of **James Carter**'s *Lo' Lazarus* included on this year's Grammy-winning Album of the Year, ***O Brother, Where Art Thou?***

August

29 The 19th MTV Video Music Awards have been rescheduled to avoid falling close to the anniversary of 9/11. In a particularly poignant opening, **Bruce Springsteen & the E Street Band** perform their new single *The Rising* (taken from his return-to-form upcoming album of the same name). But from that point, the ceremony degenerates into a lackluster and, at times, embarrassing evening. **Michael Jackson**, introduced by **Britney Spears**, who calls him her "artist of the millennium," says: "When I was a little boy in Indiana, if someone had told me that one day I would be getting as a musician the artist of the millennium award, I wouldn't have believed this. This is really amazing. I can't believe it." Neither do MTV, who have given him no such award. **Eminem** continues his, by now, predictable routine of taunting **Moby**. Despite all the hype, **Guns N' Roses** close the proceedings with an underwhelming performance. More memorably, former New York Mayor Rudolph Giuliani receives a standing ovation, and **TLC**'s **"T-Boz"** and **"Chilli"** remember **Lisa "Left Eye" Lopes**, while presenter Carson Daly announces a $25,000 scholarship in her name. The night's big winners are Eminem, with four awards (one for Video of the Year), minimalist garage-blues-blending, Detroit-based rock duo **White Stripes**, with three, and **No Doubt** and **Pink** with two apiece.

"I'm OK with it, but it'll be a drag if I don't make it 'till the next James Bond movie comes out."

Warren Zevon, on his diagnosis of inoperable lung cancer, September 12, 2002

September

7 **Coldplay**'s critically revered second album, ***A Rush Of Blood To The Head***, is at No. 1 in 11 countries: Ireland, Italy, the UK, Australia, Canada, Germany, Hong Kong, Iceland, Denmark, Norway, and Switzerland, spurred by its anthemic hit single, *In My Place*. The band is currently on a US club tour.

12 A spokesperson for **Warren Zevon** announces that the 55-year-old singer-songwriter has been diagnosed with inoperable lung cancer. Known for such songs as *Poor Poor Pitiful Me*, *Werewolves Of London*, *Mohammed's Radio*, *Lawyers Guns And Money*, and *Roland The Headless Thompson Gunner*, he will make a particularly poignant appearance on "Late Show with David Letterman" at the end of next month. A long-time fan, Letterman has regularly invited Zevon to lead the studio band in **Paul Shaffer**'s absence.

30 **Courtney Love** and Universal Music Group finally settle their differences, with the announcement that "Love and the other members of the [**Kurt**] **Cobain** estate have granted UMG permission to release new **Nirvana** packages, including a compilation album with a never-before-released track, a box[ed] set, and a rarities album." The settlement paves the way for the release of *You Know You're Right*, one of the last songs Nirvana cut before Cobain's suicide in 1994.

October

12 Following the unexpected success of his minor 1969 hit *A Little Less Conversation*, stunningly remixed by Dutch DJ **JXL** (Tom Holkenborg) and featured in a series of Nike TV ads broadcast during the World Cup, a collection

Coldplay's success crossed the ocean when the band picked up their first Grammy Award.

2002 Oct

Jam Master Jay is gunned down... Michael Jackson dangles his baby... Joe Strummer dies...

Elvis

of **Elvis Presley**'s No. 1 hits tops the US chart. The 31-track compilation (the 31st track is the bonus *A Little Less Conversation*), titled ***Elv1s – 30 #1 Hits***, tops charts in 17 territories after 4.7 million units have been shipped worldwide. Presley's records continue to sell in astonishing quantities, 25 years after his death.

30 **Run-D.M.C.**'s **Jam Master Jay** is gunned down in a recording studio on Merrick Boulevard in the Jamaica, Queens, area of New York. He is shot once in the head, and dies at the scene. Detectives have no positive leads. Jay, born Jason Mizell in Queens in 1965, began working as a DJ at the age of 13 at block parties in the Hollis neighborhood where he was raised, and went on to become the disc-spinning cornerstone of one of rap's leading pioneer acts.

19 With his solo debut album ***Justified*** and its extracted single *Like I Love You* both currently in the UK Top 10, ***NSync**'s **Justin Timberlake** announces he is pulling out of this weekend's Smash Hits Poll Winners' Party after breaking his foot. His doctors have advised him to rest for two weeks. In a statement he says, "I am sorely disappointed that I must miss any scheduled events. However, I must adhere to my physician's recommendations and rest. I look forward to being able to perform again and hope to see all my fans soon."

"I made a terrible mistake. I got caught up in the excitement of the moment. I would never intentionally endanger the lives of my children." Michael Jackson's statement after dangling his baby from a balcony, November 19, 2002

By the end of the year, *The Eminem Show* had equaled the sales of *The Marshall Mathers LP*, with eight million copies sold in the US.

November

3 **Lonnie Donegan**, known as the "King of Skiffle" dies in Peterborough, age 71. He was in the middle of a British tour – playing in Nottingham last night – when he complained of back pain. Donegan's role in the early British rock scene is inestimable: ironically, it was the emergence of the **Beatles** and the **Rolling Stones**, two bands who cited him as a major influence, that signaled his decline in popularity.

6 **Eminem**'s first movie vehicle, "8 Mile" receives its world premiere at a star-studded bash in Hollywood. The movie is loosely based on Eminem's life, and is well received by many critics. It will secure a huge $54.5 million box office take this coming weekend. Its soundtrack album features five tracks by Eminem, and contributions from other hot hip-hop talent, including **Nas**, **Jay-Z**, and fast-rising rap act **50 Cent**. Released on Eminem's new Shady label, it is already at US No. 1 and will turn triple platinum by the end of the year – adding to the seven million domestic haul of his recent album, ***The Eminem Show***.

19 **Michael Jackson** appears at the open window of his fifth-floor room at the Adlon Hotel in Berlin, and dangles his nine-month-old son, Prince Michael II, whose head is covered with a towel, over the railings. Jackson – taking a break from a $21 million lawsuit being heard in a California courtroom – is in Germany to pick up a Bambi Award for Lifetime Achievement.

December

7 Ending a triumphant 12 months, **Norah Jones** performs *Don't Know Why* and *Come Away With Me* during her debut appearance on "Saturday Night Live." Her album ***Come Away With Me*** has become the year's surprise hit, gently winning fans around the world. Still climbing the US chart after 46 weeks, it will

The night after its world premiere in Hollywood, "8 Mile" opened in the less salubrious surroundings of Eight Mile Road in Detroit's northeast side... The first anniversary of George Harrison's death was marked by the Concert for George at London's Royal Albert Hall.

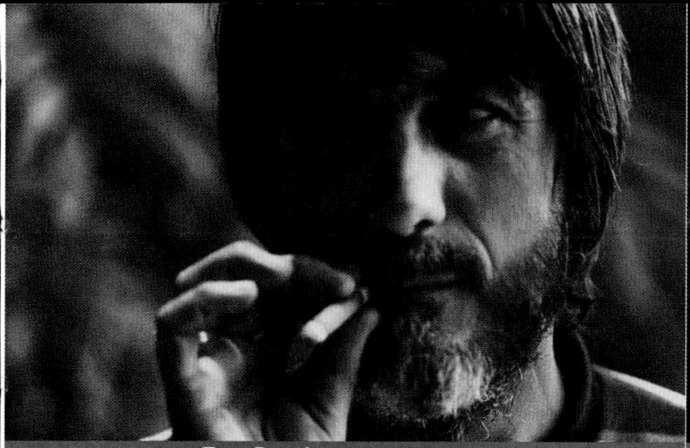
Tom Dowd

Joe Strummer

Elv1s: 30 #1 Hits **set a new record for the longest span between US No. 1 albums – 29 years, 4 months, and 7 days... Tom Dowd initially worked with Dizzy Gillespie and Charlie Parker... Future Forests, an environmental charity supported by Strummer, created a Joe Strummer Memorial Forest on the Isle of Skye after his death.**

eventually top the survey next month. Jones will sweep the Grammys, winning five awards – Record of the Year, Album of the Year, Best Female Pop Vocal Performance, Best New Artist and Best Pop Vocal Album. For once, the record company marketing has been spot on: "Sometimes in a room full of shouting, a whisper is the loudest voice."

9 Ramesh Christie is shot dead in the Toronto suburb of Vaughan while watching the making of a video by dancehall reggae star **Sean Paul**. Police believe there is no connection between the two events. Paul, who has already collaborated with **Blue Cantrell**, **De La Soul**, **DMX**, and **Jay-Z**, is currently enjoying a Top 10 hit with his dope-smoking themed *Gimme The Light* from his yet-to-be platinum album *Dutty Rock*.

9 **Ashanti** takes home eight trophies at the 2002 **Billboard** Music Awards at the MGM Grand Garden Arena in Las Vegas – including Top Female Artist, and Top R&B/Hip-Hop Artist. She accepts the latter award accompanied by her mother and Murder Inc. boss Irv Gotti.

12 **Moby** is attacked by two men in the early hours of the morning, while signing autographs outside the Paradise rock club on Commonwealth Avenue in Boston, following the annual WBCN Xmas Rave concert.

13 **Zal Yanovsky**, the one-time rhythm guitarist of the **Lovin' Spoonful**, dies six days before his 58th birthday in Kingston, Ontario. The Canadian-born Yanovsky met folkie **John Sebastian** at **Cass Elliot**'s house on February 9, 1964, to watch the **Beatles** on "The Ed Sullivan Show." They subsequently formed the **Mugwumps**, and then the Lovin' Spoonful. The combination of Sebastian's studious songcraft and Yanovsky's zany onstage personality made the group one of the hottest acts of the mid 1960s.

22 Punk icon, **Clash** co-founder **Joe Strummer** dies following a heart attack at home in Somerset, England, age 50. After the demise of punk's most formidable band in 1985, Strummer took occasional acting roles and wrote soundtrack albums (notably for director friend Alex Cox). He completed a stint as lead singer for the **Pogues** and most recently toured with his latest combo, the **Mescaleros**. After Strummer informally teamed with ex-Clash colleague **Mick Jones** at a Mescaleros gig in November, the Clash were due to reunite (after 17 years) at their induction into the Rock and Roll Hall of Fame next March.

23 **U2** frontman **Bono** (with whom **Joe Strummer** and **Dave Stewart** wrote *48864* – a tribute to Nelson Mandela) says of Strummer's death: "The Clash was the greatest rock band. They wrote the rule book for U2. It's such a shock." **Billy Bragg** adds: "Within the Clash, Joe was the political engine of the band, and without Joe there's no political Clash and without the Clash the whole political edge of punk would have been severely dulled."

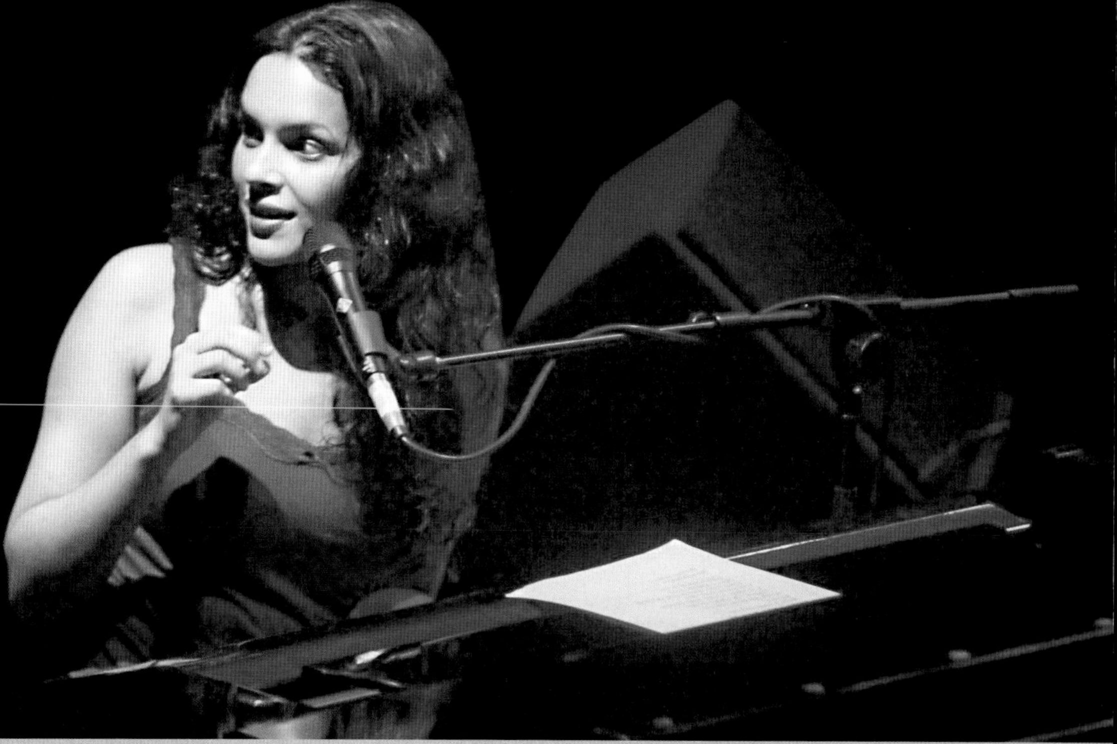
By the time Norah Jones won five Grammys in February 2003, *Come Away With Me* was on its way to five million US sales.

ROOTS **During this year: at the personal invitation of headliner Morrissey, Irish rock quintet the Thrills make their live UK debut performing at the Royal Albert Hall in London in December... hotly touted neo-psychedelic Liverpool-based rock sextet, the Corals' self-titled debut album is released by Sony... native New Zealand garage rock foursome the Datsuns record their eponymous album for V2... already critically revered by legendary producer Van Dyke Parks, singer-songwriter Alexi Murdoch makes his US national radio debut on KCRW's syndicated "Sounds Eclectic"... the reunited Folkmen (comprising Christopher Guest, Michael McKean, and Harry Shearer) perform at Carnegie Hall for the first time, an event captured on film for release next year as the folkumentary, "A Mighty Wind"... and signed to Mushroom Records in Australia, cheeky rock quartet the Androids record their first two singles, *Here She Comes* and *Do It With Madonna*...**

Index

A

B

Left to right: Little Richard's stage jacket, Talking Heads T-Shirt and Bonnie Raitt's waistcoat.

C

Left to right: Doc Pomus's saxophone, Yardbirds drum head.

D

SANDINISTA!
CLASH

IKE & TINA TURNER
REVUE
The HUMAN "BOMB SHELL"
Jimmy Thomas
Stacy Johnson
Bobby John
Tina Turner
Vernon Guy
Vanetta Fields
and their KINGS of RHYTHM Orchestra

THE DISNEY CHANNEL

Left: Jimmy Page's harmony acoustic guitar. Above: Howlin Wolf's electric guitar.

I

J

K

L

M

Above: Tom Petty's hat. Right: Snoop Doggy Dog's baseball cap.

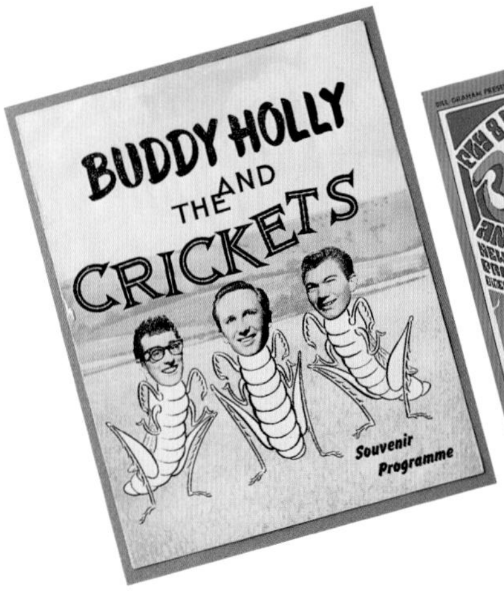
BUDDY HOLLY
AND
THE CRICKETS
Souvenir
Programme

BYRDS
FILLMORE AUDITORIUM

ARETHA
RECORDING LIVE AT FILLMORE WEST
KING CURTIS AND THE KINGPINS
TOWER OF POWER
MARCH 5 6 7

Above: Union Jack platform boots worn by Geri Halliwell (Ginger Spice), 1997.

Above: Shoes belonging to George Hunter (The Charlatans).

S

T

Left: Steve Tyler's patchwork stage shirt. Right: Al Green's clerical robe.

U

V

W

Above: Duane Eddy's electric guitar. Below: Muddy Waters's Martin acoustic guitar.

X

Y

Z

Acknowledgments

Dorling Kindersley would like to thank the following for their contributions:
Seymour Stein at the Rock and Roll Hall of Fame; James Henke and Meredith Rutledge at the Rock and Roll Hall of Fame and Museum; Larry Demellier at Sire Records; Bryan Adams; Charles Wills; Mike Evans; Tony Barton, Marshall Bromley, Carolyn Clerkin, Janice English, Phil Gilderdale, Molly Jarvis, Martin Lampon, Nicki Lampon, Ana-Maria Rivera, Karen Self, Alison Shackleton, Hayley Smith, and Anna Youle for the loan of memorabilia.

Editorial and design:
Editorial: Amy Corzine, Clare Hill, Sharon Lucas; Design: Anna Benjamin, Mark Cavanagh, Steve Knowlden, Marianne Markham, Simon Wilder; DTP: Mark Bracey, Jonathon Montague; Production: Lauren Britton, Kate Oliver; DK Picture Library: Richard Dabb, Claire Bowers; Photography: Andy Crawford.

The Authors would like to thank:
First and foremost, many thanks to midfield dynamo Tim Lister whose research, editorial skills, and uncommon good nature proved invaluable – as were his occasional dispatches from Baghdad. Special thanks and love to Jessica and Linda for their saintly patience. All at DK but especially the unrivaled Stephanie Jackson and Nicki Lampon, who together with Adèle Hayward and Karen Self, often made working on the project more fun than was necessary. Thanks also to Colin Webb, Sonya Newland, Beverley Jollands, and Tim Jollands at Palazzo and David Costa at Wherefore Art?

Many thanks to Jim Henke, the eagle-eyed curator of the Rock and Roll Hall of Fame Museum in Cleveland, and the President of the Hall, Seymour Stein. Also Quincy Jones, Rob Thomas, Russell Ash, and Christopher Davis. Special mention to the hardworking (!) team on "The Music Room": Shanon Cook, Neil Curry, Jessica Ellis, Max Ramming, Brian Streicher, Angelique Van Der Byl, and Dan Vanderkooy. Barry Lazell, Marilyn Lazell, Pete Frame (for the phrase "starry-eyed aspirant"), Peter Compton, and all at MRIB, and Kim Bloxdorf at Record Research. Mary and Rex Burrow, Mark Crampton, Paul and Julie Evans, Phil Jones, Helena de Lister, Dr. N.D. Mallary, Greg de Santis, Frances Schultz, Luther Randall, and Steve Wright.

Resources
Among a vast research resource of newspapers, magazines, books, print, and broadcasting archives, innumerable internet sites, boxed sets, and personal interviews, the following proved particularly useful:

Magazines/newspapers: **Amusement Business**, **Billboard**, **Boston Globe**, **Boston Herald**, **Cash Box**, **Circus**, **Daily Mirror**, **Daily Telegraph**, **Daily Sketch**, **Details**, **Disc & Music Echo**, **Discoveries**, **Downbeat**, **Entertainment Weekly**, **Goldmine**, **Hollywood Reporter**, **Ice**, **Interview**, **Kerrang!**, **Los Angeles Times**, **Melody Maker**, **Mojo**, **Music & Media**, **Music Week**, **Musician**, **New Musical Express**, **New York Daily News**, **New York Post**, **The New York Times**, **People**, **Performance**, **Premiere**, **Pulse**, **Q**, **Radio & Records**, **Record Business**, **Record Collector**, **Record Mirror**, **Record Retailer**, **Record World**, **Rolling Stone**, **Select**, **Smash Hits**, **Sounds**, **Spin**, **The Sun**, **Time Out**, **The Times**, **TV Guide**, **USA Today**, **Vanity Fair**, **Variety**, **VH1**, **Vox**, **Zig-Zag**, and wire reports.

Books: Joel Whitburn's indispensable range of US chart reference books, including **Top Pop Singles** and **Top Pop Albums**, **The Billboard Book of Number One Hits** (Fred Bronson), **X-Ray** (Ray Davies), **Nat King Cole** (Daniel Mark Epstein), **Aretha – From These Roots** (Aretha Franklin), **Last Train to Memphis** (Peter Garulnick), **Q** (Quincy Jones), **Lissauer's Encyclopedia of Popular Music In America** (Robert Lissauer), **Man and Music** (Michael Lydon), **Rock Stars Encyclopedia** (Dafydd Rees & Luke Crampton), **Bill Haley – The Daddy of Rock and Roll** (John Swenson), **Trouble Man – The Life and Death of Marvin Gaye** (Steve Turner).

Also, industry organizations ASCAP, BMI, BPI, MCPS, NARAS, PRS, RIAA, the Rock and Roll Hall of Fame and the Songwriters Hall of Fame.

All the quotes used at the opening of each chapter are original, except the following: page 8: Little Richard, **New Musical Express**, 1985; page 90: Brian Wilson, **The Guardian**, 1988 and Bob Dylan, **The Sunday Times**, 1984; page 218: Joni Mitchell, **Q**, 1988; page 330: Suzanne Vega and Michael Stipe, **Rolling Stone: The Decades of Rock & Roll**, 2001.

Disclaimer
A significant amount of misinformation has plagued the history of rock and pop music since its inception. In an attempt to clean up and clear up thousands of debatable "facts," the authors have made every effort to verify the accuracy of the information contained in this book. If, however, you are included in these pages (or think you ought to be) and would like to correct, corroborate, or contribute further information for subsequent editions, or if you are a particular devotee of a certain act with a detailed knowledge of its career and would like to contact the authors, please do so at:
P.O. Box 173, Barnstable, Massachusetts 02630, USA

Notes on reading this book
Chart data: any reference to a chart position for either singles or albums in the UK or US, uniquely refers to the week-ending Saturday date of the published chart (a practice not generally observed by chart compilers in the 1950s and 1960s).

Singles are shown in italics. ***Albums (including LPs, EPs, cassettes, 8-track tapes, compact discs, mini-discs, CD-ROMs, DVDs etc.) are shown in bold italics.***

Television and radio broadcasts, theatrical productions, films, and videos are shown in "double quotes."

Magazines, newspapers, books, and other literary sources are shown in bold.

This book may be best read from front to back.